Magill's
Cinema
Annual
2011

Magill's Cinema Annual 2011

30th Edition
A Survey of the films of 2010

Brian Tallerico, Editor

A VideoHound® Reference

GALE
CENGAGE Learning™

Detroit • New York • San Francisco • New Haven, Conn • Waterville, Maine • London

Magill's Cinema Annual 2011

Brian Tallerico, Editor

Project Editor: Michael J. Tyrkus

Editorial: Stephen Bridenstine, Jim Craddock, Lauren Hansz

Editorial Support Services: Wayne Fong

Composition and Electronic Prepress: Gary Leach, Evi Seoud

Manufacturing: Rhonda Dover

Gale, Cengage Learning
27500 Drake Rd.
Farmington Hills, MI, 48331-3535

ISBN-13: 978-1-55862-759-8
ISBN-10: 1-55862-759-6

ISSN: 0739-2141

Printed in Mexico
1 2 3 4 5 6 7 15 14 13 12 11

Contents

Preface

Magill's Cinema Annual 2011 continues the fine film reference tradition that defines the VideoHound® series of entertainment industry products published by Gale. The thirtieth annual volume in a series that developed from the twenty-one-volume core set, *Magill's Survey of Cinema,* the *Annual* was formerly published by Salem Press. Gale's sixteenth volume, as with the previous Salem volumes, contains essay-reviews of significant domestic and foreign films released in the United States during the preceding year.

The *Magill's* editorial staff at Gale, comprising the VideoHound® team and a host of *Magill's* contributors, continues to provide the enhancements that were added to the *Annual* when Gale acquired the line. These features include:

- More essay-length reviews of significant films released during the year
- Obituaries and book review sections
- Trivia and "un facts" about the reviewed movies, their stars, the crew, and production
- Quotes and dialogue "soundbites" from reviewed movies, or from stars and crew about the film
- More complete awards and nominations listings, including the American Academy Awards®, the Golden Globes, and others (see the User's Guide for more information on awards coverage)
- Box office grosses, including year-end and other significant totals
- Publicity taglines featured in film reviews and advertisements

In addition to these elements, *Magill's Cinema Annual 2011* still features:

- An obituaries section profiling major contributors to the film industry who died in 2010
- An annotated list of selected film books published in 2010
- Nine indexes: Director, Screenwriter, Cinematographer, Editor, Art Director, Music Director, Performer, Subject, and Title (now cumulative)

COMPILATION METHODS

The *Magill's* editorial staff reviews a variety of entertainment industry publications, including trade magazines and newspapers, as well as online sources, on a daily and weekly basis to select significant films for review in *Magill's Cinema Annual*. *Magill's* staff and other contributing reviewers, including film scholars and university faculty, write the reviews included in the *Annual*.

MAGILL'S CINEMA ANNUAL: A VIDEOHOUND® REFERENCE

The *Magill's Survey of Cinema* series, now supplemented by the *Annual*, is the recipient of the Reference Book of the Year Award in Fine Arts by the American Library Association. Gale, an award-winning publisher of reference products, is proud to offer *Magill's Cinema Annual* as part of its popular VideoHound® product line, which includes *VideoHound®'s Golden Movie Retriever* and *The Video Source Book*. Other Gale film-related products include the four-volume *International Dictionary of Films and Filmmakers, Women Filmmakers & Their Films,* the *Contemporary Theatre, Film, and Television* series, and the four-volume *Schirmer Encyclopedia of Film*. Also, be sure to visit Video-Hound on the web at *www.MovieRetriever.com*.

ACKNOWLEDGMENTS

The editor could not be prouder of the dedicated work of all of the talented contributors of *Magill's Cinema Annual 2011*. They continuously impress with their professionalism, knowledge, and dedication to the project. This year's edition is honored by the presence of eight members of the Chicago Film Critics Association, including three members of the Board of Directors. The staff at Gale, Cengage Learning—Mike Tyrkus, Jim Craddock, and Tom Burns—deserve thanks for their continued efforts on behalf of the book and the editor must finally note that he would accomplish nothing if not for the support of his beautiful wife Lauren, incredible son Lucas, and his entire network of family and friends. The work of one would never be possible without the support of many.

We at *Magill's* look forward to another exciting year in film and preparing the next edition of *Magill's Cinema Annual*. As always, we invite your comments, questions, and suggestions. Please direct them to:

Editor
Magill's Cinema Annual
Gale, a part of Cengage Learning
27500 Drake Road
Farmington Hills, MI 48331-3535
Phone: (248) 699-4253
Toll-Free: (800) 347-GALE (4253)
Fax: (248) 699-8865

The Year in Film: An Introduction

The media machine found multiple ways to define the film year of 2010 as a battle between old and new school, most significantly embodied in the awards season battle between David Fincher's *The Social Network* and Tom Hooper's *The King's Speech,* the eventual winner for Best Picture, Best Director, and Best Original Screenplay at the Academy Awards®. The race for major awards between what was seen by many as a cutting edge drama and what even its admirers would admit was an old-fashioned approach to storytelling defined the end of the year but it also served as a mirror image for another year-long conversation—the artistic viability of 3D in the wake of James Cameron's *Avatar* in 2009. Was 3D part of the new school of filmmaking or simply a fad? And, as studios continued to struggle to reach a mass audience in a new era of multiple delivery systems for popular entertainment, a surprising level of quality at the end of the year actually rose to the top of the box office with several critical favorites and Oscar® contenders beating out lowest common denominator fare. Perhaps the new school thinking should be that audiences are not as stupid as producers previously thought.

They do, however, still flock to the familiar. Only one live-action original screenplay could crack the top ten moneymakers of the year as Christopher Nolan once again redefined popular entertainment with the incredibly-challenging *Inception,* one of the most ambitious Summer movies ever made. The Leonardo DiCaprio vehicle placed sixth on the year behind *Toy Story 3, Alice in Wonderland, Iron Man 2, The Twilight Saga: Eclipse,* and *Harry Potter and the Deathly Hallows: Part 1,* in that order. Despite the promise of the box office success of critically-beloved films at the end of the year, the majority of box office blockbusters of 2010 proved yet again that moviegoers, especially families, like to know what they are in for when they open their wallets for an increasingly-expensive proposition.

As for those year-end stories, the pattern of box office success would have indicated that populist fare like *Little Fockers, Yogi Bear,* and *Gulliver's Travels* would have dominated the charts of the holiday season but they were accompanied by a surprisingly-strong array of eventual Oscar® nominees including the highest-grossing film of the Coen brothers' career (*True Grit*), the eventual winner for Best Supporting Actor and Best Supporting Actress (*The Fighter*), Harvey Weinstein's most resonant success in years (*The King's Speech*), and perhaps the weirdest movie to ever break $100 million domestically (*Black Swan*). It may sound clichéd, but the year truly ended with a diverse enough theatrical line-up that there was truly something for everyone.

The story of 2009 was arguably the battle between James Cameron (*Avatar*) and his ex-wife Kathryn Bigelow (*The Hurt Locker*) and, when the latter became the first woman to ever win an Oscar® for Best Director, some questioned whether or not it was a fluke or the beginning of a pattern. The jury is still out. While it is certainly notable that twenty percent of the Best Picture nominees for 2010 were directed by women (Lisa Cholodenko's *The Kids Are All Right* and Debra Granik's *Winter's Bone*), neither director was nominated for Best Director and neither was really a part of the conversation.

The jury would need another year to determine the artistic and even financial viability of 3D as well, even after so many proclaimed that it was the way of the future after Cameron's mega-profitable trip to Pandora. The technology would continue to be used to its best effect in animated fare like *Toy Story 3, Despicable Me, Shrek Forever After,* and *How to Train Your Dragon,* all films that ended the year in the top ten of the year's box office. But the use of 3D in live-action fare continued to prove divisive. M. Night Shyamalan's *The Last Airbender* would become the poster child for the overindulgence of the trend after it was weakly-transferred from 2D to 3D, eventually winning the Razzie for the Worst Picture of the Year (although it is worth noting that while critics and many audiences hated the film, it brought in an amazing $319 million worldwide, a number surely inflated by the 3D ticket price but nonetheless remarkable). If anything was learned in 2010 regarding 3D it was that it was not a surefire financial coup as films like *Saw 3D, Cats & Dogs: The Revenge of Kitty Galore, Gulliver's Travels, My Soul to Take,* and *Step Up 3-D* all bombed. It appears that, even in three dimensions, quality matters.

As for the critical darlings of 2010, several of the form's most influential auteurs returned with acclaimed fare including Joel and Ethan Coen (*True Grit*), Martin Scorsese (*Shutter Island*), and Roman Polanski (*The Ghost Writer*), but the critical story of the year was the knighting of a new generation of directors led by Christopher Nolan (*Inception*), Darren Aronofsky (*Black Swan*), David O. Russell (*The Fighter*), and David Fincher (*The Social Network*). Fincher watched his social-media masterpiece become one of the most critically-lauded and critically-awarded films in the history of film theory but it ultimately became the also-ran to the Weinstein machine as they proved their might yet again by pushing *The King's Speech* to not just a remarkable late awards season run but to status as a crowd favorite as well. The film's run up to Oscar® night, as it became clearer that it would supplant the Facebook Movie in the history books, made many critics apoplectic.

Perhaps the lesson to take away from all of the above is that there is no school, old or new. It is always going to be about individual movies. One can point to the success of *Alice in Wonderland* or the failure of *Gulliver's Travels* to make disparate points about the potential of 3D or the popularity of familiar family films. One can lament critically-derided junk like *Shrek Forever After* or *The Last Airbender* appearing in the top twenty financial successes of the year or note that *Inception* and *True Grit* also found entrance into that elite club. One can argue over the worth of Tom Hooper or David Fincher's films, but just as Kathryn Bigelow and James Cameron's battle in 2009 was not repeated the next year, one must assume that there will be a different shade of heavyweight bout in 2011 with new contenders and slightly different rules. For those that analyze both individual efforts and examine entire years in an art form, it is the thrill of a fight that never ends.

Brian Tallerico
Chicago, Illinois

Contributing Reviewers

Michael Betzold
Author, Publishing Professional

David L. Boxerbaum
Freelance Reviewer

Tom Burns
Publishing Professional

Dave Canfield
Professional Film Critic

Erik Childress
Professional Film Critic

Mark Dujsik
Professional Film Critic

Joanna MacKenzie
Freelance Reviewer

Matt Pais
Professional Film Critic

Matthew Priest
Freelance Reviewer

Steven Prokopy
Professional Film Critic

Brent Simon
Professional Film Critic

Peter Sobczynski
Professional Film Critic

Collin Souter
Professional Film Critic

Brian Tallerico
Professional Film Critic

Michael J. Tyrkus
Publishing Professional

Nathan Vercauteren
Freelance Reviewer

User's Guide

ALPHABETIZATION

Film titles and reviews are arranged on a word-by-word basis, including articles and prepositions. English leading articles (A, An, The) are ignored, as are foreign leading articles (El, Il, La, Las, Le, Les, Los). Other considerations:

- Acronyms appear alphabetically as if regular words.
- Common abbreviations in titles file as if they are spelled out, so *Mr. Death* will be found as if it was spelled *Mister Death.*
- Proper names in titles are alphabetized beginning with the individual's first name, for instance, *Gloria* will be found under "G."
- Titles with numbers, for instance, *200 Cigarettes,* are alphabetized as if the numbers were spelled out, in this case, "Two-Hundred." When numeric titles gather in close proximity to each other, the titles will be arranged in a low-to-high numeric sequence.

SPECIAL SECTIONS

The following sections that are designed to enhance the reader's examination of film are arranged alphabetically, they include:

- *List of Awards.* An annual list of awards bestowed upon the year's films by the following: Academy of Motion Picture Arts and Sciences, British Academy of Film and Television Arts Awards, Directors Guild of America Awards, Golden Globe Awards, Golden Raspberry Awards, Independent Spirit Awards, the Screen Actors Guild Awards, and the Writer's Guild Awards.
- *Obituaries.* Profiles major contributors to the film industry who died in 2010.
- *Selected Film Books of 2010.* An annotated list of selected film books published in 2010.

INDEXES

Film titles and artists are separated into nine indexes, allowing the reader to effectively approach a film from any one of several directions, including not only its credits but its subject matter.

- *Director, Screenwriter, Cinematographer, Editor, Art Director, Music Director,* and *Performer* indexes are arranged alphabetically according to artists appearing in this volume, followed by a list of the films on which they worked. In the *Performer* index, a (V) beside a movie title indicates voice-only work and an (N) beside a movie title indicates work as narrator.
- *Subject Index.* Films may be categorized under several of the subject terms arranged alphabetically in this section.
- *Title Index.* The title index is a cumulative alphabetical list of films covered in the thirty volumes of the *Magill's Cinema Annual,* including the films covered in this volume. Films reviewed in past volumes are cited with the year in which the film appeared in the *Annual*; films reviewed in this volume are cited with the film title in boldface with a bolded Arabic numeral indicating the page number on which the review begins. Original and alternate titles are cross-referenced to the American release title in the Title Index. Titles of retrospective films are followed by the year, in brackets, of their original release.

SAMPLE REVIEW

Each *Magill's* review contains up to sixteen items of information. A fictionalized composite sample review containing all the elements of information that may be included in a full-length review follows the outline on the facing page. The circled number following each element in the sample review designates an item of information that is explained in the outline.

1. **Title:** Film title as it was released in the United States.

2. **Foreign or alternate title(s):** The film's original title or titles as released outside the United States, or alternate film title or titles. Foreign and alternate titles also appear in the Title Index to facilitate user access.

3. **Taglines:** Up to ten publicity taglines for the film from advertisements or reviews.

4. **Box office information:** Year-end or other box office domestic revenues for the film.

5. **Film review:** A signed review of the film, including an analytic overview of the film and its critical reception.

6. **Reviewer byline:** The name of the reviewer who wrote the full-length review. A complete list of this volume's contributors appears in the "Contributing Reviewers" section which follows the Introduction.

7. **Principal characters:** Listings of the film's principal characters and the names of the actors who play them in the film.

8. **Country of origin:** The film's country or countries of origin and the languages featured in the film.

9. **Release date:** The year of the film's first general release.

10. **Production information:** This section typically includes the name(s) of the film's producer(s), production company, and distributor; director(s); screenwriter(s); cinematographer(s); editor(s); art director(s); production designer(s); music composer(s); and other credits such as visual effects, sound, costume design, and song(s) and songwriter(s).

11. **MPAA rating:** The film's rating by the Motion Picture Association of America. If there is no rating given, the line will read, "Unrated."

12. **Running time:** The film's running time in minutes.

13. **Reviews:** A list of brief citations of major newspaper and journal reviews of the film, including author, publication title, and date of review.

14. **Film quotes:** Memorable dialogue directly from the film, attributed to the character who spoke it, or comment from cast or crew members or reviewers about the film.

15. **Film trivia:** Interesting tidbits about the film, its cast, or production crew.

16. **Awards information:** Awards won by the film, followed by category and name of winning cast or crew member. Listings of the film's nominations follow the wins on a separate line for each award. Awards are arranged alphabetically. Information is listed for films that won or were nominated for the following awards: American Academy Awards®, British Academy of Film and Television Arts Awards, Directors Guild of America Awards, Golden Globe Awards, Golden Raspberry Awards, Independent Spirit Awards, the Screen Actors Guild Awards, and the Writers Guild of America Awards.

THE GUMP DIARIES ①
(Los Diarios del Gump) ②

Love means never having to say you're stupid.
—Movie tagline ③

Box Office: $10 million④

In writer/director Robert Zemeckis' *Back to the Future* trilogy (1985, 1989, 1990), Marty McFly (Michael J. Fox) and his scientist sidekick Doc Brown (Christopher Lloyd) journey backward and forward in time, attempting to smooth over some rough spots in their personal histories in order to remain true to their individual destinies. Throughout their time-travel adventures, Doc Brown insists that neither he nor Marty influence any major historical events, believing that to do so would result in catastrophic changes in humankind's ultimate destiny. By the end of the trilogy, however, Doc Brown has revised his thinking and tells Marty that, "Your future hasn't been written yet. No one's has. Your future is whatever you make it. So make it a good one."

In *Forrest Gump,* Zemeckis once again explores the theme of personal destiny and how an individual's life affects and is affected by his historical time period. This time, however, Zemeckis and screenwriter Eric Roth chronicle the life of a character who does nothing but meddle in the historical events of his time without even trying to do so. By the film's conclusion, however, it has become apparent that Zemeckis' main concern is something more than merely having fun with four decades of American history. In the process of re-creating significant moments in time, he has captured on celluloid something eternal and timeless—the soul of humanity personified by a nondescript simpleton from the deep South.

The film begins following the flight of a seemingly insignificant feather as it floats down from the sky and brushes against various objects and people before finally coming to rest at the feet of Forrest Gump (Tom Hanks). Forrest, who is sitting on a bus-stop bench, reaches down and picks up the feather, smooths it out, then opens his traveling case and carefully places the feather between the pages of his favorite book, *Curious George.*

In this simple but hauntingly beautiful opening scene, the filmmakers illustrate the film's principal concern: Is life a series of random events over which a person has no control, or is there an underlying order to things that leads to the fulfillment of an individual's destiny? The rest of the film is a humorous and moving attempt to prove that, underlying the random, chaotic events that make up a person's life, there exists a benign and simple order.

Forrest sits on the bench throughout most of the film, talking about various events of his life to others who happen to sit down next to him. It does not take long, however, for the audience to realize that Forrest's seemingly random chatter to a parade of strangers has a perfect chronological order to it. He tells his first story after looking down at the feet of his first bench partner and observing, "Mama always said that you can tell a lot about a person by the shoes they wear." Then, in a voice-over narration, Forrest begins the story of his life, first by telling about the first pair of shoes he can remember wearing.

The action shifts to the mid-1950s with Forrest as a young boy (Michael Humphreys) being fitted with leg braces to correct a curvature in his spine. Despite this traumatic handicap, Forrest remains unaffected, thanks to his mother (Sally Field) who reminds him on more than one occasion that he is no different from anyone else. Although this and most of Mrs. Gump's other words of advice are in the form of hackneyed cliches, Forrest, whose intelligence quotient is below normal, sincerely believes every one of them, namely because he instinctively knows they are sincere expressions of his mother's love and fierce devotion. ⑤

John Byline ⑥

CREDITS ⑦

Forrest Gump: Tom Hanks
Forrest's Mother: Sally Field
Young Forrest: Michael Humphreys
Origin: United States ⑧
Language: English, Spanish
Released: 1994 ⑨
Production: Liz Heller, John Manulis; New Line Cinema; released by Island Pictures ⑩
Directed by: Robert Zemeckis
Written by: Eric Roth
Cinematography by: David Phillips
Music by: Graeme Revell
Editing: Dana Congdon
Production Design: Danny Nowak
Sound: David Sarnoff
Costumes: David Robinson
MPAA rating: R ⑪
Running time: 102 minutes ⑫

REVIEWS ⑬

Doe, Jane. *Los Angeles Times.* July 6, 1994.
Doe, John. *Entertainment Weekly.* July 15, 1994.
Reviewer, Paul. *Hollywood Reporter.* June 29, 1994.
Writer, Zach. *New York Times Online.* July 15, 1994.

QUOTES ⑭

Forrest Gump (Tom Hanks): "The state of existence may be likened unto a receptacle containing cocoa-based confections, in that one may never predict that which one may receive."

TRIVIA ⑮

Hanks was the first actor since Spencer Tracy to win back-to-back Oscars® for Best Actor. Hanks received the award in 1993 for his performance in *Philadelphia.* Tracy won Oscars® in 1937 for *Captains Courageous* and in 1938 for *Boys Town.*

AWARDS ⑯

Academy Awards 1994: Film, Actor (Hanks), Special Effects, Cinematography

Nomination:

Golden Globes 1994: Film, Actor (Hanks), Supporting Actress (Field), Music.

A

AFTER.LIFE

Life is the symptom. Death is the cure.
—Movie tagline

How do you save yourself when you're already dead?
—Movie tagline

A young woman wakes up on a table with no sense of why or where. A large, sober-faced man leans over to deliver the news that she is dead, in a funeral home, and that what she feels now is only the last gasp of her soul preparing to leave her body. He says he is there to help her move on, to let go. Such a set-up could be a quiet and moving if somewhat surreal drama, even a romance. It could be a horror film, a dark fantasy, or even a morbid comedy. It could also be a mystery/thriller. It could also be a mess. *After.Life* not only mixes genres but mangles them like the car accidents that provide the victims for its confused plot. Stuck in the wreckage are Liam Neeson, Christina Ricci, and Justin Long.

Anna (Christina Ricci) a young woman in a troubled relationship wakes to finds herself in a funeral home run by local mortician Eliot Deacon (Liam Neeson). He tells her that she is dead, the result of a car accident, and that it is his job not only to prepare her for her funeral, but for her transition into the afterlife. Attempts to escape are futile as are arguments with Eliot who claims to speak to the dead. Anna slowly begins to wonder if she really is dead. As she faces her deepest fears, her heartbroken boyfriend Paul, unconvinced of her death, starts his own investigation into the accident and, ultimately, Eliot. As Paul edges closer to finding

out what really happened, Anna and Eliot prepare for her funeral and her ultimate transition.

After.Life is the feature film debut of writer/director Agnieszka Wojtowicz-Vosloo and writers Paul Vosloo and Jakub Korolczuk. Unfortunately, the team approaches this fairly straightforward and interesting story idea with a frustratingly vague sense of what they want to accomplish. As a horror film or mystery thriller, *After.Life* is too talky and cliché-ridden. As a dramatic dark fantasy, the film makes few demands on its characters creating relationships that go nowhere and predictable situations. Nobody grows or changes in this movie; nobody really learns anything.

The opening shot shows some promise, opening on Anna's slack face as Paul attempts to make love to her. As metaphors go this would be a fine one. Angry, apt to pick fights with her generally supportive boyfriend, Anna seems to be exactly what Eliot tells her she is later in the film, providing the setup for conversations about living life as opposed to just existing. But Eliot soon reveals himself as a badly-drawn, annoying cipher; there only to imperil Anna and manipulate the feelings of the audience. It is never made clear why he does what he does and, more importantly the likelihood that he could actually accomplish his gross misdeeds without getting caught never seems credible. Anna herself is thoroughly unlikeable and clueless, dead at least from the neck up, especially in her dealings with Paul, who she picks a huge fight with on, of course, the night he plans to propose to her.

None of the cast is really to blame here. The weakest link is still good. Justin Long has made a splash in horror before early in his career with *Jeepers Creepers* (2001) but has done well across a wide range of roles. He played a sci-fi obsessed fanboy in *Galaxy Quest* (1999), a stoner in the underrated *The Sasquatch Gang* (2006), and a credible leading man in *Going the Distance* (2010). The role of Paul here would be perfect for him if he had not already played virtually the same character in *Drag Me to Hell* (2009).

Liam Neeson tries his best to endow his character with a sense of motivation but to no avail. Ultimately, his physicality and understated approach save him from ignominy in a thankless role. Undertakers can make great movie monsters (or at least madmen). In Don Coscarelli's unforgettable *Phantasm* (1979), Angus Scrimm became the unforgettably menacing Tall Man. In *Dead and Buried* (1981), the great Jack Albertson turned in a powerful performance as William G. Dobbs, an undertaker obsessed with animating the dead. In *Tales from the Hood* (1995) Clarence Williams III played Funeral Director Mr. Simms with a wide-eyed ranting relish. Sadly, *After.Life* gives Liam Neeson no such dramatic opportunities. As written, the character of Eliot would be hard to play with any sort of color at all although Neeson does his best to make the dour character somewhat interesting.

Christina Ricci is naked throughout much of *After. Life*. The idea seems to be a desire to enhance the cold sterility of her environment, but her character is already too sterile. There simply is no need for such theatrics. Ricci first came to prominence as Wednesday, the little girl in the truly macabre (and very funny) *The Addams Family* (1991) and its sequels. Since then her film choices have been less mainstream. *The Ice Storm* (1997) and *Monster* (2003) notwithstanding, Ricci is better known by fans for starring in small quirky independents like *Buffalo 66* (1998), *Prozac Nation* (2001), *Pumpkin* (2002), and the underrated *Black Snake Moan* (2006). Roles in truly-wretched stuff like *Cursed* (2005) do not seem to have hurt her ability to get parts and there is always the sense with her that she may yet break out and fulfill the promise in something that has the chance to reach a wider audience.

Viewers interested in mind games of the sort that *After.Life* promises in its advertising would be well advised to try Universal Studios *Inner Sanctum* series of films from the 1940s or better yet the more modern and absolutely-brilliant *Frailty* (2001). In the final analysis, *After.Life* simply twists and turns as if it were in its own death throes when it should spiral down like a damned spirit heading towards some dark, consuming truth.

Dave Canfield

CREDITS

Anna Taylor: Christina Ricci
Eliot Deacon: Liam Neeson
Paul Coleman: Justin Long
Jack: Chandler Canterbury
Beatrice Taylor: Celia Weston
Tom Peterson: Josh Charles
Origin: USA
Language: English
Released: 2010
Production: Brad M. Gilbert, Celine Rattray, William O. Perkins III; Plum Pictures, Lleju Prods., Harbor Light Entertainment; released by Anchor Bay Films
Directed by: Agnieszka Wojtowicz-Vosloo
Written by: Agnieszka Wojtowicz-Vosloo, Paul Vosloo, Jakub Korolczuk
Cinematography by: Anastas Michos
Music by: Paul Haslinger
Sound: Coll Anderson
Editing: Niven Howie
Costumes: Luca Mosca
Production Design: Ford Wheeler
MPAA rating: R
Running time: 97 minutes

REVIEWS

Berardinelli, James. *Reelviews.* April 9, 2010.
Buckwalter, Ian. *NPR.* April 8, 2010.
Dargis, Manohla. *New York Times.* April 9, 2010.
Ebert, Roger. *Chicago Sun-Times.* April 8, 2010.
Keizer, Mark. *Boxoffice Magazine.* April 8, 2010.
Lumenick, Lou. *NY Post.* April 9, 2010.
Schager, Nick. *Slant Magazine.* April 5, 2010.
Schelb, Ronnie. *Variety.* April 8, 2010.
Sharkey, Betsy. *Los Angeles Times.* April 8, 2010.
Weinberg, Scott. *FEARnet.* April 9, 2010.

QUOTES

Eliot Deacon: "The others? They just see you as a dead body on a slab. Only I can see you as you really are."

TRIVIA

The film was shot in a mere 25 days.

AGORA

Alexandria, Egypt. 391 A.D. The world changed forever.
—Movie tagline

One woman. One city. One civilization. One planet.
—Movie tagline

In the grand scheme of human and societal evolution, math and science are certainly every bit as important if not even more so than language and the cultural arts, but their inspirations typically remain more abstruse to the average person, since the swoon of feelings—which music, film and poetry capture in such heady abundance—are much stronger than concrete thoughts. As a result, many big screen biographies that deal with important figures of such fields often bog down in pedantic speechifying, laboring to convince viewers how capital-I important everything is. With injections of overwrought emotionalism, others swing in the opposite direction—like *Creation* (2010), which, in detailing Charles Darwin's inspiration for and penning of the influential *Origin of Species,* comes across as more hysterical drama than historical drama.

A bit mannered but not ridiculously so, filmmaker Alejandro Amenábar's *Agora* has the relative advantage of being based on a noted historical figure of whom almost no audience member has heard—or if they have, then their knowledge is fairly circumscribed. The winner of seven Goya Awards®, the Spanish equivalent of the Oscars®, the film is a visually sumptuous historical drama set in Roman Egypt during the fourth century A.D., detailing the influence of Hypatia, a Neoplatonist philosopher and astronomer who served as an important teacher and adviser to Alexandria's young elite. While a modest, $38 million hit overseas, *Agora* failed to make a commercial dent Stateside, done in by a poorly conceived distribution campaign from Newmarket that did not see the movie expand into double-digit theaters until its tenth week of release, a decision which absolutely decimated any ability to build and sustain arthouse word-of-mouth.

Rachel Weisz stars as Hypatia, the daughter of respected pagan library keeper Theon (Michael Lonsdale). One of her star pupils, Orestes (Oscar Isaac), nurses a crush on Hypatia, but she spurns his publically announced affection in a manner most bizarre—presenting him a handkerchief stained with her menstrual blood. (That Orestes seems to take this in good stride is but one of many of the curious interpersonal fumblings within the narrative.) Hypatia's young, devoted personal slave, Davus (Max Minghella), is in love with her as well. Among the main characters, only Synesius (Rupert Evans) seems immune to her charms, fitting in that he eventually goes off and becomes a vicar.

Against a backdrop of rising Christian populist rhetoric, Davus falls sway to the plebian moralizing of Ammonius (Ashraf Barhom), a devout street preacher who sees wickedness in the polytheism of the day. When Alexandria's pagan council of elders sanctions a retaliatory strike against Christian rabble-rousers, their precious library is overrun and sacked, and the religious

laws of the land overturned; paganism becomes banned. Some years later, Orestes has risen to the title of prefect, but stands in conflict with Cyril (Sami Samir), a fundamentalist cleric determined to stamp out the "heresy" of science. As Christians take aim at institutions of higher learning—instruments of governmental and public strata that had for generations been used to keep them down—they impose strict new tests and standards of public morality, attempting to further turn back tolerance of different religious faiths. For those caught up in the churning change and unwilling to submit, things will not end well.

Production designer Guy Hendrix Dyas, honored by the Los Angeles Film Critics Association for his work on *Inception* (2010), could just as easily have been co-honored for his contributions here, so stirring and amazing is his work—and presumably on less than the half the budget. Working in concert with cinematographer Xavi Giménez, special effects supervisor Chris Reynolds and visual effects supervisor Félix Bergés, Amenábar and his team deliver a rapturous, visually absorbing film. Smart effects choices are complemented by high-angle camerawork that conveys a much grander palette than the actual physical spaces in which the filmmakers have to work.

Weisz turns in a fairly solid performance; she makes believable Hypatia's unyielding passion for deductive reasoning and science. Unfortunately, the script saddles her with some awkward, chatty theorizing—chiefly in conversation with her assistant Aspasius (Homayoun Ershadi)—when it needs to vouch for her intellect, and march her more directly toward conflict with Cyril and his followers. Other performances are engaging only fitfully, rising and falling on the strength of the settings surrounding them.

Co-written by Amenábar and frequent collaborator Mateo Gil, *Agora* is never less than watchable, and yet its balance of epic scale and intimate narrative seems a bit wonky and off. The filmmakers seem to want to give greater contextual mooring than your average swords-and-sandals picture, but the personal relationships within the film seem governed by gravitational forces just as elliptical and strange as the tides and planetary orbits are to the characters within the movie. As previously mentioned, Orestes remains platonically beholden to Hypatia, which seems akin to keeping on speed-dial a girl who throws a drink in your face at a high school dance. Given that the entire love triangle is unconsummated on all sides, the decision to include it at all—especially Davus' preposterous skyward prayers, "Please don't let anyone else have her!," which lends his religious conversion more than a touch of campy absurdity—seems ill conceived. The essential and awkward asexuality of the movie is repeatedly emphasized by the screenplay's insistent highlighting of it; otherwise it would not be so big a deal.

Likewise, while the rise of Christianism—which is to say the fervent embrace of Christianity as a means of political expedience—is definitely heartily explored, Amenábar seems to crucially hold back from drawing any conclusions, lest he be accused of intolerance and condescension himself. (One interesting tack that he pursues is occasionally zooming back out to a Google-Earth-type map to geographically place the action—an approach which seems to affirm and underscore the story's metaphorical underpinnings.) The persecuted of today are just always the fundamentalists of another generation, the film wanly posits, which is true by degrees but not an absolute. A failure to more fully explore this, in the form of the sincerity of Orestes, Synesius, and Davus' faiths, makes *Agora* a lackluster historical tract.

Brent Simon

CREDITS

Hypatia: Rachel Weisz
Davus: Max Minghella
Oreste: Oscar Isaac
Ammonius: Ashraf Barhoum
Synesius: Rupert Evans
Theon: Michael Lonsdale
Aspasius: Homayoun Ershadi
Cyril: Sami Samir
Origin: Spain
Language: English
Released: 2009
Production: Fernando Bovaira, Alvaro Augustin; Himenoptero, Mod Producciones, Telecinco Cinema; released by Newmarket Films
Directed by: Alejandro Amenabar
Written by: Alejandro Amenabar, Mateo Gil
Cinematography by: Xavi Gimenez
Music by: Dario Marianelli
Sound: Peter Glossop
Editing: Nacho Ruiz Capillas
Costumes: Gabriella Pescucci
Production Design: Guy Hendrix Dyas
MPAA rating: Unrated
Running time: 141 minutes

REVIEWS

Alter, Ethan. *Film Journal International.* May 25, 2010.
Burr, Ty. *Boston Globe.* July 22, 2010.
Ebert, Roger. *Chicago Sun-Times.* July 22, 2010.
Edelstein, David. *New York Magazine.* May 24, 2010.

Hornaday, Ann. *Washington Post.* July 23, 2010.
Hynes, Eric. *Village Voice.* May 26, 2010.
Long, Tom. *Detroit News.* August 13, 2010.
Phillips, Michael. *Chicago Tribune.* June 17, 2010.
Scott, A.O. *New York Times.* May 28, 2010.
Stevens, Dana. *Slate.* July 7, 2010.

QUOTES

Hypatia: "If I could just unravel this just a little bit more, and just get a little closer to the answer, then…then I would go to my grave a happy woman."

TRIVIA

The set was built on the exact same spot in Malta where many previous historical dramas were filmed including *Gladiator* (2000), *Helen of Troy* (2003), and *Troy* (2004).

AJAMI

A 2010 Academy Award® nominee for Best Foreign Language Film, and a winner of various other prizes and accolades during its many festival presentations, *Ajami* is an accomplished drama that plays as a thematically anthologized disquisition on the internecine combustibility of religious, ethnic, and caste system differences in the Middle East. Co-written and directed by Scandar Copti, a Palestinian, and Yaron Shani, an Israeli, the film is set in an impoverished, same-named neighborhood in the Tel Aviv-Jaffa metropolis, and in absorbing, non-flashy style it connects the dots of group-think and racial identity, showing how serial humiliation and a lack of open dialogue breeds separation between geographically-bound, homogenous groups, and then, almost unfailingly, bitter contempt for one another.

Running just over two hours, *Ajami* unfolds in a mix of subtitled Hebrew and Arabic in five "chapters," which introduce a variety of complicated scenarios. Winding backward and forward in time, a fuller portrait of their interrelatedness slowly emerges, bringing into starker relief the lives of its characters. *Ajami*'s tranquil opening is shattered by a drive-by shooting in which a young boy is mistakenly gunned down. The intended target of the violence is nineteen-year-old Omar (Shahir Kabaha), whose offense is that his shopkeeper uncle shot and wounded an armed extortionist with powerful clan ties. After a tribal judge renders a truce payout verdict equivalent to $57,000, Omar and his remaining family must figure out whether and how to pay for such a guarantee of their safety. Complicating this decision is Omar's clandestine relationship with Hadir (Ranin Karim), a Christian girl whose father, Abu Elias (Youssef Sahwani), owns the restaurant where he works.

Malek (Ibrahim Frege), one of Omar's younger coworkers, also has money problems. An illegal immigrant hoping to raise money for his ailing mother, Malek strikes up friendships with Omar and cook Binj (Copti again, pulling triple duty), who collectively take him under their wings. Simultaneously, Israeli police officer Dando (Eran Naim) searches for his younger brother, who has gone missing from the Israeli army and left the rest of his family stricken with grief. When Omar comes into possession of some cocaine, he senses an opportunity to make some quick money and embarks upon a misguided drug deal. His younger brother, Nasri (Fouad Habash), tags along, as does Malek, but Omar remains unaware that Abu Elias, in an attempt to save his daughter from what he deems an inappropriate relationship, is setting him up for arrest.

A sense of glancing verisimilitude slowly materializes in *Ajami* without a viewer necessarily feeling like they are being force-fed capital-A authenticity. The chief reason for this is clear, and stems from an early filmmaking decision that left room for no daylight between the scripted narrative and its interpretation: Copti and Shani put dozens if not hundreds of non-actors through a series of sometimes abstruse workshops before casting the movie. Markedly unlike anything resembling traditional auditions, this unique approach—built around physical and vocal exercises, as well as roundtable discussions of the movie's themes—helps explain the unfussy naturalness of the performances in *Ajami,* which do not much revolve around showy dialogue or dramatic emoting.

Unsurprisingly, then, the visual look and editing of the film works in lockstep with this modest methodology. Whereas many other movies with a partitioned narrative often deal in either overworked metaphor or a surfeit of affected cool that underscores a latent anxiety about the slow-building dramatic hold of the material, *Ajami* unfolds in a laidback style that is neither entirely classical, nor jittery docu-drama. It is achingly modern in the very real social divisions and fissures that it details, but its makers do not seem overly concerned with its contemporary qualities, per se. As shot by cinematographer Boaz Yehonatan Yaacov, the movie uses some panicked handheld camerawork when appropriate, but also trades heartily in more conventional framing. This allows the material room to breathe, and seem at once familiar and a bit exotic.

If there are problems in *Ajami,* one is that the movie's criminal elements—which are so integral to similarly minded interwoven fare, like Mexican import *Amores Perros* (2001), the sprawling Italian effort *Gomorrah* (2008), and Brazil's Oscar®-nominated *City of God* (2003)—notably seem like self-conscious narrative additions, tacked on for cheap effect. This can be seen in the

casual, not fully rationalized way in which Binj receives and then passes along drugs, in addition to the shooting which opens the movie and is then largely discarded as a motivating factor. (The notable exception to this is a cold-to-hot flare-up between an older Jewish man and his Arab neighbors, over the nighttime noise of a group of sheep.)

Furthermore, for all the small ways that it successfully draws in viewers, *Ajami* largely lacks a basic sense of powder-keg urgency in its puzzle box narrative, and it even avoids any real sense of humanistic conclusion. It just ends, in a place that elicits neither catharsis nor queasy, lingering disquiet. The movie's pacing sags a bit in the middle, and if the surrounding detail is all top-notch, the manner in which it is stitched together feels artificial at times. While drugs and gunplay are understandably vital in sketching conflict, the film most capably and tellingly illuminates ethnic tensions in smaller moments—as when Binj's Arab friends hassle him over moving in with his Jewish girlfriend, a woman whom they have all met and presumably know.

As a result of these faults in stitching, the film's emotional takeaway is therefore less powerful than any number of other, likeminded movies. Captivating but somewhat reserved, *Ajami* illustrates the difference between a work that is admired and one that is more deeply and lastingly felt.

Brent Simon

CREDITS

Omar: Shahir Kabaha
Nasri: Fouad Habash
Malek: Ibrahim Frege
Abu Elias: Youseff Sahwani
Hadir: Ramin Karim
Dando: Eran Naim
Binj: Scandar Copti
Origin: Israel
Language: Arabic, Hebrew
Released: 2009
Production: Mosh Danon, Thanassis Karathanos, Talia Kleinhendler; Inosan Prods., Twenty Twenty Filmproduktion, arte, Vertigo Films, Das Kleine Fernsehspiel (ZDF); released by Kino International
Directed by: Scandar Copti, Yaron Shani
Written by: Scandar Copti, Yaron Shani
Cinematography by: Boaz Yehonatan Yaacov
Music by: Rabiah Buchari
Sound: Kai Tebbel
Editing: Scandar Copti, Yaron Shani
Art Direction: Yoav Sinai

Costumes: Rona Doron
Production Design: Tony Copti
MPAA rating: Unrated
Running time: 120 minutes

REVIEWS

Anderson, John. *Wall Street Journal.* February 11, 2010.
Burr, Ty. *Boston Globe.* February 26, 2010.
Ebert, Roger. *Chicago Sun-Times.* February 18, 2010.
LaSalle, Mick. *San Francisco Chronicle.* March 12, 2010.
Richards, Jonathan. *Film.com.* April 29, 2010.
Schenker, Andrew. *Slant Magazine.* February 1, 2010.
Scott, A.O. *New York Times.* February 3, 2010.
Taylor, Ella. *Village Voice.* February 2, 2010.
Turan, Kenneth. *Los Angeles Times.* February 19, 2010.
Weissberg, Jay. *Variety.* February 3, 2010.

TRIVIA

The film was shot with all first-time actors with most of the scenes being improvised.

AWARDS

Nomination:
Oscars 2009: Foreign Film.

ALICE IN WONDERLAND

Fantastic fun for the whole family.
—Movie tagline

Box Office: $334 million

Poor Aunt Imogene (Frances de la Tour), a pitiful spinster who may never had what could rightfully be called a prime, sits expectantly amidst the goings-on in Tim Burton's *Alice in Wonderland* and waits for an imminent ideal match to transport her ever so thrillingly away. Unfortunately, after decades of crushingly layered-on loneliness she is now delusional, an assuaging fantasy having stepped in kindly because the yearned-for reality will painfully never show. In contrast, those who eagerly anticipated the film Imogene inhabits had real reason to believe they would be enchantingly transported by a seemingly-propitious pairing: Lewis Carroll's indelible, witty and wonderful realm of (at least) half-mad but totally enthralling oddballs with a cinematic auteur who is not only an impressive visual artist but also has a pronounced bent for electrically-eccentric stories that get, as Alice would say, "curiouser and curiouser."

However, what made the material that Carroll came up with to entertain his beloved "child-friend" Alice Liddell during an 1862 boating excursion so extraordinarily delightful has largely sunk out of sight. All those amusing puns and other clever contortions of language and logic are a big part of why Alice continues to loom even more impressively than she did when she partook of Wonderland's elevating edibles and elixirs. Overall, the tale Burton's film tells actually only cherry-picks from *Alice's Adventures in Wonderland* and its sequel, *Through the Looking-Glass and What Alice Found There*, and then combines them with the script's admitted biggest inspiration: Carroll's famed nonsense poem "Jabberwocky." It turns out to be much less an adaptation than what might best be called a Gothic-flavored aggregate continuation. This *Alice* is akin to the lingering grin of the otherwise-dematerialized Cheshire Cat: striking to look at, but most of what was once there is now conspicuously gone.

Burton expressed the opinion that Carroll's beloved works had a too-passive Alice merely pinball-bumping through Wonderland from one "weirdo" to another, and so he liked the idea of not only adding some psychological seriousness/depth but also a vital goal that would drive the narrative forward with a focused sense of dramatic purpose. This was referred to as "grounding" the material. So what had once been something wonderfully conjured-up within the mind of a carefree, bored child who had drifted off to sleep is here a reality, naggingly (if hazily) recalled during unquiet slumbers and destined to be revisited by this unwitting savior of a subterranean land. Alice (Mia Wasikowska) is now a nineteen-year-old freethinker who is sullenly chafing under Victorian constraints. Weighed down by the loss of a beloved, kindred spirit father and now on the uncertain cusp of adulthood, Alice will make that preordained return topple down into Wonderland, a place in which she must once again find herself so she can "find herself." (Alice had mistakenly given the wrong moniker on her previous trip to what is actually called Underland, meaning that she not only suffered from recurring nightmares but apparently also a somewhat-detrimental build-up of ear wax.)

Put on the spot and thrown off-kilter by a sudden and very public proposal of marriage, Alice needs some time to think, and consequently darts after a fascinating White Rabbit with a pocket watch and down a hole to where being off-kilter is the norm. While there, she regains her confident footing and her "muchness," enabling her to put an end to both the dragon-augmented reign of the oppressive Red Queen (Helena Bonham Carter) below ground and the plans of the ultra-starched toothy twit (Leo Bill) up above for a marital bliss that would have left her miserably bridled. She is in the end transformed, a metamorphosis underscored by the reappearance of Absolem (superbly voiced by Alan Rickman), Underland's hookah-huffing blue caterpillar, who now soars upward as a newly-emerged butterfly. It is no surprise that this Vorpal sword-wielding, Jabberwocky-slaying armored Alice who declares when back up with the upper class that it is "my life and I will decide what to do with it!" is the brainchild of screenwriter Linda Woolverton, who previously delved into distaff verve with Disney's *Beauty and the Beast* (1991) and *Mulan* (1998). Here, she has unfortunately taken what has brought singular enchantment and dragged it down into the realm of formula: a CGI-enlivened tale about coming into one's own that is meant here to empower young females, culminating in a less-than-captivating battle scene that stands out for its fantasy epic fare triteness. (The 3-D effects of the film, which was actually shot in 2-D and then converted, are not as spectacular as those in *Avatar* (2009), and some found them rather distracting.) The taste that is left in one's mouth upon leaving Underland is of something underwhelmingly ordinary.

However, even those who nodded disappointedly whenever an Underland character initially expressed the opinion that what was before them was "the wrong Alice" had to admit that Burton's *Alice* is not without its pleasures. Besides Rickman, of note is the enjoyably-morphed Matt Lucas as both Tweedledee and Tweedledum, and Stephen Fry's voicing of the Cheshire Cat. Head and shoulders above the rest, however, is Bonham Carter's Red Queen, a hugely hydrocephalic hybrid of the Queen of Hearts from Carroll's first book and the Red Queen of the second. While the actress and Burton (her real-life husband) last worked together on a film in which craniums were only partially sliced from bodies (2007's *Sweeney Todd*), here the incessant demand of the Queen is for a more thorough job. Each vile, bombastic blurt of "Off with his head!" or "Off with her head!" is emitted in much the same manner as a child projectile vomits, except what comes out here is infinitely more appealing. The Queen does indeed seem like a little girl in need of a "time out" to think about a thing or two, or perhaps a crankiness-curing nap. Bonham Carter's characterization is more than just one note, however, as viewers can clearly sense—and even sympathize with—the underlying pain that erupts in that demanding petulance, the understandable ego-deflation that comes from being stuck with a less-than-flattering, balloon-like noggin manifesting itself in autocratic bigheadedness. As the Red Queen is clearly jealous of the younger sister she usurped, Anne Hathaway's peculiar-in-her-own-way White Queen, she would surely cackle at how that character barely elicits any interest whatsoever from the audience. When the formidable and formidably-foreheaded freak (who keeps reminding one of Bette Davis' 1939 portrayal of Elizabeth I) bellows for a warm-bellied pig to soothe her aching feet, most viewers will squeal with delight at the sight.

As noticeably inflated as the potent potentate's pate is the role of the Mad Hatter, played with too little pleasing effect for all his efforts by Johnny Depp in his seventh collaboration with Burton. No longer merely the bristling and utterly bonkers tea party host, the character is now Alice's bosom friend and selfless protector, recalling the Dorothy-Scarecrow relationship in *The Wizard of Oz* (1939). (There are a number of similarities to that classic: a girl's discombobulating transportation to an exceedingly unusual, eye-poppingly-colorful but sometimes nightmarishly grim place filled with fantastic characters; the competing good and bad powerful sisters; the valiant rescue of a prisoner held in a castle; the way various people from the framing scenes are mirrored in the beings who live "Over the Rainbow" or under Nineteenth Century England.) Adding more psychological heft to the proceedings, the Hatter endures a post-traumatic stress-like flashback that allows the audience to learn of the horrors that haunt a mind already unhinged by mercury poisoning (a historically-accurate drawback to his profession). With Kabuki-white face, roaringly-orange hair and shining, insane green eyes that were enlarged during the film's lengthy post-production, Depp stands out more strikingly in a visual sense than through characterization, even though his Hatter sometimes exudes a sweet sadness that is rather affecting. He looks exactly like Elijah Wood would if that actor opted for a career in the circus instead of the cinema. An incongruous, jaw-droppingly-bad low point of *Alice* is when the Mad Hatter gets to enjoy "futterwacking vigorously" again, which sounds intriguingly risqué but is actually something off-puttingly risible. It is actually a dance in which the character's head spins around, and viewers will want to turn theirs, too—away from the screen. All the flamboyance rather overshadows Wasikowska's titular Alice, who possesses Gwyneth Paltrow-like loveliness but never remarkably compels with her performance. She is quite grave throughout, and looks almost pale enough to warrant being in one.

Through it all, Burton shoehorns as many bits of eye-enticing business (or is it sometimes merely busyness?) into his mise-en-scène as possible. There is shadowy foliage everywhere, lush and lurking, and one wonders if a branch might reach out and grab Alice like those sour-dispositioned apple trees of Oz. Hulking, enraged creatures thunderously charge through the vegetation, while others awesomely swoop down from the sky with sharp, eager talons extended. As Underland has been under siege by the Red Queen, and its landscape shows repeated evidence of her scorching fury. War has certainly not left much room for whimsy in its wake. The image of Alice climbing upon skulls to get to the Queen's castle is a particularly startling, Burtonesquely-macabre touch.

Too often, moviegoers are given good reason to grumble about how they just wasted their money on what was a lot of nonsense. Tim Burton's *Alice in Wonderland,* however, had fans of the source material grousing about the lack of it, or, at least, Carroll's version of nonsense. Utilizing a budget that exceeded $200 million to combine live action, computer generated animation, and motion capture creatures, Disney's second stab at adapting *Alice* earned over $330 million, despite the fact that most critics were left at least partially disenchanted. As in Carroll's initial book, Depp's Mad Hatter confounds Alice with a riddle to which he himself ends up having no answer. Like that stymied pair, Burton and Woolverton have failed to figure out how to make a cinematic adaptation that is as captivating as what is still cracklingly alive between the covers of Carroll's books after nearly a century and a half.

David L. Boxerbaum

CREDITS

Alice: Mia Wasikowska
The Mad Hatter: Johnny Depp
The White Queen: Anne Hathaway
The Red Queen: Helena Bonham Carter
The Knave Of Hearts: Crispin Glover
The White Rabbit: Michael Sheen
The Caterpillar: Alan Rickman
The Jabberwock: Christopher Lee
The Cheshire Cat: Stephen Fry
Tweedledee/Tweedledum: Matt Lucas
Charles Kingsleigh: Marton Csokas
Helen Kingsleigh: Lindsay Duncan
Aunt Imogene: Frances de la Tour
Hamish: Leo Bill
Origin: USA
Language: English
Released: 2010
Production: Tim Burton, Richard D. Zanuck, Joe Roth, Jennifer Todd, Suzanne Todd; Roth Films, Team Todd, Tim Burton Productions, Zanuck Company; released by Walt Disney Pictures
Directed by: Tim Burton
Written by: Linda Woolverton
Cinematography by: Dariusz Wolski
Music by: Danny Elfman
Sound: Steve Boeddeker
Editing: Chris Lebenzon
Art Direction: Stefan Dechant
Costumes: Colleen Atwood
Production Design: Robert Stromberg
MPAA rating: PG
Running time: 108 minutes

REVIEWS

Corliss, Richard. *TIME Magazine.* March 15, 2010.
Dargis, Manohla. *New York Times.* March 5, 2010.
Gleiberman, Owen. *Entertainment Weekly.* March 12, 2010.
Lane, Anthony. *New Yorker.* March 22, 2010.
Lipshutz, Jason. *Billboard.* March 6, 2010.
McCarthy, Todd. *Variety.* March 1, 2010.
Morgenstern, Joe. *Wall Street Journal.* March 5, 2010.
Mullen, Lisa. *Sight & Sound.* May 2010.
Travers, Peter. *Rolling Stone.* March 18, 2010.
Wheat, Alynda. *People.* March 15, 2010.

QUOTES

The Mad Hatter: "There is a place. Like no place on Earth. A land full of wonder, mystery, and danger! Some say to survive it: you need to be as mad as a hatter."

The Mad Hatter: "What a regrettably large head you have. I would very much like to hat it. I used to hat The White Queen, you know. Her head was so small."

TRIVIA

Director Tim Burton worked with actor Johnny Depp for the seventh time in his career on this film and it marks his sixth time working with Helena Bonham Carter.

AWARDS

Oscars 2010: Art Dir./Set Dec., Costume Des.
British Acad. 2010: Costume Des., Makeup
Nomination:
Oscars 2010: Visual FX
British Acad. 2010: Visual FX, Prod. Des., Orig. Score
Golden Globes 2011: Actor—Mus./Comedy (Depp), Film—Mus./Comedy, Orig. Score.

ALL GOOD THINGS

The perfect love story. Until it became the perfect crime.
—Movie tagline

Word of advice to couples considering marriage: Talk about the possibility of having kids before tying the knot, not after. Actually, the question of raising a family is just one thing Katie (Kirsten Dunst) does not know about David (Ryan Gosling) when they get hitched. She also does not really know the details of his mother's death when David was a young boy, or why he talks to himself, or why everyone around him believes him to be so messed up. That is not on her mind, of course, during the pair's whirlwind romance, which is portrayed with legitimate feeling by Gosling and Dunst. The actors convincingly embody two people who are so excited to have met that they are just concerned with being together now and they will shake out the small stuff later. Since *All Good Things* is inspired by New York's most notorious and unsolved missing persons case, it is fair to say that David and Katie's feel-first, think-later approach backfires.

Unfortunately, a number of promising elements in this family drama-turned-thriller also backfire before they can really pay off. For starters, director Andrew Jarecki (who tackled another story of a real-life troubled family with the documentary *Capturing the Friedmans* [2003]) and writers Marcus Hinchey and Marc Smerling craft a story that delivers rising dread but takes too long to decide what it wants to be. The movie begins with ominous imagery of dark water underneath a bridge. Above, a car pulls up to the bridge. Later, a lone figure seems to be dumping in the water bags that may contain human body parts. Other than those occasional foreboding moments, however, roughly the first half of *All Good Things* focuses on the relationship between David and Katie without providing necessary detail to their characters. What is clear: David comes from an uptight Jewish family who has become extremely wealthy and successful in the real estate business. David's father Sanford (Frank Langella) does not think much of his son but wants him in the family business anyway. David is not interested, so when he meets Katie, a cute, non-Jewish blonde whose plans to go to med school were derailed when her father passed away, the two quickly latch onto each other and onto David's interest in opening a health food store in Vermont. To Sanford's chagrin, David and Katie leave New York to open their store, which they call All Good Things.

The narrative trajectory seems to suggest a standard drama in which parents and children have different opinions. This is not at all the case. Slowly, Katie begins to get the creeps from David, who spends a lot more time smoking pot and muttering to himself than he does talking to his wife or, in particular, opening up about his traumatic past. Things do not improve after the couple moves back to New York so David can take his father up on his offer, soon after which David becomes more and more abusive to Katie. Gosling has not hit a false note in his acting life, and he effectively shifts between a socially awkward sweetheart and a scarred kid who seems to have never moved on from his painful youth. (In fact the movie shares a few similarities with *Blue Valentine* [2010], another, better film in which Gosling plays a stunted guy who cannot give his wife what she wants.) This it not enough, though, when the movie only hints at emotional damage that is never fully explored and not connected to the behavior that follows decades afterwards. Later in the film, when a major character disappears and another major character starts dressing in drag, *All Good Things* has not laid nearly enough groundwork to take such dramatic and intense left turns.

Also problematic is that the film is inspired by a real-life unsolved case. *All Good Things* fails to provide clarity as to why these events became so mysterious and why the police were unable to get to the bottom of them. Everything is about who commits the crime and how it is dramatized, whereas no parallel storyline is established to determine what made the cops struggle to uncover what the writers seem to know for sure. In fact, as the film's official biography notes, it uses both newly-discovered facts and speculation to craft its eerie tale of foggy identity and broken families. Little that happens on-screen winds up ringing true.

The film is actually based on the story of Robert Durst, who was suspected but never tried for killing his wife, who disappeared in 1982. It seems like good fodder for a documentary, and it is unfortunate that Jarecki did not make a doc that would have had more facts and compelling uncertainty about it. Sometimes *All Good Things* achieves a certain degree of poetry, such as when a therapist watches as David shrieks to uncork his bottled-up emotions or when David explains that Katie is perfect because, "There's nothing that I do that she doesn't like." Later he is very much proven wrong, but that line says a lot about the lack of connection between he and his bride and what kind of a woman this ultimately very off-center individual is looking for.

Still, what momentum the film does achieve is periodically interrupted by voiceover from David as he testifies during a trial in 2003. (Most of the movie takes place in the 1970s and 1980s.) This framing device prevents *All Good Things* from achieving the sort of rhythm and investigative pulse that would have come from a subplot about cops or reporters on the trail of the disappearance. Instead, the movie offers several well-acted scenes between Gosling and Langella as well as between Gosling and Dunst, who delivers one of her best, most controlled performances. This does not go very far, though, since this mystery simultaneously offers too much information about what may have happened and not enough about who was involved. At best, it adds up to a misfire that could have been far more chilling and thought-provoking. At worst, it is a cautionary tale for women who are not sure if their charming but possibly-disturbed significant other is endearing or just dangerous.

Matt Pais

CREDITS

David Marks: Ryan Gosling
Katie Marks: Kirsten Dunst

Sanford Marks: Frank Langella
Deborah Lehrman: Lily Rabe
Lauren Fleck: Kristen Wiig
Janice Rizzo: Diane Venora
Malvern Bump: Philip Baker Hall
Daniel Marks: Michael Esper
Jim McCarthy: Nick Offerman
Richard Panatierre: John Cullum
Origin: USA
Language: English
Released: 2010
Production: Marc Smerling, Andrew Jarecki, Bruno Papandrea, Michael London; Groundswell Productions, Hit the Ground Running Films; released by Magnolia Pictures
Directed by: Andrew Jarecki
Written by: Marcus Hinchey, Marc Smerling
Cinematography by: Michael Seresin
Music by: Rob Simonsen
Sound: Pavel Wdowczak
Music Supervisor: Sue Jacobs
Editing: David Rosenbloom, Shelby Siegel
Art Direction: Russell Barnes
Costumes: Michael Clancy
Production Design: Wynn Thomas
MPAA rating: R
Running time: 101 minutes

REVIEWS

Bernardinelli, James. *ReelViews.* December 6, 2010.
Buckwalter, Ian. *NPR.* December 6, 2010.
Chang, Justin. *Variety.* December 6, 2010.
Dargis, Manohla. *New York Times.* December 6, 2010.
Fear, David. *Time Out New York.* December 6, 2010.
Orange, Michelle. *Movieline.* December 6, 2010.
Pinkerton, Nick. *Village Voice.* December 6, 2010.
Reed, Rex. *New York Observer.* December 6, 2010.
Tobias, Scott. *AV Club.* December 6, 2010.
Travers, Peter. *Rolling Stone.* December 6, 2010.

TRIVIA

Ryan Gosling sent Kirsten Dunst flowers because he felt so bad after the scene where he had to pull her hair.

ALPHA AND OMEGA

A pawsome 3D adventure.
—Movie tagline

Box Office: $25 million

For wee watchers who snuggle up with stuffed animals at night on up to grown moviegoers who prefer more dynamic bed companions, there is nothing like a uniquely-absorbing story of uncertain outcome, captivating characters, spellbinding visuals, and a tune that cannot help but be hummed for days on end, much to the annoyance of others. More to the point, there is nothing like any of those things in *Alpha and Omega,* an innocuous, formidably-forgettable animated feature that may be useful at Pixar and DreamWorks to remind their staffs of what to avoid. It is perhaps most notable as one of the last completed projects in the long, storied career of Dennis Hopper.

With characters named Humphrey and Kate, and a love story in which the hearts of two disparate individuals gradually come to beat as one while being tested by travails amidst remote, unfamiliar environs, one cannot watch *Alpha and Omega* without recalling Humphrey Bogart's Charlie and Kate Hepburn's Rose in *The African Queen* (1952). Those responsible for *Alpha and Omega* openly admitted deriving a degree of inspiration from that indelible tale of polar opposites who meet, melt, and meld at the Equator. Wanting to give it an affectionate nod is wholly understandable. What is much harder to comprehend, however, is how those responsible for *Alpha and Omega* could have labored under the delusion that they were making a classic film of their own. The film's production notes expressed optimism that it would "appeal to both adults and children for generations to come," and was capable of providing enduring inspiration. However, despite all this straining to make a majestic mountain out of a middling molehill, *Alpha and Omega,* whether viewed in 2D or generally unspectacular 3D, ended up awfully flat.

The protagonists paired in the title are young wolves whose coupling is unthinkable in their society. Such carnivores of different strata cannot canoodle, let alone become life partners and procreate. Alpha Kate (voiced by Hayden Panettiere) is a highly-promising teenaged leader-in-the-making who possesses a strong sense of responsibility. Dreamily drooling over her lupine loveliness is contrastingly-carefree Humphrey (Justin Long), an Omega whose time is spent having fun with lightheartedly-named buddies Salty (Brian Donovan), Shakey (Kevin Sussman), and Mooch (Eric Price). This good-natured goof-off's usefulness, viewers are told, is to remind even the most austere wolves to whoop it up once in a while, and not be so quick to get their "fur in a bunch." "Silly Omegas," says Kate, although her put-down is warmed up nicely by a fond, sweet smile. Her own lot in life, however, is duty, not daffiness.

As part of that duty, Kate agrees to an arranged marriage that will ensure harmony with the encroaching Eastern wolves. For the greater good, this daughter of pack pooh-bah Winston (Danny Glover) will unite with the Alpha son of the Eastern's Tony (Hopper), thus enabling everyone to peaceably cooperate in the savage ripping apart of reindeer within Canada's Jasper National Park. (Tony is snarlingly out-of-sorts, as much from the lack of a chiropractor for his back as from the dearth of caribou for his stomach.) Unfortunately, while showoff Garth (Chris Carmack) has an impressively-hunky physique, his howl is thoroughly-embarrassing. While birds plummet from the sky (to mild comedic effect) during his mortifying attempts, Kate will not be falling for Garth.

Of course, everyone watching *Alpha and Omega* knows that Humphrey would be a better (and beneficially balancing) mate for Kate, and cupid's arrow hits them both in the form of matching tranquilizer darts to the derriere. The road to true love is a bumpy one leading to Idaho, where the two are released from cages into that state's wolf-deficient woods. The humans' hope that repopulation will result sounds mighty fine to smitten Humphrey, but Kate's one-track mind is focused on scoring a ride back to Jasper in time to prevent the fur from flying. Thus, the two derive help rather than sustenance from a golf-loving French-Canadian goose (Larry Miller) and his duck caddy Paddy (Price again), and are soon homeward bound. While their uninspired journey North through the wilds is tame enough to prevent the film's diminutive target audience from having nightmares later on, adults may find themselves nodding off for some peaceful slumbering on the spot.

As Humphrey and Kate repeatedly come to each other's aid, what has been entirely expected comes to pass: she loosens up, and he shows substance by courageously and resourcefully rising to the occasion. Despite being initially crushed by her pressing on with the plans to marry Garth, Humphrey nevertheless heroically saves Kate from being trampled to death by stampeding caribou, and mutual love is finally professed. Thus, like trepidatious, tradition-bound parents who finally drop their objections to a mixed marriage, Winston, his wife, Eve (an amusingly potent Vicki Lewis), and Tony resignedly give their consent to not one but two Alpha-Omega unions, as Garth is now both literally and figuratively more in tune with Kate's Omega sister, Lilly (Christina Ricci). As the PG film euphemistically puts it, both couples will get to happily "howl together" for years to come.

While more than a few kids may have squirmed during *Alpha and Omega* due to the onset of boredom, their accompanying caretakers may have done so because of the story's constant allusions to canine copulation, regardless of their being suitably veiled. Perhaps it all safely sailed over lower-placed heads. However, most of the humor here is unquestionably on the juveniles' level. "Why do they call this Rabbit Poo Mountain?" Garth asks at one point. "Because this is where rabbits poo," is Lilly's response. Tykes may indeed guffaw heartily. Anyone else who does so should probably seek help.

As the *Washington Post*'s Michael O'Sullivan correctly put it, *Alpha and Omega* "isn't so much howlingly bad as it is howlingly boring." (The film's music and dance sequences may qualify for both, however.) It is the first in a three-picture deal between Lionsgate and Mumbai-based Crest Animation Studios. The forthcoming follow-up, *Norm of the North* does not exactly sound like fresh material: An animal that inadvertently left its native land races to dutifully avert a disaster back home that threatens its brethren. (Instead of the endangered wolf population, the environmental concern will be melting polar ice cap.) This initial offering was made on a budget of $20 million and succeeded in grossing just past that, despite the fact that most critics responded like O'Sullivan and, taking a cue from Humphrey, lifted their leg on *Alpha and Omega*.

David L. Boxerbaum

CREDITS

Kate: Hayden Panettiere (Voice)
Humphrey: Justin Long (Voice)
Tony: Dennis Hopper (Voice)
Winston: Danny Glover (Voice)
Garth: Chris Carmack (Voice)
Lilly: Christina Ricci (Voice)
Marcel: Larry Miller (Voice)
Paddy/Mooch: Eric Price (Voice)
Eve: Vicki Lewis (Voice)
Salty: Brian Donovan (Voice)
Shakey: Kevin Sussman (Voice)
Origin: USA
Language: English
Released: 2010
Production: Richard Rick, Ken Katsumoto, Steve Moore; Crest Animation; released by Lionsgate
Directed by: Anthony Bell, Ben Gluck
Written by: Chris Denk, Steve Moore
Music by: Chris P. Bacon
Sound: Paula Fairfield
Music Supervisor: Jay Faires, Tracy McKnight
Editing: Scott Anderson
MPAA rating: PG
Running time: 88 minutes

REVIEWS

Barker, Andrew. *Variety.* September 13, 2010.
Bowles, Scott. *USA Today.* September 16, 2010.
Hale, Mike. *New York Times.* September 17, 2010.
Jones, Oliver. *People.* September 27, 2010.
Markovitz, Adam. *Entertainment Weekly.* September 17, 2010.
Nicholson, Amy. *BoxOffice.* September 16, 2010.

O'Sullivan, Michael. *Washington Post.* September 17, 2010.
Russo, Tom. *Boston Globe.* September 17, 2010.

QUOTES

Berry-Eating Wolves: "Stop the insanity! Go organic!"

TRIVIA

The film mirrors the real life story of Yellowstone National Park receiving wolves from Alberta, Canada to repopulate the park.

THE AMERICAN

Box Office: $35 million

Focus Features may have advertised Anton Corbijn's *The American* as a descendant of the *Bourne* franchise, featuring nearly every shot of star George Clooney in the previews that sold it as an action adventure. The marketing strategy both worked and backfired. The film opened with an impressive $13 million, way more than it ever would have made in its first frame if people knew that it was more of a European art movie than a shoot-em-up thriller. But viewers felt cheated and word-of-mouth hurt the film, keeping it from the audience that might have appreciated it in the first place. *The American* is an excellent piece of work, a movie with a European sensibility that just happens to star one of America's biggest stars. It fell into that odd gray area that keeps movies like this from being made by skittish producers. Neither mainstream enough for the multiplex nor deemed artistic enough for indie film lovers, *The American* was too easily dismissed by both audiences. In fact, there is reason for every audience to check out this very well-made paranoia thriller about a man coming to terms with the final days of his life and perhaps finding elements of beauty and joy in ways that he never had before.

Rowan Joffe, son of the legendary director Roland, adapted the book *A Very Private Gentleman* by Martin Booth into a very precise, somber, dark slice of character study about a man leaving a profession for which there are no exit interviews or traditional severance packages—a hitman. Clooney's title character, Jack, is introduced with a drink in one hand while the other one rests on a naked woman, but one should not get the impression that this will be some Sean Connery-esque riff on James Bond. Immediately, there is a melancholy in Clooney's eyes, as if he can sense something is wrong or something is ending. The next morning, as Jack and his lady love cross a frozen lake, he spots a set of footprints. Moments later, everyone around him is dead, including the woman and the assassins sent to kill him.

Like any hitman with a target now on his head, Jack goes into hiding while he tries to figure out who burned him. He first heads to Rome to meet with one of the few people he feels he can still trust, an old friend named Pavel (Johan Leysen), who guides him to a small Italian city and instructs him to wait it out while he figures out what exactly is going on. Rather than killing only time, why not take on another assignment? So Pavel gives Jack a job to build a high-powered weapon to ends that neither Jack nor the audience knows. All Jack knows from his lovely contact Mathilde (Thekla Reuten) is that he is supposed to build a semi-automatic weapon with the range of a rifle and a silencer. In one of many great, subtle details, Corbijn presents Mathilde three times; as a blonde, brunette, and redhead. Jack is on such shifting sands in which he can never be sure who to trust that even his contact never looks quite the same.

Jack spends most of his time doing...a lot of nothing. He walks to the café. He drinks some coffee. He works on his weapon. As he spends his time peering around every corner waiting for what could be the last trigger click he hears, Jack spends time in the sway of what many men reach to in their final days—religion and sex. The former is represented by a Priest (Paolo Bonacelli) he befriends and the latter by a prostitute (Violante Placido). Without any overt expression of it, and possibly in ways he does not even consciously understand, Jack is looking for a bit of peace and love in what he knows could be his final days. With large passages free of any dialogue at all much less the cheesy tripe that usually accompanies stories like this one, Corbijn, Joffe, and Clooney perfectly convey the story of a very, very sad man finally reaching out for a scant degree of happiness that he probably declined to himself he even wanted for decades. Watching Jack appreciate a butterfly on a beautiful girl's shoulder, one gets the impression that is the first time something of the natural world has moved him in such a way.

George Clooney gives one of his best performances here, finding the deep melancholy of a man who has become attuned to a solitary life of restraint. One gets the feeling that Jack almost identifies with the Priest and the prostitute because of the similarities they have with a hitman in that, like the Priest, Jack must live a life largely alone and, like the prostitute, he cannot get attached to his assignments. Clooney distinctly turns *The American* into a ticking clock film—perhaps he can find one more job, have one more passionate affair, or just drink a final cup of Italian coffee before the contract catches up with him. Jack seems to have given up on happiness years ago and now tries, however slightly, to find a modicum of it in his final days. Clooney, one of the best and most underrated actors working today, does an amazing amount of acting with almost no dialogue at all. The genius of the performance is in the way Jack walks the streets, the distant way he makes love to his hooker with the heart of gold, or the way he matter-of-factly builds a killing device. He completely discards his movie star persona and disappears into the character the way he has in his best performances. It reminds one of the foreign films of the 1970s in which great American stars would give themselves to talented European directors (*Last Tango in Paris* [1972], *The Passenger* [1975], more). It often took years for those films to be appreciated as well.

Brian Tallerico

CREDITS

Jack/Edward: George Clooney
Father Benedetto: Paolo Bonacelli
Larry: Bruce Altman
Clara: Violante Placido
Mathilde: Thekla Reuten
Pavel: Johan Leysen
Origin: USA, United Kingdom
Language: English
Released: 2010
Production: Anne Carey, Jill Green, George Clooney, Ann Wingate, Grant Heslov; This Is That, Greenlit, Smokehouse, Twins Financing; released by Focus Features
Directed by: Anton Corbijn
Written by: Rowan Joffe
Cinematography by: Martin Ruhe
Music by: Herbert Gronemeyer
Sound: Chris Munro
Editing: Andrew Hulme
Art Direction: Domenico Sica
Costumes: Suttirat Anne Larlbarb
Production Design: Mark Digby
MPAA rating: R
Running time: 105 minutes

REVIEWS

Ebert, Roger. *Chicago Sun-Times.* September 1, 2010.
Edelstein, David. *New York Magazine.* September 1, 2010.
Howell, Peter. *Toronto Star.* September 1, 2010.
Pais, Matt. *Metromix.com.* August 31, 2010.
Poland, David. *Movie City News.* September 1, 2010.
Puig, Claudia. *USA Today.* September 1, 2010.
Scott, A.O.. *New York Times.* September 1, 2010.
Tobias, Scott. *AV Club.* September 1, 2010.
Rickey, Carrie. *Philadelphia Inquirer.* September 1, 2010.
Zacharek, Stephanie. *Movieline.* September 1, 2010.

QUOTES

Father Benedetto: "You cannot deny the existence of hell. You live in it. It is a place without love."

TRIVIA

The tattoo on Jack's right shoulder reads "Ex Gladio Equitas," which translates as "Justice From the Sword."

ANIMAL KINGDOM

A crime story.
—Movie tagline

Box Office: $1 million

From the enduring popularity of *The Godfather* (1972) and its two sequels to the hugely influential nature of *Scarface* (1983) straight on to recent hit films like *American Gangster* (2007), the United States has an indisputable entertainment fixation with crime and families who trade in illicit behavior. Nowhere was this obsession more readily apparent than during the wildly-successful HBO run of *The Sopranos*, which engendered identification with James Gandolfini's mafia boss to a disconcerting degree, and even led 2010 Delaware Republican senatorial candidate Christine O'Donnell to wax rhapsodic about the "traditional upbringing" of the fictitious Soprano family.

Of course, florid gangster tales are not limited to the United States, as Vincent Cassel and director Jean-François Richet's César®-winning *Mesrine* (2010) double bill amply demonstrates. Adding to this recent wave of foreign felony mayhem is writer-director David Michôd's Australian import *Animal Kingdom,* winner of the Grand Jury Prize at this year's Sundance Festival, and a superb drama which slots favorably alongside fellow Down Under crime tales *Lantana* (2001) and *The Square* (2010). An involving, rangy and sneakily ambitious movie about one overwhelmed kid's attempts to escape the sad, cold shadow of fate foisted upon him by his family, the film was a solid box office performer overseas, to the tune of $4.4 million. But *Animal Kingdom* never found its footing with Stateside audiences, with distributor Sony Pictures Classics somehow unable to translate its overwhelming critical support (it received an astounding 96 percent Fresh rating on Rotten Tomatoes) into theatrical receipts of even one million dollars.

The movie unfolds against an unfussy, decidedly non-glamorous criminal backdrop of modern-day Melbourne, and opens with a heartbreakingly frank and plaintive scene in which a slightly hulking teenager, Joshua "J" Cody (James Frecheville), discovers his unconscious junkie mom, calls an estranged family member, and simply says, "Mum's gone and OD'ed, and died." With nowhere else to go, J gets taken in by his doting grandmother Janine, aka Smurf (Jacki Weaver), which would seem to be a good thing. Problem is, she is the den mother to a cabal of ne'er-do-wells, whose armed bank robberies have made them all marked men.

Pope Cody (Ben Mendelsohn) is in hiding, on the run from a gang of renegade detectives who want him dead and have no qualms with vigilante justice. His business partner and best friend, Barry Brown (Joel Eegerton), wants out of the game, recognizing that their days of old-school banditry are all but over. Another of J's uncles, the speed-addicted Craig Cody (Sullivan Stapleton), is making a fortune in the illicit substances trade, while the youngest Cody brother, Darren (Luke Ford), is seemingly just along for the ride. When tensions between family and police result in more bloodletting, J finds himself at the center of a revenge plot that threatens to ensnare innocent bystanders, including his new girlfriend Nicky (Laura Wheelwright). As one police officer, Nathan Leckie (Guy Pearce), tries to flip him and make him a protected source, J must figure out where he fits in this paranoid and vengeful underworld, and whether there is anyone he can really trust.

In his narrative feature debut, Michôd smartly trades in organic rather than artificial thrills, making a movie about the legacy of violence that does not often indulge in it. A bullet fired with no special reason seemingly holds no particular interest for him; he is more intrigued by what pulls one toward violence, in both biology and environment, and whether those tethering bonds can be escaped. So in lieu of incessant mouthing off, or an action piece set merely to satisfy some studio executive's idea of proper pacing, Michôd instead works to capture the subtle ways that men (particularly criminal-types) try to establish dominance over one another. (Early in their relationship, Pope hassles and browbeats J over washing his hands; later he leers, "Are you gay—just tell me?") Michôd also knows the value of a pregnant pause, and so is content to let a lingering, silent glance, or an extra second-and-a-half in an edit substitute for someone pushed up against a wall or backed into a corner. The result is a movie that pulses with a low hum of danger and works its way into an viewer's psyche slowly, so when those types of things do happen, they hold even more tension and importance.

As a moment's reflection upon its title suggests, the film is set in a world of eat-or-be-eaten survival, shot through with anxiety. Michôd and cinematographer Adam Arkapaw's shot selection and camerawork convey this menacing portent without ever dipping into mannered affectation.

The rest of the film's considerable pull comes from its superlative ensemble acting. Frecheville believably exudes naivety and the tuned-out eyes of a teenager who would rather be anywhere than in the situation and setting they find themselves in, and is a great anchor for *Animal Kingdom*. But his is not the only excellent performance. The lanky Mendehlson—who sort of resembles Chris Parnell by way of Wallace Shawn, or perhaps vice versa—wrings atypical hazard out of his characterization of Pope, eschewing showy affect and largely even electric temper, but slipping in smart, understated signs of a coddled man-child whose every calculation masks a disturbing sociopathy. Finally, as a quietly venomous matriarch making increasingly cold and calculated decisions about her extended family, and with whom she should cast her lot, Weaver is chilling, and worthy of wider awards consideration.

Though it initially seems a strange title fit, *Animal Kingdom* eventually proves a deadly appropriate moniker for Michôd's examination of adolescent coming-of-age amidst terrible circumstances. Evincing a rare, virtuosic combination of insight and directorial restraint, Michôd posits that there are irremovable animalistic elements and tendencies in all of us—which may go a long way toward explaining our preoccupation with violence.

Brent Simon

CREDITS

Janine "Smurf" Cody: Jacki Weaver
Det. Senior Sgt. Nathan Leckie: Guy Pearce
Andrew "Pope" Cody: Ben Mendelsohn
Barry "Baz" Brown: Joel Edgerton
Joshua "J" Cody: James Frecheville
Darren Cody: Luke Ford
Craig Cody: Sullivan Stapleton
Ezra White: Daniel Wyllie
Det. Justin Norris: Anthony Hayes
Det. Randall Roache: Justin Rosniak
Alicia Henry: Susan Prior
Justine Hopper: Anne Lise Phillips
Nicky Henry: Laura Wheelwright
Catherine Brown: Mirrah Foulkes
Gus Emery: Clayton Jacobson
Origin: Australia
Language: English
Released: 2009
Production: Liz Watts; Porchlight Films Prod., Screen Australia; released by Sony Pictures Classics, Paladin
Directed by: David Michôd
Written by: David Michôd
Cinematography by: Adam Arkapaw

Music by: Antony Partos
Sound: Philippe Decrausaz
Editing: Luke Doolan
Art Direction: Janie Parker
Costumes: Cappi Ireland
Production Design: Josephine Ford
MPAA rating: R
Running time: 112 minutes

REVIEWS

Burr, Ty. *Boston Globe.* August 19, 2010.
Colin, Covert. *Inneapolis Star Tribune.* August 26, 2010.
Corliss, Richard. *Time Magazine.* August 20, 2010.
Edelstein, David. *New York Magazine.* August 2, 2010.
Honeycutt, Kirk. *Hollywood Reporter.* August 13, 2010.
Lemire, Christy. *Associated Press.* August 12, 2010.
Long, Tom. *Detroit News.* September 3, 2010.
Schager, Nick. *Slant Magazine.* August 8, 2010.
Schwarzbaum, Lisa. *Entertainment Weekly.* August 11, 2010.
Turan, Kenneth. *Los Angeles Times.* August 12, 2010.

QUOTES

Janine Cody: "I'm having trouble trying to find my positive spin. I'm usually very good at it. Usually it's right there, and I can just have it. But I'm having trouble finding it now."

TRIVIA

The part of Janine Cody was written by writer/director David Michod for Jacki Weaver.

AWARDS

Nomination:

Oscars 2010: Support. Actress (Weaver)
Golden Globes 2011: Support. Actress (Weaver).

ANOTHER YEAR

Some might look at the title for *Another Year* and think it incomplete. *Another Year, Another Mike Leigh Movie About Quiet Desperation in Middle Class England.* At this point, art house savvy moviegoers either embrace Leigh's films or avoid them completely. His work is an acquired taste. Yet few filmmakers continually nail down the human condition, particularly the sadness that creeps into everyday life, even with those who are seemingly happy-go-lucky. Leigh is unmatched in his ability to dissect his characters' inner turmoil as well as their inner joy. His methodical approach to reaching these mostly saddened peaks may not be the recipe for a fun night out at the movies, but the ensemble of English actors often assembled for his films are almost always at the top of their game and the material itself can be hard to shake off.

Another Year opens with a typical Leigh character: A sad, lonely woman (Imelda Staunton) who cannot sleep. She sees a doctor who will not prescribe her the sleeping pills she craves, but rather a lesser prescription and the insistence that she see a counselor. It becomes clear with every pressing question that the woman's loneliness is consuming her. Her husband drinks, her son still lives at home and her daughter only comes home when she wants something. The only way out of this depression is sleep, perhaps an eternal one. A couple scenes later, this same woman is seeing the counselor and cannot remember the last time she was happy.

The counselor is one half of a happy couple, played by Ruth Sheen and Jim Broadbent. Gerri (Sheen), the counselor, is a sympathetic ear with a capacity for compassion that has its limits outside the office. Tom (Broadbent) works as an engineering geologist. They are a couple one would hope to know and have in their lives as they get older, the kind of couple who make it easy to drop in on at a moment's notice. Their lives seemed to have worked out just fine. Working a few offices away from Gerri is Mary (Lesley Manville), a highly talkative, flighty, chain-smoking alcoholic whose idea of a long-term life plan is to buy a used car.

The movie takes place over the course of a year and is broken up into four parts, one for each season. The first season is spring. For this segment, Mary is a houseguest for a night in Tom and Gerri's modest home. Mary, who believes their son Joe (Oliver Maltman) will be joining them, tries to conceal her disappointment as she learns it will just be the three of them for the evening. Mary helps herself to drink after drink just to make it through the evening and pours out personal confessions as a result. "Sometimes I feel like someone else," she says. Once the conversation turns to politics and practical matters, she finds herself unmatched intellectually by Tom. As she gets more drunk, she becomes more and more of a handful.

Mary mistakes a brief exchange with their son Joe as flirtatious. Joe is about twenty years younger than Mary, but she will not let it go. Tom and Gerri inquire Joe about his love life, which is, for the time being, non-existent. Come summer, the film's second segment, another houseguest pays Tom and Gerri a visit. Ken (Peter Wight), a husky, elder, longtime friend of the couple is also a lonely soul. When Tom and Gerri rattle off the list of attendees for the upcoming barbeque, his ears perk up when he learns Mary will be attending. When asked what Ken would do with his time of retirement, he answers "Don't know. Eat, drink, be merry." It would seem he and Mary would be a perfect couple, but he is nowhere near Mary's idea of a soulmate. She has eyes for a younger, more virile man, namely Joe, who will soon give his heart to another woman.

As autumn rolls in, the unrequited desire Mary has for Joe (or anyone who will have her) becomes increasingly desperate as her welcome slowly wears out for Tom and Gerri. Even when Joe's affections become more and more out of reach, her sense of personal boundaries become more and more blurred. Soon, Mary's visits become a source of annoyance. To add insult to injury, Tom and Gerri cheerfully acknowledge that they always thought of Mary as an "auntie" to Joe. Rarely has the sting of growing older been felt than in Manville's performance during this moment.

In the winter segment, Leigh's darker tendencies begin to surface. The rage so often felt by the central characters in his previous films takes center stage. Mary's flightiness is traded in for Tom and Gerri's hateful nephew who has lost his mother. Like Mary, he tends to solve his problems with a bottle of wine. It is here that Tom and Gerri's perpetual niceness is put to the test. While they certainly do not want to be in the same room with him much longer, they appear to have an unspoken understanding of his anger. The winter segments ends on a scene typical of Leigh's: Two characters converse quietly with long passages of silence that speak louder than anything else.

The character of Mary is a brilliant collaboration between Leigh and Manville and the sort of multi-layered creation that is typical of Leigh's films. Mary is a character who when she enters the room, no one else can get a word in edgewise and she rarely has anything to say that is worth listening to. The miracle of Leigh's writing and Manville's performance is that the viewer is drawn to her every gesture and expression. It is obvious that she is not entirely welcome in this household, but Tom and Gerri put up with it politely (another common trait of English behavior that Leigh has explored in the past).

As Tom and Gerri (whose names are eventually mocked), Jim Broadbent and Ruth Sheen are a lovely couple. Their easygoing nature and convincing relationship remind one of how deceptively easy it can look to be an actor. They are a sympathetic ear and a pair of souls to lean on in times of need and they do it selflessly, after which time they are content to be with one another, either looking at the Sunday paper or laying in bed dissecting the evening's events with warm symmetry. They may very well be the nicest people Leigh has ever put in a film. The viewer is given little history about this couple, but it hardly seems to matter. They clearly fit and probably have for decades now.

The downward spiral of Mary is one of Leigh's great triumphs as a screenwriter. The viewer sees her only through the eyes of those around her who can stand her for a long period of time. Most of her life mistakes happen off-screen, but the affects of her poor life decisions are readily apparent. In the end, it is clear that Mary is a blank slate, someone who tries to be everything to everybody who is in the room with her. Every time she has a cigarette, she explains "I don't even really smoke." She says this to at least three different people. She has little sense of herself, which makes it that much harder for anyone around her to get a sense of what makes her tick.

Another Year is one of Leigh's best films. In the end, the theme of loneliness has a harsh conclusion by way of almost bookending the first and last scene. The patient seeking sleeping pills to cure whatever ails her could very well be Mary's future self. For if there is no one around to listen, what is the point of talking to one's self? "It's good to have someone to talk to," she says rather stoically. Mary has gone from co-worker to friend to patient. The movie's final moment of a cheerful, congenial family gathering has never carried such sadness. Leigh has always been a master of effortlessly juxtaposing behavior with mood and with *Another Year,* he may have created one of the happiest and yet maybe the saddest film of his career.

Collin Souter

CREDITS

Tom: Jim Broadbent
Gerri: Ruth Sheen
Mary: Lesley Manville
Joe: Oliver Maltman
Ken: Peter Wight
Ronnie: David Bradley
Carl: Martin Savage
Jack: Philip Davis
Janet: Imelda Staunton
Katie: Karina Fernandez
Tanya: Michele Austin
Origin: United Kingdom
Language: English
Released: 2010
Production: Georgina Lowe; Thin Man; released by Sony Pictures Classics
Directed by: Mike Leigh
Written by: Mike Leigh
Cinematography by: Dick Pope
Music by: Gary Yershon
Sound: Tim Fraser

Editing: Jon Gregory
Art Direction: Andrew Rothschild
Costumes: Jacqueline Durran
Production Design: Simon Beresford
MPAA rating: PG-13
Running time: 129 minutes

REVIEWS

Bennett, Ray. *Hollywood Reporter.* July 6, 2010.
Denby, David. *New Yorker.* December 27, 2010.
Edelstein, David. *New York Magazine.* December 27, 2010.
Edwards, David. *Daily Mirror.* November 5, 2010.
Felperin, Leslie. *Variety.* July 6, 2010.
Kenny, Glenn. *MSN Movies.* December 30, 2010.
Legel, Laremy. *Film.com.* May 26, 2010.
Noh, David. *Film Journal International.* December 16, 2010.
Scott, A.O. *New York Times.* December 29, 2010.
Ultichi, Joe. *Cinematical.com.* May 28, 2010.

AWARDS

Nomination:

Oscars 2010: Orig. Screenplay
British Acad. 2010: Support. Actress (Manville), Alexander Korda Award.

THE A-TEAM

> *There is no plan B.*
> —Movie tagline

Box Office: $77 million

Joe Carnahan's *The A-Team* is an unapologetically testosterone-driven slice of macho escapism that delivers on its own terms without displaying an ounce of the ambition that could have pushed it to a wider audience in the surprisingly-crowded summer season of 2010. As the pop culture icons are preparing yet-another logic-defying mission in the final act of the film, Col. Hannibal Smith says "Overkill is underrated." It could easily have been the creative motto of the entire production. This is a film that does not merely forget subtlety; it laughs at the very concept. The potential summer blockbuster stretched suspension of disbelief to the breaking point for most critics and movie goers but if a film should be judged on how well it succeeds on its intended purpose, *The A-Team* is an enjoyable success. It may not be a masterpiece, but a film based on the television program that turned Mr. T into a star should not have had such lofty aspirations.

Most films based on characters originally created for decades-old television programs go the easy route of retelling (or in the overly common vernacular of the Hollywood agent, "rebooting") the origin story of their source for a new generation. It would not be a bad guess to assume that the 2010 version of *The A-Team* would re-imagine how the band got together, but Carnahan and writers Brian Bloom and Skip Woods get that out of the way in the opening scenes of the film, first introducing us to a captive Col. Smith (Neeson) in the hands of corrupt Mexican cops who nearly feed the grizzled veteran to their dogs. Of course, Hannibal escapes and just happens to cross paths with Bosco 'B. A.' Baracus (Quinton 'Rampage' Jackson) in the middle of the desert near the border between Mexico and Arizona. Hannibal and B.A. find unity through their Ranger tattoos and go on to rescue Lt. 'Face' Peck (Bradley Cooper) before the suave alpha male is killed by the bad guy whose wife just slept with the enemy. The trio quickly moves on to hire the possibly-insane pilot Murdock (Sharlto Copley) and "The A-Team" is born.

Carnahan's film flashes forward several years after the team has run hundreds of missions. They happen to be in Iraq as the U.S. presence there is being withdrawn and they cross paths with a C.I.A. agent named "Lynch" (Patrick Wilson)—although it is made clear that every agent comes with an alias, often Lynch, which instantly casts the G-man in shades of potential enemy—and a General named Morrison (Gerald McRaney). Lynch and Morrison ask the A-Team to run a final Iraq mission and stop the hijacking of some counterfeiting plates from Baghdad but the plates are stolen, Morrison is killed, and the legendary quartet is accused of going on an unassigned mission. The men are stripped of their rank and sent to prison, but there is no way four walls can stop The A-Team from clearing their names and enacting revenge on the people who framed them.

The Baghdad-counterfeiting mission is something of a mess. The editing is choppy and the action choreography makes it difficult to tell exactly what is going on. It was a fatal flaw for many critics, including Roger Ebert, who accused the film of being too difficult to follow in its action. However, after that Baghdad mission and through some over-the-top action sequences that follow, Carnahan seems to get a tighter grip on the proceedings. The second half of the film really is not as choppy as some critics made it out to be and a few of the action sequences, including one involving a tank "flying" to the ground and the final sequence, are actually among the best conceived and executed of the year.

As for the cast, the results are mixed. Bradley Cooper finally displays the screen charisma that agents and Hollywood producers were convinced he had years ago but that he never really fulfilled. Cooper often falls into lazy traps as an actor but he is perfectly cast here, believably playing suave, smart, and deadly. Neeson and

Wilson are actors who almost always work in every scene they take on and the case is no different here. Copley gets a few movie-stealing moments despite one of the most-fluctuating accents of the year but Jackson mumbles far more than is necessary for the role and Jessica Biel, who plays the one government agent on the boy's side, is horrendously miscast. She is not believable as a tough g-woman or as a love interest for Face. The film nearly screeches to a halt every time she appears. It is possible that no actress could have successfully survived such a testosterone-laden film but Biel was still the wrong choice.

There is not a single subtle moment in *The A-Team* but one would be hard-pressed to find one in the entirety of the run of the popular television series as well. Just as that program did for its target audience, *The A-Team* works when viewed purely as tongue-in-cheek, adrenalin-pumping, testosterone-filled lunacy. Perhaps in a summer that included such cerebrally-challenging escapism as *Toy Story 3* (2010) and *Inception* (2010), critics and audiences demanded a bit too much of a film based on an 1980s action program, but *The A-Team* did what most films based on nostalgic properties fail to do—stayed true to its source.

Brian Tallerico

CREDITS

Col. John "Hannibal" Smith: Liam Neeson
Lt. Templeton "Faceman" Peck: Bradley Cooper
Capt. "Howling Mad" Murdock: Sharlto Copley
Capt. Bosco "B.A." Baracus: Quinton "Rampage" Jackson
Capt. Charisa Sosa: Jessica Biel
Lynch: Patrick Wilson
Pike: Brian Bloom
Gen. Morrison: Gerald McRaney
Director MacCready: Henry Czerny
Chopshop Jay: Omari Hardwick
Lynch #2: Jon Hamm
Gen. Tuco: Yul Vazquez

Gammons: Maury Sterling
Himself: Dirk Benedict (Cameo)
Himself: Dwight Schultz (Cameo)
Origin: USA
Language: English
Released: 2010
Production: Stephen J. Cannell, Jules Daly, Ridley Scott, Tony Scott, Iain Smith; Dune Entertainment, Scott Free; released by 20th Century Fox
Directed by: Joe Carnahan
Written by: Skip Woods, Michael Brandt, Derek Haas
Cinematography by: Mauro Fiore
Music by: Alan Silvestri
Editing: Roger Barton
Sound: Jim May
Art Direction: Michael Diner
Costumes: Betsy Heimann
Production Design: Charles Wood
MPAA rating: PG-13
Running time: 117 minutes

REVIEWS

Childress, Erik. *eFilmCritic.com.* June 11, 2010.
Ebert, Roger. *The Chicago Sun-Times.* June 10, 2010.
Honeycutt, Kirk. *The Hollywood Reporter.* June 9, 2010.
Howell, Peter. *Toronto Star.* June 10, 2010.
LaSalle, Mick. *San Francisco Chronicle.* June 10, 2010.
Lowry, Brian. *Variety.* June 9, 2010.
Pais, Matt. *Metromix.com* June 10, 2010.
Phillips, Michael. *Chicago Tribune.* June 10, 2010.
Rich, Katey. *CinemaBlend.com.* June 10, 2010.
Roeper, Richard. *RichardRoeper.com.* June 11, 2010.

QUOTES

Lynch: "Wow, that's awesome! That looks exactly like *Call Of Duty*, doesn't it?"

TRIVIA

"Die Vergeltung" is a German word for "The Retaliation," which was also the name of the ship at the end of the movie.

B

BABIES
(Bebes)

Everybody loves...
—Movie tagline

Box Office: $7 million

Thomas Balmes' documentary *Babies* presents itself as a nature film of sorts, only instead of following animals around for an extended period of time, it follows the lives of four newborn babies in four different locations: Namibia, Mongolia, Tokyo and San Francisco. None of the babies will meet (at least, not in the movie) and the director has no grand plan for creating a narrative drive. The movie exists solely to observe the behavior of babies for eighty minutes. There is no narrator, social commentary or desire to expose a greater truth about child-rearing. The diversity of the locations themselves serve as enough of a purpose to explore the different customs and methods of raising a child, either single-handedly or as a couple.

In Namibia, a mother gives birth to what appears to be her second child. She lives in a small desert community apparently living off the land. The movie opens with her new son, Ponijao, sitting next to his older brother (presumably). They start fighting over something. Ponijao bites his older brother and his older brother pulls Ponijao's hair. Ponijao cries, thus setting off what might turn into a lifelong case of sibling rivalry. That would appear to be the case until later one day, the older brother is helping Ponijao balance a can atop his head.

In Tokyo, Japan, a couple raises little Mari, who has been blessed with many toys and parents who love her. One scene, however, shows the father shaking a rattle in the girl's face without really engaging her in the slightest. He is too busy talking on his cell phone to notice how completely disinterested she is. Later in the film, Mari sits by herself with her toys trying to make sense of the ring toy, in which rings are dropped onto a pole from largest to smallest. Frustrated, she whips the toy away and cries out of (possibly) frustration and boredom. The scene goes on for quite some time without a single parent coming in to see what could be wrong.

In Mongolia, a mother gives birth to Bayar. The camera is there for the actual birth and soon, the baby is wrapped tightly in a blanket and whisked away with its mother back to a rural farmland. Bayar has far more complicated sibling rivalry issues with his older brother (older probably by a year or two), who mercilessly taunts him by constantly throwing a small towel in his face or leaving him out in the middle of the grassland.

Finally, in San Francisco, a well-to-do couple gives birth to Hattie, who of course is living the good life with her new age parents. Hattie, though, does not respond in favor to most of her parents' choices for quality time. She dislikes the bubbles in their hot tub. She has to be reminded not to hit people via the book *No Hitting*. The funniest moment is when she makes a beeline for the door at her mother's hippie, earth mother circle group while they chant "The earth is our mother..." over and over again, all of whom have their babies in tow.

If all of this sounds like hardly the stuff of high drama, it is because it is not. Director Balmes intercuts between the four babies seemingly at random without regard for rhythm or context. This provides the most basic problem with *Babies* that could have been the same problem for such highly regarded nature films as *Microcosmos* (1998) or *Winged Migration* (2003): There is nothing here, save for the observance of babies. Unfortunately, Balmes' film does not benefit from gorgeous cinematography or the idea that the audience is witnessing something that is rarely ever captured on film, much less seen in real life.

Therefore, the unobtrusive *Babies* exists only to ogle the infants and to watch them eventually learn to walk and to make speaking sounds in the course of a year. The audience is treated to watching babies scream, poop, urinate freely, fight, cry, drool, suckle, and resist breastfeeding. In case the audience has forgotten what babies do, this film will remind them. Many will find this cute, enlightening, and entertaining, but people whose attention spans start to wander just as someone is telling their latest "guess what my baby did" story will probably run for the exit just like Hattie.

Upon its release, *Babies* was greeted with a bit of controversy involving a technicality of the filmmakers working with minors, particularly Hattie the San Francisco baby. An Associated Press story ran accusing the filmmakers of violating child labor laws, which Focus Features' James Schamus denounced. The AP story stated that according to California law, an infant can only be on camera twenty minutes a day and require a doctor's note of permission and legal permits before they can become stars. Thanks to a marketing campaign that started almost an entire year before its release, *Babies* enjoyed an above average run at the box office after it opened appropriately on Mother's Day.

Collin Souter

CREDITS

Origin: France
Language: English
Released: 2010
Production: Armandine Billot, Alain Chabat, Christine Rouxel; Canal Plus, Studio Canal, Chez Wam; released by Focus Features
Directed by: Thomas Balmes
Cinematography by: Jerome Almeras, Steeven Petitteville
Music by: Bruno Coulais
Sound: Pierre Gamet, Olivier Dandre
Editing: Craig McKay, Reynald Bertrand
Art Direction: Guillaume Lips
Production Design: Jill Coulon
MPAA rating: PG
Running time: 79 minutes

REVIEWS

Denby, David. *New Yorker.* May 17, 2010.
Ebert, Roger. *Chicago Sun-Times.* May 5, 2010.
Edelstein, David. *New York Magazine.* May 7, 2010.
Goss, William. *Orlando Weekly.* May 5, 2010.
Kois, Dan. *Village Voice.* May 4, 2010.
Puig, Claudia. *USA Today.* May 7, 2010.
Scott, A.O. *New York Times.* May 7, 2010.
Snider, Eric. *Film.com.* May 7, 2010.
Sobczynski, Peter. *eFilmCritic.com.* May 7, 2010.
Tobias, Scott. *AV Club.* May 6, 2010.

THE BACK-UP PLAN

Fall in love. Get married. Have a baby. *Not necessarily in that order.*
—Movie tagline

Box Office: $37 million

It becomes quite clear in the opening scenes of the incredibly bland comedy *The Back-Up Plan* that the film will not present one original or interesting thought. As the movie's heroine Zoe (Jennifer Lopez) awaits her sperm donation in the operating room, she narrates to the audience that she is getting impregnated by an anonymous donor because she is in her mid-thirties and still has not found "the one." On her way out of the doctor's office and in a state of euphoria since having it done, she hails a cab, not knowing that she is about to have a "Meet Cute" (that is, a cute way couples meet in innocuous romantic comedies) with another impossibly good-looking New Yorker, Stan (Alex O'Loughlin), who insists he hailed the cab first. This eventually leads to some dull flirtation, more dull "Meet Cutes" and every cliché that has ever existed in a contemporary romantic comedy.

Even the movie's title lacks ambition. Zoe has found herself living her life's "back-up plan," since romance has not worked out in her favor. Gradually, of course, her relationship with the richest street vendor of cheese one could ever meet begins to build. Zoe and Stan have one of those relationships that only exists in the movies: She runs a pet store, he sells cheese. Both can somehow afford nice New York apartments on their own. As her relationship with Stan develops, she finds it increasingly harder to tell him the truth about her predicament.

She eventually does and after a round of accusations, misunderstandings and explanations, he decides to stay with her and help her raise her kid, even though he wants to eventually have kids of his own. Meanwhile, Zoe attends a single parent support group, which of course is also attended by butch lesbians, flaky new-age women, and other stereotypes that the audience is meant to laugh at and loathe. This needless subplot eventually results in one of the least funny, most unnecessary birth scenes ever committed to celluloid. The movie also sets up its third act for a wedding comedy of sorts where it becomes plainly obvious that somebody in the wedding party will go into labor before the end of the ceremony.

The clichés along the way never cease: Zoe is a city girl and Stan is, occasionally, a farmer, which of course means the movie must contain at least one fish-out-of-water sequence. Zoe also must have a brash, sassy, know-it-all best friend who tells it like it is and who has all the answers. Also, because part of the movie takes place in a pet store, it must contain shots of dogs reacting curiously to things adults say. Put it all in a blender with flat cinematography, a true lack of character development or definition and less-than-sophisticated viewpoints on domesticity and relationships and *The Back-Up Plan* has all the earmarks of a typically safe, dreary, and completely forgettable Hollywood formula film.

This was supposed to be Jennifer Lopez's big comeback film after not having appeared in a movie since *El cantante* (2006), for which she insists she should have been nominated for an Academy Award®. The movie went completely unnoticed as did Lopez's absence from the spotlight. The lack of a Jennifer Lopez movie for years on end was hardly cause for alarm amongst film critics or the moviegoing public. Considering such forays in the previous decade like *The Wedding Planner* (2001), *Gigli* (2003), and *Monster-in-Law* (2005) (with plenty of garbage in between), the public was more likely grateful for not having her movies around anymore. Still, it remains a wonder how she still managed to select low-grade screenplays after a long hiatus, during which she could have taken a good, long, hard look at her career choices.

Yet, the movie has one pivotal scene that offers clues into Lopez's decision-making skills, a scene in which she gets to wax philosophical about the kind of woman she used to be; a scene the insufferable, mid-level diva might have written herself. If she did not write it herself, it must have been the moment while reading the script for the first time in which she realized this movie must get made and with her in it. Lopez's character Zoe, while laying in bed with Stan, talks at length about her rear end and how it looked a few years ago versus how it looks now. This is the closest the script ever comes to depth and the one moment where Lopez almost appears to be addressing the audience personally. This is the comeback role Lopez has been waiting for all these years, it seems.

Alex O'Loughlin does little to convince the audience he is anything but a second-rate Gerard Butler, who himself is a second rate John Corbett. The

otherwise competent TV director Alan Poul (whose credits include episodes of *Six Feet Under* and *Big Love*) shoots everything sitcom style. Kate Angelo's screenplay seems to have been assembled together using scenes from other bad screenplays. How do movies like this get made? Usually because of weak-kneed and short-sighted producers and screenwriters in need of a back-up plan in case an original idea fails at a pitch meeting.

Collin Souter

CREDITS

Zoe: Jennifer Lopez
Clive: Eric Christian Olsen
Olivia: Danneel Harris
Carol: Melissa McCarthy
Stan: Alex O'Loughlin
Playground Dad: Anthony Anderson
Mona: Michaela Watkins
Origin: USA
Language: English
Released: 2010
Production: Todd Black, Jason Blumenthal, Steve Tisch; Escape Artists; released by CBS Films
Directed by: Alan Poul
Written by: Kate Angelo
Cinematography by: Xavier Perez Grobet
Music by: Stephen Trask
Sound: Sean McCormack
Music Supervisor: Linda Cohen
Editing: Priscilla Nedd Friendly
Art Direction: Priscilla Elliott
Costumes: Karen Patch
Production Design: Alec Hammond
MPAA rating: PG-13
Running time: 106 minutes

REVIEWS

Barnard, Linda. *Toronto Star.* April 22, 2010.
Berardinelli, James. *Reelviews.net.* April 21, 2010.
Ebert, Roger. *Chicago Sun-Times.* April 22, 2010.
Goodykoontz, Bill. *Arizona Republic.* April 21, 2010.
Lewis, Don R. *Film Threat.* April 27, 2010.
Lumenick, Lou. *New York Post.* April 23, 2010.
O'Hehir, Andrew. *Salon.com.* April 22, 2010.
Pols, Mary. *Time Magazine.* April 22, 2010.
Rabin, Nathan. *AV Club.* April 22, 2010.
Tallerico, Brian. *MovieRetriever.com.* April 23, 2010.

TRIVIA

This was the final film for Tom Bosley.

BARNEY'S VERSION

*First he got married. Then he got married again.
Then he met the love of his life.*
—Movie tagline

Box Office: $1 million

A wonderful thing about movies is the way that they can inspire empathy for even the most hard-sell cases. Take Barney Panofsky. From various points of view, *Barney's Version* paints him as a murderer, an adulterer, an alcoholic, and a first class irascible, self-absorbed ass. His only successful venture has been as the founder and head of the aptly named Unnecessary Productions TV production company, which has as its primary show a wretched, if insanely popular and long running, soap opera, about a Canadian Mountie, "O'Malley of the North." By all accounts, Barney is just another schmuck waiting to pass, deservedly, into the dust of history, unremembered.

Yet the wonderment of *Barney's Version* is that, although Panofsky is almost all those awful things, he does not cease to be a creature who can inspire affection, love, devotion, passion, compassion, forgiveness, and wonder. Without sugarcoating him, this marvelously acted film rises to the challenge of showing the good aspects of a not-so-good man. *Barney's Version* falls short of perfection, but then again so does its subject.

Sixty-five year-old Barney Panofsky (Paul Giamatti) is looking back on life and is less than happy with what he sees, especially after a retired cop (Mark Addy) publishes a book naming him as the leading suspect in a decades-old investigation into the death of Panofsky's best friend, the would-be novelist Boogie (Scott Speedman). How Barney got to where he is remains a mystery to even himself and his memories offer few clues.

There is his first marriage to Clara Chambers Charnofsky (Rachelle Lefevre), the woman he believes he accidently got pregnant, and a subsequent series of misunderstandings and, finally, a tragedy that spins him off into a new career and into the arms of the second Mrs. Panofsky (Minnie Driver), who has a doctorate, rich parents, and a laugh that could give a hyena an earache. At the wedding, he meets, and falls head over heels, at first sight, in love with Miriam (Rosamund Pike), a guest, going as far as to leave the wedding reception to track her down after she leaves. Rebuffed, he goes back home, unable to forget her, and, gradually, over the course of time, unable to forgive himself for his own stupidity in marrying the second Mrs. P., who has an affair with the leech-like money-pit Boogie, who subsequently disappears after a drunken fight with Barney. Free at last to pursue Miriam, Barney does,

capturing her heart and seemingly well on his way to a fairy tale ending. Whether Barney is a prince, a frog, or just something in between remains to be seen. As his last stage of life is played out, the film presents a man who has had to live by his wits in a hard cruel world, only to discover he is at his wits end.

The screenplay is adapted by the late Michael Konyves from the novel by Mordecai Richler. Konyves is known primarily for being the writer of a number of badly-realized science fiction and fantasy made-for-TV movies but his work here would never suggest that. This is a marvelously compact film that that never feels less than complete in the story it tells or in the observations of the fascinating characters that inhabit it. Richler was a fascinating writer whose diverse credits included screenplays (*Fun with Dick and Jane* [1977]), well-received novels (*The Apprenticeship of Duddy Kravits* [1974]), and, as the creator of Jacob Two-Two, enduring children's fiction.

Richard J. Lewis offers workman-like direction, which is all the story really needs. A few nice flourishes offer some visual icing on the cake, but mostly the director stays out of the way of his incredible cast. Lewis, like Konyves, is primarily known for his work in television which, although far broader in dramatic scope, in no way suggests a film of this quality and magnitude was to be a later entry on his resume. This is not his debut feature film but it may very well be his ticket out of TV land if he wants it to be.

Barney's Version gives Paul Giamatti a chance to perfect a character he has played well many times and the actor knocks it out of the park. This is no romanticized, golden-hearted, gruff-only-on-the-outside cliché. Giamatti gives Panofsky things to show real fear about, real struggle with, and faults to which he exhibits a maddening cluelessness. Dustin Hoffman breezes through his role as Barney's retired cop father, the boisterous, crass, and completely lovable Izzy Panofsky. But what a sweet breeze it is. Hoffman seems to be channeling people he has known and loved and been a little embarrassed by his whole life. As Miriam, the radiant Rosamund Pike makes it easy to believe Barney would pursue her the way he does. She is every inch a brilliant woman, but she is so in virtue as well, able to love Barney at his most selfish without losing sight of herself. Lastly is the surprising Scott Speedman, offering a truly great performance in a part that could have been a complete throwaway as Boogie, the perpetually drunk, drug-addicted, philandering wastrel who also happens to be Barney's best friend.

Oddly enough, special effects are also worth mentioning here. The aging process depicted in the film is top notch, never a distraction. When aging makeup is done badly (as it is, for instance, in the highly overrated *A Beautiful Mind* [2001]) it draws attention to itself, something no effect should ever do. Here, so natural is the depiction, that the actual age of the actors is never a consideration.

Barney's Version clocks in at just over two hours and could have used a little tightening up in the editing room. But viewers may well feel that they have been privileged to see it just as it is, a little creaky, a little sentimental, but worth getting to know and maybe even loving.

Dave Canfield

CREDITS

Barney Panofsky: Paul Giamatti
Izzy Panofsky: Dustin Hoffman
Miriam: Rosamund Pike
Mrs. P: Minnie Driver
Clara: Rachelle Lefevre
Boogie: Scott Speedman
Blair: Bruce Greenwood
Constable O'Hearne: Mark Addy
Charnofsky: Saul Rubinek
Origin: Canada, Italy
Language: English
Released: 2010
Production: Robert Lantos; Serendipity Point Films, Fandango, Lyla Films; released by Sony Pictures Classics
Directed by: Richard J. Lewis
Written by: Michael Konyves
Cinematography by: Guy Dufaux
Music by: Pasquale Catalano
Sound: Lou Solakofski
Music Supervisor: Liz Gallacher
Editing: Susan Shipton
Art Direction: Michele Laliberte
Costumes: Nicoletta Massone
Production Design: Claude Pare
MPAA rating: R
Running time: 132 minutes

REVIEWS

Bartyzel, Monika. *Cinematical*. September 21, 2010.
Fear, David. *Time Out New York*. December 1, 2010.
Gordon, Rachel. *FilmCritic.com*. December 16, 2010.
Howell, Peter. *Toronto Star*. December 23, 2010.
Mandel, Nora-Lee. *Film-Forward.com*. December 3, 2010.
Neumaler, Joe. *New York Daily News*. December 3, 2010.
Rainer, Peter. *Christian Science Monitor*. December 10, 2010.
Scott, A.O. *New York Times*. December 3, 2010.

Smith, Kyle. *New York Post*. December 3, 2010.
Zacharek, Stephanie. *Movieline*. December 2, 2010.

QUOTES

Barney Panofsky: "For the first time in my life, I am truly in love."

TRIVIA

Dustin Hoffman's son Jake Hoffman plays his grandson in the film.

AWARDS

Golden Globes 2011: Actor—Mus./Comedy (Giamatti)
Nomination:
Oscars 2010: Makeup.

BEST WORST MOVIE

The story behind the worst movie ever made: "Troll 2."
—Movie tagline

In the documentary *Best Worst Movie*, film critic Scott Weinberg perfectly sums up the idea of a bad movie being good: "Bad food is bad. Bad books are bad. But bad movies are not always bad." Not always. Sometimes, the best time that can be had at the movies is when the audience is in on the fact that they are watching one of the worst films ever made. It could be because the acting is so atrocious that one wonders if an audition ever took place to begin with. It could be because the storyline is so ludicrous, the directing is so incompetent, and the production so incredibly flimsy. In the best case scenario, the movie would encompass a combination of these traits to the point where all the audience can do is laugh. *Troll 2* (1990) is such a film. *Best Worst Movie* is a documentary about *Troll 2*, the people who made it, the people who love it, and the actors who wish they could erase it from their resume.

Troll 2 is the in-name-only sequel to the forgettable horror film *Troll* (1986), a movie that, if nothing else, can lay claim to star both Julia Louis-Dreyfus and Sonny Bono. *Troll 2* was originally titled *Goblin* when the Italian filmmakers made it in Utah in the summer of 1989. The movie tells the story of a typical American family taking a vacation to the "wonderful, half-empty town" of Nilbog, where they become the prey to a gang of mutant trolls (or goblins). There is much more to the story than that, but it all has to be seen to be believed. The U.S distributors gave it the name *Troll 2*, probably to make it in some way marketable. The film went straight-to-video and was never heard from again. That is, until it started to pick up an enthusiastic cult movie audience almost randomly more than ten years later.

In the wake of the cult phenomenon, actor Michael Stephenson, who played the young boy in the film, decided to chronicle the *Troll 2* success by making a documentary film about it and by catching up with his fellow cast members. Stephenson opens *Best Worst Movie* by introducing us to a charming and funny dentist named George Hardy. George is loved by all in the small town where he lives. He is a regular at town gatherings and always has a smile on his face. But he has never told anyone about being in a movie, much less one of the worst-rated movies on the Internet Movie Database. But thanks to the wonders of late-night cable TV, George had to own up to his first and only foray into acting. "Turn it off," he would say to his friends, "It gets worse!"

Stephenson then turns the camera on himself and explains that he was so excited when he was a kid and got his first VHS copy of *Troll 2* for Christmas. As soon as he was done watching it, his dreams of being a child star evaporated. Actress Connie Young (billed in *Troll 2* as Connie McFarland) tells of the horrific reviews the movie and her performance got on Rotten Tomatoes and the Internet Movie Database ("Worst actress ever!"). She tried everything she could to erase *Troll 2* from her resume. One of *Troll 2*'s supporting actors, Don Packard (who played the crazed drugstore owner), claims that he was not acting in the movie. He was very troubled and not all there during filming.

Best Worst Movie stays mostly with George Hardy, who embraces being a cult movie personality. He shows up at all the midnight screenings and is more than happy to repeat cherished lines from *Troll 2* to all the adoring fans. The documentary also explains perfectly why bad movies carry such appeal and how a great bad movie cannot be made on purpose. It must be apparent from watching a film like *Troll 2* that the filmmakers were dead serious when they made it. Sincerity is key. Stephenson's film eventually catches up with *Troll 2*'s writer-director team, Rossella Drudi and Claudio Fragasso, respectively, who are also married and living in Italy. It becomes readily apparent that they were indeed deadly serious when they made the film and still attempt to defend it with a straight face.

Claudio even shows up to one of the many sold-out screenings in the U.S. He is greeted with great adulation from fans outside the theater, unaware that they love his movie not because it is any good, but because it is truly awful. He watches it with the crowd, completely perplexed as to why the audience is laughing when nothing that is meant to be funny is happening. Claudio remains defiant even after the reason behind the phenomenon dawns on him. When Stephenson later asks him how he feels about making one of the worst movies ever made, Claudio responds in broken English, "that's their problem. I make good movie. I keep making movies. I never stop."

Best Worst Movie is a lot of fun, although it is a bit redundant at times. Stephenson lets a few sequences run a little too long while reiterating the same point(s) over and over. Yet, nobody with a vested interest in *Troll 2* will mind. Some questions, though, remain unanswered. For instance, why has the first *Troll* film been ignored when it is arguably just as bad? Why is Claudio listed as Drago Floyd on *Troll 2*'s credits and cover box? The film could have also explained the popularity of other bad movies that have enjoyed the same kind of cult sensation, particularly the most recent success story, *The Room* (2003).

Stephenson's film has plenty of charm, poignancy, and a touch of sadness. Not everyone involved wants in on the *Troll 2* craze. Perhaps the saddest story in *Best Worst Movie* is that of Margo Prey, who played the mom. She lives with her ailing mother and tends to her every need. She talks about noises she hears at night, how she has given up acting to take care of her mother and how she would like to just get away from everybody and never be found again. There are moments like these throughout *Best Worst Movie* that gives the film its weight, making it more than a celebration of bad cinema, but a celebration of life and all its absurdities and ironies.

Collin Souter

CREDITS

Himself: George Hardy
Himself: Claudio
Herself: Margo Prey
Himself: Jason Steadman
Himself: Darren Ewing
Himself: Michael Stephenson
Origin: USA
Language: English
Released: 2009
Production: Lindsay Rowles Stephenson, Brad Klopman, Michael Stephenson, Jim McKeon; Magic Stone Productions; released by Abramorama Films
Directed by: Michael Stephenson
Cinematography by: Katie Graham, Carl Indriago
Music by: Bobby Tahouri
Sound: Geoffrey "Woody" Woodhall
Editing: Katie Graham, Andrew Matthews
MPAA rating: Unrated
Running time: 91 minutes

REVIEWS

Adams, Sam. *Salon.com.* May 14, 2010.
Baumgarten, Marjorie. *Austin Chronicle.* April 23, 2010.

Goss, William. *Cinematical.* December 17, 2009.
Hartlaub, Peter. *San Francisco Chronicle.* June 4, 2010.
Lybarger, Dan. *eFilmcritic.com.* May 19, 2010.
Pinkerton, Nick. *Village Voice.* May 11, 2010.
Shannon, Jeff. *Seattle Times.* June 17, 2010.
Schrager, Norm. *Filmcritic.com.* April 15, 2010.
Uhlich, Keith. *Time-Out New York.* May 13-19, 2010.

BIUTIFUL

Box Office: $3 million

Alejandro González Iñárritu may have ditched the crosscutting narrative trick that he used in his first three films (*Amores Perros* [2000], *21 Grams* [2003], and *Babel* [2006]) but he did not lose his relentlessly bleak outlook on life in the sometimes-tedious *Biutiful,* a film worthy of attention for a stellar lead performance from Oscar® nominee Javier Bardem (the film was also nominated for Best Foreign Language Film) but ultimately a work that betrays such incredible acting by offering little more than audience abuse. Bardem does not falter once in the lead role of Iñárritu's latest tragedy, proving yet again that he is currently one of the best actors working today, but writer/director Iñárritu seems intent on offering only the grime, dirt, and decay of humanity, even in what could have and should have been a tale that featured a modicum of last-minute redemption for its troubled hero. Addiction, abuse, death, misery—these are the only themes in which Iñárritu seems interested and it has created a cloud over his work as they have become as repetitive and monotonous as films in which only the happy, positive side of life is portrayed. *Biutiful* works as an acting showcase for a spectacular craftsman, but its faux symbolism and self-righteous sense of importance offer little more.

Uxbal (Bardem) is a low-level criminal who deals primarily with illegal immigrants. He keeps them safe and relatively-paid while making a cut on the other end from the sweatshop owners and construction site managers that need workers. Uxbal is not exactly the scum of the Earth but he is also not beyond moral reproach. In one of many bizarre subplots, Uxbal can also supposedly speak to the dead. Iñárritu never really develops this thread other than perhaps to suggest that this is a man for whom death has always been a part of the fabric of his life.

It becomes a much greater part after one too many blood-filled urinations sends Uxbal to the doctor and he is given the tragic news that he has cancer that has spread throughout his body. With treatment, he still only has months to live. Without it, as he chooses to go, one imagines it is even less. Meanwhile, the body of Uxbal's

father, who never met his son, is being disinterred and Uxbal and his brother Tito (Eduard Fernández) must take the body and have it cremated. Once again, this is pure thematic writing as Iñárritu is too coincidentally playing with how fathers leave their children since Uxbal is about to die and leave his own. Like so many elements of Iñárritu's script, co-written with Armando Bo and Nicolas Giacobone, the convenience of Uxbal's father coming back into his life in any way possible just as Uxbal is about to die is a narrative trick that betrays attempts at realism.

All that Uxbal really must determine before he joins his father on the other side is what will happen to his two young children, Ana (Hanaa Bouchaib) and Mateo (Guillermo Estrella). Their mother, Marambra (Maricel Álvarez), is a complete mess. Not only is she sleeping with Tito, but she is a manic-depressive emotional rollercoaster who also hits Mateo on occasion. Uxbal certainly has his character flaws but the driving emotional rising action of *Biutiful* is the hope that his lovely children will not end up with their disastrous mother full-time after he dies. In a bizarre screenwriting decision, Uxbal must also deal with an immense tragedy involving multiple deaths of illegal workers and the deportation of another important one in his life. Perhaps Iñárritu is suggesting that everything is fleeting for these people, including citizenship and their very lives, but it feels more like depressing material purely for the sake of inducing depression.

Despite the narrative flaws of the pretentious screenplay, Bardem does spectacular work in *Biutiful,* deserving his Oscar® nomination in a year when the Best Actor category was crowded with talent. From his opening scenes, Bardem feels completely genuine in this character's skin, not overplaying either the criminal elements or the redemption tale that could have turned him into a cliché. Nearly everything that works about *Biutiful* (Rodrigo Prieto's typically-strong cinematography deserves praise as well) can be traced back to the decisions made by Javier Bardem. Rarely has a film found resonance so solely through its star.

Iñárritu is a talented man, although it now seems clear that his partnership with Guillermo Arriaga (who wrote Iñárritu's first three films) may have been more crucial than first expected. Still, the number of strong performances in the four Iñárritu films—and Bardem's here is arguably the best of the talented lot—makes it clear that he knows how to work with actors to draw the best that he can from them. One only wishes that he would stop writing so clearly from a foundation of theme instead of plot or even character. *Biutiful* constantly feels like a film that wants to telegraph its importance through its relentlessly depressing narrative and directorial style. Instead of allowing viewers to be sucked into Uxbal's story, they see the filmmaker's fingerprints on every frame.

Brian Tallerico

CREDITS

Uxbal: Javier Bardem
Marambra: Maricel Álvarez
Tito: Eduardo Fernández
Ige: Diaryatou Daff
Hai: Taisheng ("Cheng Tai Shen") Cheng
Ana: Hanaa Bouchaib
Mateo: Guillermo Estrella
Origin: Mexico, Spain
Language: Spanish, Mandarin
Released: 2010
Production: Alejandro González Iñárritu, Jon Kilik, Fernando Bovaira; Mod Producciones, Menage Atroz; released by Universal Pictures
Directed by: Alejandro González Iñárritu
Written by: Armando Bo, Nicolas Giabone, Alejandro González Iñárritu
Cinematography by: Rodrigo Pireto
Music by: Gustavo Santaolalla
Sound: Martin Hernandez
Music Supervisor: Lynn Fainchtein
Editing: Stephen Mirrione
Art Direction: Marina Pozanco, Sylvia Steinbrecht
Costumes: Paco Delgado
Production Design: Brigitte Broch
MPAA rating: R
Running time: 147 minutes

REVIEWS

Anderson, Melissa. *Village Voice.* December 29, 2010.
Chang, Justin. *Variety.* July 6, 2010.
Honeycutt, Kirk. *Hollywood Reporter.* July 6, 2010.
Jenkins, Mark. *NPR.* December 29, 2010.
Moore, Roger. *Orlando Sentinel.* January 26, 2011.
Pais, Matt. *Metromix.com.* January 27, 2011.
Phillips, Michael. *Chicago Tribune.* January 27, 2011.
Scott, A.O. *New York Times.* December 29, 2010.
Tobias, Scott. *AV Club.* December 28, 2010.
Zacharek, Stephanie. *Movieline.* December 29, 2010.

TRIVIA

Javier Bardem in *Biutiful* is the first actor to be nominated for a Best Actor Oscar® for a performance entirely in the Spanish language.

AWARDS

Nomination:

Oscars 2010: Actor (Bardem), Foreign Film

British Acad. 2010: Actor (Bardem), Foreign Film
Golden Globes 2011: Foreign Film.

BLACK SWAN

Box Office: $84 million

One of the best films of 2010, Darren Aronofsky's *Black Swan* was critically-lauded and intensely popular (in the right circles of art movie goers) with its director's incredible precision in his approach to every element of the production and a performance so memorable that it seared itself upon the brain of everyone who saw it. Like watching the career highlight of a virtuoso dancer whose every step has been precisely choreographed and practiced to perfection, *Black Swan* never fails to be anything less than riveting filmmaking. The surreal masterpiece can be taken apart and praised contributor by contributor—from Natalie Portman's award-winning lead to Clint Mansell's stunning reinterpretation of the score from *Swan Lake* to longtime Aronofsky collaborator cinematographer Matthew Libatique's daring camera work—or merely admired as the haunting sum of its notable parts. There were few 2010 films that were as mesmerizing or riveting from first frame to the stunning final shot.

Of course, a dreamlike drama should open with an actual dream and Mark Heyman and Andres Heinz and John J. McLaughlin's script does just that as Nina Sayers (Natalie Portman) imagines herself in a terrifying production of *Swan Lake*. While most people would wake up screaming from such a dark vision, Nina wakes up smiling and tells her "mommy" (Barbara Hershey) about her prophetic dream.

Later that morning, almost as if she was birthed from Nina's dream, Aronofsky's heroine spots her future nemesis on the train to the company in which she is a member of the dance core; a background dancer hoping for her turn in the spotlight. The girl in black that Nina sees in the train car next to hers is Lily (Mila Kunis), who will shortly be introduced to the entire troupe by director Thomas Leroy (Vincent Cassel) as its newest member, a girl with a natural gift for dance (as opposed to Nina's calculated, intensely-cerebral approach to the perfect dance steps). After hearing other dancers complain that her old age demands imminent replacement, the audience is also introduced to Beth Macintyre (Winona Ryder), the fading star of the dance company who seems keenly aware that her time as Thomas' "little princess" is running short.

Nina desires nothing more than to dance the lead in *Swan Lake* but Thomas informs her that her technical skills are strong enough to be immediately cast as The

White Swan but she is missing the passion required to believably portray her evil twin, The Black Swan. After Nina rebuffs one of Thomas' advancements with a bit of unexpected bite, he casts her in the role and tries to pull her dark side to the surface; to bring The Black Swan to life.

Despite an ominous, foreboding tone, the first act and most of the second act of *Black Swan* could be interpreted as a pretty straightforward tale of a young lady giving her all to a role. Nina clearly has some body issues including references to a past problem with scratching (that may have resurfaced with an odd wound on her back) and a few shots that suggest bulimia but she seems driven to deliver the most perfect performance she can. The occasionally-disturbing-but-fleeting visions (including bloody fingers and a chunk of skin pulled from her hand) pile up into one night of lunacy, when it can be argued that Nina's "black swan" emerges. Lily comes to the apartment that Nina shares with her mother and whisks her off for a night of clubbing, drinking, dancing, and doing drugs that ends with the two ladies in a passionate night of lovemaking.

Or does it? When Lily reveals that she never went back to Nina's room at all that night, the questions of reality and insanity really come to the forefront. And as Nina's visions become increasingly violent (almost as if the sexual side of her comes out first followed by the aggressive part of her nature), it may be tempting to ask what is real and what is imagined. The miracle of *Black Swan* is that it does not matter. As Thomas Leroy says before Nina is about to go on, the key to her success is to "lose yourself." The same could be said to the audience.

Film has long been a more deliberate and explained form of fiction. It is common to see theater, ballet, opera, and other musical performances in which it is the emotion and not the literal plot that matters. Aronofsky has made a piece about ballet in which it is the grand expressions and the broad emotions created by the film that matter far more than the literal plot. An argument about "what happened to Nina" feels far less essential than it would with a less-daring director, one who felt a need to define the plot in less symbolic terms. With echoes of David Lynch, Roman Polanski, and Dario Argento, Darren Aronofsky joins a very elite club of filmmakers who can make the surreal emotionally resonant.

The symbols of *Black Swan* also culminate in a piece that can clearly be read as a companion piece to Aronofsky's *The Wrestler* (2008). As that Oscar®-nominated drama was about a man giving his physical self completely over to his craft, Aronofsky's follow-up can be read as a piece about a woman giving not just her physical or mental self but her very identity. When a

performer like Nina Sayers dives so deeply down the personal rabbit hole of trying to bring elements of her own self like her arguably-repressed sexuality to the stage, is it any wonder she mentally cracks? Artists so often are credited with disappearing into their role and *Black Swan* can be viewed as an examination of the danger of blurring that line between performer and role.

Technically, Aronofsky's film is without flaw. Matthew Libatique has been a notable cinematographer for years (working regularly with Aronofsky on films such as *Requiem For a Dream* [2000] and *The Fountain* [2006] and Spike Lee on films such as *Inside Man* [2006] and *Miracle at St. Anna* [2008]) but *Black Swan* represents the pinnacle of his achievements to date. Whether it is the camera swooping around Nina, virtually keeping time with her as if it is another dancer, or capturing the nightmare visions often associated with mirrors or other split images, the cinematography in *Black Swan* was some of the best of the year. Clint Mansell's score brilliantly distilled the music from the original ballet with his own dark vision. On a design level, Aronofsky and his collaborators cleverly avoid almost all colors other than black or white. Nina occasionally wears a light pink to distinguish her but the film is noticeably devoid of bright colors like yellow or green and only turns red at key moments. Modern films with actual color palette choices are increasingly rare. Of course, all of these technical elements require praise to be heaped back upon Aronofsky, the director who coordinated it all to perfection.

As for performances, the film belongs to Natalie Portman, who gives not only the best turn by an actress in 2010 but one of the best of the last several years. Not only is it a daringly physical exhibition but she nails the emotional arc of the character in a way that no other actress could have accomplished. As for the team that supports her, Kunis landed a few nominations during awards season for a daringly sexy and complex part. She is matched by the fascinating Barbara Hershey and the underrated Vincent Cassel, who takes the only real male speaking role in the film and plays mentor, suitor, abuser, and father figure in one film.

It might be considered boisterous or even repulsive for another film to end with the word "perfect" and to the sound of rapturous applause. In the case of *Black Swan,* it is well-deserved.

Brian Tallerico

CREDITS

Nina: Natalie Portman
Lily: Mila Kunis

Thomas Leroy: Vincent Cassel
Erica: Barbara Hershey
Beth MacIntyre: Winona Ryder
Madeline: Janet Montgomery
Origin: USA
Language: English
Released: 2010
Production: Scott Franklin, Mike Medavoy, Arnold Messer, Brian Oliver; Protozoa Pictures, Phoenix Pictures; released by Fox Searchlight Pictures
Directed by: Darren Aronofsky
Written by: Mark Heyman
Cinematography by: Matthew Libatique
Music by: Clint Mansell
Editing: Andrew Weisblum
Sound: Craig Henighan
Costumes: Amy Westcott
Production Design: Therese DePrez
MPAA rating: R
Running time: 108 minutes

REVIEWS

Corliss, Richard. *TIME Magazine.* September 10, 2010.
Dargis, Manohla. *New York Times.* December 3, 2010.
Debruge, Peter. *Variety.* September 1, 2010.
Ebert, Roger. *Chicago Sun-Times.* December 2, 2010.
Edelstein, David. *New York Magazine.* November 29, 2010.
Howell, Peter. *Toronto Star.* December 2, 2010.
Long, Tom. *Detroit News.* December 10, 2010.
Pais, Matt. *Metromix.com.* December 2, 2010.
Rich, Katey. *CinemaBlend.com.* September 10, 2010.
Voynar, Kim. *Movie City News.* December 3, 2010.

QUOTES

Nina: "I had the craziest dream last night about a girl who has turned into a swan, but her prince falls for the wrong girl and she kills herself."

TRIVIA

Alexandria was Nina's original name in the screenplay.

AWARDS

Oscars 2010: Actress (Portman)
British Acad. 2010: Actress (Portman)
Golden Globes 2011: Actress—Drama (Portman)
Ind. Spirit 2011: Actress (Portman), Cinematog., Director (Aronofsky), Film
Screen Actors Guild 2010: Actress (Portman)
Nomination:
Oscars 2010: Cinematog., Director (Aronofsky), Film, Film Editing

British Acad. 2010: Cinematog., Costume Des., Director (Aronofsky), Film, Film Editing, Makeup, Orig. Screenplay, Sound, Support. Actress (Hershey), Prod. Des., Visual FX
Directors Guild 2010: Director (Aronofsky)
Golden Globes 2011: Director (Aronofsky), Film—Drama, Support. Actress (Kunis)
Screen Actors Guild 2010: Support. Actress (Kunis), Cast
Writers Guild 2010: Orig. Screenplay.

BLUE VALENTINE

A love story.
—Movie tagline

Box Office: $5 million

Derek Cianfrance's *Blue Valentine* is the most striking debut of 2010, a daring drama that uses its set-up to illuminate the human condition instead of merely exploiting it as a cheap hook. The fact that Cianfrance's piece simultaneously tells the first and last days of a young relationship through flashbacks to happier times could easily have resulted in dramatically-false material in the hands of less-talented people. With two of the best young stars of their generation in Ryan Gosling and Michelle Williams, *Blue Valentine* not only never feels false, it is as emotionally resonant as anything released in the entire year. Billed as "a love story," Cianfrance's relationship drama finds the truth of real-life love in that it is not always what it seems. The fact is that many young couples get married for reasons of chance and circumstance and that fate does not always lead down the rosy path that so many romantic comedies have led viewers to believe that it does. Like some of the great doomed relationship dramas of the 1970s, *Blue Valentine* is heartbreaking in its believability.

Dean (Ryan Gosling) and Cindy (Michelle Williams) are clearly in the end days of their still-young relationship. As Cindy becomes more professionally-driven, Dean seems stuck in a blue-collar rut in which his favorite thing about his job is the fact that it allows him the freedom to drink at eight in the morning. They are drifting apart not through abuse, infidelity, or any of the other typical problems of the relationship drama but through the common circumstance in which two young people simply take different paths as they grow up. In an attempt to rekindle what he can surely tell is a diminishing flame, Dean plans one more night of passion with his wife at a cheesy motel complete with sexually-charged, themed rooms. Despite Cindy's protestations that she has to work early in the morning, she goes along with Dean's half-hearted attempts at romance and the two make love, drink, and even try to dance to the song that was once clearly "their song."

The next morning, Cindy has to go into work and leaves Dean alone in a sex-driven room with no windows (a cheesy place with a futuristic theme for couples without much of a future). The next morning, the inevitable happens as Dean makes a drunken mistake from which this tenuous relationship cannot survive.

While the last twenty-four hours (roughly) before Dean and Cindy's divorce plays out, Cianfrance flashes back to the days in which they met, fell in some sort of love, and got married. It turns out that Dean met and wooed Cindy while she was in the middle of another, awful relationship; one that produced a pregnancy. If Cindy had not needed a father for her coming daughter, would she have ended up with Dean? Would she have seen through his song-playing romanticism to the lack of motivation beneath and broken up with him long before the marriage license? While Dean and Cindy have a passionate affair in the flashbacks, Cianfrance never suggests that there was some amazing romance that was torpedoed by time. In fact, Dean even says in one conversation with a co-worker that he believes that men wait for the right girl to get married while women wait for the right circumstance. *Blue Valentine* seems to tell that story as Dean is passionately drawn to Cindy from the minute he sees her while Cindy almost seems to give in to his advances more than reciprocate them.

Clearly, this is complex, character-driven material and if it was not filled with such subtext regarding unstated intentions and possibly-incongruent levels of love, it would be pure cliché. *Blue Valentine* is nearly as remarkable for what it does not do as for what it does. Cianfrance never falls into the obvious pitfalls of his simple story. He never allows his two talented leads to play the plot, allowing them to work purely from their characters. And they are more than up to the challenge. Gosling gives one of the best performances of 2010 as Dean, not only never hitting one note that feels false but finding new ways to make his character believable that other actors would not have even considered. With this role, Gosling solidifies the argument that he is the best actor of his generation. And he is matched by his co-star, the mesmerizing Michelle Williams, a young lady who also finds the honesty in every line. Both of these young actors feel completely in the moment at all times, never betraying that they are purely actors playing roles but sinking into their characters in ways that other performers could not possibly hope to mimic.

Many directors, especially young voices working on their low-budget debuts, have decided to use the tragedy of love gone bad as their first project but very few have resulted in such confident, promising filmmaking. Largely due to the prodigious talents of its two leads but also thanks to a refreshing lack of melodrama and cliché from its writer/director, *Blue Valentine* may not be a

traditional love story in cinematic terms but it is one of the most memorable in years.

Brian Tallerico

CREDITS

Dean: Ryan Gosling
Cindy: Michelle Williams
Bobby: Mike Vogel
Jerry Heller: John Doman
Sam Feinberg: Ben Shenkman
Frankie Periera: Faith Wladyka
Origin: USA
Language: English
Released: 2010
Production: Lynette Howell, Alex Orlovsky, Jamie Patricof; Hunting Lane Films, Silverwood Films; released by Weinstein Co.
Directed by: Derek Cianfrance
Written by: Derek Cianfrance, Joey Curtis
Cinematography by: Andrij Parekh
Sound: Damian Canelos
Music Supervisor: Joe Rudge
Editing: Jim Helton
Art Direction: Chris Potter
Costumes: Erin Benach
Production Design: Inbal Weinberg
MPAA rating: R
Running time: 120 minutes

REVIEWS

Ebert, Roger. *Chicago Sun-Times.* January 6, 2011.
Edelstein, David. *New York Magazine.* December 27, 2010.
Hornaday, Ann. *Washington Post.* January 7, 2011.
Kelly, Kevin. *Cinematical.* July 6, 2010.
Lane, Anthony. *New Yorker.* December 28, 2010.
McCarthy, Todd. *Variety.* January 27, 2010.
Pais, Matt. *Metromix.com.* January 6, 2011.
Scott, A.O. *New York Times.* December 29, 2010.
Sharkey, Betsy. *Los Angeles Times.* December 29, 2010.
Travers, Peter. *Rolling Stone.* December 29, 2010.

QUOTES

Dean: "In my experience, the prettier a girl is, the more nuts she is, which makes you insane."

TRIVIA

The screenplay won the Chrysler Film Project contest in 2006 for $1 million in funding.

AWARDS

Nomination:

Oscars 2010: Actress (Williams)

Golden Globes 2011: Actor—Drama (Gosling),
   Actress—Drama (Williams)
Ind. Spirit 2011: Actress (Williams).

THE BOOK OF ELI

Deliver us.
   —Movie tagline

Box Office: $95 million

If the *Book of Eli* is any indication, our post-apocalyptic future will be tinged yellow-grey (causing everyone to wear shades), water will be scarce, and everyone will be in pursuit of the last copy of the bible. It is this sacred tome to which the title of the movie refers, as well as the item that Eli (Denzel Washington) has been carrying west for the last thirty years with the hopes that he will find the place where the book truly belongs. In this future everyone will also sport distressed leather attire, motorcycle gangs will continue to run amok, and society will revert to a *Deadwood*-esque free for all. This is not good news for Eli who comes face-to-face with the Al Swearengen of the apocalypse, Carnegie (Gary Oldman), a man determined on getting his hands on Eli's sacred book for he knows the mind-bending power it possesses over the masses. On a normal day, Eli would just kick Carnegie's butt, but now he's randomly started to care for another person—a young barmaid, Solara (Mila Kunis)—and his until-now seemingly-infallible ninja skills start to falter, placing his cherished book in jeopardy.

In a sea of post-apocalyptic narratives, *The Book Of Eli* falls squarely in the middle, possessing an intriguing-enough glimpse at a possible dystopian future to appease genre fans and including a mysterious enough hero to keep said fans engaged. On the downside, *Eli* feels more like a video game than a movie and the shallow writing allows for too many holes to elevate the film above the territory of *I Am Legend* (2007).

With his steely jaw, calm tenor, and muscular presence, Washington is a force on-screen as a near future hero trekking through the desert ravaged landscape of the United States. And it is his ability to command the screen that anchors the film. Eli's got a knack for staying alive, mad weapon skills, and sharpened street smarts. He has also got some pretty crazy scars and is overly-protective about a book in his possession from which he reads every day. The scars and ninja-like dexterity work to create a character that gives off the "complex" and "resilient" vibe. The book in his possession and his committed reading of it hints at his quiet side—it turns out Eli is a real thinker who would rather listen to Al

Green than wield a gun, if he can help it. There is enough attention to character creation from writer Gary Whitta to make Eli the person highly watchable and highly compelling. His acquired side-kick is not half-bad either. Shedding her sitcom persona, Kunis makes an interesting passage from abused barmaid to butt-kicking action heroine.

Whitta also does well in grounding Eli's future in our reality, creating a world that seems plausible and consequently watchable. Eli is in possession of a first generation iPod, for example, and the 2010 lifestyle that encompassed books and movies and greenery is still known —or at least mythologized—to those living in the new world order. Add to this director Albert Hughes's take on the color and texture of the film's present day America (the palpable desert heat and the agitating hue of the outside world) and you have one heck of a compelling set-up on your hands.

The problems arise in Hughes's penchant for slow-motion fight scenes and Whitta's failure to expound on why society arrived at this dismal state. Both have the film's arctic pace on their shoulders as well. The main point of contention with *Eli* is that it is boring—not in the sense that there is not anything on screen worth watching, but boring in that too often we are given nothing but shots of the protagonist walking. It is a huge relief then when Eli starts meeting fellow itinerants and is forced to start kicking their collective butts. But though they are well choreographed and fun, Eli's brand of fighting style leans toward the showy and predict-able—and truthfully there just is not enough of it to keep viewers engaged on a pure action level. Maybe it would help if he had to fight a virulent product of the apocalypse he survived? As it stands the reasons for society's unraveling are chalked up to material excess and the product of said excess seems to have been a war that caused a super bright sun. Sure, that works with the film's religious angle, if everyone is looking for the bible than it stands to reason that turning away from it in the first place was our collective undoing, but Whitta does not deliver on what exactly the sun did to people and how society fell to such depths. Most of all though, he does not plant the idea of hope early enough. It's the hope that Robert Neville holds on to in *I Am Legend* that glued audiences to the screen, the same goes for the blind hope that acts as motivator in movies like *The Road* (2009) and *Children of Men* (2006). Eli chalks his quest up to hearing a voice in his head. And in as much as his quest springs from the spiritual, in the end it just does not fly. A post-apocalyptic zombie-vampire would have been nice.

Joanna Topor MacKenzie

CREDITS

Eli: Denzel Washington
Carnegie: Gary Oldman
Solara: Mila Kunis
Redridge: Ray Stevenson
Claudia: Jennifer Beals
Lombardi: Malcolm McDowell
George: Michael Gambon
Origin: USA
Language: English
Released: 2010
Production: Broderick Johnson, Andrew A. Kosove, Joel Silver, David Valdes, Denzel Washington; Alcon Entertainment, Silver Pictures; released by Warner Bros.
Directed by: Allen Hughes, Albert Hughes
Written by: Gary Whitta, Anthony Peckham
Cinematography by: Don Burgess
Music by: Atticus Ross, Leopold Ross, Claudia Sarne
Sound: Eric A. Norris, Steven D. Williams
Music Supervisor: Deva Anderson
Editing: Cindy Mollo
Art Direction: Chris Burian-Mohr
Costumes: Sharen CQ Davis
Production Design: Gae Buckley
MPAA rating: R
Running time: 117 minutes

REVIEWS

Ebert, Roger. *Chicago Sun-Times.* January 14, 2010.
Hartl, John. *Seattle Times.* January 14, 2010.
Honeycutt, Kirk. *Hollywood Reporter.* January 11, 2010.
Lumenick, Lou. *New York Post.* January 15, 2010.
McCarthy, Todd. *Variety.* January 11, 2010.
Moore, Roger. *Orlando Sentinel.* January 13, 2010.
Morgenstern, Joe. *Wall Street Journal.* January 14, 2010.
Pais, Matt. *Metromix.com.* January 14, 2010.
Phillips, Michael. *Chicago Tribune.* January 14, 2010.
Puig, Claudia. *USA Today.* January 14, 2010.

QUOTES

Eli: "Stay on the path. It's not your concern. Stay on the path. It's not your concern."

TRIVIA

All of the stunts in the hand-to-hand fighting sequence were done by Denzel Washington himself.

THE BOUNTY HUNTER

It's a job. It isn't personal. Well, maybe a little…
—Movie tagline

Box Office: $67 million

Judgment tends to fly out the window at roughly the same speed hooch disappears down the hatch, something to which *The Bounty Hunter*'s chagrined Nicole (Jennifer Aniston) can attest. The lovely, career-obsessed woman had once chosen to pucker up with a loser co-worker, who is now gratingly obsessed with her, a regrettable course of action that (as she is quick to point out) would never have been taken had she not been impeded by inebriation. With such things having been freshly and firmly planted in viewers' minds, they could surely not be blamed for wondering during the ill-conceived proceedings if the film itself may have resulted from a case of discernment dashed by drink.

Most moviegoers who sought out *The Bounty Hunter* wished they had never caught sight of it. For their efforts, they were rewarded with the bitter resentment that comes from sitting through irritating, ineffectual lameness. Sarah Thorp's screenplay cross-pollinates triteness from romantic comedies with that of action films and creates a hybrid that bears absolutely no fruit. It is not only deleteriously predictable but also contrived and overcomplicated, with a dearth of laughs and elements that quicken the pulse solely because one finds them so exasperatingly second-rate. In addition, if there were a Nobel Prize given out for lack of chemistry, the couple here would be under strong consideration for recognition. One of the pair, Gerard Butler's Milo, is increasingly off-putting, coming across as a sneering, beard-stubbled brute. The unpleasantness of his divorce from Nicole threw him for a loop and then off of the police force and one character opines that Milo is currently in great pain. Whether or not that is true, he unquestionably is one.

The Bounty Hunter harks back with a tone-deaf ear to a type of screwball comedy from the 1930s and 1940s for which Stanley Cavell coined the term "comedy of remarriage." Films like *The Awful Truth* (1937) and *His Girl Friday* (1940) featured a couple cut off from each other by rough waters that viewers not only expected but also hoped would be bridged before the lights went back up. Amidst all the rat-a-tat-tat repartee and tit-for-tat one-upmanship, one can still clearly sense a mutual (if temporarily only grudging) appreciation that lingers between the former couple. The pair move steadily from locked horns to goo-goo eyes, entering into a sprightly, sparkling swirl of dizzying complication and eventually come out with the clear-headed recognition of a simple truth: that each just plain fits better with the other than with anyone else.

However, viewers are thoroughly convinced by what transpires during the contrastingly delight-free *Bounty Hunter* that Nicole and Milo are a match made somewhere far south of heaven. Thus, there is no reason to root for their reunification. If the two are still mad about each other, they hide it awfully well. What is wearyingly in evidence throughout the proceedings, however, is that they are steadfastly mad at each other. As the film begins, Nicole and Milo are out for a drive together, only she is stuffed in the trunk and he is overheating behind the wheel as much as the car is under the hood. What soon follows is no roll in the hay, but a rough tackle on the highway as she attempts to escape.

Take the characters played by Cary Grant in the aforementioned films, lose the looks, the grooming, the engaging personality, and just about every benefit of advancing evolution and civilization over millennia, and one has Butler's Milo. Those who were repulsed by the caveman he portrayed in *The Ugly Truth* (2009) will react similarly to this character. When this unkempt, gruff jerk, now working as a bounty hunter between swigs of booze, finds out that he can erase pressing gambling debts by hauling in his ex, he receives the script's contrivance to cause the couple's intersection with a disturbing degree of glee. Milo does a little dance of joy and proceeds to repeatedly rub his hands together as he relishes the opportunity to not only bring in his former wife but also bring her down.

Propelled by this unattractive unbridled enthusiasm, Milo soon locates Nicole at the horse races in Atlantic City, and, after sadistically enjoying her vain attempts to flee, picks the woman up, throws her over his shoulder, and delightedly dumps her in the aforementioned trunk. Later, he handcuffs her to a bed and a car door. She thanks Milo for it all by giving him a hickey—with a taser to the neck. At one point, a fuming Nicole sputters that she cannot believe she ever married the man. Neither can the audience. Thus, restraining orders seem more believably in this couple's future than another marriage license. Even after Milo and Nicole's Punch and Judy show culminates with his callously still turning her in after she moments before saved his derriere, the audience is asked to believe as they share a lip lock in lock up that they will now form a more perfect union. If they do, one entirely expects a very uncivil war will follow.

Milo's debts have a couple of goons pursuing him while he pursues Nicole as she is in pursuit of her story, and she not only has Stewart hot on her trail but also a villain (Peter Greene) who wants to put an end to both Nicole's investigation and Nicole herself. To make things more contrived and convoluted, the best man at Nicole and Milo's ill-fated wedding may be implicated by the evidence she uncovers with her former spouse's help. Few will muster enough attentiveness to try to connect all the dull dots along with the banded-together bickerers, and no one will be anywhere close to the edge of their seats during all the uninspired chases and gunplay.

Some of the dialogue, however, may unintentionally cause derisive chortling.

Made on a budget of $40 million, *The Bounty Hunter* somehow grossed over $67 million despite teeth-gnashing reviews. It was directed by Andy Tennant, who helmed *Fool's Gold* (2008) and was unfortunately not prevented from bringing similar dreck to the screen yet again. During a brief thaw, Nicole references her history with Milo with the following toast: "Here is to our big fat, ugly mistake." It could just as easily be the two stars speaking of their unwise choice to make *The Bounty Hunter,* and to avoid repeating their mistake a la Tennant they best stay away from any more of that decision-hampering hard stuff.

David L. Boxerbaum

CREDITS

Milo Boyd: Gerard Butler
Nicole Hurley: Jennifer Aniston
Stewart: Jason Sudeikis
Kitty Hurley: Christine Baranski
Irene: Cathy Moriarty
Earl Mahler: Peter Greene
Origin: USA
Language: English
Released: 2010
Production: Neal H. Moritz; Relativity Media, Original Film; released by Columbia Pictures
Directed by: Andy Tennant
Written by: Sarah Thorp
Cinematography by: Oliver Bokelberg
Music by: George Fenton
Sound: Joe White, Joseph Aspromonti
Editing: Troy Takaki
Art Direction: Kimberly Asa
Costumes: Conan Castro Jr.
Production Design: Jane Musky
MPAA rating: PG-13
Running time: 110 minutes

REVIEWS

Chang, Justin. *Variety.* March 22, 2010.
Denby, David. *New Yorker.* April 5, 2010.
Dyball, Rennie. *People.* April 5, 2010.
Ebert, Roger. *Chicago Sun-Times.* March 17, 2010.
Gleiberman, Owen. *Entertainment Weekly.* April 2, 2010.
Honeycutt, Kirk. *Film Journal International.* May 2010.
Kois, Dan. *Washington Post.* March 19, 2010.
Morris, Wesley. *Boston Globe.* March 19, 2010.
Scott, A.O. *New York Times.* March 19, 2010.
Sharkey, Betsy. *Los Angeles Times.* March 19, 2010.

QUOTES

Milo Boyd: "You see, what I do is, I hunt down criminals. Idiots who jump bail, specifically."

Also considered for the role of Nicole Hurley was Sarah Jessica Parker.

AWARDS

Nomination:

Golden Raspberries 2010: Worst Picture, Worst Actor (Butler), Worst Actress (Aniston), Worst Couple/Ensemble (Aniston and Butler).

BROOKLYN'S FINEST

Every man has a moment of truth.
—Movie tagline

This is war. This is Brooklyn.
—Movie tagline

Box Office: $27 million

In 2001, director Antoine Fuqua scored big with *Training Day,* a movie about a rookie officer (Ethan Hawke) learning the corrupt streetwise ways of a veteran narcotics cop (Denzel Washington). Fuqua must think moviegoers have a short memory, because nine years later he returned with *Brooklyn's Finest,* which represents hardly any shift in topic or situation. This time the drug dealing takes place in New York City, and Hawke has graduated to the role of the corrupt narcotics cop trying to skim money from drug raids.

Fuqua has done nothing memorable in between, but *Brooklyn's Finest* has the ponderous air of important cinema. The film boldly opens on a dark street with an extended conversation. The dialogue seems important, but it is merely a set-up for Hawke's Sal to plug his first victim and escape with a bag of cash. When he returns home, he is disappointed how little there is. He goes to confession and tells the priest he does not want God's forgiveness but God's help. Not only does he already have three kids whom he must support on a cop's meager salary, his asthmatic wife is pregnant with twins and the mold in the walls of their house is threatening her health.

The script, by Michael C. Martin, is clichéd and heavy-handed. The music is dark and thumping. The story attempts the rather common feat of portraying three cops and then bringing them together at the end. But the editing veers between two extremes—action interrupted as Fuqua cuts back and forth between his trio of protagonists in the middle of action scenes in a way that diminishes rather than heightens the tension, and long stretches where threads of the story seem to be forgotten altogether. It is a train crash of cop movie tropes.

Nonetheless, there are some memorable scenes amid the clunkers and the constant gang-banger dialogue, though some of them seem to be coming from entirely different movies. Richard Gere plays a retiring cop who must endure tragedies while training rookies in his last week. Laconic and hoping just to stay of trouble, Gere's Eddie is weary to the bone of police work. Must he really be suicidal too? The reasons why are not clear, but after the opening scene with Hawke's robbery, Eddie is shown waking up and putting a pistol in his mouth. His one solace is a prostitute he has grown to love, and a scene with her is like a flashback to Robert Altman's *McCabe and Mrs. Miller* (1971)—her whole apartment has a hazy red tinge, and Jefferson Airplane's "White Rabbit" jumps into the soundtrack.

Fuqua certainly has a quartet of fine actors to work with. The reliably-brilliant Don Cheadle has a role that is a refreshing change of pace for him, as an undercover narc whose sympathies seem to lie as much with his targets as the cops he is working for. Cheadle's Tango is hair-trigger, prickly, and cocky. He pairs up nicely with Wesley Snipes (as drug kingpin Caz), and a couple of their scenes provide some brief comic relief in a movie whose script could have used a lot more.

The lead actors have little room to roam in their tightly drawn characters. Hawke chooses to play his hyperkinetic, stressed-out live wire with a desperate energy, which is sometimes compelling. At other times his angst seems way over the top, but where else can he go? These are one-dimensional characters.

What hurts the movie the most is that it drags out to 132 minutes as if it were an epic (a half-hour could easily have been edited out) and the ending makes hardly any sense at all. The drug dealers and Tango's bosses seem to act without any logic, and the heralded ending where the three protagonists cross paths turns out to be simply putting the characters together in the same location to do entirely different things with apparently disparate groups of thugs. Much of the plotting, and especially this climax, seem random, and instead of threads being pulled together, the entire movie simply unravels in a most unsatisfying way.

Even for fans of action films, *Brooklyn's Finest* does not have the kind of big-budget bang for the buck that its contemporary competitors can muster. Fuqua prefers scenes to be shot in the dark, and he loves grit and street language. But as far as building tension, the movie is more plodding than thrilling. A flirtation with the issue of police brutality simply disappears from the script. It is as if Fuqua thought he could just add in more cop protagonists and churn out another *Training Day.* But while the film is worth a look for its quartet of excellent actors, it is cobbled together almost randomly. Perhaps the intent is simply to replicate the nonsensical, unpredictable typical day for a member of an American city's police force.

Michael Betzold

CREDITS

Eddie Dugan: Richard Gere
Sal: Ethan Hawke
Tango: Don Cheadle
Caz: Wesley Snipes
Agent Smith: Ellen Barkin
Lt. Bill Hobarts: Will Patton
Ronny: Brian F. O'Byrne
Carlo: Vincent D'Onofrio
Red: Michael K. Williams
Angela: Lili Taylor
Chantel: Shannon Kane
Origin: USA
Language: English
Released: 2009
Production: Basil Iwanyk, John Langley, Elie Cohn, John Thompson; Thunder Road Productions, Millenium Films; released by Senator Film Entertainment
Directed by: Antoine Fuqua
Written by: Michael C. Martin, Brad Caleb Kane
Cinematography by: Patrick Murguia
Music by: Marcelos Zavras
Sound: Joe White
Editing: Barbara Tulliver
Costumes: Juliet Polcsa
Production Design: Therese DePrez
MPAA rating: R
Running time: 125 minutes

REVIEWS

Anderson, John. *Variety.* March 2, 2010.
Doerksen, Cliff. *Chicago Reader.* March 4, 2010.
Ebert, Roger. *Chicago Sun-Times.* March 4, 2010.
Germain, David. *Associated Press.* March 2, 2010.
Honeycutt, Kirk. *Hollywood Reporter.* March 2, 2010.
Keough, Peter. *Boston Phoenix.* March 4, 2010.
Lengel, Kerry. *Arizona Republic.* March 4, 2010.
Phillips, Michael. *Chicago Tribune.* March 4, 2010.
Rodriguez, Rene. *Miami Herald.* March 3, 2010.
Wilonsky, Robert. *Village Voice.* March 2, 2010.

QUOTES

Det. Sal Procida: "Change that skirt. People are gonna start to think we're Catholic only on Sundays."

BURIED

Paul Conroy isn't ready to die.
—Movie tagline

170,000 sq miles of desert. 90 minutes of Oxygen. No way out.
—Movie tagline

Box Office: $1 million

Rodrigo Cortes' striking debut *Buried* was one of the more interesting releases of 2010 in that it essentially fell flat at the box office but lingered in the background of the movie consciousness from its Sundance Film Festival debut all the way through a surprising Best Original Screenplay win from the National Board of Review for Chris Sparling's script. Led by a popular star, clever concept, and strong critical acclaim, it feels like Lionsgate must have made a mistake somewhere in the marketing of *Buried,* as it was not even able to domestically return its $3 million budget. With career-best work by star Ryan Reynolds and a daring concept well-executed, *Buried* has a lingering power that will almost certainly turn it into a cult hit as viewers find it on Blu-ray and DVD.

Paul Conroy (Ryan Reynolds) is a man in an absolutely-terrifying situation. He wakes up in a coffin and a cell phone goes off at his feet, indicating to both him and the audience that he is not here accidentally. Through a series of conversations, it is revealed that Paul was a driver in Iraq and he has been taken hostage. He has been buried alive. Based on what he can hear through the coffin (and the fact that he has cell phone reception), he is probably not too deep underground but one needs not be too deep to run out of air. Between conversations with his captors, Paul tries to contact someone to help him with little success and he learns, tragically, that he is not only not the first to be in this situation in the Middle East but that it did not end so well for those buried before him. He soon is asked to take a video and ask for a ransom, but it is unclear if it will do any good or if he could even be found in time. An even-more-startling realization is that there may be no one looking for him.

Much was made about audience reaction to *127 Hours* and the squeamishness associated with its concept and it seems similar stories could have been written about Rodrigo Cortes' debut if the film had been publicized on a wider canvas. Even the mildly-claustrophobic could find their palms sweating at the very premise of a film that takes place entirely in a coffin that holds a man who is not-yet-dead. Cortes' smartest move was to stick to his guns and not allow the audience a single chance to catch its oxygen-depleting breath, choosing to include no flashbacks or set-up before or after the action of the piece. The audience spends every single minute of *Buried* in a coffin with a man running out of time and becoming increasingly aware that he is going to die. More than just an exercise in torture, the reason that *Buried* won Best Original Screenplay (besides the NBR's desire to be different every once in awhile) is that Sparling brilliantly weaves the cycles that someone would go through in a situation like this from confusion to fear to anger to hope to acceptance.

A brilliant stroke of both the script and direction of *Buried* is the complete lack of dramatic irony. The audience knows nothing that Paul himself does not know. If the film had cut to the surface or revealed details about Paul's captors, it would have deflated the fear created by being right there with the hostage. The set-up makes his desperation resonant as he tries to contact officials, loved ones, and anyone who will listen. He is running out of patience, hope, and oxygen, and *Buried* works because its creators never gives the audience a dramatic break away from Paul's plight.

Naturally, a piece like *Buried* demands a lot of its star, who will not just be in every scene but often be the only thing in frame. The increasingly-popular Ryan Reynolds has shown signs of acting ability instead of mere sex appeal in small films like *Adventureland* (2009), *Chaos Theory* (2008), and *The Nines* (2007) but often torpedoed any chance at critical acclaim with mainstream junk like *X-Men Origins: Wolverine* (2009) and *The Proposal* (2009). *Buried* features the Reynolds who actually seems interested in character over paycheck and he truly delivers, committing completely to the believability of every horrifying moment of the part. Without Reynolds' everyman believability, *Buried* would completely fall apart. Cortes and Sparling made great decisions in the film's production but none was as important as the casting of Reynolds.

The only problem with *Buried* is a common one in the horror genre in that it becomes a bit less interesting as it goes along as Cortes and Sparling are forced to stretch the running time to a typical film length. If *Buried* could have only been sixty minutes long and not infuriated full-price-paying movie goers, it could have been spectacular, but it feels like some elements were stretched a bit too thin to avoid that. *Buried* may not be the gut-punch that it could have been with less running time, but it is still a powerful punch.

Brian Tallerico

CREDITS

Paul Conroy: Ryan Reynolds
Alan Davenport: Stephen Tobolowsky
Linda Conroy: Samantha Mathis
Special Agent Harris: Erik Palladino
Dan Brenner: Robert Paterson

Jabir: Jose Luis Garcia-Perez
Origin: Spain
Language: English
Released: 2010
Production: Peter Safran, Adrian Guerra; Safran Co., Dark Trick Films, Versus Entertainment; released by Lionsgate
Directed by: Rodrigo Cortes
Written by: Chris Sparling
Cinematography by: Eduard Grau
Music by: Victor Reyes
Sound: Urko Garai
Editing: Rodrigo Cortes
Art Direction: Maria De la Camara, Gabriel Pare
Costumes: Elise De Andres
MPAA rating: R
Running time: 95 minutes

REVIEWS

Childress, Erik. *Cinematical.* February 5, 2010.
Dudek, Duane. *Milwaukee Journal Sentinel.* October 7, 2010.
Ebert, Roger. *Chicago Sun-Times.* September 23, 2010.
Hornaday, Ann. *Washington Post.* October 1, 2010.
Howell, Peter. *Toronto Star.* October 5, 2010.
Phillips, Michael. *Chicago Tribune.* September 23, 2010.
Reed, Rex. *New York Observer.*. September 22, 2010.
Rich, Katey. *CinemaBlend.com.* January 24, 2010.
Smith, Kyle. *New York Post.* September 24, 2010.
Thompson, Gary. *Philadelphia Daily News.* September 30, 2010.

QUOTES

Paul Conroy: "I need one million dollars by nine o'clock tonight or I'll be left to die in this coffin!"

TRIVIA

A total of seven coffins were used during the 17 day shoot at a Barcelona studio.

BURLESQUE

It takes a LEGEND…to make a STAR.
—Movie tagline

Box Office: $39 million

For fans of "Good Bad Movies," the kind of films that are so chock-full of unbelievable characters, ludicrous plotting, ridiculously purple dialogue, and, if one is truly lucky, an incredibly gaudy musical production number or two that they wind up becoming hilariously entertaining despite themselves, the last few years have not been particularly kind. There have been plenty of bad movies clogging the multiplexes but in most cases, they have just been ordinary, run-of-the-mill "Bad Movies" that are just bland and boring instead of endearingly goofy. And the ones that have aspired to "Good Bad Movie" status, including the dubious likes of such would-be camp classics as *The Room* (2003) and *Birdemic* (2008), have been so self-conscious about their attempts that one can practically feel them jabbing them in the ribs at every bit of campy lunacy. *Burlesque* on the other hand, is a "Good Bad Movie" through and through because it thinks that it is a "Good Good Movie" and fails so mightily in its attempts to live up to those ideals that it makes for an inadvertently-entertaining good time for viewers with a taste for such things. It is so silly, in fact, that if there was still a viable market for midnight movies, the colorful audiences who have been following *The Rocky Horror Picture Show* (1975) for decades could easily segue into *Burlesque* without even adjusting their costumes or makeup.

Pop singer Christina Aguilera stars as Ali, a small-town girl who dreams of kicking the dust of her tiny Iowa hometown off her feet and making it big as a singer. When she arrives in Los Angeles to make said dreams come true, the closest she can get is a job as a waitress in a financially-troubled, neo-burlesque lounge, helpfully named The Burlesque Lounge, run by former dancer Tess (Cher). After another dancer gets pregnant, spunky Ali demands a chance to audition to be her replacement and wows Tess and aide-de-camp/ choreographer/gay best pal Sean (Stanley Tucci) with her unexpectedly sweet moves. This raises the ire of Nikki (Kristen Bell), the show's drunken and troublemaking lead dancer ("I will not be upstaged by a slut with mutant lungs!"). When Ali is given Nikki's slot one night when the latter shows up too hammered to perform, Nikki tries to get revenge on her rival by sabotaging the musical playback that is supposed to be accompanying her. Luckily, Ali manages to burst into song and improvise an entire elaborate song-and-dance that shows off her amazing lungs and her voice. Inspired, Tess decides that Ali is her ticket to saving the club and instantly redirects the entire show overnight to feature her in a series of increasingly-lavish production numbers. Naturally, Ali becomes an instant sensation and, almost inevitably, finds herself caught in a romantic dilemma—will she go with the poor-but-honest bartender/aspiring songwriter (Cam Gigandet) or will she choose the rich-but-sleazy Marcus (Eric Dane), a real estate developer who is trying to buy the club in order to turn it into an apartment complex? Will Ali choose sincerity over money (even after she gets a load of the song that he has apparently spent years writing)? Will she somehow manages to save the club with a combination of her onstage talents and the most suspect real estate transaction to hit the big screen since *The Cocoanuts* (1929)? Will she ac-

complish all this without violating the all-important PG-13 rating?

By all rational critical standards, *Burlesque* is absolute gibberish from start to finish. The screenplay, much like at least one of its stars, contains not a single original part. The whole thing is an amalgam of *Flashdance* (1983), *Coyote Ugly* (2000), the edited-for-television version of *Showgirls* (1995), and practically every vanity film ever made by a top-selling pop singer hoping that their talents would transfer from the jukebox to the screen. At least it includes more big laughs than most of the other films of 2010, albeit nearly all of them unintentional. Then there is the inescapable fact that it is a film designed as a star vehicle for someone who, although an undeniably talented singer, simply cannot act.

Even the music, for the most part, is problematic in that practically all of the songs sound like rejects from Aguilera's retro-chic *Back to Basics* album. And yet, while *Burlesque* is undeniably terrible in every possible way and should be avoided by most rational people, it is possible for someone in the right frame of mind to feel some strange form of affection for its campy charms. The plot is so goofy, the dialogue is so gauche, and the musical numbers are so wildly overstated that those viewers on the right wavelength will find themselves embracing them. It has been a long time since a movie this blatantly ridiculous has made it to the screen and whatever its sins (and they are numerous), it is never boring. Best of all, it contains a performance from Cher that is perfectly suited to the material. Unlike Aguilera, who seems convinced that she is in a genuinely serious movie and comes off all the more badly as a result, Cher knows she is standing smack in the middle of an enormous slab of overripe cheese and responds accordingly with a turn that is just as flamboyant. In the end, she winds up stealing every scene that she is in and even many of the ones that she is not.

Look, there is no confusing *Burlesque* with anything remotely resembling Art—though the members of the Hollywood Foreign Press Association were confused enough to give it a controversial nomination for the Golden Globe for Best Picture (Musical or Comedy)—and if one was to put it up against a serious-minded work of artistic expression like *The King's Speech* (2010) or *Winter's Bone* (2010) or any of 2010's other acclaimed dramatic works, it would instantly crumble away by comparison. On the other hand, it is a hell of a lot more fun to watch than those films and that should count for something as well. Those important films may get all the acclaim and respect but when it comes to which film people will be more likely to curl up with on a typical Friday night, *Burlesque* will undoubtedly be the one whose dance card is filled far more regularly.

Peter Sobczynski

CREDITS

Tess: Cher
Nikki: Kristen Bell
Ali Rose: Christina Aguilera
Georgia: Julianne Hough
Jack: Cam Gigandet
Sean: Stanley Tucci
Alexis: Alan Cumming
Marcus Gerber: Eric Dane
Vince Scali: Peter Gallagher
Origin: USA
Language: English
Released: 2010
Production: Donald De Line; De Line Pictures; released by Sony Pictures
Directed by: Steve Antin
Written by: Steve Antin
Cinematography by: Bojan Bazelli
Music by: Christophe Beck
Sound: Richard E. Yawn
Music Supervisor: Todd Bozung
Editing: Virginia Katz
Art Direction: Chris Cornwell
Costumes: Michael Kaplan
Production Design: Jon Gary Steele
MPAA rating: PG-13
Running time: 100 minutes

REVIEWS

Childress, Erik. *eFilmcritic.com.* November 25, 2010.
Dargis, Manohla. *New York Times.* November 24, 2010.
Debruge, Peter. *Variety.* November 22, 2010.
Gonzalez, Ed. *Slate Magazine.* November 22, 2010.
Longworth, Karina. *Village Voice.* November 23, 2010.
Pais, Matt. *Metromix.com.* November 23, 2010.
Rabin, Nathan. *AV Club.* November 23, 2010.
Reed, Rex. *New York Observer.* November 23, 2010.
Tallerico, Brian. *HollywoodChicago.com.* November 24, 2010.
White, Armond. *New York Press.* November 23, 2010.

QUOTES

Ali Rose: "If I'm not 20 times better than 'boobs for brains' over there, you don't have to pay me."

TRIVIA

"You Haven't Seen the Last of Me" was performed live by Cher.

AWARDS

Golden Globes 2011: Song ("You Haven't Seen the Last of Me")
Nomination:
Golden Globes 2011: Film—Mus./Comedy, Song ("Bound to You")
Golden Raspberries 2010: Worst Support. Actress (Cher).

C

CAIRO TIME

An adventure of the heart.
　—Movie tagline

Box Office: $2 million

In a summer packed with overblown, idiotic action fare like *Salt* (2010) and *The A-Team* (2010), out of nowhere came *Cairo Time,* a quiet little love story that is devastating in its emotional precision. The film begins as Juliette (Patricia Clarkson), an American magazine writer, arrives in Egypt to visit her husband Mark (Tom McCamus), a U.N. official who organizes refugee camps in Gaza. Juliette immediately looks wary of the new environment but is excited for the opportunity. This trip to the Middle East is something she has wanted to take for many years, and now that her children are adults, she finally has the chance to travel and vacation with her husband.

That is what makes it so disappointing when Juliette arrives and learns there is a "flare up" at the camp and her husband will not be able to get away for a while. Fortunately, Juliette has an ally in Tareq (Alexander Siddig), a retired U.N. security officer who picks her up from the airport. Tareq used to work with Mark, and as Juliette lingers in Egypt waiting for her husband to get off work, Tareq, a gentle man who recently took over his father's coffee shop, demonstrates his willingness to keep Juliette company and help her explore.

Throughout *Cairo Time* is a theme of people doing what is practical and proper versus what their heart tells them to do. This is first seen when Juliette and Tareq encounter Yasmeen (Amina Annabi), a woman from Tareq's past whose husband died and who tells Tareq

that she never forgot him. Later, when Juliette asks for more detail, Tareq suggests that his feelings for Yasmeen were merely a crush. Yet in the graceful way Siddig plays the scene, it is clear that this was no crush. Tareq wears the past softly on his face, as activity in his mind triggers memories in his heart. Still, Tareq does not feel that it would be appropriate to pursue Yasmeen out of respect for her late husband.

Juliette is also aware of this conflict within her own family. Her son recently eloped, an act that was clearly damaging to his mother but one that obviously sprung from an impulsive act of love. Meanwhile, Juliette's daughter sought to do something she loved by majoring in creative writing, but consequently she now finds herself struggling to find a job. The impracticality of the major is obvious even to Tareq, who asks Juliette with concern, "How will she make a living?" Juliette worries for her daughter but seems pleased that she is trying to do something that inspires her.

Perhaps the greatest clash between passion and reason, however, occurs as Juliette and Tareq grow closer as they walk and dine around town at a relaxed pace that writer-director Ruba Nadda fashions as something in the vicinity of *Before Sunrise* (1995) and *Lost in Translation* (2003). The script is a marvel of minimalist intellectual bonding. Juliette is hungry to take in the culture but her home life has obviously rendered her underprepared—though not naïve or ignorant like the American women in Abu Dhabi in the summer's earlier atrocity, *Sex and the City 2* (2010)—for the sights, tastes, and temperature. Therefore, small gestures from Tareq take on great significance, whether he is teaching her to say "Thank you" in Arabic or proudly offering her coffee from his shop, which he half-jokingly claims is the best in Egypt. Later, Tareq goes out of his way to pick up a copy of Juliette's magazine and playfully acknowledges his lousy score on a personality quiz. Here, the relationship between these two friends shows a hint of flirtation. Juliette clearly enjoys the attention and focus she receives from Tareq, which is something she likely has not received much from her husband as years have turned into decades.

For some, *Cairo Time* will be too reserved; viewers may grow frustrated that Juliette and Tareq never throw caution to the wind to shout everything they are feeling and make a broad demonstration of their growing bond. In fact, this is part of what makes the film so lovely and bittersweet. These are not reckless movie characters. They are mature adults with legitimate values and priorities, and they are not in position to do whatever they want, whenever they want to. So whereas in those films like *Before Sunrise* and *Lost in Translation* characters can at least mentally indulge the possibility of a new, fleeting romance, the connection that develops between Juliette and Tareq only brings the context of their respective situations into focus. She is waiting for her husband, and Tareq is doing right by his old friend and colleague by helping the man's wife explore a new place. Juliette tells Tareq she promised Mark she would wait to see the pyramids with him, a commitment that lingers over the film as Juliette wonders if her husband indeed will have time to participate in their own happiness anymore.

This sense of yearning also appears as Juliette makes a new friend in Kathryn (Elena Anaya), who speaks of a man in her life who started out great but later became possessive and demanding. And when Juliette finally tries to take a bus to Gaza to see Mark, the bus is pulled over and Juliette is escorted off by Egyptian security officials. First, though, a young woman, who opened up to Juliette on the bus about not being able to spend time with her lover, gives Juliette a note to deliver to that man. Juliette aches for this woman, as well as for the Egyptian children she sees selling items in the street or working full-time. She expresses concern for the social issues these kids face; Tareq responds kindly but sternly, "You don't live here; it's complicated."

As such, the world is not simple. Life is not simple. People are brought together at inopportune times, and the wind has a way of blowing once-happy circumstances off course, even for a little while. *Cairo Time* gently captures this feeling with remarkable assuredness without pushing a large amount of background information about the characters or their cultural differences. This is a film in which the ticking clock of both the vacation and of life is always felt, but always in context of the other people and circumstances involved. This approach is not smug and never boring. Rather, it yields some beautiful and beautifully sad moments that reflect, with few words and subtle behavior, just who these characters are and how they feel. Early on in the film, Juliette returns to her hotel to discover Tareq waiting for her. She asks if he has been waiting long. He has not, he tells her. Only an hour. An hour? Most people would consider that a modest amount of time to sit around waiting for someone. Not Tareq. He is happy to burn a little time for the chance to enjoy a little with a woman who, if nothing else, provides good conversation and someone with whom to share a brief adventure.

Matt Pais

CREDITS

Juliette Grant: Patricia Clarkson
Tareq Khalifa: Alexander Siddig
Mark Grant: Tom McCamus
Kathryn: Elena Anaya
Yasmeen: Amina Annabi
Origin: Canada, Ireland
Language: English, Arabic
Released: 2009
Production: David Collins, Daniel Iron; Foundry Films, Samson Films; released by IFC Films
Directed by: Ruba Nadda
Written by: Ruba Nadda
Cinematography by: Luc Montpellier
Music by: Niall Byrne
Sound: Robert Fletcher
Editing: Teresa Hannigan
Costumes: Brenda Boer
Production Design: Tamara Conboy
MPAA rating: Unrated
Running time: 88 minutes

REVIEWS

Berardinelli, James. *Reelviews.* August 7, 2010.
Edelstein, David. *New York Magazine.* August 1, 2010.
Lumenick, Lou. *New York Post.* August 6, 2010.
Neumaier, Joe. *New York Daily News.* August 6, 2010.
Phipps, Keith. *AV Club.* August 5, 2010.
Rea, Stephen. *Philadelphia Inquirer.* August 27, 2010.
Scott, A.O. *New York Times.* August 5, 2010.
Simon, Alissa. *Variety.* September 20, 2009.
Taylor, Ella. *NPR.* August 5, 2010.
Zacharek, Stephanie. *Movieline.* August 6, 2010.

QUOTES

Tareq Khalifa: "They say that if you drink water from the Nile, you will always come back."

This movie was filmed in Cairo, Egypt for 25 days with the average temperature hovering around 50 degrees Celsius (122 degrees Fahrenheit).

CARLOS

The man who hijacked the world.
　　—Movie tagline

Epic and entertaining in equal measure, *Carlos* unfolds like a gritty cross between *The Bourne Supremacy* (2004), *Munich* (2005) and a slightly more esoteric, politically-flavored foreign language drama like *The Baader Meinhof Complex* (2009). A staggering, swaggering 340-minute triptych, filmmaker Olivier Assayas' ambitious account of the life and crimes of the Venezuelan-born "Carlos the Jackal," the preeminent celebu-terrorist of the 1970s and 1980s, began as a miniseries for French television and arrived theatrically in both its original form and a single, shorter-by-half cinematic cut. While its complex subject matter and unwieldy running time were always going to make for a tough domestic commercial sell for distributor IFC Films, the production was wildly embraced and honored by a number of critics organizations, including the Los Angeles Film Critics Association and the Hollywood Foreign Press Association's Golden Globes®—it was tabbed as the Best Foreign Language Film of the Year by both organizations—with Assayas additionally sharing Best Director honors with David Fincher for *The Social Network* (2010) from the LAFCA. A deliberate movie that remarkably still achieves considerable globetrotting, cloak-and-dagger intrigue, *Carlos* ultimately gives a fascinating aerial view of the slow-bleed effectiveness of diplomacy in snuffing out the dead-end mindlessness of extremism.

The story opens in 1973 and covers a period of almost two decades. The film introduces Carlos (Édgar Ramírez), born Ilich Ramírez Sánchez before adopting his *nom du guerre* and fighting as a pro-Palestinian militant in Jordan, as an ideology-spouting revolutionary, just a bit before he decides his anti-imperialist bona fides need the weight of more forceful action. Early on, Carlos, a married man and young father still going by his given name, wets his terrorist beak by impulsively attempting (and failing) to assassinate a pro-Israeli London businessman. This garners the attention of the Popular Front for the Liberation of Palestine (PFLP), which tasks him with several European missions, under the command of a Lebanese militant, Michel Mourkhabal (Fadi Abi Samra).

In the aftermath of one assignment gone wrong, Carlos shoots three French domestic intelligence officers and absconds to southern Yemen. There, the head of the PFLP, Wadie Haddad (Ahmad Kaabour), tabs him for an important assignment: Leading a small, hodgepodge team comprised of other Palestinian militants and German revolutionary leftists, and crashing a 1975 OPEC conference in Vienna, where he is supposed to take a selection of hostages, board a plane, and eventually bump off the Saudi oil minister.

This segment ends the first part of *Carlos,* and encompasses the majority of the second film, which easily contains the most conventional action of the three movies. Though the operation does not turn out as planned, and effectively ends his relationship with Haddad, the brash nature of the raid makes Carlos famous, and seems to ignite inside of him an ill-advised desire to wage war as much in the newspapers as in the streets—a dangerous undertaking for a wanted man. Now essentially a politically conscious mercenary for hire, Carlos' personal politics undergo a morphing and broadening to incorporate the aggrieved, righteous indignation and interests of whatever alignment or faction grants him resources and/or cover, be it the Japanese Red Army or, in many cases, the military-security apparatus of various nation-states, who seek to instigate trouble by proxy.

Despite being pursued by Interpol, Carlos, with a small band of compatriots, moves around freely, from Iraq to Syria, Romania to Libya. He finds safety for a considerable time in Budapest and East Berlin, where he hooks up with Magdalena Kopp (Nora von Waldstätten), the somewhat kinky, terrorist wife of a revolutionary colleague, Johannes Weinrich (Alexander Scheer), who eventually becomes disenchanted with "the cause." Then it is on to Sudan (and yet another woman), where Carlos' strata of nation-state protection eventually crumbles down around him.

Assayas' most recent previous film, *Summer Hours* (2009), was a perceptive but modestly scaled, very French cinematic treatise on family and mortality—in many ways the exact polar opposite of *Carlos*. His follow-up, of course, is rangy and geopolitical, bouncing around from country to country. It is a macro portrait, to *Summer Hours'* micro snapshot. Both movies, however, derive a goodly portion of their power from the unlikely magic of the quotidian—the way characters are impacted and shaped by their surroundings and the simple day-to-day actions of those around them as much as any grand single act or decision. Rather necessarily for a movie spanning twenty years, *Carlos* is full of domestic scenes with portentous but smartly sketched metaphorical weight. The same goes for later scenes of professional betrayal.

Buried in this dizzying array of names and dates, political calculations, and shifting alliances, Assayas and co-writer Dan Franck skillfully shine a light on the business of international terrorism, and all its recruitment and tradeoffs. ("If you stay with the Iraqis, you'll have to answer [for it]—I have a better offer for you," says one party.) The film makes the case that the quest for notoriety and glory drive Carlos as much as any ideology. He chafes at what he views as Western greed, yes, but Carlos is ironically as persuadable as any Wall Street broker if the money is right, and later in his career he engages roundly in weapons smuggling and money laundering, justifying them as a way to raise funds. His belief system can be altered whimsically to fit his own corporeal needs of the moment, as when the OPEC hijacking goes wrong and Carlos—much to the resentment and anger of some of his fellow revolutionaries—comes to the conclusion that martyrdom does not suit him.

In his *indieWIRE* review of the film, Todd McCarthy notes that Ramírez inhabits the title role "with the arrogant charisma of Marlon Brando in his prime," which is absolutely on-point. Both over the years and at any given moment Carlos is many different and often contradictory things: a ruthless killer and a garrulous armchair philosopher; an affectionate father and a philandering misogynist; a raging narcissist and an insecure, overcompensating introvert; a brilliant, clear-eyed strategist and an impulsive caller of foolhardy audibles; and, finally, both a savvy manipulator and a myopic pawn—well, OK, bishop—on a board too big for him to realize. And Ramírez, shaping his physical appearance to reflect his satisfaction and comfort level, or lack thereof, with his environment (at one point Haddad calls him out for getting fat), communicates all of these subtly shaded facts quite capably. His increasingly surly demeanor exemplifies someone who entered into a cause with the intention of noble service, but finds themselves, years on, increasingly willing to sacrifice principles for personal gain and comfort.

Though budgeted at only $18 million, *Carlos* was shot in Austria, France, Germany, Hungary, Lebanon, and Morocco, and this—as well as the fact that it unfolds in at least eight languages—helps give the movie an unshakeable sense of authenticity. While many films deploy myriad horizon-expanding special effects to give scope and depth, Assayas and his crew achieve a remarkable level of period specificity via an impressive array of more traditional means—practical locations, costumes, smart set dressing and the like. Production designer Francois-Renaud Labarthe deserves ample praise, while cinematographers Denis Lenoir and Yorick Le Saux intelligently do not attempt to overwhelm the viewer with stylish gimmickry (an approach that would grow tiresome quite quickly), but instead trade in an unfussy vérité style that puts the focus and attention on the characters and spaces they occupy.

By the end of his professional career as a peddler of politicized violence (he was arrested in a daring raid in 1994, not killed, as one might initially suspect), Carlos was a man of the world with neither the ability to travel nor really a home of his own, living in Sudan essentially under house arrest. His previous hosts had all come to the conclusion that Carlos' presence was not worth it. This noteworthy lesson—that the state-sanctioned manipulation and enabling of fear through sub-political means can largely be bled to death by fierce, unrelenting diplomacy—is a message that resonates even more strongly in this day and age.

Brent Simon

CREDITS

Ilich Ramírez Sánchez/Carlos the Jackal: Édgar Ramírez
Johannes Wenrich: Alexander Scheer
Magdalena Kopp: Nora von Waldstatten
Wadie Haddad: Ahmad Kaabour
Hans-Joachim Klein/Angie: Christoph Bach
Anis Naccache/Khalid: Rodney Ed-Haddad
Gabriele Korcher-Tiedermann/Nada: Julia Hummer
Joseph: Rami Farah
Youssef: Zeid Hamdan
Origin: France, Germany
Language: English, Arabic, French, German, Hungarian, Japanese, Russian, Spanish
Released: 2010
Production: Daniel Leconte; Egoli Tossell Film, StudioCanal; released by IFC Films
Directed by: Olivier Assayas
Written by: Olivier Assayas, Dan Franck
Cinematography by: Yorick Le Saux, Denis Leconte
Sound: Daniel Sobrino, Olivier Goinard
Editing: Luc Barnier, Marion Monnier
Costumes: Juergen Doering
Production Design: Francois-Renaud Labarthe
MPAA rating: Unrated
Running time: 330 minutes

REVIEWS

Burr, Ty. *Boston Globe.* October 28, 2010.
Dargis, Manohla. *New York Times.* October 15, 2010.
Ebert, Roger. *Chicago Sun-Times.* December 2, 2010.
Fine, Marshall. *Hollywood & Fine.* October 15, 2010.
Gleiberman, Owen. *Entertainment Weekly.* October 13, 2010.
Lacey, Liam. *Globe and Mail.* October 22, 2010.
Lane, Anthony. *New Yorker.* October 19, 2010.
Lewis, David. *San Francisco Chronicle.* November 4, 2010.

Morgenstern, Joe. *Wall Street Journal.* October 15, 2010.
O'Hehir, Andrew. *Salon.com.* October 14, 2010.

TRIVIA

During the entire five-and-a-half hour running time, Carlos is not once referred to as "The Jackal."

CASE 39

Some cases should never be opened.
—Movie tagline

Box Office: $13 million

Throughout time, the movies have had a morbid fascination with exploring the darker side of childhood. Not puberty, first crushes or inevitable bullying of the weak, but the kind where special parenting needs to be involved; usually the kind that involves injections and strait jackets. Bad kids come in all forms. Some are bred that way from birth. Others are born from outer space (*Village of the Damned* [1960]) or the flames of hell (*The Omen* [1976]). Then there are those that are just pure evil: Patti Duke's *Bad Seed* (1956), Macaulay Culkin's *Good Son* (1993,) or Sam Rockwell's adopted *Joshua* (2007). The central mystery behind Christian Alvart's *Case 39* is whether little Lilith is in control of her demons or if they are controlling her. The greater mystery is why another potentially evil child narrative could not offer a fresher diagnosis than sedatives for the audience.

Emily Jenkins (Renee Zellweger) works overtime on her child counseling cases. She does not even have enough time to move forward on the advances of her shrink friend, Doug (Bradley Cooper). But she is stuck on the titular situation, a young girl named Lilith (Jodelle Ferland) whose parents may be abusing her. After a late night phone call from the girl, Emily arrives just in time with her cop friend, Mike (Ian MacShane) to stop the folks from cooking her in the oven. Not wanting her to fall through the system, Emily convinces the courts to let Lilith stay with her.

An acknowledgment of love might be enough to erase the curiosity factor in Lilith's snooping around Emily's things, but odder things are afoot in the Jenkins household. Another child under her management kills his parents after a mysterious call comes through. Lilith begins to undergo dastardly personality quirks, challenging the authority of both Emily and Doug, who will regret the day he leaked his greatest fear to a child. When another mysterious death occurs, Emily begins wondering if Lilith's parents knew what they were doing when they locked themselves away from her at night.

These scenes of discovery, as they begin to overtake Emily an hour into the picture, are where *Case 39* could have found a way to distinguish itself from the pack. Instead, Ray Wright's script follows all the clichés of paranoia-driven psychodrama right down to having only one person suspect the truth at any time. Everyone else must offer reason…until they begin to suspect. Which means, everyone but the lead will be dead soon. Last year's bizarrely crafted, *Orphan* (2009), found a way to embrace its Grand Guignol sense of horror with a dark sense of humor and a wacky twist that, at the very least, removed some of the ickiness inherit in wanting to see a child destroyed for their sins. *Case 39* has no twist to speak of and is too dead-serious in its supernatural mind games to spark a sense of humor about its preposterousness.

If all Wright and Alvart wanted to offer up was the feminine—and less fanciful—version of Joe Dante's wish fulfillment segment of *Twilight Zone: The Movie* (1983), then mission accomplished. Any viewer jumping to that conclusion would be thinking far more out of the box than the filmmakers though, who use the bare minimum of scare tactics to pepper the lack of psychological suspense. Audiences can roll their eyes at phone calls of malevolent murmurs preluding death a la *The Ring* (2002), the presence of snapping dogs out of *The Omen* or the appearance of insects which have represented demonic plagues since the beginning of time. None of it is the least bit scary nor does it even approach crossing the line into simple unsettlement. In a faceoff between Emily and Lilith late in the picture it is hard to choose between which is more frightening—an *Exorcist*-like retort from the face of a little girl or an Academy-Award® winning actress busting a television while accentuating "get out of my house" with all the grace of a theater school reject trying to project breathless anxiety in a wind tunnel. Maybe that is why she gets first billing when the final credits display the cast "in order of prominence."

After sitting for years on the shelf—it was filmed in 2006 and originally scheduled for a 2008 release—*Case 39*'s trailers did a far more convincing job of misleading one's expectations than the film itself. Once you have hornets crawling out of ears and eye sockets, there is little speculation that Lilith's adolescent behavior is not subsidized by some corner of hell. Zellweger's poor Emily must struggle for people to believe her and be hamstrung with terrifying visions because some demon child needs a foster home. Can spectres from the underworld not take care of themselves? Is it their sole purpose to be born into this world and then flaunt their secret identity enough until their ultimate plan—if one exists—is crumbled by annoying a movie star? There is a bizarre fascination in exploring the unfiltered darkness of a child's soul and many well-crafted thrillers have resulted from it. *Case 39* is nothing more than a pointless retread that ranks at the bottom of the class and likely puts the evil kid movie on ice for a while.

Erik Childress

CREDITS

Emily Jenkins: Renee Zellweger
Lilith Sullivan: Jodelle Ferland
Mike Barron: Ian McShane
Douglas Ames: Bradley Cooper
Edward Sullivan: Callum Keith Rennie
Wayne: Adrian Lester
Nancy: Cynthia Stevenson
Georgia: Georgia Craig
Margaret Sullivan: Kerry O'Malley
Origin: USA
Language: English
Released: 2010
Production: Steve Golin, Kevin Misher; Anonymous Content; released by Paramount Vantage
Directed by: Christian Alvart
Written by: Christian Alvart, Ray Wright
Cinematography by: Hagen Bogdanski
Music by: Michi Britsch
Sound: David A. Cohen, Darren Brisker
Editing: Mark Goldblatt
Art Direction: Ross Dempster
Costumes: Monique Prudhomme
Production Design: John Willett
MPAA rating: R
Running time: 109 minutes

REVIEWS

Abele, Robert. *Los Angeles Times.* October 2, 2010.
Gibron, Bill. *Filmcritic.com.* September 30, 2010.
Gilsdorf, Ethan. *Boston Globe.* October 7, 2010.
Johanson, MaryAnn. *Flick Filosopher.* October 3, 2010.
Mintzer, Jordan. *Variety.* September 30, 2010.
Puccio, John J.. *DVD Town.* December 24, 2010.
Savada, Elias. *Film Threat.* October 15, 2010.
Schager, Nick. *Time Out New York.* October 6, 2010.
Swietek, Frank. *One Guy's Opinion.* October 2, 2010.
Weinberg, Scott. *Fearnet.* January 9, 2011.

QUOTES

Edward Sullivan: "They say when you're born you're given your eternal soul. The part of you that lives on…lives again. Whatever evil she is, didn't come from us. It was already there. From the moment she came into being, she brought something with her. Something older…destructive. Soul of a demon."

The film was released in the United States three years after it was completed in 2007.

CASINO JACK
(Bagman)

Honor. Integrity. Principles. Everything is negotiable.
—Movie tagline

George Hickenlooper's *Casino Jack* arrives with the unique—or unfortunate—timing of being released in the same calendar year as a documentary on the same subject matter. Just seven months prior, Alex Gibney's *Casino Jack and the United States of Money* (2010) tackled the tale of infamous government lobbyist, Jack Abramoff, in non-fiction form. Using ironic movie clips and potent soundtrack choices to underline the potentially dry layout of financial facts and business-as-usual political corruption, Gibney helped make a farce out of Abramoff's dirty dealings. By putting viewers right in the shoes of the charismatic crook, Hickenlooper manages to do just the opposite in a narrative that feels far-less-fascinating than the daily news coverage that followed this story once it broke.

Kevin Spacey plays Abramoff, who, while being indicted in the film's opening scenes, is also trying to indict viewers for his behavior. After all, those stylish blue jeans would not be on sale if he was not greasing the wheels of politicians like Tom DeLay (Spencer Garrett) with fact-finding missions to Hawaii to keep labor laws from shutting down sweatshops that manufactured them. His nickname derives from his business with Indian tribes, first for his help in keeping their casinos untaxed and then later for bilking those same clients in millions of dollars of unchecked fees. Jack's business partner, Michael Scanlon (Barry Pepper), is shown as the instigator of this scam, suggesting he "deserve[s] better" than the ceiling the law sets for lobbying a client's interests.

While Abramoff's list of shenanigans is long and winding, the film attempts to settle on his relationship with Adam Kidan (Jon Lovitz), a bumbling mattress salesman with mob connections, as a large part of his eventual downfall. Along with Scanlon, their back door endeavor to buy the Sun Cruz casinos while representing it gets Jack fired from his firm just as he is being pegged by the *Wall Street Journal* as a "super-lobbyist." Abramoff continues to extend himself through restaurants and real estate, leading him to take on more clients and live up to his newfound title and fame. But between Kidan's phony wire transfer involving Sun Cruz, the murder of its original proprietor, and the cheated Mrs. Scanlon's (Rachelle Lefevre) relationship with a snooping reporter about to hit spiteful levels, K Street is about to be taken back for the people.

Well, not exactly. Norman Snider's screenplay takes no opportunity to brand Abramoff and his ilk as the overriding ingredient in the corruption that is poisoning Washington. The Kidan chapter is merely presented as a misstep in judgment. Busting him Capone-style might seem like the usual irony for a meaty political satire except Snider's script and Hickenlooper's approach to it neither induces outrage nor recognizes where it should be reduced to comedy. It counts on Lovitz to play the buffoon for comic relief in-between trying to snipe its own version of Gibney's techniques by ushering in Spacey's gift for impressions.

Hickenlooper should be the right director to invoke the correlation between the big screen and behind-the-scenes fiascos, having crafted *Hearts of Darkness* (1991), arguably the quintessential filmmaking documentary. Where else is the combination of wannabe stars, money and sleaze more documented than in Hollywood and D.C.? And he opens on the right note with Spacey's Abramoff psyching himself up in the mirror, preaching what he believes to be an audience of one with the dubious punchline of strength about how he "works out every day." General Patton he most certainly is not.

Golden Globe® voters were confused as much as anyone by the presumed tone of the film, enough to nominate Spacey as Best Actor in the Comedy/Musical department. Tap-dancing towards laughs would be more feasible if Abramoff was more of a pathetic figure caught in a web of his own making. But this was a really smart guy who manipulated a system that has no qualms about being manipulated. This is more *Middle Men* (2010) than *In the Loop* (2009) or *Wag the Dog* (1997); films where the behavior of insiders represented an accentuated irony to the irrationality of their behavior and the public's passive reaction to their meaningless words. Outrage should be the word associated with Jack, who is instead treated with the indifference of an actual errand boy sent by grocery clerks to collect a bill. He is just doing his job in a town that is so broke it has to take on credit that it does not deserve.

Erik Childress

CREDITS

Jack Abramoff: Kevin Spacey
Pam Abramoff: Kelly Preston
Adam Kidan: Jon Lovitz
Michael Scanlon: Barry Pepper

Oscar Carillo: Yannick Bisson
Chief Poncho: Eric Schweig
Ralph Reed: Christian Campbell
Big Tony: Maury Chakin
Tom DeLay: Spencer Garrett
Emily Miller: Rachelle Lefevre
Origin: USA
Language: English
Released: 2010
Production: Gary Howsam, Bill Marks, George Zakk; Trigger Street, Rollercoaster Entertainment, An Olive Branch Productions, Vortex Words Pictures, Hannibal Pictures; released by ATO Pictures
Directed by: George Hickenlooper
Written by: Norman Snider
Cinematography by: Adam Swica
Music by: Jonathan Goldsmith
Sound: Jane Tattersall
Music Supervisor: Amy Fritz
Editing: William Steinkamp
Art Direction: Peter Emmink
Production Design: Matthew Davies
MPAA rating: R
Running time: 108 minutes

REVIEWS

Berardinelli, James. *ReelViews.* December 16, 2010.
Burr, Ty. *Boston Globe.* January 6, 2011.
Ebert, Roger. *Chicago Sun-Times.* December 30, 2010.
Hoberman, J.. *Village Voice.* December 14, 2010.
Koehler, Robert. *Variety.* September 27, 2010.
Levin, Robert. *am New York.* December 19, 2010.
Nusair, David. *Reel Film Reviews.* September 9, 2010.
Scott, A.O.. *New York Times.* December 17, 2010.
Tobias, Scott. *AV Club.* December 16, 2010.
Weinberg, Scott. *Cinematical.* September 19, 2010.

AWARDS

Nomination:

Golden Globes 2011: Actor—Mus./Comedy (Spacey).

CASINO JACK AND THE UNITED STATES OF MONEY

Come see where your democracy went.
—Movie tagline
Meet Jack Abramoff—America's greatest lobbyist.
—Movie tagline

Having previously made the excellent documentary *Enron: The Smartest Guys in the Room* (2005), a film that managed to take a sprawling and potentially confusing tale of massive greed, corruption, and financial chicanery and transformed it into a clear and concise narrative that laid out the story of what actually happened in a manner that both enlightened audiences and made them mad as hell to boot, it stands to reason that prolific documentarian Alex Gibney would be a good choice to tell the story of Jack Abramoff, the notorious political lobbyist and influence peddler whose highly questionable deed allowed him to line his pockets with millions of dollars before landing him a four-year prison sentence for fraud, tax evasion and conspiracy to bribe public officials. The trouble with the resulting film, *Casino Jack and the United States of Money* (not to be confused with another 2010 release, *Casino Jack,* a dramatized version of the story from the late George Hickenlooper featuring Kevin Spacey as Abramoff), is that unlike the Enron film, it never manages to pull its avalanche of details together into a straightforward and compelling storyline. As a result, it too often feels like an overly-detailed PowerPoint presentation gone awry that will only be fully understood by viewers who already come to it with a strong working knowledge of the subject at hand.

This is not to say that a movie, or even two, about Abramoff was a bad idea because, as the film reveals, he is one of those outsized characters that almost seem too good to be true. Although he had a childhood fascination with film that would manifest itself in odd ways later in life—he would convert to Orthodox Judaism after watching *Fiddler on the Roof* (1971) and produce and co-write the Dolph Lundgren action epic *Red Scorpion*(1989)—an admiration for Ronald Reagan would inspire him to drift into the political arena. After graduating from Brandeis University, he would become chairman of the College Republican National Committee and, along with such future stars as Karl Rove and Ralph Reed, he would help push the party further to the right on the political spectrum. He then formed his own lobbying firm and when the Republicans took control of Congress in 1994, he used his skills, influence and connections to make enormous amounts of money by pushing congressmen from both parties to support the interest of clients ranging from Third World sweatshop owners and Russian businessmen of questionable nature to pharmaceutical companies and Indian casinos, often by creating fake organizations through which he could funnel huge amounts of corporate money or by pitting unwitting clients against each other in classic *Yojimbo* (1961) style. In one especially inspired bit, his company convinced Christian groups to fund and support anti-gambling legislation against Indian tribes hoping to build their own casinos and then turned around and represented those very same tribes in their efforts to lobby Congress to overcome said legislation.

This is fascinating stuff to be sure but it has not resulted in a fascinating movie in the end. One of the chief problems is that Gibney never quite manages to invoke the spirit of outrage towards Abramoff and the system that could allow people like him to flourish. Unlike the Enron film, where the sight of the shocking lengths that a seemingly healthy and all-American company would go to in order to make enormous profits no matter what the cost was a truly eye-opening experience, the notion that the corridors of power in Washington are rife with corruption and greed is one that will not exactly shock or stun most viewers. Gibney tries to make the greater point throughout that Abramoff, while the most high-profile of the bunch thanks to his achievements and eventual conviction, was just merely one part of the increasingly blatant alliance between rich corporations and officials ostensibly elected to serve the needs of their constituents but the suggestion that this is all just business as usual in the new America winds up muting a good portion of the anger that he is trying to stir up. Gibney tries to make up for this by studding his film with any number of ironically chosen song cues and film clips to underline his case but for the most part, they only serve as cheap shots and distractions.

The biggest flaw of *Casino Jack and the United States of Money* is the relative absence of Abramoff's own presence from his own story. Although Gibney was able to interview him while in prison (he was released in December 2010), he was not allowed to film any of those interviews. In such previous efforts as the Enron film and *Gonzo: The Life and Work of Dr. Hunter S. Thompson* (2008), his overview of the life and work of the legendary journalist, Gibney was also working with projects where the central characters were unwilling or unable to be interviewed on camera but he managed to work around that problem in those cases by lashing together enough archival footage of those people to help move the narratives along. In the case of Abramoff, part of the whole point of being a lobbyist is remaining in the shadows, and while there is some tantalizing footage of his early years as he is building his power base, it mostly runs out by the time the film gets to the meatier portions. As a result, there is an unmistakable vacuum in its center that no amount of ironic stock footage, readings of his incredibly incriminating e-mails by Stanley Tucci, or talking head interviews with peripheral characters, can quite overcome. In fact, former congressman Tom DeLay, whose dealings with Abramoff helped hasten his departure from public office and who did sit for Gibney's cameras, winds up dominating the proceedings by default with his utterly shameless attitude and oily demeanor inspiring the kind of outrage that Gibney clearly wants viewers to feel—so much so, in fact, that after the film is over, many people may wonder why Gibney did not just make a movie about him instead.

Peter Sobczynski

CREDITS

Origin: USA
Language: English
Released: 2010
Production: Alex Gibney, Alison Ellwood, Zena Barakat; Participant Media, Jigsaw Productions; released by Magnolia Pictures
Directed by: Alex Gibney
Written by: Alex Gibney
Cinematography by: Maryse Alberti
Music by: John McCullough
Sound: Philip Stockton, Al(lan) Zaleski
Editing: Alison Ellwood
MPAA rating: R
Running time: 123 minutes

REVIEWS

Burr, Ty. *Boston Globe.* May 21, 2010.
Edelstein, David. *New York Magazine.* May 7, 2010.
Feeney, F.X. *Village Voice.* May 4, 2010.
Hartlab, Peter. *San Francisco Chronicle.* May 14, 2010.
Holden, Stephen. *New York Times.* May 7, 2010.
Kennicott, Phillip. *Washington Post.* May 7, 2010.
Koehler, Robert. *Variety.* January 24, 2010.
Lybarger, Dan. *eFilmcritic.com.* June 5, 2010.
Musetto, V.A. *New York Post.* May 6, 2010.
Rea, Steven. *Philadelphia Inquirer.* May 21, 2010.

CATFISH

Don't let anyone tell you what it is.
—Movie tagline

Box Office: $3 million

The documentary *Catfish* arrived in theaters sandwiched between the release of Casey Affleck and Joaquin Phoenix's faux documentary *I'm Still Here* (2010) and David Fincher's incendiary chronicling of Mark Zuckerberg's invention of Facebook, *The Social Network* (2010). *I'm Still Here* depicted actor Joaquin Phoenix changing career paths from a respected actor to an out of control hip-hop wannabe. The two-year long, highly publicized (and mostly believed) journey was later revealed after the film's release and its subsequent scathing reviews to be a performance and not at all real. *The Social Network* eventually finds Zuckerberg becoming an addict of his own creation and one of the many

millions who would live their life online through the social network Facebook, where one is able to create a whole new virtual identity while making "friends" or even enemies.

Like these films, *Catfish* is about a relationship that develops on Facebook and upon the film's release, many grew skeptical about the movie's authenticity and the motives of the filmmakers, Henry Joost and Ariel Schulman. Everyone involved insists *Catfish* is real. It is not an unreasonable question, especially considering the rise in popularity of fake documentaries (*The Last Exorcism* (2010) and *The Virginity Hit* (2010) had also been released in the same time period). But *Catfish,* while perhaps murky in its intentions, is a completely believable story and probably not uncommon in the landscape of online social networking and internet dating.

The story begins with a mostly likable filmmaker and photographer Nev Schulman, bother of filmmaker Ariel and friends with the other filmmaker Henry Joost. They all live in New York. Ariel, Henry, and Nev often film themselves in various situations, so (as they tell it) the cameras happened to be rolling while Nev developed a friendship with an eight-year-old painter in Michigan, Abby Pierce. Nev, of course, can only communicate with her through the kid's mom, Angela. Nev photographs dancers and Abby saw one of Nev's photos online and decided to paint it. Nev sent more photos and Abby made more paintings. A perfectly innocent relationship between two unlikely friends grew, with Nev talking to Abby once very briefly on the phone.

Angela also has an older daughter named Megan, an attractive, 19-year old horse enthusiast who also plays guitar. Nev and Megan's relationship grows more platonic, then romantic, then sexual. Megan posts messages on her Facebook page such as "I miss someone I don't even know." They begin texting each other (or "sexting"), talking late at night, and soon Nev wants nothing more than to meet this person and see if the fantasy he is living with this person is, in fact, real. Nev and his filmmaking friends seize an opportunity to drop in on the family unexpectedly in their Michigan home.

What happens from here on in is best left a secret. *Catfish* is not really a mystery, but it has elements of mystery within its storyline. It would not be much of a movie without that element. While the movie was mis-advertised as being a "documentary thriller" with a Hitchcockian twist, *Catfish* does have suspense in that the viewer wants to know just as much as Nev what is up with this family. When all is finally revealed, it is done so with a delicate anti-climax. Nothing is under-scored, but rather left hanging in the air for Nev and the audience to interpret in the moment.

The film's intent, contrary to the cryptic marketing campaign, is not to shock, thrill, or pull the rug out from under the viewer, but to reveal the underlying sadness of many who use social networking sites such as Facebook to live a life and to gain attention from friends and strangers. The filmmakers are sensitive toward their subjects, but they have also been accused of exploiting them. If they were exploiting these people in Michigan, their reactions to their discoveries about them would be different and more knee-jerk. Their approach in depicting them is sympathetic. Their intentions for driving out to their house is certainly suspect, especially given what they already know about this family (they got a lot of what they expected to find even before meeting them), but there is not a documentary filmmaker alive who would not seize the same opportunity to make the same kind of investigation first hand.

If *Catfish* were a hoax, it is indeed a brilliantly conceived one. The camerawork is messy, poorly lit, and home movie-like without much in the way of suspiciously pre-conceived scenes or plot points as one would find in a reality TV series. The only technical question is whether or not these little cameras actually work underwater as they appear to do in the film (why would any documentary filmmaker test that just for a throwaway "artsy" affect?). And if filmmakers were going to stage a hoax of a story, why would they choose this story?

In the end, *Catfish* is a sad and moving film. The viewer is taken on the same journey as the filmmakers and subjects. The reactions to everything are shared. Often a mystery does not warrant a repeat viewing. Once the viewer knows the end, what is the point of watching it again? But *Catfish* does reward when visited a second time. It is not a film about a twist, but about these people. If done properly, the story would probably work as a piece of narrative fiction as well. It is often said about documentaries "If this were a work of fiction, no one would believe it." Interesting how *Catfish*'s story is completely believable and there are many who do not want to believe it.

Collin Souter

CREDITS

Melody C. Roscher: Herself
Ariel Schulman: Himself
Yaniv Schulman: Himself
Angela Wesselman-Pierce: Herself
Origin: USA
Language: English
Released: 2010

Production: Andrew Jarecki, Marc Smerling, Ariel Schulman, Henry Joost; Hit the Ground Running Films, Supermarche; released by Universal
Directed by: Ariel Schulman, Henry Joost
Cinematography by: Ariel Schulman, Henry Joost, Yaniv Schulman
Sound: Coll Anderson
Music Supervisor: Sue Jacobs
Editing: Zac Stuart-Pintier
MPAA rating: PG-13
Running time: 86 minutes

REVIEWS

Burr, Ty. *Boston Globe.* September 23, 2010.
Doerkson, Cliff. *Chicago Reader.* September 24, 2010.
Ebert, Roger. *Chicago Sun-Times.* September 23, 2010.
Edelstein, David. *New York Magazine.* September 13, 2010.
Johnson, G. Allen *San Francisco Chronicle.* September 16, 2010.
Lane, Jim. *Sacramento News and Review.* September 25, 2010.
Lybarger, Dan. *eFilmcritic.com.* October 1, 2010.
Murray, Noel. *AV Club.* September 16, 2010.
Phillips, Michael. *Chicago Tribune.* September 23, 2010.
Scott, A.O. *New York Times.* September 17, 2010.

CATS & DOGS: THE REVENGE OF KITTY GALORE

Purr-fessional spy.
—Movie tagline

Box Office: $44 million

The void that has existed in film for nearly ten years was finally filled in 2010, when the long-awaited, demanded-by-no-one sequel to *Cats & Dogs* (2001) was finally released. With a different director, different writers, and almost none of the same actors playing the human characters or performing the voices of the bevy of talking animals, *Cats & Dogs: The Revenge of Kitty Galore* was unleashed into theaters and managed to erase the modest profit margin the original film made, while giving children across the country every reason they might need to not want pets.

While the stakes of the first film were relatively small—cats and dogs fighting over control of a serum that would cure human allergies to dogs—in *The Revenge of Kitty Galore,* the fate of the globe is in the paws of a grotesque hairless cat named Kitty Galore (voiced by Bette Midler), once one of the great cat spies who has since gone rogue. Since neither cats nor dogs are a fan of Kitty's attempt to rule the world, the two species join forces to save their world and that of their human owners. The new spy dog recruit from the first film, Lou the beagle (voiced by Neil Patrick Harris, taking over for Toby Maguire), is now a top agent leading the fight against Kitty. Her plan involves globally broadcasting a specific frequency designed to make all dogs transform into vicious, biting creatures so that humans will be forced into putting dogs in kennels or worse, leaving cats to rule the world.

One of the few funny aspects to *The Revenge of Kitty Galore* is the revenge angle. Kitty is plotting to commit these terrible acts not because dogs were mean to her but because humans rejected her when she lost her hair. It is never really clear how Kitty will subdue the human population, but any cat that can figure out how to rid the world of dogs should clearly be feared. The dog side of the defensive is led by Lou, Diggs (James Marsden), and Butch (an appropriately grumpy vocal turn by Nick Nolte). The feline army is led by Catherine (Chirstina Applegate), with a few other animals thrown in for good measure, including Seamus the pigeon (Katt Williams). Also lending their voices to the affair are returning voice talent Joe Pantoliano and Michael Clarke Duncan.

Of secondary concern are the human characters, such as Chris O'Donnell's police officer Shane, and comic actors Jack McBrayer and Fred Armisen, whose sole duties seem to be inserting jokes and improvising lines to beef up the sagging comedy. With a title referencing one of the cruder names in the James Bond series, it is hardly a secret that the *Cats & Dogs* movies are tired send-ups of spy movie franchises and the gadgets that populate such works. *The Revenge of Kitty Galore* truly drives home this homage with Roger Moore popping in to voice Tab Lazenby, a cat that wears a bow-tie, and there is a brief appearance by a secondary villain character with a full set of metal teeth.

Perhaps the strangest—some might say least appropriate for kids—reference occurs when Mr. Tinkles (the bad guy from the first film, still voiced by Sean Hayes) is brought into the film wearing a Hannibal Lecter-style muzzle and straightjacket. The parents of any child that gets that reference should be put in jail or at least seriously investigated. That said, the sequence with kittens getting stoned on catnip is a classic.

The biggest problem with *The Revenge of Kitty Galore* is that it feels bloated by both its special effects budget and its overly ambitious story. The first film's premise that there is a centuries' old battle between cats and dogs over who will be the favorite pet of humans seems weirdly logical by comparison. Certainly such conflicts exist between pet owners. But the idea of an evil cat attempting to take over the world or dogs using jet packs pushes the entertainment value of the concept from fantasy to ridiculous. If something in the writing improved along with the inflated conceit, the filmmakers (led by first-time feature director Brad Peyton) might have made something out of the concept. Instead, viewers are left to contend with the same old butt-sniffing jokes from nine years ago.

There is potential for heartfelt moments, but it is squandered. Diggs is a police K-9 dog who is seen as a little too aggressive for the force. O'Donnell plays his owner-officer. Although Diggs is eventually recruited by the canine spy organization to defeat Kitty, the missed opportunity to play up the bond between Diggs and his owner could not be more noticeable. Speaking of missed opportunities, any project that renders Jack McBrayer un-funny does not deserve to exist.

While the world certainly did not have high hopes for *The Revenge of Kitty Galore*, few could have anticipated the extent of the stink on this movie. While it is clear more money was spent on special effects—and the theatrical release had the added "bonus" of being projected in post-conversion 3D—what little heart the original movie had has been erased completely from this limp effort. It is likely that even children will reject this brainless exercise in adventure/comedy; at least the smart ones will.

Steven Prokopy

CREDITS

Shane: Chris O'Donnell
Chuck: Jack McBrayer
Crazy Carlito: Paul Rodriguez (Voice)
Tab Lazenby: Roger Moore (Voice)
Mr. Tinkles: Sean P. Hayes (Voice)
Catherine: Christina Applegate (Voice)
Butch: Nick Nolte (Voice)
Seamus: Katt Micah Williams (Voice)
Kitty Galore: Bette Midler (Voice)
Sam: Michael Clarke Duncan (Voice)
Peek: Joe Pantoliano (Voice)
Butch: Alec Baldwin (Voice)
Diggs: James Marsden (Voice)
Lou: Neil Patrick Harris (Voice)
Origin: USA
Language: English
Released: 2010
Production: Polly Cohen Johnsen, Andrew Lazar; Village Roadshow Pictures, CD2 Films, Mad Chance, Polymorph Films; released by Warner Bros.
Directed by: Brad Peyton
Written by: Ron J. Friedman, Steve Bencich
Cinematography by: Steven Poster

Music by: Christopher Lennertz
Sound: Christopher Aud
Music Supervisor: Julianne Jordan
Editing: Julie Rogers
Art Direction: Sandra Tanaka
Costumes: Tish Monaghan
Production Design: Rusty Smith
MPAA rating: PG
Running time: 82 minutes

REVIEWS

Biancolli, Amy. *San Francisco Chronicle.* July 30, 2010.
Biodrowski, Steve. *Cinefantastique.* August 3, 2010.
Hale, Mike. *New York Times.* July 29, 2010.
Meek, Tom. *Boston Phoenix.* July 28, 2010.
Orndorf, Brian. *eFilmCritic.com.* July 30, 2010.
Propes, Richard. *TheIndependentCritic.com.* July 30, 2010.
Puig, Claudia. *USA Today.* July 31, 2010.
Savlov, Marc. *Austin Chronicle.* July 31, 2010.
Tyrkus, Mike. *MovieRetriever.com.* July 30, 2010.
Wright, Rachel. *FlickFeast.co.uk.* November 29, 2010.

AWARDS

Nomination:

Golden Raspberries 2010: Worst Use of 3D.

TRIVIA

The film features the voice of Roger Moore who portrayed
fellow super spy James Bond.

CENTURION

Fight or die.
—Movie tagline

British writer-director Neil Marshall has a true gift for exploring the intricacies of the group dynamic. In previous works, such as *Dog Soldiers* (2002) and *The Descent* (2005), Marshall illustrates the strengths and weaknesses of a team of men or women against overwhelming odds, usually against a small army of supernatural beings. But with *Centurion*, he pits man against man—with a few ferocious women thrown in—in this story set in 117 A.D., as the Roman Empire attempts to strengthen its positions in Britain. But thanks to a group of savage Britons known as the Picts, the Romans have a near impossible time winning any battles or coming out of any battle with survivors.

The sole survivor of a Pict attack on an isolated Roman fort is Quintus Dias (Michael Fassbender), who somehow makes it across some of the roughest terrain during the most unimaginable weather to find the near-

est Roman garrison and its commander General Titus Flavius Virilus (Dominic West, portraying a slightly nicer Roman than he did in *300*), leader of the famous Ninth Legion. The general has received explicit orders to eliminate the Picts and he gathers Quintus and an army to do so. After a brutal and unmerciful Pict raid on invading Romans, a handful of survivors attempt to flee the Picts and retreat to the closest Roman outpost while being pursued by some of the greatest trackers and most ferocious killers the world has to offer.

Marshall is not capable of making a film that does not find new and innovative ways to make blood flow, splatter, and otherwise run red. With very little budget and no digital effects, the director has created a gore-filled sword-and-sandal work that feels epic in scale while maintaining an intimate connection to the core group of Roman characters. Fassbender absolutely inhabits the character of Quintus, with his battered body, sunken face, and burning will to survive. Other great performances as the Roman soldiers come from Liam Cunningham as the most brutish of the bunch, Brick, and David Morrissey as the thoughtful and cautious Bothos.

The far-more-colorful and interesting characters are the Picts, who dress in furs and bones, and wear warpaint that resembles skin peeling off the body. Little is known in history about the real-life Picts since they did not keep records of their exploits, so Marshall has the freedom to get creative. The leader of this particular Pict clan is Gorlacon (Danish actor Ulrich Thomsen). When the Romans come to his camp to rescue their captured general, Gorlacon's son (Ryan Atkinson) is accidentally killed, an incident that adds a special brand of rage to the Pict's pursuit of the Roman survivors. Two of the more interesting Pict warriors are played by woman. Russian-born Olga Kurylenko plays the mute tracker Etain, who initially helps the Romans find the Picts but turns on them as part of a trap. Marshall's real-life wife Axelle Carolyn plays the silver-haired murderess Aeron, who tends to smile as she kills. As enjoyable as it is getting to know the Roman characters, *Centurion* tends to be a lot more entertaining and certainly more bloody when the Picts are close by.

In an interesting third-act turn, Marshall introduces a love interest into the story in the guise of Arianne (Imogen Poots), a witch of sorts and banished Pict who provides food, shelter, and a hiding place for the few remaining Romans who reach her neck of the woods. Arianne and Quintus have a few sweet, enjoyable moments together in one of the film's few non-action sequences. The scene also sets the stage for the Roman characters to enjoy a rare moment of levity. Not surprisingly, humor is not a major element in *Centurion*.

The film is about the pursuit, and it is relentless in its mission to give an audience as few moments to collect itself or breath easy as possible. In his own ultra-violent style, Marshall has also fashioned a kind of antiwar movie, which occasionally takes the opportunity to draw parallels between the current war in the Middle East and the exploits of these well-armed and organized Romans against the guerilla tactics of men and women defending their homeland. It might strike some as a bit strange that Marshall wants the audience to root for an invading army rather than those protecting their homes, but perhaps that is not exactly what he is after. It is certainly a subject worthy of interpretation and discussion after watching *Centurion*.

For those fans of Marshall who prefer his more horror-oriented fare, it is difficult to believe that the sheer volume of blood and guts in *Centurion* would not satisfy even the most violence-starved moviegoer. For example, the director seemingly goes out of his way to explore fascinating new ways to sever a head. (Who ever said a head had to come off at the neck?) And whenever someone is pierced with an arrow or struck by a sword, the blood does not so much trickle out as explode from the wound. The squeamish should consider themselves warned.

With his micro-budget and a group of exceedingly talented actors in tow, Neil Marshall has conjured something that is often quite creative and adventurous, while still remaining true to its war-film roots. Add to that *Centurion*'s seemingly authentic weaponry and costumes, and the resulting film is a gloriously blood-soaked piece of entertainment.

Steven Prokopy

CREDITS

Centurion Quintus Dias: Michael Fassbender
Gen. Titus Flavius Virilus: Dominic West
Thax: J.J. Feild
Septus: Lee Ross
Bothos: David Morrissey
Gorlacon: Ulrich Thomsen
Governor Agricola: Paul Freeman
Etain: Olga Kurylenko
Brick: Liam Cunningham
Macros: Noel Clarke
Leonidas: Demitri Leonidas
Tarak: Rizwan Ahmed
Arianne: Imogen Poots
Gorlacon's Son: Ryan Atkinson
Aeron: Axelle Carolyn
Origin: United Kingdom

Language: English
Released: 2010
Production: Christian Colson, Robert Jones; Celador Films, Cloud Eight Films; released by Magnet Releasing, Warner Bros.
Directed by: Neil Marshall
Written by: Neil Marshall
Cinematography by: Sam McCurdy
Music by: Ilan Eshkeri
Sound: John Hayes
Editing: Chris Gill
Art Direction: Jason Knox-Johnston, Andy Thomson
Costumes: Keith Madden
Production Design: Simon Bowles
MPAA rating: R
Running time: 97 minutes

REVIEWS

Berkshire, Geoff. *Metromix.com.* August 26, 2010.
Biancolli, Amy. *San Francisco Chronicle.* August 27, 2010.
Blake, Bitchin. *FilmReviews.com.* August 31, 2010.
Emerson, Jim. *RogerEbert.com.* August 25, 2010.
Feeney, F.X. *Village Voice.* August 25, 2010.
Holden, Stephen. *New York Times.* August 26, 2010.
O'Hehir, Andrew. *Salon.com.* August 25, 2010.
Orndorf, Brian. *eFilmCritic.com.* August 7, 2010.
Prigge, Matt. *Philadelphia Weekly.* August 25, 2010.
Vijn, Ard. *TwitchFilm.com.* June 15, 2010.

QUOTES

Centurion Quintus Dias: "My name is Quintus Dias, I am a soldier of Rome, and this is neither the beginning nor the end of my story."

CHARLIE ST. CLOUD

Life is for living.
—Movie tagline

Box Office: $31 million

We all deal with death in different ways. Some of us look towards the heavens to pray or curse the higher power which took our loved ones from us. There are those who withdraw from the world until the pain goes away. The most popular of all these remedies is usually the credo that if we keep their memories alive they will always be with us. Whether we crack jokes at the after-funeral gathering or shed our tears in full view of friends and family, grieving is an individual mannerism. Support can ease the process but it is still very much our own. When someone then asks you to share in the grief of another, especially in the movies where people tend to escape from their daily troubles, they better be sure it is not just an attempt to manipulate you into shedding tears for someone they never knew. *Charlie St. Cloud* is so palpable in its exploitation of death that it practically reaches off the screen to stroke the tears out of us through the eyes of a character the film itself barely knows.

Charlie (Zac Efron) is a prize-winning sailor and the envy of fellow competitors in the coastal town where he is still in high school. Not for long though as he has received a sailing scholarship from Stanford. He will be leaving behind mom (Kim Basinger) and his precocious twelve-year-old brother, Sam (Charlie Tahan), to whom he promises one last summer to practice baseball. That summer does not come, however, when Charlie and Sam are hit by a drunk driver and the dreaded T-boning semi that has haunted so many unsuspecting shotgun riders in movies. Charlie survives thanks to persistent paramedic, Florio Ferrente (Ray Liotta), but Sam is gone. After his funeral, Charlie runs out to the woods and discovers that he can see his now-dead brother. And a promise is a promise.

Five years later, Charlie has neglected his scholarship to take a job as the town cemetery's groundskeeper. He has not sailed since the accident and not only still plays catch with Sam, but can actually see the ghosts of others (or, at least, the best friend with the scary eyebrows [Dave Franco, brother of James]). All eyes on sailing in the community are now on Tess Carroll (Amanda Crew), one-time competition of Charlie's who is preparing for a solo trip around the world. Tess has always been "flummoxed" by Charlie and while her coach with the definitive crusty sailor's name of Tink Weatherbee (Donal Logue) sees him as a loon and a distraction, she is nevertheless drawn to him for a final fling before heading off into the sunset. Or, in her case, the perfect storm.

It would be convenient to use Tess' impending obstacle as a metaphor for this film's collapse of ideas but that would be to suggest it was ever anything but a wandering collection of moments with nothing to center it but close-ups of Zac Efron. His baby blues are not enough to tame the lazy eye of this emotional tempest that confuses fortune cookie wisdom with psychological healing. "You should be living your life...You have been given a second chance," says Liotta's dying lifesaver despite not having seen Charlie since the ambulance and knows as much about his life as one can when having to start a conversation with "What have you been up to?" In case Charlie and Florio have forgotten as much about each other as the audience has, their big scene begins with "You're the paramedic" and "Yeah, I'm the paramedic."

The screenplay by Craig Pearce & Lewis Colick—based on the novel by Ben Sherwood—plays fast and loose with the rules of the afterlife. Charlie seems so unfazed by his new powers that he walks through the film almost bored with it. There is no joyous sense of return when his military pal appears—presumably for the first time—nor does the story develop this sensory magic to a point where Charlie is tired of being surrounded by death. Is there a penance involved for the guilt from Sam's death or is this just a device with a built-in cry button? When Kevin Bacon underwent hypnosis in *Stir of Echoes* (1999) and came back with similar powers, he solved a murder. Charlie St. Cloud is whisked away from death to start up the longest-running and worst outdoor theater performance of *Field of Dreams* (1989).

Over five years, Charlie and Sam have apparently just gone on like nothing happened. There is no emotional catharsis between the two and no talk of moving on or what could have been. When Charlie finally makes a step towards renewing his life with Tess, Sam takes him on another kind of trip. "I can feel myself disappearing," Sam says when Charlie is with her. But is this just a reflection of his subconscious shame? The film is less rooted in ruminating valuable lessons and life and death. It fails to define the ground rules of Charlie's paranormal therapy. Just what was Charlie really doing in the woods if he was alone? After life, the deceased are rarely able to have that kind of aim let alone pick up a ball and throw it.

"Weird," "misunderstood," and "wounded" are adjectives used to describe Charlie St. Cloud the person by the local girls. "Befuddled," "contrived," and "hypnotically insipid" are the ones to best describe his movie. Efron has no problems holding our attention, especially when director Burr Steers and cinematographer Enrique Chediak use close-ups of his face against a blue sky as a bridge between scenes as if filming a slideshow of discarded poster art. Charlie's story is all over the map on a very small piece of real estate begging audiences to search for its meaning through rocky coasts and misty cemeteries. Too superficial to be spiritual and too brain-dead to have a heartbeat, the comforting notion is that if you forget all about Charlie St. Cloud it will be like it never existed. And no tears will ever be shed over that.

Erik Childress

CREDITS

Charlie St. Cloud: Zac Efron
Sam St. Cloud: Charlie Tahan
Tess Carroll: Amanda Crew
Alistair Woolley: Augustus Prew

Tink Weatherbee: Donal Logue

Florio Ferrente: Ray Liotta

Clarie St. Cloud: Kim Basinger

Sully: Dave Franco

Origin: USA

Language: English

Released: 2010

Production: Marc Platt, Michael Fottrell; Relativity Media, Marc Platt Productions, Charlie Film Productions; released by Universal Pictures

Directed by: Burr Steers

Written by: Craig Pearce, Lewis Colick

Cinematography by: Enrique Chediak

Music by: Rolfe Kent

Sound: Michael Williamson, Bruce Carwardine

Editing: Padraic McKinley

Art Direction: Kevin Humenny, Geoff Wallace

Costumes: Denise Wingate

Production Design: Ida Random

MPAA rating: PG-13

Running time: 109 minutes

REVIEWS

Berardinelli, James. *ReelViews.* July 29, 2010.

Duralde, Alonso. *HitFix.* July 29, 2010.

Goss, William. *Cinematical.* July 30, 2010.

Olszewski, Tricia. *Film Threat.* July 29, 2010.

Orndorf, Brian. *eFilmCritic.com.* July 30, 2010.

O'Sullivan, Michael. *Washington Post.* July 30, 2010.

Phillips, Michael. *Chicago Tribune.* July 29, 2010.

Rich, Katey. *CinemaBlend.com.* July 30, 2010.

Scott, A.O. *New York Times.* July 30, 2010.

Tallerico, Brian. *MovieRetriever.com.* July 30, 2010.

QUOTES

Sam St. Cloud: "Nobody ever gets to see what could have been."

TRIVIA

To fill the role of Sam St. Cloud, the producers held an open online casting call and eventually settled on Charlie Tahan.

CHLOE

If the one you love was lying to you, how far would you go to find out the truth?
—Movie tagline

Box Office: $3 million

In relationships, sexiness is a plus, but it is not everything. The same often goes for movies. Director Atom Egoyan's thriller *Chloe* is quite sexy, but that is only half the battle—and ultimately, thanks to an unfortunate late-movie twist, even less than that.

The set-up is like something out of a trashy movie on late-night cable. Or merely an erotic French mystery, since *Chloe* is adapted from the French film *Nathalie* (2003). The remake focuses on Catherine Stewart (Julianne Moore), a Toronto gynecologist who has drifted from her husband David (Liam Neeson), a college professor who frequently asserts that he is not flirting with students or waitresses, merely being friendly. When Catherine suspects that David missed a flight back home—in effect leaving her alone with a house full of guests at her husband's surprise birthday party—she resorts to drastic measures. She enlists Chloe (Amanda Seyfried), a prostitute with no backstory whatsoever, to present herself to David to test his fidelity.

The film is scripted by Erin Cressida Wilson, who wrote the twisted, sexually strange *Secretary* (2002), and, in Egoyan (*Exotica* [1994], *Adoration* [2008]), has a filmmaker who has long been fascinated with the ambiguity in human communication. Where *Chloe* falters is in making its characters less interesting as they develop, not more. Without giving too much away, what initially presents itself as an erotically-charged mystery in which everyone is in a precarious position eventually just becomes a look at how a fractured family deals with a major catalyst that comes into their life. This is disappointing, as the film initially suggests an exploration of Chloe and her profession. Over dinner with friends, David and Catherine demonstrate a certain curiosity about the relatable human side of a professional sex worker. They are obviously willing to acknowledge that someone like Chloe is a woman with feelings and past experiences, not just an empty vessel meant to serve others. In the end, though, Wilson and Egoyan give far less credence to Chloe and her feelings and, in an over-the-top third act that sabotages everything that came before, uses the titular character only as a puzzling wrench who further unscrews the Stewart family.

As previously noted, for what it is worth, the way all of this goes down is quite sexy. Wilson's dialogue has a snap to it, alive with potential and doubt and excitement. The film opens with Chloe, in the movie's only voiceover, emphasizing the power of words, and the rest of *Chloe* reiterates just how titillating a verbal description of sex can be. After all, it is the stories that Catherine hears about Chloe's sexual interactions with David that fill Catherine with confused feelings that combine jealousy and arousal. This is one of many cases in which the film continually shifts the story's emotional landscape into places that are muddier but not deeper. As Catherine finds herself surprisingly intrigued by

Chloe and her stories, she becomes the first of two characters played by Moore in the same year—the second being a lesbian who becomes attracted to a man in *The Kids Are All Right* (2010)—whose newly-fluid sexuality feels merely like a contrivance of the story. How Catherine feels about opening up this Sapphic side of her is unclear, and Chloe's position in this complex love triangle only becomes more and more ridiculous as the film proceeds.

What does resonate throughout *Chloe* is Catherine feeling as if she has become invisible to David and to her ungrateful teenage son Michael (Max Theriot). He has no interest in communicating with his mother, whose orders for Michael's girlfriend Anna (Nina Dobrev) to leave the house before bed are barely acknowledged, much less obliged. Moore makes Catherine's plight sympathetic; she never comes off as an inappropriately overprotective mother, even when she watches as Anna dumps Michael via video chat. Rather, Catherine is a mother trying to prevent her men from slipping away, and all she wants is for them to be happy. As the breakup is being finalized after Michael has slammed the door on her, Catherine tells David, " I don't know what bothers me more: that he's sleeping with her or that he isn't."

Of course, who is sleeping with whom becomes a major issue in *Chloe*. It is one that winds up far less intriguing than the question of how spouses drift apart over time or how parents can maintain connections with their teenage children. *Chloe* is far from the first film to address the challenge in keeping a marriage fresh, but it occasionally finds painful poignancy in losing touch with the most important person in the world. "I love your smile," David tells Catherine. "No, you don't," she answers. A pause. His response: "When did we stop picking each other up at the airport?" These are two people who were once very close but now fail to connect emotionally or physically, a rift that is the basis for Chloe's implantation into their lives. Unfortunately, David is so oblivious that he stops being an active participant in the story, and Seyfried, very effective for the first hour or so, loses her handle on Chloe as the movie derails.

Similarly, Egoyan handles most of *Chloe* with elegance and class until the final half-hour unravels everything that made it so compellingly mysterious. Gone is the truth in the human need to feel desired and the distance that can result from busy lives set to different schedules, even within the same household. In its place is an attempt to chronicle a fantasy spun out of control that is less psychological analysis than nod to *Fatal Attraction* (1987). Complicated sexual behavior between adults always brings with it absorbing layers; the accumulation of lies and the descent of a main character into spontaneous, violent obsession is far less useful.

Matt Pais

CREDITS

Catherine Stewart: Julianne Moore
David Stewart: Liam Neeson
Chloe: Amanda Seyfried
Michael Stewart: Max Thieriot
Frank: R.H. Thomson
Anna: Nina Dobrev
Origin: Canada, France
Language: English
Released: 2009
Production: Ivan Reitman, Joe Medjuck, Jeffrey Clifford; StudioCanal, Montecito Picture Co.; released by Sony Pictures
Directed by: Atom Egoyan
Written by: Erin Cressida Wilson
Cinematography by: Paul Sarossy
Music by: Mychael Danna
Sound: Bissa Scekic
Editing: Susan Shipton
Costumes: Debra Hanson
Production Design: Phillip Barker
MPAA rating: R
Running time: 99 minutes

REVIEWS

Ebert, Roger. *Chicago Sun-Times*. March 24, 2010.
Edelstein, David. *New York Magazine*. March 26, 2010.
Hoberman, J. *Village Voice*. March 24, 2010.
McCarthy, Todd. *Variety*. Sept. 16, 2009.
Page, Janice. *Boston Globe*. March 26, 2010.
Phipps, Keith. *AV Club*. March 25, 2010.
Rothkopf, Joshua. *Time Out New York*. March 25, 2010.
Stevens, Dana. *Slate*. March 26, 2010.
Toppman, Lawrence. *Charlotte Observer*. March 26, 2010.
Weitzman, Elizabeth. *New York Daily News*. March 25, 2010.

QUOTES

Catherine Stewart: "My husband's cheating on me. At least, I think he is."

TRIVIA

Co-stars Julianne Moore and Amanda Seyfried have the same birthday.

THE CHRONICLES OF NARNIA: THE VOYAGE OF THE DAWN TREADER

Return to magic. Return to hope. Return to Narnia.
   —Movie tagline

Box Office: $101 million

C. S. Lewis' patent allegory is ill-suited to film—or, better, the budget-and-profit-minded Hollywood studio type of filmmaking. Hence the cinematic adaptations of his most famous works, the fantasy series set in the mystical land of Narnia, focus on and implant additional elements of spectacle. The series has shifted aim and tone in its previous two installments from a relatively innocent and faithful imagining of Lewis' world to a violent, generic, and hollow fantasy adventure. *The Chronicles of Narnia: The Voyage of the Dawn Treader,* which takes on the most straightforward and effective book of the series—one that on its own narrative merits strikes a fine balance between the fancy and faith—is at least a step up from its immediate predecessor *The Chronicles of Narnia: Prince Caspian* (2008). Still, it is representative of the intrinsically systemic problem of transferring such symbolic works as Lewis' *Narnia* series into something as literal as a special-effects machine.

A year after the events of the last entry, Lucy (Georgie Henley) and Edmund Pevensie (Skandar Keynes) return to Narnia with their petulant, moaning cousin Eustace Scrubb (Will Poulter) after entering a painting of a ship at sea in Eustace's home (Their older siblings Susan [Anna Popplewell] and Peter [William Moseley] are in the United States with their family, having left England because of World War II, but appear briefly in a dream). Now-King Caspian (Ben Barnes) is aboard the painted ship, the *Dawn Treader,* with a crew searching for seven lost lords and, later, their seven lost swords, which can save the populace of the Lone Islands to the east of the Narnian mainland from a great, unknown reveal that presents itself as a peasant-stealing, green mist of—as one character plainly puts it—"pure evil." The reasoning is never clear, even under mythological stipulations.

Like the book, director Michael Apted's movie does a lot of roaming as the characters hop from island to island, encountering new and strange sights, inhabitants, and moral conundrums perfectly suited to highlighting and rectifying each of the players' own character flaws. Edmund desires to rise in stature above and out of his older brother's shadow and, like Caspian, is tempted to the point of violence by a pool that grants the same gift/ curse of Midas' power/downfall. Greed also serves as the basis of temptation for Eustace, whose cries and moans of disbelief and disapproval are silenced when he becomes a dragon after pillaging some unattended treasure. The move, dictated by the source material, means Eustace, the only character with a sense of growth (Poulter plays him with the right note: just short of insufferable), undergoes his change as an anthropomorphic digital creature. The beloved Reepicheep (voiced by Simon Pegg), a stalwart, chivalrous mouse soldier, helps teach Eustace about courage and, in the process, becomes a far-too sanctimonious, bland interpretation of the character.

While Edmund and Lucy retain their blank slate status, Lucy, in her encounter with a page from a book of incantations that promises a spell for the user to become her concept of beauty, is the subject of the movie's most successful moral examination. Taking on the form of her elder sister, Lucy soon realizes that she no longer exists as Lucy. Aslan (voice of Liam Neeson) is there to teach her the lesson of discovering and embracing her own importance, as he is there at the end of the journey—at the edge of his country on the sands of in front of a massive wall of water—ready to tell them with little room for error that he is an allegorical representation (Lewis, despite his protestations, uses the same language about and sets the same terms for Aslan in the book).

As heavy-handed as the ultimate lesson of the story is ("[In your world] I have a different name. You must learn to know me by that name. This was the very reason why you were brought to Narnia," says the lion who died and was resurrected), the ones that bring the characters to a sense of redemptive wholeness (and/or holiness) miss the point, thanks to the continuing underdevelopment of the characters. The movie almost obtains a last-minute reprieve in the extraneous additions department (a trip through the cosmos with a magician [Bille Brown] stands out as particularly aimed at enticing the senses and little else) by inserting an effectively visceral battle with a sea serpent. Despite this late increase in involvement (no matter how far removed it might be from Lewis' original work), *The Chronicles of Narnia: The Voyage of the Dawn Treader* not only puts into question whether the rest of the series could be adapted to film but also whether it should.

Mark Dujsik

CREDITS

Lucy Pevensie: Georgie Henley
Edmund Pevensie: Skander Keynes
Eustace Scrubb: Will Poulter
King Caspian: Ben Barnes
Lord Drinian: Gary Sweet
Lord Rhoop: Bruce Spence
Aslan: Liam Neeson (Voice)
Reepicheep: Simon Pegg (Voice)
Susan Pevensie: Anna Popplewell
Peter Pevensie: William Moseley
Coriakin: Billie Brown
Origin: USA
Language: English

Released: 2010

Production: Andrew Adamson, Mark Johnson, Philip Stever; Dune Entertainment, Fox 2000 Pictures, 20th Century Fox, Walden Media; released by Fox Walden

Directed by: Michael Apted

Written by: Christopher Markus

Cinematography by: Dante Spinotti

Music by: David Arnold

Editing: Rick Shaine

Sound: James Boyle

Costumes: Isis Mussenden

Production Design: Barry Robison

MPAA rating: PG

Running time: 113 minutes

REVIEWS

Berardinelli, James. *ReelViews.* December 7, 2010.

Biancolli, Amy. *Houston Chronicle.* December 9, 2010.

Chang, Justin. *Variety.* December 7, 2010.

Fibbs, Brandon. *Colorado Springs Gazette.* December 8, 2010.

Kennedy, Lisa. *Denver Post.* December 10, 2010.

O'Hehir, Andrew. *Salon.com.* December 8, 2010.

Sharkey, Betsy. *Los Angeles Times.* December 10, 2010.

Snider, Eric D. *Film.com.* December 10, 2010.

Swansburg, John. *Slate.* December 9, 2010.

Vaux, Rob. *Mania.com.* December 10, 2010.

QUOTES

Coriakin: "To defeat the darkness out there, you must defeat the darkness inside yourself."

TRIVIA

The returning character, Reepicheep, is voiced by Simon Pegg who replaces Eddie Izzard from the previous installment of the series.

AWARDS

Nomination:

Golden Globes 2011: Song ("There's a Place For Us").

CITY ISLAND

Truth is stranger than family.
—Movie tagline

Box Office: $7 million

Watching *City Island* is a lot like watching an extended episode of a long-running sitcom. In most cases, such a comparison would seem to be a harsh criticism suggesting that the film in question was filled with tired storylines and hackneyed punch lines but in this particular case, it is meant in a far more complimentary manner. The comparison arises from the way that it tells a modest and unassuming story in a brisk and entertaining manner with snappy dialogue, solid direction, and excellent performances from an ensemble cast that works together so nicely that it feels that they have been together for years. The end result may not be a towering masterpiece of the cinematic form, but it is an undeniably winning work that is far more satisfying in the end than most big-budget behemoths one could mention.

The film stars Andy Garcia as Vince Rizzo, the patriarch of a decidedly dysfunctional family living in the City Island neighborhood in the Bronx. Vince goes off every few nights to what he claims is a poker game and what his wife, Joyce (Julianna Marguiles), naturally assumes is a dalliance with a mistress. In truth, Vince harbors a secret dream of one day becoming an actor and his "poker games" are actually acting classes in Manhattan in which he is partnered up with fellow aspiring actor Molly (Emily Mortimer) for a project in which each is supposed to reveal their deepest and most unspoken secret to each other as part of the scene they are to develop. As it turns out, Vince is harboring an even bigger secret than his thespian dreams and it comes to light when he discovers that his secret illegitimate son, Tony (Steven Strait), is a prisoner at the same jail where he works as a guard and is scheduled to be released soon.

Without letting him know that they are related, Vince brings Tony home to live with his family and work as hired help, much to the confusion of everyone else who wonder why he is expending so much time and energy on an apparent stranger. Then again, the rest of Vince's family has a collection of wild secrets of their own that they have been keeping from each other. Daughter Vivian (Dominik Garcia-Lorido), unbeknownst to anyone else, dropped out of college and is now working as a stripper in order to make enough money to go back to school. Son Vinnie (Ezra Miller) has become a devotee of Internet porn involving overweight women that leads to an obsession with a zaftig next-door neighbor. As for Joyce, her misguided fury at Vince's "affair" leads her to contemplate a fling of her own with none other than Tony, not realizing that he is actually Vince's son.

This is a lot of plot for any movie to juggle, especially one that aspires to be relatively lighthearted in tone, and it is true that *City Island* stumbles somewhat out of the gate in trying to introduce all of the characters while setting up the various plot strands. However, writer-director Raymond De Felitta, who won a good deal of acclaim for his earlier effort, *Two Family House* (2000), another New York-based story about an unconventional family, settles things down before long and the film begins to work. Despite the fact that the screenplay is filled to the brim with deep, dark secrets, many of which may not strike some viewers as inherently amusing, De Felitta finds an agreeably-lighthearted approach to the material that strikes just the right tone, and, even though some of it is a bit predictable (few will be surprised to discover that most of the big secrets held by the characters become exposed at roughly the same time during the climax), he throws just enough curve balls (such as the way that he handles the younger son's fascination with the hefty neighbor) to keep things interesting. He also gets a collection of good and spirited performances from a cast that bounces off of each other in an agreeable manner while each getting a moment or two of their own in which to shine—Garcia has one standout moment, a bit in which his character scores an audition for a Martin Scorsese movie that unexpectedly finds him going from brash Brandoesque posturing to exposing genuine emotions, that may just be the single best bit of acting of his entire career.

Although it received many strong reviews upon its release, *City Island* was hardly a behemoth at the box-office when it was released last spring and it is likely that the majority of its audience will wind up discovering it on cable or on DVD. In a way, this is sort of fitting because this is the kind of film whose modest charms actually play better within the cozier confines of one's living room than the average multiplex. As suggested before, the film is like a long-running sitcom and after seeing it for themselves, it is more than likely that most people who see it would be more than willing to tune in next week to see what these characters have gotten themselves into. For a film like this, that is high praise indeed.

Peter Sobczynski

CREDITS

Vince Rizzo: Andy Garcia
Joyce Rizzo: Julianna Margulies
Michael Malakov: Alan Arkin
Molly: Emily Mortimer
Tony Nardella: Steven Strait
Vinnie Rizzo: Ezra Miller
Vivian Rizzo: Dominik Garcia-Lorido
Origin: USA
Language: English
Released: 2009
Production: Andy Garcia, Zachary Matz, Raymond De Felitta, Lauren Versel; Lucky Monkey Pictures, Gremi Film Production, Filmsmith Prods.; released by Anchor Bay Films
Directed by: Raymond De Felitta
Written by: Raymond De Felitta

Cinematography by: Vanja Cernjul
Music by: Jan A.P. Kaczmarek
Sound: Jan McLaughlin
Editing: David Leonard
Costumes: Tere Duncan
Production Design: Franckie Diago
MPAA rating: PG-13
Running time: 100 minutes

REVIEWS

Adams, Sam. *AV Club*. March 31, 2010.
Anderson, Melissa. *Village Voice*. March 16, 2010.
Burr, Ty. *Boston Globe*. April 1, 2010.
Catsoulis, Jeanette. *New York Times*. March 19, 2010.
Denby, David. *New Yorker*. March 29, 2010.
Ebert, Roger. *Chicago Sun-Times*. April 1, 2010.
Lybarger, Dan. *eFilmcritic.com*. May 2, 2010.
Phillips, Michael. *Chicago Tribune*. April 2, 2010.
Puig, Claudia. *USA Today*. April 8, 2010.
Sheib, Ronnie. *Variety*. April 2, 2010.

TRIVIA

The father and daughter characters Vincent and Vivian Rizzo are played by real life father and daughter Andy Garcia and Dominik Garcia-Lorid.

THE CITY OF YOUR FINAL DESTINATION

If *The City of Your Final Destination* was on anyone's cinematic itinerary in 2010, it was most likely because it was billed as a Merchant/Ivory effort: One of the many movies produced since 1961 by Ismail Merchant and directed by James Ivory. (In fact, however, Merchant is deceased and it was produced by Paul Bradley and Pierre Proner, despite being associated with the pedigree of the Merchant/Ivory filmography.) Most of these past films were period pieces, often set in early twentieth-century England, and often literary adaptations. Their most successful, both commercially and critically, was *A Room with a View,* and, like that movie and many other Merchant/Ivory films, *The City of Your Final Destination* was written by Ruth Prawer Jhabvala (from a novel by Peter Cameron).

The story concerns the quest of a young Midwestern U.S. college literature professor, Omar (Omar Metwally) to be the first to write a biography of a writer named Jules Gund, who committed suicide for unexplained reasons after writing one critically-acclaimed book. At the urging of Omar's live-in girlfriend and colleague, Deirdre (Alexandra Maria Lara), he travels to Uruguay to seek to interview Gund's family, even though the family has denied him permission to write an authorized account. Omar just shows up one day in the villa where the family lives, and he is taken in.

The Gund family is an odd group. It consists of the dead writer's middle-aged wife, Caroline (Laura Linney); his twenty-eight-year-old mistress, Arden (Charlotte Gainsbourg); the daughter of the writer and his mistress, Portia (Ambar Mallman); the writer's aged brother, Adam (Anthony Hopkins); and the brother's younger but longtime lover, Pete (Hiroyuki Sanada). They live in a sort of desolate squalor making small sums of income off the land. Arden, the same age as Omar, is immediately smitten with him and thus approves his intent. Caroline, bitter and suspicious and protective of her ex-husband's legacy, is adamantly opposed. Adam wants to strike a deal: Get Omar to smuggle some of his mother's jewelry out of the country (a plot device that might make more sense were this a thriller, which it decidedly is not).

As one might suspect, Omar gets thrown off the track of his quest and becomes enamored of the family, especially Arden, and their situation. There are certain parallels between the young would-be biographer and his subject: both seem bored with a woman who is controlling their lives and attracted to a woman who seems weak and indecisive (Arden). But since the movie's interest lies in whether Oscar will win the family's approval for his biography, when the protagonist's own interest in the biography wanes, it is a big problem for the film.

And it is far from the only one. Movies about writers face the dilemma of how to make writing, a solo and often dull pursuit, into something more cinematically engaging. But *The City of Your Final Destination* is a movie about someone who wants to write a book about someone who once wrote a book. Not only that, but there is barely a mention of what made Gund's book so intriguing or why the author is worth a biography. Why is Gund so important to anyone, especially to Oscar? There is nary a clue. And who is Oscar other than a nobody who suddenly shows up at the family's door? Why should anyone in the Gund family care, and more importantly, why should a film audience care? Yes, there is romance a-budding, but it is as tepid and tentative as Oscar's and Arden's personalities, which is to say, far from passionate or alluring.

The movie depends heavily on viewers sharing Oscar's fascination with the Gund family, and while the suicidal author has certainly left behind (and left adrift) a motley group, there have been far stranger and certainly more dysfunctional families in movie history. And while Ivory deftly makes the scenes pretty enough, there have been plenty of more exotic settings as well.

Into the lengthy second hour of this film, it is easy to grow tired of waiting for something to happen. Then, when it does, it turns out to be an anticlimax.

As for the acting, there is some pleasure in watching Hopkins play Hopkins (non-villainous variety) and sharing a civilized martini with Linney, who with pulled-back hair and fright makeup plays a mature role rather against type (she makes Caroline even more unlikable than she needs to be). Up against these veterans, the unremarkable Metwally looks like he has wandered into an acting class, but it is not entirely his fault that his character is a cipher. At least he is alive, which is more than can be said for the writer, Gund, whom the movie is all about. If there is an intriguing mystery about him, the screenwriter forgot to supply it.

Michael Betzold

CREDITS

Omar: Omar Metwally
Adam: Anthony Hopkins
Caroline: Laura Linney
Arden: Charlotte Gainsbourg
Pete: Hiroyuki Sanada
Deirdre: Alexandra Maria Lara
Mrs. Van Euwen: Norma Aleandro
Lucy: Kate Burton
Portia: Ambar Mallman
Origin: USA
Language: English
Released: 2009
Production: Paul Bradley, Pierre Proner; Merchant-Ivory Productions, Goldcrest Features, Falkhan Entertainment Group; released by Screen Media Films
Directed by: James Ivory
Written by: Ruth Prawer Jhabvala
Cinematography by: Javier Aguirresarobe
Music by: Jorge Drexler
Sound: Robert Hein
Editing: John David Allen
Production Design: Andrew Sanders
Costumes: Carol Ramsey
MPAA rating: R
Running time: 118 minutes

REVIEWS

Burns, Sean. *Philadelphia Weekly.* July 13, 2010.
Burr, Ty. *Boston Globe.* April 27, 2010.
Holden, Stephen. *New York Times.* April 16, 2010.
Knight, Richard. *Windy City Times.* June 15, 2010.
Long, Tom. *Detroit News.* August 13, 2010.
Lumenick, Lou. *New York Post.* April 16, 2010.

MacDonald, Moira. *Seattle Times.* June 18, 2010.
Rainer, Peter. *Christian Science Monitor.* May 7, 2010.
Reed, Rex. *New York Observer.* April 14, 2010.
Richards, Jonathan F. *Film.com.* August 1, 2010.

TRIVIA

James Ivory's 24th collaboration with screenwriter Ruth Prawer Jhabvala and his first film since the death of producing partner Ismail Merchant in 2005.

CLASH OF THE TITANS

Between gods and men, the clash begins.
—Movie tagline

Box Office: $163 million

The original *Clash of the Titans* (1981) has not aged well, but remains a fun little excursion into adventure cinema of yester-year. It was a product of the early 1980s, but with the feel and spirit of an old Saturday morning matinee cliffhanger, complete with hammy acting and cheesy special effects. None of that was on purpose, of course, but that is how it is viewed today. The film represented the final bow of famed visual effects master Ray Harryhausen, whose pioneering stop-motion effects for films such as *The 7th Voyage of Sinbad* (1958) and *Jason and the Argonauts* (1963) had been highly regarded as a major step forward in the world of special effects. But when *Clash of the Titans* came out in 1981, the films of George Lucas and Steven Spielberg had already pushed the boundaries even further. Despite a cast that was game enough to go along with the material and a rousing and memorable score by Laurence Rosenthal, *Clash of the Titans* never really had a chance.

The film retains a certain charm and Beverly Cross's screenplay is still rife with possibilities for a great remake. Take away some of the stiff dialogue and the mis-step of inserting a mechanical owl into the story and *Clash of the Titans* could really fly. The storyline takes Greek mythology and boils it down into bite-size chunks just enough so that kids will be entertained enough to want to learn more about Perseus, Medusa, and all the Gods and Goddesses. There is not a whole lot about the original that needs changing for a sure-fire modern blockbuster. The structure of the story is near-perfect for it.

Yet, the remake completely misses several opportunities to make a fun, cheerful, and altogether engaging adventure film and instead delivers a typically bloated and joyless affair. The story still centers on Perseus (Sam Worthington) and how he goes from a boy unaware of his real upbringing to a man with a destiny to defeat the Gods' deadliest creation: The Kraken. In this version, he is found by a fisherman (Pete Postlethwaite) who raises him until an attack by the vengeful Hades leaves Perseus's father drowning and Perseus on a personal crusade against the Gods. This falls in line with the rest of all mortal men who have pretty much decided to give the Gods the silent treatment.

After Hades tries to scare the Olympians into worshipping the Gods again, he informs them that they have ten days before he unleashes the deadly, gigantic sea serpent the Kraken to destroy Argos. They can either face their doom or sacrifice the Princess Andromeda (Alexa Davalos) in order to save themselves. Eventually, Perseus learns of his heritage and, of course, denounces it. But once he learns of Hades' role in the death of his mother, he vows revenge and joins up with a band of warriors who will do what they can to try and defeat the Kraken, if it in fact can be defeated.

Meanwhile, the Gods hang out in what looks like a stage for a 1970s prog-rock production, with Zeus (Liam Neeson) looking as though he wandered off the set of *Barbarella* (1968). It looks too silly to be taken seriously, but *Clash of the Titans* has only serious intentions and falls flat throughout most of its quick ninety-minute running time. The movie is in too much of a hurry to tell its story, lest it should put off anyone with the attention span of a video game addict. It exists only for its action sequences, which are uninspired and belabored.

Take, for instance, the scene in which Perseus meets the winged horse Pegasus for the first time. There is little in the way of awe or wonderment when the film reveals the lovely animal. The sense of a bond between Perseus and Pegasus does not seem to exist, especially when the scene is interrupted by an attack, which is followed by an action sequence involving giant scorpions that goes on longer than almost any other scene in the film. The horse disappears until the final two reels of the film. Furthermore, the screenplay is too ahead of itself for there to be any suspense. At least in the 1981 film, the story unfolded in a way so that the characters had to figure out the story on their own. The plan to defeat the Kraken is already laid out from the get-go so that there really only remains one obstacle: Cut off the head of Medusa and do it quickly.

The film has been given stiff direction from Louis Leterrier and the actors do not help. Sam Worthington, fresh from his unjustifiable star-making turn in James Cameron's *Avatar* (2009), has nowhere to go with the role and actually looks quite bored and out-of-place. He projects little more than a pout and a sullen brood and has been written as a bit of a whiner. The rest of the cast looks either completely lost or just waiting for their check to clear.

From a marketing standpoint, this *Clash of the Titans* was not made with the performances or screenplay in mind. With the growing popularity of Rick Riordan's *Percy Jackson* books (which encompassed Greek Mythology in a contemporary storyline), it was inevitable that someone would get around to remaking *Clash of the Titans*. Yet, with the unparalleled success of *Avatar* in 3-D, the decision was made late in the game to transform *Clash of the Titans* into a 3-D movie, even though it had never been shot that way. The result looked flimsy and hardly enveloping. While the original *Clash of the Titans* seems to be best-remembered for its less than cutting edge effects, the remake will also be remembered for its use of 3-D as an ill-conceived marketing afterthought. At least the first film was made with heart.

Collin Souter

CREDITS

Perseus: Sam Worthington
Zeus: Liam Neeson
Hades: Ralph Fiennes
Poseidon: Danny Huston
Athena: Izabella Miko
Draco: Mads Mikkelsen
Acrisius: Jason Flemyng
Io: Gemma Arterton
Andromeda: Alexa Davalos
Danae: Tine Stapelfeldt
Spyros: Pete Postlethwaite
Origin: USA
Language: English
Released: 2010
Production: Basil Iwanyk, Kevin De La Noy; Legendary Pictures, Thunder Road Productions, Zanuck Company; released by Warner Bros.
Directed by: Louis Leterrier
Written by: Phil Hay, Matt Manfredi, Travis Beacham
Cinematography by: Peter Menzies Jr.
Music by: Ramin Djawadi, Mike Higham
Sound: Dominic Gibbs, James Mather
Editing: Vincent Tabaillon, Martin Walsh
Art Direction: Patricio M. Farrell, Troy Sizemore
Costumes: Lindy Hemming
Production Design: Martin Laing
MPAA rating: PG-13
Running time: 106 minutes

REVIEWS

Burr, Ty. *Boston Globe.* April 1, 2010.
Childress, Erik. *eFilmcritic.com.* April 1, 2010.
Corliss, Richard. *Time Magazine.* April 2, 2010.
Cornelius, David. *eFilmcritic.com.* April 2, 2010.
Ebert, Roger. *Chicago Sun-Times.* April 1, 2010.
Kennedy, Lisa. *Denver Post.* April 2, 2010.
Lane, Anthony. *New Yorker.* April 12, 2010.
Long, Tom. *Detroit News.* April 2, 2010.
Phipps, Keith. *AV Club.* April 1, 2010.
Weinberg, Scott. *Cinematical.com.* April 1, 2010.

QUOTES

Spyros: "One day, somebody's gonna have to make a stand. One day, somebody's gonna have to say enough."

TRIVIA

Liam Neeson agreed to star in this film because his two sons are fans of ancient Greek mythology.

AWARDS

Nomination:

Golden Raspberries 2010: Worst Sequel/Prequel, Worst Use of 3D.

CLIENT 9: THE RISE AND FALL OF ELIOT SPITZER

Money. Sex. Power. Betrayal.
—Movie tagline

Shakespeare would have certainly been impressed with the layer upon layer of complexities that led to the crushing of the career and reputation of former New York Governor Eliot Spitzer, whose crusades against over-compensated CEOs and corrupt financial institutions made him a hero to the little man and the enemy of some of the most power men in America. While the title of director Alex Gibney's latest documentary—the third he either directed or co-directed in 2010 after *Casino Jack and the United States of Money* and *Freakonomics*—implies that the focus of *Client 9* is Spitzer's sexual dalliances with high-priced prostitutes, it is in fact a more ominous tale of government and boardroom conspirators who worked together to bring down a man whose career path made him a potential leading candidate for the White House.

While Gibney certainly indulges us in some of the ins and outs of ordering a call girl online, the more interesting moments in *Client 9* are his extensive, soul-baring interview with Spitzer, who clearly seems more at ease touting his track record as both New York State Attorney General and Governor than he does talking about the impact his elicit actions had on his wife and family.

Although, at times, Spitzer does refuse comment on certain specific inquiries, when pressed with a more delicately worded question, he does eventually give an answer of substance.

Not surprisingly, Spitzer earned quite a few enemies along his journey, and many of them were bankers or the heads of investment firms, whose practices he fought passionately to stop, hoping to avoid the financial crisis that occurred not long after he resigned from office. It is no coincidence that Spitzer also appeared in the 2010 documentary *Inside Job,* a film that took a detailed, blow-by-blow account of the banking crisis that nearly tanked the economy of the United States. In that film, he made the point that the revelations about his extramarital behavior stemmed from an investigation begun at the urging of those in the financial community he sought to bring down. *Client 9* does a respectable job making the case for those accusations.

Since *Enron: The Smartest Guys in the Room* (2005), director Gibney has excelled in unraveling complicated and often-tangled stories involving the government, power brokers, and those who know how to move money, and laid out quite succinctly the corruption that binds them all. He is a master of not just finding the border of the puzzle, but also filling in every last piece until the picture is complete. His Oscar®-winning *Taxi to the Dark Side* (2007) tore the veil off government-sanctioned torture, and his superb profile of super-lobbyist Jack Abramoff, *Casino Jack and the United States of Money* (2010), revealed some of the most shameful human behavior on record. (Also in 2010, Gibney contributed a short film to the documentary anthology *Freakonomics*.)

In addition to the judicial work of Eliot Spitzer, *Client 9* takes a few minutes to tell the world about the modern version of an escort service. Surprisingly enough, Gibney reveals, if one lives in New York City and has a bit of money to play with, a hooker is not that difficult to find. One of the more interesting revelations the films gives is that the woman often identified as "Spitzer's girl," Ashley Dupre, was in fact a publicity-seeking young woman from New Jersey who had been with the former governor one time. His true "regular" girl refused to be interviewed for the documentary, so Gibney hired a pretty actress to recite in character her portion of their interview. It is an interesting technique, but it may get a bit confusing for some viewers who might think the woman on camera is the real prostitute. But those sections of the film are not nearly the most interesting.

Far more engaging are the moments in which Gibney unravels the stories of Spitzer's enemies and how they slowly converged and conspired to wreck the governor. Anyone paying attention might have seen it coming from a mile away. So by the shocking news breaks, Spitzer's foes are ready with quotes saying they knew it was only a matter of time until this bad man came tumbling down. And when Gibney finally shows the now-infamous resignation speech—Spitzer standing at the podium, clearly broken, with his wife at his side—there is almost no possible way to see Spitzer as anything other than a victim.

Eliot Spitzer earned his enemies, with his short temper and unwillingness to back down from the biggest, baddest antagonists. *Client 9* certainly does not paint him as a flawless angel of a man either, but the film does force viewers to wonder what the nation and its economic foundation would have been like if Spitzer had not been forced to exit public life for a time—he was not asked to resign—to see to the mending of his family. The movie is worth the price of admission if only for the lengthy moments of listening to Spitzer talk about his personal and professional struggles. The work is strikingly honest and gives a complete portrait of a flawed, passionate man who had the capacity and opportunity to change the world.

Steven Prokopy

CREDITS

Origin: USA

Language: English

Released: 2010

Production: Alex Gibney, Jedd Wider, Todd Wider, Maiken Baird; Jigsaw Productions, Wider Film Projects; released by Magnolia Pictures

Directed by: Alex Gibney

Written by: Alex Gibney

Cinematography by: Maryse Alberti

Music by: Peter Nashel

Sound: David Hocs

Music Supervisor: John McCullough

Editing: Plummy Tucker

MPAA rating: R

Running time: 117 minutes

REVIEWS

Anderson, Melissa. *Village Voice.* November 3, 2010.
Barsanti, Chris. *FilmCritic.com.* November 4, 2010.
Biancolli, Amy. *San Francisco Chronicle.* November 19, 2010.
Carvajal, Nelson. *cinefile.com.* November 9, 2010.
Dargis, Manohla. *New York Times.* November 4, 2010. Morris, Dave. *Eye Weekly.* November 17, 2010.
O'Hehir, Andrew. *Salon.com.* November 3, 2010.
Pakravan, Saideh. *ScreenComment.com.* November 12, 2010.
Saito, Stephen. *ifc.com.* September 12, 2010.
Schenker, Andrew. *Slant Magazine.* October 31, 2010.

QUOTES

Eliot Spitzer: "I did what I did, and shame on me."

AWARDS

Nomination:

Directors Guild 2010: Director (Gibney).

THE COMPANY MEN

> *In America, we give our lives to our jobs. It's time to take them back.*
> —Movie tagline

More than two years after the bottom fell out on the American economy, there is still not a more relatable story to the viewing audience than a man who has lost his job and must find new employment to support his family. Not as relatable: A guy who loses a $120,000 per year job and eventually faces hard truths like the possibility that he may have to sell his Porsche.

That unemployed MBA is Bobby Walker (Ben Affleck), a native Bostonian who, before becoming victim to mass layoffs at Global Transportation Systems (GTX), seems to have all the luck in the world. His wife Maggie (Rosemarie DeWitt) is incredibly kind and beautiful and his son Drew (Anthony O'Leary) and daughter Carson (Angela Rezza) are healthy and easygoing. Besides the fortune of looking like Ben Affleck, Bobby also owns a big house and drives an expensive car and enjoys luxuries like membership at a prestigious golf club, which falls right in line with his dreams of one day becoming a CEO. He certainly does not think he is in jeopardy of being laid off, particularly because his protective boss Gene McClary (Tommy Lee Jones) said that Bobby was not in danger. Gene was wrong.

Where *Up in the Air* (2009) offered a glimpse of people losing their jobs yet backed away after the initial anger, *The Company Men* proves to be a much more rewarding look at what happens after someone is fired. Bobby is ashamed to share the news with many people and becomes quickly frustrated while searching for new employment, even stooping to insult a recruiter's weight after Bobby spends two hours waiting to have an interview about a job that only pays about half of what he used to make. Maggie is immensely supportive, but she grounds Bobby too, emphasizing that the family needs to cut back and recognize that their lifestyle may be changing. She says they should consider selling the house and, if necessary, move in with Bobby's parents for a while. Bobby's response, mostly joking: He'd rather die.

Though the Walkers belong to an economic class well above the majority of the American public, *The Company Men* draws plenty of sympathy out of the universal plight of a man who wants to care for his family. Sure, Bobby needs to realize that the longer he insists he is not the kind of person that would, say, hang drywall, the longer he may be without a paycheck. Yet within that condescending perspective is the fact that everyone holds tightly to their pride and sense of success and purpose, and it is difficult to imagine taking a large professional step back for purely financial reasons. After all, in this country, populated by many overworked and underpaid people, it often feels like people are what they do. Without getting too sentimental or patronizingly fun, *The Company Men* recognizes the silver lining of termination: That, to a certain extent, a person who is laid off regains control of what direction he or she will move in next. Of course, not everyone is overworked and underpaid. There are also high-earning, not-exactly-overworked CEOs out there. At GTX, that's James Salinger (Craig T. Nelson), Gene's best friend whose preferred method of increasing his company's stock is significant downsizing. Though Gene is cheating on his wife with GTX firing specialist Sally Wilcox (Maria Bello), he has too much of a conscience to stand by while James and fellow executives collect giant checks and scope out the site of their new, huge offices, while countless employees receive agonizing, life-changing news. This results in some strong exchanges between Nelson and Jones, whose face has an automatic setting of wistful sadness. Affleck's performance is also impressively understated, as Bobby works to maintain his dignity while clearly holding back tears, and Chris Cooper has some nice scenes as Phil Woodward, a GTX employee who also does not expect to lose his job.

For all its humanity and real-life relevance, then, it is a shame that *The Company Men* so lacks perspective about how its story fits into the fabric of the country. With millions of people out of work, moviegoers could definitely use an insightful story about the hardships faced by average people at a time when floundering companies inevitably mean floundering workers. (After all, it is not only once-highly paid people on the unemployment line.) That sort of movie, however, would take a non-sugar-coated look at the type of jobs held by the majority of the nation and the emotional and financial toll taken when people may not be able to feed their kids or afford any shelter whatsoever. Sure, in a sense *The Company Men* stands up for the working man and woman by teaching Bobby that just because he does not wear an expensive suit, or a suit at all, does it mean the labor he is doing is not skilled. And that ultimately, things are just things, and the important parts of life are family and friends—jobs are just what people take in order to support the ones they love.

Yet the film unfortunately delivers those messages in the snobbish context of an upper-middle class family who, after some stress and soul-searching, must finally come to terms with the chance of falling down to middle class. The movie recognizes that CEOs most likely do not work 700 times harder than people who make 700 times less than them, but the script from director John Wells does not deconstruct a culture that continually pushes the rich and less-than-rich farther apart. The question of what remains after items like video games and in-ground pools and backyard fountains disappear applies to everyone, regardless of salary or professional connections. In this respect *The Company Men* misses an opportunity to connect all people by not including more main characters of a lower economic class. Bobby faces a troubling situation and his family must make some unfortunate sacrifices, but never do they face anything that would truly devastate their sense of security or well-being. The film's ending also revolves around a convenience that most people out of work just do not have.

Still, it is hard not to feel for Bobby when he discovers he is competing with countless other qualified applicants for one salary, or for Phil as he is told that his decades of experience and time served in Vietnam need to be tweaked on his resume so as not to make him seem old and objectionable to potential employers. These are experiences being had by people of all demographics everyday around the country (not to mention the rest of the world). *The Company Men* is an engaging, well-acted film about those issues that would be wise to cater to more than just the Rich White Man crowd.

Matt Pais

CREDITS

Bobby Walker: Ben Affleck
Phil Woodward: Chris Cooper
Gene McClary: Tommy Lee Jones
Kack Dolan: Kevin Costner
Maggie Walker: Rosemarie DeWitt
Sally Wilcox: Maria Bello
James Salinger: Craig T. Nelson
Drew: Anthony O'Leary
Carson: Angela Rezza
Origin: USA
Language: English
Released: 2010
Production: Claire Rudnick Polstein, Paula Weinstein, John Wells; Battle Mountain Films, Company Men Productions, Spring Creek Productions; released by the Weinstein Company
Directed by: John Wells

Written by: John Wells
Cinematography: Roger Deakins
Sound: Tom Williams
Music Supervisor: Ann Kline
Art Direction: John R. Jensen
Costumes: Lyn Elizabeth Paolo
Music by: Aaron Zigman
Editing: Robert Frazen
Production Design: David J. Bomba
MPAA rating: R
Running time: 109 minutes

REVIEWS

Corliss, Richard. *TIME Magazine.* December 13, 2010.
Denby, David. *New Yorker.* December 13, 2010.
Gleiberman, Owen. *Entertainment Weekly.* December 6, 2010.
Holden, Stephen. *New York Times.* December 9, 2010.
Longworth, Karina. *Village Voice.* December 7, 2010.
McCarthy, Todd. *Variety.* December 8, 2010.
Mondello, Bob. *NPR.* December 10, 2010.
Morgenstern, Joe. *Wall Street Journal.* December 9, 2010.
Murray, Noel. *AV Club.* December 9, 2010.
Rothkopf, Joshua. *Time Out New York.* December 7, 2010.

THE CONCERT

An uplifting comedy about a true band of misfits.
—Movie tagline

Impersonating a world famous orchestra isn't easy unless you have the brass to pull it off.
—Movie tagline

Classical music does not serve as the backdrop for many films, and even fewer that might be at least partially described as a romp, but that is just the case for *The Concert*, a very accessible, altogether pleasant, crowd-pleasing foreign film the kind of which Bob and Harvey Weinstein's Miramax Films used to have much luck marketing as a cinematic vacation to urban upper-income-bracket types. Still, given that its emotional catharsis arrives with considerable arm-twisting, anything more than a fleeting appreciation of the movie will depend largely on one's personal threshold for a uniquely European combination of manically-pitched humanism and overt sentimentality.

The winner of Best Original Score and Best Sound and the recipient of three other top-shelf César® nominations in its native France, *The Concert* was also an overseas box office hit, pulling in almost $24 million in theatrical receipts. Stateside, however, it was never able to catch on with arthouse audiences that seek affordable global travel through trips to the cineplex, nor pull in those who might have just discovered costar

Mélanie Laurent a year earlier, in Quentin Tarantino's *Inglourious Basterds* (2009). Releasing in the late summer, the movie topped out at just over $590,000, while never expanding beyond two dozen theaters.

Directed by Radu Mihaileanu, *The Concert* unfolds in French and Russian with English subtitles, and centers around Andrei Filipov (Aleksey Guskov), a once celebrated Russian conductor of the Bolshoi Orchestra. Now battling alcoholism and depression, he works as a janitor at the same venue over which he used to preside. His dreams seem dead. But when Filipov intercepts an urgent fax inviting the Bolshoi to step in for a last-minute cancellation by the San Francisco Philharmonic and perform in Paris at the prestigious Châtelet Theater, Filipov is seized with a desire to prove himself.

With his longtime friend Bertrand (Laurent Bateau) by his side, Filipov concocts a seat-of-his-pants plan to gather his own orchestra to go in place of the actual Bolshoi musicians. First, Filipov begrudgingly enlists the aide of Ivan Gavrilov (Valeriy Barinov), an ex-KGB officer and the former manager of the Bolshoi who destroyed his career in the first place. He then sets about assembling a varied bunch of former musicians, a sort of gypsy traveling band.

With tickets underwritten by a wealthy mogul and would-be cellist (Vlad Ivanov), the group sets off for Paris, where they are met by the Châtelet's operator, Olivier Duplessis (François Berléand), who becomes increasingly suspicious about the Bolshoi's unconventional appearance and methods, not to mention their terrible sound. With only a couple days to rehearse, Filipov tries to keep his charade going, all while spending time with a beautiful young violin virtuoso, Anne-Marie Jacquet, also known as Lea (Laurent), with whom he shares an unexpected connection.

In films like *Train of Life* (1998) and *Live and Become* (2005), Mihaileanu revealed himself to be a humanist, and someone very much interested in the commingling of cultures and ethnicities. Those same preoccupations hold true here. The themes and messages at the core of *The Concert*—hope, personal reconnection, and making the most of second chances—make for a universal viewing experience, regardless of whether one is a foreign film aficionado, or even has an appreciation of classical music. The script, credited to Mihaileanu, Matthew Robbins, and Alain-Michel Bland, economically establishes the movie's core conflicts and intersecting back stories, but otherwise proves not terribly interested in either musical detail or stretching for verisimilitude. There's a pinch of political messaging (some characters amusingly reminisce about their good old days in the Communist Party), but the story here is

a framework; it is not allegorical, exactly, but neither does it hold up to much scrutiny.

Guskov gives a good performance, and is an effective anchor for *The Concert*. He gives layers to the regrets of his life—prideful, melancholic, and roused from slumber. In what is much more of a reactive role, meanwhile, Laurent is extremely beautiful, a sort of non-threatening, perfectly Gaelic cross between Scarlett Johansson and a young Nastassja Kinski. Laurent Dailland's worshipful cinematography smartly recognizes this, and dotes on her in arresting close-up, including a dinner scene where Anne-Marie laments that this rushed, difficult concert is doomed to fail.

If the central performances of *The Concert* offer much to enjoy, there is an almost fatal miscalculation with respect to how deeply (which is to say not really at all) the movie gets into the personalities of the "scab" orchestra, and how many are new members versus returnees and old acquaintances. At its core, is the film a putting-the-band-back-together romp, or is Filipov's motley crew composed largely of new ragamuffin recruits?

On the surface, that question might not much seem to matter, but the lack of differentiating ensemble characterization feeds a general, free-floating sense of disconnect and irritation at the group's antics, for when they get to Paris the orchestra members generally behave like a marauding hoard of Viking drunkards. Only at the last minute are they rallied (finally, conveniently) with a series of text messages goading them to come together and "do it for Lea." Given just how much of the plot hinges on the group's absence from rehearsal and overall lack of professionalism, and how that is in turn impacting Filipov's own quest for redemption, this lack of clarity in their individual relationships with Filipov is fairly problematic.

The film's conclusion, set to Pyotr Tchiakovsky's stirring "Violin Concerto in D Major, Op. 35," is also more dependent on audience empathy than traditional payoff. Unfolding against a montage of footage from the concert grand finale, it paper mâchés over the fundamental dramatic questions of movie, giving air-quote closure (Anne-Marie learns of her personal identity, and Filipov's orchestra books tours around the world, flipping off their rivals, the real Bolshoi, at the airport). It is an impressionistic stab at the sort of overarching harmony talked about by characters in the film, but it also feels like a bit of a dramatic cheat.

For those, however, who are predisposed to have an interest in seeing the film—the sort of folks who ventured out to theaters and warmly received movies like *Cinema Paradiso* (1990), *Life Is Beautiful* (1998), *Chocolat* (2000), and *Casanova* (2005)—these academic-sounding quibbles will largely not matter. There is an abundance of human feeling here, and in this *Concert* they will find plenty of fortifying melodies.

Brent Simon

CREDITS

Anne-Marie: Melanie Laurent
Olivier: François Berléand
Guylene: Miou-Miou
Jean-Paul: Lionel Abelanski
Andrei: Aleksey Guskov
Aleksander: Dmitri Nazarov
Ivan: Valeriy Barinov
Bertrand: Laurent Bateau
Pyotr Tretyakin: Vlad Ivanov
Origin: France, Romania, Belgium, Italy
Language: French, Russian
Released: 2009
Production: Alain Attal; Bim Distribuzione, Oi Oi Oi Prods., Castel Films, Panache Prods.; released by Weinstein Company
Directed by: Radu Mihaileanu
Written by: Radu Mihaileanu, Matthew Robbins, Alain-Michel Blanc
Cinematography by: Laurent Dailland
Music by: Armand Amar
Sound: Bruno Tarriere, Pierre Excoffier, Selim Azzazi
Editing: Ludo Troch
Costumes: Maira Ramedhan-Levi, Viorica Petrovici
Production Design: Cristian Niculescu, Stanislas Reydellet
MPAA rating: PG-13
Running time: 120 minutes

REVIEWS

Anderson, Melissa. *Village Voice.* July 27, 2010.
Fine, Marshall. *Hollywood & Fine.* July 29, 2010.
Holden, Stephen. *New York Times.* July 30, 2010.
LaSalle, Mick. *San Francisco Chronicle.* August 6, 2010.
Rickey, Carrie. *Philadelphia Inquirer.* August 5, 2010.
Robey, Tim. *Daily Telegraph.* July 15, 2010.
Saslow, Rachel. *Washington Post.* August 6, 2010.
Smith, Kyle. *New York Post.* July 30, 2010.
Thomas, Kevin. *Los Angeles Times.* July 30, 2010.
Weissberg, Jay. *Variety.* July 7, 2010.

TRIVIA

The film won the Prix du Public Mel Oppenheim at the Cinemania Film Festival in Montreal.

AWARDS

Nomination:
Golden Globes 2011: Foreign Film.

CONVICTION

An extraordinary journey of how far we go to fight for our family.
—Movie tagline

Box Office: $7 million

The fact most capable of knocking the wind out of viewers with a surprise slam to the gut was cut from *Conviction,* and, upon reflection, that was probably a smart decision. Betty Anne Waters devoted eighteen years of her life to a long shot, tilting at windmills in an astonishingly headstrong and heartfelt manner on the chance that she might be able to extricate her beloved brother from a lifetime of wrongful imprisonment. Having little money to hire the kind of legal firepower needed to blast Kenneth Waters out of confinement, Betty Anne sallied forth herself, getting her GED, putting herself through college, and then earning a law degree, all for the sole, selfless purpose of getting him the exoneration she never doubted he deserved. Her single-minded mission had multiple costs, including the crumbling of her marriage and the decision by her two sons to go live with their father as the woman's protracted battle wore on everyone. Still, armed with the exculpating results of DNA tests that had yet to be invented when Kenny was convicted, Betty Anne eventually triumphed over police corruption, coerced perjury, and a legal system that in general can be as fallible as it is zealous. She gave her brother a new lease on life.

Then, he promptly died. Just six months after Kenny had walked out from behind the prison's barbed-wire fences, brimming with gratitude, relief and hope; he stumbled, fell, and ended up within the confines of a cemetery. The brother Betty Anne had just gotten back had been taken from her again, and this time she had no recourse. Did this cruel twist of fate make her grueling efforts seem like a tragic waste of time? Betty Anne does not think so, as Kenny died a free man who had been cleared of butchering Katharina Brow in 1980, and he and his daughter at least had a brief window of opportunity during which they could get acquainted. However, director Tony Goldwyn worried that including a mention of Kenny's demise at the end of *Conviction* would cap what had up to then been an unfathomable well of inspiration and instantaneously turn it into a depressing story about the depths of futility. After much angst-ridden debate, Goldwyn ultimately excised the item so that uplift would not be undermined. It was a wise choice to refrain from yanking the rug out from under moviegoers, which would have sent them home reeling instead of roused.

Describing *Conviction* (note the dual meaning of the title) as an uncommon love story between a brother and sister admittedly risks giving prospective viewers both the wrong impression and the willies, yet that is exactly what it is. Goldwyn provides viewers with many flashbacks to Betty Anne and Kenny's unstable childhood, during which they were basically left to their own devices. (The wholeheartedly-bracketed protagonists are played in these sequences by young Bailee Madison and Tobias Campbell.) These glimpses of the past help to explain how their resolute attachment came to be, why these two siblings, just a year apart in age, might have felt emotionally unmoored and thus anchored each other from early on with a comforting steadfastness. Their Betty Anne-and-Kenny-against-the-world bond included being pint-sized pilferers, who then trespassed onto properties where the grass seemed greener to enjoy their ill-gotten goods. They were subsequently ripped away from each other and sent to separate foster homes, a deprivation that made them determined to someday be ever-so-present in each other's lives.

One of the most commendable things about *Conviction* is that it does not lug out a bucket of whitewash and portray Betty Anne (Hilary Swank) as a sublimely-perfect superwoman, or increase pity for Kenny (Sam Rockwell) by refraining from showing how he could often be an incorrigible, smart-mouthed jerk capable of hair-triggered fury and embarrassing excess. Instead, Betty Anne is seen struggling and juggling, trying to meet daunting family and financial demands as best she can. She is often harried, runs late, misses classes, flunks tests, and is put on academic probation. When she laughs (albeit sometimes with embarrassment) at Kenny's inappropriate, ill-timed antics, viewers will likely shake their heads at what strikes one as her counterproductive indulgence. The ferociously-focused manner in which Betty Anne plows forward, eyes unwaveringly fixed on the prize, is an absolutely astounding example of fidelity, her blinders fixed so firmly in place that at time she seems delusional. Kenny shared the same blood type as the perpetrator, but with the dawning of DNA analysis, an accurate accusatory finger could now be pointed at—or away from—a specific individual. Everything hinges on these tests, and yet when it first appears that no evidence has survived to scrutinize (the state can destroy it after ten years of inactive storage), what should crush Betty Anne is determinedly dismissed by her as merely a "setback." This will likely fill those watching with equal amounts of incredulousness and sympathetic understanding. (If there is one thing Swank is good at, it is gumption.)

Even more character complexity is provided by Rockwell, whose pungent portrayal certainly risks alienating viewers' affections. An early bar scene shows a doting Kenny enjoying a cuddly dance with his infant daughter before suddenly erupting with shocking, violent excessiveness at another patron. He then tries to make amends by being equally over-the-top as the disarming life of the party. To many, the man will undoubtedly come off as the body part with which he moons those in attendance. Kenny is a cheeky, uncouth loose cannon whose actions are as unrestrained as is his devotion to loved ones. He seems liable to do anything. The audience can easily see how people could have believed that murder was not beyond the realm of possibility. However, it is likely that even those who cannot stomach Kenny will nevertheless find the injustice of his situation even harder to take.

Swank and Rockwell are utterly believable as sister and brother, the connection between the characters palpable every time Kenny praises his "baby sister" and she basks in his approval—or when she lays down the law to him with a potency he would likely take from no one else. The laudable leads are, for the most part, ably supported. Peter Gallagher does not capture the abrasiveness of the Innocence Project's famed Barry Scheck. Far better is Melissa Leo as the malevolent, disdainful lieutenant who goes after Kenny with cuffs and a shoehorn, purposefully using the latter to make him fit the crime. As the best friend who supplies Betty Anne with a hug here, a prod there, and invaluable assistance throughout as the other half of the film's dynamic legal duo, Minnie Driver provides *Conviction* with welcome comic relief. The real hoot here, however, is Juliette Lewis, a vivid scene stealer as the trashy, cagey ex-lover of Kenny's whose perjury under duress helped put him behind bars.

Made on a budget of $12.5 million, *Conviction* only earned about half of that during its limited release, despite generally good reviews. The film basically unfolds as even those unfamiliar with the case expect, but while behinds may not have been brought to the edges of seats, the way Betty Anne gave her life over to her brother for nearly two decades undoubtedly made jaws drop. Thanks to Goldwyn's shrewd decision, viewers' hearts did not do the same thing at the conclusion of *Conviction*.

David L. Boxerbaum

CREDITS

Betty Anne Waters: Hilary Swank
Kenny Waters: Sam Rockwell
Abra Rice: Minnie Driver
Nancy Taylor: Melissa Leo
Brenda Marsh: Clea DuVall
Roseanna Perry: Juliette Lewis
Rick: Loren Dean
Barry Scheck: Peter Gallagher

Mandy Marsh: Ari Graynor
Richard: Conor Donovan
Ben: Owen Campbell
Aidan: John Pyper-Ferguson
Elizabeth Waters: Karen Young
Young Betty Anne: Bailee Madison
Young Kenny: Tobias Campbell
Origin: USA
Language: English
Released: 2010
Production: Andrew Sugerman, Andrew S. Karsch, Tony Goldwyn; Omega entertainment, Oceana Media Finance, Prescience; released by Fox Searchlight
Directed by: Tony Goldwyn
Written by: Pamela Gray
Cinematography by: Adriano Goldman
Music by: Paul Cantelon
Sound: David Obermeyer
Music Supervisor: Liz Gallacher
Editing: Jay Cassidy
Art Direction: Stephanie Gilliam
Costumes: Wendy Chuck
Production Design: Mark Ricker
MPAA rating: R
Running time: 96 minutes

REVIEWS

Anderson, Melissa. *Village Voice.* October 13, 2010.
Chang, Justin. *Variety.* September 20, 2010.
Diones, Bruce. *Christian Science Monitor.* November 15, 2010.
Morgenstern, Joe. *Wall Street Journal.* October 15, 2010.
Morris, Wesley. *Boston Globe.* October 15, 2010. Phillips, Michael. *Chicago Tribune.* October 14, 2010.
Pols, Mary. *TIME Magazine.* October 14, 2010.
Rainer, Peter. *Christian Science Monitor.* October 15, 2010.
Schwarzbaum, Lisa. *Entertainment Weekly.* October 22, 2010.
Scott, A.O.. *New York Times.* October 14, 2010.
Travers, Peter. *Rolling Stone.* October 28, 2010.
Wheat, Alynda. *People.* October 25, 2010.

TRIVIA

The movie took almost 10 years to develop.

AWARDS

Nomination:
Screen Actors Guild 2010: Actress (Swank).

COP OUT
(A Couple of Dicks)

Rock out with your glock out.
—Movie tagline

Box Office: $45 million

Cop Out was a quickly forgotten action buddy comedy for most people, but for fans of the film's director Kevin Smith, it represented a curious career move for a guy who has always directed his own scripts and who had established himself as a bit of a prankster, provocateur, and cult figure. Starting with the no-budget indie hit *Clerks* (1994), Smith had been rather consistent with his material. Whether his characters are defying authority, debating pop culture, or talking openly about sexual escapades (or even performing them in the movie, as has often been the case), Smith's movies always had a heart beating beneath the layers of raunchy behavior. Even with a failure such as *Jersey Girl* (2004), one could see Smith at least making an effort to grow up, only to be pulled back to his roots with *Clerks 2* (2006) a couple years later. Love him or hate him, he is very much an auteur with his own signature touch.

Smith has never been just a director-for-hire, that is, until *Cop Out*. Perhaps it seemed like a good time for him to get out of his comfort zone and take a chance on someone else's material and even try an action sequence (something Smith has admittedly avoided his whole career). Smith himself seemed to take the project in stride and confessed the movie lacked ambition. That makes it all the more curious as to why Smith lashed back at critics who hated the movie, which most of them did. If the movie was meant to be fluff, what does it matter if the critics lambasted it for being unfunny and a time waster?

Basically, the movie announces itself as just that within the first ten minutes. Bruce Willis and Tracy Morgan play undercover cops. Willis plays Jimmy Monroe, the straight cop. Morgan plays Paul Hodges, a cop obsessed with quoting lines from movies, which he does at a mile a minute in the film's first opening scene. Paul says the lines, Jimmy names the movies. This is not a funny scene, but Smith uses it to tell his audience that *Cop Out* is "an homage" (which is French for "you better let me do this," according to Paul).

Smith sticks to that aesthetic. *Cop Out* is a parade of cop movie clichés, including (but not limited to) an angry police chief who suspends Jimmy and Paul after a bust goes haywire, two rival cops (Kevin Pollak and Adam Brody), Mexican drug runners, one of the cop's daughters marrying a shady slimeball, and cheesy synth music to go along with all the chase scenes. The plot consists of Paul and Jimmy trying to track down a couple of hold-up men who robbed a pawn shop while Jimmy was trying to sell a valuable baseball card as a means for paying for the expensive wedding of his daughter (Michelle Trachtenberg).

Once they find one of the men (Seann William Scott), they interrogate him after handcuffing him to their car and dragging him across the pavement. This inevitably leads them to the Mexican drug lords, the head of which happens to be a baseball fanatic. He makes a deal with Jimmy and Paul to get him his car back. If they do, they will get the baseball card back. Meanwhile, Paul is obsessed with the notion that his wife Debbie (Rashida Jones) might be having an affair with the next door neighbor.

Smith is clearly having fun with these conventions, but he has nowhere to go with them. They exist for Smith's occasional amusement, since he seems to have little interest in telling the story. *Cop Out* may be an homage, but there is no clear consensus between Smith and screenwriters Marc and Robb Cullen as to where the homage stops and the actual movie begins. The movie cannot decide what it ultimately wants to be. Smith often makes "meta" movies, but here he struggles with material that suggests a lack of imagination more than a keen insight into a particular genre. As a result, *Cop Out* is a meta movie with nothing to say, a cop-buddy movie without any surprises and a laborious comedy with no direction.

As for performances, Willis and Morgan go through their usual motions. Willis keeps his face straight and delivers an uninspired performance his audience expects time and again. Even a reference to *Die Hard* falls flat and feels incredibly forced. Morgan does what he has always been known for, delivering his seemingly improvised lines with confidence while the material comes to him from outer space. On the hit TV show *30 Rock*, Morgan's antics fit in perfectly with the wacked-out co-stars that populate the landscape. Here, he proves that a little of his shtick can go a long way. Only Seann William Scott offers a performance that is even remotely inspired.

Smith has always been one of the most self-deprecating filmmakers, never pretentious and always willing to own up to the fact that his movies are basically juvenile, but not dumbed down. Smith's war-of-words with his critics over *Cop Out* are all the more curious since he clearly did not put his heart and soul into this film. Had the critics attacked a personal and ambitious project of his, it might explain his outburst. It is highly unlikely that *Cop Out* will enjoy the same sudden popularity that Smith's sophomore film *Mallrats* (1996) did years after its release to similarly unkind critical response. *Cop Out* will more likely be remembered as a creative detour for Smith, who has always been a better filmmaker when he focuses on what he knows about people rather than what he knows about movies.

Collin Souter

CREDITS

Jimmy Monroe: Bruce Willis
Paul Hodges: Tracy Morgan
Dave: Seann William Scott
Barry Mangold: Adam Brody
Hunsaker: Kevin Pollak
Roy: Jason Lee
Debbie: Rashida Jones
Ava: Michelle Trachtenberg
Manuel: Mark Consuelos
Origin: USA
Language: English
Released: 2010
Production: Polly Cohen Johnsen, Marc Platt, Michael Tadross; Marc Platt Productions; released by Warner Bros.
Directed by: Kevin Smith
Written by: Robert Cullen, Marc Cullen
Cinematography by: David Klein
Music by: Harold Faltermeyer
Sound: Tim Chau
Editing: Kevin Smith
Art Direction: Jordan Jacobs
Costumes: Juliet Polcsa
Production Design: Michael Shaw
MPAA rating: R
Running time: 107 minutes

REVIEWS

Barker, Andrew. *Variety.* February 24, 2010.
Ebert, Roger. *Chicago Sun-Times.* February 25, 2010.
Jones, J.R. *Chicago Reader.* February 25, 2010.
LaSalle, Mick. *San Francisco Chronicle.* February 26, 2010.
Phillips, Michael. *Chicago Tribune.* February 25, 2010.
Puig, Claudia. *USA Today.* February 26, 2010.
Rechtshaffen, Michael. *Hollywood Reporter.* February 24, 2010.
Scott, A.O. *New York Times.* February 25, 2010.
Tobias, Scott. *AV Club.* February 25, 2010.
Tallerico, Brian. *MovieRetriever.com.* February 26, 2010.

QUOTES

Paul Hodges: "This is the stuff that my mom would tell friends about me, 'My son is genius, my son is a genius.'"

TRIVIA

Due to scheduling conflicts, long-time Kevin Smith regulars Jason Mewes and Ben Affleck couldn't be in the movie.

COUNTDOWN TO ZERO

Demand zero.
    —Movie tagline

Countdown to Zero is documentarian Lucy Walker's attempt to revitalize the movement to put an end to the nuclear arms race once and for all. Both this and 2006's *An Inconvenient Truth* were produced by Lawrence Bender, and, like that film, this one knows its audience. It realizes that an independently released documentary is likely to play to moviegoers already predisposed to opposing nuclear weapons and rather than wasting its time convincing viewers of their evils, focuses instead on the pressing need for immediate action to rid the world of them. Even viewers who think they may have the appropriate amount of concern regarding such things, will find this documentary's wake-up call fairly sobering.

At the start and periodically throughout *Countdown to Zero*, Walker presents a quote from John F. Kennedy's 1961 U.N. speech: "Every man, woman, and child lives under a nuclear sword of Damocles, hanging by the slenderest of threads, capable of being cut at any moment by accident, or miscalculation, or by madness." These unnerving words serve as the driving force behind the film, as well as the means by which its argument is divided, as it proceeds to provide examples supporting the very real existence of all three dangers.

When one ponders the nuclear perils of our time, the threat of terrorism is probably the first thought that comes to mind. And apart from a few scenes early on, in which terrorism experts insist that if Al-Qaeda had access to a nuclear weapon, they would not hesitate to use it, *Countdown to Zero* does not spend much time covering the "madness" angle. The film does, however, go into a fair amount of detail as to the shocking ease with which someone looking to acquire the materials necessary to build one could do so. A nuclear weapon requires either highly enriched uranium or plutonium. And though the facilities and know-how required in producing those have always been extremely difficult to come by, *Countdown to Zero* demonstrates that these days, getting hold of the finished product is not nearly as hard as one would hope. The former Soviet Union has a large supply of poorly documented and guarded nuclear materials that amateur thieves have successfully stolen and then attempted to sell numerous times. Those materials can be easily smuggled out of that region via a country like Georgia and U.S. ports are ill-prepared to detect them, if subsequently brought here. The lack of proper international oversight of the materials, combined with the vulnerability of the world's shipping and transportation hubs, constitutes the "miscalculation" portion of the film's argument. It then goes on to cover the degree to which an accidental nuclear explosion is astoundingly possible and, on a few occasions since the notorious Cuban Missile Crisis, has actually come close to happening. It asserts that often the system of checks and balances put into place to prevent such an occur-

rence is so complicated as to render the overall process completely incomprehensible to any single person, which is a hazard unto itself.

For the most part, *Countdown to Zero* is quite effective. Though like many documentaries attempting to cover the development of a topic over the course of many years, it has some difficulties maintaining a consistent tone. It is an understandable challenge balancing grainy, archival film of nuclear explosions from the 1940s and 1950s with stock footage and news reels of world events in the 1960s, 1970s and 1980s and tastefully-lit interviews with leaders of the present. Add to that some computer animation depicting the mechanics behind a nuclear warhead and its potential urban blast radius, along with a surprisingly modern mixtape of songs by The Cure, UNKLE, Radiohead, and Pearl Jam, and the result is a movie that at times, looks, sounds and feels somewhat disorienting. Though conversely, the film also suffers some when it settles too comfortably into a series of talking heads. Dignitaries such as Tony Blair, Jimmy Carter, Robert McNamara and Mikhail Gorbachev are certainly all authorities on the nuclear arms race and any serious, modern meditation on the subject ought to include their thoughts. But when heard as a group, their views—which all tend to fall along very similar, cautionary lines—begin to fade into one another. But once in awhile, Walker presents the "Father of the Atomic Bomb," J. Robert Oppenheimer, in striking black and white, as he provides chillingly matter-of-fact answers to unsettling questions about mankind's inevitable downfall, at the likely hands of his own creation. It is in these moments that *Countdown to Zero,* by placing his forewarnings amidst modern examples as to the increasing likelihood of such an occurrence, is at its most successful.

At first glance, the title *Countdown to Zero* seemingly refers to the counting down of a nuclear weapon's launch timer. But as the documentary nears its conclusion, the viewer learns that it also possesses a second meaning, as most experts agree that the only safe world is one in which *zero* nuclear weapons exist. And though throughout history, much has been made of the dangers should nuclear weapons fall into the "wrong hands," this film places the bulk of the responsibility on America. A quote from Iranian President Mahmoud Ahmadinejad stands out: "If nuclear weapons are good, why can't I have them? And if they're bad, why do you have them?" Here, the quote is used not to underline Ahmadinejad's madness but to illuminate the fact that the U.S. and former Soviet Union (who, combined, currently possess the vast majority of the world's nuclear arsenal) must lead by example. And thankfully, whereas some documentaries on a bleak subject such as this are content merely to scare and leave viewers throwing up their hands in hopelessness, this one is not. *Countdown to Zero* encouragingly reports that the planet's total number of nuclear warheads today has decreased significantly from its high in 1985. And in its closing scenes, the figures presented throughout the film are heard supporting a unified will to do away with all nuclear weapons completely and then proposing possible solutions for doing so. And thus, *Countdown to Zero* ends on a note that is inspiring, rather than simply terrifying.

Matt Priest

CREDITS

Narrator: Gary Oldman
Origin: USA
Language: English
Released: 2010
Production: Lawrence Bender; Participant Media, World Security Institute; released by Magnolia Pictures
Directed by: Lucy Walker
Cinematography by: Robert Chappell, Gary Clarke, Bryan Donnell, Nick Higgins
Music by: Peter Golub
Sound: Michael Boyle, Alexander Marshall
Music Supervisor: Matt Biffa
Editing: Brad Fuller, Brian Johnson
MPAA rating: PG
Running time: 90 minutes

REVIEWS

Anderson, John. *Wall Street Journal.* July 30, 2010.
Gleiberman, Owen. *Entertainment Weekly.* July 21, 2010.
Hornaday, Ann. *Washington Post.* July 23, 2010.
Jenkins, Mark. *NPR.* July 22, 2010.
Murray, Noel. *AV Club.* July 22, 2010.
O'Hehir, Andrew. *Salon.com.* July 22, 2010.
Rizov, Vadim. *Village Voice.* July 20, 2010.
Rodriguez, Rene. *Miami Herald.* August 4, 2010.
Savlov, Marc. *Austin Chronicle.* July 30, 2010.
Turan, Kenneth. *Los Angeles Times.* July 30, 2010.

QUOTES

John F. Kennedy: "The weapons of war must be abolished before they abolish us."

COUNTRY STRONG

It doesn't matter where you've been as long as you come back strong.
—Movie tagline

Box Office: $17 million

The often-boozy and occasionally-sordid lives of musicians, both real and composited, have over the years proven a fairly fertile ground for big screen adaptation. From *Coal Miner's Daughter* (1980) and *Great Balls of Fire!* (1989) to *Ray* (2004), *Beyond the Sea* (2004), *Walk the Line* (2005), and *Crazy Heart* (2009), the opportunity to portray performers who as often as not hold sway over actual live audiences seems to hold an inescapable attraction for Hollywood creative types every bit as much as ticket-buyers—lending credence to the old saw that all actors would rather be rock stars, and rock stars in turn want to be actors.

The latest film to avail itself of such a showcase opportunity is *Country Strong,* a fictionalized look at an on-the-mend superstar country crooner who, fresh out of rehab and still suffering the scars of a recent miscarriage, sets out on an emotionally risky and financially dubious three-city mini-tour, to try to reclaim her place in the spotlight. An ensemble character study masquerading as a star vehicle for Gwyneth Paltrow, the movie comes across as a schizophrenic collision of two unlikely tones and feelings—at once incredibly authentic in its setting and surrounding atmosphere, and yet breathtakingly artificial in the story it peddles.

Written and directed by Shana Feste, the film centers around Kelly Canter (Paltrow), a six-time Grammy Award® winner. When her manager-husband, James (Tim McGraw), pulls her out of rehab before she is ready, he compensates by throwing an opening guest slot on the bill of the traveling road show to Beau Hutton (Garrett Hedlund), a talented part-time singer-songwriter and orderly at the care facility with whom Kelly has developed a strong relationship. While Kelly is still clearly fragile, James seems more invested in his new protégé, Chiles Stanton (Leighton Meester), a beauty-queen-turned-singer and sort of "country Barbie" focused almost entirely on the end result of fame rather than the focus and hard work required to attain it. As the four characters variously orbit one another, Kelly has a breakdown of sorts at her first show and then no-shows at her second gig, setting the stage in improbable fashion for a concert in Dallas, the scene of her biggest personal troubles.

Despite its unabashedly commercial bent and middle-America target demographic, *Country Strong* need not automatically be designed to elicit sighing critical derision. But it certainly courts it in the manner it willfully disregards and disrespects modern consideration of the problem ostensibly at its core. Even excepting a lot of needless smoke and mirrors about Beau—is he really a sponsor with a rooted investment in Kelly's sobriety, or just an on-the-side romantic interest—the film is utterly insincere about the manner in which it treats serious issues of alcoholism and addiction, especially as it relates to Kelly's marriage. It would be one thing if Kelly and James were careerist-minded codependents. But Feste goes to the extra trouble of making theirs a relationship dating back to high school, and then crucially does not delve into James' behavior as a twenty-year partner in Kelly's disease and acting out. Whether or not one is intimately familiar with the notion of enabling, this has the result of rendering the movie's entire narrative underpinning ridiculous and unrealistic. In *Country Strong*, alcoholism is just a bright and shiny shawl, to be worn flamboyantly in a couple scenes and conveniently tucked away for others, when it suits the purposes of the story.

Thankfully, the film's music is much better. Paltrow has sung in movies previously, most notably in *Duets* (2000) and *Infamous* (2006), and, of course, off-screen she is married to Coldplay singer Chris Martin. As Kelly, her musical performances are spirited and believable, and play well equally to country and non-country music fans alike. Hedlund and Meester, meanwhile, provide a number of credible ballads, especially in the form of "Give in to Me," a deep-fried cockeyed seduction.

Apart from the mostly original tunes, the performances and the shading of most of the characters are by far the strongest part of *Country Strong*. As with her debut film, *The Greatest,* (2010) Feste is as invested in having characters who are a bit uncomfortable with one another and their surroundings as she is in material narrative conflict. The result is something a bit left-of-center; rather pleasantly, developments do not always align with expectation. If she badly fumbles the major personal predicament at its core, Feste convincingly establishes a country milieu, and also nicely sketches out Chiles in particular. While on the surface little more than an upstart bimbo challenger to Kelly (with whom the audience is supposed to more clearly identify), Chiles is given a back story, rife with insecurities, which smartly and tidily informs her behavior.

Additionally, Feste exhibits a strong working touch with actors, as each of the main quartet deliver robust, engaging turns. Hedlund evidences much more charisma and screen presence than in *Tron: Legacy* (2010). Meester is button-cute, and communicates ably how Chiles is quietly aware of her shortcomings. And country music star McGraw, who showed promise in *The Blind Side* (2009), may not have the same traditional acting training as his peers, but he is smart enough to understand how to maneuver his dependably rural, decent-guy persona around the screen. (It is interesting to note, too, that he does not sing in the movie, though he does appear on the soundtrack, in a duet.)

Then there is Paltrow. Ever since her Academy Award®-winning turn in *Shakespeare in Love* (1998),

she has taken a road less frequently traveled, mixing small but not always conventionally "Oscar® bait" movies with larger films that were not necessarily built around her (perhaps negligible) opening-weekend selling power. In *Country Strong*, she plays Kelly wonderfully, while largely, if not entirely, avoiding the trap of histrionics associated with many screen portrayals of alcoholics. While Feste injects one misguided party-girl scene into the proceedings, Paltrow strives to present Kelly as more latently troubled and morose, most notably embodied in a scene with a leukemia-stricken child, as part of fulfilling a Make-a-Wish Foundation obligation. While some behind-the-scenes profile management highlights the crass nature of this visit as little more than spin control to repair Kelly's damaged image, Paltrow plays the sequence in heartbreakingly straightforward and open fashion, shining a light on the Kelly Canter that the audience does not much see—the Kelly Canter existing in the years leading up to the warped, not entirely convincing narrative that *Country Strong* flogs. A more honest examination of the reasons for her pain and struggles with alcohol, hinted at but never truly elucidated here, would provide for a much more interesting film.

Brent Simon

CREDITS

Kelly Canter: Gwyneth Paltrow
James Canter: Tim McGraw
Beau Hutton: Garrett Hedlund
Chiles Stanton: Leighton Meester
Origin: USA
Language: English
Released: 2010
Production: Tobey Maguire, Jenno Topping; Maguire Entertainment, TVM; released by Screen Gems
Directed by: Shana Feste
Written by: Shana Feste
Cinematography by: John Bailey
Editing: Conor O'Neil
Costumes: Stacey Battat
Music by: Michael Brook
Sound: Sean McCormack, Kami Asgar
Production Design: David J. Bomba
MPAA rating: PG-13
Running time: 112 minutes

REVIEWS

Berkshire, Geoff. *Metromix.com*. December 22, 2010.
Chang, Justin. *Variety.* December 22, 2010.
Duralde, Alonso. *HitFix.* December 22, 2010.

Eisenberg, Eric. *Cinemablend.com.* December 22, 2010.
Grierson, Tim. *Screen International.* December 22, 2010.
Honeycutt, Kirk. *Hollywood Reporter.* December 22, 2010.
Kit, Zorianna. *Huffington Post.* December 29, 2010.
Longworth, Karina. *L.A. Weekly.* December 22, 2010.
Puig, Claudia. *USA Today.* December 21, 2010.
Sharkey, Betsy *Los Angeles Times.* December 22, 2010.

QUOTES

Kelly Canter: "Don't be afraid to fall in love. It's the only thing that matters in life."

TRIVIA

The appearance of Beau Hutton was based on real life singer-songwriter Hayes Carll .

AWARDS

Nomination:

Oscars 2010: Song ("Coming Home")
Golden Globes 2011: Song ("Coming Home").

THE CRAZIES

Fear thy neighbor.
—Movie tagline

Box Office: $39 million

George A. Romero's original *The Crazies* (1973) was dismissed in its day as a re-hash of the director's highly influential *Night of the Living Dead* (1968). Instead of the dead rising from the grave and wreaking havoc on the American landscape, this film featured average Americans slowly going insane and killing one another thanks to a chemical outbreak. The difference, aside from the obvious story elements, was in the commentary. *Night of the Living Dead* was (among other things) a statement on America's passive nihilism in the face of tumultuous times and world changing events. *The Crazies,* in contrast, was a response to the hysteria and violence that broke out in the face of protests (particularly Kent State). On the surface, both films appear to have roughly the same storyline, but any astute viewer of the horror genre would know that Romero was and is always after bigger game.

This begs a series of questions regarding the 2010 remake of *The Crazies* and why it was made. Romero himself has an Executive Producer credit on the project, so it must stand to reason that he approves of it (he is highly vocal about his disdain for the new wave of zombies that can run, as they did in the 2004 remake *Dawn of the Dead*). The newer version of *The Crazies*

could have easily been a commentary on our own times. Pick a hot topic or societal trend and *The Crazies* can probably deconstruct it. The filmmakers instead banked on the idea of *The Crazies* as just a straightforward horror film, which is not without merit. In fact, the result is surprisingly solid.

It takes place in a small, rural town where sheriff David Dutten (Timothy Olyphant) has just had to gun down a town regular for walking out onto a field at a ballgame and brandishing a shotgun. He might have been drunk, the sheriff suspects, but the man did just try and kill him point blank. Later, when the lab tests come back, it turns out that the poor guy did not have a single drop of alcohol in him. Soon, more freakish killings slowly start to take place, each one more unexplainable than the last until, finally, the town is under siege by military haz-mat units hell bent on containing the pandemic and gunning down anyone who looks suspicious, which could very well be the entire town.

The movie stays with the sheriff David, his pregnant wife Judy (Radha Mitchell), his friend and fellow deputy Russell (Joe Anderson) and for a brief time, teenager Becca (Danielle Panabaker). David and Judy become separated once it is believed she might be carrying the virus that turns normal people into crazies. She turns out to be fine, of course, but that particular plot point helps the movie establish an important point: If she seems to be okay, perhaps there was another reason they took her in. As the characters react suspiciously to everyone they meet, so does the audience. After all, the crazies here are not zombies. They are regular people in a catatonic state doing horrific things.

The Crazies alternates between horror and thriller while effectively staging some well-crafted action-horror sequences involving a bone cutter, a pitchfork, an oil change facility, and a car wash. It moves quickly from sequence to sequence without giving the audience much time to breathe. Director Breck Eisner keeps the pace going fast enough so that the viewer has little time to stop and think about practicalities and plot holes. Perhaps most importantly, he keeps the horror aficiona-dos from looking beneath the surface for Romero-esque satire. It does not exist, nor does it necessarily need to. This remake of *The Crazies* is its own film.

A movie like this could succeed on a technical level and still fail if the actors did not appear to be in step with the material, or try to rise above it. Luckily, Eisner's movie has a cast that keeps the movie grounded in reality. With a title like *The Crazies*, one wonders how the movie managed to be so level-headed. Timothy Olyphant and Radha Mitchell are a believable couple and one the viewer will want to see get through this mess. Joe Anderson also downplays his role as the best friend who, slowly but surely, becomes just as dangerous as the people they are running from.

Eisner also gets a lot of help from his cinematographer Maxime Alexandre, who takes advantage of the wide open vistas of the landscape, effectively giving the sense of limitless possibilities as to what could happen next, while showing that there really is nowhere safe to run. Mark Isham's minimal score recalls his equally haunting and melancholy take on the similarly themed *The Mist* (2007), giving the film more of an overall feeling of dread and sadness than shock and horror.

The Crazies does run out of steam in the last act, but it remains a solid thriller in its own right, which is certainly more than most horror remakes can claim. Sometimes it takes just the right elements to make a justifiably cynical audience forget their baggage and enjoy the ride. When a movie such as this or the 2004 remake of *Dawn of the Dead* carries a namesake of such high pedigree, it can ruin its chances of ever being taken seriously. Why not just call it something else? Danny Boyle's film *28 Days Later* (2003) sure had a lot in common with Romero's *The Crazies* and nobody seemed to mind. Good horror is good horror, no matter what the name.

Collin Souter

CREDITS

David Dutton: Timothy Olyphant
Judy Dutton: Radha Mitchell
Pvt. Billy Babcock: Joe Reegan
Russell Clank: Joe Anderson
Becca Darling: Danielle Panabaker
Origin: USA
Language: English
Released: 2009
Production: Michael Aguilar, Rob Cowan, Dean Georgaris; Participant Media, Imagenation Abu Dhabi FZ, Road Rebel, Penn Station; released by Overture Films
Directed by: Breck Eisner
Written by: Ray Wright, Scott Kosar
Cinematography by: Maxime Alexandre
Music by: Mark Isham
Sound: Laurent Kossayan
Editing: Billy Fox
Art Direction: Gregory A. Berry
Costumes: George L. Little
Production Design: Andrew Menzies
MPAA rating: R
Running time: 101 minutes

REVIEWS

Abele, Robert. *Los Angeles Times.* February 26, 2010.
Bunch, Sonny. *Washington Times.* February 26, 2010.
Corliss, Richard. *Time Magazine.* February 26, 2010.
Harvey, Dennis. *Variety.* February 25, 2010.
Hoffman, Jordan. *UGO.* February 25, 2010.
Phillips, Michael. *Chicago Tribune.* February 25, 2010.
Puig, Claudia. *USA Today.* February 26, 2010.
Rechtshaffen, Michael. *Hollywood Reporter.* February 25, 2010.
Tallerico, Brian. *HollywoodChicago.com.* February 26, 2010.
White, Armond. *New York Press.* March 3, 2010.

QUOTES

David Dutton: "Do you wanna give up? You wanna sit here and die tell me, and I will sit here and die with you."

TRIVIA

The makeup process to transform an actor into a "crazie" lasted up to three hours.

CREATION

How he saw the world changed it forever.
      —Movie tagline

With Charles Darwin's theory of evolution under attack once again by religious fundamentalists, it seems an auspicious time to make a new film about the man. *Creation* purports to be the story of how Darwin's *The Origin of Species* came to be written. To make drama out of such a narrative, screenwriter John Collee and director Jon Amiel take a little bit of information from Darwin's biography—skewed already in the historical novel *Annie's Box* by Randal Keynes—spin it into a frenzy of melodrama, and boil it until it is sufficiently frothy.

To its credit, the movie does get right to the point of the enduring conflict over evolution versus Biblical creationism. "You killed God," Thomas Huxley (Toby Jones), a colleague, tells Darwin (Paul Bettany) bluntly in an early scene, while urging him to write a book about his ideas that would decimate the prevailing theory of creation, as presented in the book of *Exodus*.

Darwin is depicted in *Creation* as initially afraid of publishing his revolutionary theories and tortured by the crisis of faith his mind has caused him to experience. He is even made deathly ill by his dilemma, distressed that he could cause such widespread disbelief in God that his theory will destroy the structure of civilization. In his actual life, Darwin was at times physically fragile, but that was due to overwork and had little to do with the familial stress *Creation* milks for all it is worth.

To add to the conflict imagined in this telling, *Creation* pits the increasingly haunted scientist against his own wife, Emma (Jennifer Connelly), and his children. His wife is worried he will be destroyed by his heretical ideas if they become famous, and she is also a pious believer who turns to religion as she turns away from her bedeviled husband. Over the course of this rather insular family drama, Darwin also becomes estranged from his favorite daughter. This extremely narrow focus on his personal life allows *Creation* to abandon most of the careful, nuanced storytelling necessary for a good biography and make the movie into an emotional roller-coaster ride. Darwin is driven mad to the point of exhaustion; his very sanity and life at stake.

Certainly this tack allows the filmmakers to avoid the trap of a dry, intellectual drama about a colorless historical figure, but *Creation* so overdramatizes the imagined crises Darwin's theory precipitates that it becomes an outrageously over-the-top psychological horror film, complete with scenes of children in distress and a marriage in disarray. That there is little historical evidence for such a narrative does not bother the filmmakers one bit. In dream and nightmare sequences, Darwin is attacked by embodiments of all kinds of fears, including, in one memorable hallucination, an office full of the very creatures he has studied throughout his career.

Bettany has little choice but to go along for the ride, discarding all dignity in playing this character as an extremely eccentric victim of society's religious fervor. His eyes go buggy as his brain cooks in its own juices. At one point, Darwin is even straightjacketed and undergoes water torture in an attempt to cure his brain-induced disease. He suffers the loss of friends. Perhaps the intent is to show that society will persecute someone for unorthodox thinking, but there is no evidence this happened to Darwin. This is a movie which abandons all decorum to force-feed its audience a story concocted from a Hollywood screenwriting template.

It is difficult to believe that the man Bettany portrays so hysterically could be a man capable of such an intellectual achievement. It is hard to buy the story line and the portrait of scientist driven to his limits by a family and personal crisis because of writing a book. Thus it is difficult to care about this Darwin. The movie almost suffocates with domestic anguish and inexcusably puts a dying child at the heart of the story, when it could have been something quite different—an expansive portrayal of the adventurous scientist whose eyes were opened by his travels around the world.

Connelly, a fine actress too often cast in the role of the wife of a smart man, has her options constricted as well, and her Emma comes across as an unsympathetic, narrow-minded shrew. Is it really necessary to make Darwin into a victim in order to bring home the revolutionary character of his ideas? It seems more like a calculated studio ploy for a big payback, but despite its controversial subject matter, *Creation* was a flop, so the

gamble did not pay off. Perhaps that is because the script was more paint-by-numbers than inspired, and the filmmakers did not reach for any grand ideas. In moviedom as in the natural world, it is survival of the fittest, and *Creation* is inexcusably weak.

Michael Betzold

CREDITS

Charles Darwin: Paul Bettany
Emma Darwin: Jennifer Connelly
Rev. Innes: Jeremy Northam
Thomas Huxley: Toby Jones
Joseph Hooker: Benedict Cumberbatch
Parslow: Jim Carter
Annie Darwin: Martha West
Origin: United Kingdom
Language: English
Released: 2009
Production: Jeremy Thomas; Ocean Pictures, BBC Films, HamWay Films, Recorded Pictures Company; released by Newmarket Films
Directed by: Jon Amiel
Written by: John Collee
Cinematography by: Jess Hall
Music by: Christopher Young
Sound: John Midgley
Editing: Melanie Oliver
Art Direction: Bill Crutcher
Costumes: Louise Stjernsward
Production Design: Laurence Dorman
MPAA rating: PG-13
Running time: 108 minutes

REVIEWS

Chen, Jeffrey. *Real Talk Movie Reviews.* July 10, 2010.
Goss, William. *Cinematical.* January 23, 2010.
Hall, Phil. *Film Threat.* July 7, 2010.
Levin, Robert. *Critic's Notebook.* January 22, 2010.
Loder, Kurt. *MTV.* January 22, 2010.
Morgenstern, Joe. *Wall Street Journal.* January 21, 2010.
Richards, Jonathan F. *Film.com.* July 9, 2010.
Travers, Peter. *Rolling Stone.* January 24, 2010.
Tynan, Alice. *The Vine.* July 13, 2010.
Weaving, Simon. *Screenwize.* July 8, 2010.

QUOTES

Charles Darwin: "Suppose the whole world stopped believing that God had any sort of plan for us?"

TRIVIA

Real life couple Paul Bettany and Jennifer Connelly played the on-screen couple Charles and Emma Darwin.

CROPSEY

The truth is terrifying.
    —Movie tagline

What if your urban legends were real?
    —Movie tagline

Few things are as compelling as a good urban legend. Much has been made in recent years about the complex needs that drive the desire to believe in these tall tales. Yet surprisingly little has been said about the opposite, which is also true. Urban legends are fun to believe in individually, but only for a little while. Part of the listener is always happy to get back to reality. Nobody really wants to live in a world where hook-handed murderers stalk them on dates, or where spiders hatch out of beehive hairdos. *Cropsey* is fascinating because it looks at people who have been forced to accept that the urban legend they were raised with may indeed have been true after all, offering viewers a chilling look at how easily human community breaks down under such pressure and, among other things, how those least able to defend themselves (small children and the mentally and physically challenged) end up prey to tall tales, shoved aside into the dark corners of society's minds.

Filmmakers Joshua Zeman and Barbara Brancaccio grew up on the famed New York Staten Island hearing stories about Cropsey, an escaped mental patient/lunatic/Satanist/murderer/ghost that supposedly haunted the woods and abandoned institutional buildings that were once part of the Willowbrook Mental Institution. But what started as stories, designed to frighten children home after dark, took a terrifying turn into real life when the boogeyman the children of Staten Island feared was given a face and a name. A 1987 manhunt triggered by the disappearance of thirteen year-old Jennifer Schweiger led police to a former Willowbrook patient, Andre Rand, who had indeed lived in the woods around the time of the disappearance. Even as the public raged over a front page photo of the drooling almost catatonic Rand being led away in handcuffs, five other missing children were identified as having ties to the case and soon the urban legend machine geared up again.

Going back to Staten Island, Zeman and Brancaccio uncover disturbing discrepancies about the police investigation, the two trials, and the history of Willowbrook itself. In the rush to judgment it certainly seems that a fair trial was all but impossible for Rand. It also seems that police ignored other possibilities and were quick to buy into theories linking Rand to The Process, an obscure religious group, in support of the Satanist conspiracy theories that came to epitomize the thinking of many law enforcement officers and psychotherapists gone wrong in the eighties and early nineties.

The documentary also reminds that horrible living conditions and abuse of patients at Willowbrook provided the breakthrough story for a young reporter named Geraldo Rivera and that, despite public outcry, the institution remained virtually unchanged until it was closed down years later due at least in part to budget cuts. Many patients were left simply to fend for themselves and took to living in the tunnels that adjoined various buildings on the heavily wooded Willowbrook grounds. Among those people living in the woods was Andre Rand. Several of the cases of missing children in that area remain unsolved.

Both trials of Rand ended in foregone guilty verdicts. Skillfully, through interviews with police officers, community members, and victim advocates, as well as communications with Rand himself, the filmmakers uncover predetermined ideas that have forever poisoned the well of public investigation into what may have happened to all those children all those years ago. The scariest truth here is that it is much easier to lock one man up and give the boogeyman a face than to imagine there might be a more upstanding seemingly normal member of the community responsible for the crimes.

The filmmakers also manage to explore the fun side of even such a dark urban legend by taking viewers on a late night tour of the tunnels and living spaces on the abandoned Willowbrook estate. As they encounter teens out for their own adventures the circle seems somewhat complete. Andre Rand is not even known by name by many of them. He has become a nameless phantom/ghost/Satanist/escaped lunatic again that daring teens and daters can whistle past in the dark.

Co-directed by Brancaccio and Zeman, the documentary seems to strive slightly for profundity. It hardly needs to. Ominous music and a *Dateline*-esque style of narration threaten to cheese up the proceedings. It would also have helped matters greatly if Rand had consented to an interview. In the end, this is far more than just another well-done true crime documentary. The questions arising from viewing will haunt virtually anyone long after the closing credits going far beyond the question of the innocence or guilt of Rand. Zeman and Brancaccio are right on the mark when they posit their footage and the facts of the case as pointing toward a collective horror story. *Cropsey* is as close as it gets in real life.

Dave Canfield

CREDITS

Origin: USA
Language: English
Released: 2010
Production: Zachary Mortensen, Joshua Zeman, Barbara Brancaccio; Antidote Film, Afterhours Productions, Ghost Root; released by Cinema Purgatorio

Directed by: Joshua Zeman, Barbara Brancaccio
Written by: Joshua Zeman
Cinematography by: Chad Davidson
Music by: Alexander Lasarenko
Editing: Tom Patterson, Anita Gabrosek
Sound: Tom Efinger
MPAA rating: Unrated
Running time: 84 minutes

REVIEWS

Anderson, John. *Variety*. July 6, 2010.
Brody, Richard. *New Yorker*. June 4, 2010.
Catsoulis, Jeanette. *New York Times* June 4, 2010.
Lovece, Frank. *Film Journal International*. June 8, 2010.
Lumenick, Lou. *New York Post*. June 4, 2010.
McWeeny, Drew. *HitFix*. July 10, 2010.
Mondello, Bob. *NPR*. June 3, 2010.
Olsen, Mark. *Los Angeles Times*. July 8, 2010.
Rapold, Nicolas. *Village Voice*. June 1, 2010.
Schager, Nick. *Slant Magazine*. June 10, 2010.

TRIVIA

At the 2009 Tribeca Film Festival, this film garnered the Hammer to Nail's Grand Jury Prize for best documentary.

CYRUS

John met the woman of his dreams. Then he met her son.
—Movie tagline

Box Office: $7 million

While it is debateable that the filmmaking brothers Mark and Jay Duplass invented the film sub-genre "mumblecore," their debut feature *The Puffy Chair* (2005) was certainly the first of its ilk to gain widespread critical acceptance and a modest audience. The brothers' technique of filming on digital video with little more than a plot outline for a screenplay and unknown actors—sometimes Mark Duplass himself—improvising nearly all of the dialogue became more refined with their twist on horror movies, *Baghead* (2008). But unlike improv-heavy comedies by directors such as Judd Apatow, Adam McKay, and Christopher Guest, the Duplass brothers seem more intent on using their actors to explore the emotional depths of their fragile characters rather than simply go for laughs.

Using recognizable actors for the first time in their short career, the Duplass brothers have sacrificed little of their handheld visual style that often feels like the camera is seeking out the most satisfying material and worthy performances. The result is *Cyrus,* a work that finds the means to be charming, powerfully awkward, and completely entertaining by refusing to see the dividing line between comedy and drama. Master improvisation artist John C. Reilly plays John, a man still reeling from his divorce from ex-wife Jamie (Catherine Keener) seven years earlier. She has clearly moved on with most of her life but still feels somewhat responsible for John's sad, lonely condition. She and her fiancé Matt (the perfectly deadpan Matt Walsh) invite John to a party, hoping he will meet a woman.

What happens instead defines who John is for the audience. After a series of colossally awful attempts to talk to women at the party in which John spills his guts all over the floor about his station in life, he meets a woman that actually finds him honestly refreshing. While most party goers avoid him, Molly (Marisa Tomei, in full sweetheart mode) actually comes on to John. To many men, this might send up the red flag, but he is so moved that a woman as beautiful as Molly would even look at him, he does not care.

The missing piece to the puzzle of Molly comes in the form of her chubby, 21-year-old son Cyrus (Jonah Hill, with a serial-killer, close-cropped haircut and collection of plaid shirts), still living at home and sharing what might be described as a borderline inappropriate closeness with his mom. And while John is willing to see if this unlikely trio could make for an unconventional but happy family, he soon discovers that Cyrus is a master manipulator, who does everything from faking night terrors and panic attacks to moving out briefly to make his mother's attentions swing from John back to him.

In the hands of another director or a larger, more controlling studio, *Cyrus* might have been turned into a typical exercise in these two men engaging in juvenile one-upmanship whenever Molly was not looking—not unlike what Reilly did with Will Farrell in *Step Brothers* (2008). But the Duplass brothers seem to actively loathe the predictability of the Hollywood comedy and have, instead, gone for emotional honesty. More importantly, they trust their actors to breathe life into these characters and allow real feelings to emerge from all three characters.

By using improvisation, the film has achieved something resembling real life. This is especially true when Jonah Hill is on-screen, displaying vulnerability but with a dark edge that he has never even hinted at in other movies. Cyrus is a complicated, layered (often scary) person, and Hill rises to the acting occasion to let viewers understand his fear of losing his mother. Not to alienate fans of Hill's comedic work, he still manages to come up with some of the film's best shocking lines and funniest moments. The film's only true weak spot is the

Molly character, who could have used a little more insight into her motivations for continuing to treat her son like he is a little boy at times. Tomei pulls it off without Molly coming across as creepy, but the character is the least developed of the three.

The most fascinating aspect of *Cyrus* is how the Duplass brothers build the characters gradually and make the audience realize that these are three damaged people that could therapeutically benefit from being in each other's lives at this juncture. All three are at turning points, and it actually stings to watch these would-be friendships fall apart at one point in the story. While most films might have allowed the story to build to an ultimate showdown between John and Cyrus, this one veers off in a remarkably welcome direction that, again, reflects what might actually happen in the real world. *Cyrus* has plenty of sweet, humorous moments throughout, but it is the more somber and honest moments that give it depth and staying power upon repeat viewings. This is the kind of movie that takes up residence in the heart and stays there through every weird second of its running time.

Steven Prokopy

CREDITS

Cyrus: Jonah Hill
John: John C. Reilly
Molly: Marisa Tomei
Jamie: Catherine Keener
Tim: Matt Walsh
Roger: Tim Guinee

Origin: USA
Language: English
Released: 2010
Production: Michael Costigan; Scott Free, Dune Entertainment; released by Fox Searchlight
Directed by: Jay Duplass, Mark Duplass
Written by: Jay Duplass, Mark Duplass
Cinematography by: Jas Shelton
Music by: Michael Andrews
Sound: Mack Melson
Music Supervisor: Marguerite Phillips
Editing: Jay Deuby
Costumes: Roemehl Hawkins
Production Design: Annie Spitz
MPAA rating: R
Running time: 91 minutes

REVIEWS

Carvajal, Nelson. *Cinefile.com.* June 25, 2010.
Ebert, Roger. *Chicago Sun-Times.* June 23, 2010.
Fear, David. *Time Out New York.* June 14, 2010.
Goss, William. *Orlando Weekly.* July 7, 2010.
LaSalle, Mick. *San Francisco Chronicle.* June 25, 2010.
O'Hehir, Andrew. *Salon.com.* June 16, 2010.
Orndorf, Brian. *efilmcritic.com.* June 20, 2010.
Pais, Matt. *ChicagoMetromix.com.* June 24, 2010.
Puig, Claudia. *USA Today.* June 19, 2010.
Taylor, Ella. *Village Voice.* June 15, 2010.

AWARDS

Nomination:
Ind. Spirit 2011: Actor (Reilly).

D

DATE NIGHT

On April 9th one night can change your life.
—Movie tagline

Box Office: $99 million

Phil (Steve Carell) and Claire Foster (Tina Fey) have a stable life in New Jersey. They work a lot, as a tax consultant and realtor, respectively. They have two energetic, well-adjusted kids, Oliver (Jonathan Morgan Heit) and Charlotte (Savannah Paige Rae). The spouses even regularly take time to schedule a date night, which always finds them at the same restaurant, ordering the same salmon and potato skins and talking to the server who knows them by name. It is an exhausting, routine existence, and that is the problem.

The Fosters are exactly the sort of people who need a wild night to shake things up, and in the very-funny and surprisingly-sweet *Date Night*, that is just what they get. The evening begins with simple intentions: Phil and Claire are dressing up and re-injecting spontaneity into their lives. That means traveling an hour from home in New Jersey into Manhattan to boldly try, sans reservation, the hot new seafood restaurant Claw. It is the sort of place that is so pretentious and enamored of its own exclusivity that the maître d' (Nick Kroll) answers the phone, "This is Claw. You're welcome." Phil and Claire are rudely dismissed when they try to acquire a table. Phil even endearingly tries to negotiate by offering that he wants the night to be special for he and his wife. No dice. The Fosters may have put a lot of significance on reclaiming the fire in their marriage, but Claw does not care.

So Phil and Claire do what perhaps any desperate married couple would do while surrounded by younger people in a trendy spot that will not even serve them a drink: They steal another couple's reservation and snag a prime table. Soon, the two are, just as they had hoped, enjoying expensive wine and goofy conversation that has nothing to do with kids or plans for the next day. They are just a happy couple having fun, a state many married couples and maybe some unmarried couples may need to strive to achieve. Of course, *Date Night* is a screwball comedy that is about to get screwy, so the dream date does not last. Tough guys Collins (Common) and Armstrong (Jimmi Simpson) show up at the table and demand to talk to Phil and Claire outside about serious business, thinking that the Fosters are actually the Tripplehorns, the name on the reservation they stole.

It is not long before the Fosters are running for their lives, breaking into apartments and strip clubs, and experiencing more excitement than they have in years, and likely more danger than they have in their entire lives. Their underlying fear is that they have become like their friends Brad (Mark Ruffalo) and Haley (Kristen Wiig), who are splitting up because, as Brad tells Phil in confidence, "We're not even a couple anymore; we're like excellent roommates." This is as depressing as it gets for a married couple, recognizing that the passion and love that once was there is gone, replaced by something platonic. So even as Phil and Claire are being shot at and stealing cars and running for their lives all over town, there is the sense that, as long as they survive, they will probably be glad that their routine has finally been mixed up a bit.

All this action would not mean much if not balanced by comedy, and *Date Night* is loaded with funny people putting just the right warmth and silliness into an increasingly outrageous situation. Carell, so deft at playing socially awkward Michael Scott on NBC's *The Office*, and Fey, the perfect, vulnerable straight woman on NBC's *30 Rock*, are complementary not just as a couple who strives to function together but comedians who bounce off each other with precision and affection. "Honey, are you breathing?" Phil asks Claire in a panic after a near-escape from Collins and Armstrong. "Only in!" screams Claire in a perfectly executed bit of comic timing. Better still is that Carell and Fey are surrounded by an almost overqualified cast of versatile performers, including Mark Wahlberg as Holbrooke, Claire's former client with an aversion to shirts, and James Franco and Mila Kunis, pitch-perfect as Taste and Whippit, the criminal couple whose reservation the Fosters stole but whose magic—while Taste and Whippit transition from bickering to impassioned smooching—the Fosters soon envy. Add on minor roles for Taraji P. Henson, William Fichtner, Ray Liotta, and Leighton Meester and *Date Night* is overloaded with familiar faces playing roles much smaller than usual, to generally strong effect.

The joy in the film's comic spunk and excellent performances does not come through as well in the action sequences, unremarkably executed by director Shawn Levy (*Night at the Museum*, [2006], *The Pink Panther*, [2006]), whose films are normally much worse. These scenes are fine and escalate the mayhem that turns the Fosters' night from special to unforgettable. Yet as cars are speeding through New York streets or guns are firing away, the actors' rapport and the wit of Josh Klausner's script becomes minimized in favor of action that is far less unique. Perhaps slightly less emphasis on scampering and shooting would allow for more character development on the edges and make the high-level conspiracy into which the Fosters are thrown feel less generic.

No harm done, though, as *Date Night,* a charming romp about the need to keep a relationship fresh, unfolds with such a light, amusing touch that it is easy to spend the entire movie smiling and simply glad to spend time with these characters. That is far from expected in a film starring Carell, whose big-screen work outside of *The 40-Year-Old Virgin* (2005) has been pretty lousy, or Fey, whose sole starring role was in the uneven comedy *Baby Mama* (2008). Perhaps it is appropriate, though; after all, *Date Night* is about a husband and wife rediscovering their ability to play together and surprise each other, and the film's pleasant surprise is that Carell and Fey are not just a great team but can truly anchor a studio comedy with the right material. When most action-comedies are being cast with people like Jennifer Aniston and Gerard Butler (who appeared earlier in the year in the atrocious *The Bounty Hunter* [2010]), Carell and Fey, and *Date Night,* are nothing short of refreshing.

Matt Pais

CREDITS

Clara Foster: Tina Fey
Phil Foster: Steve Carell
Holbrooke Grant: Mark Wahlberg
DA Frank Crenshaw: William Fichtner
Brad Sullivan: Mark Ruffalo
Taste: James Franco
Katy: Leighton Meester
Detective Arroyo: Taraji P. Henson
Haley Sullivan: Kristen Wiig
Joe Miletto: Ray Liotta
Whippit: Mila Kunis
Collins: Common
Oliver: Jonathan Morgan Heit
Charlotte: Savannah Paige Rae
Claw Maître D': Nick Kroll
Armstrong: Jimmi Simpson
Origin: USA
Language: English
Released: 2010
Production: Shawn Levy, Tom McNulty; 21 Laps Entertainment, Dune Entertainment III, Media Magik Entertainment; released by 20th Century Fox
Directed by: Shawn Levy, Josh Klausner
Written by: Tina Fey, Josh Klausner
Cinematography by: Dean Semler
Music by: Christophe Beck
Sound: Steve Cantamessa, Joshua Anderson
Editing: Dean Zimmerman
Art Direction: Peter Rogness
Costumes: Arlynn Abseck
Production Design: David Gropman
MPAA rating: PG-13
Running time: 88 minutes

REVIEWS

Ebert, Roger. *Chicago Sun-Times.* April 7, 2010.
Longworth, Karina. *Village Voice.* April 6, 2010.
Morris, Wesley. *Boston Globe.* April 9, 2010.
Phillips, Michael. *Chicago Tribune.* April 8, 2010.
Puig, Claudia. *USA Today.* April 11, 2010.
Rabin, Nathan. *AV Club.* April 8, 2010.
Rickey, Carrie. *Philadelphia Inquirer.* April 9, 2010.
Rothkopf, Joshua. *Time Out New York.* April 8, 2010.

Scott, A.O. *New York Times.* April 9, 2010.
Stevens, Dana. *Slate.* April 8, 2010.

QUOTES

Phil Foster: "He turned the gun sideways! That's a kill shot!"

TRIVIA

There is one additional bonus scene after the final credits.

DAYBREAKERS

The battle between immortality and humanity is on.
—Movie tagline

Box Office: $30 million

Daybreakers is a somewhat imaginative entry into the vampire genre with some things to recommend it: A novel premise, the revelation of a startling cure for vampirism, and a great cast. Add to that the visual style of Australian filmmaking team of directors Michael and Peter Spierig and the result is a vampire film that should stand head and shoulders above recent genre efforts. But the film falters, most notably in the last act, when it becomes clear that the blood type of *Daybreakers* is clearly B.

The film takes place in a world where vampires have conquered the human race and remade society in their own image. Remaining humans are scarce and as extinction looms and blood becomes harder to find starved vampires find themselves physically and mentally devolving into a bestial cannibalistic life form that threatens to destroy all life on the planet. Desperate, they set their top scientific minds on finding a blood substitute. One such scientist, Dr. Edward Dalton (Ethan Hawke), is anxious to find the substitute for his own reasons, most notably, because he, like some others of his kind, is sympathetic to humanity, and wants to find a way the two races can peacefully co-exist.

A chance encounter with a group of rebel human survivors puts him in touch with their leader Lionel 'Elvis' Cormac (Willem Dafoe), a former vampire who says he has found the cure for vampirism. Opposing Dalton and the humans is the primary corporate supplier of blood, Bromley Marks, led by Charles Bromley (Sam Neill) and Dalton's estranged brother Frankie (Michael Dorman), a soldier whose job it is to round up humans.

The problems with this plot are innumerable. If there are good and bad vampires then what is the problem with becoming one? What need of a cure? If there are good and bad vampires why are they not openly at war with one another long before the action in *Daybreakers* takes place? *Daybreakers* also reveals vampires as distinctly more fragile than their human counterparts. Humans are shown knocking vampires unconscious and holding their own in other physical confrontations. Again this begs the question of why anyone would want to be a vampire. Immortality would certainly be a draw but as *Daybreakers* shows in its opening scene the monotony of an earthly eternity can drive even a vampire mad.

The search for individual meaning and identity as well as connection with the other is only hinted at in this film which is a shame considering how much effort is expended in building a visually interesting vampire universe in which the characters travel and live. There are glimpses of vampire coffee shops, self-darkening cars for travel during daylight hours, billboards displaying vamp products, and lively civic debate on how humans should be treated. But there is not enough of this material. Everything has been retro-fitted toward the vampire lifestyle but it seems as hollow as an open grave and so the film fails to establish vampire society or vampire life in general as in any appreciable way different than its human counterpart.

Daybreakers is mainly interested in borrowing visual elements from what has gone before making it functionally impossible to watch without thinking of *Blade* (1998), or *Underworld* (2003). The film is shot in a steely blue light that looks great (especially given the vampire's naturally reflective eyes). But even this stylistic flourish simply serves to remind that *Daybreakers* could have been more. It fails to be as fun as genre counterparts and certainly fails to be as thoughtful as it could have been. The Spierigs also indulge a taste for empty theatrics when they end the film with a deus ex machina rescue.

The special effects here are slightly cheap looking. Severed heads do not look real enough, the dark lighting hides a bit too much of the action at times and, even though the scenes involving the vampiric cure are impressive, they showcase the problem this movie has in moving viewers. *Daybreakers* simply fails to assume an identity. It contains social commentary, moments of horror, humor, action, and gore, but it is none of these in the sum of its parts. One scene is indeed moving, as we watch a de-vampirized character stare in wonder at the sun, but that sort of emotional depth, which should have tied the film together as we follow the conflict to the inevitable showdown, seems wasted here.

As mentioned the film does have a great cast. Ethan Hawke is fine as Edward Dalton and it would be remiss not to mention the grand time Sam Neill has as wicked CEO Charles Bromley. Neill is one of those actors who always seems out on loan from some fabled land where great character types are kept. He rarely fails to elevate mediocre material. He could have simply chewed the scenery here but instead downplays Bromley investing him with a sense of loneliness; a disconnect that seems to suggest an awareness of the loss associated with becoming a vampire. His is the most satisfactorily other-worldly performance.

The highly distinguished Willem Dafoe is mostly wasted here in a role that feels like outtakes from Kris Kristofferson's performance in *Blade* and yet he manages to bring to life lines like, "Living in a world where vampires are the dominant species is about as safe as bare backing a five-dollar whore." Relative newcomer Michael Dorman manages to breathe some life into the character of Dalton's brother Frankie even though, like most of the secondary characters in *Daybreakers*, the writing virtually forces him to play to type.

In their first feature, *Undead* (2003), the Spierig Brothers showed considerable talent for doing a lot with a little. *Undead* was funny, frightening, and rose above the zombie herd through sheer gonzo force, throwing one jaw dropping genre-mashing bit of screwy plot development after another. The end result was far too enjoyable to dismiss. With *Daybreakers* they do little with a lot more. Some will find it enough but most will have the sense of a story that settles for less.

Dave Canfield

CREDITS

Lionel Cormac: Willem Dafoe
Edward Dalton: Ethan Hawke
Charles Bromley: Sam Neill
Christopher Caruso: Vince Colosimo
Audrey Bennett: Claudia Karvan
Alison Bromley: Isabel Lucas
Frankie Dalton: Michael Dorman
Origin: USA, Australia
Language: English
Released: 2009
Production: Chris Brown, Brian Furst, Sean Furst; Film Finance Corp, Paradise Films; released by Lionsgate
Directed by: Michael Spierig, Peter Spierig
Written by: Michael Spierig, Peter Spierig
Cinematography by: Ben Nott
Music by: Christopher Gordon
Sound: Wayne Pashley
Editing: Matt Villa
Art Direction: Bill Booth
Costumes: George Liddle
Production Design: George Liddle

MPAA rating: R
Running time: 98 minutes

REVIEWS

Biodrowski, Steve. *Cinefantastique Online.* May 11, 2010.
Catsoulis, Jeanette. *New York Times.* January 8, 2010.
Ebert, Roger. *Chicago Sun-Times.* January 6, 2010.
Frappier, Rob. *Screenrant.* January 7, 2010 .
Phillips, Michael. *Chicago Tribune.* January 7, 2010.
Pinkerton, Nick. *Village Voice.* January 5, 2010.
Puig, Claudia. *USA Today.* January 10, 2010.
Seaver, Jay. *EFilmCritic.com.* January 14, 2010.
Yamato, Jen. *Movies.com.* January 12, 2010.
Zacharek, Stephanie. *Salon.com.* January 8, 2010.

QUOTES

Charles Bromley: "Do you like being a vampire?"

TRIVIA

According to an *Entertainment Weekly* article, this film was shot in 2007.

DEAR JOHN

Love can transform us in ways we never could have imagined.
—Movie tagline

Box Office: $80 million

Six of author Nicholas Sparks' fifteen published works have been adapted to film with moviegoers forced to endure stories of Leukemia, Alzheimer's Disease, and the general shuffling off of mortal coils as bookends to his tales of found love. If the axiom that laughter is the best medicine holds true, one must wonder what damage could be caused by prolonged exposure to the opposite in Sparks' melodramas? Sparks writes romance for adolescents and not adults; fairy tales for martyrs through the eyes of a Junior High student experiencing those feelings for the first time and confused at how to interpret it or what to say. The shame is that *Dear John* had to feel the brunt of Sparks' trademarks during its second half because for close to an hour it actually feels more like a Lasse Hallstrom film than just another tearjerker.

John Tyree (Channing Tatum) just wanted to get in some surfing during his leave from the U.S. Army. He did not expect to look upon the face of an angel like Savannah Curtis (Amanda Seyfried) nor make a daring rescue of her handbag by jumping off a pier into the ocean. This act of kindness earns him a beer and a two-week love affair with the girl every male in the area harbors some sort of crush on. Randy (Scott Porter) passive-aggressively needles John's military background to knock him back as the wrong guy for her and less obvious is the quieter Tim (Henry Thomas) who offers him a ride home and makes brotherly warnings not to break her heart.

Every film based on a Nicholas Sparks novel demands an affliction of the moment and *Dear John* turns to autism, although less as an obstacle to be overcome and more as a device to help define its two lead characters. The widowed (or abandoned) Tim has a son with the disease and Samantha dotes on him to the extent that she wants to open up a stable for autistic children. On top of that, John's father (Richard Jenkins) is diagnosed with the same by Samantha, who recognizes the symptoms of obsessive repetition and withdrawn emotions. Since Tim's child is portrayed as an active, happy tyke and John's dad a sad sack, her diagnosis must be taken with a degree of disbelief and that is enough for her new beau to punch out three of her friends in a moment of frustration about his father.

Dear John is only a disease-of-the-week story in passing while it attempts to concentrate on the long-distance relationship between its lovers. With a year left on his rotation, John and Samantha exchange countless letters solidifying their romance after her initial doubts that "a lot can happen in twelve months." As the film begins in August of 2001, most viewers will not need three guesses as to what is on the horizon. To the film's credit, it chooses not to linger upon the after-effects of this first of many tragedies-to-come and tries to treat it along the lines of *From Here To Eternity* (1953) when an unprovoked attack temporarily hinders our couple. While it is subtly-handled, this factual plot twist does spin *Dear John* to where it finally jumps the rails for good.

For about the first fifty minutes of the running time, there is a tolerability to the budding romance. The story goes on auto-pilot through the requisite getting-to-know-you montages and has an easygoing, non-offending away about it. When the complications begin to rise with a fever pitch, the audience is faced with the backtracking prospect that they have no idea who these people really are. They are physically appealing for sure, but what really makes them tick and why do they even like each other? Their only personality traits stem from how they respond to others. Samantha is a no-vices saint who rides horses with the autistic kid while John cannot relate to his dad under the same shadow and keeps leaving him in the lurch on lasagna night.

The film's more empathetic tale resides with this secondary relationship, wedged in to produce tears rather than build the story. Samantha should be the third wheel to John and his father since thanks to Richard Jenkins' earnest portrayal of a withdrawn soul who has lost connection with his son. Jenkins finds something genuine in the film that is not present when the young lovers are alone. Samantha's experience with autism could have made her the bolt that helps bonds the paternal conflict. And therein lies a love story based in understanding, appreciation, and filling the hole left in John's heart since growing apart from his father and joining the military to get away from it all. In the progressively emotionless central union, it becomes difficult to listen to Seyfried's Samantha go on and on about how her life was hell being without John while he was off risking his life in the Middle East when most would not consider riding horses and going to college being the equivalent of eternal damnation.

Lasse Hallstrom is no stranger to sentimentality throughout his career and has usually succeeded when earning those heartstring tugs through characters motivated by life and their own desires. In *Once Around* (1991), *What's Eating Gilbert Grape* (1993), and *The Cider House Rules* (1999) the stories are often equally balanced between their characters and a moral backdrop; two sides of the same coin influencing each other. The first half of *Dear John* has the feel if not the actual feelings of what Hallstrom excels at before Sparks' prose flips the coin and lays it on so thick in the final fifty minutes that it would not be out of the realm for asteroids and global warming to wedge apart the beautiful people. Even when the film finally lives up to its name and delivers the eponymous letter, the reasons behind it are masked in music drowning out the voiceover. If the movie cannot be bothered to elucidate on the fate of its characters, why should we bother to care either? Unless an immediate reaction after ingesting more Nicholas Sparks is to go to the doctor.

Erik Childress

CREDITS

John Tyree: Channing Tatum
Savannah Lynn Curtis: Amanda Seyfried
Tim Wheddon: Henry Thomas
Capt. Stone: Keith D. Robinson
Mr. Tyree: Richard Jenkins
Noodles: D.J. Cotrona
Rooster: Cullen Moss
Starks: Gavin McCulley
Randy: Scott Porter
Origin: USA
Language: English
Released: 2010

Production: Marty Bowen, Wyck Godfrey, Ryan Kavanaugh; Relativity Media, Temple Hill Productions; released by Screen Gems

Directed by: Lasse Hallstrom

Written by: Jamie Linden

Cinematography by: Terry Stacey

Music by: Deborah Lurie

Sound: Jonathan S. Gaynor

Music Supervisor: Happy Walters

Editing: Kristina Boden

Art Direction: Mark Garner

Costumes: Dana Campbell

Production Design: Kara Lindstrom

MPAA rating: PG-13

Running time: 105 minutes

REVIEWS

Ebert, Roger. *Chicago Sun-Times*. February 4, 2010.
Honeycutt, Kirk. *Hollywood Reporter*. February 2, 2010.
Jones, J.R. *Chicago Reader*. February 4, 2010.
Lowry, Brian. *Variety*. February 2, 2010.
Page, Janice. *Boston Globe*. February 4, 2010.
Pais, Matt. *Metromix.com*. February 4, 2010.
Puig, Claudia. *USA Today*. February 4, 2010.
Rickey, Carrie. *Philadelphia Inquirer*. February 4, 2010.
Sharkey, Betsy. *Los Angeles Times*. February 4, 2010.
Tobias, Scott. *AV Club*. February 4, 2010.

QUOTES

Savannah Curtis: "The saddest people I've ever met in life are the ones who don't care deeply about anything at all."

TRIVIA

Opened at number one at the box office, ending the seven week run of *Avatar*.

DEATH AT A FUNERAL

On April 16th, no one will rest in peace.
—Movie tagline

Box Office: $43 million

Before the figurative body of Frank Oz's 2007 original is even cold, here is an Americanized retread of an already partially American production. *Death at a Funeral*, which retains screenwriter Dean Craig, actor Peter Dinklage (reprising his role as a mysterious, out-of-place guest), and each and every major gag from the original, is hardly necessary and yet almost as successful a comedy as its originator.

In its English countryside manor setting, Oz's film had the advantage of juxtaposing the quiet, reserved conceit of a British comedy of manners with the broader, baser sensibilities of the "gross-out" comedy so prevalent in the American cinema of the decade or so before it. Director Neil LaBute also (predictably, given his background in the theater) handles the material like a chamber play, and his staging is such that allows the cast—each member infusing their own spin on the characters in between the showcase joke sequences—to play freely.

The similarities start from the outset with an animated opening credit sequence that apes the original's and surpasses it in detail, watching a hearse traverse the streets of Los Angeles to a home where a funeral is about start. One of the dead man's sons, Aaron (Chris Rock), awaits its arrival and is as outraged as possible in his grief to discover that the delivered body is not that of his father. Starting a string of pop culture references that will dominate much of the apparent ad-libbing from the cast, Aaron calls the body of the dead Asian man in front of him "Jackie Chan."

The mix-up by the scatter-brained undertaker (Kevin Hart) is the first of many mishaps to befall this most grievous and depressing of occasions. After setting up that tone and expectation, Craig's screenplay spends a notable amount of time on establishing the basics of the characters, their relationships, and whatever not-inconsiderable baggage accompanies them.

Aaron's wife Michelle (Regina Hall) is consoling to her husband but also reminds him that it is the last day of her menstrual cycle, meaning they will have to have sex some time that day—funeral or not. Michelle's almost single-minded focus on becoming pregnant comes from her mother-in-law Cynthia (Loretta Devine), who pushes the point even when discussing her dead husband. A grandchild would surely help her grief and give her a reason to continue living, she supposes.

Cynthia is the first of many in attendance shocked and disappointed to learn that Aaron will be saying the eulogy, when, after all, there is a successful writer already in the family: Aaron's brother Ryan (Martin Lawrence). Aaron is quick to point out to anyone who is critical of the decision that he too is a writer. "We all write checks," his uncle Duncan (Ron Glass) stabs, while Ryan reassures him that it is Aaron's nine-month seniority that has prompted the choice of speaker.

Uncle Duncan's children are Elaine (Zoë Saldaña) and Jeff (Columbus Short), a pharmacology student who has concocted a new drug cocktail that is like "acid mixed with acid." Elaine's boyfriend Oscar (James Marsden) is nervous about meeting her father again, so Elaine, unknowing of the true hallucinogenic contents in her brother's pill bottle, gives Oscar what she believes to be medication for anxiety.

Marsden and Short, in their inherently disparate portrayals, are the funniest performances in the movie. Marsden plays the all-too familiar joke of a person unwittingly high with skilled physical comedy, interacting with the locale (diving his head into bushes that are, by his reasoning, "so green" and playing with the lutes of angel statues) and props (wrapping his head in toilet paper like a mummy or mouthing words with a magnifying glass in front of his face) at every opportunity. His most absurd moment of comic inspiration comes from a faux baritone rendition of "Amazing Grace" to Cynthia, before becoming startled by her feathery headpiece.

Meanwhile, Short is subdued in his delivery, displaying an adept sense of comic timing. It is especially evident in a pair of verbal double-takes (when he realizes what Oscar has taken and following that revelation to Elaine with an equally calm "yikes") and a moment in which he changes his answer from "no" to "yes," with multiple words in one breath.

The other guests consist of Derek (Luke Wilson, who plays slimy well), an old boyfriend of Elaine's, his friend Norman (Tracy Morgan, whose insistence on stream-of-consciousness rants misses the point of the character's necessary hypochondria), and Uncle Russell (Danny Glover, who snarls and repeats his famous line about getting old from the *Lethal Weapon* series). Then there is Frank (Dinklage), who slides into frame and whose voice appears out of the blue, trying to talk to Aaron in private. When he finally has the chance, he reveals that he was Aaron's father's lover, although the revelation is unspoken and learned through a visual gag (Aaron's POV shifts from his father's possessions of a statute of nude men wrestling to a book about the singer Madonna to yet another statue of grappling, naked men).

With the exposition out of the way, Craig's script turns into a series of off-kilter jokes. Since they are the same, usually predictable bits from the original film, a familiar audience is doubly aware of what will happen. These set-piece gags are only as successful in this version as the members of the cast who participate in them.

A disgusting scatological joke, involving Norman trying to help Russell get to the bathroom in a hurry, is literal toilet humor. Whereas the shock value of the punch line of a hand (and later, through too-excited washing, face) covered in excrement is heightened in the original by the character's concern with his health, it is even further downgraded here—without Norman's phobia of disease highlighted—to only Morgan's reaction. The obvious impropriety of the body falling out of the coffin remains intact, while the hectic attempt to silence Frank and the ensuing complications that result in the possibility of the titular scenario is the movie's most successful sequence, mostly due to the contrasting dynamic between Rock, Lawrence, Short, and Morgan.

Not without its moments of laughter, *Death at a Funeral* is mainly a commendable effort on the part of its cast to make the material its own.

Mark Dujsik

CREDITS

Aaron: Chris Rock
Norman: Tracy Morgan
Ryan: Martin Lawrence
Cynthia: Loretta Devine
Duncan: Ron Glass
Uncle Russell: Danny Glover
Michelle: Regina Hall
Oscar: James Marsden
Elaine: Zoë Saldaña
Jeff: Columbus Short
Brian: Kevin Hart
Derek: Luke Wilson
Frank: Peter Dinklage
Reverend Davis: Keith David
Origin: USA
Language: English
Released: 2010
Production: Chris Rock, Sidney Kimmel, William Horberg, Share Stallings, Laurence Malkin; Parabolic Pictures, Sidney Kimmell Entertainment, Stable Way Entertainment, Wonderful Films; released by Screen Gems
Directed by: Neil LaBute
Written by: Chris Rock, Dean Craig
Cinematography by: Rogier Stoffers
Music by: Christophe Beck
Sound: David A. Cohen, Ron Eng
Editing: Tracey Wadmore-Smith
Art Direction: Chris Cornwell
Costumes: Maya Lieberman
Production Design: Jon Gary Steele
MPAA rating: R
Running time: 92 minutes

REVIEWS

Berardinelli, James. *Reelviews.net.* April 15, 2010.
Burr, Ty. *Boston Globe.* April 16, 2010.
Covert, Colin. *Star Tribune.* April 15, 2010.
Ebert, Roger. *Chicago Sun-Times.* April 14, 2010.
Groen, Rick. *Globe and Mail.* April 16, 2010.
Johanson, MaryAnn. *Flickfilosopher.com.* April 19, 2010.
Putman, Dustin. *Dustinputman.com.* April 15, 2010.
Rabin, Nathan. *AVclub.com.* April 15, 2010.

Snider, Eric D. *Ericdsnider.com.* April 16, 2010.
Thompson, Gary. *Philadelphia Daily News.* April 15, 2010.

QUOTES

Aaron: "Let me get this straight: our father was romantically involved with a guy that could fit in his pocket, and you're mad because he's white?"

TRIVIA

Peter Dinklage was the only actor to reprise his role from the original 2007 British version of the film.

DESPICABLE ME

Superbad. Superdad.
—Movie tagline

Box Office: $252 million

Animated films have to try harder than ever these days to catch the public eye as well as the child's heart and imagination. It is not enough that the film have celebrity voices and 3-D effects, the two most common traits of any animated film in the last ten years, save for Pixar, who always know how to cast the right voices, not necessarily the most popular. The ad campaigns also have to begin much earlier. It is not unusual for a teaser trailer to appear in theaters eight months to a year before the animated film in question is released to the public. Universal Pictures' *Despicable Me* played the game accordingly, making sure its name was out there in the public eye long before its release date. Although it is not based on any previously-known source material, the film had been treated almost like an event.

It is hardly worthy of such build-up, but it is certainly not the worst or most undeserving film to receive such treatment. It is, in the end, just a fun little animated movie that will be enjoyed more in the moment than upon reflection. It does not pander to kids, nor does it make parents feel out-of-touch, bored, or intolerant. Furthermore, to its great credit, it does not go the way of the pop culture reference in order to get a decent joke (although it does go for the occasional fart joke). *Despicable Me* is never actually despicable and not the least bit groundbreaking. It is simply a time-killer, but not a bad one.

The 'Me' in the title refers to rogue evil genius Gru (voiced by Steve Carell), who is past his prime and on the verge of losing his title of Most Evil Person Alive. Vector (voiced by Jason Segel), a skinnier, younger, more virile scientist has taken over the mantle. Both of them sit in the waiting room of the owner of an evil bank, Mr. Perkins (voiced by Will Arnett), who informs Gru

that he will not be able to grant him a loan to finance the capturing of the moon, which appears to be the only thing left on or near the planet Earth that has not been taken over or stolen by a mad scientist.

Gru knows that Vector has assembled a machine that can shrink anything to the size of an insect. His only chance of securing a loan is to show Mr. Perkins that he has the shrinking machine, which will then shrink the moon down to the size of a baseball. After many feeble attempts to steal the machine out of Vector's house—sequences that appear to be inspired by the antics of Mad Magazine's Spy vs. Spy—Gru happens to see three little girls selling cookies and gaining admittance into Vector's house. Once Gru learns they are orphan girls, he gets the idea to adopt them and use them as bait.

The three girls vary in age and live with the unlikable Miss Hattie (voiced by Kristin Wiig) at her House For Girls. Gru makes himself out to be a Nobel Prize-winning dentist as a means of convincing Miss Hattie to let him adopt the girls and his plan works. As Margot (voiced by Miranda Cosgrove), Edith (voiced by Dana Gaier) and Agnes (voiced by Elsie Fisher) move in, it does not take any kind of genius to see where the story goes from here. Gru's evil plan seems less and less interesting as he eventually succumbs to the charms of these three kids and becomes more of a father figure to them.

Gru is no stranger to looking after small ones since he is surrounded in his lair by several hundred indecipherable yellow minions to help him carry out his evil work. The seemingly cute little goofballs who look like something created in a Nerf® factory speak their own form of gibberish and act like a cross between *The Simpson*'s Itchy and Scratchy, Joe Dante's *Gremlins*, and the green aliens in Pixar's *Toy Story* movies. Gru's own childhood is explored as well in flashbacks that show him trying to win the approval of his always unsatisfied mother (voiced by Julie Andrews).

What *Despicable Me* lacks in momentum, it makes up for in charm and wit. Many of the hyperactive gags feel lifted from Tex Avery or Warner Brothers cartoons (having the girls sleep in hollowed-out bombs is a great touch). The pace is just about right for the material and the sentimental side of the storyline builds gradually and earns its touching moments at the end, even if it botches them completely just before the credits. Directors Pierre Coffin and Chris Renaud do the best they can to justify the use of 3-D with fun results. However, the closing credits sequence will likely fall flat on a 2-D screen as the little yellow minions try to make their way out into the audience as far as they can.

Credit must also go to the cast, who do a terrific job of making the audience forget who is supplying the audio. Carrell, Segel, Wiig, and Russell Brand (who plays Gru's assistant) make an effort to bring some flavor to their performances instead of easily coasting on their own personas, which so many Hollywood actors end up doing, usually with bad results. Likewise, the three kids are engaging, realistic (in terms of behavior), and funny. This greatly helps *Despicable Me* to be an above average concoction that could have benefitted from a couple more screenplay re-writes to give the story a bit more of a punch, but in its moment, it goes down easily enough.

Collin Souter

CREDITS

Gru: Steve Carell (Voice)
Vector: Jason Segel (Voice)
Margo: Miranda Cosgrove (Voice)
Dr. Nefario: Russell Brand (Voice)
Agnes: Elsie Fisher (Voice)
Edith: Dana Gaier (Voice)
Mr. Perkins: Will Arnett (Voice)
Fred McDade: Danny McBride (Voice)
Gru's Mom: Julie Andrews (Voice)
Tim: Jemaine Clement (Voice)
Miss Hattie: Kristen Wiig (Voice)
Tourist Dad/Carnival Barker: Jack McBrayer (Voice)
Tourist Mom: Mindy Kaling (Voice)
Scientist: Ken Jeong (Voice)
Dave the Minion: Chris Renaud (Voice)
Various Minions: Pierre Coffin (Voice)
Origin: USA
Language: English
Released: 2010
Production: John Cohen, Janet Healy, Christopher Meledandri; Illusion Entertainment Group; released by Universal Pictures
Directed by: Chris Renaud, Pierre Coffin
Written by: Ken Daurio, Cinco Paul
Music by: Hans Zimmer
Sound: Dennis Leonard
Editing: Gregory Perler, Pamela Ziegenhagen-Shefland
Art Direction: Eric Guillon
Production Design: Yarrow Cheney
MPAA rating: PG
Running time: 95 minutes

REVIEWS

Burr, Ty. *Boston Globe.* July 8, 2010.
Childress, Erik. *eFilmcritic.com.* July 8, 2010.
Corliss, Richard. *Time Magazine.* July 9, 2010.
Ebert, Roger. *Chicago Sun-Times.* July 8, 2010.
LaSalle, Mick. *San Francisco Chronicle.* July 8, 2010.
Phillips, Michael. *Chicago Tribune.* July 8, 2010.
Robinson, Tasha. *AV Club.* July 8, 2010.
Scott, A.O. *New York Times.* July 9, 2010.
Smith, Kyle. *New York Post.* July 9, 2010.
Turan, Kenneth. *Los Angeles Times.* July 8, 2010.

QUOTES

Vector: "When I'm done with Gru, he's gonna be begging for mercy!"

TRIVIA

The NBC logo can be found in Gru's lair on the top of the Jumbotron.

AWARDS

Nomination:

British Acad. 2010: Animated Film
Golden Globes 2011: Animated Film.

DEVIL

Bad things happen for a reason.
—Movie tagline

Box Office: $34 million

From its opening moments, sporting upside-down aerial views of the city of Philadelphia and soon after a narration offering tell-tale remembrances of a religious fable from a character's childhood, *Devil* unmistakably establishes itself as a topsy-turvy parable. The long, warped route to a feel-good philosophical conclusion that asserts evil as the path to good somehow bypasses the plot's most obvious thematic setup: Hell is other people.

For there is no exit for the movie's central characters, a quintet of anonymous types, defined in the credits and through the dialogue by their age (for the women) or their profession (for the men). Only one has a name listed (because "Unemployed Veteran" is either too specific or too politically charged), and his primary characteristic of brooding silence makes his character the least likely to offer any details about himself.

The premise is simple: Five strangers are trapped in an elevator. The movie's narrator, a superstitious but correct security guard named Ramirez (Jacob Vargas) hints to the audience that this is no ordinary inconvenience due to a mechanical failure. His repetitious suggestions of otherworldly intent and malice turn from foreshadowing to spoiling and then to redirection. Everything Ramirez says will happen does indeed happen, and, as destined by the movie's advertising tagline, it happens for a reason.

That reason is more important to screenwriter Brian Nelson (working from a story by producer M. Night Shyamalan, who has approached this theme of redemptive fatalism throughout his own films to varying success) than the claustrophobic setup and setting. Even before the five find themselves inside the building housing the tight space where they will be confined for the majority of the movie, the voice-over by Ramirez spells out the entire rationale for their imprisonment. One of them is the Devil incarnate, his mother would tell him as a child, intending to punish them one last time in the physical world before snagging their souls to Hell. It always began with a suicide, to "pave the way" for the Devil's arrival, and in the end of the story of a so-called "Devil's Meeting," all of those trapped would be dead.

After also introducing Detective Bowden (Chris Messina), a recovering alcoholic whose wife and son were killed in a hit-and-run car accident in which the driver was never found and who also arrives at the scene of the Devil's mischief because of a suicide, Nelson finally shows the soon-to-be ensnared. The camera wanders the lobby and holds on them longer than the rest: a salesman (Geoffrey Arend), an old woman (Jenny O'Hara), a young woman (Bojana Novakovic), a security guard (Bokeem Woodbine), and Anthony (Logan Marshall-Green), the war veteran who makes a last-minute dash to join the others in their unsuspected date with destiny.

Director John Erick Dowdle and cinematographer Tak Fujimoto make extensive use of a subjective camera to illuminate how the strain between the characters grows from an initial nervous discomfort to panicked suspicion. The salesman ogles the young woman and finds the older woman looking on in scorn. The elevator stops suddenly and all look to and question the guard, who has no idea why it has stopped and no radio to call for help. Everyone's cell phones are without a signal. Ramirez and his partner Lustig (Matt Craven) can speak to the passengers from the monitoring station via the intercom but cannot hear any sound on their end. An elevator music version of "Don't Sit Under the Apple Tree" begins to play, to the frustration of all but the salesman who sings along (to the annoyance of the rest).

The salesman speaks directly to his role as the comic relief. The guard is tough but anxious in enclosed spaces (due to a childhood incident being locked in the trunk of a car), and the veteran is silent but intense. The young woman, according to the salesman, is well-to-do but, on her end, will not admit to it, and the older woman is judgmental. Once the lights start to flicker and soon black out, Nelson ensures the audience never forgets

four of them are red herrings. Someone attacks the young woman—a bloody mark like a bite or serrated blade appears on her back—and the accusations fly. The salesman is acting creepy. The veteran is too quiet. The guard appears the strongest of them. The older woman clearly does not like any of the others. Perhaps the young woman made the wound herself. One by one, suspects are eliminated through their deaths, and Ramirez, spotting the image of a diabolical face on the monitor of the camera in the elevator, immediately suspects the Devil's hand is involved.

Inside the elevator, the characters are monotonous in their characterizations and accusations. Outside the elevator, Ramirez's constant narration states each new plot point (the innocent who help will die and the last the Devil kills will die in front of the person they love the most) or question of faith (on the previous parenthetical points: because the Devil does not like his authority questioned, and to make skeptics of everyone who witnesses). Both undermine the tension of the constricted scenario. Dowdle's insistence on revealing details to the audience before the characters mirrors the effect of the voice-over (an overhead shot of the building's engineer [Joe Cobden] on the roof of the car ruins the reveal for the characters—a slow appearance of a pool of blood inside an interior light cover). Neither Dowdle nor Nelson believes in the possibility of the minimalist setup of *Devil*. There is as much potential for fear in the ordinary as there is in the unknown and in spelling out the specifics of the supernatural force at play, it becomes commonplace.

Mark Dujsik

CREDITS

Det. Bowden: Chris Messina
Salesman/Vince: Geoffrey Arend
Mechanic/Tony: Logan Marshall-Green
Young Woman/Sarah: Bojana Novakovic
Old Woman: Jenny O'Hara
Guard/Ben: Bokeem Woodbine
Ramirez: Jacob Vargas
Elsa Nahai: Caroline Dhavernas
Lustig: Matt Craven
Origin: USA
Language: English
Released: 2010
Production: M. Night Shyamalan, Sam Mercer; Media Rights Capital, Night Chronicles; released by Universal Pictures
Directed by: John Erick Dowdle
Written by: Brian Nelson
Cinematography by: Tak Fujimoto

Music by: Fernando Velazquez
Sound: Glen Gauthier
Editing: Elliot Greenberg
Art Direction: Nigel Churcher
Costumes: Erin Benach
Production Design: Martin Whist
MPAA rating: PG-13
Running time: 80 minutes

REVIEWS

Barsanti, Chris. *Filmcritic.com.* September 17, 2010.
Berardinelli, James. *ReelViews.* September 19, 2010.
Hall, Phil. *Cinematical.* September 17, 2010.
Harvey, Dennis. *Variety.* September 17, 2010.
Moore, Roger. *Orlando Sentinel.* September 17, 2010.
Orndorf, Brian. *BrianOrndorf.com.* September 17, 2010.
Snider, Eric D. *Film.com.* September 17, 2010.
Tallerico, Brian. *HollywoodChicago.com.* September 17, 2010.
Vaux, Rob. *Mania.com.* September 17, 2010.
Weinberg, Scott. *FEARnet.* September 17, 2010.

QUOTES

Ramirez: "You must consider that one of these people might be the Devil."

TRIVIA

The film is based on the classic folktale "The Devils Meeting."

DIARY OF A WIMPY KID

It's not a diary. It's a movie.
—Movie tagline

Box Office: $64 million

With the consistent success of the *Harry Potter* movie franchise and with various other wannabes in its wake trying for the same success story, it was only a matter of time before Hollywood would turn its attention to a less ambitious, but almost as successful book series, *Diary of a Wimpy Kid.* Jeff Kinney's modest, yet irresistible literary scribblings became a welcome antidote for the elementary school/tween crowd in need of characters they could relate to in situations that seemed plausible and rooted in reality. Like Judy Blume before him, Kinney had created a series of books that would probably never feel dated or "of their time," but instead touched on universal adolescent themes that would resonate with readers for generations to come. Most people, young and old, have at one time or another, felt like a Wimpy Kid.

The titular hero here is Greg Heffley (Zachary Gordon), an 11-year-old who is about to embark on his first year of middle school. His relentlessly tormenting older brother Roderick (Devon Bostick) offers him sage advice: "Don't get noticed by anyone." Greg knows early on that there exists a hierarchy in middle school. Everyone there is on a popularity scale of 1 to 200 or so. Greg sees himself around #19, a comfortable enough position, so long as he keeps flying below everybody else's radar. With his boisterous and all-too-childlike best friend Rowley (Robert Capron) always in tow, it will not be easy.

Every single day is a challenge for Greg. His gym coach sadistically pits the scrawny kids against the older kids who have grown well beyond their initial growth spurt. When Greg decides to show up at school in his own particular style, he is mortified to find his friend Rowley has shown up wearing the exact same thing, which results in relentless teasing from their classmates. When Greg and Rowley decide to get jobs as safety patrol boys in hopes they will seem more confident and respected, they learn that they have signed their popularity death warrant. Their friendship gets put to the test when Rowley inadvertently becomes more popular than Greg. And so on and so on.

Like the books, the movie is made up of episodic events rather than being driven by one central plot. In that respect, the movie works in much the same way as Bob Clark's much-celebrated *A Christmas Story* (1983), complete with childhood taunts based on middle school folklore and legend. In this case, a mysterious piece of rotten cheese that has been sitting on the basketball court for years becomes a source of social suicide to anyone who dares to touch it. To have the dreaded "Cheese touch" is the equivalent to having an easily communicable disease. This little narrative device resurfaces periodically and might be the closest the movie has to any real plot point. *Diary of a Wimpy Kid*, much like middle school itself, is only about surviving these social obstacles.

While the movie fails on any pure emotional level, it remains a breeze to sit through, mainly because of its capable young cast. Zachary Gordon is a natural and a good choice for Greg (who exists as the next best thing to a stick figure illustration in the books). He has great timing and he never comes off as overly coached or bratty. Likewise, Robert Capron, as his goofy friend Rowley, has the right amount of childishness and affability to help make Greg's worries and efforts seem that much more trivial. These two almost seem like the live version of the main characters in the animated *Monster House* (2006).

The movie is lovingly reverential of the source material, but almost to a fault. The book itself has a scrappy feel and is a literal take on a kid's diary. It is hand written on notebook lines and is interspersed with simple sketches only a kid could draw. The movie sporadically references that style almost as a way of underscoring its punchlines. This is obviously a means of demonstrating to its target audience that the filmmakers understand the material and have read it thoroughly, lest they should suffer the wrath of the book's unsatisfied fanbase.

Director Thor Freudenthal and his four screenwriters (Jackie Filgo, Jeff Filgo, Jeff Judah and Gabe Sachs) never try to expand the material beyond what the source dictates. While it might be a mistake to try and skew it to a style that would remind one of TV's overly precious *The Wonder Years*, it would have been nice if the creators here had tried for an alternate tone once in a while. Instead, the movie labors under such notions as having someone flying through the air in slow motion because it seems funnier that way. As a result, the movie is a little too much like an after school Nickelodeon show for its own good.

Yet, *Diary of a Wimpy Kid* is not a chore to watch. It goes down fairly easy. If parents watch it with their kids, they might be surprised to find how much they remember from their own middle school experiences and how certain behaviors and rituals have never changed. Kids can always find a reason to be cruel to one another and they can always survive even the most belittling torment, so long as there is someone lower than them on the totem pole. At some point in adolescence, friendship is based more on going to a friend's house to hide rather than to play. Jeff Kinney clearly understands this. The filmmakers understand it as well, up to a point.

Collin Souter

CREDITS

Angie: Chloe Grace Moretz
Frank: Steve Zahn
Susan: Rachael Harris
Greg Heffley: Zachary Gordon
Rodrick: Devon Bostick
Rowley: Robert Capron
Origin: USA
Language: English
Released: 2010
Production: Nina Johnson, Bradford Simpson; Color Faree; released by 20th Century Fox
Directed by: Thor Freudenthal
Written by: Jeff Filgo, Jackie Filgo, Jeff Judah, Gabe Sachs
Cinematography by: Jack N. Green
Music by: Julia Michels
Sound: Elliott L. Koretz

Music Supervisor: Elliott L. Koretz
Editing: Gary Burritt
Art Direction: David Dowling
Costumes: Monique Prudhomme
Production Design: Brent Thomas
MPAA rating: PG
Running time: 94 minutes

REVIEWS

Burr, Ty. *Boston Globe.* March 18, 2010.
Ebert, Roger. *Chicago Sun-Times.* March 18, 2010.
Honeycutt, Kirk. *Hollywood Reporter.* March 18, 2010.
Lowenstein, Lael. *Variety.* March 18, 2010.
Pais, Matt. *Metromix.com.* March 18, 2010.
Phillips, Michael. *Chicago Tribune.* March 18, 2010.
Puig, Claudia. *USA Today.* March 18, 2010.
Schwarzbaum, Lisa. *Entertainment Weekly.* March 17, 2010.
Taylor, lla. *Village Voice.* March 16, 2010.
Whipp, Glenn. *Associated Press.* March 18, 2010.

QUOTES

Rodrick Heffley: "You never sign up for anything at school. You fly below the radar! That way you never raise anybody's expectations."

TRIVIA

Robert Capron's real life mother plays his screen mother in the movie.

DINNER FOR SCHMUCKS

Takes one to know one.
—Movie tagline

Box Office: $73 million

Paul Rudd and Steve Carell have proven to be two of the most likable and reliable comic actors working since they were a part of the adored ensemble casts of *Anchorman: The Legend of Ron Burgundy* (2004) and *The 40-Year-Old Virgin* (2005). Both men have the ability to take strong—or even standard—source material and make it stronger with brilliantly conceived improvisation. Watching the seemingly endless outtakes on either film's DVD is to open a treasure trove of lines and gags just as funny as what was used in the finished film. So, expectations were understandably high for their latest pairing in *Dinner for Schmucks,* directed by Jay Roach, who helmed all three *Austin Powers* (1997-2002) movies, as well as *Meet the Parents* (2000) and *Meet the Fockers* (2004).

Dinner for Schmucks does a solid job of keeping an audience smiling and even giggling, although the full-on belly laughs are few and far between. Considering the comic lineage Rudd and Carell share, that actually seems like a negative comment, and in some ways it is. The film comes across as a sugar-coated remake of the downright dark French comedy *The Dinner Game* (1998), and frankly, this somewhat limp remake could have used a touch of evil. For example, in the original film, Rudd's character has perfected the act of being a bastard. In *Schmucks,* Rudd's Tim is a sweetheart of a guy, who loves his girlfriend Julie (Stephanie Szostak) and wants to get ahead at his company so he can pay for a lifestyle he cannot afford in his current position. His boss (Bruce Greenwood) offers Tim the opportunity to get a promotion, the caveat being that Tim must bring a remarkable idiot to a coveted dinner at the boss' house: The man who brings the best moron wins.

It just so happens that Tim ran into a prime candidate with his car and his name is Barry (Carell), an IRS auditor whose hobby is constructing dioramas of famous paintings or scenes from history using costumed dead mice in place of humans. And while watching Barry construct one of his creations is mesmerizing, his enthusiasm for his hobby and life is what gets him a seat at the dinner table, where he seems like Tim's ace in the hole.

The trouble with *Dinner for Schmucks* is not with the performances. Rudd and Carell are practically tearing ligaments, stretching themselves to the limit to turn this poorly scripted movie into something worth paying money for. These men can work magic with the right material, for the right director, but they do not ever seem to click with Roach. And the blame for this comic shortfall can go squarely on Roach's shoulders, since every single performer in this movie is giving their all, including the remarkable Jemaine Clement as the self-obsessed artist Kieran. Clement is great in this movie, and the moments with him and Carell are the best in the film. Also quite good is Zach Galifianakis as Barry's co-worker Therman, the man who stole Barry's wife and a master of mind control (which is different than brain control, apparently). When the film does finally roll around to the actual dinner, the laughs are almost non-stop. The final thirty minutes of *Dinner for Schmucks* make a lot of the film's ills a whole lot easier to handle.

The great scenes at the movie's end do not balance out the overloaded contrivances from the rest of the story, including Tim and Barry having to spend a couple days together during some of Tim's most important life-turning points—troubles with the girlfriend, issues landing an important client, and Darla (Lucy Punch), a woman he slept with three years earlier, still stalking him. Punch is a great British comic talent, but watching her play a character so ridiculous and grating ruins the tone of the film. *Schmucks* is peppered with moments like that, and the cumulative effect is that it waters down what should have been a much better film.

The *Dinner for Schmucks* screenplay from David Guion and Michael Handelman is undeniably weak. One can almost feel director Roach taking the story's framework, throwing it to the actors, and saying, "Do something with that." And for the most part, they rise to the occasion—Rudd and Carell might have ground to petition the Writers Guild of America for screenwriting credit. As much as one might assume Rudd takes on the straight-man role here, that is not exactly the case. His reactions to Carell and the other fools that cross his path are as much a part of what produces laughs as the more overt physical comedy from Carell and company. There are few actors that can pull that off as convincingly as Rudd, whose fans may ultimately look to *Schmucks* as a placeholder between better films in his more recent filmography.

Steven Prokopy

CREDITS

Barry: Steve Carell
Tim Conrad: Paul Rudd
Darla: Lucy Punch
Lance Fender: Bruce Greenwood
Therman: Zach Galifianakis
Caldwell: Ron Livingston
Kieran Vollard: Jemaine Clement
Julie: Stephanie Szostak
Chuck: Rick Overton
Origin: USA
Language: English
Released: 2010
Production: Laurie MacDonald, Jay Roach, Walter F. Parkes; Paramount Pictures, Dream Works SKG, Spyglass Entertainment, Parkes/McDonald, Everyman Pictures; released by Paramount Pictures
Directed by: Jay Roach
Written by: Michael Handelman
Cinematography by: Jim Denault
Music by: Theodore Shapiro
Sound: Kenneth McLaughlin, Michael O'Farrell
Editing: Alan Baumgarten, Jon Poll
Art Direction: Chris Burian-Mohr, Lauren E. Polizzi
Costumes: Mary Vogt
Production Design: Michael Corenblith
MPAA rating: PG-13
Running time: 113 minutes

REVIEWS

Bowen, Kevin. *ScreenCommnet.com.* July 30, 2010.
DeFore, John. *Hollywood Reporter.* July 16, 2010.
Ebert, Roger. *Chicago Sun-Times.* July 28, 2010.

Kois, Dan. *Village Voice.* July 27, 2010.
LaSalle, Mick. *San Francisco Chronicle.* July 30, 2010.
O'Hehir, Andrew. *Salon.com.* July 29, 2010.
Phillips, Michael. *Chicago Tribune.* July 29, 2010.
Puig, Claudia. *USA Today.* July 31, 2010.
Savlov, Marc. *Austin Chronicle.* August 6, 2010.
Scott, A.O. *New York Times.* July 29, 2010.

QUOTES

Barry: "When life gives you lemons, you make lemonade. Unless you don't have any water or sugar. And then you just eat the lemons, and the rind will give you diarrhea."

Barry: "Well, I try to look at the bright side. I guess you could say I'm an eternal optometrist."

TRIVIA

Sacha Baron Cohen was originally cast to play the lead role.

THE DISAPPEARANCE OF ALICE CREED

Sometimes a great thriller requires a small army of actors, a team of writers, and a seasoned director at the helm. But in the case of the British production *The Disappearance of Alice Creed* all that is necessary are three performers, one room, and a first-time writer/director to make a compelling and usually-plausible kidnapping drama. Right from the first moments, this film proves itself to be unique. Rather than opening with the kidnapping of the title character (Gemma Arterton), the audience is allowed to witness the methodical building of the sparse, darkened, soundproof, ultra-secure room where Alice will be held after being abducted by Vic and Danny (Eddie Marsan and Martin Compston, respectively).

Once Alice is brought into the room, she is stripped naked—the film occasionally indulges in exploitation—and dressed in ordinary sweats. The kidnappers remain masked in her presence and speak as infrequently as possible, only coming into the room where she is being held to feed her and have her make ransom videos. The entire operation initially comes across as fairly professional, but as time passes and a series of both predictable and out-of-nowhere twists occur, the plan slowly begins to unravel, and director J Blakeson masterfully ratchets up the tension. If the plan goes off without a hitch, the kidnappers are two million pounds richer, but that would also make for a dreadfully boring film.

The Disappearance of Alice Creed is a difficult film to discuss in specifics since largely everything that is revealed in its second and third acts would be considered spoiler material. But in broader terms, it is safe to say that the relationship between the two kidnappers is not all that it appears, nor was the selection of Alice as a target a random choice. The audience does eventually discover both how Vic and Danny met and concocted this scheme, since it is clear early on that they are not exactly lifelong friends. Vic is older and has probably done something like this before, while Danny is barely in his twenties and is prone to sympathizing with Alice's predicament.

Having proven himself a fine and versatile actor in a variety of films (such as *Vera Drake* [2004], *Happy-Go-Lucky* [2008], *Sherlock Holmes* (2009), and *V for Vendetta* (2006)), Marsan is a master at playing characters so tightly wound they appear ready to explode, and Vic is no exception. Every small mistake or deviation from the carefully-diagrammed plan is met by Vic with rage. Compston, on the other hand, is a pliable, charming actor who plays Danny as a young man eager to please both his partner and his beautiful victim, and in the process manages to anger both.

The real surprise in terms of acting is the previously-untested Gemma Arterton, who does a remarkable job presenting Alice as both utterly terrified and quietly intelligent as she assesses her situation with little information and makes a few plans of her own in an attempt to escape. Until playing Alice, Arterton had smaller supporting roles in major studio films, including being a Bond girl in *Quantum of Solace* (2008) and popping up as a pretty face in *Clash of the Titans* (2010) and the only major female role in *Prince of Persia: The Sands of Time* (2010). But her Alice is a fully realized character with a working brain who finds ways to play her two kidnappers off of each other using both brains and beauty.

It's fun watching how the dynamic between the three characters shifts during the course of what is essentially a filmed play—although *Alice Creed* was never a staged work. Characters who begin the film filled with anxiety and fear slowly drift into moments of confidence and bravery. While the cool-as-a-cucumber Vic eventually cracks under the weight his actions and the stakes, and this leads this seemingly stable man to become a ticking time bomb.

Whether or not someone watching this film may enjoy it or not may depend entirely on one's ability to buy into the premise of *Alice Creed* in the first few minutes. Once the kidnapping is complete and the ransom plan is clear, it's difficult to envision a viewer buying into the premise and then allowing disbelief to come creeping back in. This is not to say that some of the plot turns are not ridiculous, but if one is willing to put aside a certain amount of believability, the strong performances and simple-yet-effective directing have an undeniable sway. This is not reality filmmaking, but there is a boldness to Blakeson's approach to his material that is impressive and memorable. Although far from a great film, *The Disappearance of Alice Creed* is a promising debut and an encouraging exercise in showing that British crime dramas do not all have to be about truckloads of gangsters in sharp suits blowing each other's heads off. Simplicity is the key here.

Steven Prokopy

CREDITS

Alice Creed: Gemma Arterton
Danny: Martin Compston
Vic: Eddie Marsan
Origin: United Kingdom
Language: English
Released: 2009
Production: Adrian Sturges; CinemaNX; released by Anchor Bay Entertainment
Directed by: J. Blakeson
Written by: J. Blakeson
Cinematography by: Philipp Blaubach
Music by: Marc Canham
Sound: Srdjan Kurpjel
Music Supervisor: Claire Freeman
Editing: Mark Eckersley
Art Direction: Sally Black
Costumes: Julian Day
Production Design: Ricky Eyres
MPAA rating: R
Running time: 100 minutes

REVIEWS

Biancolli, Amy. *San Francisco Chronicle.* August 6, 2010.
Edwards, David. *Daily Mirror.* April 30, 2010.
Hale, Mike. *New York Times.* August 5, 2010.
Loinaz, Alexis. *metromix.com.* August 5, 2010.
Savlov, Marc. *Austin Chronicle.* August 6, 2010.
Schenker, Andrew. *Slant Magazine.* August 1, 2010.
Seaver, Jay. *efilmcritic.com.* July 20, 2010.
Snider, Eric. *cinematical.com.* April 29, 2010.
Weinberg, Scott. *FearNet.com.* September, 16, 2009.
Weisberg, Sam. *ScreenComment.com.* August 2, 2010.

QUOTES

Vic: "Wake up Ms. Creed, it's breakfast time!"

DISTRICT 13: ULTIMATUM
(Banlieue 13: Ultimatum)

Although using the same formula, *District 13: Ultimatum* fails to recapture the rapid pacing, resourceful plotting, and focused energy of its predecessor. Even going as far as repeating key plot and character moments of *District B13* (2004) with slightly different specifics, the sequel is like a photocopy made from a machine with low toner. One might infer a sense of pride on the part of the filmmakers in the duplication of the original's successful blueprint. Instead, it comes across as pure, simple laziness.

The movie begins with a recap of the final scene of the first film. Captain Damien Tomaso (Cyril Raffaelli) and idealist loner Leïto (David Belle) have returned to the titular neighborhood, a poor, criminally infested ghetto walled off from the rest of Paris, after averting its destruction. Always the optimist, Leïto hopes things will change; Damien promises to do his part by upholding whatever law may arise. Three years later, the titles state, the government has changed while nothing else has.

At once a trite thematic statement of how quickly hope can turn to the status quo and, more appropriately, an idle plot device, that statement is the first indication that screenwriter Luc Besson (who also co-wrote the first film) has eliminated the need to explore whatever developments may have arisen due to prior events. It is the first hint that, just as nothing has changed for District 13 and its inhabitants, there will be little variation to the setup of the story and its details this time around.

Just like the ticking clock of a government-planted bomb threatening the destruction of the neighborhood in the first, Damien and Leïto once again confront a conspiracy within the government to destroy District 13. This time, however, it involves Walter Gassman (Daniel Duval), the head of the city's special services, who frames a local gang for the murders of two police officers. The President (Philippe Torreton) wants to ensure the liberty, equality, and fraternity of even the most troublesome members of Paris society; Gassman sees them as vermin needing extermination. Plus, the empty space provided by leveling a major area of the district will perfectly accommodate his plan to construct new high-rises and will earn him a handsome personal commission for laying the groundwork (The company desiring the space is Harriburton, proving that a certain American company with questionable ties to a previous administration is still an easy target).

The movie incorporates many familiar elements. The second scene employs a free-flying, omniscient camera as a tour guide for the wheeling and dealing inside the ward. Kids carry submachine guns, dog-fights are prevalent, and the gangs continue to hold on to their territory with violence and drug-running (They smuggle them into the main part of the city by hiding them in watermelons). No, nothing has changed. Leïto is a patient freedom fighter, attempting to tear down that wall one small hole at a time. He also has the police with whom to deal, although his free-running antics this time are less parkour and more well-timed dodging. In one sequence, Leïto jumps across rooftops, slides down ladders, and runs through alleys avoiding a seemingly endless supply of Gassman's employees, who pop up anywhere Leïto happens to bound to next.

Damien is once again undercover; although this time he is in drag to take down a hedonistic drug dealer. Again his stealthy maneuvers (leading each goon into a room to take them down one at a time) lead to chaos, and his backup proves less than a quarter as efficient as he is on his own.

Picking up behind the camera, director Patrick Alessandrin composes the action sequences in such a way that the audience registers each death-defying leap, every vicious punch (including an incongruous instant-replay moment that shows in slow motion how Damien drops one thug into a table), and all the wild gunplay. What's lacking is a sense of excitement, as the reliability of the dynamics of the sequences turn them routine. Damien and Leïto's enemies regularly attack one at a time, in that age-old and inexplicable cliché. At least Gassman's right-hand man (Pierre-Marie Mosconi) is taken down without much fuss, leading to one of the movie's few deviations from its established habits.

Another flaw of the film is the more complex plot. While simple in its own terms, Besson spends an inordinate amount of time getting the heroes from point A to point B in relation to their understanding of the evidence of Gassman's evildoings. False video proof airs on television as the true version changes hands, and Damien and Leïto stop mid-prison break to connect the dots that the script has already established multiple times.

The climactic brawl inside the Army's central command center, where Gassman and the president enter into one final debate between democratic ideals and the shady distortion of them, brings together the protagonists and the leaders of the major gangs inside District 13. They are all disposable types (with Tao [Elodie Yung] as a minor exception), lending nothing but a string of jokes aimed at a downed thug. The ultimate resolution of the story, which fulfills the villain's plan without his intent, displays no development in Damien and Leïto's comprehension. If they once believed the situation would change for the better and were left disillusioned by the results, what possible rationale do they have to believe this option will work? Why would this resolution be any better than last time?

There is no believable resolution, yet *District 13: Ultimatum* tries to convince viewers that things are looking up for the heroes' democratic principles. It is a hollow promise that is at least on par with the rest of the movie.

Mark Dujsik

CREDITS

Damien Tomasso: Cyril Raffaelli
Leito: David Belle
Walter Gassman: Daniel Duval
President of the Republic: Philippe Torreton
Tao: Elodie Yung
Roland: Pierre-Marie Mosconi
Origin: France
Language: French
Released: 2009
Production: Luc Besson; Europacorp, TF-1 Films, CIBY 2000; released by Magnet Releasing
Directed by: Patrick Alessandrin
Written by: Luc Besson
Cinematography by: Jean-Francois Hensgens
Music by: Alexandre Mahout
Sound: Alain Feat, Guillaume Bouchateau
Editing: Julien Rey
Costumes: Jelena Djordjevic
Production Design: Hugues Tissandier
MPAA rating: R
Running time: 101 minutes

REVIEWS

Dargis, Manohla. *New York Times.* February 5, 2010.
Gibron, Bill. *Filmcritic.com.* April 27, 2010.
Miller, Brian. *Village Voice.* February 2, 2010.
Morris, Wesley. *Boston Globe.* February 19, 2010.
Rea, Steven. *Philadelphia Inquirer.* February 5, 2010.
Safaya, Rubin. *Cinemalogue.com.* March 5, 2010.
Schager, Nick. *Slant Magazine.* February 1, 2010.
Sobczynski, Peter. *eFilmCritic.com.* February 26, 2010.
Tallerico, Brian. *MovieRetriever.com.* February 5, 2010.
Tobias, Scott. *AV Club.* February 4, 2010.

TRIVIA

The filming lasted just 14 weeks.

DOGTOOTH
(Kynodontas)

The Greek entry for Best Foreign Language Film at the Academy Awards® became a surprising nominee on the big morning, competing against much more high-profile entries like Susanne Bier's *In a Better World* (2011) and Alejandro González Iñárritu's *Biutiful* (2010). The surprise registered by most pundits was not a commentary on the quality of Giorgos Lanthimos' satirical drama but on the fact that the Academy rarely nominated films this subversively twisted in a category that typically went to crowd-pleasers. The concept of *Dogtooth* may at first seem similar to M. Night Shyamalan's divisive *The Village* (2004), a certain kind of crowd-pleaser, but co-writer/director Giorgos Lanthimos (who wrote the film with Efthymis Lanthimos) has much different dramatic intents (and accomplishes quite a bit more). With a piece that sometimes feels like dark satire and other times like tragic cultural commentary or even a horror film, *Dogtooth* is certainly one of the more unique films to ever be nominated for an Academy Award®.

Known only as Father (Christos Stergioglou) and Mother (Michele Valley), the parents of *Dogtooth* have gone to extremes to shelter their three nearly-adult children (Aggeliki Papoulia, Mary Tsoni, and Christos Passalis) from the world. They not only keep them prisoner on their compound-like estate but they have warped their view of the world, teaching them new meanings for words and forcing them to fear anything beyond the walls that essentially keep them prisoners. The children are even told that they have a brother on the outside who has been ostracized for his disobedience. When a stray cat wanders onto the premises, the son kills it and the father uses its arrival to add another layer of fear, pretending that the missing brother was killed by a cat. He teaches the children to get on their knees and bark like dogs to scare away any potential feline predators.

As deeply twisted as things obviously are, the domestic balance of this twisted clan may have remained in place if not for that pesky thing that often challenges attempts to subvert normal human development—sexuality. Realizing that the oldest son could present problems if his sexual needs are not fulfilled, the father brings home a woman for him to fornicate with. The intruder into this bizarre world, a worker at the father's company named Christina (Anna Kalaitzidou), shakes things up by turning to one of the daughters for sexual release in exchange for small things like hair gel and awakens in her a desire to escape. The final image of *Dogtooth* is perfect in that it is both one of the most mundane and yet also one of the most disturbingly memorable ones of 2010.

Lanthimos film reminds one of the subversive works of Michael Haneke and his explorations of the twisted stories behind the estate walls in films like *Benny's Video* (1992) and *Funny Games* (1997). This talented Greek director has a similar way of twisting familiar (and often

familial) imagery to dark means. Even in their moments of silence, one can sense something is very wrong at the core of the family in *Dogtooth* and the extreme events like the cat-killing, the children barking like dogs, the father's vengeance on the woman who disrupted his bizarre experiment, and a disturbing scene involving a character shattering her own teeth have immense power by their matter-of-fact placement in a domestic setting. Lanthimos strikes the perfect balance by neither playing the piece too horrifically to be taken seriously nor erring on the side of melodrama or overly symbolic screenwriting. Much like Haneke's films and some of Lars von Trier's, what the audience is meant to take away from a disturbing affair like *Dogtooth* is never underlined, although, unlike the other some of von Trier's films, it never feels like Lanthimos is intending to shock merely for the sake of it. The excellence of *Dogtooth* is in its restraint. The film is free of sentimentality, overt symbolism, moralizing, or outright horror. It is merely a character study of a truly disturbing group of characters. It is easy to make a statement on film but much more difficult to make a film that asks audiences to make their own such as *Dogtooth*. It is a work both open to long coffee house discussions on its meaning and purely enjoyable on its own terms without dissection.

In other words, it is not the kind of fare usually embraced by the Academy Awards® when it comes to Best Foreign Language Film. As of this writing, it seemed unlikely that something as extremely dark as *Dogtooth* could walk away with the actual Oscar®, but just the nomination was a pleasant surprise for a film that defied audience expectations every time it was presented.

Brian Tallerico

CREDITS

Father: Christos Stergioglou
Mother: Michele Valley
Son: Christos Passalis
Oldest Daugter: Aggeliki Papoulia
Younger Daughter: Mary Tsoni
Christina: Anna Kalaitzidou
Origin: Greece
Language: Greek
Released: 2009
Production: Yorgos Tsourgiannis; Greek Film Center, Boos Productions; released by Kino International
Directed by: Yorgos Lanthimos
Written by: Yorgos Lanthimos, Efthimis Filippou
Cinematography by: Thimios Bakatakis
Sound: Landros Ntounis

Editing: Yurgos Mavropsaridis
Art Direction: Elli Papageorgakopoulou
Production Design: Stavros Hrysogiannis
Costumes: Elli Papageorgakopoulou
MPAA rating: Unrated
Running time: 94 minutes

REVIEWS

Berkshire, Geoff. *Metromix.com.* June 24, 2010.
Ebert, Roger. *Chicago Sun-Times.* July 8, 2010.
Hillis, Aaron. *Village Voice.* May 26, 2010.
Jones, J.R.. *Chicago Reader.* March 19, 2010.
Orange, Michelle. *Movieline.* June 23, 2010.
Pais, Matt. *Metromix.com.* July 12, 2010.
Schager, Nick. *Slant Magazine.* March 17, 2010.
Scott, A.O.. *New York Times.* June 25, 2010.
Tobias, Scott. *AV Club.* June 24, 2010.
Weinberg, Scott. *Cinematical.* September 21, 2009.

QUOTES

Father: "Soon your mother will give birth to two children and a dog."

TRIVIA

The fifth Greek film ever to be nominated for an Oscar® and the first one since 1977's *Iphigenia.*

AWARDS

Nomination:

Oscars 2010: Foreign Film.

DON McKAY

Some secrets are better left buried.
—Movie tagline

Sometimes to appreciate the uniqueness of filmmakers like Joel and Ethan Coen, one must unfortunately look upon those who try to capture their style and fail. It is not unlike the spate of wannabes who desperately tried to cash in on Quentin Tarantino's fancy crime-and-character based dialogue or the Wachowski's new style of action in the wake of *The Matrix* (1999). The Coens have waded in and out of various genres while still maintaining a level of educated quirk in their speech and always know when a slap of shocking violence was appropriately-timed, even when it seemed inappropriate. Tim Blake Nelson overshot his skills as a director by trying to go toe-to-toe with that style in *Leaves of Grass* (2010) and Michael Winterbottom discovered that even with novelist Jim Thompson as the guide in *The Killer Inside Me* (2010), dark comedy and violence do not blend if the audience is napping in-between. Jake Goldberger's *Don McKay* might not seem like part of that school at first. And by the end, it is clear Goldberger has got a lot to learn.

Thomas Haden Church plays the title character, a high school janitor who receives a letter from his hometown asking for a visit. It was written by Sonny (Elisabeth Shue), an old sweetheart of Don's whom he hasn't seen in twenty-five years. Don returns to the home she grew up in and discovers that this is more than just a social call. Sonny is dying and she does not just want to see him one last time; she wants to spend her remaining days with him. He has never been able to forget Sonny and now that she is offering herself body and soul to him for an albeit-brief respite from his mundane existence, what does he have to lose?

Coming home again, they say, is never easy. Sonny's caretaker, Marie (Melissa Leo), is hardly a soothing presence to anyone but her. It only takes a second meeting for her doctor, Lance (James Rebhorn), to express his displeasure with Don's sudden reappearance into Sonny's life. Then there is the matter of an old crime that Don is connected with and may be directly responsible for him leaving town in the first place. "You said you would call me back in five minutes and it's been twenty-five years," says his old friend, Otis (Keith David), whom Don contacts when a new crime has been committed.

Don McKay's plot may contain numerous secrets and begins to play its games rather early on, but is miles apart from a film like *Shutter Island* (2010), where apparent hints only amplify a second experience. A return to *Don McKay* only distances one further from its characters and amplifies the phoniness of its opening act. What appears as a potentially-moving setup for a romantic weepy about lost chances is buried by Shue's none-too-cautious performance. Upon her very first moments, Shue engulfs Sonny in the mannerisms of a teenage girl who cannot wait to unveil the big secret she is carrying inside.

Don is the guilty one though. No spoiler alert necessary as the plot thickens at the twenty-minute mark and the next forty are dedicated to the wavering anxiety over whether an incident has been covered up, who did it if it has, who knows, and if an incident even happened at all. The action is a long way from *Diabolique* (1955) and treading through a watered-down *Blood Simple* (1984) with only the occasional appearance of M. Emmet Walsh as a cab driver to even make such a direct comparison. Murder (or attempted murder) turns to blackmail when the final act introduces a left-field motive (which also may not exist) for Don's summons back to town, resulting in double-crosses that get so convoluted that the players cannot even keep track of their true intentions anymore.

Perhaps *Don McKay* was intended as straight comedy in the guise of a crime film, but it can never keep a straight tone from scene-to-scene. Lacking the gravitas of the absurdity in *The Ice Harvest* (2005) or the nervous fun of films that revel in the history of the genre like *Head Above Water* (1996) and *Kiss Kiss Bang Bang* (2005), Goldberger's efforts get more confused with the exponential ticking of a dud time bomb. One character disappears from sight entirely with no further explanation as if the actor missed the day he was to show on-set to answer a phone call. By the time the final act revs up its revelations into practically all-out farce with a character casually handing another an axe to take care of business, the film is long past the point of caring who lives, who dies and for what. Joel and Ethan Coen obviously can inspire new generations of filmmakers, although it may be impossible to learn all the tricks that keep their work so out of the ordinary. One thing is for certain though. Trying to capture that magical mixture of comedy and violence is anything but simple.

Erik Childress

CREDITS

Don McKay: Thomas Haden Church
Sonny: Elisabeth Shue
Marie: Melissa Leo
Samuel: M. Emmet Walsh
Otis Kent: Keith David
Mel: Pruitt Taylor Vince
Dr. Lance Price: James Rebhorn
Origin: USA
Language: English
Released: 2009
Production: Jim Young; Animus Films; released by Image Entertainment
Directed by: Jake Goldberger
Written by: Jake Goldberger
Cinematography by: Phil Parmet
Music by: Steven Bramson
Editing: Andrew Dickler
Sound: Michael Mcdonald
Costumes: Andrew Poleszak
Production Design: Aleta Shaffer
MPAA rating: R
Running time: 87 minutes

REVIEWS

Brenner, Jules. *Filmcritic.com.* April 1, 2010.
Dargis, Manohla. *New York Times.* April 2, 2010.
Fine, Marshall. *Hollywood & Fine.* March 30, 2010.
Kendrick, James. *Q Network Film Desk.* June 29, 2010.
Morris, Wesley. *Boston Globe.* April 1, 2010.
Nelson, Rob. *Variety.* September 1, 2009.
Orndorf, Brian. *DVDTalk.com.* July 24, 2010.
Schwarzbaum, Lisa. *Entertainment Weekly.* April 7, 2010.
Sobczynski, Peter. *eFilmCritic.com.* April 8, 2010.
Verniere, James. *Boston Herald.* April 1, 2010.

DOWN TERRACE

You're only as good as the people you know.
    —Movie tagline
It's about to kick off.
    —Movie tagline

"You're only as good as the people you're with." This truism is chilling enough without being applied to immediate family. *Down Terrace* takes it to heart and then breaks the hearts of viewers who have spent the better part of an hour and half watching laughing, sometimes hysterically, and finally realizing that the joke may very well be on them. Directed with a naturalistic (almost nihilistic) directness by Ben Wheatley, this British dramedy offers an uncomfortably real slice of dysfunctional small town family life in the employ of the London mob using the stuff of low-level gangsterism to trigger old resentments, new feuds, and revealed secrets. The end result is tonally mixed but still powerful and worth viewing by anyone who enjoys quirky crime cinema.

Bill (Robert Hill) is the patriarch of a low-level crime family operating out of a small home in a rural English town. Having just gotten out of jail, along with his oldest son, the bookish Karl (Robin Hill), he makes it his business to track down the informant that landed him in jail. This standard crime drama beginning is complicated by the fact that the family business, operated by his wife Maggie (Julia Deakin) and an assortment of decidedly incompetent family and friends, has been on the rocks for some time, attracting unwanted attention from the London HQ. When Karl reveals he and his girlfriend of one year Valda (Kerry Peacock) are about to be surprise parents the timing is less than ideal. So is the rampant paranoia and suspicion beginning to take over the family. As chaos descends and bodies pile up, the only question is who will come out on top.

Down Terrace has been billed as comedy and indeed it is very funny in spots. But this is one of those occasions when viewers may wish the film had been less funny and more focused on the rich relationships sketched out by director Ben Wheatley and star Robin Hill; both do double duty as credited co-writers. Crime drama has been used to unpack family dysfunction before but the setting of *Down Terrace,* a rural small English town, sets this film slightly apart. Such a setting makes it seem more like the stuff of real life, removing the film from the clichés of glamour and easy wealth often associated with the gangster genre. This is a family simply trying to survive much less make a big score. *Down Terrace* does offer some original takes on cinematic gangster clichés, but the film is ultimately populated with human beings shot through with uncertainties about their roles in life and their collective shock that the life they have chosen has led them to where they are. When it works it is a thing of beauty.

The writing is reminiscent of the complex novels of Tana French, and television shows like *The Wire* (2002-2008) and *The Sopranos* (1999-2007). *Down Terrace* only just misses such excellence by aiming for one too many screwball scenarios. But it does manage to be entertaining even when it drifts. A local hitman shows up at the family home to perform a hit for Bill only to arrive with a small child in tow, unable to find a babysitter. When Bill gets tired of menacing everyone around him, he keeps himself company with his guitar. Karl just wants everyone to get along but only has the tools his broken family has given him; tools that are mainly good for hurting and threatening others, which he lacks the self confidence to use. Almost all the characters in the film are fleshed out way beyond where they needed to be and that is one of the really endearing things about *Down Terrace.*

Bill and Karl are played by real life father and son Robert and Robin Hill and their chemistry together is dangerous, showcasing a real-life dynamic of being able to bond and blow-up over the smallest of things. Robert Hill has only scant credits to his name but absolutely aces the part of an aging, befuddled small town gangster/ father evoking a fear rooted in his own growing sense of uselessness, a deep, if misplaced, pride in his work ethic, and a wild-eyed inner rage at the incompetence of his own flesh and blood.

Julia Deakin is, as usual, a revelation as the mousey mother Maggie. She plays her cards carefully giving Maggie hidden depths and a fearful, almost-Shakespearian edge. In the end, this film belongs to co-writer and star Robin Hill, who tackles a very difficult part and manages to convey Karl's growing dissatisfaction with family and his heartbreak over where the family business has finally led him. He conveys an uncomfortable level of humanity that refuses to be reined in by filmic or social expectations. He is a worm of a man, raised by worms, and fearful he may become food for them. When informed of the pregnancy he panics. When forced to bury the body of a friend he barely seems to feel anything. When forced with a final decision he is heartbroken but blind. In the end, he lost

himself long ago and is unable to do more than imitate the despicable characters that have guided him thus far.

Down Terrace will likely be remembered as much for its gruesome ending as for the many surprising laughs that lighten the tension. It serves as, if not exactly a cautionary tale, a genuinely interesting take on the crime film.

Dave Canfield

CREDITS

Bill: Robert Hill
Karl: Robin Hill
Maggie: Julia Deakin
Uncle Eric: David Schaal
Garvey: Tony Way
Valda: Kerry Peacock
Michael Smiley: Michael Smiley
Berman: Mark Kempner
Origin: USA
Language: English
Released: 2010
Production: Andy Starke; Mondo Macabro Movies, Baby Cow Productions, Magnet Releasing; released by Magnolia Pictures
Directed by: Ben Wheatley
Written by: Robin Hill, Ben Wheatley
Cinematography by: Laurie Rose
Music by: Jim Williams
Sound: Rob Entwhistle
Editing: Robin Hill
MPAA rating: R
Running time: 93 minutes

REVIEWS

Halfyard, Kurt. *Twitch Film.* October 15, 2010.
Holden, Stephen. *New York Times.* October 15, 2010.
James, Rob. *Total Film.* July 29, 2010.
Leader, Michael. *DenofGeek.com.* Jul 30, 2010.
O'Hehir, Andrew. *Salon.com.* October 22, 2010.
Scheib, Ronnie. *Variety.* March 24, 2010.
Simonson, CJ. *Collider.com.* December 2, 2010.
Simpson, Don. *smellslikescreenspirit.com.* October 14, 2010.
Staunton, Terry. *Radio Times.* August 2, 2010.
Thomas, Kevin. *Los Angeles Times.* October 14, 2010.

DUE DATE

Check yourself before you wreck yourself.
    —Movie tagline

Box Office: $100 million

"I'd watch that guy read the dictionary." That phrase, often uttered about great actors and comedians is meant to comment on their ability to elevate mediocre material. Turned around, that same phrase applies to *Due Date,* which despite the solid efforts of two gifted performers, plays like a dictionary, which is to say it plods through a series of unconnected events reaching a foregone conclusion. Robert Downey Jr. and Zach Galifianakis do manage some big laughs, but they are stuck in a road film that goes to too many places its viewers have gone before.

High strung Peter Highman (Robert Downey Jr.) has five days to get to Los Angeles so he can sit in on the birth of his first child. It should be no problem. But when he meets the obnoxious disaster magnet and wannabe actor Ethan Tremblay (Zach Galifianakis) he quickly finds himself stuck in traveler's Hell. A simple conversation with Ethan (and his own anger issues) gets Peter tasered and put on a no-fly list. Having lost his money, luggage and ID, Peter is now forced to accept Ethan's offer of a ride. Thus begins the endless string of inappropriate behaviors, questions, and male bonding that result from two men with nothing in common being forced together. Accompanied only by the ashes of Ethan's dad in a coffee can and Ethan's French Bulldog for company, Peter begins to wonder if survival is in the cards, much less making it to the birth on-time.

The comparison to John Hughes' far-superior *Planes, Trains and Automobiles* (1987) is unavoidable here. *Due Date* clearly lifts a central plot device from that film as well as any number of other gags. Of course, Ethan crashes the car. Of course, the two get stoned together and bond through it. Of course, Ethan had Peter's wallet the whole time. And, of course, there was a tragic mystery surrounding Ethan that will win over our sympathies in the end. Director Todd Phillips even reveals that mystery to us by having Downey remember a number of previous moments from the film just as Steve Martin's character, Neal Page, did in the earlier film.

Of course, Phillips (*Road Trip* [2000], *Old School* [2003], *The Hangover* [2009]), should be exactly the director to subvert such a holiday standard via removing the sentiment and creating a comedic masterwork of discomfiture. But what Phillips did so well in *The Hangover* seems to be the very thing that trips him up here. Viewers will get the sense that Phillips felt almost obligated to make a deeper film this time out. It would all be forgivable just for the chance to watch two major talents coast through those situations, giving them their own unmistakable creative stamp. Where *Due Date* falters most is in trying too hard to actually be a movie of some substance. Peter and Ethan, for instance, are both fundamentally harsh, unlikeable characters stuck in a script that lacks the sort of nuances that would attract empathy. Viewers will probably wonder more than once if Peter's wife and son would be better off if Peter just died in a blazing wreck instead of getting home. Ethan is stupid in a way that a real life person simply never is. These two deserve each other, and, instead of playing off that, *Due Date* offers a number of, admittedly well-played and reasonably-well written, moments where the two men learn to meet each other halfway and see the humanity in each other. But *Due Date* never connects any of its serious moments with the funny ones. This road movie rides like an idiot trying to drive stick, jerking from one mode to the next without any real care for where it might be headed.

There are some really funny bits. One, involving the way Ethan gets to sleep at night and the effect this has on his dog, will separate viewers into those who get this kind of comedy and those who are simply outraged or grossed out. Another brilliant moment has Peter picking a fight with a teller at a Western Union only to realize that the man is a war vet confined to a wheelchair. Said veteran then proceeds to beat Peter into a pulp. Are viewers supposed to laugh or be horrified? This kind of comedy via discomfort works best when the film in question lets the audience decide for themselves and that is exactly what viewers get here. Sadly, the rest of *Due Date* fails to approach this level of sophistication, swinging from the wildly improbable (Ethan successfully breaking Peter out of a border guard crossing holding room) to just what one would expect (Ethan accidently brews coffee with his dad's ashes which everyone drinks before realizing their mistake).

This talented pair of actors, given their chemistry, and the right material, could have single-handedly revived the road movie or at least given cinema another worthy buddy team 'ala Gene Wilder and Richard Pryor. They are that good. But *Due Date* suffers heavily from an underdeveloped script, a surprisingly timid approach by a director who should have followed his instinct for bodily humor a step farther, and an inability to sit back and just enjoy the ride. Phillips needs to take Ethan's advice, "You better check yourself, before you wreck yourself."

Dave Canfield

CREDITS

Peter Highman: Robert Downey Jr.
Ethan Tremblay/Ethan Chase: Zach Galifianakis
Sarah Highman: Michelle Monaghan
Jim: Jamie Foxx
Marshall: RZA
Heidi: Juliette Lewis

Lonnie: Danny McBride

Origin: USA

Language: English

Released: 2010

Production: Daniel Goldberg, Todd Phillips; Warner Bros., Legendary Pictures, Green Hat Films; released by Warner Bros.

Directed by: Todd Phillips

Written by: Todd Phillips, Alan R. Cohen, Adam Freedland, Adam Sztykiel

Cinematography by: Lawrence Sher

Music by: Christophe Beck

Sound: Cameron Frankley

Music Supervisor: George Drakoulias

Editing: Debra Neil-Fisher

Art Direction: Shepherd Frankel

Costumes: Louise Mingenbach

Production Design: Bill Brzeski

MPAA rating: R

Running time: 95 minutes

REVIEWS

Dargis, Manohla. *New York Times.* November 4, 2010.

Debruge, Peter. *Variety.* October 29, 2010.

Ebert, Roger. *Chicago Sun-Times.* November 3, 2010.

Kendrick, Ben. *ScreenRant.* November 5, 2010.

Lemire, Christy. *Associated Press.* November 2, 2010.

Martinovic, Paul. *DenofGeek.com* November 1, 2010.

McCarthy, Todd. *Hollywood Reporter.* October 29,2010.

McWeeney, Drew. *HitFix.* November 1, 2010.

Vejvoda, Jim. *IGN Movies.* November 3, 2010.

Zacharek, Stephanie. *Movieline.* November 5, 2010.

QUOTES

Ethan Tremblay: "My father loved coffee, and now we loved him as coffee."

TRIVIA

Maternity day was the code name for when the movie shipped to theaters.

E

EASY A

The rumor-filled totally FALSE account of how I ruined my flawless reputation.
—Movie tagline

Let's not and say we did.
—Movie tagline

$58 million

In the late 1990s and early 2000s, when teen movies were abundant and Freddie Prinze Jr. was mysteriously considered a movie star, classic novels and plays were frequently given a modern spin. The goal seemed to be that contemporary audiences in the PG-13 demographic could chuckle at a romantic comedy and pretend to have learned something in the process. George Bernard Shaw's *Pygmalion* became *She's All That* (1999), starring Prinze Jr. William Shakespeare's *Othello* provided a starring role for Josh Hartnett in *O*. Edmond Rostand's *Cyrano de Bergerac* became the Shane West vehicle *Whatever It Takes* (2000). Shakespeare's *The Taming of the Shrew* became *10 Things I Hate About You* (1999). With the exception of the latter film, which benefited from breakout turns by Joseph Gordon-Levitt and Heath Ledger, most of these movies were not much good, but they had a breezy, 1980s-style flavor that could sometimes float by on easygoing superficiality and a likable supporting cast member or two.

Aiming to reboot the trend is *Easy A,* a charming romantic comedy that constantly strains credibility but nearly gets by on the shoulders of its cast and a quick-thinking sense of humor. The premise might work if it made any sense. Olive (Emma Stone) is gorgeous and emotionally mature, not to mention packed with wit at

the speed of *Juno* (2007) and a best friend, Rhiannon (Aly Michalka), who is arguably even more stunning than Olive. Yet apparently these two are overlooked outcasts at Ojai North High School in Ojai, California, where attitudes are still so behind the times that sexual activity, even by wallflowers, is immediately transmitted around the whole school and devoured as delicious gossip.

In reality, pals like Olive and Rhiannon would run their school; in *Easy A* the gals are loners. So Olive does not really mind when she embraces Rhiannon's false assumption that Olive had sex, and uptight Christian conservative Marianne (Amanda Bynes), who overheard the conversation from a bathroom stall, spreads that fib around the school as truth. No harm done, Olive thinks. Even if her classmates think she is a promiscuous harlot like Hester Prynne—conveniently Olive's English class currently is reading Nathaniel Hawthorne's *The Scarlet Letter*—Olive knows deep down that she is not. She is merely taking advantage of the social cache that falls on anyone in school believed to have knocked boots.

Already first-time feature screenwriter Bert V. Royal has written the story into a corner, revolving the film around a character who, regardless of her claims of feeling invisible, seems largely unaffected by her high school existence and does not fit into any of the boxes the movie creates for her. Meanwhile, the film is paced so misguidedly fast it seems as if Royal needed to polish off the script before an oven timer sounded. Many, many relationships between characters are addressed and tossed aside. Most egregiously batted around is a running romantic interest for Olive in Todd (Penn Badgley), who missed an opportunity to kiss Olive years ago but is never on screen for long enough in the present to register as a main character. Similar mistakes are made in the rushed, condescending treatment of Marianne's pro-abstinence group and the personal life of Olive's favorite teacher Mr. Griffith (Thomas Haden Church), which comes out of nowhere in a failed attempt to turn comic relief into the source of a major plot point.

The reason *Easy A* does not spin out of control as much as Olive's lie is that Stone fully asserts her developing star power. She turns Olive, regardless of her far-fetched presentation as a hopeless outsider, into a spunky role model who is not afraid of her sexuality but does not, contrary to popular belief, spread it all over town. Stone makes cleverness sexy and winning, particularly when sharing a laugh with her incredibly likable parents played by the always-excellent Stanley Tucci and Patricia Clarkson. Even in a throwaway scene, like when Olive mocks the way Marianne sharpens her pencils, Stone's lively performance gives *Easy A* a lot of personality.

That spark appears sporadically thanks to a number of one-liners that generate something that was not terribly common in those late-1990s teen movies: Actual jokes that earn audible laughter. When Olive tells her mom she was sent to the principal, mom, a delightfully upbeat spirit grounded by Clarkson's warmth, responds sweetly and naively, "Did you win a medal or something?" In response to a rumor that she hooked up with three guys at once in a Jacuzzi, Olive says snidely, "Uh, that sounds like a lot of work," a quick and funny way to dismiss the rumor and acknowledge its inherent silliness. The film thus works better as a comedy than as a social commentary about the double standard that perceives promiscuous guys as heroes and promiscuous girls as much-discussed, to take a word from Marianne and her friends' protest signs, "sluts."

This is partly because *Easy A* spends more time trying to be hip and insightful than actually being hip and insightful. Characters constantly recognize clichés such as teen stories in which the main character's plight is mirrored by the book he or she is reading in class. That does not make the film smart; it just means Royal tried to talk his way out of using a cliché. And direct references to 1980s films like *Sixteen Candles* (1982) and *The Breakfast Club* (1985), as Olive claims she longs for her life to mirror a 1980s movie, ignore those films' stereotypical conception of teenagers. A girl as savvy as Olive would be less likely to long for John Cusack or Judd Nelson than to dream of her own Ben Gibbard or Ryan Gosling, present-day indie romantic figures who signify that chivalry and intellectual cool do still exist.

Ultimately, most viewers will not remember many of these details in *Easy A*, which whooshes by in a 90-minute blur that is frequently amusing but increasingly frustrating in its inability to settle down and focus. Stone may be a keeper, but Olive's adulthood is a major hole in her own movie, which at heart reminds why teenagers cling so tightly to gossip: It feels good to be included, and even if there is little honesty in high school rumors, lies are frequently more interesting than truth anyway.

Matt Pais

CREDITS

Olive Penderghast: Emma Stone
Woodchuck Todd: Penn Badgley
Micah: Cam Gigandet
Marianne: Amanda Bynes
Rosemary Penderghast: Patricia Clarkson
Dill Penderghast: Stanley Tucci
Principal Gibbons: Malcolm McDowell
Mrs. Griffith: Lisa Kudrow
Mr. Griffith: Thomas Haden Church
Pastor: Fred Armisen
Marianne's Mom: Stacey Travis
Rhiannon: Alyson Michalka
Brandon: Dan Byrd
Rhiannon: Alyson Michalka
Origin: USA
Language: English
Released: 2010
Production: Zanne Devine, Will Gluck; Olive Bridge Entertainment, Screen Gems; released by Sony Pictures
Directed by: Will Gluck
Written by: Bert V. Royal
Cinematography by: Michael Grady
Music by: Brad Segal
Sound: Jon Wakeham
Music Supervisor: Wende Crowley
Editing: Susan Littenberg
Art Direction: Bo Johnson
Costumes: Mynka Draper
Production Design: Marcia Hinds
MPAA rating: PG-13
Running time: 92 minutes

REVIEWS

Cordova, Randy. *Arizona Republic.* September 15, 2010.
Ebert, Roger. *Chicago Sun-Times.* September 15, 2010.
Holden, Stephen. *New York Times.* September 16, 2010.
Honeycutt, Kirk. *Hollywood Reporter.* September 10, 2010.
Hunt, Kristin. *Premiere.com.* September 17, 2010.
Jones, Kimberley. *Austin Chronicle.* September 17, 2010.
Morgenstern, Joe. *Wall Street Journal.* September 17, 2010.
Phipps, Keith. *AV Club.* September 16, 2010.

Puig, Claudia. *USA Today.* September 17, 2010.

Weitzman, Elizabeth. *New York Daily News.* September 16, 2010.

QUOTES

Marianne: "You've made your bed…I just hope for your sake, you've cleaned the sheets."

TRIVIA

The website freeolive.com mentioned in the film actually leads to the film's official website in real life.

AWARDS

Nomination:

Golden Globes 2011: Actress—Mus./Comedy (Stone).

EAT PRAY LOVE

Let yourself go this August.
—Movie tagline

Box Office: $80 million

The strongest, most involving characters in *Eat Pray Love* do not include the protagonist. They are a pair of men she meets along the way, going through a similar sense of regret, a kindred feeling of being lost in the world, and the same idea that a change of location can alter more than one's geographic coordinates.

The heroine of the movie is Liz Gilbert (Julia Roberts), a New York writer who leaves the Western Hemisphere to spend a year travelling to Italy, India, and Indonesia after a difficult divorce and failed love affair. As Liz, Roberts can only attain the artifice of depression the role requires in its bones. In one scene, she sobs, kneels, and prays, and there is no sincerity in the moment.

Compare her performance to those of Richard Jenkins and Javier Bardem. These two, playing men she meets at an ashram outside of Kolkata and in a town on Bali, respectively, have far less screen time, serve primarily as a means to further Liz's spiritual and interpersonal instruction, and only reveal enough about their characters' histories as is essential to correlate to Liz's own. In spite of this inherent short-changing, Richard (Jenkins) and Felipe (Bardem) actually give a feeling of continual struggle with the past.

Liz's struggle is one of the past coming back to haunt her, as realized with director Ryan Murphy's concrete technique of flashbacks to her former life when she is feeling sad and lonely. She cannot move past feelings of guilt over divorcing her aimless but devoted husband Stephen (Billy Crudup) or a hope for improving her relationship with actor David (James Franco). Hence, Murphy shows Liz and Stephen at their wedding reception—he, the happiest man in the room, and she, barely not yet miserable—followed by Liz achieving an amiable reconciliation with a phantom Stephen. Since the real Stephen is unlikely to forgive Liz, Richard opines, her only goal is to forgive herself. Murphy envisions this scenario in the afore-described blunt, literal terms.

The relationship with David is even less defined. At the end of the prologue showing Liz's life in New York, she leaves David sitting on his front stoop. Their romance has shifted from lustful love into unhappiness in one cut, which contrasts how David once folded her laundry with a spring in his step to now doing so with a grimace. For all intents and purposes, the image of David alone on the steps is the end of their story. Instead, the screenplay by Murphy and Jennifer Salt (based on the memoir by Elizabeth Gilbert) continues with David as a present and past boundary to Liz's spiritual recovery. David, as a character, is a dead issue once Liz first travels to Rome, yet there are more flashbacks depicting how her relationship with David deteriorated than how her marriage with Stephen fell apart.

When Liz arrives in Rome, the movie is at its travelogue best. She rents a run-down loft, meets fellow traveler Sofi (Tuva Novotny), and hires a tutor (Luca Argentero) to teach her Italian. There are language lessons (including a montage of what gestures mean), fine dining experiences (Murphy hungrily lingers on a plate of spaghetti as Liz indulges), and the enjoyment of "The sweetness of doing nothing" (Liz eating breakfast and reading the newspaper on the floor while dressed in a newly purchased negligee). This act (the first of the title's obvious three-act division) works as a sort of wish-fulfillment for the audience.

Oddly, it is when Liz progresses beyond the sensual and into the spiritual that the movie feels most self-indulgent. In Kolkata, Liz attempts to lead the meditative life and is stymied by her own obsession with the past. Here, the problematic flashbacks take over the narrative, and Roberts' performance cannot keep up with emotional intake they so heavily imply. Jenkins is the foundation of this act, highlighted by a monologue in which Richard talks about his drunken past, told—it should be emphasized—without flashback. Here is real trauma on display, even if Richard has the tendency to speak in "bumper sticker," as Liz puts it. She is never critical about her own inclination to talk in a similar way.

To a lesser extent, Felipe, whom Liz meets, hates, then loves in Bali on the last stop in her vacation-cum-therapy, is also in turmoil. He, like Liz, is divorced and, unlike Liz, has a college-aged son named Leon (Tj Power). They meet in a way more attuned to a generic romantic comedy—he runs her off the road while distracted by a song—and Felipe begins to show his wounds in ways slightly more subtle than a monologue. He cries while sending off Leon from the son's visit, and when Liz suggests that she cannot disrupt the balance in her life she has found through prayer by furthering a relationship with him, Felipe begins to encroach her decision through his own rationalization why her choice is wrong.

Bardem's performance is prudent in the way it is sympathetic to Felipe's heartache and aware of how his reaction to it might make him an ill fit for Liz. It is consequently unfortunate how neatly the movie resolves each of the character's personal dilemmas in such conventional ways. It is also unfortunate that Robert Richardson's cinematography denies the movie the sense of a true travelogue by homogenizing each locale with a glossy, nonspecific finish.

Eat Pray Love suffers from the blank slate of its central protagonist. She and, hence, the movie rarely feel sincere in intention or genuine about character growth.

Mark Dujsik

CREDITS

Elizabeth Gilbert: Julia Roberts
Felipe: Javier Bardem
Richard: Richard Jenkins
Delia: Viola Davis
Steven: Billy Crudup
David: James Franco
Sofi: Tuva Novotny
Giovanni: Luca Argentero
Leon: Tj Power
Origin: USA
Language: English
Released: 2010
Production: Dede Gardner; Plan B Entertainment, Red Om Films, Syzygy Productions; released by Columbia Pictures
Directed by: Ryan Murphy
Written by: Ryan Murphy, Jennifer Salt
Cinematography by: Robert Richardson
Music by: Dario Marianelli
Sound: Drew Kunin
Music Supervisor: P.J. Bloom
Editing: Bradley Buecker
Art Direction: Charley Beal

Costumes: Michael Dennison
Production Design: Bill Groom
MPAA rating: PG-13
Running time: 133 minutes

REVIEWS

Connolly, Matthew. *Slantmagazine.com.* August 12, 2010.
Gang, Alison. *San Diego Union-Tribune.* August 12, 2010.
Johanson, Mary Ann. *Flickfilosopher.com.* August 13, 2010.
MacDonald, Moira. *Seattle Times.* August 12, 2010.
Morgenstern, Joe. *Wall Street Journal.* August 13, 2010.
O'Hehir, Andrew. *Salon.com.* August 12, 2010.
Phillips, Michael. *Chicago Tribune.* August 12, 2010.
Rea, Steven. *Philadelphia Inquirer.* August 13, 2010.
Scott, A.O. *New York Times.* August 12, 2010.
Stevens, Dana. *Slate.com.* August 12, 2010.

QUOTES

Liz Gilbert: "Maybe my life hasn't been so chaotic. It's just the world that is and the only real trap is getting attached to any of it. Ruin is a gift. Ruin is the road to transformation."

THE ECLIPSE

If there is life after death—love lives on.
—Movie tagline

Ciarán Hinds plays Michael Farr, a drifting widower who gets tangled up with all types of ghosts in *The Eclipse*, Conor McPherson's haunting, slow-burn romantic thriller. Still reeling from his wife's untimely death and raising their two children solo, a post as a lackey for a local literary festival puts Michael in the path of Lena Morrelle (Iben Hjejle, who some may recognize from 2000's *High Fidelity*), a horror writer obsessed with the supernatural, and Nicholas Holden (Aidan Quinn), an egomaniacal novelist desperate on re-enacting the one night stand the two scribes shared when they last met. But playing the hypotenuse in this bizarre love triangle is only part of Michael's trouble; he's also seeing specters. The resulting maelstrom of creepy apparitions combined with drunken lovers' spats forces Michael to come to terms with the grief he is kept bottled-up since his wife passed away and finally think about moving on.

In less-talented hands this coupling of romantic drama with the otherworldly to create a romantic paranormal thriller might end up reeking of Hollywood gimmick (read: forceful soundtrack and ghosts appearing in medicine cabinet mirrors). But writer-director McPherson cleverly eschews all possible pitfalls, creating instead a character-driven romance about grief and acceptance that just happens to be peppered with downright heart-stopping moments of horror. The result is a unique hybrid that satisfyingly lulls with gorgeous cinematography, a vivid soundtrack and standout performances only to wind audiences with appearance by the supernatural (bloody eyes and reaching dead fingers and all) when they least expect it.

How McPherson succeeds in ramping up the suspense in *The Eclipse* without allowing the film to come off as a standard horror flick is the result of his careful balance of all production elements, leading off with skilled camera work. McPherson carefully orchestrates a distance between the camera and his actors. At times reminiscent of something out of Hitchcock, cinematographers Ivan McCullough's angles and placement are all about removed observation. Michael in effect becomes a subject in addition to being a character in the film and the feeling of watching a real, organic life unfold on screen not only heightens Michael's directionlessness, but also elevates the believability of what he is experiencing. This realness extends even further with a jarringly realistic (sounding at least) fight scene that leaves the viewer feeling and hearing every painful and embarrassing blow.

McPherson also pays careful attention to atmosphere, providing sweeping views of the sea side gothic town where Michael lives among towering castles, crumbling graveyards, and empty country lanes. His mundane sad life is infused with a sense of eerie anticipation as he is perpetually overshadowed by ancient churches, overcome by small town silence and bound by the locale's vast nothingness. Everything around Michael seems out of his control, from his jack of all trades volunteer assignment that pulls him from home late at night to ferry an author hither and yon, to the vastness of the house he shares with his children and where they seem engulfed. All in all the perfect life for a ghost to visit. Non-character dependent camera pans around Michael's home, shots of his daughter being almost swallowed by the kitchen furniture and Michael drifting through rooms in his lonely house almost beg for monsters to jump out of dark corners, but McPherson's knack for pacing keeps all ghosts at bay until the audience is ready to release their held breaths. Even the soundtrack, which works so well to imbue the town with its inviting otherworldliness and whose inclusion is carefully chosen, does not warn on expected cue.

Ultimately, it is the quiet and nuanced performances that give this film its strength of presence. Each actor inhabits their character so completely it is impossible not to fall into step with them. Hjejle's Lena is a soft presence on screen, but one laced with the hint of much dragging baggage. The result is an enticing and mysterious performance. It is through her that we understand how writers exercise their personal demons as well as the importance of writing as catharsis and mood stabilizer. Aidan Quinn shines as a midcareer self-important author whose self-consciousness dictates his reprehensible behavior. But it is really Hinds who commands the screen. To call Michael complex would be trite. Really he is lost and covered with layers of emptiness and grief and frustration and somehow Hinds manages to convey this without making Michael pitiable. This role is unique and in need of an actor capable of maintaining its prerequisite delicate balance. Hinds makes it look effortless, elevating this potentially under the radar indie film to a noteworthy showcase of fine acting.

Joanna Topor MacKenzie

CREDITS

Michael Farr: Ciaran Hinds
Nicholas Holden: Aidan Quinn
Lena Morelle: Iben Hjejle
Malachy McNeill: Jim Norton
Thomas: Eanna Hardwicke
Sarah: Hannah Lynch
Origin: Ireland
Language: English
Released: 2009
Production: Robert Walpole; Treasure Entertainment; released by Magnolia Pictures
Directed by: Conor McPherson
Written by: Conor McPherson, Billy Roche
Cinematography by: Ivan McCullough
Music by: Fionnuala Ni Chiosain
Sound: Ronan Hill
Editing: Emer Reynolds
Costumes: Consolata Boyle
Production Design: Mark Geraghty
MPAA rating: R
Running time: 88 minutes

REVIEWS

Abele, Robert. *Los Angeles Times.* March 25, 2010.
Dargis, Manohla. *New York Times.* March 26, 2010.
Fear, David. *Time Out New York.* March 24, 2010.
Lumenick, Lou. *New York Post.* March 26, 2010.
Martin, Philip. *Arkansas Democrat-Gazette.* May 1, 2010.
Morgenstern, Joe. *Wall Street Journal.* March 26, 2010.
Pinkerton, Nick. *Village Voice.* March 24, 2010.
Scott, A.O. *New York Times.* March 29, 2010.
Tallerico, Brian. *MovieRetriever.com.* April 15, 2010.
Weber, Bill. *Slant Magazine.* March 22, 2010.

EDGE OF DARKNESS

Some secrets take us to the edge.
—Movie tagline

Few escape justice. None escape vengeance.
    —Movie tagline

Box Office: $43 million

Martin Campbell's *Edge of Darkness* begins and ends like the simple revenge tales made popular by Charles Bronson but tries to be a labyrinthine conspiracy mystery in the middle. This narrative agenda is the product of its original source material: a six-part, British mini-series of the same name from 1986. Unfortunately, the film's two hour running time is not sufficient to coherently compress the complicated plot that the original mini-series had five hours to slowly, subtly, and satisfyingly unspool. The compression of the original's complex plot results in an insufficiently realized mystery that is hard to understand and harder to care about. The viewer is left longing for more Charles Bronson and less mystery.

As though recognizing the plot-compressing task ahead of it, the film wastes no time getting started. With an admirable (and unintentionally hilarious) narrative economy, the film provides the viewer with the absolute minimum of dialogue and character development necessary to establish the loving-but-estranged relationship between grizzled widower cop Thomas Craven (Mel Gibson) and his only child Emma (Bojana Novakovic) before the bullets begin to fly. Within seconds of reuniting at the train station, Emma is experiencing violent dry heaves. Minutes later, at home, she is vomiting blood. As father and daughter hurry though the front door to head to the hospital, she reveals that "there's something I should have told you Dad…" but she is prevented from saying more as a man in a ski mask materializes out of the darkness and spectacularly shotguns her to death. As Craven cradles her bloodied corpse, screaming in anguish and rage, the scene shifts to Craven sitting in his couch, staring blankly into the distance, hearing nothing as his old partner (Jay O. Sanders) tries to get through to him. They killed the only thing ex-Marine and cop Craven cares about and he will gun his way to vengeance no matter where it leads.

However, what the viewer receives for the next 90 minutes is an intricate, densely plotted conspiracy thriller which, because of the film's running time, unfolds like a John LeCarre novel on fast forward. Emma was employed at a shadowy national defense contractor named Northmoor and she appears to have been involved in a security breach of the facility involving three now-dead environmental activists. Craven starts digging and a large cast of characters with complicated, sinister, and only partially-explained connections to one another are rapidly introduced. There is Emma's co-worker and boyfriend, David Burnham (Shawn Roberts), who clearly knows more than he is letting on but is reluctant to share his knowledge with Craven. There is co-worker Melissa (Catarina Scorsone), who is terrified of her employer to near hysteria. There is the overly cordial and creepy head of Northmoor, Jack Bennet (Danny Huston), who gives himself away by asking Craven what it feels like to have a child murdered. Also involved is a corrupt United States Senator (Damian Young), two vaguely identified U.S. government operatives (Denis O'Hare and David Aaron Baker), and a mysterious, philosophical assassin named Jedburgh (Ray Winstone). Jedburgh quickly makes contact with Craven, hinting at a bigger picture he cannot yet see and feeding him enigmatic clues. Even with Jedburgh's help, Craven has a tough job ahead of him as at least two separate cover ups, one by Northmoor and one by the U.S. government, are taking place.

The problem is that there simply is not enough screen time to develop these characters, relationships, and plot into a compelling, understandable whole. Winstone does well enough with his character but his role feels streamlined, as if significant portions of his character ended up on the cutting room floor. The viewer never gets enough of a sense of who he is to understand or care about what he does. This is frustrating since what little there is of Jedburgh in the film hints at a rich and intriguing character, easily the most interesting of the film. Similarly, Huston's villain is a cipher, not given enough screen time or dialogue to develop his motives. The film attempts to solve the dilemma of compressing five hours of plot into two hours by having the characters explain the plot to one another instead of revealing the plot through the actions of the characters. However, not even the explanations make things clear to the viewer as the dialogue-heavy scenes between Craven and Jedburgh are so fast and dense that it is very difficult to understand what is being said. Maddeningly, this is, in part, purposeful, as Jedburgh is supposed to both help Craven but also throw in sufficient vagueness for the character to remain enigmatic and keep the viewer guessing (which he succeeds all too well at). As a result of the film's failure to fully articulate its mystery, the viewer is not really able to meaningfully participate in the solving of the mystery. Instead, the viewer is left waiting around for the mystery to be explained so that the film can get to the satisfyingly cheap thrills of the revenge thriller which the film does exceedingly well.

Late in the film, Craven is asked by Northmoor's slick, arrogant attorney who he thinks he is. "I'm the guy with nothing to lose who doesn't give a shit!" Craven snarls in response and the film really comes alive on the few occasions where it allows him to demonstrate this passion. When a speeding car has shockingly and horrifically sped over a witness Craven has just finished interviewing, the car turns around to finish Craven off and, as the car accelerates towards him, Craven charges towards the car, emptying his clip into the windshield. Once Craven finally sorts out all of the shadowy subterfuge and figures out who is responsible for his daughter's disappearance, refreshingly, he simply walks up to the front door of the house and starts shooting until everyone inside is dead.

Few actors do righteous rage as well as Gibson and the film receives a jolt of energy whenever he is allowed to cut loose. Campbell's tight direction combines with Gibson's furious performance to focus that rage to great effect. There simply is not enough of it. It is rare indeed to suggest that a film would be better if it spent more time in the gutter but *Edge of Darkness* does the gutter so well and the rest so inadequately, that that is exactly where it belongs.

Nate Vercauteren

CREDITS

Thomas Craven: Mel Gibson
Darius Jedburgh: Ray Winstone
Bennett: Danny Huston
David Burnham: Shawn Roberts
Moore: Denis O'Hare
Emma Craven: Bojana Novakovic
Whitehouse: Jay O. Sanders
Melissa: Catarina Scorsone
Senator Jim Pine: Damian Young
Millroy: David Aaron Baker
Origin: United Kingdom, USA
Language: English
Released: 2010
Production: Tim Headington, Graham King, Michael Wearing; BBC Films, Icon Productions, Warner Bros., GK Productions; released by Warner Bros.
Directed by: Martin Campbell
Written by: William Monahan, Andrew Bovell
Cinematography by: Phil Meheux
Music by: Howard Shore
Sound: Bub Asman, Alan Robert Murray
Editing: Stuart Baird
Art Direction: Gregory A. Berry
Costumes: Lindy Hemming
Production Design: Tom Sanders
MPAA rating: PG-13
Running time: 126 minutes

REVIEWS

Berardinelli, James. *Reel Views.* January 27, 2010.
Ebert, Roger. *Chicago Sun-Times.* January 27, 2010.
Lane, Anthony. *New Yorker.* February 8, 2010.
Lowry, Brian. *Variety.* January 24, 2010.
Phillips, Michael. *Chicago Tribune.* January 28, 2010.
Phipps, Keith. *AV Club.* January 27, 2010.
Pinkerton, Nick. *Village Voice.* January 26, 2010.
Scott, A.O. *New York Times.* January 29, 2010.
Travers, Peter. *Rolling Stone.* January 29, 2010.
Zacharek, Stephanie. *Salon.com.* January 28, 2010.

QUOTES

Thomas Craven: "Everything's illegal in Massachusetts."

TRIVIA

This movie is Mel Gibson's first lead role since the movie *Signs* in 2002.

ENTER THE VOID

Told entirely from the physical and spiritual point of view of a junkie protagonist, *Enter the Void* sweeps and swoops through red light Japan on a quest that may leave many viewers in the dust and feeling understandably dirty. Writer/director Gaspar Noe has never been known for making accessible movies. His deeply disturbing portrait of madness, *I Stand Alone* (1998), and his graphic deconstruction of violent rape, *Irreversible* (2002), left many critics and viewers shocked and outraged and defenders wrestling with the notion that he may be best-described as a technically-adept purveyor of pretentious art house exploitation. But this visually-arresting film clearly means to do more (as do all Noe films) than shock and is liable to provide a substantial answer to such critiques. For all the excess that Noe indulges in, he is clearly attempting a visceral assault not unlike that of *Requiem for a Dream* (2000), where viewers are meant to feel more than think, even as he plunges them headlong into one provocative scenario after another.

An impossible-to-follow, neon assault of flashing multicolored text, severe rave music, and what sounds like a clicking projector races viewers through the opening (and closing) credits. This filmic device conveys much about the exploitive nature of the world the film takes place in and viewers are finally invited via the single word "ENTER" to a relatively tranquil and almost laconic scene where a man beckons a woman onto a balcony overlooking Japan. As a plane passes overhead, he asks her what Japan "…looks like from up there," to which she replies, "I'd be scared, of dying, of falling, into the void." He says, "I hear that you fly when you die."

The rest of the film seems to play out visually upon this metaphysical anxiety. The young man and woman are Oscar (Nathaniel Brown) and Linda (Paz de la Huerta), brother and sister. She leaves the apartment, he gets high, and calls a friend who has loaned him a copy of *The Tibetan Book of the Dead*. The friend comes by and they discuss the book and the idea of reincarnation and venture to a club where Oscar is shot by police as he brokers his first drug deal. What follows is an impressive array of out of body point-of-view vignettes in which the soul or consciousness of Oscar flies back and forth over the city, through timescapes and memories, until he himself is reincarnated as the baby of Linda and the friend who loaned him the book.

The initial sequence of his drug trip is spectacular in the way it conveys an addict's tripping point of view. But as direct as *Enter the Void* is about illicit pleasures, it goes to even greater lengths to portray the pains that drive people toward them and, more importantly, toward the isolation that they create. Noe has made a film that is all about connectedness. Part of the shifting sense of time involves the constant replay of memories. Viewers repeatedly see the car accident in which Oscar and Linda were orphaned, the pact that they later make with one another to never leave the other. Viewers also see the interconnectedness of their suffering and struggles with that of others.

An abortion (presented in great detail) affects not only Linda but her philandering boyfriend who begins to ponder what it means to be loved by someone enough that they want to have a child with him. The friend who has introduced Oscar to drugs (giving Oscar the needed cash to bring his sister to Japan where they can be reunited) struggles with his responsibility for the shooting that killed Oscar. His own struggles with drug abuse signal his own decline. Through it all is the omnipresent spirit of Oscar who watches and never turns away, no matter how degraded the memory or current timeline becomes. He is present, giving lie to the despair that threatens always to grip at his friends who are so tempted to give up, believing that they are alone, lost forever.

Considering the incredibly violent and disturbing nature of some of his imagery, it is perhaps fair to suggest that his work will always be embraced by a core of people who value such cinema for shock value alone. There is certainly a word of warning appropriate here for any viewer that is sensitive to sexual imagery. There is rampant and graphic, even pornographic, imagery offered here, particularly during a lengthy sequence near the end in which a variety of sexual acts are showcased.

At his most shocking, Noe still presents primary characters who are decidedly and fundamentally sympathetic. His void is far less of a destination where images, sounds, chemical highs, and sexual escapades simply provide momentary distraction from despair but a way station where the most intense of pleasures are still merely shadows of what his characters hope for. For Noe, moans of sexual pleasure and his most graphic image—that of the end of a penis ejaculating into a vagina from the inside—fade, tellingly, into a scene in which a woman cries out in the pangs of childbirth and his protagonist is reborn.

Gaspar Noe is making films at a time when the hyper-violent and sexually-charged imagery he often uses can pass by with nary a blip on the cultural radar. But those who long ago dismissed him as a purveyor of exploitation dressed up in art house clothes will have a hard time doing so here, even if *Enter the Void* is like all other Noe films in the jarring way that it assaults viewers with a highly questionable intensity.

The employ of co-writer Lucile Hadzihalilovic gives a solid hint of how hard Noe reaches out towards transcendence. Her own director /writer debut *Innocense* (2004) offered up coming-of-age imagery in an often startling mélange of natural symbols and metaphors that, while on the surface seemed almost too obvious, were rendered with a stunning clarity and celebratory beauty. Noe has made a film that can hardly be called beautiful, is certainly not for everyone, and may even be morally objectionable, but there is little doubt that the neon void of our own cultural landscape does well to consider the way excess does not negate the embrace of meaning, it just clouds it.

Dave Canfield

CREDITS

Linda: Paz de la Huerta
Little Linda: Emily Alyn Lind
Oscar: Nathaniel Brown
Alex: Cyril Roy
Little Oscar: Jesse Kuhn
Victor: Olly Alexander
Mario: Masto Tanno
Bruno: Ed Spear
Origin: France
Released: 2009
Production: Olivier Delbosc, Marc Missonnier, Pierre Buffin, Brahim Chioua, Vincent Maraval; Fidelite Films, Wild Bunch, BUF; released by IFC Films
Directed by: Gaspar Noe
Written by: Gaspar Noe
Cinematography by: Benoit Debie
Sound: Ken Yasumoto
Music by: Thomas Bangalter
Editing: Gaspar Noe, Marc Boucrot, Jerome Pesnel

Costumes: Nicoletta Massone, Tony Crosbie
Production Design: Kikuo Ohta, Jean Carriere
MPAA rating: Unrated
Running time: 161 minutes

REVIEWS

Abele, Robert. *Los Angeles Times.* September 23, 2010.
Burr, Ty. *Boston Globe.* November 11, 2010.
Chaney, Jen. *Washington Post.* November 12, 2010.
Dargis, Manohla. *New York Times.* May 23, 2009.
Faraci, Devin. *CHUD.* July 6, 2010.
Gleiberman, Owen. *Entertainment Weekly.* October 13, 2010.
Gonsalves, Rob. *eFilmCritic.com.* October 4, 2010.
Longworth, Katrina. *Village Voice.* September 21, 2010.
McWeeny, Drew. *HitFix.* September 20, 2010.
Nelson, Rob. *Variety.* May 23, 2009.

QUOTES

Oscar: "Do you remember that pact we made? We promised to
never leave each other."

TRIVIA

Director Gaspar Noé wanted the film to be shown at 25 frames
per second instead of the normal 24 resulting in two
different run times that differ by as much as seven minutes.

EXIT THROUGH THE GIFT SHOP

The incredible true story of how the world's
greatest street art movie was never made...
—Movie tagline
The world's first street art disaster movie.
—Movie tagline

Box Office: $3 million

Entertaining, insightful, inspiring, and cautionary
are all adjectives that apply equally to this great
documentary which looks at street art and street art
practitioners from behind-the-scenes and then switches
gears midway to ask the question that critics of the form
should have been asking all along, "Does it really matter
if this stuff is art or not?" The idea here is that most
street art practitioners could care less about the theory
of what they do. Art or not, they do it because they feel
compelled. *Exit Through the Gift Shop* is a warts-and-all
look at that naiveté and how little it matters to the
masses that have turned street art into a thriving cottage
industry.

Decidedly eccentric, Los Angeles-based shopkeeper
Thierry Guetta always has a camera in his hand. A
chance meeting with his street artist cousin gives him

the opportunity to meet and casually film some of street
art's most-famous up-and-comers as they graffiti, stencil,
sticker, and sculpt their way into infamy. Only one artist
eludes him, the world famous Banksy, whose provocative images helped build and define the form as it
emerged from the architectural shadows into a respected
mode of artistic self-expression. It would seem to be a
hopeless cause but when Thierry, with the help of other
artists, finally does locate Banksy the two hit it off and
arrive at a tenuous agreement. Banksy will allow himself
to be filmed as long as his identity remains hidden and
Thierry agrees to help him with his installations. *Exit
Through the Gift Shop* would have made for a compelling documentary if it had stopped there. But this is a
film that goes way beyond expectations offering twists
and turns, role reversals aplenty, and an increasingly-
amused, even satirical, eye on the art form and scene it
examines. Thierry goes off to edit a film together having
never done so before and comes back to Banksy with an
incoherent mess. Banksy offers to take over the footage
if he himself can start turning the camera on Thierry
who has now been playing at being a street artist for
quite a while. "Put together a small show and let me
document it," says Banksy.

This is where it gets weird, wonderful, and where
Exit Through the Gift Shop takes a final tail-swallowing
spin. Thierry takes this suggestion to do a show of his
own art and blows it up to nuclear proportions. He
mortgages the house, sells everything, hires a staff, and
proceeds to fill a warehouse with hundreds upon
hundreds of original pieces, most of them not so subtly
aping the art styles he has spent countless hours filming.
Of course, by now, Banksy has already put on his own
very successful commercial exhibition and street art has
emerged from the shadows to become a highly sought
after commodity.

But now Banksy is forced to confront the 800 lb.
gorilla in the room, a wonderful irony since he himself
used a live, painted elephant in his own show. As Thierry prepares his show, Banksy begins to wonder if he
has created a Frankenstein, a monster that may devour
street art altogether. When the show does happen, Thierry, who now calls himself Mr. Brainwash, becomes an
overnight sensation, achieving commercial success
beyond his wildest dreams, leaving Banksy and the other
artists in the film shaking their bemused heads.

Much of the art showcased in *Exit Through the Gift
Shop* is wonderfully whimsical, employing not only
skilled artifice but highly sophisticated communicational
dynamics. In one piece by Banksy there is a naked man
depicted so that he is dangling from a real window ledge.
While the husband looks angrily out the window just
out of view, and the wife stands in the background horrified, the naked man demurely covers his privates. Not

hard to imagine are the myriad ways that actual passersby, caught up by the highly visible scene, are emotionally and intellectually, even spiritually, engaged.

Few of the Mr. Brainwash pieces seem to do more than skim the surface of profundity, calling into question whom the joke is ultimately on. Street art has always been based on an ability to turn heads and draw attention before the inevitable white washing of the cultural wall. Where Thierry fits in seems to be a mystery that even Banksy himself, hidden behind a trademark hoodie is reticent to answer. Ultimately, *Exit Through the Gift Shop* seems most comfortable leaving the value of art in the hands of the people who are asked to purchase it, to support the artistic community. The only other major character in the film is Mrs. Guetta. At the end of the film we learn that she is indeed still married to Thierry, still devoted to their family and ultimately, most surprisingly, the film saves the biggest surprise for last. There are no bad guys here. Just people lost in the landscape, covering it with beauty, using art to connect, financially survive, and find a place in the world.

Exit Through the Gift Shop is more than a documentary; it is a story of how art functions to serve people, building human community while suggesting new roles and life directions, even amongst the most iconoclastic.

Dave Canfield

CREDITS

Narrator: Rhys Ifans
Origin: United Kingdom
Language: English
Released: 2010
Production: Jaime D'Cruz; Paranoid Pictures; released by Oscilloscope Laboratories
Directed by: Banksy
Cinematography by: Thierry Guetta
Music by: Geoff Barrow
Sound: Jim Carey
Editing: Chris King, Tom Fulford
MPAA rating: R
Running time: 87 minutes

REVIEWS

Burr, Ty. *Boston Globe.* April 22, 2010.
Caldwell, Thomas. *Cinema Autopsy.* June 3, 2010.
Debruge, Peter. *Variety.* January 26, 2010.
Ebert, Roger. *Chicago Sun-Times.* April 29, 2010.
Fuchs, Cynthia. *PopMatters.* April 16, 2010.
Gleiberman, Owen. *Entertainment Weekly.* April 14, 2010.
Lane, Anthony. *New Yorker.* April 26, 2010.
Michel, Brett. *Boston Phoenix.* April 21, 2010.

Turan, Kenneth. *Los Angeles Times.* April 16, 2010.
Vognar, Chris. *Dallas Morning News.* May 7, 2010.

QUOTES

Thierry Guetta: "I don't know how to play chess, but to me, life is like a game of chess."

AWARDS

Ind. Spirit 2011: Feature Doc
Nomination:
Oscars 2010: Feature Doc.

THE EXPENDABLES

Choose your weapon.
—Movie tagline

Box Office: $103 million

In the heyday of the Reagan-era action heroes, there were really only two film types associated with the stars who got top billing in them: the gloriously over-the-top scoops of carnage that made no apologies for their muscle-laden stars ability to mow down as many foreign (and domestic) threats to their country or families as possible—and the just plain ol' bad. The latter made up the majority while films like *Commando* (1985) and *Rambo: First Blood Part II* (1985) found a way to boost blood-lusting adrenaline for revenge to the next level and remain pleasures to this very day, guilty or not. Therefore, the prospect of teaming up as many action heroes as humanly possible, in a brand of *Ocean's Eleven* (2001) casting and throwback to the era when big violence reigned and everything else got out of the way or got blown up, is as juicy as a giant steak with all the trimmings. When it is rolling, *The Expendables* brings out all the best elements expected from a great, big, dumb action spectacular. In-between those moments though, it also brings out many of the worst, and, if nothing else, should serve as its own evidence for future film students in why only some of the stars associated with these films made it out alive.

Sylvester Stallone was intent to bring this idea to life and naturally gives himself top billing as Barney Ross, the leader of a mercenary crew that is made up of a few relics but mostly newer tough guys. His right-hand man, Lee Christmas (Jason Statham) is more fond of the blade than the gun. Ying Yang (Jet Li) is the tiny Asian who gets to display his martial arts skills more on his own men than the bad guys. Toll Road (Randy Couture) has cauliflower ear, Hale Caesar (Terry Crews) is the giant black man and Gunner Jensen (Dolph Lundgren) is the loose cannon on the team with a thirst for extra-senseless violence; a thirst no doubt developed by watching Dolph Lundgren in *Universal Soldier*

(1992). After laying waste to some Somali pirates in the opening scene, they try returning home to their everyday lives. For Christmas, it means trying to reacquaint with Lacy (Charisma Carpenter) while Barney needs to get a tattoo finished with former merc-turned-artist, Tool (Mickey Rourke).

Life does not intercede for long as Barney is already looking into their next mission with the unknown Mr. Church (Bruce Willis). Dubbed practically a suicide mission by Barney's chief rival, Trench (Arnold Schwarzenegger), the team is expected to hit the island of Vilena to overthrow corrupt dictator General Garza (David Zayas) and his CIA puppet master James Munroe (Eric Roberts). Their contact-in-destructive-philanthropy is the general's daughter, Sandra (Giselle Itié), who doesn't share her father's ideology of drugs and money—just painting, whether it be portraits or the faces of his soldiers. Despite almost finishing the job on just a scouting mission and being guilted into returning by Tool, Barney's team suits up for the operation.

With a cast this notable, the action could just be spared if it meant spending more time with these personalities. Except personality is in short supply. Characters are, by and large, superfluous to *The Expendables*. Stallone and Statham get the lion's share of screen time and they do the bare minimum to boost their chemistry when getting center stage. As for the rest, none are given any significant get-to-know-them time and their dialogue (co-scripted by Stallone and *Doom* (2005) writer David Callaham) cannot be strained to reach the level of forced banter when camaraderie should be at a maximum. As much fun as it is to see the original owners of Planet Hollywood on screen together for the first time, even as mere cameos, it is actually a detriment to the rest of the cast. In just one scene, Stallone, Schwarzenegger, and Willis show us how they were able to stick around as A-list stars for so long. A natural combination of direct timing, charisma, and mockery, the trio have an instant rapport with themselves and the audience making the rest of the lot (particularly Statham who, without the accent, would have likely gone the way of *The Perfect Weapon*'s (1991) Jeff Speakman) look expendable.

Barney, Christmas, and the others sneak into the backyard of a presidential palace under the noses of an entire army and plant enough explosive charges to take out ten completed Death Stars before being detected. The action scenes carry little stake as to their success or failure. *The Expendables* ends with a twenty-minute climax of carnage unrivaled since the eighty-plus solo kills of the finale of *Commando* (1985). The carnage gets so thick at times that it is hard not to laugh when someone actually yells "stop" to spare someone. Stallone, the director, is actually pretty good at paying off the ac-

tion if not setting the initial stage for it. Edited with just enough real estate to see who is throwing a punch and who is feeling its bone-breaking wrath, the sheer volume of mano-a-mano and gun-a-mano is relentless to the point that one forgets that there ever was a point.

The Expendables does not classify into the growing trend of "so bad it's good" enterprises no matter how guilty one might feel about liking it. The plotting is sloppy, the chemistry joins a parade of 2010 films (*The Losers*, *Red*) that fail to compete with the same year's *The A-Team*, and the performances range from bland to downright abysmal. It cannot be easy to assemble a cast of such recognition (in name, if not career choices) but for a film that boasts to "have them all" in reference to action stars, there are conspicuous absences. With a martial artist, extreme fighter, champion kickboxer, and a wrestler in tow, who needs Steven Seagal and Jean Claude Van Damme? But if Stallone really wanted to make the film more playful and not so deadly serious, he would have been better off getting Chuck Norris and playing off his third career as the toughest man in the world or even Dwayne "The Rock" Johnson who was passed the torch of the new action hero by none other than Schwarzenegger himself in *The Rundown* (2003). Instead he wound up with Steve "Stone Cold" Austin whose character "does not share that moral dilemma" about hitting women; a trait best removed for a guy once charged with spousal abuse.

Whatever awareness Stallone may have tried to bring with Rambo's annihilation of Burma is doubly suspect here with the strong-arms of the red, white, and blue laying waste to a tiny island and then handing over some cash to "help get things growing around here." But, "You've done so much," they are told before withdrawing for good. "So much" may be overemphasizing Stallone's accomplishments here. Perhaps the real tag line of the film should be Barney's response to the query, "How are you here?" "I just am," he says. *The Expendables* may not be the big, juicy steak Stallone promised, but occasionally meat loaf just hits the spot; even with the inevitable indigestion.

Erik Childress

CREDITS

Barney Ross: Sylvester Stallone
Hale Ceasar: Terry Crews
Toll Road: Randy Couture
James Monroe: Eric Roberts
Gunnar Jensen: Dolph Lundgren
Yin Yang: Jet Li
Lee Christmas: Jason Statham
Tool: Mickey Rourke
Dan Paine: Steve Austin
Mr. Church: Bruce Willis

Trench: Arnold Schwarzenegger

Lacy: Charisma Carpenter

Agent Will Sands: Nick Searcy

Gen. Garza: David Zayas

The Brit: Gary Daniels

Sandra: Giselle Itié

Origin: USA

Language: English

Released: 2010

Production: Kevin King, Avi Lerner, John Thompson, Kevin King Templeton; Millenium Films, Nu Image Films, Road Rebel, Rogue Marble; released by Lionsgate

Directed by: Sylvester Stallone

Written by: Sylvester Stallone, David Callaham

Cinematography by: Jeffrey L. Kimball

Music by: Brian Tyler

Sound: Toninho Muricy, Paul Ledford

Music Supervisor: Selena Arizanovic

Editing: Ken Blackwell, Paul Harb

Art Direction: Daniel Flaksman, Andy Thodes

Costumes: Lizz Wolf

Production Design: Franco-Giacomo Carbone

MPAA rating: R

Running time: 103 minutes

REVIEWS

Bayer, Jeff.. *Scorecard Review.* August 17, 2010.
Goss, William. *Cinematical.* August 12, 2010.
Hornaday, Ann. *Washington Post.* August 13, 2010.
Levy, Shawn. *Oregonian.* August 13, 2010.
Miller, Neil. *Film School Rejects.* August 12, 2010.
Rabin, Nathan. *AV Club.* August 12, 2010.
Roeper, Richard. *RichardRoeper.com.* August 13, 2010.
Scott, A.O. *New York Times.* August 13, 2010.
Sobczynski, Peter. *eFilmCritic.* August 13, 2010.
Tallerico, Brian. *MovieRetriever.com.* August 13, 2010.

QUOTES

Tool: "I promised myself, I'm gonna die for something that counts."

TRIVIA

The role of Hale Ceasar was originally offered to Wesley Snipes, Forest Whitaker, and 50 Cent before director Sylvester Stallone settled on former NFL player Terry Crews.

AWARDS

Nomination:

Golden Raspberries 2010: Worst Director (Stallone).

EXTRAORDINARY MEASURES

Don't hope for a miracle. Make one.
—Movie tagline

Box Office: $12 million

When retelling a true story, filmmakers should always ask themselves, "Would this story be better served by a documentary than a narrative film with factual stretch marks?" Sometimes the answer may not be clear until it is too late. That seems to have been the case with *Extraordinary Measures,* an earnest drama whose good intentions do not translate to the moving, convincing tale of triumph over tragedy that its true story warrants. Part of the blame starts with star Brendan Fraser. As John Crowley, a man who will stop at nothing to help his two kids fight Pompe—a form of muscular dystrophy that yields an expected life span of about nine years—Fraser simply does not have the required acting chops. Whether John is behaving impulsively and out of character or breaking down into tears, Fraser's performance almost always seems forced. This removes the movie's potential for emotional truth and too often makes it seem like a poorly executed attempt to deliver a painful drama to a mainstream audience.

Extraordinary Measures is the first production of CBS films, which may be why the film is over-lit and unsubtle like a TV movie. It also may be why it feels so methodical in moving from scene to scene, as if a commercial break is not far off, without ever truly getting inside the story in a real way. As *Extraordinary Measures* begins, John and his wife Aileen (Keri Russell) are paying $40,000 each month to support their two children with Pompe—8-year-old Megan (Meredith Droeger) and 6-year-old Patrick (Diego Velazquez). There is little in life that is truer than the steps parents will take to protect their children, and the horror of potentially losing them. That is what makes the script by Robert Nelson Jacobs, adapted from the book *The Cure* (2006) by Geeta Anand, so disappointing in its frequent need to overdramatize.

This is no more evident than in the character of Dr. Stonehill (Harrison Ford, who executive produced), a composite of the real scientists with whom the real John Crowley worked to develop a new enzyme to battle Pompe. This is a movie about children in need and the urgency of science; Stonehill's personality should not be the focus. Yet *Extraordinary Measures* overcompensates and makes Stonehill a salty, twice-divorced workaholic who is difficult to get along with and can only work while listening to loud classic rock. From a writing perspective, these are shortcuts to character development, turning Stonehill into not a complex person but a fictional character with a few quirks. John calls him "really eccentric," which is not true. Stonehill is just a grouchy character cooked up by a movie that incorrectly thinks it needs a grouch to keep things interesting.

Instead, Stonehill's gruffness is more of a distraction. It is given screen time that should be given to Megan and Patrick, both of whom are presented as relentlessly upbeat, perky kids, as if the movie is afraid to confront the children's own fears and feelings about their disease. Obviously, *Extraordinary Measures,* which begins by noting that its story is "inspired by true events," is not trying to devastate viewers with the many challenges faced by children whose muscles are deteriorating. However, by keeping Megan and Patrick and their ailments at arm's length, showing little more than their decreasing ability to throw a ball or piece of bread to a duck, the film seems unwilling to actually look its subject straight in the eye. Consequently, little information is really offered about Pompe, and there is never the feeling that someone watching *Extraordinary Measures* is experiencing the Crowley's agonizing struggle along with them.

Still, even people bored by science will be drawn in by the film's most surprisingly effective thread, focusing on what must be done to get Stonehill's enzyme project up and running and keep it going. Early on, John and Aileen race to establish their own foundation and raise as much money as possible. This is delivered quickly, montage-style, but it works as an indication of how determination and timely action can get things done in pressing situations. Likewise, when John and Stonehill must sell their company to a larger company so investors do not shut them down, it speaks to the medical industry's all-important bottom line. It does not matter how advanced the science is; if no one signs the checks, the research does not continue and the drug does not get made.

In many of these scenes, too, *Extraordinary Measures* botches its grip on the story's sad timeline and persistent complications. There is just too much of Stonehill growling lines like, "Nobody's gonna tell me how to run my lab!" and "I already work around the clock!" Later, when the film taps into something credible about John's lack of objectivity in serving as an executive on a project that may help his own children, it ultimately backs away from the conflict of interest—and its implications on the success of the project. The resulting message is that medical research can, in fact, be driven by personal interest, regardless of any clash with FDA guidelines. That is nice to think but harder to believe.

What is most believable is the long nights John and Aileen spend at the hospital, worrying about their kids and, no matter how badly Fraser delivers the line, the fact that John, "can't just sit around and wait for my kids to die." The same cannot be said for Stonehill teasingly calling New Jersey-native John "Jersey" or Stonehill storming out of an important meeting, seemingly just to provide the film with more conflict. The story about how John and Aileen Crowley worked tirelessly to foster science that could help their kids and many, many others does not need to be spruced up, and it definitely does not need to close to the tune of Eric Clapton's

song "Change the World" (1996). There is a big difference between the sorrow and uplift of life and the way it is sometimes presented on screen, and *Extraordinary Measures* unfortunately takes too much realism out of reality.

Matt Pais

CREDITS

Dr. Robert Stonehill: Harrison Ford
John Crowley: Brendan Fraser
Aileen Crowley: Keri Russell
Sal: Dee Wallace
Dr. Kent Webber: Jared Harris
Jurgen Axelsson: Patrick Bauchau
Marcus Temple: Courtney B. Vance
Pete Sutphen: Alan Ruck
John Crowley, Jr.: Sam Hall
Megan Crowley: Meredith Droeger
Patrick Crowley: Diego Velazquez
Origin: USA
Language: English
Released: 2010
Production: Carla Santos Shamberg, Michael Shamberg, Stacey Sher; Double Feature Films; released by CBS Films
Directed by: Tom Vaughan
Written by: Robert Nelson Jacobs
Cinematography by: Andrew Dunn
Music by: Andrea Guerra
Sound: Gregg Baxter
Music Supervisor: Eric Craig
Editing: Anne Coates
Art Direction: John Richardson
Costumes: Deena Appel
Production Design: Derek R. Hill
MPAA rating: PG
Running time: 105 minutes

REVIEWS

Ebert, Roger. *Chicago Sun-Times.* January 20, 2010.
Morris, Wesley. *Boston Globe.* January 22, 2010.
Phillips, Michael. *Chicago Tribune.* January 21, 2010.
Rickey, Carrie. *Philadelphia Enquirer.* January 22, 2010.
Robinson, Tasha. *AV Club.* January 22, 2010.
Rodriguez, Rene. *Miami Herald.* January 21, 2010.
Scott, A.O. *New York Times.* January 22, 2010.
Scott, Mike. *New Orleans Times-Picayune.* January 22, 2010.
Stevens, Dana. *Slate.* January 21, 2010.
Zacharek, Stephanie. *Salon.com.* January 22, 2010.

QUOTES

Dr. Robert Stonehill: "Scientists get all sensible and careful when they get old. Young ones like risk, not afraid of new ideas…and you can pay 'em less."

TRIVIA

This was the first film in 27 years to star Harrison Ford and not feature his name first in the credits.

F

FAIR GAME

Wife. Mother. Spy.
—Movie tagline

Box Office: $9 million

The tale of Valerie Plame is shameful for two reasons. First, she was callously revealed to be a C.I.A. agent/spy in the *Wall Street Journal* by a source seeking to discredit and silence Plame's husband, Professor Joseph Wilson, who spoke openly against the war in Iraq soon after it began. Second, the press covering the Plame case were fed the equivalent of journalistic junk food to sidetrack them from the real story, which was that revealing a clandestine operative's name is considered treason in the law books of the United States—punishable by death. When *Fair Game* director Doug Liman does not allow himself to get too sidetracked from Plame's shameful treatment by her government and the media, this movie is a powerful thought-provoking film.

While Naomi Watts (who plays Plame) is a talented actress, she has never been one of those names who can simply get cast in a film and it instantly becomes a better work. In films such as *Mulholland Dr.* (2001), *21 Grams* (2003, in which she co-starred with her *Fair Game* husband Sean Penn), *Eastern Promises* (2007), and *Funny Games* (2007), Watts has illustrated that her true strength is rising to meet the challenge of complex and challenging material. She has never been the kind of actor to make a film better, but she often makes one more palpable; *Fair Game* is proof of that.

Watts portrays Plame as a woman only happy when she is working harder than those around her, someone who is often the smartest person in the room. She was one of the C.I.A.'s leading experts on the Middle East, often taking trips to the region and securing quality intelligence for the agency and the Bush administration, which was eager to find a reason to invade Iraq throughout 2002 and early 2003. The search for weapons of mass destruction was going nowhere, but a lead cropped up stating that Iraqi leader Saddam Hussein might be purchasing potential nuclear fuel rod casings from Africa. Knowing her husband had many contacts in the region, Plame enlisted Wilson (Sean Penn) to investigate. He was paid nothing for the assignment. He returned saying the lead was unsubstantiated, but when President Bush gave his speech justifying the invasion of Iraq, he said the African purchase was proof of the existence of WMD. This convoluted story led Wilson to write an article in the *New York Times* laying out his investigation and calling the "evidence" for the U.S. invasion lies. The Bush administration was not amused.

The first half of *Fair Game* is laid out so beautifully by Liman that it is easy to forget where the story is going. Many have complained about the film's factual accuracy. For those worried about such things, pretend the movie is 100 percent fiction. It holds up nicely as a smart, briskly-paced thriller, not quite to the level of Liman's *The Bourne Identity* (2002) or *Mr. & Mrs. Smith* (2005), but he is going for something more reality based, so having Plame rappel down the side of building in S&M gear would not be appropriate. The film's most heartbreaking moments occur immediately after her status as a spy is revealed, and all of the men and women she called co-workers are forced by protocol to shut her out, literally and figuratively. Then, the leaks about her role in the C.I.A. begin. Some claim she was nothing more than a glorified secretary, while others maintain her work was shoddy. When in truth, even when the president made false statements about WMDs, Plame did her duty and kept her mouth shut like a good soldier.

The second half of *Fair Game* is a little less focused, but not without merit. Arguments erupt between the husband and wife. As both of their reputations get trashed in the press, the strain gets more pronounced. At times, Penn seems to be overcompensating in his performance as if to somehow balance out Watts' more dialed-back and, frankly, better work. Still, it is difficult to find fault with Penn as an actor. As ramped up as his performance may be, he consistently makes it easy to sit back and watch him gesture and scream a lot. Plame seeks advice from her stoic father, Sam (Sam Shepard), and while his advice is muddled and the scene underwritten, it is tough to pass up a chance to see Shepard chew up a little scenery.

Perhaps too succinctly, the film makes Scooter Libby (David Andrews) overly villainy and the scapegoat for all the Bush administration's bad behavior. But if the tactic is good enough for the White House, it is certainly good enough for screenwriters Jez Butterworth and John-Henry Butterworth, who based their adaptation on both Wilson's and Plame's respective books on these events. Director Liman does an admirable job adding drama to a story whose ending most of us already know. There are perhaps a few too many speeches and declarations of love and loyalty between the couple at the end of the movie, but by that point, a heartbreaking story of a patriotic government worker has already been told.

Fair Game tends to wander a bit too often from Plame's story to Wilson attempting to reclaim his good name, but since the mud-slinging hit both of them, there is not really a way around that. There is just something inherently more tragic about Plame's situation and Watts rises once again to capture her desperation to keep both her family and reputation intact. This is solid work from everyone involved. The film ends with video of the real Valerie Plame testifying during a Congressional investigation concerning her ordeal, and it is wise and necessary that the final lines of the film come from the victim of this story, if only to remind the audience that this all happened to a real person.

Steven Prokopy

CREDITS

Valerie Plame: Naomi Watts
Joseph Wilson: Sean Penn

Bill: Noah Emmerich
Fred: Ty Burrell
Jim Pavitt: Bruce McGill
Sam Plame: Sam Shepard
Scooter Libby: David Andrews
Diana: Brooke Smith
Dave: David Denman
Hamed: Khaled Nabawy
Joe Turner: Kristoffer Ryan Winters
Ari Fleischer: Geoffrey Cantor
Origin: USA, United Arab Emirates
Language: English
Released: 2010
Production: Jez Butterworth, Akiva Goldsman, Doug Liman, Janet Zucker, Jerry Zucker; River Road Entertainment, Weed Road Pictures; released by Summit Entertainment
Directed by: Doug Liman
Written by: Jez Butterworth, John Henry Butterworth
Cinematography by: Doug Liman
Music by: John Powell
Music Supervisor: Julianne Jordan
Editing: Christopher Tellefsen
Art Direction: Kevin Bird
Costumes: Cindy Evans
Production Design: Jess Gonchor
MPAA rating: PG-13
Running time: 106 minutes

REVIEWS

Honeycutt, Kirk. *Hollywood Reporter.* October 20, 2010.
Jones, J.R. *Chicago Readers.* November 4, 2010.
Mick LaSalle. Mick, *San Francisco Chronicle.* November 5, 2010.
Pinkerton, Nick. *Village Voice.* November 3, 2010.
Puig, Claudia. *USA Today.* November 13, 2010.
Rocchi, James. *IFC.com.* May 20, 2010.
Savlov, Marc. *Austin Chronicle.* November, 5, 2010.
Scott, A.O. *New York Times.* November 4, 2010.
Weber, Bill. *Slant Magazine.* November 1, 2010.
Younkin, Craig. *ScreenComment.com.* October 29, 2010.

TRIVIA

The film originally included Nicole Kidman and Russell Crowe attached to the leading roles.

FASTER

Slow justice is no justice.
—Movie tagline

Box Office: $23 million

Of all the modern performers who transitioned into acting via what might best be described as nontraditional means, Dwayne Johnson may slot second to only Mark Wahlberg in terms of the smoothness and long-view deftness of his changeover. After earning a football scholarship to the University of Miami but blowing out his knee and derailing a possible career in the NFL, Johnson turned to professional wrestling, where his broad-shouldered physique, megawatt smile and amiable personality (in addition to his preternaturally arched brow) made him a natural star. The catchphrase of his in-the-ring alter-ego, "Do you smell what The Rock is cooking?," caught on even with non-wrestling fans, and soon Johnson found Hollywood calling.

Johnson kept his wrestling moniker for his mainstream film debut, which was a heralded cameo turn in *The Mummy Returns* (2001). He played the same character in a successful spin-off, *The Scorpion King* (2002), surrounded by the sorts of special effects indulgence which helps guarantee adolescent rear-ends in seats. When it came time to at least partially hang up his wrestling tights, Johnson still went by The Rock in more square-jawed action fare like *Walking Tall* (2004) and *Doom* (2005), while also dabbling in more comedic-inflected work like *The Rundown* (2003), and the ensemble film *Be Cool* (2005). Then, while still mixing in a series of TV cameos that played upon his wrestling persona, The Rock slowly, methodically became Dwayne Johnson, costarring in Richard Kelly's art house phantasmagoria *Southland Tales* (2006) before headlining the football drama *Gridiron Gang* (2006) and pivoting into wide-appeal family fare like *The Game Plan* (2007), *Race to Witch Mountain* (2009), and *Tooth Fairy* (2010).

All of which is important to consider when one encounters *Faster,* the sort of stone-faced, no-frills, graphic action film that the managers of a less-reasonably plotted career would have foisted upon a hulking, physically adept, would-be movie star much, much earlier, and then rode reliably into the ground with nothing but slight, differently-costumed iterations on a theme. Arriving earlier in the decade, before almost all of the aforementioned films, *Faster* would have come across as slapdash and derivative, and roundly dismissed, with likely gleeful derision. Arriving in 2010, it sparkles and shines to no greater degree as either wildly original or even notably superlative in its execution, but it at least has the advantage of tapping into a reservoir of goodwill attached to its good-natured star. Viewers, then, will shrug, not tag any lasting dissatisfaction to Johnson, and merely await the star vehicle that better serves his talents.

Newly freed after a decade in prison, Driver (Johnson) sets out to cut a swath of retribution through dusty California, with little more than an old black Chevelle, a snub-nosed revolver and a considerable hit list of those he intends to give dirt naps. The reason behind the bullet-bald Driver's tunnel-vision rage is the death of his brother in a bank heist gone wrong, which also factors into his own imprisonment. Bodies quickly start to drop, and Driver is soon on the local news. On his trail are a druggie, soon-to-retire lawman known only as Cop (Billy Bob Thornton) and his partner Cicero (Carla Gugino). As he works down his list, Driver comes into the crosshairs of Killer (Oliver Jackson-Cohen), a pointlessly elegant hitman-for-hire who seems to have taken on his professional calling only after having himself worked his way down a very long to-do list.

There can absolutely be a certain mad, cathartic appeal to assembly-line commercial product like *Faster*—movies embraced with the intensity of feeling rather than reason or intellectual appreciation—but that is unfortunately not the case here. Paying emphatic homage to Sergio Leone's *The Good, the Bad and the Ugly* (1967) (Ennio Morricone's pioneering theme even serves as the ringtone for Killer's cell phone), Tony and Joe Gayton's script refers to its main characters only by their roles/archetypes, yet, perhaps unsurprisingly, does not delve in any substantive way into the issues of redemption or letting go of the past that might give this vengeance tale a greater (read: any) emotional mooring. In fact, the entire Killer plotline feels like distracting, superficial "color" (hopelessly jaded, he consults with his therapist by Bluetooth), and a third act twist on this front only feels like an even more meaningless gambit, pure screenwriter affectation.

Director George Tillman, Jr. made an impact with the bristling, engaging *Notorious* (2008), but in *Faster* he slides back into a much lower gear, despite much noise and artificial energy. The action scenes are sleek and kind of coldly efficient, but not wildly memorable. With cinematographer Michael Grady, Tillman tries to affect a change in mood by shifting lens filters, hue and camera angles, but the movie's plotting and stolid dialogue do not always support this interpretation of *Faster* as a vibrant, hip, quicksilver thing.

Excepting the ridiculousness of his hairdo (which seems to be a cousin's of Al Pacino's cockatoo coif in *88 Minutes* [2008]), Thornton gives fairly good twitchy dramatic engagement as Driver's barking pursuer. But Jackson-Cohen chiefly comes across as a pretty boy, just another in a long line of lanky, easy-on-the-eyes drama school Brits who seem like the United Kingdom's answer to the Abercrombie & Fitch catalogue. Meanwhile, though Johnson's physicality provides the necessary underpinning for this type of role and film, his innate charisma is like an engine. And endless, constipated brooding of the sort that Driver requires is like leaving that engine idling. It does not come naturally to

Johnson, such stasis—which is something that *Faster* tries laboriously and vociferously to make its audience forget. Unfortunately, however, it is empty noise.

Brent Simon

CREDITS

Driver: Dwayne Johnson
Cop: Billy Bob Thornton
Killer: Oliver Jackson-Cohen
Cicero: Carla Gugino
Lily: Maggie Grace
Marina: Moon Bloodgood
Warden: Tom Berenger
Evangelist: Adewale Akinnuoye-Agbaje
Sergeant Mallag: Xander Berkeley
Telemarketer: Courtney Gains
Baphomet: Lester "Rasta" Speight
Grone: Mike Epps
Origin: USA
Language: English
Released: 2010
Production: Tony Gayton, Liz Glotzer, Martin Shafer, Robert Teitel; Castle Rock Entertainment, TriStar Pictures, CBS Films, State Street Pictures; released by CBS Films
Directed by: George Tillman Jr.
Written by: Joe Gayton, Tony Gayton
Cinematography by: Michael Grady
Music by: Clint Mansell
Sound: Michael Ferdie
Editing: Dirk Westervelt
Art Direction: Andrew E. W. Murdock
Costumes: Salvador Perez
Production Design: David Lazan
MPAA rating: R
Running time: 98 minutes

REVIEWS

Cole, Stephen. *Globe and Mail.* November 24, 2010.
Ebert, Roger. *Chicago Sun-Times.* November 23, 2010.
Fine, Marshall. *Hollywood & Fine.* November 24, 2010.
Grierson, Tim. *Screen International.* November 23, 2010.
Holden, Stephen. *New York Times.* November 24, 2010.
Honeycutt, Kirk. *Hollywood Reporter.* November 23, 2010.
Koehler, Robert. *Variety.* November 23, 2010.
Kois, Dan. *Washington Post.* November 24, 2010.
Pais, Matt. *Metromix.com.* November 23, 2010.
Phillips, Michael. *Chicago Tribune.* November 23, 2010.

QUOTES

Driver: "God can't save you from me!"

TRIVIA

Actress Salma Hayek was originally cast, but later resigned before shooting began.

THE FIGHTER

Box Office: $78 million

The most crucial fight of boxer Micky Ward's life was waged and won outside the ring, and is the most stirring thing one witnesses in David O. Russell's laudable, fact-based *The Fighter,* a multiple Oscar® nominee, including nods for Best Director and Best Picture. Watching Micky come into his own as an individual within his dysfunctional family at long last is what gratifies most, his finally standing up for himself and letting loose pent-up, festering feelings making one rejoice far more than his knocking down of any opponent with yet another agonizingly-delayed, viscera-rearranging wallops. That was Ward's wont in both his personal life and pugilistic pursuits, taking what seemed like an eternity to rise up and take control of the situation, appearing to be no match for what he was up against before ultimately bursting forth with a decisiveness that he had up to that point given ample reason to believe was not in the offing. Observing this shy, soft-spoken man achieve some much-needed self-determination, successfully endeavoring to loosen (but not sever) the ties that detrimentally bind him to a clan of enervating, exasperating, motormouth pieces of work, will likely elicit an even more thoroughly thrilled "It's about time!" from viewers than his culminating title triumph over Shea Neary in 2000.

As this man who passively puts off confrontation and yet yearns to excel in brutal competition, Mark Wahlberg lays back and draws the audience in with a quiet magnetism. On the other hand, first-time Oscar® nominee Christian Bale threatens to dazzle that audience to a frazzle, almost spasming off the screen to grab those watching, with his showy, hyperkinetic, sometimes humorous, and, sadly, harrowingly-accurate depiction of Dicky Eklund, the elder half-brother who had preceded Micky into pugilism and became his childhood hero. Thus, when Dicky stresses that he and his sibling have distinctly different styles as fighters, the statement rings just as true for the aptly polar-opposite techniques employed by the actors who portray men who also possess manifestly-dissimilar personalities.

As it has been so often in life, Micky's showier sibling is the one commanding attention as *The Fighter* begins. Dicky is in the depths of delusion, once hailed as "The Pride of Lowell" after going the distance with Sugar Ray Leonard and now a manifestly-manic, cocaine-KO'd clownish caricature of what he once was and thinks he still is. He is sadly unable to pinpoint exactly how many years ago the highlight of his life occurred. Dicky's physique is emaciated, his eyes dart and pop and his half-goofy, half-unsettling, rotten-toothed smile would look perfect scrawled upon a Halloween pumpkin. He can at once be disarmingly dynamic and wince-inducingly tragic. Dicky comes off as a narcotically-addled narcissist as he struts through the streets of his Massachusetts home town thinking that the HBO cameras there to document his downfall are actually covering a pie-in-the-sky comeback he cannot stop jabbering on about. The film they are shooting is, however, not a fairy tale, but a cautionary one. Micky has a real fight coming up, but even as he walks along smiling with his boastful, beloved brother's arm around his shoulders, he is heavily recessed in the shadow of a spectacle.

It must have been tough for Micky to avoid feeling like a mere stand-in for Dicky, the family's second-best place marker until their once-and-supposedly-future star could stop training his kid brother and shine once again. It is all too clear in *The Fighter* that Dicky is the apple of his mother's eye, and that both of hers are astonishingly blind to the seriousness of his situation. One keeps thinking that it would help Micky if Alice (Oscar® nominee Melissa Leo) did not so incessantly crow how "my Dicky" taught Micky everything he knows, especially since the person she is praising keeps holding up his brother's fight preparations by holing up in a neighborhood crack house. Alice is a formidably-potent force of nature, often exhibiting a defiantly-glowering, sour expression and always sporting a hairstyle so thoroughly stiffened by hairspray that her chain smoking seems liable to not only cause cancer but a conflagration. As Micky's manager, she is sure she knows what is best, but when Alice (and Dicky) selfishly guilt him into proceeding with a clearly-inadvisable mismatch with a much bigger fill-in fighter (if he does not, it is pointed out, no one gets paid), the audience—along with Micky himself—can certainly not be blamed for having their doubts about her mothering abilities. Is it any wonder that Micky so often refers to her instead as "Alice"?

Russell provides viewers with a multitude of shots in which Micky is sighing and shaking his head in dismayed disbelief, holding his tongue and brooding about how he will ever be able to simply do what is best for him. Indispensable help arrives in the fetching form of Charlene Fleming (Oscar® nominee Amy Adams), a bartender with a mouth as salty as the rim of any margarita glass. How appropriate that this moxie-filled angel of mercy with the tattoo-revealing bare midriff excelled at high jumping in school, as she is the one who lends Micky the gumption he needs to get up and over what

dauntingly stands in his way. She lovingly leads him to a full recognition of the unavoidable truth: dutifully obeying his family's dictates was getting him nowhere. Charlene is that rare lady in Micky's life, one with an assuaging, keen interest in listening and learning what he thinks and feels. When he opens up to her, laying bare his disappointment, embarrassment, and frustration, it is deeply affecting. At times they ease into each other and convey a great deal through a shared gaze in utter silence, which is certainly in stark contrast to—and a blessed departure from—what is both familiar and familial. One of the film's most electrically charged (and highly amusing) scenes is the one in which Charlene, arm entwined with her man's with purposeful conspicuousness, boldly enters into hostile territory and faces off against—and gloriously mouths off to—a fundamentally-threatened Alice. Micky's tough cookie deliciously ends up giving even better than she gets when attacked by a snake pitfull of the matriarch's decidedly-inelegant, venomously-vituperative daughters.

Micky owes it to himself to grab onto a highly-promising opportunity to get paid year-round to train, but it is hard to do so with fingers that are bashed while getting in between his lunkheadedly afoul-of-the-law brother and the Lowell police. "I didn't do nothin'," Micky says after the cop who arrests him bashes his hand and potentially his hopes. However, "nothin'" is actually what he should have done instead of his ill-advised dutiful dash to rescue Dicky, something he was strenuously warned not to do by Charlene, his put-upon father, George Ward (highly-enjoyable Jack McGee), and new trainer, Sgt. Mickey O'Keefe (who plays himself in his acting debut). Thereafter, the state became his brother's keeper for a stretch, during which time the humiliating HBO expose airs and forcibly rips away every last carefully-clung-to vestige of both Alice's denial and Dicky's dissemblance. Movingly, the addict is able to see the painful truth about his life with a clarity he has not experienced in ages. Redemption can now begin. Dicky rising once and for all from amongst the smoky haze of burning crack and ashes of his self-immolated life makes for uplifting viewing. However, while he is shown pulling the plug on the prison's screening of his sad saga, Dicky has in reality been unable to stop its continuation since then with an arrest for cocaine possession as recently as 2006—not to mention a charge of assault and attempted murder in 2008.

In a real sense, Micky had also been imprisoned, and it is powerfully poignant when he finally and fully has his freeing say. He takes charge at last, aiming to properly put all his ducks in a row—even the daffiest ones. Micky rightfully feels that he, not Dicky, should currently and deservedly be the family's boxing focal point. He would just like his dreams to not be derailed or stifled but instead shared in by every last person around him who claims to care and want to help. "I thought you were my mother, too," is a statement that actually asks a question, and when a stunned and remorseful Alice embraces her weeping son, viewers will likely also have trouble maintaining composure.

Sports Illustrated heralded *The Fighter* as not only "the best sports movie of the decade," but one of the best of the last thirty years since Martin Scorsese's *Raging Bull* (1980). A dream project of producer/star Wahlberg about one of his heroes when he himself was growing up tough not too far away in Dorchester, this film was for years like a deciduous tree that perennially shed stars and directors like leaves. The actor's brother Donnie Wahlberg, Brad Pitt. and Matt Damon all reportedly fell away over time from the role of Dicky, and director Darren Aronofsky departed, as well. (An attempt was made to entice Scorsese at one point, but he politely declined to revisit the ring.) Russell, who has cinematically dealt with familial dysfunction before, was justly praised for his work here, which keeps the story alive and affecting with shifts between—and combinations of—things that are hellishly hard, humorous, and heartrending. By the 1990s, working class Lowell, like Dicky, had seen better days, and many noted the way Russell and cinematographer Hoyte Van Hoytema convincingly convey the wear and tear of economic decline.

Made on a budget of $25 million, *The Fighter* was a modest financial success but a much bigger critical one, and awards nominations started piling up. Critics especially sang the praises of Bale's extraordinary, transformative performance, for which the actor thinned both his physique (although not as drastically as his ghastly sixty-three pound weight loss for 2003's *The Machinist*) and his hair, and they understandably predicted Oscar® gold. However, Leo's dragon lady who figuratively breathes fire and literally blows cloud after cloud of smoke, as well as Adams' pleasingly-pugnacious departure, also deservedly garnered recognition. Last but not least, Wahlberg's tremendously sympathetic, largely-internal work as Ward was thankfully not overlooked. After all, nothing that transpires inside or outside the ring in *The Fighter,* even during the film's climactic underdog victory featuring the sight of everyone Micky loves the most both literally and figuratively in his corner, is as deeply gratifying to watch as the man's long-overdue unburdening.

David L. Boxerbaum

CREDITS

"Irish" Mickey Ward: Mark Wahlberg
Dickie Eklund: Christian Bale
Charlene: Amy Adams
Alice: Melissa Leo
George Ward: Jack McGee
Cathy "Pork" Eklund: Bianca Hunter
Cindy "Tar" Eklund: Erica McDermott
Sgt. Mickey O'Keefe: Himself
Origin: USA
Language: English
Released: 2010
Production: Ryan Kavanaugh, Todd Lieberman; Mandeville Films, Relativity Media; released by Paramount Pictures
Directed by: David O. Russell
Written by: Scott Silver, Paul Tamasy, Eric Johnson
Cinematography by: Hoyte Van Hoytema
Music by: Season Kent, Happy Walters
Sound: Odin Benitez
Editing: Pamela Martin
Art Direction: Laura Ballinger
Costumes: Mark Bridges
Production Design: Judy Becker
MPAA rating: R
Running time: 115 minutes

REVIEWS

Ansen, David. *Newsweek.* December 6, 2010.
Corliss, Richard. *TIME Magazine.* December 13, 2010.
Debruge, Peter. *Variety.* November 15, 2010.
Gleiberman, Owen. *Entertainment Weekly.* December 17, 2010.
Hornaday, Ann. *Washington Post.* December 17, 2010.
Lane, Anthony. *New Yorker.* December 20, 2010.
Morgenstern, Joe. *Wall Street Journal.* December 10, 2010.
Rainer, Peter. *Christian Science Monitor.* December 10, 2010.
Scott, A.O.. *New York Times.* December 9, 2010.
Torre, Pablo S.. *Sports Illustrated.* December 20, 2010.
Travers, Peter. *Rolling Stone.* December 9, 2010.
Turan, Kenneth. *Los Angeles Times.* December 10, 2010.
Wheat, Alynda. *People.* December 20, 2010.

QUOTES

Mickey Ward: "I'm the one who's fighting. Not you, not you, and not you."

TRIVIA

Melissa Leo was cast as the mother of Mark Wahlberg and Christian Bale's characters despite being only 11 and 14 years older than the two actors.

AWARDS

Oscars 2010: Support. Actor (Bale), Support. Actress (Leo)
Golden Globes 2011: Support. Actor (Bale), Support. Actress (Leo)

Screen Actors Guild 2010: Support. Actor (Bale), Support. Actress (Leo)

Nomination:

Oscars 2010: Director (Russell), Film, Film Editing, Orig. Screenplay, Support. Actress (Adams)

British Acad. 2010: Orig. Screenplay, Support. Actor (Bale), Support. Actress (Adams)

Directors Guild 2010: Director (Russell)

Golden Globes 2011: Actor—Drama (Wahlberg), Director (Russell), Film—Drama, Support. Actress (Adams)

Screen Actors Guild 2010: Support. Actress (Adams), Cast

Writers Guild 2010: Orig. Screenplay.

A FILM UNFINISHED

In 1942 the Nazi propaganda machine was hard at work. 70 years later, the deceit is finally unmasked.
—Movie tagline

Usually, but not always, when footage that has thought to have never existed suddenly surfaces, it is cause for either celebration, reflection or reexamination of history (or all three). Often, it is related to an artist's work, but every once in awhile, it is related to an already enormous historical document of great importance. Such is the case with *A Film Unfinished,* a documentary by Yael Hersonski, which encompasses new, never-before-seen footage of the Holocaust, both in black-and-white and, perhaps more startlingly, in color.

The discovered film in question is a soundless piece of Nazi propaganda simply titled "The Ghetto." The film was found in an underground vault along with hundreds of similar Nazi-based film reels, yet it distinguishes itself by being the one reel of film to depict the Jews in the Warsaw ghetto as living a peaceful existence, or so the Nazis would hope. The footage was shot not long before the atrocities would occur. The mystery then becomes: How does this help the Nazis? Why film it? Hersonski states (via narrator Rona Kenan), that the film would help the cause of Holocaust deniers and anyone who would defend the Third Reich. It has often been said that Hitler knew the power of cinema to help any cause, which is one of the reasons why he hired filmmaker Leni Riefenstahl to be his documentarian.

But Hersonski juxtaposes the newfound footage with other shots of the same Ghetto that showed the harsh realities. Among the scenes staged for "The Ghetto" are moments of Jews playing cards in a luxurious apartment, serving tea, and wearing nice clothes. There is even a scene of the inhabitants enjoying a lavish party in a ballroom, the flowers for which were actually taken from a graveyard just outside of town. Ac-

companying this footage is a diary of Adam Czerniakow, Chairman of the Judenrat in Warsaw (read by Janusz Hamerszmit), who was forced to help stage these scenes. Czerniakow kept an exhaustive diary of his role in the filming. There are also Holocaust survivors offering their input on the Ghetto footage and how they were sometimes beaten by the German filmmakers if they messed up a shot.

Until the 1960s, nobody knew who made this film. A lead was discovered on one document that traced back to a cameraman who went to great lengths to erase his involvement. The cameraman, Willy Wist, had since stopped making movies altogether and instead found work as a scrap metal merchant. He burned copies of the films he made during the war, but is the only one who has been exposed for helping to create them. A taped recording of Wist's testimony is heard wherein he claims that he had no idea what was in store for him when he got to the Ghetto, but that he had orders to just film it.

Along with Wist's testimony and Czerniakow's diary, *A Film Unfinished* also has readings from reports written by Heintz Auerswald, wherein he explains point blank his observations on the socio-economical conditions of the Ghetto. Furthermore, Dr. Emanuel Ringenblum, a historian, assembled many personal, secret journals that the Jews were encouraged to write during their time in the Ghetto. But perhaps the most revealing and startling footage found is that of staged events being filmed multiple times from multiple angles until the filmmakers were satisfied.

Gradually, as *A Film Unfinished* reveals more and more footage, it gets harder and harder to watch. Shots of circumcisions, Jews being led into steam baths and layers of corpses on the sidewalks are just a few of the harrowing images captured. The film shows take after take after take of Jews walking by corpses with their heads held high. The intent of "The Ghetto" film becomes clearer and clearer. The message the Nazis eventually wanted to send out to the world was that Jews live a life of luxury and they are ignorant of the horrors around them and often turn their noses up at them.

A Film Unfinished is an undeniably strong piece of work. Hersonski and Editor Joëlle Alexis take on the daunting task of assembling this footage into a cohesive narrative while underlining its importance. Hersonski employs re-enactments of Wist giving his testimony, but they are never obtrusive or distracting. They are beautifully photographed in dark shadows by cinematographer Itai Ne'eman, as are the shots of the survivors sitting in a theater watching the same footage.

While there does not seem to be any attempt to help make this particular story of the Holocaust relevant to present day times, it does send a clear message about the nature of media manipulation and trickery. Such practices are still employed today, albeit more subtly. Still, media outlets and politicians are careful to stay one step ahead of their opponents and critics. Hersonski never attempts to make this connection, which does the film a slight disservice. Nevertheless, *A Film Unfinished* shows and tells the viewer just enough in ninety minutes what this footage means and why the story of the Holocaust still matters.

Collin Souter

CREDITS

Narrator: Rona Kenan
Origin: Germany, Israel
Language: English, German, Hebrew, Polish, Yiddish
Released: 2010
Production: Noemi Schory, Itay Ken-Tor; Belfilms; released by Oscilloscope Laboratories
Directed by: Yael Heronski
Written by: Yael Heronski
Cinematography by: Itai Neeman
Music by: Ishai Adar
Sound: Aviv Aldema
Editing: Joelle Alexis
MPAA rating: Unrated
Running time: 88 minutes

REVIEWS

Barsanti, Chris. *Filmcritic.com.* August 19, 2010.
Burr, Ty. *Boston Globe.* September 23, 2010.
Catsoulis, Jeannette. *New York Times.* August 18, 2010.
Cole, Stephen. *Globe and Mail* September 24, 2010.
Hertz, Leba. *San Francisco Chronicle.* September 30, 2010.
McCarthy, Todd. *Variety.* July 6, 2010.
O'Sullivan, Michael. *Washington Post* September 24, 2010.
Rea, Steven. *Philadelphia Inquirer.* October 14, 2010.
Rodriguez, Rene. *Miami Herald.* November 4, 2010.
Schwarzbaum, Lisa. *Entertainment Weekly.* August 11, 2010.

FISH TANK

Live, love and give as good as you get.
—Movie tagline

Every year it seems that a new talent or fresh face will come along to help break up the monotony of all the pre-packaged "yes" men yelling action and magazine cover models passing as actors. *Fish Tank* wastes no time in providing viewers with two. Katie Jarvis, reportedly discovered while having a public argument, announces her presence with authority right up front ridiculing some wannabe dancers gyrating their bodies without an ounce of soul behind it. Thanks for highlighting this discovery goes to writer/director Andrea Arnold who has already established herself with her Oscar®-winning short, *Wasp* (2003) and Cannes Jury Prize winning feature, *Red Road* (2006), but with *Fish Tank* confirms a major talent that needs to be paid attention by more than just those handing out trophies.

Fifteen-year-old Mia (Jarvis) lives in the public housing projects of Essex. School is off the table because of her attitude and her days are spent sneaking off to empty rooms to practice her dance moves. When she does come home it is to a cacophony of swearing and insults between herself, little sister Tyler (Rebecca Griffiths), and mother (Kierston Wareing), each appearing to invade a space they would rather have just to themselves. Welcomed into this domain though—at least by mom—is handsome new boyfriend, Connor (Michael Fassbender).

He does not look upon Mia as an adversary. Instead, like any new addition to an established household, he tries to win her favor by playing to her guarded level and slowly bringing her to trust him. Sensing someone willing to talk to her rather than scream at her, Mia is drawn to Connor's potential as a regular addition to her family, somewhat unaware that further feelings may be stirring in her. When he gives her a piggy-back ride and she rests her head on his shoulders is it merely her first touch of a real man or the longing for a father figure she has spent her whole life missing? Their relationship will be tested throughout as Mia begins opening herself up to experiences other than her daily routine and Connor's connection to the home becomes further complicated.

These are characters not prone to plotting their next move or reacting from hidden agendas. They live from moment-to-moment and it is impossible to cement a label on their moral intentions. Mia is most definitely the pursuer; that of her own dancing dreams providing an escape and her feelings towards Connor. He is seen as a positive influence in every aspect of her life (the house is cleaner, mom is less vocal) and we become too busy appreciating Mia's change in attitude that it is easy to neglect how her feelings are going to come out on the other end. In the beginning, Mia is presented as the symbolic counterpart to a chained-up horse she once tried to set free; dancing amidst a wallpaper of palm trees and sunsets. Connor treats her like some wild mare, carefully gaining her trust so as not to scare her away and as Arnold shows us a flock of birds changing direction, there is hope that Mia is going to find her way.

Katie Jarvis announces her presence with authority right up front, berating a group of wannabes in the street for their lackluster dance moves; unafraid to be one against the world. Looking like a prizefighter with her grey hoodie, there is never a moment on screen when she is not in the center ring. Fassbender shows considerable charm here and real movie star appeal but it is Jarvis' face that registers most effectively. Her front of anger projected at anyone within earshot gives way to vulnerability that greater reflects that she is still a young girl. "You're what's wrong with me," Mia shouts at her mother perhaps projecting a flash of her own future. As she thaws to a potential brighter one, the betrayal she discovers of her skills reduced to an object fantasy is hopefully not the one which will define the future of the actress playing her, because this is the introduction of a promising career indeed.

Fish Tank is the equivalent of the female *What's Eating Gilbert Grape?* (1993) minus the quirky characters. A rawer and less glamorized coming-of-age tale than last year's *An Education* (2009), Andrea Arnold is more interested in tales of her own backyard where glitz does not offer a holiday and most roads appear to be abandoned territory. As she did with *Red Road*, Arnold offers a view of only one corner of the world where reconciliation and potential sexual predatory converge. The heroines of both films resort to rash schemes to expose their tormentors and provide a kind of everyday suspense where people worth caring about get in over their heads. Mia's moves as a dancer are not the sort to garner attention from professionals, nor is that the point; those shown by both Jarvis and Arnold are far more impressive and build to an emotional catharsis that actually makes the viewer smile as he or she leaves them to whatever their next move might be.

Erik Childress

CREDITS

Connor: Michael Fassbender
Billy: Harry Treadway
Mia Williams: Katie Jarvis
Joanne: Kierston Wareing
Tyler: Rebecca Griffiths
Keira: Sydney Mary Nash
Liam: Jason Maza
Origin: United Kingdom
Language: English
Released: 2009
Production: Kees Kasander, Nick Laws; BBC Films, U.K. Film Council, Limelight; released by IFC Films

Directed by: Andrea Arnold
Written by: Andrea Arnold
Cinematography by: Robbie Ryan
Sound: Joachim Sundstrom
Music Supervisor: Liz Gallacher
Editing: Nicolas Chaudeurge
Art Direction: Christopher Wyatt
Costumes: Jane Petrie
Production Design: Helen Scott
MPAA rating: Unrated
Running time: 123 minutes

REVIEWS

Bradshaw, Peter. *The Guardian.* May 15, 2009.
Ebert, Roger. *Chicago Sun-Times.* February 3, 2010.
Edelstein, David. *New York Magazine.* January 11, 2010.
Fine, Marshall. *Hollywood & Fine.* January 11, 2010.
Johanson, Mary Ann. *Flick Filosopher.* March 9, 2010.
Morgenstern, Joe. *Wall Street Journal.* January 22, 2010.
O'Hehir, Andrew. *Salon.com.* January 13, 2010.
Phillips, Michael. *Chicago Tribune.* February 4, 2010.
Scott, A.O. *New York Times.* January 15, 2010.
Tallerico, Brian. *MovieRetriever.com.* February 5, 2010.

QUOTES

Mia: "Can you give Keeley a message for me? Tell her I think her old man's a cunt!"

TRIVIA

Katie Jarvis was cast in the lead role of Mia after the casting director spotted her fighting with her boyfriend in a train station.

FOR COLORED GIRLS

Many voices. One poem.
—Movie tagline

Box Office: $38 million

Film and theater are two distinct mediums. The forms have found themselves more intertwined over the years as successful theatrical productions have been adapted into features and vice versa, but the fact is that they have different strengths and weaknesses. On occasion, a brilliant piece of theater can make it to the screen with its dramatic power intact (*Glengarry Glen Ross* [1992], *Chicago* [2002]), but more often the transition merely serves to amplify the fact that not every powerful play makes a powerful film. The latest such example can be found in writer/director Tyler Perry's *For Colored Girls,* an adaptation of Ntozake Shange's powerful choreopoem *For Colored Girls Who Have Considered*

Suicide When the Rainbow is Enuf, a landmark theater event in 1974. Despite a few strong performances in the hit-and-miss ensemble, it is clear why it took almost four decades and several aborted attempts by other filmmakers to get Shange's work committed to celluloid. While it retains some of the inherent power of its source merely because it would be difficult not to, Perry never finds the narrative cohesion necessary to be one of those stand-out stage-to-screen adaptations.

On stage, *For Colored Girls* was merely a series of monologues or poems—confessions, life lessons, inner thoughts, and personal stories from a group of women who felt like they were finding their voice for the first time. The immediacy of a choreopoem in which the audience is directly addressed by the emotionally-charged actress often just a few feet in front of them simply cannot be replicated by the colder process of filmmaking. Recognizing this, Perry has taken the structure of *For Colored Girls* and deconstructed it, taking several of the characters and pieces from Shange's work and crafting them into an intertwined narrative, adding other roles, relationships, and a few dramatic twists in an attempt to not only turn theater into film but turn poetry into prose. Perry's piece too often gets caught in the gray area in between the multiple forms he has tried to weave into one piece. The seams are simply too unrefined.

For Colored Girls tells the nine interconnected stories of Crystal (Kimberly Elise), Jo (Janet Jackson), Juanita (Loretta Devine), Tangie (Thandie Newton), Yasmine (Anika Noni Rose), Kelly (Kerry Washington), Nyla (Tessa Thompson), Gilda (Phylicia Rashad), and Alice (Whoopi Goldberg). All of the characters are either directly related or through minimal degrees of separation. For example, Alice is the mother of Nyla and Tangie, who lives across the hall from Crystal, who works for Jo, and so on. Crystal has a horribly-abusive husband. Tangie is aggressively promiscuous. Yasmine trusts the wrong man. Jo has fallen into a loveless marriage with a man who happens to be homosexual. Every character in *For Colored Girls* comes with a significant, life-changing drama. Perry's film touches on physical abuse, murder, rape, addiction, possible insanity, promiscuity, abortion, homosexuality, and more. There is enough melodrama in *For Colored Girls* for an entire season of most television soap operas.

The melodramatic structure of Perry's film ends up being its biggest drawback. With so many emotionally-charged plotlines, the mega-successful writer/director is forced to insert another draining dramatic scene nearly every five minutes. Hearing about the pain of life through monologue is much different than seeing it visualized on film. It gets numbing as it becomes clear that each moment of intense pain will be followed by another in just a few minutes. And it creates an odd structure in that each connecting scene loses power by virtue of merely being a way to push the audience to another manipulative moment. It borders on emotional pornography with the sex scenes of the adult genre replaced by tears. Life undeniably and tragically turns out like it does in *For Colored Girls* (even darker, actually) for some women, but it lessens the film's relation to the spectrum of life to merely be presented with the melodrama of it.

Luckily for everyone involved, there are a few actresses in *For Colored Girls* who find the humanity beneath the heartstring-pulling. Anika Noni Rose (*Dreamgirls* [2006]) and Kimberly Elise (*Diary of a Mad Black Woman* [2005]) are both stellar, finding complete honesty in their complex roles. Tyler Perry is often critically-derided, but his theatrical background has given him an underrated skill with actresses such as Taraji P. Henson (great in *I Can Do Bad All by Myself* [2009]) and Angela Bassett (*Meet the Browns* [2008]). In fact, Perry stumbles the most as a filmmaker when he eschews an actual actress and casts himself in the Madea films. Here, Rose, Elise, Thandie Newton, and Phylicia Rashad can be added to the list of quality Perry performances that fail to get the praise they deserve.

Sadly, each of the excellent performances in *For Colored Girls* has a counterpart that falls flat, although usually due to a script that never allows a character to gain realistic traction. Elise and Rose found a way to make it work but Jackson, Goldberg, Washington, and Devine distinctly did not. And the men, including Omari Hardwick, Michael Ealy, and Hill Harper, are purely plot devices. They are simply there to make the monologues feel less theatrical.

For Colored Girls is part-theater piece, part-poem, and part-melodrama while being proof that multiple parts can often fail to form a cohesive whole. Elise and Rose nearly save the film but the question has to become if anyone could have done more with a piece of theater that never supported the transition from stage to screen. It is impossible to say if a filmmaker other than Tyler Perry could have made it work, but we know that this version does not.

Brian Tallerico

CREDITS

Joanna/Red: Janet Jackson
Juanita/Green: Loretta Devine
Crystal/Brown: Kimberly Elise
Tangie/Orange: Thandie Newton
Yasmine/Yellow: Anika Noni Rose
Nyla/Purple: Tessa Thompson

Kelly/Blue: Kerry Washington

Alice/White: Whoopi Goldberg

Gilda: Phylicia Rashad

Rose: Macy Gray

Beau Willie: Michael Ealy

Carl: Omari Hardwick

Origin: USA

Language: English

Released: 2010

Production: Paul Hall, Roger M. Bobb; Tyler Perry Studios, 34th Street Films; released by Lionsgate

Directed by: Tyler Perry

Written by: Tyler Perry, Frederique Gruyer

Cinematography by: Alexander Grusynski

Music by: Aaron Zigman

Sound: Damian Canelos

Music Supervisor: Joel High

Editing: Maysie Hoy

Art Direction: Roswell Hamrick

Costumes: Johnetta Boone

Production Design: Ina Mayhew

MPAA rating: R

Running time: 134 minutes

REVIEWS

Adams, Thelma. *Us Weekly.* November 3, 2010.
Anderson, Melissa. *Village Voice.* November 2, 2010.
Dargis, Manohla. *New York Times.* November 5, 2010.
Ebert, Roger. *Chicago Sun-Times.* November 4, 2010.
Gonzalez, Ed. *Slant Magazine.* October 29, 2010.
Phipps, Keith. *AV Club.* November 4, 2010.
Pols, Mary F. *TIME Magazine.* November 4, 2010.
Rich, Katey. *CinemaBlend.com.* November 4, 2010.
Rickey, Carrie. *Philadelphia Inquirer.* November 4, 2010.
Schwarzbaum, Lisa. *Entertainment Weekly.* November 3, 2010.

QUOTES

Juanita: "I got a real dead loving here for you now, because I don't know anymore how to avoid my own face wet with my tears! Because I had convinced myself that colored girls have no right to sorrow!"

TRIVIA

This is the first R-rated film directed by Tyler Perry.

FOUR LIONS

Four Lions is a deft comic balancing act. With seeming ease, co-writer/director Chris Morris examines the causes, players, and effects of terrorism, planned and perpetrated by a quintet of men who claim Islam as their religion and whose incompetence is limitless. Their motives are shady at best, rallying in incoherent vitriol against "Zionism," "capitalism," "consumerism," "moderates," and a slew of other targets of buzz words individually and, in imaginatively conspiratorial ways, collectively. At one point, Barry (Nigel Lindsay), a convert to Islam whose rage is the greatest of the group, claims, "Jews invented spark plugs to control global traffic," when his car (which he himself repaired) breaks down.

The sentiment of that statement and others like it in the film exists in the world; it is without any kind of logic based in reality but makes perfect sense in the mind of people like Barry. Morris and co-screenwriters Jesse Armstrong and Sam Bain accept all of these components in the creation of their characters and commit an act of *reductio ad absurdum* on their arguments for committing atrocities and, to a certain extent, their very existence. They are living only to die violently with bombs strapped to their chests, hoping to kill as many people as possible in doing so. The end result, in their minds, is a "fast pass" to Heaven—a comparison to a theme park made by the group's de facto leader Omar (Riz Ahmed). "Would you rather be in the queue or on the rides," he asks Waj (Kayvan Novak), the most simple-minded of the crew, who bases his knowledge of Islam on the content of a children's book. Whether he has actually read it or not is left open to debate.

The film opens (after Waj's failed attempt to make a pre-emptive video statement about an attack, using a toy assault rifle and misunderstanding the concept of forced perspective to make it appear larger) with Omar and Waj about to join a terrorist training camp in Pakistan to become "proper mujahideen." Meanwhile, Barry recruits Hassan (Arsher Ali), a college student who performs a prank bombing (confetti explodes from his belt) at a community town hall meeting where Barry is a participant on the panel, to join him and Faisal (Adeel Akhtar) in preparing real explosives for an attack.

They are all helpless and hopeless (with the exception of Omar—which is why he is their leader, by default). Waj mistakes chickens for rabbits, and Omar easily befuddles him into believing his brain is his heart when he has doubts about the morality of killing himself to kill others. Hassan, when not rapping about *jihad* in painfully simple rhyming schemes, is most upset about having to repeat a class and later dances with an absentminded neighbor (Julia Davis) in the room where the group is building their bombs. Faisal buys a garage-full of bleach from the same store, using different voices to disguise himself (his own, an impression of a member of the Irish Republican Army, and a woman, despite his beard), and he rigs a crow with explosives in an attempt to train it to take his place in any upcoming attack. Whenever one of his comrades-in-arms points a camera at him, Faisal quickly tosses a cardboard box over his head to avoid the possibility of identification.

Barry, meanwhile, envisions a plan to blow up a local mosque, believing it would incite moderates to violence and bring about the "end of days" (which he believes is near, since there are "women talking back" and "people playing stringed instruments"). Despite his insistence on their ultimate wrong-headed goal, Omar serves as the relative voice of reason here, explaining that Barry's plan is like the losing party in a fistfight punching himself in the face in a futile attempt to win. It is a funny line, and then Morris and company take it one step further, forcing Barry to argue his case for attacking Muslims by literally executing Omar's metaphor. His resulting bloody nose does not hinder him from making a video statement claiming responsibility ahead of time for a hypothetical mosque bombing.

Their motivations are detached from religion. Omar's brother Ahmed (Wasim Zakir), a fundamentalist in traditional clothing who refuses to enter Omar's home as long as his brother's wife Sophia (Preeya Kalidas) is in the same room, cites opinions from scholars on the repudiation of violence and warns his brother to heed that wisdom. Barry decries the mosques as breeding grounds for "spies" that have lost their way, scolding Hassan for attending at all. In removing Islam directly from the equation, Morris instead forces the audience to examine these men in a clear light, with fresh eyes.

Most disquieting is Omar's relationship with his family. Sophia and their son Mahmood (Mohammad Aqil) know Omar's plan to achieve martyrdom. Mahmood jokes that his face will be in Heaven "before his head hits the ceiling." When in doubt, after Faisal accidentally detonates himself in an attempt to transport explosive materials (the survivors debate whether or not he attained martyrdom and, if not, who to blame or, if so, who to congratulate), Sophia and Mahmood enliven his spirits. It is his duty to ensure that the remaining squad blow themselves up properly. Omar tries to pass on his philosophy to his son by using the moral certainty of the story of *The Lion King* (1994) to explain his actions at the camp in Pakistan (though he must change the plot to fit his devastating error). The scenes are simultaneously funny and unsettling in the way the characters treat the entire scenario as an everyday, ordinary concern.

Morris accomplishes a similar tone in the observation of law enforcement, who are also, in their own way, inept, stressing their ineffectiveness through their proclivity to racially profile. Despite having security footage of Faisal prematurely detonating a crow, the police raid Ahmed's home, because—the only discernable reason—he has the outward appearance of a

Muslim. The concept of profiling is also taken to ridiculous extreme at the London Marathon, the site of Omar, Barry, Waj, and Hassan's planned strike, where the participants are dressed in costume. A pair of snipers learns their target is a bear. They pass over Omar, dressed as a bright orange, furry mascot for a cereal, for man dressed as a Wookiee. Later, another squad shoots Waj's hostage in a kabob shop, because he also happens to be of Arab descent. They are innocent victims killed simply because they look a certain way.

The climax of the film at the marathon alone is a delicate feat. Continuing the handling of the fanatical protagonists without any respect, ultimately, Morris treats the effects of terrorism with solemnity. There are flashes of irreverence (the bear debate and a haplessly helpful man who tries to save Barry with the Heimlich maneuver only to trigger his bomb), but in the end, the sober reality *Four Lions* presents is clear: snicker at the fools they may be, but even these idiots still have the capability of getting the last laugh.

Mark Dujsik

CREDITS

Omar: Rizwan Ahmed
Waj: Kayvan Novak
Faisal: Adeel Akhtar
Barry: Nigel Lindsay
Hassan: Arsher Ali
Sofia: Preeya Kalidas
Alice: Julia Davis
Ahmed: Wasim Zakir
Mahmood: Mohammad Aqil
Origin: United Kingdom
Language: English
Released: 2010
Production: Mark Herbert, Derrin Schlesinger; Film4, Wild Bunch, Warp Films, Optimum Releasing; released by Drafthouse Films
Directed by: Christopher Morris
Written by: Jesse Armstrong, Christopher Morris, Sam Bain
Cinematography by: Lol Crawley
Editing: Billy Sneddon
Music by: Phil Canning
Sound: Darren Banks
Art Direction: Julie Ann Horan
Costumes: Charlotte Walter
Production Design: Dick Lunn
MPAA rating: R
Running time: 97 minutes

REVIEWS

Burr, Ty. *Boston Globe*. November 5, 2010.
Kennedy, Lisa. *Denver Post*. November 26, 2010.

Lewis, David. *San Francisco Chronicle.* November 12, 2010.
Phillips, Michael. *Chicago Tribune.* November 12, 2010.
Rabin, Nathan. *AV Club.* November 4, 2010.
Roberts, Rex. *Film Journal International.* November 4, 2010.
Schager, Nick. *Slant Magazine.* October 31, 2010.
Scott, A.O. *New York Times.* November 4, 2010.
Stevens, Dana. *Slate.* November 11, 2010.
Zachaerk, Stephanie. *Movieline.* November 3, 2010.

QUOTES

Hassan: "I'm a martyr, you're all squashed tomatoes."

TRIVIA

The UK "terror threat" level was raised to "severe" due to non-specific "chatter" the same day of the premiere of *Four Lions.*

AWARDS

Nomination:

British Acad. 2010: Alexander Korda Award.

FRANKIE & ALICE

Turn back, look forward.
—Movie tagline

The list of character and narrative ingredients in *Frankie & Alice* reads like an Oscar®-bait game of Mad Libs—a stripper with multiple personalities, plus infanticide, racial tension, and psychiatric breakthrough, all based on a true story—so of course it is not too surprising that Halle Berry, who won a Best Actress Academy Award® for *Monster's Ball* (2001), headlines *Frankie & Alice,* a decently executed but fairly transparent star vehicle and psychological drama based on the harrowing life events of Frankie Murdoch, a woman suffering from multiple personality disorder in early 1970s Los Angeles.

The film opens with Frankie (Berry), a go-go dancer, shaking her backside in a gold lamé skirt and halter top in a cage suspended high up the air, teasing extra dollars out of the clientele by wriggling out of her underwear only to then reveal an extra pair. Moments later, she is backstage working deep into a crossword puzzle, and offering advice to the club's new girl on how to effectively compartmentalize her personal and private lives. After an abortive romantic rendezvous with the club's deejay, Frankie experiences a mental breakdown, and winds up in the middle of the street.

She is taken to a hospital, where Dr. Joe Oswald (Stellan Skarsgård), a kindly, unconventional and somewhat scatterbrained psychiatrist, conducts a basic examination but is forced to discharge her. After later showing up and causing a scene at the wedding of socialite Paige Prescott (Emily Tennant), however, Frankie voluntarily commits herself, and submits to the somewhat quirky care of Dr. Oswald. In talking with Frankie about these frequent blackout spells, he quickly ascertains that she might have multiple personalities and, even discovering that the Everly Brothers' "Bye Bye Love" is an aural trigger, Dr. Oswald sets out to coax signed "contracts" of treatment with each of what turn out to be Frankie's two other identities.

The additionally peculiar rub is that besides a genius-level child persona, Frankie's other personality, Alice, is a racist Southern belle. Dr. Oswald solicits more information from Frankie's mother, Edna (Phylicia Rashad), and sister, Maxine (Chandra Wilson), but receives little cooperation. Trying to push Frankie toward healthful reintegration without triggering the Alice persona to take over, he eventually uncovers the source of Frankie's trauma—a clandestine teenage relationship involving Pete (Scott Lyster), Paige's brother.

Despite its fairly intense subject matter, the movie retains a fatalistic and sometimes surprising streak of dark humor that serves it well. Frankie is not presented as a raving lunatic, but rather a weary woman who is trying to come to terms with a disease she of course does not completely understand. When Dr. Oswald, attempting to console Frankie after delivering his diagnosis and explaining his course of treatment, tells her that she is not alone, Frankie takes a drag on her cigarette before cracking a smile and replying, "Well, no shit." There are also a couple double entendres involving Ding-Dongs, a confectionary treat to which Frankie is partial.

Still, the much-labored over screenplay (in taking nearly a decade to wind its way to the screen, an astounding six writers share screenplay credit, and another two different scribes net story recognition) has trouble cracking the spine of the racial conflict and bigotry at the center of Frankie's splintering into multiples. The film's grand revelation, in the form of a much-teased flashback, centers on a forbidden love affair between a teenage Frankie (Vanessa Morgan) and Pete, but all the other social factors that inform this predicament are shunted off to the side, and packed away.

Furthermore, the movie's ending, while pointing the audience in an emotionally satisfying direction with Stevie Wonder's bopping, upbeat "Higher Ground" and a textual coda that neatly wraps things up, sidesteps the hard lift of Frankie's familial reconciliation with Edna and Maxine. One reasonably presumes this would be a huge part of any treatment of multiple personality disorder, so its absence in turn feels like a colossal copout.

In an effort to compensate for a fairly meager budget that effectively hampers any large-scale period piece production design work by Linda Del Rosario and Richard Paris, director Geoffrey Sax leans more heavily on vintage hairstyles, costumes, and musical choices to try to convincingly convey the era. Likewise, cinematographer Newton Thomas Sigel—whose work has encompassed everything from high-end commercial product to more quirky, character-based films—reaches into his deep bag of professional tricks to come up with saturated film stocks and different looks in the movie's copious flashbacks, laboring intensely to create lines of demarcation between the past, the present inside the hospital, and the present outside the hospital. All of this works, up to a certain point, but also unfortunately serves to highlight, by comparison, the deficiencies within the story's telling.

Much can be written or said about Berry's performance, and some might attempt to dismiss the film out of hand by characterizing her work as at times a bit over-the-top, especially when she slips into the scared "Genius" persona. Point-blank, such criticism comes almost across-the-board from those with no working knowledge of borderline or split personality disorders, and it seems credible that splintering would in fact result in more affected tones and behaviors. In this respect, Berry captures the creeping confusion of someone beset with mental instability, but scared to put a name to it.

Either way, however one parses the drama, it cannot deeply be argued that anything other than the two lead performances are at the heart of *Frankie & Alice*. While Berry undeniably has the showcase role, Skarsgård is a delight as Dr. Oswald, communicating the awakened impulses of someone who is both professionally fascinated by this unique case study in front of him, and also moved to help as a human being. What most works about *Frankie & Alice* are their delightful scenes and the connection they share, as well as a sense that Frankie and Dr. Oswald are truly working the problem together, not as the afflicted party and someone treating her with knowledge-from-on-high.

Brent Simon

CREDITS

Frankie Murdoch: Halle Berry
Dr. Joseph "Oz" Oswald: Stellan Skarsgard
Edna Murdoch: Phylicia Rashad
Maxine Murdoch: Chandra Wilson
Clifton: Adrian Holmes
Dr. Warren Backman: Brian Markinson
Annabelle Prescott: Christine Schild

Paige (16 years old): Emily Tennant
Bobby: James Kirk
Paige (8 years old): Megan Carpentier
Dr. Strassfield: Matt Frewer
Frankie (16 years old): Vanessa Morgan
Pete: Scott Lyster
Origin: Canada
Language: English
Released: 2010
Production: Vincent Cirrincione, Simon DeKaric, Halle Berry, Hassain Zaidi; Access Motion Picture Group, Cinesavvy; released by Freestyle Releasing
Directed by: Geoffrey Sax
Written by: Cheryl Edwards, Marko King, Mary King, Jonathan Watters, Steve Blair
Cinematography by: Newton Thomas (Tom) Sigel
Music by: Andrew Lockington
Sound: Gord Anderson
Editing: David Richardson
Costumes: Ruth E. Carter
Production Design: Linda Del Rosario, Richard Paris
MPAA rating: R
Running time: 100 minutes

REVIEWS

Berkshire, Geoff. *Metromix.com.* December 9, 2010.
Brevet, Brad. *RopeofSilicon.com.* December 16, 2010.
Clifford, Laura. *Reeling Reviews.* January 24, 2011.
Debruge, Peter. *Variety.* November 18, 2010.
Granger, Susan. *SSG Syndicate.* January 19, 2011.
Hazelton, John. *Screen International.* December 11, 2010.
Levy, Emanuel. *EmanuelLevy.com.* December 21, 2010.
Orange, Michelle. *Movieline.* December 8, 2010.
Schwarzbaum, Lisa. *Entertainment Weekly.* December 1, 2010.
Travers, Peter. *Rolling Stone.* December 17, 2010.

QUOTES

Edna Murdoch: "I've always tried to do the best I could for Frankie. I've only done what was right!"

AWARDS

Nomination:

Golden Globes 2011: Actress—Drama (Berry).

FREAKONOMICS

Six rogue filmmakers explore the hidden side of everything.
—Movie tagline

Freakonomics is the first of its kind: an anthology film made up of five different documentaries from five different directors. The anthology format has almost always made for an uneven viewing experience. Some of the short films in the piece work, some do not. *Paris, je t'aime* (2007) seems to be the only example thus far of an anthology film that worked for almost all of its running time. For an anthology documentary to be artistically successful, the subjects have to have a unifying theme, in this case, the ways in which incentives for financial gain can alter human behavior, for better or for worse. The six filmmakers are accomplished and well-suited to the material. The film is based on the best-selling book *Freakonomics: A Rogue Economist Explores the Hidden Side of Everything* by economist Steven D. Levitt and journalist Stephen J. Dubner, who also appear in the film.

It opens with Levitt and Dubner explaining their thesis and how their bestseller came to be, using a real estate scheme as an example of how sellers do not make as much on a commission as a buyer is led to believe, but who must appear as though they do. This is the first of many sidebar sequences in the film that appear sandwiched between two larger pieces. The sidebars are directed by Seth Gordon and employ much in the way of animation. Other subjects include reasons why a teacher might help students cheat on a test and how ice cream was once thought to be a major cause of polio. These mini-segments are enjoyable enough, with Levitt and Dubner driving the commentary along.

The first major short film is *A Roshanda by Any Other Name,* from Morgan Spurlock, whose engaging personality and keen sense of the absurd helped make *Super Size Me* (2004) truly memorable and worth repeat viewings. Here, Spurlock looks at some of the potential side effects of naming a child. One example shows a woman who wanted to name her child Tempest, but misspelled it "Temptress." The child ended up living up to that name and being very promiscuous. Another parent named his first child "Winner" and his second child "Loser." The boys each led lifestyles that were the complete opposite of their namesakes (Loser went to college while Winner went to prison). But Spurlock points out that giving your child a predominantly African American name can alter their chances of landing a first-rate job. One notable experiment yielded a result in which men who had names such as Greg were more likely to get a phone call from a prospective employer over someone with a name like Tyrone.

With *Pure Corruption,* Alex Gibney takes on the subject of sumo wrestling and how the purity on-stage bares no resemblance to the backroom deals and thievery that takes place behind-the-scenes. Sumo wrestling has religious overtones to it in terms of the rigorous training and its spiritual nature. It is taken very seriously on that level, but Gibney finds a mafia-like lawlessness behind the curtain. Among other ways of cheating, those who train together have been known to throw their games in order to help a fellow wrestler get ahead.

Eugene Jarecki's *It's Not Always a Wonderful Life* focuses on Levitt's research in the area of crime and how certain sociological changes helped affect the crime rates in America. Perhaps the most notable finding in Levitt's studies was how the Roe v. Wade Supreme Court ruling which legalized abortion ultimately affected the crime rate in America. Because of the legalization, women in impoverished parts of the country had fewer kids who would eventually go on to lead a life of crime. The long-term effects of Roe v. Wade would be felt twenty years later in the 1990s.

Finally, with *Can aA 9th Grader Be Bribed to Succeed?,* directors Heidi Ewing and Rachel Grady turn their cameras toward the Chicago Public School system and how an experiment by the University of Chicago helped failing students get better grades by paying them a certain amount of money every time they had an above average report card. Each student gets $50 a month to keep their grades up and maybe even a ride home in a stretch limo Hummer if they go above and beyond. For some students, the experiment is a success and shows that money can buy graduation. Others simply give up and accept the idea of never graduating. This particular segment has echoes of another documentary from 2010, Davis Guggenheim's *Waiting For "Superman."*

Freakonomics is, as one might expect, a mixed bag. Spurlock's is the most entertaining and most focused piece on delivering alarming facts with a humorous edge. Gibney's sumo wrestling film tends to meander a bit, trying to make several points at once. Jarecki's is the least successful. The use of Frank Capra's *It's a Wonderful Life* as a counter-point to the subject of crime seems only half thought out and Melvin Van Peebles is hardly the most engaging narrator. Ewing and Grady's film is solid enough, although of the four, it seems like the one that would benefit the most from a full-length feature treatment. Its characters are interesting and worth following around a bit longer.

The main problem with *Freakonomics* as a whole is that it does not feel grounded in anything. Levitt and Dubner, who often come off as a bit snide and self-satisfied, are on hand to explain why they found these items fascinating enough to spend a year researching and writing about them, but the end result feels like channel surfing during an episode of *60 Minutes*. Certainly, there are enough interesting facts and topics here to warrant a viewing out of curiosity, but once it ends, the viewer is left wondering what one is supposed to do with all this new information.

Collin Souter

CREDITS

Narrator: Melvin Van Peebles

Origin: USA

Language: English

Released: 2010

Production: Chad Troutwine, Dan O'Meara, Chris Romano; Cold Fusion Media, Green Films Co.; released by Magnolia Pictures

Directed by: Seth Gordon, Morgan Spurlock, Alex Gibney, Eugene Jarecki, Rachel Grady, Heidi Ewing

Written by: Seth Gordon, Morgan Spurlock, Alex Gibney, Eugene Jarecki, Jeremy Chilnick, Peter Bull

Cinematography by: Bradford Whitaker, Daniel Marracino, Darren Lew, Junji Aoki, Ferne Pearlstein, Tony Hardmon, Rob Vanalkemade

Music by: Jon Spurney, Peter Nashel, Pete Miser, Paul Brill

Sound: Brian Fish, Bill Chesley

Editing: Luis Lopez, Tova Goodman, Sloane Klevin, Doug Blush, Michael Taylor

MPAA rating: PG-13

Running time: 86 minutes

REVIEWS

Anderson, John. *Variety.* May 3, 2010.

Burr, Ty. *Boston Globe.* September 30, 2010.

Corliss, Richard. *TIME Magazine.* October 2, 2010.

Douglas, Edward. *comingsoon.net.* September 28, 2010.

Gleiberman, Owen. *Entertainment Weekly.* September 29, 2010.

Kois, Dan. *Village Voice.* September 28, 2010.

Lockerby, Loey. *Kansas City Star.* October 8, 2010.

Robinson, Tasha. *AV Club.* September 30, 2010.

Rodriguez, Rene. *Miami Herald.* October 20, 2010.

Sobczynski, Peter. *eFilmcritic.com.* October 1, 2010.

THE FREEBIE

A one night experiment in infidelity.
—Movie tagline

Actress Katie Aselton has been associated with the independent film movement known as "mumblecore" through both her appearance in the highly-acclaimed *The Puffy Chair* (2005) and her marriage to one of the most recognizable faces of the subgenre, Mark Duplass (director of *Cyrus* [2010], star of *Humpday* [2009]), with whom she co-stars on FX's *The League* (2009-2010). As Aselton's star continued to rise, she took a chance by sitting in the director's chair for the semi-successful *The Freebie,* well-intentioned, interesting character study about planned infidelity. The final product makes it clear that Aselton knows how to work with actors, drawing the best performance yet from the underrated Dax Shepard, but that she still has some work to do when it comes to fleshing out a subject to

the length of a feature film. With drastic tone changes and character behavior that does not feel quite genuine, *The Freebie* often feels like a work-in-progress; there are things to like about said work, but it is not quite complete.

The Freebie raises the interesting point that it is the very act of infidelity not the lying or betrayal often associated with it that could tear a couple apart. Darren (Shepard) and Annie (Aselton) are a happy couple with few problems. As people often do, they have become so busy with everyday life (not to mention their love of ending the day with crossword puzzles instead of coitus) to maintain a healthy sex life. When they discover that is has been months since they last had sex, the two come up with a plan that nearly anyone would know is a very bad idea—they will each have a free night to do whatever they choose with whomever they choose. The idea is that they will come back with their sexual spark renewed and ready to light their own relationship on fire. Of course, they agree to ask no questions before or after and the mystery surrounding what exactly happened on the night of the "freebie" eats the couple alive. Darren wonders why Annie came home at six in the morning. Annie wonders how far Darren went and why he seems so depressed. In her smartest move, Aselton does not show the audience the key events. She cuts away right after Annie begins to make out with a bartender in a bathroom and right after Darren begins to engage in heavy petting with a local waitress but it is unclear just how far either went, making the mystery and questions between the couple those of the audience's as well.

Where Aselton falters is in fleshing out the emotional core of the piece—how this couple relates before and after the fact. She was wise to limit time spent on the night in question but she also short shrifts the pre- and post-game, turning them into what feels like plot devices instead of honest human interaction. The opening act is not nearly long enough, jumping right into the conversation about sowing wild oats when it would have been wise to at least spend some time with Annie and Darren to observe their chemistry. They seem so happy and content that the night of unquestioned infidelity feels more like a writer's device than anything that would come naturally out of their relationship. It is not that it is unbelievable, merely that is given no time to become so and, therefore, creates a falsity at the core of the entire piece.

The aftermath is handled even more briskly. In a misguided move, Aselton starts playing with chronology after the crucial conversation, moving quickly to the morning after and then back to the night of and so on. There is a stronger version of *The Freebie* without the chronological tricks. But that version would still have to offer more of the emotional minefield in the days after. Aselton and Shepard go from loving and supportive to distant and downright suicidal in the blink of an eye and it feels forced. Aselton almost seems like she is rushing for a running time of under eighty minutes, giving the characters and their predicament no time to breathe and resonate. The two actors get a fantastic scene right at the end where everything is laid bare and they confront each other on the events of the crucial night, both saying things that they may not come back from as a couple. Both actors are spectacular in this scene, one that nearly makes the film worth seeing on its own. One only wishes that it was a part of a more complete story instead of a film that still feels like an outline for a more rewarding drama.

Brian Tallerico

CREDITS

Darren: Dax Shepard
Ken: Ken Kennedy
John: Sean Nelson
Jessica: Bellamy Young
Annie: Katie Aselton
Lea: Leonora Gershman
Emily: Marguerite Phillips
Scott: Scott Pitts
Origin: USA
Language: English
Released: 2010
Production: Adele Romanski; released by Phase 4
Directed by: Katie Aselton
Written by: Katie Aselton
Cinematography by: Benjamin Kasulke
Music by: Julian Wass
Sound: Gene Park, Sean O'Malley
Music Supervisor: Marguerite Phillips
Editing: Nat Sanders
Production Design: Jessica Anisman
MPAA rating: R
Running time: 78 minutes

REVIEWS

Berkshire, Geoff. *Metromix.com.* September 15, 2010.
Goldstein, Gary. *Los Angeles Times.* September 30, 2010.
Holden, Stephen. *New York Times.* September 17, 2010.
Hynes, Eric. *Time Out New York.* September 15, 2010.
LaSalle, Mick. *San Francisco Chronicle.* October 28, 2010.
MacDonald, Moira. *Seattle Times.* October 7, 2010.
Pais, Matt. *Metromix.com.* November 10, 2010.
Pinkerton, Nick. *Village Voice.* September 14, 2010.
Rich, Katey. *CinemaBlend.com.* September 16, 2010.
Schenker, Andrew. *Slant Magazine.* September 12, 2010.

FROM PARIS WITH LOVE

Two agents. One city. No merci.
—Movie tagline

Box Office: $24 million

From Paris with Love is an utterly routine low-budget action film not to be confused in any way with the James Bond classic, *From Russia with Love* (1963). Produced by Lionsgate, purveyor of cheap, cartoonish action films, *From Paris with Love* shares none of the earlier film's wit, style, or ambition and is a forgettable, standard issue entry into its catalogue that generates no memorable action or amusement.

From Paris with Love's story coasts on the usual array of tired buddy action film cliches. Jonathan Rhys-Meyers plays James Reece, an ambitious, by-the-book, desk-bound aide to an American Ambassador in Paris. Chomping at the bit to do something more important than draft his ambassador's daily schedule and play chess with him (lazy script shorthand to indicate that Reece is smart), Reece has surreptitiously been doing low-level assignments for the CIA on the side. Not content with planting the occasional bug or switching license plates for vehicles to be used by real spies, Meyers pleads with his CIA superior to let him do real spy work. He soon gets a whole lot more of that than he bargained for in the form of Charlie Wax, a wildcard lone wolf government operative with a penchant for shooting first and asking questions later. Reece is assigned the task of getting Wax through French customs and once he has arrived at the airport, he gets a sense of the nature of the agent he has been assigned to help and the trademark lack of subtly that has surely served Wax well as an inconspicuous agent in foreign, hostile cultures.

Once Reece has successfully extricated Wax from customs they go out to what Reece thinks is dinner at a Chinese restaurant but what is, in fact, a front for a cocaine operation. He knows this because mid-conversation Wax pulls out a pistol and presses it to the head of his waiter and asks where the cocaine is stored. This instigates a shootout involving every occupant of the restaurant and *From Paris with Love*'s comedic action-adventure roller coaster ride begins with the reluctant and nervous Reece unhappily accompanying the wise cracking Wax from set-piece shoot-out to set-piece shoot-out throughout Paris. Soon, of course, the tweedy, chess-playing diplomat is packing heat and punching people out. According to Wax, their assignment is to destroy a drug cartel that has been implicated in the overdose of the niece of the Ambassador. However,

Reece quickly learns that there is far more to the mission than meets the eye and that even with his chess-playing prowess he will struggle to keep up with terrorist plots and multiple double crosses that emerge as the result of his and Wax's investigations.

From Paris with Love's lazy and clichéd plot is not the point, of course, and exists merely as a vehicle for delivering the action—the reason for the film to exist. Unfortunately, that action is boring and cheap, consisting almost exclusively of cheap-to-film shoot-outs and a couple of car explosions which avoid the expensive CGI required by imaginative and exhilarating action sequences. With the *Transporter* series, *Crank* series, and other films, Lionsgate has filled the quasi straight-to-video action film niche that its forbear Cannon did in the 1980s. However, the action in *From Paris with Love* looks like it is from a Cannon film. The action is state of the art 1989, with lots of slow motion shootouts featuring waves of indistinguishable gunmen standing in the middle of rooms spraying Uzis and getting dispatched with over-the-top blood squibs. *From Paris with Love* is the kind of movie where there is a shoot out in a restaurant and the chefs come out shooting. The film's action is as lazy and unimaginative as its story. The most amusing exemplification of the film's laziness is Travolta's appearance. Although he's playing a deadly government operative who seeks to solve every challenge with instantaneous violence and routinely dives through windows and off the sides of buildings, Travolta did not deem it necessary to get in shape for the role and sports a sizable gut throughout the film, wearing a leather jacket and scarf that try in vain to conceal it. Hilariously, whenever Travolta is required to do anything marginally athletic it cuts to slow motion. Executing a Jet Li jump kick might justify slow-motion but hitting a thug with a baseball bat (about the most athletic activity Travolta is required to engage in) should not require camera tricks. Travolta is a thoroughly unconvincing badass, with his large gut and bald head, he is less Bond or Bourne and more Brando's Colonel Kurtz from *Apocalypse Now* (1979). Meyers fares a bit better, resembling, with his pencil thin mustache and fussy complaints, Malcom McDowell as a stressed-out accountant-cum-reluctant-action-hero.

Unable to distinguish itself as spectacle with its cheap, run of the mill action, *From Paris with Love*'s only hope to set itself apart is as a buddy comedy a la *48 Hours* (1982), *Lethal Weapon* (1987), *Bad Boys* (1995), *Rush Hour* (1998), and *Pinapple Express* (2008). Travolta is supposed to be the hilarious, wise-cracking wild man and Rhys-Meyers his exasperated straight man, but the film's terrible script gives them nothing clever to say, forcing them to recite comically intended dialogue that thinks it is a lot cooler than it actually is. *From Paris with Love*'s comedy-bereft script makes the comedic interplay of Bruce Willis and Danny Aielo in *Hudson Hawk* (1991) look like a side-splitting Laurel and Hardy classic by comparison.

Not every action film has to be an innovative CGI spectacular like *Avatar* (2009) but it also does not have to be this formulaic and uninspired, either. The *Transporter* and *Crank* films, while by no means classics, at least showed that a modestly budgeted action film could compensate for its limited budget with humor and style. *From Paris with Love* lacks both and departs from the viewer's mind even as it is playing.

Nate Vercauteren

CREDITS

Charlie Wax: John Travolta
James Reece/Richard Stevens: Jonathan Rhys Meyers
Ambassador Bennington: Richard Durden
Nichole: Amber Rose Revah
Caroline: Kasia Smutniak
M. Wong: Yin Bing
Origin: France
Language: English
Released: 2010
Production: Luc Besson, India Osborne; Europacorp, M6 Films, Grive Prods., Apipoulai Productions; released by Lionsgate
Directed by: Pierre Morel
Written by: Adi Hasak
Cinematography by: Michel Abramowicz
Music by: David Buckley
Sound: Frederic Dubois
Music Supervisor: Alexandre Mahout
Editing: Frederic Thoraval
Costumes: Olivier Beriot
Production Design: Jacques Bufnoir
MPAA rating: R
Running time: 92 minutes

REVIEWS

Barker, Andrew. *Variety.* January 28, 2010.
Baumgarten, Marjorie. *Austin Chronicle.* February 12, 2010.
Ebert, Roger. *Chicago Sun-Times.* February 3, 2010.
Edelstein, David. *New York Magazine.* January 31, 2010.
Holden, Stephen. *New York Times.* February 5, 2010.
Morris, Wesley. *Boston Globe.* February 5, 2010.
Pinkerton, Nick. *Village Voice.* February 2, 2010.
Pols, Mary. *TIME Magazine.* February 5, 2010.
Smith, Kyle. *New York Post.* February 7. 2010.
Tobias, Scott. *AV Club.* February 4, 2010.

James Reece: "I'm not your driver. I'm your partner."

TRIVIA

The film features cameo appearances by John Travolta's wife Kelly Preston and Luc Besson, who developed the story.

FROZEN

No one knows you're up there.
    —Movie tagline

In Adam Green's *Frozen,* three young people bribe their way onto a ski lift at a resort only to find themselves stranded mid-mountain dozens of feet up in the air as the resort closes down for the week during a freezing blizzard. What could have been a taut tale of survival against all odds is instead merely a series of gross-out action sequences pieced together with long stretches of utterly cardboard dialogue. Characters sit and talk and something bad happens. They talk some more and something worse happens. Then the unthinkable happens, the characters talk some more. During a screening of *Frozen* at the 2010 Sundance Film Festival audience members supposedly cried, threw up, and had to abruptly leave the theater. Producers evidently took that to mean they had a good film on their hands. What they had and have is a movie full of wholly uninteresting characters with nothing to say and way too much time on their hands with which to say it.

Writer director Adam Green's previous projects include the old-school slasher redux *Hatchet* (2006) and the far-superior tale of psychological suspense *Spiral* (2007). Green is an interesting talent who seems bent on making a mark in the horror genre but though both these films demonstrate that he knows how to mine a simple premise, *Frozen* seems anti-climactic from the word go.

There is no doubt the concept of the film was approached ambitiously. Green uses no sound stages, CGI, or green screens choosing instead to actually dangle his cast high above a mountainside at an actual resort midwinter. Green himself, along with his director of photography Will Barratt did much of the actual filming from an adjacent lift chair.

The film is also reasonably well cast Emma Bell (*Gracie* [2007], *Death in Love* [2008]) is best known for her TV work on shows like *Law & Order* and *The Bedford Diaries,* offers a perfectly fine performance as Parker O'Neil. Shawn Ashmore whose recurring role as Bobby Drake/Iceman in the *X-Men* films has made him a recognizable bit player is far better than the role he is given here. *The Quiet* (2005) and *The Ruins* (2008) both showcased him far better. Lastly, and most interest-ingly, Green cast Kevin Zeggers, who, though best known for his breakout performance in *Transamerica* (2005), has appeared in solid horror fare chocking up TV appearances in *The X-Files* and *Goosebumps* as well as film roles in underrated films including *In the Mouth of Madness* (1995), *Wrong Turn* (2003), and *Dawn of the Dead* (2004).

A high point of *Frozen* are the cringe-inducing special effects. In one scene, a character does the inevitable, simply dropping out of the chair to the ground below in a futile attempt to escape, only to snap both legs. In another, a character must pull a frozen hand free of the lift bar only to leave behind a chunk of ragged frozen skin. In still another, wolves, which evidently run wild at this particular resort, show up on-cue to engage in a series of grisly attacks. Green shows some restraint here, managing to generate some genuine chills through sound effects. Later shots of the wolves eating their victim and a dead body are expertly handled, truly gross and disturbing, and, most of all, provocative in what they tell viewers might happen during any possible getaway.

But an ongoing list of *Frozen*'s many assets—an ambitious talented director, a strong cast and solid effects—make the film's fatal flaw even more noticeable. *Frozen* is badly written, so badly written in fact, that it plays exactly as if Green put only enough down on paper to get himself and his cast and crew out into the snow to see if the film could actually be made in the way he was envisioning. Put more simply, the film plays like a simplified, self-indulgent exercise in technique and genre.

Many recent horror films have used winter as a backdrop: *Dead Snow* (2009), *The Thaw* (2009), *Wind Chill* (2007), and *The Last Winter* (2006) among them. Any of these are better than *Frozen* which sees its winter environs strictly in terms of the gore conventions they can satisfy. In a larger sense, the characters are indeed *Frozen* in their lives unable to get past feelings they have for one another or unable to surmount the obstacles that block them from their desires. A smarter film that was truly interested in telling a compelling story would have found a way to make the scenery stand in for these central conflicts. Instead, stranded is exactly how viewers are likely to feel as they slowly realize that nobody in *Frozen* is going to resolve anything. These seem like people who have never suffered, thereby learning nothing from their suffering, in an environment as compelling as white noise.

Dave Canfield

CREDITS

Dan: Kevin Zegers
Lynch: Shawn Ashmore

Parker: Emma Bell

Shannon: Rileah Vanderbilt

Rifkin: Adam Johnson

Jason: Ed Ackerman

Ryan: Chris York

Origin: USA

Language: English

Released: 2010

Production: Peter Block, Cory Neal; A Bigger Boat, Ariescope Pictures; released by Anchor Bay Films

Directed by: Adam Green

Written by: Adam Green

Cinematography by: Will Barratt

Music by: Andy Garfield

Sound: Douglas Cameron, Douglas Cameron

Editing: Ed Marx

Art Direction: Richard T. Olson

Costumes: Barbara Nelson

Production Design: Bryan McBrien

MPAA rating: R

Running time: 94 minutes

REVIEWS

Burr, Ty. *Boston Globe.* February 5, 2010.
Catsoulis, Jeannette. *New York Times.* February 5, 2010.
Daley, Ryan. *Bloody Disgusting.* January 31, 2010.
Debruge, Peter. *Variety.* January 28, 2010.
Faraci, Devin. *CHUD.* January 24, 2010.
Kennedy, Lisa. *DenverPost.com.* February 5, 2010.
Lang, Rebecca. *Minneapolis Star Tribune.* February 4, 2010.
Lumenick, Lou. *New York Post.* February 5, 2010.
Reed, Rex. *New York Observer.* February 2, 2010.
Schrager, Norm. *Filmcritic.com.* September 28, 2010.

QUOTES

Joe Lynch: "Hmmm, smell that mountain air. You know what it smells like? Cancer."

TRIVIA

Writer/director Adam Green named all of the characters after his close friends.

FURRY VENGEANCE

He came. He saw. They conquered.
—Movie tagline

Box Office: $18 million

As these words are being written, it has been less than four months since *Furry Vengeance* debuted in theaters but in that short period of time, it has already staked a claim for itself as one of the worst movies to come along in recent memory. At the *Rotten Tomatoes* website, it maintains an 8 percent "Fresh" rating, only one percentage point above the likes of such maligned items as *The Bounty Hunter* (2010) and *The Last Air-bender* (2010), with only six of the eighty reviews collected offering anything remotely positive to say about it. Over at *IMDB*, the news is even grimmer; not only does it currently have a lowly average viewer rating of 2.2 out of a possible 10, it is #83 on their list of the Bottom 100 movies of all time, a ranking that puts it above such legendary losers as *Battlefield Earth* (2000) and *Gigli* (2002). To some observers, the idea that a film primarily intended for younger viewers could inspire such vitriol may seem somewhat unlikely but if ever there was a film deserving of all these brickbats and many, many more, rest assured that it is this one.

Brendan Fraser, Hollywood's go-to guy for hack-neyed and borderline-embarrassing family-film premises, stars as Dan Sanders, a genial but apparently clueless dope who uproots his family—wife Tammy (Brooke Shields) and obnoxious son Tyler (Matt Prokop)—from the hustle and bustle of Chicago to the woods of Oregon to oversee the construction of a supposedly eco-friendly housing development that is nevertheless dooming countless acres of pristine woodland in the process. As it turns out, the local wildlife is not particularly enthused about this development and have banded together to fight back with Dan serving as the focus of their efforts. This leads to an endless series of scenes in which Dan is repeatedly brutalized or soaked in some kind of unsavory substance and then cannot convince anyone that the animals are responsible for his mishaps. Eventually, Dan learns of his company's evil plans for the area and the animals and decides to do the right thing by uniting with the creatures. It all comes to a head at a public relations event thrown by Dan's company where he, his newly united family, and the animals confront his evil boss (Ken Jeong) in an orgy of heartfelt speeches, property destruction, and animal poop—mostly the latter.

As bad as *Furry Vengeance* may sound in theory, it is nothing compared to the mind-numbing horror of actually sitting through it. This is one of those movies that is actually so rotten that it does not even inspire the anger that usually accompanies a typically bad film. Viewers are more likely to stagger away from it in a state of pure stupefaction, wondering how it could have possibly gotten produced and released in the first place. Director Roger Kumble, the auteur behind such modern comedy classics as *The Sweetest Thing* (2002), *Just Friends* (2005), and *College Road Trip* (2008), handles the material as though it were an exceptionally-frantic cartoon, an approach that might have been acceptable if the film was in fact animated but which comes across as utterly excruciating when done in live-action. The actors have taken a similar approach with their contributions and the result is a collection of some of the most cringe-inducing performances ever collected under the auspices of a single film. Fraser (who also served as one of the film's executive producers) is so relentlessly awful here that he may have single-handedly destroyed whatever reputation as a serious actor he may have still maintained, the sadly misused Shields looks utterly embarrassed in all of her scenes, and, as the evil boss, Ken Jeong solidifies his standing as one of the least funny personalities to currently be gracing the silver screen. Even the slapstick is mishandled in such a way that it comes across as more sadistic than silly—during the opening scene, the animals straight-up murder Fraser's predecessor—and feels wildly inappropriate for what is supposed to be a film aimed at younger viewers.

Furry Vengeance is a complete failure on every possible artistic and aesthetic level and even the easiest-to-please viewers will find sitting through it to be a chore. Upon reflection, there are maybe three good things about it at best. For one thing, unlike a lot of recent terrible family films, it was not presented in 3D. For another, unlike a lot of recent and terrible family films, it at least manages to restrain itself by not allowing the animals to talk. Finally, and most importantly, unlike a lot of recent and terrible family films, it proved to be such a enormous flop at the box office that it is pretty much a certainty that the threat of *Furry Vengeance 2* has been more or less eradicated for good.

Peter Sobczynski

CREDITS

Dan Sanders: Brendan Fraser
Tammy Sanders: Brooke Shields
Tyler Sanders: Matt Prokop
Neal Lyman: Ken Jeong

Principal Baker: Samantha Bee
Riggs: Rob Riggle
Origin: USA, United Arab Emirates
Language: English
Released: 2010
Production: Keith Goldberg, Robert Simonds; Imagenation Abu Dhabi FZ, Participant Media; released by Summit Entertainment
Directed by: Roger Kumble
Written by: Michael Carnes, Josh Gilbert
Cinematography by: Peter Lyons Collister
Music by: Ed Shearmur
Sound: Greg Steele, Mike Wilhoit
Music Supervisor: Patrick Houlihan
Editing: Lawrence Jordan
Art Direction: E. David Cosier
Costumes: Alexandra Welker
Production Design: Stephen Lineweaver
MPAA rating: PG
Running time: 92 minutes

REVIEWS

Burr, Ty. *Boston Globe.* April 29, 2010.
Cheney, Jen. *Washington Post.* April 30, 2010.
Hale, Mike. *New York Times.* April 30, 2010.
Hewitt, Chris. *St. Paul Pioneer Press.* April 30, 2010.
Linden, Sherri. *Hollywood Reporter.* April 30, 2010.
Lumenick, Lou. *New York Post.* April 30, 2010.
Pais, Matt. *Metromix.com.* April 29, 2010.
Puig, Claudia. *USA Today.* April 29, 2010.
Taylor, Dawn. *Cinematical.* April 30, 2010.
Tobias, Scott. *AV Club.* April 29, 2010.

QUOTES

Neal Lyman: "Bruce Lee from the grave!"

TRIVIA

The Brendan Fraser role was initially offered to both Steve Carell and Jeremy Piven.

G

GET HIM TO THE GREEK

Arriving this summer (hopefully).
—Movie tagline

Aaron Green has 72 hours to get a Rock Star from London to L.A. Pray for him.
—Movie tagline

Box Office: $61 million

Rock stars are not lovable losers. They are self-destructive, wealthy icons who are more often envied for the vicarious thrills they provide than pitied for the loneliness that sometimes comes with their grueling schedules and constant temptations. That is why Aldous Snow (Russell Brand), an English rocker whose idiocy never gets in the way of his arrogance, does not make a particularly compelling main character for a movie. Yet *Get Him to the Greek,* a spin-off feature from the better *Forgetting Sarah Marshall* (2008) thrives anyway. The reason, simply put, it is funny more often than it is not.

In the film's opening sequence, Aldous suffers a major career setback when his new song "African Child"—whose music video is a blatantly and hilariously offensive comparison between Aldous' problems and those of an African child—is called the worst thing to happen to Africa since apartheid. Then Aldous' girlfriend Jackie Q (Rose Byrne), a Lily Allen-esque pop singer with an even fouler mouth, leaves him. Suddenly, the once-great rock star has little left going for him besides memories and the support of his mum (Dinah Stabb), from whom he clearly still needs encouragement. So Aldous, who has not performed in three years, does

not exactly have any scheduling conflicts when low-level record employee Aaron (Jonah Hill) comes to London. His task is to escort Aldous to New York for a *Today Show* appearance and then fly to Los Angeles, where the singer will perform a concert celebrating the tenth anniversary of his live album, recorded at the historic Greek Theatre.

That assignment proves surprisingly difficult for Aaron, who quickly and easily is overwhelmed by Aldous' taste for debauchery and complete lack of structure. "Change it to the next one," Aldous tells Aaron casually about both their flights and their limos. Much hedonistic mayhem ensues involving booze, drugs, and Aaron, who thinks he is broken up with his girlfriend Daphne (Elizabeth Moss), drunkenly having sex with a girl in a bathroom. In this scene and many others, Hill mines a lot of amiable comic energy from this fish out of water situation. Duos as mismatched as Aldous and Aaron are nothing new to the big screen, but the paired actors do not always work as well together as Brand and Hill. (The two worked together previously in *Forgetting Sarah Marshall*, in which Hill played a different, far-more-irritating character.) They convince that Aaron would envy and succumb to the rock star lifestyle of one of his idols, and that Aaron's awkwardness and completely different sense of scale would remind Aldous that life can be experienced without mind-altering substances.

Of course, that is where *Get Him to the Greek* loses some of its buzz. In small doses in *Forgetting Sarah Marshall,* Aldous was a hysterical buffoon, well-intentioned but selfish and stupid. Using Aldous as one of the stars of this film, writer-director Nicholas Stoller (who directed the previous venture) gives him a sense of regret and alienation that does not suit him. Sure, it is understandable that a rock star would feel shut off from any legitimate human connection when life is nothing but a series of drunken episodes and one-night stands. Still, turning Aldous soft and suggesting that his partying is only a way to mask his fear does not convince. To a degree, it replicates a problem found in the third act of other films produced by Judd Apatow like *Knocked Up* (2007). Viewers inevitably sense that everything is going to turn out nice and easy for everyone, logic and emotional consequences be damned. The result is less suspense, less credibility.

Nevertheless, a lot of the appeal of *Get Him to the Greek* comes from its laid-back blend of raunchiness and good-hearted sweetness. When Aaron first meets Aldous, the rocker introduces himself by saying, "I'm Aldous Snow, the rock star." This is as foolishly arrogant as a musician can be. Brand plays it so lightly, though, that somehow Aldous becomes more likable because of his ego. This is also because it is clear that, deep down, he is not a bad guy. On the phone with Jackie, Aldous refers to Aaron as "some affable nitwit." There is fondness in that insult. It is a testament to the underlying down-to-earth qualities of the main characters and that, despite their differences, they appreciate each other's company.

For viewers looking for more than laughs, *Get Him to the Greek* is an easy film to criticize. It is episodic and possesses a crude streak that sometimes causes jokes to miss the mark. In one particularly misguided scene, Aaron's boss Sergio (Sean Combs) orders Aaron to sleep with a groupie named Destiny (Carla Gallo), who is in a Pussycat Dolls cover band. Destiny also has shaved her pubic hair into the shape of a microphone and asks Aaron if he wants to sing "hairy-oke." That is a lazy joke, and a bad one. *Get Him to the Greek* is at its funniest when its outrageousness comes from an endearing place. The sequence with Destiny, on the other hand, is crass and out of place. The same goes for a scene when, after Aldous forces Aaron to insert a balloon of heroin in his anal cavity before a flight, Aaron wipes his soiled hand on a leaf after the procedure. Funny? Not really. Just gross.

The absence of *Forgetting Sarah Marshall* writer and star Jason Segel is evident in the superficiality and relative aimlessness of *Get Him to the Greek,* which loses focus by the time Aldous, Aaron, and Daphne ponder a threesome in a scene straight out of *Chasing Amy* (1997). And little is gained from Aldous' detour to Las Vegas to try to reunite with his estranged father (Colm Meaney). Yet the feeling that another good laugh is always on its way helps keep the film's silliness charming. Whether it is Aaron vocally imitating the twisted sounds of the

Mars Volta or Jackie Q speaking on behalf of her vagina as she talks to Aldous on the phone, *Get Him to the Greek* presents characters whose quirks feel both ridiculous and deliberately drawn; not that characters ever really take precedence over comedy. The film's title, unlike its predecessor, merely refers to a location-based mission, not something as emotional as getting over an ex. The goal is just good, goofy laughs, and the movie gets it done.

Matt Pais

CREDITS

Aaron Greenberg: Jonah Hill
Aldous Snow: Russell Brand
Jackie Q: Rose Byrne
Daphne Binks: Elisabeth Moss
Sergio Roma: Sean Combs
Lena Snow: Dinah Stabb
Destiny: Carla Gallo
Jonathan Snow: Colm Meaney
Origin: USA
Language: English
Released: 2010
Production: Judd Apatow, David L. Bushell, Rodney Rothman; Apatow Productions, Relativity Media, Spyglass Entertainment; released by Universal Pictures
Directed by: Nicholas Stoller
Written by: Nicholas Stoller
Cinematography by: Robert D. Yeoman
Music by: Lyle Workman
Sound: George Anderson
Editing: William Kerr, Michael L. Sale
Costumes: Leesa Evans
Production Design: Jan Roelfs
MPAA rating: R
Running time: 109 minutes

REVIEWS

Burr, Ty. *Boston Globe.* June 4, 2010.
Ebert, Roger. *Chicago Sun-Times.* June 2, 2010.
Goodykoontz, Bill. *Arizona Republic.* June 2, 2010.
Phillips, Michael. *Chicago Tribune.* June 3, 2010.
Rodriguez, Rene. *Miami Herald.* June 3, 2010.
Scott, A.O. *New York Times.* June 4, 2010.
Smith, Kyle. *New York Post.* June 4, 2010.
Stevens, Dana. *Slate.* June 3, 2010.
Tobias, Scott. *AV Club.* June 3, 2010.
Zacharek, Stephanie. *Movieline.* June 3, 2010.

QUOTES

Aldous Snow: "This is it, Aaron. This is rock 'n' roll. Did you enjoy the party?"

GET LOW

Every secret dies somewhere.
—Movie tagline

Box Office: $9 million

Aaron Schneider's *Get Low* begins with a haunting and mysterious sequence. A house deep in the forest burns wildly in the dead of night. A man bursts through a window and flees into the pitch blackness. Although the film that follows is about the life of that man and the circumstances of the fire, it does not succeed in offering anything as powerful or intriguing as its wordless opening until the very end, at which point it is too late. In between, the film tries to be both a comedy and a drama and, despite a nuanced and powerful performance by Robert Duvall, ends up succeeding as neither. Not funny enough to succeed as a comedy and too corny to succeed as a drama, *Get Low* ends up being uncomfortably close to a Hallmark Channel holiday special, albeit with really good actors.

Felix Bush (Robert Duvall) has lived in the Tennessee wilderness as a hermit for forty years. Legends and tall tales have developed in the nearby town to explain his status. "He's crazy." "He's a killer." Everyone has a story about him and the story usually ends in violence. He is the local bogeyman and, when the film opens, children dare each other to step onto his porch. (When one does and Felix abruptly appears, the boy is so scared that he vomits.) Felix's isolation is interrupted when the Reverend Gus Horton (Gerald McRaney) comes and tells him that an acquaintance has died. This gets Felix contemplating his own mortality and soon he is in the town with a wad of cash asking the Reverend Horton about having funeral, but with a unique twist. He wants the funeral while he is still alive. Why? Because he wants everyone who has heard a story about him to come and tell it before he "gets low." Finding this most irregular, Horton turns him down. However, Felix's request is overheard by Buddy (Lucas Black), apprentice to the local undertaker, Frank Quinn (Bill Murray), and soon Buddy is at Felix's home (after surviving a near miss from Felix's shotgun) telling him that they would be more than happy to accommodate his wishes. Felix comes up with the novel solution of financing his funeral by offering, for one dollar per ticket, a raffle of his land after his death. Soon Felix is the talk of the town and

the money is pouring in from his bemused community, filling up a coffin in the funeral home with one dollar bills. While Felix is in town getting barbered and fitted for his "funeral" suit he encounters widow Mattie Darrow (Sissy Spacek), the sister of a woman he once knew. They resume their acquaintance from long ago and, for a short while, it appears as though a romance might blossom between the two. Then Mattie notices a photograph of her sister on Felix's wall and inquires as to what he may have had to do with her death.

Get Low vividly evokes the atmosphere of its rural, depression era Tennessee setting. The sets and costumes ooze with authenticity and make the viewer feel as though he or she is in the backwoods in the 1930s. The film also benefits from an excellent cast. Sissy Spacek is superb as the kind-hearted but angry and confused Mattie. Bill Murray is great as a funny, cynical alcoholic fighting the temptation of all the dollar bills Felix's raffle is bringing into his funeral home. Bill Cobbs shines as Reverend Charlie Jackson, who is the one person who knows Felix's secret and is weary of having repeatedly told Felix what he needs to do to get right with God over the years. And Lucas Black does a good job with a rather generic role. As might be expected, much depends on Duvall. And, unsurprisingly, the veteran actor does a superb job. With many of his acting contemporaries dead, long-retired, or settled comfortably into paycheck grandfather roles, Duvall, like the great Michael Caine, is, at nearly eighty, still interested in taking chances and challenging himself as an actor. Duvall delivers a magnificent performance and invests Felix with as much passion and complexity as any of his great roles over his long and storied career. The viewer simply wishes that the script gave him a more complicated character to play and better dialogue for that character to say.

Indeed, from its setting, characters, and tone, it is clear that *Get Low* would like to be a whimsical period piece in the vein of Frank Darabont; equal parts funny and moving. The film's tag line, "A True Tall Tale," makes this goal explicit. Unfortunately, the central conceit of this tale, though true, is hokey and lame, like all those British movies about pot growing pensioners and grandmas posing in nudie calendars. Having a funeral while you are still alive is the kind of "crazy" that might be the centerpiece of a frisky episode of the *Golden Girls*. This could be forgivable if the film compensated with a hilarious script but it does not. The script lays on the whimsy thick but not so much the funny. For example, when Felix is asked, "how are you" his response, "I am," is neither profound nor funny, though the script intends it to be both. When Quinn is assisting Felix shop for clothes, Quinn asks "How are you fixed for underwear?" Felix: "I don't wear none."

Quinn: "Too much information." If the viewer finds this hilarious, then *Get Low* is the movie for them.

As for the drama, it turns out that Felix has a reason for wanting his funeral while he is still alive and it is not because he wants to hear what stories others have to tell about him but because he has a story to tell them. In a rather improbable climax, Felix collects the town together and reveals his story from a platform via a microphone. The story explains what happened in the burning house forty years ago and why it has resulted in Felix's self-imposed exile ever since. His motive for finally revealing his story is to demonstrate his immense shame to the community and to beg for its forgiveness. Unfortunately, this climax is underwhelming because the punishment Felix has imposed upon himself seems disproportionate to the wrong he feels he has committed. Felix seems more the victim of circumstances than a purposeful wrong doer deserving the exile and shame to which he has sentenced himself. A more ambitious and daring film would have made Felix more morally culpable. However, the delivery of the story by Duvall is nonetheless moving and powerful, owing to Duvall's immense skill as an actor and is the only part of the movie, aside from its very beginning, that comes alive. An actor of Duvall's exceptional abilities could read *Curious George* and make it as riveting as Shakespeare and Duvall's speech makes the viewer wish that the whole of *Get Low* was "story hour" with Duvall, instead of one hundred minutes of lightweight schmaltz. *Get Low* is worth seeing as a showcase for one of America's greatest actors, but, in all other respects, it is a film that will quickly depart from the viewer's mind.

Nate Vercauteren

CREDITS

Frank Quinn: Bill Murray
Mattie Darrow: Sissy Spacek
Rev. Charlie Jackson: Bill Cobbs
Felix Bush: Robert Duvall
Buddy Robinson: Lucas Black
Rev. Gus Horton: Gerald McRaney
Carl: Scott Cooper
Kathryn: Lori Beth Edgeman
Origin: USA
Language: English
Released: 2009
Production: Dean Zanuck, David Gundlach; Butchers Run Films; released by Sony Pictures Classics
Directed by: Aaron Schneider
Written by: Chris Provenzano, C. Gaby Mitchell
Cinematography by: David Boyd

Music by: Jan A.P. Kaczmarek
Sound: Shirley Libby
Music Supervisor: Evyen Klean
Editing: Aaron Schneider
Art Direction: Korey Micheal Washington
Costumes: Julie Weiss
Production Design: Geoffrey Kirland
MPAA rating: PG-13
Running time: 102 minutes

REVIEWS

Burr, Ty. *Boston Globe. August 6, 2010.*
Ebert, Roger. *Chicago Sun-Times.* August 4, 2010.
Hornaday, Ann. *Washington Post.* August 13, 2010.
Leydon, Joe. *Variety.* September 14, 2010.
Murray, Noel. *AV Club.* July 29, 2010.
Pols, Mary. *TIME Magazine.* July 30, 2010.
Rea, Stephen. *Philadelphia Inquirer.* August 13, 2010.
Savlov, Marc. *Austin Chronicle.* August 13, 2010.
Scott, A.O. *New York Times.* July 29, 2010.
Travers, Peter. *Rolling Stone.* July 28, 2010.

QUOTES

Frank Quinn: "I sold twenty-six of the ugliest cars in the middle of December with the wind blowing so far up my ass I was farting snowflakes into July."

TRIVIA

"Burly Beard" was the code name used on the film prints when it shipped to theaters.

AWARDS

Ind. Spirit 2011: First Feature
Nomination:
Ind. Spirit 2011: Support. Actor (Murray)
Screen Actors Guild 2010: Actor (Duvall).

THE GHOST WRITER

Read between the lies.
—Movie tagline

Box Office: $16 million

Whether it is in the service of a deeply felt personal project or a simple genre exercise, there are few pleasures for the cineaste more exquisite than to sit down to watch a movie and realize almost instantly that they are in the hands of a master filmmaker working at the top of their game. This sensation has become increasingly rare in recent years but it is certainly there in *The Ghost Writer,* the latest work from the great Roman Polanski. At first blush, the notion of a director of his stature adapting the pulpy best-seller by Robert Harris, the kind of book that is usually only read by people to kill time during long plane flights, might seem like a waste of his talents. However, within a few minutes, those apprehensions are quickly erased because not only is the film a smart and engrossing political thriller, it is also a Roman Polanski film through and through and, with the obvious exception of *The Pianist* (2002), it is also his best work in years.

Ewan McGregor stars as an unnamed former journalist who now makes a living ghost-writing the autobiographies of famous people who lack the time, energy, or literary talent to do it for themselves. As the story opens, he is summoned by his agent to a top-secret meeting where he is offered the job of completing work on the memoirs of former British Prime Minister Adam Lang (Pierce Brosnan) in the wake of the mysterious death of the previous ghost writer. He agrees and is quickly jetted off to America to work on the book in a remote beach house off Martha's Vineyard that Lang is using while embarking on an East Coast lecture tour meant to burnish his credentials as a retired statesman. When he arrives, he finds the place under virtual lockdown with access to the only copy of the book handled by Lang's personal assistant, Amelia (Kim Cattrall). When he reads it, he is even more mystified because the book is the kind of terminally boring and self-serving slog that men in Lang's position tend to write. Lang finally arrives to begin work on the book, accompanied by his cool and reserved wife Ruth (Olivia Williams), but he and the ghost have hardly begun when an unexpected bombshell threatens to disrupt everything: Lang's former foreign minister (Robert Pugh) takes to the air to accuse him of approving a plan to kidnap four alleged Pakistani terrorists in order to hand them over to the C.I.A. to be tortured, a move that resulted in the death of one of them.

While Lang's people close ranks in order to figure out whether he should return home to England and face the music for his alleged misdeeds or stay put in America where he cannot be touched for those potential crimes by the International Criminal Court, the ghost finds himself being pressed upon by his publisher, who now want the book even quicker in order to capitalize on all the unexpected publicity, from Adam, who implores him to write a couple of press releases to send out to the media ("That makes you an accomplice"), from Ruth, whose interest in him seems to be growing outside the dictionary definition of "professional," and from his own nagging suspicion that something strange is going on. During his own private investigation, he learns that not only are there inconsistencies surrounding the death of the previous ghost, it seems that his predecessor

discovered a shocking bombshell about Lang's past and may have hidden it somewhere inside the manuscript. Now, not only is the ghost trying to uncover what that revelation might have been, he now finds himself being pursued by shadowy figures who presumably assume that he has discovered the secret and who want to do to him what they did to his predecessor.

The story of *The Ghost Writer* did not originate with Polanski, but there are certain elements and ideas that obviously must have struck a chord with him when he read the book. While one probably should not read too much into this, the notion of a famous person in a foreign land faced with the prospect of being forced home to face the music for his alleged past misdeeds is one that presumably and perversely resonated with him on some level. More importantly, the character of the ghost is an ideal example of the typical Polanski male protagonist—a smart and solitary man who thinks that he is smart enough to navigate his way through a corrupt and confusing world and the mysteries contained within but who winds up watching impotently from the sidelines as things get worse and worse despite his best efforts. What is impressive here is the way that he and Harris, who co-wrote the screenplay, have managed to deftly juggle these more personal elements within the confines of a narrative that is tricky and twisty while always playing fair with audiences and which somehow manages to serve both as a timeless thriller and as a biting and up-to-the-minute piece of political commentary as you will find in a non-documentary film. (Suffice it to say, any connections between Adam and Ruth Lang and Tony and Cheri Blair are pretty much anything but coincidental.) On the directing side of things, Polanski demonstrates once again that he is without a doubt one of the living masters of the form. He keeps the potentially convoluted plot humming along without getting bogged down in details and is seemingly incapable of coming up with an uninteresting visual. His extended suspense set-pieces are little miracles of filmmaking craft and he knows how to punctuate scenes with welcome bits of weird humor to release the tension that he has been slowly but surely building up. And he wraps it all up with a final shot that is one of the most haunting and memorable moments of his entire career.

Although Polanski is pretty much the star of *The Ghost Writer*, this is a film that is aided immeasurably by the contributions of virtually all of the participants across the board. Cinematographer Pawel Edelman, who worked with Polanski on *The Pianist* and *Oliver Twist* (2005), does a masterful job of capturing the sodden and swampy atmosphere of Lang's beach retreat and lends a slick and stylish edge to the extended scenes of cat-and-mouse that make up much of the second half of the film. Although the first half of the film contains virtually no score, the second half, which is more along the lines of pure cinema anyway, contains work from Alexandre Desplat that does such an effective job of moving things forward that Alfred Hitchcock himself would have given his eye teeth to have access to it for one of his own thrillers. The performances are also quite striking all around. Some have complained that McGregor comes across as bland and bloodless in the early scenes but that is kind of the point—his character is there not to impose his own personality but to have someone else's imposed on him—and when he takes control in the latter stages of the story, he comes into his own as well. Among the other leads, Brosnan is also quite good as the ersatz Tony Blair and Olivia Williams pretty much steals the film outright with a sexy and sinister turn that is the best thing she has done since *Rushmore* (1998). There are also a lot of nifty one-scene turns from actors ranging from Eli Wallach and Tom Wilkinson to, of all people, Jim Belushi in a hilarious bit as the book publisher trying to get something of value for the book that he has unwisely paid ten million dollars for.

There are only two minor elements in *The Ghost Writer* that do not quite pan out. Although she does not do anything technically wrong, Kim Cattrall is not very convincing as Lang's British extra-personal secretary and stands out like a sore thumb in most of her scenes. Likewise, despite the Herculean efforts of the crew, the film never quite manages to make the German locations where it was shot look remotely like Martha's Vineyard. (Although this does add another certain sense of dislocation to the proceedings, it is clearly not the kind that Polanski had in mind.) Those quibbles aside, this is one of the very best films of 2010—a superlative bit of contemporary filmmaking that is simultaneously funny, gripping, topical, and formally exquisite—and serves as another reminder that Roman Polanski is no mere ghost and remains one of the finest living filmmakers working today.

Peter Sobczynski

CREDITS

The Ghost: Ewan McGregor
Adam Lang: Pierce Brosnan
Amelia Bly: Kim Cattrall
Ruth Lang: Olivia Williams
Paul Emmett: Tom Wilkinson
Sidney Kroll: Timothy Hutton
John Maddox: James Belushi
Vineyard Old Man: Eli Wallach
Roy: Tim Preece
Rick Ricardelli: Jon Bernthal

Richard Rycart: Robert Pugh
Origin: France, Germany, United Kingdom
Language: English
Released: 2010
Production: Robert Benmussa, Roman Polanski, Alain Sarde; France 2 Cinema, RP Films, Elfte Babelsberg Film, Runteam; released by Summit Entertainment
Directed by: Roman Polanski
Written by: Roman Polanski, Robert Harris
Cinematography by: Pawel Edelman
Music by: Alexandre Desplat
Sound: Thomas Desjonqueres
Editing: Herve De Luze
Art Direction: David Scheunemann
Costumes: Dinah Collin
Production Design: Albrecht Konrad
MPAA rating: PG-13
Running time: 128 minutes

REVIEWS

Anderson, John. *Wall Street Journal.* February 19, 2010.
Burr, Ty. *Boston Globe.* March 4, 2010.
Dargis, Manohla. *New York Times.* February 19, 2010.
Denby, David. *New Yorker.* March 1, 2010.
Ebert, Roger. *Chicago Sun-Times.* February 25, 2010.
Elley, Derek. *Variety.* February 16, 2010.
Howell, Peter. *Toronto Star.* March 5, 2010.
Larsen, Josh. *Larsen on Film.* March 24, 2010.
Phillips, Michael. *Chicago Tribune.* February 22, 2010.
Turan, Kenneth. *Los Angeles Times.* February 18, 2010.

QUOTES

The Ghost: "You wouldn't happen to know if there are any flights leaving the airport tonight, would you?"

TRIVIA

Despite being set largely in Massachusetts, the film was shot in Germany since director Roman Polanski is unable to enter the United States.

THE GIRL ON THE TRAIN

(La fille du RER)

The Girl on the Train is a work of historical imagination. The acclaimed French director Andre Techine (*Wild Reeds* [1994]), working from a script he wrote with Odile Barski and Jean-Marie Besset, has taken a real incident from the news of recent years and conceived a story that grows around the central character, a young woman who claims the comforting attention of being a victim. The film is based on a 2004 incident in a Paris suburb in which a woman who was not Jewish claimed to be the victim of an anti-Semitic attack by immigrants from northern Africa. The report caused a media sensation and a minor international incident, causing Israeli prime minister Ariel Sharon to call on Jews to flee Europe to escape the scourge of rampant anti-Semitism expressed in such attacks. There was only one problem: the young woman faked the assault, taking real incidents as a template on which to project her own version of victimization.

It is a fascinating subject for a film, but full of pitfalls. Techine and his co-writers have wisely avoided a historical recreation; the bizarreness of the incident argues against doing so and thus risking descent into a political and psychological swamp. *The Girl on the Train* suggests rather than explains its protagonist's motivation, for there is no really coherent explanation that makes sense. The real-life story is merely a jumping-off point for a re-imagining of what kind of person in what kind of circumstances would do such a thing.

The result is a character study and psychological thriller steeped in mystery that is never fully resolved. Rather than a young mother (the real incident included the concocted story that a baby stroller was overturned), Techine's movie gives us a young- twenty-something skateboarder, Jeanne (Emilie Dequenne), who acts like she is even younger. She is encountered midstream, without much back story, as an unemployed post-graduate of some level of education which is never made clear. Instead of going to Italy for the summer as planned, she is broke and at a loss. Her mother, Louise (the great Catherine Deneuve), runs a home day care center and urges Jeanne, on whom she dotes, to apply for work that is beyond her skills. Louise indulges the notion that her daughter is talented, but, in fact, Jeanne has no real skills, skating through life without expending much effort, a recognizable representative of her generation of people at loose ends, with no place to go.

She is wooed by a blunt-spoken, handsome wrestler, Franck (Nicolas Duvauchelle), who pursues her with rough charm and cleverness. The quickly blossoming romance, by the way, includes the best scene yet filmed on online chatting, a scenario that often results in clumsy or laughable cinematography. Techine and Julien Hirsch, however, handle it deftly. The two young chatters use web cams and we see them looking at each other as if through a window at times while alternate images make clear they are at separate computers. This is an imaginative representation of what such encounters are all about: the illusion of intimacy. It is just one of many scenes that use small, telling details to convey an utterly convincing sense of reality. *The Girl on the Train* is very skillfully constructed, though the constant images of trains passing by seems a bit overdone—but even that makes the point that the ubiquitous presence of trains creates a world in which anonymous public space provides a backdrop for narcissistic impulses.

The entire first part of the film, entitled "Circumstances," has nothing to do with the incident and nothing much that seems to explain it, but it does depict a mess in Jeanne's life, as Franck first proposes marriage to her and then proves to be not at all the man he seems to be. We are also introduced to various members of a prominent Jewish family, headed by a prominent media-savvy attorney, Samuel Bleistein (Michel Blanc), who is an old flame of Louise's and for whom Jeanne aspires to work. When the film abruptly shifts into the fake attack in part two, entitled "Consequences," it comes as a complete surprise; it has not been foreshadowed at all, but seems to be an impulsive act fueled by the content of a historical show on TV that Jeanne watches with her mother just when she is at her most vulnerable.

The Girl on the Train has an unusually subtle script; it leaves it up to the viewer to speculate on what exactly were Jeanne's motivations. Clearly, she craved the kind of special attention only available to recognized cultural victims; it is as if she rewrote her life story to take on the mantle of a persecuted (and specially treated) minority. In doing so, she becomes the unlikely friend of the most orthodox of the Bleisteins, a young boy who is both pious and honest.

Though not completely satisfying, *The Girl on the Train* is a psychologically and cinematically ambitious movie. It may frustrate those viewers who like everything wrapped up in neat little bows, but for those who do not mind a little mystery, it will come as an unexpectedly delightful present.

Michael Betzold

CREDITS

Jeanne: Emilie Dequenne
Samuel Bleistein: Michel Blanc
Judith: Ronit Elkabetz
Louise: Catherine Deneuve
Nathan: Jeremy Quaegebeur
Alex: Mathieu Demy
Franck: Nicolas Duvauchelle
Origin: France
Language: French, Hebrew
Released: 2009
Production: Said Ben Said; France 2 Cinema, SBS Films; released by Strand Releasing
Directed by: Andre Techine
Written by: Andre Techine, Odile Barski, Jean-Marie Besset

Cinematography by: Julien Hirsch
Music by: Philippe Sarde
Sound: Jean-Paul Mugel
Editing: Martine Giordano
Costumes: Khadija Zeggai
Production Design: Michele Abbe
MPAA rating: Unrated
Running time: 105 minutes

REVIEWS

Atkinson, Michael. *IFC.com.* June 1, 2010.
Dargis, Manohla. *New York Times.* January 22, 2010.
Ebert, Roger. *Chicago Sun-Times.* April 21, 2010.
Hunter, Alan. *Daily Express.* June 4, 2010.
Jenkins, David. *Time Out.* June 2, 2010.
Morris, Wesley. *Boston Globe.* April 30, 2010.
Rea, Steven. *Philadelphia Inquirer.* April 23, 2010.
Reed, Rex. *New York Observer.* January 19, 2010.
Tallerico, Brian. *HollywoodChicago.com.* April 23, 2010.
Vance, Kelly. *Easy Bay Express.* March 17, 2010.

THE GIRL WHO KICKED THE HORNET'S NEST

(Luftslottet som sprängdes)

Box Office: $5 million

The end of a remarkable Swedish trilogy, that started with the one-two punch of *The Girl With the Dragon Tattoo* (2009) and *The Girl Who Played with Fire* (2009), *The Girl Who Kicked the Hornet's Nest* signals something far more than the end of an often-thrilling yarn involving many large-than-life characters. Like enigmatic heroine, Lisbeth Salander (Noomi Rapace) herself, this is a film that is, sometimes to a fault, unwilling to be labeled, never marrying the disparate story elements and stylistic components that lead to a 147-minute running time. But the things it does do well, it does very well. One of those things is bringing the character of Lisbeth Sander to fascinating, fluid life. The neater trick, however, lies in bringing to life what Salander herself is up against. Talky, sometimes frustratingly so, *The Girl Who Kicked the Hornet's Nest* is also intelligent, provocative, and, when it does move into action mode, exciting.

The film picks up precisely where *The Girl Who Played with Fire* left off. Lisbeth Salander has been shot in the head after an unsuccessful attempt to kill her estranged father, Russian defector, Zalachenko (Georgi Staykov). Her injuries leave her all but bedridden as her archenemy recovers down the hall. Now that the police have her under guard it is only a matter of time before she is formally charged, and, most probably, returned to

the care of her abusers, The Section, a completely hidden intelligence unit of the Swedish government that needs to keep her quiet in order to prevent exposure. Her chief ally, journalist Mikael Blomkvist (Michael Nyqvist), believes she is innocent and has begun to uncover the conspiracy. But even as her circle of defenders grows, enemies close in: The Section, her murderous half brother Ronald Niederman (Micke Spreitz), a blonde giant who cannot feel pain, the psychiatrist who wants her recommitted, and, most dangerously, the system itself, which has failed her for her entire life and is on the verge of doing so again—fatally.

There are nods, often heavy-handed ones, to various genres all through both the book and film series. For instance, Salander is constantly pitted against villains that feel more the stuff of fiction than she does. That Rapace is able to project that sense of reality about Lisbeth even when she is up against a closeted serial killer in his secret basement torture chamber under his beautiful tract house, is a testament not only to her abilities but to the source material which has larger goals in mind than simply satisfying genre conventions for readers or future viewers.

Among those goals is shining a light on abuse issues, racism, and governmental corruption. Larsson was attempting in his books to broaden the genre in which he was writing. These films attempt the same sort of shift. None of the three wholly succeed but the goal is an admirable one. Still, the structure of this massive story reminds viewers constantly that what they think of in terms of evil conspiracies is, after all, often the work of individual people working out of laziness, incompetence, or arrogance as much as out of the desire to actually hurt anyone. The members of The Section are merely self-appointed patriots willing to settle for whatever collateral damage need be to establish their political goals. For every spy, pedophile in hiding, or serial killer in the story there are countless petty bureaucrats "just doing their job." As if to underline this fact, Salander shows up to the big courtroom scene in full Goth Punk regalia; individuality writ large in the most faceless environment imaginable. Otherwise, the courtroom scene could almost be called boring, except for the opportunity to watch such banal corrupt individuals and modes of governance brought thoroughly to their knees. As filtered by the conventions of genre fiction as the character of Salander is, this is what brings her into the real world and makes her story seem to matter.

The biggest cinematic issue here is one of adaptation. In the books, all the characters exist within an emotional space carefully created by Larsson to humanize the improbable events and intrigue that surround them. As the movies truncate the books such characters are robbed of that context and, as often as not, fail to register as they enter and exit the story. There are so many such characters that this becomes a major distraction, reminding viewers that they are, after all, only watching a movie. Only when the film is wholly present with Salander or perhaps Blomkvist does the viewer have a sense of what is at stake. With the emphasis on so much dialogue about what to do with Lisbeth, when the action sequences do kick in they feel almost as if they are part of another film.

A sequence near the end of the film featuring the blonde giant Neiderman is a good example. After unexpectedly finding her half brother hiding out in a warehouse that was part of her unwanted estate from Zalachenko, the newly freed Salander finds herself locked in a deadly battle. No weapons at hand she must fight the giant with her wits leading him on a chase with a much unexpected end. The point is that nowhere in the sequence, indeed nowhere in anywhere of the films, does Salander come off like a superhero. She usually wins her battles because other people underestimate her due to her small size and waifish features, or as often as not because of dumb luck. She is resourceful and gifted with a photographic memory, but not superhumanly so, and so the Goth Punk figure of rebellion evinced by the poster art for *The Girl Who Kicked the Hornet's Nest* is actually simultaneously both a heroine and a damsel-in-distress.

Perhaps the biggest strength of Steig Larsson's thrilling trilogy is the lesson Salander learns about trusting others and operating out of hope rather than despair. It seems a tall order for any film, but for those who are inspired by the character of Lisbeth Salander, whether by her willingness to finally trust or her obvious need for help, the film does indeed encourage viewers to find their own roles in the fight.

Dave Canfield

CREDITS

Lisbeth Salander: Noomi Rapace
Mikael Blomkvist: Michael Nyqvist
Annika Giannini: Annika Hallin
Holger Palmgren: Per Oscarsson
Erika Berger: Lena Endre
Nils Bjurman: Peter Andersson
Christer Malm: Jacob Ericksson
Malin Erikson: Sofia Ledarp
Dr. Peter Teleborian: Anders Ahlbom
Dr. Jonasson: Aksel Morisse
Alexander Zalachenko: Georgi Staykov
Ronald Niederman: Micke Spreitz

Origin: Sweden
Language: Swedish
Released: 2010
Production: Soren Staermose; Yellow Bird Films; released by Music Box Films
Directed by: Daniel Alfredson
Written by: Ulf Rydberg
Cinematography by: Peter Mokrosinski
Music by: Jacob Groth
Sound: Nalle Hansen, Anders Horling
Editing: Hakan Karlsson
Costumes: Cilla Rorby
Production Design: Maria Haard, Jan Olof Agren
MPAA rating: R
Running time: 146 minutes

REVIEWS

Carpenter, Fr. Chris. *Movie Dearest.* October 18, 2010.
Dargis, Manhola. *New York Times.* October 29, 2010.
Ebert, Roger. *Chicago Sun-Times.* October 28, 2010.
Fuchs, Cynthia. *PopMatters.* November 29, 2010.
Gleiberman, Owen. *Entertainment Weekly.* October 27, 2010.
Jenkins, David. *Time Out.* November 29, 2010.
Kennedy, Lisa. *Denver Post.* October 29, 2010.
McDonaugh, Maitland. *Film Journal International.* October 28, 2010.
O'Hehir, Andrew. *Salon.com.* October 28, 2010.
Rainer, Peter. *Christian Science Monitor.* November 1, 2010.

TRIVIA

Director Daniel Alfredson cast his father Hans Alfredson in the role of Evert Gullberg.

THE GIRL WHO PLAYED WITH FIRE
(Flickan som lekte med elden)

Box Office: $8 million

Most movie thrillers these days, good or bad, are fairly preposterous creations filled with improbable coincidences, implausible characters, and ridiculous plot developments. The major difference between the two is that the good ones are those that are done in such a skillful and exciting manner that most viewers find themselves ignoring or overlooking the contrivances and improbabilities at least until they reach the parking lot while the bad ones have them nitpicking every single flaw while still sitting in their seats. The three Swedish-made film adaptations of the late author Stieg Larsson's enormously popular Millennium Trilogy, produced in their native country in 2009 and released Stateside in 2010 to capitalize on the success of the books and to pave the way for the eventual English-language versions, offer perfect examples of this particular theory. The first, *The Girl with the Dragon Tattoo* (2010), told a story that was wildly convoluted and patently unbelievable but it told said story in such a bold and forceful manner that the flaws were forgiven. On the other hand, the final entry in the trilogy, *The Girl Who Kicked the Hornet's Nest* (2010), told a story that was just as nutty but lacked the energy and stylistic flair of *Dragon Tattoo* and as a result, it turned out to be a boring, dreary, and disappointing mess. As for *The Girl Who Played with Fire,* the second film in the franchise and the one under discussion here, it hits a happy medium between the other two in a way that befits its position as the middle chapter—the storytelling is not as smooth as its predecessor and it is not quite as successful in selling the increasingly improbable plot developments that eventually begin to jam things up in the final reels but it is done in an entertaining enough manner to make it sort of worth watching.

Picking up roughly a year after the events of *The Girl with the Dragon Tattoo* the film begins with muckraking journalist Mikael Blomkvist (Michael Nyqvist) back at the helm of *Millennium* magazine and hotshot computer hacker Lisbeth Salander (Noomi Rapace) returning to Sweden after spending time abroad. Mikael is working on a piece with a pair of ambitious young journalists about sex trafficking involving underage girls and men in high political office but before the piece can be published, Mikael's two collaborators are brutally murdered. At the same time, Lisbeth visits her monstrous court-appointed guardian, who used to brutally rape her until she turned the tables on him via a blackmail video, to remind him to continue to keep up his end of their bargain but he also turns up dead before long. When Lisbeth is implicated in both crimes and a manhunt for her begins as she goes on the run, both she and Mikael begin to investigate the crimes separately, occasionally connecting with each other via computer, and uncover shocking information regarding not only the murders but also Lisbeth's own family secrets and why it seems that virtually every person in Sweden with any sort of power seems hell-bent on using it to try to destroy her life one way or another.

Despite being about thirty minutes shorter than its predecessor, *The Girl Who Played with Fire* somehow feels slower and clunkier by comparison at times. Part of this may be due to the switch of directors from the original's Niels Arden Opley to Daniel Alfredson. Alfredson does an okay job of translating the material from the page to the screen but he does not do as good of a job of recreating it in cinematic terms as Opley—

his direction is roughly the equivalent of Larsson's prose and that is not exactly a compliment. A bigger problem is that the story inexplicably takes one of the key elements that made *The Girl with the Dragon Tattoo* so fascinating to watch—the intriguing relationship that developed between Mikael and Lisbeth—and renders it moot by keeping them apart from each other for virtually the entire running time. However, the biggest problem is that the story simply is not very interesting this time around and is riddled with plot holes and huge implausibilities—the vast conspiracies swirling around Lisbeth begin to strain the bounds of credulity and the presence of a hulking secondary villain who is apparently impervious to all forms of pain threatens to loosen whatever tenuous grasp the story has in reality and send it spinning off into second-tier James Bond territory.

What ultimately saves *The Girl Who Played with Fire* from itself and makes it worth seeing despite the numerous imperfections is the same thing that helped transform the first film from just a solidly made thriller into an absolute must-see and that is the central performance of Noomi Rapace as Lisbeth. Not since Anthony Hopkins slipped into the part of Hannibal Lecter has there been such an impressive merging of actor and role as there is with Rapace and Lisbeth. No matter how ridiculous the story gets or how brutalized her character is throughout, Rapace dominates the proceedings with a strong, sexy, and determined presence that lights up the screen in a way that few others have done in recent memory. She takes a character that could have easily come across as too good to be true and transforms her into a living, breathing person who can effortlessly win even the most hardened audience members to her side with either the click of her mouse or the zap of a Taser. The film may be titled *The Girl Who Played with Fire,* but it is Rapace who brings the real heat to what might have otherwise been just another lukewarm potboiler.

Peter Sobczynski

CREDITS

Lisbeth Salander: Noomi Rapace
Mikael Blomkvist: Michael Nyqvist
Holger Palmgren: Per Oscarsson
Erika Berger: Lena Endre
Nils Bjurman: Peter Andersson
Annika Giannini: Annika Hallin
Christer Malm: Jacob Ericksson
Malin Erikson: Sofia Ledarp
Origin: Sweden
Language: Swedish

Released: 2010

Production: Soren Staermose; Yellow Bird Films; released by Music Box Films

Directed by: Daniel Alfredson

Written by: Jonas Frykberg

Cinematography by: Peter Mokrosinski

Music by: Jacob Groth

Sound: Anders Horling, Nalle Hansen

Editing: Mattias Morheden

Costumes: Cilla Rorby

Production Design: Maria Haard, Jan Olof Agren

MPAA rating: R

Running time: 125 minutes

REVIEWS

Ebert, Roger. *Chicago Sun-Times.* July 8, 2010.
Edelstein, David. *New York Magazine.* July 8, 2010.
Gonsalves, Rob. *eFilmcritic.com.* July 6, 2010.
Gronvall, Andrea. *Chicago Reader.* July 8, 2010.
Honeycutt, Kirk. *Hollywood Reporter.* July 1, 2010.
Orndorf, Brian. *BrianOrndorf.com.* July 7, 2010.
Phillips, Michael. *Chicago Tribune.* July 8, 2010.
Robinson, Tasha. *AV Club.* July 8, 2010.
Scott, A.O. *New York Times.* July 9, 2010.
Tallerico, Brian. *MovieRetriever.com.* July 9, 2010.

TRIVIA

Boxer Paolo Roberto plays himself in the film after appearing as a character in the original novel.

THE GIRL WITH THE DRAGON TATTOO

(Män som hatar kvinnor)

Box Office: $10 million

In his native Swedish Stieg Larsson's global bestselling novel is titled *Men Who Hate Women*. Concededly *The Girl with the Dragon Tattoo*, as the book is known here in the United States, has a nicer ring to it, but it is the former title—and the edgy tension between the sexes that it references—that director Niels Arden Oplev was channeling when he approached his adaptation of Larsson's book, turning an otherwise-mediocre novel into an unrelenting hard-boiled thriller.

To recap for those who have yet to get their hands on one of the millions of copies of the book sold domestically, *The Girl with the Dragon Tattoo* is an at times over-written, unnecessarily detailed whodunit that teams a young-and-disturbed female Goth computer hacker, Lisbeth Salander (Noomi Rapace) with an older, recently-indited-for-libel journalist, Mikael Blomkvist

(Michael Nyqvist), for some crime-solving and a little bit of hooking-up. Both are hired to search for a long-missing member of the Vagner family, an old-moneyed Swedish clan whose hidden secrets are as expansive as their family tree. Of course they can't help but fall into bed together while sleuthing. But in addition to a crime thriller, Larsson also penned a novel about depraved, violent sex perpetrated by the men Larsson references in his original title who hate the women he writes about. More often than not that woman is Lisbeth, and Larsson is as interested in getting into her head to understand what her victimization has done to her as he is with the case she is working on. The result is a book that is part crime fiction and part perverse character study.

Wading through this narrative are screenwriters Nikolaj Arcel and Rasmus Heisterberg, who wisely do away with Larsson's lengthy character back stories and focus instead on Lisbeth's run-ins with skeezy men. In terms of pace this is a good thing. Gone are Mikael's career history and the convoluted attempts at explaining why Lisbeth is the way she is (who would not be withdrawn and angry after all that abuse?). Arcel and Heisterberg get through the set-up quickly, introducing us to Mikael at the end of his trial and to Lisbeth who has been following him around after being hired to do a background check on him for the Vagner Corporation. Before long, Mikael is meeting with Vagner to discuss a private investigator job opportunity and Lisbeth is facing the first of her many sexual assaults. Soon the two of them are drawn into the twisted world of the Vagner family. Arcel and Heisterberg move the story along at a nice clip, focusing on the mystery and building tension. But no matter how far you scoot to the edge of your seat while watching, it is hard not to notice that their approach reeks too much of Larsson's love of the eerily perverted. Lisbeth endures quite a bit of trauma at the hands of men throughout the story and with a lot of Larsson's exposition done away with there is no buffer to her assaults. While these scenes work to establish her guarded, weary, and violent disposition it is hard not to wonder if the minutes-long rape and assault scenes are necessary, or if they tread toward the gratuitous.

Of course Arcel and Heisterberg only provided the foundation for these scenes, how they were realized falls entirely to Oplev—and he does not shy away from any of Larsson's disturbing imagery. In his finer moments he channels Ingmar Bergman in the way he perceives the sparse, cold Swedish landscape. But otherwise he tends to favor the screenwriters' predilection toward the over-the-top. Lisbeth's intense rape scene leads its way into her less intense, but still disturbing, revenge scene and each one of the murders she and Michael investigate are laid out in full gory detail. And though it can be argued that Oplev is just reveling in the edginess that foreign filmmaking is afforded in relation to its American counterpart, there are moments where the *Girl with the Dragon Tattoo* portrays gruesomeness for its own sake, making the film feel eerie in a dirty way and walking the increasingly thinning line between narrative development and exploitation.

Though it is hard to pinpoint why exactly the universe hates Lisbeth so much, it is awesome to watch her materialize on screen and take her revenge. Rapace imbues Lisbeth with angry eyes and a brisk attitude. She is bad-assed-and-clever, damaged-and-exciting and stands out among the glamorized versions of kick-ass leading ladies that Hollywood has produced. Her chemistry with Michael is organic, but also on her own terms. Hers is also exactly the kind of leading role any actress would kill for, so it is easy to understand why so many Hollywood starlets were vying for the role in the American remake (that eventually went to Rooney Mara). The great part of Rapace is that she does not look like any of them: she is pierced, boy-skinny, rough, and though there is a pull about her, it has everything to do with her fierce presence on-screen, not her outfit.

Joanna Topor MacKenzie

CREDITS

Mikael Blomkvist: Michael Nyqvist
Lisbeth Salander: Noomi Rapace
Henrik Vanger: Sven-Bertil Taube
Dirch Frode: Ingvar Hirdwall
Cecilia Vanger: Marika Lagercrantz
Harriet Vanger: Ewa Froling
Martin Vanger: Peter Haber
Origin: Sweden, Denmark, Germany
Language: Swedish
Released: 2009
Production: Soren Staermose; Yellow Bird Films; released by Music Box Films
Directed by: Niels Arden Oplev
Written by: Rasmus Heisterberg, Nicolaj Arcel
Cinematography by: Jens Fischer, Eric Kress
Music by: Jacob Groth
Editing: Anne Osterud
Sound: Peter Schultz
Costumes: Cilla Rorby
Production Design: Niels Sejer
MPAA rating: Unrated
Running time: 152 minutes

REVIEWS

Bradshaw, Peter. *The Guardian.* March 15, 2010.
Dargis, Manohla. *New York Times.* March 19, 2010.
Ebert, Roger. *Chicago Sun-Times.* March 18, 2010.
Lane, Anthony. New Yorker. March 22, 2010.
Linden, Sheri. *Hollywood Reporter.* March 9, 2010.
Nashawaty, Chris. *Entertainment Weekly.* February 27, 2009.
Patterson, John. *Village Voice.* March 16, 2010.
Phillips, Michael. *Chicago Tribune.* March 18, 2010.
Sharkey, Betsy. *Los Angeles Times.* March 18, 2010.
Tallerico, Brian. *MovieRetriever.com.* March 17, 2010.

QUOTES

Mikael Blomkvist: "What has happened to you? How did you turn out this way? You know everything about me. I don't know sh*t about you. Not a damn thing."

TRIVIA

Actress Nina Norén plays the role of Agneta Salander, the mother of Lisbeth Salander. She is in fact the real life mother of actress Noomi Rapace who plays Lisbeth.

AWARDS

British Acad. 2010: Foreign Film
Nomination:
British Acad. 2010: Actress (Rapace), Adapt. Screenplay.

GOING THE DISTANCE

A comedy about meeting each other halfway.
—Movie tagline

Box Office: $18 million

In theory, virtually every romantic comedy should feature two characters that look good together, played by actors who have the chemistry to convince as a real couple. Sadly, that is rarely the case. More often, in terrible, terrible films like *The Ugly Truth* (2009), two unlikable characters have no believable spark, and the performers—in this case Katherine Heigl and Gerard Butler—go together like chocolate and chicken.

That is one reason why *Going the Distance,* a romantic comedy staring Drew Barrymore and Justin Long, feels like such a breath of fresh air. Of course, the film has an advantage in its casting: Barrymore and Long are a real-life on-again, off-again couple. The actors, who also appeared in *He's Just Not That Into You* (2008), do not need the prep time pre-shooting that most onscreen pairs normally need to develop a rapport. They already have one. Of course, some real-life couples fizzle when starring together such as Ben Affleck and Jennifer Lopez in *Gigli* (2003). In the case of Barrymore and Long, however, they have an easygoing, fun dynamic that nicely suits the playful *Going the Distance.*

The set-up is a bittersweet one, built around the concept of finding big, real love at an inconvenient time. Garrett (Long) is a New York record label employee who has never really committed to a relationship. Erin (Barrymore) is a Californian finishing a summer internship at a fictional newspaper, the *New York Sentinel*. A few hours after Garrett's girlfriend (an uncredited Leighton Meester) dumps him for being too wishy-washy about her—his answer to whether or not he is invested in her is a trailing off "Sure…"—he picks up Erin at a bar. First, he accidentally interrupts her arcade game and buys her an apologetic beer. This leads to them teaming up for bar trivia and Erin meeting Garrett's pals Box (Jason Sudeikis) and Dan (Charlie Day), who are both rarities in the romantic comedy world in that each is funny and asked only to provide some amusing dude support throughout the film.

Soon, Garrett and Erin have spent much of her last six weeks in New York together, culminating with an Italian dinner during which Garrett proudly, half-jokingly, acknowledges that the restaurant does, in fact, have real cloth napkins. The spot also only offers one kind of wine, served in a jug, but the new couple has such an appealing sense of humor about themselves and life that they roll with whatever silliness comes their way. Meanwhile, Barrymore and Long present the giddy excitement of two people who are incredibly happy they have met and can get to know each other.

If that comfortable bliss lasted without interruption, there would be no movie. After briefly contemplating breaking up, Erin and Garrett agree to maintain their relationship long-distance when she returns to California to finish graduate school at Stanford. Here, *Going the Distance* is already onto something that most modern romantic comedies cannot achieve. Rather than set up an elaborate, far-fetched problem for two exaggerated personalities, the film is stripped down to an issue countless viewers can relate to: being separated from an important person due to career and geography, and hoping that the desire to make things work will be enough to actually have that happen. The script from first-time screenwriter Geoff LaTulippe also features many laugh-out-loud moments that play off quirky character traits in the process. As Garrett and Erin sit on his bed for the first time, anticipating a kiss, in the next room Dan turns on "Take My Breath Away," a memorable song from Garrett's favorite movie *Top Gun* (1986). The timing and good-natured goofiness of this gesture gets a laugh, as does Dan playing "(I've Had) The Time of My Life" from *Dirty Dancing* (1987) the next morning, which lightens the mood and removes any awkwardness felt by Garrett and Erin after sleeping together the night they met.

Going the Distance is filled with these nuggets of cheerful romance, yet just when the movie seems ready to rise into the top tier of recent romantic comedies it delivers a scene that feels uncomfortably and unwisely forced into the film. It feels as if a studio executive read the script and determined that every twenty minutes or so a scene or a joke needed to be added to make the movie more outrageous and less mature. As a result, Garrett has a stale, stupid run-in with a fake tanning machine. Garrett and Erin are caught having sex by Erin's brother-in-law Phil (Jim Gaffigan), who is mostly in the movie to perpetuate an unfunny running joke about his unusual sexual habits with his wife, Erin's protective sister Corinne (Christina Applegate).

In between these scenes, though, *Going the Distance* glides easily along with its leads, who constantly capture the pain of being apart from a loved one and the heightened emotion of being with that person for just a few days every few months. Miscommunication and jealousy appear, but the film never devolves into a series of idiotic miscommunications or mistakes. Mostly, this is a story about believable people making mature decisions, while also finding sweetness in both platonic friendship and lovers who also genuinely feel like best friends. That is not supported by Dan walking an old woman across the street while talking to her about the hazards of masturbation, or Box's ridiculous goal of sleeping with older women who will be transported back to the late 1970s or early 1980s as a result of his mustache. "This is not a mustache," he says. "It's a time machine." No, it is a mustache. The movie is the time machine, bringing viewers back to an experience that happens all too rarely this decade: seeing movie characters who care about their jobs and their families and also care about each other, deliver both humor and genuine romance while trying to put all of the good things in their life on the same page.

Matt Pais

CREDITS

Erin: Drew Barrymore
Garrett: Justin Long
Dan: Charlie Day
Box: Jason Sudeikis
Will: Ron Livingston
Brianna: Kelli Garner
Corinne: Christina Applegate
Phil: Jim Gaffigan
Ron: Rob Riggle
Hugh: Matt Servitto
Amy: Leighton Meester

Origin: USA

Language: English

Released: 2010

Production: Adam Shankman, Jennifer Gibgot, Garrett Grant; New Line Cinema, Offspring Entertainment; released by Warner Bros.

Directed by: Nanette Burstein

Written by: Geoff LaTulippe

Cinematography by: Eric Steelberg

Music by: Mychael Danna

Sound: Michael Barosky

Music Supervisor: Dana Sano

Editing: Peter Teschner

Art Direction: Peter Rogness, John J. Kasarda

Costumes: Catherine Thomas

Production Design: Kevin Kavanaugh

MPAA rating: R

Running time: 102 minutes

REVIEWS

Gleiberman, Owen. *Entertainment Weekly.* September 1, 2010.
LaSalle, Mick. *San Francisco Chronicle.* September 3, 2010.
Moore, Roger. *Orlando Sentinel.* September 1, 2010.
Morris, Wesley. *Boston Globe.* September 3, 2010.
Phillips, Michael. *Chicago Tribune.* September 2, 2010.
Pols, Mary. *TIME Magazine.* September 3, 2010.
Puig, Claudia. *USA Today.* September 3, 2010.
Scott, A.O.. *New York Times.* September 2, 2010.
Tobias, Scott. *AV Club.* September 2, 2010.
Williams, Joe. *St. Louis Post-Dispatch.* September 3, 2010.

QUOTES

Corinne: "He's thousands of miles away from here. You don't know what he's doing right now. He could be in some bar, doing shots with some sexy bartender dry humping her."

TRIVIA

Writer Geoff LaTulippe based the film's story on a real-life long-distance relationship between the film's producer David Neustadter and a former girlfriend.

THE GOOD, THE BAD, THE WEIRD

The genre known in some circles as "Gun fu" suggests a mix of martial arts and gunplay. Forget the high kicks, think more high caliber. Gun fu is a genre epitomized first and foremost by the stylized use of firearms. Nobody blinks at the wire work in martial arts cinema that gives actors the ability to defy gravity and create dazzling hand-to-hand combat. Likewise, Gun fu offers physically impossible or at least highly impractical

gun play that takes the energy of classic shoot 'em ups and action movies to new highs. Gun fu at its best is a wide eyed playground for anyone who has ever cocked their own thumbs, jumped through the air, and shouted "Pow!" as they hit another playmate's imaginary bullet in mid-air.

The Good, the Bad, the Weird takes place circa 1930 and tells the story of three men as they race across the Manchurian desert in search of buried treasure. Park Chang-yi aka The Bad (Byung-hun Lee) is a ruthless bandit hired to steal a treasure map from a Japanese government official traveling by train, unaware that Yoon Tae-goo aka The Weird (Kang-ho Song) has been hired to steal it back from him. After a huge shootout and the derailment of the train, Park Do-won aka The Good (Woo-sung Jung), a bounty hunter shows up in pursuit of The Bad allowing The Weird to escape with the map pursued by still another group—government soldiers. Abandoning plans to sell the map on the black market, The Weird sets out to find the treasure for himself. With everyone in pursuit, the film becomes, basically, one long, spectacular series of chases and shootouts ending with the three being the only ones to reach the treasure site which turns out to be a boarded up hole in the earth.

Inspired by Sergio Leone's revered *The Good, the Bad and the Ugly* (1966), and directed by Jee-woon Kim, *The Good, the Bad, the Weird* is a rollicking adventure that lives up to its name, offering something for any action movie fan and paying homage to the spaghetti western without becoming a mere ape of it. Known as *Joheun nom nabbeun nom isanghan nom* in its native South Korea, *The Good, the Bad, the Weird* may have a chance when all is said and seen to enter the pantheon of Gun fu that includes revered films such as *Hard Boiled* (1992) and *A Better Tomorrow* (1986). But its western milieu and self-awareness seem to put it firmly in the camp of more recent efforts like Takashi Miike's *Sukiyaki Western Django* (2007) and the American *Shoot 'Em Up* (2007). In short, it is a tongue-in-cheek riff that often goes where no suspension of disbelief would dare.

Jee-woon Kim's first film, the darkly comic *The Quiet Family* (1998), besides being a disquieting surreal gem on its own, helped launch the international reputation of Asian Horror and the career of Takashi Miike. But it was *A Tale of Two Sisters* (2003), remade later stateside as *The Uninvited* (2009), that cemented his place in film history. Densely atmospheric and worthy of the title Hitchcockian, *A Tale of Two Sisters* may have been the finest modern day Asian horror film to emerge from its era.. But fans expecting the director to confine himself to the horror genre were equally blown away by the gangster drama *A Bittersweet Life* (2005). If moving from horror to gangster drama, both having their attendant violence, seemed like not that much of a leap then the move into Gun fu was certainly startling. His latest film, *I Saw the Devil* (2010), has been picked up for distribution stateside and promises fans another fine return to the horror form that established him as a director to watch.

Kim was smart enough to tackle this technically complex action film with very experienced and distinguished players. Song Kang-ho will be most familiar to American world cinema enthusiasts having previously seen him in films like Bong Joon-ho's *Thirst* (2009) and *The Host* (2006), as well as the widely regarded *Lady Vengeance* (2005), *Memories of Murder* (2003), and *Sympathy for Mr. Vengeance* (2002). His normally meek demeanor is stretched here to accommodate broad comic relief without sacrificing the sympathetic edge that he has powerfully evoked in the past. Viewers who failed to catch Byung-hun Lee in *G.I Joe: The Rise of Cobra* (2009) can see his talents on much better display. Lastly, Woo-sung Jung made his biggest impression stateside in *The Warrior* (2001).

Asian action cinema and martial arts long ago set the standard for action film in general. Gun fu brings a twist to that which, in the long run, like almost any other group of genre conventions, has to be proven to stand the test of time. Thankfully, Jee-woon Kim abandons neither the demands of storytelling nor the need of the audience to identify with his characters in this film. A mark of distinction here is that although *The Good, the Bad, the Weird* takes some wild shots it generally hits what it aims at, and it aims to do a little more than just dazzle the eye.

The quality of violence in these films is striking as much as it is graphic. If John Woo can be said to have perfected the idea of the poetry of violence then perhaps Gun fu offers the necessary adolescent antidote of fun to a world cinema that is increasingly part of a smaller world, highly influential and being consumed by a younger and younger audience through anime, manga and even stateside children's cinema. The term gun "play" is used for a reason: the use of guns to extend the heart and soul into adventurous battle landscapes where the good and the bad and the weird can reinforce that guns are good for play and little else.

Dave Canfield

CREDITS

Do-won/The Good: Woo-sung Jung
Chang-yi/The Bad: Byung-hun Lee
Tae-goo/The Weird: Kang-ho Song
Man-gil: Seung-su Ryu

Pan-joo Kim: Young-chang Song
Origin: Korea
Language: Korean
Released: 2008
Production: Jee-woon Kim, Jae-weon Choi; CJ Entertainment, Grimm Pictures; released by IFC Films
Directed by: Jee-woon Kim
Written by: Jee-woon Kim, Min-suk Kim
Cinematography by: Mo-gae Lee
Music by: Yeong-gyu Chang
Sound: Kim Wook
Editing: Na-yeong Nam
Costumes: Yu-jin Gweon
Production Design: Hwa-seong Jo
MPAA rating: R
Running time: 139 minutes

REVIEWS

Abele, Robert. *Los Angeles Times.* April 29, 2010.
Burr, Ty. *Boston Globe.* April 29, 2010.
Gronvall, Andrea. *Chicago Reader.* May 7, 2010.
Howell, Peter. *Toronto Star.* August 6, 2010.
Hale, Mike. *New York Times.* April 23, 2010.
Lybarger, Dan. *eFilmCritic.com.* July 24, 2010.
Murray, Noel. *AV Club.* April 22, 2010.
Rea, Steven. *Philadelphia Enquirer.* May 6, 2010.
Schrager, Norm. *FilmCritic.com.* April 9, 2010.
Verniere, James. *Boston Herald.* April 29, 2010.

QUOTES

Park Do-won: "Every Korean has a sad story."

TRIVIA

This movie was the most expensive in South Korean cinema history as of 2009.

THE GREATEST

In *The Greatest,* Carey Mulligan plays Rose, an American teen whose boyfriend dies in a car crash just a few weeks into their relationship and right after the first time they have sex. The problem is that Rose did not think virgins could get pregnant. But lo and behold she is, and with nowhere else to go, she shows up on her dead boyfriend's parent's doorstep looking for a place to stay because she is keeping the baby and wants to know more about her baby-daddy. Bennett's (Aaron Johnson of *Kick-Ass* [2010]) bereft parents are played by Pierce Brosnan and Susan Sarandon and they channel the clichéd dichotomy of parents grieving the loss of a child. Allen (Brosnan) is trying to hold it together and Grace (Sarandon) falls apart every chance she gets. Despite their compromised emotional states, they let Rose stay, giving her a room across the hall from their younger son Ryan, a confused druggie high schooler played by Johnny Simmons who resents living in his older brother's shadow. For the next six months the makeshift family tries to coexist while hashing out all their death/ grief issues, dealing with their personal demons and having a "whose breakdown is the best" contest (Simmons wins, by the way). A lot of the calculated antics that are present throughout the film are unavoidable, this is a dead child story after all, but instead of shining as a well-cast "from the ashes a new family is born" film, *The Greatest* comes off as a clunky, melodramatic, and underwritten exercise that amounts to showcasing famous actors crying.

Shana Feste's film starts out with such potential. Bennett's death scene (this is not a spoiler, it happens right away and sets the mood for the film) is jarring and the initial scenes of his family processing his death—namely Grace's waking-up-and-crying and Allen's not sleeping at all—are touching and intriguing, but once Rose joins the brood things get a little confusing. First off is the question of why she has come to stay at all. Toward the end of the film we can piece together the fact that her hippie mother—whom we see briefly at Bennett's funeral—is not only in rehab, but also an opportunistic jerk who should not be around babies (or other people). But that still leaves questions. Does Rose have no other family? Friends? What is it exactly that makes her dead boyfriend's parents the right choice for living companions? Rose's presence is justified through the flashbacks of her time spent with Bennett, which play throughout the narrative and help solidify their earnest and urgent teen love. But since Rose is the only one who triggers these scenes, at times it is hard not to wonder if this is supposed to be a film about Rose's singular-yet-brief relationship with Bennett—as opposed to involving all the other cast members.

It is also difficult to believe that time flies as fast as it does in *The Greatest*. No sooner does Rose move in than she is sporting a hefty baby bump, talking about baby names, and going into labor. The characters around her however seem to be stuck in the same week. A product of grief no doubt, but it does not allow the audience to put what they are seeing into any type of perspective.

Then there are the side plots that just feel piled-on and unnecessary, like Ryan's drug use as well as his grief counseling gone bad, Grace's irrational need for closure and Allen's old flame that keeps coming around. None of these are given tremendous attention in the hopes, one can assume, that they not take over the plot and to showcase just how messy life is. People have affairs and do drugs well before considering the fact that one of

their loved ones might not be around tomorrow. Why treat these messy human moments with kid gloves screenwriter and director Shana Feste seems to be asking—it only makes it more real if the characters have to deal with everything all at once, right? It is not a bad approach; the layered nature of the story does open itself up for complex characterization and plot. Unfortunately, due to poor balance, this short film just feels cluttered with tangents more than anything else. Rose and Allen bond at a random high school party, Ryan learns that the girl he is crushing on is a fake and Grace visits the man accused of killing her son way too much. Though all these moments have potential for intrigue and some even let Simmons shine in the film's least heavy-handed performance, all they really amount to are building blocks for cry-fests that lead to a resolution that is as harried as it is unlikely.

Joanna Topor MacKenzie

CREDITS

Allen Brewer: Pierce Brosnan
Grace Brewer: Susan Sarandon
Rose: Carey Mulligan
Ryan Brewer: Johnny Simmons
Bennett Brewer: Aaron Johnson
Joan: Jennifer Ehle
Ashley: Zoe Kravitz
Jordan Walker: Michael Shannon
Lydia: Amy Morton
Origin: USA
Language: English
Released: 2009
Production: Lynette Howell, Beau St. Clair; Silverwood Films, Irish DreamTime; released by Paladin
Directed by: Shana Feste
Written by: Shana Feste
Cinematography by: John Bailey
Music by: Christophe Beck
Sound: Michael Baird
Music Supervisor: Manish Raval, Tom Wolfe
Editing: Cara Silverman
Art Direction: Bradley Schmidt
Costumes: Luca Mosca
Production Design: Judy Rhee
MPAA rating: R
Running time: 99 minutes

REVIEWS

Burr, Ty. *Boston Globe.* April 8, 2010.
Goldstein, Gary. *Los Angeles Times.* April 1, 2010.
LaSalle, Mick. *San Francisco Chronicle.* April 8, 2010.

Murray, Rebecca. *About.com.* April 12, 2010.
Reed, Rex. *New York Observer.* March 31, 2010.
Rickey, Carrie. *Philadelphia Inquirer.* April 8, 2010.
Schenker, Andrew. *Slant Magazine.* March 29, 2010.
Tallerico, Brian. *HollywoodChicago.com.* April 9, 2010.
Thompson, Gary. *Philadelphia Daily News.* April 8, 2010.
Travers, Peter. *Rolling Stone.* April 1, 2010.

QUOTES

Rose: "I knew this boy…who was really wonderful to me."

TRIVIA

Writer/director Shana Feste wrote the script during a three month stint as a nanny in Southern California.

GREEN ZONE

Chief Warrant Officer Roy Miller is done following orders.
—Movie tagline

Box Office: $35 million

Like the Oscar®-winning *The Hurt Locker* (2009), *Green Zone* is about demolitions experts in Iraq. The two films could serve as bookends for the long-running war there, but the latter's release date seems weirdly out of sync with the national mood. Whereas *The Hurt Locker,* which came out in early 2009, is not argumentative about the war, while detailing its human repercussions and even its seductive nature for one bomb squad leader, *Green Zone,* though not released until 2010, centers on the deception that got America bogged down in Iraq in the first place. It is a movie that seeks to settle scores that have long needed settling.

Green Zone seems six or seven years overdue—unlike Paul Greengrass's *United 93* (2006), which quickly picked over a nation's recent terrifying wound well before it had even started to heal. Sharing the you-were-there pseudo-documentary feel of that earlier unflinching fact-based masterpiece, Greengrass's new film ultimately suffers from its willingness to launch from known facts into rampant speculation. In the end, it turns a blazing political diatribe into a standard action movie.

The premise is bold and almost breathtaking. Matt Damon plays an Army officer whose purpose is to find and destroy Saddam Hussein's weapons of mass destruction immediately after the invasion of Iraq. Damon's Roy Miller is a good soldier, trying to do his duty, who starts out believing wholeheartedly in his mission. When his targets keep coming up empty, he becomes irked at what he believes is the bad intelligence that is ruining his job. Then it begins to dawn on him that he is just a pawn in a big game based on a big lie: there are no weapons of mass destruction to be found.

As a case study in the disillusionment of a loyal American, *Green Zone* is powerful. Damon's plight reflects that of many Americans who came to realize that we had gone to war for reasons that didn't match up with propaganda. This is a portrait that is full of the weight of the military personnel who had to find a reason to continue their fight after realizing the fight was based on a false premise. As such, *Green Zone* is a venting of spleen. One critic even called it a raised finger pointed in the direction of George W. Bush.

But Greengrass's problem is that while the lie has now been revealed, the way the lie was manufactured and sold is still murky. So he has invented a fictitious plot to explain a known fact, and that plot is heavy with shadowy movie-type conspirators and action figures. And the resolution of Miller's conflict must involve car chases, urban warfare, and shootouts.

In *United 93,* Greengrass also had to invent a scenario to explain activities not completely known—how the passengers of the doomed airline wrested control from the terrorist hijackers. But because it is so thoroughly grounded in known fact, the action is completely plausible. Not so here. It is far more likely that the WMD canard did not proceed as a highly cinematic conspiracy. So Greengrass had to concoct his own.

In this version of what might have taken place, Greg Kinnear plays a Pentagon information officer who is trying desperately to keep the war story spinning his way, Amy Ryan plays a big-time Washington reporter who has been duped by the official disinformation campaign, and Brendan Gleeson plays a CIA operative who is willing to let Miller go rogue and discover the truth, which has to do with some important Middle Eastern sect leaders who have been manipulated as part of the cover story. Miller's quest for the truth involves risky infiltration and clandestine meetings, and the official military loyalists willing to wipe out the dissenter Miller in order to get the truth known. The plot plays out as elaborate wishful thinking, with the lie exposed and the record set straight. It is not as elaborate a wartime revenge fantasy as was played out in *Inglourious Basterds* (2009), but it is not far from that order of magnitude. If we could rewrite history so that the bad guys get their due, Greengrass imagines, it would go something like this.

The split personality of *Green Zone*—part diatribe, part wartime action/adventure—ended up making near-zero impact on the box office and critical radar. The war-weary American public (and the rest of the world, too) had little interest in revisiting the nonexistent WMD issue. Not for lack of chutzpah nor for lack of cinematic firepower and sincerity, but simply for carrying through an idea that strained credibility more than the WMD fabrication itself, this time Greengrass falls flat, but it is a rather spectacular fall, and worth seeing just for the effort.

Michael Betzold

CREDITS

Roy Miller: Matt Damon
Clark Poundstone: Greg Kinnear
Lawrie Dayne: Amy Ryan
Major Briggs: Jason Isaacs
Martin Brown: Brendan Gleeson
Origin: France, Spain, United Kingdom, USA
Language: English
Released: 2010
Production: Tim Bevan, Eric Fellner, Lloyd Levin; Working Title Films, Relativity Media, Studio Canal, Antena 3; released by Universal Pictures
Directed by: Paul Greengrass
Written by: Brian Helgeland
Cinematography by: Barry Ackroyd
Music by: John Powell
Sound: Oliver Tarney
Music Supervisor: Peter Myles
Editing: Christopher Rouse
Art Direction: Mark Bartholomew
Costumes: Sammy Sheldon
Production Design: Dominic Watkins
MPAA rating: R
Running time: 114 minutes

REVIEWS

Dinning, Mark. *Empire Magazine.* March 9, 2010.
Ebert, Roger. *Chicago Sun-Times.* March 11, 2010.
Edelstein, David. *New York Magazine.* March 8, 2010.
Hoberman, J. *Village Voice.* March 9, 2010.
Lacey, Liam. *Globe and Mail.* March 12, 2010.
Lane, Anthony. *New Yorker.* March 8, 2010.
Offer, Avi. *NYC Movie Guru.* March 13, 2010.
Pais, Matt. *Metromix.com.* March 11, 2010.
Phillips, Michael. *Chicago Tribune.* March 11, 2010.
Stevens, Dana. *Slate.* March 11, 2010.

QUOTES

Martin Brown: "You cannot just hand this country over to an exile no one's ever heard of, and a bunch of interns from Washington."

TRIVIA

Morocco served as the shooting location for scenes set in downtown Baghdad. Real life Iraq and Afghanistan veterans were cast to play the soldiers in Matt Damon's WMD unit.

AWARDS

Nomination:

Screen Actors Guild 2010: Stunt Ensemble.

GREENBERG

He's got a lot on his mind.
—Movie tagline

Box Office: $4 million

A basic characteristic of most good films is that it successfully creates a protagonist for whom the audience can root. And though in this case, "root" is too strong a word, *Greenberg*'s greatest feat is that viewers find themselves wishing its eponymous main character well, despite him giving them hardly any reason to do so. Like most movies by writer/director Noah Baumbach (including *The Squid and the Whale* [2005] and *Kicking & Screaming* [1995]), its narrative aims feel modest. Rather than watching its characters power through the most dramatic moments of their lives, viewers are, instead, simply dropped into their stories at seemingly random points. And instead of undergoing major shifts in character over the course of these films, the protagonists usually evolve in small and subtle ways. So it is impressive, then, that while Roger Greenberg (Ben Stiller) shuffles unassumingly through this movie, somewhere along the way, viewers end up caring about what happens to him.

The title character is a forty-year-old carpenter from New York, who suffers from numerous neuroses, including, presumably, a form of OCD. He has been recently released from a psychiatric hospital and has returned to his hometown of Los Angeles, to regroup for six weeks at his brother's family's home while they are on vacation abroad. Roger has been charged with keeping an eye on the house and dog, but it feels as if those responsibilities were created primarily to keep his mind occupied, as his brother's capable, personal assistant, Florence (Greta Gerwig), is also available and has been asked to stop in from time to time.

Roger's family and friends hope his visit will inspire him to make a fresh start, but he appears paralyzed by his new surroundings, rather than invigorated by them. It seems that the smallest foreign details assault his senses and set his mind reeling, whether that be the noise of an airplane overhead or the sight of neighbors carousing in the pool. From day to day, he is unable to accomplish little more than writing angry letters to corporations and a bit of work on a doghouse he is building. And a visit to a laid-back, typically Californian party—where those who once served as his peers appear strikingly comfortable with their aging and shifts in priories—crystallizes the gap he is feeling between his current place in life and that of others his age. But he stubbornly defends his state, proclaiming proudly that he is "really trying to do nothing right now," a statement that strangely wins him admiration from Florence, who says she prefers that over a subscription to the societal pressures that normally accompany adulthood. The irony, of course, is that Roger is not at all comfortable with himself, and it is Florence who seems blissfully, naively content with who/where she is, despite lacking ambitions toward a family, career, etc. This bewilders Greenberg and causes him to awkwardly pursue a relationship with her, one to which she never really agrees, but stumbles into passively nonetheless.

Roger's biggest problem is that he insists on constantly sabotaging his own potential happiness, at the first sight of someone else's. And he often goes about that in such spectacular fashion, as to extinguish everyone else's too. After reconnecting with two of his once-best friends, Ivan and Eric (Rhys Ifans and Mark Duplass), we learn that years ago, they played together in a promising band that was offered a major recording contract. But without ever giving convincing reasons, Greenberg torpedoed the deal and effectively ended the group. And to this day, it appears that they still have not forgiven him, even if they have come to expect nothing less. Up until now, this has been Greenberg's lot in life. And as the film progresses, it is conceivable that Florence is doomed to sink with him or instead, perhaps capable of opening him up to the small pleasures life has to offer.

Greenberg marks a new milestone in Ben Stiller's career, who in the past, has commonly played the affable straight man, using his crinkled smirk, sharp comedic timing and his characters' poor luck to win audience affection. But here, he embraces the physical person he is becoming—looking shaggy, graying and somewhat haggard—and boldly portrays Roger as a serious killjoy, nearly daring us to turn our backs on him. Gerwig is also fantastic in her highest profile role to date. Her eyes sparkle without an ounce of cynicism and there is a real effortlessness about her character which renders the performance behind it nearly invisible. Also deserving of mention is the refreshingly unobtrusive work of the movie's technical artists, including Harris Savides' highly naturalistic cinematography and the sparse, plaintive score by LCD Soundsystem's James Murphy (who interestingly enough, avoids lyrics here, though he is usually heard singing about the struggle to maintain relevance whilst aging).

Again, *Greenberg* is a film with simple ambitions, but one that achieves them quietly. And much of the credit belongs to Baumbach, who specializes in presenting a quirky personality that can seem awfully strange at first, then refining viewer point of view until the character begins to feel familiar and in this case, surprisingly sympathetic. Though of all his films, *Greenberg* manages this the most inconspicuously. And by the final frame, the viewer realizes that the bulk of the transformation has taken place not on-screen, but within his own frame of reference, which is an accomplishment worth commending.

Matthew Priest

CREDITS

Roger Greenberg: Ben Stiller
Florence: Greta Gerwig
Ivan Schrank: Rhys Ifans
Sara: Brie Larson
Muriel: Juno Temple
Eric Beller: Mark Duplass
Beth: Jennifer Jason Leigh
Rich: Dave Franco
Philip Greenberg: Chris Messina
Origin: USA
Language: English
Released: 2010
Production: Jennifer Jason Leigh, Scott Rudin; Scott Rudin Productions; released by Focus Features
Directed by: Noah Baumbach
Written by: Noah Baumbach
Cinematography by: Harris Savides
Editing: Tim Streeto
Art Direction: Curt Beech
Music by: James Murphy
Sound: Paul Hsu
Costumes: Mark Bridges
Production Design: Ford Wheeler
MPAA rating: R
Running time: 107 minutes

REVIEWS

Ebert, Roger. *Chicago Sun-Times.* March 24, 2010.
Hoberman, J. *Village Voice.* March 16, 2010.
McCarthy, Todd. *Variety.* February 14, 2010.
Phillips, Michael. *Chicago Tribune.* March 25, 2010.
Rea, Steven. *Philadelphia Inquirer.* March 26, 2010.
Schwarzbaum, Lisa. *Entertainment Weekly.* March 19, 2010.
Scott, A. O. *New York Times.* March 19, 2010.
Stevens, Dana. *Slate.* March 18, 2010.

Travers, Peter. *Rolling Stone.* March 19, 2010.
Zacharek, Stephanie. *Salon.com.* March 18, 2010.

QUOTES

Roger Greenberg: "Dear Starbucks, in your attempt to manufacture culture out of fast food coffee you've been surprisingly successful for the most part. The part that isn't covered by 'the most part' sucks."

TRIVIA

Actors originally considered for the lead roles included Amy Adams, Mark Ruffalo, and Maggie Gyllenhaal.

AWARDS

Nomination:

Ind. Spirit 2011: Actor (Stiller), Actress (Gerwig), Cinematog., Film.

GROWN UPS

Boys will be boys…some longer than others.
—Movie tagline

Back then they were too young to know better. Now they have no excuse.
—Movie tagline

Box Office: $162 million

Someone once said that one's favorite cast from *Saturday Night Live* can be directly attributed to their time in Junior High School. Whether this was meant as an implication to the show's tendency to connect with juvenile humor or praise for its edgier satire restructuring our ideas of what is funny during our formative years is left to speculation. Pratfalls and gross-out humor certainly found their place on the show, but few have taken and parlayed it into a career more successfully than Adam Sandler. While that success has afforded him the opportunity to work with distinguished filmmakers tackling more unique dramatic (and humor-based) challenges such as Paul Thomas Anderson's *Punch-Drunk Love* (2002), James L. Brooks' *Spanglish* (2004), and Judd Apatow's *Funny People* (2009), his bread-and-butter with his followers has always been the goofball persona. Now with fellow friends and goofballs, many from his days on *Saturday Night Live,* Sandler is out to definitively show that what may have been funny in seventh grade is not quite as funny when you get older. And maybe never was.

As kids, five little boys won Coach "Buzzer" (Blake Clark) his first and only basketball championship. Now as men they get the phone call that the coach has died and they will gather once again for his funeral. Lenny Feder (Adam Sandler) is a Hollywood agent with a fashion designer wife in Roxanne (Salma Hayek) and two spoiled kids obsessed with video games and being served. Eric Lamonsoff (Kevin James) specializes in lawn furniture and is married to Sally (Maria Bello) who is still breastfeeding their four year-old son. Kurt McKenzie (Chris Rock) is a stay-at-home dad who is constantly he is berated by his mother-in-law (Ebony Jo-Ann while his pregnant wife, Deanne (Maya Rudolph) works. Rob Hilliard (Rob Schneider) is a new-age guru on his fourth wife, Gloria (Joyce Van Patten), who is usually mistaken for his mother. And Marcus Higgins (David Spade) is the single guy of the group.

For the weekend after the funeral, Lenny has rented a lake house for them all even though he is under pressure to leave for Milan the next day for a fashion show. In the meantime, he is hoping to get his boys interested in the beauty of the outdoors and reconnect with his pals. They fall into the old habits of ribbing and slapping each other while occasionally letting out a nugget of casual regret about their marriages. Thrown into the mix are not only Rob's daughters; the statuesque beauties Jasmine (Madison Riley) and Amber (Jamie Chung), and the less attractive Bridget (Ashley Loren) who appears to be more in line with his short, goofy-haired gene pool, but also their old court rivals including Dickie Bailey (Colin Quinn) who never left town and still holds a grudge that Lenny's game-winning shot should have been disallowed. Nothing would please him more than a rematch.

Lurking right out front in *Grown Ups* is a really interesting, if overtly familiar, tale about adulthood, parenthood, and so many other hoods; a tale that likely would have had a wonderful polish by, say, someone like James L. Brooks or Judd Apatow. Unfortunately it has been helmed by Dennis Dugan, a Sandler loyalist ever since *Happy Gilmore* (1995) that has gone on to direct the star in *Big Daddy* (1999), *I Now Pronounce You Chuck & Larry* (2007), and *You Don't Mess with the Zohan* (2008). While none of those titles leap out as mature works, maybe this was an opportunity for Dugan to join his fellow goofballs in living up to the title. Leopards of any age apparently still do not change their spots and all of Dugan's missteps in comic timing and lazy bargain-basement humor undercut the film every time it hopes to connect as something more.

Humor being the most subjective of any criticism, *Grown Ups* is counting on more of a grade school mentality to achieve its laughs. The aforementioned breastfeeding is just a taste of what is in store and the concept of branching out subscribed to by Dugan, Sandler and co-writer Fred Wolf is to repeat their jokes beyond a degree of ad nauseum. A four year-old boy breastfeeding once or twice not enough? How about a third time when the milk is squirted in an adult's face? James' Eric embarrasses himself peeing on a boat, so why not a second time in a children's pool and then again joined by his friends. Jokes paid at the expense of Van Patten's age are too numerous to count and Chris Rock, one of the smartest stand-up comedians of his generation, is reduced to doing toe puns and proving once again that putting him in PG-13 comedies is akin to casting a unich.

The complete lack of interest in real-world problems leaves *Grown Ups* completely edge-free. One character does go on a rant about life, claiming that the second act is "where the depth comes in." That may be the funniest line of the whole film as characters gather in the film's third act to air their grievances in an impromptu therapy session that would be satire if we were not supposed to take their disclosures somewhat to heart. The overtly syrupy, score-laden moments cue us into postponing our laughter while Roxanne accidentally scars her daughter Becky's (Alexys Nycole Sanchez) belief system, Rob blows up about his past marriages, and Eric borrows a character secret from, of all movies, *The Great Outdoors* (1988) without irony. If the writers were interested in making this more *City Slickers* (1991) and less *Wild Hogs* (2007), they may have found value in continuing little Becky's empathetic approach towards death. Instead they split the difference and leave out what could have been a very poignant scene between father and daughter to wedge in more height and fart jokes.

Grown Ups does manage to squeeze out the occasional laugh as about one-in-four quips between the guys lands a less obvious target. When left to their own devices — ones that do not involve shrewish reaction shots and breast pumps—the women even get to play a little welcome relief in-between the male shenanigans. Far out in its favor is that none of the guys, no matter how one-dimensional, are unlikable. The real-life friendships casually grace their performances leading one back to the assertion that some films are not as interesting as their actors having lunch together. Since Dugan does not possess the chops to take advantage of Sandler's talents—which drift more to the paternal here—he may as well have just stripped down everything altogether and followed the five of them along for an actual weekend trip. Maybe then audiences could determine who amongst them have truly grown up.

Erik Childress

CREDITS

Lenny Feder: Adam Sandler
Eric Lamonsoff: Kevin James
Kurt McKenzie: Chris Rock
Rob Hilliard: Rob Schneider
Marcus Higgins: David Spade
Roxanne Chase-Feder: Salma Hayek
Sally Lamonsoff: Maria Bello
Deanne McKenzie: Maya Rudolph
Malcolm: Tim Meadows
Geezer: Norm MacDonald
Gloria: Joyce Van Patten
Bailey: Colin Quinn
Pastor: Tim Herlihy
Mama Ronzini: Ebony Jo-Ann
Coach Buzzer: Blake Clark
Wiley: Steve Buscemi
Jasmine: Madison Riley
Amber: Jamie Chung
Bridget: Ashley Loren
Becky: Alexys Nycole Sanchez
Origin: USA
Language: English
Released: 2010
Production: Adam Sandler, Jack Giarraputo; Happy Madison Productions, Relativity Media; released by Columbia Pictures, Sony Pictures Entertainment
Directed by: Dennis Dugan
Written by: Adam Sandler, Fred Wolf
Cinematography by: Theo van de Sande
Music by: Rupert Gregson-Williams
Sound: David Wyman, Thomas Causey
Music Supervisor: Michael Dilbeck, Brooks Arthur
Editing: Tom Costain
Art Direction: Alan Au
Costumes: Ellen Lutter
Production Design: Perry Andelin Blake
MPAA rating: PG-13
Running time: 102 minutes

REVIEWS

Bowles, Scott. *USA Today.* June 24, 2010.
Ebert, Roger. *Chicago Sun-Times.* June 24, 2010.
Lemire, Christy. *Associated Press.* June 24, 2010.
Morris, Wesley. *Boston Globe.* June 23, 2010.
Pais, Matt. *Metromix.com.* June 24, 2010.
Phillips, Michael. *Chicago Tribune.* June 24, 2010.
Pinkerton, Nick. *Village Voice.* June 22, 2010.
Simon, Brent. *Screen International.* June 24, 2010.
Tallerico, Brian. *HollywoodChicago.com.* June 25, 2010.
Tobias, Scott. *AV Club.* June 24, 2010.

QUOTES

Lenny Feder: "We needed to be here. Our kids were turning into snotty, spoiled, little…this is what we needed."

TRIVIA

Adam Sandler, David Spade, Rob Schneider, and Chris Rock were all castmates at "Saturday Night Live" in the 1990s.

In almost every scene of the movie, Adam Sandler wears a different New England area college shirt or hat. Adam Sandler originally wrote the screenplay in the mid-1990s with actor Chris Farley in mind. Kevin James assumed the role after Farley's untimely death in 1997 postponed production for more than a decade.

AWARDS

Nomination:

Golden Raspberries 2010: Worst Support. Actor (Schneider).

GULLIVER'S TRAVELS

Black is the new big.
—Movie tagline

Something big is going down.
—Movie tagline

Box Office: $41 million

Jonathan Swift's *Gulliver's Travels* has captivated readers for almost three hundred years, while this latest adaptation of the classic tome had trouble doing so over eighty-eight minutes. The book's titular character, who never took anything close to a blissfully-uneventful pleasure cruise, seemed entirely insignificant when juxtaposed with the giants of Brobdingnag, but this film, even when not compared with Swift's towering, indelible source material, strikes one as something that only reaches the height of triviality. While the author aimed for savage satire that might enlighten mankind, the filmmakers set their sites infinitely lower, instead aiming the anus of a falling Gulliver so that it slams down on a Lilliputian who thereafter ceases to be visible up the cavernous crease. Not much else in the film strikes one as possessing great depth. Mildly amusing but never particularly engaging, it is utterly forgettable in the end—something that would doubtlessly not be said by that decidedly unlucky citizen of Lilliput.

Swift, who himself enjoyed employing scatological and generally bawdy humor, might very well be giggling from the grave at that part of *Gulliver*, but the remainder is capable of sending him right back to his six-feet-under slumber. The film is probably not something that would quite agonize the author enough to start him spinning in that grave, even though his highly-creative and potent poking fun at the human race has been severely abridged to something that merely facilitates some negligible adventure and romantic comedy. There is also some psychobabbling reassurance that anyone, when encouraged to believe in themselves, can rise to the occasion and achieve what had seemed well out of their reach. The film's moral message is likely sufficient to at least make Swift shake his head once more at such misguided folly.

At one point, this Lemuel Gulliver (Jack Black, once again nearly acting his eyebrows off) is seen shaking his head and lamenting, "I got nothin'," which unfortunately is not especially far off-the-mark concerning both the character and this actor devoid of a worthwhile script. Gulliver describes himself as one of the "little people," monotonously toiling amongst the big shots in the Big Apple, a lowly clerk who emerges from the bowels of the *New York Tribune* and delivers mail to those whose ambitions have taken them onwards and upwards toward importance. Having already toiled in this manner for a decade, Gulliver exhibits no sign of having any such fire in his flabby belly to attain anything loftier. There is, however, warmth in his heart for the newspaper's lovely travel editor Darcy Silverman (sweet Amanda Peet), only Gulliver does not have enough confidence to ask her out. Suit-and-tie-clad whippersnapper Dan (T.J. Miller), who vaults from being Gulliver's newly-hired subordinate to his boss overnight, opines that his runty colleague-in-a-rut's life has most likely topped-out at the bottom. This prods Gulliver to at least try to work up his courage concerning Darcy. One ineffectual, misunderstanding-laden encounter later, Gulliver walks away with an abruptly-acquired writing assignment instead of plans for a long-yearned-for assignation. He creates a wholly-plagiarized portfolio of writing samples, things cobbled together from the accomplishments of others that will be sure to please. That is actually what the film does, as well, taking the fundamentals of Book One and just a bit of Book Two of Swift's *Gulliver*, and adding numerous elements from, and references to, well-known popular culture sources.

Darcy compliments inadvertent-go-getter Gulliver for "putting himself out there" as he heads down to the Bermuda Triangle to write a fluff piece for the paper, but neither realize just how exceedingly "out there" he will soon find himself. Sucked up into a colossal, watery vortex when gorgeous blue serenity turns into a tempestuous, supernatural squall, Gulliver wakes upon the shore of Lilliput to incredulously find himself lashed down and surrounded by hordes of equally-astonished and scarily-small people. This is, of course, the image that is familiar to everyone, although viewers will be hard-pressed to remember a previous version in which the character's feet are clad in Converse, or where he goes on to refer to anyone as "dude" or "lame-ass."

The relatively gigantic man goes from being deflatingly referred to as "the beast" to the more preferable "Our savior, the beast" after heroically hosing down a castle fire with a bladderful of urine. A number of critics failed to recognize this as one of the few things faithfully derived from Swift's text, pointing it out as an example of screenwriters Joe Stillman and Nicholas Stoller being needlessly, childishly lowbrow. It is true that Gulliver's good deed was not previously commemorated in the form of a risqué ice sculpture fountain. Gulliver also valiantly wades into the waves and defeats the imminently-invading armada of neighboring Blefuscu, splashing around like a little boy imaginatively playing in an immense bathtub. All hail Gulliver and thereafter gratefully do his bidding, except for supercilious General Edward (a funny bone-tickling Chris O'Dowd), who could not be more exasperated—and threatened—by the land's new focal point of valor. Gulliver is clearly and understandably enjoying being the new, exceptionally big, Big Man on Campus, but the general is hell-bent on cutting him down to size.

The most enjoyable sequence in this *Gulliver* is when he gets the Lilliputians to act out gripping scenes purportedly from his own impressive past that he actually has lifted from the likes of the original *Star Wars* trilogy and *Titanic* (1997). Humorously, a sputtering General Edward is incredulous that anyone is buying it all; particularly that Gulliver somehow rose not only from the deep but the dead after the unsinkable ship famously went under. While the faux star of the show reclines most appropriately in a La-Z-Boy, the rapt, highly-moved, and idolatrous Lilliputian audience that includes King Theodore (always welcome Billy Connolly) and Queen Isabelle (Catherine Tate and her cleavage) pointedly shush the disgusted general as if his voicing of doubts is ungracious, outrageous blasphemy.

There is so much else, however, that merely garners a Lilliputian level of interest. The film's fleeting visit to Brobdingnag seems merely tacked on so that a doll-sized Gulliver can be put first in a diaper and then in a dress by a less-than-angelic young lass, something which may make kids chortle just enough to wake their parents. Borrowing this time from *Cyrano de Bergerac,* Gulliver feeds beguiling sweet nothings (actually lyrics from Prince's 1986 hit song, "Kiss") to reticent commoner Horatio (blandly-likable Jason Segel) so he can woo and win the woman up on the balcony who is also well above his station, Princess Mary (Emily Blunt). Their burgeoning, forbidden romance is admittedly rather sweet, but while their own hearts may quicken whenever they meet, those in the audience will remain decidedly palpitation-free. (It is, however, satisfying to see her detour from an intended bloodless betrothal to General Edward, who brings a smile to audience members—but definitely not to the princess—with effusive but ridiculously underwhelming professions of adoration, such as when he gushes, "I find you absolutely satisfactory!") Likewise, when the plot's machinations deposit Darcy in Lilliput so that Gulliver can chivalrously rescue her, redeem himself with honesty, and consequently get his own seemingly-unattainable gal, it is pleasant but certainly not stirring. In an exceedingly blatant example of outright pilfering from Michael Bay's cash cow *Transformers* films, Gulliver valiantly engages in an inane battle-to-the-wedgie with traitorous, treacherous General Edward. Apparently lacking any ideas—original or otherwise—about how to then wrap things up, the film is padded with a wince-inducing, choreographed spectacle to the tune of Edwin Starr's pacifistic anthem, "War." Only in the sense that the credits roll soon after does this number qualify as a showstopper.

Made on a budget of $112 million, *Gulliver's Travels* was a huge box office disappointment for 20th Century Fox, domestically grossing only about a third of that amount. As many noted, the 3D effects raised the price of admission but not the entertainment value. Most reviews were negative (more than one declaring it "not too Swift"), with many critics sincerely aghast. Swift's satiric tour de force has been certainly been drained of that force. One cannot help but think, therefore, of the aforementioned scene in which sky-high Gulliver provides relief by relieving himself upon the burning royal abode below. In more ways than one, watered-down can be used to describe what transpires in this negligible adaptation of a complex, enduring masterwork.

David L. Boxerbaum

CREDITS

Lemuel Gulliver: Jack Black
Princess of Lilliputia: Emily Blunt
Horatio: Jason Segel
Darcy: Amanda Peet
King of Lilliputia: Billy Connolly
Queen of Lilliputia: Catherine Tate
Dan: T.J. Miller
Blefusian Princess: Nikki Harrup
Harold James: Ian Porter
Nigel: Richard Laing
General Edward: Chris O'Dowd
Origin: USA
Language: English
Released: 2010
Production: Jack Black, Ben Cooley; Davis Entertainment Company, Electric Entertainment; released by 20th Century Fox

Directed by: Rob Letterman
Written by: Nicholas Stoller, Joe Stillman
Cinematography by: David Tattersall
Music by: Henry Jackman
Editing: Alan Edward Bell
Sound: Derek Vanderhorst
Art Direction: Robert Cowper, Phil Harvey
Costumes: Sammy Sheldon
Production Design: Gavin Bocquet
MPAA rating: PG
Running time: 85 minutes

REVIEWS

Debruge, Peter. *Variety.* December 22, 2010.
Ebert, Roger. *Chicago Sun-Times.* December 22, 2010.
Honeycutt, Kirk. *Hollywood Reporter.* December 22, 2010.
Morgenstern, Joe. *Wall Street Journal.* December 24, 2010.
Morris, Wesley. *Boston Globe.* December 24, 2010.
O'Sullivan, Michael. *Washington Post.* December 25, 2010.
Rainer, Peter. *Christian Science Monitor.* December 30, 2010.
Scott, A.O. *New York Times.* December 23, 2010.
Sharkey, Betsy. *Los Angeles Times.* December 25, 2010.
Travers, Peter. *Rolling Stone.* January 6, 2011.

QUOTES

Lemuel Gulliver: "There's no small jobs—just small people."

TRIVIA

Actors originally considered for roles in the film include Taylor Lautner and Sarah Michelle Gellar.

Despite being based on the book *Gulliver's Travels*, author Jonathan Swift received no mention in the credits.

AWARDS

Nomination:

Golden Raspberries 2010: Worst Actor (Black).

H

HARRY BROWN

The law has limits. He doesn't.
—Movie tagline

Every man has a breaking point.
—Movie tagline

One man will take a stand.
—Movie tagline

Box Office: $1 million

Harry Brown is another slick, sleazy exploitation item in which a seemingly mild-mannered person is pushed too far and goes on a violent rampage of revenge and retribution against the punks that have harmed him and his loved ones. This would be perfectly fine if it were willing to simply accept its standing, but as it goes about its blood-soaked way, it seems determined to convince viewers that it is more profound and introspective. As a result, there is a bizarre disconnect from the movie that *Harry Brown* would like to be—a thoughtful drama about a man forced to re-embrace the violent tendencies that he has suppressed for most of his life—and the movie that it is, which is essentially a retread of one of the lesser *Death Wish* (1974) sequels in which audiences are directed to cheer every time one of the bad guys bites the big one in a spectacularly grisly manner. The end result is a grim, squalid, and depressing bummer that is even more frustrating because it contains a highly impressive performance by Michael Caine amidst all the dreck that is far better than the film really deserves.

At first glance, Harry Brown (Caine) seems as modest and unassuming as his name. He is an aging pensioner and recent widower who lives in a run-down London council flat that is under constant siege from violent drug-dealing punks who go about their depravations in broad daylight because they know that the other residents are too scared to stand up to them. For years, Brown has been just as cowed as his neighbors but when his best friend is murdered by the thugs after drunkenly standing up to them and the cops seem unable or unwilling to do anything about bringing the killers to justice, he realizes that he has nothing left to lose and begins to knock them off one-by-one, using the long-dormant skills that he picked up as a soldier fighting in Northern Ireland decades earlier. Meanwhile, a good-hearted cop (Emily Mortimer) begins investigating the rapidly-mounting body count and while she is initially sympathetic towards Harry and his plight, she becomes increasingly suspicious that this seemingly mild-mannered old duffer may know more than he is letting on.

One does not have to be much of a film scholar to realize that director Daniel Barber and screenwriter Gary Young are consciously trying to invoke the vigilante classic *Death Wish*—a film that is actually smarter and more thoughtful than most people tend to give it credit for—with this effort. But, as it goes about its blood-soaked way, it begins to feel more like the vastly-inferior *Death Wish II* (1982) in the sleazy and manipulative ways in which it stacks the decks for viewers to root for Harry to brutalize the baddies by making them so odious and beyond the pale that even Sister Helen Prejean (from *Dead Man Walking* [1995]) herself would have cheerfully pulled the trigger on them if given the chance. Things get so nasty and sadistic after a while that even those who happen to get a kick out of this particular subgenre may feel the need for a shower. Unfortunately, Barber and Young are so busy trying to think of nasty ways to hurt people that they let the story go to hell as it lurches to a climax that somehow manages to simultaneously come off as ridiculously implausible and achingly predictable.

However, while *Harry Brown* cannot be recommended as a whole, it cannot be dismissed entirely either because of the startlingly effective central performance by Michael Caine. In the early scenes, he is completely convincing as a once-proud man now cowed by the world around him and devastated by the loss of his wife, his friend, and the neighborhood he once knew. Later on, he is equally convincing as a hard man who will go to any lengths to get vengeance on those who have wronged him—at times, he may strike some viewers as an older version of the character that he played so memorably in the revenge classic *Get Carter* (1971). While *Harry Brown* probably will not be playing a big part of any Michael Caine career retrospectives in the immediate future, it cannot be denied that he does an exceptional job here. It is too bad that nobody else involved with the film was willing or able to step up in the same way. If they did, perhaps the end result might have been worthy of the effort that Caine clearly put into it.

Peter Sobczynski

CREDITS

Harry Brown: Michael Caine
D.I. Frampton: Emily Mortimer
D.S. Hicock: Charlie Creed-Miles
Sid Rourke: Liam Cunningham
S.I. Andrew Childs: Iain Glen
Leonard Attwell: David Bradley
Marky Hathaway: Jack O'Connell
Noel Winters: Ben Drew
Origin: United Kingdom
Language: English
Released: 2009
Production: Matthew Vaughn, Kris Thykier, Matthew Brown; Prescience, Framestore Features; released by Samuel Goldwyn Films
Directed by: Daniel Barber
Written by: Gary Young
Cinematography by: Martin Ruhe
Music by: Martin Phipps, Ruth Barrett
Sound: Simon Hayes
Music Supervisor: Matt Biffa
Editing: Joe Walker
Costumes: Jane Petrie

Production Design: Kave Quinn
MPAA rating: R
Running time: 103 minutes

REVIEWS

Burr, Ty. *Boston Globe.* June 10, 2010.
Dargis, Manohla. *New York Times.* April 30, 2010.
Dujsik, Mark. *Mark Reviews Movies.* April 29, 2010.
Ebert, Roger. *Chicago Sun-Times.* April 29, 2010.
Levy, Shawn. *Oregonian.* May 20, 2010.
Phillips, Michael. *Chicago Tribune.* April 29, 2010.
Reed, Rex. *New York Observer.* April 28, 2010.
Tallerico, Brian. *MovieRetriever.com.* April 30, 2010.
Tobias, Scott. *AV Club.* April 29, 2010.
White, Armond. *New York Press.* April 28, 2010.

QUOTES

Harry Brown: "I don't reckon you've got long. Seen that before. Gut wound. The slug's probably torn right through your liver."

TRIVIA

This film is director Daniel Barber's feature length film debut.

Actor Michael Caine was originally drawn to the film because of the similarities between himself and the character Harry Brown including past military service and a connection to the same London neighborhood.

HARRY POTTER AND THE DEATHLY HALLOWS: PART 1

The end begins.
—Movie tagline

Box Office: $294 million

When it was originally announced that Warner Bros. was planning to split J.K. Rowling's seventh and final Harry Potter novel, *Harry Potter and the Deathly Hallows*, into a two-part film event, the initial reaction from fans and pundits alike was a mixture of skepticism followed by, what could possibly be best described as, relief. The decision is almost a textbook example of the concept of "win-win." For Warner Bros., they get to turn seven novels into eight movies, giving them both a year-end holiday 2010 cliffhanger and a big summer 2011 finale, two brand spanking new chapters in what has become the most financially successful film franchise of all time. For Potter fans, they get more of what they covet and have less reason to bemoan the inevitable textual cuts that occur in the book-to-film adaptation process since they get a whole extra movie to revel in the plot lines that would've been deleted in a single *Deathly Hallows* film. And, particularly, for David Yates, the acclaimed British director who directed the past two Potter films (*Order of the Phoenix* and *Half-Blood Prince*) and both parts of *Deathly Hallows*, the decision to split the final book in two has resulted in the best Harry Potter film he's helmed to date. So, actually, that's win-win-win.

It might seem odd that something as logistical and arbitrary as the choice to break up *Deathly Hallows* into two films had such a positive effect on Yates' first *Deathly Hallows* film, but take a look at the history of the Potter films so far. Chris Columbus turned the two shortest and most simplistic Potter novels (*Sorcerer's Stone* and *Chamber of Secrets*) into short, simplistic, milquetoast spectacles that reproduced Rowling's text without adding anything extra. Alfonso Cuarón's *Prisoner of Azkaban* was a leap-forward in terms of movie-making— moody, emotional, visually stunning—even though it was lacking on a story level, and Mike Newell brought an even, yet underwhelming directorial hand to one of the most structurally sound Potter movies, *Goblet of Fire*. All in all, as J.K. Rowling's novels became longer, deeper, and more intricately plotted, the quality of the visual filmmaking in Warner Bros. adaptations improved exponentially. However, the new exciting filmmakers increasingly struggled to bring Rowling's sprawling plotlines to the big screen. This conflict—visual vs. narrative—came to a head in Yates' first Potter movie, *Order of the Phoenix*, where the narrative storytelling, for the first time, really and truly took a back seat to everything else. Thus began Yates' era as the Harry Potter director who was simply making films for Harry Potter fans. And, while that doesn't sound bad on the surface, in reality, it resulted in movies where storytelling was thrown to the side in favor of breathlessly recreating moments from the books. Character arcs, emotion, exposition, plot—all were ignored while Yates found himself in the regrettable position of having to fit twenty pounds of movie into a five-pound bag. *Order of the Phoenix* and *Half-Blood Prince* are both movies told in short-hand, where Yates seems to be relying on his Potter-informed audience to fill in the massive holes while he flimsily assembles his shanty-town of set-pieces into movies.

However, thanks to the decision to expand this final chapter into two films, *Deathly Hallows: Part 1* is the first Potter movie where it seems like Yates has been able to give the story some space to breathe, and the result is, frankly, a breath of fresh air. *Harry Potter and the Deathly Hallows: Part 1* opens with the new Minister of Magic, Rufus Scrimgeour (Bill Nighy), telling the wizarding world to remain calm—everything is under control— while the evil Lord Voldemort (Ralph Fiennes) terrorizes magicians and muggles alike following the death of his

old nemesis, Albus Dumbledore (Michael Gambon). Voldemort's immediate plan for the future is simple and to the point: kill Harry Potter, the one person who might still have a chance of taking down the Dark Lord. Meanwhile, Harry Potter (Daniel Radcliffe) has a similar goal. He's done with school, done with Quidditich, done with trying to win the House Cup. His new raison d'etre? Kill Voldemort by destroying seven magical repositories known as horcruxes, which contain the splintered fragments of Voldemort's twisted soul. This kill-or-be-killed tension might seem a bit dark for what is, ostensibly, a kid's movie, but the Potter movies have been skewing darker ever since *Prisoner of Azkaban*, and the directness of the character motivations gives the story a weight and an urgency that was lost in the maze of subplots surrounding the earlier Potter films. With his purpose set, Harry, his best pals Ron Weasley (Rupert Grint) and Hermione Granger (Emma Watson), and the Voldemort-hating resistance, the Order of the Phoenix, set out from Harry's safe haven in suburban Privet Drive and plunge into the dangerous magical world outside.

After a nasty flying ambush—which brings us the first of several character deaths—Harry and his pals arrive safely at the Weasley family home, where Ron's clan is preparing for a wedding and Rufus Scrimgeour appears to fulfill Dumbledore's last will and testament by bequeathing several gifts to Harry, Ron, and Hermione. While the trio debates the true purpose of Dumbledore's gifts and attempts to figure out the locations of the remaining horcruxes, Voldemort and the "is-he-isn't-he-evil" Severus Snape (Alan Rickman) step up their pursuit of Potter. It all comes to a head at the Weasley family wedding, when Voldemort's Death Eaters ambush the festivities, and the uber-fugitives Harry, Ron, and Hermione have to run for their lives. The friends escape to London where they hide out in the former headquarters of the Order of the Phoenix and, with the help of the house elves Kreacher and Dobby, they discover that one of the horcruxes, an enchanted locket, is in the possession of the sinister Dolores Umbridge (Imelda Staunton), i.e. the disgustingly pink bad guy from *Harry Potter and the Order of the Phoenix*. The problem is—to get to the horcrux, Harry and friends have to break into Umbridge's place of employment—the heavily guarded Ministry of Magic. The break-in scene is one of the most tense and purely exciting sequences in any of the Potter movies, and it stands as a great example of what Yates is able to accomplish when he has some time to tell a story. The Ministry job is a mini-heist film, dropped into the center of *Deathly Hallows: Part 1*, and, as Yates plays with the genre conventions, you can feel him having the same exuberant fun that exudes from

Rowling's pages during the best sequences in the Potter novels.

Following the heist, Harry, Ron, and Hermione flee with their newly stolen horcrux into the English countryside, hiding out in the wilderness as Voldemort's growing army of followers search endlessly for the fugitives. The "camping" sections were among the most criticized passages in Rowling's widely praised seventh novel, with some complaining that the trio's rural wanderings went on for far too long, but Yates, again, wisely uses this downtime, with his leads isolated and alone, to give us some of the best character development that we've seen yet in the Potter movies. Yes, the wilderness scenes bring the breakneck pace of the wedding escape and the Ministry heist to a halt, but, to steal a line from Madison Avenue, it's a "pause that refreshes." More than any other sequence in Yates' previous Potter movies, this is the moment where Radcliffe, Grint, and Watson stop acting like exposition engines and really become Harry, Ron, and Hermione. The scenes are awkward, tense, and filled with seven years of personal history between these characters and, even in the scenes that don't appear in the books, such as the Harry/Hermione impromptu dance scene, these are moments where the characters really feel as if they were pulled right out of Rowling's text.

Out in the woods, the horcrux locket quickly begins working its evil magic on the trio, corrupting their thoughts in the same way that the One Ring made Gollum purr "My Precious." The immediate results of this psychological manipulation are the departure of Ron—who is tricked into believing that Harry and Hermione have the hots for one another—and a series of visions that send Harry searching for clues at Godric's Hollow, his childhood home where his parents are buried. After a Voldemort ambush and the timely return of Ron, Harry and company destroy the locket and make their way to visit Xenophilius Lovegood (Rhys Ifans), father of their Hogwarts pal Luna, who tells them of the legend of the Deathly Hallows. Harry discovers that his visions have been tracking Voldemort's quest for the Hallows, three magical items that can help Voldemort escape death forever—the Elder Wand, an invisibility cloak, and a resurrection stone. It turns out that Dumbledore was in possession of the Elder Wand for years and, as Voldemort speeds to the wizard's tomb to claim the first Hallow, Harry and friends are captured by Voldemort's Death Eaters, led by Bellatrix Lestrange (Helena Bonham Carter), a dire situation that they only escape thanks to the death of a major character. Then—*Exeunt Omnes*—the story will continue in *Deathly Hallows: Part 2.*

Deathly Hallows: Part 1 is definitely Yates' best Harry Potter film to date, but does that mean it's a good movie or just an improvement on the director's past track record? It's debatable. While there is a beautiful human heart and some wonderful tension driving the film, in terms of storytelling, the movie is still totally incoherent to anyone who is not previously versed in Potter-isms. It's hard not to agree with Roger Ebert, who said in his review of *Deathly Hallows*: it "is a handsome and sometimes harrowing film, and will be completely unintelligible for anyone coming to the series for the first time." So, while, yes, this is still a Potter film made for Potter fans, one has to compliment Yates for working so hard to bring new and different dimensions to *Deathly Hallows*. His previous films have relied almost entirely on Potter shorthand—assuming that people know what a house-elf or the Half-Blood Prince is—but *Deathly Hallows* blends that sense of the overly familiar with a gleeful beating heart and some wonderful genre filmmaking to make a Potter film that feels like a hybrid between a work of fan art and an honest-to-god movie. The Harry Potter films have, for too long, seemingly forgotten that they should be movies first and everything else second. And, while it stumbles along the way, *Harry Potter and the Deathly Hallows: Part 1* thankfully acknowledges its movie-making roots and gives us a boy wizard who is more than just an adaptation—he's a pretty great movie hero as well.

Tom Burns

CREDITS

Harry Potter: Daniel Radcliffe
Hermione Granger: Emma Watson
Ron Weasley: Rupert Grint
Lord Voldemort: Ralph Fiennes
Bellatrix Lestrange: Helena Bonham Carter
Rufus Scrimgeour: Bill Nighy
Mr. Ollivander: John Hurt
Severus Snape: Alan Rickman
Draco Malfoy: Tom Felton
Lucius Malfoy: Jason Isaacs
Albus Dumbledore: Michael Gambon
Aberforth Dumbledore: Ciaran Hinds
Minerva McGonagall: Maggie Smith
Ginny Weasley: Bonnie Wright
Alastor 'Mad-Eye' Moody: Brendan Gleeson
Rubeus Hagrid: Robbie Coltrane
Remus Lupin: David Thewlis
Rita Skeeter: Miranda Richardson
Dolores Umbridge: Imelda Staunton
Gellert Grindelwald: Jamie Campbell Bower
Xenophilius Lovegood: Rhys Ifans
Griphook: Warwick Davis

Luna Lovegood: Evanna Lynch
Fenrir Greyback: Dave Legeno
Nymphadora Tonks: Natalia Tena
Victor Krum: Stanislav Ianevski
Vernon Dursely: Richard Griffiths
Neville Longbottom: Matthew Lewis
Kingsley Shacklebolt: George Harris
Percy Weasley: Chris Rankin
Origin: United Kingdom, USA
Language: English
Released: 2010
Production: David Barron, David Heyman; Heyday Films, Warner Bros. Pictures; released by Warner Bros.
Directed by: David Yates
Written by: Steve Kloves
Cinematography by: Eduardo Serra
Music by: Alexandre Desplat, Matt Biffa
Editing: Mark Day
Sound: James Mather
Art Direction: Andrew Ackland-Snow
Costumes: Jany Temime
Production Design: Stuart Craig
MPAA rating: PG-13
Running time: 146 minutes

REVIEWS

Gronvall, Andrea. *Chicago Reader.* November 18, 2010.
Howell, Peter. *Toronto Star.* November 17, 2010.
Kenny, Glenn. *MSN Movies.* November 18, 2010.
Kois, Dan. *Village Voice.* November 16, 2010.
Long, Tom. *Detroit News.* November 18, 2010.
McCarthy, Kevin. *BDK Review.* November 18, 2010.
Rainer, Peter. *Christian Science Monitor.* November 18, 2010.
Roeper, Richard. *RichardRoeper.com.* November 18, 2010.
Stevens, Dana. *Slate.* November 18, 2010.
Travers, Peter. *Rolling Stone.* November 18, 2010.

QUOTES

Lord Voldemort: "I must be the one to kill Harry Potter!"

TRIVIA

Bill Weasley is played by Domhnall Gleeson, who is the son of cast member Brenden Gleeson.

AWARDS

Nomination:

Oscars 2010: Art Dir./Set Dec., Visual FX
British Acad. 2010: Makeup, Visual FX.

HATCHET II

Victor Crowley lives again.
    —Movie tagline

Hold on to all of your pieces.
    —Movie tagline

When Adam Green made the rounds at horror festivals in 2006, he attempted to make the case that slasher films were not all that they used to be. If not being dragged straight into the video market without a theatrical release or softened for a PG-13 rating, the genre was being spoofed to death in films like the *Scream* trilogy (1996, 1997, 2000) and *Behind the Mask: The Rise of Leslie Vernon* (2006). Green hoped to go back to what fans really loved—gratuitous gore and nudity—and gave rise to his own Victor Crowley, who was being laid claim to as the next horror icon. Taken at such face value, Green's *Hatchet* (2006) was clearly what it wanted to be—a self-aware, bare-bones throwback with a focus on quality kills above all else. There has not been a lot of talk since then of Mr. Crowley or any anticipation for his return except maybe in the darkest corners of genre fan basements. But Green has returned to remind us of his mass-murdering brute and delivers much of the same all while taking a step back in his own ambitions to revive the genre he so clearly loves.

The original's sole survivor, Marybeth, was so traumatized by her encounter with Crowley that she morphed from actress Tamara Feldman to Danielle Harris, the latter known for her pre-teen run-ins with another past-his-prime icon, Michael Myers in *Halloween 4: The Return of Michael Myers* (1988) and *Halloween 5* (1989). Marybeth finds her way out of the swamps of New Orleans, where Crowley stalks hunters and tourists alike, to seek the help of Reverend Zombie (Tony Todd), a local charlatan with an intimate knowledge of the madman's curse. After a refresher course on the legend from the first film, the Reverend recaps that Crowley was a deformed child who was killed by his own father (Kane Hodder, also playing Victor) with an accidental hatchet to the face while trying to save him from a fire set by some local punks.

Adding to the legend, Victor's father cheated on his dying mother with the house nurse and was subsequently cursed to have a child with severe issues. Once that business is out of the way, *Hatchet II* introduces its new round-up of potential victims; a collection of interchangeable, gun-toting hillbillies all chasing a small purse offered by the Reverend for Crowley's head. Mr. Zombie has other plans to sever the Crowley curse though and insists that Marybeth bring along her Uncle Bob (Tom Holland) for they both may have a greater connection to the killer than they realize.

The setup sounds fun enough with the appearance that Green is upping the stakes for his sequel in an *Aliens* (1986), or at least *Jaws 2* (1978), kind of way with more horror action and a higher body count. This potential is very short-lived though as Green cannot help but follow the old standard formula of watching pairs split-up and then meet a particularly gruesome end without putting up much of a fight. Not once during *Hatchet II* is this scenario put to good use to build suspense sequences of any ingenuity nor create even an all-out smorgasbord massacre where working together turns out to be just as bad an idea as going it alone.

Not that anyone is expecting A-level star power or even B-level acting from the likes of a film named after a tool. With Green expecting a somewhat wink-wink nod to the kind of material that invites C-level thespians, the comic aspects of *Hatchet II* come off rather forced, drawing attention to actors unable to bridge its intentions. Tony Todd does his usual gravelly-voiced, gravity-laden speechifying. Parry Shen, a victim in the first film returns as a twin brother devised to be the most overt comic relief and reminds us that he was better off left for dead. Danielle Harris may only need to scream and cry, but her line readings of any necessity should not have the audience calling out "CUT!" Tom Holland, a respected horror director responsible for 1980s horror favorites, *Fright Night* (1985) and *Child's Play* (1988), surely will see the film and instruct his casting directors never to hire the guy who played Uncle Bob. Only A.J. Bowen passes the test in finding just the right note and attitude to play in the middle of all this carnage and legend phooey, so Green rewards him by putting him in the sex scene with Alexis Peters.

Directors who ride their own ideas back-to-back with little-to-no ambition in-between projects do not deserve the same kind of respect as those who branch out and take a break from their babies. Eli Roth and his back-to-back *Hostel* films is a perfect example. Adam Green is not one of those guys, however, and really upped his game with the spare, but ambitious thriller *Frozen* (2010), about three friends trapped on a ski lift. It was clever, well-performed and found room for some nail-biting set pieces in a situation that invites playing the "what would we do?" game. (There is a fun, blink-and-you-miss-it call back wrapping up that film here.) *Hatchet II* is more an unnecessary throwback to a time before *Frozen* when Adam Green was just getting noticed with a number of clever short films and ends up countering the leap he had just made.

Erik Childress

CREDITS

Marybeth: Danielle Harris
Reverend Zombie: Tony Todd
Victor Crowley: Kane Hodder
Justin: Parry Shen

Uncle Bob: Tom Holland
Tony: R.A. Mihailoff
Layton: AJ Bowen
Cleatus: Ed Ackerman
Avery: Alexis Peters
Jack Cracker: John Carl Buechler
Origin: USA
Language: English
Released: 2010
Production: Cory Neal, Sarah Elbert, Derek Curl; Dark Sky Films, Ariescope Pictures; released by MPI Media Group, Dark Sky Films
Directed by: Adam Green
Written by: Adam Green
Cinematography by: Will Barratt
Music by: Andy Garfield
Sound: Bobby Fisk
Editing: Ed Marx, Ed Marx
Costumes: Heather Allison, Heather Allison
Production Design: Bryan McBrien, Bryan McBrien
MPAA rating: Unrated
Running time: 89 minutes

REVIEWS

Ebert, Roger. *Chicago Sun-Times.* September 30, 2010.
Gilchrist, Todd. *Cinematical.* September 28, 2010.
Hynes, Eric. *Time Out New York.* September 29, 2010.
Johanson, MaryAnn. *Flick Filosopher.* October 5, 2010.
Leydon, Joe. *Variety.* September 27, 2010.
O'Sullivan, Michael. *Washington Post.* October 1, 2010.
Rabin, Nathan. *AV Club.* September 30, 2010.
Swietek, Frank. *One Guy's Opinion.* September 30, 2010.
Weinberg, Scott. *FEARnet.* October 3, 2010.
Wilson, Chuck. *Village Voice.* September 28, 2010.

QUOTES

Rev. Zombie: "You gotta be f**king kidding me!"

TRIVIA

Over 120 gallons of fake blood were used in *Hatchet II* as compared to only 55 gallons of blood in *Hatchet I.*

After numerous attempts to edit down to an R rating, the filmmakers decided to circumvent the MPAA and strike a special deal with AMC Theaters to release the film unrated. It was pulled after only two days.

HEREAFTER

Box Office: $32 million

A narrative triptych about the universality of what inarguably is the greatest curse of human consciousness—of knowing we are all born to expire, but not knowing what lies beyond mortal life—*Hereafter* is a quietly-expressive drama that, as with director Clint Eastwood's *Invictus* (2009), for some audiences will skate either dangerously close to or just over the line of portentousness. A decidedly unhurried, almost European-style drama, the film achieves its hold in a manner most old-fashioned: through the slow build of an audience's investment in characters. And yet a lot of *Hereafter*'s emotional punch also ultimately depends on off-screen elements and not what unfolds within the story—what sort of sensitivity and emotional mindset a viewer brings to its viewing, and how much interest they might have in considering a celebrated, octogenarian filmmaker reflect, in proxy fashion, on his own mortality. Given the movie's autumnal euthanizing at the box office, it is clear that for many adult audiences that a basic qualifying condition of entertainment was not met.

Hereafter opens in a Southeast Asian resort town in 2004, where a vacationing, well-known French television news reporter, Marie Lelay (Cécile de France), finds her romantic getaway interrupted by a massive tsunami. Swept away and knocked unconscious by the waves, she is jerked back to life from an otherworldly vision by two strangers. Shaken by this near-death experience, Marie returns home and tries to slip back into some sort of rhythm and routine, even taking a professional sabbatical, ostensibly to work on a book about François Mitterrand. She remains haunted, however.

In San Francisco, meanwhile, George Lonegan (Matt Damon) attempts to resist the habitual cajoling of his well-meaning brother Billy (Jay Mohr) to again try to make financial use of his psychic gifts, which allow him to communicate with the dead. Even accidentally brushing up against someone can offer a glimpse of their tortured past or doomed future, making normal relationships extremely difficult, to say the least. To cope, George has retreated into a simple laborer's job, though he finds his asceticism tested when he meets a young woman, Melanie (Bryce Dallas Howard), in a night-school Italian cooking class.

Finally, in London, a pair of twin boys, Jason and Marcus (George and Frankie McLaren), go to extraordinary lengths to care and cover for their junkie mother Jackie (Lyndsey Marshal), all to stave off the intervention of social services. When a terrible accident befalls his brother, Marcus is eventually shipped off to a foster home, where his loving new parents try to care for him as best they can. Irretrievably disconsolate, however, Marcus starts trying to seek out someone who can help him make contact with Jason.

Hereafter represents a notable departure for Oscar®-nominated, British-born screenwriter Peter Morgan.

From *The Last King of Scotland* (2006) and *The Queen* (2006) to *The Other Boleyn Girl* (2008) and *Frost/Nixon* (2008), much of the rest of Morgan's work (particularly in the Hollywood realm) has centered around specifically corroded or crumbling power structures, and the tension of their embodying individual's relationship with accountability and/or modernity. *Hereafter* is a much more stagey and broadly classical tale, a thematic exercise less driven by the narrative urgency characteristic of most Hollywood films, and more interested in exploring the unspoken but often shared thoughts that compel individual action. And despite the underlined nature of its melancholic solitude vis-à-vis via its protagonist's last name (which sounds a lot like "alone again"), *Hereafter* is a movie with uncommon amounts of tenderness. It is a ruminative work through and through, professionally mounted and full of very small, relatable human moments that speak to silent yearnings.

On the other hand, for all the engaging atypicality of its unadorned style, *Hereafter* is rigidly structured—perhaps too much so, intercutting in such a formal, paced fashion between its three discrete stories that the inevitable intertwining of them seems even more yawningly predictable. Digressions into pseudoscientific intrigue do not help, either. When a wandering Marie visits a reclusive Alpine academic, Dr. Rousseau (Marthe Keller, seemingly reading her lines from off-screen cue cards), who hints at some sort of government-media partnership in the conspiratorial silencing of those able to communicate with the deceased, the movie flirts with a headlong turn into something more active and intriguing (an actual investigation!), only to just as quickly and strangely abandon the plot, and have Marie pen her own same-named book on her experience with the hereafter. Such moments feel like an insincere way to merely mark time, until the characters can be brought together in the final reel, at a book publishing and marketing convention.

For both better and worse, Eastwood's directorial approach, particularly over the past decade, has been marked by an unfussy simplicity and straightforwardness. In his eyes, moviemaking is no more necessarily difficult or honorable than any number of other professions, and so he trusts explicitly in his casting choices, figuring them to be professionals who will deliver professional work. Sometimes, though, an actor's character choices need redirection or momentary muddying, so as to signal interior conflict or tumult. There is precious little of that in *Hereafter*, which contributes to a potentially dismissive reading of the material as simply too boring if one is neither in the mood nor has the inclination to bear with the movie's moroseness.

Technically, too, Eastwood's choices figure prominently into one's level of acceptance or squirrelly dissatisfaction with *Hereafter*. Working on what has to be the most CGI-infused film of his career, Eastwood delivers an opening tsunami sequence that is as amazing as anything Roland Emmerich or Michael Bay could dream up. It is gripping, and a prime example of the power and emotional value of special effects serving an actual story, rather than arbitrarily attempting to overwhelm an audience with novelty.

On the other hand, George's psychic readings are staged matter-of-factly, almost to a fault. When he grasps the hand of a grieving person, there is a brief jolt or flash of light, and sometimes the glimpse of a shadowy figure. Clearly the audience is meant to identify these connections as sincere and honest, and Eastwood seems intent on not overloading these segments with goading atmosphere, as so many films either with or about psychic mediums do. Yet the vacuumed-clean absence of almost any tension here helps undercut not only the scene-to-scene drama, but also the film's presentation of George as fraught and broken. To understand and empathize with the burden of his gift, to equate it with a sort of unusually symptomatic terminal illness, is to render more relevant and poignant the film's conclusion. Directorially, Eastwood misses some opportunities to do this—to bind together more strongly the shared nature of his characters' plights, and thus their defacto attachment to an audience.

Performances are at the heart of *Hereafter*'s appeal, and also some of its problems. The real-life McLaren twins, acting neophytes with the ability to approximate mournful visages but little more, pull effectively on heartstrings at times, but also lack the ability and range to pull off proactivity and guile, especially when Marcus finally makes contact with George. Damon ably conveys a sort of emotional constipation, even if the one-note material paints him into a bit of a corner, and Howard, in her small role, is excellent with silent reaction and connection.

It is De France, however, who most shines in *Hereafter*. If familiar at all to mainstream American audiences, it is likely for her starring role in the slick foreign language horror thriller *High Tension* (2005), or perhaps the remake of *Around the World in 80 Days* (2004), which are each about as far away as one can get, thematically, from her nuanced work here. An American actress—Sandra Bullock or Gwyneth Paltrow, say—even just approximating a vaguely European accent and persona, or the casting of an international star like Penélope Cruz, would each have undeniably done wonders for *Hereafter*'s box office appeal. It is a credit to Eastwood's respect for the material, and the fact that distributor Warner Bros. took a hands-off approach in demanding any changes in this regard, that *Hereafter* retains its worldliness. That helps the film feel at the very least genuine and honest in its thematic disquisition, even if its metaphysical ruminations are not exactly of the flavor that most easily spell mainstream embrace.

Brent Simon

CREDITS

George Lonegan: Matt Damon
Marie LeLay: Cecile de France
Marcus/Jason: Frankie McLaren
Christos: Richard Kind
Melanie: Bryce Dallas Howard
Billy: Jay Mohr
Marcus/Jason: George McLaren
Didier: Thierry Neuvic
Jackie: Lyndsey Marshal
Candace: Jenifer Lewis
Dr. Rousseau: Marthe Keller
Origin: USA
Language: English
Released: 2010
Production: Clint Eastwood, Kathleen Kennedy, Robert Lorenz; Kennedy/Marshall, Malpaso Productions; released by Warner Bros.
Directed by: Clint Eastwood
Written by: Peter Morgan
Cinematography by: Tom Stern
Music by: Clint Eastwood
Sound: Bub Asman, Walt Martin
Editing: Joel Cox, Gary D. Roach
Art Direction: Tom Brown, Patrick M. Sullivan Jr.
Costumes: Deborah Hopper
Production Design: James Murakami
MPAA rating: PG-13
Running time: 129 minutes

REVIEWS

Chang, Justin. *Variety.* October 11, 2010.
Ebert, Roger. *Chicago Sun-Times.* October 19, 2010.
Edelstein, David. *New York Magazine.* October 11, 2010.
Morgenstern, Joe. *Wall Street Journal.* October 15, 2010.
O'Sullivan, Michael. *Washington Post.* October 22, 2010.
Rainer, Peter. *Christian Science Monitor.* October 22, 2010.
Schwarzbaum, Lisa. *Entertainment Weekly.* October 13, 2010.
Scott, A.O. *New York Times.* October 15, 2010.
Stevens, Dana. *Slate.* October 22, 2010.
Tallerico, Brian. *HollywoodChicago.com.* October 13, 2010.

TRIVIA

This film was shipped to theaters with the codename "Heaven's Playground."

Filming was interrupted for a month in December 2009 when Matt Damon left to shoot *The Adjustment Bureau*.

AWARDS

Nomination:

Oscars 2010: Visual FX.

HOLY ROLLERS

In 1998, 1 million ecstasy pills were smuggled into the USA by a group of Hasidic Jews.
—Movie tagline

Holy Rollers uses its opening declaration, "Inspired by true events," as a crutch to rest a sense of significance upon a story that holds little weight apart from its fact-based origin. Telling the true story of a drug ring that employed Hasidic Jews as couriers to smuggle the psychoactive drug ecstasy from Amsterdam through Canada and into Brooklyn in 1998, the screenplay by Antonio Macia is a collection of vague scenes that does little to illuminate the procedural side of the operation and only delves a bit deeper into the root causes of its protagonist's reasoning for partaking in illegal activity, the familial divide that erupts, and the ethical conflict that arises within him as a result.

He is Sam Gold (Jesse Eisenberg), the twenty-year-old elder child of the family, who works with his father Mendel (Mark Ivanir) at the patriarch's fabric store. On the path to becoming a rabbi, with weekly lessons in the Torah, he arranged to be married to Zeldy (Stella Keitel), a local young woman whom Sam sees regularly walking to and from home with her family but to whom he cannot speak before congregation leader Rebbe Horowitz (Bern Cohen) grants permission (he still tries after synagogue services, though his younger sister Ruth [Hallie Kate Eisenberg, Jesse's real-life younger sister] forces him to walk away from the situation before anyone notices the breach of etiquette).

Sam is an impatient young man and quite an insecure one, especially in matters of money. Early on, Macia shows him at work in the store, arguing with a customer over the cost of a purchase. His father had agreed to a discounted price, and Sam attempts to raise it to what he considers a more appropriate sum. Mendel corrects his son and, after the disagreement, explains his business philosophy: Keep prices low and customers loyal and plenty. He reminds Sam that he still runs the shop, of his place as Mendel's employee and, more importantly, son. Giving and showing respect are of highest value to the family and, more broadly, the community in which they live.

The same kind of dispute is happening next door to the Gold home. The Zimmerman brothers, Yosef (Justin Bartha) and Leon (Jason Fuchs), are at odds in their way of living. While Leon is a favorite at rabbinical school, Yosef has dismissed custom (unlike Sam and Leon, he does not have *payis*—long sideburns—and wears bright, white sneakers) in favor of a criminal life. Yosef recruits Sam to become a drug mule for Jackie Solomon (Danny A. Abeckaser), a dealer with an Israeli drug cartel, under the guise that they are bringing in "medicine" for rich people.

Two drives compel Sam to accept the job, even when he discovers the true nature of the imported goods. First is his desire for wealth, and the pay is good. Second is the sex drive of a young man who cannot even speak to the woman to whom he is unofficially engaged and who spies out his window to watch pornographic movies on Yosef's television. Likewise, when Jackie's girlfriend Rachel (Ari Graynor) tries to shake Sam's hand, he physically withdraws from her, repeating to her, "I respect you." It is less a statement of explanation to her than it is a reminder of denial to himself.

While the relationship between the two urges is left ambiguous, one can only assume he sees the first as a means to the second. His anxiety to meet and speak with Zeldy in part comes from a fear that his family does not come from satisfactory financial means, so he must show he is a worthy potential husband or marry before she and her family discovers his family's lack of money. When Leon later becomes engaged to Zeldy, Sam immediately criticizes his friend's own monetary weakness as a prospect.

His narrow-minded focus on money as the primary driving force of success in life and sex leads to Sam's eventual fall from grace, and Macia and director Kevin Asch treat the cliché fairly literally. Sam's new life of aiding in drug trafficking not only means a rejection of his family (Mendel disowns Sam after he buys a new stove for his mother [Elizabeth Marvel]), community, and faith—essentially leaving him without an identity—but also of *HaShem*. The movie emphasizes the point by a including a voiceover that repeats the Rebbe's teaching on the story of the shame of Adam and Eve in the Garden of Eden when they realize they are naked as Sam reaches the pit of despair (it should be noted that Eisenberg, despite the script's narrow development of Sam, maintains a genuine fragility that adds a layer of depth).

All must "know where we stand in relation to *HaShem,*" the Rebbe highlights the lesson; "We can move closer or further away." This simplistic message of the right path and the wrong one is consistent with the lack of exploration of characterization and situation within *Holy Rollers*.

Mark Dujsik

CREDITS

Sam Gold: Jesse Eisenberg
Yosef: Justin Bartha
Rachel: Ari Graynor
Jackie: Danny A. Abeckaser
Mendel Gold: Mark Ivanir
Elka Gold: Elizabeth Marvel
Leon: Jason Fuchs
Zeldy: Stella Keitel
Rebbe Horowitz: Bern Cohen
Ruth: Hallie Kate Eisenberg
Origin: USA
Language: English
Released: 2010
Production: Danny A. Abeckaser, Tory Tunnell, Per Melita, Jen Gatien; Deerjen Films, Lookbook Films, Safehouse Pictures, Gulfstream Films; released by First Independent Pictures
Directed by: Kevin Asch
Written by: Antonio Macia
Cinematography by: Ben Kutchins
Music by: MJ Mynarski
Sound: Bryan Dembinski
Editing: Suzanne Spangler
Art Direction: Adam Sober
Costumes: Jacki Roach
Production Design: Tommaso Ortino
MPAA rating: R
Running time: 89 minutes

REVIEWS

Addiego, Walter. *San Francisco Chronicle.* June 11, 2010.
Burr, Ty. *Boston Globe.* June 4, 2010.
Chang, Justin. *Variety.* January 26, 2010.
Ebert, Roger. *Chicago Sun-Times.* June 2, 2010.
Kelly, Christopher. *Dallas Morning News.* June 10, 2010.
Lovece, Frank. *Film Journal International.* May 20, 2010.
Macdonald, Moira. *Seattle Times.* June 24, 2010.
Rabin, Nathan. *AV Club.* May 20, 2010.
Schager, Nick. *Slant Magazine.* May 17, 2010.
Zacharek, Stephanie. *Movieline.* May 20, 2010.

TRIVIA

Jesse Eisenberg and Hallie Kate Eisenberg are siblings in real life. In the movie, the two play siblings as well.

The filmmakers cast many real-life Satmar Hasidim as extras in the film who would provide many unscripted moments of prayer and blessings.

HOT TUB TIME MACHINE

Kick some past.
—Movie tagline

Box Office: $50 million

The number of worthwhile films that have successfully combined pee, poop, and projectile puke with poignancy can surely be counted on one hand, and *Hot Tub Time Machine,* which is just such a shamelessly-tasteless yet touching treat, has a character that would be just perfect for the task. Sporting fewer appendages but far more attitude than one would ideally want in a hotel bellboy, one-armed Phil (Crispin Glover) lets fly both seething testiness and the guests' luggage. The time-traveling film's most inspired moments are those that continually seem to promise an explanation for how Phil got that way, creating in both the characters and the audience a curiosity and sense of anticipation that is admittedly macabre but utterly delightful. Finally, there is the snowplow sideswiping that appallingly satisfies, followed by a fountain of spurting blood and punctuated by the film's final, book-ending view of vomit. However, after all the retching and the wretched excess, the plot has been propelled back from a spoofing of the 1980s to an agreeably-altered future, and a decidedly-sunnier Phil has sensation in his good-as-new reattached arm. Certainly by the end of *Hot Tub Time Machine,* many viewers also found themselves feeling something—besides a degree of queasiness.

Even more weighty and challenging to handle than the suitcases with which Phil struggles is the emotional baggage being carried into middle age by a trio of formerly-fast friends. The three have not only been separated over time but also noticeably crushed by its passage. Adam (a suitably-drained John Cusack) is a world-weary salesman who insures people against loss and is no stranger to it himself. Most recently, numerous items have been wrested from him by a peeved and rather petty girlfriend's sudden exit from his life. "What did you do?" asks his sister's doughy, basement-dwelling son, Jacob (Clark Duke), and his tone suggests there may be good reason to suspect culpability on Adam's part. "I didn't do anything," is the reply after a pause, and it is unclear whether Adam is genuinely mystified or stubbornly skirting the harsh truth that his pain is all-too self-inflicted.

Nick (sweetly-appealing Craig Robinson of NBC's *The Office*), who had aspired to be more than just an aspiring musician, feels like he is literally reaching the bottom of his own personal quicksand as his searching, gloved fingers delve into the rear end of a pooch at the pet care outfit where he has ended up working. That the animal's flourishing owner recalls the now-past pinnacle of Nick's life clearly makes him feel even more like the stuff that covers the BMW keys removed during the canine cavity search. What is worse, Nick suspects that the women for whom he settled down has cuckolded him, adding to the emasculation of agreeing to hyphenate his name with hers.

Worst off of all, however, is licentious Lou (scene-stealing Rob Corddry of Comedy Central's *The Daily Show*), a gleefully-unbridled hoot of a character who perhaps should best be required by law to wear a muzzle and a condom at all times. While his once-long locks have left him, the man's adolescent inanity remains deep-rooted. Lou is stuck in 1980s salad days that included greens and mushrooms never found in any salad, plus gallons of booze and plenty of head-banging rock 'n' roll. Viewers probably do not want to know exactly how he earned the nickname "Violator," but are quickly convinced of Lou's capacity to have earned it. The drunken night he literally puts pedal to the metal and nearly kills himself in an enclosed garage is what forces these variously-stunted guys uneasily back together.

To cheer Lou up, they return to a ski resort initially recalled with self-assuaging imperfection as a place of carefree abandon they had enjoyed before everything went downhill. Never mind that it is also the scene of the painful, pivotal Winterfest '86, when Adam broke up with his blisteringly-hot girlfriend (Lyndsy Fonseca) and got stabbed in the eye for it, Nick gave a poor performance onstage that crippled his career, and Lou was scarred less by the beatings he suffered at the hands of ski patrol goons than by the fact that his two buddies failed to back him up. Along for the ride is nerdy Jacob, who does not seem to have a life outside of Second Life and, even there, he is in prison. He will act as a kind of geek Greek Chorus, commenting exasperatedly on the adult's missteps and misbehavior.

No one will miss the symbolism when it is observed that the years have been as unkind to their destination as they have been to Adam, Nick, and Lou. It is decidedly rundown and in urgent need of restoration, with hot tubs that were once overflowing with delight now containing formerly lively critters in the slow process of decay. When one of those tubs is suddenly filed with both water and a beckoning golden glow, the characters, soothing their sorrows with alcohol-fueled, head-swirling revelry, are magically transported back via ridiculously-retro special effects to that fateful weekend in 1986. There, they find "I want my MTV!" ads, cassette Walkmen and brick-sized cell phones, legwarmers and *Miami Vice*-inspired styles, mullets and Jheri curls—plus an oh-so tempting chance to reroute their lives toward fulfilling futures. Moviegoers who lived through the 1980s will likely react to the film's myriad period references with smiles elicited by both wistfulness and embarrassed incredulity. They will also certainly chuckle at the irony of Cusack, who came to prominence during the decade on display here, playing a character who bitterly dismisses it as having merely given rise to "Reagan and AIDS."

Males who have reached an age when both hair and expectations have painfully begun falling by the wayside will surely feel melancholic twinges of empathy during all the briskly-paced, F-bomb-filled, sometimes off-puttingly off-color absurdity. Admittedly, the cryptic hot tub repairman (Chevy Chase, a walking example of 1980s film iconography like Glover, Cusack, and William Zabka of 1984's *The Karate Kid*) warns the quartet what alterations of the future may result if they dare to even slightly modify the past. Jacob wants to see history repeated exactly to ensure he will even exist in the future, and gets the cornea-scorching sight of Lou conceiving him with his slutty mom (Collette Wolfe) for his efforts. Still, most viewers found themselves rooting for rewriting, for the men to bat aside the persistent talk of that darn, dire 'Butterfly Effect' with as little reservation as they would some tiresomely-pesky gnat.

Made on a budget reported variously as either $36 million or $50 million, *Hot Tub Time Machine* grossed just over the latter amount and garnered generally good reviews. The film ends by showing the new and improved 2010 lives that have resulted for everyone after some time-traveling tinkering, developments that are enthusiastically toasted. It is pleasing to leave them this way—and to exit before anyone is tempted to overindulge one last time and hurl.

David L. Boxerbaum

CREDITS

Adam: John Cusack
Lou: Rob Corddry
Nick: Craig Robinson
Phil: Crispin Glover
Blaine: Sebastian Stan
The Repairman: Chevy Chase
April: Lizzy Caplan
Jennie: Lyndsy Fonseca
Jacob: Clark Duke
Kelly: Collette Wolfe
Origin: USA
Language: English
Released: 2010
Production: John Cusack, Grace Loh; Lakeshore Entertainment, New Crime Productions; released by MGM
Directed by: Steve Pink
Written by: Josh Heald
Cinematography by: Jack N. Green
Sound: Michael Williamson
Editing: Luben Izov
Art Direction: Kevin Humenny
Costumes: Dayna Pink

Music by: Christophe Beck
Production Design: Bob Ziembicki
MPAA rating: R
Running time: 101 minutes

REVIEWS

Alter, Ethan. *Film Journal International.* May 2010.
Harvey, Dennis. *Variety.* March 29, 2010.
Kois, Dan. *Village Voice.* March 24, 2010.
Morgenstern, Joe. *Wall Street Journal.* March 26, 2010.
Phillips, Michael. *Chicago Tribune.* March 25, 2010.
Pols, Mary. *TIME Magazine.* March 25, 2010.
Schwarzbaum, Lisa. *Entertainment Weekly.* March 24, 2010.
Scott, A.O. *New York Times.* March 26, 2010.
Sharkey, Bets. *Los Angeles Times.* March 26, 2010.
Travers, Peter. *Rolling Stone.* April 15, 2010.

QUOTES

Adam: "One little change has a ripple effect and it affects everything else. Like a butterfly floats its wings and Tokyo explodes or there's a tsunami, in like, you know, somewhere."

TRIVIA

Actor John Cusack decided to star in the film after simply hearing the title of the film and bursting into laughter.

HOW DO YOU KNOW
(Everything You've Got)

Box Office: $30 million

There is no denying that, for as infrequently as he makes movies, writer/director James L. Brooks is one of the modern masters of the tragic-comedy. In works such as *Terms of Endearment* (1983), *Broadcast News* (1987), and *As Good As It Gets* (1997), Brooks has made audiences weeping almost as often as he has them laughing. And many times, the laughter comes through the tears. While early commercials for *How Do You Know* made it appear to be more of a straight-ahead, cookie-cutter, romantic comedy—something Brooks has never done prior—the film is actually a surprisingly strong effort about three 30-something characters in transition. Everything they have been doing with their lives up to this point must suddenly and unexpectedly change, and none of these course diversions into unknown waters is by choice. This is Brooks' comfort zone.

The entry point into this story is Lisa (Reese Witherspoon), an Olympic-grade softball player who lives in Washington, D.C., and is forced off the team by a new coach because she is too old (she just turned thirty), and

there are younger players he would like to bring onboard. For her entire adult life, Lisa has been defined by her gift on the field, and now she has no idea where to go from here. Witherspoon does a convincing job playing a woman who is not only unsure where her life is headed, but is also completely unaware how attractive she is. She is in the early stages of dating major league baseball pitcher Matty (Owen Wilson), a laid-back, nice-enough guy who considers being "mostly monogamous" with Lisa a major step toward being a better boyfriend. There is never a scene between them in which it is not clear that Lisa considers Matty a work in progress, and the realization that she has only ever dated athletes makes Lisa all the more restless about her station in life.

What is fascinating about the way Matty is written is that he is so blissfully ignorant of his shortcomings when it comes to relationships, that he approaches his life with Lisa like another competitive sport that he must win. He throws elaborate parties and gives her expensive gifts, and demands credit whenever he moderately succeeds at getting something remotely right. Wilson plays Matty to perfection as the quintessential dope who still possesses a few layers worth uncovering to get to the real guy. As much as this character may not seem like much of a stretch for Wilson, he actually spins Matty with subtle differences from characters he has played in the past. The man is struggling to overcome the expected jock lifestyle for the love of a woman. It is a noble effort that will undoubtedly fail.

Into Lisa's unsettled life comes a phone call from a complete stranger named George (Paul Rudd), who has been given her number by a mutual friend thinking a blind date might be in order. The initial call is to apologize for not calling sooner, and to let Lisa know that he is already seeing someone. But after George's girlfriend dumps him when he is blindsided with the news that he is being targeted in a federal investigation tied to financial improprieties at his company—owned by his father Charles (Jack Nicholson)—George calls Lisa again to actually make a date. George is fully aware he did nothing illegal, but with evidence mounting against him and the burden of federal prosecutors on his heels, he walks into his first date with Lisa, and the results are both catastrophic and hilarious.

Brooks has done something brave with *How Do You Know*—his first film since *Spanglish* (2004)—by hiring three lead actors from whom audiences have not seen this kind of depth, despite them all being highly capable performers. The movie is absolutely ruled by Witherspoon, who has certainly proven herself on the dramatic and comedic fronts in roles as varied as Elle Woods in *Legally Blonde* (2001) and June Carter in *Walk the Line* (2005), but what she is doing here is quite different. She is playing a normally confident woman filled with anxiety and uncertainly. Far from a glamour role, Witherspoon is called upon to play Lisa as a real person and it suits her talents perfectly.

The back half of *How Do You Know* is even less conventional than the first part, and that is a good thing. Brooks is not trying to make a standard-issue romantic-comedy here, although a smattering of bad, even underwhelming, jokes pop in from time to time. Despite this sometimes distracting need to make viewers laugh throughout the film, Brooks also wants to present us with three characters whose lives need to change for the betterment of their souls, and he conveys this through some great conversations, especially between George and Lisa.

The result is that the audience gets to know these characters by simply watching them with each other for prolonged exchanges. In a couple of nicely-realized sequences, George and Lisa sit in his new, cramped apartment and simply talk. These are the scenes in which Rudd truly shines. George's world is collapsing around him, but something about being with this woman soothes him. Most people in the world know that Rudd is a gifted comic actor, but it has been years since he has climbed into a character so completely and made viewers care so much about him.

If there is one egregious problem with *How Do You Know*, it is that Nicholson does not seem as invested in his underwritten character as he normally does in other Brooks films. He is not exactly phoning it in, but the level of commitment is absent most of the few times he is on-screen. Still, a scene between father and son, where a decision has to be made about which of the two is going to jail, is kind of perfect as Nicholson's Charles tries to sweet talk his son into taking one for the team. But that legendary Nicholson charm is completely absent from this film. Even playing the nastiest villains, Nicholson typically makes audiences love him (or love to hate him). But here, he is simply a self-absorbed cad who would rather see his son go to prison than admit to the authorities what he did and face the humiliation and consequences.

While Brooks has earned his reputation as a great writer by avoiding romantic-comedy trappings that feel like sins against humanity in many other films, *How Do You Know* still comes down to which man Lisa will choose—and, of course, whether or not George will go to jail. But by the time he gets to that point, Brooks has earned this pass by having steered his characters clear of so many other such clichés on the way to the finale. Even the way, Lisa's decision is handled is done with a bit more sophistication than the immature "Rom-Com" junk that comes out every year.

Brooks spares audiences a movie loaded with music montages, shopping sprees, or formula-driven elements that drive 99 percent of all such works. This is a movie about adults whose lives are changing at a time when they probably thought such changes were a thing of the past. The highest compliment one could pay a film like *How Do You Know* is that the characters are so interesting and richly drawn that it would be wonderful to see how these folks turn out five or ten years down the road. In the end, the movie is not trying to teach people how to fall or be in love; it wants viewers to realize that sometimes love can lift one above the worst things in life. It sounds corny, yes, but with this level of acting and writing skill on hand, it still works.

Steven Prokopy

CREDITS

Lisa Jorgenson: Reese Witherspoon
Manny: Owen Wilson
George: Paul Rudd
Charles: Jack Nicholson
Annie: Kathryn Hahn
Tom: Dean Norris
Waiter: Brian O'Halloran
Terry: Shelley Conn
Ryan: Domenick Lombardozzi
Ron: Mark Linn-Baker
Sally: Molly Price
Tower: Daniel Benzali
Al: Lenny Venito
Dylan Laurie: Ron McLarty
Origin: USA
Language: English
Released: 2010
Production: Julie Ansell, Laurence Mark, James L. Brooks, Paula Weinstein; Gracie Films, Columbia Pictures, Road Rebel; released by Sony Pictures
Directed by: James L. Brooks
Written by: James L. Brooks
Cinematography by: Janusz Kaminski
Music by: Hans Zimmer
Music Supervisor: Nick Angel
Editing: Richard Marks
Sound: D. Chris Smith
Art Direction: John Demeo, Will Riley, Anthony Dunne
Costumes: Shay Cunliffe
Production Design: Jeannine Oppewall
MPAA rating: PG-13
Running time: 116 minutes

REVIEWS

Biancolli, Amy. *San Francisco Chronicle.* December 17, 2010.
Dargis, Manohla. *New York Times.* December 16, 2010.

Debruge, Peter. *Variety.* December 15, 2010.
Ebert, Roger. *Chicago Sun-Times.* December 15, 2010.
Jones, Kimberley. *Austin Chronicle.* December 17, 2010.
Moore, Roger. *Orlando Sentinel.* December 15, 2010.
Persall, Steve. *St. Petersburg Times.* December 16, 2010.
Puig, Claudia. *USA Today.* December 17, 2010.
Rodriguez, Rene. *Miami Herald.* December 15, 2010.
Rothkopf, Joshua. *Time Out: New York.* December 14, 2010.

QUOTES

Lisa: "When you're in something you got to give it everything you have or else what are you doing?"

TRIVIA

Bill Murray was actually considered for the role of the father but turned it down.

HOW TO TRAIN YOUR DRAGON

Box Office: $218 million

The tension between art and commerce exists in almost all modern mainstream American films, but it is frequently particularly acute in animation, where, outside of the brand respect and reputation that Pixar has built up, the desperate need to please tends to devour most thoughtful storytelling silences or moments of quieter reflection, and fill them instead with the patter of desultory dialogue. Ditching by moderate degrees this rampant, jokey, rib-nudging tone, as well as any strained attempts at referential pop culture asides, *How to Train Your Dragon* aims for more heartfelt and straightforward emotional connection, and the result—a well-deserved Academy Award® nominee for Best Animated Feature—is an adventuresome, compelling coming-of-age story that also delivers rapturous visual beguilement.

Released in late March to overwhelmingly positive critical response, *How to Train Your Dragon* pretty much ruled the animated box office roost until the May arrival of *Shrek Forever After* (2010). It exhibited strong word-of-mouth staying power, as evidenced by a $44 million opening weekend, and sophomore and junior frames that only saw 34 and 14 percent drop-offs, respectively. With a hearty foreign box office gross of over $275 million and a worldwide cumulative haul of nearly half a billion dollars, the film also established an appealing protagonist and rich background setting, so it is no surprise that a sequel for 2013 is already in the works.

Co-directed by Dean DeBlois and Chris Sanders, who previously collaborated on *Lilo & Stitch* (2002), the movie unfolds in a mythical world of burly Vikings and winged beasts, in a seaside town described as "the meridian of misery." Overshadowed by his stocky warrior father Stoick (Gerard Butler), gangly teenager Hiccup (Jay Baruchel) finds that he does not quite fit in with his tribe's longstanding tradition of dragon-slaying, which for over three centuries has been the local unit of heroic measurement. The will to participate is there, but Hiccup is all knees and elbows, as his apprenticeship with blacksmith Gobber (Craig Ferguson) confirms. Hiccup also has anthropological curiosities that none of his fellow Vikings seem to share. He wants to engage the dragons, but capture, study and understand them—a notion that seems foreign to all those around him.

A too-frantic opening sequence, with Hiccup narrating the action under a massive dragon siege aimed at the burgh's livestock, eventually gives way to more mannered, subdued storytelling. At the insistence of his father, Hiccup is enrolled in an age-appropriate dragon-fighting class, where he meets up with tomboy Astrid (America Ferrera) and a gaggle of other kids, including Snotlout (Jonah Hill), Fishlegs (Christopher Mintz-Plasse), and twins Tuffnut and Ruffnut (T.J. Miller and Kristen Wiig, respectively). As their instructors go about teaching them, in a very hands-on, fend-for-yourself manner, the different attack styles and weaknesses of various breeds of dragons, it appears Hiccup will remain the brunt of his village's jokes forevermore.

Hiccup's world is turned upside down, however, when one of his contraptions snares a legendary species, the elusive and deadly Night Fury. Emotionally unable to kill him, Hiccup instead inventively mends the creature's wing, carefully makes nice with him, and comes to name him Toothless. They slowly bond, and Hiccup eventually uncovers biological truths that challenge his brood to see the world from a different point-of-view. When Hiccup and Toothless' fragile friendship is threatened by the rapacious emergence of a queen dragon, they must work together to save the village and its inhabitants.

Distributor DreamWorks had enormous success adapting William Steig's book into *Shrek* (2001) and its subsequent sequels, so it is perhaps less of a surprise than it might seem on the surface that *How to Train Your Dragon* is loosely based on a children's novel of the same name by Cressida Cowell. Working from a screenplay co-written with William Davies, directors DeBlois and Sanders avoid topicality and instead invest more heartily into feeling, which gives the movie an impression more timeless than timely. If one wanted to reach for a political metaphor—about, say, the folly of fighting first and asking questions later, and assuming all dragons to be both at once enemies and the same as one another—there is certainly more than enough material to bear out that reading. It is softly peddled, though, and not heavy-handed in the least.

Chiefly, *How to Train Your Dragon* is a story of adolescent uplift and empowerment, and its success comes in its deft balancing of tone, and how the action is used to sincerely amplify legitimate feeling rather than merely overwhelm them or serve as a placebo. The mythos of the terrible, bloody-thirsty dragons is a bit at odds with what an audience sees, since such care is taken to present the movie's opening dragon attack as more of a town-rallying sport than mortal menace. Still, *How to Train Your Dragon* is deeply humanistic, and among its pleasurable narrative takeaways are the not insignificant notions that curiosity and knowledge are good things, that children must eventually be allowed to choose their own paths, and that the outside world must sometimes be engaged with on its own terms rather than simply battled in brutish, head-on fashion.

Visually, the film is an absolute treat. Its creature design allows for a fairly robust range of dragons, many of whom retain an air of goofy if pugnacious relatability without coming off as too cute, like concept sketches for stuffed animals. Exhibiting the sleek angles of a luxury automobile, Toothless dips perhaps just a bit too overtly into cutesy affectation with some of his mischievous, leonine behavior, but nonetheless reminds one in warm and favorable ways of Stitch, albeit with less gnashing vocalization.

The film's backgrounds are full of layered lushness that help draw in and envelop an audience, particularly adults. The richness of the Vikings' natty beards and muscle mass stand in contrast to the detail of hair on their arms, or the textured moss on scattered seaside rocks. Noted veteran cinematographer Roger Deakins was brought in on the movie as a special visual consultant, a unique adjunct capacity in which he also served on *Wall-E* (2008), and his experience and counsel is especially evident in the interplay of light and shadow throughout the film, especially in Toothless' hideaway lair—a parcel of valley land with a strikingly clear lake, rimmed by stone walls. Deakins' work, along with that of DeBlois, Sanders, production designer Kathy Altieri, and art director Pierre-Olivier Vincent, is top-notch, full of involving detail that helps create a realistic world in which this fantastical action takes place.

The movie's 3-D presentation is also exceedingly well integrated, possessing an innate awareness of the emotional possibilities of the add-on viewing experience. The action sequences pop, and connect in visceral fashion, but never in a way that pulls one far outside of the narrative. Most notable are several thrilling point-of-view perspective shots in a handful of amazing climb-and-dive sequences involving Toothless. Composer John

Powell's score soars particularly during these spirited moments, which underscore the adolescent daydream of flight, and deliver a powerful, enjoyable reminder of the elemental hold of moviemaking.

Spot-on vocal performances help seal the deal, too. The most theatrical of the bunch is by far Butler, who turns up his accented Scottish growl to an "11" on the amp; it may at first blush seem too much, but one comes to realize that it reflects Stoick's larger-than-life nature, and the shadow that he casts over his son. Baruchel, meanwhile, has a reedy natural timbre that mimics his physicality, upon which his character's look is also based. It works well in conveying everything from Hiccup's hemming emotional uncertainty and confusion to his equivocation through self-effacing asides. Amongst the group of supporting players, Ferrera truly stands out, delivering a forceful turn as a girl whose headstrong spunkiness is earned, not merely some throwaway screenplay descriptor.

Brent Simon

CREDITS

Hiccup: Jay Baruchel (Voice)
Stoick: Gerard Butler (Voice)
Astrid: America Ferrera (Voice)
Snotlout: Jonah Hill (Voice)
Fishlegs: Christopher Mintz-Plasse (Voice)
Gobber: Craig Ferguson (Voice)
Ruffnut: Kristen Wiig (Voice)
Tuffnut: T.J. Miller (Voice)
Origin: USA
Language: English
Released: 2010
Production: Bonnie Arnold, Kristine Belson; Vertigo Entertainment; released by DreamWorks Animation
Directed by: Christopher Sanders, Dean DeBlois
Written by: Christopher Sanders, Dean DeBlois
Music by: John Powell
Sound: Randy Thom
Editing: Maryann Brandon, Darren T. Holmes
Production Design: Kathy Altieri
MPAA rating: PG
Running time: 98 minutes

REVIEWS

Cole, Stephen. *Globe and Mail.* March 26, 2010.
Ebert, Roger. *Chicago Sun-Times.* March 25, 2010.
Gleiberman, Owen. *Entertainment Weekly.* March 10, 2010.
Honeycutt, Kirk. *Hollywood Reporter.* March 12, 2010.
Puig, Claudia. *USA Today.* March 25, 2010.
Rea, Steven. *Philadelphia Inquirer.* March 25, 2010.

Sharkey, Betsy. *Los Angeles Times.*. March 25, 2010.
Smith, Kyle. *New York Post.* March 26, 2010.
Tallerico, Brian. *MovieRetriever.com.* March 29, 2010.
Taylor, Ella. *Village Voice.* March 24, 2010.

QUOTES

Hiccup: "This is Berk. It snows nine months out of the year, and hails the other three. What little food grows here is tough and tasteless. The people that grow here, even more so. The only upsides are the pets. While other places have ponies, or parrots…we have dragons."

TRIVIA

A Dreamworks employee's computer screen saver of a black leopard inspired the film's creators to make Toothless more feline in appearance instead of more wolf like.

AWARDS

Nomination:

Oscars 2010: Animated Film, Orig. Score
British Acad. 2010: Animated Film, Orig. Score
Golden Globes 2011: Animated Film.

HOWL

The obscenity trial that started a revolution. The poem that rocked a generation.
—Movie tagline

James Franco's searing, tour-de-force performance in *127 Hours* (2010) earned him the critical acclaim that translates to awards at the end of the year, including an Oscar® nomination for Best Actor. It was the kind of part that elevates an actor from one tier of received scripts and desired collaborators to the next and it came on the heels of several highly-acclaimed turns in diverse works such as *Pineapple Express* (2008) and *Milk* (2008). But there was another Franco performance that landed in art houses just a few months earlier that which, when combined with his take on the saga of Aron Ralston, further displayed the remarkable range of one of the best actors of his generation. Taking on a very different true-life story, Franco portrayed the legendary beat poet Allen Ginsberg in Rob Epstein and Jeffrey Friedman's unusual hybrid drama *Howl*. The filmmakers behind the documentaries *The Celluloid Closet* (1995) and *Paragraph 175* (2000) approach Ginsberg's celebrated and controversial poem from several angles, animating portions of it, including large chunks of the text read straight to a captive audience, and recreating the courtroom battle to determine whether or not it was obscene (with an odd panoply of recognizable actors that turn the scenes into an odd guessing game of who will be hitting the witness chair next). The hybrid approach may have seemed essential due to the fluctuating styles within the poem itself and downright reverent considering the influence of the work over an entire generation but it results in a final product that never quite finds its footing or personality. Franco's performance is once-again great and the power of the source material still resonates but every time Epstein and Friedman drift from that source, most notably in the misguided courtroom scenes, the film sags.

Howl works itself around Ginsberg's 1955 poem, offering a bit of a glimpse into other aspects of his life in the 1940s and 1950s, but focusing clearly on his writing and its impact. Ginsberg debuted the poem in October of 1955 and the reading at which he did so serves as the centerpiece of the film. The drama includes read portions of *Howl* but also veers off into animated portions of Ginsberg's vision that bring the work to life in ways that the Beat Generation never could have imagined. And might have argued were not needed.

One of the fatal flaws of the admittedly ambitious *Howl* is that the film is never stronger than when Franco is merely standing on that stage reading the material directly without lyrical interpretation or the dramatic emphasis of film. Not all forms of artistic expression are easily translated from one to another and translating poetry to celluloid requires overcoming some unique challenges that *Howl* does not always manage. The decision to animate *Howl* may have seemed promising on paper, but when one closes their eyes and merely conjures their own visions to associate with Ginsberg's words, the poem has a power that film cannot match. Despite the freedom of animation, the filmmakers' decisions can never match the creativity of the mind's eye.

The animated portions of *Howl* are nowhere near as damaging to the overall product as the filmmakers' desire to recreate the 1957 obscenity trial against City Lights Bookstore co-founder Lawrence Ferlinghetti, the man who first published the poem in 1956. The trial has undeniable relevance in the debate over what can be deemed obscene and it is historically important but not necessarily of the same cloth when it comes to the artistic power of the piece or what drove Ginsberg. The film never connects the dots between Franco's part of the film and the courtroom probably because Ginsberg could not accurately be portrayed as a free speech fighter; he was merely thrust into that role by virtue of his artistic drive. Consequently, the courtroom scenes feel nearly from another film, a fact that is underlined by an odd group of recognizable faces including Jon Hamm as the defense attorney, David Strathairn as the prosecuting attorney, Bob Balaban as the judge, and Allesandro Nivola, Mary-Louse Parker, Jeff Daniels, and Treat Williams as witnesses. None of them are bad, but one wonders if the courtroom sequences might not have felt so out of place if they were cast with unknowns. It is not as if the rest of the film features such a cavalcade of known actors and actresses, making one also wonder if the budget was spent filming the courtroom scenes.

Despite its structural flaws, the great work by James Franco elevates *Howl* to a position of value. He glides in and out of scenes in the film with ease and finesse, perfectly portraying a man driven by his own creative energy. Poets, especially those of the Beat Generation, have typically been turned into film clichés typified by the standard expectations spawned by the word hippie but Franco somehow finds the humanity in Ginsberg even though he has little time to do so between animated sequences and courtroom melodramatics. He alone brings value to *Howl* and does the legacy of one of the Beat Generation's most important voices proud.

Brian Tallerico

CREDITS

Allen Ginsberg: James Franco
"Himself": Allen Ginsberg
Ralph McIntosh: David Strathairn
Jake Ehrlich: Jon Hamm
Judge Clayton Horn: Bob Balaban
Professor David Kirk: Jeff Daniels
Gail Potter: Mary-Louise Parker
Mark Schorer: Treat Williams
Luther Nichols: Alessandro Nivola
Jack Kerouac: Todd Rotondi
Neal Cassady: John Prescott
Peter Orlovsky: Aaron Tveit
Origin: USA
Language: English
Released: 2010
Production: Elizabeth Redleaf PRO, Christine Kunewa Walker, Robert Epstein, Jeffrey Friedman; Werc Werk Works, Telling Pictures, Rabbit Bandini Prods.; released by Oscilloscope Laboratories
Directed by: Robert Epstein, Jeffrey Friedman
Written by: Robert Epstein, Jeffrey Friedman
Cinematography by: Edward Lachman
Music by: Carter Burwell, Hal Willner
Sound: Jan McLaughlin
Editing: Jake Pushinsky
Art Direction: Russell Barnes
Costumes: Kurt and Bart
Production Design: Therese DePrez
MPAA rating: Unrated
Running time: 84 minutes

REVIEWS

Butler, Robert W. *Kansas City Star.* October 22, 2010.
Childress, Erik. *eFilmCritic.com.* January 31, 2010.
Covert, Colin. *Minneapolis Star Tribune.* October 14, 2010.
Hoberman, J. *Village Voice.* September 21, 2010.
Jones, J.R. *Chicago Reader.* October 8, 2010.
LaSalle, Mick. *San Francisco Chronicle.* September 23, 2010.
O'Hehir, Andrew. *Salon.com.* January 28, 2010.
Phillips, Michael. *Chicago Tribune.* September 30, 2010.
Phipps, Keith. *AV Club.* September 23, 2010.
Stevens, Dana. *Slate.* September 24, 2010.

THE HUMAN CENTIPEDE: FIRST SEQUENCE

Their flesh is his fantasy.
—Movie tagline

The Human Centipede is a very sick but often very funny and profoundly disturbing horror shocker that manages to emerge from a crowded field of wannabe exploitation films at a time when just what constitutes an exploitation film is under question. The increased studio interest in hyper-violent horror fare spurred initially by the success of the *Saw* (2004-2010) films, *Hostel* (2005), and higher budget glossy gross outs like *The Texas Chainsaw Massacre* (2003), *Grindhouse* (2007), and *Machete* (2010) has seemingly put to rest the validity of the argument that exploitation film can be defined primarily by looking at how much one costs to make. Of course, the fallback position is that exploitation films are best defined as films which exploit in a morally negative sense, tainting the viewer via their gratuitous use of sex, violence, and generally disgusting imagery.

In the commentary to the Blu-ray release of the film, director/writer Tom Six explains the beginning of *The Human Centipede* as an embrace of horror film clichés. Two American tourists become lost and stranded in the woods on the way to a night on the town and seek refuge during a storm at an isolated home which proves to be inhabited by a madman. He drugs them, and they wake to find themselves strapped to hospital beds in an underground laboratory/operating theater.

Of course, it is at this point that the film, by careful design, ceases to resemble those broadly drawn clichés. Marketing hyperbole aside *The Human Centipede* is hardly as graphic as one is led to expect it will be from the trailers and the fan-press hype. Certainly, aspects of the film provoke intense discomfort and disgust but the film also offers up an irreverent sense of humor integrated in often surprisingly subtle ways, lampooning the horror genre, and the very idea of the exploitation film itself, while still fully taking in and offering a path for empathy to the human suffering that is never far from the camera's eye.

The madman in question is the reclusive Dr. Heiter, self-proclaimed expert on the separation of Siamese Twins. Long-retired, he has taken up a narcissistic mission, to create a human centipede using three subjects to form a head, a midsection and a tail—all joined via the gastric digestive tract and hobbled at the knees to facilitate obedience.

The complexity of *The Human Centipede* is showcased in the way viewer disgust lies as much, if not more, with the debasement of personhood by Heiter as it does with the physical details of the surgery and subsequent existence of the victims, which are both handled with surprising visual delicacy. As if to underline its intent, the film constantly invites viewers to look outside the house at the bucolic natural setting of the woods, and consider the peaceful tranquility that lies just outside the front door. The universe, in other words, may be indifferent to these victims, but we are close to them, closed in with them, far from indifferent toward them.

After successfully joining his victims together, Heiter, takes them into his backyard. There, dressed in his Nazi Doctor coat and sunglasses and carrying a riding crop, he issues various commands. The scenario is so reminiscent of a World War II concentration camp that the fact his subjects are an Asian man and two American women seems almost an afterthought. The fact that the Japanese man constantly talks but cannot be understood underscores Heiter's contempt at the same time it brings to mind the idea of geopolitical conflicts and cinematic exploitation. That Heiter has no real interest in what his centipede may say is revealed early on when we see Heiter kissing a mirror to congratulate himself on his sadistic surgical success. So how much more moving is it that the same Japanese man who has had to lick Heiter's jack boots humbles himself before his captor, thrusting the viewer directly into the horror of man's undying need for contact as he cries, "God. Are you God? [*laughing*] I'm just a puny insect. I cast out my parents, left my child. But dear God that's how I've lived and this is my punishment. I want to believe that I'm still a human being." [*crying*].

The two women who form the midsection and tail, dressed only in diaper-like attire, would be ripe subjects for crass sexual exploitation by the camera, but not once in the entire film does Six show any sexual interest in their nakedness. Instead, we are constantly haunted by close-ups of their faces and especially their eyes as they experience a wide range of emotions. Rage, anger, disgust, compassion, defiance all pass through them as they struggle to survive a form of torture. As the end section dies at the film's conclusion, Six gives viewers an image of two human hands clasped, comforting one another, connecting in a way that gives the lie to all

Heiter has done. It makes Six's vision of suffering and the film's ending all the more awful to behold. The camera pans away to the bucolic outdoors once more.

Scenes like these seem less stitched together as a glorious whole than they should in a true masterpiece. If Six seems content to allow his film to wander to and fro it can hardly be said he does so to no effect. *The Human Centipede* is a solid, disturbing evocative film that can wear the moniker of exploitation without fear of dismissal for those willing to truly consider it.

This is a film about people, not nations, or ideologies. As such it is amazing to see Six navigate the territory that gives his film emotional resonance. Instead of over-relying on either gore or shock he signals from the get-go that this is a movie that will attempt to engage the suffering of its characters. Even for those who find his purpose in doing so ambiguous it can hardly be argued that viewers are not meant to take the suffering of Heiter's victims seriously. Like Heiter himself, Six has created something that seems oddly-stitched and yet it is undeniably human.

Dave Canfield

CREDITS

Dr. Heiter: Dieter Laser
Lindsay: Ashley Williams
Jenny: Ashlynn Yennie
Katsuro: Akihiro Kitamura
Det. Kranz: Andreas Leupold
Origin: Netherlands
Language: English, German, Japanese
Released: 2010
Production: Ilona Six, Tom Six; Six Entertainment; released by IFC Films
Directed by: Tom Six
Written by: Tom Six
Cinematography by: Goof de Koning
Music by: Patrick Savage, Holeg Spies
Editing: Nigel De Hond
Sound: Eilam Hoffman
Production Design: Thomas Stefan
MPAA rating: Unrated
Running time: 92 minutes

REVIEWS

Abrams, Simon. *Slant Magazine.* April 26, 2010.
Catsoulis, Jeannette. *New York Times.* April 30, 2010.
Douglas, Edward. *ComingSoon.net.* April 28, 2010.
Ebert, Roger. *Chicago Sun-Times.* May 5, 2010.
Gilchrist, Todd. *Cinematical.* October 27, 2009.
Kohn, Eric. *indieWIRE.* April 21, 2010.

Longworth, Karina. *Village Voice.* April 27, 2010.
McDonagh, Maitland. *MissChickFlick.* April 30, 2010.
Mendelson, Scott. *Huffington Post.* April 27, 2010.
Wesley, Morris. *Boston Globe.* May 7, 2010.

QUOTES

Katsuro: "God. Are you God? I'm just a puny insect. I cast out my parents, left my child, dismissed their love and led a selfish life. Just like an insect. No, my existence is even lower than insects, but…but dear God…that's how I've lived, and this is my punishment."

TRIVIA

A joke writer/director Tom Six made with friends about punishing child molesters by stitching their "mouth to the ass of a fat truck driver" was the initial inspiration for the film.

I

I AM LOVE
(Lo sono l'amore)

Box Office: $5 million

Tilda Swinton continues to make the case that she must be considered in any discussion of the best living actresses as she is once again (after *Julia* [2009] last year) the best thing about a film she stars in, Luda Guadagnino's *I Am Love*. The fact that Swinton shines in Guadagnino's luscious melodrama should come as no surprise as the film was so clearly designed as a cinematic love letter to the multi-talented actress. It is a vehicle built for Swinton, one that plays to her strengths while framing her like a classic movie star at all times. It is a sensuous, beautiful drama that was easily one of the most visually sumptuous pieces of 2010. Sadly, like a lot of art that focuses so purely on the aesthetic beauty, *I Am Love* is a bit hollow. The overly mannered, soap-opera level dialogue and melodramatic plot are balanced by stunning design elements (including Oscar®-nominated costume design from Atonella Cannarozzi along with lovely cinematography by Yorick Le Saux and gorgeous music provided by John Adams) but only barely, making for an odd critical tug of war. In an era when so many movies look the same, it is difficult to completely dismiss one as lovely to look at as *I Am Love,* but it is essentially a very well-made melodramatic soap opera. It is a technical beauty in pursuit of a story that too often strikes cliché and contrivance.

The film is visually stunning from the very beginning with a lovely extended sequence in Milan that introduces the Recchi family, an extremely wealthy clan of upper-class socialites. These are beautiful people with beautiful homes and beautiful possessions. The drama begins at a birthday party for the aging patriarch, Edoardo (Gabriele Ferzetti). Instead of announcing that he will bequeath his business to his beloved son Tancredi (Pippo Delbono), he decides that his offspring will have joint partnership with his grandson Edoardo Jr. (Flavio Parenti). Edoardo believes that Tandcredi is a smart, good man, but not as headstrong or passionate as his grandson. The push-and-pull between the intellectually right decisions and what the heart wants will permeate the rest of the film. The rest of the family includes Tancredi's other son named Gianluca (Mattia Zaccaro), a daughter named Elisabetta (Alba Rohrenbacher), and Edoardo Sr.'s wife Allegra (Marisa Berenson). Most of the family serves as lovely background but Rohrenbacher is effective.

The changing face of this family that has clearly enjoyed social prominence for decades or even centuries is represented by Tancredi's wife Emma (Swinton). Emma is a Russian immigrant who married into the family years earlier but is also clearly an outsider. It is notable that Guadagnino cast such a striking woman to play the role, someone who is clearly not Italian and stands out among the rest of the cast, although Swinton speaks the language perfectly. Emma meets a chef at the birthday luncheon named Antonio (Edoardo Gabbrielllini). Sometime later, the patriarch has died and Emma is faced with two life-changing events. First, she discovers that her daughter Elisabetta is a lesbian, which does not upset the woman as much as arguably lead her to reassess her own view of passion and taking risks to find hers. She does when she reencounters the handsome Antonio, a man who strikes her as the opposite of her straight-laced husband. He is a force of nature, the new passion in Emma's life that she seems unable to avoid. Their affair is discovered by Edoardo Jr. and it leads to tragedy.

I Am Love is a visually striking film from the Italian mansions of the Recchi family to the natural landscapes in which many of Emma and Antonio's romantic moments take place. Guadagnino knows how to frame a scene like a work of art and how to light and costume Tilda Swinton like she is his Mona Lisa. And she gives more than just a typical art model. She takes Emma in interesting directions that most of her colleagues would have never even considered, completely conveying both her original tedium and the passion awakened within her along with the sincere emotion of the final act.

Oh, that final act. Sadly, *I Am Love* starts with such opulence and visual beauty that it has nowhere to go but over-the-top as the film reaches its melodramatic peaks. As John Adams' score becomes oppressively loud and the histrionics kick in, it becomes clear that the supporting cast is really nothing more than a series of plot devices. Even Antonio is a cipher when one considers the importance of his character. The emotions never register beyond being another part of the artistic fabric of the film. The melodrama feels as rehearsed and well-chosen as the costumes, which is a flaw for a film that feels designed to tell a moving story. *I Am Love* is a beautiful trip, but never the emotionally memorable one that it could have or should have been.

Brian Tallerico

CREDITS

Emma Recchi: Tilda Swinton
Edoardo Recchi Sr.: Gabriele Ferzetti
Elisabetta Recchi: Alba Rohrwacher
Eva Ugolini: Diane Fleri
Mr. Kubelkian: Waris Ahluwalia
Allegra Recchi: Marisa Berenson
Edoardo Recchi Jr.: Flavio Parenti
Antonio Biscaglia: Edoardo Gabbriellini
Tancredi Recchi: Pippo Delbono
Ida Roselli: Maria Paiato
Gianluca Recchi: Mattia Zaccaro
Origin: Italy
Language: English, Italian, Russian
Released: 2009
Production: Luca Guadagnino, Tilda Swinton, Alessandro Usai; Mikado Films, First Sun; released by Magnolia Pictures
Directed by: Luca Guadagnino

Written by: Ivan Cotroneo, Walter Fasano, Luca Guadagnino, Barbara Alberti
Cinematography by: Yorick Le Saux
Music by: John Adams
Sound: Riccardo Spagnol, Francesco Cucinelli, Francesco Liotard
Editing: Walter Fasano
Costumes: Antonella Cannarozzi
Production Design: Francesca Balestra Di Mottola
MPAA rating: R
Running time: 119 minutes

REVIEWS

Burr, Ty. *Boston Globe*. July 8, 2010.
Dargis, Manohla. *New York Times*. June 18, 2010.
Ebert, Roger. *Chicago Sun-Times*. June 24, 2010.
Hillis, Aaron. *Village Voice*. May 26, 2010.
Lemire, Christy. *Associated Press*. June 23, 2010.
Long, Tom. *Detroit News*. July 2, 2010.
Schwarzbaum, Lisa. *Entertainment Weekly*. June 16, 2010.
Stevens, Dana. *Slate*. June 25, 2010.
Weissberg, Jay. *Variety*. June 18, 2010.
Wise, Damon. *Empire Magazine*. April 8, 2010.

TRIVIA

Actress Tilda Swinton had to learn both Italian and Russian for her role in the movie.

AWARDS

Nomination:

Oscars 2010: Costume Des.
British Acad. 2010: Foreign Film
Golden Globes 2011: Foreign Film.

I LOVE YOU PHILLIP MORRIS

Do some time with the one you love.
    —Movie tagline
A story so incredible, it could only be true.
    —Movie tagline
The Conman who wouldn't go straight.
    —Movie tagline

Box Office: $2 million

John Requa and Glenn Ficarra's *I Love You Phillip Morris* is such an unusual comedy-drama hybrid that most studios would have probably struggled when it came to marketing and promoting the picture even without the financial woes that befell the film's original company. After an international release, the film sat on the shelf for months waiting for a stateside game plan before Roadside Pictures picked it up and unexpectedly released it not only in the prime of the holiday season but pushing it for potential awards. The fact-based comedy features one of the most daring performances of the year in one of Jim Carrey's career-best turns but Requa and Ficarra cannot quite figure out what they have here. The story of a man who went to unusual extremes in the pursuit of both wealth and love fluctuates from wacky comedy to drama to even romance and the writers of *Bad Santa* (2003) cannot quite handle the tone changes in their directorial debut. Carrey delivers enough to warrant a look but the script never comes together to fully showcase his performance the way one hopes it will and a particularly-dramatic turn in the final act truly sinks the overall piece.

Carrey plays con man Steven Jay Russell, a notoriously-daring thief who started with insurance fraud and eventually moved on to the kind of theft that has kept him in prison to this day. During one of his stints behind bars, Russell meets Phillip Morris (Ewan McGregor)—no relation to the legendary tobacco company—a sweet, gentle man who Steven instantly wants to protect. The two fall in love and eventually become a couple outside of prison. To try to keep Phillip in the life of opulence that he thinks he deserves, Steven turns up the volume on his life of fraud, even rising to the ranks of C.F.O. of a major company, which he uses to embezzle nearly a million dollars before getting caught again. As Steven succeeds in one escape after another, each more daring then the one that came before, Phillip learns the depth of his identity fraud and their love affair fractures.

I Love You Phillip Morris tries to be several movies at once and the odd hybrid works for two acts on the strength of Carrey's accomplished work. Jim Carrey used to take risks with daring, unusual films like *The Truman Show* (1998), *Man on the Moon* (1999), and *Eternal Sunshine of the Spotless Mind* (2004), but has settled into a lackluster period over the last several years with lazy junk like *The Number 23* (2007) and *Yes Man* (2008). His work here harkens back to the actor Carrey used to be as he perfectly balances the love story with the broad comedy of his larger-than-life character. McGregor and co-star Leslie Mann are also effective (although it is becoming remarkably-clichéd for Mann to play roles like this one), but this is Carrey's show from beginning to end.

When a writer sets up a shell game like *I Love You Phillip Morris*—a script that is founded on love but also based in the cynical world of gay jokes and identity fraud—the final act can be a particularly tricky maneuver and here is where *I Love You Phillip Morris* shoots itself in the foot. The film goes from an ironic and cynical

spin on *Catch Me If You Can* (2002) with a dose of unabashed romanticism into something much more manipulative. It turns out that Steven's previous lover (Rodrigo Santoro) dies of AIDS and Requa and Ficarra stage a deathbed scene that punctures the tires of the entire movie. What was (at times) delightful crashes to the ground and simply cannot get back up again, especially when the script is required to perform similar acts of manipulation as it comes to a conclusion. Essentially, *I Love You Phillip Morris* is a promising film without an ending; two-thirds of a movie with either creators who never figured out how to close the film or a post-production process that mangled their intentions as the film struggled to be released.

Steven Jay Russell may be too complicated a man to fully capture in film. He is not the typically suave con man usually brought to life and he is larger-than-life without being blown to the size of a movie screen. And yet there is a serious mental problem at play in the mind of a man who would threaten the life he had created out of love by pretending to be a C.F.O., fully aware that his house of cards would collapse. There could have been a daring (and long) film about the many faces of Russell but *I Love You Phillip Morris* is not ambitious enough to be that film. Instead, it is merely a showcase piece for a great actor proving that he still has the talent he displayed more consistently in the late 1990s and early 2000s. Like the film itself, Carrey's chameleonic skill is something that most critics never thought they would see again.

Brian Tallerico

CREDITS

Steven Russell: Jim Carrey
Phillip Morris: Ewan McGregor
Debbie: Leslie Mann
Jimmy: Rodrigo Santoro
Origin: France, USA
Language: English
Released: 2010
Production: Andrew Lazar, Far Shariat; Europacorp, Mad Chance; released by Freestyle Releasing
Directed by: Glenn Ficarra, John Requa
Written by: Glenn Ficarra, John Requa
Cinematography by: Xavier Perez Grobet
Music by: Nick Urata
Sound: Paul Urmson
Music Supervisor: Gary Calamar
Editing: Tom Nordberg
Art Direction: Helen Harwell
Costumes: David C. Robinson

Production Design: Hugo Luczyc-Wyhowski
MPAA rating: R
Running time: 100 minutes

REVIEWS

Anderson, John. *Variety.* May 19, 2009.
Anderson, Melissa. *Village Voice.* November 30, 2010.
Bayer, Jeff. *Scorecard Review.* December 18, 2010.
Bradshaw, Peter. *The Guardian.* Mar. 19, 2010.
Ebert, Roger. *Chicago Sun-Times.* December 9, 2010.
Lane, Anthony. *New Yorker.* December 8, 2010.
Pais, Matt. *Metromix.com.* December 9, 2010.
Puig, Claudia. *USA Today.* December 2, 2010.
Sharkey, Betsy. *Los Angeles Times.* December 2, 2010.
Stevens, Dana. *Slate.* December 6, 2010.

QUOTES

Steven Russell: "I love you, Phillip Morris! I love you!"

TRIVIA

Based on the real life story of Steven J. Russell.

AWARDS

Nomination:

Writers Guild 2010: Adapt. Screenplay.

I SPIT ON YOUR GRAVE

It's Date Night.
    —Movie tagline

Day of the Woman—October 8, 2010.
    —Movie tagline

The original *I Spit on Your Grave* (1978) has earned its place in horror infamy among fans and detractors for being one of the most brutally realized revenge films of its time. Just short of a pornographic depiction of various forms of rape, the film was equally explicit in its payback with violence including disembowelment and emasculation of the worst kind. In the thirty years since, the extremes attached to it have included everything from being a pro-feminist statement to a morally repugnant fantasy. The necessity to revisit this material for a new generation must come into question unless the filmmakers have decided to tackle the underlying themes and explore them in a new time when torture and score-settling have taken on greater meaning. Director Steven R. Monroe only saw the sadistic violence on the surface and is determined to make sure today's audiences see it too.

The story is pretty much the same thirty-two years later. Attractive young writer Jennifer Hills (Sarah Butler) has rented a cabin in the woods to, as she says, write her first book. Stopping for some gas, she embarrasses and teases station attendant Johnny (Jeff Branson) for his suggestive flirtation. When plumbing issues have her call upon mentally challenged handyman Matthew (Chad Lindberg), she rewards his service with a spontaneous smooch. When Johnny and his boys, harmonica-playing Andy (Rodney Eastman) and video camera-operating Stanley (Daniel Franzese), hear about this they are determined to pay this big-city girl a visit.

At what appears to be either a pre-dawn or extended evening terrorizing, the four guys harass Jennifer in her cabin until she is able to escape into the forming daylight where Sheriff Storch (Andrew Howard) is on his morning hunt. It turns out that this seemingly life-saving officer is really the Edward Herrmann to these Lost Boys and joins in on what becomes an attempt for Matthew to lose his virginity. Jennifer is abused further by Johnny and the Sheriff until she catatonically must stumble naked through the woods before they can finish her off for good. Disappearing for a full month, the rapists begin to be taunted by relics of their day with Jennifer and will eventually come face-to-face with this avenging angel who may have spent her time studying up on the *Saw* films.

Violence in its many film forms has become an acceptable vice for audiences looking to vicariously project their own frustrations at the evils of this world. More so than even sex, viewers enjoy a certain level of retribution toward cinematic enemies that one could not possibly inflict nor wish for in the everyday pattern of law, order, and evidence. When that level is combined with sexual gratification or exploitation, it is then where critics must take a deeper look at the Freudian implications of what audiences are actually expected to enjoy. Employing that tactic to get within the gray matter is why some of the best revenge films of this ilk like *The Virgin Spring* (1960) and *Straw Dogs* (1971) have stood the test of time. Even the former's more bloody updating, *Last House on the Left* (2009)—a superior version of the original—paused to include believable sentiment and contemplation over the consequences of acting within the moment to protect an innocent girl. *I Spit on Your Grave* is even more premeditated than its inspiration despite being a meditation on nothing.

Full of phallic close-ups on gun barrels and gas pumps, Monroe almost announces himself as a co-conspirator to the rapists' ideology that they have what Jennifer needs and she should be thanking them for giving it to her. Nobody ever wants to give credence to the "she had it coming" defense as she walks around in revealing clothing and jogs around in an outfit that leaves little to the imagination. Stuart Morse's screenplay invites such discussion though not by lingering on her fashion decisions but by turning Jennifer into the atypical horror film character who makes one questionable move after another. Beginning by isolating herself in hillbilly woods, Jennifer investigates abandoned houses and strange noises in the night without protection unhindered by the possibility of wild animals (either the bear or hairy male variety) lurking about. Forget about sympathy for the crime against her gender, if Jennifer was a character in a *Friday the 13th* or other cheap slasher film would the core audience not be welcoming her demise for her not erring on the side of caution?

The 1978 film is not without its defenders from that core audience who see the good, see the bad, and invite the ugliness when warranted. The remake's decision to include a fifth antagonist in the Sheriff serves to extend both the initial assault and provide an extra body for Jennifer to abuse herself when the flip-flop is on the other foot. Within this warped view of small town justice, the Sheriff is not just the supposed peacekeeper but also a family man with a pregnant wife and a daughter named Chastity. "Daddy always makes breakfast before Church," his little girl says over the phone while Jennifer is in the other room being gagged. The myriad of things that Monroe and Morse appear to be investing in this overt bit of hypocritical irony makes one wonder just how far their heads are buried up their simplistic views of middle-American moral outrage. Presented as such the Sheriff may just be a self-admitted "God-fearing" man with a good family that is so offended by the big city (aka: liberal) "whore" who drinks and smokes them marijuana cigarettes that he had to teach her a lesson; albeit in a place where new big city people cannot be spawned.

Jennifer may not use her sexuality to the extent she did in 1978 to ensnare her attackers and her tortuous schemes are certainly more creative despite opening herself up to identification for her crimes by pulling a stunt straight out of *Fatal Attraction* (1987). Still, this is a film intent on giving viewers twenty minutes of sexual assault and thirty minutes of vengeance (with some of that assault going the other way) up front and personal from the direct point of view—rape-to-revenge—of the bad guys. This is not a horror film. It is a snuff film with slightly better production values; though even that can be questioned from script-to-direction with laughable instances that include one of the worst mace scenes ever and the Sheriff berating Stanley that a videotape can be used as evidence a month after he allowed the same idiot to film the entire incident. It is a shame someone did not do the same to Mr. Monroe after making his debut.

Brian Tallerico

CREDITS

Jennifer Hills: Sarah Butler
Andy: Rodney Eastman
Johnny: Jeff Branson
Stanley: Daniel Franzese
Matthew: Chad Lindberg
Sheriff Storch: Andrew Howard
Earl Woodason: Tracey Walter
Origin: USA
Language: English
Released: 2010
Production: Lisa M. Hansen, Paul Hertzberg; Cinetel Films; released by Anchor Bay Films
Directed by: Steven R. Monroe
Written by: Stuart Morse
Cinematography by: Neil Lisk
Music by: Corey A. Jackson
Sound: Bobby Fisk
Editing: Daniel Duncan
Costumes: Bonnie Stauch
Production Design: Dins W.W. Danielsen
MPAA rating: R
Running time: 108 minutes

REVIEWS

Anderson, Jason. *Toronto Star.* September 23, 2010.
Dujsik, Mark. *Mark's Movie Reviews.* October 7, 2010.
Ebert, Roger. *Chicago Sun-Times.* October 7, 2010.
Gonzalez, Ed. *Slant Magazine.* October 3, 2010.
LaSalle, Mick. *San Francisco Chronicle.* October 7, 2010.
O'Hehir, Andrew. *Salon.com.* October 7, 2010.
Pinkerton, Nick. *Village Voice.* October 5, 2010.
Rothkopf, Joshua. *Time Out New York.* October 6, 2010.
Tobias, Scott. *AV Club.* October 7, 2010.
Weinberg, Scott. *Daily-Reviews.* October 3, 2010.

TRIVIA

This film was given zero stars by Roger Ebert. He also gave the original *I Spit On Your Grave* (1978) zero stars.

THE ILLUSIONIST
(L'illusioniste)

Sylvain Chomet's brilliant follow-up to his internationally-acclaimed *The Triplets of Belleville* (2003), *The Illusionist* is a charming, surprisingly-moving slice of whimsy that serves a multi-faceted tribute to the road life of the performer, fathers and daughters, and the work of the legendary Jacques Tati. The story goes that Tati's daughter Sophie gave the unproduced screenplay, which Tati intended to direct as a live-action feature, to

Chomet at Cannes in 2006 and it took the talented animator until 2010 to bring his version of it to the big screen. The result was a bit controversial given the dedication and the mystery surrounding the background of the screenplay but it was also widely-acclaimed, going as far as to land an Oscar® nomination for Best Animated Film, beating out much-more high-profile choices like *Despicable Me* (2010) and *Tangled* (2010). *The Illusionist* is a reminder of the beauty of traditional animation, containing some of the most strikingly gorgeous imagery of 2010 in the pursuit of a lovely tale about the magic of life.

Chomet turns Tati's arguably semi-autobiographical piece of work into a tribute to the director as well, crafting a lead character that looks exactly like Tati's legendary Mr. Hulot, an aging magician watching the popularity of his art fade with the years. He travels from small venue to smaller venue and plays to crowds more interested in emerging rock musicians than a rabbit coming out of a hat. When he does find a loyal audience at a pub, they are usually drunk enough to be entertained by the magic of a light switch. The magician's time is fading as his art form becomes less popular. As his journey starts to end, another is beginning. He meets a young girl named Alice and is instantly drawn to her, at first probably because she is thrilled by his tricks. He takes her under her wing and travels with her to the big city where he performs and she explores the world around her. She discovers magic and wonder in a new dress, an act of kindness to one of the performers who live in their tenement, and, eventually, a young man. The magician performs his greatest trick by caring for her and in doing so opening up the world's magic to a young woman.

A vast majority of *The Illusionist* contains no dialogue at all. It plays more like a silent film with a lovely score and imagery that says more than words ever could. *The Triplets of Belleville* was refreshingly zany and wacky and there are a few bits of broad humor here (a bit in which the title character tries to make money washing a car is priceless) but *The Illusionist* is much more lyrical than his last film. It is a gentle, quiet tale with visual treats that add up to emotional depth instead of traditional character development or riveting plot twists. Animation has become such a playground for writers looking to prove their value to adults with pop culture references, that it is almost shocking to see a piece from the medium that feels timeless and will never be dated. It is a visual treat with a different level of beauty than Pixar or DreamWorks films. Honestly, one should have difficulty even comparing it to *Toy Story 3* (2010) as the films use such different techniques to different ends.

The minor controversy surrounding the film deserves mention. After its release, some critics and historians noted that Jacques Tati also had a daughter who he discarded and ignored and that the film should more accurately be read as an ode or apology to her. Whatever historical relevance one takes from *The Illusionist* in terms of Tati's intentions is not particularly relevant to the success of the film. It works whether or not one has seen all of Tati's films and knows his complex back story or whether or not one has never even heard of the man.

The lush landscapes, the detailed expressions of the characters, even the broad caricatures of the lively supporting personalities—every element of *The Illusionist* blends together into something that is nearly transcendent in its beauty. There are stills and shots from the film that could easily be sold in a gallery. It is great art judged frame by frame but it is the cumulative power of the piece that is truly remarkable. It is one of those films that sneaks up on the viewer, quietly drawing them in and walloping them with the emotion of the final act. And it is so by proving the form's vitality through old-fashioned artistry instead of a new technological advancement. One only hopes that it does not take as long for Sylvain Chomet to make another.

Brian Tallerico

CREDITS

The Illusionist/French Cinema Manager: Jean-Claude Donda (Voice)
Alice: Eilidh Rankin (Voice)
Origin: United Kingdom, France
Language: French
Released: 2010
Production: Bob Last, Sally Chomet; Django Films, CineB; released by Sony Pictures Classics
Directed by: Sylvain Chomet
Written by: Sylvain Chomet
Music by: Sylvain Chomet
Sound: Carl Goetgheluck
Production Design: Jacques Arhex
Art Direction: Bjarne Hansen
Running time: 78 minutes

REVIEWS

Atkinson, Michael. *Boston Phoenix.* January 27, 2011.
Burr, Ty. *Boston Globe.* January 27, 2011.
Dargis, Manohla. *New York Times.* December 30, 2010.
Ebert, Roger. *Chicago Sun-Times.* January 13, 2011.
Felperin, Leslie. *Variety.* January 5, 2011.
Howell, Peter. *Toronto Star.* January 20, 2011.

Jones, J.R.. *Chicago Reader.* January 21, 2011.
O'Hara, Helen. *Empire Magazine.* August 19, 2010.
Pais, Matt. *Metromix.com.* January 15, 2011.
White, Armond. *New York Press.* December 24, 2010.

TRIVIA

When Sylvain Chomet adapted the original screenplay, he moved the setting from Prague to Edinburgh, the home of his animation studio.

AWARDS

Nomination:

Oscars 2010: Animated Film
Golden Globes 2011: Animated Film.

I'M STILL HERE

(I'm Still Here: The Lost Years of Joaquin Phoenix)

One day short of a week after the theatrical release of *I'm Still Here,* director Casey Affleck revealed that it was also appropriate to credit him as a "co-conspirator" for the film. Joaquin Phoenix, the subject of the faux documentary, had not suffered a nervous breakdown. He had not retired from acting, and in fact, Affleck, as quoted in an article of the *New York Times* published on the paper's website the day before the film's wider theatrical release, said Phoenix's work in *I'm Still Here* is "the performance of his career."

The opinion is sound; Phoenix fooled many. The rest had their doubts. Most treated it as a joke, even though neither Affleck nor Phoenix had stated openly that it was one. In that way, if the pair wanted to expose a parasitic nature of entertainment "journalism" that chews up a celebrity's personal problems and spits out the star when finished, they have succeeded in real life, if not precisely in the capsule of Phoenix's act that is the film. It is not as though the statement is earth-shattering, either.

The question on which critics, journalists, and other interested parties focused on about the film—just as with the real-life circus act that broke out following Phoenix's announcement—was toward its authenticity or lack thereof. The puzzle was more important than the content of the film, unlike *Exit Through the Gift Shop* (2010), another documentary with questionable dependability, which concentrated its overarching thematic intent within the confined context of the film. Real or hoax, the audience knows exactly the point of that film. Now that both Affleck and Phoenix on the *Late Show*

with David Letterman, whose appearance on the same show in February 2009 solidified his phony public persona featuring unkempt hair and beard, black suit and tie, and plastic, thick-rimmed sunglasses to accompany an air of aloofness, have admitted the film to be "performance art," the question of its purpose and meaning is at once more intelligible and incoherent.

I'm Still Here begins in late 2008, when Phoenix announces his retirement from acting to an entertainment news network after a staged reading in honor of the recently deceased Paul Newman. While preparing for the show, Phoenix establishes the narcissism of a celebrity personality. He complains that Affleck, who has the leading role in the reading, gets to have scenes with the likes of Tom Hanks, while Phoenix only reads opposite of Danny DeVito (whose stand-in for rehearsals is comical just in contrasting appearance). This should not be Affleck's night, Phoenix scolds his friend and brother-in-law (Affleck married Phoenix's sister Summer in 2006). After all, this is Phoenix's final acting gig, which he is more than happy to share with every available star in attendance, including Danny Glover and Sean Penn (with whom he shares an awkwardly lengthy embrace), just so the attention is on him.

Phoenix's performance in the film is fearless not due to his dedication to staying in character for public appearances, interviews with reporters, and the *Late Show* but in how unappealing this persona is in the "private" moments with friends or alone. The character in certain ways must reflect the person. The unbridled egotism of the façade wanting to steal the thunder of Affleck's success is only the start. After retiring, Phoenix adopts the nickname "J.P." and decides to concentrate on a career in music, specifically hip-hop.

J.P. has a sense of entitlement to success in his new field and success for J.P. is measured by fame. In his previous vocation, J.P. was famous, which Affleck establishes using a montage of award show footage (culminating with Phoenix's Golden Globe win for Best Actor for his portrayal of Johnny Cash in *Walk the Line* [2005]) and talk shows featuring repetitive answers from the actor. Perhaps Phoenix's clear boredom with the tedious promotional process is a major factor in creating a character that keeps himself and the press on their toes during interviews. At one point, he describes the job of an actor as being a "puppet," a role that—as seen in those interviews—goes beyond the process of making a film.

The rapper J.P. has expectations for his new career. All he must do is contact a famous producer, who will immediately sign him based on his name. Only Sean "P. Diddy" Combs responds, although he is skeptical of J.P. The reports that Phoenix's retirement and subsequently apparent nervous breakdown are a prank are a major part of the film's story. Finally hearing some of J.P.'s songs, Combs grimaces, nods his head to the beat, has his assistant skip ahead tracks, and ultimately does the wisest but kindest thing he can do: turns down but encourages J.P.'s "talent."

It is an outrage for J.P. that anyone believes that his career change is not sincere or that he does not deserve a recording contract. He verbally abuses his friend and general assistant Anton (Antony Langdon), after suspecting that Anton went to the press with the rumor that the whole thing is a ruse. Anton proceeds to sneak into J.P.'s room and defecate on his face.

While the attack on Phoenix and Affleck's intended targets is vague at best, the depiction of the destructive nature of an insecure, ego-driven personality is the film's most successful, uncomfortable achievement. There are staged encounters with prostitutes, snorts of cocaine, and venomous verbal assaults on his acquaintances. The real results of the chicanery include a moment in which a now overweight J.P. can barely tie his own shoes while sitting, due to his protruding stomach, and a vomiting fit after a failed musical performance.

J.P. does not come across well, and, by extension, neither does Phoenix. *I'm Still Here* is at once a humbling depiction of celebrity and, in supposing grander aspirations, an arrogant display of the same sort of excess it satirizes. In the context of the film, the final image of J.P. walking down a river in Panama (which was, in reality, Hawaii) with his back turned to the camera as the water slowly rises over his head is symbolic of a creative man getting in over his head in his groundless ambition. In actuality and in reference to the film, the metaphor still works.

Mark Dujsik

CREDITS

Himself: Joaquin Phoenix
Himself: Casey Affleck
Anton: Antony Langdon
Himself: David Letterman
Himself: Edward James Olmos
Himself: Ben Stiller
Origin: USA
Language: English
Released: 2010
Production: Joaquin Phoenix, Casey Affleck PROD, Amanda White PROD; They are going to kill us productions; released by Magnolia Pictures
Directed by: Casey Affleck
Cinematography by: Magdalena Gorka

Music by: Rayston Langdon, Tom Waits, Kathleen Brennan, Christopher H. Knight
Sound: Dolby Digital
Editing: Peggy Eghbalian, Dody Dorn
MPAA rating: R
Running time: 108 minutes

REVIEWS

Burr, Ty. *Boston Globe.* September 10, 2010.
Corliss, Richard. *Time.com.* September 6, 2010.
Ebert, Roger. *Chicago Sun-Times.* September 7, 2010.
Edelstein David. *Nymag.com.* September 7, 2010.
Gang, Alison. *San Diego Union-Tribune.* September 9, 2010.
Lemire, Christy. *Dallas Morning News.* September 9, 2010.
Macnab, Geoffrey. *Independent.co.uk.* September 7, 2010.
Rodriguez, Rene. *Miami Herald.* September 8, 2010.
Turan, Kenneth. *Los Angeles Times.* September 10, 2010.
Wilmington, Michael. *Chicago Tribune.* September 8, 2010.

QUOTES

Joaquin Phoenix: "Do the snow angel, dude. I can reach you, do the f**king snow angel. Dude, do the f**king snow angel. Do the snow angel, man. Do the f**king snow angel, dude. Do the f**king snow angel!"

TRIVIA

In the film, there is a scene where Joaquin Phoenix is sitting with his father drinking beers. This man is not Joaquin Phoenix's father, but actually the real-life father of actors Casey Affleck and Ben Affleck.

INCEPTION

The dream is real.
—Movie tagline
Your mind is the scene of the crime.
—Movie tagline

Box Office: $293 million

Daniel Burnham is a name little known outside the realm of municipal planners, but amidst much late nineteenth century metropolitan disorder, the architect put forth a powerful and compelling vision of what an American city should look like and how it should function, crafting enormously influential urban plans for Chicago, Washington, D.C., San Francisco, Cleveland, and even Manila. Explaining his penchant for thinking outside the box and attempting to reconcile concepts often thought popularly to be contradictory, he once famously said, "Make no little plans, for they have no magic to stir men's blood. Make big plans, aim high in hope and work."

Filmmaker Christopher Nolan is a man for whom Burnham would no doubt have much admiration, so linked are their ways of thinking. The modern cinematic landscape is chockablock full of both auteur-minded writer-directors who handcraft gorgeous little intensely personal baubles (Wes Anderson, Noah Baumbach, and Sofia Coppola, to name but a few of many), as well as mastercraft-level technicians who stand astride massive productions which command nine-figure budgets. There is no one else working today quite like Nolan, however—someone who is functioning effectively and simultaneously in both realms, fashioning bracing, sociologically relevant and unapologetically mainstream high-wire entertainments.

Inception, Nolan's Oscar®-nominated follow-up to the lauded, Academy Award®-winning *The Dark Knight* (2008), is a staggeringly-ambitious shot across the bow of cinematic complacence, a bold play in the joint espousal and defense of the belief that Hollywood films can and should try to push the envelope intellectually as much as technologically, in an effort to matter in deeper, more substantive ways than merely how much money they can separate from wallets. At a time when so many movies are either sequels, wan spinoffs, franchise reboots, or take as their source material comic books and videogames, *Inception* is a power hitter's swing for the fences, exciting in a way because of its very overreach and flaws.

Whatever one ultimately thinks about it—and one will think about it, that much is certain—*Inception* is a film with an original idea at its core. That is the type of story for which cinephiles should root, on a certain level. And, inspiringly, that idea was widely embraced, both critically and at the box office. Nolan's film was a worldwide commercial smash, pulling in $531 million overseas. More notably, it was the fifth-highest grossing Stateside release of 2010, at $293 million—a figure over $130 million greater than the next highest originally-scripted, live-action non-sequel.

A father of two separated by legal problems from his children, Cobb (Leonardo DiCaprio) is a successful, high-tech freelance operative who specializes in cutting-edge corporate espionage, entering people's dreams to uncover business secrets—and in certain cases peddling them mental "insurance," to protect against would-be raiders just like himself. *Inception* opens in a dream-within-a-dream, where Cobb and his trusted lieutenant Arthur (Joseph Gordon-Levitt) are attempting to put the cerebral con moves on a Japanese energy mogul, Saito (Ken Watanabe). Plans go awry and get even more complicated when Cobb's dead wife, Mal (Marion Cotillard) (it is not for nothing that her name is French for "pain" and "trouble"), pops up and imposes herself upon all the action of the subconscious.

Wishing to crush his more dominant rival, Saito makes Cobb an offer: He will take care of the immigration hurdles preventing him from returning to the United States if, instead of merely stealing information, Cobb and his crew can perform the inordinately more difficult and dangerous task of actually planting a corruptive thought in the mind of Robert Fischer (Cillian Murphy), who stands to inherit all of the business holdings of his dying tycoon father (Pete Postlethwaite). Cobb accepts, in spite of Arthur's reservations. In need of a new "architect" to build the complicated dreamscapes they will inhabit, Cobb turns to his father-in-law Miles (Michael Caine), who recommends Ariadne (Ellen Page), a super-talented design student. Rounding out Cobb's "dream team" (a pun the movie avoids, rather shockingly) are Eames (Tom Hardy), an expert forger and impersonator, and Yusuf (Dileep Rao), a sedatives expert whose concoctions will allow the group to stay in enough of a trance to delve deep into several different layers of dreams.

As Ariadne familiarizes herself with the logistics of dreamscape construction, Cobb, Eames, and Arthur work up a plan of attack. The approach they seize upon involves trying to boil down the idea of Robert breaking up his father's company to its most elemental form, and something born of a desire for positive catharsis rather than rooted in revenge. To get back out of the mental depths required for the idea to stick, the group also has to devise and rely on an elaborate series of choreographed "kicks" that will wake them up in unison at the proper times. Almost immediately after they trigger their grand scheme on a transatlantic flight, however, they run into problems. Militarized projections of Robert's subconscious, which has been trained to defend against attacks, swarm the group, turning *Inception* into something of a wonky, intellectualized action film cross-pollinated with a psychological Möbius strip. Cobb, meanwhile, finds his slipping hold on reality further tested by an increasingly manic Mal, who he literally cannot get out of his head.

That Nolan's film is so open to re-visitation, study, and interpretation is undeniably chief amongst its strengths. One can return to it multiple times, with significant reward. Yet *Inception* also has both an idea and the courage of its own convictions, something a lot of glossy Hollywood summer product does not. It does not shy away from esoterica or the imponderability of the human condition, even within the confines of its big, high-concept conceit. So while the same type of overblown set piece thrills of your average pedigreed slam-bang thriller exist herein—in this case including a cityscape that imaginatively folds in on itself and an amazing gravity-free hallway battle between Arthur and some armed goons, filmed on a 100-foot hallway set that rotated a full 360 degrees—there is a substantive weight to the manner in which Nolan attempts to balance inspiration, contemplation and action. The result, quite literally, keeps one on the edge of their seat, sometimes struggling (but always enjoyably) to keep up.

Perhaps a bit unsurprisingly, the performances take a back seat to the moviemaking. DiCaprio is intense and professional, very solid, while Hardy, so outrageous in *Bronson* (2009), is slick and contained. His ample charisma stripped down to an occasional series of sardonic asides, Gordon-Levitt is mainly defined through his sartorial preciseness, befitting for his role as Cobb's detail-oriented point man. As the quavering-voiced Mal, Cotillard steals scenes; she comes across like a coiled snake, and one is never quite sure where her penchant for acting out is going to take a given scene. Other characters fill their roles reliably, but *Inception* is not necessarily what one might call an actor's showcase.

Individually and collectively, the film's technical work shines. Because of the sheer volume in which he trades, composer Hans Zimmer has worked up more than his share of blustery, insipid scores throughout the years, but here he delivers music that is by turns ominous, grandly evocative, and delightfully off-kilter. Production designer Guy Hendrix Dyas and cinematographer Wally Pfister, Nolan's collaborator on every film of his since *Memento* (2000), also turn in superlative work, creating and capturing a world in which each dream sub-level has its own subtly different look and feel.

One thing that is at least nagging if not truly outright damning about *Inception* is that it does not possess a conventional antagonist. The intensity of feeling of this somewhat coldly clinical criticism dissipates a bit with subsequent viewings, but the movie's muddled third act still suffers for it. There is, too, still a chasm between what Nolan clearly believes to be the emotional pulse or heartbeat of the film, Cobb's relationship with Mal, and how that storyline actually plays out. The horse-gallop pace of *Inception* is cool and aggressively streamlined, and all its action and effects-driven bells and whistles—the sizzle that sells the steak—are fun, to be sure. But there remains a lingering feeling that the movie would be even more radical were it to slow down a bit and dig deeper into Cobb and Mal's early life together. Nolan gets into this some with sub-dreamworld time structures, in which time expands exponentially, but by playing cute he misses a chance to extract even richer tension from how Cobb and Mal's relationship might have suffered a more natural dissolution after fifty "dream" years together.

Still, there is undeniably a sort of dumbstruck, exultant entanglement that comes from watching *Inception* if one submits to it with a properly open mindset. Thematically, the movie returns to many of the same preoccupations of Nolan's previous films: misbegotten criminality, the faultiness of memory, the unforeseen and often nasty consequences of violence or impulsive acting out, and whether one's identity is inherently one's own or instead part of a grander living organism, and dependent on the perceptions of outsiders.

At its core, *Inception* is a distillation and examination of obsession, and a reminder of the crumbling ruination that awaits those for whom the strongest preoccupation of the present lies in memories of the past. When hell breaks loose and the gun-toting henchmen of Robert's militarized subconscious attack, Cobb urges his comrades to simply follow their laid-out plan, down into the next dream level. When things further deteriorate, it is then eventually Ariadne who urges not some line-in-the-sand last stand, but instead a course of action that could best be described as a sort of prescribed audible. "Push forward," Nolan seems to be saying. "That is the nature of man, of relationships, of all that is worth achieving, of humankind's social and societal evolution." Oh, and out of dangerous, netherworld dream states, too, of course. Films need not be huge in scope to illuminate or explore the human condition. Little, spare films can be wonderful. But that is not Nolan's place. He has gained access to canvas by the hectometer, and seems evermore invigorated by it.

Brent Simon

CREDITS

Cobb: Leonardo DiCaprio
Saito: Ken Watanabe
Ariadne: Ellen Page
Arthur: Joseph Gordon-Levitt
Mal: Marion Cotillard
Eames: Tom Hardy
Fischer: Cillian Murphy
Browning: Tom Berenger
Professor: Michael Caine
Nash: Lukas Haas
Maurice Fischer: Pete Postlethwaite
Yusef: Dileep Rao
Origin: USA
Language: English
Released: 2010
Production: Christopher Nolan, Emma Thomas; Legendary Pictures, Syncopy; released by Warner Bros.
Directed by: Christopher Nolan
Written by: Christopher Nolan
Cinematography by: Wally Pfister

Music by: Hans Zimmer

Sound: Edward Novick

Editing: Lee Smith

Art Direction: Frank Walsh

Costumes: Jeffrey Kurland

Production Design: Guy Hendrix Dyas

MPAA rating: PG-13

Running time: 148 minutes

REVIEWS

Anderson, John. *Wall Street Journal.* July 16, 2010.

Chang, Justin. *Variety.* July 5, 2010.

Ebert, Roger. *Chicago Sun-Times.* July 15, 2010.

Edelstein, David. *New York Magazine.* July 12, 2010.

Howell, Peter. *Toronto Star.* July 13, 2010.

Lemire, Christy. *Associated Press.* July 13, 2010.

O'Hehir, Andrew. *Salon.com.* July 15, 2010.

Scott, A.O. *New York Times.* July 15, 2010.

Tallerico, Brian. *MovieRetriever.com.* July 14, 2010.

Turan, Kenneth. *Los Angeles Times.* July 15, 2010.

QUOTES

Cobb: "Dreams feel real while we're in them. It's only when we wake up that we realize something was actually strange."

TRIVIA

Kate Winslet, James Franco, Taylor Swift, and Evan Rachel Wood were all originally considered for lead roles in the film.

AWARDS

Oscars 2010: Cinematog., Sound, Sound FX Editing, Visual FX

British Acad. 2010: Prod. Des., Sound, Visual FX

Screen Actors Guild 2010: Stunt Ensemble

Writers Guild 2010: Orig. Screenplay

Nomination:

Oscars 2010: Art Dir./Set Dec., Film, Orig. Screenplay, Orig. Score

British Acad. 2010: Cinematog., Director (Nolan), Film, Film Editing, Orig. Screenplay, Orig. Score

Directors Guild 2010: Director (Nolan)

Golden Globes 2011: Director (Nolan), Film—Drama, Screenplay, Orig. Score.

INSIDE JOB

> *The global economic crisis of 2008 cost tens of millions of people their savings, their jobs, and their homes. This is how it happened.*
> —Movie tagline

> *The film that cost $20,000,000,000,000 to make.*
> —Movie tagline

Box Office: $4 million

Charles Ferguson's brilliant *Inside Job,* a film nominated for the Best Documentary Oscar®, opens with what might first seem like an unusual aside regarding an economic crisis in Iceland. Slowly, it dawns on the American viewer that what happened in that far-off land is a tempest in a teapot, a perfectly encapsulated example of what happened and is happening to the U.S. economy in the late 2000s through today. Iceland went from total stability to near-anarchy in the blink of an eye and can be used as a perfect parallel to what has happened as the United States has discarded all systems of checks and balances, pulling the rug out from under millions of Americans who watched their bubbles burst.

In one of the best documentaries of the last decade, *No End in Sight* (2007), Ferguson expertly disseminated the days leading up to the war in Iraq and did so in a way that both taught people who already felt they knew everything about the conflict and spoke to people completely unaware of the military industrial complex. Just as he did with that spectacular film, the best documentary on the Iraq War yet produced, Ferguson has again distilled a very complex subject in a way that makes it accessible without dumbing it down in the slightest. *Inside Job* is a snapshot of a system completely destroyed by internal decay—the American economy.

Matt Damon expertly narrates the film, which is comprised of mostly a series of interviews, including many of the major players in the crisis from all angles including politicians, academics, financial analysts, and the men and women (although mostly men) who essentially fiddled as Rome burned. The general thesis of *Inside Job* is that when the banks were deregulated, no one was left watching the store. Or, to put it more disturbingly, it was to no one's profit to stop the runaway train headed toward economic collapse. The film makes crystal clear that many, many people took advantage of a system for short-term gain, either not realizing the impact their decisions and practices would have long-term or, sadly, realizing it and just not caring. As financial deregulation became the norm, it made it easier for everyone on Wall Street and beyond to make millions and who among them could stand up and say that profits needed to stop to prevent a bleak future, especially for the average worker? And those who did stand up were ignored or worse.

Banks bet against their own customers, lenders became predators for their own clients, rating agencies were either corrupt or incompetent (or both), and an incredibly large number of people in power came to it with immense conflicts of interests. Looking back, it is crystal clear that the 2000s were a ticking time bomb headed to an economic depression. Why did no one sound the alarms? Well, a few people did and Ferguson gets fascinating insight from them and how they were soundly ignored. More remarkably, as he did with *No End in Sight,* Ferguson gets several of the responsible parties, including those who looked the other way or actively profited on the decline, to speak on camera and, unlike some other economic documentarians of late, he pulls no punches, even going as far as to call some of them out on their blatant lies. He does not allow for the revisionist history that some of these men would like to purport but he also never comes off as overly aggressive like Michael Moore sometimes can and he never appears on camera. It is simply enjoyable to hear someone intelligently follow up with the right comment or question to get deeper into the matter. If only there were more modern journalists with the intelligence and interviewing skills of Charles Ferguson.

The reason *Inside Job* is as accomplished as it is is that one can always sense the strong, guiding hand behind the film while also not feeling like they are being preached to or at the will of showman. Like a brilliant lecture by an award-winning professor, Ferguson creates films that are never dry but always informative. He knows, as he did with the Iraq War, just the right opinions, stats, angles, and sound bites to play to not just to tell a story he needs to expose but entertain and educate at the same time. *Inside Job* should be required viewing for any documentarian trying to figure out how to distill a complex subject into something that does not feel dry as a bad lecture or simple as a *Dateline NBC* special. There are plenty of documentarians who have followed the Moore model in an attempt to become entertainers and there are many on the other end of the spectrum that are great educators. Charles Ferguson is both, as well as a great filmmaker.

Brian Tallerico

CREDITS

Narrator: Matt Damon
Origin: USA
Language: English
Released: 2010
Production: Charles Ferguson, Audrey Marrs; Representation Pictures, Screen Pass Pictures; released by Sony Pictures Classics
Directed by: Charles Ferguson
Written by: Charles Ferguson
Cinematography by: Kalyanee Mam, Svetlana Cvetko
Music by: Alex Heffes

Sound: David Hocs, Michael Jones, David Mendez
Music Supervisor: Sue Jacobs
Editing: Chad Beck, Adam Bolt
MPAA rating: PG-13
Running time: 120 minutes

REVIEWS

Byrge, Duane. *Hollywood Reporter.* October 1, 2010.
Denby, David. *New Yorker.* October 11, 2010.
Edelstein, David. *New York Magazine.* October 4, 2010.
Hoberman, J. *Village Voice.* October 5, 2010.
Howell, Peter. *Toronto Star.* October 28, 2010.
Nelson, Rob. *Variety.* October 1, 2010.
Phillips, Michael. *Chicago Tribune.* October 14, 2010.
Rickey, Carrie. *Philadelphia Inquirer.* October 28, 2010.
Scott, A.O. *New York Times.* October 8, 2010.
Turan, Kenneth. *Los Angeles Times.* October 14, 2010.

AWARDS

Oscars 2010: Feature Doc.
Directors Guild 2010: Director (Ferguson)
Writers Guild 2010: Doc. Screenplay.

IRON MAN 2

Box Office: $312 million

When, towards the end of *Iron Man 2,* a psychological assessment characterizes hero Tony Stark as a narcissist and a self-destructive loose cannon, Robert Downey Jr. as Stark can only nod in vigorous assent. *Iron Man 2* demonstrates again that we like our heroes supremely confident and quite a bit off-center. Downey has come to specialize in playing almost all of his roles with this same reckless attention-deficit-disorder personality; mumbling to himself, spouting off rapid-fire non sequiturs, posing cleverly on the very edge of sanity.

Downey now has not one, but two blockbuster franchises going simultaneously, playing the lead roles of both Iron Man and Sherlock Holmes. In fact, it is testament to the mass appeal of Downey's wonderfully off-kilter heroism. There is a sort of mad genius personality he projects, teetering on the edge of mastery and insanity simultaneously, that works for both the old British sleuth (reconceived as an action hero by Guy Ritchie in the 2009 film) and the newer comic-book persona equally well. One could almost interchange each of these character's mannerisms and personalities—and lose little also in swapping them out for almost any other Downey character, such as the eccentric reporters in *The Soloist* (2009) and *Zodiac* (2007), proving conclusively that that this actor is in tune with the zeitgeist. And, judging by the $133 million that *Iron Man 2* took home in opening-weekend box office, none of his characters is more in synch with the times than the comically conceited, witty, and wildly self-important Stark.

Stark is an unapologetic capitalist entrepreneur, whose Iron Man suit has revolutionized warfare, rendering the U.S. government and military rather limp and superfluous. In front of oily, taunting Congressional leaders (including one played by Gary Shandling) he boasts he has "privatized peace"—and indeed, he has with his save-the-world intervention that ended the first film. Stark delights in his power to have his way, throwing wild parties, extravagant tech expos, and childish tantrums when he cannot immediately bed whatever woman he wants (in this case it is a new brainy and super-cool assistant played by Scarlett Johansson).

Stark is having tremendous fun being a superhero (with the notable exception of the blood poisoning his suit's energy source is causing, a minor annoyance that he can solve by the simple expedience of inventing and synthesizing an entirely new element). Downey is having fun playing Stark, and almost everyone else seems to be having a ball too. There is Johansson as the typical cinematic brainy, kick-ass sexpot with a withering pouty-lipped stare (she is clearly reveling in the teasing super-woman possibilities the role presents her). Samuel L. Jackson settles without much effort into his familiar, smooth, laid-back, omniscient, bad-ass persona as the eye patch-wearing head of S.H.I.E.L.D., a powerful but shadowy intelligence unit. Sam Rockwell is a wildly inappropriate weapons dealer who seems more like some kind of ditzy game show host—his power has gone to his head and shaken loose a few marbles; it is a real lark for Rockwell (and, at least for him, a change of pace). Don Cheadle does his winsome buddy part as charmingly and reliably as ever, yet he, too, doesn't need to stretch much. They are all playing their roles as high camp and so is the over-the-top movie, as directed by the reliably campy Jon Favreau.

The only contributor who seems uncomfortable, and sometimes even like a fish out of water, is Gwyneth Paltrow, who seems to be straining to fit into her role as Stark's partner Pepper Potts, who runs his business empire and—we are guessing but not quite sure—the personal end of his emotional fireworks machine. Downey and Paltrow try to fight cute in the midst of action scenes, but their banter is more wearisome than attractive, and there is so little chemistry between the stiffly backboned Paltrow and the wind-up-toy Downey that it is not clear until the very end that they are romantically attached. Perhaps Paltrow has played in so many period dramas that she is a bit out of her element trying a turn as a tightly wound modern-day female CEO. The casting, thus, is mainly a walk in the park for

most, but a nightmare in the fun house for the rather underwritten leading lady, who has to share the stage by a completely overly endowed Johannson character, who has no trouble upstaging Paltrow's rather woefully drawn and characterized role—the sultry Johannson can triumph with a single withering glance, while Paltrow can puff and whine without any influence at all on her supposed companion, the easily distracted Stark.

Iron Man 2 is best when, as mostly happens, it does not take itself seriously. Superhero fatigue worsens when the comic-book spin-offs take themselves deadly seriously. Here, there is not a lot of complexity in the effort to cook up a complicated save-the-world plot, thankfully. Mickey Rourke has to carry the villain's part (with a wacky assist from Rockwell), and it is hard to work up much loathing for him. He looks like a deadly alien or a sort of dangerously sinister Transformer with arms that spout destructive laser beams like whips: an apocalyptic gunslinger walking down Main Street, which happens to be the Grand Prix track at Monaco, where he has just popped Stark's big celebrity bubble. His Russian accent is all over the map, and his character is patently absurd—a Terminator physicist motivated by a desire to revenge his father, who was betrayed by Stark's father. To be fair, Rourke can deliver even when the script leaves big holes. His white-streaked hair is all pinned up at one point, like a punk queen at a Goth prom.

It is too bad that the script by Justin Theroux, riffing on Stan Lee's Marvel Comics series, is not really clever—it is mostly just clever talk to a pointless end. Like many movies these days, the characters in this movie suffer from an embarrassment of technological riches. When not one, but two, three, four, and maybe more main characters can command a virtual army of supercomputer wizardry, when everyone is able to manipulate and distort reality, the movie tends to lapse into a rather enervating video game. Stark has the greatest powers of all, waving his hands in the air to command computerized holographic tasks from a virtual assistant whose powers make his progenitor, Hal, of *2001: A Space Odyssey* (1968), look hopelessly wimpy and out-of-date. One does not have to work that hard at a convincing plot when one can let computer technology take over and even stage its own battle. Except for the clanking of the metal suits, it thus becomes a bit of a bore. In this action movie, the action seems like an afterthought, the banter has the most kinetic energy, and the characters have a field day playing mostly caricatures of their typical characters in other movies.

Despite the endless banter, the film does end up taking itself way to seriously, in its technologically overbearing video-game simulations. It is, in fact, rather comic in a sad way how the typically ironic and overly imaginative comic-book franchise has had to become "serious entertainment."

Michael Betzold

CREDITS

Tony Stark/Iron Man: Robert Downey Jr.
Pepper Potts: Gwyneth Paltrow
Col. James "Rhodey" Rhodes/WarMachine: Don Cheadle
Ivan Vanko/Whiplash: Mickey Rourke
Natasha Romanoff/Black Widow: Scarlett Johansson
Justin Hammer: Sam Rockwell
Nick Fury: Samuel L. Jackson
U.S. Marshal: Kate Mara
Christine Everhart: Leslie Bibb
Howard Stark: John Slattery
Agent Phil Coulson: Clark Gregg
Sen. Stern: Garry Shandling
Maj. Allen: Tim Guinee
Rebecca: Helena Mattsson
Hogan: Jon Favreau
Jarvis: Paul Bettany (Voice)
Origin: USA
Language: English
Released: 2010
Production: Kevin Feige; Marvel Entertainment, Fairview Entertainment; released by Paramount Pictures
Directed by: Jon Favreau
Written by: Justin Theroux
Cinematography by: Matthew Libatique
Music by: John Debney
Sound: Keith Sasser, Christine T. Silverman
Editing: Richard Pearson
Art Direction: Page Buckner
Costumes: Mary Zophres
Production Design: J. Michael Riva
MPAA rating: PG-13
Running time: 117 minutes

REVIEWS

Childress, Erik. *eFilmCritic.com.* May 6, 2010.
Ebert, Roger. *Chicago Sun-Times.* May 5, 2010.
Edelstein, David. *New York Magazine.* May 3, 2010.
Honeycutt, Kirk. *Hollywood Reporter.* April 27, 2010.
Howell, Peter. *Toronto Star.* May 6, 2010.
Lane, Anthony. *New Yorker.* May 3, 2010.
Schwarzbaum, Lisa. *Entertainment Weekly.* May 5, 2010.
Scott, A.O. *New York Times.* May 6, 2010.
Travers, Peter. *Rolling Stone.* May 4, 2010.
Turan, Kenneth. *Los Angeles Times.* April 7, 2010.

QUOTES

Tony Stark: "Because I'm your nuclear deterrent. It's working. We're safe. America is secure. You want my property? You can't have it. But I did you a big favor."

Tony Stark: "Contrary to popular belief, I know exactly what I'm doing."

TRIVIA

This is Jon Favreau's first sequel as both a director and an actor.
The filmmakers hired famed animator Genndy Tartakovsky to draw the storyboards for the film's action sequences.

AWARDS

Nomination:

Oscars 2010: Visual FX.

IT'S KIND OF A FUNNY STORY

Sometimes what's in your head isn't as crazy as you think.
—Movie tagline

Box Office: $6 million

It's Kind of a Funny Story is a decidedly erroneous title. It belies the movie's more successful accomplishment, despite much-different intentions on behalf of co-screenwriters and directors Anna Boden and Ryan Fleck and the unfortunate expectations that arise from the name. This is not a "funny" story by any means that one might associate with the titular phrase. It is not ironic. It is not facetious. It is not serendipitous. It is not strange, unique, or abnormal. For all the quirkiness of the movie's ancillary characters, the dreamy internal diversions of its central character, and a far-too-pat resolution made possible by a pair of supporting characters, *It's Kind of a Funny Story* is an accurate portrayal of a teenager suffering from depression due to the onslaught of real pressures and perceived failures. When Boden and Fleck's screenplay (based on a novel of the same name by Ned Vizzini) examines the causes and effects of 16-year-old Craig's (Keir Gilchrist) struggle to soothe his mental state, there is a durable sense of honesty that nearly outweighs the attempts at frivolity.

Craig's search for serenity begins after he has a dream—one he has had many times as of late. In it, he rides his bike to the Brooklyn Bridge and steps out across the beams above traffic. Typically, he awakens before falling, but this time, he does not. Sensing something is wrong, he calls a suicide hotline, visits an emergency room, and demands that he is admitted into the psychiatric ward. Because of renovations, the hospital places Craig in the adult ward under the care of Dr. Eden Minerva (Viola Davis) for a week-long trial period.

Craig befriends Bobby (Zach Galifianakis, finding just the right balance between comic relief and heartache), a secretive, supportive, and suicidal patient, and Noelle (Emma Roberts), a cutter whose rationale is never explained and whose scars are rarely discussed. His mother Lynn (Lauren Graham) believes this is the right step for her son, while his father George (Jim Gaffigan) is not fazed in the slightest by his son's self-institutionalization, instead disappointed that Craig has yet to fill out an application for a summer business course that George believes will help his son achieve the career he wants for the boy.

There is a dichotomy to the movie's elements—how they serve a narrative or tonal purpose and how they relate to Craig. On the one hand, for example, is Noelle. She is such an underdeveloped character that her only purpose is a goal for Craig (i.e., once he has mastered his problems, he will—as they say—get the girl). That superficial role becomes even more pronounced when Craig must choose between Noelle and Nia (Zoë Kravitz), with whom he has been smitten for years and the girlfriend of his best friend Aaron (Thomas Mann).

On the other is Bobby, whose years-long battle with psychological problems serves as a mirror to Craig's own—given more years and life experiences. Bobby has lost his family: his wife (Mary Birdsong) has divorced him, and he has only rare encounters with his young daughter, in front of whom his ex-wife insults him for his problems. The hospital is set to release Bobby at the end of the week, and while he must interview for placement in a group home, he is convinced it will lead to denial—a state in which he lives, denying even that the woman is his ex-wife.

Craig is on the same route of projecting failure upon his own life and fulfilling his projection. In a clever flurry of montage, Boden (who also acted as the movie's editor) and Fleck follow the mental acrobatics Craig must do in order to justify why he is conflicted about the summer business class application. It is not a matter of whether or not he even wants to attend the class; he has convinced himself of a "damned if you do/damned if you don't" scenario. He assumes his application will be rejected, and from there, Craig jumps years down the line of rejection after rejection, ending with him in the same place he is now: alone and depressed. The results, he assumes, will be the same whether he applies or not.

His bleak look into the future is one of a few sequences of insight into Craig's psyche. It and the dream that opens the movie fit squarely into the end of developing Craig's character—the way his focus on how others perceive him as a person and his actions overshadow any desire he might have to do or not do

something. Through some of the therapy sessions in the ward, Craig discovers an artistic acumen, so the fantasy scenes continue. One travels through an animated version of a sketch of a city by Craig, which he compares to his mind, and another features Craig leading patients, nurses, and orderlies in a rendition of Queen and David Bowie's "Under Pressure," severely edited (even to the point of excising lyrics that are thematically precise) and set as a glam rock music video. A piano version of "Where Is My Mind?" by the Pixies also appears as a melodic joke.

These sequences emerge to simplify, not expand; they are mere flourishes of style. Boden and Fleck's final narrative diversion arrives in Craig narrating his own denouement with Noelle and his family—arguing he is not cured while the pictures imply otherwise.

Apart from Bobby and Noelle, the occupants of the ward play like a cavalcade of craziness. From Craig's roommate Muqtada (Bernard White), who refuses to leave their room, to Solomon (Daniel London), who has developed super-sensitive hearing after dropping too much acid while belonging to a Hasidic gang of rollerbladers, the background characters are as responsible for setting the tone as the scenes in Craig's imagination.

Then again, that is only half of the divided mood of *It's Kind of a Funny Story*. The aim for a light-hearted touch waters down the pain at the heart of its characters.

Mark Dujsik

CREDITS

Craig: Keir Gilchrist
Bobby: Zach Galifianakis
Noelle: Emma Roberts
Dr. Minerva: Viola Davis
Dr. Mahmoud: Aasif Mandvi
Nia: Zoë Kravitz
Lynn: Lauren Graham
George: Jim Gaffigan
Aaron: Thomas Mann
Bobby's Ex: Mary Birdsong
Muqtada: Bernard White
Solomon: Daniel London
Origin: USA
Language: English
Released: 2010
Production: Ben Browning, Kevin Misher; Focus Features, Wayfare Entertainment; released by Focus Features
Directed by: Anna Boden, Ryan Fleck
Written by: Anna Boden, Ryan Fleck
Cinematography by: Andrij Parekh

Music by: Broken Social Scene
Sound: Noah Vivekanand Timan
Music Supervisor: Andrea Von Foerster
Editing: Anna Boden
Art Direction: Michael Ahern
Costumes: Kurt and Bart
Production Design: Beth Mickle
MPAA rating: PG-13
Running time: 101 minutes

REVIEWS

Burr, Ty. *Boston Globe.* October 8, 2010.
Hornaday, Ann. *Washington Post.* October 8, 2010.
Larsen, Josh. *Naperville Sun.*. October 14, 2010.
Moore, Roger. *Orlando Sentinel.* October 6, 2010.
Phillips, Michael. *Chicago Tribune.* October 7, 2010.
Putman, Dustin. *DustinPutman.com.* October 7, 2010.
Rea, Steven. *Philadelphia Inquirer.* October 8, 2010.
Schager, Nick. *Slant Magazine.* October 3, 2010.
Weinberg, Scott. *Cinematical.* September 11, 2010.
Zacharek, Stephanie. *Movieline.* October 6, 2010.

QUOTES

Dr. Eden Minerva: "Lord, grant me the serenity to accept the things I cannot change; courage to change the things I can; and wisdom to know the difference."

J

JACK GOES BOATING

A pair of smartly-modulated lead performances shore up the orchestrated gloom of *Jack Goes Boating,* a hushed drama that represents the feature film directorial debut of Oscar®-winning actor Philip Seymour Hoffman. A thinly drawn, morose wallow in indie-style shoe-gazing that cannot escape the confining shackles of its theatrical roots, the movie lacks enough sharp-tack detail to connect as a realistically-rooted portrait of wounded-soul adult love, or enough of a genuine emotional punch to score as a searing, ensemble piece musing on life's accumulated miseries and misfortune. After its January premiere at the Sundance Film Festival, the movie was released by Overture Films in September, but never gained traction as either an awards contender or art house hit.

Hoffman stars as the title character, an oafish, quasi-dreadlocked limo driver who tries to hold his ineffable, swallowed sadness at bay with the good-vibe positivity of reggae music, which he keeps in constant rotation on his beat-up Walkman. At the urging of his coworker and friend Clyde (John Ortiz), Jack awkwardly, elliptically pursues another brokenhearted New Yorker, Connie (Amy Ryan), who is the colleague of his wife Lucy (Daphne Rubin-Vega) at a funeral home. After a fitful start to the pair's courtship, there is a dinner party double date arranged to diminish the awkwardness and pressure of any romantic connection. Alcohol and marijuana come out, and lingering extramarital resentments between Clyde and Lucy burst wildly to the surface, making for an explosively uncomfortable evening for all involved.

Jack Goes Boating is adapted by Bob Glaudini from his own stage play, a work originally produced by LAByrinth Theater Company, in which Hoffman, Ortiz, and Rubin-Vega all starred. The appeal of this relatively straightforward story in movie form is predicated on thematic acceptance—an embrace of the noodling exploration of the private lives of those for whom life has not turned out as they might have wished. (If the film had more of a pulse, Tom Petty's "Even the Losers" could serve as its theme song, focusing as it does on the quest for love by those with shattered or all-consuming pasts.) But for all the sense of detail in the actors' choices here, there is not a strongly sketched enough sense of awakened need powering the characters' decisions.

In works like *Boogie Nights* (1997), *Happiness* (1998), and *Love Liza* (2002), Hoffman crafted involving portraits of sad-sack loneliness and despair that belied his adroitness as a bombastic scene-stealer in films like *Almost Famous* (2000), *Charlie Wilson's War* (2007), and *Pirate Radio* (2009). *Jack Goes Boating* shares in common with those three aforementioned movies, as well as James Mangold's *Heavy* (1996), a character with an almost pathological introversion. Jack is wrecked, bereft of focus. Possessing an intuitive understanding of space and depressed body language, Hoffman delivers a very watchable performance, as does Ryan.

Yet while it ably communicates the pain informed by their respective isolations, there is not enough of a sense of quiet longing and libidinal yearning to give viewers a sustained and cathartic rooting interest in Jack and Connie's romance. Connie is something of a cipher, a romantic life preserver for Jack. And even as it charts a course toward love's bloom, the movie's conveyance of desire and ambition (romantic and otherwise) remains blunted and vague. One feels less that they are changing and instead that changes are merely happening to them. The more dramatically conventional marital strife between Clyde and Lucy, meanwhile, only distracts from Jack and Connie's uncertain stirring (admittedly a smaller, more difficult target), and dilutes the film's value as a dual character study.

Directorially, Hoffman eschews vanity (not that the character of Jack offers much in this realm) and opts for an unfussy visual scheme that does not attempt to overly manipulate viewer compassion via the close-up. Costume designer Mimi O'Donnell, Hoffman's longtime girl-friend and the mother of his three children, works mostly in grey, brown, black and other muted, heavy shades. Similarly, production designer Thérèse DePrez and art director Matteo De Cosmo craft dank and/or claustrophobic spaces, lending the movie a further correlative despondence.

That the dramatic stakes are small except to the characters who live them—working towards the third-act dinner, Jack tries to file an application for a new job with the Metro Transit Authority, takes swimming lessons from Clyde for a planned summer date, and learns how to cook since Connie has never had anyone fix her a meal—is not the most damning problem. But while *Jack Goes Boating* is certainly tonally of a piece, Hoffman does not seem comfortable impressing a more aggressively focused telling of the material, as evidenced by everything from an indulgence of circuitous arguments by Clyde and Lucy to the last shot of the movie, which features a curious cutaway from the main characters. In an attempt to goose up the film's affected, free-floating melancholy, Hoffman slathers on a jazz score and throws in a few montages, but to little lasting effect. "Everybody hurts," R.E.M. once opined. True, but not all portraits of wallflower pain are created equal.

Brent Simon

CREDITS

Jack: Philip Seymour Hoffman
Clyde: John Ortiz
Connie: Amy Ryan
Lucy: Daphne Rubin-Vega
Dr. Bob: Thomas McCarthy
Origin: USA
Language: English
Released: 2010
Production: Marc Turtletaub, Peter Saraf, Beth O'Neil; Big Beach; released by Overture Films
Directed by: Philip Seymour Hoffman

Written by: Bob Glaudini
Cinematography by: W. Mott Hupfel III
Music by: Grizzly Bear, Evan Lurie
Sound: Jeff Pullman, Christof Gebert
Music Supervisor: Sue Jacobs
Editing: Brian A. Kates
Art Direction: Matteo De Cosmo
Costumes: Mimi O'Donnell
Production Design: Therese DePrez
MPAA rating: R
Running time: 90 minutes

REVIEWS

Honeycutt, Kirk. *Hollywood Reporter.* January 25, 2010.
Kennedy, Lisa. *Denver Post.* October 1, 2010.
Long, Tom. *Detroit News.* October 1, 2010.
Ramos, Steve. *Milwaukee Journal Sentinel.* October 7, 2010.Rickey, Carrie. *Philadelphia Inquirer.* September 30, 2010.
Schenker, Andrew. *Slant Magazine.* September 12, 2010.
Schwarzbaum, Lisa. *Entertainment Weekly.* September 22, 2010.
Scott, A.O. *New York Times.* September 17, 2010.
Tallerico, Brian. *HollywoodChicago.com.* September 24, 2010.
Thompson, Gary. *Philadelphia Daily News.* September 30, 2010.

QUOTES

Connie: "In a bathtub, I imagined I was with you."

TRIVIA

Actor/Director Philip Seymour Hoffman was very familiar with the role of Jack since he was reprising the role he had originated on Broadway.

AWARDS

Nomination:

Ind. Spirit 2011: Support. Actor (Ortiz), Support. Actress (Rubin-Vega), First Screenplay.

JACKASS 3D

Box Office: $117 million

Building upon its branded small screen entertainment of scandalously inadvisable staged stunts and gross-out gags, *Jackass: The Movie* (2002) grossed $79 million in theaters upon its release. Audiences, mostly young and mostly dudes, turned out to bear witness to a plotless collection of hijinks involving reckless golf cart rides, self-administered paper cuts, the insertion of a toy car into a willing participant's anus, and another guy traversing a tightrope over a pond full of alligators with raw chicken stuffed in his underwear. With its healthy spread of fecal humor (as winkingly noted by the film's title), *Jackass Number Two* (2006) delved even further into sickening silliness, with outrageous sequences which included a leeched eyeball, a sheathed penis used as a puppet to entice a snake, and the manual stimulation of a horse and imbibing of its after-effects.

Informed by a highly entertaining sensibility at once punkish and entirely amiable, *Jackass 3-D* similarly provides a wild and wooly showcase for these throwback vaudevillian instincts taken to their modern, masochistic logical extremes. The movie—which pulled in $50 million-plus in its debut weekend, over $20 million more than its best previous bow—is, like its predecessors, a cinematic act of willful provocation, designed to try to make audiences as queasy as the cameramen who have the sometimes unfortunate task of capturing such choreographed mayhem amidst all the jostling, effluvium, and other bodily fluids. Yet the film is also a conceptually inventive high-wire comedy that consistently evokes a forward-leaning suspense born of equal parts shock, horror, and gobsmacked amazement. If it is first and foremost clamorous juvenilia, it still actually says something important about human nature and some of the baser impulses that bind us all together.

In addition to returning director Jeff Tremaine, *Jackass 3-D* reunites good-humored ringleader Johnny Knoxville, Bam Margera, Ryan Dunn, Jason "Wee-Man" Acuña, Preston Lacy, Chris Pontius, Ehren McGhehey, Dave Englund and, of course, tattooed wildman Steve-O, who regularly submits to some of the series' most dangerous stunts. In a nod to its small screen roots, the film opens with an animated segment featuring Mike Judge's Beavis and Butt-Head characters, who once shared a spot on MTV with the original *Jackass*. The movie then launches into a litany of discrete sketches. While there is a certain attention paid to the sequencing, any sincere attempt at carving out a story through line is pretty much impossible. So a narrative encapsulation does best by simply listing some of the film's more shocking and memorable moments, which include, variously, a game of beehive tetherball, a massive jet engine being used to propel all manner of debris into the path of unlucky human targets, Steve-O drinking the collected workout sweat of Lacy, Knoxville battling an angry bull, the cast marveling at a dart gun powered by flatulence, and McGhehey having a tooth yanked out by a speeding Lamborghini.

The work of originating series director of photography Dimitry Elyashkevich, along with co-credited cinematographers Lance Bangs and Rick Kosick, each back from the second film in the series, goes a long way toward establishing *Jackass 3-D*'s loose-limbed appeal. Their work shuns authorial subjectivity in favor of informality. Thus, the movie feels like a warm, inviting, slickly collected greatest-hits package of adolescent bedlam. The massively choreographed set pieces that open and close the film—as well as a human duck-hunt with paintball guns, and fetishistically presented, boxing-glove physical assaults, the latter rendered in slow-motion—also make nice use of three-dimensionality without sacrificing the basic nature of the gags. In other interstitial sequences, Tremaine and his collaborators utilize forced point-of-view camerawork to capture cast members urinating on one another.

A couple segments involve meticulously staged gags meant to make one gag, as with a diarrhetic defecation staged to resemble a model-sized volcanic eruption. Others, meanwhile, are in the tradition of Allen Funt's far more genteel *Candid Camera*, and involve gauging public responses to strange or socially awkward moments. The best of these hidden-camera bits in *Jackass 3-D* involve the diminutive Acuña. In one short sketch, the four-foot-tall Acuña returns in place of the identically dressed, tall, obese Lacy, after the latter asks a man outside a store to hold his dog while he runs indoors. In another set-up, an argument between Acuña and another midget builds into an elaborately staged bar-fight that is then broken up by a legion of dwarf cops, leaving the daytime clientele of the heretofore sleepy little watering hole utterly bewildered by what they have just witnessed.

At its core, though, *Jackass 3-D* and its filmic predecessors are each about young men testing their own outer limits (in this case, of decency, endurance, and violability), a theme that has through the ages been central to much great literature. That these exercises are wildly juvenile is not contestable, but to focus merely on that fact is to fail to recognize the quiet genius of this series. One of the two best examples of this is a mock-prison escape, set to Eddy Grant's "Electric Avenue," through a narrow, obstacle-ridden passageway with live, charged 950k-volt stun guns hanging down from the ceiling. The other, featured prominently in the movie's trailer, is a sequence in which Steve-O is launched, via a massive bungee cord, dozens if not a hundred feet into the air in a port-a-potty full of human waste. In these bits, the participants psyche themselves and each other up before diving into the task at hand; Steve-O draws one of the movie's biggest laughs when he sighs and asks, simply, "Why do I have to be Steve-O?"

Given such literal toilet humor, it is certainly not surprising that Tremaine gets no credit as a "normal" filmmaker, particularly since he has not really attempted to expand his filmography beyond the *Jackass* movies and the franchise's roster of related small screen offshoot projects. Yet his gift for comedic construction can be glimpsed in any number of ways, from the framing of stunts to savvy use of background detail, as when

Knoxville and Dunn appear off to the side as enthusiastic fans when a professional kicker lines up a field goal shot a mere five yards away from a near-naked Lacy, clad in underpants and painted yellow to resemble a football goalpost. Within gag set-ups there is also a smart use of editing, too. A joke involving a giant, spring-loaded papier-mâché hand that levels those in its path invokes comedy's "rule of three," getting more sublimely ridiculous with each staging.

It helps, of course, that the cast members are all friends off screen (Knoxville and his colleagues spearheaded a physical intervention that got Steve-O into rehab, where he kicked a nasty drug problem), which totally shines through. As always, the *Jackass* crew also ropes in some interesting outside co-conspirators to take part in its shenanigans. Filmmaker Spike Jonze, who is a producer on the *Jackass* series, appears briefly, and its roster of other low-key cameos this time around includes Seann William Scott, Will Oldham, Rivers Cuomo, and quadriplegic Mark Zupan, of *Murderball* (2005).

In the end, though, *Jackass 3-D* strikingly captures fraternal camaraderie and the bonds born of shared suffering—even though in this case, the participants are habitually hazing themselves, basically. That thick-or-thin jocularity, believe it or not, infuses most of *Jackass 3-D*'s dumb pranks with a gilded sense of ennobled purpose, along with a general impression that a large part of the movie's audience has grown (if not exactly grown up) with its cast members, and lived a little vicariously through their scars and battles with excrement.

Brent Simon

CREDITS

Himself: Johnny Knoxville
Himself: Bam Margera
Himself: Steve-O
Himself: Ryan Dunn
Himself: Jason "Wee Man" Acuña
Himself: Chris Pontius
Himself: Preston Lacy
Himself: Ehren McGhehey
Himself: Dave Englund
Origin: USA
Language: English
Released: 2010
Production: Jeff Tremaine, Spike Jonze, Johnny Knoxville; MTV Films, Dickhouse; released by Paramount Pictures
Directed by: Jeff Tremaine
Written by: Preston Lacy
Cinematography by: Dimitry Elyashkavich, Lance Bangs, Rick Kosick

Sound: Cordell Mansfield
Music Supervisor: Ben Hochstein
Editing: Seth Casriel, Matthew Probst, Matthew Kosinski
Art Direction: Seth Meisterman
Production Design: James Peter Blackmon, Seth Meisterman
MPAA rating: R
Running time: 94 minutes

REVIEWS

Chang, Justin. *Variety.* October 14, 2010.
Dargis, Manohla. *New York Times.* October 15, 2010.
Fine, Marshall. *Hollywood & Fine.* October 18, 2010.
Gleiberman, Owen. *Entertainment Weekly.* October 16, 2010.
Kois, Dan. *Washington Post.* October 15, 2010.
Lemire, Christy. *Associated Press.* October 14, 2010.
Morris, Wesley. *Boston Globe.* October 17, 2010.
Phillips, Michael. *Chicago Tribune.* October 21, 2010.
Rechtshaffen, Michael. *Hollywood Reporter.* October 14, 2010.
Stevens, Dana. *Slate.* October 15, 2010.

QUOTES

Johnny Knoxville: "Dave doesn't get it. The more you freak out like that, the more you get stung."

TRIVIA

The segment before the film was created by Mike Judge and featured his characters Beavis and Butt-Head.

The filmmakers shot the slow motion scenes with Phantom high-speed cameras and 3D equipment at speeds up to 1,000 frames per second.

JOAN RIVERS: A PIECE OF WORK

Box Office: $3 million

There have been any number of worshipful hagiographies of showbiz types, from the dreadful and inert, like *The Boys: The Sherman Brothers' Story* (2009), to the slickly entertaining, like *The Kid Stays in the Picture* (2002), which was admittedly a lot of fun and itself a work of pop-art despite, almost unfathomably, being narrated by its star. Rare, though, is the nonfiction celebrity film that has the participatory blessing of its subject and yet still finds room to ably showcase all the disagreeableness, shortcomings and contradictions of its pin-up personality, along with presumably what makes them popular in the first place.

Such is the case, though, with co-directors Ricki Stern and Anne Sundberg's fantastically beguiling *Joan Rivers: A Piece of Work,* which premiered at the 2010 Sundance Film Festival. Its title both a reference to Rivers' wild and catty persona as well as a winking nod to the catalogue of plastic surgery procedures which have left her looking like some sort of twisted human mash-up of a Barbie doll and a mountain lion, the film is a rousing portrait of unconquerable work ethic and wit that also never shortchanges the humanity of its subject.

Much like *The Eyes of Tammy Faye* (2000)—which centered on Tammy Faye Bakker, the cofounder of PTL cable TV ministries and a demigod of the Reagan-era electric church—this documentary is a fascinating, and oddly cathartic, from-the-ground-up reconstruction of an American pariah. It does not matter what one thinks of Rivers before viewing; in fact, there is actually more image-inverting revelatory reward for those who know her not as a groundbreaking comedienne during the heyday of Johnny Carson but instead only as a shrill red carpet emcee, pitchperson for tacky jewelry and all-around media whore. Amidst all its bouncy irreverence, *A Piece of Work* is a brutally frank look at her vulnerabilities and quiet charitableness. The more one sees Rivers as a cartoonish joke before viewing, the more the joke is on them.

The film charts a year in the life of Rivers, seventy-five years old at the time of filming, as she works a string of small club gigs, prepares a one-woman show for its Edinburgh debut, goes on a book tour, competes alongside her daughter Melissa on NBC's *Celebrity Apprentice,* pitches various lecture series and eventually submits to a roast on Comedy Central. On this purely surface level, the movie is an entertaining snapshot of defiant energy and maniacal focus, qualities of Rivers which keep her multiple assistants and manager of several decades, Billy Sammeth (who is now embroiled in a lawsuit against her alleging defamation and the obligation of back wages), on their toes, and struggling to keep up.

Like Richard Pryor, Rivers is profane and reckless, a peddler of commingled harsh truths and shock for shock's sake. When she first broke into stand-up, she would end her routine talking about the Hollywood casting couch, and close by saying, "Remember, my name is Joan Rivers…and I put out." She keeps this and all her jokes on index cards, stored in thin, library card-size filing cabinets with cryptic, alphabetized subject lists scrawled on the front ("New York/No Self Worth" reads one). Rivers is also a workaholic; looking through date-book calendars of years past she gets caught up in a moment of nostalgia, and confesses that her nightmare is the blinding white from an open fold of blank pages.

If *A Piece of Work* does not grill its subject like a district attorney or dig down into her issues with the depth and directness of a therapist, the emergent portrait of Rivers is still full-bodied and crystal clear, courtesy of exceedingly smart narrative pivot points chosen by the filmmakers and editor Penelope Falk. Rivers is upfront and candid about her anxieties, vanity and neediness, but the audience does not come to learn of the suicide of her husband, Edgar Rosenberg—and how, in unlikely fashion, she and Melissa achieved a sort of therapeutic peace by costarring together as themselves in *Starting Again* (1994), a TV movie which addressed their grief and guilt—until 25 minutes into the film. A couple other personal revelations follow a similar trajectory. More ploddingly conventional nonfiction movies would have shoved this material into the foreground, but *A Piece of Work* ties them into the fabric of Rivers' still lively if tumultuous working life, making for an experience in which the viewer's opinion of her takes several intriguing twists and turns.

The only area the film pulls punches where it could have mined more interesting nuggets of insight is in the arena of Rivers' cosmetic procedures and body image. Though obviously whip smart (she is a graduate of Barnard College), Rivers evidences an unhealthy and seemingly unexamined preoccupation with the notion that men are attracted *solely* by beauty, and in particular an attempt to hold onto a look which might be considered age-inappropriate. (It is an intriguing comparative parallel that Rivers, like the aforementioned, frighteningly mascara-ed Bakker before her, has deep-seated issues with appearance.) While her struggles with bulimia go un-discussed or commented upon, Rivers is more or less open about her many plastic surgeries, Botox appointments (at one rehearsal for her play she shows up with her face swollen to twice its normal size) and love of makeup. Both she and the movie, however, are more circumspect about the motivations behind them, which likely stem from childhood issues. Getting into this a bit certainly would not have hurt. If anything, it would have made her even more relatable, which later material detailing her liberal charitable giving does.

Early in the film, thumbing through a proposed pilot script, looking hungrily for lines that are hers, Rivers says, "I can't find me anywhere." The genius of *Joan Rivers: A Piece of Work* is that it locates the unruly soul of its subject, amidst her voracious professional appetites, nutty behavior, foibles, and contradictions. She is more than a little wounded, but she shows up day in and day out and keeps dancing as fast as she can, because that is all that she knows how to do.

Brent Simon

CREDITS

Herself: Joan Rivers
Herself: Melissa Rivers

Himself: Billy Sammeth
Origin: USA
Language: English
Released: 2010
Production: Ricki Stern, Seth Keal, Annie Sundberg; Break Thru Films; released by IFC Films
Directed by: Ricki Stern, Anne Sundberg
Written by: Ricki Stern
Cinematography by: Charles Miller
Music by: Paul Brill
Sound: Seth Keal
Editing: Penelope Falk
MPAA rating: R
Running time: 84 minutes

REVIEWS

Dargis, Manohla. *New York Times.* June 11, 2010.
Ebert, Roger. *Chicago Sun-Times.* June 17, 2010.
Edelstein, David. *New York Magazine.* June 7, 2010.
Gleiberman, Owen. *Entertainment Weekly.* June 9, 2010.
Harvey, Dennis. *Variety.* June 7, 2010.
LaSalle, Mick. *San Francisco Chronicle.* June 10, 2010.
McDonald, Moira. *Seattle Times.* June 18, 2010.
O'Sullivan, Michael. *Washington Post.* June 18, 2010.
Pais, Matt. *Metromix.com.* June 16, 2010.
Phillips, Michael. *Chicago Tribune.* June 17, 2010.

JONAH HEX

> *Revenge gets ugly.*
> —Movie tagline

Box Office: $11 million

Plagued with an inexperienced director (Jimmy Hayward) left to dangle while nearly half his film was reshot by a studio flunkie (Francis Lawrence of *Constantine* [2005] and *I Am Legend* [2007]), *Jonah Hex* runs a paltry 73 minutes sans credits and plays as if it was edited on shuffle mode from somebody's DVD player. The title character (Josh Brolin) was a Confederate soldier in the Civil War who drew the ire of Commander Quentin Turnbull (John Malkovich). As punishment, his wife and child were burned alive and he was left baring the brand of his nemesis on his face. Left for dead, Jonah somehow crossed over and came back from the other side with the ability to talk to corpses and now finds work as a bounty hunter. President Grant (Aidan Quinn) has recently been briefed that Turnbull is alive and well—after the prologue spoke of his demise—and is on his way to making "the weapon." Grant tells his men to seek out Jonah and enlist his services for a full pardon; an iffy proposition for a man who fought for

the South not for his politics but because he "didn't like the government telling [him] what to do."

Jonah does not have much else to do except Lilah (Megan Fox), visiting her at the brothel and warding off advances to ride the Earth with him. He cannot resist the chance to exact revenge though and sniffs out Turnbull's trail thanks to a couple of dead folk including Quentin's son Jeb (Jeffrey Dean Morgan, WB's current go-to guy for lesser-known comic book characters from *Watchmen* [2009] to *The Losers* [2010]), the best friend he killed in defiance of some questionable orders. Turnbull and his allies, including tattooed Irishman Burke (Michael Fassbender), have been in pursuit of some "pretty orange balls" that are capable, when shot out of a cannon, to wipe out entire towns. Can Jonah Hex make it to the Potomac in time for the Fourth of July fireworks? Time is running out on him and the movie.

As with most comic book heroes, there have been several incarnations of Jonah Hex over the years. Precisely what incarnation this cinematic version is supposed to be is anybody's guess. Leaving behind the issues where the scarred cowboy encountered zombies or was transported into the 21st century, the motion picture writers (Mark Neveldine and Brian Taylor, responsible for *Gamer* [2009], *Pathology* [2008], *Crank* [2006], and its sequel) have nevertheless introduced their own ghoulish device in giving Hex resurrection powers. This element will have some viewers playing chicken-and-the-egg with the marvelous ABC show *Pushing Daisies,* which also featured a character who solved crimes by talking to the dead, albeit on a time limit.

Watching talented actors fumble through a maze of half-baked plotting and full-baked incoherence pulls focus away from how bored Malkovich looks or how little screen time Megan Fox has until the climax needs a hostage. Instead, audience attention is aimed at how disjointed scenes do not fit together and picking out what looks to be a product of a reshoot and what was actually meant for this disaster. Often it is as the audience has been thrown directly into the second half or chapter of a film where all the relationships had already been established between villainous Southerners, whores, and entire Indian villages. Anything uniquely distinguishing about this Western hero from his powers to weaponry that includes double-barrels of Gatlings on the side of his horse to specially-made dynamite crossbow handguns is gone as quickly as they are introduced.

There have been films over time that were messed with in the editing room at the whim of a studio or witless producers trying to cluelessly improve it over the wishes of its director or to maximize its profit margin. *Jonah Hex* is more than a bit of a quandary though. Even at an obviously trimmed 90 minutes, how much worse could it have been than at its current 73? The extra time would not have eased the silliness over lines like "America needs a Sheriff" or a weapon with an actual Washington Capital-shaped target sight that fits perfectly over the building at the precise distance it would need in order to trace it. But at least it might have seemed like an actual movie with pacing, definition, and rational action. The film was clearly trimmed down to a PG-13 rating, enhancing the overall lack of credibility with scenes like a man's head being forced into a spinning propeller only to have his dead body presented with nothing more than a small bleeding wound. The film ends with what feels like an alternate conclusion that should have been saved for the DVD's deleted scenes instead of cross-cut with the current climax as if it were some mind's eye flashback that does not fit in the current journey's timeline. It is merely a final false note for a project that cost over $50 million but only resulted in seventy-three minutes of running time, the majority of which forces the viewer to demand his or her time back.

Erik Childress

CREDITS

Jonah Hex: Josh Brolin
Quentin Turnbull: John Malkovich
Lilah: Megan Fox
Doc Cross Williams: Michael Shannon
Burke: Michael Fassbender
Pres. McKinley: Aidan Quinn
Prospector: David Patrick Kelly
Travis Hex: Luke James Fleischmann
Cassie: Julia Jones
Lieutenant Evan: Will Arnett
Jeb Turnbull: Jeffrey Dean Morgan
Origin: USA
Language: English
Released: 2010
Production: Akiva Goldsman, Andrew Lazar; Legendary Pictures, Mad Chance, Weed Road Pictures, DC Entertainment, Warner Bros.; released by Warner Bros.
Directed by: Jimmy Hayward
Written by: Mark Neveldine, Brian Taylor
Cinematography by: Mitchell Amundsen
Music by: Marco Beltrami, Mastodon
Sound: Craig Henighan
Editing: Kent Beyda
Art Direction: Jonah Markowitz, Seth Reed
Costumes: Michael Wilkinson
Production Design: Tom Meyer
MPAA rating: PG-13
Running time: 84 minutes

REVIEWS

Chang, Justin. *Variety.* June 17, 2010.
Ebert, Roger. *Chicago Sun-Times.* June 17, 2010.
Howell, Peter. *Toronto Star.* June 17, 2010.
Pais, Matt. *Metromix.com.* June 17, 2010.
Phillips, Michael. *Chicago Tribune.* June 17, 2010.
Phipps, Keith. *AV Club.* June 17, 2010.
Rea, Steven. *Philadelphia Inquirer.* June 17, 2010.
Sharkey, Betsy. *Los Angeles Times.* June 18, 2010.
Sobczynski, Peter. *eFilmCritic.com.* June 17, 2010.
Verniere, James. *Boston Herald.* June 18, 2010.

QUOTES

Jonah Hex: "To burn down a hospital. Your father was gonna kill all those people, just to make a point. I couldn't stand for that. I'm surprised you could."

Jonah Hex: "They say that a man with revenge in his heart should dig two graves. One for his enemy and one for himself. I guess mine's just gonna have to wait."

TRIVIA

Matthew McConaughey and Emile Hirsch were both considered for roles in the film.

AWARDS

Nomination:

Golden Raspberries 2010: Worst Actress (Fox), Worst Couple/Ensemble (Brolin's Face and Fox's Voice).

THE JONESES

Some families are too good to be true.
—Movie tagline

They're not just living the American dream, they're selling it.
—Movie tagline

Can you keep up?
—Movie tagline

Box Office: $1 million

In *The Truman Show* (1998), Truman Burbank (Jim Carrey) does not know that his entire life has been manufactured for a television show. His neighbor is an actor. His office building's elevator is not really an elevator. The sky is fake. Even his wife Meryl (Laura Linney) is an actress who has been planted in the show to sell products while developing no legitimate emotional connection to anyone around her.

Though it does not revolve around a TV show, writer-director Derrick Borte's *The Joneses* may as well be a spin-off movie for Truman's wife. The Joneses look like a family, but they are not related. They are four incognito marketing reps, hired to pretend to be a family and implant themselves in a random affluent suburb where they will show off their cars and golf clubs and workout gear and watch as their envious, $100,000-household neighbors whip out their wallets to, yes, keep up with the Joneses. This is a cinch for fake mom Kate (Demi Moore), fake daughter Jenn (Amber Heard) and fake son Mick (Ben Hollingsworth), but for fake dad Steve (David Duchovny), this is his first time. A single, 45-year-old ex-car salesman who failed as a golf pro, Steve has yet to harden towards the job and is the only Jones to seek any honest human connection with his imaginary family members.

On the surface, *The Joneses* has a great hook for a satire of American overconsumption and the notion that, when too much emphasis is put on material goods, the things people own end up owning them. Yet Borte's script, based on a story by Randy T. Dinzler, goes far too soft in articulating the human side of the Joneses' work. What begins as a sharp indictment of superficial success eventually feels like trying to cut steak with a butter knife, with similarly ineffective results.

Where *The Joneses* should be ruthless it is needy. Mick lacks interest in his job and semi-vaguely confesses to his friend Naomi (Christine Evangelista) that his family only throws a party so they can show off what they own. Jen cares less about her productivity than satisfying her more primal urges, at first hopping in the sack naked with Steve—who does not even have a chance to reject her before Kate pulls her out of the bed—and later with a married man, throwing the Joneses' overall credibility into question with their cold boss KC (Lauren Hutton). Steve, meanwhile, starts falling for Kate, leaving her as the only member of the household with her eyes on the prize.

A movie about the buyers quickly becomes about the sellers and their own disinterest in their hollow work. To counteract the Joneses' emotional struggles Borte offers the plight of the Joneses' neighbors Larry (Gary Cole) and Summer Symonds (Glenne Headly), who live in a big, beautiful house that is not quite as big and not quite as beautiful. Larry and Summer have no children and have not been happy in years; soon, Larry has taken Steve's advice that the secret to a happy marriage is a "steady stream of gifts," while paying little attention to what that does to his bank account. Though there is certainly merit in the destructive force of an overactive credit card, this plotline feels shoehorned in to make a statement that lacks the necessary punch. Rather than capturing his characters' desperation and inability to show emotion through anything other than material offerings, Borte soft-peddles a lighter brand of pathetic, commercially-driven hunger. When the situation

ultimately turns tragic, the effect is a thematic sledge-hammer without any force.

The film cuts deepest in small moments, when items are used as replacements for people and feelings. Not long after buying the expensive lawnmower with a built-in TV, Larry sits outside his house at night watching that tiny screen, preferring to be alone in his yard than inside with the wife with whom he no longer shares a connection. Instead of admiring her neighbors' sense of style and moving on, Summer notes, "I could die for that dining set." For the Symondses, inanimate objects are filling a void left by people. Since the Joneses are so overflowing with objects they do not actually own, perhaps it is inevitable that they would feel the opposite and strive to get closer to other people.

The problem is that this realization is not the criticism of American commerce that *The Joneses* at first purports to be. It becomes a surprisingly corny story about the need for family and friends, which eventually features an earnest crisis of conscience and a romantic subplot that completely spins the film away from even the mildest satire. Maybe this should not be all that surprising, considering how easily the Joneses themselves fit into the role of *The Joneses*. Based on how incredibly expensive it must be to finance the fake family's operation for an entire year, the type of irresponsible behavior in which Jen in particular specializes would theoretically not be tolerated by a corporation with its eye on the bottom line. Yet there are few, if any, consequences for members of the Jones family as a result of their disinterest in their jobs. It also does not seem like anyone has considered the emotional toll that can be expected by pretending to be someone else. Steve seems very shaken up after an old friend recognizes him at a restaurant and Steve has to act like the friend is mistaken. That kind of thing must happen all the time to these "employees," so they would probably train for that in orientation. After the incident, however, Steve, who is clearly too compassionate for this line of work, looks like he needs a hug.

For too much of *The Joneses,* the quartet gradually tries to recapture their sense of humanity and/or personal fulfillment without much concern for the cutthroat job they're engaged in. The film begins as something not far from a *Twilight Zone* episode. It concludes as something closer to a cute TV movie with a lot of product placement and nothing very specific to say about a society that focuses on things instead of the people who buy them.

Matt Pais

CREDITS
Steve: David Duchovny
Kate: Demi Moore

Jenn: Amber Heard
Larry: Gary Cole
Billy: Chris Williams
KC: Lauren Hutton
Mick: Ben Hollingsworth
Naomi: Christine Evangelista
Summer: Glenne Headley
Origin: USA
Language: English
Released: 2009
Production: Andrew Spaulding, Kristi Zea, Derrick Borte, Doug Mankoff; Premiere Pictures, Echo Lake Productions; released by Roadside Attractions
Directed by: Derrick Borte
Written by: Derrick Borte
Cinematography by: Yaron Orbach
Music by: Nick Urata
Sound: Mary H. Ellis
Music Supervisor: Sue Jacobs
Editing: Janice Hampton
Art Direction: Paul D. Kelly
Costumes: Renee Ehrlich Kalfus
Production Design: Kristi Zea
MPAA rating: R
Running time: 93 minutes

REVIEWS

Ebert, Roger. *Chicago Sun-Times.* April 14, 2010.
LaSalle, Mick. *San Francisco Chronicle.* April 16, 2010.
Mohan, Marc. *Portland Oregonian.* April 15, 2010.
Ogle, Connie. *Miami Herald.* April 15, 2010.
Phillips, Michael. *Chicago Tribune.* April 15, 2010.
Puig, Claudia. *USA Today.* April 18, 2010.
Rea, Steven. *Philadelphia Inquirer.* April 16, 2010.
Schwarzbaum, Lisa. *Entertainment Weekly.* April 15, 2010.
Tobias, Scott. *AV Club.* April 15, 2010.
Weitzman, Elizabeth. *New York Daily News.* April 16, 2010.

QUOTES

Steve Jones: " I'd love to give this my full attention, but I'm gonna go see Larry—tell him I'm gay."

TRIVIA

Most of the background students in the high school scenes were actual junior and senior students at Kell High School in Marietta, Georgia.

JUST WRIGHT

In this game every shot counts.
—Movie tagline

Box Office: $22 million

Light-hearted romance has hit such a low point with recent films like *The Bounty Hunter* (2010) and *Life as We Know It* (2010) that relative successes must be recognized. So, for the record: *Just Wright* is not an excruciatingly terrible movie, nor does it feature exclusively annoying characters. Still, this love story lacks credibility around every turn and has about as much chemistry and sexual energy as a documentary about architecture.

In a performance that would need several improvements to rise to a description like "bland," Queen Latifah plays Leslie Wright, a cheerful, 35-year-old physical therapist who has something going for her that most modern romantic heroines do not: she has pride in who she is and does not base her happiness around whether or not she has a man in her life. Leslie is not ashamed of her beaten-up car or her body, which is considerably fuller than that of her god-sister Morgan (Paula Patton), whose major goal in life is to marry a basketball player. So Morgan is happy when, thanks to a meet-cute with New Jersey Nets star guard Scott McKnight (Common), diehard Nets fan Leslie scores an invite to Scott's birthday party and brings Morgan along. At first Morgan fakes a lack of interest; Scott continues to pursue her. Soon, the two are appearing in photo spreads in celebrity magazines and Morgan is sitting courtside while her new man runs the floor. Then, to the chagrin of his mom (Phylicia Rashad), Scott pops the question and Morgan has what she has always wanted, while Leslie, as usual, remains on the sideline.

To call Scott and Morgan's courtship a whirlwind romance would imply that their relationship revolves around anything other than her loving his lifestyle and him loving her appearance. Scott is presented as a down-to-earth, intelligent guy, yet one of the movie's major logical canyons is the way Scott so fully and carelessly falls for Morgan, who blatantly lies about volunteer work and possesses so little personality that even one conversation would be enough for any smart guy to see that she is solid in the looks department but that is it. Scott, apparently, is blinded by beauty, so much so that he does not even stand up for his own interests. Shortly after he gets engaged, Scott suffers a knee injury—while exerting maximum effort during the NBA All-Star game, no less, which may explain why most real-life stars exert none at all during the contest—that threatens to knock him out for the rest of the season, if not hinder his chances of re-signing with the Nets and have a successful career ahead of him. His best chance of recovery lies with Bella Goldsmith (Kim Strother), who is known as the best physical therapist in the league and is often called "the miracle worker." Of course, as soon as Morgan sees that Bella is a stunningly beautiful woman,

Bella disappears and Leslie becomes Scott's new therapist.

That Morgan automatically and jealously claims Bella, who is white, is a "ho" evokes curiosity about Morgan's potential racial bias, but the movie does not address this. Nor does it address why Scott says absolutely nothing about the fact that his fiancé fired the one woman who might be able to get his physical health and career back on track. Instead, the script by Michael Elliott constantly hinges on contrivances like this to move the plot along, at the cost of characters who all turn out to be far less bright and interesting as they initially appear.

Obviously *Just Wright* is squirming to push Scott and Leslie together. If only the two had even the slightest spark between them. Multiple times throughout the film Leslie expresses frustration that men only want her as a friend and not a romantic partner. Yet just because Leslie is nice does not mean that she has a good personality, and just because she has confidence does not mean she has charisma. Leslie and Scott never seem like more than buddies hanging out, so their inevitable romantic pairing feels false instead of sweet. Latifah and Common, both actors who began as rappers, have been friends off-screen for years. Their easygoing but sexless onscreen rapport recalls Sandra Bullock and Ryan Reynolds, real-life friends who brought spunk but not a believable relationship to the mediocre 2009 romantic comedy *The Proposal*.

With some laughs and some palpable romantic connections *Just Wright* might have been a low-key tweak of *Cinderella*, (1950) as the evil god-sister (Morgan) acts in her own selfish interest and the prince (Scott) must eventually discover the previously overlooked beauty (Leslie) in front of him. That does not imply particularly positive things about the amount of originality found in *Just Wright*, however. The movie's lack of interest in developing its characters or allowing them to make understandable decisions results in a story that does not have much to offer outside of its restrained tone. It does benefit from an underplayed turn from Common, who allows Scott to come off as a smooth, good guy who has not let fame or fortune turn him into a jerk. The actor previously has not had much to chew on in the movies. He has been relegated to small roles as generic tough guys in films like *American Gangster* (2007) and *Date Night* (2010), but he shows promise when allowed to soften into a personality closer to the rapper's own demeanor. Scott's continuous obliviousness towards Morgan's intentions and behavior, though, prevents him from being as likable and fleshed out as he could be.

Again, despite all the narrative stumbles and complete lack of passion, *Just Wright* is more tolerable than many recent cinematic love stories simply because it is a calm, nice movie. The world needs more romantic comedies with strong female characters like Leslie Wright, as well as more romantic leads played by African American actresses. However, these movies also need to leave a positive impression, not just the absence of negative one. *Just Wright* may not be an irritating slap in the face, but it is the equivalent of a shrug after a forgettable date.

Matt Pais

CREDITS

Leslie Wright: Queen Latifah
Scott McKnight: Common
Morgan Alexander: Paula Patton
Leslie's mother: Pam Grier
Leslie's father: James Pickens Jr.
Angelo: Mehcad Brooks
Nelson: Michael Landes
Scott's mother: Phylicia Rashad
Bella Goldsmith: Kim Strother
Origin: USA
Language: English
Released: 2010
Production: Debra Martin Chase, Queen Latifah, Shakim Compere; Flavor Unit Entertainment; released by Fox Searchlight Pictures
Directed by: Sanaa Hamri
Written by: Michael Elliot
Cinematography by: Terry Stacey
Music by: Lisa Coleman, Wendy Melvoin
Sound: Damian Canelos
Music Supervisor: Julia Michels
Editing: Melissa Kent
Art Direction: Robert Pyzocha
Costumes: David C. Robinson
Production Design: Stephanie Carroll
MPAA rating: PG
Running time: 100 minutes

REVIEWS

Anderson, Melissa. *Village Voice.* May 11, 2010.
Baumgarten, Marjorie. *Austin Chronicle.* May 14, 2010.
Burr, Ty. *Boston Globe.* May 14, 2010.
Ebert, Roger. *Chicago Sun-Times.* May 12, 2010.
Moore, Roger. *Orlando Sentinel.* May 12, 2010.
Phillips, Michael. *Chicago Tribune.* May 13, 2010.
Orange, Michelle. *Movieline.* May 14, 2010.
Scott, Mike. *New Orleans Times-Picayune.* May 14, 2010.
Tobias, Scott. *AV Club.* May 13, 2010.
Wilson, Calvin. *St. Louis Post-Dispatch.* May 14, 2010.

TRIVIA

Singer John Legend has a cameo appearance as the Nets fan cheering courtside when McKnight is injured.

K

THE KARATE KID

*A challenge he never imagined. A teacher he
never expected.*
—Movie tagline

Box Office: $177 million

How appropriate that the first scene of *The Karate
Kid* shows a door frame upon which the titular character's height has been marked at various milestone's in
his short life, as moviegoers who fondly remember the
original 1984 version had serious doubts about this new
"Kid" measuring up. After all, the mere utterance of
"Wax on, wax off" can make such adults wax nostalgic
about what has been described as a karate version of
Rocky (1976) targeted at teenagers. (Indeed, John G.
Avildsen directed both iconic productions.) The story of
the string bean and the sensei that so satisfyingly ended
with a put-upon young man's triumph over his tormentors on the mat put Ralph Macchio on the map, not to
mention the poster-clad walls of countless love-struck
young ladies. It also garnered a surprise—but well-
deserved—Oscar® nomination for Noriyuki "Pat"
Morita.

The unexpected hit gave hope (realistic or not) to
the bulkless bullied, many of whom became convinced
that the way to stop getting belted all the time was to
work toward a black one at the nearest dojo. Enrollment
in karate soared, and whether respect was ever eventually
won, the self-esteem of many a high-kicking kid shot up
to previously-unattained levels. Maybe they could even
succeed in attracting a girl as adorable as Elisabeth Shue's
"Ali-with-an-i." Whoever they eventually wound up
with, those minors who sought major miracles from

their own real-life Miyagi stand-ins resultantly now have
kids of their own, and accompanied them to the
multiplex with mixed emotions. Would this remake that
admittedly might thrill and inspire a new generation be
a crass besmirchment of that favorite film from their
own youth? For most, skepticism turned to surprise as
they found themselves once again rooting hard for the
beleaguered underdog, who here supplants his inept
karate skills with expert kung fu. Sure, the original film
could still whoop this one, but the remake nevertheless
rises to the occasion and puts up an unexpectedly good
fight.

With pride-fueled, nepotistic zeal, Will Smith and
his wife Jada Pinkett Smith endeavored to give their son
Jaden a leg up in the business with a possible *Karate Kid*
franchise. (The couple serves as two of the film's eleven
producers.) When Jaden first appeared on screen
alongside his father in *The Pursuit of Happyness* (2006),
this sire of a star was a handsome little guy with a winning personality. That the description still applied to
Jaden when he made this film at the age of eleven is
interestingly both a plus and a minus for the production.
Although Macchio was twenty-three when he portrayed
Daniel LaRusso in the original, he still looked like a
reedy teen. Thus, the actor was well-cast as a New Jersey
high schooler transplanted in Southern California who
is having trouble putting down roots because he keeps
getting beat up by dirt-biking peers who fight sadistically dirty. This time around, the protagonist has not
only been age-regressed to just twelve years old, but
Smith, being small of stature and slight of build, looks
even younger than that. Thus, his fish-out-of-water Dre
Parker seems alarmingly like a minnow with

psychotically-gnashing preteen sharks relentlessly on his tail. On the one hand, adults now queasily watch callow Dre's drubbings by more powerful and seemingly-unhinged schoolmates with a parental sense of outraged revulsion. Yet, that very repugnance paradoxically tends to draw many further into the proceedings, rooting perhaps in spite of themselves and at least as hard as their offspring for the just comeuppance they know is coming—responsibly refereed, of course.

Sympathy for this *Karate Kid* is also intensified by his having to adjust to surroundings that are far-more-foreign. Dre's widowed mother, Sherry (a funny, tart, and terrific Taraji P. Henson) must relocate all the way from the Midwest (Detroit, Michigan) to the Far East (Beijing, China) in order to remain employed. While she doggedly tries to put the best face on their move, the dubious look on her son's mug reveals resentment about what he has had to leave behind and apprehension about what lies ahead. As a result of these feelings, charmingly affable and often humorous Dre can sometimes be something of a petulant pipsqueak, but this seems not only authentic but wholly understandable. After his first shockingly-vicious trouncing at the hands of Tormentor-in-Chief Cheng (a scarily-potent Zhenwei Wang), made infinitely more humiliating by the presence of Mei Ying (Wenwen Han), the sweet violin prodigy he would much rather impress, Dre's resulting physical and emotional pain leads to a tearful eruption toward his mother that is quite affecting. The poor kid just wants his old life back.

Like Daniel before him, Dre is bailed out of acute distress by his apartment building's initially distant handyman, who shows up at just the right moment with a surprising display of self-defense adroitness. However, it is actually only surprising this time around to the kid and the antagonists, as even those viewers unacquainted with the earlier movie wholly anticipated some formidable kung-fu fighting from Mr. Han since he is played by none other than martial arts legend Jackie Chan. (This is one of his best performances, quietly piquing interest without all the trademark mugging and flashy stunts.) Back in 1984, audiences' mouths fell open in delighted amazement when Morita's Miyagi expertly dispatched a horde of hoodlums who were not only a fraction of his age but also much bigger, broader and beefier. Seeing an actor known solely to most as kooky elfin Arnold from television's *Happy Days* do that is quite different from Chan simply doing the expected, and thus that delicious, electrifying element of surprise has been excised from this pivotal scene.

There are other sequences in which this *Karate Kid* falls short while aiming to both respectfully replicate the original film and stand on its own two feet. Daniel had become frustrated by the car waxing, fence painting, and other refurbishing chores Miyagi made him do, as they seemed totally unrelated to the acquisition of skills that would prevent toughs from giving one a good shellacking. They were meant to strengthen and add flexibility to his muscles before then being astonishingly adapted to useful karate techniques. Here, while the endless throwing down and hanging up of a light jacket teaches a heedless kid adherence to his mom's wishes, it does not believably do much to segue into skills. Another comparative weakness: what amounts to an ultra-chaste crush between Dre and Mei Ying lacks interest compared to the heady exhilaration of a high school romance.

There are other problems, as well, such as travelogue-like interludes that likely made the remake's Chinese investors and the Board of Tourism quite happy but only helped the film become unhappily long. (The cinematography is, however, quite arresting.) However, in spite of this *Karate Kid*'s shortcomings, there is here, as before, a captivating chemistry between the two likeable leads, a poignant mutually-healing relationship between a suffering son who lost his father and a grieving father who lost his wife and son. Through Han's teaching of a time-honored discipline, as much a way of conducting one's life as of defending it, Dre and the audience walk away with some deep things to think about after the film's rousing, pleasing, instant replay-augmented finale. Made on a budget of $40 million, the film kicked aside its competition to gross $359 million worldwide, and garnered favorable reviews. Reported talk of sequels, however, should be tempered by memories of the increasingly regrettable ones that followed the original film.

David L. Boxerbaum

CREDITS

Dre Parker: Jaden Smith
Mr. Han: Jackie Chan
Sherry Parker: Taraji P. Henson
Meiying: Wenwen Han
Master Li: Rongguang Yu
Cheng: Zhenwei Wang
Origin: USA
Language: English
Released: 2010
Production: James Lassiter, Jada Pinkett Smith, Will Smith, Ken Stovitz, Jerry Weintraub; China Film Group, Jerry Weintraub Productions, Overbrook Entertainment; released by Columbia Pictures
Directed by: Harald Zwart
Written by: Christopher Murphey
Cinematography by: Roger Pratt
Music by: James Horner

Sound: Steve Ticknors
Editing: Joel Negron
Costumes: Han Feng
Production Design: François Séguin
MPAA rating: PG
Running time: 140 minutes

REVIEWS

Atkinson, Michael. *Sight & Sound.* August 2010.
Burr, Ty. *Boston Globe.* June 11, 2010.
Chang, Justin. *Variety.* June 7, 2010.
Diones, Bruce. *New Yorker.* June 28, 2010.
Gleiberman, Owen. *Entertainment Weekly.* June 25, 2010.
Lovece, Frank. *Film Journal International.* July 2010.
Orange, Michelle. *Village Voice.* June 9, 2010.
Scheck, Frank. *Hollywood Reporter.* June 4, 2010.
Scott, A.O. *New York Times.* June 11, 2010.
Wheat, Alynda. *People.* June 21, 2010.

QUOTES

Mr. Han: "Being still and doing nothing are two very different things."

Dre Parker: "Mom, look. In China, everything is old. There's old houses, old parks, old people. Look, this guy is at least four hundred years old."

TRIVIA

The filmmakers decided to maintain the title *The Karate Kid* for continuity sake despite the martial arts portrayed in the film being a form of kung fu.

KICK-ASS

Have fear. They're here.
—Movie tagline
A new breed of superheroes will be revealed.
—Movie tagline

Box Office: $48 million

On the title track of his breakthrough 1977 album *The Stranger*, Billy Joel sang about the many different faces ("Some are satin, some are steel, some are silk and some are leather") a person can assume depending on the situation, and nowhere is this notion of slippery, guileful identity truer than in adolescence, when insecurity and cocksureness can commingle to often weird effect. That sense of inner conflict, that teenage collision of bristling ambition and crippling stasis, is at the heart of *Kick-Ass*, adapted from Mark Millar and John Romita, Jr.'s comic book of the same name.

Unlike many of its superhero film brethren, *Kick-Ass* does not take as its central figure the victim of a radioactive spider bite or cosmic rays, nor a gloomy, misunderstood genius or the refugee of a doomed alien world. Instead, it centers on a regular teenage guy with no special access or powers, and not much of a grandly-sketched plan beyond something that is merely different than the status quo. The result, under director Matthew Vaughn, is a film with vim, much color, and a distinct, streamlined personality, no doubt, but also one whose punchy connection recalls the effects of a piece of that paper-wrapped, nickel-priced bubble gum of yester-year—an ultra-sweet, sugary rush that fades quickly, and is apt to leave one feeling a bit queasy.

Bespectacled comic book fanboy Dave Lizewski (Aaron Johnson) is a seemingly average teenage virgin, consumed with fantasies of his teacher, and unsure of how to even approach any girls his own age. His imagination, however, is verdant. Sick of his crime-riddled hometown, in which bad guys seemingly get away with everything, Dave decides to become a real-life superhero. As would any good crime fighter, he works up a new identity (Kick-Ass), procures a suit and mask (in this case via mail-order), and starts training, keeping all of this secret from friends Marty and Todd (Clarke Duke and Evan Peters, respectively).

Lacking superpowers or a billionaire's bankroll, however, it quickly becomes apparent Dave is doing little more than acting out a first-grader's playground fantasies. When Kick-Ass confronts some carjackers, he receives a massive beat down—a humiliation that, owing to the fact that he is found without his clothes, somehow finally helps endear him to Katie Deauxma (Lyndsy Fonseca), on whom Dave has long had a crush.

After recuperating, an undeterred Dave again sets out to fight crime, and when an amateur cell phone video of his exploits becomes a viral sensation, his life changes forever. As a subculture of even more bumbling copycats springs up, Dave manages his burgeoning Internet popularity but again gets himself in a tough situation. He is rescued by a pair of crazed, costumed vigilantes—eleven-year-old Mindy Macready, aka Hit Girl (Chloe Grace Moretz), and her mild-mannered ex-cop father, Damon, aka Big Daddy (Nicolas Cage), who has been training Mindy for a special revenge mission her entire life. Individually and collectively, their exploits draw the attention of criminal kingpin Frank D'Amico (Mark Strong), and Frank's attention-starved son Chris (Christopher Mintz-Plasse) eventually develops an alter ego, Red Mist, in order to forge an alliance with Kick-Ass and win his father's approval.

While not the first film to aim for laughs alongside superhero hijinks—other such efforts have included James Gunn and Craig Mazin's *The Specials* (2000), as well as studio fare like *My Super Ex-Girlfriend* (2006) and *Superhero Movie* (2008)—*Kick-Ass* may well be the most robust and indefatigably single-minded in its execution. Vaughn, working from a screenplay coauthored with his *Stardust* (2007) collaborator Jane Goldman, peppers his dialogue with snarky asides, but also leaves room around the movie's edges for plenty of bewilderment and exasperation from its characters, which helps give *Kick-Ass* a convincing sense of organic pop. They may be doing outrageous things, but all of these characters occupy the same world.

Occasionally, the film seems poised to break through and land some blows of grander cultural critique, but each time it backs away. Despite its novelty on a certain level, in significant ways it feels like it shares the main problem of many comic book film adaptations, or at least those not involving Christopher Nolan—of being overly beholden to the source material, where a surfeit of cool is always the prime directive.

Kick-Ass dances along a razor's edge of contradictions, at once glossy and colorful as well as graphic and brutal. In this regard, it is somewhat akin to slickly shot, hyper-idealized Internet pornography; it pursues titillation through shock and overload. Its makers would argue that its audience is inherently in on the joke, and therefore there is no moral hazard, but one need not be a fusty retiree to harbor conflicted thoughts about the nature of the impact of such gleefully inflicted violence on younger, more impressionable minds. The film garners big reactions from playing with superhero conventions, and subverting expectation in over-the-top ways (an as-yet-untrained Kick-Ass getting the snot beaten out of him; Big Daddy shooting a bulletproof-vest-clad Hit Girl in order to teach her how to take a bullet; and Hit Girl viciously slaying people), but as often as not these thrills come across as fleeting, piecemeal amusements.

It is as a wild, hormonally charged distillation of adolescent male fantasy—of setting wrongs right, of getting the girl—that the movie scores its points. Yet as it shifts into more pronounced third-act confrontations, *Kick-Ass* begins to feel like little more than just another slick exercise in product placement and masturbatory action excess, albeit a bit differently framed. Vaughn's film entertains much more often than not, but does not evoke deeper reflection or ask its audience to do anything other than jeer at the spectacle of it all. In the end, that is disappointing and, because of the nature of its violence, a bit unnerving.

Apart from its adrenalized packaging and some colorful production design by Russell De Rozario, what most helps *Kick-Ass* viscerally connect is its cast. As the protagonist, Dave can be neither one-note ineffectual nor all awakened machismo, and British-born Johnson

nicely captures all the gangly, jumbled, and frequently at-odds energy of his character and quest, which is all about putting the cart before the horse. It is a performance that is all the more laudable when one sees Johnson's very different turn in *Nowhere Boy* (2010), playing a young John Lennon.

Robbing the show, though, is Moretz. As written, the character of Hit Girl is a natural scene-stealer—a tiny, prepubescent girl dispatching burly henchmen with decapitating twirls. But Moretz, while skilled with a well-timed quip, also locates a bit of her character's driving adolescent desire to please a parent, even though the material she is given in this vein is perfunctory. It is a flint of tangible human yearning, in a colorful movie driven, perhaps excessively and failingly so, by its own goading instinct to please.

Brent Simon

CREDITS

Dave Lizewski/Kick-Ass: Aaron Johnson
Damon Macready/Big Daddy: Nicolas Cage
Mindy Macready/Hit Girl: Chloe Grace Moretz
Katie Deauxma: Lyndsy Fonseca
Frank D'Amico: Mark Strong
Chris D'Amico/Red Mist: Christopher Mintz-Plasse
Detective Vic Gigante: Xander Berkeley
Marty: Clark Duke
Todd: Evan Peters
Mrs. Lizewski: Elizabeth McGovern
Erika Cho: Sophie Wu
Big Joe: Michael Rispoli
Tre Fernandez: Randall Batinkoff
Lobby Goon: Jason Flemyng
Mr. Lizewski: Garrett M. Brown
Angie D'Amico: Yancy Butler
Origin: USA
Language: English
Released: 2010
Production: Adam Bohling, Brad Pitt, David Reid, Kris Thykier, Matthew Vaughn; Marv Films, Plan B Entertainment; released by Lionsgate
Directed by: Matthew Vaughn
Written by: Matthew Vaughn, Jane Goldman
Cinematography by: Benjamin Davis
Music by: Marius De Vries, Ilan Eshkeri, Henry Jackman, John Murphy
Sound: Danny Sheehan
Music Supervisor: Ian Neil
Editing: Jon Harris, Eddie Hamilton, Pietro Scalia
Art Direction: John King
Costumes: Sammy Sheldon

Production Design: Russell De Rozario
MPAA rating: R
Running time: 117 minutes

REVIEWS

Dargis, Manohla. *New York Times.* April 16, 2010.
Groen, Rick. *Globe and Mail.* April 16, 2010.
Hornaday, Ann. *Washington Post.* April 16, 2010.
Kennedy, Lisa. *Denver Post.* April 16, 2010.
Lane, Anthony. *New Yorker.* April 19, 2010.
Long, Tom. *Detroit News.* April 16, 2010.
Puig, Claudia. *USA Today.* April 15, 2010.
Rainer, Peter. *Christian Science Monitor.* April 23, 2010.
Tallerico, Brian. *HollywoodChicago.com.* April 16, 2010.
Vognar, Chris. *Dallas Morning News.* April 16, 2010.

QUOTES

Mindy Macready: "I'm just f**king with you Daddy! Look, I'd love a Benchmade model 42 butterfly knife."

Dave Lizewski: "With no power, comes no responsibility. Except, 'that' wasn't true."

TRIVIA

The role of Big Daddy went to Nicolas Cage after the filmmakers considered both Daniel Craig and Mark Wahlberg.

THE KIDS ARE ALL RIGHT

Nic and Jules had the perfect family, until they met the man who made it all possible.
—Movie tagline

Box Office: $21 million

Lisa Cholodenko's Oscar®-nominated portrait of the modern American family was a major player in the 2010 awards season, winning the Golden Globe for Best Comedy, garnering great praise for the script co-written by Cholodenko and Stuart Blumberg, and notching multiple nominations for a fantastic ensemble led by Academy Award® nominees Annette Bening and Mark Ruffalo but also successful due to notable contributions from Julianne Moore, Mia Wasikowska, and Josh Hutcherson. *The Kids Are All Right* succeeds by not focusing on the differences between the family it presents and the more common nuclear one, but the similarities. Even more importantly, Cholodenko and Blumberg's excellent script works in the space between stated action and the subconscious: the subtext that drives so much human interaction but that is so hard to put into fictional form. Most film characters operate purely on surface-level intentions like "saving the world," "getting the girl," or "stopping the killer," but the real world operates more on subconscious behavior, something rarely translated as successfully to the big screen as it was in *The Kids Are All Right,* a film in which people make fascinating decisions for reasons they do not fully even understand. Dramatically rewarding and with one of the most impressive ensembles of 2010, *The Kids Are All Right* was one of the best films of the year.

Nic (Annette Bening) and Jules (Julianne Moore) have a reasonably happy partnership. They are certainly not set up as the healthiest lesbian couple in town as Nic seems to practically mock Jules' latest attempts at starting her own career (this time it is landscaping but one gets the impression that she has had some failed ventures in the past) as the film opens and possibly with good reason. But Nic and Jules are certainly not presented as a couple in crisis. Nic may work too hard and drink a bit too much red wine with dinner and Jules may be a little flighty and noncommittal but they have common problems of a common couple, they just happen to be lesbians with two teenage children—a sweet, waif-like girl named Joni (Mia Wasikowska) and a slightly rebellious younger boy named Laser (Josh Hutcherson).

Joni (named after the legendary singer/songwriter Joni Mitchell) has just turned eighteen, and, therefore, can now find her birth father, which she shares with Laser. Joni seems more concerned about the impact that finding their "donor" will have on their mothers but Laser is the one pressuring her to make the call. It is never explicitly stated why Laser wants to find his dad, but a brief subplot involving a truly moronic friend that he spends time with, who clearly has different values, seems to imply that Laser needs not just a role model or mentor but a new person with whom to hang out who does not get kicks from peeing on stray dogs. After some brief debate, Laser and Joni contact Paul (Mark Ruffalo), an earthy restaurant owner with subtle shades of commitment phobia (he has a gorgeous girlfriend who makes it crystal clear that she would be more if he asked and the decisions to not have a family will play strongly into the sometimes-misread finale of the film). The three get along but it is actually Joni who is more drawn to her biological father and wants to not only see him again but bring him home to meet their mothers.

Nic seems the most instantly threatened by Paul's arrival into their family unit, which makes sense given that she is presented as the more protective of the two mothers. Despite their apprehension, the two women meet with and get along with the likable, affable Paul. One of the joys of Cholodenko and Hutcherson's character-driven script is that it does not set Paul up like the traditional interloper who sets out to destroy a family unit. In fact, he seems to be consciously aware (as anyone would be) that he is the outsider to this clan and tries not to rock the boat. After Jules goes to landscape Paul's home, the boat gets definitely rocked as the two begin a heated sexual affair in the first of two plot points to aggravate some critics and viewers of the film, some of who believed that the film was too actively presenting sexuality as a choice instead of a biological dictum through the fact that Jules jumps into Paul's bed. In fact, Cholodenko brilliantly sets up the subconscious reasons behind the affair through a seemingly harmless and mostly comical exchange earlier in the film in which Jules and Nic explain to Laser that they watch gay male porn because in that they can see an outward display of attraction. Outward displays are what are missing in Jules and Nic's partnership and Jules finds that in Paul, someone who clearly makes her comfortable if not just through the fact that he looks like her children. It is not as if Jules jumps into the loving arms of a male stranger to whom she is sexually drawn—she finds passion through someone who feels close to a part of her family already. There is a notable difference for those willing to see it.

Even more divisive was the finale of *The Kids Are All Right,* which a shocking number of intelligent people falsely read as being anti-male or even anti-traditional family. Neither is the case. The fact that Paul is left on the sidewalk and away from his children after the affair is revealed is not a statement against his behavior with Jules but more a commentary on the simple, undeniable fact that those who have families on which to rely when the chips fall are better off than those who do not. Not everything works out. Not everyone is forgiven. And Cholodenko also does not intend the final scenes as final judgment on Paul or to suggest that he will never have contact with his children again—in fact, Joni wearing a motorcycle helmet in the final scenes added to this viewer's feeling that she would contact her biological pop somewhere down the road. Part of the brilliance of the film is that Cholodenko never demonizes Paul and those who bemoaned the lack of forgiveness in the finale were hoping for a pat resolution that simply would not have fit with the realism of the rest of the script.

Cholodenko and Blumberg's script is especially notable for writing five distinct arcs, something increasingly rare in a world where most screenwriters focus on one lead protagonist. All five of the central characters in *The Kids Are All Right* feel fully-realized, not only thanks to the screenplay but with credit due to one of the best ensembles of the year. Annette Bening walked away with the most acclaim brilliantly playing a woman who arguably has begun to take the life she has for granted. Like so many married people, gay or straight, she has too easily dismissed her life partner and pays the price for that,

but Bening never turns Nic into the cold villain that she would have been in the hands of so many lesser actresses. She finds a way to display the warmth under the sometimes-harsh exterior. Late in the film, Bening is given a showcase scene—a sequence involving, like a few of the best in the film, a meal, that also includes a song and a revelation—that other actresses die for and she knocks it out of the park. She goes through a dozen emotions in one long scene and every one of them feels genuine and of-the-moment.

Bening's highly-acclaimed work should not lessen the contributions of the other four members of the cast. Julianne Moore taps into that reservoir of energy that has helped her to so many great performances and imbues Jules with a beautiful combination of passion and self-doubt. Mark Ruffalo matches the women, perfectly drawing a man who has not only not even come to terms with what he wants from life but not yet even asked the question (and, once again, that is not meant as judgment, merely as character trait). Many critics and viewers pointed to Ruffalo's turn here as the one they had been waiting for after his breakthrough work in *You Can Count On Me* (2000) (although one could also argue he has been underrated in the decade since, delivering great turns in *Zodiac* [2007] and *The Brothers Bloom* [2008]). The adults got the praise they deserved, but it too often went unnoticed that Wasikowska and Hutcherson gave two of the most believable young-adult turns of the year as well.

Films as funny, heartfelt, and genuine as *The Kids Are All Right* are rare. Ones that can match believable comedy with a pitch-perfect ensemble come along even less often. However one reads Cholodenko's artistic intent—whether or not her film should be read as a commentary on the new American family or merely appreciated as a character-driven comedy with an incredible ensemble—*The Kids Are All Right* stands up as one of the 2010 films that is certainly much better than just all right.

Brian Tallerico

CREDITS

Jules: Julianne Moore
Nic: Annette Bening
Paul: Mark Ruffalo
Joni: Mia Wasikowska
Laser: Josh Hutcherson
Jai: Kunal Sharma
Tanya: Yaya DaCosta
Luis: Joaquin Garrido
Clay: Eddie Hassell

Sasha: Zosia Mamet

Origin: USA

Language: English

Released: 2010

Production: Gary Gilbert, Jeff Levy-Hinte, Celine Rattray, Daniela Taplin Lundberg, Jordan Horowitz; Antidote Film, Plum Pictures; released by Focus Features

Directed by: Lisa Cholodenko

Written by: Lisa Cholodenko, Stuart Blumberg

Cinematography by: Igor Jadue-Lillo

Music by: Craig Wedren, Nathan Larson

Sound: Jose Antonio Garcia

Editing: Jeff Werner

Art Direction: James Pearse Connelly

Costumes: Mary Claire Hannan

Production Design: Julie Berghoff

MPAA rating: R

Running time: 104 minutes

REVIEWS

Burr, Ty. *Boston Globe.* July 15, 2010.
Edelstein, David. *New York Magazine.* July 5, 2010.
Hornaday, Ann. *Washington Post.* July 16, 2010.
Keough, Peter. *Boston Phoenix.* July 15, 2010.
LaSalle, Mick. *San Francisco Chronicle.* July 8, 2010.
Lowe, Justin. *Hollywood Reporter.* January 27, 2010.
Nelson, Rob. *Variety.* January 26, 2010.
Phillips, Michael. *Chicago Tribune.* July 8, 2010.
Scott, A.O. *New York Times.* July 9, 2010.
Sharkey, Betsy. *Los Angeles Times.* July 8, 2010.

QUOTES

Paul: "It's hard enough to open your heart in this world. Don't make it harder."

TRIVIA

The song "The Kids Are Alright" by The Who inspired the title of the movie.

AWARDS

Golden Globes 2011: Actress—Mus./Comedy (Bening), Film—Mus./Comedy

Ind. Spirit 2011: Screenplay

Nomination:

Oscars 2010: Actress (Bening), Film, Orig. Screenplay, Support. Actor (Ruffalo)

British Acad. 2010: Actress (Bening), Actress (Moore), Orig. Screenplay, Support. Actor (Ruffalo)

Golden Globes 2011: Actress—Mus./Comedy (Moore), Screenplay

Ind. Spirit 2011: Actress (Bening), Director (Cholodenko), Film, Support. Actor (Ruffalo)

Screen Actors Guild 2010: Actress (Bening), Support. Actor (Ruffalo), Cast

Writers Guild 2010: Orig. Screenplay.

THE KILLER INSIDE ME

Disproving the auteur theory, Michael Winterbottom has made a directorial career out of variety with little connective tissue between his films. In fact, it sometimes feels like the popular British filmmaker is purposefully jumping from genre to genre in an attempt to "do it all." From adaptations of classic novels (*Jude* [1996], *A Cock and Bull Story* [2006]) to films set in war-torn areas of the world (*Welcome to Sarajevo* [1997], *In This World* [2002]) to music-driven works (*24 Hour Party People* [2002], *9 Songs* [2004[), he revisits concepts but promises something unique every time. He has such a diverse resume that when it was announced that he was tackling the incredibly-popular Jim Thompson 1952 noir classic *The Killer Inside Me,* no one was surprised. However, when the film unspooled at the 2010 Sundance Film Festival, to say people were surprised would be putting it mildly. Walk-outs, audible boos, and complaints to the festival about even booking the film greeted Winterbottom's controversial thriller, proving yet again that nothing provokes the same response as extreme violence.

Portrayed by the genial, easygoing Casey Affleck, Texan Sheriff Lou Ford seems like the kind of boyish lawman that is easy to trust. And it is just as easy to see why women would be drawn to this man. He not only seems harmless but downright protective. The two women that fall into his dementia are Joyce Lakeland (Jessica Alba) and Amy Stanton (Kate Hudson), a pair of characters on the ends of the spectrum of noir femininity in that Joyce is a prostitute and Amy is a schoolteacher. Both will end up victims of Lou's brutality.

It starts with Joyce, who has been having an affair with Elmer Conway (Jay R. Ferguson), the son of an important businessman named Chester (Ned Beatty). Lou goes to her to try and convince her to leave town instead of creating trouble for the Conways. Joyce physically threatens the seemingly-harmless Lou and he pins her down and smacks her hard on the ass. It turns out that the misogynistic act actually turns Joyce on and the two start a twisted, sadomasochistic sexual relationship. Of course, this means that Ford has a problem as his new girlfriend was supposed to be out of town. He figures out a way out of the situation that not only puts him back in a comfortable position of power but satisfies dark urges that he has been battling since he was a child. In the most graphic scene of 2010, Lou pummels

Joyce in the face until she is barely recognizable. Alba reportedly walked out of the theater at Sundance upon viewing this scene, the one that sent many viewers over the edge to work on nasty letters to Robert Redford.

Joyce survives—and it seems like one of the reasons Winterbottom detailed the beating in such brutality is because her survival could otherwise make it seem less psychopathic were it not so grotesque to view—and stays in a coma as Lou unravels over the course of the rest of the film. He juggles trying to keep his house of lies from crashing while also satisfying his reinvigorated murderous desires. Lou has to kill again and again and it is only a matter of time before his schoolteacher sweetheart falls victim. Fantastic character actors including Elias Koteas, Simon Baker, Tom Bower, Brent Briscoe, and Bill Pullman pop up in small-but-effective roles and Alba and Hudson do vastly superior work to the romantic comedy junk that have littered their resumes of late.

Despite featuring some of the most shocking imagery of the year, it is false to label *The Killer Inside Me* as "violence for the sake of violence." That would be missing the point. Audiences responded so strongly in Park City not only because they are not used to seeing extreme violence at the typically-friendly Sundance but because most noirs focus on femme fatales and stylish sexuality over the darker elements of their stories. Winterbottom recognizes that Thompson is painting a portrait of a man for whom sex is simply not important. Closer to *Henry: Portrait of a Serial Killer* (1986) or *American Psycho* (2000) than *Double Indemnity* (1944), *The Killer Inside Me* is an extremely violent film for a reason. It turns the conventions of noir in a new direction, away from sexuality and into the dark recesses of the mind of a maniac and it dares to ask if perhaps a film about a lunatic should be stomach-turning and hard-to-watch after all. Winterbottom has taken the pitch black elements of noir seriously and dared viewers to follow into the darkness.

For two acts and part of the third, *The Killer Inside Me* is riveting, but the film culminates in a misguided scene that is easily one of the biggest mistakes of Winterbottom's career. Winterbottom and writer John Curran (the director of *The Painted Veil* [2006] and *Stone* (2010) felt a need to match the extremity of earlier moments with a ridiculously over-the-top climax. The ending approaches operatic lunacy as Lou Ford's world explodes around him. By that point, many audience members will have given up on this unique take on a timeless genre; another stand-out entry in the resume of one our most interesting modern filmmakers.

Brian Tallerico

CREDITS

Lou Ford: Casey Affleck
Amy Stanton: Kate Hudson
Joyce Lakeland: Jessica Alba
Howard Hendricks: Simon Baker
Billy Boy Walker: Bill Pullman
Chester Conway: Ned Beatty
Joe Rothman: Elias Koteas
Sheriff Bob Maples: Tom Bower
Elmer Conway: Jay R. Ferguson
Johnnie Pappas: Liam Aiken
Deputy Jeff Plummer: Matthew Maher
Bum/Stranger: Brent Briscoe
Origin: USA
Language: English
Released: 2010
Production: Bradford L. Schlei, Andrew Eaton, Chris Hanely; Revolution Films, Stone Canyon, Muse; released by IFC Films
Directed by: Michael Winterbottom
Written by: John Curran
Cinematography by: Marcel Zyskind
Music by: Mark Tildesley, Lynette Meyer, Melissa Parmenter, Joel Cadbury
Sound: David O. Daniel
Music Supervisor: Chadwick Brown
Editing: Mags Arnold
Production Design: Rob Simmons
Costumes: Lynette Meyer
MPAA rating: R
Running time: 108 minutes

REVIEWS

Andrews, Nigel. *Financial Times.* June 3, 2010.
Baumgarten, Marjorie. *Austin Chronicle.* July 30, 2010
Gleiberman, Owen. *Entertainment Weekly.* June 16, 2010.
Hillis, Aaron. *Village Voice.* May 26, 2010.
Levy, Shawn. *Oregonian.* July 22, 2010.
Long, Tom. *Detroit News.* July 2, 2010.
McCarthy, Todd. *Variety.* January 26, 2010.
Neumaier, Joe. *New York Daily News.* June 18, 2010.
Phillips, Michael. *Chicago Tribune.* June 24, 2010.
Rea, Steven. *Philadelphia Inquirer.* July 1, 2010.

QUOTES

Billy Boy Walker: "A weed is just a plant out of place."

TRIVIA

Tom Cruise, Katherine Heigl, Natalie Portman, Emily Blunt, Anne Hathaway, and Amanda Seyfried were all originally considered for roles in the film.

KILLERS

Marriage…give it your best shot.
—Movie tagline

Perfect husband. Perfect target.
—Movie tagline

Box Office: $47 million

Reputation is often as important to a filmmaker's career as success. Certain hack workers may dismiss their critics. As long as the checks keep rolling in on the next for-hire project, they can brush off such negativity and never seek to improve any significant style or the basic fundamentals of storytelling. Bad comedy directors are a dime-a-dozen, some more successful than others in catching a franchise or a star at the right time and are able to parlay that into scripts that might be high concept for them but are little more than the same old shtick in less than capable hands. Robert Luketic is such a director.

Lightning struck for Luketic with *Legally Blonde* (2001), a 21st century example of a bad 1980s movie. He then parlayed that success into snuffing out the potential satire of tabloid fandom with a typical romantic triangle in *Win a Date with Tad Hamilton* (2004) and brought Jane Fonda out of retirement only for us to want her to go right back and take Jennifer Lopez with her after *Monster-In-Law* (2005). At the South by Southwest Film Festival premiere of his botched Vegas blackjack scheme film, *21* (2008), Luketic referred to it as an "action film." Compared to his previous trio of films, anything not based on a sitcom convention or featuring people running may have electro-shocked the filmmaker into the definition of the word that typically comes after "lights" and "camera" but not what constitutes an actual work of action. That is never more clear than after experiencing his latest "action comedy," *Killers*.

Reuniting with the star of his aptly titled *The Ugly Truth* (2009), Katherine Heigl stars as Jen, an American with the kind of dating problems that only befall tall, blonde, chesty women in the movies. She is on vacation in France with her parents (Tom Selleck and Catherine O'Hara) when she meets the shirtless Spencer (Ashton Kutcher) in an elevator. Walking in the same direction, awkwardness turns into plans for a dinner date, except while Jen is headed to the pool, Spencer is carrying out a mission to blow up a helicopter. Yes, the shirtless wonder is actually a member of some forgettable organization and they gave him a "license to kill," as he will reveal once his cover is blown. That is not before he falls in love with Jen and disavows his loyalty to his handler, Holbrook (Martin Mull), to spend wedded bliss in the suburbs.

Spencer keeps his secretive past from Jen while working in home furnishings. Her friends take his distance as some kind of premature itch in their marriage. Even the father-in-law is suspicious that he might have some action on the side. Spencer might be stepping out permanently though when he discovers a contract has been put out on his head; a fact Jen inadvertently walks into during a fight with one of his co-workers. Now on the run, Spencer is forced to come clean while the "quiet life" once embraced by Jen is being disrupted by fistfights, car chases, lots of bullets, and an ill-timed pregnancy test.

In James Cameron's *True Lies* (1994), Arnold Schwarzenegger was a CIA agent unbeknownst to his mousy wife as both pursued different types of action on the side. The differences between an action maestro like Cameron and someone who has not progressed beyond just pronouncing the word like Luketic are night and day. A skilled satirist or one who might recognize and anticipate the comic possibilities past a fifteen-words-or-less concept pitch would have targeted the easygoing stability of the suburbs and turned it upside down. Someone more adept at playing up the thriller angle would have played up the irony of sleeper cells in your backyard from your own team as much harder to track and more unsettling. Merging the two would require someone capable of elevating the baseline material they started with or having an eye to hire the right people for the job.

Ashton Kutcher has fitted his career on being a handsome goofball, usually adding a couple octaves to his delivery when his character is in crisis mode and needs to express outrage or dissatisfaction. When toning down his mode of comedy, Kutcher has shown hints of a vulnerable puppy dog side that makes him irresistible to women and more tolerable as an actor. Those shades are evident here in the early scenes. In secret agent form, Kutcher just needs to speak softly and offer a crooked smile to attract attention without actually attracting it. He is not the most convincing James Bond in the world, seemingly having more to hide behind than his smile as the gigolo-like huckster in *Spread* (2009) than as someone with a license to blah. But he plays off others nicely, especially in scenes with Tom Selleck, who has discovered just the right level of deadpan comic sincerity over the years. When the action finally kicks in forty-five minutes into the film, one can almost see Luketic pushing Kutcher into that goofy mentality and any investment in his character as the impetus for this mayhem is dropped with a loud thud.

Grinding the film to a halt at every opportunity is Katherine Heigl's shrill, uninspired performance. From the very opening as she fawns over Spencer like some teenage Justin Bieber fan, Heigl creates not so much a character as a screaming pawn moved into various moods around the board who never becomes an active participant. Jen is so oblivious to what is going on it is as if Luketic insisted she not notice Spencer punching out a guy right behind her on a dance floor or not blink an eye at the giant knife he happens to be carrying when she needs her dress sliced open so that her ignorance in the second half would lend credence to the film's reality. Heigl's entire character beat is to discover she is pregnant, get mad at the hubby trying to save them ("bullets before babies"), and then try to divorce herself away from this new life the way Uma Thurman did when she "saw those two bars" on the pregnancy test in *Kill Bill: Vol. 2* (2004).

Reality is the least of the film's numerous problems. Luketic and screenwriters Bob DeRosa and T.M. Griffin may want to note that using the process of elimination to spot the secret villain requires more than two potential suspects to keep audiences caring. Invoking the name of Cary Grant even in passing is not wise, especially when one of the most suave actors of all time showed everyone how to do this very same material in *Charade* (1963). Luketic's action scenes would like to replicate the close proximity of Paul Greengrass' Bourne pictures, but they cannot even compare to original *Bourne Identity* (2002) director Doug Liman and his tightly destructive methods from *Mr. & Mrs. Smith* (2005), another much better illustration of marital secrets and life contracts.

Erik Childress

CREDITS

Spencer Aimes: Ashton Kutcher
Jen Kornfeldt: Katherine Heigl
Vivian: Katheryn Winnick
Henry: Rob Riggle
Mac Bailey: Kevin Sussman
Mr. Kornfeldt: Tom Selleck
Mrs. Kornfeldt: Catherine O'Hara
Holbrook: Martin Mull
Mrs. Bailey: Alex Borstein
Origin: USA
Language: English
Released: 2010
Production: Jason Goldberg, Scott Aversano, Mike Karz, Ashton Kutcher; released by Lionsgate
Directed by: Robert Luketic
Written by: Ted Griffin, Bob DeRosa

Cinematography by: Russell Carpenter
Music by: Rolfe Kent
Sound: Michael Babcock
Editing: Mary Jo Markey
Costumes: Johanna Argan
Production Design: Missy Stewart
MPAA rating: PG-13
Running time: 100 minutes

REVIEWS

Abele, Robert. *Los Angeles Time.* June 4, 2010.
Anderson, John. *Newsday.* June 4, 2010.
Berkshire, Geoff. *Metromix.com.* June 4, 2010.
Catsoulis, Jeannette. *New York Times.* June 4, 2010.
Morris, Wesley. *Boston Globe.* June 4, 2010.
Nelson, Rob. *Variety.* June 4, 2010.
Phillips, Michael. *Chicago Tribune.* June 4, 2010.
Scheck, Frank. *Hollywood Reporter.* June 4, 2010.
Schwarzbaum, Lisa. *Entertainment Weekly.* June 4, 2010.
Sobczynski, Peter. *eFilmCritic.com.* June 4, 2010.

QUOTES

Spencer Aimes: "We've been married for three years and we've never been more than five minutes away from your parents. They're always coming over and your dad's all…all…well, uh, this is how the Kornfeldt's load the dishwasher. And, mow the lawn clockwise 'cause that's the Kornfeldt way. Take this piece of coal, stick it up your kiester, squeeze it real tight like we do, and you'll and make a Kornfeldt diamond."

TRIVIA

Ashton Kutcher accidentally knocked out a stunt man during filming.

AWARDS

Golden Raspberries 2010: Worst Actor (Kutcher).

THE KING'S SPEECH

When God couldn't save the King, the Queen turned to someone who could.
—Movie tagline

It takes leadership to confront a nation's fear. It takes friendship to conquer your own.
—Movie tagline

Box Office: $84 million

Tom Hooper's *The King's Speech* was one of the most beloved and lauded films of 2010, landing twelve Oscar® nominations on its way to what many assumed would be a win for Best Picture of the year. The film is best viewed and appreciated as an old-fashioned reminder of what people love about the movies as opposed to the more cynical, cerebral films that took off with critics in the same year like *Inception* (2010), *Black Swan* (2010), and *The Social Network* (2010). It is not meant as an insult to suggest that *The King's Speech* would not have been drastically different ten, twenty-five, or even fifty years ago. It is clearly conceived, designed, and executed as a throwback to the kinds of films that have won Oscars® for Best Pictures for the last century. It is a crowd-pleasing tale of a man swallowing his pride and asking for help to effectively rule a country in a time of crisis. The film came along at just the right time, tapping something in viewers that made it one of the most beloved works of the year. The fact that it was a little overrated in some circles will almost certainly be borne out by history but that can be left for time to tell.

David Seidler's acclaimed script opens with a speech by Prince Albert, Duke of York (Colin Firth) at the end of the Empire Exhibition at Wembley Stadium in 1934. With his halted, terrified stammering, it is instantly clear that the man will not be a popular, confident leader in the days of the new form of the wireless radio. The next scenes make clear that poor "Bertie" has dealt with a number of experts and physicians in an attempt to fix his stutter but has been greeted with ineffective advice like smoking to clear the lungs and trying to speak through a mouthful of marbles without choking to death. The Prince's wife Elizabeth (Helena Bonham Carter) tracks down a most-unusual specialist; an outgoing Australian actor named Lionel Logue (Geoffrey Rush) and convinces her husband to give him a shot. At first, Bertie's well-known short fuse and general frustration/embarrassment lead to little progress and some immature screaming. Logue is convinced that he can fix the Prince's stutter and impresses his new client and her wife by recording Albert on a record speaking *Hamlet* with fluid ease. Lessons begin and an unusual friendship even develops.

As the royal son is learning to use his diaphragm and bounce on to certain words in order to get them out, his monarchy is about to go through a tumultuous time. Bertie's father King George V (Michael Gambon) passes away and the crown gets passed down to the new King Edward VIII (Guy Pearce), a truly troubled soul who Seidler's film presents as a weak-willed man more interested in the love of a divorcee (Eve Best), a no-no according to the church, than leading his country in a time of impending war. (In fact, there were rumors that Edward VIII was sympathetic to Hitler, a fact that Seidler's script somewhat glides over on its way to getting Bertie in the big chair with less historical controversy.) King Edward VIII steps down and it is

time for King George VI to be crowned. Both the coronation and a speech on the eve of World War II would be major moments for the new King to show off his improved speech and lead the people as he was fated to do.

The King's Speech does nothing wrong. Some critics and awards group have mistaken doing nothing wrong for doing something spectacular. There is a fine difference. It is the difference between a good, crowd-pleasing film like *The King's Speech* and the ambitious works that truly stand the test of time and influence generations. It is hard to see Tom Hooper's film being influential in any way (other than perhaps in the way Oscar® campaigns are run and Oscar® bait is greenlit). While the confident production values and strong performances throughout *The King's Speech* are worthy of praise, it never transcends its old-fashioned sentimentality to become something more impressive. It is nothing that viewers have not seen before and it is surprisingly cold, a film that works in the crowd-pleasing instant but does not linger in the memory long after the credits roll. It is a good movie that some have mistaken for great.

The best thing about *The King's Speech* is the lead performance by the likable Colin Firth that is definitely Oscar® material (it is worth noting that the talented actor has delivered nomination-worthy performances two years in a row after his equally excellent work in *A Single Man* [2009]). Firth completely sells the complexities of a man forced to deal with a deeply personal issue in public. Lineage has placed this man in a position of power whether or not he ever had even the slightest desire to be there. As war approaches and it becomes clearer that the United Kingdom is going to need a royal leader to guide them through some dark times, Albert's more-confident brother fades into obscurity while the new King George steps up. He is simultaneously fearful and made confident by the important role he now realizes he must play. Firth is excellent in these complex moments of tentative leadership. And he has perfect chemistry with Geoffrey Rush, a fellow Oscar® nominee displaying his pitch-perfect comic timing. With limited screen time, Rush perfectly brings Logue to life, selling his familial warmth and creativity in ways that other actors may have ignored. Helena Bonham Carter was also nominated for an Oscar® but her work was a bit too understated for this critic. She is certainly not bad but does nothing that most actresses would not have done with the same role. The film is also nicely rounded out in terms of ensemble by an excellent cast in minor roles including Guy Pearce, Michael Gambon, Timothy Spall (doing a somewhat-overcooked Winston Churchill impression), and the ageless Derek Jacobi.

The technical elements are uniformly strong. Cinematography by Danny Cohen offers some unusual framing and angles to provide enough personality to keep *The King's Speech* from becoming a dry period piece visually. The great composer Alexandre Desplat landed a well-deserved fourth Oscar® nomination for his lovely score (and third in the last three years), although this critic would have preferred his more ambitious work from *The Ghost Writer* (2010) had gotten the nod. Art direction, editing, costume design—all of the behind-the-scenes elements were well-orchestrated by director Hooper, a filmmaker more well-known for his award-winning TV mini-series (*Elizabeth I* [2005], *John Adams* [2008]) before this film catapulted him into household name status and an Oscar® nomination for Best Director (he won the equivalent prize from the Directors Guild of America).

The King's Speech is an entertaining, well-made movie that deserves praise but the onslaught of awards attention at the beginning of 2011 shocked some critics who felt that there were more ambitious, impressive works released in the previous twelve months. It is certainly rare to see a movie that does nothing notably wrong, but merely doing nothing wrong should not be mistaken for doing something great. If a film is going to be crowned the best of the year, it should be a true leader, not merely a competent one.

Brian Tallerico

CREDITS

King George VI: Colin Firth
Lionel Logue: Geoffrey Rush
Queen Elizabeth: Helena Bonham Carter
Edward VIII: Guy Pearce
Dr. Cosmo Lang: Derek Jacobi
Winston Churchill: Timothy Spall
King George V: Michael Gambon
Myrtle Logue: Jennifer Ehle
Stanley Baldwin: Anthony Andrews
Wallis Simpson: Eve Best
Origin: United Kingdom
Language: English
Released: 2010
Production: Emile Sherman, Gareth Unwin, Iain Canning; Bedlam Production, See Saw Films, Aegis Film Fund, Weinstein Company, U.K. Film Council; released by Weinstein Company
Directed by: Tom Hooper
Written by: David Seidler
Cinematography by: Danny Cohen
Music by: Alexandre Desplat

Sound: Lee Walpole
Music Supervisor: Maggie Rodford
Editing: Tariq Anwar
Art Direction: Netty Chapman
Costumes: Jenny Beavan
Production Design: Eve Stewart
MPAA rating: R
Running time: 111 minutes

REVIEWS

Alter, Ethan. *Hollywood Reporter.* November 25, 2010.
Corliss, Richard. *TIME Magazine.* September 14, 2010.
Debruge, Peter. *Variety.* September 5, 2010.
Ebert, Roger. *Chicago Sun-Times.* December 16, 2010.
Kohn, Eric. *indieWIRE.* November 22, 2010.
Lane, Anthony. *New Yorker.* November 22, 2010.
Mondello, Bob. *NPR.* November 29, 2010.
Pais, Matt. *Metromix.com* December 16, 2010.
Rich, Katey. *CinemaBlend.com.* November 27, 2010.
Turan, Kenneth. *Los Angeles Times.* December 2, 2010.

QUOTES

King George VI: "If I am King, where is my power? Can I declare war? Form a government? Levy a tax? No! And yet I am the seat of all authority because they think that when I speak, I speak for them."

TRIVIA

Both Timothy Spall and Michael Gambon had previously portrayed the roles of Winston Churchill and King Edward VII respectively.

AWARDS

Oscars 2010: Actor (Firth), Director (Hooper), Film, Orig. Screenplay
British Acad. 2010: Actor (Firth), Film, Orig. Screenplay, Support. Actor (Rush), Support. Actress (Bonham Carter), Orig. Score, Alexander Korda Award
Directors Guild 2010: Director (Hooper)
Golden Globes 2011: Actor—Drama (Firth)
Ind. Spirit 2011: Foreign Film
Screen Actors Guild 2010: Actor (Firth), Cast
Nomination:
Oscars 2010: Art Dir./Set Dec., Cinematog., Costume Des., Film Editing, Sound, Support. Actor (Rush), Support. Actress (Bonham Carter), Orig. Score
British Acad. 2010: Cinematog., Costume Des., Director (Hooper), Film Editing, Makeup, Prod. Des., Sound
Golden Globes 2011: Director (Hooper), Film—Drama, Screenplay, Support. Actor (Rush), Support. Actress (Bonham Carter), Orig. Score
Screen Actors Guild 2010: Support. Actor (Rush), Support. Actress (Bonham Carter).

KISSES

Irishman Lance Daly's *Kisses* took a long trip to get to the United States from across the pond and, even after it did finally land stateside in July 2010 it could only muster a measly $80k, never playing wider than 11 screens. It is noble and impressive that the rising indie studio Oscilloscope could even get the film to American shores, but it is also odd that it did not catch on with a wider audience in much the way that another Irish import did just a few years earlier when the excellent *Once* (2007) made over $20 million internationally. Playing at festivals in the States as early as 2008, *Kisses* seemed primed to be the next word-of-mouth art house sensation but then it sat in the Atlantic pipeline for years and the foreign film market changed. The slide of the economy has impacted even the way films are brought overseas and even the most successful ones have a tough time making a profit after a studio factors in distribution and marketing costs. Companies are taking less risks in 2010 than they were in 2007 and, somehow, *Kisses* became seen as a risk. That was a mistake. This delightful, charming, enjoyable little gem should have found a larger audience and likely will on DVD (once again, thanks to Oscilloscope, one of the few companies that seem to be taking chances and finding success with films like *Howl* [2010], *The Exploding Girl* [2010], and *Exit Through the Gift Shop* [2010]). *Once* and *Kisses* have more in common than an accent. They are both films about everyday people and an uncommon relationship that sneaks up on the viewer with genuine heartfelt emotion.

The beating heart of *Kisses* lies in the performances of Shane Curry and Kelly O'Neill, giving two of the most genuine and believable child performances that have come out of any country in quite some time. One could argue that Curry and O'Neill are merely playing variations on themselves, but that does not lessen the power of what they accomplish here. It is not meant as a commentary on their range or future potential as actors but they are both brilliant here, conveying exactly the emotion and dreamlike wonder that the film needed to succeed. Curry and O'Neill play Dylan and Kylie, respectively, two kids living on the edge of middle-to-lower class Dublin. They are at that undefined age when childlike play still takes up a large portion of the day but also when real-life concerns have clearly become a part of their lives. They are also at that crucial age when a friendship between a boy and a girl often segues into something a bit more. It is not even well-defined beyond the fact that she has something of a crush on him and he feels a bit protective of her. Their story is not a typical childhood romance despite a title that may hint at such a film. In fact, it is a very atypical road movie.

The journey for Dylan and Kylie begins when the former decides that he has been threatened and hit by his father for the final time. There is one too many physical altercations and the headstrong young man packs up things and decides that the time has come to run away from home. Kylie also has the face and manner of a girl who has probably been toughened by childhood trauma and she wants to escape her domestic nightmare as much as the cute boy who lives down the street. When Dylan heads for Dublin, she tags along. The two sleep in the streets and have unpredictable encounters along the way to the big city.

A childhood road movie with romantic undertones surely sounds like the material of a bad Rob Reiner comedy (and perhaps the corny nature of the film's "pitch" scared off distributors from the true value of the movie) but the actual movie is not nearly as clichéd as it may sound in print. In one of director Lance Daly's more clever moves, *Kisses* starts in black-and-white and color slowly seeps into the picture as the pair get closer to Dublin. It is a small touch but a lovely one, almost like the two children are going over the rainbow. To children like Kylie and Dylan, Dublin probably does hold more excitement than Emerald City. Daly's film contains music by Bob Dylan, a surreal appearance by the excellent actor Stephen Rea, and some beautiful cinematography—all elements that help the movie rise above its potential coming-of-age treacle. But the most important element, besides the excellent child performances, is screenwriting that feels genuine instead of forced. The story of Dylan and Kylie should have been heard and seen by more theater goers in 2010 but films this good have a way of finding their audience. *Kisses* surely will.

Brian Tallerico

CREDITS

Kylie: Kelly O'Neill
Dylan: Shane Curry
Dylan's father: Paul Roe
Dylan's mother: Neili Conroy
Down Under Dylan: Stephen Rea
Origin: Ireland
Language: English
Released: 2008
Production: Macdara Kelleher; Fastnet Films; released by Oscilloscope Pictures, Inc.
Directed by: Lance Daly
Written by: Lance Daly
Cinematography by: Lance Daly
Music by: GoBlimpsGo
Sound: Robert Flanagan
Editing: J. Patrick Duffner
Art Direction: Andrew Manson
Costumes: Leonie Pendergast

Production Design: Waldemar Kalinowski
MPAA rating: Unrated
Running time: 76 minutes

REVIEWS

Bennett, Ray. *Hollywood Reporter.* July 19, 2010.
Cole, Stephen. *Globe and Mail.* November 12, 2010.
Holden, Stephen. *New York Times.* July 16, 2010.
Means, Sean. *Salt Lake Tribune.* October 9, 2010.
Parkinson, David. *Empire Magazine.* July 17, 2009.
Ramos, Steve. *Boxoffice Magazine.* July 16, 2010.
Schwarzbaum, Lisa. *Entertainment Weekly.* July 14, 2010.
Taylor, Ella. *Village Voice.* July 13, 2010.
Turan, Kenneth. *Los Angeles Times.* July 16, 2010.
Verniere, James. *Boston Herald.* August 5, 2010.

AWARDS

Nomination:

Ind. Spirit 2011: Foreign Film.

KNIGHT AND DAY

Box Office: $76 million

Knight and Day starts out with the simple idea of a woman getting taken for a long-and-convoluted ride by a rogue agent who may or may not be out of his mind. He uses her to smuggle something called a "zephyr" onto a plane and out of harm's way. He ends up on the plane with her and while she is in the bathroom freshening up, he kills virtually everyone else on-board who is trying to kill him (not just every passenger on this otherwise empty flight, but the pilots as well). Of course, he would not commit this act if he did not also know how to fly and land the plane as well, which he eventually does in Wichita, Kansas. He does this in such an easygoing and confident manner, the woman cannot help but feel simultaneously scared of and drawn to him and the audience feels the same.

The woman is June Havens (Cameron Diaz), an expert car restorer who is en route to retrieve a special auto part for a very special car. The man is Roy Miller (Tom Cruise) and he is simply trying to keep this "zephyr" out of the hands of government officials who might tamper with it in the wrong way. What is this "zephyr"? According to its inventor, scientist Simon Feck (Paul Dano), it is a source of energy as great as the sun and just as perpetual. Agent Fitzgerald (Peter Sarsgaard) would like nothing more than to retrieve and sell it.

The film works very well for the first hour or so, as Cruise and Diaz go from one dizzying action set piece to another. The screenplay, written by Patrick O'Neill, is careful not to tell us too much about Cruise's character, yet the movie makes a point of showing him getting lost in a video game and looking intently at rows of action fantasy figures, perhaps establishing that he might be living a fantasy of his own making. The verbal back-and-forth between Cruise and Diaz on the plane before the action starts is charming and pure Hollywood chemistry between two impossibly good looking people who often do more to please the eye than the intellect.

During that first hour, *Knight and Day* stays true to that aesthetic. It does not take itself too seriously and it is pretty much aware that its star power will carry it through its silly plot. James Mangold cuts the action sequences together in a confident and slick manner, utilizing the increasingly popular method of cutting the action quickly so as not to let the audience think too much about what just happened. Because Diaz spends much of the story drugged up on a serum, the story shifts from location to location without much logic, a frequently used plot device that actually works better than it should. Cruise is the most charming he has been in a long time and Diaz is considerably less annoying than usual. Up to a point, everything about this summertime popcorn trifle is done right.

But then about half-way through, something happens. The tone shifts a bit. The character of Roy Miller shows his other sides. He explains everything. The movie does likewise and suddenly, it all stops being fun. O'Neill's screenplay actually follows through on the plot of the zephyr instead of whether or not Cruise's character may be something of a mentally unfit loose cannon. What could have been (and almost was) an interesting action film and character study about a straight woman trying to reason with a delusional oddball is instead a standard *Charade* (1963) wannabe that plays more to its weaknesses than its strengths.

The tonal shift in the film's second act is what ultimately bogs the film down. Director Mangold—who proved he could do a strong character study with *Walk the Line* (2005) and a solid action Western with *3:10 to Yuma* (2007)—tries mightily to regain the momentum of the film's first half by going back to the outrageous action sequences (a later one involving a running of the bulls in Spain) and also trying to sell the audience on Roy Miller's mental state. Furthermore, Diaz's character comes off as inconsistent and after a while, she becomes merely a plot device that has her acting in a way that the screenplay demands in order to move the film forward. The movie becomes too serious for all the wrong reasons.

It is certainly not the cast's fault, although Sarsgaard and Viola Davis (who plays the CIA director) certainly deserved better roles. It is also not clear if the screenplay had one kind of aspiration that the final movie failed to live up to, especially since the movie seems so confident in itself every step of the way. At its best, *Knight and Day* feels as breezy and alluring as the tropical island where these two characters end up more than once. At its worst, it is simply too forgetful and schizophrenic. There are certainly worse kinds of summertime escapist films and the fact that this one works as much as it does is certainly more than could be said for the similarly executed *Killers* (2010), which came out a few weeks prior, or *The Bounty Hunter* (2010) a few months before that. Saying it is better than those two films may seem like faint praise, but if all three were watched in one sitting, *Knight and Day* would come out looking like *North By Northwest* in comparison.

Collin Souter

CREDITS

June Havens: Cameron Diaz
Roy Miller: Tom Cruise
Fitzgerald: Peter Sarsgaard
April Havens: Maggie Grace
Antonio: Jordi Molla
Director George: Viola Davis
Simon Feck: Paul Dano
Rodney: Marc Blucas
Molly: Celia Weston
Frank: Dale Dye
Origin: USA
Language: English
Released: 2010
Production: Todd Garner, Cathy Konrad, Steve Pink, Joe Roth; New Regency Pictures, Regency Enterprises, Pink Machine, Wintergreen Productions, Tree Line Films; released by 20th Century Fox

Directed by: James Mangold
Written by: Patrick O'Neill
Cinematography by: Phedon Papamichael
Music by: John Powell
Sound: Lee Orloff, Paul Massey, David Giammarco
Editing: Michael McCusker, Quincy Z. Gunderson
Art Direction: Gregory A. Berry
Costumes: Arianne Phillips
Production Design: Andrew Menzies
MPAA rating: PG-13
Running time: 109 minutes

REVIEWS

Burr, Ty. *Boston Globe.* June 22, 2010.
Cabin, Chris. *Filmcritic.com.* June 24, 2010.
Childress, Erik. *eFilmcritic.com.* June 23, 2010.
Covert, Colin. *Minneapolis Star Tribune.* June 23, 2010.
Ebert, Roger. *Chicago Sun-Times.* June 22, 2010.
O'Hehir, Andrew. *Salon.com.* June 23, 2010.
Phillips, Michael. *Chicago Tribune.* June 22, 2010.
Pols, Mary F. *Time Magazine.* June 25, 2010.
Tobias, Scott. *AV Club.* June 22, 2010.
Turan, Kenneth. *Los Angeles Times.* June 22, 2010.

QUOTES

Milner: "They'll tell you I'm mentally unstable and violent and dangerous and it will all sound very convincing."

TRIVIA

Actress Celia Weston plays the mother of Tom Cruise's character despite being only ten years older than him in real life.

L

THE LAST AIRBENDER

Four nations, one destiny.
—Movie tagline

Box Office: $132 million

The Last Airbender is not merely bad or boring but offensive. The film is so badly written and so badly cast that even special effects sequences (which are awkwardly shoe-horned in left and right) have no real impact. Viewers might just as well pick up a kaleidoscope to obtain the same sort of experience, except that it would be important to imagine a really annoying group of people constantly interrupting the jumbled display of colors.

Better yet, viewers could pick up the excellent animated series that M. Night Shyamalan's summer blockbuster is based on and discover the central and most obvious flaw. This film adaptation departs from the original (always a risky move creatively—especially when the original is much loved and quite well done) for no good reason, bearing the unmistakable marks of a director who, of late, has needed more creative input from others. Ponderously self-important, boring, nonsensical; all of these are fair descriptions of *The Last Airbender*. But after the somewhat likable-yet-muddled *Lady in the Water* (2006) and the complete debacle that was *The Happening* (2008), it becomes tempting to use another adjective in describing this latest effort: arrogant. This is a movie that plays exactly as if someone said, "I know better than you what you will like. Watch this, because I said so."

The four kingdoms of the world are each ordered around the element that those of that kingdom are adept at manipulating. Holding them in balance is the Avatar, a being whose special link to the world of the spirit has given him the ability to master all of the elements. But one hundred years ago, the Avatar, a young man named Aang, disappeared, leaving the nations to themselves, and the hostile fire nation decided to seize the opportunity to conquer the others, imprisoning all who can manipulate the other elements.

When Katara (Nicola Peltz) and Sokka (Jackson Rathbone), members of a Southern Water Tribe, discover a young boy imprisoned in a massive underground ice prison they help free him and discover he is Aang (Noah Ringer), last of the Air Benders and destined to become the Avatar. Swearing to protect him, they embark on a dangerous journey to the other kingdoms to help him master the remaining elements and assume his rightful place. Pursued by the Fire Nation, led by the Fire Lord Ozai (Cliff Curtis), his exiled son Prince Zuko (Dev Patel), and Commander Zhao (Aasif Mandvi), the trio have little time and little chance, but no choice but to fight for the restoration of balance among the elements.

Except for the lead, young newcomer Noah Ringer, this is a horribly miscast film. Part of the problem is that Shyamalan has taken on source material that features Asians and Native Americans and chosen to ignore the question of race altogether. If *The Last Airbender* were anymore culturally diverse it would feature a race of space aliens. The point is that, as great as it is to promote the idea of cultural diversity, it is best done by actually representing cultures rather than simply having skin types onscreen. Viewers do not get much of a sense of identity for any of the tribes. The three good guy tribes and the bad guy tribes are presented in the simplest of visual terms for no particular reason other than being badly cast that way. This is what makes Shyamalan vulnerable to critics that have cried "racist" although there is clearly no racist intent on his part.

It should also be noted that other than Ringer, who is blessed with a certain physical grace and a likable-if-simplistic natural screen presence, Shyamalan wastes the considerable talent at his disposal. Dev Patel, best known for his dynamic turn in *Slumdog Millionaire* (2008) seems trapped by the demands of a character whose constant rage requires all the range of a painting, as do his older costars Aasif Mandvi (*The Proposal* [2009]) and Cliff Curtis (*Whale Rider* [2002], *Sunshine* [2007]). The less said about Jackson Rathbone the better. He is a good actor. A better representation of his abilities can be found in the low-budget horror film *Dread* (2009). But his performance here is teeth-gratingly bad, a fact that is exacerbated by writing that limits him to exclamations, exposition, and cheesy bits of comic business.

M. Night Shyamalan has three absolutely masterful films under his belt. *The Sixth Sense* (1999), *Unbreakable* (2000), and *The Village* (2004). It is less a question of whether or not he is a gifted filmmaker than what exactly has gotten in the way of his making the most of his obvious gifts. Cynics have long ago written him off as the purveyor of second rate *Twilight Zone* style twist-ending storytelling but his feel for composition, his use of color, and his obvious ability to draw viewers in to the emotional lives of his characters leaves hope that he will get back to the business of telling good stories soon.

It is sad to say that Shyamalan evinces none of those qualities here, imbuing the action sequences in his first action film with a leaden quality that never provokes wonder and feels cribbed from better sources and cramped all the way through. Moments hint at what could have been. The escape from the Fire Nation ship in the beginning of the film is reasonably well done. The scenery is generally spectacular and the many supernatural creatures are brought to life beautifully but none of it gels into a single solid scene. Lastly, the post-production 3D effects are so murky they render the film virtually unwatchable. This film is offensive not just because it is bad but because it seems almost arrogantly so. It is difficult to place blame for this at the feet of anyone but the director.

At their best, anime and manga storytelling forms embrace a sort of wide-eyed innocence and an energy that can captivate viewers open to simple play. But *The Last Airbender* is adaptation at its worst, draining the life out of or outright ignoring what originally gave it to the thing being adapted in favor of that which at best reflects the vision of a misguided creative visionary pandering to the basest instincts that commercial cinema can embrace.

Bring on the fast food and cheap toys, quick, before any wonder seeps into young hearts.

Dave Canfield

CREDITS

Aang: Noah Ringer
Katara: Nicola Peltz
Sokka: Jackson Rathbone
Prince Zuko: Dev Patel
Commander Zhao: Aasif Mandvi
Firelord Ozai: Cliff Curtis
Uncle Iroh: Shaun Toub
Old Man: Randall Duk Kim
Princess Yue: Seychelle Gabriel
Origin: USA
Language: English
Released: 2010
Production: Scott Aversano, Sam Mercer, M. Night Shyamalan, Frank Marshall; Nickelodeon Movies, Blinding Edge Pictures, Kennedy/Marshall; released by Paramount Pictures
Directed by: M. Night Shyamalan
Written by: M. Night Shyamalan
Cinematography by: Andrew Lesnie
Music by: James Newton Howard
Sound: Chris Munro
Editing: Conrad Buff
Art Direction: Richard Johnson
Costumes: Judianna Makovsky
Production Design: Philip Messina
MPAA rating: PG
Running time: 103 minutes

REVIEWS

Biodrowski, Steve. *Cinefastastique.* July 3, 2010.
Corliss, Richard. *TIME Magazine.* July 2, 2010.
Debruge, Peter. *Variety.* June 30, 2010.
Ebert, Roger. *Chicago Sun-Times.* June 30, 2010.
Lasalle, Mick. *San Francisco Chronicle.* July 2, 2010.
McWeeny, Drew. *HitFix.* July, 1, 2010.
Orr, Christopher. *The Atlantic.* July 2, 2010.
Scott, A.O.. *New York Times.* June 30, 2010.
Sorrento, Matthew. *Bright Lights Film Journal.* July 2, 2010.
Turan, Kenneth. *Los Angeles Times.* July 1, 2010.

QUOTES

Uncle Iroh: "There are reasons each of us are born. We have to find those reasons."

TRIVIA

The film is an adaptation of the animated series *Avatar: The Last Airbender*. The filmmakers opted to drop the word

'Avatar' from the title to avoid confusion with James Cameron's 2009 film *Avatar*.

AWARDS

Golden Raspberries 2010: Worst Picture, Worst Support. Actor (Rathbone), Worst Director (Shyamalan), Worst Screenplay, Worst Use of 3D

Nomination:

Golden Raspberries 2010: Worst Support. Actor (Patel), Worst Support. Actress (Peltz), Worst Couple/Ensemble (Cast), Worst Sequel/Prequel.

THE LAST EXORCISM

Believe in him.
    —Movie tagline

Box Office: $41 Million

The Last Exorcism takes advantage of one of the horror genres most enduring and effective scenarios: that of the skeptic plunged into the very real possibility of the supernatural, thus invoking a wide array of quality horror cinema including *Night of the Demon* aka *Curse of the Demon* (1957), *The Haunting* (1963), *The Blair Witch Project* (1999), and *Drag Me to Hell* (2009). Good performances and some chilling atmosphere will be enough to save it for most horror fans or those already geared to explore the relationship of horror and religion but the film is liable to have a hard time converting skeptics due to an ending that many found forced and a sometimes-meandering storyline.

A crisis of faith and of conscience has led Reverend Cotton Marcus (Patrick Fabian) to stop performing the exorcisms that have helped him earn a living in and around the bayous of Baton Rouge, Louisiana. Unsure of how he will support his wife and son once he moves away from the church, he agrees to perform one last exorcism with a documentary crew in tow, exposing the behind-the-scenes bag of tricks he long ago adopted as tools of his trade.

Choosing a request at random from a pile of letters, Rev. Marcus, together with documentary producer/director Iris Reisen (Iris Bahr) and cameraman Dave Moskowitz (Adam Grimes), travel to the Sweetzer farm where Louis Sweetzer (Louis Herthum), a middle-aged widower with two children, Caleb (Caleb Landry Jones) and Nell (Ashley Bell), claims to need an exorcism for his daughter.

The Last Exorcism sets up its characters well, especially Rev. Marcus who comes across as a man in a complex state, deeply at odds with the chicanery that has supported him thus far while at the same time able

to engage in a disturbing degree of self deception in order to put food on the table. At one point he brags that if he wanted to he could preach a recipe for banana bread and that nobody in his holy rolling congregation would notice. He proceeds to do just that which is, of course, pretty amusing to behold, but is also mixed into a film where Cotton rationalizes about the possibility that he somehow does his exorcism clients some psychological good.

The Last Exorcism does one of its neatest tricks in following Marcus through the process of planting hidden speakers in Nell's bedroom, and preparing other props designed to fool customers into believing they are witnessing actual casting out of demons. A trick crucifix emits smoke, demons wail on cue and the bed shakes. Most importantly, Rev. Marcus will get paid after the show. That show, at the expense of the Sweetzer family is indeed a good one and the film is careful not to mock the Sweetzers and their beliefs, setting Louis up, at least initially, as a stern-but-loving and reasonably intelligent man, who is simply at his wit's end in trying to deal with his daughter's mysterious condition.

Patrick Fabian is very good as Rev. Cotton Marcus, straddling the line between spiritual cynicism and the desire to still do some good in this world while he sorts out what he truly believes, managing to make Cotton likable and trustworthy even as he reveals his own dark secrets and flaws. As for the possibly possessed Nell Sweetzer, comparisons here to the title character from *The Exorcism of Emily Rose* (2005) are absolutely fair but do little to tarnish Bell's dynamic performance which moves from wide-eyed innocence to catatonia to malevolent fury throughout *The Last Exorcism* and which is shot entirely with handheld cameras with no special effects to augment it. Her transformation is, if anything, even more startling and disturbing in that the audience remains in doubt for the vast majority of the film about the exact nature of her plight.

At first it appears as if the ritual has worked. The team leaves the farm with Nell's state seemingly much improved. But later that night she unexpectedly appears in Marcus' hotel room. What *The Last Exorcism* does next is so truly unsettling precisely because it is so ambiguous. There are horrific encounters with Louis who may or may not be abusing Nell. Caleb's face is slashed. Until the end, Nell herself never seems to quite cross the line over into what cannot be explained away via mental illness or some abuse syndrome. In short, *The Last Exorcism* finds its idea of horror as something that can take place in the world whether Nell is possessed or not. In either case, evil is something that cannot be understood or reasoned with, or scared away through fake exorcisms.

The ending of *The Last Exorcism* was controversial for most audiences. At one point, Marcus and the team find a series of disturbing artworks by Nell. This old convention has been used in a variety of horror films in a myriad of ways over the years. Here the artwork seems designed to specify the manner in which each character will meet their end. Such a device when used well, as newcomer director Daniel Stamm does here, will make its import felt most keenly precisely when it will have the most impact. By carefully staging and pacing his film's violent moments, Stamm reinforces not only the danger his characters are in through the use of this device but the idea that they might still have some control over their own destiny. The picture implicating Rev. Marcus shows him walking towards a large fire arms outstretched. Is he being swallowed up by an angry God having offered too little repentance too late? Devoured by the devil? The ambiguity of Cotton Marcus' situation is compelling, especially since he is now revisiting his faith, determined to face the evil on its own terms. When this actually happens in the film it is clunky, but many viewers will find it oddly moving and, thought about on its own terms for any length of time, alternately uplifting and deeply disturbing. Either way, the film is must-see viewing for anyone interested in the mix of horror and religion.

Dave Canfield

CREDITS

Cotton Marcus: Patrick Fabian
Louis Sweetzer: Louis Herthum
Iris Reisen: Iris Bahr
Nell Sweetzer: Ashley Bell
Gerald: Tony Bentley
Dave Moskowitz: Adam Grimes
Caleb Sweetzer: Caleb Landry Jones
Origin: USA
Language: English
Released: 2010
Production: Marc Abraham, Thomas A. Bliss, Eli Roth, Eric Newman, Thomas A. Bliss; Studio Canal, Strike Entertainment, Louisiana Media Productions, Arcade Pictures; released by Lionsgate
Directed by: Daniel Stamm
Written by: Huck Botko, Andrew Gurland
Cinematography by: Zoltan Honti
Music by: Nathan Barr
Sound: Michael Baird, B.J. Lehn
Editing: Shilpa Khanna
Costumes: Shauna Leone
Production Design: Andrew Bofinger

MPAA rating: PG-13
Running time: 90 minutes

REVIEWS

Anderson, John. *Variety.* June 25, 2010.
Fuchs, Cynthia. *PopMatters.* September 5, 2010.
Gingold, Michael. *Fangoria.* August 3, 2010.
Hartlaub, Peter. *San Francisco Chronicle.* August 27, 2010.
McDonagh, Maitland. *Miss FlickChick.* September 19, 2010.
McWeeney, Drew. *HitFix.* August 27, 2010.
Neumaier, Joe. *New York Daily News.* August 26, 2010.
Newman, Kim. *Empire Magazine.* September 1, 2010.
Puig, Claudia. *USA Today.* August 26, 2010.
Punter, Jennie. *Globe and Mail.* August 27, 2010.

QUOTES

Cotton Marcus: "Is that regular water?"

TRIVIA

No special effects were used when Ashley Bell wildly contorted her body. She did them on her own as she has hypermobility.

The movie was shipped to theaters under the code name "Scrutiny."

AWARDS

Nomination:

Ind. Spirit 2011: First Feature, Support. Actress (Bell).

THE LAST SONG

Do you ever really forget your first heartbreak?
—Movie tagline

A story about family, first loves, second chances and the moments of life that lead you back home.
—Movie tagline

Box Office: $62 Million

As the newly hatched sea turtles scramble for the safety of saltwater in *The Last Song,* is that a look of confused indecision one detects on their faces? Surely no one could blame them for wondering which way to go, what with the ocean in one direction and a tear-soaked saga transpiring back up the dunes. *The Last Song* is yet another lachrymose story of love from Nicholas Sparks, whose bittersweet bestsellers are as sure to cause crying as any onion. Some say they also stink about as much, especially (but by no means exclusively) males who tend to find the proceedings to be nauseatingly-maudlin mush. Never mind that every new work that emanates from Sparks is so undeniably reminiscent of all the old ones. Apparently some people appreciate such formulaic familiarity, finding comfort in knowing upfront that the basic blueprint they responded to so positively in the past has been utilized once again. With tissues at the ready, they proceed to swallow the soggy sameness with enthusiastic, emotion-choked gulps.

That two Sparks films were released in quick succession during early 2010 did nothing to dissipate the cumulative mustiness. Worse still, striking similarities between the relatively superior *Dear John* (2010) and *The Last Song* helped make things seem even more rehashed than usual. For example, a young couple first connects on the beach in both films. Problematic relationships between parents and their offspring figure prominently in the two productions. The reading-aloud in voiceover of letters aims mightily in both to extract dew from one's tear ducts. There are also other parallels, including, as with every story from Sparks, the necessity for a hearse to be standing by. In short, *The Last Song* seemed like a warmed-over second helping of fare that, at least to some, seemed pretty stale to begin with.

In an attempt to stretch her talents and push her career beyond the borders of tween-favorite Hannah Montana, seventeen-year-old Miley Cyrus' handlers felt that the time was now ripe for her to hit a wider range of notes in *The Last Song*. As Ronnie, a twice-arrested, potently sullen, piano prodigy goth girl, Cyrus largely skims the surface of the role like a stone tossed upon the film's strikingly photographed seascapes. She succeeds in doing a great deal of eyebrow and lip acting, scowling and sneering her way through it all to such an extent that premature lines may result which will ultimately be helpful in her transition to more mature roles.

As Ronnie and her younger brother, Jonah (a quirky Bobby Coleman), journey from the Big Apple to the Peach State with their soon-to-remarry mom (Kelly Preston), they traverse a lengthy bridge that soon seems symbolic of reconciliation needed within the family. There is, after all, a particularly sizeable schism between the teenager and her father, Steve (Greg Kinnear), whom she is grudgingly going to stay with at the shore for the summer. It is since the patriarch ditched his family to pursue a career of classical composing for the piano that his resentful daughter's life has run aground. Ronnie is now churlishly smart-of-mouth but no longer fleet-of-finger, obstinately refusing to play. She has gone so far as to turn down an offer from prestigious Juilliard to spite the dad who deserted them. This similarly talented man with whom, one surmises, Ronnie might otherwise be as close as keys A and B, aims to change her mind, and will patiently endure her petulance to do so.

Ronnie may be decidedly hard on her dad, but she quickly develops a soft spot for the aforementioned baby turtles prior to their hatching, resolutely watching over them as a salivating raccoon tenaciously lurks nearby. She is joined in her efforts by towering, sun-kissed beach volleyballer/aquarium volunteer Will (Liam Hemsworth), with whom she is quite cold upon meeting. Of course, Ronnie soon melts as Will is revealed to be a hunk with a heart. While keeping an eye on the eggs, Ronnie and Will also furtively eye each other, and her steadfastly sour puss becomes plastered with an adoring smile. She emerges from her crusty shell, no longer so akin to a turtle of the snapping variety. Sure Ronnie still says, "I hate you" to her father, but now the edge has been sanded off those words by an accompanying, warm grin.

Miley's minions will, of course, be most concerned with the young lovers' prospects for happiness, which, like the tides, rise and fall both repetitively and predictably. However, of all the film's ups and downs, the one most likely to move everyone to at least some degree is when Steve slumps to the sand, a heretofore secret-sufferer of terminal cancer. Before the character's demise in Sparks' latest sappy snuff film, Kinnear delivers an authentic, graceful portrayal of a guilt-ridden man out to not only mend figurative fences with his children but also restore a stained glass window to the local church he mistakenly believes he burned to the ground. (Will ends up not only possessing sinew that has a profound effect upon Ronnie but also secrets that clear up the latter matter.) Coleman's Jonah is also affecting when beside himself over his father's impending inexorable demise. With its unified fragments of glass, the window is obviously a symbolic representation of both the reintegration of a shattered man and his reconnection with his family members. When light shines through the finished product at Steve's funeral, Ronnie responds with a tender, "Hi Daddy!" Those watching will either sob or scoff.

Made on a budget of $20 million, *The Last Song* was propelled by Hannah Montana fans and Sparks devotees toward a gross of $62.9 million despite predominantly negative reviews. Sparks' films featuring longer-in-the-tooth lovers have not done as well as ones like this with fresher faces, which is why *True Believer* starring Zach Efron will be next to gush down the pipeline, the sixth cinematic adaptation of the author's fifteen books with still more of both reportedly on the way.

David L. Boxerbaum

CREDITS

Veronica Miller: Miley Cyrus
Steve Miller: Greg Kinnear
Will Blakelee: Liam Hemsworth

Tom Blakelee: Nick Searcy
Kim Miller: Kelly Preston
Jonah Miller: Bobby Coleman
Scott: Hallock Beals
Origin: USA
Language: English
Released: 2010
Production: Jennifer Gibgot, Adam Shankman; Offspring Entertainment, Touchstone Pictures; released by Walt Disney Pictures
Directed by: Julie Anne Robinson
Written by: Nicholas Sparks, Jeff Van Wie
Cinematography by: John Lindley
Music by: Aaron Zigman
Sound: Jonathan S. Gaynor, Randle Akerson
Music Supervisor: Buck Damon
Editing: Nancy Richardson
Art Direction: Scott A. Meehan
Costumes: Louise Frogley
Production Design: Nelson Coates
MPAA rating: PG
Running time: 107 minutes

REVIEWS

Anderson, Melissa. *Village Voice.* March 31, 2010.
Brody, Richard. *New Yorker.* April 12, 2010.
Morgenstern, Joe. *Wall Street Journal.* April 2, 2010.
Morris, Wesley. *Boston Globe.* March 31, 2010.
Nelson, Rob. *Variety.* April 5, 2010.
Newman, Kim. *Sight & Sound.* June 2010.
Schwarzbaum, Lisa. *Entertainment Weekly.* April 9, 2010.
Scott, A.O.. *New York Times.* March 31, 2010.
Sealy, Shirley. *Film Journal International.* May 2010.
Vilkomerson, Sara. *People.* April 12, 2010.

QUOTES

Steve Miller: "Love is fragile. And we're not always its best caretakers. We just muddle through and do the best we can. And hope this fragile thing survives against all odds."

Kim: "We're not perfect. Any of us. We make mistakes, we screw up but then we forgive and move forward."

Steve Miller: "Sometimes you have to be apart from the people you love, but that doesn't make you love them any less. Sometimes it makes you love them more."

TRIVIA

Miley Cyrus and Liam Hemsworth began their widely publicized relationship together while the film was in production.

AWARDS

Nomination:

Golden Raspberries 2010: Worst Actress (Cyrus).

LEAP YEAR

Anna planned to propose to her boyfriend on February 29th. This is not her boyfriend.
—Movie tagline

Box Office: $25 million

The first major movie of 2009 was *Bride Wars*, a terrible comedy that made its female characters look like marriage-obsessed idiots. In 2010, the first major movie released was *Leap Year,* a comedy that made its similarly marriage-obsessed female protagonist look nearly as foolish. Perhaps one day someone will do a study evaluating the correlation between these films and people who spend the first week of the year swearing off marriage forever.

This is not hyperbole as much as an irritated curiosity that results from watching the pathetic romantic comedy *Leap Year,* which does nothing but humiliate its heroine until the film's premise itself has been proven completely absurd. The plot, which would have been insensitive to women fifty years ago, revolves around Anna (Amy Adams), a high-strung Boston native who specializes in staging apartments for realtors to make the units more attractive to potential buyers. "Most people don't know what they want until I show it to them," says Anna, a control freak with more than a streak of entitlement. For four years Anna has been dating Jeremy (Adam Scott), a cardiologist who is introduced and dismissed in a way that asserts he is not a character worth knowing. When, to Anna's surprise, the special dinner Jeremy planned features earrings, not an engagement ring, Anna decides to take matters into her own hands. Jeremy is heading to a medical conference in Dublin, Ireland, where apparently a centuries-old tradition dictates that every four years, on Leap Day, women are permitted to propose to their boyfriends. Conveniently, February 29th is only a few days away, so Anna hops on a plane to take advantage of the tradition—which her dad Jack (John Lithgow) claims brought together Anna's grandma and grandpa—and turn her boyfriend into a fiancé.

Any impetuous romantic spirit that is supposed to result from Anna's quest is tarnished by the sheer sexism implied in the situation. For starters, the dynamic between Anna and Jeremy plays on gender stereotypes suggesting that men are distant and afraid of commitment and women are pushy and desperate to settle down. Worse, Anna's excitement over the Irish tradition implies that she would not be able to propose to Jeremy at any other time or in any other place. Certainly a woman proposing to her boyfriend is not the norm. That does not make it wrong. What is wrong is that the entire concept of *Leap Year* hinges on its otherwise intelligent, professional main character dropping everything and booking an international trip just for the tiny window of opportunity to foster an engagement faster than she believes her boyfriend wants it.

Of course, based on the way the film pushes Jeremy aside, it is clear that Anna will soon have another romantic option. That comes in the form of Declan (Matthew Goode), a bartender and innkeeper in Dingle, Ireland, where Anna winds up after her flight to Dublin makes an emergency stop in Wales. (And after Anna hires a tiny fisherman's boat to take her the rest of the way, but only makes it to Dingle due to terrible storms.) During these travels, Anna seems less concerned for her own life than the prospect that her marriage proposal plans will be thwarted. Curious priorities, to say the least.

It is no big surprise how things play out. Anna hires Declan to drive her to Dublin. Declan constantly gives Anna a hard time. Anna suffers an endless array of emotional and physical embarrassment, including blowing out the power in Declan's inn, stepping in cow dung while wearing $600 shoes and, after accidentally pushing Declan's car down a hill and into a lake, naively trying to hitchhike with the first van she sees, only to have her expensive Louis Vuitton luggage stolen. These ordeals do not result in any laughs, nor do they make Anna and Declan particularly endearing. The scenes simply degrade Anna while Declan either gets angry at the impact on him or chuckles at the misfortune caused to his traveling companion.

Needless to say, the bitter banter between the two is meant to be a throwback to screwball comedies of the 1930s and 1940s, in which a man and woman appeared to hate each other all the way up until the time when they realize they are in love. The problem with *Leap Year* is that it thinks resentment and attitude are enough to make this approach charming. They are not. A film like this needs wit and pep between its two mismatched potential lovebirds, but Declan calling Anna's plan to propose "a load of poo" is far from clever. These two snipe at each other to no great impact or amusement. Rather, their rapport proves only that they get on each other's nerves, not that there is some dormant romantic connection waiting to come alive when Anna realizes Declan is actually charming and sweet—whereas Jeremy is distracted and uninterested in settling down.

Goode, so good in films like *Match Point* (2005) and *The Lookout* (2007), fails to give Declan enough charisma to match his smugness. Adams, meanwhile, who by the release of *Leap Year* had already begun whittling away at her unofficial "America's Next Sweetheart" title with a shrill turn in *Julie and Julia* (2009), has no chance of providing enough sweetness to balance out Anna's erratic need to get engaged. As she is flying on the plane originally meant for Dublin, she tries to calm herself during major turbulence by screaming, "I'm getting engaged! I'm getting engaged! I'm not going to die without getting engaged!" That is not appealing, just sad. Not because she is excited at the possibility of becoming engaged; it is because she is fixated on the title, not the guy in position to earn it.

Yes, *Leap Year* has echoes of, to name just one, the romantic comedy *Forces of Nature* (1999), but originality is not its problem. *Leap Year* simply never turns its tale of one woman's frantic grasp for a new marital status into a sincere love story. It is far more preoccupied with populating the film with Irish stereotypes and multiple situations for a senseless American woman like Anna to misunderstand Irish culture and mispronounce Irish names. This type of shallow, insulting attempt at humor is nothing new for the screenwriting team of Deborah Kaplan and Harry Elfont, who, among other travesties, wrote *Made of Honor* (2008), an awful romantic comedy that tried to draw humor from Scottish stereotypes. But just because *Leap Year* is more of the same does not make the film or its perspective on gender and romance any easier to swallow.

Matt Pais

CREDITS

Anna: Amy Adams
Declan: Matthew Goode
Jeremy: Adam Scott
Jack: John Lithgow
Libby: Kaitlin Olson
Origin: USA
Language: English
Released: 2010
Production: Gary Barber, Jake Weiner, Roger Birnbaum, Jonathan Glickman, Chris Bender; Benderspink, Spyglass Entertainment; released by Universal Pictures
Directed by: Anand Tucker
Written by: Harry Elfont, Deborah Kaplan
Cinematography by: Newton Thomas Sigel
Music by: Randy Edelman
Sound: Leslie Shatz, Gabriel J. Serrano
Music Supervisor: Ian Neil
Editing: Nick Moore
Costumes: Eimer Ni Mhaoldomhnaigh
Production Design: Mark Geraghty
MPAA rating: PG
Running time: 100 minutes

REVIEWS

Ebert, Roger. *Chicago Sun-Times.* January 6, 2010.
Goodykoontz, Bill. *Arizona Republic.* January 6, 2010.

Lumenick, Lou. *New York Post.* January 8, 2010.
Morris, Wesley. *Boston Globe.* January 8, 2010.
Ogle, Connie. *Miami Herald.* January 8, 2010.
Phillips, Michael. *Chicago Tribune.* January 7, 2010.
Rabin, Nathan. *AV Club.* January 7, 2010.
Savlov, Marc. *Austin Chronicle.* January 8, 2010.
Scott, A.O. *New York Times.* January 8, 2010.
Weitzman, Elizabeth. *New York Daily News.* January 7, 2010.

QUOTES

Anna: "What are you, the Lucky Charms leprechaun?"

TRIVIA

The number listed for Anna's social security on her apartment
application is 987-6543-20.

LEAVES OF GRASS

Edward Norton gives his all to a challenging dual
role, but Tim Blake Nelson's *Leaves of Grass* fails to rise
to the black comedy ranks of which it clearly aspires. As
Joel and Ethan Coen have become increasingly acclaimed
they have also become increasingly influential with
darkly humane comedies like *Don McKay* (2010) and
Down Terrace (2010) attempting that daring balance of
illegal behavior and likable characters such as what the
Coens found in gems like *Raising Arizona* (1987) and
Fargo (1996). Nelson's *Leaves of Grass* wears its Coen
brothers inspiration like a badge, playing with the
awkward silences and unusual characters in the way that
it believes the Coens would have done were they given
the same source material with which to play. While
imitation may be the sincerest form of flattery, there is a
reason that the Coens have reached the peak of acclaim
that has garnered them so many awards—what they do
is nowhere near as easy as it looks. Imagining Edward
Norton in an actual Coen film can lead a movie fan's
imagination to spin with glee, but Nelson cannot find
the right balance between the dark and the light; the
comedy and the plot. He loses his way by forgetting
that quirky characters cannot exist merely for the sake of
quirk and that they need to also be believable, likable,
and, most of all, interesting.

Bill Kincaid (Norton) is the most popular professor
at Brown University. When he is not spouting his
philosophical theories from the front of a classroom, he
is being wooed by both horny co-eds and Harvard
University, representatives of which offer him not only
full-time employment but also the chance to essentially
found his own institute. Bill is a popular guy. So is his
brother Brady (also Norton), but for very different
reasons. Brady heads a very impressive marijuana operation, loves his black lights, and stays in touch with the
Kincaid matriarch (the required casting when it comes
to aging hippie naturally played by Susan Sarandon)
that Bill discarded with his Oklahoma accent.

The two brothers are reunited (and the film springs
to life for at least a reel) due to a plan on Brady's part to
take advantage of the fact that he is identical to his
intellectual sibling. Brady's partner (Tim Blake Nelson)
calls Bill and tells him that he has been murdered by
crossbow, something that is apparently more common in
the South than one might believe. The lie tricks Bill
back to his Oklahoma home and into the machinations
of a complex plot involving a nefarious Tulsa drug lord
(played by, of all people, Richard Dreyfuss, who falls
completely flat in the film's worst scene, one from which
the film never really recovers). It is actually a relatively
clever plot in that Brady needs an alibi. Who better to
provide it than the identical twin that his entire
hometown seems to have forgotten exists? Of course,
there is no movie unless the best laid plans fall flat, and
a movie like *Leaves of Grass* rarely comes together
without a love interest, so it is unsurprising when the
lovely Keri Russell pops up as, of course, a local high
school English teacher with excellent chemistry with the
smarter Kincaid.

Debuting in 2009 at the Toronto Film Festival,
Leaves of Grass struggled to find distribution and a solid
release date, never getting a wide release and grossing
less than $70,000 during a very limited release. The film
has some deep structural flaws but the shame of the
whole endeavor is that it also features excellent work by
Norton; an actor who has fumbled significantly more
than the meteoric rise of his star status initially suggested he ever would. Norton seems more vital and alive
than he has in years, clearly invigorated by being able to
not only play to his dark sense of humor but to do so in
not one, but two distinct roles. He brilliantly distinguishes the brothers, not merely taking the easy route of
"city mouse, country mouse" that the script could have
easily supported. The scenes in which they are first
reunited are nearly spectacular. Norton and Norton find
the rhythm and the film seems like it is about to come
together. The scenes that feature both brothers are easily
the film's greatest, although they are fewer than one
would hope. Moments between Norton and Russell also
hint at a better film as the two work well off of each
other. Nearly every film would be better with the underrated Ms. Russell in the cast.

The lesson of *Leaves of Grass* is a cinematically
important one in that movies are not the sum of their
parts. Individual scenes in this piece work. Performances
are generally strong, especially from the leads. But there
is a tone and a pace to black comedy that is essential to
its overall success and this is where Nelson drops the

ball as a director. *Leaves of Grass* has a love story arc yet is not romantic. It has a violent drug story arc but is never really dramatic. And it is, ultimately, a comedy and is never really that funny. Perhaps it is appropriate that *Leaves of Grass* plays like a pothead's version of something deep that is only revealed to be shallow when he sobers up.

Brian Tallerico

CREDITS

Bill/Brady Kincaid: Edward Norton
Janet: Keri Russell
Pug Rothbaum: Richard Dreyfuss
Daisy Kincaid: Susan Sarandon
Ken Feinman: Josh Pais
Colleen: Melanie Lynskey
Bolger: Tim Blake Nelson
Buddy Fuller: Steve Earle
Origin: USA
Language: English
Released: 2009
Production: Tim Blake Nelson, Edward Norton, John Langley, Elie Cohn, Bill Migliore; Millenium Films, Class 5 Films, Langley Films; released by First Look Studios
Directed by: Tim Blake Nelson
Written by: Tim Blake Nelson
Cinematography by: Roberto Schaefer
Music by: Jeff Danna
Sound: Steve Aaron
Music Supervisor: Randall Poster
Editing: Michelle Botticelli
Art Direction: Rob Simons
Costumes: Caroline Eselin
Production Design: Max Biscoe
MPAA rating: R
Running time: 104 minutes

REVIEWS

Denby, David. *New Yorker.* March 29, 2010.
Ebert, Roger. *Chicago Sun-Times.* March 29, 2010.
Edelstein, David. *New York Magazine.* March 29, 2010.
Genzlinger, Neil. *New York Times.* September 17, 2010.
Harvey, Dennis. *Variety.* September 18, 2009.
Honeycutt, Kirk. *Hollywood Reporter.* September 18, 2009.
Hynes, Eric. *Movieline.* September 22, 2010.
Lumenick, Lou. *New York Post.* September 17, 2010.
Schager, Nick. *Slant Magazine.* March 29, 2010.
Uhlich, Keith. *Time Out New York.* March 31, 2010.

TRIVIA

Writer/director Tim Blake Nelson wrote the two main characters specifically to be played by Edward Norton.

LEBANON

An opening shot of a vast field of sunflowers against a bright blue horizon is the unlikely start to one of the tensest and most effective war dramas of recent years. Directed and written by Samuel Maoz and based on his own war experiences, *Lebanon* seems to squeeze the drama of an entire war into the cramped confines of a single tank manned by a few soldiers. It makes for harrowing POV cinema. The comparisons that have floated around it linking it to Wolfgang Petersen's *Das Boot* (1981) are more than justified. Horrifying in the deepest sense of the word, *Lebanon,* winner of the Golden Lion at the 66th Venice International Film Festival, will almost certainly establish for Maoz a place in the history of war cinema.

It is the first battle of Lebanon, June 1982, and a lone group of soldiers, a paratrooper platoon and tank, are ordered on what should be a simple in-and-out mission to search a small town, leveled by the air force, for the few enemy combatants who might have survived. Unable to see anything outside except through the narrow viewer attached to their gun the four-man tank crew find themselves plunged into a chaos. War is commanders who see them as nothing more than cannon fodder to further their own ambitions, despotic mercenaries anxious to torture prisoners, a supposedly empty city inexplicably full of hostile forces and a tank—their only means of shelter from the constant gunfire—that is rapidly becoming inoperable. As they fight for survival, each man must make decisions, to obey or not obey orders, to give aid or not give aid to prisoners, to kill or not to kill when it will endanger civilians. In war, they discover the enemy is within as well as without.

Part of the genius of *Lebanon* is the POV which is almost always from within the impossibly tight space of the tank itself or thru the targeting crosshairs which are used time and again to suggest the limited vision soldiers have in time of war, and the incapability of contextualizing what war shows men about their fellows—be they enemy or not. At one point the glass lens across the crosshairs even becomes splintered calling to mind the fragile state of the soldiers who watch the world through it. Viewers see women searching for children, the embittered faces of civilians caught in the cross fire, and the whole hellish host of suffering that greets them whichever way they point the viewfinder.

Utilizing a masterful mix of filmmaking techniques *Lebanon* never feels less than dangerously close to the edge of sanity as Moaz and his fellow filmmakers find ways to ratchet up the tension even when viewers will be convinced it cannot be done. A close-up of a drop of oil spilling into a puddle on the tank floor signifies not only that the tank itself is in mortal danger but gives viewers the chance to see a desperate face reflected in the puddle. A dead comrade is dropped inside the tank until he can be airlifted out, providing a profound irony in that the one who least needs rescue is carried to safety through a haze of white light pouring through the hatch, leaving his living comrades behind in the dark and smoke. The enemy combatant responsible for the death of that soldier is placed in the tank for safekeeping. Babbling away in a language that none of the tank crew understands, his plight and his guilt mixes with theirs in an almost palpable sense of isolation. Whether by camera placement, the written word, special effects, lighting, or especially sound, which at times is deafening, the sense that the film is in expert hands is clear.

Maoz only has one other credit, a documentary, *Total Eclipse* (2000). It was not well-reviewed and certainly could not have prepared viewers to expect this. Likewise his uniformly excellent cast who will be completely unfamiliar to anyone not versed in Israeli cinema. *Lebanon* is liable to drop like a bomb on anyone of any political persuasion or opinion about the Middle East. It is, first and foremost, a frayed nerve, the cinematic equivalent of the famous fence-grasping bomb-amputated arms in *All Quiet on the Western Front* (1930). An earthy richness pervades the visual tone of *Lebanon,* evoking classic war cinema even as the film itself pushes out to new boundaries.

If the film has a central conceit, it is the willingness of Maoz to sell out the higher command when he needs to create some of the drama. Seriously punishable offenses like constantly disobeying direct orders or telling an officer to go f**k himself feel a little tossed into the mix, a little too "movie-like." Not so for the special effects which are never anything but riveting and repulsively realistic. Maoz is careful to make the gore count for something. In one sequence, a woman shellshocked and almost certainly deafened by the tank attack searches for her daughter whom viewers know is almost certainly dead. She is just one more maddened shriek amid the wail around her. Viewers will be thankful to be spared the sight of the child's body but the sight of the mother is almost worse.

A moment of silence falls corpselike at one point in the film signaling—what? Each man must decide: to grieve, offer compassion, to despair, or seek forgiveness. *Lebanon* seems to suggest that war itself is too big for any one man to change but also that what any one man does in war can change him, and those immediately around him, forever.

Dave Canfield

CREDITS

Assi: Itay Tiran
Hertzel: Oshri Cohen
Yigal: Michael Moshonov

Jamil: Zohar Strauss
Shmulik: Yoav Donat
Origin: Israel, France, Germany
Language: English, Arabic, Hebrew
Released: 2009
Production: Moshe Edery, Leon Edery, Einat Bikel, Uri Sabad; Paralite Films, Arte France, Ariel Films; released by Sony Pictures Classics
Directed by: Samuel Maoz
Written by: Samuel Maoz
Cinematography by: Giora Bejach
Music by: Nicolas Becker
Sound: David Liss, Tobias Fleig, Jan Petzold
Editing: Arik Lahav-Leibovici
Costumes: Hila Bargiel
Production Design: Ariel Roshko
MPAA rating: R
Running time: 93 minutes

REVIEWS

Burr, Ty. *Boston Globe.* September 9, 2010.
Ebert, Roger. *Chicago Sun-Y Times.* August 26, 2010.
Hoberman, J. *Village Voice.* August 3, 2010.
Merry, Stephanie. *Washington Post.* August 27, 2010.
Richards, Jonathan F. *Film.com.* September 22, 2010.
Schager, Nick. *Slant Magazine.* August 1, 2010.
Scott, A.O. *New York Times.* August 6, 2010.
Scott, Mike. *Times-Picayune.* December 18, 2010.
Turan, Kenneth. *Los Angeles Times.* August 12, 2010.
Weaving, Simon. *Screenwize.* November 13, 2010.

LEGEND OF THE GUARDIANS: THE OWLS OF GA'HOOLE

> *On his way to finding a legend...he will become one.*
> —Movie tagline

Box Office: $55 Million

The most surprising element of *Legend of the Guardians: The Owls of Ga'Hoole* is the unabashedly political aspect of the movie. Without venturing into any kind of specific allegory (although the buildup to World War II is perhaps most on the mind of Kathryn Lasky's *Guardians of Ga'Hoole* book series, at least as emphasized in this adaptation of the first three books), the story envisions a world of moral absolutes—pure evil and even purer good, patriots and traitors, and the horror of battle in the telling along with the thrilling necessity of war in the actual portrayal.

The fact that the tale is told through the words and actions of computer-generated owls, who live in an overly lit but photorealistic world of beautiful woods and haunting wastelands, is only demonstrative of its target audience. That such a simplistic, almost irresponsible worldview is aimed at children is the disheartening part. The combination of the naïve, the immature, and the thoughtless leads to a dramatically dull narrative.

Lasky and screenwriters John Orloff and Emil Stern employ the hero's journey—that old, reliable staple of narrative—in the story of young Barn Owl Soren (voice of Jim Sturgess). Captured by the dastardly Metalbeak (voice of Joel Edgerton) and his mate, the bewitching Nyra (voice of Helen Mirren), Soren and his older brother Kludd (voice of Ryan Kwanten) learn of the malevolent plans afoot at the St. Aegolius Academy for Orphaned Owls, a euphemistic name for a work and training camp for stolen owlets.

Those deemed inferior are brainwashed in a process called "moon blinking" (i.e., sleeping at night) and sent to mine the pellets of other owls for magical metal flecks. The superior "Pure Ones" (i.e., barn owls) are instructed in the ways of war. While Kludd appreciates the attention of Nyra and stays behind, Soren escapes to seek out the mythical Guardians from the rousing stories he has heard and acted out over and over again.

The Guardians live in the grand Ga'Hoole Tree located on the shores of the Sea of Hoolemere, and the number of owl-related puns thankfully decreases greatly after the introduction of these two locales (although one of Soren's eventual assistants Digger [voice of David Wenham], a Burrowing Owl, manages to fill in a few jokes that fit the same motif). The homes and hideaways of the heroes fit the same angelic nature as their inhabitants, awash in the golden hues of the "magic hour" with the characters lit unnaturally by a bright, white digital spotlight that endows them with halos (an odd cinematic convention consigned upon nocturnal creatures). Meanwhile the rocky canyons of Metalbeak's lair are shadows and soft lights (made especially dark by the application of post-production stereoscopic 3-D).

The blatant nature of the settings is an echo of the overarching thematic aims, the clear-cut narrative, and the basic qualities of the characters. Along the preordained path of Soren's quest, he discovers his mandatory helpers. Besides the twitchy Digger, who, in addition to his ineffective jokes, does what his name implies, there is the Great Grey Owl Twilight (voice of Anthony LaPaglia), a minstrel poet who sings—with successful comic effect—of the band of adventurers' impending doom. The Elf Owl Gylfie (voice of Emily Barclay), another owl able to resist Metalbeak's philosophy of a master race of the *Übereule* (if one continues the allegorical connection to World War II), flees from Metalbeak's

fortress with Soren. Digger, Gylfie, and Soren's younger sister Eglantine (voice of Adrienne DeFaria) exhibit disproportionately large eyes, and their traditionally cute appearance is nearly the full extent of their characterizations. Appearance lends much to the rest of minimally developed players. The fearsome Metalbeak sports a dead eye and—appropriately enough—a metallic mask. The rebellious Kludd has a sort of mohawk arrangement to his feathers. The long neck of Nyra emphasizes her seductive appeal to Kludd. The animators bestow upon them an impeccable anthropomorphic flair.

They are, though, as hollow as the story. Only Kludd, with his latent jealousy of his parents' attention to Soren and desire for recognition of his own successes, suggests any level of ambiguity. He lies somewhere between the script's preferred ease of the moral qualifiers of "good" and "evil." Presented with difficulty in portraying his clashing motivations (fierce individualism vs. loyalty to family), the movie sides him with the villains, willing, during an anticlimactic fight between brothers in a burning forest, to deceive Soren with feelings of fraternity before trying to kill him. Similarly, Allomere (voice of Sam Neill), one of the Guardians, voices his opposition to battle or at least demands evidence that Metalbeak is planning to conquer the Owl Kingdoms, and in the end, he is revealed as a collaborator. Rationality, in the movie's view, is akin to appeasement, which is not only philosophical treachery but also a very real form of it.

Upon arriving at the Ga'Hoole Tree, Soren meets his hero the Screech-owl Ezylryb (voice of Geoffrey Rush), looking quite the opposite of the warrior he envisioned when hearing stories of the Guardians. Wizened and scarred, Ezylryb tries to douse Soren's passion for combat with testimonies of reality, and director Zack Snyder then goes on in the final battle at Metalbeak's stronghold (complete with the baffling but still debilitating effects of the metal specks) to highlight the visceral excitement of flying, clawing warfare with his by-then tiresome use of slow motion.

The moments of higher "camera" speed do emphasize the detail of animation (a flight through a torrential rain storm is particularly striking). At times, the care and craft on the technical end of *Legend of the Guardians: The Owls of Ga'Hoole* is breathtaking, and it also serves as an emphasis on the lack of those qualities in the screenplay.

Mark Dujsik

CREDITS

Soren: Jim Sturgess (Voice)
Kludd: Ryan Kwanten (Voice)

Gylfie: Emily Barclay (Voice)

Digger: David Wenham (Voice)

Nyra: Helen Mirren (Voice)

Boron: Richard Roxburgh (Voice)

Allomere: Sam Neill (Voice)

Ezylryb: Geoffrey Rush (Voice)

Noctus/Grimble: Hugo Weaving (Voice)

Otulissa: Abbie Cornish (Voice)

Marella: Essie Davis (Voice)

Metalbeak: Joel Edgerton (Voice)

Twilight: Anthony LaPaglia (Voice)

Mrs. Plithliver: Miriam Margolyes (Voice)

Echidna: Barry Otto (Voice)

Eglantine: Adrienne DeFaria (Voice)

Origin: USA, Australia

Language: English

Released: 2010

Production: Village Roadshow Pictures, Animal Logic Film; released by Warner Bros.

Directed by: Zack Snyder

Written by: Emil Stern, John Orloff

Music by: David Hirschfelder

Editing: David Burrows

Sound: Wayne Pashley

Production Design: Simon Whiteley

MPAA rating: PG

Running time: 90 minutes

REVIEWS

Barker, Andrew. *Variety.* September 19, 2010.

Graham, Adam. *Detroit News.* September 24, 2010.

Hall, Sandra. *Sydney Morning Herald.* September 30, 2010.

Kois, Dan. *Washington Post.* September 24, 2010.

Lovece, Frank. *Film Journal International.* September 23, 2010.

Nusair, David. *About.com.* September 24, 2010.

Putman, Dustin. *DustinPutman.com.* September 21, 2010.

Schrodt, Paul. *Slant Magazine.* September 23, 2010.

Vaux, Rob. *Mania.com.* September 23, 2010.

Webster, Andy. *New York Times.* September 23, 2010.

QUOTES

Soren: "We need to find the Guardians. They're the only ones who can save us!"

TRIVIA

This was director Zack Snyder's first non-R rated film.

LEGION

When the last angel falls, the fight for mankind begins.
—Movie tagline

Box Office: $40 million

Legion plays as if writer Scott Stewart and his co-conspirator Peter Schink, a film editor turned screenwriter and a wanted man for assembling such atrocities as *Barb Wire* (1996), *Detroit Rock City* (1999), and the Chuck Norris canine cop comedy, *Top Dog* (1995), started by watching James Cameron's *The Terminator* (1984). The film inspired them to attempt to get away with a similar first act, only this time with angels instead of robots. The archangel Michael (Paul Bettany) has fallen to Earth a couple of days before Christmas, cuts off his wings and loads up an arsenal in defiance of a mission tasked by God himself. It seems that the Lord Almighty is tired of the humans he created. Enough is enough and he is sending his army of angels to exterminate mankind.

Stewart and Schink decided to toast their God, one James Cameron, and continued to offer him tribute by making the fail-safe to man's extinction an unborn child. Michael's assignment was to end the pregnancy of a diner waitress named Charlie (Adrianne Palicki). She works not at Big Jeff's, but at a hole in the middle of the desert known as Paradise Falls. It has a cook in Percy (Charles S. Dutton), an owner in Bob (Dennis Quaid), and his son, a mechanic named Jeep (Lucas Black). How they stay in business is anyone's guess since their only patrons appear to be people who are lost like Kyle (Tyrese Gibson), a family (Jon Tenney, Kate Walsh, and Willa Holland) whose car broke down and an old woman (Jeanette Miller) who is really a possessed demon-angel that climbs on the ceiling and attacks customers.

There is a natural temptation to play along with the filmmakers and gleefully laugh at their outrageous construct. Who needs legitimate quality in the basic food groups of filmmaking and storytelling when mocking its inherent flaws becomes a viable means of entertainment? That may be a fun parlor game when watching with your friends and an entire audience is in on the joke. When left alone in its own elements though, a film like *Legion* can be a deadly soul-sucking experience.

Unsure of whether they wanted to write an end-of-the-world countdown on humanity's vices, a claustrophobic horror film about the trapped-and-outnumbered ragtag group of the last survivors, or a bullets-blazing action film, the writers went for broke and mashed them all together. And is it ever broke. The opening quotation from Psalms ("Come, ye children, listen to me. I will teach you the fear of the lord.") should not fool audiences into thinking that the filmmakers did their homework. The biblical quote is soon followed by one from Charlie's mom about God being tired of all the B.S. that will not be found as easily by a Google search anytime soon despite the efforts by Stewart and Schink to make it stick by repeating the exact same speech as a bookend on the fade out. A film less concerned with special effects might have focused a little more on the archetypes at the diner; the stranded yuppies and their teasingly promiscuous daughter, the criminal reformed by fatherhood and the Job who lost everything in pursuing his dream. Without six seasons of television to expand upon these lost souls or writers who can make them interesting enough to root for in a half-hour's time, the film better be scary or kinetic enough to give us a reason to remain involved.

There have been some monumentally dumb fantasy films in the last few years including the deceased physics of *The Time Traveler's Wife* (2009) and the fractured Greek mythology of *Percy Jackson & the Olympians: The Lightning Thief* (2010). *Legion* may just take the cake in terms of outright incompetence and stupidity. It is not like the theologically challenged Stewart and Schink were devoid of angel studies in motion pictures. If *Wings of Desire* (1987) was too foreign for their tastes, there was always its American counterparts, *City of Angels* (1998), *Michael* (1996), or even *Date with an Angel* (1987). There was also plenty to skim through on the apocalyptic side with Kevin Smith's *Dogma* (1999) or *The Prophecy* trilogy (1995, 1998, 2000) with Christopher Walken in the role of the murderous Angel Gabriel. Ten years removed from the last film in that series, demand has never been so low for a reboot in sheep's clothing. The adaptation of the *Hellblazer* comic, *Constantine* (2005), was equally ridiculous but had the benefit of an over-the-top graphic novel sensibility. No one is going to mistake *Legion* with the spirit of a comic book that made it past a first issue and no movie fan can take a film seriously that uses a literal deus ex machina to save its heroes.

Erik Childress

CREDITS

Archangel Michael: Paul Bettany
Archangel Gabriel: Kevin Durand
Bob Hanson: Dennis Quaid
Kyle Williams: Tyrese Gibson
Percy Walker: Charles S. Dutton
Jeep Hanson: Lucas Black
Sandra Anderson: Kate Walsh
Charlie: Adrianne Palicki
Howard Anderson: Jon Tenney
Audrey Anderson: Willa Holland

Gladys Foster: Jeanette Miller
Origin: USA
Language: English
Released: 2010
Production: David Lancaster, Michel Litvak; Bold Films; released by Screen Gems
Directed by: Scott Stewart
Written by: Scott Stewart, Peter Schink
Cinematography by: John Lindley
Music by: John Frizzell
Sound: Martin Lopez, Steven Ticknor
Music Supervisor: Chris Douridas
Editing: Steven Kemper
Costumes: Wendy Partridge
Production Design: Jeff Higinbotham
MPAA rating: R
Running time: 100 minutes

REVIEWS

Abele, Robert. *Los Angeles Times.* January 22, 2010.
Collis, Clark. *Entertainment Weekly.* January 22, 2010.
Doerksen, Cliff. *Chicago Reader.* January 27, 2010.
Hale, Mike. *New York Times.* January 22, 2010.
Hardy, Ernest. *Village Voice.* January 27, 2010.
Koplinski, Charles. *Illinois Times.* January 30, 2010.
Leydon, Joe. *Variety.* January 22, 2010.
Orange, Michelle. *Movieline.* January 27, 2010.
Pais, Matt. *Metromix.com.* January 22, 2010.
Uhlich, Keith. *Time Out New York.* January 22, 2010.

QUOTES

Kyle Williams: "I don't give a f**k how long she been dead—the bitch just walked on the ceiling. She ain't staying in here."

TRIVIA

The tattoos that appear on Michael are based on Enochian, a supposed language of the angels derived in the sixteenth century.

LET ME IN

Innocence dies. Abby doesn't.
—Movie tagline

Box Office: $12 million

If the jab of this spring's colorful, wildly over-the-top graphic novel adaptation *Kick-Ass* (2010) represented her bawdy coming-out party, *Let Me In* is the bracing uppercut follow-up that shows viewers Chloe Moretz, still now just fourteen years old, is more than just a one-punch wonder, or some piece of adolescent stunt casting.

A remake of Tomas Alfredson's moody Swedish film *Låt den rätte komma in* (*Let the Right One In* [2008]), in which a bullied boy strikes up a fragile relationship with the strange new girl in his apartment complex, only to discover she is a vampire, the film—in both its evocative, quiet precision and well-timed scares—undercuts all sighing, dismissive expectations born of its one-sentence plot logline. It is a uniquely gripping and unnerving horror-drama hybrid rooted in delicate performances, of which Moretz's star-confirming turn is paramount.

Unfortunately, *Let Me In* was never able to translate its rapturous critical reception into commercial lucre. Against a crowded slate of October genre competition that included fellow horror entries *Case 39* (2010), *My Soul to Take* (2010), *I Spit on Your Grave* (2010), *Paranormal Activity 2* (2010), and *Saw 3D* (2010)—all films with the additional marketing advantage of franchise value, bigger stars, a name director, or the pedigree of an unrated shock-remake—this cerebral offering could simply not find an audience willing to let it in, grossing just over $12 million in theaters. It is a discomfiting fate that compares frustratingly to *Let the Right One In,* which received similarly positive reviews but could likewise never punch through and overcome the genre snobbery of art house filmgoers who would otherwise likely respond favorably to its superb storytelling and acting.

Let Me In unfolds in Los Alamos, New Mexico, in the early 1980s, although its period piece setting is really of no special significance. Meek, rail-thin middle school student Owen (Kodi Smit-McPhee) is a social outcast who, in the confines of his room, acts out dark fantasies as a way to escape the pain of his parents' impending divorce, and being bullied at school. When mysterious, 12-year-old Abby (Moretz) and her gruff dad (Richard Jenkins) move in next door, Owen forms a profound bond with his young new neighbor, who is like no one he has met before.

Arguments emanate from her apartment (arguments probably a lot like the ones he has heard his parents have), and Owen silently seeks out the companionship of someone he likely believes to be his shadow self. The embers of a friendship are stoked. At Abby's urging, Owen even takes a stand against his schoolyard persecutors, though it initially grants him only a momentary reprieve and the looming threat of more retaliation.

As news of a string of strange, grisly murders spreads, and a policeman (Elias Koteas) investigates them, Owen finally learns the full truth about his new friend—that Abby is actually a vampire, and her dad is not her father at all, but instead a caretaker guardian who does Abby's bidding and, in the bluntest terms

possible, collects blood for her. Faced with this tangible horror but at the same time drawn to the one person who has shown him kindness, Owen faces tough choices.

Writer-director Matt Reeves is ostensibly working from John Ajvide Lindqvist's script for *Let the Right One In,* and his bestselling novel of the same name, but he retains the artfully deliberate pacing and, indeed, even much of the same shot selection from Alfredson's film, all while upping the gore quotient a bit. His experience on *Cloverfield* (2008) with helping to construct a visual scheme that is chaotic and jumbled yet still emotionally involving is richly evident in this work. Cinematographer Greig Fraser, who captured the sunny, open-plain and outback beauty of New Zealand and Australia, respectively, in *Out of the Blue* (2007) and *The Boys Are Back* (2009), here trades in wintry desolation and skittishness. The camerawork is not entirely handheld, but predominantly so, working in a lurking mode and featuring obstructed frames. The utter physical absence of authority and protective figures in Owen's life (his father is a disembodied voice on the phone, and his mother's face never actually appears in the movie) further highlight this piercing compositional isolation.

Crucially, though it does not meet the auteurist criterion of an original work, Reeves recognizes that, current commercial appetites of the *Twilight* franchise "tween" set notwithstanding, this is not really a vampire movie in any typical sense, but rather a movie about loneliness. Though the source material is of foreign origin, he seems to have an acutely personal and sincere connection to it. In artful and economic fashion, *Let Me In* absolutely nails the lingering, character-molding anxiety of adolescent humiliation and degradation, and in doing so breaks one's heart while simultaneously quickening one's pulse.

Pain and apprehension abound for the young characters at the center of the film, but their choices and behavior are always informed by pragmatic, credible circumstances. The same thick panic over abandonment that Owen feels in his stomach over his parents' perhaps benign neglect renders him incapable of turning away from what he knows to be a bad situation with Abby. Likewise, Abby and her guardian are tethered together by fused bitterness, affection, recrimination, and need. Even Owen's chief tormenter, Kenny (Dylan Minnette), is eventually revealed to himself be the target of his older brother's heckling.

It is also worth saying that since film is first and foremost a director's medium, one of the marks of a truly gifted filmmaker lies in getting a good performance out of actors, particularly younger actors without as much of a base of experience to fall back upon. While Moretz was already at the top of her game in *Kick-Ass,*

Smit-McPhee was far less convincing in *The Road* (2009), another spare and ruminative work studded with violence. The fact that Reeves is able to get perfectly modulated performances out his young charges—something different for Moretz, encompassing flinty bits of animalistic rage, and something serene and heartrendingly forlorn from Smit-McPhee—without compromising their essential senses of innocence is a great credit to his talent.

Lest this all sound a bit too touchy-feely and esoteric, it is worth stressing that there is a palpable sense of danger and a visceral pop to *Let Me In*. It is predominantly a work of tension, lonesomeness, and dread. But when there is horror to be shown Reeves does not shy away, capturing it at times with a balletic fluidity (as with the natatorium comeuppance of Kenny and his cabal of bullying acolytes), but mostly with a CGI-infused viciousness and brutality, as separate walkway and bathroom kills attest. Composer Michael Giacchino's score, meanwhile, further abets this crafty balance; it is a chilly, atonal thing, giving off a vibe at once tranquil and menacing, with a few flashes of shock.

Interestingly, and hearteningly, *Let Me In* also leaves somewhat ambiguous the issue of Abby's motivations, of whether her protective instincts for Owen relate to a rekindled connection to her own human mortality, a more selfish desire to corrupt and manipulate—indebting Owen to her in a manner that provides her with her next caregiver—or some commingled combination of the two. She is a monster, yes, it is true. The animalistic nature of her behavior affirms that. But she was also human once, and the movie trusts the strength of its material and everyone involved—Moretz, the rest of its actors, and its audience—to leave room for debate around the edges as to just how self-serving her choices and actions are.

At once tender and brutal, *Let Me In* is a transfixing elegy the likes of which the supernatural horror genre rarely produces. It is a chilling, engrossing film rooted in recognizably human behavioral patterns, no matter that one of its characters is not human. Reeves' movie stands as an ultra-rare case of an American studio remake of a foreign film that does not merely strip away its useful conceit and leave everything else special about it sitting up on cinderblocks, in an effort to kowtow to popcorn thrills. No matter its box office reception, *Let Me In* is a treat for both protective fans of the original Swedish movie and newcomers alike.

Brent Simon

CREDITS

Owen: Kodi Smit-McPhee
Abby: Chloe Grace Moretz
The Father: Richard Jenkins
The Policeman: Elias Koteas
Owen's Mother: Cara Buono
Virginia: Sasha Barrese
Mark: Jimmy Pinchak
Kenny: Dylan Minnette
Origin: USA
Language: English
Released: 2010
Production: Guy East, Donna Gigliotti, Nigel Sinclair; Hammer Film Productions; released by Overture Films
Directed by: Matt Reeves
Written by: Matt Reeves
Cinematography by: Greig Fraser
Music by: Michael Giacchino
Editing: Stan Salfas
Sound: William Files, Douglas Murray
Art Direction: Guy Barnes
Costumes: Melissa Bruning
Production Design: Ford Wheeler
MPAA rating: R
Running time: 115 minutes

REVIEWS

Covert, Colin. *Minneapolis Star Tribune*. September 30, 2010.
Debruge, Peter. *Variety*. September 12, 2010.
Edelstein, David. *New York Magazine*. October 4, 2010.
Fine, Marshall. *Hollywood & Fine*. September 30, 2010.
Kennedy, Lisa. *Denver Post*. October 1, 2010.
Means, Sean. *Salt Lake Tribune*. October 8, 2010.
Morgenstern, Joe. *Wall Street Journal*. September 30, 2010.
Phillips, Michael. *Chicago Tribune*. September 30, 2010.
Scott, A.O. *New York Times*. October 1, 2010.
Tallerico, Brian. *HollywoodChicago.com*. October 1, 2010.

QUOTES

The Policeman: "What do you mean a little girl? How little?"

TRIVIA

The word "Vampire" is only said once in the movie.

LETTERS TO JULIET

What if you had a second chance to find true love?
   —Movie tagline

The greatest love story ever told…is your own.
   —Movie tagline

Box Office: $53 million

While Sophie (Amanda Seyfried) tries to decide between two men, one her fiancé and the other a complete stranger, to find true love throughout a point-by-point rundown of the standard outline of plot and character developments that have come to give the term "romantic comedy" a bad name, there is a genuinely romantic story playing in the background. Why screenwriters Jose Rivera and Tim Sullivan set out to write a romance, found a worthwhile one, and then decided to toss it to the side while two less appealing characters acted out the motions of hate growing into love is a mystery. Sophie, a passive observer in her most consequential moments, is the heroine, while Claire (Vanessa Redgrave), a woman who fifty years ago met the love of her life and now wants to seek him out, is a side player to her own story.

Sophie is torn between her inattentive, self-centered, and neglectful boyfriend Victor (Gael García Bernal) and a priggish, dispassionate, and easily irritated Brit named Charlie (Christopher Egan). She is tied to Victor through loyalty and the past and to Charlie through the fact that he is the only other man her age that she meets and the requirements of the script. Neither forges the material of a suitable love story, especially in a movie that cites perhaps the greatest one in the English language—from its title all the way through to using a balcony for no discernable reason in the final scene.

The two meet after Sophie and Victor travel to Verona, Italy, for a "pre-honeymoon." Victor quickly becomes obsessed with visiting potential suppliers for a restaurant he is opening in their hometown of New York, and Sophie takes the opportunity to do some sightseeing on her own.

She stops at "Casa di Giulietta," the alleged home of the inspiration for Juliet Capulet of William Shakespeare's *Romeo and Juliet,* where she notes women writing letters and placing them on the wall beneath the balcony. Following the letters after their daily collection, Sophie discovers the "Segretarie di Giulietta," a group of women who write responses to each and every letter on the wall. With Victor still busy, she spends some time with them, finds a fifty-year-old letter hidden in a nook beneath a loose brick, and writes a response.

Claire penned the letter five decades ago while in art school. In love with a young man but aware she had obligations at home and that her parents would never approve, she ran away—their plans for marriage shattered. She regrets the decision and wants to apologize for leaving him without any notification. Charlie is her grandson, whom she raised since his parents died in a car accident when he was a child, and he objects to her plan to search for her old love. He feels the hunt for a successful meeting negates the importance of her present family, and he worries his grandmother might be devastated if they cannot find her old flame. The man might, after all these years, even be dead.

The game between Sophie and Charlie starts the moment he learns she wrote the response. Sophie is thrilled her letter got such a reaction, but Charlie immediately shoots down her joy. They hate each other once they realize their role in relation to Claire, so it is only quaintly appropriate that they share Claire's journey to find the one Lorenzo Bartolini that stole her heart out of the almost eighty around the Siena area. If he seems cold and unromantic, Claire tells Sophie, the young woman should know, beneath that exterior, he has a "warm, passionate heart." The hatred between Sophie and Charlie grows into begrudging indifference, which becomes uncomfortable attraction—exchanged smiles in the rearview mirror while driving to the next prospect. The next step is true love, and the screenplay ensures that any possibility of the emotion being reciprocated by both parties at the same time is drawn out until the movie's final, awkward, and strained moments.

Meanwhile Claire's story rolls out in quick comic snippets and montages, as she meets one Lorenzo Bartolini after another—none of whom are the one she loved so long ago. They flirt with her, asking that she return if she does not find her Lorenzo or pronouncing they would never let her go if they were him. One curses the year she and Lorenzo met because it was the same year he met his wife. One wife implores that Claire take her husband. In the clamor and confusion of the search, Redgrave stands poised and graceful in a performance of sensory recall that transcends the primary plot opposite of her character. When she finally finds her Lorenzo (Franco Nero), they embrace, and the camera holds on Claire's face, which stares open-eyed at the back of his head. It is a subtle choice—one that recalls an earlier conversation in which Claire remembers Lorenzo, not by sight, but by smell.

One happy ending must lead to another, and after forestalling a declaration of love by either Sophie or Charlie for the other, the screenplay continues to keep them apart. After Sophie returns to New York and ends her relationship with Victor, she and Charlie meet again at Claire and Lorenzo's wedding. For no reason other than an unnecessary complication, Charlie is accompanied by Patricia (Ashley Lilley), a cousin who shares the same name as an ex-girlfriend. This leads Sophie to leave the reception but only climb to a nearby balcony, a move that holds no logic. Then again, *Letters to Juliet* holds very little logic, in making the truly romantic and what should be central story the secondary one.

Mark Dujsik

CREDITS

Sophie: Amanda Seyfried
Claire: Vanessa Redgrave
Charlie Wyman: Christopher Egan
Lorenzo Bartolini: Franco Nero
Victor: Gael García Bernal
Lorraine: Marcia DeBonis
New Yorker magazine editor: Oliver Platt
Viticoltore: Giordano Formenti
Patricia: Ashley Lilley
Origin: USA
Language: English
Released: 2010
Production: Mark Canton, Erik Feig, Caroline Kaplan, Patrick Wachsberger, Ellen Barkin; Applehead Productions; released by Summit Entertainment
Directed by: Gary Winick
Written by: Jose Rivera, Tim Sullivan
Cinematography by: Marco Pontecorvo
Music by: Andrea Guerra
Sound: Ken Ishii
Music Supervisor: John Houlihan
Editing: Bill Pankow
Art Direction: Stefano Ortolani
Costumes: Nicoletta Ercole
Production Design: Stuart Wurtzel
MPAA rating: PG
Running time: 105 minutes

REVIEWS

Berardinelli, James. *ReelViews.* May 11, 2010.
Biancolli, Amy. *San Francisco Chronicle.* May 14, 2010.
Ebert, Roger. *Chicago Sun-Times.* May 12, 2010.
Johanson, MaryAnn. *Flick Filosopher.* May 17, 2010.
Moore, Roger. *Orlando Sentinel.* May 12, 2010.
Phillips, Michael. *Chicago Tribune.* May 13, 2010.
Phipps, Keith. *AV Club.* May 13, 2010.
Rich, Katey. *CinemaBlend.com.* May 13, 2010.
Schager, Nick. *Slant Magazine.* May 13, 2010.
Tallerico, Brian. *HollywoodChicago.com.* May 14, 2010.

QUOTES

Victor: "It's not a mushroom, okay. It's a truffle."

TRIVIA

The on-screen couple Vanessa Redgrave and Franco Nero are in fact a real life couple.

LIFE AS WE KNOW IT

A comedy about taking it one step at a time.
—Movie tagline

Box Office: $53 million

Those responsible for birthing the charmless and familiar *Life as We Know It* could have used some friends to offer them a morning-after pill. Witless, pitiful, and downright annoying for its entire running time, it is the ugly offspring of about a half-dozen wretched romantic comedy plots and wannabe feel-good exercises.

Three years ago, Holly (Katherine Heigl) and Eric (Josh Duhamel), who prefers to go by his surname, Messer, were set up on a blind date by their mutual friends, Alison (Christina Hendricks) and Peter (Hayes MacArthur). He shows up unshaven and late, on a motorcycle, taking booty calls from another woman. She is angered and calls it off. As best friends of the happy couple it is a mystery why their paths never crossed before this night. No matter though as they are doomed to be in each other's lives after Peter and Alison get married and have a child. One unfortunate evening, a car crash occurs and baby Sophie is left without parents. Lucky for her but unlucky for viewers, the will has chosen Holly and Messer to be the legal guardians. They even get to live in the lovely suburban home left behind; only with each other.

The scene is set for the travails of a snippy couple who do not like each other to battle over their lack of parenting skills and commitment to their growing responsibilities at work. Messer is hoping to get his shot at directing a big league television sportscast. Holly owns her own bakery restaurant and was hoping to catch the attention of divorced pediatrician Sam (Josh Lucas), who regularly frequents her store. Advice from the neighborhood parents run the checklist of how little time they have for each other and their own wants. Plus they have to put up a good front for the social services worker (Sarah Burns) who drops in to make sure the subjects of her new case are not complicating things by sleeping together. She should not have to worry about such things because she is in a movie. And in movies, men and women who start off hating each other never wind up in bed together, right?

Holly and Messer do not need a baby handbook courtesy of Dr. Spock, just the standard cinema rulebook that has already predetermined their fates. It would give them more time to learn the baby basics, realize they will not always hate each other, and stop forcing an audience to sit through every cliché in the book with characters neither interesting nor smart enough to forgive the proverbial journey and earn its happy outcome. Whatever points director Greg Berlanti earns for not inducing injections of cloy with close-ups of the tyke doing something cute, he loses twice over by hanging the child out to dry as a mere prop for this pair to act like imbeciles around.

In a bathroom emergency, Holly uses Messer's hat as an impromptu diaper despite the fact that she is already hovering the baby over a toilet; the second baby poop joke she is subject to. The first ends up on her face for the neighbors to see. In preparation for his shot in the director's booth, Messer leaves the kid under the care of a cab driver whom he may have just met. Their haggling over game tickets for compensation may suggest he is a regular driver, but as he is never heard from before or after this scene it is just one of many questions that debuting screenwriters Ian Deitchman and Kristin Rusk Robinson should be answering under the hot lights at a police station. Even the social worker who narrowly avoids the most obvious pot brownie gag in film history encourages Holly to drive faster and more reckless in order to enact the non-honored cliché of racing down the one you love to the airport while endangering your child in the backseat.

Messer and Holly are not imbeciles based on their hyper-manic, ill-advised behavior towards their adopted situation. Who would not have a few questions or make a few mistakes, even with planned parenthood? Because *Life as We Know It* does not treat the predicament with any respect, it lowers its protagonists down to a sub-human or fictional level where goofball antics replace the truth of the issue. These are children; not in the manner of the man-child syndrome evident amongst the bachelor trio of *Three Men and a Baby* (1987) nor the metaphorical kind seen in the psyche of the adults in *Little Children* (2006). Holly and Messer are written with the mental capacity of kids who are bothered even though the other is not touching them and still hitting on the playground to express emotions they are not capable of yet comprehending.

Katherine Heigl, after the greatest success of her film career (*Knocked Up* [2007]), went out of her way to badmouth not being part of the boys club she accused Judd Apatow and company of creating around her humorless character. Since then her choices have left a trail of shrill, un-dateable nitwits in worthless star vehicles *27 Dresses* (2008), *The Ugly Truth* (2009), *Killers* (2010), and now this, leaving little mystery to whether Apatow was really the one responsible for her humorless side. It might be time for her to get out her copy of *Knocked Up* and take notes on a filmmaker who paid enough attention to write real characters dealing with the same type of situation.

By the end of *Life as We Know It*, the only chunk of wisdom that prospective parents, cool uncles, and general moviegoers hoping for something different will take away comes from one of the couple's neighbors that applies more to a viewing of this film than child-rearing. "Imagine a prison. Now don't change anything."

Erik Childress

CREDITS

Holly Berenson: Katherine Heigl
Eric Messer: Josh Duhamel
Sam: Josh Lucas
Alison Novack: Christina Hendricks
DeeDee: Melissa McCarthy
Peter Novack: Hayes Macarthur
Josh: Will Sasso
Janine Groff: Sarah Burns
Origin: USA
Language: English
Released: 2010
Production: Paul Brooks, Barry Josephson; Village Roadshow Pictures, Gold Circle Films, Josephson Entertainment; released by Warner Bros.
Directed by: Greg Berlanti
Written by: Ian Deitchman, Kristin Rusk Robinson
Cinematography by: Andrew Dunn
Music by: Blake Neely
Sound: Mary Ellis
Editing: Jim Page
Art Direction: Austin Gorg
Costumes: Debra McGuire
Production Design: Maher Ahmad
MPAA rating: PG-13
Running time: 113 minutes

REVIEWS

Berardinelli, James. *ReelViews*. October 8, 2010.
Goss, William. *Cinematical*. October 8, 2010.
Holden, Stephen. *New York Times*. October 8, 2010.
Johanson, MaryAnn. *Flick Filosopher*. October 8, 2010.
Kenny, Glenn. *MSN Movies*. October 7, 2010.
McGranaghan, Mike. *Aisle Seat*. October 12, 2010.
Morgenstern, Joe. *Wall Street Journal*. October 7, 2010.
Phipps, Keith. *AV Club*. October 7, 2010.
Rich, Katey. *CinemaBlend.com*. October 7, 2010.
Snider, Eric D. *EricDSnider.com*. October 8, 2010.

QUOTES

Eric Messer: "Just because you accept help from someone, doesn't mean you have failed. It just means you're not in it alone."

TRIVIA

Josh Duhamel, who is originally from North Dakota, plays the character Messer who prominently wears a University of North Dakota "Fighting Sioux" T-shirt in the film.

LIFE DURING WARTIME

In *Life During Wartime,* director Todd Solondz pursues his by-now-customary themes, including mercenary, twisted, and bizarre love and family relationships, and, of course, his favorite topic, pedophilia by presenting a quasi-sequel to *Happiness* (1998) with different actors playing the same roles from Solondz's most-acclaimed and commercially-successful work. If anything, Solondz has mellowed somewhat since that film—the unconventional sequel proceeds with his expected sequences of bizarre, at first seemingly disconnected one-on-one conversations, but unlike *Happiness* the narrative moves along in somewhat lackluster fashion, not at all like a series of incendiary moments, but more like a growing pileup of head-scratchers amounting to a numbing ache.

The plot, intricate and somewhat indecipherable at times but in the end rather pedestrian, centers around three adult sisters in a dysfunctional family. Trish (Allison Janney) is a single mom with a boy, Timmy (Dylan Riley Snyder), about to be Bar Mitzvahed, and an older son, Billy (Chris Marquette), away at college. Trish has told Billy his father is dead. In fact, he is a convicted child molester (Ciaran Hinds) who has been locked away and is being released from prison as the film opens. The pedophile is a heavy-breathing, sweaty mass of emotional turmoil—surprisingly, since this is a Solondz film, one of the most stereotypical abusers imaginable. Meanwhile, Trish has latched onto Harvey (Michael Lerner), an ordinary-looking nice guy whom she falls head over heels in love with just because he is not a creep. When Timmy finds out the truth about his father and quizzes his mother about what pedophilia is, she tells him to scream if a man ever touches him. The scene has Solondz's trademark frankness, but it also telegraphs the film's key development rather blatantly. And it is not a very clever one, either.

The movie spends a lot of time with Trish's virginal-looking sister Joy (the very unglamorous-looking Scottish-born actress Shirley Henderson). Joy is trying to recover from the emotional death grip of relationships with a number of despicable men, whom she encounters in real conversations or in dreams and flashbacks, and their interactions are mostly unintelligible. It is clear only that Joy is a very weak, troubled soul. By way of contrast, her sister Helen (Ally Sheedy) is a strong-willed free spirit who complains that others keep accusing her of being bossy and manipulative (which she clearly is). Helen's character seems something of a throwaway or a filler.

Charlotte Rampling also has a minor part that seems quite expendable. She plays a self-described monster who picks up a man in a bar; in what is supposed to be

some kind of a joke, after sexual calisthenics he takes money out of her purse, as if she is some sort of prostitute in reverse. It is a singularly disagreeable scene, typical of Rampling's unusual choices in roles.

In *Life During Wartime,* one experiences the sad spectacle of a daring, sometimes brilliant filmmaker spinning his wheels—this is a vehicle that is definitely stuck in the same old muck. Solondz has nothing new to say about love relationships, dysfunctional families, or pedophilia that he has not already said before—in much more compelling fashion. What was once daring and unique now, sadly, looks rather commonplace. Attempts at ironic comedy mostly fall flat this time around, and that results in a rather dreary ride.

This kind of film needs outrageous scenes to spice it up, but Solondz's ability to outrage by set-piece conversations has dwindled. The main problem is that the characters do not seem real as much as they are constructed as types just to make the points the writer-director wants to drive home. But what are those points? People are cruel, manipulative, bad at communicating, weak, arrogant, and absurd.

Because the roles must fit a template of sorts rather than freely flow out of realistic experience, the performances mostly seem stiff and unyielding. This is not mainly the fault of the actors; they must play the hands they are dealt. Janney does best, given the fact she is given the most likable and sympathetic character, and the one that seems closest to being believable.

Similarly, the scenes are staged and shot in a way that seems contrived, though some (especially the dream sequence in which Joy walks through a city at night and enters a vacant café which the waitress seems to believe is crowded) are bizarre enough to be quite effective. More such black-comic dream sequences would have made the movie more tolerable, but instead of smoothly integrating such escapism, Solondz insists, as always, in making his audiences tolerate the non-cinematic along with the watchable, as if enduring the worst in both characterization, behavior, and staging must be part of the bitter pill he makes viewers swallow. *Life During Wartime,* after all, cannot be easy. Solondz now has become like a very klutzy anti-Almodóvar, and this film is pure masochism.

Michael Betzold

CREDITS

Joy Jordan: Shirley Henderson
Trish Maplewood: Allison Janney
William Maplewood: Ciaran Hinds
Timmy Maplewood: Dylan Riley Snyder

Billy Maplewood: Chris Marquette
Andy: Paul Reubens
Harvey Weiner: Michael Lerner
Mark Weiner: Rich Pecci
Helen Jordan: Ally Sheedy
Allen: Michael K. Williams
Jacqueline: Charlotte Rampling
Wanda: Gaby Hoffman
Mona Jordan: Renee Taylor
Origin: USA
Language: English
Released: 2009
Production: Christine Kunewa Walker, Derrick Tseng; Werc Werk Works, Fortissimo Films; released by Sony Pictures
Directed by: Todd Solondz
Written by: Ally Sheedy, Todd Solondz
Cinematography by: Edward Lachman
Music by: Doug Bernheim
Sound: Heriberto Rosas
Editing: Kevin Messman
Art Direction: Matteo De Cosmo
Costumes: Catherine George
Production Design: Roshelle Berliner
MPAA rating: R
Running time: 96 minutes

REVIEWS

Anderson, John. *Wall Street Journal.* July 30, 2010.
Butler, Robert W. *Kansas City Star.* October 1, 2010.
Cole, Stephen. *Globe and Mail.* August 27, 2010.
Covert, Colin. *Minneapolis Star Tribune.* August 19, 2010.
Hall, Stan. *Oregonian.* August 26, 2010.
Hornaday, Ann. *Washington Post.* August 6, 2010.
Long, Tom. *Detroit News.* August 13, 2010.
Meyers, Jeff. *Metro Times.* August 26, 2010.
Rickey, Carrie. *Philadelphia Enquirer.* August 12, 2010.
Upchurch, Michael. *Seattle Times.* August 13, 2010.

QUOTES

Joy about her ex-husband Allen: "Once a perv, always a perv."

TRIVIA

The film titles comes from the name of a Talking Heads song.

AWARDS

Nomination:
Ind. Spirit 2011: Screenplay, Support. Actress (Janney).

LITTLE FOCKERS

Kids bring everyone closer, right?
—Movie tagline

Maybe kids will bring them closer?
—Movie tagline

Box Office: $146 Million

Before the 2000 hit *Meet the Parents,* there was a little known micro-budgeted film upon which it was based, also called *Meet the Parents* (1992). Those lucky enough to have seen this treasure in its very limited Chicago art house run may remember cringing in horror and laughing heartily at the mostly believable mishaps of the young man meeting his socially clueless in-laws. The people on-screen seemed real and no joke felt belabored. At one point, the father asks the young man how he manages his money. He replies rather nervously, "Oh, you know…a penny saved is a penny earned." The father gets out of his chair and storms out of the room, clearly upset by this response. "What did I say?" he asks his fiancé sheepishly. "Dad's mother was named Penny. He keeps her ashes in an urn. He never got over her death." There is no score underlining the joke; just the uncomfortable silence in the room adding to the tension. Sadly, this film remains unavailable on DVD.

The remake paled in comparison, but still had its share of laughs. Ben Stiller was the obvious choice for the put upon Greg and Robert De Niro was appropriate enough to play the intimidating soon-to-be father-in-law. With these two at the helm, the remake and their sequels would inevitably lack the believability of the original, since these two prominent Hollywood figures are too familiar to be relatable. Furthermore, the unnecessary addition to make the dad a former CIA agent who can dig up information on anything and anybody would add contrivances to what should be an easy storyline and giving Greg the last name Focker would eventually become one of the most tired verbal gags in film history, hence the title of the third installment, *Little Fockers.*

It is now ten years after the original remake and the Fockers now have two twin children, both aged five. Greg is still a nurse, but with more responsibility as a pharmaceutical rep in charge of selling the latest erectile dysfunction medicine. His wife, Pam (Teri Polo), is still an indistinguishable non-character, this time helping to raise the two kids. Jack and Dina Byrnes (De Niro and Blythe Danner) are still married. The Focker parents, Bernie (Dustin Hoffman) and Roz (Barbra Streisand), appear to be separated. Bernie is obsessed with finding his "true north" by taking flamenco dance lessons in Spain while Roz hosts a tacky sex therapy show.

The story this time, which feels like a bunch of random ideas for a story thrown together with no throughline, involves Jack realizing after a cardiac arrest that Greg Focker is the only proper patriarch for the Byrnes family. For reasons unknown, Jack is hiding his heart attack from his family, but confides in Greg and asks him to be the family's "God-focker," a joke that gets six tries in one scene in case the audience did not hear it the first time. Greg agrees. Meanwhile, the Fockers are having a new house built for them that will hopefully be ready in time for their twins' fifth birthday party.

Of course, some misunderstandings involving infidelity must be forced into the narrative (again, the term "narrative" is used loosely here). One of Greg's partners in the promotion of the erectile dysfunction medicine is the flirtatious and mysteriously named Andi Garcia (a joke that goes nowhere and is just as well, since she is played by the equally vapid Jessica Alba). They go to a business seminar together, work late and are eventually spied upon by Jack, who now sees Greg as an inappropriate patriarch for his family lineage. Meanwhile (and there are a lot of "meanwhiles" here), the rich philanthropist Kevin (Owen Wilson) is still after Pam's heart and now sports a large tattoo of her on his backside. He shows up at every family function and even offers to host the kids' birthday party himself.

One last meanwhile: the kids are being tested to get into a high-end progressive education institution, Early Human School, the Harvard of kindergarten. Running this facility is Prudence, played by Laura Dern, who is the only actor in the entire ensemble who is actually using (and therefore wasting) her talents here. This plot is only worth mentioning because the film is titled *Little Fockers,* which would indicate that the kids are a big part of the storyline. In fact, the kids have very little to do with anything that is going on.

Everybody involved in this film is on autopilot. De Niro's Jack Byrnes is barely the domineering presence he was in the first film. The tension between he and Greg is all but sucked out of the storyline, only to be forced back in once Jack gets an idea in his head that Greg and Andi Garcia are having an affair. Stiller and Wilson are both simply collecting paychecks. But perhaps most shockingly of all, the film is directed by Paul Weitz, who in the past has directed remarkably-perceptive and wonderfully-acted humanist comedies, such as the original *American Pie* (1999), *About a Boy* (2002), and *In Good Company* (2004). What could have possibly attracted him to this bottom-feeder material?

Little Fockers is one of those comedies that only exists for its tired comedic set-pieces without any regard for whatever made the original so successful. Every set-up for every gag is belabored and drawn out in case the audience cannot possibly see the joke coming. Once the words "erectile dysfunction medicine" are uttered, it is only a matter of time before the wrong person takes them. Once one of the kids reveals he has a small pet

lizard, one counts the minutes for it to become a catalyst for a chain of slapstick comedic events. And anytime there are two characters in an undesirable, but perfectly innocent, situation involving genitalia (in this case, Greg giving Jack a shot in the groin for taking the erectile dysfunction meds), a child must walk through the door.

But why is Jack even taking the meds in the first place? The screenplay by John Hamburg and Larry Stuckey would have the audience believe that Jack really wants to help spice up his own love life with his wife, who is trying to work some role-playing into their sex, at the advice of Roz Focker's TV show. Does this not go against Jack's own narrow way of thinking? No matter. The writers believe this movie cannot exist without this gag. Combine that with uninspired bits involving enemas, blood, and projectile vomiting and that sums up *Little Fockers* in a nutshell.

What is especially disheartening about these three films (*Meet the Fockers* came out in 2004) is how little faith they each have in their audience. The theme of meeting one's in-laws, having the in-laws meet and then having the entire family around to help raise children (which would have been the logical story here, but never really happens) are universal. There is no need for any sub-plots involving the CIA. There is no need to drive any joke involving the word "Focker" into the ground three times over. And there is certainly no need for a climactic fist fight between Jack and Greg with a tired *Jaws* joke thrown in. All one needs are real characters facing real situations and the audience will still be on their side, relating to all of it and wincing in recognition.

But *Little Fockers* and its two predecessors ignore that simple formula and end up achieving even less. Nobody comes to any great understanding here. The film is not about anything. Its vacant theme is tantamount to one person saying "Oh, when I saw you through the window, it looked like you two were having sex. But you weren't. And now I don't dislike you anymore." The end.

Granted, the original, little-seen 1992 film ended on a truly dark note and was also devoid of any real emotional or thematic breakthrough. But at least it knew what was funny and how to construct original jokes. It is too bad that the film exists in limbo and can only be seen through means of pure luck. Greg Glienna, who wrote, produced, directed and starred in the original, is still credited as an Original Creator in these films (along with co-writer Mary Ruth Clarke). He and his collaborators deserve better. Hopefully, after Universal makes all the cash they can from this franchise, they will allow the original to be seen by the public once again, even if just as an extra DVD in a Special Edition. Those unfortunate to have had to sit through anything as shrill and empty as *Little Fockers* should be somehow compensated.

Collin Souter

CREDITS

Greg Focker: Ben Stiller
Jack Byrnes: Robert De Niro
Pamela Focker: Teri Polo
Dina Byrnes: Blythe Danner
Rozalin Focker: Barbra Streisand
Kevin Rawley: Owen Wilson
Bernie Focker: Dustin Hoffman
Samantha Focker: Daisy Tahan
Henry Focker: Colin Baiocchi
Gustavo: Sergio Calderon
Andi Garcia: Jessica Alba
Prudence: Laura Dern
Origin: USA
Language: English
Released: 2010
Production: Robert De Niro, John Hamburg; DW Studios, Everyman Pictures
Directed by: Paul Weitz
Written by: Larry Stuckey, John Hamburg
Cinematography by: Remi Adefarasin
Music by: Stephen Trask
Sound: Eric Lindemann
Editing: James Andrykowski
Art Direction: Sue Chan
Costumes: Molly Maginnis
Production Design: William Arnold
MPAA rating: PG-13
Running time: 98 minutes

REVIEWS

Burr, Ty. *Boston Globe.* December 21, 1010.
Jones, J.R. *Chicago Reader.* December 22, 2010.
Kenny, Glenn. *MSN Movies.* December 21, 2010.
Long, Tom. *Detroit News.* December 22, 2010.
McCarthy, Tom. *Hollywood Reporter.* December 20, 2010.
Pinkerton, Nick. *Village Voice.* December 21, 2010.
Pols, Mary F. *TIME Magazine.* December 21, 2010.
Rickey, Carrie. *Philadelphia Inquirer.* December 21, 2010.
Smith, Kyle. *New York Post.* December 22, 2010.
Weitzman, Elizabeth. *New York Daily News.* December 22, 2010.

TRIVIA

Dustin Hoffman almost didn't reprise his role as Bernie Focker due to creative issues until Universal Pictures convinced him to at least shoot six scenes.

AWARDS

Golden Raspberries 2010: Worst Support. Actress (Alba)
Nomination:

Golden Raspberries 2010: Worst Support. Actress (Streisand), Worst Screenplay.

THE LOSERS

You don't give them orders. You just turn them loose.
—Movie tagline
Anyone else would be dead by now.
—Movie tagline

Box Office: $23 million

It has been well-documented, and often quite accurately, that Hollywood studios these days are as much in the business of not making movies as they are of actually making films, which is a pithy way of saying that the deemed inherent risk in green-lighting an original screenplay can make the perceived loyal and built-in fan base of virtually any sort of source material seem alluring by comparison. That certainly seems to characterize the thinking behind *The Losers*, yet another entry in Hollywood's recent binge of graphic novel adaptations. An intermittently punchy but essentially pointless ball of color and noise, the film delivers an unmemorable rendering of a very standard and familiar soldiers-of-fortune revenge tract.

Releasing in late April, *The Losers* beat fellow manly 2010 mercenary tales *The A-Team* (2010) and *The Expendables* (2010) to the big screen by two and four months, respectively, yet could not convert that jumpstart to its financial advantage, grossing less in its entire two-month domestic theatrical run (under $24 million) than each of those movies did in their debut weekends. It could be the comparative lack of franchise name recognition or star power, or the fact that, despite its considerable mayhem, the movie is saddled with enough judicious cutaways to ensure a PG-13 rating, which renders it seemingly inauthentic and free of consequence. Either way, audiences agreed a bit too readily with the title and consigned it to commercial anonymity in rapid fashion.

On a mission deep in the Bolivian jungle, Clay (Jeffrey Dean Morgan), the leader of an elite U.S. Special Forces unit, refuses a radio order that would result in the collateral damage death of two dozen children. For this transgression, he and the rest of his commando team—Rogue (Idris Elba), Jensen (Chris Evans), Pooch (Columbus Short), and Cougar (Óscar Jaenada)—are immediately cut loose, and subjected to a massive air strike meant to rub them out. Betrayed and presumed dead, the group makes plans to even the score with the higher-up who authorized the attack, a shadowy enemy from within known only as Max (Jason Patric).

As the company regroups and tries to figure out a way back into the United States, one night Clay meets a gorgeous woman (Zoe Saldana). He is not as lucky as he believes, as it turns out she would rather kill him than make love. A hotel room smash-up befitting a debauched rock band ensues, and said lethal beauty is eventually revealed as Aisha. An enigmatic operative with her own agenda, Aisha makes clear her willingness to help bankroll the return of Clay and friends, as long as they let her in on the action. Takedown-style vengeance ensues, against the backdrop of Max and his henchman Wade (Holt McCallany) trying to bribe and intimidate international sources to get a weapon that will allow them to stage what from the outside will look like a foreign terrorist incident, and kick-start a new front in the global war on terror.

From other bawdy ensemble action flicks that wear their over-the-top gaudiness proudly on their sleeve, like *The Big Hit* (1998) and *Smokin' Aces* (2007), to all sorts of pedestrian straight-to-video 1980s action thrillers featuring corrupt government villains, *The Losers* has plenty of antecedents, though in and of itself that is not the reason for its failure to engage. Rather, *The Losers* suffers from basic creative entropy; of how to marry intriguing style and content on a very fundamental level.

The Vertigo/DC Comics title ran for thirty-two issues from August 2003 to early 2006, and the muscular visual style of British writer Andy Diggle and artist Mark Simpson (aka Jock), gets translated to screen fairly devotedly, as director Sylvain White displays a music video sensibility throughout, employing an expressive color palette alongside various whip pans, flash edits and up-tempo music. This sort of madcap style worked much better for the dance sequences in White's well received *Stomp the Yard* (2007). Here, the work of he and his conspirators—cinematographer Scott Kevan, editor David Checel, and composer John Ottman—while technically of a piece, has an effect that is more deflating than leavening.

In visually and tonally draining the story of any grittiness, White places a greater burden of audience engagement upon screenwriters Peter Berg and James Vanderbilt, whose adaptation lacks enough colorful flourishes to give the movie a zany, carefree sense of flight. That it lacks pretensions is cold comfort, for there is no depth either. All the characters and conflicts herein are one-note, and third-act betrayals and revelations are easily apparent only twenty to twenty-five minutes into the movie. For those who insist on attempting to parse the narrative, and find meaning in its conflict, Max's motivations eventually become problematic, too, since there is never a clear sense of whether he is truly working for only himself or as part of a larger, breakaway government plot.

Unsurprisingly, *The Losers*' performances do not amount to much. Morgan and Elba are gruff and gruffer, but there is not quite enough machismo pop to the dialogue to make their alpha dog characterizations very interesting. There are two exceptions, however. With the starring role in *Captain America* (2011) on deck, Evans is quietly distinguishing himself as not only a solid leading man, but also an enjoyable, raffish presence in movies like this and *Scott Pilgrim vs. the World* (2010). Jensen is the guy who figures he is going to get hit or shot, so he might as well enjoy himself while doing his job, and Evans brings a pinch of self-deprecating fatalism to the proceedings, particularly in a scene involving his infiltration of a company as a computer repairman.

The other notable exception is Patric, a talented actor too frequently given to dourness. In playing an eccentric nut-job whose sociopathic tendencies have seemingly been exacerbated by bureaucratic enablement, he gets to truly cut loose for the first time in years, but even his scene-chewing villainy is not enough to redeem *The Losers*.

Brent Simon

CREDITS

Clay: Jeffrey Dean Morgan
Roque: Idris Elba
Aisha: Zoe Saldana
Pooch: Columbus Short
Jensen: Chris Evans
Cougar: Óscar Jaenada
Max: Jason Patric
Wade: Holt McCallany
Origin: USA
Language: English
Released: 2010
Production: Joel Silver, Akiva Goldsman, Kerry Foster; Dark Castle Entertainment, DC Entertainment, Weed Road Pictures; released by Warner Bros.
Directed by: Sylvain White
Written by: Peter Berg, James Vanderbilt
Cinematography by: Scott Kevan
Music by: John Ottman
Sound: Larry Long, Mark Larry
Music Supervisor: Amine Ramer
Editing: David Checel
Art Direction: Erin Cochran
Costumes: Magali Guidasci
Production Design: Aaron Osborne
MPAA rating: PG-13
Running time: 97 minutes

REVIEWS

Dargis, Manohla. *New York Times.* April 23, 2010.
Debruge, Peter. *Variety.* April 21, 2010.

Ebert, Roger. *Chicago Sun-Times.* April 22, 2010.
Gleiberman, Owen. *Entertainment Weekly.* April 22, 2010.
Honeycutt, Kirk. *Hollywood Reporter.* April 21, 2010.
Howell, Peter. *Toronto Star.* April 23, 2010.
Kois, Dan. *Village Voice.* April 20, 2010.
Morris, Wesley. *Boston Globe.* April 22, 2010.
Puig, Claudia. *USA Today.* April 22, 2010.
Sharkey, Betsy. *Los Angeles Times.* April 23, 2010.

QUOTES

Jensen: "Did you know that cats can make one thousand different sounds and dogs can only make ten? Cats, man. Not to be trusted."

Jensen: "That's right bitches; I got a crossbow!"

TRIVIA

The "Girls of America" dolls that Jensen and Cougar were assembling in the Bolivian factory reappear in a later scene when Roque drops through the ceiling of a store and falls next to a product display for those very same dolls.

The film features art from the original *Losers* comic series on which it is based as well as new illustrations by the original artist Jock.

LOTTERY TICKET

Winning is just the beginning. Surviving is another story.
—Movie tagline

Box Office: $24 million

Lottery Ticket is almost too innocuous to knock. It seems like its greatest ambition is to be a broad, urban comedy version of *29th Street* (1991), which is to say that it does not aim very high. There is, of course, nothing wrong with concocting a lighthearted comedy out of the fantasy of winning a $370 million lottery, but why is it that screenwriters can barely tap into the drama of such an event without resorting to clichés or melodrama? *Lottery Ticket* is about as ambitious as its title would suggest. Even the movie's location (the projects) looks about as destitute as Stepford. Whatever statement it might have wanted to make about the economy in 2010 is muted by a lack of authenticity. Every time a character claims they have nothing, the audience is forced to simply take their word for it, even though evidence points to the contrary.

The movie tells the story of Kevin (Bow Wow), a good kid fresh out of high school who aspires, realistically, to become an assistant manager at Foot Locker. His long-term dream is to one day start his own shoe company. His closet is stacked with product that could easily make him the Carrie Bradshaw (of *Sex and the City*) of the urban sect. His best friend Benny (Brandon T. Jackson) is not nearly as ambitious, but he is loyal. Kevin lives with his Grandmother (Loretta Devine) who sends him out on errands, not the least of which is her daily lottery ticket. At the moment, the jackpot is up to $370 million and every drug store has customers around the block. Kevin decides not to partake, seeing it as a cynical ploy to get more money out of the pockets of hardworking people.

This little enclave where Kevin resides is, of course, packed with characters only found in movies. There is the old hermit, Mr. Washington (Ice Cube), who never leaves his apartment and uses Kevin as an errand boy. There is a four-pack of friends who follow Kevin's every move, but do not seem to have lives of their own. Nikki (Teairra Mari), the neighborhood's main hottie, struts down the streets knowing full well the impression she is making and is not shy about exploiting it for all its worth (she freely name-drops when talking about her sexual escapades). Lorenzo (Gbenga Akinnagbe) is the main thug who gets his way just by staring down at his victims. When he sees Kevin in his Foot Locker outfit, he demands three pairs of the new Nike Air Jordans for him and his posse.

Eventually, this demand leads to Kevin getting fired from Foot Locker and having a cheap Chinese food lunch with his longtime female friend, Stacie (Naturi Naughton). She gives him a fortune cookie inscription with lucky numbers on the back. When he finally gets around to buying his Grandma's lottery ticket, he reluctantly buys one for himself at the insistence of the store owner. The numbers on that fortune cookie are, of course, prophetic and Kevin finds himself the winner of $370 million.

As much as he and his Grandmother try to keep it a secret, it is only a matter of minutes before everyone in the neighborhood finds out and wants a piece of it. Somehow, a local gangster named Sweet Tee (Keith David) agrees to give Kevin a cash advance of the money before he cashes in the ticket so that he may go on a big date sooner than later. Kevin takes the bag of cash and goes on a spending spree with his friends. He does not cash in the ticket just yet because the screenplay demands that he hang into it so he can lose it to Lorenzo.

Lottery Ticket is told in broad comic terms. Almost every supporting performance is playing to the back of the room. While it does not rely on slapstick as much as other comedies of its kind, it relies too heavily on current pop culture references to serve as punch lines, a surefire way to make a movie feel dated long after its release. As the movie builds to its predictable third act, the comic mugging gets traded in for melodrama as

Kevin and his friend Benny have a heated argument over loyalty and what having this kind of money means to them. Again, the question arises: How come nobody attempts a good drama about winning the lottery? They only ever seem to come up with lame comedies with equally lame dramatic points on the subject.

Nothing that happens in *Lottery Ticket* will come as any great shock. Characters' pasts are revealed and they come into the fray when the screenplay demands it. The actors all appear to be going through the motions of the storyline, with only an occasional bit of charm. Director Erik White, who wrote the story with screenwriter Abdul Williams, fills the frame with an abundance of sunlight and good cheer that it makes the projects actually look like a fun place to live. Are there not worse neighborhoods in America that could use that money? Why not make a movie about them?

Collin Souter

CREDITS

Kevin Carson: Bow Wow
Benny: Brandon T. Jackson
Sweet Tee: Keith David
Jimmy: Terry Crews
Stacie: Naturi Naughton
Mr. Washington: Ice Cube
Giovanni: Bill Bellamy
Minister: Mike Epps
Grandma: Loretta Devine
David Semaj: Charlie Murphy
Lorenzo: Gbenga Akinnagbe
Nikki: Teairra Mari
Origin: USA
Language: English
Released: 2010
Production: Matt Alvarez, Mark Burg, Broderick Johnson, Andrew A. Kosove, Oren Koules; Alcon Entertainment, Cube Vision; released by Warner Bros.
Directed by: Erik White
Written by: Abdul Williams, Erik White
Cinematography by: Patrick Cady
Music by: Teddy Castellucci
Sound: Whit Norris
Music Supervisor: Dave Jordan, JoJo Villanueva
Editing: Harvey Rosenstock
Art Direction: Matteo De Cosmo
Costumes: Sandra Hernandez
Production Design: Roshelle Berliner
MPAA rating: PG-13
Running time: 95 minutes

REVIEWS

Anderson, Jason. *Toronto Star.* August 19, 2010.
Childress, Erik. *eFilmcritic.com.* August 20, 2010.

Goodykoontz, Bill. *Arizona Republic.* August 19, 2010.
Honeycutt, Kirk. *Hollywood Reporter.* August 13, 2010.
Lybarger, Day. *Moviemaker Magazine.* August 20, 2010.
Phillips, Michael. *Chicago Tribune.* August 19, 2010.
Puig, Claudia. *USA Today.* August 19, 2010.
Rabin, Nathan. *AV Club.* August 19, 2010.
Russo, Tom. *Boston Globe.* August 19, 2010.
Weitzman, Elizabeth. *New York Daily News.* August 20, 2010.

QUOTES

Benny: "You were supposed to get her number. Not doo-doo."

TRIVIA

Hip-hip artist Nicki Minaj auditioned for the role of Nikki Swayze but it ended up going to fellow recording artist Teairra Mari.

LOVE AND OTHER DRUGS

Box Office: $32 Million

It is not hard to subscribe to the theory that just about all prescription drugs are bad for people in some way. This need not be based within any religious practice nor any formal medical training aside from what can be learned on Web M.D. The manner in which drugs are handed out and taken like candy these days makes wondering if an avoidance of them all these years could actually boost one's immune system rather than create a momentary pusher's fix for feelings that are supposed to be absolutely natural. Whether or not love is a natural contagion you can catch or just another chemical reaction akin to consuming large quantities of chocolate is one for the writers to romanticize. To combine the two against the backdrop of the apparent rise of the pharmaceutical soft sell is an intriguing concept. The execution, on the other hand, of Edward Zwick's *Love and Other Drugs*, is akin to watching *Love Story* (1970) plopped into the middle of *Thank You For Smoking* (2005). And, surprisingly, the love story turns out to be far more interesting.

Jamie Randall (Jake Gyllenhaal) can sell anything. However, when he cannot keep his libido in check at work, he is fired and jumps headlong into becoming a sales rep for Pfizer. Tasked with cluing in and even bribing medical offices, Jamie is pushing Zoloft as the new Prozac; fewer side effects, even if some of the harsher ones have not been "proven." On a visit to the office of Dr. Knight (Hank Azaria) where Jamie has hooked up with a giddy secretary (Judy Greer), he sits in on an impromptu breast examination of Maggie Murdock

(Anne Hathaway). When she discovers he is not an intern, she is outraged, but after he turns on the apology charm she agrees to meet him for coffee at the shop where she works.

Thus begins a torrid sexual affair that Maggie prefers to keep as is. She has been hurt before (by Jake's Prozac competitor no less, played by Gabriel Macht) when the guy was unwilling to commit to her complications with Parkinson's Disease or his own as a married man. Yes, it turns out that Maggie is not just another pill-popper. She actually has Stage One Parkinson's, which gives her the occasional tremor or—when off her meds—tightness in her extremities that make everyday tasks a problem. Viagra makes Jamie an even bigger star within the company and on the fast track towards the apparent center of sales—Chicago. With Jamie becoming more aware of the progressive reality of Maggie's ailment, he needs to sell himself on just how good a person he actually is.

If *Love and Other Drugs* could be given a prescription itself it would be one for Saphris, a newly approved drug for the treatment of bipolar disorder. Alternating between the love story and whatever statement it wants to make about the drug industry is only one of the areas where the screenplay by Charles Randolph, Marshall Herskovitz, and Edward Zwick wildly shifts gears. It also finds different plateaus and valleys within their respective storylines that make it hard to maintain an emotional consistency. What begins as an expose inspired by the book *Hard Sell: The Evolution of a Viagra Salesman* by Jamie Reidy quickly gets left behind for a half-baked bit of soul-searching for its lead character. While the arc of the recent *The Social Network* (2010) was for its fast tracking ingénue to admit he was a jerk, this becomes the discovery of one man's inner goodness. But is his journey about coming to the realization that the product he is pimping is dangerous or that he can still love the sexual dynamo who continues shaking well after she orgasms?

Not to make light of Parkinson's, of course, but it becomes the third lead of the film; the literal disease of the week that takes over the film to somehow preach the idea that there are bigger problems than mood swings to solve. Zwick films a whole scene with Hathaway brought to a Parkinson's support group intent to see the bright side of things. The montage of the couple flying back and forth searching for treatment begins to take away from what, up to a certain point, was becoming a really well-written relationship story. The scenes between Gyllenhaal and Hathaway are such a cut above the standard rut of romantic comedies that an audience could have easily forgiven forgoing the lessons in pharmaceutical malfeasance. Gyllenhaal has never been this loose and fun with a role and Hathaway is luminescent and believ-

able as a woman cautious enough to keep her distance but ready to jump at a chance for pleasure when she sees it.

And then there is the case of Jamie's brother, Josh (Josh Gad), who as the film opens has made countless millions. But after breaking up with his lady, Josh spends the rest of the film as an unshaven slob who hangs around his big brother hoping a little of his sexual power will rub off on him. Beware any film designed as a comedy that then has to bring in someone like this to provide comic relief. The Josh character is such an abrasive distraction that every time he appears one hopes are that this is the big tragedy scene where he overdoses on Jamie's samples. Gad, who played his character in the disastrous *21* (2008) in precisely the over-exemplified manner here, destroys the vibe of the film with every appearance as if he were improvising lines stolen from a *Van Wilder* (2002) sequel and creating embarrassing moments straight out of *American Pie* (1999). A scene where he is caught masturbating to a sex tape made by Jamie and Maggie serves no purpose in this film. It is not a bridge, not part of a montage, and has no distinguishing arc to anyone except to remind us that the character is worthless and out-of-place. If love is so powerful for a guy to walk away from millions of dollars to live like a freeloader, then the screenplay better be prepared to treat him seriously enough to form Jamie's progression to a one-woman man.

Money becomes the 800-pound gorilla in the film that nobody seems to speak about after Josh's early bragging. The rest of Jake's family, including George Segal and Jill Clayburgh as mom and dad, get one scene and are forgotten; the suggestion of some serious trims that also leave subplots involving the Macht rival and Oliver Platt's partner hanging. As this is the shortest film Zwick has ever released, we might actually welcome his usual two-hour plus cuts in the hopes that it might actually be the story everyone wanted to tell. Jason Reitman's *Thank You For Smoking* (2005) was flawed but was at least confident in the tonal shift of its character from cancer-pusher to becoming a better father. Its view of the tobacco industry was clear and never felt like just a conveniently hot-button backdrop for its lead character. The screenplay here is confused in its condemnation of Pfizer and its products after its grabbing opening act. Showing a homeless man become a three-step callback joke from bum-to-job interviewee after popping Prozac is unfunny, simplistic, and counters the film's themes by becoming what it preaches against—a commercial for the pill's strengths.

The portrait of the film's women deserve more scrutiny than the charges being leveled at the makers of *The Social Network*. That film had college groupies and party girls. These women are supposed to be adults and yet are all portrayed as oversexed male fantasies ready to give it up easier than those on Rohypnol. Even big, fat, insecure Josh gets a girl to drop her top for him by flattering her with less-than-gentleman-like behavior. Women in the audience though will find it hard to avoid wooing over Jake. And their dates will be too distracted by Hathaway's generous displays of flesh to care. At least the scenes between these two ring with authenticity and almost make the film worth recommending.

But there are so many better films as a whole that make up the sum of *Love and Other Drugs'* best parts. *Garden State* (2004) was all about the thawing of a generation raised on prescriptions. *Up in the Air* (2009) recently portrayed a charming workaholic who found solace in wanting to settle down with a vibrant woman. The little seen Sundance gem, *Dopamine* (2003), explored the possibility that love was indeed a drug embedded in our brains rather than our hearts. Even the Kids in the Hall feature, *Brain Candy* (1996), was a more effective satire on the subject. By the end of Zwick's film, it is easy to remember another comedy about another smart professional; one on the fast track of an industry's subsection whose talents could be better used to help truly sick people and not just ones that need to feel better about themselves. And along the way he meets a woman whose breasts take center stage at first sight until she can see him for what he is and he changes because of her. Even *Doc Hollywood* (1991) is another film that is better than *Love and Other Drugs*.

Erik Childress

CREDITS

Jamie Randall: Jake Gyllenhaal
Maggie Murdock: Anne Hathaway
Dr. Knight: Hank Azaria
Bruce Winston: Oliver Platt
Dr. James Randall: George Segal
Dr. Ted Goldstein: Scott Cohen
Josh Randall: Josh Gad
Lisa: Katheryn Winnick
Helen Randall: Natalie Gold
Cindy: Judy Greer
Trey Hannigan: Gabriel Macht
Nancy Randall: Jill Clayburgh
Origin: USA
Language: English
Released: 2010
Production: Pieter Jan Brugge, Marshall Herskovitz, Scott Stuber, Edward Zwick, Charles Randolph; Bedford Falls, Fox 2000 Pictures, New Regency Pictures, Regency Enterprises, Stuber Productions; released by 20th Century Fox

Directed by: Edward Zwick
Written by: Edward Zwick, Charles Randolph, Marshall Herskovitz
Cinematography by: Steven Fierberg
Music by: James Newton Howard
Sound: Edward Tise
Music Supervisor: Randall Poster
Editing: Steven Rosenblum
Art Direction: Gary Kosko
Costumes: Deborah Lynn Scott
Production Design: Patti Podesta
MPAA rating: R
Running time: 113 minutes

REVIEWS

Berardinelli, James. *ReelViews.* November 23, 2010.
Chang, Justin. *Variety.* October 27, 2010.
Edelstein, David. *New York Magazine.* November 22, 2010.
Hassenger, Jess. *Filmcritic.com.* November 23, 2010.
Longworth, Karina. *L.A. Weekly.* November 22, 2010.
McWeeny, Drew. *HitFix.* November 17, 2010.
Pais, Matt. *Metromix.com.* November 23, 2010.
Orndorf, Brian. *BrianOrndorf.com.* November 23, 2010.
Phillips, Michael. *Chicago Tribune.* November 23, 2010.
Weber, Bill. *Slant Magazine.* November 22, 2010.

QUOTES

Jamie Randall: "Sometimes the things you want the most don't happen and what you least expect happens. I don't know—you meet thousands of people and none of them really touch you. And then you meet that one person and your life is changed."

TRIVIA

Director Edward Zwick encouraged his stars to watch romantic films as well as improvise their sex scenes before hand while fully clothed in order to get the best results when it came time for the actual shoot.

AWARDS

Nomination:

Golden Globes 2011: Actor—Mus./Comedy (Gyllenhaal), Actress—Mus./Comedy (Hathaway).

LOVE RANCH

When it comes to love…everyone pays a price.
—Movie tagline

A story about money, power, murder…and the one thing that makes the world go round.
—Movie tagline

In 2010, the subject of corporate greed and its inevitable downfall permeated the cinematic landscape throughout the latter half of the year. With films such as *The Social Network, Casino Jack* (and its documentary on the same subject), and *Inside Job* as well as countless other films that had the subject of unemployment and financial ruin somewhere in the background of a storyline, it seemed as though Hollywood and the indies wanted to tap into a tried and true rags-to-riches-to rags story as a way of reflecting on the current times (while still asking the American public for their hard-earned dollar). If the storylines were not lifted directly out of the current headlines, they were allegories or flashbacks to another time and another place where the same story existed on a smaller, or in the case of *Love Ranch,* seedier scale.

Taylor Hackford's *Love Ranch* opens with the images of flashing lights and champagne toasts while the character of Grace Bontempo (Helen Mirren) says via voice-over, "Selling love will make you rich, my mother always said. Just don't put your heart into it." The story takes place in 1976. Grace is married to Charlie (Joe Pesci). Together, they run the Mustang Ranch just outside Reno, Nevada. The bordello is somewhat protected by the law and attracts bottom-feeder johns. The place, which Charlie has nicknamed the Love Ranch, is flourishing, but of course, Charlie is seeking another revenue stream. He takes up managing a boxer named Armando Bruza (Sergio Peris-Mencheta), who has fought Muhammed Ali.

Two things are about to impede the success of the Ranch. First, Grace has cancer and is not going to tell Charlie until the time is right. With Charlie, though, there is no right time. And, second, Church people are filing petitions to have the Ranch closed and will likely win the battle. Charlie is one to ignore danger signs and eventually invites Armando to stay at the ranch to train. Grace is furious at Charlie for his spending habits and so-called business practices and she lets him know it. Grace appears to have the upper hand no matter what, even with the prostitutes, who break into meaningless catfights, which she has to break up. Charlie and Grace bicker and fight like any married couple, but they also know how to kiss and make up. Amidst all the ugliness of their chosen profession, there appears to be great love and understanding between them.

Charlie also owns a trailer park, where Armando eventually has to train. Charlie has bigger dreams for the place. He wants to turn it into the next Love Ranch. While Charlie makes television appearances and carries out physical threats against anyone who even remotely double-crosses him, a bond begins to grow between Armando and Grace, who at first resents his presence. She becomes his trainer and confides in him every problem with her marriage. Eventually, they fall in love.

Hackford's direction is as assured as it ever has been and he still knows how to get great performances out of his actors, but Mark Jacobson's screenplay is all over the map. The relationship between Grace and Armando feels forced and unconvincing. No doubt, liberties were taken with the true story the movie attempts to depict, but even their love-making scene feels like an element wedged into the narrative just so filmgoers will have something tantalizing to talk about once the film is over. Grace is the logical focal point in the storyline, but it lacks a momentum. The Love Ranch itself is a horrid place where seemingly nothing pleasant ever happens, even if pleasure is meant to be the service of choice. Is the audience really supposed to care whether or not it stays open?

Mirren (Hackford's wife in real life) has always made the most of the roles she plays (even in 2010's dull and dreary *Red,* she refused to phone it in). She tries in earnest to give Grace her tough-as-nails demeanor while showing signs of a bruised and battered heart beneath the surface. Occasionally, there are signs of a great-as-usual performance, but not often enough. The casting of Pesci, however, is unimaginative. He is basically doing a variation of roles he has played in the past, most notably *GoodFellas* (1990) and *Casino* (1995). Every scene in which he appears lacks any element of surprise. When he gets mad, he punctuates his profanity with punches. As Armando, Peris-Mencheta is a welcome presence and the only true heart of the story. Once his limelight fades due to unforeseeable physical circumstances, however, the story takes more conventional turns. Gina Gershon, who plays the ranch's main prostitute, is completely wasted as usual.

Even when couched in any sort of present-day allegory, *Love Ranch* ultimately lacks purpose. As a story about the dangers of excess, it lacks a compelling figure of greed. As a love story, it is too hopeless and contrived to invest in. As a piece of noteworthy entertainment, the only thing worth really investigating is if the film indeed broke the record for the number of times the F-word is uttered (probably not, but it like that was the goal here). *Love Ranch* certainly has elements of an interesting story and a documentary could probably do it some justice, but Hackford's film is a mixed bag of good intentions in an ugly and senseless universe.

Collin Souter

CREDITS
Grace Bontempo: Helen Mirren
Charlie Bontempo: Joe Pesci

Christina: Scout Taylor-Compton

Mallory: Taryn Manning

Sheriff Cortez: Gil Birmingham

Armando Bruza: Sergio Peris-Mencheta

Irene: Gina Gershon

Samantha: Bai Ling

Origin: USA

Language: English

Released: 2010

Production: David Bergstein, Taylor Hackford, Marty Katz, Lou DiBella; Capitol Films, Aramid Entertainment, Anvil Films Production, Rising Star; released by E1 Entertainment

Directed by: Taylor Hackford

Written by: Mark Jacobson

Cinematography by: Kieran McGuigan

Music by: Chris P. Bacon

Sound: William Sarokin

Editing: Paul Hirsch

Art Direction: Mark Alan Duran

Costumes: Melissa Bruning

Production Design: Bruno Rubeo

MPAA rating: R

Running time: 117 minutes

REVIEWS

Anderson, Melissa. *Village Voice.* July 29, 2010.

Barsanti, Chris. *Film Journal International.* June 25, 2010.

Ebert, Roger. *Chicago Sun-Times.* June 28, 2010.

Ellingson, Annlee. *Moving Pictures Magazine.* June 29, 2010.

Holden, Stephen. *New York Times.* July 2, 2010.

Howell, Peter. *Toronto Star.* June 30, 2010.

Morris, Wesley. *Boston Globe.* July 1, 2010.

Rabin, Nathan. *A/V Club.* June 30, 2010.

Reed, Rex. *New York Observer.* July 7, 2010.

Tallerico, Brian. *MovieRetriever.com.* June 30, 2010.

TRIVIA

This film marks the second time that actress Helen Mirren has worked with her husband director Taylor Hackford.

M

MacGRUBER

The ultimate tool.
—Movie tagline

Box Office: $8 million

The *Saturday Night Live* sketch that inspired *MacGruber* begins and ends the same way every time. MacGruber (Will Forte), a parody of the cult do-it-yourself hero of the television series *MacGyver*, is confined in a room with his cohorts—a time bomb ticking away. It explodes. In between those two necessary points is the opportunity to insert the show's guest host as another assistant and display MacGruber's total lack of competency and situational awareness.

In general, the short format is, with few exceptions, best left as is, and *MacGruber* suffers from the extension. Forte, John Solomon, and director Jorma Taccone's script hardly halts from joke-telling. Indeed, the entire premise of the plot is a familiar retread of the old action movie standby: A nuclear device controlled by a megalomaniacal villain.

That scoundrel's name sets the tone and class for most of the movie's humor. He is Dieter Von Cunth (Val Kilmer), a name that is pronounced three different ways throughout the course of the movie—always with a soft vowel sound. The first takes the soft, lisping end of the spelling. The second employs a hard, voiced "Z" sound. The third is downright obscene. There is no rule that states a tasteless joke is deficient simply because of its nature, and this movie proves that. Its funniest moments are of a vulgar variety, although that might simply be a matter of odds since the majority of the gags fit into that category.

The villain's name, for one, is at least amusing the first time a character utters it. No matter how many variations of that surname arise (intentional distinctions from Taccone or unintentional divergences on the part of the cast), the blunt force of its primary impact cannot be matched. The subsequent iterations, which are typically repeated multiple times throughout a given scene, begin not only to pale in comparison but also to lose the effect. The gag grows annoying and quickly, too.

One of the classic "rules" of comedy is the so-called 'Rule of Three,' which states a repeated joke can only be funny three times before it grows stale, and even that rule assumes the joke is funny the first time. The same screenplay that offers endless intonations of the name Cunth at least understands the spirit of this rule in certain moments and has the astuteness to adapt it.

If done at all, the most successful jokes in the movie are repeated only once. MacGruber, after accidentally killing his entire squad before they can begin their mission to stop Cunth, begs that Lt. Dixon Piper (Ryan Phillippe) team up with him, otherwise Col. James Faith (Powers Boothe) will remove him from the mission. His pleas turn to sobs. His sobs bring him to his knees. While there, he offers sexual favors of widely varying kinds, and no sooner than Piper shuts the door that the camera reveals MacGruber with his pants around his ankles. The editing mirrors the dialogue exchanges, which never pause between jokes and certainly never when MacGruber realizes he has misspoke, revealed too much, or otherwise made a fool of himself.

The series of steps that lead MacGruber to that vulnerable position are repeated once—and only once—with Faith, and even then, it is comic shorthand—a quick callback to his string of offered sex acts. Another recurring bit involves MacGruber and Faith, who repeat the same three lines of dialogue, which add up to MacGruber leaving "the game," Faith stating "the game has changed," and MacGruber pointing out that the players of said game have stayed the same.

The exchange pushes a clichéd metaphor to its breaking point, recalling the heated conversations of countless action movie heroes and their superiors. From the opening sequence, a dead-serious sequence in which Cunth and his goons steal a nuclear warhead in sandy Siberia, Taccone and cinematographer Brandon Trost employ the pristinely lit polish of a traditional, big-budget Hollywood action film of the late 1980s and 1990s (heavenly whites blinding through windows, the monotone pallet of the Pentagon, a few solemnly gray and one rainy scene at a cemetery).

The look of the movie is a joke unto itself, reflecting MacGruber's own dated attire (jeans, plaid shirt, vest, and boots), haircut (a flowing mullet), taste in music (soft rock of the 1980s), and device to listen to said songs (a removable but cumbersome car radio, which he carries everywhere). In spite of the movie's overall appearance, the only direct satirical jab at the genre comes in the form of a sex scene. Starting with pans across candles in a bedroom and rhythmic cuts of close-ups of MacGruber and his partner Vicki St. Elmo (Kristen Wiig) kissing and caressing, it suddenly drops the façade, as MacGruber thrusts in a mechanical pattern and makes horrifying grunts of pleasure. The joke is repeated once more with MacGruber and the ghost of his dead fiancée Casey (Maya Rudolph).

That discrepancy between fantasy and reality is the crux of the character of MacGruber, who proves himself to be the opposite of the description in his personnel file. The mileage of success for such a character is short, and strangely, the screenplay only directly references the nominal inspiration for the character in one moment, in which MacGruber sets up a trap for arriving guards: a paper cup full of water that drops on the first one who opens the door. Without a solid through-line of purpose, the jokes in *MacGruber* that work are few and far between.

Mark Dujsik

CREDITS

MacGruber: Will Forte
Vicki St. Elmo: Kristen Wiig
Dieter Von Cunth: Val Kilmer
Lt. Dixon Piper: Ryan Phillippe
Col. James Faith: Powers Boothe
Casey: Maya Rudolph
Origin: USA
Language: English
Released: 2010
Production: John Goldwyn, Lorne Michaels; Relativity Media, Broadway Media; released by Universal Pictures
Directed by: Jorma Taccone
Written by: Will Forte, Jorma Taccone, John Solomon
Cinematography by: Brandon Trost
Music by: Matthew Compton
Editing: Jamie Gross
Production Design: Robb Wilson King
Music Supervisor: Happy Walters
Art Direction: Steven Maes
Costumes: Susanna Puisto
MPAA rating: R
Running time: 90 minutes

REVIEWS

Berardinelli, James. *Reelviews.* May 21, 2010.
Burr, Ty. *Boston Globe.* May 21, 2010.
DeFore, John. *Hollywood Reporter.* March 16, 2010.
McCann, Ruth. *Washington Post.* May 21, 2010.
Moore, Roger. *Orlando Sentinel.* May 20, 2010.
Putman, Dustin. *Dustinputman.com.* May 21, 2010.
Rea, Steven. *Philadelphia Inquirer.* May 22, 2010.
Smith, Kyle. *New York Post.* May 21, 2010.
Sobczynski, Peter. *Efilmcritic.* May 22, 2010.
Vaux, Rob. *Filmcritic.com.* May 20, 2010.

QUOTES

MacGruber: "MacGruber don't play like homie, and homie don't play that game."

TRIVIA

MacGruber is the fifteenth feature film to be based on a *Saturday Night Live* sketch.

MACHETE

He was given an offer he couldn't refuse…
—Movie tagline

Yesterday he was a decent man living a decent life. Now he is a brutal savage who must slaughter to stay alive.
—Movie tagline

Box Office: $26 million

Sandwiched between Robert Rodriguez and Quentin Tarantino's feature length contributions to 2007's *Grindhouse* were three delicious strips of cheesy celluloid: previews for make believe B-movies coming soon to a 1970s theater near you. The tastiest looking of these, *Machete,* featured a handlebar-mustached Mexican badass on a very Charles Bronson-eque mission of revenge. Featuring intentionally low-rent special effects, generous female skin, and over-the-top action, the preview succeeded in being both fall-out-of-your-seat hilarious and the best movie of all time that no one would ever get to see. Now, however, *Machete* is a real film and has the unenviable task of living up to the outrageous trailer that inspired it. Unfortunately, the feature length *Machete* is unable to sustain the energy of its 90-second preview, however, if the viewer can tolerate the momentum killing lulls between action sequences *Machete* offers up some decent B-movie cheese.

Machete starts out exactly the way it should, wasting no time establishing a setting, plot, or characters. A grim faced Federale, Machete (Danny Trejo), tears through the Mexican desert at one hundred miles an hour. His purpose: rescuing a woman who has been kidnapped. His orders: exactly the opposite. Machete's partner screamingly pleads with him from the passenger's seat not to defy orders. Machete's superior officer commands him by walkie-talkie to obey orders and stop. Machete slams the car through the wall of the house in which the woman is being held (his partner is instantly killed in a cascade of bullets; Machete is untouched). Machete strides through the building, killing everyone in his path with his titular blade (most memorably twirling 360 degrees and decapitating five thugs standing in a circle around him). But, alas, it is a trap. Shanghaied by the supposed kidnap victim, Machete helplessly watches as his arch nemesis, crime lord Torrez (Steven Seagal) decapitates his wife just for laughs. Left for dead and emotionally shattered, Machete fades into the anonymous life of a day laborer.

Meanwhile, the reelection campaign of the rather conservative Texas state senator McLaughlin (Robert De Niro) is not going well. Senator McLaughlin is so conservative that he patrols the border with a gang of right-wing terrorists (led by Don Johnson) who are murdering illegal immigrants. The viewer is introduced to the senator as he personally guns down an immigrant on camera for a right-wing fundraising commercial. Despite his efforts, however, McLaughlin is down in the polls and his sleazy aide, Booth (a fabulous Jeff Fahey), decides to pick a Mexican day laborer at random to attempt to "assassinate" the senator (a set up to generate sympathy votes in which the senator will be superficially wounded, and the Mexican assassin double-crossed and murdered before he can reveal anything). Unfortunately for Booth, McLaughlin, the right wing terrorists and Torrez (who, it turns out, is behind everything), that randomly selected day laborer is Machete.

Machete's greatest strength is its rogue's gallery of a cast which is a B-movie aficionado's dream and makes the film worthy of viewing all on its own. One of the great pleasures of the film is its gleeful eschewing of contemporary Hollywood action casting conventions. The median age of the principal male cast is sixty-three. Rather than a 25-year-old ripped pretty boy, *Machete*'s action hero is pushing 70, cannot really run, and cannot really act (Trejo delivers every line with an identical facial expression and identical emotionless monotone that makes Charles Bronson look like Alec Guinness). Fahey, plays his sinister-yet-hapless (he cannot even control his oversexed wife, June [Alicia Marek], and daughter, April [Lindsey Lohan], let alone manage a labyrinthine conspiracy) senatorial operative to the hilt, sporting a gray-streaked mullet that has to be seen to be believed (only in a Rodriguez film would the aide to a conservative Texas state senator possess a mullet). Seagal proves that, just like Elvis, an actor can have nearly twenty-five years and forty movies of practice and still not be able to act worth a lick. Indeed, Seagal puts as little effort into acting in this film as any actor in any film ever. When Machete sticks his machete into Seagal's ample gut at the film's climax, Seagal responds as if someone has lightly tapped him on the shoulder and asked him for the time. Cheech Marin shines as the decidedly non-pacifist catholic priest, Padre. "God forgives, but I don't," he comments before graphically shooting his would be assassin's head off. Lohan spends half of her screen time naked, the other half in a nun's habit, gunning white supremacists down with dual-wielded pistols. The actors have a lot of fun with their cartoonish roles and much of *Machete*'s pleasure comes from simply watching them interact with one another.

Obviously, the point of *Machete* is not its plot, which is a purposeful revenge flick cliché designed to connect one over-the-top action scene to another. Cornered in a hospital by a gang of Booth's henchmen, Machete plunges his hand into the gut of one of the men, tugs out his entrails like a fire hose and then dashes through a window gripping the intestine like a rope to swing him through the window of a lower floor to safety. Searching Booth's home for evidence against the senator, Machete encounters Booth's horny wife and daughter, which leads to a mother-daughter-Machete three-way in the backyard swimming pool. Apprehended by corrupt cops, Machete patiently bides his time in the back of their cruiser, waiting until one of the cops casually mentions that he thought the "other" cop had frisked Machete before casually inserting his machete through the back of the seat and through the driving officer (employing about as much force as putting a card into an ATM machine). The car flips, catches on fire and explodes, sending Machete flying towards the camera in low rent, slo-mo. When *Machete* cuts to the action, it delivers the B-movie goodness.

The problem is that there is simply not enough of it. Despite its excellent cast and cheese ball action, *Machete* simply cannot sustain the momentum of the preview that inspired it. It might seem unreasonable to expect a 105-minute low budget movie to sustain the energy of a 90-second preview, however, Rodriguez proved he could do exactly that with his full length entry to *Grindhouse, Planet Terror,* which featured a relentless pace which *Machete* lacks. Every action movie has its lulls. The key is either to make the lulls interesting (and, consequently, not really lulls at all) with an intriguing plot and good dialogue (as Rodriguez did with *Sin City* [2005]) or, failing that, as infrequent and short as possible, like a Warner Brother's cartoon as he did with *Planet Terror*. A film as ridiculous as *Machete,* like a shark, has to keep swimming or it dies and *Machete* either needed to be thirty minutes shorter or have had a dozen more action sequences.

Nate Vercauteren

CREDITS

Machete: Danny Trejo
Booth: Jeff Fahey
Sen. McLaughlin: Robert De Niro
Torrez: Steven Seagal
Luz: Michelle Rodriguez
Padre Benito del Toro: Cheech Marin
April: Lindsay Lohan
Sartana: Jessica Alba
Von: Don Johnson
Julio: Daryl Sabara
Osiris Ampanpour: Tom Savini
Earl McGraw: Michael Parks
Culebra Cruzado: Tito Larriva
Cherry Darling: Rose McGowan
Jorge: Gilbert Trejo
Sniper: Shea Whigham
June: Alicia Marek
Origin: USA
Language: English
Released: 2010
Production: Robert Rodriguez, Quentin Tarantino, Rick Schwartz, Elizabeth Avellan, Aaron Kaufman; Troublemaker Studios, Dune Entertainment, Dune Entertainment III, Overnight Films; released by 20th Century Fox
Directed by: Robert Rodriguez, Ethan Maniquis
Written by: Robert Rodriguez, Alvaro Rodriguez
Cinematography by: Jimmy Lindsey
Music by: John Debney

Sound: Ethan Andrus
Editing: Robert Rodriguez, Rebecca Rodriguez
Costumes: Nina Proctor
Production Design: Christopher Stull
MPAA rating: R
Running time: 105 minutes

REVIEWS

Baumgarten, Marjorie. *Austin Chronicle.* September 3, 2010.
Burr, Ty. *Boston Globe.* September 3, 2010.
Corliss, Richard. *TIME Magazine.* September 2, 2010.
Derakshani, Tirdad. *Philadelphia Inquirer.* September 3, 2010.
Holden, Stephen. *New York Times.* September 2, 2010.
Leydon, Joe. *Variety.* September 1, 2010.
O'Sullivan, Michael. *Washington Post.* September 3, 2010.
Phillips, Michael. *Chicago Tribune.* September 2, 2010.
Tobias, Scott. *AV Club.* September 2, 2010.
Travers, Peter. *Rolling Stone.* September 2, 2010.

QUOTES

Machete: "Machete don't text."

TRIVIA

Danny Trejo originated the character Machete in the *Spy Kids* film series, making *Machete* his fifth appearance as the eponymous character.

AWARDS

Golden Raspberries 2010: Worst Support. Actress (Alba).

MADE IN DAGENHAM

1968. It's a man's world. But not for long...
—Movie tagline

This well-intentioned, spirited, but paint-by-the-numbers period piece concerns a group of female factory workers in 1960s Britain who collectively served as the focal point of the nation's movement of equal pay for women. The fairly standard means of telling this significant story is saved in many ways by an exceptional cast, headed by Sally Hawkins as young wife and mother Rita O'Grady, the unlikely leader of the 187 union ladies working at the Ford Motor Company assembly plant in Dagenham who demanded that their jobs as car seat upholstery sewers be re-qualified from "unskilled" labor to "skilled," resulting in better pay.

As she proved in director Mike Leigh's *Happy-Go-Lucky* (2008), Hawkins has a magnetic charm and expressive face that makes audiences root for whatever her cause might be. In the hands of director Nigel Cole—who had a similar approach to his *Calendar Girls*

(2003)—the entire story leans too hard on being cutesy and the fire in the belly of this film is kept rather dim as a result, which is not to say it does not spark up now and again.

Rita must learn to stand up for herself, but considering she has difficulty talking to her son's ruthless teacher, this is more of a challenge than it might seem. One unlikely ally—both with the teacher and Ford Motor Company—is Lisa (Rosamund Pike), the wife of Ford's Head of Industrial Relations Peter Hopkins (Rupert Graves), who Rita meets at the school where both of their children attend. Lisa is one of the few completely-realized characters outside of Rita. She is a beautiful, poised, university-educated woman who is told by her husband to keep her supportive thoughts on the female workers to herself and stick to being the perfect wife and hostess. The frustrated life of this trophy wife is one of the most moving elements of *Made in Dagenham*.

One of the film's few sympathetic male characters is the women's supervisor and union representative Albert Passingham (Bob Hoskins), who covertly guides Rita through the process of meeting with both the head of the union and the Ford executive throughout the negotiation process and the inevitable worker's strike that follows. Hoskins is at his sly best as a man working very hard to appear to support his employer while wishing to honor the women he has grown to be friends with over the years. From him, Rita learns quickly when it is safe to ask for something unprecedented and when it is not, and she is shocked to learn that even the head of her own union balks at her attempts at equal pay. The film also exposes a kind of collusion that went on between union leaders who were supposed to be fighting for these women's demands and the automaker who threatened to pull out of the community if they were forced to make this adjustment.

Particularly impressive is Miranda Richardson's take on Barbara Castle, the British Secretary of State for Employment and Productivity, a modern woman who is in a position to actually make the equal pay demand a national issue. Perhaps, the combination of having a woman in this job was serendipitous at the time, but it certainly makes this story a lot more interesting. Richardson's take on Castle is wonderfully realized as someone frustrated with the all-male status quo around her and seeing this strike as a means to make her mark on society. Her motives are not entirely selfless, but that does not mean she cannot be useful either. Another notable performance comes from Geraldine James as Connie, the matriarch of the female workforce at the factor, whose ill husband demands she makes a choice between working and taking care of him. Through her dilemma, the true price these women paid by sticking to their principles becomes clear.

There is never any doubt how these events will turn out (the Equal Pay Act was made law in 1970), but director Cole is able to extract suitable levels of drama from this story and make it a largely enjoyable experience. Unfortunately, the film also feels dumbed-down for public consumption and relies too much on speeches that probably did not happen and words that were probably never spoken. Plus, while there certainly were pressures at home while the women were on strike, that fact does not make for particularly compelling movie moments. Rita's husband, Eddie (Daniel Mays), complaining about how the blokes treat him badly because of his wife's actions, sounds not like a dramatic character but a whiner. Still, *Made in Dagenham* is largely a pain-free viewing experience, and gives a nice reminder about a simple style of British filmmaking from the 1990s that is not seen much any longer.

Steven Prokopy

CREDITS

Lisa: Rosamund Pike
Barbara Castle: Miranda Richardson
Rita O'Grady: Sally Hawkins
Connie: Geraldine James
Albert: Bob Hoskins
Robert Tooley: Richard Schiff
Eddie: Daniel Mays
Harold Wilson: John Sessions
Peter Hopkins: Rupert Graves
Origin: United Kingdom
Language: English
Released: 2010
Production: Elizabeth Karlsen, Stephen Woolley; Audley Films, BBC Films, HanWay Films, LipSynch Prods., Number 9 Films; released by Sony Pictures Classics
Directed by: Nigel Cole
Written by: Billy Ivory
Cinematography by: John de Borman
Music by: David Arnold
Editing: Michael Parker
Sound: Ian Wilson
Production Design: Andrew McAlpine
MPAA rating: R
Running time: 113 minutes

REVIEWS

Anderson, Melisssa. *Village Voice.* November 17, 2010.
Baumgarten, Marjorie. *Austin Chronicle.* January 7, 2011.
Bennett, Ray. *Hollywood Reporter.* September 11, 2010.
Biancolli, Amy. *San Francisco Chronicle.* November 24, 2010.
Ebert, Roger. *Chicago Sun-Times.* November 23, 2010.

Holden, Stephen. *New York Times.* November 18, 2010.
Meek, Tom. *Boston Phoenix.* November 23, 2010.
O'Hehir, Andrew. *Salon.com.* November 18, 2010.
Orndorf, Brian. *eFilmCritic.com.* December 18, 2010.
Travers, Peter. *Rolling Stone.* November 18, 2010.

QUOTES

Barbara Castle: "Credence? I will give credence to their cause. My god! Their cause already has credence. It is equal pay. Equal pay is common justice, and if you two weren't such a pair of egotistical, chauvinistic, bigoted dunderheads, you would realize that."

TRIVIA

Sandie Shaw who sings the film's title song actually worked in the Ford plant at Dagenham prior to the events portrayed in the film.

AWARDS

Nomination:

British Acad. 2010: Costume Des., Makeup, Support. Actress (Richardson), Alexander Korda.

MAO'S LAST DANCER

Before you can fly you have to be free.
—Movie tagline

Box Office: $4 million

While dance is never long absent from the big screen, it is typically confined to explicitly youth-oriented pictures, like *Honey* (2003), *You Got Served* (2004), *Dirty Dancing: Havana Nights* (2004), *Step Up* (2006) and its sequels, *Stomp the Yard* (2007), and, of course, Disney's lucrative *High School Musical* films, which migrated from the small screen to cineplexes with a hugely successful 2008 release, the third release in the franchise. The year 2010, however, saw something of an unexpected focus on ballet, with Darren Aronofsky's critically touted slice of manic, grand guignol ballerina competitiveness, *Black Swan*, garnering awards attention, and the more quietly earnest, straightforward drama *Mao's Last Dancer* wooing art house audiences.

A tastefully packaged and visually-appealing movie that is inoffensive almost to a fault, director Bruce Beresford's biopic demonstrates some of the strengths and many more of the weaknesses of what might be called "cinema of personal affiliation." While not an outright hagiography, the movie, adapted by screenwriter Jan Sardi from Li Cunxin's bestselling autobiography of the same name, feels for much of its nearly two-hour running time polite to the point of inertness. It would

likely connect in more dramatically robust fashion if it allowed for more arguments to be had and hurt feelings to linger, and its makers more fully appreciated the distinction between aching sincerity and dramatic conflict. While a fairly solid Stateside art house performer in its autumnal release via Samuel Goldwyn, the movie was a smash hit in Beresford's native Australia, where it grossed over $14 million of its almost $16 million international haul.

A crosscut opening establishes young Li Cunxin's backstory. In 1972, he is taken from his peasant home and overworked parents (Joan Chen and Shuang Bao Wang) in the rural Shadong province by Mao Tse-Tung's government, in order to study ballet in Beijing, and work to eventually represent China on the world stage. Separated from his family and enduring countless hours of practice, Li struggles to find peace or happiness with the new life that has been chosen for him.

Gaining confidence from a kind (if politically incorrect) mentor, Chan (Yu Qi Zhang), who slips him clandestine videotapes of Mikhail Baryshnikov, Li continues to work hard, improves, and eventually wins a short-term artistic scholarship trip to America. Upon arriving in Houston in 1981, Li (Chi Cao, making his acting debut) quickly comes to realize that all of the stories of unimaginable squalor that he has been fed about America by his Communist handlers are not quite on point. The friendly artistic director of the local ballet, Ben Stevenson (Bruce Greenwood), takes him under his wing, and Li dazzles his hosts with his adaptability to a different dancing style.

Li then meets a fellow would-be dancer, Liz Mackey (Amanda Schull), and falls for her. When the expiration of his student visa looms, the pair marry in an effort to allow for Li to stay in the country. While Chinese embassy diplomats aim to force his return, Stevenson and an immigration lawyer, Charles Foster (Kyle MacLachlan), work to try to smooth things over, even if Stevenson has misgivings about Li staying.

For its first hour or so, *Mao's Last Dancer* coasts along as a sort of reverse travelogue, at a not unpleasant yet still strangely subdued clip. A large part of this is because the movie seems designed to entirely avoid all conflict and unpleasantness. Even when Li encounters racial bigotry, it is folded into the narrative as an unseen scene and dealt with as a joke, with Stevenson offering a cheery alternative explanation of the word "chink" to a baffled Li. Owing to this fact, there is not much drama early on. It is only when the looming calendar date of Li's departure becomes more of an issue that the movie finally gets a kick in the pants, and starts to work to induce any sort of grander, more complex or inquisitive feelings about Li's life and fate.

Similarly, Beresford seems content to trade in a fairly unfussy directorial style. In his eleventh collaboration with cinematographer Peter James, the pair settles on a streamlined visual scheme that highlights open lighting and medium-distance framing. While the bulk of the film was shot in Australia, smart location work in China and Houston at least helps give *Mao's Last Dancer* a bit of production value and outwardly expressed style for which the filmmakers otherwise do not assertively reach.

Given that Cao is a dancer in the Birmingham Royal Ballet, it is not surprising that the movie most connects during its handful of ballet sequence showcases, choreographed by Graeme Murphy. Yet Cao is also fairly solid in his more straightforward scenes, at least insofar as he captures the wide-eyed nature of a complete cultural innocent.

One of the great paradoxes of narratives that are based on life stories is that supporting characters are often reduced to broad strokes; stand-ins designed only to serve the plot or hero's journey, as is certainly the case here. Greenwood wrings some nice moments out of his portrayal of Stevenson, but most of the actors are not given strong enough material to establish their characters' bond to Li. This is most particularly striking as it relates to Li and Liz; their marriage is allowed one argument, and then just kind of dissipates in ethereal fashion. It is not until later in the movie that the audience is left to intuit the full nature of Li's relationship with the woman who becomes his second wife, Mary McKendry (Camilla Vergotis).

While not absolutely crucial to the story, the film's failure to delve substantively into Li's personal life—indeed, its unwillingness to even consistently engage on this front—amounts to a sort of patronizing nativism, since it has the unfortunate side effect of reducing Li from a fully fleshed-out human being to just someone who should be valued for their artistic skill, and therefore a pawn in Sino-American relations. There is some sense of how ballet comes to blossom in Li's eyes, and mean something to him, but not really a particularly penetrating sense of how the fortitude he displays in making the decision to stay in the United States came to be. *Mao's Last Dancer* does not have the heft of a movie about a political awakening, but neither are any of the love affairs, with either Liz or Mary, sketched deeply enough to give the movie a lasting sense of lift.

While these shortcomings, along with a rather predictable finale of familial reconnection, may come across as damning to some viewers, they nonetheless help the movie play like catnip to a certain boomer "smart house" set—loyal PBS and Discovery Channel viewers who see a lot of independent and foreign films but nonetheless embrace conventional narrative payoffs and simply do not like their multicultural tales of uplift too messy or rough around the edges. For this audience, the relative blandness and lack of deeper or lasting conflict in *Mao's Last Dancer* is actually an asset.

Brent Simon

CREDITS

Ben Stevenson: Bruce Greenwood
Charles Foster: Kyle MacLachlan
Niang: Joan Chen
Elizabeth Mackey: Amanda Schull
Counsel Zhang: Ferdinand Hoang
Cynthia: Penne Hackforth-Jones
Dilworth: Aden Young
Judge: Jack Thompson
Cunxin Li: Chi Cao
Mary McKendry: Camilla Vergotis
Dia: Shuang Bao Wang
Chan: Yu Qi Zhang
Origin: Australia
Language: English, Mandarin
Released: 2009
Production: Jane Scott, Great Scott; Roadshow Films, Hopscotch Films; released by Samuel Goldwyn
Directed by: Bruce Beresford
Written by: Jan Sardi
Cinematography by: Peter James
Music by: Christopher Gordon
Sound: David Lee
Editing: Mark Warner
Art Direction: Bernardo Trujillo, Elaine Kusmishko
Costumes: Anna Borghesi
Production Design: Herbert Pinter
MPAA rating: PG
Running time: 117 minutes

REVIEWS

Byrnes, Paul. *Sydney Morning Herald.* October 5, 2009.
Demara, Bruce. *Toronto Star.* May 13, 2010.
Long, Tom. *Detroit News.* August 27, 2010.
Lumenick, Lou. *New York Post.* August 23, 2010.
Morgenstern, Joe. *Wall Street Journal.* August 19, 2010.
Morris, Wesley. *Boston Globe.* August 19, 2010.
Rainer, Peter . *Christian Science Monitor.* August 27, 2010.
Rea,Steven. *Philadelphia Inquirer.* August 19, 2010.
Reed, Rex. *New York Observer.* August 18, 2010.
Tallerico, Brian. *MovieRetriever.com.* August 20, 2010.

MARMADUKE

Live large.
  —Movie tagline

Box Office: $33 million

The talking dog comedy *Marmaduke* opens with (among other things) the titular character farting in his owners' bed. The dog then looks at the audience and states with glee, "I know it's juvenile, but it's all I've got." This confession speaks volumes about the material that is to come, for *Marmaduke* exists for purely cynical reasons and not because anybody with a good conscience thought that this innocuous, one-panel comic strip would make for a great film. In fact, those very words might have been spoken at a round-table pitch meeting with every scared employee shouting out whatever they thought their bosses wanted to hear. The climate of fear is alive and well in Hollywood, as just about every executive has been trained like dogs to rollover, beg, and fetch anything established in the pop culture universe that has yet to be put to celluloid. They can now cross *Marmaduke* off the list.

The storyline has many signs of fatigue and desperation on the part of the unfortunate writers. Marmaduke (voiced by Owen Wilson) is an oversized Great Dane who lives with the Winslows, a typical white-bread suburban family consisting of Mom (Judy Greer), Dad (Lee Pace), teenage daughter Barbara (Caroline Sunshine), and little Brian (Finley Jacobson). Marmaduke, the character, talks to the viewer in a first-person narrative even though nobody around him can hear him or see his lips move (this basically follows the rule of most talking animal movies, which is just as well). He is generally a good dog, but nicknames his owner "Dr. No" because of all the rules of the household and because of how rarely he says yes to his kids.

The dad, Phil, works for an organic dog food company called Barks, which has just decided to move him and his family from Kansas to California so that he may launch a new campaign to sell the company's dog food. The family is reluctant to go, especially Marmaduke, who is set in his ways. It does not take long for the dog to make friends at the local dog park, where Phil has meetings with his new boss, Tom Twombly (William H. Macy). Marmaduke gets to know the hierarchy of dogs pretty quick. There are the mutts: Raisin (voiced by Steve Coogan), Guiseppe (Christopher Mintz-Plasse), Mazie (Emma Stone), Thunder (Damon Wayans, Jr.), and Lightning (Marlon Wayans). Like high school, there are cliques as well, such as airhead twin dogs, drama queens, and dogs who trip out on magic mushrooms. Bosco (Kiefer Sutherland) runs the park and has a girlfriend, Jezebel (voiced by Stacey "Fergie" Ferguson), whom Marmaduke takes a liking to, against the advice of his mutt friends. The mutts hang out in an abandoned garage where they dance and enjoy being dogs. They also fear a lone, disgruntled stray named Chupadogra (voiced by Sam Elliott).

Meanwhile, Phil eventually hits upon a big idea to have his own dog be a part of the ad campaign for Barks Dog Food. Being in California, it is only fitting that surfing should come into play and it just so happens, there are dogs who love to surf (or who can be trained to surf, if there are many dog trainers who have the patience for that). Marmaduke is enlisted to compete in a surfing competition, which will somehow promote organic dog food. This seems like cruel and unusual punishment for any dog and the movie does little to convince the audience otherwise. Nevertheless, this is necessary to help foreshadow and set up one of the most pointless, ill-conceived third acts in recent memory in which a random water main breaks, the ground opens up and Marmaduke and friends get trapped in an overflowing sewer. Meanwhile, Phil learns he has a lot to learn about being a dad (never mind being a dog owner).

There are a lot of young, talented actors as well as some veterans contributing their voice talents here for an easy paycheck, but there is no denying the white elephant in the room is William H. Macy, who actually has to show up on-set to play the boss. Macy has nothing interesting to do and nothing funny to say. One can only hope this does not lead to more forgettable roles for such a distinguished and always likable actor.

Director Tom Dey is on his own downward spiral, however, after a promising start with the surprisingly-charming *Shanghai Noon* (2001). Since then, he has had his name on some of the most truly awful films of the last decade (*Showtime* [2002] and *Failure to Launch* [2006]). *Marmaduke* will not help, but so goes the career of a director for hire. When work comes, no matter how unappealing, it would be foolish not to take it. That is how films such as these get made. The committee agrees it has commercial potential, voice actors who really could not care less get hired, and a director who just wants to keep his or her house, takes the job. In the end, the poor audience (particularly the parents who want better choices for their kids) is left with a movie that not only opens with a fart joke, but ends with one as well.

Collin Souter

CREDITS

Debbie Winslow: Judy Greer
Phil Winslow: Lee Pace
Don Twombly: William H. Macy
Brian Winslow: Finley Jacobsen
Barbara Winslow: Caroline Sunshine
Marmaduke: Owen Wilson (Voice)
Mazie: Emma Stone (Voice)
Giuseppe: Christopher Mintz-Plasse (Voice)

Raisin: Steve Coogan (Voice)

Carlos: George Lopez (Voice)

Thunder: Damon Wayans, Jr. (Voice)

Bosco: Kiefer Sutherland (Voice)

Jezebel: Stacy Ferguson (Voice)

Lightning: Marlon Wayans (Voice)

Chupadogra: Sam Elliott (Voice)

Origin: USA

Language: English

Released: 2010

Production: John Davis, Tom Dey; Regency Enterprises, Davis Entertainment Company, Intrigue; released by 20th Century Fox

Directed by: Tom Dey

Written by: Vince Di Meglio, Tim Rasmussen

Cinematography by: Greg Gardiner

Music by: Christopher Lennertz

Editing: Don Zimmerman

Sound: Chuck Michael

Art Direction: Don MacAulay

Costumes: Karen Matthews

Production Design: Sandy Cochrane

MPAA rating: PG

Running time: 88 minutes

REVIEWS

Douglas, Edward. *Comingsoon.net.* June 3, 2010.
Ebert, Roger. *Chicago Sun-Times.* June 3, 2010.
Goss, William. *Cinematical.* June 4, 2010.
Holden, Stephen. *New York Times.* June 4, 2010.
Lybarger, Dan. *eFilmcritic.com.* June 5, 2010.
Morris, Wesley. *Boston Globe.* June 4, 2010.
Neumaier, Joe. *New York Daily News.* June 4, 2010.
O'Sullivan, Michael. *Washington Post.* June 4, 2010.
Phipps, Keith. *AV Club.* June 3, 2010.
Smith, Kyle. *New York Post.* June 4, 2010.

TRIVIA

Although Marmaduke never talked in the original comics but in the film, Owen Wilson provides the voice for the titular character through digitally enhanced lip-synching.

AWARDS

Nomination:

Golden Raspberries 2010: Worst Support. Actor (Lopez).

MEGAMIND

A superhero movie with a mind of its own.
—Movie tagline

His brain is off the chain.
—Movie tagline

The superhero movie will never be the same.
—Movie tagline

Box Office: $147 million

Brides have traditionally been the ones going forth with "something old, something new, something borrowed, something blue" as they hope for a propitious future. However, *Megamind*, DreamWorks' 2010 animated comedy, did the same thing, heading to theaters in possession of items that trace back to various sources and time periods, some slick 3D effects, and a prominent dash of cerulean in the form of its titular character's skin tone. The studio was certainly looking forward to good fortune (preferably in the hundreds of millions) once viewers laid their eyes on the film down the aisle of their nearest theater, and things worked out fairly well. Made on a budget of $130 million, *Megamind* opened at number one and was a box office success. The surprisingly sympathetic and rather endearing nature of its sky blue-hued protagonist was largely responsible for its success, a supervillain with an oversized noggin full of really bad (in every sense of the word) ideas who also has a heart that is rather touchingly aching for acceptance. He is actually more like an unruly child who settles for the eliciting of negative attention because it seems to be the only kind he can get.

Megamind (voiced by Will Ferrell, reportedly in place of both Ben Stiller and Robert Downey, Jr.) is definitely not the film's only character with a big head. His nemesis, superhero Metro Man (Brad Pitt), is a preening, puffed-up paragon of virtue whose feet are literally kissed while he shows off to the delight of the fawning, fanatical citizens of Metro City. A grateful public has built a shrine-like museum to honor their savior, featuring a statue out front that could probably have given the Colossus of Rhodes an inferiority complex. In any event, it will certainly do nothing to make Metro Man's own ego any smaller.

It is not hard to figure out why the blue, skinny, and bald Megamind's eyes are colored green, as he is bitterly jealous of the handsome, buff, admirably coiffed "goody two-shoes" whose behind he would love to kick just once. However, their continual, competitive clashes have invariably gone the good guy's way and, worse still, with ease. As babies, both were sent hurtling toward Earth in protective pods from planets that were about to be destroyed. Metro Man lucked into landing in the lap of luxury with a family that warmly embraced his angel-faced preciousness. Megamind, already behind the eight ball due to his atypical appearance, inauspiciously crashed onto the grounds of a prison for the criminally gifted. The unusually toned tyke is referred to as an "it."

Thus Megamind is raised on the decidedly wrong side of the tracks, and the inmates fill his ample cranium with all that is sure to put him on the wrong side of the law. However, he does try to better himself during studies at a school for exceptional youngsters, only there he is chagrined to find himself in the eclipsing shadow of Metro Man, who is the grade school equivalent of a Big Man on Campus. Eager attempts to get noticed and win over the other kids with his brilliant mind merely get him in trouble and thought of as a bad boy. As a result, Megamind feels he has no choice but to play the only role fate has offered him—and he will do it to the hilt. Fueled by frustration and hurt feelings, he will become one hell of a hellion, devoting his life to acting up with the sole goal of bringing Metro Man down.

Describing someone as a "bad villain" sounds like redundancy, but in Megamind's case it is aptly descriptive. His intelligence and electric enthusiasm lead to grandiose plans that always seem to short-circuit, and thus Metro Man maintains the upper hand and swats him away with it. Megamind's incessant attempts to get his counterpoint's goat by kidnapping the hero's girlfriend, plucky-and-savvy television news reporter Roxanne Ritchie (Tina Fey), are no longer capable of fazing even her. (She is quite reminiscent of Reese Witherspoon's Susan from the DreamWorks offering, *Monsters vs. Aliens*.) Megamind is like Wile E. Coyote to Metro Man's Road Runner. Every new scheme is the one that will finally work out as planned, but the results—much to his demoralized disgust—are always the same. Despite his wicked ways (again, he really seems to be more of a misunderstood, misguided menace), one cannot help but feel sorry for the poor guy. As this underdog is trying so excruciatingly hard, and gets so excited every time things at least seem to be working out, one wishes that maybe just once he would not underachieve. One day, much to everyone's incredulity (particularly his own), Megamind not only triumphs over but apparently terminates Metro Man, and then finds that he should have been more careful about what he had wished for all those years.

There is no fractious fun to be had without friction, which requires an opponent one can continually go up against. The self-declared "evil overlord" becomes the color of his complexion because the completeness of his victory robbed him of the chance to gratifyingly lord it over his long-time rival. Now a bored rebel waxing nostalgic for when he still had a cause, Megamind decides to create a new, ever-so-worthy opponent. Commandeering Roxanne's doughy cameraman Hal (Jonah Hill), who himself knows about things that disappointingly fizzle thanks to an ineffectual pursuit of his comely colleague, Megamind transforms him into superhero Tighten. As with Dr. Frankenstein, things go horribly awry. Unable to get the fetching journalist as either Hal or Tighten, Megamind's now formidably-frustrated creation opts like he had for a malevolent outlet. Who will step into the vacuum where virtue always used to stand and deliver?

Megamind goes from acting like an enfant terrible to a mensch because he too has fallen for Roxanne while taking the form of mild-mannered museum curator Bernard. As she gives him a transformative hug, the audience peers over her shoulder to see a sweet look on his face of heretofore-unknown pleasure. When it is pointed out by Megamind's loyal but leery Minion (effective David Cross), a bizarre robot/ape/fish-in-a-fishbowl hybrid, that Evil never gets the girl, Megamind replies, "Maybe I don't want to be the bad guy anymore." He has come to truly care for her, and when his true identity is revealed to a shocked and repulsed Roxanne, his shattered mortification is quite affecting. It makes one root all the harder for him to prevail, which a love-bolstered Megamind does by chivalrously rescuing both her and Metro City from Tighten's grip. Megamind may not be your stereotypical, lantern-jawed hero, but look how dependable the guy who fits that description was when the chips were really down. Apparently, between the whitest of knights and the vilest of blackguards, there are not only many shades of grey, but at least one of blue.

While all of this will linger on in Megamind's memory for some time to come, it will likely not do the same for viewers. Still, most will find it to be diverting fun while it lasts. Many will probably also find the production to be too much of a derivative pastiche. In particular, it has been supplied with an endless number of homage-paying elements originating from the *Superman* saga. These include (but are not limited to): the manner of, and reason for, both Megamind and Metro Man's arrival on Earth; a Lois Lane-like reporter; a Jimmy Olsen-esque cameraman; and Megamind's loopy incarnation as Marlon Brando's Jor-El from Richard Donner's 1978 telling of the Man of Steel's story. Museum and City Hall-related havoc recall *Batman* (1989) and *The Dark Knight* (2008). Then, when Minion asks, "What happens when she finds out who you really are?" and the "she" is named Roxanne and the "you" is an odd-looking someone speaking through a person capable of making a more acceptable impression, it is clear that there has also been some borrowing from *Cyrano de Bergerac* incarnations like *Roxanne* (1987). With viewers also reminded of things more recently seen in *The Incredibles* (2004) and *Despicable Me* (2010), *Megamind* ended up seeming to many like a referential retread.

Nevertheless, Ferrell's commendable voice work enables viewers to both feel Megamind's pain and delight in his funny bone-tickling superciliousness and penchant for mispronunciation. (For example, the way he says Metro City rhymes with atrocity.) To paraphrase an oft-quoted line from *Jerry Maguire* (1996), he truly has the audience at hello, which is another word Megamind is incapable of uttering correctly. By getting those watching to align themselves with the (supposedly) bad guy and wish him well throughout, *Megamind*'s creators succeed in their aim to "upend" the traditional superhero movie, which lands here rather nicely on a bulbous, blue head.

David L. Boxerbaum

CREDITS

Minion: David Cross (Voice)
Megamind: Will Ferrell (Voice)
Metro Man: Brad Pitt (Voice)
Roxanne Ritchie: Tina Fey (Voice)
Titan: Jonah Hill (Voice)
Origin: USA
Language: English
Released: 2010
Production: Lara Breay, Denise Nolan Cascino; Pacific Data Images; released by DreamWorks Animation
Directed by: Tom McGrath
Written by: Alan Schoolcraft, Brent Simons
Music by: Lorne Balfe, Hans Zimmer
Production Design: David A.S. James
Editing: Michael Andrews
Sound: Erik Aadahl, Ethan Van der Ryn
MPAA rating: PG
Running time: 95 minutes

REVIEWS

Chang, Justin. *Variety.* November 8, 2010.
Diones, Bruce. *New Yorker.* November 22, 2010.
Ebert, Roger. *Chicago Sun-Times.* November 3, 2010.
Gleiberman, Owen. *Entertainment Weekly.* November 12, 2010.
Holden, Stephen. *New York Times.* November 4, 2010.
Morris, Wesley. *Boston Globe.* November 5, 2010.
O'Sullivan, Michael. *Washington Post.* November 5, 2010.
Phillips, Michael. *Chicago Tribune.* November 4, 2010.
Puig, Claudia. *USA Today.* November 4, 2010.
Rainer, Peter. *Christian Science Monitor.* November 5, 2010.

QUOTES

Megamind: "Let's stop wasting time and call your boyfriend in tights, shall we?"
Megamind: "All men must choose between two paths. Good is the path of honour, friends, and family. Evil...well, it's just cooler."
Megamind: "Where did you park the invisible car?"

TRIVIA

Alternative titles for the film included "Master Mind" and "Oobermind" before they settled on *Megamind*.

This film is Brad Pitt's first foray into voice acting since the 2003 film *Sinbad: Legend of the Seven Seas*.

MESRINE

The excellent French actor Vincent Cassel starred in a pair of high-octane imports that often played at the same theater and can be succinctly viewed as one continuous piece—*Mesrine: Killer Instinct* and *Mesrine: Public Enemy #1*. The films tell the combined story of the major events in the life of the legendary Jacques Mesrine, a notorious criminals in the 1960s and 1970s who took credit for dozens of bank robberies, murders, and other illegal activities. Not unlike a French version of *Scarface* (1983) or *Public Enemies* (2009), *Mesrine* attempts to detail a larger-than-life figure without losing either the real man underneath the bombast or the infamous deeds that made him a household name in France. Despite having two films to do so, director Jean-Francois Richet still has a tough time distilling the episodic nature of the story he is trying to tell into something that feels like more than the sum of his parts. It takes a large amount of skill (that of Michael Mann or Brian De Palma) to turn an anti-hero into something more than a loathsome human being. Richet never quite answers the key question to the entire experience of *Mesrine*—why should viewers care?

Vincent Cassel has been an excellent actor for years, stealing scenes as far back as *La Haine* (1995) and giving great performances in a diverse array of films including *The Crimson Rivers* (2000), *Irreversible* (2002), *Ocean's Twelve* (2004), *Sheitan* (2006), and *Eastern Promises* (2007). The *Mesrine* films were released in France in 2008 but, as with most European films of late, they took some time crossing the Atlantic and added up to a hell of a year for Cassel as they came out shortly before he would steal scenes yet again in the Best Picture-nominated *Black Swan* (2010). With all of this acclaimed work in the last fifteen years, Cassel's work in *Mesrine* stands as his towering achievement. He is charming, riveting, and perfect in every moment, making both films worth seeing through his efforts alone.

Mesrine: Killer Instinct opens with an overweight, older Jacques Mesrine (Cassel) hurriedly packing and planning an escape that appears to go very badly before the film then jumps back what is clearly several decades to the 1950s and a much younger protagonist. Mesrine is serving in Algeria and forced to make an ugly decision involving torture. He chooses an alternate way out of it, impressing upon the audience that this is a man who instinctually knew how to handle himself in extreme and violent situations. Mesrine comes home and attempts to live a normal life but finds himself attracted to crime and is pretty damn good at it. The majority of Richet's first film is a tug-of-war within Jacques Mesrine to live a straight life or embrace his success as a criminal powerhouse. It leads to a somewhat anticlimactic, episodic structure in that it is clear that every time Mesrine tries to go straight it is only a matter of time before he slides back into the underworld. Otherwise, there would not be a movie.

Killer Instinct culminates in a prison break that is truly riveting and the best sequence in both films, but it takes too long to get there, feeling bloated to push the set-up for the second film into a reasonable running time of its own. The plot sags in the middle as Richet seems to be going by the numbers. And those numbers are not pretty. Mesrine, as presented, was a scumbag. Cassel does his best to make him engaging and it's to the actor's credit that he accomplishes as much as he does in that regard, but it is unclear how the audience is supposed to feel when they watch Mesrine beat his wife and shove a gun in her mouth in front of his child. The film never recovers from such intense moments to allow viewers to then root for Mesrine as he is escaping capture. And *Killer Instinct* wastes some extremely talented supporting actors including Cecile de France and Gerard Depardieu.

By the time, *Mesrine: Public Enemy #1* kicks into gear, Jacques Mesrine is a bank-robbing machine. At one point he is robbing one bank when he sees a vulnerable one across the street and decides to go for two in one day. The message is clear—Mesrine was a man who just as often went with the flow of his instincts as he planned his criminal acts. With a whole film designed to serve as the climax to the story of Jacques Mesrine, the insanity of this lunatic's life is turned up to eleven. At one point, he even pulls a gun in a courtroom and takes a judge hostage. Once again, the very bad behavior gets repetitive and a bit numbing. Cassel is even better in the second film (making it arguably the best performance of his career), but one has to wonder if there is not a much stronger version of this man's life story cut down to the length of an average feature. Once again, great supporting actors (this time it is Mathieu Amalric, Ludivine Sagnier, and Anne Consigny) are wasted by the film's episodic structure.

The entirety of *Mesrine* is such an inconsistent, haphazard affair that the strengths and flaws of the two films can be judged as one. By telling the story of a madman with such intensity, Jean-Francois Richet has given a great actor a great showcase but has lost what holds a feature together into a riveting piece overall, much less two.

Brian Tallerico

REVIEWS

Andrews, Nigel. *Financial Times.* August 7, 2009.
Berning, Beverly. *culturevulture.net.* August 29, 2010.
Cline, Rich. *Shadows on the Wall.* August 7, 2009.
Gilchrist, Todd. *Cinematical.* October 5, 2010.
Hunter, Allan. *Daily Express.* August 7, 2009.
Major, Wade. *Boxoffice Magazine.* October 29, 2010.
Newman, Kim. *Empire Magazine.* July 31, 2009.
Quinn, Anthony. *Independent.* August 7, 2009.
Rothkopf, Joshua. *Time Out New York.* September 1, 2010.
Smith, Neil. *Total Film.* July 31, 2009.

MESRINE: KILLER INSTINCT
(L'instinct de mort)

Please refer to the essay for *Mesrine*. The two films *Mesrine: Killer Instinct* and *Mesrine: Public Enemy #1* were reviewed together as components of a complete entity. Cast, crew, and other information has been listed separately in order to avoid confusion.

CREDITS

Jacques Mesrine: Vincent Cassel
Jeanne Schneider: Cecile de France
Guido: Gerard Depardieu
Jean-Paul Mercier: Roy Dupuis
Paul: Gilles Lellouche
Sofia: Elena Anaya
Sarah: Florence Thomassin
Mesrine's father: Michel Duchaussoy
Mesrine's mother: Myriam Boyer
Origin: France, Canada, Italy
Language: French
Released: 2008
Production: Thomas Langmann; Remstar, La Petite Reine, Novo RPI; released by New American Vision
Directed by: Jean-Francois Richet
Written by: Jean-Francois Richet, Abdel Raouf Dafri
Cinematography by: Robert Gantz
Music by: Marco Beltrami
Sound: Jean Minondo
Editing: Herve Schneid
Costumes: Virginie Montel
Production Design: Emile Ghigo

MPAA rating: R
Running time: 114 minutes

TRIVIA

The characters of Sylvia and Jeanne were originally slated to be played by Eva Green and Marion Cotillard respectively.

MESRINE: PUBLIC ENEMY #1

Please refer to the essay for *Mesrine*. The two films *Mesrine: Killer Instinct* and *Mesrine: Public Enemy #1* were reviewed together as components of a complete entity. Cast, crew, and other information has been listed separately in order to avoid confusion.

CREDITS

Jacques Mesrine: Vincent Cassel
Sylvia: Ludivine Sagnier
Francois Besse: Mathieu Amalric
Michel Ardouin: Samuel Le Bihan
Charlie Bauer: Gerard Lanvin
Commissaire Broussard: Olivier Gourmet
Avocate: Anne Consigny
The Millionaire: George Wilson
Father: Michel Duchaussoy
Origin: France
Language: French
Released: 2008
Production: Thomas Langmann; La Petite Reine, Remstar, Novo RPI; released by New American Vision
Directed by: Jean-Francois Richet
Written by: Jean-Francois Richet, Abdel Raouf Dafri
Cinematography by: Robert Gantz
Music by: Marco Beltrami, Marcus Trump
Sound: Jean Minodo
Editing: Bill Pankow
Costumes: Virginie Montel
Production Design: Emile Ghigo
MPAA rating: R
Running time: 134 minutes

QUOTES

Mesrine's millionaire hostage: "A revolutionary would have put a bullet through my head without even asking for a cent. A gangster asks for a ransom, picks up his money and releases me."

MICMACS
(Micmac a tire-larigot)

Box Office: $1 million

Micmacs, the latest effort from the legitimately visionary French filmmaker Jean-Pierre Jeunet, the man behind such cult favorites as *Delicatessen* (1991), *The City of Lost Children* (1995), and *Amelie* (2001), is a film filled with enough visual wonders to fill up at least three conventional full-length features with enough left over for a substantial deleted scenes section on the DVD. The trouble is that it also contains a story that barely stretches out enough to serve one. Since Jeunet is one of the most visually inventive directors at work today, this approach sort of works for a while but at a certain point, even his most devout fans are likely to feel so overwhelmed by the onslaught of dazzle and the relative paucity of everything else that they may feel that it is proof perfect that there can indeed be too much of a good thing.

The film opens a few decades ago in North Africa as a French soldier is blown up while trying to defuse a land mine. This man is the father of Bazil (Dany Boon), who is introduced in modern-day France where he is working in a video store and obsessively watching the Howard Hawks classic *The Big Sleep* (1946). At that precise moment, a violent car chase has broken out in the streets outside and a stray bullet hits Bazil and lodges in his head. Faced with an impossible decision—removing the bullet could cause permanent paralysis and leaving it in could cause him to die at any moment—Bazil's surgeon flips a coin and decides based on that to leave the bullet in. After a lengthy hospital stay, Bazil attempts to return to his former life but discovers that, in the interim, he has lost both his job and his apartment—in fact, the only remnants of his earlier life that he is able to retrieve are his beloved hat and the casing from the bullet that now resides in his head.

Unable to find any real work, Bazil is reduced to panhandling in order to survive when he is discovered and taken in by a quirky group of people living in the local junkyard that includes a human cannonball, a guy obsessed with being in the *Guinness Book of World Records* (Jeunet regular Dominique Pinon), and a contortionist (Julie Ferrier). One day, he happens to stumble upon the arms manufacturer that supplied both the mine that killed his father and the bullet that changed his life forever. He is then inspired to devise a plan utilizing the unique skill sets of his newfound friends to destroy both the company and the two loathsome men in charge, one of whom, Nicolas Thibault de Fenouillet (André Dussollier), has been using part of his ill-gotten fortune to purchase a collection of body parts taken from the cadavers of deceased historical figures.

As anyone who has seen any of Jeunet's previous films can quickly surmise, the plan involves any number of elaborately conceived and executed tricks and stunts straight out of the Rube Goldberg playbook—after all, this is the same guy who once conceived of a sequence in *The City of Lost Children* in which a single teardrop shed by a little girl kicks off a chain reaction that winds up saving her life two minutes later. The whole film is filled with scenes like this, one even allows for the brief appearance of a bit from *Delicatessen,* and virtually every single frame is so crammed to bursting with little visual details worth savoring that one could freeze it at any given moment and simply study what is on the screen as they might a work of art in a museum. At a time when most filmmakers have chosen to simply bludgeon viewers with elaborate but impersonal orgies of visual effects instead of enchanting them with imagination, Jeunet must be applauded for his ceaseless efforts to present audiences sights that they have never seen—or even *contemplated* seeing—before.

The trouble with *Micmacs* is that Jeunet is so enamored of his visual pyrotechnics this time around that he has allowed them to utterly dominate the proceedings. Yes, his earlier films were also jam-packed with such things but he always managed to balance things out with reasonably compelling storylines, characters, and ideas that allowed viewers to feel as though they had been served a full cinematic meal—even the film generally regarded as his weakest to date, his franchise-freezing American debut *Alien Resurrection* (1997) has more going on in it than one might expect from such a thing. Jeunet presumably devised this story as a sort of whimsical modern-day fable but what starts off as simple soon turns simple-minded and he winds up adding in an awful lot of padding, including an extra helping of whimsy, to get it up to a proper length. Sometimes an ambitious filmmaker will make a short subject and then expand it into a feature film—this, on the other hand, is a feature film that might be better served if it were contracted into a short subject. Another key problem with the film is that while Bazil's cause inspires a certain amount of sympathy from viewers, Bazil himself does not because Jeunet has drawn him in such a thin and undistinguished manner that it is difficult to work up much interest in him personally. Frankly, the only character who really stands out amidst the clutter is the monstrous Fenouillet because of all the characters on display, his is the only one to display an actual personality instead of just a bunch of quirky tics masquerading as such.

Micmacs is not a very good movie but at the same time, it is not a boring one and it cannot easily be dismissed because it is indeed a feast for the eyes at a time when people are starving for new and unique energy. The trouble is that with this particular feast, every course is a dessert and while that may sound like a fabulous idea in theory, most viewers are likely to come away from it wishing that there had been something a little more substantial included on the menu. Perhaps it will play better on home video where it can be seen in smaller chunks that will allow people to savor the visuals and then back away until another time when the proceedings get to be too much.

Peter Sobczynski

CREDITS

Bazil: Dany Boon
Nicolas Thibault de Fenouillet: André Dussollier
Placard: Jean-Pierre Marielle
Tambouille: Yolande Moreau
Francois Marooni: Nicolas Marie
Francasse: Dominique Pinon
Caoutchouc: Julie Ferrier
Calculette: Marie-Julie Baup
Origin: France
Language: French
Released: 2009
Production: Frédéric Brillion, Jean-Pierre Jeunet, Gilles Legrand; Epithète Films, Tapioca Films, Warner Bros., France 2 Cinéma, France 3 Cinéma; released by Sony Pictures Classics
Directed by: Jean-Pierre Jeunet
Written by: Jean-Pierre Jeunet, Guillaume Laurant
Cinematography by: Tetsuo Nagata
Music by: Raphael Beau
Editing: Herve Schneid
Sound: Gérard Hardy
Costumes: Madeline Fontaine
Production Design: Aline Bonetto
MPAA rating: R
Running time: 105 minutes

REVIEWS

Adams, Sam. *Salon.com.* May 28, 2010.
Honeycutt, Kirk. *Hollywood Reporter.* May 24, 2010.
Miller, Brian. *Village Voice.* May 26, 2010.
Nelson, Rob. *Variety.* May 21, 2010.
Pais, Matt. *Metromix.com.* June 3, 2010.
Reed, Rex. *New York Observer.* May 26, 2010.
Robinson, Tasha. *AV Club.* May 27, 2010.
Scott, A.O. *New York Times.* May 28, 2010.
Tallerico, Brian. *MovieRetriever.com.* June 4, 2010.
White, Armond. *New York Press.* May 26, 2010.

MIDDLE MEN

Money. Sex. Murder. Greed. Corruption.
—Movie tagline

In 1995, music was still bought in record stores. There was a VCR in every house. And you couldn't buy anything online…until they came along.
—Movie tagline

Business is a lot like sex…getting in is easy, pulling out is hard.
—Movie tagline

For Internet pornography users, pop-up ads are a major turnoff. Those pesky ads always seem to appear at the wrong time and serve little purpose other than to take attention away from the desired content and kill the mood. In a way, *Middle Men* is like one continuously appearing pop-up ad. The film, inspired by the story of the first businessmen to bring adult-oriented sexual content onto the Internet, constantly loses focus and distracts from its central idea. It is too bad, since that idea is ripe for a film adaptation. Whether or not they will admit it, the entire world cares about sex, and bringing an accessible source of inspiration for self-love is a brilliant idea that inherently favors business values over family ones.

In this erratic action-comedy-drama, that lesson falls on Jack Harris (Luke Wilson), who is a happy family man in Houston one minute, a hedonistic purveyor of pornography in Los Angeles the next. Jack first goes to L.A. to help a sick friend with a nightclub but quickly connects with Wayne (Giovanni Ribisi) and Buck (Gabriel Macht). It is 1997, and the two pals and habitual drug users have begun selling pornography on the Internet. They have no idea how to run a business, but they quickly make millions and team up with the Russian mob, who then proceed to violently beat them for not paying their debts on time. Jack's role is to get Wayne and Buck organized and help them charge users of their pornographic websites without getting the guys killed in the process.

The storyline is based in truth—the film stems from the career of businessman Christopher Mallick, one of the film's producers—and well-connected to a topic with universal appeal: sex. In places, *Middle Men* amusingly captures this truth, whether it is an opening montage of young boys throughout the decades being caught masturbating by their mothers or a late-and-underdeveloped subplot focused around Islamic terrorists' fixation on Audrey Dawns (Laura Ramsey), a porn star with whom Jack falls into a committed and completely unconvincing relationship. The joke is that even religious fundamentalists have basic human needs for physical satisfaction, and what a political coup it would be for the FBI to be able to use a porn star to identify the location of terrorists while they surf the web on her X-rated site.

Unfortunately, the movie never develops a clever rhythm from its world of high-rolling, arousing entrepreneurship. In fact, it never develops a rhythm at all, thanks to a remarkably-oppressive voiceover by Jack that narrates roughly the first half-hour of the movie and continually pops up throughout the remainder to explain even the most obvious points. When dangerous acquaintances put Jack's life in jeopardy, clearly the dilemma pressing on any father who is involved in the life of his children would be the threat of leaving his kids without a dad. Yet as this is happening, there is Jack's voiceover again, explaining that this is how he feels. Director/co-writer George Gallo demonstrates this tendency to overcompensate throughout *Middle Men* as characters have unnecessary flashbacks. As a result, shades of gray in Jack and many of his associates are gradually pushed into black-and-white portrayals of good people in bad situations or nasty people briefly hiding their true colors.

What results is a movie about clueless people in over their heads that appears to have been made by clueless people in over their heads. Gallo and co-writer Andy Weiss reduce Jack's wife Diana (Jacinda Barrett) into an uptight nag who is sidelined by Jack's new life and ultimately forced to decide whether or not to dismiss the pain endured as a result of her husband's infidelity. It is a very similar role to the one Barrett played in *The Last Kiss,* (2006) and her character's one-dimensionality fails to provide the film with the necessary emotional element beneath all the sleaze.

That is not to say that *Middle Men* is without its scenes of freewheeling, testosterone-pumping entertainment or that the film is not based around a fascinating paradox. The porn industry is pushed to the fringes of society and scorned by many religious leaders and politicians, yet frequently those people in power are exposed for their own secret perversions, and the booming business of sexual content is as American as American business gets. At times, *Middle Men* threatens to be a breezy cautionary tale about the temptations of this kind of world.

Still, shaky characterizations and the film's devolution into a frantic action movie about the mafia are the reasons why *Middle Men* would have worked so much better as a documentary. Sticking to what really happened as the multi-multi-multi-billion dollar per year porn industry developed online, that movie would have had the same intrigue of a major business idea and a controversial explosion of content that many deem obscene. The movie just would have been focused and informative instead of choppy and absurd, a classification most applicable towards *Middle Men* once Jack begins his relationship with Audrey. Wilson, an actor who has shown little emotional range outside of his standout roles in writer-director Wes Anderson's *Bottle Rocket* (1996) and *The Royal Tenenbaums,* (2001) fails to competently depict the change in Jack's personality as he becomes wrapped up in a world of power, money and sex. Thus, he never seems like a major player in the L.A. porn community, and his quick-moving bond with Audrey, a gorgeous and much younger starlet who would be way out of Jack's league if he were not mega-wealthy, feels nothing but phony.

It is one of many elements of *Middle Men,* regardless of what actually happened to Christopher Mallick, that appears to have completely discarded truth for the sake of telling a story that writers Gallo and Weiss thought would be more interesting and exciting. This is a story about pornography and unimaginable amounts of money and sex being sent all over the world. There is no fabrication necessary.

Matt Pais

CREDITS

Jack Harris: Luke Wilson
Wayne Beering: Giovanni Ribisi
Buck Dolby: Gabriel Macht
Diana Harris: Jacinda Barrett
Audrey Dawns: Laura Ramsey
James: Terry Crews
Nikita Sokoloff: Rade Serbedzija
Curt Allmans: Kevin Pollak
Jerry Haggerty: James Caan
Louie La La: Robert Forster
Origin: USA
Language: English
Released: 2010
Production: William Sherak, Jason Shuman, Christopher Mallick, Michael Weiss; Blue Star Entertainment, Oxymoron Entertainment; released by Paramount Pictures
Directed by: George Gallo
Written by: George Gallo, Andy Weiss
Cinematography by: Lukas Ettlin
Music by: Brian Tyler
Sound: Michael B. Koff
Music Supervisor: Tricia Holloway
Editing: Malcolm Campbell
Art Direction: Douglas Cumming
Costumes: Sharen CQ Davis
Production Design: Bob Ziembicki
MPAA rating: R
Running time: 99 minutes

REVIEWS

Lumenick, Lou. *New York Post.* August 6, 2010.
McCarthy, Todd. *Variety.* February 18, 2010.
Orange, Michelle. *Movieline.* August 6, 2010.
Phillips, Michael. *Chicago Tribune.* August 5, 2010.
Puig, Claudia. *USA Today.* August 7, 2010.
Rabin, Nathan. *AV Club.* August 5, 2010.
Savlov, Marc. *Austin Chronicle.* August 6, 2010.
Schwarzbaum, Lisa. *Entertainment Weekly.* August 6, 2010.
Scott, A.O. *New York Times.* August 5, 2010.
Wilonsky, Robert. *Village Voice.* August 4, 2010.

QUOTES

Jack Harris: "Hey do we wanna get the money or do we wanna break this guy's legs? I say we get the money, you know?"
Wayne Beering: "We take some pictures from some magazines, we scan them, we upload them onto the Internet, and we make some money."

TRIVIA

This film is based on the real life story of Christopher Mallick who serves as a producer on the film.

MONSTERS

After six years, they're no longer aliens. They're residents.
—Movie tagline
Now, it's our turn to adapt.
—Movie tagline

At first glance, *Monsters* seems like the inevitable clone that arrives in the wake of two successful genre films, *Cloverfield* (2007) and *District 9* (2009), two alien invasion films that attempted to take the concept to a more realistic level while still showcasing top-notch special effects. Both films work beautifully for different reasons. *Cloverfield* saw everything from the point of view of someone's video camera while *District 9* used the idea of alien invasion and co-habitation as an allegory on apartheid. The trailer for *Monsters* suggests an apocalyptic thriller with a Hollywood scale budget and big visual and visceral pay-offs, in spite of it being distributed by an indie studio. To suggest that the trailer is a bit misleading would be a massive understatement.

The movie's opening exposition makes its allegory perfectly clear: N.A.S.A. discovered a form of alien life within our solar system. A probe was sent to collect samples, but crashed upon re-entry over South America. The alien life forms spread throughout and rendered the upper half of the continent an "Infected Zone." The aliens still need to be contained and there now exists a giant wall between North and South America to contain the "creatures." With the subject of illegal immigration being a hot political topic over the past several years, it is not hard to see the filmmaker's allegorical intentions.

What *Monsters* lacks in cleverness for an allegory, it more than makes up for in something else that is actually quite hard to define.

There are two characters: a photojournalist and the daughter of a rich newspaperman. The man, Andrew (Scoot McNairy), reluctantly agrees to help guide a woman, Samantha (Whitney Able), to the coast of Mexico where she will be picked up and taken back home to the States. Andrew works for her father's publication and has been waiting his whole career to get photos of great importance. What should have been a simple train ride from the hospital (where they met) to the coast ends up being a much longer, more complicated journey after the train suffers engine failure. With still several kilometers to go, Andrew and Samantha must try and make it on foot.

Their best bet for getting Samantha back to America is a ferry boat that leaves the next day. Naturally, after a fun night out on the town (yes, they still have fun here, even with the constant military and alien presence), they get robbed and Samantha's passport disappears, presumably stolen by a local. The man who sold her the ferry ticket offers to get her home by land, which will be far more dangerous. With little to no money left, Samantha offers him her engagement ring as payment. From there, Andrew and Samantha travel through various infected zones, jungles, and areas ravaged by giant aliens.

As the movie progresses, there is an anticipation of something big and scary, but *Monsters* is really about these two people and their developing relationship. Andrew and Samantha have an easygoing chemistry between them and they are both well aware of their mutual attraction. Both have complications back home: She has a fiancé, he has a kid from a previous marriage and prefers being single. They have conversations about mundane things, such as dolphins and how cool it might be to work in a gas station. *Monsters* is certainly more in the spirit of a Mumblecore indie than the alien invasion blockbuster its ads (let alone its title) made it out to be.

This will likely be a major disappointment for those who expected more of the latter. *Monsters* shows signs of almost delivering on the action, but most of the time, Andrew and Samantha are arriving in the aftermath of an attack. The creatures, when they are shown, are like giant squids that move slowly and without purpose. One scene in which it is revealed that these creatures lay their eggs in the trees evokes *The Ruins* (2008), which also took place in Central America, but the idea is treated as a sidebar. The final sequence will likely be a make-or-break moment for the viewer. Some will come to love its poetic simplicity. Others will be completely put off by it.

Whatever people's expectations may be, taken on its own merit, *Monsters* is a wonderful surprise. Writer/director Garreth Edwards, who filmed the movie on location without permission from officials and with a reported budget of only $200,000, crafts quite an interesting hybrid of a film. Using natural locales in Central America with hardly anything in the way of extra set-decorating, *Monsters* achieves an authenticity that is both beneficial to the storytelling, but also eye opening as a travelogue. The background people in the film are not really extras, but actual citizens walking into the shot. At the same time, Edwards and his cast create two believable characters that have more of an invested interest in their own growing relationship than in the dangers and the carnage that surrounds them. Strangely enough, the audience does, too.

Monsters is a movie that really should not work, and there is certainly a case to be made that it does not, but Edwards' dual intentions for the project as well as his shooting strategies are so noble and daring that the viewer cannot help but just go with it. Credit certainly goes to Able and McNairy, who carry the film effortlessly. The movie does not make any startling points or arguments about illegal immigration, but it does tell a good story about these people and the aliens look very good for a film that was made for under $1 million. *Monsters* may not have any memorable "monsters" in it, but when was the last time someone made an alien invasion movie where the two central characters and their love story were the most interesting part?

Collin Souter

CREDITS

Andrew Kaulder: Scoot McNairy
Samantha Wynden: Whitney Able
Origin: United Kingdom
Language: English
Released: 2010
Production: Allan Niblo, James Richardson; Vertigo Films, Magnet Releasing; released by Magnolia Pictures
Directed by: Gareth Edwards
Written by: Gareth Edwards
Cinematography by: Gareth Edwards
Music by: Jon Hopkins
Sound: Ian MacLagan
Music Supervisor: Lol Hammond
Editing: Colin Goudie
Production Design: Gareth Edwards
MPAA rating: R
Running time: 97 minutes

REVIEWS

Barsanti, Chris. *Filmcritic.com*. October 28, 2010.
Burr, Ty. *Boston Globe*. November 4, 2010.

Catsoulis, Jeannette. *New York Times.* October 29, 2010.
Ebert, Roger. *Chicago Sun-Times.* November 18, 2010.
Morgenstern, Joe. *Wall Street Journal.* October 29, 2010.
Murray, Noel. *AV Club.* October 28, 2010.
O'Hehir, Andrew. *Salon.com.* October 28, 2010.
O'Sullivan, Michael. *Washington Post.* November 5, 2010.
Phillips, Michael. *Chicago Tribune.* November 19, 2010.
Rea, Steven. *Philadelphia Inquirer.* November 11, 2010.

TRIVIA

The film was shot on an extremely minimal budget with a two-person crew in real-life locations.

MORNING GLORY

Breakfast TV just got interesting.
—Movie tagline

Box Office: $31 million

There is a terrible shortage of top-quality female leads for romantic comedies right now. Pass on Jennifer Aniston and Katherine Heigl and Kate Hudson and Anne Hathaway, none of whom can elevate material that is lousy, which these days the material often is. Drew Barrymore is a welcome presence, anchoring lively films like *Going the Distance* (2010), but she is more of a familiar comfort than a game-changer. Cozy and likable, yes, but not exactly fresh.

Rachel McAdams, on the other hand, could save the romantic comedy genre. She will not actually save it; the actress (*Mean Girls* [2004], *Sherlock Holmes* [2009]) does not make movies frequently enough, nor does she always play the same part. She "could" save it though, if she wanted. Granted, good writing and suitable co-stars and so forth are important, too, but McAdams has that surprisingly elusive attribute known as charm, and it is a powerful thing. At a time when most female leads are written as cold control freaks (see practically every Katherine Heigl movie) or pretty nitwits with a lot more looks than personality (most Jennifer Aniston films), McAdams can play an ambitious career woman who wants love too and make the character both impressively professional and romantically appealing.

That is exactly what McAdams does in *Morning Glory,* a delightful little pick-me-up of a movie about a morning news show that feels, in many ways, very much like a morning news show. It is frequently loose and funny and even a little kooky, occasionally dipping into schmaltz and struggling to maintain its momentum. Overall, though, it is something worth watching, and something that would not be objectionable to see again.

In the film, McAdams plays Becky, who is cheerful and bouncy like a ponytail, which is also this 28-year-old TV producer's preferred hairstyle. Becky, who is tied to her Blackberry and has no time to invest in a relationship, is a workaholic, but a bubbly one. Since she was 8 years old she dreamed of being on NBC's *The Today Show*, and her work ethic dictates that she is not going to relax until that is exactly where she lands. That does not prevent her from being fired from her producer job on *Good Morning, New Jersey,* but it is not long until Jerry Barnes (Jeff Goldblum), an executive at the fictional network IBS' morning show *Daybreak,* hires Becky to improve the ratings of a program that always ranks fourth in its time slot.

That is a tall order; the show is hosted by Colleen Peck (Diane Keaton), a diva who has seen more than a dozen other people in the executive producer role Becky fills, and Paul McVee (Ty Burrell), a creep who shortly after meeting Becky asks if he can photograph her feet and post the pictures on his blog, "Sexy Feet." It is a ridiculous exchange that is not indicative of the generally sharp, affectionate writing in Aline Brosh McKenna's script. Then the movie clicks in a scene that McAdams absolutely devours, in the effortlessly sweet way that a crafty actress like her consumes light material. On her first day, in her first meeting, Becky is bombarded with issues about which she needs to make decisions immediately. Initially, it seems she may be overwhelmed by the onslaught of varied and occasionally strange questions, such as what ethnicity the baby that the show uses for a piece on baby food should be. Then Becky rifles off answers to every question in a flurry of confident authority, fires Paul, and immediately earns the respect of her co-workers and starts a buzz about herself in the building. That is how you begin a job, and McAdams totally owns the scene.

Unlike most romantic comedies, and at its heart *Morning Glory* falls into that category without being confined by it, the film's central pairing is a work relationship, not a romantic one. That occurs between Becky and Mike Pomeroy (Harrison Ford, ever comfortable as a salty grouch), a veteran broadcast newsman of more than forty years who is up to his elbows in Emmys, Pulitzers, and Peabody Awards. He does not let anyone forget this. Though she embarrassed herself the day of her job interview when she saw Mike in the elevator and professed her incredible fandom, Becky recruits Mike as Colleen's new co-anchor and, to the surprise of the *Daybreak* staff, he accepts. "You're here for the money," Becky says, bluntly recognizing the gruff, old-school reporter's agenda while probably hoping he will protest otherwise. No dice: "That is correct," he responds. So as Becky works to move the show in the right direction, Mike constantly declines to be a team player, capitalizing on contract stipulations that allow him final approval of promotional spots and the ability to refuse any story he does not feel like doing. And he does not feel like doing most of the slightly-to-considerably-less-than-hard-news pieces featured on a show like *Daybreak*. This provides plenty of opportunities for McAdams and Ford to jaw at each other, and the combination shines; he is a pretentious grump who is really fighting to still consider himself relevant, and she is a go-getter who sees no reason why news can not have some entertainment mixed in, where appropriate. They are constantly at odds, and the relationship has a lot of old-fashioned spunk. He is egotistical, she says. "I'm on-air talent!" he screams back, proving her right.

With a lot of time devoted to Mike's rough demeanor and, eventually, his not very interesting personal life, Keaton has little to do, and the romance between Becky and fellow producer Adam Bennett (Patrick Wilson) feels underwritten. That is a shame, since Wilson puts heart into a role that asks him only to flash a great smile, and he has chemistry with McAdams. She sells Becky's lack of relationship pizzazz even though this woman's tendency to get flustered and ramble around romantic possibilities just seems like a mandate by the genre, not a necessary element to an otherwise intelligent and well-adjusted character. Likewise, a scene in which Becky's colleagues drool over Adam and another when Becky's co-workers buy her T-shirts proclaiming "Yes, I accept" to wear to the meeting in which they expect she will get a promotion, are out of place here. *Morning Glory* comes to life because it is carried by capable actors playing entertaining personalities, and the film only gets dragged down by scenes in which generic romantic comedy clichés pop up to offer nothing but phony contrivance and awkward attempts at goofy comedy.

The film does a nice job, though, in its examination of the age-old debate between news and entertainment, particularly in a modern climate in which a media operation that clings too tightly to outdated approaches and principles will quickly find itself full of integrity and off the air/newsstand/etc. Becky has standards, and she does not seek to turn *Daybreak* into a mockery. Yet she understands the morning news format's room to play around a little, and the development of the show from a ratings stalwart into a limber and increasingly popular diversion offers contagious, amusing energy, regardless of how believable or unbelievable it may be. With Becky's help, the show finally establishes a sense of fun and purpose, and the movie experiences the same effect along with it.

Thankfully, this also brings a number of laughs, a result of both the film's eccentric personalities and funny scenes that are handled with a mostly casual hand by director Roger Michell (*Notting Hill* [1999]). Mike refuses to say the word "fluffy." Weatherman Ernie

Appleby (Matt Malloy) becomes the show's go-to guy to try extreme activities, including screaming his way down a rollercoaster on live TV. In a scene that plays better on screen than it does on paper, a snafu in the graphics department accidentally implies that Jimmy Carter is a sex offender. Many of the laughs in the film would not work if *Morning Glory* did not float along on such good vibrations, but McAdams brings such cheerful vivacity to Becky, and Ford provides much-needed oomph to a role he has played many times before, that a mild grin will likely sit on the faces of most viewers throughout the movie. The film does not so much reassure about finding love as it permits Becky to not apologize for working hard and expect that a significant other will understand her commitment. Yet work-life balance is necessary, the movie admits, as Mike regrets spending so much time away from his family and Adam requests that Becky detach from her Blackberry every so often. It is something with which many viewers who are tied to their computers, iPhones, iPads, and any other form of technology they can get their hands on will be extremely familiar.

Morning Glory is not reinventing any wheels. The short-lived FOX sitcom *Back to You* (2007-2008) dealt with bickering anchors on a news program, and a morning show producer played by Katherine Heigl also searched for love and professional success in *The Ugly Truth* (2009). However, that film offered a sexist view of working women (Heigl's character must lighten up to get her guy and ultimately seems to care much more about romance than her career) and nothing but brash, objectionable characters. *Morning Glory* has warmth in it, like a just-hot-enough cup of coffee that gets the day going. The buzz may not last terribly long, but its brief boost is still enjoyable and very welcome.

Matt Pais

CREDITS

Mike Pomeroy: Harrison Ford
Colleen Peck: Diane Keaton
Becky Fuller: Rachel McAdams
Jerry Barnes: Jeff Goldblum
Adam Bennett: Patrick Wilson
Lenny Bergman: John Pankow
Paul McVee: Ty Burrell
Ernie Appleby: Matt Malloy
Becky's mom: Patti D'Arbanville
Origin: USA
Language: English
Released: 2010
Production: J.J. Abrams, Bryan Burk; Bad Robot; released by Paramount Pictures

Directed by: Roger Michell
Written by: Aline Brosh McKenna
Cinematography by: Alwin Kuchler
Music by: David Arnold
Sound: Tom Nelson
Editing: Nick Moore, Daniel Farrell, Steven Weisberg
Art Direction: Alex DiGerlando, Kim Jennings
Costumes: Frank Fleming
Production Design: Mark Friedberg
MPAA rating: PG-13
Running time: 107 minutes

REVIEWS

Burr, Ty. *Boston Globe.* November 10, 2010.
Ebert, Roger. *Chicago Sun-Times.* November 10, 2010.
Gleiberman, Owen. *Entertainment Weekly.* November 10, 2010.
Jones, Kimberley. *Austin Chronicle.* November 12, 2010.
Moore, Roger. *Orlando Sentinel.* November 9, 2010.
Phillips, Michael. *Chicago Tribune.* November 11, 2010.
Reed, Rex. *New York Observer.* November 9, 2010.
Tobias, Scott. *AV Club.* November 9, 2010.
Toppman, Lawnrece. *Charlotte Observer.* November 12, 2010.
Zacharek, Stephanie. *Movineline.* November 10, 2010.

TRIVIA

The film was shot on the set of an actual television studio and featured many real-life film and television crew members playing fictional crew members in the film.

THE MOST DANGEROUS MAN IN AMERICA: DANIEL ELLSBERG AND THE PENTAGON PAPERS

The sad truth is that, as urgent as certain historical events seem, they often tend to fade from public consciousness quickly, as do the lessons which might have been learned from careful study of them. Documentary filmmaking seems a chief ally in the fight against such historical shortsightedness, especially these days when information floods in at an overwhelming rate. In the case of *The Most Dangerous Man in America: Daniel Ellsberg and the Pentagon Papers*, a documentary collects the facts behind a story so big it seems almost impossible that anyone would ever forget it and manages to do so in the best tradition of its form, creating a picture that is emotionally compelling, intellectually disturbing, and oddly reminiscent of where the American public still stands in 2010. War is something that nations can be (and often are) lied into, and often the people doing the lying hide behind the very principles they say they

are using war to defend. Yet it is conversely true that people can, if they choose, simply tell the truth to those in power until truth becomes undeniable. The story of Daniel Ellsberg is the story of what must be risked in order for men to have freedom. The relevancy of that story lies in the fact that what must be done by individuals has not changed.

On June 13, 1971, the *New York Times* began publishing portions of the *United States-Vietnam Relations, 1945-1967: A Study Prepared by the Department of Defense,* a top secret report that had been leaked to them by U.S. military analyst Daniel Ellsberg revealing the heretofore secret history of the Vietnam War. The documents detailed, comprehensively, the lies and deceptions across five separate presidencies from Truman all the way to Johnson that led to the conflict and strongly suggested that America's primary reason for continued involvement lay at the feet of leaders who were more than willing to sacrifice lives simply to save face. The truth was staggering and boiled down to, among other things, the existence of an unaccountable imperial presidency. When a court injunction against the *Times,* the first ever heard in a Federal court, demanded they cease publication, the story was picked up by the *Washington Post.* When an injunction against the *Post* was issued, the Pentagon Papers were then read into the record during a congressional filibuster. The government's charges against Ellsberg were finally dismissed when it was revealed that the government had, among other things, secretly wiretapped Ellsberg for as long as two years prior to the release of the documents and had broken into his psychiatrist's office post-publication to assess the level of threat he presented. Soon after, congress cut off funding for the war and Nixon resigned from office. In the intervening decades, Ellsberg has championed various anti-war efforts and social causes encouraging others to speak out against government duplicity and work towards laws which will hold government accountable.

Judith Ehrlich whose Award-Winning *The Good War and Those Who Refused to Fight It* (2000) (TV) chronicled dissent by conscientious objectors, teams here with Rick Goldsmith whose Oscar®-nominated *Tell the Truth and Run: George Seldes and the American Press* (1996) also embraced the story of one man against power run amok. Co-writing with first time writer Laurence Lerew and Michael Chandler of PBS standouts *The American Experience* (1995) and *Frontline* (1998-2001), the pair put together a definitive portrait of a man determined to see change in himself as much as anything else and it is indeed inspiring to watch Ellsberg recount the process by which he moved from hawkish young intellectual to fervent anti-war activist. "I accepted the basic premises within the government that being allied with America was good for you, good for the other people and that there was an idealistic aspect to it. [ie; the war]. In Vietnam we were protecting, supposedly democracy or the possibility of democracy against a Stalinist dictatorship."

But Ellsberg's real-life journey through that belief system let him down and Ehrlich and Goldsmith expertly use the tools of their trade to show how. Archival footage is combined with a wide range of present day voice over and interviews to highlight Ellsberg's discovery of the Gulf of Tonkin lie that President Johnson used to step up the conflict. While in Vietnam, Ellsberg is shown a chart logging hundreds of patrols in the country. Picking one to accompany at random, he is told that it, like the vast majority of the others, is simply a fabrication created to generate the hopeful statistics that Washington and the White House demand regarding the war. Once dragged out of his ivory tower by his own conscience, the film now begins to link to the people that helped Ellsberg sort through where he now found himself ideologically and to connect that back to his humanity in order to determine the way he would then live. Rather than offer a shrill denouncement of lies in high places, *The Most Dangerous Man in America: Daniel Ellsberg and the Pentagon Papers* traces the path of a disillusioned soul who must move from follower to leader and in so doing moves from leader to symbol.

At one point in the film, a shot of the Washington monument in the distance, lit up at night, is suddenly transformed by the realization that the camera is next to the Vietnam War Memorial. As the light sweeps by, the darkness is swallowed by the reflection of thousands of names which then fall back into shadow leaving the viewer where they started. Far from simply recounting the facts around a historical event or even tracing the path of one man's conscience, this is a film in which history itself, collective and individual, cries out to be known, embraced, grappled with and surrendered to. Nominated for the 2010 Academy Award® for Best Documentary Feature *The Most Dangerous Man In America: Daniel Ellsberg and the Pentagon Papers* is must-see viewing in an age glutted with demagoguery posing as documentary.

Dave Canfield

CREDITS

Narrator: Daniel Ellsberg
Origin: USA
Language: English
Released: 2009
Production: Judith Ehrlich, Rick Goldsmith; Insight Productions, ITVS, Kovno Communications; released by First Run Features

Directed by: Judith Ehrlich, Rick Goldsmith
Written by: Michael Chandler, Judith Ehrlich, Rick Goldsmith, Lawrence Lerew
Cinematography by: Vicente Franco, Dan Krauss
Music by: Blake Leyh
Sound: Rick Goldsmith, Nick Bertoni
Editing: Michael Chandler, Rick Goldsmith, Lawrence Lerew
MPAA rating: Unrated
Running time: 92 minutes

REVIEWS

Burr, Ty. *Boston Globe.* February 12, 2010.
Colvert, Colin. *Star Tribune.* April 8, 2010.
Denby, David. *New Yorker.* September 7, 2009.
Ebert, Roger. *Chicago Sun-Times.* March 24, 2010.
Gibron, Bill. *Popmatters.com.* July 19, 2010.
Goldstein, Gary. *Los Angeles Times.* September 24, 2009.
Hornaday, Ann. *Washington Post.* February 12, 2010.
Jenkins, Mark. *NPR.org.* February 4, 2010.
Lasall, Mick. *San Francisco Chronicle.* February 18, 2010.
Vognar, Chris. *Dallas Morning News.* April 22, 2010.

AWARDS

Nomination:

Oscars 2009: Feature Doc.

MOTHER
(Madeo)

> *She'll stop at nothing.*
> —Movie tagline

The great Jong-ho Bong continues to solidify his reputation as one of the world's most-interesting filmmakers with the excellent *Mother,* a near-masterpiece that was nominated for multiple awards around the world in 2009 and 2010. This riveting thriller/drama would be the career peak for most filmmakers twice Bong's age but it faces stiff competition from his even-superior *Memories of Murder* (2003) and *The Host* (2006). Like those two internationally-acclaimed films, *Mother* plays with audience expectations of a genre in a refreshing and daring way. Bong finds a way to take traditional appellations—the procedural *Memories of Murder,* monster movie *The Host,* and Hitchcockian thriller *Mother*—and spin them into something that feels original. His films not only have such unexpected twists and turns that they work completely as pure escapism but they are also so clearly the product of a confident filmmaking voice, an increasing rarity in a medium that feels more like a machine every year.

The archaic system that requires countries to submit only one film for the Oscar® for Best Foreign Language

Film led to something of a problem for Korea in 2009 (the year *Mother* was first eligible) as they had Bong's work and an amazing piece by his colleague: Park Chan-wook's *Thirst* (2009). Most people, having already seen Park's stunning vampire thriller, were stunned that there could be a better film after hearing the announcement that *Mother* was the chosen submission (it was, sadly, not nominated). It may not be "better" necessarily but it is easy to see why *Mother* won out in some voter's eyes. It's mesmerizing, memorable stuff.

One key element of *Mother* played differently in the film's home country—the casting of Hye-ja Kim in the title role. The star of the film is a multi-talented actress, who won the Los Angeles Film Critics Award for her work here, but her casting was somewhat shocking in Korea as she has been compared to the Doris Day of her people and this story takes this matriarchal figure to some daring and dark places. Kim plays a woman only referred to as "Mother," the single parent of a mentally-handicapped young man named Yoon Do-joon (Bin Won). The two live a simple, relatively-sheltered life in a small town but Do-joon has begun to hang out with a questionable young man named Jin-tae (Ku Jin). In the film's opening scene, the tough Jin-tae and the gentle Do-joon chase down and assault a few men that they believe nearly hit Do-joon with their car. It may seem like an aside but violence and protection will be major themes of Bong's unfolding story.

The action of the piece begins on a drunken evening as Do-joon follows a young girl home from a bar. Do-joon has had too much to drink and he starts by staring at the girl, then talking to her, and then…Bong shows her disappear into the shadows and Do-joon continuing up a path. The next morning, the girl's brutally-murdered body is found slumped on a roof right where Do-joon saw her last. After a brief investigation, the cops become convinced that Do-joon killed the girl and put him in jail. Do-joon's decreased mental faculty makes it easy to think that he could be railroaded into a prison cell by a corrupt system, but Bong cleverly keeps audiences guessing as to the young man's guilt or innocence.

His mother does no such guessing. For a variety of reasons, including standard maternal connection along with Do-joon's capacity to make bad decisions and even revealed guilt over something she did early in his life, Do-joon's mother never wavers in her belief that her son should not be imprisoned. Whether or not he is guilty is not as important a fact as it would be for most other filmmakers. What is more essential is that this mother simply needs her son back in her life both because of how much he relies on her and that he is one of the few things she connects to as well. They are co-dependent in dangerously-close and possibly-incestuous ways. Conse-quently, she is willing to go down whatever dark alley she needs to in order to guarantee his release: innocent or otherwise.

While a mother's journey for her son's release from prison sounds like the stuff of a Lifetime TV movie, but *Mother* is much darker than its brief summary might make it out to be. It is not a search for justice or truth as much as it is a character study of a woman with an unhealthy but protective relationship with her son.

The performances here are uniformly excellent, especially the riveting lead by Hye-ja Kim, but this is Joon-ho Bong's movie in every sense of the way that truly great filmmakers put their personal stamp on their films merely by virtue of their skilled direction. Like the best thriller directors, Bong leads the viewer through his emotional maze of a story, staying just one step ahead at all times, revealing little elements of his story carefully so the viewer is eager to catch up. Only after the trip does the viewer realize that it was not the destination but the twisted journey that was essential to this fantastic film.

Brian Tallerico

CREDITS

Hye-ja: Hye-ja Kim
Yoon Do-joon: Bin Won
Jin-tae: Ku Jin
Origin: Korea
Language: Korean
Released: 2009
Production: Woo-sik Seo, Tae-joon Park; CJ Entertainment, Barunson; released by Magnolia Pictures
Directed by: Joon-ho Bong
Written by: Joon-ho Bong, Eun-kyo Park
Cinematography by: Kyung-Pyo Hong
Music by: Byeong-woo Lee
Editing: Sae-kyoung Moon
Sound: Tae-young Choi
Costumes: Se-yeon Choi
Production Design: Seong-hie Ryu
MPAA rating: R
Running time: 128 minutes

REVIEWS

Burr, Ty. *Boston Globe.* March 18, 2010.
Dargis, Manohla. *New York Times.* March 12, 2010.
Ebert, Roger. *Chicago Sun-Times.* March 25, 2010.
Elley, Derek. *Variety.* May 17, 2009.
Kennedy, Lisa. *Denver Post.* April 16, 2010.
Lane, Anthony. *New Yorker.* March 8, 2010.
Morgensetern, Joe. *Wall Street Journal.* March 12, 2010.

Simon, Brent. *Shared Darkness.* March 5, 2010.
Sobczynski, Peter. *eFilmCritic.com* April 2, 2010.
Stevens, Dana. *Slate.* March 12, 2010.

TRIVIA

South Korea's official submission to the 82nd Academy Award's Foreign Language category in 2010.

AWARDS

Nomination:

Ind. Spirit 2010: Foreign Film.

MOTHER AND CHILD

Box Office: $1 million

In *Mother and Child,* an embittered woman named Karen (Annette Bening)—who, at fifty-one, has never gotten over giving up, at fourteen, her unwanted child for adoption—undergoes one of the most remarkable character transformations in film history. Bening, who seems to have taken up specializing in unglamorous, unsmiling, downright bitchy roles, plays a woman so hate-filled and suspicious that her own housekeeper wins more affection and gifts from her ailing, dying mother than does Karen. And Karen angrily rejects every overture from a kind-hearted coworker (Jimmy Smits) who, for some reason that defies logic, is attracted to her. Do not underestimate movie magic. By film's end, Karen has suddenly married her suitor, become devoted to her housekeeper's young daughter (who she formerly thought was a brat and a thief), and is perfectly loving grandmother material.

Karen's unbelievable character arc is rivaled only by that of the daughter she abandoned and never knew. Applying for a job at a law firm, Elizabeth (Naomi Watts) says she prefers to be supervised by a man because "Women find me threatening. I'm not in the sisterhood." She emphasizes how much she values her independence, and soon she demonstrates to her boss, Paul (Samuel L. Jackson), how confident and self-centered she is by practically demanding sex and then also bedding down a married neighbor the next morning. Elizabeth shows no signs of being capable of caring for anyone but herself, but by movie's end she too is transformed into the ultimate self-sacrificing mother.

Joining Karen and Elizabeth in the throes of motherhood crisis is a third woman, Lucy (Kerry Washington), who wants to adopt a child with her husband. Lucy is all superheated earnestness and fine character, but her husband balks after the birth mother, a sassy twenty-year-old college grad, interviews them

and makes it clear she is also in charge. The men in this movie conveniently appear, disappear, and accept the women's decisions without debate. Even the usually flamboyant Jackson plays down his character, looking rather buttoned-down and uptight and humbly pledging whatever Elizabeth wants.

Writer-director Rodrigo Garcia has the right stuff for Lifetime channel sentiment, and it is no surprise he earned his chops directing for television. Watching the movie, a viewer can almost see the arrows connecting the plot lessons. The subject, motherhood, is almost sacrosanct, so Garcia sometimes gets away with his amateurish plot. One longs for the wry knowingness of Pedro Almodovar, who has tackled the subject of motherhood before without falling into cliché. Instead, there is such sentimentality, redemption, and moral rectitude that *Mother and Child* is like a trip to the confessional.

Bening's Karen is a real picture of human wreckage. She writes letters daily to her abandoned child, telling her, "I know in my heart that we will meet someday." She is guilt-ridden yet unsympathetic to others, and Bening makes her so repulsive in manner and appearance that it is a complete mystery why any man would ever appear and rescue her. But rescue is a motif in *Mother and Child,* as characters need redemption in so many ways. And they get it.

Along with her part in *The Kids Are All Right* (2010), Bening seems to be specializing in shrewish, largely unlikable mothers. She seems content playing very unglamorous parts with a dare-you-to-hate-me kind of conviction. Though these are challenging, against-the-grain roles for a onetime Hollywood leading lady to play, there is almost no produced empathy that any moviegoer needs to have for a protagonist. As for Watts, she somehow manages to make her underwritten character into more than a cliché of the self-absorbed career woman with vixen tastes. Elizabeth manages to be sympathetic even when she is at her worst morally because Watts has a smiling, sunny presence from the start that allows the viewer to recognize that Elizabeth is not really dastardly, just enjoying life as a sort of live-for-today romp.

There is a good topic for a movie here, one about the ways in which changing attitudes toward adoption have changed women's roles as mothers and expanded their choices. And that is the movie Garcia is trying to make, but he is way too heavy-handed and simplistic to make his lessons go down palatably. One nun seems to handle all adoptions in Los Angeles, and the plot neatly resolves racial assignment, too complicated an issue in adoption for the single-minded *Mother and Child* to do anything but punt on. "Motherhood should be so much simpler than that," Lucy's mother blurts out at one point—and it is apparent that Garcia, for all the posturing in his plot, thinks so too.

Michael Betzold

CREDITS

Karen: Annette Bening
Elizabeth: Naomi Watts
Lucy: Kerry Washington
Paul: Samuel L. Jackson
Paco: Jimmy Smits
Ray: Shareeka Epps
Dr. Stone: Amy Brenneman
Tom: David Morse
Joseph: David Ramsey
Sister Joanne: Cherry Jones
Steven: Marc Blucas
Julian: Ahmed Best
Ada: S. Epatha Merkerson
Leticia: Lisa Gay Hamilton
Maria: Tatyana Ali
Origin: USA
Language: English
Released: 2009
Production: Julie Lynn, Lisa Marie Falcone; Cha Cha Cha Films, Mockingbird Pictures, Everest Entertainment; released by Sony Pictures Classics
Directed by: Rodrigo Garcia
Written by: Rodrigo Garcia
Cinematography by: Xavier Perez Grobet
Music by: Ed Shearmur
Sound: Peter J. Devlin
Editing: Steven Weisberg
Costumes: Suzie DeSanto
Production Design: Christopher Tandon
MPAA rating: R
Running time: 125 minutes

REVIEWS

Bell, Josh. *Las Vegas Weekly.* June 24, 2010.
Braun, Liz. *Jam! Movies.* May 14, 2010.
Caldwell, Thomas. *Cinema Autopsy.* July 4, 2010.
Ebert, Roger. *Chicago Sun-Times.* May 20, 2010.
Gang, Alison. *San Diego Union-Tribune.* August 11, 2010.
Groen, Rick. *Toronto Globe and Mail.* May 14, 2010.
Hartl, John. *Seattle Times.* May 20, 2010.
Keller, Louise. *Urban Cinefile.* June 12, 2010.
Rainer, Peter. *Christian Science Monitor.* May 14, 2010.
Scott, Mike. *New Orleans Times-Picayune.* June 30, 2010.

TRIVIA

In real life, Annette Bening is only ten years older than Naomi Watts despite playing mother and daughter in the film.
Naomi Watts filmed all her scenes in a mere eight days.

AWARDS

Nomination:

Ind. Spirit 2011: Support. Actor (Jackson), Support. Actress (Watts).

MY SON, MY SON, WHAT HAVE YE DONE

The mystery isn't who. But why.
—Movie tagline

A man wakes up one morning, inexplicably kills his mother and barricades himself inside his house with a couple of hostages. A veteran cop arrives on the scene and finds himself trying to negotiate with the man and keep things calm and orderly while the street fills with cops, media, and other onlookers. As time goes by, the cop interviews a couple of people who know the man and, through flashbacks to what they tell him, begins to piece together a picture of exactly who the guy is and why he would commit such a seemingly unthinkable act. This is a scenario that has been enacted so many times in TV shows and movies that it seems impossible that anyone could bring anything fresh to it. And yet, that is exactly what maverick filmmaker Werner Herzog has done with his latest effort, *My Son, My Son, What Have Ye Done,* and the result is easily the most fascinatingly police procedural to come along since *The Bad Lieutenant: Port of Call New Orleans* (2009), Herzog's previous bizarre take on the cop movie genre.

As with that earlier film, it quickly becomes clear that Herzog has no interest in following the standard rules of the genre and is more interested in using the familiar framework as a jumping-off point for one of his patented meditations on the mysteries of madness and the myriad ways that it affects the affected. This is why he skips over all the expected action beats and moments of conventional tension that one might find in a hostage drama set in a suburb of San Diego in order to present sequences that take viewers to such far-flung locales as Peru, Mexico, Calgary, and an ostrich farm where, in one unforgettable moment, a pair of eyeglasses makes a journey from a character's jacket pocket to the throat of an ostrich and back again. None of these scenes may have much to do with the central story but once they are seen, it is essentially impossible to imagine the film without them.

As the hostage taker, Michael Shannon creates an indelible portrait of a man walking the thin tightrope between lunacy and enlightenment and is ably supported by an eclectic supporting cast that features Willem Dafoe as the lead cop, Chloe Sevigny as the fiancée, Udo Kier as a theater director who had to let our hero go for behaving too weirdly to star in a production of *Elektra* (and whose eyeglasses make that aforementioned trip), Michael Peña as a younger cop who has seen too many of the movies and TV shows featuring the kinds of clichés and turgid plotting that Herzog is rejecting here, Brad Dourif as a racist ostrich farmer, Verne Troyer as a dwarf, and Grace Zabriskie as the overly coddling mother who winds up getting run through with a sword for her troubles.

Because *My Son, My Son, What Have Ye Done* was executive-produced by David Lynch, some viewers may have gone into the film expecting the union of him and Herzog to produce a cinematic freak out of epic proportions and come away slightly disappointed that it was not as completely insane as they might have hoped. (It appears that Lynch's participation extended no further than supplying some funding and providing some actors from his stable of regulars, including Grace Zabriskie and Brad Dourif.) However, while it may not be as completely bizarre as one might have hoped, it is still an uncommonly compelling film to watch. In a time when movies are becoming more homogenized than ever, Werner Herzog is one of those rare individuals who lives to supply his audiences with sights that they have never before seen or even contemplated and whether one loves or hates *My Son, My Son, What Have Ye Done*—and to judge from the reviews, there appears to have been no middle ground in terms of critical response—no one who sees this extraordinary work can deny that he has done just that once again.

Peter Sobczynski

CREDITS

Det. Hank Havenhurst: Willem Dafoe
Brad McCullum: Michael Shannon
Ingrid: Chloe Sevigny
Det. Vargas: Michael Peña
Lee Meyers: Udo Kier
Uncle Ted: Brad Dourif
Mrs. McCullum: Grace Zabriskie
Mrs. Roberts: Irma P. Hall
Miss Roberts: Loretta Devine
Midget: Verne Troyer
Origin: USA
Language: English
Released: 2009
Production: Eric Bassett; Industrial Entertainment, Absurda (a David Lynch Company); released by Paper Street Films
Directed by: Werner Herzog
Written by: Werner Herzog, Herbert Golder
Cinematography by: Peter Zeitlinger

Music by: Ernst Reijseger
Sound: Greg Agalsoff
Editing: Joe Bini, Omar Daher
Costumes: Mikel Padilla
Production Design: Tyson Estes, Danny Caldwell
MPAA rating: Unrated
Running time: 87 minutes

REVIEWS

Dargis, Manohla. *New York Times.* December 11, 2009.
Ebert, Roger. *Chicago Sun-Times.* April 8, 2010.
Gang, Alison. *San Diego Union-Tribune.* August 11, 2010.
Goldstein, Gary. *Los Angeles Times.* December 18, 2010.
Hoberman, J. *Village Voice.* December 8, 2009.
Jones, J.R. *Chicago Reader.* January 3, 2011.
Murray, Noel. *AV Club.* December 10, 2009.
Musetto, V.A. *New York Post.* December 11, 2009.
Shannon, Jeff. *Seattle Times.* April 8, 2010.
Tallerico, Brian. *MovieRetriever.com.* April 9, 2010.

QUOTES

Brad McCullum: "Some people act a role, others play a part!"

TRIVIA

This film marks the fourth collaboration between Werner Herzog and Brad Dourif.

MY SOUL TO TAKE

Only one has the power to save their souls.
—Movie tagline

Box Office: $14 million

My Soul to Take is a film that would be completely ignored if not for the fact that it is the first film that Wes Craven has written and directed since the under-rated *New Nightmare* (1994). Fifteen years later, Craven delivers one of the weakest, most muddled screenplays of his career and even though he manages to dress it up with some solid technique and a good cast, his sense for suspense is undercut by one of his most boring creations. The man who gave us Papa Jupiter and his brood (*The Hills Have Eyes* [1977]), Freddy Krueger (*A Nightmare on Elm Street* [1983]), and the slasher from *Scream* (1996), can only conjure a monster best-described as a horror version of Hagrid from the Harry Potter series. Not even Robbie Coltrane himself could have breathed life into this grunting hobo who is unimaginatively called "The Ripper" and not even Harry Potter could cast a spell to make audiences remember this movie after they leave the theater.

The Ripper first haunted the small town of Riverton sixteen years ago, killing seven people before he was captured and presumably killed. He swore to come back, to hunt down and kill the Riverton children born on that same night. As the teenagers get ready to celebrate their sixteenth birthdays, they begin dying one-by-one. Is it the Ripper who may have escaped and has been living in the woods all this time? Is it his spirit reincarnated in someone else? No one knows but one of the kids, nicknamed Bug (Max Thieriot), has been plagued by nightmares of the murders, seeing them as they happen, and joins with his nerdy friend Alex (John Magaro) and the others hoping to find out the answer before the last of the Riverton seven dies.

Max Thieriot has lately distinguished himself with a small role in Atom Egoyan's *Chloe* (2009) but is better known as the typical teen hearthrob of stuff like *Kit Kiteredge: An American Girl* (2008), *Jumper* (2008), *Nancy Drew* (2007), *The Pacifier* (2005), and *Catch That Kid* (2004). He is a capable actor, but there is simply little to work with in the character of Bug. As written, the character simply slips into whatever mode the action requires of him. He is hardly even a real person.

Bug's friend Alex is played by John Magaro, a charismatic up-and-comer with an unnerving stare and decent-enough acting chops to have scored meaningful roles in interesting projects like *The Box* (2009), *Assassination of a High School President* (2008), *The Life Before Her Eyes* (2007), and *The Brave One* (2007). Magaro is stuck with a role (indeed an entire movie) that feels like leftovers from *Scream* and limited most of the time to expositing through dialogue what Craven should have found a way to show his audience. When the killer is finally identified as the disembodied personality of the original killer working through Alex, Magaro does a fine job of conveying the switch but the scenes are so talky that any sense of tragedy leading up to Magaro's death is undercut by the cheesiness of it all.

The teens are, for the most part, reasonably well-drawn and presented even when they veer into cliché (stuck-up bitch, stupid jock, outsider, etc.) but the film really has nothing for them to do but fulfill those stereotypes prior to getting killed. Despite their best efforts, the cast are all as faceless as the Ripper himself. The murders are faceless too. In *Scream,* in fact in almost all of Craven's horror films, the art of the kill was perfectly designed to elicit audience response. Viewers could count on having fun, being disturbed, getting grossed out. Here the payoffs are mundane in the extreme. So is the retrofitted 3D which is basically nonexistent, popping up here and there only to fall flat back into the screen where it smudges the overall look of the film. It is so bad that viewers should wait until they can see *My Soul to Take* in a standard format rather than subject themselves to it.

Things that fail to work in this film are altogether more frustrating because of the things that do. Craven still has a handle on how to build suspense. The entertaining Zena Grey (*Snow Day* [2000], *Max Keebles Big Move* [2001], *The Shaggy Dog* [2006]), is genuinely interesting as Penelope, the school's resident born-again, but is killed off far too early to do more than register her presence in a couple of standout character bits. Also, a nature presentation by Alex and Bug involving a rare species of bird is one of the funniest moments in film this year and there are a number of scares that do succeed.

A short list of Craven films and characters reveals not only memorable monsters but insightful social commentary and an engaged intellect. Often, his best work has reached back into his difficult childhood and emergence from the strict religiosity that kept him from discovering film earlier. *The People Under the Stairs* (1991) is his masterpiece in that regard. *My Soul to Take* seems disengaged in the extreme, like Bug himself, and more of an attempt to create another franchisable boogie man than tell a memorable story or to exorcise any personal demons.

Dave Canfield

CREDITS

Adam "Bug" Heller: Max Thieriot
Fang: Emily Meade
Brandon O'Neal: Nick Lashaway
Jerome King: Denzel Whitaker
Chandelle King: Shareeka Epps
Abel Plenkov: Raul Esparza
Det. Frank Paterson: Frank Grillo
Penelope Bryte: Zena Grey
Alex Dunkelman: John Magaro
Brittany Cunningham: Paulina Olszynski
May: Jessica Hecht
Principal Pratt: Dennis Boutsikaris
Origin: USA
Language: English
Released: 2010
Production: Wes Craven, Anthony G. Katagas, Iya Labunka; Relativity Media, Rogue, Corvus Corax Productions; released by Rogue Pictures
Directed by: Wes Craven
Written by: Wes Craven
Cinematography by: Petra Korner
Music by: Marco Beltrami
Sound: Betsy Blankenbaker, Todd Toon
Music Supervisor: Ed Gerrard

Editing: Peter McNulty, Todd E. Miller
Art Direction: Jack Ballance, Brianne Zulauf
Costumes: Kurt and Bart
Production Design: Adam Stockhausen
MPAA rating: R
Running time: 107 minutes

REVIEWS

Goldstein, Gary. *Los Angeles Times.* October 15, 2010.
Harvey, Dennis. *Variety.* October 8, 2010.
Kendrick, Ben. *Screen Rant.* October 7, 2010.
Mendelson, Scott. *Huffington Post.* October 8, 2010.
Miska, Brad. *Bloody Disgusting.* October 8, 2010.
Moore, Roger. *Orlando Sentinel.* October 8, 2010.
Morris, Wesley. *Boston Globe* October 9, 2010.
Salisbury, Brian. *Hollywood.com.* October 8, 2010.
Snider, Eric D. *Film.com.* October 11, 2010.
Zimmerman, Samuel. *Fangoria.* October 8, 2010.

QUOTES

The Ripper: "Fear ye, the Ripper!"

TRIVIA

Set the record for the lowest opening gross of a 3D film to date upon release.

N

NANNY McPHEE RETURNS

(Nanny McPhee and the Big Bang)

Who's your nanny?
—Movie tagline

Box Office: $29 million

In favor of *Nanny McPhee Returns* (or *Nanny McPhee and the Big Bang,* as it is called in the United Kingdom) is the fact that Nanny McPhee (Emma Thompson) does nothing as drastic as threatening to boil a baby alive, as she did when introducing herself to the children of the original movie in 2005. Instead, McPhee uses her magical cane to coerce the three children, one niece, and one nephew of Isabel Green (Maggie Gyllenhaal) to inflict physical pain on their own bodies. They pull their own hair, poke at their own eyes, and throw themselves to the floor. Worst of all, for the youngest of the Green children Vincent (Oscar Steer), is the act of knocking the beloved letters from their father (Ewan McGregor), who is off to war, into the fire. McPhee, of course, freezes time and stops the letters from falling at the last moment, and she has taught them a lesson (to stop fighting)—the first of five she plans to instill upon her charges.

McPhee, based on the character Nurse Matilda introduced in a trio of books by Christianna Brand, was and remains an oddity—a teacher who uses terror and intimidation to straighten out the behaviors of the children under her watch. She begins a witch-like figure, complete with warts, uni-brow, swollen nose, a jagged tooth that extends past the lip, and a plump frame beneath an all-black ensemble. With each moral she teaches, McPhee loses one of her unflattering physical characteristics in a simple dissolve. She is the ugly duckling, awaiting her gradual transition into one who looks more like Thompson as a result of her methods.

The trouble starts when Vincent, Norman (Asa Butterfield), and Megsie's (Lil Woods) cousins Cyril (Eros Vlahos) and Celia (Rosie Taylor-Ritson) arrive from London to stay at the Green's farm. Spoiled, sarcastic, and upset with the separation from their parents, the cousins ridicule the Green children's home (as Cyril sees it, they live in "the land of poo," or "the British museum of poo") and destroy the jar of jam they had made for their father (after saving months of sugar rations). On the other hand, Vincent, Norman, and Megsie mock their cousins' elitist attitudes and throw Celia's clothes in the mud.

Isabel is overwhelmed at work at the local candy store where her boss, Mrs. Docherty (Maggie Smith), is senile and now at home with another two children for whom to care. Her brother-in-law Phil (Rhys Ifans) is attempting to sell the family farm—the same where Isabel and the children live—as a way to appease his gambling debts, although Isabel must agree to such a sale. Phil is hounded by "hit women" and "lady heavies" Misses Topsey (Sinead Matthews) and Turvey (Katy Brand), who, in their respective guttural and high-pitched voices, threaten to remove one of his kidneys and later stuff him like a taxidermy subject if he does not pay.

With her usual threat of "When you need me but do not want me, then I must stay; when you want me but no longer need me, then I have to go," McPhee enters into the Greens' cluttered, melancholy lives, hardly making things better. When Phil sabotages the barn and scatters the family's money-earning piglets, it is simply not enough that the children learn the third lesson on their own and work together. McPhee casts a spell that the pigs climb trees, cartwheel, flip, perform a synchronized swimming routine a la Esther Williams and crew in *Bathing Beauty* (1944), and otherwise avoid the children, whose despairing frustration shifts into amused frustration.

The pairing of pastoral joviality with the sinister machinations involved in Phil's subplot (during which he turns from bumbling nitwit into despicable fiend) and the possibility of wartime death and destruction is uneven in the hands of director Susanna White. The delivery of a telegram in a yellow envelope from the War Office is an affecting moment, undermined entirely by Norman's unwavering belief that the news his father has been killed in action is false. Norman and Cyril travel to London with McPhee, where Cyril confronts his father (Ralph Fiennes), a powerful force in the War Department, and learns—again, on his own—to stand up for himself.

With McPhee on the sidelines, scolding her belching bird friend Mr. Edelweiss for eating the putty from her windows, the children do most of the growing on their own, and this change is in the movie's favor. On the quest to the city, Norman and Cyril develop a bit more than the one-dimensional caricature of Celia and the mere state of existence of Vincent and Megsie. The solidifying of the children's new, deeper bond comes with the appearance of an unexploded bomb dropped by an "enemy plane" (The movie hints at the Second World War without getting into any specifics). After Mr. Docherty (Sam Kelly), the town's air raid warden, faints, they must work together to diffuse the situation (using the military's trusty pamphlet, euphemistically titled "Three steps to an explosion-free day").

In writing less of her titular character into the story, Thompson's screenplay for *Nanny McPhee Returns* makes a slightly more palatable experience than its predecessor. Even so, the jarring dichotomy of the movie's tone—a battle between the darling and the dangerous—weakens that mild success.

Mark Dujsik

CREDITS

Nanny McPhee: Emma Thompson
Isabel Green: Maggie Gyllenhaal
Uncle Phil: Rhys Ifans
Lord Gray: Ralph Fiennes
Mrs. Docherty: Maggie Smith
Norman Green: Asa Butterfield
Megsie Green: Lil Woods
Vincent Green: Oscar Steer
Cyril Gray: Eros Vlahos
Celia Gray: Rosie Taylor-Ritson
Rory Green: Ewan McGregor
Mr. Docherty: Sam Kelly
Miss Topsey: Sinead Matthews
Miss Turvey: Katy Brand
Blenkinsop: Daniel Mays
Origin: United Kingdom, France, USA
Language: English
Released: 2010
Production: Tim Bevan, Lindsay Doran, Eric Fellner; Three Strange Angels, Working Title Films, Studio Canal, Relativity Media; released by Universal Pictures
Directed by: Susanna White
Written by: Emma Thompson
Cinematography by: Mike Eley
Music by: James Newton Howard
Sound: Simon Hayes
Editing: Sim Evan-Jones
Art Direction: Suzanne Austin, Gary Jopling, Nick Dent
Costumes: Jacqueline Durran
Production Design: Simon Elliott
MPAA rating: PG
Running time: 109 minutes

REVIEWS

Basile, Annette. *Filmink.com.au.* March 23, 2010.
Gritten, David. *Daily Telegraph.* March 25, 2010.
Neumaier, Joe. *New York Daily News.* August 19, 2010.
Phillips, Michael *Chicago Tribune.* August 19, 2010.
Putman, Dustin. *Dustinputman.com.* August 18, 2010.
Russo, Tom. *Boston Globe.* August 20, 2010.
Schager, Nick. *Village Voice.* August 18, 2010.
Smith, Robert W. *Kansas City Star.* August 19, 2010.
Whipp, Glenn. *Los Angeles Times.* August 20, 2010.
Wilson, Jake. *Age.* March 25, 2010.

QUOTES

Mrs. Docherty: "You seem to have forgotten the way she works. When you need her but do not want her, then she must stay. When you want her, but no longer need her, then she has to go. I know from personal experience."
Nanny McPhee: "I am Nanny McPhee. Small C, Big P."

NEVER LET ME GO

Box Office: $2 million

Henry David Thoreau regretted that "the mass of men lead lives of quiet desperation," whereas mink and muskrat caught in the teeth of a trap would rather gnaw off their own feet than remain stoically stuck. Giving a new depth of disturbing meaning to "quiet desperation" are the young characters of *Never Let Me Go,* who are more akin to sheep on their creepily-compliant way to the slaughter. As the *Boston Globe*'s Wesley Morris noted, the film could aptly have shared a title with 1991's *The Silence of the Lambs.*

Everyone on Earth is, of course, doomed from the start. Death can sometimes be ducked due to luck or delayed by the intervention of modern medicine, but it patiently waits and has yet to be denied. What remains mercifully unknown until the finish line comes into view is the length of each person's term before they will be terminated, and in which of the myriad ways the deed will be done. However, the protagonists of *Never Let Me Go* know all too well what has been blessedly left blank for all of those in the real world and most of those who populate the dystopian alternate one originally created by Kazuo Ishiguro for his 2005 critically-acclaimed bestselling novel. At a distressingly tender age, they are hit with the stunningly-brutal facts of their lives: they are utilitarian clones, flesh and blood incubators for steadily-maturing parts destined for the failing bodies of those who came to be as a result of old-fashioned sensuality rather than new-fangled science. At about the time most lives get underway in earnest is when their pre-ordained decline toward death will begin, gradually giving up their vital organs until they oh-so-euphemistically "complete."

It is horrific stuff of which *Never Let Me Go* speaks, but the tale being told is less ghoulish science fiction than it is thoughtful guidance concerning our own reality. This story of love, friendship, and loss can be seen as an unsettling, morose metaphor, meant, director Mark Romanek asserted, to make viewers appreciate that there are at least some choices and chances during their own all-too-fleeting and frighteningly-finite lives. Thus, there is actually an uplifting message to be found in the film, but it has an exceedingly tough time shining through the unrelenting, chilly gloom that hangs over the proceedings.

As twenty-eight-year-old Kathy H. (Carey Mulligan) begins telling her story in voiceover, viewers unacquainted with Ishiguro's work are unaware that she is wistfully recalling her past while nearing the limits of a foreshortened future. They do not realize what she is, what has already been ripped away from her, and what will soon be literally ripped out of her. Kathy is not just clinging to her memories because they are cherished, but because they are the only things that have permanence in her existence. The audience is transported back past curiosity-piquing mentions of worthy but wearisome work as a "carer" for those making "donations" to her childhood, which was spent at an isolated British boarding school that is infused with a curious strangeness.

Some things are ordinary enough, like the puppy love triangle between young Kathy (a lovely find named Isobel Meikle-Small), best friend Ruth (Ella Purnell), and the object of their affection, Tommy (Charlie Rowe). There is also little surprising about the way some students relish tormenting a sensitive peer, repeatedly pushing Tommy's buttons until he erupts in rages and they in derisive laughter. (While Kathy is sympathetic, Ruth seems to get a callous kick out of it all.) They seem like normal kids, so why, viewers wonder, do some people seem repulsed by them, at times even averting their eyes? Then there is the steely headmistress (Charlotte Rampling) who stresses that they are "special," implores them to remain healthy, and rapturously rants about "forward thinking." (As the institution's name is Hailsham, some may be reminded of Dickens' manipulative Miss Havisham.) After the firing of the only "guardian" (an effective Sally Hawkins) who ever dared to reveal to the children the truth about themselves and what is inevitably to come (which, depending on how one wants to look at it, is either laudably decent or misguidedly destructive), they clap at the announcement like the thoroughly-indoctrinated innocents that they are. The audience cannot help wondering about the scanners across which the children so matter-of-factly swipe their wrists. The powers that be have shockingly stooped so low as to create ghastly tall tales meant to ensure that the kids never stray from the premises. Beat up cast-off items are periodically brought in for them from the outside world, for which the students are oddly overjoyed. (One thinks later: secondhand things are thought sufficient for second-class beings.)

By the time Kathy, Ruth and Tommy leave the halls of Hailsham for a somewhat less restrictive clone cloister cozily named "The Cottages," they have grown into the well-cast Mulligan, Keira Knightley, and Andrew Garfield. This part of *Never Let Me Go,* a film which never exceeds a speed beyond wafting, is especially sluggish. An excursion to peek at Ruth's supposed "original" is utterly anticlimactic—for her and for viewers. Kathy continually suppresses her steadfast true love for Tommy as he remains in the aggressive clutches of Ruth, her best friend that only a masochist could seem to love. To give her heart a distracting purpose beyond achingly pining, devotion that might be appreciated and also warm her in the face of the cold reality ahead, Kathy pursues becoming a carer.

With the ominous word "completion" printed upon the screen, the final phase of both *Never Let Me Go* and the characters' lives begin. All along, they—and the audience—know how things had to end, yet Kathy, Ruth, Tommy and those watching still cannot help but wish things were otherwise, that there would be a way to at least slow the merciless slide toward a societally-sanctioned butchering. Having already given up some of her organs, a repentant and quickly-fading Ruth endeavors to provide Kathy and Tommy with some eleventh-hour happiness. There had been rumors of a possible deferral of three or four years for couples who could prove that they are truly in love, ascertained, Tommy had theorized, by examining the supposedly soul-revealing artwork they had created at Hailsham for the mysterious "gallery" maintained by Madame Marie-Claude (Nathalie Richard). The scene in which the last-ditch hopes to which Kathy and Tommy have been desperately clinging are dashed—there are no deferrals, and never were—is quite affecting. Also moving is the sight of Tommy's subsequent demise, with Kathy, luminously looming like an agonized angel, determinedly holding it together in his waning moments to try to transmit strength she possesses and comfort she does not.

By the time Kathy wraps up the film in a coda equating their all-too-brief time with loved ones with our own (rather unfortunately muddying the all-important difference of free will with which the real world navigates the road toward termination), it is clearly hoped that it will all have most-appropriately ripped viewers' hearts out. (Speaking of which, the shell that once was Ruth simply being deserted on an operating table after she flatlines, her eyes left as open as her chest, strikes one as a beastly way for humanity to thank her for dispensing the indispensable.) However, while there was audible sniffling in theaters, it did not quite seem to be the despair of the intimately involved. Especially with its decided accent on atmosphere and acceptance rather than action, too many moviegoers found quietly-unfolding, ceaselessly-solemn, Merchant Ivoryesque *Never Let Me Go* to be depressing, listless, and ultimately somnolent. Critical reaction was mixed. Made on a budget of $15 million, it earned just $2.3 million and was never able to break out of limited release. Having a hard time warming to the bleak proceedings, replete with grey, desolate, windswept visuals guaranteed to trigger melancholia and the gathering together of one's coat, is wholly understandable. There is also an undeniable emotional remoteness—for some an impenetrability—as the characters constantly and carefully keep stuffed way down within themselves what could be utterly immobilizing so they can cope and trudge on. It far exceeds the oft-noted British stiff upper lip. What some saw as sublime, Herculean stoicism, struck others as perplexing or even irritating passive acceptance, while still others found it simply dull, expressionless storytelling. (A notable, heartrending exception is Tommy's anguished letdown meltdown.)

There were no escape attempts a la *Logan's Run* (1976) in Ishiguro's source material, a work seemingly permeated with aesthetics favored by the country in which the author was born before moving to England with his family as a small boy. (Incidentally, could it possibly be mere coincidence that screenwriter Alex Garland now has an interest in penning the proposed remake of that sci-fi classic?) Romanek referred in interviews to Japanese concepts such as yugen—"the calm surface that belies deep, strong currents underneath"—and the reverent, sorrow-tinged recognition of beauty's impermanence in mono no aware and wabi sabi. Whatever the film's challenges or flaws, watching young people come to an end just when they should be coming into their own cannot help but give one pause. Kathy, Tommy, and Ruth have convinced themselves that they are performing a unique, valuable service, and do so with a graceful dignity. It is sobering, if not quite devastating, to watch them go so gently into that good night.

David L. Boxerbaum

CREDITS
Kathy: Carey Mulligan
Tommy: Andrew Garfield
Ruth: Keira Knightley
Miss Emily: Charlotte Rampling
Miss Lucy: Sally Hawkins
Miss Geraldine: Kate Bowes Renna
Arthur: Oliver Parsons
Keffers: David Sterne
Young Kathy: Isobel Meikle-Small
Young Ruth: Ella Purnell
Young Tommy: Charlie Rowe
Madame Marie-Claude: Nathalie Richard
Origin: United Kingdom
Language: English
Released: 2010
Production: Alex Garland, Andrew Macdonald, Allon Reich; DNA Films Ltd., Film4, Dune Entertainment; released by Fox Searchlight Pictures
Directed by: Mark Romanek
Written by: Alex Garland
Cinematography by: Adam Kimmel
Music by: Rachel Portman
Sound: Glenn Freemantle, Jim Greenhorn
Music Supervisor: George Drakoulias, Randall Poster
Editing: Barney Pilling
Art Direction: Paul Cripps, Denis Schnegg
Costumes: Rachel Fleming, Steven Noble
Production Design: Mark Digby

MPAA rating: R
Running time: 103 minutes

REVIEWS

Bowles, Scott. *USA Today*. September 15, 2010.
Corliss, Richard. *TIME Magazine*. September 13, 2010.
Debruge, Peter. *Variety*. September 13, 2010.
Denby, David. *New Yorker*. October 4, 2010.
Gleiberman, Owen. *Entertainment Weekly*. September 17, 2010.
Handy, Bruce. *Vanity Fair*. October 2010.
Jones, Kristin M.. *Film Comment*. September/October 2010.
Phillips, Michael. *Chicago Tribune*. September 23, 2010.
Rainer, Peter. *Christian Science Monitor*. September 24, 2010.
Thomas, Louisa. *Newsweek*. September 20, 2010.

QUOTES

Kathy: "It had never occurred to me that our lives, so closely interwoven, could unravel with such speed. If I'd known, maybe I'd have kept tighter hold of them and not let unseen tides pull us apart."

Kathy: "We all complete. Maybe none of us really understand what we've lived through, or feel we've had enough time."

TRIVIA

In order to film her driving scenes, Carey Mulligan had to first learn how to drive, eventually failing the driving test and forcing the production to shoot her scene on a private road.

AWARDS

Nomination:

Ind. Spirit 2011: Cinematog.

THE NEXT THREE DAYS

What if you had 72 hours to save everything you live for?
—Movie tagline

Box Office: $21 million

The Next Three Days has the decided misfortune of having been released in the immediate wake of Tony Goldwyn's excellent and similarly-themed *Conviction* (2010). Both films tell the story of a person wrongly convicted of murder and the ferocious efforts of a loved one to get them out of prison. In *Conviction*'s believable and moving story, the vehicle of escape is the court system and a decade-plus journey of the protagonist from GED to legal degree. In Paul Haggis's wildly implausible thriller, the vehicle of escape is a Prius and a pistol. The idea of a community college professor engineering his wife's escape from the Pittsburgh city jail is not, by itself, an insurmountable barrier to the

viewer's suspension of disbelief. After all, with meticulous planning and a lot of luck, almost anything is possible and *The Next Three Days* could have compensated for its implausible premise with a subtle and realistic jailbreak plan along the lines of the classic *Papillion* (1973). Unfortunately, the film's script goes in exactly the opposite direction and *The Next Three Days* delivers an escape about as believable as Charles Bronson's *Breakout* (1975).

An alternative title for the film might be "The Thoroughly Unbelievable Railroading by Fate of Lara Brennan." A series of events so completely bizarre conspire to seal Lara's (Elizabeth Banks) doom that the only logical interpretation would seem to be that it is the product of a frame job. In fact, she is the victim of an incredible set of circumstances that, though the product of pure chance, happen to play out in exactly the way they need to in order to tighten a noose around her throat. An argument with her boss at work escalates to a shouting match. Later that day, the boss is murdered in a parking ramp during a random burglary by a female thief, her head caved in with a fire extinguisher. The killer drops the cylinder to the ground and it rolls to a stop next to Lara's car. As the thief exits the ramp, the wife enters the parking garage and the two accidently collide, somehow smearing a small circle of the boss's blood onto the back of her coat (so that it is conveniently invisible to Lara). Somehow, Lara manages not to see her dead boss in a pool of blood but does see the cylinder on the floor next to her car. She picks it up (putting her finger prints all over it) and tosses it aside. She then drives off, just as a witness tidily enters in time to see her leaving the scene. The cops determine that she is the killer within twelve hours and are at her door arresting her just as she notices the blood on her jacket. The sad reality is that a far-more-plausible explanation for a wrongful conviction in America in 2010 is that depicted in the true life *Conviction* and hundreds of other real life wrongful conviction cases just like it: lazy and corrupt cops, coerced confessions, witnesses blackmailed into lying and overzealous prosecutors. No matter, the script for *The Next Three Days* is not concerned with making Lara's conviction realistic since its only purpose is that of a straightforward plot device to send an innocent person to jail for a very long time.

Three years later, Lara's English professor husband John Brennan (Russell Crowe) is facing exhausted legal appeals and an increasingly depressed wife whose son is starting to forget about her. When she attempts suicide, Brennan decides on an alternative, decidedly illegal route of getting his wife out of prison. Brennan contacts legendary escape artist Damon Pennington (Liam Neeson) who, despite having broken out of seven prisons is not only not in prison but agrees to meet with Brennan to talk about a book Brennan alleges to be writing about escapists. When Pennington quickly realizes that there is no book and that Brennan is talking about a real break-out, the ex-con not only continues to talk to him but, incredibly, allows Brennan to continue recording him as he provides specific, multiple felony-generating advice as to how to break someone out of the Pittsburgh jail. The invaluable information the master of escape imparts? Have the whole plan in place before the escape. Have a timetable and get out of town fast. Obtain false identification documents and a have lot of money available.

Initially the film flirts with reality as Brennan's amateur efforts at obtaining a fake passport ends with a beat down and a rip-off and his attempt to use a "bump key" he learned how to make on the internet on the jail elevator results in an alarm going off and a stomach churning scene in the warden's office where Brennan tries to persuade the thoroughly un-fooled warden that the figure on the video screen inserting the bump key into the elevator lock is not him. "Who," the warden wisely asks, "is going to raise your son if both of his parents are in jail?" Brennan is released and promptly vomits off the side of the nearest railing. After this, however, realism is left behind and things go largely according to Brennan's plan. This is unfortunate because his is not a very believable plan. After watching an instructional video on YouTube, Brennan fashions a lock pick out of a tennis ball which allows him to break into a mail van—twice—in broad daylight to first obtain and then replace a copy of his wife's medical records so he can get her transferred from the jail to a hospital. Later, when Lara's final appeal is denied faster than expected and she is going to be transferred to prison, Brennan is caught off guard because he has not yet sold his home to provide the necessary funds for the escape. Brennan solves this problem by ripping off a meth house at gunpoint. This is supposed to demonstrate that he is willing to do whatever it takes to get his wife out of jail but his determination does not make it any more plausible that a man who was asking the pawn store owner two days earlier "to show him where the bullets go" in the gun he has just purchased will be capable of subduing three armed and hardened criminals, shooting one of them to death in the process and then setting the place on fire on his way out the door.

It is also surprising that he can succeed in these endeavors because, on a selective, plot-required basis, he is matched by a police force possessing extra sensory perception (except, of course, in discerning that his wife is innocent in the first place). Minutes after the police arrive at the destroyed meth house, a witness calls and reports that a dead man has just been rolled out of a Prius. Lieutenant Nabulsi (Lennie James) instantly knows that the dead body is linked to the meth lab and narrows the list of possible suspects down to convicted felons. He instructs his subordinate to search for any Prius registrations in the name of convicted felons. There are only two in the entire state he is informed, a murderer and rapist and the murderer is in jail. "How about the murderer's husband?" the lieutenant somehow knows to instantly ask. Based on this and nothing more, the lieutenant immediately goes to Brennan's house. Finding no car there he decides to forgo a warrant and illegally enters the house. From the home's emptiness (Brennan has sold most of his furniture) and the presence of a cork board on the wall with a few scraps of torn, blank paper pinned to it, Nabulsi instantly and supernaturally surmises exactly what's going on. Not only is the husband responsible for the meth lab attack, he has a plan to free his wife and that plan is being executed at that exact moment. As, the police and assorted detectives flood the hospital, Lieutenant Nabulsi rushes there as well. Brennan, undeterred by the police's awareness of his plan, manages to subdue two armed guards and extricate his wife from her hospital bed. Nabulsi races towards the elevator John and Lara have just entered but just misses them, raising his gun to fire as the elevator doors shut. Once outside, Lara and John melt into the crowd. All appears lost for the police but fortunately Nabulsi is looking in the right direction at the right time and sees them getting on the train. Unable to get to the train on time, the super hero cop not only calls ahead for the train to be stopped at the next station, he then pursues the train by running down the tracks behind it. Running into pitch blackness with oncoming trains and an electrified third rail certainly goes above and beyond the call of duty. It is a wonder Pittsburgh has any crime at all.

Despite the lieutenant's Jack Webb worthy efforts, Brennan and his wife manage to make it to Brennan's friend's house where the couples' son waits. There they learn that yet another obstacle has been put in their path. Brennan's friend Nicole (Olivia Wilde) has unexpectedly taken their son to the zoo! Will they choose to preserve the timetable essential to their escape even if it means abandoning their child or will they risk backtracking to pick him despite the near certainty of their capture?

The Next Three Days is well directed by Paul Haggis and superbly edited by Jo Francis and their combined efforts lend a real sense of urgency and excitement to the film. Its acting is uniformly excellent with Russell Crowe leading a seasoned ensemble including Elizabeth Banks, Liam Neeson, Brian Dennehy, and Daniel Stern. The film has everything going for it except a believable escape story. But, of course, that is everything. An escape movie is only as good as the escape it portrays and *The*

Next Three Days' blueprints would have never gotten Brennan past the front door.

Nate Vercauteren

CREDITS

John Brennan: Russell Crowe
Lara Brennan: Elizabeth Banks
Damon: Liam Neeson
George Brennan: Brian Dennehy
Nicole: Olivia Wilde
David: Jonathan Tucker
Mouse: RZA
Lt. Nabulsi: Lennie James
Det. Quinn: Jason Beghe
Erit: Moran Atias
Elaine: Nazanin Boniadi
Mike: Ty Giordano
Luke: Ty Simpkins
Grace Brennan: Helen Carey
Meyer Fisk: Daniel Stern
Origin: USA
Language: English
Released: 2010
Production: Olivier Delbosc, Paul Haggis; Lionsgate, Fidelite Films; released by Lionsgate
Directed by: Paul Haggis
Written by: Paul Haggis, Fred Cavaye, Guillaume Lemans
Cinematography by: Stephane Fontaine
Music by: Alberto Iglesias, Danny Elfman
Editing: Jo Francis
Sound: Lon Bender
Costumes: Abigail Murray
Production Design: Laurence Bennett
MPAA rating: PG-13
Running time: 122 minutes

REVIEWS

Burr, Ty. *Boston Globe.* November 18, 2010.
Chang, Justin. *Variety.* November 13, 2010.
Ebert, Roger. *Chicago Sun-Times.* November 17, 2010.
Hornaday, Ann. *Washington Post.* November 18, 2010.
Jones, Kimberly. *Austin Chronicle.* November 24, 2010.
Pols, Mary. *TIME Magazine.* November 20, 2010.
Rea, Stephen. *Philadelphia Inquirer.* November 18, 2010.
Scott, A.O. *New York Times.* November 18, 2010.
Tobias, Scott. *AV Club.* November 18, 2010.
Travers, Peter. *Rolling Stone.* November 18, 2010.

QUOTES

Lara Brennan: "I don't think I can last another twenty years."
Damon Pennington: "No prison in the world is airtight."

TRIVIA

Writer/director Paul Haggis shares the same birthday with Olivia Wilde.

NIGHT CATCHES US

United by revolution, divided by the past.
   —Movie tagline

Telling a personal story against a widely-known political backdrop can be a delicate balancing act. Many filmmakers have lost sight of the truth of their characters and emphasized the social and cultural canvas on which they were working instead. Conversely, many character studies set in tumultuous times feel false in that they tell a story that might be seen as minor compared to what was going on around it. And then there are the films that fall deep into the gap in-between, losing the believability of character and also failing to adequately transport the viewer to a time filled with unrest. Tanya Hamilton's *Night Catches Us* is an ambitious piece, especially for a debut director, and features two very strong lead performances from a pair of underrated actors, but it never comes together as character study nor social commentary. It is caught in the middle, failing to resonate.

The great Anthony Mackie (*Half Nelson* [2006], *The Hurt Locker* [2009]) plays Marcus, a man returning to his neighborhood in Philadelphia in the 1970s just a few years after the peak of the Black Power Movement forced him into a decision that still has open emotional wounds for everyone involved. The death of his father may be what initially brings him home, but there are also clearly broken fences in the relationships of his life that he would like to mend. One such relationship involves the gorgeous Patricia (Kerry Washington), a woman directly impacted by the decision that Marcus made years earlier. While others ostracize and outwardly threaten Marcus for the acts he took that led to the death of one of their own, Patricia does not act the same, even though it left her a widow and a single mother. She definitely does see him as a symbol of a past that she would like to forget but the two have unresolved feelings for one another that makes it impossible to completely close the chapter on their younger days.

Of course, the parallel between the ghosts of the past in the Black Power Movement and the fact that racial tension still simmers in Marcus and Patricia's neighborhood is clear. When it comes to issues like civil rights, the past can never be completely put in a box and placed on a shelf. It remains a daily part of the character's lives. As Marcus and Patricia are trying to mend the fences in their life, the world around them is about to explode in a violent climax and the message that skeletons of racial tension are never completely buried is a quietly understated.

Thematically, *Night Catches Us* works. Looked at from a distance, it is easy to admire Hamilton's low-key efforts to merge the personal and the political. The problem is that film does not exist purely thematically and the individual elements, most notably the dialogue and the paper-thin supporting characters, deflate Hamilton's noble attempts. When her script focuses directly on the saga of Marcus and Patricia and the film allows Mackie and Washington to show their skills as two of the most interesting actors of their generation, the movie works. These two have a complex relationship that melds past pain, present passion, and future problems and Mackie and Washington are typically excellent. Anthony Mackie has been a scene-stealer for years and more directors should give him meaty roles like this one. As for Washington, she is often the best thing about the films on her resume, giving underrated performances even in lackluster works like *Lakeview Terrace* (2008) and *I Think I Love My Wife* (2007) while also serving as a strong supporting actress to Oscar® winners in *Ray* (2004) and *The Last King of Scotland* (2006). Most of what works about *Night Catches Us* can be directly attributed to these two actors.

The dialogue is more problematic. It is difficult not to react incredulously upon hearing a child read lines like "They're all around us. Ghosts. They're everywhere." It is simply not how people in the real world speak, and the majority of the supporting cast has that air of falsity, as if even they are aware that they are characters in a movie, rarely feeling genuine. It is a failure of the piece that the community, so essential to the drama at the core of the relationship in the movie that feels genuine, never comes to life. The story of Marcus and Patricia is believable, but never the world in which it is set. It is an incredible challenge for even the most veteran directors to amply balance the lyrical with the realistic, the historic with the melodramatic. While the results are mixed at best, the attempt by a first-time director bodes well for future projects by Tanya Hamilton.

Brian Tallerico

CREDITS

Marcus Washington: Anthony Mackie
Patricia Wilson: Kerry Washington
Dwayne "DoRight" Miller: Jamie Hector
Det. David Gordon: Wendell Pierce
Bostic Washington: Tariq Trotter
Iris Wilson: Jamara Griffin

Jimmy Dixon: Amari Cheatom
Origin: USA
Language: English
Released: 2010
Production: Ron Simons, Sean Costello, Jason Orans, Gigantic Pictures; Simonsays Entertainment, Gigantic Pictures; released by Magnolia Pictures
Directed by: Tanya Hamilton
Written by: Tanya Hamilton
Cinematography by: David Tumblety
Music Supervisor: Dave Golden
Sound: Wil Marsisak
Editing: Affonso Goncalves, John Chimples
Costumes: Maren Reese
Production Design: Beth Mickle
MPAA rating: R
Running time: 88 minutes

REVIEWS

Anderson, John. *Variety.* July 7, 2010.
Anderson, Melissa. *Village Voice.* November 30, 2010.
Ebert, Roger. *Chicago Sun-Times.* December 9, 2010.
Grierson, Tim. *Screen International.* June 29, 2010.
Morgenstern, Joe. *Wall Street Journal.* December 2, 2010.
O'Hehir, Andrew. *Salon.com.* December 2, 2010.
Pais, Matt. *Metromix.com.* December 9, 2010.
Phillips, Michael. *Chicago Tribune.* December 9, 2010.
Rickey, Carrie. *Philadelphia Inquirer.* October 21, 2010.
Travers, Peter. *Rolling Stone.* December 2, 2010.

AWARDS

Nomination:

Ind. Spirit 2011: First Feature.

A NIGHTMARE ON ELM STREET

All you have to do is dream...
    —Movie tagline
Never sleep again.
    —Movie tagline
Welcome to your new nightmare.
    —Movie tagline

Box Office: $63 million

Wes Craven's original *A Nightmare on Elm Street* (1984) terrified people. It made them "genuinely" afraid to go to sleep. For many, many viewers that film was the single most unsettling horror movie experience of their young lives. The inevitable franchise could almost be forgiven for quickly dissipating into quasi-farce based on that, especially since several of the sequels contain outstanding suspense and or horror sequences and Craven's highly underrated *New Nightmare* (1994) brought Freddy Krueger back in real style, addressing fandom, the terror inherent in parenting and the horror genre itself. If *Freddy vs. Jason* (2003) seemed like a money grab it was at least a fun one. But this reboot, though well cast, and approached with some care, generates scant scares, even though it aims for them constantly, delivering instead dissonant musical stabs and characters jumping into frame. This film is the equivalent of being woken up out of a pleasant reverie by someone tripping loudly over a piece of furniture in the dark. During the experience you have trouble remembering where you are and the instigator of your confusion clearly has no idea what they are doing.

The film has a dynamic, well-photographed, and disturbing opening sequence in which an exhausted teen being stalked by Freddy grapples with the killer in the dreamscape as his friends in the real world watch him seemingly cut his own throat. The moment is disturbingly violent and lurches between planes of reality with all the power of the original film's opening sequence. After starting out strong, the film falters, more or less repeating the plot of the original with a plot twist that could have saved the project if it had been exploited properly. But the only thing being exploited here are the fans who have been eagerly anticipating the reinvention of one of cinema's great villains.

The plot twist is a variation on Freddy's origins. It hinges on the conceit that we are asked to consider whether or not he might have been innocent and has come back as a spirit of justice rather than as one of mere vengeance. The film also ups the ante on exactly what Freddy may have done to all those kids to get all those parents so upset that they burned him to death. Maybe the kids lied, or maybe Freddy was/is just a vile child-molesting murderous thug. If *A Nightmare on Elm Street* (2010) spent more time developing its characters and this central conflict, it could have been a great film.

First-time feature director Samuel Bayer and writers Wesley Strick (*Arachnophobia* [1991], *Cape Fear* [1991]) and Eric Heisserer would rather payout a constant-and-weak stream of homages to Craven's original. Thus their version is like a slot machine that seems to give out a huge coin payoff until you realize that all of the coins are pennies. This is especially sad given that the ending of this film is so much better than that of the original. The fact that Freddy was a child molester (not just a killer of children) was glossed over by the initial franchise, probably deliberately, by those who felt the violence already gave them a big enough public relations nightmare. But this film addresses the topic head-on, offering an ending that gives Freddy Krueger a chance to reveal his own desperation to be perceived as powerful.

Performances in this film are hard to judge, centered as they are on generally-weak dialogue. Rooney Mara (*Youth in Revolt* [2009], *The Social Network* [2010]) shines as the withdrawn Nancy and Kyle Gallner (*The Haunting in Connecticut* [2009], *Jennifer's Body* [2009]) seems born to play the pharmaceutically-challenged Quentin Smith. Both manage to embody the struggles of victims of childhood sexual abuse consistently and well. The real problem, surprisingly, is Jackie Earle Haley (*Little Children* [2006], *Watchmen* [2009], *Shutter Island* [2010]) whose thuggish Freddy is saddled with lots of unfunny one-liners and a voice so deep it verges on monotone. Even so, Haley does a remarkable job of bringing the character to life. By the end of the film, Krueger has been reborn. Haley is the sole reason fans might look forward to a sequel here. Given a little bit more latitude in his portrayal by the studio (who clearly over-thought this aspect of the reboot), he could craft an absolutely unforgettable character.

The physical redesign of Freddy works very well. This makeup is pure, real-life burn victim, never less than disturbing to behold and remarkably responsive to Haley's expressionistic facial tics and movements. It roots Freddy in the physical reality of his horrific death while giving him a wraithlike demonic aspect that has always been the character's strongest selling point visually.

But make no mistake. Everything else in this film is borrowed, bashed and butchered in an effort to throw bones to potential customers anxious to buy back in to the Krueger-verse. The mind really does boggle at trying to understand how Bayer could borrow so many images from the series and manage to strip virtually every one of them of the suspense, the dread, the timeless fairy-tale energy that brought back fans again and again even when the original film's stories were downright silly. Watched back-to-back with almost any of the original *Nightmare* films, this one comes off as tepid, or worse, lost in development hell where forgettable characters, a complete lack of suspense or style, a forgettable score, and a replacement of the earlier film's Grimm's fairy tale atmosphere with a leaner, meaner, but ultimately indifferent sense of seen-it-before ultra-violence lurk around every corner.

Dave Canfield

CREDITS

Freddy Krueger: Jackie Earle Haley
Nancy Holbrook: Rooney Mara
Quentin: Kyle Gallner

Jesse: Thomas Dekker
Dean Russell: Kellan Lutz
Kris: Katie Cassidy
Dr. Gwen Holbrook: Connie Britton
Alan: Clancy Brown
Origin: USA
Language: English
Released: 2010
Production: Michael Bay, Brad Fuller, Andrew Form; Platinum Dunes; released by New Line Cinema
Directed by: Samuel Bayer
Written by: Wesley Strick, Eric Heisserer
Cinematography by: Jeff Cutter
Music by: Steve Jablonsky
Sound: Charlie Campagna
Editing: Glen Scantlebury
Art Direction: Craig Jackson
Costumes: Mari-An Ceo
Production Design: Patrick Lumb
MPAA rating: R
Running time: 95 minutes

REVIEWS

Corliss, Richard. *TIME Magazine.* April 29, 2010.
Ebert, Roger. *Chicago Sun-Times.* April 28, 2010.
Fuchs, Cynthia. *PopMatters.* April 30, 2010.
Goldman, Eric. *IGN Movies.* April 30, 2010.
Hall, Peter. *Hollywood.com.* April 29, 2010.
Harvey, Dennis. *Variety.* April 29, 2010.
McDonagh, Maitland. *Film Journal International.* April 29, 2010.
Scott, A.O. *New York Times.* April 30, 2010.
Sobczynski, Peter. *eFilmCritic.com.* April 29, 2010.
Topel, Fred. *Can Magazine.* April 30, 2010.

QUOTES

Freddy Krueger: "You really shouldn't fall asleep in class."
Freddy Krueger: "Remember me?"

TRIVIA

This is the first *Nightmare* film not to feature Robert Englund in the role of Freddy with Jackie Earle Haley taking over the iconic role.

NORTH FACE
(Nordwand)

Philipp Stölzl's *North Face* is a taut, thrilling, and heartbreaking 90 minute mountain climbing film trapped in a 120 minute format. With nearly unbearable suspense, the film chronicles the real life 1936 attempt by four men to be the first to summit the deadly Swiss mountain, Eiger, via its notorious North Face (known as the "murder wall" for the number of climbers' lives it has claimed). Had the film confined its narrative to their climb and trusted that that story was compelling enough to sustain it, *North Face* would have been a classic climbing film like *Touching the Void* (2003). Instead, the film unwisely undercuts its climbing story with a Nazi subplot and love story that cannot compete with the action on the mountain.

As terrestrial exploration literally ran out of new ground to discover by the early part of the twentieth century, explorers searching for immortalizing "firsts" shifted their gaze from outward to upward. This is an impulse that is still alive and well today, though with understandably rather diminishing results. ("I'm waiting for the first barefoot runner on the summit of Everest, or the first one hopping into the South Pole on a pogo stick," Werner Herzog amusingly observes in his documentary *Encounters at the End of the World* [2007]). *North Face* takes the viewer back to a time when there were still significant firsts to yet be had.

The climbing sequences of *North Face* are tautly directed by Stölzl, crisply edited by Sven Budelmann, and breathtakingly shot by cinematographer Kolja Brandt. These elements combine to convey the incredible scope and beauty of the Eiger, the daunting challenge of its ascent and, when injury and bad weather intervene, the climbers' desperate struggle for survival. When a loose rock incapacitates Austrian climber Willy Angerer (Simon Schwarz), the ascent turns into an emergency descent and, when a blizzard rolls in, from emergency descent to against-the-odds quest for survival. Terrain that was ascended easily under sunny conditions becomes another matter entirely in a roaring blizzard with frozen fingers, exhausted arms, and half the team immobilized by frost bite and injury. The film excels at these scenes with Stölzl's riveting direction and Budelmann's tight editing creating a Hitchcockian level of suspense. *North Face* is the kind of film the viewer is weary from tension after seeing. Had the film started with the men at the base of the mountain and stayed with them as they made their attempt, the film would be a classic of the genre. However the film does not start with them nor does it stick with them once they begin.

Instead the film begins long before the climb in a newsroom in Berlin with a long, boring editorial meeting between the paper's editor and Nazi enthusiast, Henry Arau, (an excellent Ulrich Tukur), and his staff. Arau believes that a great story is to be had if two of Germany's best climbers, Toni Kurz (Benno Fürmann) and Andreas Hinterstoisser (Florian Lukas), can be induced to summit the Eiger via its North Face as a means of demonstrating Aryan superiority prior to the 1936 Olympics in Berlin. Arau cares little for climbing itself and when he learns that his young, attractive secretary, Luise Fellner (Johanna Wokalek), is a childhood friend of the climbers, he deploys her to her home town in Bavaria to persuade them to make the climb.

Luise travels home and reunites with Toni and Andreas. She reminds them that other climbers will be shortly making the North Face attempt, knowing that this will kindle the fires of competition within them. Also kindled are the embers of an apparently unrequited past romance between Luise and Toni. Persuaded by the desire to be first, Toni and Andreas soon head to the base of the Eiger to begin their assault. Simultaneously, Luise and Arau arrive at the luxurious hotel below the Eiger. As Toni and Andreas begin the grueling, dangerous task of ascending the mountain with Austrians Angerer and Edi Rainer (Georg Friedrich), Luise and Arau monitor their progress from the luxury of the hotel, enjoying exquisite meals, discussions about Aryan superiority and piano-playing sessions.

This results in a parallel narrative that undermines the suspense on the mountain by annoyingly crosscutting from the superbly executed story on the mountain the viewer cares about to the boring, unremarkable story at the hotel which the viewer does not. As four desperate men struggle for survival on one of the deadliest mountains known to man, employing every ounce of some of the best climbing skills in the world to return to safety, the scene shifts to Luise looking for her love on the mountain through a hotel viewing glass. As Andreas's frostbitten fingers desperately try to curl around a rock, trying to obtain a purchase that is necessary for all of their survival, the film cuts to the dinner debate musings of a windbag Nazi propagandist. The obvious dichotomy the film is attempting to establish with these two narratives is the moral purity of those climbing the mountain for its own sake versus the moral corruption of those cynically exploiting that climb to promote a racist ideology with Luise caught between both worlds. The problem is that the film's run-of-the-mill script simply cannot match the action on the mountain. The non dialogue-dependent climbing sequences succeed spectacularly while the dialogue-dependent hotel sequences fall spectacularly flat.

It is quite possible that Toni and Andreas's climb was viewed as a vehicle for promoting Aryan superiority by the German press and that an unfulfilled and deeply touching romance existed between Toni and Luise but the film simply does not have the writing depth to make these elements convincing or compelling. The reason to see the film is its thrilling and beautiful climbing sequences which, though made to compete with a pair of lackluster sub plots, nonetheless make the film worthy of viewing.

Nate Vercauteren

CREDITS

Toni Kurz: Benno Fürmann
Anreas "Andi" Hinterstoisser: Florian Lukas
Luise Fellner: Johanna Wokalek
Willy Angerer: Simon Schwarz
Edi Rainer: Georg Friedrich
Henry Arau: Ulrich Tukur
Origin: Germany
Language: German
Released: 2008
Production: Boris Schoenfelder, Danny Kruasz, Rudolf Santschi, Benjamin Herrmann; Dor Film-West Produktiongesellschaft GmbH; released by Music Box Films
Directed by: Philipp Stölzl
Written by: Philipp Stölzl, Christoph Silber, Rupert Henning, Johannes Naber
Cinematography by: Kolja Brandt
Music by: Christian Kolonovits
Editing: Sven Budelmann
Sound: Heinz Ebner
Costumes: Birgit Utter
Production Design: Udo Kramer
MPAA rating: Unrated
Running time: 126 minutes

REVIEWS

Burr, Ty. *Boston Globe.* February 12, 2010.
Ebert, Roger. *Chicago Sun-Times.* February 24, 2010.
Elley, Derek. *Variety.* August 13, 2008.
Gronvall, Andrea. *Chicago Reader.* February 25, 2010.
Holden, Stephen. *New York Times.* January 29, 2010.
Miller, Brian. *Village Voice.* January 26, 2010.
Musetto, V.A. *New York Post.* January 29, 2010.
Phillips, Michael. *Chicago Tribune.* February 25, 2010.
Savlov, Marc. *Austin Chronicle.* April 30, 2010.
Tobias, Scott. *AV Club.* January 28, 2010.

QUOTES

Luise Fellner: "When you're at the bottom—Toni once told me—at the foot of the wall, and you look up, you ask yourself: How can anyone climb that? Why would anyone even want to? But hours later when you're at the top looking down, you've forgotten everything. Except the one person you promised you would come back to."

NOWHERE BOY

The extraordinary untold story of John Lennon.
    —Movie tagline

Box Office: $1 million

Nowhere Boy is less a musical biopic about the origins of The Beatles than it is an exquisite coming-of-age story of an angry, brooding teenager, who just happens to turn out to one day become John Lennon. Aaron Johnson (*Kick-Ass*) is absolutely brilliant as the teenage Lennon. His portrayal of the soon-to-be-Beatle is instantly recognizable as an angst-ridden young everyman who has seen everyone he loves either lie to or leave him. He doesn't want to conquer or change the world at this point, he just wants to be wanted and have a place in it. As a result, the bravado he begins to display after getting the itch to play rock and roll is more a defense mechanism than a belief in his abilities. If you're expecting the definitive biopic of the early days of The Beatles, you may be disappointed with *Nowhere Boy*. (In fact, there are only a few actual performances by the band that would eventually become the Fab Four.) But, if a rich and eloquent examination of the core identity behind that band is more to your liking, then you'll be pleasantly surprised by *Nowhere Boy*.

The film begins by establishing Lennon's home life with his strict, very proper Aunt Mimi (Kristin Scott Thomas) and his more free-spirited Uncle George (David Threlfall). John is obviously very fond of his uncle and is devastated when he suddenly dies, leaving a void in his life that he seems unable to fill by himself. Aunt Mimi's cold and emotionless response to George's death signals a turning point for John (at least in terms of the dramatic arc of the film) as he begins to search for a more "maternal" influence in his life. This leads him to seek out his mother, Julia (Anne-Marie Duff), who left him with Mimi when he was just five years old. He begins a secret relationship with Julia during which she nurtures his creativity and instills in him a love of music. Mimi ultimately discovers the relationship and vehemently disapproves, ostensibly to protect John. This leads to revelations regarding both of the women's relationship with John. It is here that the emotional depth of *Nowhere Boy* shines. Of course, during all of this, John befriends a young man named Paul (Thomas Brodie Sangster), meets someone named George (Sam Bell), and lays the groundwork for the group that will eventually become The Beatles. But this is all secondary to the relationships with his mother and aunt.

Based on Julia Bard's (John's half-sister) memoir, *Imagine This: Growing Up with My Brother John Lennon*, screenwriter Matt Greenhalgh is telling, at times, the story of a love triangle between Mimi, Julia, and John more so than the formative years of a teenage John Lennon. While there are some oedipal slants to John's relationship with Julia (she does, after all, represent the wild, raucous world of rock and roll that Mimi is so staunchly opposed to), she's more a "mate" for John and

less the strict "mother" that Mimi represents. Or, as Richard Corliss more succinctly puts it in *TIME Magazine*: "One woman represents the propriety John needs to escape, the other the underlying danger in unfettered emotion. John has to choose between the two tendencies or find a blend of them both." After the loss of his uncle, John is lost, searching for an identity. Ultimately, he is torn between the two worlds that Mimi and Julia represent until this disjointed family cathartically airs old family business and each member is allowed a sort of spiritual rebirth. The dramatic reliance on the complexities of each of John's relationships is, as Manohla Dargis elaborates in the *New York Times*, "the film's best and boldest move...[in] how it brings maternal love and sexual desire into play with artistic longing and youthful ambition."

Throughout the film we're meant to surmise that the mental anguish John is feeling during these formative years is what made him the man he ultimately became. However, the temptation to assign some other significance to these revelations simply because he grew up to be a Beatle is an unnecessary one since, at its core, *Nowhere Boy* is a fine dramatic story of a confused teenager searching for an identity in its own right, regardless of its subject's destination in life. Some of the credit for this belongs to director Sam Taylor-Wood for depicting the Liverpool in which Lennon grew up so perfectly and without resorting to any "ah ha" moments such as a pass by Penny Lane or other cutesy visual Beatles cues. True, there's a quick glimpse of the Strawberry Field Orphanage at the beginning of the film, but that seems more in line with defining the "nowhere" state that young John will soon find himself than a precursor to songwriting genius or a nod to Beatles fans. Some credit also belongs to screenwriter Greenhalgh for refraining from including what could have become an overly-melodramatic series of winks to the audience amidst a clichéd Hallmark movie tragedy of a lost, confused boy. More credit may be due editor Lisa Gunning, who expertly paces the film without ever overstaying a moment. There are some expertly cut cross-timeline scenes that give the film emotional depth, allowing the dramatic high points to resonate long after their individual scenes have passed. But what truly makes *Nowhere Boy* a resounding success is Aaron Johnson's performance as John. He embodies Lennon from the first frame and makes him likeable, sympathetic, and occasionally reprehensible. As Owen Gleiberman noted in *Entertainment Weekly*, Johnson initially "seems too morose to be John Lennon, but then the Lennon personality—the wit, the casual cruelty—emerges [and] by the end of *Nowhere Boy*, [you] feel you know John Lennon better than you ever did."

Nowhere Boy was widely released near October 9, 2010 (a date that would have marked Lennon's 70th birthday had he not been assassinated on December 8, 1980). But this is no mere toss-off biopic designed to cash-in on a milestone anniversary. It may possibly be one of the greatest musical biographies ever made (it certainly seems more honest, genuine, and heartfelt than by-the-book films like *Ray* or *Walk the Line*), not to mention that it may be the best movie ever made about The Beatles. And the truly amazing thing surrounding that fact is that the Beatles are never actually mentioned in the film. In fact, the film ends with the group leaving for Hamburg where they would hone their skills to become the band that eventually drew the attention of Brian Epstein and then the world; also, the other would-be Beatles that make appearances in the film are referred to only by their first names: Paul and George.

Other films that depicted the group's origin (such as *The Birth of the Beatles* [1979] or *Backbeat* [1994]) focused on the group's early years but tended to start once John met Paul, who then introduced John to George and so on, while all the time reverently adhering to the homogenized Beatles mythos. *Nowhere Boy*, however, gives a unique and unfettered insight into the psyche of the man who started the group and may actually provide a better understanding of his music than if it had featured more of it. As Claudia Puig, observed in *USA Today*, the film "helps us understand the underpinnings of Lennon's music as well as his idealism and lifelong desire to rebel against social strictures. It is a profoundly compelling portrait of the emotional turmoil that plagued Lennon, contributed to his art and no doubt complicated his personal life" (which is probably something we're all uniquely able to relate to). The thing that Beatles fans may ultimately take from *Nowhere Boy* could be, as Roger Ebert noted in the *Chicago Sun-Times*, "that if Julia had always been there for him, he might not have been there for us."

Michael J. Tyrkus

CREDITS

John Lennon: Aaron Johnson
Aunt Mimi Smith: Kristin Scott Thomas
Julia: Anne-Marie Duff
Paul: Thomas Brodie Sangster
Uncle George Smith: David Threlfall
Bobby: David Morrissey
George: Sam Bell
Pete: Josh Bolt
Marie: Ophelia Lovibond
Origin: United Kingdom
Language: English
Released: 2009
Production: Robert Bernstein, Kevin Loader, Douglas Rae; Film 4, U.K. Film Council, Northwest Vision, HanWay Films, LipSynch Prods.; released by Weinstein Company
Directed by: Sam Taylor-Wood
Written by: Matt Greenhalgh
Cinematography by: Seamus McGarvey
Music by: Alison Goldfrapp, Will Gregory
Sound: John Midgley, Martin Trevis
Music Supervisor: Ian Neil
Editing: Lisa Gunning
Art Direction: Charmian Adams, Kimberley Fahey
Costumes: Julian Day
Production Design: Alice Normington
MPAA rating: R
Running time: 98 minutes

REVIEWS

Burr, Ty. *Boston Globe*. October 14, 2010.
Calhoun, Dave. *Time Out*. December 18, 2009.
Corliss, Richard. *TIME Magazine*. October 8, 2010.
Dargis, Manohla. *New York Times*. October 7, 2010.
Ebert, Roger. *Chicago Sun-Times*. October 13, 2010.
Gleiberman, Owen. *Entertainment Weekly*. October 8, 2010.
Hunter, Allan. *Daily Express*. December 18, 2009.
Orange, Michelle. *Movieline*. October 6, 2010.
Phipps, Keith. *AV Club*. October 7, 2010.
Puig, Claudia. *USA Today*. October 15, 2010.

QUOTES

John: "There's just no point hating someone you love."

AWARDS

Nomination:

British Acad. 2009: Support. Actress (Duff), Support. Actress (Scott Thomas).

O

―――――■―――――

OCEANS

Explore the depths of our planet's oceans. Experience the stories that connect their world to ours.
—Movie tagline

Box Office: $19 million

Even the stunning creativity of today's most innovative CGI artisans can never best the sublime stuff that Mother Nature has been coming up with for eons. They are, after all, pretenders, while she is the real deal. Even though her singular accomplishments have sustained mankind for so long, a too-unappreciative human race now runs the risk of unconscionably and perhaps irreparably damaging them. To mark the 40th anniversary of environmental awareness-raising Earth Day, Disney-Nature showcased some of the lady's finest—and most imperiled—work in *Oceans,* a mesmerizing follow-up to its box office-dominating documentary, *Earth* (2007). Filmed all over the world using 35mm and digital cameras, the $80 million production grossed a less-than-hoped-for $19.4 million domestically despite critical praise. Still, its worldwide take made it a financial success, and *Oceans* became one of the highest-grossing nature documentaries of all time.

Oceans does not drown viewers with a tidal wave of facts, but is rather a meditative mood piece aiming to persuade through the eliciting of strong emotion. Trying to immerse audiences in everything there is to know about the subject during a reasonable running time would have been a futile endeavor. (This is especially true considering the final cut does not even span ninety minutes.) Instead of something overstuffed and replete

with a litany of Latin names that might make eyes glaze over, directors Jacques Perrin and Jacques Cluzaud chose to present something uniquely alluring that instead made eyes open wide in wonderment.

Under certain circumstances, being told that one is about to be "swimming with the fishes" is a terrifying threat. Here, however, it is a delightfully kept promise, as the development and use of new underwater photographic technology provide a closer and clearer look at aquatic life than ever before. One can almost feel the textures of skin and shells, as well as the grit and rocks of the ocean floor. This encounter feels so intimate that absentmindedly reaching to towel off as the credits roll would be wholly understandable. What is revealed with crystal clarity at what were previously-murky depths is so breathtaking that viewers may, like the film's marine mammals, also feel a periodic need for a little air. Things are so intriguing down there, however, that most who are taking it all in would only grudgingly depart the deep.

There is a dazzling display of whimsy beneath the waves. How many people had previously even heard of a crab named Sally Lightfoot? How about the Sweetlips fish, or the Elephant Man-like Asian Sheepshead Wrasse? Then there is also the red-and-white Australian sea slug that rhythmically undulates like the dreamily-flipping skirt of a flamenco dancer. There is also the amazing Leafy Sea Dragon, which looks like an overgrown sea horse with a bad case of kelp. Garden Eels appear like something that just germinated from the sandy bottom. The audience learns that obliviously seeking shelter near a craggy-faced, lethally-disguised Stonefish is one of the worst mistakes—and probably the last—a creature can make. Observing such oddities, it certainly does seem, as Pierce Brosnan's smoothly-delivered, contemplative voiceover states, as if "nature has given everything a try."

Indeed, there are many shots in *Oceans* capable of eliciting ocular orgasm, if that utterly apt description is not too racy a term with which to describe a family film. Especially spectacular is watching whales and other creatures swirling up from below and predatory birds simultaneously dive-bombing from above for a massive, frenzied sardine feast. The film is the first to capture the sight of a blue whale feeding, which took twenty-eight-weeks-worth of watchful waiting on the part of the film's amazingly-patient camera crews. It is astonishing that a half-block long, 120-ton behemoth can move with such beautiful grace. Along with such images that inspire awe are those calculated to bring forth affectionate aws from viewers with resultantly-melting hearts, including nuzzling mothers and babies, adorably-waddling penguins, playfully-barking sea lions, or a scrambling batch of baby turtles. The fact that those last two are picked off (albeit swiftly and without visible blood or agonized struggle) may sober up some smiling faces, particularly those of the younger set. Children may, however, remain sufficiently buoyed by the sight of a clownfish like that in *Finding Nemo* (2003).

Oceans is indeed as much about vulnerability as it is about variety, and man's indifference is held up as the most dreadful of killers. While a section of the film emphasizes how various creatures symbiotically coexist, the point is made that the most evolved species of all is doing the most damage to creatures great and small around him, selfishly fouling, overfishing, and perhaps forever fragmenting fragile ecosystems to which he is inexorably connected and upon which his own continued healthful existence depends. (The shot of a curious sea lion swimming in sickening juxtaposition to a submerged discarded shopping cart is haunting.) "The animals themselves cannot stand up for their survival," it is stated: their future—and in turn our own—"depends upon us." It is clearly hoped that viewers will no longer be content to remain passively neutral at the shoreline, but will have been both enticed to roll up their pants legs for an enjoyable wade in the waves and induced to roll up their sleeves and fight the good fight.

David L. Boxerbaum

CREDITS

Narrator: Pierce Brosnan
Origin: France, Spain, Switzerland
Language: English
Released: 2009
Production: Jacques Perrin, Nicolas Mauvernay, Romain Le Grand; Galatee Films, Notro Films, JMH-TSR; released by DisneyNature

Directed by: Jacques Perrin, Jacques Cluzaud
Written by: Jacques Perrin, Jacques Cluzaud
Cinematography by: Simon Christidis, Luc Drion, Laurent Fleutot, Philippe Ross, Luciano Tovoli
Music by: Bruno Coulais
Sound: Jerome Wiciak, Philippe Barbeau
Editing: Vincent Schmitt, Catherine Mauchain
Production Design: Jean Rabasse
MPAA rating: G
Running time: 102 minutes

REVIEWS

Catsoulis, Jeannette. *New York Times.* April 22, 2010.
Gleiberman, Owen. *Entertainment Weekly.* April 22, 2010.
Hammond, Pete. *Boxoffice.* April 22, 2010.
Lacey, Liam. *Globe and Mail.* April 21, 2010.
Morris, Wesley. *Boston Globe.* April 22, 2010.
Puig, Claudia. *USA Today.* April 21, 2010.
Saslow, Rachel. *Washington Post.* April 23 2010.
Smith, Kyle. *New York Post.* April 22, 2010.
Turan, Kenneth. *Los Angeles Times.* April 22, 2010.
Weissberg, Jay. *Variety.* November 12, 2009.

ONDINE

The truth is not what you know. It's what you believe.
—Movie tagline

The question at the heart of *Ondine* is whether the mysterious, young woman, literally fished from the sea, is a mythical creature with fantastic origins and preternatural abilities or an entirely ordinary lass, upon whom a fisherman and his young daughter place extraordinary expectations. No matter which way writer/director Neil Jordan chooses, the final revelation is bound to underwhelm. The disappointment is in the very existence of a decision.

As such, the buildup to the final truth is as enigmatic as the character to which the title refers, and Jordan establishes that mystery with selective disclosure and convenient happenstance. For the character—with either outcome—it is a matter of self-preservation, so there is no uncertainty in the reasoning why she lies to or hides the truth from her new acquaintances. In return, though, they impose upon her demands she cannot fulfill. Either way she is confined by the true nature of her kind—mythological or human.

There is a more sinister view of the actions of Syracuse (Colin Farrell), the fisherman who pulls the young woman who calls herself Ondine (Alicja Bachleda) out of the Celtic Sea while going about his job. Syracuse, a joke around town due to his past alcoholism (dubbed

"Circus" by nearly everyone, including his few friends and loved ones), has much to prove to himself and to others. He has tried and is, at the movie's start, failing. His marriage to Maura (Dervla Kirwan) has dissolved. His daughter Annie (Alison Barry) lives with her mother and her new boyfriend Alex (Tony Curran, whose character is, refreshingly, a fairly decent man). Annie is also suffering from kidney failure; she undergoes regular dialysis treatment and is in need of a transplant soon. Syracuse lives alone in his mother's old house on the coast, isolated from civilization. Success in his trade is dwindling.

Syracuse, over two and a half years sober, is in a transitional period when he frees Ondine from his fishing net, and so, it seems, is she. She claims partial amnesia, saying she does not remember her name or how she ended up in the water in the first place. Even so, she does not want anyone except Syracuse—and only him because she really has no choice—to see her. While Annie is in the middle of her latest treatment, Syracuse romanticizes his finding of Ondine as a story a bedtime story a father would tell his daughter. Annie, disappointed by the lack of detail but intrigued by the possibilities, is reminded of the myth of the selkies, seals that can transform into humans by shedding their skin. She quickly becomes an expert on the subject, filling in the details for her father and his new guest. Meanwhile another stranger (Emil Hostina) wanders the southwestern Irish coast looking for Syracuse's "water baby," as Maura calls the mystery lady with a sharp tinge of jealousy. To Annie, the man is Ondine's selkie husband, the only man according to the myth who has the right to take her away from her new home.

The alluded struggle between Syracuse and Ondine's "husband" is representative of the conflict between fantasy and reality in Jordan's screenplay. Both men intend to use the woman for the own means, and both are willing to set her aside when their own interests are threatened. When Syracuse has the opportunity to take custody of Annie under the condition that Ondine is not around, he summons the courage (i.e., falls off the wagon) to excise the woman from his life. Believing she is a mythical water creature, he abandons her on an island, an act of cruelty no matter who or what she is. Her individual identity is none of Syracuse's concern, and, in spite of loosely twisting a mystery around the facts of her character, Ondine is no concern of Jordan's either when Syracuse returns to retrieve her from that island, Ondine helplessly and submissively returns to him without a hitch. Ondine alternately refers to herself as a selkie and flat-out states she is not one. A private conversation—when there is no need to conceal details—with her "husband" is infuriating in its cryptic abstracts ("You speak their language now," and "The sea

spit you out," he asks). In constructing the riddle of Ondine's past and species, Jordan downplays the reality of her situation as a woman deprived of humanity and the circumstances of those around her, whether it is Annie's dwindling health or Syracuse's current state of crushing regret.

What is important is the sewing of a fairy tale—a story of "Forever," "Once upon a time," and "Happily ever after," as Syracuse so succinctly puts it while discussing his relationship with Ondine. Here be hopes and wishes, song (Ondine's, which seems to attract fish to Syracuse's net) and swimming lessons (for Annie, who never learned how to), gossipy townsfolk and a helpful priest (Stephen Rea). A tragic death leads to opportunity for Annie. Syracuse's drunken outburst and desertion are a chance to learn the priest's ultimate lesson: one must work at happiness. When that lush Irish coast becomes a grainy, tinted nightmare as Ondine's "husband" invades their dreams or home in the straightforward climax, it is as close to a blunt sense of menace about Ondine's predicament as Jordan musters.

The details of the ultimate turn are almost irrelevant, and the revelation of the truth behind the eponymous character in *Ondine* is dishonest and would be no matter which of the two alternatives Jordan chose. It is merely an exercise in the writer/director manipulating the circumstances to arrive at a mystery.

Mark Dujsik

CREDITS

Syracuse: Colin Farrell
Ondine: Alicja Bachleda
Alex: Tony Curran
Vladic: Emil Hostina
Maura: Dervla Kirwan
Priest: Stephen Rea
Annie: Alison Barry
Origin: USA, Ireland
Language: English
Released: 2009
Production: Neil Jordan, James Flynn, Ben Browning; Octagon Films, Wayfare Entertainment, Little Wave Productions; released by Magnolia Pictures
Directed by: Neil Jordan
Written by: Neil Jordan
Cinematography by: Christopher Doyle
Music by: Kjartan Sveinsson
Sound: Brendan Deasy
Music Supervisor: Becky Bentham, Abbie Lister
Editing: Tony Lawson
Art Direction: Mark Lowry

Costumes: Eimer Ni Mhaoldomhnaigh
Production Design: Anna Rackard
MPAA rating: PG-13
Running time: 110 minutes

REVIEWS

Alter, Ethan. *Film Journal International.* May 12, 2010.
Cabin, Chris. *Filmcritic.com.* June 3, 2010.
Dudek, Duane. *Milwaukee Journal Sentinel.* June 24, 2010.
Gonzalez, Ed. *Slant Magazine.* May 31, 2010.
Phipps, Keith. *AV Club.* June 3, 2010.
Rea, Steven. *Philadelphia Inquirer.* June 11, 2010.
Sobczynski, Peter. *EFilmCritic.com.* June 11, 2010.
Tallerico, Brian. *MovieRetriever.com.* June 11, 2010.
Turner, Matthew. *ViewLondon.* March 3, 2010.
Weinberg, Scott. *Cinematical.* April 22, 2010.

QUOTES

Syracuse: "She sings to the fishes and he catches them."

TRIVIA

Director Neil Jordan reportedly chose little known Polish actress Alicja Bachleda in order to have a fresh face in the lead role.

127 HOURS

There is no force more powerful than the will to live.
　　—Movie tagline

Every second counts.
　　—Movie tagline

Box Office: $17 million

For most of the 1990s and 2000s, Danny Boyle was an extremely well-respected director, widely known in film schools and among savvy cineastes. But his notoriety reached a whole new level with the rather unlikely commercial embrace of *Slumdog Millionaire* (2008), which went from studio orphan (initial distribution rights holder Warner Bros. wanted to release it straight-to-video before eventually selling off its stake in the film to Fox Searchlight) to eight-time Academy Award®-winner, grossing over $140 million in the United States and $378 million worldwide.

Part of Boyle's gift as a director is also his curse. If the concept of a varied, renaissance-man existence died off sometime in the 19th century, no one bothered to tell him. While many other directors mine a thematic seam, or at least specialize broadly in a certain genre, Boyle skips to and fro, always with the indefatigable optimism and energy of a caffeinated front-row college student. Despite his enormous technical facility, he seems to regard cinema first and foremost as a means through which to explore life in all its altered states and sudden curveballs. Story matters, yes, but not as much as the manner in which his characters react to the extreme polarities of their situations and surroundings.

All of this is necessary preface to any discussion of *127 Hours* because it is so vividly on display in the adaptation of Aron Ralston's at once threadbare and remarkable 2004 memoir *Between a Rock and a Hard Place,* about a hiker who survived five days in the wilderness and made it back to civilization only by cutting off his own arm and then walking eight miles before being rescued. Telling the tale of an extraordinary true-life survival can make for engaging screen drama that does not automatically leave a deep emotional footprint. Boyle's film, though, is surprisingly and concurrently a subjective rumination on loneliness and social need as well as a wild, passionate act of pure cinema. While retaining his characteristic florid pop exuberance, Boyle also crafts a work that is reflective of how the intensity of certain experiences can open one up in tangential ways heretofore unable for the effected to have guessed.

James Franco stars as Ralston, a 28-year-old thrill-seeking outdoor enthusiast who decides to spend his day off work biking into the Utah desert and checking out an isolated, off-the-map slot gorge in Canyonlands National Park. Bopping along to an upbeat soundtrack of his own devising, Aron happens upon two other hikers, Kristi (Kate Mara) and Megan (Amber Tamblyn), and spends a bit of time flirting and hanging out with them before going on his way. Such is the siren call of nature to Ralston—not even the allure of skinny-dipping in an underground hot spring with a pair of beautiful girls can long distract him from his quest.

Negotiating a tricky space, though, Aron slips, falls, and gets his arm partially crushed and then pinned between a massive boulder and the canyon's wall. Stuck, and with little in the way of provisions and no effective way to leverage himself out, Aron cycles through various attempts to extricate himself. He finds psychological release in recording a running, rambling diary with his camcorder, enjoys the fifteen minutes of sunlight that crest over his chalkstone prison each morning at 9:30, and flashes back upon memories of both family and an old girlfriend, Rana (Clémence Poésy). Eventually, though, Aron comes to the decision that the only way out of his predicament and the canyon is to leave behind the part of him that is stuck. With only his cheap pocket knife, he gets to work cutting off his arm near the elbow.

Boyle and his screenwriting collaborator, Simon Beaufoy, take what is a fairly simple, straightforward and potentially static story—a veritable movie-of-the-week conceit that could be used merely to provide some white noise and a few clucks of amazement—and instead dizzy it up into something dynamic and wholly cinematic. Beaufoy's gift with off-center humor, previously on ample display in *The Full Monty* (1997), combined with Boyle's own devilish playfulness, commingle to give *127 Hours* all sorts of surprising moments of levity and engaging irony. Bill Withers' "Lovely Day" pops up at a surprising moment, and when Aron's parched fantasies yearningly return to a bottle of Gatorade left in his car, an assortment of fizzy classic cola commercials are edited into the mix. Together, Boyle and Beaufoy channel Aron's dark predicament into wistful and self-effacing daydreams, including a talk show appearance replete with mock laugh track.

Visually, Boyle has a well-earned reputation for kinetic showmanship, and he again pulls some familiar levers here. An assaultive opening, inclusive of split-screens and a smart juxtaposition of man and nature, pitches the audience headlong into Aron's canyon adventuring. Later, a thunderous rainstorm hallucination, massive in every way, puts the audience alongside Aron as he struggles to get his bearings. In technique and tone, by opening up the story of a trapped man in creative ways, Boyle shrewdly highlights his interior struggle. The sound design (from Glenn Freemantle) and editing (by Jon Harris) are paramount in not only establishing this parallel identification, but also the movie's of-the-moment bona fides and authenticity. And if Boyle is the whip-cracking chariot driver, cinematographers Enrique Chediak and Anthony Dod Mantle, along with composer A.R. Rahman, are his masterful horses. The former deal in saturated, burnt-orange frames and sometimes woozy tones, while Rahman, another *Slumdog Millionaire* collaborator, delivers an engaging score.

Boyle has another fantastic filmmaking partner in Franco. The talented young actor captures Ralston's casual, no-harm self-centeredness and courting of danger, along with his resourcefulness, and splintered vulnerability. It is a delicate and masterful performance, because so much of its engagement and power comes not from dialogue or even the hold of darting eyes, but from a larger countenance—sizing up the hopelessness of a situation and trying to remain hopeful, and focused.

While the film traverses a different trajectory, it bears more than a few similarities in common with *Into the Wild* (2007), in that both movies were adapted from celebrated books whose protagonists in many ways seemed to prefer wilderness and all its rugged, beautiful impediments over the shallow comforts and niceties of modernity. The movie also recalls *Cast Away* (2000), with its focus on isolated personal ingenuity.

When the "Big Scene"—the arm-cutting sequence that was the subject of more than a handful of stories about film-going patrons passing out when the film screened in theaters—finally arrives, it courses with a visceral energy that summons the jarring pain of accidentally biting down on aluminum foil. And yet, oddly, this is not the most memorable scene of *127 Hours*. That would probably be Aron attempting to remain upbeat while recording what he knows might well be a goodbye message to his family.

There will be many viewers who will never see *127 Hours* because of their fear or trepidation over one grim scene. It is easily understandable, the pat dismissal of the movie as "not my type of story." And yet *127 Hours* is an inherently human story—of not just wild, do-it-yourself survival, but also the enlightenment and clarity of purpose that can result from forced delirium.

Brent Simon

CREDITS

Aron Ralston: James Franco
Rana: Clémence Poésy
Megan: Amber Tamblyn
Kristi: Kate Mara
Sonja Ralston: Lizzy Caplan
Mrs. Ralston: Kate Burton
Aron's Friend: Sean Bott
Mr. Ralston: Treat Williams
Origin: USA
Language: English
Released: 2010
Production: Danny Boyle, Christian Colson, John Smithson; Cloud Eight Films, Everest Entertainment, Darlow Smithson Productions, Dune Entertainment III, Pathe; released by Fox Searchlight Pictures
Directed by: Danny Boyle
Written by: Danny Boyle, Simon Beaufoy
Cinematography by: Enrique Chediak, Anthony Dod Mantle
Music by: A.R. Rahman
Sound: Glenn Freemantle
Music Supervisor: Ian Neil
Editing: Jon Harris
Art Direction: Christopher R. DeMuri
Production Design: Sattirat Larlarb
Costumes: Suttirat Larlarb
MPAA rating: R
Running time: 94 minutes

REVIEWS

Ebert, Roger. *Chicago Sun-Times.* November 11, 2010.
Farber, Stephen. *Hollywood Reporter.* September 7, 2010.

Grierson, Tim. *Screen International.* November 1, 2010.
Morgenstern, Joe. *Wall Street Journal.* September 11, 2010.
Murray, Noel. *Chicago Reader.* November 12, 2010.
O'Hehir, Andrew. *Salon.com.* September 16, 2010.
Rocchi, James. *MSN Movies.* November 4, 2010.
Scott, A.O. *New York Times.* November 4, 2010.
Stevens, Dana. *Slate.* November 4, 2010.
Tallerico, Brian. *HollywoodChicago.com.* October 16, 2010.

QUOTES

Aron Ralston: "Mom, Dad, I really love you guys. I wanted to take this time to say the times we've spent together have been awesome. I haven't appreciated you in my own the way I know I could. Mom, I love you. I wish I'd returned all of your calls, ever. I really have lived this last year. I wish I had learned some lessons more astutely, more rapidly, than I did. I love you. I'll always be with you."

TRIVIA

Director Danny Boyle and lead actor James Franco were allowed to view the actual footage from Aron Ralston's daily video diary in order to accurately portray the events in the film.

Cillian Murphy was director Danny Boyle's first choice to play Aron Ralston.

AWARDS

Ind. Spirit 2011: Actor (Franco)

Nomination:

Oscars 2010: Actor (Franco), Adapt. Screenplay, Film, Film Editing, Song ("If I Rise"), Orig. Score

British Acad. 2010: Actor (Franco), Adapt. Screenplay, Cinematog., Director (Boyle), Film Editing, Sound, Orig. Score, Alexander Korda Award

Golden Globes 2011: Actor—Drama (Franco), Screenplay, Orig. Score

Ind. Spirit 2011: Director (Boyle), Film

Screen Actors Guild 2010: Actor (Franco)

Writers Guild 2010: Adapt. Screenplay.

THE OTHER GUYS

Box Office: $119 million

The basic foundation of *The Other Guys* is clever enough. Officers Terry Hoitz (Mark Wahlberg) and Allen Gamble (Will Ferrell) are "the other guys," L.A.P.D. desk jockeys whose behind-the-scenes jobs keep them off the streets and out of the sort of trouble that Hoitz would love to be getting into. Gamble, a forensic accountant (who audited his own parents as a preteen), is happy with the occasional paper cut, but when hot shot action cops Danson (Dwayne Johnson) and Highsmith

(Samuel L. Jackson) are killed in the line of duty, Hoitz sees a chance for him and Gamble to become the new team in town as they stumble into an investigation involving shady investment capitalist David Ershon (Steve Coogan). Soon, guns are blazing, cars are crashing and the goofy pair is in way over their heads.

Adam McKay's film has some funny one-liners and situations including a bit in which the over-zealous Hoitz is stuck in his dead-end desk job because of a career-killing case of mistaken identity involving Derek Jeter and a gun. His hatred of Gamble leads to banter that can only be described as jaw-dropping. Gamble is married to a woman he calls the "battle axe," who is in reality the doting and completely-hot Sheila (Eva Mendes). But whether Gamble is being fooled into using his gun to let off a "desk pop" at the office or barfing his guts out in an office waste basket declaring, "I got so drunk last night I think I mistook a tube of toothpaste for astronaut food" or having his real gun, then his wooden gun, and finally his rape whistle, confiscated by the Captain (Michael Keaton), the film over-delivers gut-busters that invite a closer look at the careers of everyone involved.

At his comedic best, Will Ferrell has always brought a certain heart to his roles. Smaller parts in *Zoolander* (2001), *Old School* (2003), and a plethora of cameos in other films done soon after his departure from *Saturday Night Live* made great use of his zaniness but false starts in *A Night at the Roxbury* (1998) and *The Ladies Man* (2001) already had true believers nervous about whether their hero would find his rightful place in the big screen comedic pantheon. Ferrell clearly had the chops to do more than wail and run around in his underwear. The excellent and very funny *Elf* (2003) had been a huge hit but it was Ferrell's leading role in *Anchorman: The Legend of Ron Burgundy* (2004) that made fans breathe a sigh of relief: Ferrell was probably going to be around for a long time and he was likely to introduce viewers to more original characters. *Talledega Nights: The Ballad of Ricky Bobby* (2006) was a solidly-amusing, sometimes-hilarious follow-up.

But then came the missteps. *Kicking and Screaming* (2005) had already wound up in the bargain bin, and his next two big comedic starrers showed little of the creativity that had won him so many fans. In fact it can be effectively argued that his characters in *Blades of Glory* (2007) and *Semi-Pro* (2008) are almost identical: unlikeable blowhard has-beens that are desperate to be cheered on as they take one last undeserved shot at glory. It began to seem that Ferrell might be bit of a one or two trick pony. Then came *Step Brothers* (2008) that while funny seemed like a skit that had been stretched out to feature length. Lastly the simply-awful *Land of the Lost* (2009) showed a completely-miscast Ferrell desperately trying to convince audiences that he could be a brilliantly stupid scientist.

A list of Mark Wahlberg's worst movies includes *Planet of the Apes* (2001), *The Happening* (2008), *Max Payne* (2008), and *The Lovely Bones* (2009). These are monuments to the worst cinema can offer and Wahlberg is truly awful in them. But a list of his best films balances the scales admirably: *The Departed* (2006), *Boogie Nights* (1997), and *Three Kings* (1999). Wahlberg has other good and bad roles under his belt as well but oddly enough, in neither list will you find a comedy—until now. Wahlberg dances through this role, sometimes literally, with a lightness and feel for comedy he hinted at in guest stints on *SNL* and small roles in films like *Date Night* (2010) and *I Heart Huckabees* (2004). The role of Hoitz gives him free reign to take his own tough guy persona in for questioning. "I'm a peacock, I gotta fly!" he cries and does so wonderfully holding his own opposite much more experienced comedy heavyweights.

Dwayne Johnson and Samuel L. Jackson are, of course, perfectly cast as the blowhard action heroes and viewers may even find themselves wishing that their roles had been bigger especially with Jackson screaming lines like "If I want you to talk I'll stick my hand up your ass and work your mouth like a ventriloquist dummy!" Also having a great time here is Michael Keaton as Captain Gene Mauch who inexplicably quotes the band TLC. Mostly wasted is Steve Coogan who is given almost nothing to do but mug his way through a thankless role as the cardboard corporate schmuck.

If Ferrell has had moderate success away from McKay in dramedies ala *Melinda and Melinda* (2004), *Winter Passing* (2005), and *Stranger Than Fiction* (2006), McKay has yet to distinguish himself on the big screen without Ferrell. But if movies like *The Other Guys* are the continued result of their regular collaboration, then that is far from a bad thing.

Dave Canfield

CREDITS

Allen Gamble: Will Ferrell
Terry Hoitz: Mark Wahlberg
Christopher Danson: Dwayne Johnson
P.K. Highsmith: Samuel L. Jackson
David Ershon: Steve Coogan
Sheila Gamble: Eva Mendes
Francine: Lindsay Sloane
Capt. Gene Mauch: Michael Keaton
Fosse: Damon Wayans Jr.
Jane: Paris Hilton
Det. Evan Martin: Rob Riggle

Roger Wesley: Ray Stevenson
Chritinith: Natalie Zea
Jimmy: Bobby Cannavale
Pamela Boardman: Anne Heche
Herself: Brooke Shields (Cameo)
Herself: Rosie Perez (Cameo)
Himself: Derek Jeter (Cameo)
Narrator: Ice-T
Origin: USA
Language: English
Released: 2010
Production: Patrick Crowley, Jimmy Miller, Will Ferrell, Adam McKay; Relativity Media, Gary Sanchez Prods., Mosaic Media Group, Columbia Pictures; released by Sony Pictures Entertainment
Directed by: Adam McKay
Written by: Adam McKay, Chris Henchy
Cinematography by: Oliver Wood
Music by: Jon Brion
Sound: Tom Nelson
Music Supervisor: Erica Weis
Editing: Brent White
Art Direction: Jim Gloster
Costumes: Carol Ramsey
Production Design: Clayton Hartley
MPAA rating: PG-13
Running time: 107 minutes

REVIEWS

Corliss, Richard. *Time Magazine.* August 6, 2010.
Gilchrist, Todd. *Cinematical.* August 18, 2010.
Huddleston, Tom. *Time Out.* September 15, 2010.
Kolan, Patrick. *IGN Movies AU.* September 7, 2010.
O'Hehir, Andrew. *Salon.com.* August 6, 2010.
Morris, Anthony. *The Vine.* September 7, 2010.
Pinkerton, Nick. *Village Voice.* August 3, 2010.
Puig, Claudia. *USA Today.* August 5, 2010.
Scott, A.O. *New York Times.* August 6, 2010.
White, Armand. *New York Press.* August 6, 2010.

QUOTES

Allen Gamble: "At age 11, I audited my parents. Believe me, there were some discrepancies, and I was grounded."

Allen Gamble: "This meal is terrible…it tastes like roasted dog a-hole. I asked myself, 'Who would slow roast a dog's asshole and feed it to me?' You would."

TRIVIA

Rob Riggle plays a police officer who gives a safety presentation to schoolchildren featuring tasers, similar to his role in the 2009 film *The Hangover*

On the poster with Mark Wahlberg and Will Ferrell, 10712 is the badge number for both of them.

OUR FAMILY WEDDING

To have and to hold...'Til dads do us part.
—Movie tagline

Box Office: $20 million

It has been a long time since 1967's *Guess Who's Coming to Dinner?*, and, in the years since then, interracial marriage has become much more commonplace and thus has lost its power to shock, or to be an amusing subject in and of itself. But director Rick Famuyiwa, who shares scriptwriting credits, still gives it a shot, updating and giving the familiar subject a new twist, making the couple a Mexican American woman and an African American man. This may be a way to make the prejudices more acceptable to portray on-screen, by leaving white racists out of the picture completely, but it does not make the prejudices any less odious or any more credible.

To start the animosity rolling, the fathers of the piece (Forest Whitaker and Carlos Mencia) meet movie-cute—one is a tow truck driver (Mencia) and tows the other's (Whitaker) car. They immediately start trading racially-tinged insults. Since there is no plausible reason for these two families to have a feud, the motivations have to be contrived. So they are.

It does turn out that the fine dramatic actor Forest Whitaker has some comedic chops as well. He is the only actor in the film who can make his character carry through his predictable bits effectively; Whitaker makes believable transitions from cool to flustered to angry and then back to cool. When the fathers argue about their respective cultural wedding traditions, Whitaker's Brad Boyd makes up a position and then struggles to defend it; it is amusing to watch him try to struggle out of his own trap. His counterpart as the Mexican American dad as played by Carlos Mencia, a TV comedian, is no match for Whitaker; Mencia cannot carry a comedic skit in a movie context—like many stand-up comics, his shtick relies on insults and exaggerations, and he comes off mostly inane. America Ferrera, a television actress, plays the bride and shines in several poignant scenes, but carries off her role mostly by being agreeable and charming. There is no real passion between her and her fiancée (Lance Gross), so when their families, inevitably, cause them to doubt their love, their break-up and subsequent makeup are dull and utterly unmoving.

Just as predictable as the comic bits are the film's eventual doldrums, as it runs out of wind in melodramatic stretches that descend into great sappiness. For awhile, the movie just meanders before reaching the inevitable conclusion. With nothing original up its sleeve, *Our Family Wedding* is an unremarkable undertaking in most respects.

The direction, cinematography, dialogue, and music are all cable-TV quality at best—the soundtrack of unremarkable song snippets sounds more like a movie was made and then a deejay hired to match appropriate tunes to scenes. There are a few promising, small skits—like a family softball game that trades on humiliation. However, the game doesn't make any sense—random people seem to be pitching—and turns into slapstick. Almost every opportunity to make hay of a scene is squandered.

The wedding does not come soon enough, because at least it relieves the filmmakers of the burden of trying to carry through a plot line, since the direction is quite obvious. The wedding could become a disaster, but instead it is awash in cheap sentiment and forced happy endings. Just as everyone earlier seems to argue for no coherent reasons, everyone suddenly gets along for no good reason. Nothing outrageous occurs; the movie plays it safe and refrains from erupting into the usual Hollywood wedding anarchy, which is the only way this movie could have transcended its hackneyed boundaries. *Our Family Wedding* does not even have the courage to follow through on its own trivial, contrived tensions. The climax proves to be a letdown; the movie seems to forget it is supposed to be a comedy.

In the end, the critics were right; this film is a lazy mess. It fully earns the adjectives most bestowed on it during its brief theatrical run. Whitaker escapes the movie unscathed; playing a light-night romantic deejay, he is a fine actor trapped in a film and a role that is way beneath his talents.

Michael Betzold

CREDITS

Bradford Boyd: Forest Whitaker
Miguel Ramirez: Carlos Mencia
Lucia Ramirez: America Ferrera
Marcus Boyd: Lance Gross
Angela: Regina King
Momma Cecilia: Lupe Ontiveros
Diane Boyd: Anna Maria Horsford
Wendell Boyd: Warren Sapp
Origin: USA
Language: English
Released: 2010
Production: Edward Saxon, Steven J. Wolfe; Sneak Preview Entertainment; released by Fox Searchlight
Directed by: Rick Famuyiwa
Written by: Rick Famuyiwa, Wayne Conley, Malcolm Spellman
Cinematography by: Julio Macat
Music by: Transcenders
Sound: Lori Dovi
Editing: Dirk Westervelt

Art Direction: Colin de Rouin
Costumes: Hope Hanafin
Production Design: Linda Burton
MPAA rating: PG-13
Running time: 101 minutes

REVIEWS

Anderson, Jason. *Toronto Star.* March 12, 2010.
Coyle, Jake. *Associated Press.* March 9, 2010.
Ebert, Roger. *Chicago Sun-Times.* March 11, 2010.
Groen, Rick. *Globe and Mail.* March 12, 2010.
Hills, Aaron. *Village Voice.* March 9, 2010.
Long, Tom. *Detroit News.* March 10, 2010.
Moore, Roger. *Orlando Sentinel.* March 10, 2010.
Morris, Wesley. *Boston Globe.* March 12, 2010.
Puig, Claudia. *USA Today.* March 12, 2010.
Sharkey, Betsey. *Los Angeles Times.* March 12, 2010.

P

PARANORMAL ACTIVITY 2

Box Office: $85 million

On the surface, *Paranormal Activity 2* appears identical in form to its predecessor, holding true to the old maxim, "If it isn't broke, don't fix it." A demonic spirit haunts a house. The owners document it on video. A text preface purports the footage to be real, thanking the local police and family members of the victims of the supernatural force for allowing the use of the "found" recordings.

Whereas *Paranormal Activity* (2007), which did not find a major theatrical release until 2009 after success on the festival circuit, limited midnight screenings, and an ingenious "Demand It" marketing campaign (so effective, it is a registered trademark for the promotional web service it and this movie employed), used its minimalistic, one-camera gimmick to allude to the eerie as much as or even more than show it, the sequel increases the number of cameras to show nearly the entire house and its front and rear exteriors. The setup, which gives the appearance of a reality television show, is barebones compared to the large majority of Hollywood productions yet excessive when weighed against the previous film. It must also, then, cheat to attempt the same suggestive power the first film accomplished so well.

While the audience was only privy to the same visual and aural information the original's protagonists (Katie Featherston [as Katie] and Micah Sloat [as Micah], reprising their roles here, since the events of the sequel take place before and during the timeline of the

first film) received (except in one notable instance in which they accidentally left the camera on, leading to the film's most elaborate special effect sequence involving a Ouija board), that is not the case in this movie. Instead, paternal family head Daniel Rey (Brian Boland) suspects a robbery in his home, during which every room except for his and his wife Kristi's (Sprague Grayden) young son Hunter (William Juan and Jackson Xenia Prieto) has been torn apart, and installs an elaborate security camera system throughout.

Such extensive coverage (six mounted cameras and one handheld one) means the mystery is gone. When there is a tap at a window, a door opens or closes without anyone present, or the family dog begins to bark at the air in front of it, instead of a walk into the unknown from one of the characters, it is simply a matter of cutting to the camera in the living room, the kitchen, or Hunter's bedroom respectively. The trepidation of wandering in the dark is absent here, replaced by static views of parlor tricks shot in the blue tint of night-vision cinematography (by Michael Simmonds), accompanied by the recognizable timestamp in the lower right-hand side of the frame and titles stating which night of the disturbance it is.

The special effects are far too reminiscent of the movie's predecessor and lack their skill. An invisible hand grabs and drags Hunter and Kristi at different times, which echoes the same instance it happened to Katie the first time. Daniel's daughter from his first marriage Ali (Molly Ephraim) pulls out an Ouija board with her friend Brad (Seth Ginsberg) with no odd occurrence except the spelling of her baby brother's name. The dog is lifted up and attacked by the same imperceptible creature. All of the demon spirit's actions are accompanied by a telltale bass rumble on the soundtrack, and a few require a constant scanning of the nearly still frame to spot a movement at just the right moment.

Paranormal Activity's writer/director Oren Peli managed the hiding of important events by the virtue of using a single camera, while the sequel's director Tod Williams and editor Gregory Plotkin play loose with selective camera choices. The shock of Kristi's yanked-by-the-feet trip across the floor, down the stairs, and into the unwatched basement becomes almost comical in the way Plotkin must incorporate three of the stationary cameras multiple times for Williams' staging, which downplays the initial shock (very low, considering it has happened to Hunter—in an admittedly less violent fashion—already), to finish. While Kristi's ride into the basement is seen as it happens, the attack on the dog is obscured from view by a wall, when there is a better camera angle available from which to see it (The multiple-camera scenario raises a subconscious strain upon the entire suspension of disbelief for the whole affair that was never present before: why would someone edit a real, discovered document in such a knowingly deceptive way?). When it switches over to the handheld camera (e.g., during Ali's investigation of a now-possessed Kristi and Daniel's trip into the basement), the movie does manage a few tense, claustrophobic moments.

In between the nighttime sequences, screenwriters Michael R. Perry, Christopher Landon, and Tom Pabst reveal little about the characters beyond their relationship to each other, with the sole exception being the mild comic relief provided by the Reys' religious maid Martine (Vivis), who begins saying prayers and burning incense before anyone suspects an evil presence might be behind the odd happenings in the house and returns when Daniel has exhausted no options. Otherwise, the script spends time expanding the mythology behind the pattern of the shared paranormal experiences of sisters Kristi and Katie and unnecessary background information about the first movie. The movie's concept of a major revelation is showing who put a cryptic, damaged photo in Katie and Micah's attic.

After the huge financial success of *Paranormal Activity*, a sequel was inevitable, and *Paranormal Activity 2*, while containing a few chilling moments, is a rushed retread that, in attempting to recapture the experience of the original film, misses the point.

Mark Dujsik

CREDITS
Daniel Rey: Brian Boland
Ali Rey: Molly Ephraim

Kristi Rey: Sprague Grayden
Katie: Katie Featherston
Micah: Micah Sloat
Martine: Vivis
Brad: Seth Ginsberg
Hunter: Juan Prieto, Jackson Xenia Prieto
Origin: USA
Language: English
Released: 2010
Production: Jason Blum, Oren Peli; Blumhouse Productions, Solana Films, Room 101; released by Paramount Pictures
Directed by: Tod Williams
Written by: Christopher Landon, Michael R. Perry, Tom Pabst
Cinematography by: Michael Simmonds
Sound: Zsolt Magyar
Editing: Gregory Plotkin
Costumes: Kristen M. Burke
Production Design: Jennifer Spence
MPAA rating: R
Running time: 91 minutes

REVIEWS

Bell, Josh. *Las Vegas Weekly.* October 22, 2010.
Berardinelli, James. *ReelViews.* October 23, 2010.
Johanson, MaryAnn. *Flick Filosopher.* October 29, 2010.
Moore, Roger. *Orlando Sentinel.* October 21, 2010.
O'Hehir, Andrew. *Salon.com.* October 22, 2010.
Orndorf, Brian. *BrianOrndorf.com.* October 22, 2010.
Phillips, Michael. *Chicago Tribune.* October 22, 2010.
Weinberg, Scott. *FEARnet.* October 22, 2010.
Vaux, Rob. *Mania.com.* October 23, 2010.
Zacharek, Stephanie. *Movieline.* October 22, 2010.

QUOTES

Katie: "It wasn't Witchy! It made her feel better."

TRIVIA

The film was sent to theaters labeled "Sharpie 79."

PERCY JACKSON & THE OLYMPIANS: THE LIGHTNING THIEF

Box Office: $89 million

As the Harry Potter film series winds down to a close, it is inevitable that studios would make any number of bad attempts to co-opt the Hogwarts fanbase. *Percy Jackson & the Olympians: The Lightning Thief* is certainly meant to play like Harry Potter with swords instead of wands. Instead it plays like the Jonas Brothers with foam swords instead of guitars. Director Chris Columbus (*Harry Potter and the Sorcerer's Stone* [2001], *Harry Potter and the Chamber of Secrets* [2002]), offers a surprisingly bland $95 million adaptation of a somewhat enjoyable children's novel series by Rick Riordan. The lightness of the source material may account for the in-comparison to the Potter series scant two-hour runtime. But the film reaches out for an epic feel anyway and that is its major problem. The oldest story in the current version of Hollywood is that of the effects-laden road to the same old boring place.

Someone has stolen the lightning bolt of Zeus (Sean Bean) and the angry God becomes convinced that the thief is Poseidon's (Kevin McKidd) half-human son Percy Jackson (Logan Lerman). To avert a God war that could destroy the Earth, Percy must find and return the lightning in ten days. Escaping to Camp Half-Blood he discovers other demi-gods. His teacher Mr. Brunner (Pierce Brosnan) is really a Centaur, his crippled best friend Grover (Brandon T. Jackson) a satyr. He begins his training only to discover that his mother Sally (Catherine Keener) has been kidnapped by Hades (Steve Coogan), who wants the lightning for his own reasons. Joined by Grover and his beautiful classmate Annabeth (Alexandra Daddario), Percy embarks on a dangerous journey that will bring him face-to-face with one mythic hurdle after another. Whether battling Medusa (Uma Thurman) or huge Minotaurs, Percy's biggest battle will be confronting his absentee father and assuming responsibility for the awesome power his heritage puts at his fingertips.

The screenplay takes the predictable Cliff Notes ap-proach to condensing Riordan's 400-page book, which is somewhat understandable as screenwriter Craig Tit-ley's only other credit assuming full authorship is *Con-spiracy Theory: Did We Land on the Moon* (2001). His other credits include (and somehow this seems oddly ap-propriate) story credits for *Scooby-Doo* (2002) and *Cheaper by the Dozen* (2003). Not so understandable, and certainly not forgivable, is the wasting of so much talent in an effort to lend the proceedings some gravitas.

The cast includes so many heavyweights that the real wonder is how anyone thought the younger members of the cast could keep up. We never believe for a minute that any of them could be Godlings and we never get a sense of them moving into their new identi-ties with any authority. The heavyweights are all left playing to them and, except for Kevin McKidd (*Hideous Kinky* [1998], *Dog Soldiers* [2002], *De-Lovely* [2004]) as Poseidon, none of them have a character arc of any description. Brosnan appears worldly-wise as Chiron, Thurman vamps it up as Medusa, and Bean acts hurt and angry just like he did in *The Lord of the Rings: The Fellowship of the Ring* (2001). (Joe Pantoliano has a good

bit as Percy's mother's jerk boyfriend but it barely rises above the level of cameo and plays completely to type.) In short, there is a lack of surprises here on all counts. The normally-reliable Coogan is the best thing here and delivers his dialogue with exactly the sort of saturnine cluelessness that gets easy grins.

Cinematographer Stephen Goldblatt manages to turn in the big budget look that was a foregone conclusion. Cynics will remember him for his work on the huge bust *Batman and Robin* (1997) but the man has actually had an extraordinary career that includes a variety of unique films including *Outland* (1981), *The Hunger* (1983), *The Cotton Club* (1984), *Young Sherlock Holmes* (1985), and the surreal minor gem *Joe Versus the Volcano* (1990). He also leant his talents to the first two *Lethal Weapon* films. Sadly, such style is not really needed here nor is it given any real room to assert itself. *Percy Jackson* hampers Goldblatt, one of its finest talents, by forcing him to virtually remake Harry Potter visually, putting Columbus's familiar style up-front and taking a backseat just when the film could have used the creativ-ity he was able to show in his other far, far better work.

The special effects fail to pick up the slack for the most part as well. A dynamic opening scene offers an impossibly huge Poseidon rising from the depths of the ocean. It is well done, perfectly lit, offering a solid bal-ance of filmmaking technique. But it still fails dramati-cally in comparison to the dated-but-spectacular Neptune sequence in *Jason and the Argonauts* (1968). And this sequence is one of the most captivating. For all the action and mythic pixel overkill there, surprisingly little wonder makes it onscreen here, giving *Percy Jackson & the Olympians: The Lightning Thief* a decidedly direct-to-video or made-for-TV quality.

The movie industry is built on promises. When a film promises to be the next great franchise (especially the next great children's franchise), even the most cyni-cal viewer wants to believe it might be. The best films fulfill that promise by opening the door to a world that seems already there, writ whole. How much more important is it then, that when adapting established book series, the films have, at least, their own sense of style. The characters, the storyline, and even the admit-tedly occasionally-effective effects here seem borrowed virtues. There is no mythic quality here; an unforgivable sin for a movie that aims to point viewers toward Olympus.

Dave Canfield

CREDITS

Percy Jackson: Logan Lerman
Mr. Brunner/Chiron: Pierce Brosnan

Medusa: Uma Thurman
Zeus: Sean Bean
Poseidon: Kevin McKidd
Athena: Melina Kanakaredes
Sally Jackson: Catherine Keener
Hades: Steve Coogan
Grover: Branden T. Jackson
Annabeth: Alexandra Daddario
Origin: Canada, USA
Language: English
Released: 2010
Production: Michael Barnathan, Karen Rosenfelt, Mark Morgan, Guy Oseary, Mark Radcliffe; 1492 Pictures, Fox 2000 Pictures, Imprint Entertainment, Sunswept Entertainment, TCF Vancouver Productions; released by 20th Century Fox
Directed by: Chris Columbus
Written by: Craig Titley
Cinematography by: Stephen Goldblatt
Music by: Christophe Beck
Sound: Robert Shoup
Editing: Peter Honess
Art Direction: Sandra Tanaka
Costumes: Renee April
Production Design: Howard Cummings
MPAA rating: PG
Running time: 118 minutes

REVIEWS

Ebert, Roger. *Chicago Sun-Times.* February 10, 2010.
Fine, Marshall. *Huffington Post.* February 12, 2010.
Hall, Peter. *Cinematical.* February 12, 2010.
Holden, Stephen. *New York Times.* February 12, 2010.
Lumenick, Lou. *New York Post.* February 12, 2010.
Maurstad, Tom. *Dallas News.* February 11, 2010.
O'Sullivan, Michael. *Washington Post.* February 12, 2010.
Puig, Claudia. *USA Today.* February 15, 2010.
Robinson, Tasha. *AV Club.* February 12, 2010.
Turan, Kenneth. *Los Angeles Times.* February 12, 2010.

QUOTES

Percy Jackson: "Oh I wish I could spend all day in the water instead of this place."

Percy Jackson: "Don't the Gods see their kids?"

Poseidon: "I know I'm not the father you always wanted. But if you ever need me, I'll be there for you. In your thoughts, in your dreams."

TRIVIA

The goddess Athena never had any children in traditional Greek mythology.

PIRANHA 3D

There's something in the water.
—Movie tagline

This summer 3D shows its teeth.
—Movie tagline

Don't scream…just swim!
—Movie tagline

Box Office: $25 million

Piranha 3D—a remake of Joe Dante's *Piranha* (1978), a B-grade *Jaws* (1975) from Roger Corman—is a movie made with the 3-D concept in mind, as opposed to it being an afterthought conversion to the format. This is both a plus and a minus in terms of how 3D is used. On the one hand, the movie is a more genuine artifact. More thought was put into how to use 3D to the movie's advantage (for better or for worse). The downside, though, is that with each 3D movie that gets released, the filmmaking process has taken an uncomfortable turn to a trend that has more to do with artifice than art (not that "art" is the first word that springs to mind when talking about a horror movie about killer fish, but the point still stands). Filmmakers now make their stylistic choices based on a marketing ploy rather than what is best for the film.

But as one would expect just from looking at the poster, *Piranha 3D* is more of a "show" than a "movie" and as a show, it works just fine. It revels in bottom-feeder pay-offs one used to expect when attending a drive-in exploitation triple feature. It has plenty of "blood, beasts, and breasts" (to borrow from sleaze movie expert Joe Bob Briggs). Even the film's editor goes by the singular name "Baxter." It all spills forth right in the viewer's face with reckless abandon. In fact, the movie has plenty to be remembered for and the 3D is probably the least of these things. In standard 2D, the sight of someone getting their hair tangled in a motor boat engine as it revs up will have the same effect on the viewer.

Director Alexandre Aja establishes the tongue-in-cheek attitude right at the start as the movie opens with Richard Dreyfuss fishing in a lake and noticing some strange rumbling in the water (*Jaws* fans will be happy to know that the character is not listed as Matt Hooper, although he is humming "Show Me the Way to Go Home"). The poor guy is soon devoured in a gigantic whirlpool before being chomped to death by hundreds of bloodthirsty piranha. Thus starts the investigation by law enforcement, underwater explorers, and marine biologists as to how this could happen. Meanwhile, spring break partygoers have descended upon Lake Victoria for mindless dancing, drinking, and stripping, blissfully unaware of the piranha outbreak.

As usual, the main characters are teenagers. Jake Forrester (Steven R. McQueen) is a good kid whose mom trusts him to look after his two younger siblings while she investigates the fish attack. He reluctantly agrees, since he has accepted a job to tag along with an exploitation videographer, Derrick Jones (Jerry O'Connell), a character no doubt patterned after *Girls Gone Wild* provocateur Joe Francis. Jake's girl-next-door female friend Kelly (Jessica Szohr) is also vying for his attention. Jake decides to pay off the kids and have them look after themselves while he goes off to show Derrick around Lake Victoria, where he will eventually be joined by Kelly.

Julie Forrester, Jake's mom (inexplicably played by Elizabeth Shue), partners up with Deputy Fallon (Ving Rhames) to try and solve the mystery behind the grizzly death of the fisherman. A group of underwater explorers are also brought in to search the deep crevices below in hopes of finding clues. Once it becomes perfectly clear that an army of deadly piranha is hell-bent on devouring anyone who goes for a swim, it is up to a goofy marine biologist (Christopher Lloyd) to figure out why and up to law enforcement to close the lake. Meanwhile, the kids whom Jake is supposed to look after have decided to take a boat to Stoney Island in Lake Victoria and have a little adventure of their own.

Of course, trying to stop a spring break party in mid-flow proves futile and soon the flesh-eating fish are treated to a smorgasbord of human pickings resulting in a bloodbath that invites comparisons to the last half hour of Peter Jackson's *Dead-Alive* (1993). Elsewhere, Jake, Kelly, a couple of nude models, and filmmaker Derrick Jones are on a boat, also dealing with the piranha who are helping themselves to whomever falls first into the water, no doubt grateful for not having any bikinis getting caught in their teeth.

Piranha 3D is an exploitative free-for-all. The nude scenes go on for a long time on purpose, leading one to believe that this is a film created strictly for men. That would appear to be true until one moment in the film when a certain part of the male anatomy becomes a main course. Flesh gets eaten right off the bone, skin gets ripped off and hundreds of morons fall to their deaths after being warned to vacate the premises immediately. They get what is coming to them and the audience does, too, although people who bought a ticket probably did not expect to have 3D vomit spewed upon them.

In the wake of the film's release, director James Cameron (*Avatar* [2009]) attacked the filmmakers and their choices on how to utilize 3-D, mistakenly referring to the silly gimmick as an art form. Admittedly, some of the 3D choices are not very strong. The overhead shot of piranha devouring is not very effective and often the shots looks flimsily constructed, much in the same way non-3D movies look after the conversion process. This may work to the film's advantage in 2D when such

flaws are not as apparent. Whether or not 3D can be seriously considered an art form will always be up for debate, a discussion which could get all the more interesting if they plan on remaking Cameron's own *Piranha II: The Spawning* (1981).

Collin Souter

CREDITS

Sheriff Julie Forester: Elisabeth Shue
Novak: Adam Scott
Jake Forrester: Steven R. McQueen
Derrick Jones: Jerry O'Connell
Kelly: Jessica Szohr
Paula: Dina Meyer
Todd Dupree: Cody Longo
Mr. Goodman: Christopher Lloyd
Deputy Fallon: Ving Rhames
Matt Boyd: Richard Dreyfuss
Origin: USA
Language: English
Released: 2010
Production: Alexandre Aja, Mark Canton, Marc Toberoff, Gregory Levasseur; Weinstein Company, Chako Films Company, IPW; released by Dimension Films
Directed by: Alexandre Aja
Written by: Alexandre Aja, Josh Stolberg
Cinematography by: John R. Leonetti
Music by: Michael Wandmacher
Sound: Michael B. Koff
Editing: Baxter
Art Direction: Marisa Frantz
Costumes: Sanja Milkovic Hays
Production Design: Clark Hunter
MPAA rating: R
Running time: 88 minutes

REVIEWS

Biodrowski, Steve. *Cinefantastique*. August 20, 2010.
Floyd, Nigel. *Time Out*. August 19, 2010.
Katzman, Joshua. *Chicago Reader*. August 26, 2010.
Lemire, Christy. *Associated Press*. August 19, 2010.
Rechtshaffem, Michael. *Hollywood Reporter*. August 19, 2010.
Scott, A.O. *New York Times*. August 23, 2010.
Schager, Nick. *Slant Magazine*. August 20, 2010.
Sobczynski, Peter. *eFilmcritic.com*. August 22, 2010.
Tallerico, Brian. *HollywoodChicago.com*. August 20, 2010.
Weinberg, Scott. *FEARnet.com*. August 20, 2010.

QUOTES

Mr. Goodman: "The piranha hunt in packs. The first bite draws blood, blood draws the pack."

Deputy Fallon: "This is the Lake Victoria police department. The sheriff has declared an emergency!"

Novak: "There are thousands of them and they are pissed!"

TRIVIA

The movie poster paid homage to the classic *Jaws* movie poster replacing the shark with a giant piranha.

The film was shot in 2D but was converted in post-production to 3D using a patented conversion process.

PLEASE GIVE

Box Office: $4 million

Please Give is an apt title for Nicole Holofcener's fourth film. Audiences might ask the director: please give me a stronger plot, more fully realized characters, and a clearer point of view. Like Holofcener's other movies, *Please Give* focuses on the eccentricities of upper-middle class New Yorkers, and the intent seems to be to poke fun at or criticize such folks' bleeding-heart sympathies that somehow combine with their crass commercialism. If this were the subject of biting satire, the intent might yield a pleasing bite. But Holofcener's script ends up backing down even from its own rather milquetoast ambitions.

As in Holofcener's other films, Catherine Keener plays the director's foil. This time, she is Kate, a woman approaching middle age with angst and qualms. She and her husband, Alex (Oliver Platt), who seems more of a thinly-sketched idea than a real person, run a business in which they pay low prices to the grieving children of just-deceased people who have stuffed their homes with 1950s-era furnishings that their offspring find useless and of no value. They are delighted when Kate takes the junky stuff off their hands, little suspecting that Kate knows the couches and lamps and tables have a kitschy retro value; she and Toby will sell them at a Midtown furniture store at a huge markup. That is how they make their living, but how they have arrived at this point is opaque.

In the increasingly popular—and incredibly lazy—screenwriting style of the day, Kate and Alex have absolutely no back story. We know nothing about their marriage other than that it has entered a dull period of jaded over-familiarity, and we know zilch about why they have chosen this craven enterprise as their joint business. The latter would help, because the central point the film hammers home is that Kate has become increasingly wracked with guilt over their soulless enterprise. But why? Near the film's beginning—a sloppily edited pastiche of almost inscrutable moments introducing the characters—we discover Kate is ex-

tremely generous to homeless people she meets on the street yet penurious when it comes to spending money on her fifteen-year-old daughter, the self-doubting Abby (brilliantly played by Sarah Steele). Gradually, over the course of the movie, Kate's guilt deepens to the point where she becomes tortured and morose and practically suicidal. But there is no discernible reason. Kate does not experience a character arc so much as a character slouch. Nothing happens to her to cause this moral crisis.

Keener fails to give the character her customary spark, but it is not primarily her fault. Her personality is leaden, which makes the movie dull. She becomes wearier and wearier of the burden of the enterprise she has chosen. Yet this moral dilemma has as little depth as the rest of the movie. It plays more like a menopausal bad mood than a genuine existential dilemma.

It quickly becomes noticeable that Holofcener's script not only is populated by thinly sketched characters; it also tends to have matching good and bad pairs. Thus, Kate is guilt-stricken, yet Alex is completely guilt-free. Their next-door neighbor is a ninety-one-year grandmother, Andra (Ann Guilbert), who is bitchy and disagreeable, but another older woman comes into the movie, and she is kind and sweet. Andra's two daughters are also opposites: Mary (Amanda Peet) is shallow, cold, and cruel beyond belief; her younger sister, Rebecca (Rebecca Hall) is forgiving, understanding, and big-hearted. All of them are more caricatures than characters.

The flimsy plot, such as it is, revolves around waiting for the grandmother to die in the apartment she has leased next door from Kate and Alex; when she does, they plan to knock out a wall and expand. So the movie consists mainly of waiting for this to happen. Time is filled in with an extremely dull-and-senseless affair between Alex and Mary, while her sister finds a nice man who woos her sweetly. But the male characters are little more than ciphers.

Some critics compared the film to middle-period Woody Allen, but Allen would have been much more barbed than this. Imagine as well what a director like Pedro Almodóvar would have done with this material. Instead, Holofcener does next to nothing. Her notion of a conclusion is to suddenly patch things up simplistically. For inexplicable reasons, the grandmother's death reconciles the two sisters, a development that springs impossibly from nowhere, as does the reconciliation between husband and wife (an easy one, since the wife never knows of the affair). But even more simplistic and unmotivated is that Kate's guilt is suddenly assuaged for no discernible reason, and it is resolved, moreover, by buying her daughter an expensive pair of jeans (and by the convenient disappearance of her favorite homeless client). Kate's concerns were shallow to begin with, but the script toys for a bit with making them life-threatening. Yet in the end they are brushed away by the crass commercialism she never really questions all that seriously. It seems like just a bout of mild moral qualms in a life easily rationalized by the notion that she states repeatedly: If she was not doing this kind of business, someone else would. So what?

Maybe the movie is about being uncomfortable in one's own skin. It opens with shots of unglamorous breasts being pressed under glass for mammograms (Rebecca's job is as the technician in an office that performs them). Kate makes disparaging remarks about her aging body; daughter Abby has a severe case of acne; the two sisters are always fighting about skin color and sun exposure; and Mary has a job giving facials (and apparently sex as well). It is somehow apt that almost everyone in this film is concerned about skin, because that is about as far as the movie goes: skin-deep and not much further.

Michael Betzold

CREDITS

Kate: Catherine Keener
Mary: Amanda Peet
Alex: Oliver Platt
Rebecca: Rebecca Hall
Andra: Ann Guilbert
Abby: Sarah Steele
Mrs. Portman: Lois Smith
Eugene: Thomas Ian Nicholas
Origin: USA
Language: English
Released: 2010
Production: Anthony Bregman; Likely Story; released by Sony Pictures Classics
Directed by: Nicole Holofcener
Written by: Nicole Holofcener
Cinematography by: Yaron Orbach
Music by: Marcelo Zarvos
Sound: Stuart Deutsch
Editing: Rob Frazen
Art Direction: Lauren Fitzsimmons
Costumes: Ane Crabtree
Production Design: Mark White
MPAA rating: R
Running time: 91 minutes

REVIEWS

Bell, Josh. *Las Vegas Weekly.* June 16, 2010.
Butler, Robert W. *Kansas City Star.* June 17, 2010.

Cohen, Keith. *Entertainment Spectrum.* June 20, 2010.
Collin, Robbie. *News of the World.* June 12, 2010.
Harley, Kevin. *Total Film.* June 11, 2010.
Kisonak, Rick *Film Threat.* June 16, 2010.
Martin, Philip. *Arkansas Democrat-Gazette.* June 18, 2010.
MacDonald, Moira. *Seattle Times.* June 17, 2010.
O'Connell, Sean. *Hollywood News.* June 18, 2010.
Young, Graham. *Birmingham Post.* June 16, 2010.

QUOTES

Abby: "Ok, you like this? Do you have eyes on your face?"

TRIVIA

Author Sarah Vowell makes a brief cameo appearance as a shopper after the character Kate is seen reading Vowell's book *Assassination Vacation.*

AWARDS

Ind. Spirit 2011: Robert Altman Award
Nomination:
Ind. Spirit 2011: Screenplay
Writers Guild 2010: Orig. Screenplay.

PREDATORS

The hunt is on.
      —Movie tagline

Box Office: $52 million

The cinematic world has no shortage of movies about teams of roughnecks assembled by outside forces to achieve a common goal that, if accomplished, will earn them some sort of reward, freedom or recognition. Sometimes, the members of said team are criminals; other times, they are military types or private contractors with specialties in weapons, explosives, hand-to-hand combat, or flower arranging. Ever the equal-opportunity employers, *Predators* producer Robert Rodriguez and director Nimród Antal have pulled together a motley crew that draws its members from all of these backgrounds, dropped them on a planet that is most definitely not Earth, and pitted them against an alien race whose sole purpose seems to be improving the way they fight against and kill anything that is not them.

If this scenario sounds remotely familiar, that is because *Predators* is a sequel of sorts to the John McTiernan-directed *Predator* (1987), starring Arnold Schwarzenegger. (Rodriguez decided to pretend that the sequel, *Predator 2* [1990], and the pair of *Alien vs. Predator* films [2004, 2007] never happened.) Rather than cast a group of thick-necked action types, the *Predators* filmmakers have opted for hiring strong actors, led by

Adrien Brody's Royce, to sell this story as equal parts science-fiction thriller and character study.

The characters are literally dropped into the story, as they fall onto this mystery jungle planet one-by-one as if they have been tossed from a plane. Most of them get their wits about them in mid-plummet to notice they are wearing parachutes with ripcords that seem to function just fine. Although many come from different nations, the factor each of the characters have in common is that most are military-trained. Since Royce is the American, he gets to be in charge. It does not take the team long to realize that they are being hunted by an extremely deadly unseen force on what they describe as a "game preserve" planet. Other members of the team include Alice Braga as the token badass Israeli assassin, Oleg Taktarov as a Russian ex-military, Danny Trejo as a Mexican professional kidnapper, Louis Ozawa Changchien as a Yakuza, Mahershalalhashbaz Ali as an African soldier, the scene-stealing Walton Goggins as a death-row inmate, and Topher Grace as a geeky doctor, who seems suspiciously out of place in this situation.

With his earlier films *Kontrol* (2003) and *Armored* (2009), director Antal proved that he can take a solid B-movie plot and provide the necessary strong cast, energy, violence, and compromised morals to make something highly entertaining. *Predators* feels like Antal finally got the chance to cut loose in this candy store and involve himself in a world that he clearly has been a fan of since being bowled over by the original film as a youngster. It is a rare pleasure to be able to sense a director's enthusiasm quite as palpably as Antal's shines through this material. This experience does not always mean the resulting film will be good, but it certainly is a step in the right direction to know the filmmaker feels a sense of responsibility to make a movie worthy of its predecessor.

Viewers learn early on that even the lives of the most familiar faces are not necessarily safe. Antal is also not above surprising them by introducing characters and plot twists in places where most filmmakers would consider it strange. For example, Laurence Fishburne shows up in *Predators* at about the halfway point as Noland, a character whose very existence introduces a great deal of information to the story at a point when the audience might be expecting the action to start ramping up, which it does soon after. Antal is without a doubt a strong director with an undeniable sense of pacing and raising the stakes with each new action sequence, but it is his refusal to always conform to conventional storytelling methods that gets him into trouble as often as it throws unexpected curve balls.

Predators as a whole feels like a great first two-thirds of a longer film, with a missing third act that truly would have driven it into the stratosphere of greatness. That is a shame because the film's parting images, which may have been intended to set up a sequel, look like the beginning of a truly awesome climactic battle that we never see. Even so, the performances—particularly from Brody, Braga, and Fishburne—are so loaded with gravity that it is difficult to dismiss the entire film because of a poorly-executed conclusion. Antal and Rodriguez do an admirable job introducing new twists to the predator myth, including several new varieties of the alien hunters and some beautifully-designed weaponry, while still paying tribute to the original predator from the original film.

The other problematic issue with the film is the script's unquenchable desire to over-explain everything. *Predators* might have been a whole lot more intriguing with a few less answers. With very little information, these seemingly smart characters figure out an awful lot. And as enjoyable as he is, Fishburne's Noland character seems invented for no other purpose than to answer the questions the team members could never have figured out on their own. Even still, there is enough creativity and spirit pushing through to the surface in *Predators* to warrant checking it out.

Steven Prokopy

CREDITS

Royce: Adrien Brody
Noland: Laurence Fishburne
Edwin: Topher Grace
Isabelle: Alice Braga
Cuchillo: Danny Trejo
Stans: Walton Goggins
Mombasa: Mahershalalhashbaz Ali
Nikolai: Oleg Taktarov
Hanzo: Louis Ozawa Changchien
Origin: USA
Language: English
Released: 2010
Production: Elizabeth Avellan, John Davis, Robert Rodriguez; Troublemaker Studios, Davis Entertainment Company; released by 20th Century Fox
Directed by: Nimród Antal
Written by: Michael Finch, Alex Litvak
Cinematography by: Gyula Pados
Music by: John Debney
Sound: Paula Fairfield, Carla Murray
Editing: Dan Zimmerman
Costumes: Nina Proctor
Production Design: Caylah Eddleblute, Steve Joyner
MPAA rating: R
Running time: 107 minutes

REVIEWS

Abrams, Simon. *Slant Magazine.* July 8, 2010.
Biancolli, Amy. *San Francisco Chronicle.* July 9, 2010.
Ebert, Roger. *Chicago Sun-Times.* July 7, 2010.
Edwards, David. *Daily Mirror.* July 9, 2010.
Holden, Stephen. *New York Times.* July 8, 2010.
Holtreman, Vic. *ScreenRant.com.* July 8, 2010.
Puig, Claudia. *USA Today.* July 10, 2010.
Rechtshaffen, Michael. *Hollywood Reporter.* July 8, 2010.
Wallick, Buz. *DreadCentral.com.* July 8. 2010.
Weinberg, Scott. *Fearnet.com.* July 9, 2010.

QUOTES

Royce: "We're being hunted. The cages. The soldier. All of us. All brought here for the same purpose. This planet is a game preserve. And we're the game. In case you didn't notice, we just got flushed out. They sent the dogs in, just like you if you were stalking boar or shooting quail. They split us apart and they watched. Testing us."

TRIVIA

Despite initial rumors that he would direct the film, Robert Rodriguez produced the film through his Troublemaker Studios, shooting a majority of the film in his native Texas in order to receive a tax credit.

PRINCE OF PERSIA: THE SANDS OF TIME

Defy the future.
—Movie tagline

Box Office: $91 million

The perceived prejudice when it comes to video games being adapted into feature length cinematic excursions is one of the few that has earned its rightful scorn. The *Mortal Kombat* (1995), *Tomb Raider* (2001), and *Resident Evil* (2002) series are just part of a nearly full exhibit of time-wasters. In some ancient scroll there is probably the revelation of a curse that has befallen the translation of this entertainment once the tomb of the *Super Mario Brothers* (1993) was unearthed for live-action consumption. What else could possibly explain why so many producers, writers, and directors have been unable to capture the guns-a-blazing, butt-kicking simplicity of a video game? And if there is not already, someone would be wise to summon the unholiest of presences to place one in the wake of *Prince of Persia: The Sands of Time,* an epic bore of an adventure in the loosest sense of the term.

The story opens with a street urchin named Dastan (Jake Gyllenhaal) who is adopted by the almighty King (Ronald Pickup) after the boy stands up to his guards.

The addition to their family is hardly challenged by the King's brother and trusted advisor, Nizam (Ben Kingsley) or elder son, Tus (Richard Coyle), though second son Garsiv (Toby Kebbell) clearly shares some animosity towards him for some unexplained reason. Growing into warriors, the sons take point on an attack on the holy city of Alamut believed to be creating weapons for their enemies. Dastan jumps the gun on a backdoor strategy and thus secures the victory for his family despite an objective that now appears dubiously misguided.

The only weapon anyone can seem to find is one that the Princess Tamina (Gemma Arterton) is trying to smuggle out; a fancy dagger that Dastan intercepts and keeps as a trophy. At the victory party where Tamina is to be promised in marriage to Tus, a gift presented to the King is poisoned. As Dastan is the one who handed it to him, he is instantly blamed for his death and flees for his life with Tamina leading the way. While evading capture, Dastan comes upon a neat trick instilled within the dagger. Press the ruby top and the possessor can turn back time just long enough to correct an error in judgment or avoid unwanted piercing by sharp objects. Just as long as the magical Sands of Time remain in the crystal handle. Perhaps a motive now exists for the invasion after all.

The reasoning behind the plot is sketchy both as a grand master plan and in terms of some modern political allegory about our own country's impulses for invasion. For simple plotting purposes, the story's not-so-secret villain wants the dagger in order to control time and snatch the lineage of power away from his family. How this translates into killing the King in present time is anyone's guess since the task would just have to be repeated once time is reversed. To put it into modern terms, it is the equivalent of the machines killing John Connor in the future and then still sending a Terminator back to do it in 1984. The point is it remains a stupid plan in any year, but not nearly as misguided as trying to turn the loose structure of a video game into a testimonial on the failed hunt for weapons of mass destruction. "You need more then intuition to occupy a holy city," says a father to his son in a scene that would not have been out of place amidst the patriarchal attitudes reflected in Oliver Stone's *W.* (2008).

The adherence of *Prince of Persia* to the running, jumping, and climbing aesthetic of the video game may as well be taking place on a treadmill or in a grade school gymnasium. Special effects were designed to make the impossible possible and occasionally ease the poor burden on the stuntmen breaking their bones to live out death-defying feats before our very eyes. The recent art of parkour appears to make a cameo in the action sequences, but there is so little sense of scope that all that is seen are close-ups of fast moving bodies with frequent slow-motion shots enhanced by CGI wizardry. There is no need for a pause button here since if the viewer missed something he actually wanted to see or hear, it will come around again soon enough.

The mantra of repetition is the credo of screenwriters Boaz Yakin, Doug Miro, and Carlo Bernard but even it is inconsistent. For example, one of Dastan's allies turns out to be the comic relief stamp of Alfred Molina's Sheik Amar who informs him twice during their encounters about the deadly accuracy of his knife-throwing henchmen. When Amar wants to stop an escaping bandit through his ostrich races, he cautions Seso (Steve Toussaint), his champion of the impalement arts, not to throw because he "might kill a bird." That is an easy enough continuity error to catch if one's ears have not been turned off for good with the monotony over who has the dagger, who wants the dagger, what the dagger is and who was been entrusted to protect it. When *Pirates of the Caribbean: Dead Man's Chest* (2006) stuffed a trilogy's worth of exposition out of characters' pasts and their motivations for obtaining either a compass, a key, or what is in the chest, their writers did it with a unique wit using Jack Sparrow's nefarious logic to purposely disorient viewers to his intentions. *Prince of Persia*'s walk-a-mile descriptions of the plot will have gamers searching for their controller so they can fast forward to the action only to be disappointed again.

The camera movements in the first ambush suggest the pan-and-scanning of a video game map and the performances from the leading man and lady seem far more dependent on recreating the sheen of today's virtual renditions than actually giving the characters some semblance of life. Gyllenhaal projects frequent goofy grins as if his motor skills cannot help but display the disbelief that he is being paid for this non-performance. As for Arterton's own mouth, it is a beautiful one, as is the rest of her face. But it is her lips doing all the sneering over-acting to register the Princess' contempt in nearly every scene. She might be able to fool lusty fanboys with that accent for a while, but like Gyllenhaal, big budget spectacles are clearly not a good fit for her.

For all the nonsensical talk about destiny written into the script and across the very screen, if such were the truth in store for our heroes, would there really be a magical element that would erase said fate with the push of a button? The destiny of *Prince of Persia* is to wallow under the boots and sandals of so many superior or just plain fun swashbuckling entities both young and old. Technology may have replaced good old-fashioned stunt work, but it will be easy to reevaluate knee-jerk criticisms of Stephen Sommers' *Mummy* films and *Pirates of the Caribbean: At World's End* (2007) since they are films that managed to explore a brand of old-world excite-ment with some ingenuity in-between the special effects. Director Mike Newell, better known for more character-based entities like *Four Weddings and a Funeral* (1994) and *Donnie Brasco* (1997), displayed a touch of flair for blending that touch with spectacle for an already-established franchise in *Harry Potter and the Goblet of Fire* (2004). With paper-thin characters from top-to-bottom and a complete avoidance of anything resembling the kind of action sequence one might want to story-board, Newell is nothing more than a guy on the dock lucky enough to be chosen for a day's work.

Those whose faculties have not been deadened by the nothingness of this film will never include it within a continent's throw of the Indiana Jones series that clearly inspired it and even shared a collaborator. It may shock anyone still around for the closing credits that Steven Spielberg's editor since *Close Encounters of the Third Kind* (1977), Michael Kahn, is listed as one of the three entrusted with this footage. One can only work with the lack of choreography and all the close-ups in the action scenes that they are given. During a scene where Tamina closes off Dastan during a narrow pathway chase with Alfred Molina bringing up the rear and offers clear passage in exchange for the treasured dagger, we can assume that Kahn's whole purpose on the project was to eliminate any forthcoming in-joke to *Raiders of the Lost Ark* (1981) to ward off any comparison whatsoever. In the same year when the remake of *Clash of the Titans* (2010) had already set the bar pretty low, to watch *Prince of Persia* limbo right under it makes one long for possession of the fabled dagger if only to erase memories of the action-adventure genre from the year.

Erik Childress

CREDITS

Prince Dastan: Jake Gyllenhaal
Princess Tamina: Gemma Arterton
Nizam: Ben Kingsley
Sheik Amar: Alfred Molina
Garsiv: Toby Kebbell
Seso: Steve Toussaint
Tus: Richard Coyle
King Sharaman: Ronald Pickup
Origin: USA
Language: English
Released: 2010
Production: Jerry Bruckheimer; released by Walt Disney Pictures
Directed by: Mike Newell
Written by: Doug Miro, Carlo Bernard, Boaz Yakin
Cinematography by: John Seale

Music by: Harry Gregson-Williams

Editing: Mick Audsley, Michael Kahn, Martin Walsh

Sound: Timothy Nielsen

Costumes: Penny Rose

Production Design: Wolf Kroeger

MPAA rating: PG-13

Running time: 116 minutes

REVIEWS

Burr, Ty. *Boston Globe.* May 27, 2010.

Denby, David. *New Yorker.* May 24, 2010.

Ebert, Roger. *Chicago Sun-Times.* May 27, 2010.

Phillips, Michael. *Chicago Tribune.* May 27, 2010.

Roeper, Richard. *RichardRoeper.com.* May 28, 2010.

Schwarzbaum, Lisa. *Entertainment Weekly.* May 26, 2010.

Sharkey, Betsy. *Los Angeles Times.* May 27, 2010.

Tallerico, Brian. *MovieRetriever.com.* May 29, 2010.

Uhlich, Keith. *Time Out New York.* May 26, 2010.

Utichi, Joe. *Cinematical.* May 14, 2010.

QUOTES

Prince Dastan: "What temple? This is a pile of stones and rocks!"

Tamina: "It's gone. Protect the dagger no matter the consequences; that was my sacred calling. That was my destiny."

TRIVIA

Both Orlando Bloom and Zac Efron were rumored to star as Dastan, before the part in the end went to Jake Gyllenhaal whom director Mike Newell stated he had known since he was 7 years old and always wanted for the part.

A PROPHET

(Un prophète)

Box Office: $2 million

Like Boaz Yakin's *Fresh* (1994), Jacques Audiard's *A Prophet* places a powerless protagonist in a seemingly impossible dilemma and then reveals how by manipulating his adversaries like chess pieces, he maneuvers himself out of that dilemma. How much the viewer enjoys Audiard's superbly-directed film will depend on the value he or she assigns to how masterfully the chess pieces are manipulated versus how much he or she cares about the protagonist manipulating them.

A Prophet does an excellent job of seemingly checkmating its unfortunate protagonist. Malik El Djebena (Tahar Rahim) is a young Frenchman of Arabic descent sentenced to six years in prison for assaulting a police officer. Once he arrives at his new home he faces the depressing reality that prisons are the same everywhere. The prison is ruled by murderous gangs segregated by race and ethnicity. The prison guards and authorities are, at best indifferent, and at worst corrupt. In Malik's prison, Muslims and Corsicans vie for power. The Corsicans are ruled by a white-haired sociopath kingpin named César Luciani (a deceptively grandfatherly-looking Niels Arestrup). This is the hellish environment in which Malik must struggle to survive, a world completely devoid of compassion, consisting only of victims and victimizers. Audiard's prison is about as far from the romantic depiction of prison in *The Shawshank Redemption* (1994) as it is possible to get.

Malik's arrival coincides with the arrival of another Arab prisoner, Reyeb (Hichem Yacoubi), who has been placed in the prison temporarily as he awaits a trial in which he is to testify as a witness. César and his murderous underlings want him dead to prevent that testimony from taking place but they cannot get close to him. When César learns that Reyeb has propositioned Malik in the shower (marijuana in exchange for oral sex) he provides the friendless and powerless Malik with a choice that is not a choice at all: kill Reyeb or we kill you. This proves to be a fateful ultimatum for all involved parties.

Unsurprisingly, Malik accepts his assignment and soon he is alone with Reyeb with a concealed razorblade in his mouth, trying to work up the courage to do the last thing in the world he wants to do. This scene between Malik and Reyeb is a masterpiece of suspense and heartbreak as Malik tries to delay his decision while the blade in his mouth forces that decision by cutting into his mouth, causing him to bleed, threatening to reveal his deception. The unsuspecting Reyeb does not make Malik's dilemma any easier by being surprisingly gentle and kind. The attack, when it inevitably comes, is spectacularly savage, prolonged and traumatic for both Malik and the viewer.

Once Malik completes his grim task, César begrudgingly provides him with protection, making him the group's menial servant while continually reminding Malik that he thinks nothing of him and he lives at his whim: "He's not one of us. Let him clean up if you want. But when he's done, he's out. Dirty Arab!" However, Malik is far more intelligent and cunning than his master's reflexive racism allows for and understands his environment and masters far better than they know. Malik views his new position, degrading as it is and unasked for though it may have been, as an opportunity to use his users even more than they are using him and one of the great pleasures of the film is seeing the clever and subtle ways he extricates himself from his trap while setting a trap for his tormentors, using their greed, arrogance, and racism against them. What outwardly appears to be simply a desire to improve himself through education, learning how to read (ironically a suggestion of Reyeb), enables Malik to learn Corsican which allows him to understand everything that is said around him (the Corsicans' racism does not allow them to entertain the notion that an Arab might be intelligent enough to learn their language and so they speak freely around him thinking he cannot understand). When Malik's short sentence enables César to arrange day passes for him, which allow him out of the prison during the day, Malik not only completes the dangerous and unsavory assignments César forces him to do, but uses the opportunity to increase his own power by initiating his own criminal enterprises on the side; the proceeds of which enable Malik to buy his way into the Muslims' gang and secure their protection. And what seems to be an order that will forever cement César's hold on Malik (an order to assassinate César's superior on the outside) turns out to be the key to Malik's freedom. Step by step, piece by piece, Malik ingeniously reverses the check mate, engineering his rise and César's fall, all under the watchful, distrustful gaze of his wrathful master. Indeed, although the central relationship of the film is between Malik and César (both performances are brilliant), there is nothing resembling trust or respect between the two. César could not have more contempt for his servant or care less about how the tasks he forces him to complete might jeopardize Malik's own morality or well being. Malik: "Want to know how I feel?" César: "I couldn't care less." Later, he emphasizes this by partially digging out Malik's eye with a spoon.

A Prophet's only flaw is that it never provides a particularly-compelling reason to identify with Malik or care about his fate. Malik is a cipher and the film's script does not provide him with the depth necessary to make him much more than a hand moving chess pieces. Since the film is otherwise superior in all respects, it is likely that this lack of depth is intentional on Audiard and fellow screenwriter Thomas Bidegain's part to illustrate how an unformed teenage personality is molded into that of a sophisticated criminal by the ruthless environment in which it is forced to develop. Indeed, Malik has not only engineered his escape and exacted revenge on the criminals that entrapped him but has become a criminal kingpin in his own right. The end of the film is presented as a triumph and, by the grim standards of the world it depicts, it is. However it is hard to celebrate it as a success for Malik. He has survived and prospered but one wonders how long it will be before he is giving a choice to someone else that is not a choice at all.

Nate Vercauteren

CREDITS

César Luciani: Niels Arestrup
Malik El Djebena: Tahar Rahim
Ryad: Adel Bencherif
Prof: Gilles Cohen
Pilicci: Antoine Basler
Jordi: Reda Kateb
Reyeb: Hichem Yacoubi
Vettori: Jean-Philippe Ricci
Sampiero: Pierre Leccia
Origin: France, Italy
Language: Arabic, French
Released: 2009
Production: Lauranne Bourrachot, Martine Cassinelli, Marco Cherqui; Celluloid Dreams, Bim Distribuzione, Why Not Productions, Chic Films, Page 114; released by Sony Pictures Classics
Directed by: Jacques Audiard
Written by: Jacques Audiard, Thomas Bidegain
Cinematography by: Stephane Fontaine
Music by: Alexandre Desplot
Sound: Brigitte Taillandier, Brigitte Taillandier, Francis Wargnier
Editing: Juliette Welfing
Costumes: Virginie Montel
Production Design: Michel Barthelemy
MPAA rating: R
Running time: 155 minutes

REVIEWS

Baumgarten, Marjorie. *Austin Chronicle.* March 19, 2010.
Dargis, Manohla. *New York Times.* February 26, 2010.
Ebert, Roger. *Chicago Sun-Times.* March 3, 2010.
Edelstein, David. *New York Magazine.* February 12, 2010.
Murray, Noel. *AV Club.* February 25, 2010.
Nelson, Rob. *Village Voice.* February 23, 2010.
O'Hehir, Andrew. *Salon.com.* February 25, 2010.
Rea, Steven. *Philadelphia Inquirer.* March 12, 2010.
Turan, Kenneth. *Los Angeles Times.* February 26, 2010.
Travers, Peter. *Rolling Stone.* February 25, 2010.

TRIVIA

Writer/director Jacques Audiard hired former convicts as advisers and extras to ensure the authenticity of the prison experience.

AWARDS

British Acad. 2009: Foreign Film
Nomination:
Oscars 2009: Foreign Film
Golden Globes 2010: Foreign Film
Ind. Spirit 2010: Foreign Film.

R

RABBIT HOLE

The only way out is through.
—Movie tagline
Love will get you through.
—Movie tagline

Box Office: $2 million

There is no road map of relativity for the loss of a young child. It is not something for which anyone can utter the overused phrase "I know how you feel" unless they have too experienced the pain of not dying before an offspring. No parent should watch their child die. And the lack of ability to relate to such a horrendous experience has created more than a few melodramatic pieces of cinema over the years, films that felt designed more to manipulatively tug at the heartstrings than create anything genuine because to approach such a subject truthfully is to approach something emotionally devastating. One of the most remarkable things about John Cameron Mitchell's excellent *Rabbit Hole* is how little of it could be called manipulative. It is a genuine drama in a subgenre that rarely produces such emotionally believable, character-driven material and it is helped ably not only by Mitchell's surprisingly restrained approach to storytelling but his incredible ability to coax spectacular performances from a fantastic ensemble. Headlined by what would have be considered near the top of any conversation regarding the best work of Oscar® winner Nicole Kidman's acclaimed career, *Rabbit Hole* was one of the best dramas of 2010.

Where most other writers focus on the immediate aftermath or even the act of the death of a child to commonly-manipulative ends, David Lindsay-Abaire, working from his own play, takes on the more-challenging emotional minefield of a couple dealing with such a tragedy months after the horrifying event. As relatives turn to other events in their own lives, support groups become repetitive, and even the young man responsible for the death of Becca (Nicole Kidman) and Howie's (Aaron Eckhart) son Danny plans the next chapter in his life, the parents seem stuck in stasis. Howie stays up late watching videos of happier times while Becca cannot stand the constant reminders of Danny that she sees everywhere. She even got rid of the family dog, blaming it for the accident. If Becca needs help transitioning, Howie needs help with closure. Lindsay-Abaire's wonderful screenplay dares to suggest that perhaps parents could respond differently to the loss of a child and not devolve into screaming, melodramatic fights. There is tension in Becca and Howie's relationship but the film seems understanding of their different responses when it could have easily condemned one or the other, turning him or her into a villain.

Becca finally gives up on therapy after hearing one too many times that Heaven needed another angel but Howie continues to go and finds himself drawn closer to another grieving mother (Sandra Oh) who also finds herself without her better half. A dangerous flirtation ensues. Meanwhile, Becca's sister (Tammy Blanchard) seems to be moving on with her life, something that aggravates Becca without her even consciously understanding why. It does not help Becca's family situation that she seems constantly at odds with her mother Nat (Dianne Wiest), a woman who wants to reach out and identify with Becca considering that she too lost a son, but her daughter refuses to see the common ground of having an adult child overdose on drugs as her brother did and the tragedy that befell her family. One day, Becca spots Jason (Miles Teller), the young man who accidentally destroyed her life when he hit Danny with his car. Becca begins to stalk Jason, following him home from school until the shy teenager confronts her and the two begin an awkward friendship. Jason is writing a comic book called *Rabbit Hole* about a vision of myriad universes, including, although it is never directly stated, one in which he never drove down that road and emotionally devastated his own life as well.

On paper, *Rabbit Hole* sounds like a medley of melodramatic clichés, but Lindsay-Abaire and Mitchell take an extremely restrained approach. Mitchell, who employed a much more manic style in his *Hedwig and the Angry Inch* (2001) and *Shortbus* (2006) shows remarkable cinematic restraint with his third film, shooting several scenes without flourish at all and sometimes even with a static camera that invokes a fly-on-the-wall aesthetic. Mitchell clearly knew that the strength of the material and the performances he drew from the cast would carry the film without the extreme visual tricks of his previous films. And so he allows the focus to rest on the ensemble, doing so much by doing little.

The performances are uniformly stellar. Since winning her Oscar® for *The Hours* (2002), Nicole Kidman has made a few ill-advised career decisions including junk like *The Stepford Wives* (2004), *Bewitched* (2005), and *The Invasion* (2007), and it is spectacular to see her back in prime form, delivering such a nuanced performance that an Academy Award® nomination seemed inevitable (and, thankfully, she was not snubbed). Kidman imbues Becca with just the right amount of grief, refusing to devolve into the histrionics that would have been tempting for lesser actresses. She recognizes that Becca feels immense pain but does not express it in the way that most movie characters seem required to do. She does it with a downward gaze, a withering glance, and a pursed lip. It is truly one of the best performances of 2010 and were it not the year of "Bening vs. Portman" (for *The Kids Are All Right* [2010] and *Black Swan* [2010], respectively), Kidman's performance would have received far more widespread recognition than it did.

Kidman is not alone. Aaron Eckhart does some of the most emotionally complex and subtle work of his career as his typically-suave exterior requires a bit of breaking down. He handles the key moments with enough acting expertise that he earned an Independent Spirit Award nomination. Dianne Wiest delivers one of her career's best performances with a subtle, beautiful piece of work as a woman who tries to build a bridge to her distant daughter but finds herself pushed even further away. The entire cast, including newcomer Teller

and supporting turns by Oh and Blanchard, deserves praise.

The death of a child is the kind of manipulative device that rarely produces cinema that feels genuine. It is a common subject for cheap writers using emotional tricks to pull at the heartstrings. What is so remarkable about *Rabbit Hole* is how, through a combination of the contributions of an award-worthy ensemble, an honest screenplay, and restrained direction, the film never once feels manipulative. Two-thousand and ten was a year for intellectual dramas like *The Social Network* (2010) and *Inception* (2010), which made the raw, heartbreaking honesty of *Rabbit Hole* all the more resonant.

Brian Tallerico

CREDITS

Becca: Nicole Kidman
Howie: Aaron Eckhart
Nat: Dianne Wiest
Jason: Miles Teller
Izzy: Tammy Blanchard
Gaby: Sandra Oh
Auggie: Giancarlo Esposito
Rick: Jon Tenney
Origin: USA
Language: English
Released: 2010
Production: Gigi Pritzker, Nicole Kidman, Per Saari PRO, Leslie Urdang, Dean Vanech; Olympus Pictures, Blossom Pictures, Odd Lot Entainment, Lionsgate
Directed by: John Cameron Mitchell
Written by: David Lindsay-Abaire
Cinematography by: Frank DeMarco
Music by: Anton Sanko
Sound: Jan McLaughlin
Music Supervisor: Robin Urdang
Editing: Joe Klotz
Art Direction: Ola Maslik
Costumes: Ann Roth
Production Design: Kalina Ivanov
MPAA rating: PG-13
Running time: 91 minutes

REVIEWS

Ansen, David. *Newsweek.* December 13, 2010.
Charity, Tom. *CNN.com* December 17, 2010.
Corliss, Richard. *TIME Magazine.* December 13, 2010.
Debruge, Peter. *Variety.* September 15, 2010.
Edelstein, David. *New York Magazine.* December 20, 2010.
Phillips, Michael. *Chicago Tribune.* December 23, 2010.
Rich, Katey. *CinemaBlend.com.* December 7, 2010.
Rocchi, James. *MSN Movies.* December 16, 2010.

Turan, Kenneth. *Los Angeles Times.* December 16, 2010.
Weinberg, Scott. *Cinematical.* September 19, 2010.

TRIVIA

This film was shot in 28 days.

This is the first film produced by Nicole Kidman in which she also has a leading role.

AWARDS

Nomination:

Oscars 2010: Actress (Kidman)

Golden Globes 2011: Actress—Drama (Kidman)

Ind. Spirit 2011: Actor (Eckhart), Actress (Kidman), Director (Mitchell), Screenplay

Screen Actors Guild 2010: Actress (Kidman).

RAMONA AND BEEZUS

A little sister goes a long way.
—Movie tagline

Box Office: $26 million

Ramona and Beezus is an increasingly-rare breed of film that long ago was not so rare: A G-rated, live action film aimed at kids that does not have anything computer generated in a single shot, nor is it in 3-D. Rarer still, it presents kids as real kids and adults as real adults. While the movie is about a precocious young girl and her over-active imagination and how she copes with being a middle child, it is not a kids' fantasy where kids get the upper hand and adults wind up with egg on their faces. It is about finding that balance in being a nine-year-old who has to "grow up" while still having childlike impulses. The film is nowhere nearly as heavy-handed or as brilliant as the similarly-themed *Where the Wild Things Are* (2009), but it still depicts childhood and all of its benchmarks realistically and with intelligence.

The movie is based on a series of books by Beverly Cleary, a series which still enjoys a modest popularity among young readers, in spite of the fact that many of them were published fifty or more years ago. Like many of her books, *Ramona and Beezus* takes place on Klickitat Street in Portland, Oregon. The characters have names that today sound too cute and may be a little dated in pure Youth Literature terms. Yet, this is a film that does not make any attempt to comment on how times have changed since Cleary wrote her books, nor does it need to. It stays focused on the themes of the books themselves, that of childhood struggles and changes that are universal, no matter what decade.

Ramona and Beezus is more about Ramona, really. Most of the story is told from her point of view while also delving into her active imagination. When she hangs from the monkey bars, she imagines herself dangling above large streams of water emitting gigantic waves alongside towering mountains. It is her way of testing her own bravery. "If you cannot be brave during recess," she states, "how can you do it when it really counts?" In school, she gets in trouble for making up words like "terrific" and "funner" instead of using the important spelling bee words she is supposed to use at least once a day during school hours, at the insistence of her sensible schoolteacher, Mrs. Meacham (Sandra Oh).

Her home life appears to be made up of little more than Good Cheer. Her parents Robert and Dorothy (Bridget Moynahan and John Corbett) are a nice middle-class couple and her older sister Beezus (Selena Gomez) is a teenager facing her first real crush while trying to shake off the name her sister gave her a long time ago (her real name is Beatrice). Ramona also has a little baby sister named Roberta and an Aunt Bea (Ginnifer Goodwin) who lives nearby and is like another older sister. Living next door to her is handsome and hunky Hobart (Josh Duhamel), an old high school fling still pining for Bea, which periodically gives the movie a romantic comedy flavor.

Why make a movie about a person whose life is clearly idyllic? To a typical nine-year-old, life is anything but. Her father has just lost his job and it is quite possible the bank will take the house (which Ramona imagines in literal terms). The awkwardly-dressed Ramona gets blamed for just about every mishap that takes place in her world when it remains clear that nothing was her fault. In fact, she is almost always trying to help. Her older sister tries mightily to look cool while trying to win the heart of Howie (Jason Spevack), but when an incident involving Ramona's lemonade stand results in Beezus spitting juice all over Henry, the anger towards Ramona's existence in Beezus' life becomes clearer.

If none of this sounds like the stuff of high drama, it is because director Elizabeth Allen and screenwriters Laurie Craig and Nick Pustay treat the material with an appropriate amount of detachment. This is a film not unlike *A Christmas Story* (1983) or *Diary of a Wimpy Kid* (2010). It is an anecdotal film using the benchmarks of childhood as its through-line. The writers have borrowed storylines from more than one of the *Ramona* books and have therefore successfully given the audience a glimpse into the life of a nine-year-old, one that will resonate with kids as well as adults.

The appealing cast helps tremendously. As Ramona, Joey King gives a confident and pitch-perfect performance. She does not come off as over-coached or too cute. Her performance is charming while still being grounded in reality. Ginnifer Goodwin and Josh Du-hamel make the most of their moments together, especially a scene in which they sit in a car and talk while Ramona and her friend wash it on the outside. The scene is surprisingly leisurely and convincing for a film of this type. The worst that can be said for the cast is that John Corbett comes off a little too wholesome at times and could stand to take it down a notch or two.

Director Allen has the same problem many directors in this realm have, which is letting the score run overtime to try and punctuate every comical build-up or mishap. Thankfully, those moments are few and far between. Allen seems otherwise perfectly in tune with the material. Unlike *Diary of a Wimpy Kid* earlier in the year, *Ramona and Beezus* does not shy away from darker moments of childhood, such as the first brush with death. At a time when many films aimed at younger viewers try to become more and more fantastical by having a protagonist discover magical powers that will help save the world, *Ramona and Beezus* reminds the viewer that childhood can, in itself, be a series of fantastical discoveries and that sometimes the world's biggest problems can be solved with a simple lemonade stand.

Collin Souter

CREDITS

Ramona Quimby: Joey King
Beezus Quimby: Selena Gomez
Bob Quimby: John Corbett
Dorothy Quimby: Bridget Moynahan
Aunt Bea: Ginnifer Goodwin
Uncle Hobart: Josh Duhamel
Mrs. Meacham: Sandra Oh
Henry Huggins: Hutch Dano
Howie Kemp: Jason Spevack
Grandma Kemp: Janet Wright
Susan: Sierra McCormick
Origin: USA
Language: English
Released: 2010
Production: Denise Di Novi, Alison Greenspan; Walden Media, Di Novi Pictures, Fox 2000 Pictures; released by 20th Century Fox
Directed by: Elizabeth Allen
Written by: Laurie Craig, Nick Pustav
Cinematography by: John Bailey
Music by: Mark Mothersbaugh
Sound: Shane Connelly
Music Supervisor: Julia Michels
Editing: Jane Moran
Art Direction: Shannon Grover

Costumes: Patricia Louise Hargreaves
Production Design: Brent Thomas
MPAA rating: G
Running time: 103 minutes

REVIEWS

Anderson, Jason. *Toronto Star.* July 23, 2010.
Biancolli, Amy. *Houston Chronicle.* July 23, 2010.
Buckwalter, Ian. *NPR.* July 23, 2010.
Ebert, Roger. *Chicago Sun-Times.* July 22, 2010.
Lumenick, Lou. *New York Post.* July 23, 2010.
Phipps, Keith. *AV Club.* July 22, 2010.
Schager, Nick. *Village Voice.* July 20, 2010.
Schwarzbaum, Lisa. *Entertainment Weekly.* July 21, 2010.
Snider, Eric D. *Film.com.* July 23, 2010.
Whipp, Glenn. *Los Angeles Times.* July 22, 2010.

QUOTES

Mrs. Meacham: "I hope you are enjoying third grade. You may be here for a while."

Beezus: "Ramona, you're your own person. You don't care about coloring inside the lines."

TRIVIA

When Ramona started talking as an infant, she couldn't say "Beatrice." She said "Beezus" instead, which is explained in the television show and book.

[REC] 2

Fear revisited.
—Movie tagline

Picking up mere minutes from the end of the original Spanish production *[REC]* (2008)—remade by Hollywood as *Quarantine* (2009)—this equally freaky and terrifying sequel from writers/directors Jaume Bal-agueró and Paco Plaza centers on a sealed-off apartment complex at the mercy of what appears to be a virus that turns its victims into raging, flesh-eating maniacs that either kill their victims or spread their disease by biting them. In the original film, the plot unfolded through the camera lens of television reporter Angela Vidal (Manuela Velasco) and her crew following a group of fire-fighters sent to the ground-zero apartment complex in the early stages of the outbreak. The tension created through this hand-held, first-person narrative was palpable, and the use of shadows and light often limited to the bulb atop the camera provided classic horror scares that made audiences as terrified of what they could not see as what they could.

Since the final shot of *[REC]* was of Angela being dragged off into the darkness by an unknown evil force behind the virus, the filmmakers have replaced her camera with multiple cameras attached to the helmets of a SWAT team sent into the apartment building to take control of the situation. They bring with them a Ministry of Health medical officer Dr. Owen (Jonathan Mellor), who hopes to collect evidence of this unknown virus for study and turns out to know a little more about the force that has gripped the residents. What's fascinating about the filmmakers' approach to returning to and expanding this world that they created originally is that the audience actually does learn more about the source of this horrific phenomenon without straying too far from the context they set up in the first movie. There are definitely a few surprises that reveal themselves and the plot takes some turns that may have some rolling their eyes. Still, fans of the first film will probably go right along for the ride they began two years earlier. Unlike many inferior sequels, played back to back, *[REC]* and *[REC] 2* would make an excellent double feature.

Not having to deal with the slow-building tension of watching the disease spread as they did in the first film, Balagueró and Plaza dive right into the scares that come courtesy of not just zombie-like attacks but also from more faith-based terrors that hint that possession might be a factor in this onslaught. *[REC] 2* owes as much of a debt to *The Exorcist* (1973) as the first film did to *28 Days Later* (2002) or any George Romero-directed zombie movie. Since the infection-based attacks start right up this time around, the movie is relentless in its pacing, giving the viewers almost no time to breathe between intense moments of chaos.

The one exception to this occurs at the film's halfway point when the action is abruptly and deliberately interrupted when the SWAT team comes face to face with three teens wielding a video camera of their own. It turns out that the kids broke into the apartment complex through the sewer between it and the building next door. So, for a brief, interesting interlude, the timeline reverses itself just enough to bring us back to the moment when the two groups run into each other. The teens are a strong addition because, unlike the SWAT team members, they seem to have distinct personalities that allow audiences to have some identification with the characters.

[REC] 2 also finds clever ways to bring back characters from the original film (including the aforementioned Angela), either because the filmmakers never quite dealt with the fate of every single apartment dweller the first time around, or because the residents are now infected, so they return as blood-thirsty cannibals. Despite expanding the action slightly—and momentarily—outside the apartment building, the film still effectively maintains an undeniable claustrophobic feeling. And for fans of original, spectacularly gory kills, there are plenty of those for true horror-philes.

While most moviegoers, and in particular horror fans, might be tired of the faux-documentary/found-footage approach to genre, Balagueró and Plaza breathe some fresh life into the practice and do so in a way that actually seems feasible in the context of this outrageous and brutal story. It was clever to use picture-in-picture technology on occasion to show the vantage points of two SWAT team members at the same time. The filmmakers do not overuse it or allow it to become distracting or confusing, and they make the most of what some might say is a limiting way to tell any story. *[REC] 2* is one of the rare and wonderful examples of the horror sequel surpassing an already strong original. The scares are ramped up, the story digs deeper into the mythology established in the first film, and the performances are more focused, without being afraid to cut loose into the slightly insane every so often.

Steven Prokopy

CREDITS

Rosso: Pablo Rosso
Angela Vidal: Manuela Velasco
Dr. Owen: Jonathan Mellor
Jefe: Oscar Sanchez Zafra
Larra: Ariel Casas
Martos: Alejandro Casaseca
Mire: Andrea Ros
Ori: Alex Batllori
Tito: Pau Poch
Origin: Spain
Language: Spanish
Released: 2009
Production: Julio Fernandez; Castelao Proucciones, Filmax Entertainment; released by Magnet Releasing
Directed by: Jaume Balagueró, Paco Plaza
Written by: Jaume Balagueró, Paco Plaza, Manu Diez
Cinematography by: Pablo Rosso
Sound: Oriol Tarrago
Editing: David Gallart
Art Direction: Gemma Fauria
Costumes: Gloria Viguer
MPAA rating: R
Running time: 84 minutes

REVIEWS

Adams, Sam. *Philadelphia Citypaper.* September 23, 2009.
Berkshire, Geoff. *Metromix.com.* July 8, 2010.
Biancolli, Amy. *San Francisco Chronicle.* July 16, 2010.
Brown, Todd. *TwitchFilm.com.* September 25, 2009.
Catsoulis, Jeannette. *New York Times.* July 8, 2010.

Greenwood, Paul. *Alone in the Dark.* May 28, 2010.
Nelson, Rob. *Village Voice.* July 6, 2010.
Seaver, Jay. *efilmcritic.com.* July 25, 2010.
Shoyer, Scott. *Cinefantastique.* July 13, 2010.
Weinberg, Scott. *Fearnet.com.* September 14, 2009.

TRIVIA

Manuela Velasco wore exactly the same clothes that she wore in the original film.

RED

> *Still armed. Still dangerous. Still got it.*
> —Movie tagline
>
> *There's no substitute for experience.*
> —Movie tagline

Box Office: $90 million

With retirees making up a growing segment of the movie-going population in an industry still obsessed with appealing to a younger demographic, the eventual release of a movie like *Red* seemed all but inevitable. Take the action/caper movie formula, populate the protagonists with a bunch of very experienced kick-ass good guys, give them the customary one last assignment, and fill the roles with box-office draws and cinema buff favorites like Morgan Freeman, Helen Mirren, John Malkovich, and Bruce Willis, and you have something that is a mere tiny twist away from formulaic but original enough to launch a decent publicity campaign.

Comics and graphic novels have inspired many a recent movie, and *Red* is based on the D.C. Comics series by Cully Hamner and Warren Ellis. The protagonists are ex-C.I.A. agents who know too much about the agency's most closely-guarded secrets. When professional assassins attempt to kill retired agent Frank Moses (Willis), he "gets the band back together," by reuniting Marvin (Malkovich), Joe (Freeman), and Victoria (Mirren) in an attempt to stay alive and find who's trying to kill former agents. Meanwhile, Frank begins a tentative relationship with Sarah (Mary-Louise Parker), the woman who he formerly only flirted with while discussing his pension but who may now also be in danger by their loose association. Karl Urban co-stars as a villain and Ernest Borgnine steals a few scenes as a records keeper. Brian Cox and Richard Dreyfuss also join in on the geriatric fun.

Originality of plot is not this film's strong suit; the performers are. They all appear to be having a blast and not taking the proceedings too seriously, and neither should the audience. This is comic-book-style fun for the still youthfully-inclined geriatric set, and others who enjoy a genre romp with actors who know that their craft is primarily to entertain.

The characters, who thought they had retired but are thrown back together under dire circumstances, must rely on their smarts and cleverness to survive a situation where the tables have been turned. Some people they trusted at the agency have become their pursuers. Each, of course, has special skills and knowledge, and all possess the kind of wit and coolness under pressure expected from movie-star spies and action figures. Their action stunts get an automatic boost in pizzazz due to the unlikelihood of such maneuvers at their age. That is the main laugh device in this script by Erich and Jon Hoeber.

Red is directed by Robert Schwentke (*Flightplan* [2005] and *The Time Traveler's Wife* [2009]). He keeps things moving along at a fairly frenetic pace. Critics who liked *Red* appreciated that it did not get too bogged down in trifling details; others wished it might have bothered to allow a bit more complexity. But clearly Schwentke knew he was driving an entertainment vehicle rather than some cinema classic, and he keeps the juices flowing.

The genuine star power saves *Red* from being just another high-octane blockbuster. It is genuinely and oddly satisfying seeing Mirren, she of the high-minded and historically weighty roles, blow someone away (you expect that from Willis, but not from her or Freeman)—if body counts and typical action-flick mayhem are your cup of tea. Mirren lets her hair down and shows her versatility as an actress, though, quite frankly, none of the material is much of a challenge for this cast.

Historically, Hollywood has not found roles with much range for older women, while men can attempt just about anything at any age. *Red* has a strange casting stew, but it makes for a well-cooked popcorn-flavored meal, if one does not come to the movie with expectations to be anything more than entertained. Remember, as well, that this generation of actors and the corresponding generation of audience members grew up in the 1960s or thereabouts, and so they are primed for a plot that views the government bureaucracies with suspicion. Not that these protagonists are anti-Establishment rebels—far from it—it is the powerful forces of evil that have become corrupt. Nothing too surprising there.

Critics were particularly divided in their regard for the plot—some calling it cheesy, others disjointed, still others inconsistent and nonsensical—but generally one does not go to this type of movie to be edified or to have the brain challenged. Take it all in the spirit that Malkovich, who once again, as in *Secretariat* (2010), has oodles of fun with an unlikely role as a victim of high-level paranoia, and it should work on a visceral level. As with Mirren and her bazooka, this film is not aiming much higher—it is zeroing in for the quick kill. A bit more script doctoring, or perhaps a bit more subtlety behind the camera, might have elevated it nearer genuine blockbuster territory. With the dangerously excitable retiree-age population still going strong in Hollywood, it would not be against the grain to expect more of the same in the near future.

Michael Betzold

CREDITS

Frank Moses: Bruce Willis
Joe Matheson: Morgan Freeman
Marvin Boggs: John Malkovich
Victoria: Helen Mirren
William Cooper: Karl Urban
Sarah: Mary-Louise Parker
Ivan Simanov: Brian Cox
Stanton: Julian McMahon
Alexander Dunning: Richard Dreyfuss
Gabriel Loeb: James Remar
Henry: Ernest Borgnine
Cynthia Wilkes: Rebecca Pidgeon
Origin: USA
Language: English
Released: 2010
Production: Lorenzo di Bonaventura, Mark Vahradian; released by Summit Entertainment
Directed by: Robert Schwentke
Written by: Erich Hoeber, Jon Hoeber
Cinematography by: Florian Ballhaus
Music by: Christophe Beck
Sound: Glen Gauthier
Music Supervisor: Julianne Jordan
Editing: Thom Noble
Art Direction: Brandt Gordon
Costumes: Susan Lyall
Production Design: Alec Hammond
MPAA rating: PG-13
Running time: 111 minutes

REVIEWS

Gook, Ben. *The Vine.* October 25, 2010.
Jenkins, Davd. *Time Out.* October 20, 2010.
Meyers, Jeff. *Metro Times.* November 16, 2010.
Miraudo, Simon. *Quickflix.* October 22, 2010.
Puig, Claudia. *USA Today.* October 14, 2010.
Robey, Tim. *Daily Telegraph.* October 22, 2010.
Scott, A.O.. *New York Times.* October 15, 2010.
Scott, Mike. *Times-Picayune.* October 27, 2010.
Utichi, Joe. *Film4.* October 20, 2010.
Zane, Alex. *Sun Online.* October 22, 2010.

QUOTES

Marvin Boggs: "Frank, I never thought I'd say this again. I'm getting the pig!"
Marvin Boggs: "I remember the Secret Service being tougher."
Sarah Ross: "I was hoping not to get kidnapped. Or drugged. I was hoping you'd have 'hair.' So it looks like none of our dreams are coming true at the moment."

TRIVIA

The title of the film *RED* is actually an acronym for "Retired, Extremely, Dangerous."

AWARDS

Nomination:
Golden Globes 2011: Film—Mus./Comedy.

RED HILL

> *Revenge just rode into town.*
> —Movie tagline

Every year produces an unexplainable trend or two at the art house cinema and one of the most interesting ones of 2010 had to be a proliferation of Australian thrillers on the American indie scene. Once known for its cinematic output of increasingly quirky, flashy films like *Strictly Ballroom* (1992) and *The Adventures of Priscilla, Queen of the Desert* (1994), 2010 saw a surprising number of Australian films that could only be called dark including *The Square* (2010), *Animal Kingdom* (2010), and Patrick Hughes' unusual western/horror hybrid *Red Hill* a film with enough interesting set pieces and a strong enough central performance to barely carry it but one that never fulfills on the promise like the other two Aussie flicks that made a bigger splash at the art house this year (and, consequently, never found quite the same praise as *Square* or the Oscar®-nominated *Kingdom*).

Like so many of the thrillers that so clearly inspired it, *Red Hill* essentially tells the tale of a young man who picks the very wrong day to start his new job. Said employment involves being a constable in the small town of Red Hill, one that seems so inconsequential that it makes perfect sense that Shane Cooper (Ryan Kwanten of HBO's *True Blood*) would choose it when his pregnant wife's doctor suggests they reduce stress to ensure the safety of their unborn child. Of course, Shane comes with baggage, including a shooting gone wrong in which he was blamed for not firing on a kid even though the child was armed and the overly decent young man probably should have taken it as a sign when he could not find his gun on the first morning of his new job.

After a brief introduction to the police force and a few other residents of Red Hill, the concise action of the film kicks in as it is revealed that the deadly and disfigured Jimmy Conway (Tom E. Lewis) has recently escaped from prison and is headed to Red Hill for revenge. It turns out that the Sheriff there, known as Old Bill (an appropriately-grizzled Steve Bisley), put Jimmy away and he will do whatever it takes to return the favor, even if it means killing a majority of the population to do so. Bill arms all the men in town who then take up various lookout positions, and await Jimmy's arrival. The new guy is given the main route into Red Hill, assuming that Jimmy will take a more subtle approach. Everyone knows what they say about assumptions.

After a brilliant introduction to Jimmy that features a shotgun pointed at the obvious hero of the piece, Shane falls into a ravine and is presumed dead. As he works his way back to town, Jimmy wreaks havoc in a way not unlike what Michael Myers did to Haddonfield in the original *Halloween* (1978). With his blank stare, homicidal streak, and unmoving scowl, Jimmy resembles a slasher icon like Mr. Myers more than a typical thriller villain. And the way he dispatches most of the population of Red Hill is more reminiscent of the subgenre of horror so popular in the late 1970s and 1980s. The film alternates between horror and western in a way not unlike what John Carpenter did with such success in the prime of his career. Rarely has a film been more clearly inspired by another filmmaker as *Red Hill* is by the early work of John Carpenter. The man who directed *Halloween* worked variations on the *Rio Bravo* (1959) model repeatedly—good guys inside, bad guys outside—in films like *Assault on Precinct 13* (1976) and even *The Thing* (1982). *Red Hill* follows the same format.

But it does so without quite the same degree of success found in the best of Carpenter's filmography. Kwanten is surprisingly good as the male lead, mixing humanity with enough tough-guy believability to play an effective action hero, but Hughes cannot maintain the pace needed for a "one bad night" piece like *Red Hill*. The pace sags in the middle act as Shane finds his way back to town and the viewer realizes that they are essentially watching a slasher movie disguised as a thriller or modern western. *Red Hill* is a promising hybrid of the kind that has not been seen in some time but it never quite pays off on its potential. It is worth seeing for its narrative drive as it is increasingly rare to find talented horror directors who do not weigh their material down with twists, turns, and technical tricks, but

one hopes the next Australian import connects a little more completely from beginning to end.

Brian Tallerico

CREDITS

Shane Cooper: Ryan Kwanten
Jimmy Conway: Tom E. Lewis
Old Bill Jones: Steve Bisley
Slim: Christopher Davis
Barlow: Kevin Harrington
Alice Cooper: Claire Van Der Boom
Origin: Australia
Language: English
Released: 2010
Production: Patrick Hughes, Al Clark; Hughes House Films; released by Strand Releasing
Directed by: Patrick Hughes
Written by: Patrick Hughes
Cinematography by: Tim Hudson
Music by: Dimitri Golovko
Editing: Patrick Hughes
Sound: Frank Lipson
Costumes: Nicola Dunn
Production Design: Enzo Iacono
MPAA rating: R
Running time: 97 minutes

REVIEWS

Abele, Robert. *Los Angeles Times.* November 4, 2010.
Berkshire, Geoff. *Metromix.com.* November 3, 2010.
Brunette, Peter. *Hollywood Reporter.* November 5, 2010.
Catsoulis, Jeannette. *New York Times.* November 4, 2010.
Fear, David. *Time Out New York.* November 5, 2010.
Murray, Noel. *AV Club.* November 4, 2010.
Pinkerton, Nick. *Village Voice.* November 2, 2010.
Reed, Rex. *New York Observer.* November 3, 2010.
Schwarzbaum, Lisa. *Entertainment Weekly.* November 3, 2010.
Stratton, David. *At the Movies.* November 17, 2010.

THE RED RIDING TRILOGY

Evil Lives Here.
—Movie tagline

Based on the crime novels by David Peace, which follow the Yorkshire Ripper murders from their disturbing inception to their grizzly conclusion, and adapted for the screen by Tony Grisoni (*Fear and Loathing in Las Vegas* [1998]) the *Red Riding Trilogy* (*Red Riding: 1974*, *Red Riding: 1980*, and *Red Riding: 1983*) was originally intended for British television. Its premiere at the New York Film Festival directed it toward a cinema premier on our side of the pond—as did the fact that the eerie triptych reads like a mind-numbing collaboration between *The Wire*'s David Simon and David Fincher's work on *Zodiac* (2007). In reality each of the films is helmed by a different director, but each one aspires to channel Simon's knack for turning the police procedural on its ear and Fincher's ability to create and maintain nail-biting tension. That all three succeed to various degrees is noteworthy, but it is not the technical elements that will keep viewers awake long after the credits roll.

Before the three films play themselves out audiences will witness a lot of bloodshed. Girls and women will die at the hands of the Ripper, crooked cops will kill suspects as well as each other, innocent men will be tortured, priests shot, houses will burn, lives will be ruined and even a rat and a few swans will perish (on the upside there is one wedding, but it does not look like a lot of fun). In addition to murderous horror, the films are marked by an oppressive setting (turns out that the rainy expanse of Yorkshire is a far cry from the polished cosmopolitan milieu of London) and some pretty stand-out acting, all of which work together to turn this television procedural into a gripping cinematic experience.

The first installment, *Red Riding: 1974*, directed by Julian Jarrold (*Kinky Boots* [2005] and *Brideshead Revisited* [2008]) introduces us to cub reporter Eddie Dunford (Andrew Garfield in a stellar performance), assigned a story about a missing girl who never made it home from school. Back in his native Yorkshire for his father's funeral, Eddie approaches his assignment as a chance to get a leg up in the newspaper biz. After the girl is found brutally murdered in a drainage ditch with swan wings sewn to her back, Eddie takes his piece in another direction. With the help of a local male prostitute (B.J., played by Robert Sheehan) and his very own "Deep Throat," Eddie uncovers a string of disappearances involving schoolgirls that he believes may be linked. As he sets upon investigating the connection between them, he in turn uncovers a deadly ring of duplicitous dealings involving everyone from local authorities to the working class Yorkshire parents of the departed. Of course, Eddie gets swept up along the way and suffers for it and it is his undoing that makes *Red Riding: 1974* such a standout in the trilogy. Eddie's romantic notions about good and evil and his uncorrupted take on his job and belief in the law set him up as a character audiences cannot help but root for, the very type that viewers want to see win in all crime movies.

Shot in grainy super 16 millimeter Jarrold creates an engrossing vintage atmosphere. Everything about the production is meticulous, so not only is it easy to get lost in the locale and in Eddie's investigation, there is an immediacy about the narrative that transcends bellbottoms and shag haircuts. But it is not one built on gore. In as much as there is violence and in as much as the audience is exposed to death, it's the tension that really wears away at the senses. As the audience witnesses Eddie's downward spiral and as his poking around gets him closer to powerful and scary people, it is the anticipation of what lies before him that has the viewer averting his eyes and the hope of Eddie getting to the bottom of the truth that keeps eyes glued to the screen.

In the same way that *The Wire* exposed the interconnected layers of the seedy underbelly of Baltimore's social and law enforcement agencies, so too does *Red Riding: 1980*, the second installment of the trilogy. Unfortunately, there are times when the layers get the better of the film, taking audiences away from the immediacy created in *Red Riding: 1974* and confusing matters with politics and cover-ups. Turning away from the kidnappings and murders themselves, director James Marsh (*Man on Wire* [2008]) focuses our attention on the police force assigned to the Yorkshire Ripper murders. Many more girls and women have disappeared since 1974, but officials are no closer to solving the case. Yorkshire is in a state of panic and to combat negative perception, local law enforcement appoints a task force to head up the matter. Leading this crew is Peter Hunter (Paddy Considine in a complex and nuanced performance), a good cop in a crowd of deplorable ones, who is sidelined at every turn by politicos as well as some of the police force insiders who seem to be placed in his way just to keep him from uncovering anything. Like Eddie, Peter is also grappling with his personal demons, which end up contributing as much to his undoing as his involvement with the case.

The action in *Red Riding: 1980* remains for the most part in the steely office buildings and cold gray interrogation rooms assigned to the special investigative squad headed by Peter. And though the film has a more procedural feel to it, Marsh maintains a firm grasp on the pervasive threat of the Ripper. Peter's stubborn determination and his late-night visits to crime scenes continue the eerie feel of its predecessor. Though *Red Riding: 1980* does not possess as much meaty substance as Eddie's investigation, Marsh compensates by shifting his focus to the characters and their surroundings. We see Peter and his team dwarfed by lifeless office buildings and often encased in metal elevator cars, both indicative of their inability to penetrate the very law enforcement system that is employing them as well as the ability of said organization to keep them walled-off from the truth.

Finally, in *Red Riding: 1983* Anand Tucker (*Shopgirl* [2005], *Hilary and Jackie* [1998]) brings the haunting story of the Yorkshire Ripper to a close. When another local girl disappears, the Ripper makes headlines again. And though the police may turn a blind eye, a chubby local washed-up lawyer, John Piggott (Mark Addy) becomes convinced that the men in police custody who have been charged with the murders—and who mysteriously all end up dying—are innocent. His involvement conveniently coincides with the sudden remorse of Detective Maurice Jobson (David Morrissey) who has had a hand in the Ripper cover-up since the start. The result is a slightly cluttered resolution to a trilogy that started out with such great promise.

In many ways Tucker was tasked with the hardest part of the *Red Riding* series since the wrap-up hinges on a somewhat trite confluence of events and since the narrative is interspersed with a comes-out-of-nowhere moral-compass voice-over provided by *Red Riding: 1974*'s B.J. But Tucker adds depth by plopping his characters in a jarring, sepia-tinged world where it seems to always be raining, immersing them in a relentless environment that would push anyone to a breaking point, and by leading his actors to grounded-and-engaging performances. Though some of his montages are artier than the subject matter necessitates, the foundation of intrigue created by the earlier installments makes them easy to overlook while waiting to learn the identity of the ripper. *Red Riding: 1983* relies heavily on the first part of the trilogy and Tucker repeatedly references Eddie and his naive quest for righteous truth and love in the various clue-laden flashbacks that his segment possesses. In reconnecting with Eddie, the viewer is reminded of the strengths of *Red Riding: 1974*: the streamlined one-man-versus-a-killer narrative and the personal—and therefore approachable and more immediate—plight of our hero. And though John is an intriguing entry into this final installment, he pales in comparison to Eddie and in seeing him again the viewer is reminded of the standout nature of the first film in *The Red Riding Trilogy* more than the strengths of the piece as a whole.

Joanna Topor MacKenzie

REVIEWS

Burr, Ty. *Boston Globe.* February 18, 2010.
Denby, David. *New Yorker.* February 8, 2010.
Dargis, Manohla. *New York Times.* February 5, 2010.
Orndorf, Brian. *BrianOrndorf.com.* February 3, 2010.
Phipps, Keith. *AV Club.* February 4, 2010.
Pinkerton, Nick. *Village Voice.* February 2, 2010.
Rickey, Carrie. *Philadelphia Inquirer.* March 11, 2010.
Stevens, Dana. *Slate.* February 5, 2010.
Tallerico, Brian. *MovieRetriever.com.* March 12, 2010.
Vognar, Chris. *Dallas Morning News.* March 26, 2010.

TRIVIA

The film title comes from both the traditional tale of Red Riding Hood and the film's location in Yorkshire, England which is divided into three sections or ridings.

RED RIDING: 1974

Please refer to the essay for *The Red Riding Trilogy.* The three films *Red Riding: 1974, Red Riding: 1980,* and *Red Riding: 1983* were reviewed together as components of a complete entity. Cast, crew, and other information has been listed separately in order to avoid confusion.

CREDITS

John Dawson: Sean Bean
Bill Molloy: Warren Clarke
Eddie Dunford: Andrew Garfield
Maurice Jobson: David Morrissey
Bob Craven: Sean Harris
Paula Garland: Rebecca Hall
BJ: Robert Sheehan
Tommy Douglas: Tony Mooney
Jack Whitehead: Eddie Marsan
Martin Laws: Peter Mullan
Origin: United Kingdom
Language: English
Released: 2009
Production: Andrew Eaton, Anita Overland, Wendy Brazington; Boxing Cat Films; released by Freestyle Releasing
Directed by: Julian Jarrold
Written by: Tony Grisoni
Cinematography by: Rob Hardy
Music by: Adrian Johnston
Sound: Danny Hambrook
Editing: Andrew Hulme
Art Direction: Julie Ann Horan
Costumes: Natalie Ward
Production Design: Cristina Casali
MPAA rating: Unrated
Running time: 102 minutes

QUOTES

Eddie Dunford: "Little girl goes missing, the pack salivates. If it bleeds it leads, right?"

RED RIDING: 1980

Please refer to the essay for *The Red Riding Trilogy.* The three films *Red Riding: 1974, Red Riding: 1980,* and *Red Riding: 1983* were reviewed together as components of a complete entity. Cast, crew, and other information has been listed separately in order to avoid confusion.

CREDITS

Peter Hunter: Paddy Considine
Helen Marshall: Maxine Peake
Eddie Dunford: Andrew Garfield
Maurice Jobson: David Morrissey
John Nolan: Tony Pitts
Martin Laws: Peter Mullan
BJ: Robert Sheehan
Bob Craven: Sean Harris
Tommy Douglas: Tony Mooney
Bill Molloy: Warren Clarke
Philip Evans: James Fox
John Dawson: Sean Bean
Jack Whitehead: Eddie Marsan
The Ripper: Joseph Mawle
Origin: United Kingdom
Language: English
Released: 2009
Production: Anita Overland, Wendy Brazington, Andrew Eaton; released by IFC Films
Directed by: James Marsh
Written by: Tony Grisoni
Cinematography by: Igor Martinovic
Music by: Dickon Hinchliffe
Sound: Paul Davies
Editing: Jinx Godfrey
Art Direction: Sami Khan
Costumes: Charlotte Walker
Production Design: Tom Burton
MPAA rating: Unrated
Running time: 93 minutes

RED RIDING: 1983

Please refer to the essay for *The Red Riding Trilogy.* The three films *Red Riding: 1974, Red Riding: 1980,* and *Red Riding: 1983* were reviewed together as components of a complete entity. Cast, crew, and other information has been listed separately in order to avoid confusion.

CREDITS

John Piggott: Mark Addy
Maurice Jobson: David Morrissey
Martin Laws: Peter Mullan

BJ: Robert Sheehan
Bob Craven: Sean Harris
Tommy Douglas: Tony Mooney
Judith Jobson: Lisa Howard
Bill Molloy: Warren Clarke
Eddie Dunford: Andrew Garfield
John Dawson: Sean Bean
Michael Myshkin: Daniel Mays
Origin: United Kingdom
Language: English
Released: 2009
Production: Andrew Eaton, Anita Overland, Wendy Brazington; released by IFC Films
Directed by: Anand Tucker
Written by: Tony Grisoni
Cinematography by: David Higgs
Music by: Barrington Pheloung
Sound: James Harrison
Editing: Trevor Waite
Art Direction: Katie MacGregor
Costumes: Caroline Harris
Production Design: Allison Dominitz
MPAA rating: Unrated
Running time: 100 minutes

REMEMBER ME

Live in the moments.
—Movie tagline

Box Office: $19 million

It is almost impossible to discuss *Remember Me,* an affectionately-observed romance, without exploring the ending. It is undoubtedly exploitative, having no basis in what has come before except in the preordained machinations of Will Fetters' screenplay. In the shock of using a national tragedy in such an unexpected way, though, director Allen Coulter's film achieves—even if in a mild way—the sensation of unanticipated tragedy. The buildup of images in its climactic sequence, establishing the time and space placement of the movie's rebellious hero, is a punch in the gut.

The rebel is Tyler Hawkins (Robert Pattinson), a college student in New York with shades of Holden Caulfield. He chain smokes. He spends his time with younger sister Caroline (Ruby Jerins), of whom he is fiercely protective, building up her ego and supporting her desire to be an artist. He does not have a major. He is undecided, he tells Ally Craig (Emilie de Ravin), a fellow student in one of his classes. "About what," she asks; "Everything," he answers. There is more than a hint of the famous dialogue exchange in *The Wild One*

(1953), although Tyler is not rebelling against whatever society may throw at him.

Instead, Tyler has rejected the expectations of his own station in life, especially those set up by his lawyer father Charles (Pierce Brosnan). When the police arrest Tyler and his roommate Aidan (Tate Ellington) after Tyler tries to stop a fight in an alleyway, mouths off to, and grabs the police sergeant on the scene, Tyler refuses to call his father. When Aidan does in his stead, Tyler makes it clear to Charles that he does not need his father's help. Tyler blames Charles for the suicide of his older brother Michael, who killed himself shortly after starting work at their father's law firm, and cannot stand the way he treats his surviving children. While at lunch after visiting Michael's grave, Caroline begins to tell the family about her artistic ambitions, and Charles cuts her off to ask for sugar for his coffee.

Charles may test his children, but Ally's father Neil (Chris Cooper), who is also—in one of the script's clearest contrivances—the man who arrests Tyler and Aidan, is downright antagonistic. He clings to Ally—the result of his wife's murder in the film's prologue. In spite of their family's tragic history, Neil never becomes a sympathetic figure, primarily because Fetters writes him as an obstacle. Aidan wants Tyler to date and reject Ally to get back at Neil. Tyler wants nothing to do with the revenge scheme (which is forgotten almost immediately after it is suggested) but finds Ally attractive and asks her out to dinner. From the start, Neil is a hurdle for Tyler to jump. After Neil slaps his daughter when she suggests he is failing her as a father because of regret for not saving his wife, he becomes the same for Ally.

The beginning of Tyler and Ally's coupling is difficult to accept for the surrounding complications and foreshadowing of their eventual problems. Once Fetters overcomes the set up, Tyler and Ally become worthwhile characters. They talk about their past struggles; they listen to one another. Pattinson is a charmer as the tortured Tyler, and de Ravin never succumbs to playing this young woman with a troubling past and home life as a victim.

The screenplay leads Tyler, his family, and Ally down the hard road of redemption. The trip makes most of its stops in the relationship between Tyler and Charles, which erupts in a vocal fight during a meeting with Charles' employees. Charles tries to convince his son that he loves his children. He provides for them anything and everything they need, although Tyler will have none of that. It is not just about money and status for Tyler. Brosnan has a tricky role as Charles, a man obsessed with work and seemingly ignorant of his children's lives, and he accomplishes sympathy in a single moment. While on the phone with Tyler to discuss Caroline's

upcoming art show, Charles acknowledges that it is his son's twenty-second birthday. Immediately after, is a shot of the look on Charles' face, and Brosnan imbues it with an unspoken but palpable sense of fatherly tenderness. It is an instantaneous glance, yet it speaks volumes about Charles.

Coulter and the cast play the characters for who they are and find the genuine conflict within and amongst them. This is why Neil does not fit in the picture; his existence in the script is only to force conflict. He does, breaking into Tyler's apartment, choking him, and making the young man realize he needs to tell Ally the truth about how the two came to meet. This leads to a minor separation, resolved with such haste that it only emphasizes how false the contrived setup for their relationship is in the first place.

The cast smoothes the rough spots with sincere performances, and just when things start to look on the rise for Tyler and his loved ones, Fetters drops the floor beneath them. Tyler arrives at his father's office. Allie makes breakfast for his return. Charles brings Caroline to school. Caroline sits in her classroom, and the teacher writes the date on the chalkboard: September 11, 2001. Tyler stares out the window, and the camera makes a sweeping pull back to reveal he is on one of the upper floors of one of the World Trade Center towers.

Fetters does not trick the audience in arriving at the reveal, although he is not entirely forthright about it. After initially setting the date as "Ten years later" than 1991, the screenplay makes vague references to the time of year (The students are not in school because of break). It is clearly structured to keep the audience out of the loop. The impressive, simulated crane shot showing the towers is upsetting, and Coulter handles the aftershock of the implied attack as tastefully as can be expected in slow motion reaction shots of the survivors' faces.

The wide shot of the towers is followed by a sudden cut to black. The coda that follows, showing how everyone in Tyler's life has changed, rings false. Early in the film, Tyler quotes Gandhi to emphasize the importance of one's actions in life, yet here, the characters are changed, not by what Tyler has done, but by the fact of his death. Charles becomes closer to Caroline, and Ally can finally ride the train where her mother was murdered. It also negates the effect of the revelatory shot by reining the focus back to the specifics of the characters.

It is too pat to condemn *Remember Me* for the finale, considering that the film works as an endearing romance until that point. The ending aspires for too much significance, and in an indirect way, the film achieves some by raising the debate of if, when, how, and to what end the events of September 11, 2001 should be presented.

Mark Dujsik

CREDITS

Tyler Hawkins: Robert Pattinson
Ally Craig: Emilie de Ravin
Neil Craig: Chris Cooper
Helen Craig: Martha Plimpton
Diane Hirsch: Lena Olin
Charles Hawkins: Pierce Brosnan
Alyssa Craig at 11: Caitlyn Rund
Caroline: Ruby Jerins
Aidan: Tate Ellington
Origin: USA
Language: English
Released: 2010
Production: Nick Osborne, Trevor Engelson; Underground Films and Management; released by Summit Entertainment
Directed by: Allen Coulter
Written by: Will Fetters, Jenny Lumet
Cinematography by: Jonathan Freeman
Music by: Marcelo Zarvos
Sound: Ken Ishii
Music Supervisor: Alexandra Patsavas
Editing: Andrew Mondshein
Costumes: Susan Lyall
Production Design: Scott P. Murphy
MPAA rating: PG-13
Running time: 113 minutes

REVIEWS

Berardinelli, James. *Reelviews.net.* March 11, 2010.
Dargis, Manohla. *New York Times.* March 12, 2010.
Ebert, Roger. *Chicago Sun-Times.* March 10, 2010.
Fibbs, Brandon. *Colorado Springs Gazette.* March 10, 2010.
Jakicic, Cathy. *Milwaukee Journal Sentinel.* March 11, 2010.
Johanson, MaryAnn. *Flickfilosopher.com.* March 10, 2010.
Orndorf, Brian. *Brianorndorf.com.* March 11, 2010.
Phillips, Michael. *Chicago Tribune.* March 11, 2010.
Putman, Dustin. *Dustinputman.com.* March 9, 2010.
Tobias, Scott. *AVclub.com.* March 11, 2010.

QUOTES

Tyler: "Gandhi said that whatever you do in life will be insignificant. But it's very important that you do it. I tend to agree with the first part."

TRIVIA

The Roth family was the original name of the Hawkins family.

AWARDS

Nomination:
Golden Raspberries 2010: Worst Actor (Pattinson).

REPO MEN

You. Upgraded.
—Movie tagline
Consider them your final notice.
—Movie tagline

Box Office: $14 million

Repo Men is a satire in search of an angle for its relevant topic, a futuristic noir glossed to an uncharacteristic shine, an action movie that only achieves visceral thrills through its excessive-but-stylish bloodletting, and merely a mediocre experience overall. The concept comes from co-screenwriter Eric Garcia's novel *The Repossession Novel* (written concurrently with the screenplay), the same title used by the movie's hero Remy (Jude Law) in his quickly-composed exposé on his former profession. Writing on an old mechanical typewriter, Remy tells the audience his story, with a few philosophical flourishes, some sidesteps for character development, and a continual voiceover.

Remy works for the Union, a privatized health care corporation that sells its clients artificial organs ("artiforgs" or "forgs" for short). If a person's kidney begins to fail, the Union can replace it. If cholesterol has started to take its toll on the heart, the company can provide a replacement for that as well. The new organs function even better than the originals. Beth (Alice Braga), a singer at a bar Remy frequents and who becomes his partner in crime later, even has replacement eyes that can change color, presumably from just by thinking about it.

The catch for the buyer is in the contract, especially if one is unable to pay in full upfront. At that point, there is the option of an installment payment plan with interest, naturally. If and when a customer is unable to keep up with payments, people like Remy enter the picture—after a "kind" ninety-six-day grace period. All of this exposition is presented with the appropriate level of slimy, questionable business ethics by Liev Schreiber, who plays Remy's boss Frank. He has the compassionate sale down to a routine: "Do it for your family," he says; "Do it for yourself."

What Frank or his team of salespeople does not mention to prospective purchasers is the fact that, after that grace period has expired, Remy or someone in his position will find a delinquent payer and remove the organ or organs from their body—not before asking the person if he or she would like an ambulance for after the procedure. The absurdity of the inquiry within the context is the only truly devious piece of humor, especially when one of Remy's customers, a music producer (RZA) Remy admires, asks if the paramedics will replace his heart. "Not with your credit," Remy chuckles in response.

In a piece of irony that closes the first act, Remy is injured on the job, and the Union gives him a new, artificial heart. He attempts to continue his work but finds—in an unstated but obvious joke—that his heart is no longer in it. His wife (Carice van Houten) leaves with their son (Chandler Canterbury), and he moves in with best friend and co-worker Jake (Forest Whitaker). Soon, Remy falls behind on payments and is on the run from the Union, including Jake, with Beth.

Set in the near future, director Miguel Sapochnik's dystopian, science-fiction cityscapes might be the movie's least-developed element. After a few establishing shots that ape the identity (cluttered skyscrapers and towering, video billboards) and achieve none of the personality of the Los Angeles of *Blade Runner* (1982), production designer David Sandefur settles in for bright suburban homes and florescent-lit, glass-encased office spaces and a security-laden airport juxtaposed with the dark, grimy interiors of a freighter and abandoned apartment buildings, junkyards, and underground rooms.

Garcia and Garrett Lerner's script structures the second act as a routine chase that alternates locations between light and drab. Remy and Beth travel to the black market, where a young girl (Tiffany Espensen) acts as the surgeon on duty to repair "artiforgs." They attempt to block scanners at the airport while playing off Beth's bleeding leg, fighting and killing security guards who catch on to the ruse in an enclosed office space.

Remy's moral compass is a strange one. He finds himself on the run from the Union because he can no longer remove artificial organs and more-than-likely kill their previous owners, because now he sees them as people with names and families. Somehow, though, he takes no issue in smashing a former co-worker's skull with a typewriter or shooting an incapacitated guard in the head.

The chase section of the movie is the weakest of its acts, and it soon makes way for an assault on the Union's headquarters in an attempt to wipe his and Beth's record clean, freeing them from the system and pursuit. It is an extended sequence of overblown violence and gore and, in the grotesque purity of its intentions, the movie's strongest part. The highlight is a battle in a hallway that shifts from gunplay to knife fight to using whatever is available. Someone pulls out a hammer. Remy swings a

saw in slow motion, the camera spinning around from its point of view until it finds flesh to cut.

More slicing follows, as Remy and Beth engage in sensual surgery to free themselves from the company's grasp while still staying alive. The scene fulfills, in a bizarre way, Remy's initial description of the result of his work on his clientele as the "horizontal mambo," confusing his metaphor to blend sex and death. Less credible is the way Remy turns the example of Schrödinger's cat (used properly at first to complement Remy's own paradoxical situation) into a rallying cry for survival.

The final act of *Repo Men* is only comparatively effective when placed against the intriguing, ultimately hollow satirical elements of the first and the dull cat-and-mouse game of the second. Garcia and Lerner are not even content to leave well enough alone, ending on an inexcusable revelation of fantasy—just to add insult to inferiority.

Mark Dujsik

CREDITS

Remy: Jude Law
Jake: Forest Whitaker
Beth: Alice Braga
Carol: Carice van Houten
Frank: Liev Schreiber
Peter: Chandler Canterbury
Little Alva: Tiffany Espensen
Origin: USA, Canada
Language: English
Released: 2010
Production: Mary Parent, Scott Stuber; Mambo Film Productions, Stuber Productions; released by Universal Pictures
Directed by: Miguel Sapochnik
Written by: Eric Garcia, Garrett Lerner
Cinematography by: Enrique Chediak
Music by: Marco Beltrami
Sound: Glen Gauthier
Editing: Richard Francis-Bruce
Art Direction: Dan Yarhi
Costumes: Caroline Harris
Production Design: David Sandefur
MPAA rating: R
Running time: 111 minutes

REVIEWS

Anderson, John. *Washington Post*. March 19, 2010.
Buckwalter, Ian. *Npr.org*. March 18, 2010.
Holden, Stephen. *New York Times*. March 19, 2010.

LaSalle, Mick. *San Francisco Chronicle.* March 19, 2010.
Moore, Roger. *Orlando Sentinel.* March 18, 2010.
Murphy, Kathleen. *Msn.com.* March 19, 2010.
Phipps, Keith. *AVclub.com.* March 18, 2010.
Putman, Dustin. *Dustinputman.com.* March 17, 2010.
Rodriguez, Rene. *Miami Herald.* March 17, 2010.
Vaux, Rob. *Mania.com.* March 18, 2010.

QUOTES

Remy: "At the end, a job is not just a job, is who you are, and if wanna change who you are, you have to change what you do."

TRIVIA

In several fight scenes, Forest Whitaker utilizes the skills he acquired while studying Filipino Kali for several years under masters such as Dan Inosanto and Richard Bustillo.

RESIDENT EVIL: AFTERLIFE

(Resident Evil: Afterlife: An IMAX 3D Experience)

She's back...and she's bringing a few of her friends.
—Movie tagline

Box Office: $60 million

Resident Evil: Afterlife, the fourth installment of the surprisingly-resilient action-horror franchise (which has included *Resident Evil* [2002], *Resident Evil: Apocalypse* [2004], and *Resident Evil: Extinction* [2007]) based on the popular videogame series, is not so much a movie in the classical sense as it is a sensation machine designed expressly to momentarily entertain its presumed target audience of ADD-afflicted 14-year-old boys with a non-stop barrage of things that they presumably want to see in a film—blood, guts, guns, hot babes, explosions, mutants, fight scenes that violate all known laws relating to physics and gravity and, as the late, great Joe Bob Briggs would have put it, absolutely no plot to get in the way of the story. From an artistic perspective, this may not be the loftiest goal imaginable for a film but it is a goal nevertheless and one that the film manages to achieve thanks to a lot of energy, style, and a healthy awareness of its own absurdities.

Once again, Milla Jovovich stars as Alice, the genetically-enhanced ass-kicker who wanders the post-apocalyptic Earth looking to bring down the remaining elements of the fearsome Umbrella Corporation, the multi-national conglomerate that essentially destroyed humanity by accidentally releasing a deadly virus that turned most people into zombies while searching for the ever-dwindling numbers of healthy survivors. After leading a siege on Umbrella headquarters in Japan with an army of clones, she heads off to Alaska in search of Arcadia, a town that is supposedly infection-free. She does not find it but does run across the now-amnesiac Claire Redfield (Ali Larter), one of the few survivors of the previous film, and the two make their way back to Los Angeles. There, they come across a small group of survivors holed up inside a maximum-security prison surrounded by increasingly-impatient zombies—in a nifty coincidence, one of the survivors turns out to be Claire's brother (Wentworth Miller). These people have heard tales of Arcadia as well and it turns out to be not a town but a ship anchored just off the coast. The rest of the film consists of their efforts to escape the prison and the various zombies and mutants chasing after them in order to get to the ship because, after all, there is no possible way that it could be a trap or anything. Sure, the three previous films all found Alice falling into an Umbrella-laid trap in the final reel but that couldn't possibly happen this time around. Right?

Resident Evil: Afterlife is about as brain-dead as the zombies at its core, but it works reasonably well as mindless exploitation entertainment. Part of this is because while Paul W.S. Anderson, who wrote and produced all four entries in the series and returns to the director's chair for the first time since the 2002 original, seems incapable of telling a story that even flirts with coherence, he certainly knows how to come up with arresting individual moments that catch the eye—besides the gorgeous opening clone attack, there is also an equally-spectacular moment in which Alice leaps off the roof of the prison to make an escape while hundreds of zombies are seen in the background doing likewise. Part of this is because while the introduction of 3-D might seem to be a signal of a series that is otherwise out of ideas, it is actually used pretty well here, if only because the film was conceived and shot in the format (utilizing the same camera system designed and used by James Cameron for *Avatar* [2009]) instead of undergoing a cheap conversion at the last second.

The film manages to demonstrate a certain sense of humor about itself without stepping over the line into the hard-sell irony of such recent pseudo-exploitation flicks as *Piranha 3D* (2010) or *Machete* (2010)—beyond the inherent goofiness of the material, there are also sly in-joke references (such as having Wentworth Miller, best known for starring in the television series *Prison Break*, as the only confined person in an otherwise abandoned prison) and nudges at genre conventions (the funniest and cruelest being a set-up for a possible Alice shower scene that never quite occurs, though it does lead to an extended fight in which she battles a giant mutant while getting soaked from the pipes that are getting smashed in the fracas). A lot of it is because of the continued presence of Milla Jovovich as Alice. Sure, the role may not be the most challenging in the world and hardly shows the acting chops that she has demonstrated in films like *The Claim* (2000) and *Stone* (2010) but she throws herself into it with such conviction and fierce determination that her performance pretty much stands as an object lesson in the power and importance of screen charisma and how it can make or break a film.

Make no mistake, *Resident Evil: Afterlife* is utter nonsense from start to finish and unless you are a fan of the earlier installments or a Jovovich obsessive, there is probably no burning reason to see it. That said, it has no greater aim than to provide viewers with ninety minutes of cheerfully ridiculous monster movie thrills and to that extent, it does succeed—so much so, in fact, that when the final scenes turn into an extended set-up for a presumed *Resident Evil 5* the idea seems more like a promise than a threat. In other words, the film is a load but, all things considered, it turns out to be the good load after all.

Peter Sobczynski

CREDITS

Alice: Milla Jovovich
Claire Redfield: Ali Larter
Chris Redfield: Wentworth Miller
Bennett: Kim Coates
Luthor West: Boris Kodjoe
Albert Wesker: Shawn Roberts
Jill Valentine: Sienna Guillory
Wendell: Fulvio Cecere
Origin: USA
Language: English
Released: 2010
Production: Paul W.S. Anderson, Jeremy Bolt, Don Carmody, Bernd Eichinger, Samuel Hadida, Robert Kulzer; Constantin Film Produktion, Davis Films, Impact Pictures; released by Sony Pictures
Directed by: Paul W.S. Anderson
Written by: Paul W.S. Anderson
Cinematography by: Glen MacPherson
Music by: Tomandandy
Sound: Stephen Barden
Editing: Niven Howie
Art Direction: Brandt Gordon
Costumes: Denise Cronenberg, Azalia Snail
Production Design: Arvinder Grewal
MPAA rating: R
Running time: 97 minutes

REVIEWS

Barker, Andrew. *Variety.* September 11, 2010.
Clark, Shaula. *Boston Phoenix.* September 16, 2010.
Gonsalves, Rob. *eFilmcritic.com.* September 13, 2010.
McDonagh, Maitland. *Film Journal International.* September 10, 2010.
O'Neill, Phelim. *The Guardian.* September 9, 2010.
Ordona, Michael. *Los Angeles Times.* September 13, 2010.
Rabin, Nathan. *AV Club.* September 10, 2010.
Scheck, Frank. *Hollywood Reporter.* September 10, 2010.
Snider, Eric D. *Film.com.* September 10, 2010.
White, Armond. *New York Press.* September 13, 2010.

QUOTES

Alice: "Day 6, 1800 hours, Los Angeles. No signs of life, not even the undead. They must have burned with the city. But what about the rest?"
Albert Wesker: "I'm what you used to be. Only better."

TRIVIA

"Afterlife" is the same working title that was used in the previous movie before it became "Extinction."
The highest grossing Canadian film of all time with international receipts totaling $300 million.

RESTREPO

One platoon, one valley, one year.
—Movie tagline

Box Office: $1 million

The opening minutes of the documentary *Restrepo* shows four soldiers of Battle Company, Second Platoon, one week before being deployed for fifteen months to a location CNN once called "the most dangerous place in the world," the Korangal Valley in Afghanistan. The home video shot in 2007 shows the four men about as gung-ho as one would expect four soldiers would be who have not actually seen war, or more specifically, have not been shot at several times per day, every day. They are hungry for action, eager to kill, and there is an undeniable camaraderie that will carry on through their time in Afghanistan despite the fact that one of them will be dead in a matter of weeks.

Directors Tim Hetherington, a cinematographer on *The Devil Came on Horseback* (2007) about the genocide in Darfur, Sudan, and Sebastian Junger, writer of the novel on which the film *The Perfect Storm* (2000) was based, spare us the death of the man whose name serves as the title of this film, but they do not spare much else. *Restrepo* is a terrifying, revealing, and raw look at the war in Afghanistan, that follows that playful video with a horrific firefight that is nearly impossible to follow through the dust, smoke, and screaming that follows the initial explosion that rocks the vehicle in which the filmmakers are riding. It does not take long for men of all ranks and backgrounds to come around the same essential question: What are we doing here? And their reaction after being on the receiving end of a few too many Taliban attacks is usually something in the neighborhood of "We aren't ready" or "We're like fish in a barrel." Talking-head interviews with twenty or so of the men who had spent time at the Korengal Outpost while the documentarians were on hand are open and honest and provide a more level-headed evaluation of their wartime experience than the in-the-fight footage shot in Afghanistan. The contrast between the two sets of interviews is often quite drastic.

Some of the more interesting moments are a combination of the routine and the chaotic. Weekly meetings with the elders of the valley seem to move forward at times, but more often they retreat into frustration and name calling. As if to demonstrate the pointless nature of these meetings, the cameraman focuses on one of the elders attempting to make sense of a juice box he has been given to drink. The conversation is going on around him, but no one is really paying attention to each other. Other moments in *Restrepo* are downright heartbreaking, as is one sequence that shows the platoon going in to access the damage done by American bombers in an area said to be infested with Taliban. While it appears the mission was successful, we also see that many civilians—including women and children—are seriously hurt. The look of frustration and sadness on the soldiers' faces is one they do not try and hide. Many of them tell the filmmakers that the mission was a personal low point in their lives.

Hetherington and Junger spent a year imbedded with the Second Platoon, and it is difficult to think of a wartime documentary that has ever featured this much action. One higher-ranking officer explains that the soldiers in this particular region are seeing as much concentrated fighting as the armed forces in World War II and Vietnam saw under the worst of circumstances, and that is not difficult to believe. The highlight for these men was the opportunity to build a new outpost on top of a former enemy position and name it after their fallen comrade Juan "Doc" Restrepo, 20, who was shot twice in the neck early in his tour of duty. We see the men during their downtime, as well, talking about family, playing guitar and singing, even dancing. But a large portion of their time is spent remembering those who did not make it this far. Toward the film's closing moments, the filmmakers show a succession of close-ups of some of the men, all of whom appear to be on the verge of tears. But whenever a period of sadness overcomes the platoon, someone in command steps up

and reminds its members that their mission is to "mourn and get over it."

The filmmakers opt not to provide narration or their own comments about anything they have captured. Minimal title cards give us only what we need to know about location and the identities of the soldiers talking. *Restrepo* is a stripped-down, no-frills documentary whose impact is undeniable. Clearly, the men in front of the camera got comfortable with the crew around them since they never bother to clean up their language or seem to care what impression the cameras might be capturing. A discussion about literally shooting an enemy to bits seems to have a pair of soldiers especially giddy. But the cumulative effect of these scenes in one of the truest portraits of life in the modern military that has ever been assembled. It is as scary as it is humorous, and there is no denying that seeing these young men keep sane under conditions and in a location that would drive most insane is a powerful thing. But the haunting concern after watching a movie like *Restrepo* is wondering how anyone will know if the United States has even won this war. The looks in the eyes of the locals says that even if the Taliban is driven out, the damage the military has done to the population may be irreparable. This is tough but essential viewing.

Steven Prokopy

CREDITS

Origin: USA
Language: English
Released: 2010
Production: Tim Hetherington, Sebastian Junger; Outpost Films; released by National Geographic Cinema Ventures
Directed by: Tim Hetherington, Sebastian Junger
Cinematography by: Tim Hetherington, Sebastian Junger
Sound: Coll Anderson
Music Supervisor: Ray Garcia
Editing: Michael Levine
MPAA rating: R
Running time: 92 minutes

REVIEWS

Baumgarten, Marjorie. *Austin Chronicle.* July 30, 2010.
Connolly, Matthew. *SlantMagazine.com.* June 22, 2010.
Ebert, Roger. *Chicago Sun-Times.* June 30, 2010.
Jones, J.R. *Chicago Reader.* June 30, 2010.
Nayman, Adam. *EyeWeekly.com.* July 14, 2010.
Nelson, Rob. *Village Voice.* June 15, 2010.
Pais, Matt. *Metromix.com.* July 1, 2010.
Prigge, Matt. *Philadelphia Weekly.* June 29, 2010.
Rothkopf, Joshua. *Time Out New York.* June 24, 2010.
Scott, A.O. *New York Times.* June 25, 2010.

AWARDS

Nomination:

Oscars 2010: Feature Doc.
Directors Guild 2010: Director (Hetherington and Junger)
Ind. Spirit 2011: Feature Doc.

ROBIN HOOD

Box Office: $105 million

Arrows have been flying across the frames of Robin Hood retellings for close to a century, hitting their mark silently until the era when soundtracks could add all the thwacks. In fact, skirmishes between the outlaw hero and his oppressive foes have required so many of the pointed wooden projectiles over the years that one is taken aback each time to see any English forests still standing—Sherwood or otherwise. While it certainly would have been anachronistic to have the Sheriff of Nottingham whip out a pistol in medieval times to fire at his elusive quarry, Ridley Scott and Russell Crowe (in their fifth collaboration) were able in 2010 to take aim at Robin Hood and, in their own misguided way, pump him full of lead.

This is not the traditional, effervescently-charming and cheeky chap in green tights and a jauntily-feathered cap who has captured the imagination with his buoyant bedeviling of unjust authority, thrillingly thwarting them as he robs from the rich and gives to the poor. There is no high-watt, raffish grin either, but instead the firmly-set jaw of a grimly noble revisionist Robin in a grimy tunic and chain mail, the latter only partly accounting for his heaviness. As portrayed by Crowe, there is not only no joie, but also very little zestful vivre. Although Sean Connery looked far more into autumn when he made 1976's *Robin and Marian*, he was actually about the same age then as Crowe is now. Yet, Connery's seemingly-older Robin possesses much more magnetism. The contrast is even more striking between Crowe's portrayal and that of the exuberantly-acrobatic Douglas Fairbanks in 1922's *Robin Hood,* not to mention Errol Flynn in *The Adventures of Robin Hood* (1938), who was the absolute definition of dashing and the best of them all. Compared to Crowe, Fairbanks and Flynn seem both maniacally-positive and positively-manic.

The spring has been taken out of Robin's step here by a newly-invented tale imagining from whence he sprang. Through this ill-conceived origin story, viewers are afforded the dubious pleasure of getting to know him back before he became so exhilarating and enthralling. This Robin may be admirable, but there is precious little allure. Brian Helgeland's script mightily resolves to graft the (as far as anyone has ever been able to determine) fictitious character onto historical fact. With a "Suppose...?" here and a "What if...?" there, Robin is made to stand taller than any tree in Sherwood before beginning in earnest to present the poor with stolen riches, Robin not only unites his countrymen to repel would-be French conquerors but darn-near also provides them with the monumental Magna Carta. Serious-minded, grandiose fare? Yes. Scintillating fun? Not hardly.

When the audience first encounters Robin, he is merely an archer accompanying Richard the Lionheart (Danny Huston) back from the Crusades. However, the last name the character has been given, Longstride, makes him sound like someone destined to command-ingly come to the fore. As Richard's protracted military expeditions have not only drained a lot of blood from Muslims in the Holy Land but also much money from his subject's pockets, he decides on his way home to make a forceful withdrawal of wealth from a French castle. A fatal arrow to the neck takes all the fun out of this for the monarch, but before it does, viewers are presented with a chaotic and cacophonous, throng-choked and mud-mired display, an onslaught replete with fireball explosions and air thick with arrows. Scott is, of course, quite skilled as far as spectacle is concerned, but, especially as the film wears on, the battle scenes acquire a tiresome sameness and seem as interminable as the Crusades themselves. Even Robin expresses battle fatigue early on, along with what seems like a post-9/11 reminder that not all followers of Islam are worthy of condemnation and vengeance in the name of God. After contrivedly coming into possession of not only the dead king's crown but also the sword of mortally-wounded Sir Robert Loxley (Douglas Hodge), Robin promises to honor the latter's dying request to return the weapon to elderly Sir Walter Loxley (Max von Sydow). Besides, the inscription naggingly tries to trigger memories in Robin that stubbornly remain out of reach.

Meanwhile (and as the *New York Times'* A.O. Scott correctly stated, "there is a whole lot of meanwhile in this crowded, lumbering film"), insolent Prince John (Oscar Isaac) is unquestionably ready to mount his French mistress (Léa Seydoux), but the throne of England is something else entirely. His mother, Eleanor of Aquitaine (Eileen Atkins), never thought he was much of a son, and worries what sort of ruler he might become. When Richard's demise is revealed and John is crowned, the new king proceeds to alienate his country's already-strapped citizens with additional, callously-oppressive taxation. John refuses the counsel of fair-minded William Marshal (a suitably-august William Hurt), and instead mistakenly trusts his follicularlychallenged lifelong friend Sir Godfrey (Mark Strong). Godfrey is a two-faced (both of them glowering) meanie in cahoots with the King of France (Jonathan Zaccai), who is hoping to conquer a destabilized England. Traitorous Godfrey is not only the one who slayed Sir Robert, but he later hacks off more of the Loxley family tree by sadistically skewering poor old Sir Walter. Even though von Sydow's character is blind, the actor's effective and affecting portrayal provides him with a twinkle in his eyes that is especially welcome in this film. Strong succeeds in making viewers feel a rising desire to punch Godfrey in his oyster-slurping mouth. (One just bets the scoundrel scarfs down escargot whenever possible, too.)

When Robin arrives in Nottingham at the Loxleys', the Marion (Cate Blanchett) he meets bears startlingly little resemblance to the character's previous incarnations. She may be in distress, struggling to keep the place running despite poverty and pilferers, but she is no damsel: not Maid Marion but Lady Loxley, widow of Sir Robert. The woman is neither heart-meltingly radiant nor demure but one ice-cold cookie, gutsy and dogged and deferring to no one. Early on, when the dastardly Sheriff of Nottingham (Matthew Macfadyen) makes a pass at her, Marion bites him. Later in the film, when she is almost raped by a soldier, the only penetration that takes place is her knife into his neck. In the film's climactic beach battle scene (which weirdly features troop transport vessels reminiscent of WWII's D-Day), Marion rather improbably shows up as a weapon-wielding avenger in disguise, hell-bent on stopping what has been passing for Godfrey's heart. When Walter asks Robin to keep up a pretense of being Sir Robert so that husbandless Marion will not resultantly lose her land, she gives the useful imposter plenty of wary, warning looks—and threatens to slice off his manhood should he get any ideas of taking the charade too far. One certainly marvels at her profound pluck, but then consequently it is hard to worry a great deal about her and impossible to be beguiled—at least for viewers. As for Robin, he potently procures much-needed seed with the help of Friar Tuck (Mark Addy) and plants it in her fields with the assistance of his other merry men: Little John (Kevin Durand), Will Scarlet (Scott Grimes), and Alan A'Dayle (Alan Doyle). Marion begins to thaw, and a romance supposedly blossoms. Anyone able to perceive a scintilla of heat between this Robin and Marion deserves a prize.

Thus, it is seriousness of purpose and a realistic depiction of place that rules in this *Robin Hood,* not any electric ebullience or romance. In addition, one is struck by the decided deficiency of mischievous wit. Made on a budget of $200 million, the film only succeeded in grossing just over half of that. When it opened the prestigious Cannes Film Festival, the audience was reportedly underwhelmed and silent as the credits rolled. Most critics expressed disappointment, despite being impressed with the cinematography and ample evidence of painstaking production design. Comparing what was expected to be in the offing with what they actually got, many felt like victims of bait and switch. The *New York Times'* review of the 1922 version spoke of a "tremendous spectacle," which, as previously mentioned, Scott also provides, but in addition something that met expectations for "unbridled delight." Writing of the 1938 film, the newspaper glowingly proclaimed "that here, romantics, is a tale of high adventure, where blood is spilled and arrows fly, villains scowl and heroes smile, swords are flashed and traitors die—a tale of pageantry, brave words and comic byplay." There was delicious "derring-do" by a Robin Hood who is "quick for a fight or a frolic." Imagine if anyone had suggested to Crowe that his Robin should do a little of that frolicking: the person would likely have had to duck a fist. (The actor did become volcanically vexed when questioned about his character's variable accent.)

The clear aim here was for what producer Brian Grazer called "the *Gladiator* version of *Robin Hood,*" and elements are included that those involved clearly hoped would also give this film Maximus appeal. Crowe once again portrays the able bodied (if beefier) man with close-cropped hair and beard who is thrust forward by extraordinary circumstances to become an inspiringly resolute and righteous champion of the people. After crucially uniting his countrymen with a high-minded appeal, this solid and stolid Robin leads them to a triumph over the French, gives treasonous Godfrey his deadly due, and then spearheads the drawing-up of the Magna Carta's historic fundamental protections from heedless royalty run-amuck. (Flashbacks from Robin's newly-remembered past unconvincingly reveal old ties between the protagonist, Marshal, Sir Walter, and Robin's late father, the latter said to have been a "visionary and philosopher" who literally lost his head while stalwartly pressing for a document similar to the Magna Carta years before.) Robin becomes, as the film's production notes declare, "an eternal symbol of freedom for his people." Impressive laurels, especially for an individual who was never actually involved in any of it, largely kept from doing so by the fact that he never existed.

Only in this turgid production's last moments does King John, feeling jealous and threatened, put a price on the head of Robin Hood and all who help him, finally making him into the character that has succeeded in intriguing so many for so long. "And so the legend begins" then appears on the screen, ending the film where most viewers would much rather it had started.

David L. Boxerbaum

CREDITS

Robin Hood: Russell Crowe
Maid Marion: Cate Blanchett
Sheriff of Nottingham: Matthew Macfadyen
William Marshall: William Hurt
Sir Godfrey: Mark Strong
Friar Tuck: Mark Addy
Will Scarlet: Scott Grimes
Little John: Kevin Durand
Eleanor of Aquitaine: Eileen Atkins
Prince John: Oscar Isaac
King Richard: Danny Huston
Alan A'Dayle: Alan Doyle
Sir Robert Loxley: Douglas Hodge
Sir Walter Loxley: Max von Sydow
Isabella: Léa Seydoux
King Philip: Jonathan Zaccai
Origin: United Kingdom, USA
Language: English
Released: 2010
Production: Brian Grazer, Ridley Scott, Russell Crowe; Image Entertainment, Relativity Media; released by Universal Pictures
Directed by: Ridley Scott
Written by: Brian Helgeland
Cinematography by: John Mathiesen
Music by: Marc Streitenfeld
Sound: Nerses Gezalyan
Editing: Pietro Scalia
Costumes: Janty Yates
Production Design: Arthur Max
MPAA rating: PG-13
Running time: 140 minutes

REVIEWS

Alter, Ethan. *Film Journal International.* July 2010.
Chang, Justin. *Variety.* May 17, 2010.
Edelstein, David. *New York.* May 24, 2010.
Gleiberman, Owen. *Entertainment Weekly.* May 21, 2010.
Lane, Anthony. *New Yorker.* May 24, 2010.
Longworth, Karina. *Village Voice.* May 12, 2010.
Morgenstern, Joe. *Wall Street Journal.* May 14, 2010.
Scott, A.O.. *New York Times.* May 14, 2010.
Travers, Peter. *Rolling Stone.* May 27, 2010.
Wheat, Alynda. *People.* May 24, 2010.
Wigley, Samuel. *Sight & Sound.* July 2010.

QUOTES

Robin Longstride: "If you thought it was hard getting wages from him when he was alive, try getting wages from a dead king."

Godfrey: "In the name of King John, pay or burn."

TRIVIA

Russell Crowe was 45 when he played Robin Hood, making him the oldest person to ever play the role.

AWARDS

Nomination:

Screen Actors Guild 2010: Stunt Ensemble.

THE RUNAWAYS

> *It's 1975 and they're about to explode.*
> —Movie tagline

Box Office: $4 million

When The Runaways released their self-titled debut in 1976, they were the first and only all-female band making a name for themselves playing loud, sexed-up, guitar-heavy music. But the group did not come about naturally; it was conceived with commercial intentions that were readily apparent to most music fans. So their success was modest and their career short-lived, even though their music would later prove to be groundbreaking. That is often the experience of trailblazers in pop culture, so it is just as often that their untold stories make terrific subjects for feature films years later. It is disappointing, then, that in the case of *The Runaways,* the story behind the band is apparently far-less-intriguing than the legacy the band left behind.

Although The Runaways were a five-piece band, the producers of the film chose to focus on its two most notable—and polarized—personalities: Joan Jett (Kristen Stewart), the leather-clad, axe-wielding tomboy, and Cherie Currie (Dakota Fanning), the glamorous, sun-kissed lead vocalist. At the start of the film, both restless teens struggle to find their place in a world that does not quite suit them. They are consistently disappointed by family members, classmates, and suitors and retreat deeper and deeper into their love of music for solace. Even there, they are met with resistance, as Jett is denied electric guitar lessons by her teacher on account of her gender and Currie is pelted off the talent show stage at school for a strange and fully-committed Bowie routine. Only Kim Fowley (Michael Shannon), the legendary producer, promoter, and L.A. scenester, recognizes the makings of an explosive recipe when he sees one. So when he is approached by Jett, hawking the idea of an "all-girl rock band," the notorious svengali sets the two of them up, along with three other local, wannabe rockers. He then proceeds to sculpt and mold the band's image, sound, and manifesto, before sending them out on a number of skin-thickening road gigs. Eventually, The Runaways get signed, record a brash and noisy debut album, gain pockets of notoriety here and there and embark on a tour of Japan, diving head first into the rock n' roll lifestyle.

Though screenwriter/director Floria Sigismondi does not give Stewart and Fanning much dialogue beyond that of any normal hard-partying teenager, they make nice use of physicality—both off-stage and on—to flesh out characters that are believable as both teenage outcasts and rock goddesses. Jett's flinty stare and gum-chomping swagger feels like a natural evolution for Stewart, who is most known for her gloomy turn in *The Twilight Saga* (2008-2012). But Fanning is perhaps more surprising here. As Currie, she suddenly conveys a world-weary maturity and awareness of sensuality one could not have anticipated from the actress of *War of the Worlds* (2005) and *Charlotte's Web* (2006). However, in much the same way that the girls are little match for Fowley's overpowering personality, the brilliant actor portraying him (Michael Shannon of *Revolutionary Road* [2008] and *Bug* [2006]) steals nearly every scene he shares with the band. Some of the film's most invigorating moments take place early on, as The Runaways rehearse in a trash-ridden trailer, while Fowley—6'3" and in make-up—rants, raves and leaps about, intimidating and inspiring them as if running a boot camp for girls preparing to enter the man's world of rock n' roll. Unfortunately, as the band hits the road and he is relegated to the roll of manager-by-phone, the film begins to sorely miss the vivacity he was bringing to it.

Soon, a story that started off with interesting characters collapses into a series of standard-issue, music biopic clichés. Once The Runaways achieve some minor success and their fascination with rock n' roll begins to wear off, the excitement and energy of the film's first half go with it. The girls shun their families, lose themselves in sex and drugs, fall prey to egos and in-fighting and inevitably, break-up. In the right hands, typical cinematic situations such as those can still be engrossing, as long as the protagonist's humanity remains the focus. But Sigismondi used to direct music videos and the moment The Runaways become an honest-to-goodness band, it feels as though her past instincts lunge for the controls, setting them to "music video autopilot." So, although the concert scenes crackle with life, the drug binges look sufficiently psychedelic and the soundtrack has rock attitude to burn, the script is hard-pressed to find many remaining traces of character. Ultimately, Jett goes on to find solo success with hits like "I Love Rock n' Roll" and "Bad Reputation." But by the time the movie gets around to her reconciliation with Currie via call-in radio show (a real-life event that was downright made for the movies, if ever there was

one), the viewer's wish for their renewed friendship has mostly waned.

The problem with all this, of course, is that the path the film follows is fairly representative of The Runaways' actual story. Fowley's initial conception of the band essentially revolved around putting instruments in the hands of jailbait, in a commercially-crass attempt to capitalize on female objectification and empowerment simultaneously. But the bulk of the music-listening public recognized it for what it was and dismissed it as such. And the girls eventually joined the long list of rock clichés they had hoped to shake up. But over time, their place in history has been cemented and their impact has grown immensely, paving the way for artists such as Hole, The Go-Go's, and The Donnas. And the band is often now viewed as an important milestone in the course of the music industry's slow acceptance of women as rock artists. So it is their thirty-year legacy that continues to garner more interest than the story of their two-year existence. And in losing sight of its characters along the way, this film does not do much to convince otherwise.

Matt Priest

CREDITS

Joan Jett: Kristen Stewart
Cherie Currie: Dakota Fanning
Lita Ford: Scout Taylor-Compton
Sandy West: Stella Maeve
Robin: Alia Shawkat
Tammy: Hannah Marks
Kim Fowley: Michael Shannon
Donald Currie: Brett Cullen
Marie Harmon: Tatum O'Neal
Origin: USA
Language: English
Released: 2010
Production: Art Linson, John Linson; River Road Entertainment, Linson Entertainment; released by Apparition
Directed by: Floria Sigismondi
Written by: Floria Sigismondi
Cinematography by: Benoit Debie
Sound: Edward Tise
Music Supervisor: George Drakoulias
Editing: Richard Chew
Costumes: Carol Beadle
Production Design: Eugenio Caballero
MPAA rating: R
Running time: 109 minutes

REVIEWS

Burr, Ty. *Boston Globe.* April 9, 2010.
Ebert, Roger. *Chicago Sun-Times.* March 17, 2010.
Harvey, Dennis. *Variety.* January 26, 2010.
Longworth, Karina. *Village Voice.* March 16, 2010.
Phillips, Michael. *Chicago Tribune.* March 18, 2010.

Rabin, Nathan. *AV Club.* March 18, 2010.
Sharkey, Betsy. *Los Angeles Times.* March 19, 2010.
Stevens, Dana. *Slate.* March 19, 2010.
Weitzman, Elizabeth. *New York Daily News.* March 18, 2010.
Zacharek, Stephanie. *Salon.com.* March 18, 2010.

QUOTES

Cherie Currie: "Like she's ever worn anything twice? Anyway, you should be more worried about her finding out about how old your skanky boyfriend is."

Kim Fowley: "I like your style. A little Bowie, a little Bardot, and a look on your face that says I could kick the sh*t out of a truck driver."

TRIVIA

The actors cast in the roles of the bandmembers spent an entire month before filming began to rehearse and record The Runaways' songs.

S

SALT

Who is Salt?
   —Movie tagline
Salt will not be stopped.
   —Movie tagline

Box Office: $118 million

Salt is a film that could not be more preposterous if it tried and it is always trying. Like most of the eminently forgettable blockbuster extravaganzas of late, it is filled with clichéd characters, ridiculously over-scaled action sequences that defy all known limitations of physics, and a storyline that is so patently silly and confusing that the biggest challenge for the actors seems to be in trying to keep a straight face as the absurdities pile higher and higher. The difference is that in addition to these elements, *Salt* also has, in Philip Noyce, a director who knows how to deliver the action goods with a certain amount of style and grace and, in Angelina Jolie, a star who so thoroughly commands the screen that it is impossible to imagine anyone else in the part. Thanks to their efforts, what could have been just another live-action cartoon instead becomes one of the more effective action films in recent memory.

Jolie stars as CIA field agent Evelyn Salt and as the film opens, she has just been captured by the North Koreans before eventually being sprung by an effort spearheaded by her German arachnologist boyfriend, Mike (August Diehl) and brokered by her agency superior, Ted Winter (Liev Schreiber). When the story picks up two years later, Salt is working out of Washington D.C. and is about to go home to Mike to celebrate their anniversary when a Russian named Orlov

(Daniel Olbrychski) walks into the building and announces that he wants to defect, he is dying of cancer and that he has important information that he wants to reveal so that he can die with a clean conscience. Salt gets the job of interviewing him to see if he has any information of value and during the interrogation, Orlov spins a wild story that connects Lee Harvey Oswald, *The Brady Bunch,* and a vast network of Russian sleeper agents that have been training since childhood for the time when they would be unleashed and cause enough chaos to bring America to its knees and reestablish Russia as the one true superpower. In fact, one of those sleeper agents is scheduled to assassinate the president of Russia in New York City the very next day, when he is scheduled to speak at the funeral of the recently deceased American vice-president. Salt finds the entire story to be ridiculous and is about to turn Orlov over to another interrogator when he unexpectedly reveals the name of the agent set to perform the assassination—Evelyn Salt.

This revelation does not go over particularly well with Salt's co-workers despite her protests of innocence. While Ted is willing to give her a chance to explain, by-the-book agency rival Peabody (Chiwetel Ejiofor) wants to put her in immediate custody until things can get sorted out. Before anything can happen, Orlov makes a break for it and in the confusion, Salt, realizing that Mike is now in imminent danger, takes advantage of the situation and escapes from the locked-down building with the help of a weapon constructed out of a trash can, a fire extinguisher, and the contents of a first aid kit. When she returns home, Mike is gone and after a second narrow escape from the authorities, she dyes her hair black to escape detection and makes her way to

New York and the funeral to either prevent or pull off the assassination. No fair revealing what happens from this point on except to note that before the film ends, there will be any number of impossible escapes, several elaborate disguises, several additional assassination attempts, a threatened nuclear strike, wildly unexpected plot developments (one involving the crucial deployment of spider venom), and a shocking last-minute reveal that most viewers will be able to figure out the moment they see the cast list.

With its ridiculously convoluted story and its attempt to revive the Russkies as the biggest baddies around, *Salt* feels like it was inspired from a long-forgotten novel of the kind that one would normally only see people reading while in the middle of long plane flights. On the bright side, it seems evident that screenwriter Kurt Wimmer knows just how absurd the story is and plays up to that at certain points—note how Salt is always able to come across a convenient rack of hats or clothes that she can not only randomly pilfer at a moment's notice when the need arises but somehow manages to look like a supermodel with the results of her blind grabs every single time. What is interesting, though, is how director Phillip Noyce, whose previous efforts have included the Jack Ryan epics *Patriot Games* (1992) and *Clear and Present Danger* (1994), has chosen to approach the admittedly flamboyant material in a relatively straightforward and realistic manner—well, as straightforward and realistic as can be achieved under the circumstances. Instead of staging his action sequences as live-action cartoons in which every shot is augmented by some form of CGI, he goes for an old-school approach that favors the practical effects and snappy stunt work that used to bring action films to life back in the day. There are still plenty of sequences that stretch the boundaries of credibility (especially during Salt's truck-hopping freeway escape and a later sequence in which she hurtles herself down what appears to be the world's biggest elevator shaft) but thanks to Noyce's comparatively grounded take on the material, they never stretch the boundaries too far. Noyce is also an economical storyteller as well and in a time when even something as frivolous and inessential as *The Sorcerer's Apprentice* (2010) somehow requires two hours of screen time to tell its non-existent story, it is to his credit that he can take a story as overstuffed as this one and bring it in at a blissfully-lean 97 minutes.

Of course, the most impressive visual effect on display in *Salt* is Angelina Jolie, whose strong and smart performance is the other anchor that keeps the film from floating off into total silliness. Because it is in the service of an unabashedly pulpy action thriller, her acting will most likely be overlooked in most quarters but she really does an excellent job of taking such a potentially implausible character and turning her into someone quasi-believable. Yes, she is convincing enough in the scenes in which she is running and jumping and pounding the stuffing out of the luckiest stuntmen around but she is equally convincing during the admittedly rare character-driven moments as well. In fact, even though the question of where Salt's loyalties really lie is probably answered a little quicker than need be, Jolie manages to supply the character with enough of a sense of ambiguity that even the most cynical, seen-it-all-before viewers may be second-guessing themselves at certain points. Jolie is such a perfect fit for the role, in fact, that it is interesting to note that this project was originally designed as a star vehicle for Tom Cruise and the lead role underwent gender reassignment when he turned it down and she signed on instead. *Salt* might have worked with Cruise in the lead but Jolie's presence adds a certain something that cannot be denied and which separates it from most other summer action epics as clearly as, well, Cruise's own *Knight and Day* (2010).

Peter Sobczynski

CREDITS

Evelyn Salt: Angelina Jolie
Ted Winter: Liev Schreiber
Peabody: Chiwetel Ejiofor
Vassily Orlov: Daniel Olbrychski
Mike Krause: August Diehl
Origin: USA
Language: English
Released: 2010
Production: Lorenzo di Bonaventura, Sunil Perkash; Relativity Media, di Bonaventura Pictures, Columbia Pictures, Wintergreen Productions; released by Columbia Pictures
Directed by: Phillip Noyce
Written by: Kurt Wimmer, Brian Helgeland
Cinematography by: Robert Elswit
Music by: James Newton Howard
Sound: Paul Hsu, Philip Stockton, Warren Shaw
Editing: Stuart Baird, John Gilroy
Art Direction: Teresa Carriker-Thayer
Costumes: Sarah Edwards
Production Design: Scott Chambliss
MPAA rating: PG-13
Running time: 91 minutes

REVIEWS

Chang, Justin. *Variety.* July 19, 2010.
Corliss, Richard. *Time Magazine.* July 22, 2010.
Ebert, Roger. *Chicago Sun-Times.* July 22, 2010.
Longworth, Karina. *Village Voice.* July 20, 2010.

Pais, Matt. *Metromix.com.* July 22, 2010.
Phillips, Michael. *Chicago Tribune.* July 22, 2010.
Phipps, Keith. *AV Club.* July 22, 2010.
Puig, Claudia. *USA Today.* July 22, 2010.
Reed, Rex. *New York Observer.* July 21, 2010.
White, Armond. *New York Observer.* July 21, 2010.

QUOTES

Evelyn Salt: "Im not a goddamn Russian spy."

TRIVIA

It was reported that Angelina Jolie performed most of her own stunts in this film.

The original screenplay had a male lead to be played by Tom Cruise which was subsequently rewritten for a female lead after Cruise backed out.

AWARDS

Nomination:

Oscars 2010: Sound.

SAW 3D: THE FINAL CHAPTER

The traps come alive.
—Movie tagline

Box Office: $46 million

Since making its blood-soaked debut in 2004, the *Saw* horror film franchise has thoroughly dominated the Halloween moviegoing period to such an extent that even a seasonally apropos title such as Rob Zombie's remake of *Halloween* (2007) moved its release date to the end of summer in order to avoid being steamrolled by the Jigsaw juggernaut. Last year, however, in a twist far more shocking than anything that the films had been coming up with, *Saw VI* (2009) surprised observers by proving to be a relative non-starter at the box-office. Observers came up with numerous theories as to why this happened—the chief ones being the surprise success of the concurrently released genre entry *Paranormal Activity* (2009) and a backlash against the incredibly lazy and slapdash *Saw V* (2008), a film that even hardcore fans of the series looked upon with disdain—but for the most part, its failure to take off seemed to derive mostly from a growing sense of boredom with its combination of stomach-churning splatter, pseudo-profound yet utterly inane dialogue and narrative structures so ridiculously complicated that *Inception* (2010) seemed like a miracle of linear construction by comparison. Therefore, one might have hoped that if the producers were interested in keeping the franchise going, they would

make an effort with their next follow-up by trying to inject some fresh creative blood into the proceedings. Instead, they have simply offered up another helping of the same old slop garnished with two of the more familiar gimmicks utilized by horror series on the ropes—the addition of 3D and the solemn promise that this entry is absolutely, positively going to be the last one—and the result, the imaginatively titled *Saw 3D* (which theoretically sounds a little fresher than *Saw VII*), may well be the most useless and creatively bankrupt of the lot.

Because the storylines for the films have grown so convoluted over time that anyone hoping to make heads or tails out of them not only has to have seen all the previous installments but needs to have seen all of them exactly five minutes before watching the new one (neither of which is recommended, by the way), anyone without a working knowledge of the saga is advised to check out at this point as nothing that follows is likely to make any sense. Like most of the other films, *Saw 3D* tells two parallel stories that sort of collide together in the last few minutes in a rush of blood, guts, and breathless exposition. In the first, the psychotic Lt. Mark Hoffman (Costas Mandylor), a cop who somehow became the secret accomplice of the Rube Goldberg-inspired serial killer Jigsaw (Tobin Bell, who gets top billing here despite making little more than a cameo appearance—perfectly understandable when one recalls that his character definitively shuffled off this mortal coil at the end of *Saw III* (2006)), is obsessed with hunting down and killing Jigsaw's widow (Betsy Russell), the only one who knows his murderous secret, while simultaneously being pursued by an internal affairs agent (Chad Donella) with whom he also has a past marked with violence. In the other, Sean Patrick Flannery plays Bobby Dagan, a survivor of one of Jigsaw's previous traps, who has become a successful self-help guru after writing a book about surviving his harrowing ordeal. As it turns out, Bobby made the whole thing up and as punishment for his misdeeds, he is abducted and forced to undergo a grueling and gruesome series of hoops that generally end up with his friends and loved ones being folded, spindled, and mutilated before his eyes. There is also the suggestion that there may be another Jigsaw accomplice running around making murderous mischief, a suspicion that is bolstered by the return of Dr. Gordon (Cary Elwes), the lone survivor of the original *Saw.*

As with the other films in the series, no one really cares about whether *Saw 3D* tells a story that is interesting, original, or even borderline coherent, least of all the screenwriters themselves. The only thing of interest for most viewers is the quality and quantity of the elaborately violent set-pieces that the filmmakers have come up with this time around. While the quantity of kills is certainly high—it seems as if blood and body parts are being shed every five minutes or so—the quality is once again sadly lacking as the grisly inventiveness of the original has once again devolved into a series of ugly sequences that somehow manage to simultaneously come across as utterly repellent and utterly banal. This time around, the three members of a romantic triangle are forced to reduce their ranks by one via power saws, the wound left by a recently amputated foot is cauterized by a steam pipe, a quartet of skinheads are done in by a car rigged to decimate them all, an annoying publicist has pipes shoved through her throat, a lawyer has her eyes and mouth gouged out, our hero is forced to pull out his own teeth in order to discover clues that have been etched on them and the closest thing the film has to a sympathetic character—the author's sweet and unsuspecting wife—winds up getting roasted alive for her troubles. As for the 3D component, it only detracts from the proceedings because the combination of the reduced brightness that is an unavoidable byproduct of the process combined with the already dark and murky visual aesthetic established by the series, in which virtually all the action takes place at night and in darkened rooms or grubby warehouses, results in a film that is literally almost impossible to watch at times. The only good thing about that is that there is absolutely nothing on display here that any sentient and life-affirming viewer would want to subject their eyes to in the first place.

While watching a shabby and squalid bag of goods like *Saw 3D,* it seems almost impossible to believe that it is the offspring of a film that was respected enough to earn slots at both the Sundance and Toronto International Film Festivals and was hailed by audiences and most critics as a clever and resourceful work that effectively merged gore and psychological tension into a gruelingly effective genre exercise. That said, whatever inventiveness it might have once maintained has long since been spent as the series has devolved into the kind of utterly useless trash that gives horror movies a bad name and which seemingly exists only to provide beer money for the likes of Costas Mandylor and Betsy Russell. The best thing about *Saw 3D* is that it does conclude in a way that sort of brings everything full circle in a manner that suggests that the saga is finally coming to its long-overdue end. On the other hand, it does leave itself a bit of wiggle room in case it winds up making enough money to cause the producers to reconsider their decision and stretch things out

even further. This, it should be noted, is the only thing about *Saw 3D* that could remotely be described as scary.

Peter Sobczynski

CREDITS

Dr. Lawrence Gordon: Cary Elwes
Bobby Dagen: Sean Patrick Flanery
Mark Hoffman: Costas Mandylor
Jill Tuck: Betsy Russell
Joyce Dagen: Gina Holden
Jigsaw/John: Tobin Bell
Det. Matt Gibson: Chad Donella
Origin: USA
Language: English
Released: 2010
Production: Gregg Hoffman, Oren Koules, Mark Burg; Twisted Pictures; released by Lionsgate
Directed by: Kevin Greutert
Written by: Marcus Dunstan, Patrick Melton
Cinematography by: Brian Gedge
Music by: Charlie Clouser
Editing: Andrew Coutts
Sound: Greg Chapman
Art Direction: Peter Grundy
Costumes: Alex Kavanagh
Production Design: Anthony Ianni
MPAA rating: R
Running time: 90 minutes

REVIEWS

Gonzalez, Rob. *Slant Magazine.* October 29, 2010.
Hale, Mike. *New York Times.* October 29, 2010.
Michel, Brett. *Boston Herald.* October 29, 2010.
Nelson, Rob. *Variety.* October 29, 2010.
Newman, Kim. *Empire Magazine.* October 29, 2010.
O'Hehir, Andrew. *Salon.com.* October 29, 2010.
Pais, Matt. *Metromix.com.* October 28, 2010.
Schager, Nick. *Village Voice.* October 29, 2010.
Snider, Eric. D. *Cinematical.* October 29, 2010.
Weinberg, Scott. *FEARnet.* October 29, 2010.

QUOTES

Dr. Gordon: "Bravo! To be able to sustain such a traumatic experience and, uh…and yet find a positive in that grizzly act. It's a remarkable feat, indeed. Remarkable…if not a little perverse."
Hoffman: "You wanna know the only thing that's wrong with killing you, Jill? I can only do it once."

TRIVIA

The producers opted to convert the seventh *Saw* film to 3D after they viewed the original *Saw* film converted to 3D.
With a budget hovering around $17 million, *Saw 3D* is the

most expensive *Saw* film to date due the complexity of shooting in 3D.

AWARDS

Nomination:

Golden Raspberries 2010: Worst Use of 3D.

SCOTT PILGRIM VS. THE WORLD

An epic of epic epicness.
    —Movie tagline

Get the hot girl. Defeat her evil exes. Hit love where it hurts.
    —Movie tagline

Box Office: $32 million

Few directors have their finger quite as firmly on the pulse of youth and geek culture as Edgar Wright. But with this third offering, *Scott Pilgrim vs. the World*, Wright has stepped slightly out of his comfort zone as a collaborator and, for the first time, is not working with his usual stars Simon Pegg and Nick Frost, stars of Wright's first two films *Shaun of the Dead* (2004) and *Hot Fuzz* (2007), as well as the British television series *Spaced* (1999-2001). The results are a high-energy, furiously-edited mix of inventive images, and deadpan comedic performances, along with action sequences and other visual cues that appropriately resemble those found in the video games of the 1980s. Adapting Bryan Lee O'Malley's comic series with co-writer Michael Bacall, Wright has not simply resorted to cramming pop culture references into the mouths of twenty-something actors. Instead, he has distilled ambitious ideas with a rapturous celebration of raging hormones, pop rock music, and retro graphics into fun in its purest form.

Young Scott Pilgrim (Michael Cera) has his heart and loyalties torn between his on-the-verge-of-success band, Sex Bob-omb, and the girl of his dreams, Ramona (Mary Elizabeth Winstead), who has a small army of six evil ex-boyfriends (and one ex-girlfriend) that Scott must defeat one at a time before she can safely date him. Along his journey through these martial-arts-flavored confrontations, Scott consults his friends and family, and dodges his own jilted ex-girlfriends, including Knives (Ellen Wong). In many ways, the story of Scott's relationship with his bandmates Kim Pine and Stephen Stills (Alison Pill and Mark Webber, respectively) is as important to the film's entertainment value as the action scenes with the seven evil exes. The band sequences also make it clear that Scott's commitment issues are not exclusively the property of the women in his life.

Wright introduces a gallery of interesting characters even before the evil exes. The most interesting among them is Scott's gay roommate Wallace Wells (Kieran Culkin), a gossip fiend who gives Scott a steady stream of mostly dead-on relationship advice and can turn a straight man gay in a matter of minutes. Wallace also acts as something of a Greek chorus of cynicism and humor, commenting on every character that passes before his eyes. Also turning in a memorable performance as Wallace's gossip partner is Anna Kendrick as Scott's sister Stacey, a judgmental creature who seems on hand merely for comic relief. While it may seem that *Scott Pilgrim vs. the World*'s main objective is to get its titular character from fight to fight (Brandon Routh, Chris Evans, and Jason Schwartzman are three of the more notable names playing evil exes), Wright has cleverly made the aftermath of each action sequence a time when Scott can reflect on what negative personality trait he shares with the ex he has just defeated.

Taking its cue from the source comic books, the film's visual style and narrative structure are presented in a choppy, manically-edited format, resembling the panels in a comic book with each frame representing a change in the action or new location. Wright has essentially abandoned conventional cinematic storytelling devices and given us a collage of names and faces that make up Scott's life. The fight scenes could easily be interpreted as metaphor rather than actual knock-down, drag-out battles. The audience is seeing the world through Scott's eyes, and as a result, we are getting his impressions of the world around him, in which Ramona's exes represent a threat. While the visually-thrilling fight sequences are always hilarious—the exes explode into a rain of gold coins when defeated—they are inevitably the least interesting sections of the film. Far more engaging are Scott and Ramona's discussions about the trail of dejected ex-lovers that both have left in their wake over the years, and how they as a couple will attempt to avoid repeating their past mistakes with each other.

The much-reported video game references that may have scared some potential audience members are actually not game-specific, and those that are referencing arcade games that were played only in arcades nearly thirty years ago. They in no way dominate the dialogue or visual landscape of the movie by any measure. What *Scott Pilgrim vs. the World* does reveal is that Edgar Wright is more of a craftsman than he has been given credit for in the past. His apparent talent prior to this movie seemed to be limited to paying tribute to particular genres (such as zombie films or buddy-cop action movies), but Wright's true gift has always been his ability to be inclusive. An audience member does not need to understand genre films, video games, or comic books to appreciate his works. He can breathe joy and a sense of the mischievous into any subject, and only he would envision Cera taking a hero's stance and becoming an action star. *Scott Pilgrim vs. the World* is more than bright lights and pretty colors. It is front loaded with great adventures, catchy music, heightened emotions, and a hero that is not always likable, but is usually worth rooting for.

Steven Prokopy

CREDITS

Scott Pilgrim: Michael Cera
Ramona Flowers: Mary Elizabeth Winstead
Wallace Wells: Kieran Culkin
Lucas Lee: Chris Evans
Stacey Pilgrim: Anna Kendrick
Kim Pine: Alison Pill
Todd Ingram: Brandon Routh
Gideon Gordon Graves: Jason Schwartzman
Roxy Richter: Mae Whitman
Envy Adams: Brie Larson
Julie Powers: Aubrey Plaza
Stephen Stills: Mark Webber
Knives Chau: Ellen Wong
Origin: USA
Language: English
Released: 2010
Production: Eric Gitter, Nira Park, Marc Platt, Edgar Wright; Marc Platt Productions, Big Talk Productions, Closed on Mondays Entertainment; released by Universal Pictures
Directed by: Edgar Wright
Written by: Edgar Wright, Michael Bacall
Cinematography by: Bill Pope
Sound: Greg Chapman
Music Supervisor: Nigel Godrich, Kathy Nelson
Editing: Jonathan Amos, Paul Machliss
Art Direction: Nigel Churcher
Costumes: Laura Jean Shannon
Production Design: Marcus Rowland
MPAA rating: PG-13
Running time: 112 minutes

REVIEWS

Biancolli, Amy. *San Francisco Chronicle.* August 13, 2010.
Biodrowski, Steve. *CinefantastiqueOnline.com.* August 14, 2010.
Brown, Todd. *TwitchFilm.net.* August 12, 2010.
Holtreman, Vic. *ScreenRant.com.* August 13, 2010.
Jones, Kimberley. *Austin Chronicle.* August 13, 2010.
Nunziata, Nick. *Chud.com.* July 30, 2010.
Phillips, Michael. *Chicago Tribune.* August 11, 2010.
Rodriguez, Rene. *Miami Herald.* August 11, 2010.
Weinberg, Scott. *Cinematical.com.* August 13, 2010.
Wilonsky, Robert. *Village Voice.* August 11, 2010.

QUOTES

Ramona V. Flowers: "We all have baggage."

Stacey Pilgrim: "Next time, we don't date the girl with eleven evil ex-boyfriends."

Scott Pilgrim: "If I peed my pants would you pretend that I just got wet from the rain?"

TRIVIA

Writer/director Edgar Wright decided to cast Michael Cera in the lead role after watching him in episodes of *Arrested Development.*

THE SECRET IN THEIR EYES

(El secreto de sus ojos)

Box Office: $6 million

Juan Jose Campanella's *The Secret in Their Eyes* did not open stateside until 2010 but it did so on the heels of a shocking win for 2009's Best Foreign Language Film at the Academy Awards®. With a unique (and deeply-flawed) process that allows films to be submitted by countries for eligibility without a domestic release, Best Foreign Language Film often produces winners that cannot be seen by the viewing public until after taking home the most coveted trophy in film. With two of the most acclaimed films of the last several years in competition and nominated—Jacques Audiard's *A Prophet* (2010) and Michael Haneke's *The White Ribbon* (2009)—very few people were expecting a relatively-unheralded Argentinian thriller to take the prize but the ensuing controversy over a win in the category that many deem archaic (and too-often-incorrect) overshadowed the fact that Campanella's film is near great. It may not be the instant masterpiece of Audiard's or Haneke's and should not have beaten either film for any prize, but it is still an accomplished procedural with a deep emotional undercurrent that keeps it riveting from first frame to last.

Based on a novel by Eduardo Sacheri known as *La Pregunta de Sus Ojos* in its native tongue, *The Secret in Their Eyes* is an unusual thriller in that it is not so much of a mystery. In fact, the audience discovers the identity of the villain of the piece early and, not unlike David Fincher's brilliant *Zodiac* (2007), the rest of the film is more about the impact of the crime and its investigation than who actually committed it. Told largely in flashback and with numerous asides regarding both the dynamics of a close friendship and another built around unrequited love, Campanella's script (co-written by Eduardo Sacheri) is a structurally-daring one. The balancing act he maintains between the personal and procedural is what elevates the film above so many clichéd and predictable modern mysteries.

Benjamin Esposito (a brilliantly-subtle Ricardo Darin) has retired from the police force and is working on his first novel. He has chosen to follow the classic dictum of "write what you know" and wants to tell the story of the most important case of his life. To both help fill in any gaps in his memory and rekindle a relationship he wishes had never ended, he visits the gorgeous Judge Irene Menendez-Hastings (the stunning Soledad Villamil), a woman he worked the case with when they were both much younger. The majority of the film takes place in Espositio's book/flashback, but present-day asides often take place to remind viewers that this is a case with lingering power.

The case in question is that of a horrendous rape and murder in 1974. Victim Liliana Colotto had just been married and had her whole life ahead of her. Esposito and his alcoholic friend Pablo Sandoval (Guillermo Francella) tell the woman's husband Ricardo Morales (Pablo Rago) that they will do whatever it takes to find the man who has ruined his life. While looking through Liliana's photo albums, Esposito notices a man who has been caught by the camera a few times staring at the beautiful young lady. Ricardo makes a phone call and tragically learns that the man, whose name is Isidoro Gomez (Javier Godino), recently moved to Buenos Aires, where Ricardo lived with his new bride. The dots seem to be further connected when Esposito and Sandoval try to track down Gomez and he flees. When they finally do get their hands on him (after an amazing soccer stadium sequence), arrest him, and get a terrifying confession, a corrupt system kills any chance for true justice. Unanswered questions still haunt Benjamin and Irene twenty-five years later and the book clearly cannot be complete without knowing what happened to the shattered Ricardo and the maniacal Isidoro.

Juan Jose Campanella expertly weaves so many different films into one story with *The Secret in Their Eyes* that the true impact of the overall work is not really felt until the final credits. He deftly switches time periods and thematic focuses as the film works in and out from the procedural elements of how to find a brutal killer with the personal stories of Benjamin's friendship with the increasingly-difficult Pablo and the love he clearly feels for Irene. Issues of age and Benjamin's inability to express his true feelings for Irene kept them apart in the 1970s and it seems like the way his story ended with her has haunted him as much as the case that got away.

Darin and Villamil are both spectacular with honest chemistry and complete believability in every moment.

Buoyed by the very strong lead performances, as Campanella jumps from genre to genre (thriller, romance, procedural, mystery, drama), he never loses sight of his characters. *The Secret in Their Eyes* is about the ripple effect caused by one horrendous act, something that carries through multiple lives and over decades. Where so many other filmmakers would have dove head first into the clichés and the melodrama of the story, Campanella almost entirely avoids the potential pitfalls of his story. Ultimately, the piece is not as ambitious as *A Prophet* or *The White Ribbon* but it is a searing, accomplished mystery/thriller that lingers in the viewer's mind long after its running time. Clearly, long enough for voters filling out their Oscar® ballots.

Brian Tallerico

CREDITS

Benjamin: Ricardo Darin

Irene: Soledad Villamil

Sandoval: Guillermo Francella

Morales: Pablo Rago

Gomez: Javier Godino

Origin: Argentina, Spain

Language: Spanish

Released: 2009

Production: Gerardo Herrero, Mariela Besuievski, Juan Jose Campanella; Tornasol Films SA, 100 Bares; released by Sony Pictures Classics

Directed by: Juan Jose Campanella

Written by: Juan Jose Campanella, Eduardo Sacheri

Cinematography by: Felix Monti

Music by: Federico Jusid

Sound: Jose L. Diaz

Editing: Juan J. Campanella

Art Direction: Marcelo Pont Vergés

Costumes: Cecilia Monti

MPAA rating: R

Running time: 127 minutes

REVIEWS

Dargis, Manohla. *New York Times.* April 16, 2010.
Denby, David. *New Yorker.* April 12, 2010.
Holland, Jonathan. *Variety.* March 3, 2010.
Keller, Louise. *Urban Cinefile.* May 29, 2010.
O'Connor, Clint *Cleveland Plain Dealer.* May 20, 2010.
Phillips, Michael. *Chicago Tribune.* April 22, 2010.
Rea, Steven. *Philadelphia Inquirer.* April 29, 2010.
Sharkey, Betsy. *Los Angeles Times.* April 15, 2010.

Stevens, Dana. *Slate*. April 16, 2010.
Young, Deborah. *Hollywood Reporter*. March 3, 2010.

QUOTES

Pablo Sandoval: "A guy can change anything. His face, his home, his family, his girlfriend, his religion, his God. But there's one thing he can't change. He can't change his passion."

Ricardo Morales: "If you keep going over the past, you're going to end up with a thousand pasts and no future."

TRIVIA

This is the second Argentine film to win an Academy Award® for Best Foreign Language Film.

Also, the first Argentinean movie released on Blu-ray.

AWARDS

Oscars 2009: Foreign Film

Nomination:

British Acad. 2010: Foreign Film.

THE SECRET OF KELLS
(Brendan and the Secret of Kells)

When the 2010 Academy Award® nominations for Best Animated Feature Film were announced, the one that left almost everyone scratching their heads was *The Secret of Kells*. Not because of the movie's quality, but because outside of hardcore cineastes in New York, Los Angeles, and a few other urban centers, no one had even heard of the film, which received a quiet, one-theater qualifying run prior to awards voting. Though the distinct category has only been around less than a decade, apart from *The Triplets of Belleville* (2003), *Persepolis* (2007), and two films from Japanese maestro Hayao Miyazaki (*Spirited Away* [2002] and *Howl's Moving Castle* [2005]), nominations for the Best Animated Film Oscar® have been dominated by mainstream efforts, some of which have been decidedly unadventurous. While *The Secret of Kells* will never be mistaken for a popcorn-audience blockbuster, its deserving recognition by the Academy of Motion Picture Arts & Sciences does show a heartening willingness to embrace and reward the different possibilities of the medium.

In medieval times, young, orphaned Brendan (Evan McGuire) lives in the Abbey of Kells, a remote Irish outpost where, under the watchful eye of his uncle, Abbot Cellach (Brendan Gleeson), he dutifully helps work to fortify the abbey walls. Joyless and stern, Cellach is obsessed about preparing for the impending attack of Viking marauders, who are later represented as faceless intruders with garbled voices. But grand adventure beckons for Brendan when a celebrated master illuminator, Aidan (Mick Lally), arrives from a foreign land carrying a legendary-but-unfinished book, *The Book of Iona*, brimming with amazing artistry as well as secret wisdom and powers.

To help complete the magical manuscript, Brendan breaches the abbey's walls for the first time, heading into the forest to pick a batch of special inkberries for Aidan. There, he meets a mysterious shape-shifting fairy, Aisling (Christen Mooney), who saves him from wolves and also discloses painful secrets about her own family and childhood. When Aidan reveals that both his failing eyesight and the additional lack of a special, lost charm prevent him from completing his text, Brendan, with the barbarians closing in, gets a chance to showcase his own latent artistic vision. While he cannot completely save his village, Brendan and Aidan escape with the book, and eventually get a chance to strike a blow for the power of enlightenment.

Directed by Tomm Moore, with a co-directing credit assigned to Nora Twomey, the movie is not a conventional hero's journey, or even a rigidly structured tale. (In fact, it takes a digressive bit of third act wandering to push it over the 75-minute mark.) The story here is a fable, and best thought of as a carriage through which to ravishingly realize a tangential moral lesson. And on this front, *The Secret of Kells* succeeds wildly, capturing in aggregate the heady pleasures of surging imagination and artistic pursuit perhaps more vividly than any animated film of the past five or six years.

Visually, the film is something truly special—idiosyncratic without being flashy, informed by all the curlicued borders and ornate (some might say ostentatious) craftsmanship of medieval lettering the same sort of which are featured in Brendan's tome. It is a style that suits the material quite well, rooted in a juxtaposition of geometric shapes and a dazzling array of colors. Some of the background compositions are a mini-cubist delight, and the abbey's coterie of scribes, with their hunched necks and disproportionate bodies, reflect the skewed, looming perception of adults that adolescents often have. Moore also does a fascinating thing with light, sometimes indicating the flickering play of through-the-clouds sunlight with transparency, meaning little fragmented bits of the forest "shine" through Brendan when he goes to get the inkberries. It is small details like this that make the movie so rapturously engaging.

Perhaps most notably, though, *The Secret of Kells* does not funnel its narrative through a single, subjective stylistic point-of-view. It is instead powered by a spry, fitful, and imaginative visual scheme which allows for backgrounds to subtly shift and morph depending on a character's emotional state and point-of-view. In this way, the movie recalls the manner in which an entire narrative could be built around the changing shadows dancing across a child's bedroom wall.

This means lots of fantastical colors (a verdant green forest, and the menacing use of reds and blacks when the Vikings attack), but there is also a mostly black-and-white segment, where Brendan does battle with a serpent-like creature, that strongly recalls the refreshingly simplistic and straightforward adaptations of Edward McLachlan's *Simon in the Land of Chalk Drawings* and Crockett Johnson's *Harold and the Purple Crayon*. While its scenes are certainly of a piece, Moore and his collaborators intuitively understand animation's capacity as an intensely expressive medium, where fleeting visual cues can inform and affect an emotional response much more readily and honestly than a staid exchange of dialogue.

To this final point, it is worth noting that Moore understands the construction of a story in addition to just a visual scheme. Bruno Coulais' music unfolds in an involving swirl, and the movie's vocal performances are also engaging. As the somber, lecturing Cellach, Gleeson perfectly captures the weight of adult responsibility. Moore also lets his younger players be young, as both McGuire and especially Mooney give multiple line readings that are not polished to a fine sheen of singular emotion, but instead encompass natural adolescent ambivalence. It is a striking distinction when compared to the sentimental herding of so many animated films. But then again, the same thing can be said of *The Secret of Kells* as a whole; it is striking and pleasantly different, unfolding to its own rhythms.

Brent Simon

CREDITS

Abbot Cellach: Brendan Gleeson (Voice)

Brother Aidan: Mick Lally (Voice)

Brendan: Evan McGuire (Voice)

Aisling: Christen Mooney (Voice)

Brother Tang: Liam Hourican (Voice)

Origin: Ireland, Belgium, France

Language: English

Released: 2009

Production: Paul Young, Didier Bruner, Viviane Vanfleteren; Les Armateurs, France 2 Cinema, Cartoon Saloon, Vivi Film; released by GKIDS

Directed by: Tomm Moore, Nora Twomey

Written by: Fabrice Ziolkowski

Cinematography by: Fabienne Alvarez-Giro

Music by: Bruno Coulais

Editing: Alvarez-Giro

Sound: Kairen Waloch

Art Direction: Ross Stewart

MPAA rating: Unrated

Running time: 75 minutes

REVIEWS

Burr, Ty. *Boston Globe.* March 18, 2010.
Ebert, Roger. *Chicago Sun-Times.* April 1, 2010.
Gleiberman, Owen. *Entertainment Weekly.* March 10, 2010.
Long, Tom. *Detroit News.* April 23, 2010.
Morgenstern, Joe. *Wall Street Journal.* April 2, 2010.
Nesselson, Lisa. *Screen International.* February 2, 2010.
Rea, Steven. *Philadelphia Inquirer.* March 18, 2010.
Rechtshaffen, Michael. *Hollywood Reporter.* March 4, 2010.
Scott, A.O. *New York Times.* March 5, 2010.
Turan, Kenneth. *Los Angeles Times.* April 1, 2010.

QUOTES

Brendan: "Aidan is my friend. I'm helping him make the most incredible book in the whole world! He says it will turn darkness into light. Wait until you see it!"

Aidan: "When they come, all we can do is run and hope that we are fast enough."

AWARDS

Nomination:

Oscars 2009: Animated Film.

SECRETARIAT

> *The impossible true story.*
> —Movie tagline

Box Office: $60 million

John Malkovich, while being a daring, very good actor, is not the first person who comes to mind when thinking about casting a sports movie. When his character is first introduced in *Secretariat,* he is hilariously incompetent at hitting a golf ball off a driving range. That makes sense. Athleticism and ease with animals are not the qualities one associates with Malkovich's game.

But at least the choice of Malkovich, being so highly unorthodox, enlivens what is otherwise a by-the-book Disney biopic. *Secretariat* knows it is a winner and takes few chances. The film centers on the crowd-pleasing saga of how a Colorado housewife (daughter of a horse racing family) takes over after the illness and death of her father, recognizes something special in one of her young horses, and against all odds (foremost among them sexism in the horse racing industry and a severe financial crisis at the family farm) rides the colt's stunning success as the only Triple Crown winner in the last sixty years. Strong lady and great horse—that is not a formula worth betting against.

Especially not when the protagonist is portrayed by the always-pleasing, highly-professional Diane Lane. Lane, a veteran of daring roles in commercially-questionable films in which she often has played the wronged woman or the bad girl, now proves she can handle the perhaps easier role of a strong-willed, beautiful, smart, kind, and almost faultless central character whose judgment is (almost implausibly) always right and who has a will of steel. She manages this while commuting by air to mother her brood of teenagers and preadolescents. Apparently, her husband (Dylan Walsh) has a lot of money and infinite patience. Playing it safe, the film at one point or two approaches the question of family conflict but then backs away from it like a hot potato. Nothing is allowed to interrupt the easy trajectory of an underdog's triumph against all odds.

Lane is characteristically appealing, and tries to give nuances to her role, but she is not given much to work with in the lackluster, risk-free script by Mike Rich and William Nack and the play-it-safe direction by Randall Wallace. The story of a female owner's utter conquest over a male world of competitive sports is a natural, but crisis points are all smoothly resolved, and Lane's Penny Chenery does not seem to grow in her role or experience any doubts—she is all confidence and chutzpah right from the start, just like her never-troubled horse.

The film handles the question of Malkovich's incongruity by making him into a clownish worrywart seemingly barely involved with any hands-on interaction with the steed. At one point late in the film, he actually confesses to being afraid the horse will bite him if he touches his snout! The movie never shows him doing anything that approaches what a trainer actually does; he merely stands by and watches him race. But he does mouth French Canadian epithets, hilarious observations, and sarcastic comments. The only one not playing his part button-down straight, Malkovich is by far the most enjoyable aspect of the movie, the unlikelihood of his character and the nearly trademarked daring of his performance balancing out the utter blandness of everything else in the movie. (He is almost a satire of his own movie.) This is old-style Disney not even trying to masquerade as new-style Disney. It is squeaky clean, formulaic, uncontroversial, and audience-pleasing.

Comparing this to the last significant horse movie, *Seabiscuit,* is probably unfair. For one thing, *Seabiscuit* drew on the dramatic up-and-down trajectory of a horse with a real underdog saga that galvanized a nation; by comparison, Secretariat went straight to the top like a bullet, won his last race by an unfathomable margin, and (despite the movie's rather lame and unconvincing attempts to somehow link his fame to antiwar protests) never came close to capturing the undivided attention of a nation. This film's attempt to create an arrogant, hateful rival horse and owner cannot match the authenticity of *Seabiscuit*'s epic showdown against a really worthy foe emblematic of aristocracy. But most of all, the comparison is unfair because the film *Seabiscuit* was based on a phenomenally-reported and beautifully-told book, by Laura Hillenbrand, that interweaved the compelling stories of three lonely, brave, and flawed men. By contrast, *Secretariat* is the authorized film version of Chenery's own story, and, if there were any wrinkles in it, they have certainly been ironed out. In good sports dramas, underdog triumphs and feminist sagas, there are usually ups and downs, but *Secretariat* presents one wild ride straight to the top—heady stuff, too be sure, but nothing that provides a real jolt of surprise, nuance, or shades of gray.

Michael Betzold

CREDITS

Penny Chenery: Diane Lane
Lucien Laurin: John Malkovich
Jack Tweedy: Dylan Walsh
Bill Nack: Kevin Connolly
Bull Hancock: Fred Dalton Thompson
Miss Ham: Margo Martindale
Chris Chenery: Scott Glenn
Pancho Martin: Nestor Serrano
Kate Tweedy: Amanda Michalka
Sarah Tweedy: Carissa Capobianco
Ogden Phipps: James Cromwell
Hollis Chenery: Dylan Baker
Eddie Sweat: Nelsan Ellis
Ronnie Turcotte: Otto Thorwarth
Christopher Chenery: Julie Weiss
Origin: USA
Language: English
Released: 2010
Production: Mark Ciardi, Gordon Gray, Pete DeStafano; Fast Track Productions, Mayhem Pictures; released by Walt Disney Pictures
Directed by: Randall Wallace
Written by: Mike Rich, William Nack
Cinematography by: Dean Semler
Music by: Nick Glennie-Smith
Sound: Kami Asgar, David O. Daniel, Kevin O'Connell

Editing: John Wright
Art Direction: Sarah Boardman
Costumes: Michael T. Boyd
Production Design: Thomas E. Sanders
MPAA rating: PG
Running time: 123 minutes

REVIEWS

Biancolli, Amy. *Houston Chronicle.* October 8, 2010.
Busch, Jenna. *Huffington Post.* October 11, 2010.
Hall, Corey. *Metro Times.* October 22, 2010.
Kennedy, Lisa. *Denver Post.* October 8, 2010.
Lane, Jim. *Sacramento News & Review.* October 16, 2010.
Long, Tom. *Detroit News.* October 8, 2010.
Martin, Philip. *Arkansas Democrat-Gazette.* October 15, 2010.
Rainer, Peter. *Christian Science Monitor.* October 8, 2010.
Savada, Elias. *Film Threat.* October 15, 2010.
Stevens, Dana. *Slate.* October 8, 2010.

QUOTES

Penny Chenery: "This is not about going back. This is about life being ahead of you and you run at it! Because you never know how far you can run unless you run."

Penny Chenery: "My father's legacy is not his money. My father's legacy is the will to win."

TRIVIA

The real life Penny Chenery was always on the set during filming except for her daily afternoon nap.

The Triple Crown trophy that appeared in the film was the actual trophy on loan from the Kentucky Derby Museum.

SEX AND THE CITY 2

Carrie on.
　—Movie tagline

Box Office: $95 million

Imagining itself a great, sincere advocate of empowerment for certain groups of the downtrodden of society, *Sex and the City 2* instead promotes derision of the same groups based on stereotypes and insincere portrayals of strength. One need look no further than the event that sets in sluggish motion the continuing story of the quartet of friends from the HBO show of the same name. Carrie Preston nee Bradshaw (Sarah Jessica Parker), Samantha Jones (Kim Cattrall), Charlotte York Goldenblatt (Kristin Davis), and Miranda Hobbes (Cynthia Nixon) attend a wedding in which, as Charlotte puts, Carrie's "gay best friend" (Willie Garson) is marrying Charlotte's "gay best friend" (Mario Cantone).

It is a "gay wedding" Carrie's husband John (Chris Noth) continues to dub the upcoming ceremony, much to Carrie's scolding. That is until a partial extent of the same-sex wedding is revealed, most noticeably, apart from the all-white façade, a men's choir singing show tunes. Now, Carrie is more than pleased to call it a "gay wedding." This is before Liza Minnelli appears as herself to officiate and act as the entertainment for the reception (singing an awkward rendition of Beyonce's "Single Ladies"). The reason for her unlikely appearance is, as Miranda (supposedly the most open-minded and tolerant of the group until she is decidedly not) supposes: "Any time there's this much gay energy in one room, Liza manifests."

As quickly as it arrives (and before it even does), writer/director Michael Patrick King reduces the wedding—not to mention any political statement that the mindful inclusion of such an unnecessary sequence holds with it—to a simplistically identifiable and pigeonholed string of clichés. The betrothed couple, whose names are less important than their status as "gay best friend" to one of two of the female leads or just "the gays," are, hence, similarly observed. This is how they and anyone else outside the close-knit foursome's circle fit into the bigger scheme of the movie, which, in that way, is a fairly accurate reflection of their selfish, egotistic nature—both individually and collectively.

The two best friends are neutral in relation to the four friends' unit. They neither help nor hinder the survival of their lifestyle, and they only provide fodder for jokes and a story for Carrie's writing career, represented by an upcoming book on marriage and her nigh incessant voiceover narration, which provides King's screenplay a transitional device that is as obnoxious as it is undemanding. The hindrances to the women's lives include family. John has more desire to stay in and watch television instead of joining Carrie at social functions or going out for dinner. Charlotte's children cause her the most pain, crying for her or placing painted handprints on the backside of a vintage dress she wears while baking (Carrie consoles her with an "I'm sorry" that sounds more attuned to a death in the family, saying nothing about the wisdom of wearing a vintage dress while working in the kitchen). Miranda has had enough of her job, so she quits, giving her more time to spend with her own family, who quickly begin to annoy her.

Samantha's aggravation is cultural. After attending the movie premiere of a former lover/client (she's a publicist) Jerry "Smith" Jerrod (Jason Lewis), one of the film's producers Sheikh Khalid (Art Malik) wants Samantha to visit his new luxury hotel in Abu Dhabi to help plan a new marketing campaign. Fed up with living in a "poor country" like the United States (economic troubles affect them in no way: Carrie maintains her old apartment for the occasional writing excursion, and Miranda says she will just get another job whenever the urge strikes her to name a couple of examples), Samantha wants to go someplace rich with the only three people she knows will appreciate it as much as she will (and who can and want to drop their lives and any mountain-out-of-a-molehill problems within them).

So the quartet travels to Abu Dhabi, where no expense is spared: flying in a first class section where each passenger has her own cubicle, each having her own private car for transportation and butler to wait on any and every need, and so on. Throughout, the actresses giggle and pretend to be giddy at their fortune, singing karaoke, making observations about the status of Muslim women (stating the *niqab* covering their faces symbolizes that they do not have a voice, directly after discussing another woman who has chosen not to wear one but before discovering a gathering of women who wear the latest fashions from New York under their burqas), and finding bargains and kind men in the market.

Problems inevitably arise that they blow out of proportion, like when Carrie kisses old beau Aidan Shaw (John Corbett). Insult after insult, *Sex and the City 2* might reach its most infuriating point when Charlotte and Miranda give a patronizing toast to women who do not have their advantages. Those women are the real heroes, the two opine, but apparently the possibility—horror of horrors—of the four friends being bumped down to coach on the flight home is where the real drama lies.

Mark Dujsik

CREDITS

Carrie Bradshaw: Sarah Jessica Parker
Samantha Jones: Kim Cattrall
Charlotte York: Kristin Davis
Miranda Hobbes: Cynthia Nixon
Mr. Big: Chris Noth
Steve Brady: David Eigenberg
Harry Goldenblatt: Evan Handler
Jerry "Smith" Jerrod: Jason Lewis
Anthony Marantino: Mario Cantone
Stanford Blatch: Willie Garson
Lydia: Penélope Cruz
Sheikh Khalid: Art Malik
Aidan Shaw: John Corbett
Herself: Liza Minnelli (Cameo)
Origin: USA
Language: English
Released: 2010
Production: Michael Patrick King, John P. Melfi, Sarah Jessica Parker, Darren Star; New Line Cinema; released by Warner Bros. Pictures
Directed by: Michael Patrick King

Written by: Michael Patrick King
Cinematography by: John Thomas
Editing: Michael Berenbaum
Music Supervisor: Julia Michels
Sound: Michael Hilkene
Costumes: Patricia Field
Production Design: Jeremy Conway
MPAA rating: R
Running time: 146 minutes

REVIEWS

Berardinelli, James. *ReelViews.* May 27, 2010.
Diluna, Amy. *New York Daily News.* May 25, 2010.
Edelstein, David. *New York Magazine.* May 23, 2010.
Gonzalez, Ed. *Slant Magazine.* May 24, 2010.
Johanson, MaryAnn. *Flick Filosopher.* May 27, 2010.
Maurstad, Tom. *Dallas Morning News.* May 26, 2010.
Phillips, Michael. *Chicago Tribune.* May 26, 2010.
Puig, Claudia. *USA Today.* May 27, 2010.
Rich, Katey. *CinemaBlend.com.* May 25, 2010.
Zacharek, Stephanie. *Movieline.* May 27, 2010.

QUOTES

Miranda Hobbes: "Sometimes, as much as I love Brady, being a mother just isn't enough. I miss my job."
Samantha Jones: "Everyone knows you don't hire a hot nanny, it's the law!"

TRIVIA

The film was shipped to theaters with the codename "Heart of the Desert."
The film was not actually shot in Abu Dhabi since the government there deemed the film "too sexual."

AWARDS

Golden Raspberries 2010: Worst Actress (Parker, Nixon, Cattrall, Davis), Worst Sequel/Prequel, Worst Couple/Ensemble (Cast)

Nomination:

Golden Raspberries 2010: Worst Picture, Worst Support. Actress (Minnelli), Worst Director (King), Worst Screenplay.

SHE'S OUT OF MY LEAGUE (Hard 10)

How can a 10 go for a 5?
—Movie tagline

When she's this hot, You get one shot.
—Movie tagline

Box Office: $32 million

The comedy *She's Out of My League* represents another in a long series of films that are either produced and/or directed by Judd Apatow or inspired by films that bear his name. It remains a mystery how there has yet to be an official name for these kinds of movies or the casts that keep showing up in them. Any comedy that features Seth Rogan, Jonah Hill, Michael Sara, Paul Rudd, Jason Segal, Leslie Mann, Steve Carrell, Jay Baruchel, Danny McBride, Craig Robinson, Christopher Mintz-Plasse, Bill Hader, or James Franco can most certainly fall into the category of Apatow-esque. Yet these movies have no official name beyond maybe "Bromance" or "Raunch-mantic comedy." Past incarnations of this sort of habitual casting include The Rat Pack of the 1960s and the Brat Pack of the 1980s. At a time when just about everything in pop culture needs to be boiled down to a simple one or two word description or abbreviation, the above actors and those in their circle have remained somewhat nameless.

Perhaps it is because these talented writers and actors have maintained a relatively steady flow of mostly quality work that people have decided to just let them be without a nickname. *She's Out of My League* certainly tries mighty hard to be one of the pack, but ends up being a bit of an outcast. It has the elements of Apatow inspired work: sweetness, raunchy behavior, male bonding, and the idea of a slacker having a meaningful relationship with someone clearly out of his league (all common traits in this sub-genre). But like its protagonist, it lacks the confidence and the charisma to convince anyone that it can score better than a five or a six on the quality scale.

The main character, Kirk (Jay Baruchel), works with his buddies at an airport security station where they pass the hours by hitting on any gorgeous woman who happens to pass through. Kirk is too nice a guy to attempt that sort of thing, but when the woman of the film's title, Molly (Alice Eve), mistakenly leaves her cell phone behind before boarding the plane, Kirk must return it to her, which he does, after she invites him and a friend to attend a party she has planned. When she and Kirk finally meet, it appears that they like each other, but Kirk just knows this mutual interest cannot possibly extend beyond friendship. She is considered a "9.5." He brands himself a "5." His friends tell him that he cannot possibly do better than a "7," because nobody ever jumps more than two spaces.

But as it turns out, Molly is looking to date a guy whom she feels safe with rather than repeat the mistakes she has made in the past with guys who are more in her league. Kirk remains skeptical about her advances, but also respectfully goes along with them. Kirk is also dealing with a recent break-up, which has been made worse by the fact that his ex remains a loyal friend of his family and even brings around her new boyfriend to show off. Kirk eventually decides to just go with the situation and use it to his advantage in order to show that he has moved on from the break-up and has even upgraded.

Things get predictably complicated, though, when Kirk and Molly introduce each other to their families. Kirk gets basically no support from any of his family members, either in the case of the break-up or this new girlfriend. His hulking, dim-witted older brothers go out of their way to humiliate him and even his ex-girlfriend tries to lure him away from Molly. On the flipside, Molly's parents make an unexpected visit to her apartment just as Molly and Kirk are about to have sex for the first time. Kirk cannot bring himself to get up off the couch for fear of his arousal being exposed. This leads to an awkward exchange that ends with him running out of the apartment with little explanation.

But the real complication comes when Kirk demands to know why he has been made the target of her affections when she can clearly do better. Here, the movie shows signs of intelligence and sophistication that the rest of the material cannot sustain. During the confrontation, Kirk sees himself as some sort of pawn in the grand scheme of things. He feels she will eventually wise up and realize he is out of her league and will dump him. She convincingly refutes this, but he remains convinced that this relationship is doomed and he should just get out before he gets hurt.

Unfortunately, the movie is unable to sustain its premise with enough intelligence to even out the raunchy material. Instead of exploring this relationship even further, director Jim Field Smith goes for cheap gags and belabors them. One scene has Kirk getting his pubic hairs trimmed by a friend so his genitals can be more appealing. There seems to be no real reason for this gag other than the writers felt they had an obligation to one-up the hilarious chest waxing scene in Apatow's comedy *The 40-Year-Old Virgin* (2005), arguably the catalyst for this entire sub-genre. A finale in an airport also goes on way too long and with needless sight gags and unfunny scenarios.

The movie is not without its charming moments. Jay Baruchel can play this part in his sleep, but he still makes it easy for the audience to be on his side. *She's Out of My League* is simply missing a few crucial ingredients to help make it a success. Apatow's movies will never win awards for originality, but they work because he lets his capable cast run loose with the material. They are seasoned improvisers and very funny. *She's Out of My League* does not have that luxury, although the cast tries their best. One can see them trying, which brings to mind an old comedy rule: If the viewer can see them trying, then it cannot be that funny.

If writers Sean Anders and John Morris and the cast instead tried to figure out why this relationship between these two people was interesting, that at least would be something.

Collin Souter

CREDITS

Kirk Kettner: Jay Baruchel
Molly: Alice Eve
Stainer: T.J. Miller
Devon: Nate Torrence
Patty: Krysten Ritter
Cam: Geoff Stults
Marnie: Lindsay Sloane
Jack: Mike Vogel
Origin: USA
Language: English
Released: 2010
Production: Eric Gold, Jimmy Miller, David B. Householter; Mosaic Media Group; released by Dreamworks Pictures
Directed by: Jim Field Smith
Written by: Sean Anders, John Morris
Cinematography by: Jim Denault
Music by: Michael Andrews
Sound: Andrew Decristofaro
Music Supervisor: Deva Anderson
Editing: Daniel Schalk
Art Direction: Jim Gloster
Costumes: Molly Maginnis
Production Design: Clayton Hartley
MPAA rating: R
Running time: 106 minutes

REVIEWS

Anderson, John. *Variety.* March 8, 2010.
Doerksen, Cliff. *Chicago Reader.* March 12, 2010.
Ebert, Roger. *Chicago Sun-Times.* March 11, 2010.
Gleiberman, Owen. *Entertainment Weekly.* March 10, 2010.
Graham, Adam. *Detroit News.* March 12, 2010.
Hale, Mike. *New York Times.* March 12, 2010.
Phillips, Michael. *Chicago Tribune.* March 11, 2010.
Rickey, Carrie. *Philadelphia Inquirer.* March 12, 2010.
Sharkey, Betsy. *Los Angeles Times.* March 12, 2010.
Tallerico, Brian. *MovieRetriever.com.* March 12, 2010.

QUOTES

Stainer: "Nooo, no. I hate her. In fact, the day you broke up with her I marked that down on my calendar as a day of rejoicement. I'm going to celebrate it with a cake with her face on it, but instead of eating it, we smash it."

TRIVIA

Trevor Eve and Sharon Maughan who play Molly's parents in the film also happen to be Alice Eve's parents in real life.

SHREK FOREVER AFTER

It's ain't ogre…til it's ogre.
—Movie tagline
Bake no prisoners.
—Movie tagline
What the Shrek just happened?
—Movie tagline

Box Office: $239 million

It has been nearly a decade since Dreamworks' *Shrek* (2001) steamrolled into the animation game with its imagination-filled reworking of what audiences could expect from animation. At a time when Pixar was just on the precipice of becoming the animated studio of record and the traditional two dimensions of Disney were being challenged left and right, *Shrek* was in its own atmosphere—hilarious, edgy, and good enough to steal the first Animated Feature Oscar® away from its Disney competitors. Naturally, the sequels came. With such a bitter taste left by the overstuffed-and-charmless *Shrek the Third* (2007), a bit of revisionist history took place. Suddenly, the original did not seem as special and became remembered as nothing more than a collection of pop culture references with an all-star voice cast. An even harsher turnaround occurred over *Shrek 2* (2004) as many forgot what a great success it was with critics as with audiences who made it the second highest grossing film ever—in its initial U.S. run—at the time. The makers of the reported final chapter of the series have apparently listened to the complaints over this decline. But while they have restored some of the heart and avoided creating another cash-grab monstrosity, *Shrek Forever After* is a rather humorless affair without the storytelling prowess to engage audiences the way they once were.

Shrek (Mike Myers) is finally settling into fatherhood. He is greeted every morning by the love of his life, Fiona (Cameron Diaz) and his three small ogre children. His best friend, Donkey (Eddie Murphy) and his flock of jackass/dragon hybrids join them for meals. Puss in Boots (Antonio Banderas) shares Shrek's heroic story over dessert every single day. Shrek can barely find time for a mud bath and misses the days when he could still terrify people instead of the passersby who now take a tour through the forest of Far Far Away to get a look at the domesticated creature.

Some vacation time may be on the horizon though when Shrek meets Rumpelstiltskin (Walt Dohrn) who offers him a single day to return to his roots with no wife or kids; just Shrek and his menacing roar to jump out at people for twenty-four hours. The catch is simple enough; to grant a day, Shrek has to give up a day from his life. What he does not know is his new conjurer pal was once in line to rescue Princess Fiona himself and take control of the entire kingdom in a deal with her desperate folks. As in a deal with the devil of any size, Rumpelstiltskin takes the day in which Shrek was born, thus negating an entire life that led to family and friendship. Unless he can reacquaint himself into Fiona's world by the end of the day and seal true love's kiss, Shrek will be no more.

The plot is kind of an appropriate metaphor for what has become of this franchise. Not that there's any suspense as to whether or not Shrek would actually be erased from existence, but it is enough to hope that emotional attachment with the character could actually return when the moment of truth arrives. The actual truth, unfortunately, is by just investing ourselves within Shrek's rediscovery we begin sharing the point of view of Fiona and the rest of the characters who have forgotten the kinship they once held in high regard. So much potential is lost in the opportunity to make something out of a dealmaker bent on a kingdom of his own control while Rumpelstiltskin just wanders in and out of the story as an obstacle rather than a worthy adversary. Having exhausted all the short jokes on Lord Farquaard in the original, any chance of mockery is an afterthought. Devoid of trying to repeat themselves, there is still an astonishing absence of anything fresh in the humor department. Murphy's Donkey, once a comic creation that ranked with the best of animated sidekicks is left drifting to sing pop tunes instead of producing laughs. The only constant bit of hilarity since being introduced in chapter two is Banderas' Puss in Boots, now earning chuckles as a winded fat cat who may actually be worth revisiting in a reported spinoff film but now is just temporary relief in a flat tale.

The addition of 3-D to the proceedings is the only element that can be classified as new and brings nothing except to a couple of flying scenes that were recently done with more style and excitement in the studio's *How to Train Your Dragon* (2010). It is disconcerting to see this series, once a beacon of originality both visually and in storytelling falling back on the current technology craze to draw in fans. The kids will be entranced regardless, though thankfully with the gross-out jokes toned down and shoved into the first few minutes, may be searching for something else to laugh at. Perhaps at their parents who may be using those 3-D glasses as a shield to pretend that they are still awake during this final chapter.

Erik Childress

CREDITS

Shrek: Mike Myers (Voice)
Princess Fiona: Cameron Diaz (Voice)
Donkey: Eddie Murphy (Voice)
Puss in Boots: Antonio Banderas (Voice)
Rumpelstiltskin: Walt Dohrn (Voice)
Artie: Justin Timberlake (Voice)
Queen Lillian: Julie Andrews (Voice)
Rapunzel: Maya Rudolph (Voice)
Merlin: Eric Idle (Voice)
Cookie: Craig Robinson (Voice)
Good Looking Ogre: Jon Hamm (Voice)
Gretchen: Jane Lynch (Voice)
Cinderella: Amy Sedaris (Voice)
Lempke: Ryan Seacrest (Voice)
Witch: Kathy Griffin (Voice)
Alice: Kirsten Schaal (Voice)
Doris the Ugly Stepsister: Larry King (Voice)
Mabel the Ugly Stepsister: Regis Philbin (Voice)
Origin: USA
Language: English
Released: 2010
Production: Teresa Cheng, Gina Shay; released by DreamWorks Animation
Directed by: Mike Mitchell
Written by: Josh Klausner
Cinematography by: Yong Duk Jhun
Music by: Harry Gregson-Williams
Editing: David Teller
Sound: Erik Aadahl
Production Design: Peter Zaslav
Art Direction: Max Boas
MPAA rating: PG
Running time: 93 minutes

REVIEWS

Anderson, John. *Variety* April 22, 2010.
Biancolli, Amy. *Houston Chronicle.* May 21, 2010.
Holden, Stephen. *New York Times.* May 21, 2010.
Michel, Bret. *Boston Phoenix.* May 20, 2010.
Pais, Matt. *Metromix.com.* May 20, 2010.
Pols, Mary. *Time Magazine.* May 20, 2010.
Rea, Steven. *Philadelphia Inquirer.* May 20, 2010.
Scheck, Frank. *Hollywood Reporter.* April 22, 2010.
Sharkey, Betsy. *Los Angeles Times.* May 20, 2010.
Tallerico, Brian. *HollywoodChicago.com.* May 21, 2010.

QUOTES

Shrek: "There's a stack of freshly made waffles in the middle of the forest! Don't you find that a wee bit suspicious?"

Donkey: "Please eat my face last and send my hooves to my momma!"

TRIVIA

The performance of writer Walt Dohrn as Rumpelstiltskin during pre-production storyboard meetings was so good, he was cast in the role for the actual production.

SHUTTER ISLAND

Someone is missing.
—Movie tagline

Box Office: $128 million

Martin Scorsese's brilliant *Shutter Island* was surprisingly pushed from the awards season of 2009 and the rumor was that it was because Paramount believed they would be wiser to focus their Oscar® energy on *Up in the Air* (2009) and leave the thriller for campaigning at the end of 2010. Released in February, *Shutter Island* became a surprisingly commercial film (making nearly $300 million worldwide, the highest total of Scorsese's career) with a few intense critical proponents but was completely shut out of the 83rd Annual Academy Award® Nominations, leaving pundits to wonder what might have happened if the film had stuck to its original release date or been pushed an entire calendar year (or not fallen to third place on Paramount's radar as they spent their energy on successful campaigns for *The Fighter* [2010] and *True Grit* [2010]). With technical elements that are beyond criticism, a strong ensemble headed by one of the best actors of his generation, and a gleeful energy courtesy of one of the form's best directors, *Shutter Island* is a breakneck trip through a cinematic funhouse that will stand the test of time even without the Oscar® nominations.

The 1950s-set film based on Dennis Lehane's (*Mystic River*) best-selling novel opens with the arrival of U.S. Marshal Teddy Daniels (Leonardo DiCaprio) and his new partner Chuck Aule (Mark Ruffalo) on the titular body of land, a remote location that holds a mental hospital for the criminally insane. It is not coincidental that Teddy is introduced looking pale, sick, and deep into his own eyes in a mirror. Not only will Teddy's journey involve a number of self-discoveries but he will never look quite healthy. Immediately on their arrival, Teddy and Chuck can sense that things are not as they seem. The guards are nervous around them. They ask for their weapons. Even the patients, one of whom was featured prominently in the ads "shushing" Teddy, seem ill at ease. Teddy and Chuck soon learn that a patient named Rachel Solando has gone missing in the middle of the night. Ms. Solando drowned her three children and then set them up at the kitchen table as if nothing was amiss. She is a patient of the hospital but believes that she is still at home as the doctors and nurses play out an elaborate charade for her mental benefit. Rachel's shoes are still in her room and none of the witnesses who should have seen her escape did so. As Dr. Cawley (Sir Ben Kingsley) tells the Marshalls, it is as if Rachel merely disappeared through the walls.

Almost immediately, Teddy begins to have disturbing flashbacks to his recent service in World War II. Images of bodies piled up at concentration camps and dying Nazi soldiers seem to come to Teddy violently and unexpectedly, adding to the sense that the Marshal may have some mental issues of his own to deal with once he finds Ms. Solando. As Teddy and his partner interview faculty, staff, and the patients at the hospital trying to find Solando's whereabouts, his focus begins to shift to something much more conspiratorial. The violent ward in which few people have been allowed and where patients seem to be kept like rats threatens to hold secrets to both the island's past and how Teddy is related to it. To any viewer paying thematic attention, it is clear that Teddy is investigating not merely a disappearance. As visions of nightmarish Nazi behavior haunt him, he refuses to make the same mistake on Shutter Island and convinces himself that the island is the center of nefarious activities that he is fated to stop.

As Teddy dives deeper into the rabbit hole of the island, his own past and related mental issues come into clearer focus. He meets one Rachel Solando (Emily Mortimer), only to cross paths with another (Patricia Clarkson), a woman claiming to know the deep secrets of the island. He stumbles upon a patient (Jackie Earle Haley) who blames him for his incarceration in the violent ward. And he continues to have disturbing flashbacks not only to WWII but to a relationship with a woman (Michelle Williams) who is eventually revealed to be his wife. When it is discovered that she died in a fire possibly set by a current resident of the hospital's most dangerous ward, Daniel's tenuous grip on sanity appears to unravel and the film builds to an amazing climax on the top floor of a lighthouse.

Whatever may be said about the impact of its technical display, no one can deny the talent of the team that Scorsese assembled to bring *Shutter Island* to life. These are quite simply some of the most talented men and women in their respective fields and, in most cases, people that Scorsese has worked with before, often to Oscar® glory. Dante Ferretti's stunning art direction of the island's buildings from the stark hospital to the deeply-symbolic lighthouse is flawless; as is the way the legendary cinematographer Robert Richardson shoots them. Ferretti, Richardson, costume designer Sandy Powell, editor Thelma Schoonmaker, and, of course, Martin Scorsese—this is a team of technical all-stars and their expertise shows in every remarkable frame of *Shutter Island*. It is truly one of the Academy's greatest shames of the year that they could not find room at the table to nominate even one of them. They work together to create a piece that is mesmerizing from first frame to last.

The story contained within those frames threw some viewers and even a few critics off by virtue of its twisting and turning narrative, one that features a twist that many saw coming but left others feeling cheated. It is difficult to praise a film for its value upon repeat viewing, but being aware of the twist ending in no way diminishes the final product. In fact, knowing Teddy's past and how he has coped with it (or not, as the case may be) almost makes the action of the film more fascinating. It helps that Teddy is played by one of the best actors of his generation delivering arguably his best performance to date. DiCaprio is perfect, riding Scorsese's technical rollercoaster without losing the emotion of his character. DiCaprio has often been accused of having a young face for the adult characters he plays but one no longer sees the child star in Teddy Daniels' shattered visage. This was one of the best performances of 2010; a work that possibly lost some of its year-end acclaim by virtue of its thematic similarity to DiCaprio's turn in the highly-acclaimed *Inception* (2010), in which he also played a man taking a mind's journey to deal with tragic issues surrounding his wife.

DiCaprio takes up most of every frame and deserves most of the acting praise, but Scorsese has assembled a fascinating cast of supporting players to join him. One-scene wonders like Haley and Clarkson make lasting impressions while more prominent players like Ruffalo and Kingsley never falter. It is clear that Scorsese can likely assemble whatever cast he wants and the decisions made regarding who would take the trip to *Shutter Island* were very smart ones.

When a cast and crew's efforts appear without flaw, much of the praise must come back to the feet of the man who directed them. Martin Scorsese was long ago recognized as one of the best living filmmakers and he proves why yet again with his remarkable sense of pacing. Every technical element, even Robbie Robertson's perfect choices as musical supervisor, comes together to create something almost like a nightmare on celluloid of the kind that deserves comparison to the best of this mini-genre including Alfred Hitchcock's *Vertigo* (1958) and Stanley Kubrick's *The Shining* (1980). Ironically, neither of those films were adequately appreciated upon their release either.

Brian Tallerico

CREDITS

Teddy Daniels: Leonardo DiCaprio
Chuck Aule: Mark Ruffalo
Dr. John Cawley: Ben Kingsley
Dolores Chanal: Michelle Williams
Rachel Solando: Emily Mortimer
Dr. Jeremiah Naehring: Max von Sydow
George Noyce: Jackie Earle Haley
Andrew Laeddis: Elias Koteas
Rachel 2: Patricia Clarkson
Origin: USA
Language: English
Released: 2009
Production: Bradley J. Fischer, Martin Scorsese, Mike Medavoy, Arnold W. Messer; Phoenix Pictures, Appian Way, Paramount Pictures, Sikelia Productions; released by Paramount Pictures
Directed by: Martin Scorsese
Written by: Laeta Kalogridis
Cinematography by: Robert Richardson
Sound: Peter Hliddal
Music Supervisor: Robbie Robertson
Editing: Thelma Schoonmaker
Art Direction: Max Biscoe, Robert Guerra, Christina Wilson
Costumes: Sandy Powell
Production Design: Dante Ferretti
MPAA rating: R
Running time: 148 minutes

REVIEWS

Anderson, John. *Wall Street Journal.* February 19, 2010.
Childress, Erik. *eFilmCritic.com* February 18, 2010.
Hornaday, Ann. *Washington Post.* February 19, 2010.
Kennedy, Lisa. *Denver Post.* February 19, 2010.
Lane, Anthony. *New Yorker.* February 22, 2010.
Long, Tom. *Detroit News.* February 19, 2010.
McGranaghan, Mike. *Aisle Seat.* February 20, 2010.
Puig, Claudia. *USA Today.* February 18, 2010.
Sharkey, Betsy. *Los Angeles Times.* February 18, 2010.
Tobias, Scott. *AV Club.* February 18, 2010.

QUOTES

Teddy Daniels: "I gotta get off this rock, Chuck. Get back to the mainland. Whatever the hell's going on here, it's bad. Don't worry partner, they're not gonna catch us."
Dr. John Cawley: "We don't know how she got out of her room. It's as if she evaporated, straight through the walls."

TRIVIA

This is Martin Scorsese's highest grossing film to date.
This film marks the fourth collaboration between director Martin Scorsese and Leonardo DiCaprio. Previous collaborations include *Gangs of New York* (2002), *The Aviator* (2004), and *The Departed* (2006).

SKYLINE

Don't look up.
—Movie tagline

Soon, our first encounter will become our last stand.
—Movie tagline

Box Office: $21 million

For every effective or unique idea that *Skyline* has, the movie discovers many more ways to negate each one in the execution. On a purely logistical level, the project is an ambitious one. Directors Colin and Greg Strause (dubbing themselves the "Brothers Strause" in the credits, because—one can only deduce—they figure the "Strause Brothers" sounds too pedestrian) envision an alien invasion from a relatively-reduced perspective. Save for several establishing shots of downtown Los Angeles, a few wide shots of other major cities (New York, London, and Sydney) near the end of the movie to establish the full extent of the attack, and the bizarre denouement aboard one of the extraterrestrial ships, the story takes place exclusively in, around, or on the roof of a single apartment complex (where Greg Strause called home during filming, to be specific).

Considering the simple locale, there is an admirable sense of scale to the assault from a group of invaders, gatherers, and genocidal recyclers. The Strauses achieve that scope on a comparatively minor budget (a reported $500,000 for actual filming), with an overwhelming proportion spent on the efficient, often convincing visual effects (stated at $10 million). Beyond screenwriters Joshua Cordes and Liam O'Donnell's minimalist setup, the effects, and an intriguing alien design, though, *Skyline* primarily comes across as a ninety-minute demo reel for the Strause brothers' visual effects company Hydraulx.

The aliens themselves, while having the appearance of generic, earth-toned monsters, are an intriguing bunch. Signaling their arrival on Earth with orbs of blue light, they hypnotize anyone who sees the glow and nab people with outstretched tentacles or vacuum them up in a swirling vortex to the larger ships hovering above the city. Their make-up is part organic and part technology. Even the massive ships appear to be living, sentient beings, and they are, for all intents and purposes unstoppable. When a group of jet fighters and bombers attack one of those giant crafts (watched through a telescope and following one bomber, a microcosm of the bigger battle that echoes the one-building story), they fire a nuclear weapon at it. The vessel crashes into the ground, only to be repaired by swarms of the smaller, drone-like creatures/ships.

The script develops the symbiotic relationship of the aliens and their dichotomous nature no further than that and other visual clues. The aliens' "eyes" are like LED bulbs of the same eerie blue that fell to Earth, and they use recently removed human brains as the primary energy source for pre-manufactured creatures. Still, these aliens and their mysterious origins are far more involving than the human characters, whose traits are as thin as the paper upon which their lines are written.

Indeed most of them are defined by the relationship to others, starting with Jarrod (Eric Balfour), an artist (a shot of his old drawings in a notebook and nothing else establish this) traveling to Los Angeles with his girlfriend Elaine (Scottie Thompson) to celebrate Jarrod's friend Terry's (Donald Faison) birthday. Other than his artistic leanings, Jarrod is a nice guy, a characteristic set up when he helps a woman with a baby reach her luggage in the overhead compartment of the plane after they land. Elaine is pregnant, and Terry is rich, working in the movie industry in the field of visual effects (vague mentions of "the director" calling about "the robot sequence" are as far as descriptions about his job go). Also around when the invaders show up are Terry's girlfriend Candice (Brittany Daniel), his assistant/woman-on-the-side Denise (Crystal Reed), and the building's doorman Oliver (David Zayas), and that is as far as characterizations go for any of them.

Save for two (and one only exempt on a metaphysical level), they are expendable. A medium-sized (on the scale of these creatures) behemoth crushes Denise during an attempted getaway by car (the timing of the moment, coming before any conscious decision can be made on the part of the audience as to the inevitability of some sort of action from the aliens, is a shock), and Terry, surprisingly—given his importance in the early part of the movie—suffers a similar fate, a slow-motion appreciation of how the monsters grab their victims. The Strause brothers speed up their digital camera for a slow-down effect quite often for little dramatic effect, although it certainly highlights the details of the effects, especially in a particularly ridiculous moment as Jarrod and Elaine dodge an incoming, damaged jet, which proceeds to plow into one of the mid-sized aliens.

None of it, though, is preparation for the finale. After Jarrod pummels one of the smallish creatures to death with his bare hands (after breaking the hypnosis twice, Jarrod is, at times, prone to mild anger and feels strong, which suddenly turns into rage and preternatural strength), he and Elaine are pulled into one the ships, where Jarrod's brain maintains his mind/soul/character once it has been transplanted into an alien grunt. It is a peculiar and decidedly anticlimactic ending—one that hopes too much for a sequel to explore the implications of what transpires. For a movie with so many elements derivative of other genre films, that *Skyline* would save the concept with the most potential until the very end is its biggest disappointment.

Mark Dujsik

CREDITS

Jarrod: Eric Balfour
Terry: Donald Faison
Elaine: Scottie Thompson
Candice: Brittany Daniel
Oliver: David Zayas
Denise: Crystal Reed
Origin: USA
Language: English
Released: 2010
Production: Kristian James Anderson, Liam O'Donnell, The Brothers Strause; Black Monday Film Services; released by Universal Pictures
Directed by: Greg Strause, Colin Strause
Written by: Joshua Cordes, Liam O'Donnell
Cinematography by: Michael Watson
Editing: Nicholas Wayman-Harris
Music by: Matthew Margeson
Sound: Greg Hedgepath, Gary Krause
Production Design: Drew Dalton
Costumes: Bobbie Mannix
MPAA rating: PG-13
Running time: 94 minutes

REVIEWS

Berardinelli, James. *ReelViews.* November 13, 2010.
Fletcher, James. *FILMINK.* November 11, 2010.
Foster, Simon. *SBS Film.* November 11, 2010.
Orndorf, Brian. *Sci-Fi Movie Page.* November 12, 2010.
Phillips, Michael. *Chicago Tribune.* November 12, 2010.
Schager, Nick. *Slant Magazine.* November 12, 2010.
Snider, Eric D. *EricDSnider.com.* November 18, 2010.
Sorrento, Matthew. *Film Threat.* November 28, 2010.
Vaux, Rob. *Mania.com.* November 12, 2010.
Weinberg, Scott. *FEARnet.* November 12, 2010.

QUOTES

Jarrod: "What are you going to do when all the blinds fall down? It's not exactly like we have a lot more bedsheets!"
Elaine: "I hate L.A."

TRIVIA

Colin and Greg Strause independently financed this film without any assistance from any major studios.
While filming cost a mere $500,000 the over 800 visual effects shots cost an additional $10 million.

THE SOCIAL NETWORK

You don't get to 500 million friends without making a few enemies.
—Movie tagline

Box Office: $97 million

The social networking website Facebook is an entertaining enough way of passing the time on the computer in lieu of playing Minesweeper or doing actual work, but who would have suspected that there was any sort of entertainment value to be had from a recounting of its development beginning in the fall of 2003 and the lawsuits that would eventually emerge as the result of its improbable success? And yet, despite the unpromising nature of the material, *The Social Network* is a knockout of a film—an utterly fascinating and compelling work that combines classical dramatic storytelling, a cutting-edge visual style, and a steely intelligence equal to that displayed by any of its hyper-brainy characters into a breathlessly-exciting epic that is the closest thing to an instant classic to come along in a while, and one whose qualities will ring loud and clear even to those who have never "friended" anyone before in their lives.

The anti-hero at the center of this story is Mark Zuckerberg (Jesse Eisenberg), a nineteen-year-old Harvard undergraduate whose genius with computers is outdone only by his complete disregard for tact or basic social skills. This is apparent in the astonishing opening scene in which a date with his girlfriend, Erica (Rooney Mara), descends into an arrogant and condescending rant—not that he notices at all—that is only ended when she finally gives up and dumps him with the brutal (and brutally accurate) observation: "You're going to go through life thinking that girls don't like you because you're a nerd. It'll be because you are an asshole." Drunk and despondent, Mark goes back to his dorm room and over the course of one evening, he vengefully whips up a computer program that ranks the relative hotness of all the women on campus. This stunt, which winds up crashing the university's computer network due to the amount of traffic, earns him academic probation and the animosity of every female in school, but it also earns him the attention of a trio of would-be campus entrepreneurs, the uber-WASP twin brothers Cameron and Tyler Winklevoss (both played by Armie Hammer with the assistance of CGI trickery and a body double) and friend Divya Narendra (Max Minghella). They have devised the idea for a Harvard-exclusive social website and want Mark to design it. He takes the job, but instead of working on that project he has an idea for a similar Harvard-only social networking site, and, with the $1,000 investment of friend and future business partner Eduardo Saverin (Andrew Garfield), he launches thefacebook.com a few months later.

The site is an immediate hit on campus and both Mark and Eduardo are stunned to discover that their own social standing has been boosted as a result—the former nerds now have groupies of their own. Needless to say, the Winklevi, as Mark dubs them, and Divya are outraged over what they see as an outright theft of their idea and send off a cease-and-desist order. In response, Mark, who insists that all he did was come up with a better idea than the one he was given, ignores it and begins spreading thefacebook to other campuses with equal success. Eventually, the site comes to the attention of Sean Parker (Justin Timberlake), the slick co-founder of Napster who sees that it is about to become the next big thing on the Internet and wants in on it. While Eduardo doggedly tries to find additional monies for the site the old fashioned way, Sean woos Mark with fancy meals, hot clubs, and the promise of oodles of money to come. (To be fair, Parker is the one who suggests shortening the name to just Facebook.) Before long, the guy who once claimed he was not in it for the money has dropped out of school, moved the company to California and begun a series of moves that would cut the loyal Eduardo out of the picture and result in his only friend filing a $600 million dollar lawsuit against him in addition to the one filed by the Winklevoss brothers.

The Social Network is one of those live-wire movies that is so bursting at the seams with excitement and invention that viewers will practically be levitating in their seats the first time that they see it. Everything clicks on all cylinders here from Aaron Sorkin's whip-smart screenplay, which probably contains three times the amount of dialogue of a typical contemporary film, to David Fincher's masterful direction, at once incredibly self-assured and remarkably subtle, to the exuberant performances from the entire cast to the behind-the-scenes contributions of such people as cinematographer Jeff Cronenweth and composers Trent Reznor and Atticus Rose. Sorkin's screenplay is a miracle in the way that it takes what could have been an indigestible combination of impenetrable jargon and unlikable characters and transforms it into a classic tale of greed, ambition and jealousy that never dumbs things down, never takes the easy way out and which contains more great individual scenes than any movie in recent memory. As for Fincher, he has mostly cut down on the visual pyrotechnics that have marked his previous films but thanks to his sheer directorial skill and his obsessive attention to detail, he has still managed to create an uncommonly exciting film with nary a wasted moment—this is exceptionally impressive when one considers the fact that virtually every scene consists of nothing more than several people either talking computer jargon or giving depositions. Already responsible for some of the best movies of recent times, this may well be his crowning achievement to date.

The most fascinating thing about *The Social Network*—the thing that makes it truly great—is the intriguing way in which Sorkin and Fincher present the character of Mark Zuckerberg. In the hands of other filmmakers, the temptation might have been to show him strictly as a clear-cut villain who runs roughshod over his former friends and colleagues in the single-minded pursuit of wealth, fame, and power while depicting Eduardo as the innocent pushed to the side. In fact, the depiction of Zuckerberg created by Sorkin's writing, Fincher's empathic direction, and Eisenberg's incredibly nuanced performance is something far more complex and complicated. Yes, he is rude, pushy and completely lacking in social graces but these seem to be traits that have been hardwired in him since birth and that he is helpless to understand or change. Yes, his actions involving the development and expansion of Facebook may have been cold and ruthless, especially in his dismissal of former friend Eduardo, but if it were not for those moves, Facebook almost certainly would not be what it is today. Since he demonstrates little interest in either the money or glamour of running a wildly successful company, what drives Zuckerberg remains a tantalizing mystery that the film never spoils by offering up a convenient scene in which someone explains all of his motivations. Instead, after nearly two hours of being shown as a heartless and emotionless geek, the film takes pains to instill him with some humanity in the extraordinary final sequence in which he sits all alone and does something almost achingly human—this is a moment that could have come off as painfully ironic, especially with *Baby, You're A Rich Man* playing on the soundtrack, but it instead plays as arguably the most nakedly emotional moment in Fincher's entire oeuvre.

At once timely and timeless and bristling with energy from start to finish, *The Social Network* is more than just a great movie—it is the kind of full-throttle experience that reminds even the most jaded moviegoers of how much fun and excitement the cinema can provide when in the hands of people who know what they are doing. Some of the early reviews of the film have gone so far as to compare it to another film chronicling the meteoric rise of a media mogul, a little thing called *Citizen Kane* (1941), and while it may be a bit too soon to be making such comparisons, few films in recent memory, both in terms of ambition and execution, have deserved it as much as this one does. Hell, even Mark Zuckerberg himself might get a kick out of it as well, though it remains to be seen if he will go so far as to "like" it.

Peter Sobczynski

CREDITS

Mark Zuckerberg: Jesse Eisenberg
Sean Parker: Justin Timberlake
Eduardo Saverin: Andrew Garfield

Dustin Moskovitz: Joseph Mazzello
Marylin Delpy: Rashida Jones
Christy Lee: Brenda Song
Divya Narendra: Max Minghella
Cameron Winklevoss/Tyler Winklevoss: Armie Hammer
Billy Olsen: Bryan Barter
Erica Albright: Rooney Mara
Chris Hughes: Patrick Mapel
Gage: David Selby
Peter Thiel: Wallace Langham
Origin: USA
Language: English
Released: 2010
Production: Dana Brunetti, Michael DeLuca, Cean Chaffin, Scott Rudin; Columbia Pictures, Relativity Media, Trigger Street; released by Sony Pictures
Directed by: David Fincher
Written by: Aaron Sorkin
Cinematography by: Jeff Cronenweth
Music by: Trent Reznor, Atticus Ross
Sound: David Hughes, Marc Weingarten
Editing: Kirk Baxter, Angus Wall
Production Design: Donald Graham Burt
Art Direction: Curt Beech, Keith Cunningham, Robyn Paiba
Costumes: Jacqueline West
MPAA rating: PG-13
Running time: 120 minutes

REVIEWS

Childress, Erik. *eFilmCritic.com.* October 1, 2010.
Ebert, Roger. *Chicago Sun-Times.* September 29, 2010.
Edelstein, David. *New York Magazine.* October 4, 2010.
LaSalle, Mick. *San Francisco Chronicle.* September 30, 2010.
Morgenstern, Joe. *Wall Street Journal.* September 30, 2010.
Phipps, Keith. *AV Club.* September 30, 2010.
Rickey, Carrie. *Philadelphia Inquirer.* September 30, 2010.
Stevens, Dana. *Slate.* October 1, 2010.
Tallerico, Brian. *HollywoodChicago.com.* September 30, 2010.
White, Armond. *New York Press.* September 29, 2010.

QUOTES

Mark Zuckerberg: "I think if your clients want to sit on my shoulders and call themselves tall, they have the right to give it a try—but there's no requirement that I enjoy sitting here listening to people lie."

Erica Albright: "You are probably going to be a very successful computer person. But you're going to go through life thinking that girls don't like you because you're a nerd. And I want you to know, from the bottom of my heart, that that won't be true. It'll be because you're an a**hole."

Sean Parker: "We lived on farms, then we lived in cities, and now we're going to live on the internet!"

TRIVIA

Director David Fincher told his principal actors that they could not meet their real-life counterparts until after filming wrapped.

Screenwriter Aaron Sorkin has a small cameo role as an ad executive, a role that director David Fincher insisted he play.

AWARDS

Oscars 2010: Adapt. Screenplay, Film Editing, Orig. Score
British Acad. 2010: Adapt. Screenplay, Director (Fincher), Film Editing
Golden Globes 2011: Director (Fincher), Film—Drama, Screenplay, Orig. Score
Writers Guild 2010: Adapt. Screenplay

Nomination:

Oscars 2010: Actor (Eisenberg), Cinematog., Director (Fincher), Film, Sound
British Acad. 2010: Actor (Eisenberg), Film, Support. Actor (Garfield)
Directors Guild 2010: Director (Fincher)
Golden Globes 2011: Actor—Drama (Eisenberg), Support. Actor (Garfield)
Screen Actors Guild 2010: Actor (Eisenberg), Cast.

SOLITARY MAN

Ben loves his family almost as much as he loves himself.
—Movie tagline

Box Office: $4 million

The real-life illness of Oscar® winner Michael Douglas (along with the perceived critical and commercial failure of his return to one of his most well-known roles in Oliver Stone's *Wall Street: Money Never Sleep* [2010]) tragically overshadowed the year-end acclaim that he should have received for his lead turn in Brian Koppelman's excellent *Solitary Man.* With a strong supporting cast to drive him and what feels like a personally-relevant character to play, Douglas does some of the best work of his career in this dramedy about a man who has constantly been given second, third, and tenth chances by friends and family but has run out of time and chances simultaneously.

Ben Kalmen (Michael Douglas) is almost defiantly self-centered. He is the kind of man who blames the person he has wronged for feeling that way instead of possibly questioning that perhaps he did something wrong. He does not say so directly in the film, but one gets the sense that he has mastered the slimy line "I'm sorry you feel that way," which is the classic retort of the man who can never recognize the possibility that he should actually just feel sorry for doing the wrong thing. He knows that he cannot change so has simply given up trying, even after being presented by the kind of life-changing news that often makes men reassess their impact on the people in their lives. It may sound cliché, but Ben has become the title of the film about him—a *Solitary Man*—because of a series of incredibly-misguided personal and professional decisions, many of them involving his libido. This smooth-talking businessman has always found a way to close the deal and keep his relationships at least tenuously connected but forgiveness is becoming harder to swindle. Ben has a clearly well-worn pick-up routine in which he asks young ladies with inexperienced boyfriends what they are "getting out of the transaction." The irony is that Ben has never once cared what anyone got out of a transaction with him other than Ben himself.

Ben is a used car salesmen who has been trying to start a new dealership but has found that bad business decisions in the past may not be forgiven this time. It turns out that he is also about to make some bad personal decisions to match his professional ones. He remains casual friends with his ex-wife Nancy (Susan Sarandon), a woman who it seems probably hated Ben at one point but now sees so clearly through him that she may have something closer to pity or at least begrudging acceptance. Ben also has a friendship with daughter Susan (Jenna Fischer), but her anger has not yet distilled to pity, partially because her father so commonly lets down his grandson just as he did his own offspring. Ben's girlfriend (Mary-Louise Parker) mistakenly sends her beau on a college trip with her ridiculously-beautiful daughter (Imogen Poots) and the man commits what could be considered the ultimate sin in a relationship. It is hard to mend fences after sleeping with your girlfriend's daughter. Finally, Ben tries to maintain a pair of friendships—one old one with a settled-down reminder of his better days (Danny DeVito) and one new one with a reminder that his younger ones are way behind him (Jesse Eisenberg). Richard Schiff and Olivia Thirlby pop up in small roles. It may sound like Ben has a number of connections in his life but he has no true relationships.

The opening scenes of *Solitary Man* feature a terrifying medical diagnosis for Ben so it is natural for the viewer to assume that a clichéd tale of a cad coming to terms with his flaws before his death is about to unfold. Thankfully, Brian Koppelman did not write that movie. There are a few very hard lessons learned, but Koppelman avoids melodrama at every moment when lesser writers would have dove into that writing pool head first. Instead, he allows Douglas to craft a character study and the actor completely rises to the occasion. In the hands of a lesser actor, Ben would have been such a reprehensible jerk that viewers would not have been able to bear the film's running time but Douglas finds a way to make him, if not charming, at least relatable. He feels

real. And one has to wonder if the mistakes made in real-life past relationships did not impact the believability of Douglas' performance. Seeing him play old friends with an actual old friend (DeVito) adds to the sense that the reason Douglas took such a big bite out of this role is because he saw something he had tasted before. The entire supporting cast deserves praise, especially Fischer and Poots. In perhaps the film's greatest irony, *Solitary Man* may be about a loner finding out that he has run out of support, but it features one of the best ensemble performances of the year.

It could be argued that *Solitary Man* is a bit more episodic than it needed to be and even that Koppelman could have used a bit more drama to give the piece some emotional weight but the film features such believable character development that these are minor complaints. Even the one-scene characters that pop in and out of Ben's life feel genuine. It takes true skill to craft a film with so few moments that seem scripted. Michael Douglas may have had real-life drama that pulled attention away from it but history will go back to this underrated gem and mark it as one of his best works.

Brian Tallerico

CREDITS

Ben: Michael Douglas
Nancy: Susan Sarandon
Jimmy: Danny DeVito
Jordan: Mary-Louise Parker
Cheston: Jesse Eisenberg
Steve Heller: Richard Schiff
Susan Porter: Jenna Fischer
Allyson: Imogen Poots
Maureen: Olivia Thirlby
Origin: USA
Language: English
Released: 2010
Production: Steven Soderbergh, Paul Schiff, Heidi Jo Markel; Millenium Films, Smartest Man Productions; released by Anchor Bay Films
Directed by: Brian Koppelman
Written by: Brian Koppelman
Cinematography by: Alwin Kuchler
Music by: Michael Penn
Editing: Tricia Cooke
Sound: Lon Bender
Costumes: Jenny Gering, Ellen Mirojnick
Production Design: Rob Pearson
MPAA rating: R
Running time: 90 minutes

REVIEWS

Anderson, Melissa. *Village Voice.* May 18, 2010.
Chang, Justin. *Variety.* May 17, 2010.

Ebert, Roger. *Chicago Sun-Times*. June 10, 2010.
Edelstein, David. *New York Magazine*. May 17, 2010.
Honeycutt, Kirk. *Hollywood Reporter*. May 17, 2010.
Lane, Anthony. *New Yorker*. June 1, 2010.
Pais, Matt. *Metromix.com*. June 10, 2010.
Phillips, Michael. *Chicago Tribune*. June 10, 2010.
Schwarzbaum, Lisa. *Entertainment Weekly*. May 19, 2010.
Travers, Peter. *Rolling Stone*. May 20, 2010.

TRIVIA

This film marks the first time Michael Douglas and Danny DeVito have starred together since *The War of the Rose* (1989).

The Johnny Cash song "Solitary Man" plays at the beginning of the film.

SOMEWHERE

Box Office: $2 million

At a time when most American films all but assault their audiences, either with noisy special effects or with storylines in which virtually every single bit of plot or character development is spelled out and underlined in ridiculous detail so as to prevent viewers from having to do any thinking for themselves, a film like Sofia Coppola's *Somewhere* is a true anomaly. This is a quiet film in every sense of the word. There is barely a word of dialogue for the first fifteen minutes or so and after that point, it is anything but gregarious. Beyond that, it is quiet and restrained in terms of tone—incidents are allowed to play out without being goosed along by rapid-fire editing and plot points and character connections are left to be inferred by viewers instead of being explicitly explained to them. For viewers who prefer to have every little detail handed to them, this may prove to be a frustrating experience but for those willing to accept it for what it is and to fall under the delicate spell that Coppola has woven, it is a haunting and surprisingly touching experience that is simply one of the best films of 2010.

The film follows several days in the life of Johnny Marco (Stephen Dorff), a movie star who is clearly at odds with himself and his existence. Although he has reached a certain pinnacle of success in his field—he lives at the Chateau Marmont, the famous Hollywood hotel perhaps best known for being the place where John Belushi had his fatal overdose, and when he is not being whisked off to press junkets or makeup tests for an upcoming project, he spends most of his time smoking, drinking, and partying with the countless beautiful women who come into his orbit—he is in the midst of a profound state of alienation towards virtually everything in his life. Nothing gets a reaction out of him, not

the twin pole dancers who perform a strange, ritualized routine in his room that he can barely stay awake through nor even a drunken stumble down the stairs that results in a broken arm. Clearly he has grown weary of his life of lazy privilege but not weary enough to be inspired to do much about it. He is the kind of guy who cannot decide whether it would be worse if the car that seems to be following him one day contains members of the dreaded paparazzi or if it does not.

Johnny's routine is shaken up, however mildly, by the arrival of Cleo (Elle Fanning), his 11-year-old daughter from a failed marriage, for a short visit that is unexpectedly lengthened because of a crisis involving her mother. Although one might expect Cleo to be a spoiled brat reveling in the spoils of privilege, she instead comes across as a remarkably self-possessed young woman who is willing and able to occasionally take advantage of the perks of her position but who has not allowed such things to overtake her life in the way that they have with her father. For his part, Johnny clearly cares for her and goes through the motions of being a good dad but even there, he still seems unwilling or unable to make even the most basic human connections—when he makes a remark about Cleo's surprising skills on an ice rink, she patiently reminds him that she has been practicing for three years. Over the course of their extended time together, she easily begins to slip into his lifestyle and he winds up taking her along to Milan for a trip that involves a visit to a bizarre Italian awards show and a stay in yet another luxury hotel. The two do bond over the trip but Johnny is still not inspired to change his self-absorbed ways and Cleo is aware enough to recognize this and register her sense of disappointment in him and his behavior without saying a word.

Like all of Coppola's previous films—*The Virgin Suicides* (2000), *Lost in Translation* (2003), and *Marie Antoinette* (2006)—*Somewhere* is less concerned with giving viewers a conventional narrative than in presenting characters who are vaguely dissatisfied with lifestyles that most people would give anything to have for themselves and observing them as they go about their lives in their own personal gilded cages. Given the current socioeconomic climate, asking audiences to sympathize with a central character who spends his time slouching through his big-shot lifestyle might seem to be a little too much to bear but as she has done in her earlier efforts, she deftly manages to overcome this enormous hurdle in order to create a story that winds up being far more moving than one might expect. One smart move on her part is to avoid the easy moments of catharsis that one might expect from this kind of story—there are no scenes in which the bonding between father and daughter becomes overt (the closest the film comes to this is a moment is when the two rock out together while playing *Guitar Hero*) or of Johnny realizing that he needs to shape up and become a better dad. In fact, Coppola takes an extremely minimalist route throughout—the entire story takes place in the present tense over the course of a few days and there are no moments in which the back story regarding Johnny's life, career, and prior relationship with Cleo is regaled through endless expository dialogue—and trusts that viewers will be able to fill in the necessary blanks for themselves. The performances from Dorff and Fanning do an incredible job of helping to sell this particular take on the material in the way that they effortlessly manage to establish a convincingly distant father-daughter relationship without having to spell things out. It is easily the best work that Dorff has ever done and it establishes Fanning as a young actress to watch who seems capable of giving even her gifted older sister Dakota a run for the money.

It is an intriguing approach for such a film, one that will remind some viewers of the ennui-ridden works of acclaimed Italian filmmaker Michelangelo Antonioni, and it winds up paying off beautifully in the end because Coppola brings a couple of things to the table that lend the film some much-needed traces of humanity. For starters, she manages to present Johnny's life in a way that feels emotionally and spiritually empty while still conveying the genuine allure of a lifestyle in which booze and babes are always available, people are employed to do nothing but make sure that famous people get from point A to point B and elevator rides can be shared with the likes of Benicio Del Toro. (In this, she is aided immeasurably by the gorgeous cinematography from Harris Savides that manages to make everything look simultaneously inviting and desolate.) At the same time, Coppola also demonstrates a wry sense of humor towards the excesses of show business and how people deal with them in different ways. Most importantly, Coppola creates an aura of absolute authenticity that can be felt in every scene. Obviously, Coppola herself is the daughter of a famous film personality and presumably spent a good chunk of her childhood on movie sets and in hotel rooms observing her father dealt with his fame. This is not to say that the film is autobiographical per se but there is not a single scene that does not feel as if it had not been genuinely lived through in one form or another at some point.

Because it takes place almost entirely within hotels, deals with show business personalities, and centers on a relationship between a jaded older man and a younger woman, some viewers might dismiss *Somewhere* as nothing more than a rehashed version of *Lost in Translation* and suggest that Coppola is already repeating herself only four films into her directorial career. There are unmistakable thematic connections between the two films but *Somewhere* deals with the material in such a

fascinating and distinctive manner that it never feels like a rehash. Smart, knowing, and compulsive watchable, this is a small treasure of a film—the equivalent of a perfect short story—and once again confirms that Sofia Coppola is one of the best American filmmakers working today.

Peter Sobczynski

CREDITS

Johnny Marco: Stephen Dorff
Cleo: Elle Fanning
Sammy: Chris Pontius
Rebecca: Michelle Monaghan
Origin: USA
Language: English
Released: 2010
Production: G. Mac Brown, Roman Coppola; American Zoetrope; released by Focus Features
Directed by: Sofia Coppola
Written by: Sofia Coppola
Cinematography by: Harris Savides
Music by: Phoenix
Sound: Richard Beggs, Michael Kirchberger
Editing: Sarah Flack
Costumes: Stacey Battat
Production Design: Anne Ross
MPAA rating: R
Running time: 97 minutes

REVIEWS

Ansen, David. *Newsweek.* January 5, 2011.
Denby, David. *New Yorker.* December 27, 2010.
Dujsik, Mark. *Mark Reviews Movies.* December 21, 2010.
Ebert, Roger. *Chicago Sun-Times.* December 22, 2010.
Keough, Peter. *Boston Phoenix.* December 28, 2010.
Larsen, Josh. *Larsen on Film.* December 21, 2010.
Pais, Matt. *Metromix.com.* December 21, 2010.
Phipps, Keith. *AV Club.* December 21, 2010.
Reed, Rex. *New York Observer.* December 22, 2010.
White, Armond. *New York Press.* December 22, 2010.

THE SORCERER'S APPRENTICE

It's the coolest job ever.
    —Movie tagline

Box Office: $63 million

One of the wonderful things about the advent of CGI has been the great flowering of the fantasy film genre. Similar to the superhero film, pre-CGI film for the most part lacked the capacity to depict the fantastic elements which define the genre and, consequently, fantasy films were either consigned to B-movie schlock-dom or not made at all. CGI changed all of that, allowing the genre to finally receive its due with rich, imaginative films such as *The Lord of the Rings* trilogy (2001-2003), the *Harry Potter* series (2001-2011) and *Pan's Labryinth* (2006). *The Sorcerer's Apprentice,* however, is the dark side of this renaissance, an unimaginative and unapologetically derivative attempt to cash in on the genre of the moment. *The Sorcerer's Apprentice* is to *The Lord of the Rings* what *Battlestar Gallactica* (1978) was to *Star Wars* (1977).

The film, created by producer Jerry Bruckheimer, director John Turteltaub and Disney—the team behind the execrable *National Treasure* films (2004, 2007)—is a generic affair through and through. Loosely based on the classic Mickey Mouse *Fantasia* (1940) short, the live-action film zips through a labored prologue that jams in so much convoluted back story that is feels as if there has been a previous film (or four) in the series. It is 780 AD and the wizard Merlin (James Stephens) has three apprentices: Balthazar Blake (Nicolas Cage), Veronica Gorloisen (Monica Belucci), and Maxim Horvath (Alfred Molina). Merlin is engaged in mortal combat with his ancient enemy, Morgana le Fay (Alice Krige). Maxim secretly joins forces with Morgana and betrays Merlin at a critical moment allowing Morgana to fatally wound him. She next turns her sights on Balthazar. To save Balthazar, Veronica casts a spell absorbing Morgana into her body and, before Morgana can slay Veronica from within, Balthazar imprisons both of them in the innermost layer of a Matryoshka doll prison called the Grimhold. The dying Merlin gives Balthazar a dragon ring which will identify a chosen one, the Prime Merlinian (yes, the Prime Merlinian), who will be Merlin's successor. The Prime Merlinian is the only being who can destroy Morgana. Balthazar's role is to search the world for the Prime Merlinian while safeguarding the Grimhold from evil Sorcerers intent upon freeing Morgana. Balthazar advances through the ages battling and imprisoning Sorcerers trying to free Morgana, while traveling the world over trying to get the ring to fit on children's fingers. Finally, in 2010, the Prime Merlinian is found in the person of Dave Stutler (Jay Baruchel), a nebbish physics student. Unfortunately, shortly after his discovery, Dave inadvertently releases the outermost Sorcerer imprisoned in the Grimhold, Maxim, and, once free, Maxim finds his own apprentice, Drake Stone (Toby Kebbell), to assist him in attempting to steal the Grimhold from Balthazar and release Morgana.

The irony is that once the film rushes through this back story, moving so quickly that it is difficult to understand exactly who is who and what the story is, there is almost no plot to the rest of the film. Once the hurried prologue concludes, the film follows a simple and boring pattern: Balthazar tries to persuade Dave of his responsibility as the Prime Merlinian and train him as a Sorcerer. Dave is hesitant about assuming his role. Dave is attacked by Maxim and Drake and rescued by Balthazar. Like the end of an ongoing children's cartoon, Maxim and Drake always escape at the end of their attack so that the cycle can be repeated. At the film's climax, the formula is inverted and Dave assumes the mantle of the Prime Merlinian and rescues Balthazar. Throw in a boring romantic subplot between Dave and his classmate Becky Barnes (Teresa Palmer) and that is the entirety of *The Sorcerer's Apprentice*'s story.

The Sorcerer's Apprentice does deliver the requisite eye candy. From a technical standpoint, the film is as impressive as any other high-budget modern fantasy film. CGI convincingly renders Balthazar's flying mount, a Chrysler Building eagle sculpture magically transformed into a living creature. An evil mage freed from the Grimhold turns a costumed dragon in a Chinatown parade into a real dragon with impressive results. When magical fire bursts from the dragon's mouth it looks like the real thing. The film dutifully recreates the famous animated sequence from *Fantasia* with a convincingly realistic live-action rendering (that nonetheless fails to capture any of the magic, mystery, and imagination of the original). This would have been heady stuff in 1995 but fantasy films need to do more in 2010 than simply convincingly depict the fantastic. Fantasy films, like any other film, must feature interesting stories and intriguing characters the audience cares about. With its simplistic, cartoon structure, generic story and one-dimensional characters, *The Sorcerer's Apprentice* does not even attempt to do this. Admittedly, *The Sorcerer's Apprentice* is a kid's movie but so are the rich and complex *Lord of the Rings* and *Harry Potter* films and that is the standard to which *The Sorcerer's Apprentice* must be held.

The film's failings are not the actors' fault and what little originality the film does have is a result of their efforts to lend some personality and individuality to their underwritten and generic roles. Despite the run-of-the-mill dialogue their characters are forced to exchange, Baruchel and Cage share a winning comic chemistry and its fun just to watch them interact (and one wonders about the movie that might have been made with the two actors with a script that did not utterly emasculate itself in the interest of playing it completely safe). Baruchel manages to make his weak comic dialogue far more amusing that it deserves to be through sheer acting ability. And, for once, the nerdy physics student is played by an actor who looks like a nerdy physics student rather than the generically handsome pretty boy that Disney must have surely been tempted to cast. He sounds like a nerdy physics student as well as Baruchel gives him a wonderful, nervous, halting diction reminiscent of Crispin Glover's George McFly from *Back to the Future* (1985). Cage is excellent as well, doing the most he can with a razor-thin character. His character has been saddled with a less interesting version of the dilemma faced by Rutger Hauer in *Ladyhawke* (1985). In that film, Hauer's character and his lover have been cursed so that one is in human form while the other is in animal form. When day turns to night, they switch places, able only to be together in human form for a few fleeting seconds. Similarly, Balthazar cannot free the woman he loves from the Grimhold because doing so would also mean freeing Morgana. This has some dramatic potential but the script does not allow Cage to explore it other than having him look longingly at the Grimhold a few times. Alfred Molina has a good time hamming it up and slumming just as he did in Bruckheimer's other 2010 release, *Prince of Persia* and the wicked charm he is able to impart his generic, one note villain is enjoyable.

However, children are the primary audience for *The Sorcerer's Apprentice* and they are unlikely to appreciate the film for the effort the actors put in to making their purposefully generic characters marginally interesting. And the actor's efforts are not enough for the adult viewer to compensate for the film's otherwise complete lack of originality. Bruckheimer and company have succeeded in creating a formulaic, thoroughly-derivative fantasy film that adds absolutely nothing to the genre. There is more imagination going on in the corner of a single frame of a Guillermo Del Toro movie than the entirety of *The Sorcerer's Apprentice*'s 111-minute running time.

Nate Vercauteren

CREDITS

Balthazar Blake: Nicolas Cage
Dave Stutler: Jay Baruchel
Maxim Horvath: Alfred Molina
Veronica: Monica Bellucci
Drake Stone: Toby Kebbell
Merlin: James Stephens
Morgana: Alice Krige
Becky Barnes: Teresa Palmer
Origin: USA
Language: English
Released: 2010

Production: Jerry Bruckheimer; Saturn Films, Broken Road, Junction Entertainment, Jerry Bruckheimer Films, Walt Disney Pictures; released by Walt Disney Pictures
Directed by: Jon Turteltaub
Written by: Matt Lopez, Doug Miro, Carlo Bernard
Cinematography by: Bojan Bazelli
Music by: Trevor Rabin
Sound: Tod A. Maitland, George Watters
Music Supervisor: Jeanette Surga
Editing: William Goldenberg, George Watters
Art Direction: David Lazan, David Swayze
Costumes: Michael Kaplan
Production Design: Naomi Shohan
MPAA rating: PG
Running time: 111 minutes

REVIEWS

Baumgarten, Marjorie. *Austin Chronicle.* July 17, 2010.
Chang, Justin. *Variety.* July 9, 2010.
Corliss, Richard. *TIME Magazine.* July 15, 2010.
Ebert, Roger. *Chicago Sun-Times.* July 13, 2010.
Morris, Wesley. *Boston Globe.* July 13, 2010.
O'Sullivan, Michael. *Washington Post.* July 14, 2010.
Rickey, Carrie. *Philadelphia Inquirer.* July 13, 2010.
Robinson, Tasha. *AV Club.* July 13, 2010.
Scott, A.O. *New York Times.* July 13, 2010.
Travers, Peter. *Rolling Stone.* July 13, 2010.

QUOTES

Balthazar: "I have been searching all over the world for you. You're going to be a force for good and a very important sorcerer. But for now, you're my apprentice."
Balthazar: "Love is a distraction. Sorcery requires complete focus."

SOUL KITCHEN

Life is what happens to you while you are busy making other plans.
—Movie tagline

Internationally-renowned filmmaker Fatih Akin is a German director of Turkish descent who uses his diverse ethnic background to fascinating dramatic ends as a director in such acclaimed films as *Head-On* (2004) and *Edge of Heaven* (2007), the winner for Best Screenplay at the Cannes Film Festival. That latter work created waves around the world and was an emotionally draining, complex gauntlet for the viewer. It is not uncommon for filmmakers around the world to follow up intense emotional experiences with something a bit lighter on its feet and that is precisely what the excellent Akin did with *Soul Kitchen,* a work that was mistakenly too easily written off as an inconsequential lark. It is, without question, the least challenging of Akin's imports just by its very tone, set-up, and comedic style, but it is a great character-driven comedy. It is yet another excellent film from a director that would be a household name if foreign films created that kind of thing in the United States any more. Not yet even forty, Fatih Akin continues to cement his place as one of the world's most interesting filmmakers with *Soul Kitchen*.

Co-writer Adam Bousdoukos, who owned a tavern at which Akin was a regular customer that served as the inspiration for the film, stars as Zinos, the troubled manager of a Hamburg restaurant named Soul Kitchen. With a large warehouse-type interior, Soul Kitchen serves mediocre food to a working-class clientele and seems destined to go nowhere in culinary terms. When Zinos' girlfriend Nadine (Pheline Roggan) leaves for a job in Shanghai, it inspires Zinos to take some action and alter the lack of passion and creativity in his restaurant. Fate intervenes at Nadine's going-away party. The chef of the high-end restaurant, a cantankerous fellow named Shayn (Birol Unel), gets fired after nearly stabbing a guest who asked that his gazpacho be heated up. Zinos senses in Shayn what his restaurant is missing and hires the culinary wizard for the Soul Kitchen. As the restaurant is going through several changes, Zinos' brother Illias (Moritz Bleibtreu) gets out of prison on a work release program and starts working at Soul Kitchen. He begins a tentative romance with a snarky waitress named Lucia (Anna Bederke) and starts DJing at the restaurant as it becomes the trendy place to be. As Soul Kitchen becomes a more prized property, a former schoolmate of Zinos (Wotan Wilke Möhring) makes moves to steal it and take the success for himself.

On paper, *Soul Kitchen* surely sounds like a bad sitcom. It does have a variety of larger-than-life personalities and something of a wacky sense of humor, but Akin takes the episodic script and completely makes it work. This is a film about community more than food or music. It is about how those elements bring unusual personalities together and how they bounce off each other to create unified fronts like successful restaurants. All of Akin's films pulse with energy and *Soul Kitchen* is no different. He is a rare filmmaker who can take ordinary moments that would fall flat in the hands of most other directors and make them feel remarkable. There is one stand-out, remarkable sequence in which Illias and Lucia begin to flirt at a dance club that is truly spectacular. Even the typical food/dance montages have more energy than most films of this ilk. And Akin is great with actors, drawing personality from even the smallest supporting characters. Akin's cast of characters feels completely three-dimensional moments after they are introduced. If anything is underdeveloped it is co-

writer Bousdoukos' work as Zinos, a character who feels a bit too much like the straight guy of the piece and ends up a bit of a cipher at the center. For the most part, *Soul Kitchen* does not quite transcend its episodic, sitcomish set-up as much as embrace it and make it as enjoyable as possible. Fatih Akin is like a great chef, taking multiple, diverse ingredients and combining them in a way that makes them taste new.

Soul Kitchen was a hit internationally, bringing in over $17 million overseas, but could only muster a hair over $275k in the United States, only playing as wide as 23 screens. The foreign film market continues its downward slide in the States, as one imagines a film like *Soul Kitchen* would have caught on with an appreciative art house audience a decade ago in ways that just do not seem as feasible in 2010. Fatih Akin still has a ways to go before he gets the household name status that his talent deserves.

Brian Tallerico

CREDITS

Zinos Kazantsakis: Adam Bousdoukos
Illias Kazantsakis: Moritz Bleibtreu
Nadine Kruger: Pheline Roggan
Shayn Weiss: Birol Unel
Lucia Faust: Anna Bederke
Anna Mondstein: Dorka Gryllus
Frau Schuster: Catrin Striebeck
Herr Meyer: Jan Fedder
Thomas Neumann: Wotan Wilke Möhring
Origin: Germany
Language: German
Released: 2009
Production: Klaus Maeck, Fatih Akin; Dorje Film, Pyramide Productions, Corazon International; released by IFC Films
Directed by: Fatih Akin
Written by: Adam Bousdoukos, Fatih Akin
Cinematography by: Rainer Klausmann
Sound: Kai Luede, Richard Borowski
Music Supervisor: Klaus Maeck, Pia Hoffman
Editing: Andrew Bird
Costumes: Katrin Aschendorf
Production Design: Tamo Kunz
MPAA rating: Unrated
Running time: 98 minutes

REVIEWS

Holden, Stephen. *New York Times.* August 20, 2010.
Lane, Anthony. *New Yorker.* August 30, 2010.
Morgenstern, Joe. *Wall Street Journal.* August 27, 2010.
Morris, Wesley. *Boston Globe.* August 26, 2010.

Pais, Matt. *Metromix.com.* September 9, 2010.
Phillips, Michael. *Chicago Tribune.* September 9, 2010.
Punter, Jennie. *Globe and Mail.* August 13, 2010.
Stevens, Dana. *Slate.* August 20, 2010.
Turan, Kenneth. *Los Angeles Times.* September 2, 2010.
Zacharek, Stephanie. *Movieline.* August 18, 2010.

SPLICE

She is not supposed to exist.
  —Movie tagline

Science's newest miracle…is a mistake.
  —Movie tagline

She's not human…not entirely.
  —Movie tagline

Box Office: $17 million

Splice, like the scientists in it, races to get where it wants to go, but, unlike those scientists, goes somewhere very worthwhile, offering up a darker than dark, decidedly adult fairy tale featuring adults who act like children and a child who epitomizes Shakespeare's line from *King Lear,* "How sharper than a serpent's tooth it is to have a thankless child!" Gory, insightful, and blessed with one of the more remarkable monsters in recent cinema *Splice* is a movie that can appeal to both the thoughtful and casual fan of horror or science fiction but is finally a fantasy, writ large upon the backdrop of ongoing concerns about what science can do and what it should be allowed to do.

Clive (Adrian Brody) and Elsa (Sarah Polley) are hotshot genetic engineers whose experiments in gene splicing have led to the development of Fred and Ginger, two oversized wormlike creatures who may hold the secrets to cure whatever ails mankind. But when they are denied permission to use the human DNA needed for their experiments by the pharmaceutical company that funds them in lieu of the need to generate profits, they begin conducting their own clandestine research, which leads to the unexpected result of Dren.

Dren is a hybrid creature who starts out looking like a huge tadpole with a stinger, only to quickly grow legs and display an unnerving sentience. At first cared for like a baby animal Dren quickly grows more and more human. Elsa is delighted, but Clive grows disturbed, sensing in Dren something all too familiar. Soon Clive and Elsa are at complete odds with each other over what should be done with their creation which threatens to destroy not only their careers but their marriage. Meanwhile, Dren grows and grows and changes. What is Dren? More importantly, what is Dren becoming?

The film's central flaw is in the script which calls on everyone to accept the existence, rapid growth, high

intelligence, and uncannily human characteristics of Dren just a little too readily. Ultimately, what Dren represents would bring even the most arrogant and self-absorbed person, much less a scientist, to their knees. The casting of Adrien Brody and Sarah Polley as the scientific couple is key here. They offer nuance and believability to roles that could have seemed merely shrill backdrops to the film's outstanding special effects.

But if the physical aspects of Dren develop in a blur, the emotional/psychological aspects are handled incredibly well. Dren herself is played by two separate actors whose performances are augmented with computer technology. Dren's formative years are handled by Abigail Chu, who has since gone on to roles in *Scott Pilgrim vs. the World* (2010) and *Camp Rock 2: The Final Jam* (2010). From adolescence onward, Dren is portrayed by French actor Delphine Chaneac, hardly a newcomer yet largely unknown and making an absolute breakthrough impression here. Both actresses take us through a seamless panoply of childhood emotional development from formative bonding all the way through adolescent rebellion and sexual awakening.

By the time Dren has undergone a final terrifying transformation, coming to dominate and ultimately conquer her parents in a stunning pair of confrontations, viewers will be left with a breathtaking assortment of topics for conversation, consideration, and soul searching. To call *Splice* a horror film is like calling *Frankenstein* (1931) an angsty melodrama. It is a movie for our times whether we are scientists, parents, or at the behest of corporate concerns.

However jarring and surreal viewers may find various plot points in *Splice,* writer/director Vincenzo Natali is known for exactly that sort of approach to storytelling. His first feature film *Cube* (1997) told the story of seven strangers waking up in and trying to escape a mysterious booby-trapped maze. His follow-up *Cypher* (2002) was an underrated Kafkaesque thrill ride that invoked the intelligent science fiction fantasy of Phillip K. Dick while embracing genre sensibilities. The decidedly surreal if more problematic *Nothing* (2003) was a comedy concerning two childhood friends who, after a very bad day in which jobs and relationships and reputations and finally their home is lost, suddenly realize the world outside their front door has vanished, leaving only an endless white expanse.

Splice bravely and quite compellingly takes the focus off of science itself asking why we do the science that we do. When Oppenheimer looked at the Atomic blast he and his fellow researchers had made possible he uttered the now famous line from the Vedas "I am become death, the destroyer of worlds." He saw himself Godlike in his creation and it horrified him. As bad as the bomb seemed at that moment there was the concurrent realization that it could not have existed unless it had been harnessed by something worse.

Dave Canfield

CREDITS

Clive Nicoli: Adrien Brody
Elsa Kast: Sarah Polley
Barlow: David Hewlett
Dren: Delphine Chaneac
Gavin Nicoli: Brandon McGibbon
Joan Chorot: Simona Maicanescu
Child Dren: Abigail Chu
Origin: USA
Language: English
Released: 2010
Production: Steven Hoban; Copper Heart Entertainment, Gaumont; released by Warner Bros.
Directed by: Vincenzo Natali
Written by: Vincenzo Natali, Doug Taylor, Antoinette Terry Bryant
Cinematography by: Tetsuo Nagata
Music by: Cyrille Aufort
Sound: Bernard Bats, Joel Rangon
Editing: Michele Conroy
Art Direction: Joshu de Cartier
Costumes: Alex Kavanagh
Production Design: Todd Cherniawsky
MPAA rating: R
Running time: 107 minutes

REVIEWS

Biodrowski, Steve. *Cinefantastique.* June 4, 2010.
Chang, Justin. *Variety.* January 27, 2010.
Dargas, Manohia. *New York Times.* June 3, 2010.
Ebert, Roger. *Chicago Sun-Times.* June 2, 2010.
Fuchs, Cynthia. *PopMatters.* June 11, 2010.
Gingold, Michael. *Fangoria.* June 2, 2010.
Gonslaves, Rob. *eFilmCritic.* June 7, 2010.
Kennedy, Lisa. *Denver Post.* June 4, 2010.
Lasalle, Mick. *San Francisco Chronicle.* June 3, 2010.
Phipps, Keith. *AV Club.* June 3, 2010.
Schwarzbaum, Lisa. *Entertainment Weekly.* May 26, 2010.

QUOTES

Clive Nicoli: "Why the f**k did you make her in the first place? Huh? For the betterment of mankind? You never wanted a normal child because you were afraid of losing control."

TRIVIA

Delphine Chaneac shaved her head for the film in order to play the creature Dren.

THE SPY NEXT DOOR

Spying is easy, babysitting is hard.
　　—Movie tagline
Part spy, part babysitter, all hero.
　　—Movie tagline

Box Office: $24 million

This latest installment in the "aging action hero takes on the penultimate assignment of his career: babysitting" genre, finds action superstar Jackie Chan facing off against three suburban brats, all the while trying to apprehend a dubious, cartoonish international criminal bent on global domination. In *The Spy Next Door* Chan plays Bob Ho an elite Chinese spy on loan to the CIA who is assigned to stop Russian mobster Poldark (Magnus Scheving) from taking control of the world's oil supply. For a seasoned-and-stealthy martial artist like Ho, however, trading blows with a wannabe world dominator is a piece of cake; it is his life outside of the office that is giving him trouble.

While maintaining a fake profile as a cubicle-inhabiting peon and making his home in a suburban neighborhood, Bob fell for Gillian (Amber Valletta), his blond, single soccer-mom neighbor and, as unbelievable as it seems, she likes him back. The problem is that her three kids, perpetual eye-rolling teen Farren (Madeline Carroll), computer nerd middle-grader Ian (Will Shadley), and preschooler Nora (Alina Foley), do not feel the same way. They are determined to stop the budding romance between their mom and their wet noodle neighbor any way they can. Of course, just when Ho is presented with the perfect opportunity to win over Gillian's brood (namely a few days spent babysitting the kids solo) Poldark escapes from prison. The result leaves Ho with a nightmare of a work-life balance situation.

It is too bad then that the film does not capitalize on this nervous energy—and the inherent narrative drive—that such a predicament could offer. A zippy story that finds Ho desperately trying to figure out how to outrun assassins while trying to get the kids to school on time seems like a no-brainer. Unfortunately, *The Spy Next Door* is a sleepy tale, one where Ho is miraculously afforded the opportunity to focus on one task at a time. Grand-scale crime takes a breather while our ninja assassin grapples with bedtimes, breakfasts, and break-downs. The infuriating kids, in their turn, are peacefully tucked away at school every time Poldark rears his head. The result is a compartmentalized narrative from the screenwriting team of Jonathan Bernstein, James Greer, and Gregory Poirier and a languid pace from director Brian Levant. The screenwriters tend toward lengthy scenes full of mediocre jokes and Levant indulges them, making sure that the forced false-hilarity of shopping for princess costumes on Halloween does not become overshadowed by Chan's martial arts high jinks. Instead, the ample legroom allotted to each narrative thread creates a drawn-out, slow movie where each storyline is easily forgettable and the ninety-minute running time feels like an eternity.

The dragging pace is only amplified by the completely unbelievable set-up, clichéd characters, and forced comedy that pepper the movie. Chan as a secret spy is not such a hard morsel to digest, but Chan as romantic hero is (sorry, Jackie). As charming as he is when he is wowing audiences with his martial arts skills, no amount of cute mugging makes up for the non-existent chemistry between him and Valletta (though both try hard to cover for it). To add insult to injury, this lack of organic camaraderie carries over into Bob's life at the CIA. Billy Ray Cyrus and George Lopez as Ho's CIA counterparts (Cyrus playing the southern charmer and Lopez the sneaky boss) are entirely ramshackle and outlandish and their stiff delivery of flimsy jokes just makes their performances that much more frustrating. Even the youngest viewer could discern that this motley crew is not what CIA operatives look and act like. Still, their awkward shenanigans are nothing compared to the flat and completely clichéd portrayal of villains Poldark and his lusty counterpart Creel (Katherine Boecher). From their over- the-top accents, to the drawn out fitting-in in America gags assigned to them, not only are they not interesting, it is impossible to believe that they have brain matter enough between them to come up with a plan to dominate anything.

The only saving grace in *The Spy Next Door* are the Chan-choreographed fight scenes but there are not nearly enough of them. As viewers have come to expect from Chan, each fight scene incorporates his trademark wacky resourcefulness. Chan is seen flattening bad guys with bikes, belts, and even the occasional kid. He dances around his opponents, exuding charisma and confidence and it is so much fun to watch him in action that it is easy to temporarily forget that once he is through it is back to the film's tedious plot.

Joanna Topor MacKenzie

CREDITS

Bob Ho: Jackie Chan
Farren: Madeline Carroll
Nora: Alina Foley
Ian: Will Shadley
Glaze: George Lopez
Colton James: Billy Ray Cyrus
Gillian: Amber Valletta

Tatiana Creel: Katherine Boecher
Poldark: Magnus Scheving
Origin: USA
Language: English
Released: 2010
Production: Robert Simonds; Relativity Media, Robert Simonds Production; released by Lionsgate
Directed by: Brian Levant
Written by: Jonathan Bernstein, James Greer, Gregory Poirier
Cinematography by: Dean Cundey
Music by: David Newman
Sound: Mike Wilhoit
Music Supervisor: Season Kent, Happy Walters
Editing: Lawrence Jordan
Art Direction: Bryce Perrin
Costumes: Lisa Jensen
Production Design: Stephen Lineweaver
MPAA rating: PG
Running time: 94 minutes

REVIEWS

Anderson, Melissa. *Village Voice.* January 12, 2010.
Demara, Bruce. *Toronto Star.* January 15, 2010.
Germain, David. *Associated Press.* January 13, 2010.
Gronvall, Andrea. *Chicago Reader.* January 14, 2010.
Lowenstein, Lael. *Variety.* January 11, 2010.
O'Sullivan, Michael. *Washington Post.* January 15, 2010.
Puig, Claudia. *USA Today.* January 14, 2010.
Scott, A.O. *New York Times.* January 15, 2010.
Simon, Brent. *Screen International.* January 11, 2010.
Zacharek, Stephanie. *Salon.com.* January 14, 2010.

QUOTES

Bob Ho: "I've brought down dictators. How bad can three kids be?"
Colton James: "That man's so crooked, he could eat nails and poop corkscrews."

TRIVIA

A montage of Jackie Chan film clips plays during the opening of this film.

AWARDS

Nomination:

Golden Raspberries 2010: Worst Support. Actor (Lopez), Worst Support. Actor (Cyrus).

THE SQUARE

Some things can't be buried.
—Movie tagline

The Australian noir thriller *The Square* came up from "Down Under" with critical comparisons to the

Coen Brothers' movies, especially *Blood Simple* (1984). In some ways, the comparison is apt, but the Edgerton Brothers' taut thriller is quieter, more subdued fare. And the plot is not quite as complicated. But it is still well worth seeing as a prime example of the subgenre in which ordinary people can take one moral misstep and then slide far down the slippery slope into the abyss of nefarious acts compelled by unintended consequences.

Nash Edgerton directed *The Square* and his brother, Joel, co-wrote the script. It is actually the ninth film Nash Edgerton has helmed, but he has far more credits as a stuntman (for instance, in the recent *Knight and Day* [2010], as well as in innumerable Australian productions). In this film, he leaves the stunts to others, but Joel Edgerton is a prominent member of the cast.

The script thrusts the viewer into the life of protagonist Ray Yale (David Roberts), a developer who is working on a potentially lucrative job that involves building a big concrete square-shaped (thus the otherwise-inscrutable title) patio for a new upscale resort hotel on the outskirts of Sydney. Yale's life is rapidly becoming far more complicated. For reasons not entirely explained, he gets himself enmeshed in kickbacks and debts in order to get the job done—and unexpected events from bad weather to labor unrest are delaying the project, adding to his stress. But that is nothing compared to his domestic troubles. For no good reason we can understand he is unhappy with his wife and having an affair with a younger, married woman, Carla (Claire van der Boom). Carla is pressuring Ray to run away with her, and the pressure gets turned up when she finds a stash of cash in her attic. Her husband, Greg (Anthony Hayes), is involved in some criminal enterprise—it is never made quite clear exactly what—and she grabs the money to finance her imagined new life with Ray.

Ray has no choice but to go along with her scheme if he wants to keep her, and apparently the other option of returning to his domestic situation does not seem tolerable. Carla and Ray do not seem like the desperate, criminal types. In fact, they are ordinary to the point of near blandness. Some critics rightly pointed to the lack of sizzle in their affair, and it is true we never really see their passion nor get an explanation of what is the basis of their attraction. There are hints that Carla's husband is a mean, no-good guy (his hair is as grungy as his manner and his buddies), and the successful, enterprising, older Ray seems responsible in comparison. Roberts plays him as a perpetually-harassed soul with a somewhat blank expression.

Carla and Ray live in a small town along a river and know that the money's disappearance will arouse suspicions, so they hire a sleazy guy named Billy (Joel

Edgerton) to torch and burn down the home of Carla and Greg, figuring Greg will believe the money was lost in the fire. But in the first of a series of tragic consequences, they learn too late that Greg's mother is asleep in the house. The caper goes down while both Ray and Carla are picnicking with their families in a Christmas ceremony. Santa floats down the river in a boat, but as a choir sings carols, Santa doffs his suit and changes into his firefighters' gear. With the added impact of the strangeness (to Northern Hemisphere viewers) of a Christmas outdoor town picnic, the well-cut scene immerses the viewer into the horror Ray and Carla have fallen into. It is a marvelous, terrifyingly wrought scene.

And their problems only get deeper. Ray is besieged by blackmail notes, and he does not know who has figured out his role in the fire. Greg finds the bag that had held the cash, without the loot, in the smoldering remains of their home, and starts to suspect Carla. Ray is pursued, has nightmares, makes desperate bad choices that leave him with more blood on his hands, etc.—the innocent corrupted by one terrible misdeed. The murkiness of how Greg got the money in the first place is frustrating to the viewer, yet it adds to the atmosphere of the ubiquitous threat that dogs Ray.

There are some definite Coen-like touches, particularly in a bizarre scene involving a swimming dog. The idea is that even the two families' pets are somehow affected by how the peace of their suburban life has unraveled. There is not much humor, though—only a little irony when the local police chief exults that small-town life has suddenly turned interesting. And, very much like the Coens, the bodies pile up in a spectacular climax that seals the permanent fate of the haunted—a sort of never-ceasing moral retribution.

Like many Australian, British, and Irish movies that make it to the United States, *The Square* could use subtitles here. It is hard to understand the dialogue or to really grasp the fine points of how some of the characters (particularly Greg's friends) are involved. It turns out the plot is not all that intricately constructed, but it is full of red herrings. With stronger lead characters, more sizzle, and pungent dialogue, especially between the lovers, *The Square* could have been a minor classic heralding the arrival of some Aussie rivals to the Coens. As it is, however, this is still a must-see film for fans of innovative Noir thrillers.

Michael Betzold

CREDITS

Ray: David Roberts
Billy: Joel Edgerton

Greg "Smithy" Smith: Anthony Hayes
Barney: Kieran Darcy-Smith
Jake: Peter Phelps
Gil Hubbard: Bill Hunter
Carla: Claire van der Boom
Martha: Lucy Bell
Leonard: Brendan Donoghue
Wendy: Lisa Bailey
Smithy's Mate: Luke Doolan
Origin: Australia
Language: English
Released: 2008
Production: Louise Smith; New South Wales Film & Television Office, Blue-Tongue Films, Film Depot; released by Apparition
Directed by: Nash Edgerton
Written by: Joel Edgerton, Matthew Dabner
Cinematography by: Brad Shield
Music by: Francois Tetaz
Sound: Peter Grace
Editing: Nash Edgerton, Luke Doolan
Art Direction: Angus MacDonald
Costumes: Sally Sharpe
Production Design: Elizabeth Mary Moore
MPAA rating: R
Running time: 105 minutes

REVIEWS

Anderson, Melissa. *Village Voice*. April 6, 2010.
Bacchus, Alan. *Daily Film Dose*. May 11, 2010.
Buckmaster, Luke. *In Film Australia*. August 7, 2008.
Ebert, Roger. *Chicago Sun-Times*. April 28, 2010.
Fine, Marshall. *Huffington Post*. April 8, 2010.
Morris, Wesley. *Boston Globe*. April 16, 2010.
O'Hehir, Andrew. *Salon.com*. April 9, 2010.
Pais, Matt. *Metromix.com*. April 8, 2010.
Rainer, Peter. *Christian Science Monitor*. April 9. 2010.
Scott, A.O. *New York Times*. April 19, 2010.

STEP UP 3D

Two worlds. One dream.
—Movie tagline

Take the biggest step of all in 3D.
—Movie tagline

Box Office: $42 million

Step Up 3D arrived in theaters in early August 2010, roughly eight months after James Cameron's 3D fantasy epic *Avatar* became the highest grossing movie in history (at least at the time of this writing), largely thanks to its groundbreaking 3D effects. Naturally, Hollywood took this to mean that 3D was a bona fide attention-getter and money maker. The 3D gimmick had been enjoying a modest resurgence in popularity for a few years before *Avatar*, but that film certainly was the turning point in how films would be distributed, at least for the first year or so after its success. The 3D gimmick would also help further increase the price of a single ticket with some theaters charging up to $16 a head, even for films that were after-the-fact conversions to 3D, such as *Clash of the Titans* (2010) and *The Last Airbender* (2010).

Step Up 3D, the first dance film of its era to receive the 3D treatment, is a film that was conceived specifically for this format. With complete belief in itself, it puts the flashy gimmicks and popular trends first (assuming breakdancing is still a popular trend) and characters and storyline a distant, distant second. This falls in step with most other dance movies, dating back to the Golan-Globus *Breakin'* films of the 1980s where plot did not matter much. With *Step Up 3D*, the third in the franchise, the plot matters even less, in spite of the fact that it took two screenwriters to create it. This is a movie that boldly asks its audience for more of its hard-earned money and one that is poised to deliver the goods, no matter how silly and inept the rest of it looks in the process.

The story has many central characters, but the only carry-over character from any of the *Step Up* movies is the young college-bound Moose (Adam G. Sevani) from *Step Up 2: The Streets* (which itself had only one carry-over character from the first *Step Up* film and who is nowhere to be seen here). He and his best friend Camille (Alyson Stoner) are new to the campuses of New York University. After a scuffle in the streets in the movie's first unofficial dance-off (there are plenty of "official" ones later in the movie) where Moose shows off his moves to an impressed crowd, he finds himself associating with a street dancing gang who call themselves The Pirates, led by would-be documentary filmmaker and hunky dancer Luke (Rick Malambri).

The Pirates—all nine of them—live in a loft where they practice dance moves, graffiti, video editing, and jumping from roof-to-roof. The thought of getting a job to help pay for spray paint, bunk beds, and a giant wall of boomboxes has not occurred to these people and because of that lapse in judgment, the bank is threatening to take the loft away from them unless they can make up the last six months worth of rent. There is a major dance competition taking place within the next month and if they win that prize money, they can keep their little dance bunker. "They can't do this!" Luke protests to the real-estate broker, who is, of course, well within his right.

The group's main competition is The House of Samurai, a rival dance group led by Julien (Joe Slaughter), who is hell-bent on destroying The Pirates and their little commune. They face off in various dance-offs that either look like they take place in Thunderdome or result in giant slip'n'slides. Helping to win these dance-offs is not only Moose, but Natalie (Sharni Vinson), the female love interest of Luke, who takes her in to live with The Pirates, not taking into account that there is now another unemployed mouth to feed. "Everyone here knows what it's like to be a nomad," he tells her. The plot (such as it is) thickens when videos of The Pirates' dance practices leak online, much to the delight of The House of Samurai. Luke and Natalie's relationship deepens as she becomes enamored with his film-making skills and his love of staring into space. Meanwhile, Moose, who has been hiding his ambitions as a dancer from everyone around him, is found out by his friend Camille, who encourages him to follow his dream of becoming a double major (dance and electrical engineering). Of course, these two can never be "just friends."

While it is impossible to take this story seriously, it is also hard to not enjoy this ridiculous movie as a piece of so-bad-it's-good cinema. The acting is bad and the writing is worse ("You're BFAB," Luke says to Moose. "Born From A Boombox!"). But dance movies are easy targets for ridicule, one of the reasons being that the stars are generally not trained actors, but professional dancers and/or choreographers who got lucky enough to land an acting gig. They will never win Oscars®, but they can be fun to watch when they do not actually speak. One scene, in particular, attempts to hark back to the old days of Gene Kelly or Fred Astaire and Ginger Rogers, when Moose and Camille do a one-take dance number up a city sidewalk, utilizing every aspect of the scenery with ease. While the sentiment behind the scene is certainly forced, the intent of the scene is genuine and a welcome relief from the glitz and other forms of cheesiness thus far.

As for the 3D effects, the filmmakers do their damndest to make sure the audience gets its money's worth by infusing many of the dance numbers with elements such as bubbles, frozen slushees, balloons and, inevitably, water being splashed onto the audience and dripping down the shot. The dance scenes themselves are well-framed and edited to make it an immersive experience, though it will likely look incredibly silly on a non 3D television screen, but then, so will the rest of the movie. *Step Up 3D* may be a bad movie, but it certainly has more confidence than most mediocre movies out there.

Collin Souter

CREDITS

Moose: Adam G. Sevani
Luke: Rick Malambri
Natalie: Sharni Vinson
Cable: Harry Shum Jr.
Jenny: Ally Maki
Camille: Alyson Stoner
Julien: Joe Slaughter
Origin: USA
Language: English
Released: 2010
Production: Erik Feig, Jennifer Gibgot, Adam Shankman, Patrick Wachsberger; Offspring Entertainment, Summit Entertainment; released by Touchstone Pictures
Directed by: John M. Chu
Written by: Amy Andelson, Emily Meyer
Cinematography by: Ken Seng
Music by: Bear McCreary
Sound: Matthew Price
Music Supervisor: Buck Damon
Editing: Andrew Marcus
Art Direction: Mario R. Ventenilla
Costumes: Kurt and Bart
Production Design: Devorah Herbert
MPAA rating: PG-13
Running time: 106 minutes

REVIEWS

Anderson, Jason. *Toronto Star.* August 6, 2010.
Burr, Ty. *Boston Globe.* August 5, 2010.
Childress, Erik. *eFilmcritic.com.* August 6, 2010.
Goss, William. *Cinematical.com.* August 6, 2010.
Hale, Mike. *New York Times.* August 6, 2010.
Lybarger, Dan. *MovieMaker Magazine.* August 7, 2010.
Phillips, Michael. *Chicago Tribune.* August 5, 2010.
Rea, Steven. *Philadelphia Enquirer.* August 5, 2010.
Uhlich, Keith. *Time Out New York.* August 4, 2010.
Weitzman, Elizabeth. *New York Daily News.* August 6, 2010.

QUOTES

Luke: "You up for a little competition?"
Moose: "I was born to be the Ashley to your Mary-Kate."

STONE

Some people tell lies. Others live them.
    —Movie tagline

Box Office: $2 million

The prologue of *Stone,* a brief glimpse into the earlier home life of the movie's central character, at first appears a throwaway scene. Then it becomes clear that the introduction to Jack Mabrey (Robert De Niro) is a thematic anchor—one that grounds the material in the realm of understandable, recognizable human behavior. It is essential ballast to Angus MacLachlan's screenplay, which drifts from the specifics of Jack's character to the sociopolitical landscape of his rural surroundings (amplified by aural montages of talk radio snippets) and ultimately to a contrast of his spiritual state against the others in his life. MacLachlan's script is comprehensive and ambitious yet lacking in balance, favoring indulgence in the philosophical reflections of a few (some of them phony) over the bitter, blunt story of its characters' aimless lives.

In the preface, Jack (played as a younger man by Enver Gjokaj, channeling De Niro's icy stare in his short moments on screen) sits watching golf on television—a drink in one hand, the other resting behind his head. His wife Madylyn (played by Frances Conroy in the movie's present, with Pepper Binkley as the younger incarnation) puts their daughter down for a nap, sits on the bed, and drowns in the buzzing of a bee at the window. The sound—stated directly later in the movie as an example of the voice of God—brings a revelatory moment. She is leaving her husband, Madylyn works up the courage to tell Jack, adding, "You keep my soul in a dungeon," to make the reason as all-encompassing as possible. His response is to run upstairs and threaten to throw their child out the window. She stays, and they sit outside watching the girl play.

Neither speaks about it then, and De Niro and Conroy give the sensation that very little else has been said between them in the decades since. Their life is routine after forty-three years of marriage. He goes off to work as a parole officer at a correctional facility—weeks away from retirement—while she stays at home—perhaps having company over for a card game now and again. After work, she reads a passage from the Bible before dinner, and they sit outside on the porch in their rocking chairs at night, where Jack listens to more talk radio, oblivious to any conversation Madylyn might try to start.

Their daughter has started her own family but is getting divorced, a fact that Jack tries to keep quiet or dismiss immediately once it has been raised. Divorce is not "normal" in his book, and normality, or at least the appearance of it, is the key to understanding Jack. Maintaining appearances is the reason he used his daughter to keep his wife in a proverbial dungeon. He is attempting to control the circumstances to the best of his ability.

Another master manipulator enters Jack's life. His name is Gerald "Stone" Creeson (Edward Norton), in prison and soon to be up for parole after helping to plan the robbery of his grandparents, which resulted in their murders and the burning down of their home. He is innocent of the latter two crimes, Stone contends, and a jury believed it.

Compared to Jack's complex motivation, Stone's is entirely straightforward: He wants out of prison. After testing the waters with Jack's methods, using clever platitudes ("I don't want no beef with you," Stone says, "I want to be a vegetarian") or a sense of righteous anger (suggesting Jack wants to keep him locked up), Stone gradually learns the expectations of the parole board through their conversations. Jack hears the inmates' stories day after day; a montage shows them saying the same things: they have found religion, regret their actions, and apologize for their wrongdoing. So Stone does the same, searching the prison library's religion section for some guidance/excuse (the one he decides upon is the one that suggests truth can be found by listening to one's surroundings, calling back the bee buzzing from the prologue and recalled at the end as Jack ignores the same droning invitation to enlightenment).

Whether Stone is sincere in his transformation is left to doubt by story's end. Norton's dead eyes, his character's lack of regret for his true involvement in the murder/arson charges he avoided in court, his insistence on having his wife Lucetta (Milla Jovovich, playing yet another manipulating character who, in her case, uses sex as a game she has loaded in her favor to win) seduce Jack, and his defiant display of success after he is granted parole suggest he has not reformed. His sincerity, though, is another matter; Stone does acknowledge his crime and finds a sense of peace in understanding his cold, uncaring nature. He does not regret his actions and prods Jack, a man of similar denial, to consider his own.

The dialogue between Jack and Stone takes on the tenor of a duel. Director John Curran's pacing escalates their own internal struggles with identity projected into these exchanges to a physical confrontation following the mysterious destruction of the Mabrey's home (an unresolved puzzle, either the work of a vengeful Stone, a desperate Madylyn, or faulty wiring, although more than likely the second option). Indeed, the scenes following Stone's release from jail take on the tone of an average thriller, although it is a logical progression.

The problem lies in Curran and MacLachlan's concentration on the spiritual fight within and between Jack and Stone. Not only does it simplify the context of their respective character flaws to a matter of either gaining or rejecting an external kind of redemption, it also muddles the narrative. The focus becomes more about what the characters are saying as opposed to what they are doing to each other through their words. The difference is subtle and *Stone,* which begins as a strong character study, becomes bogged down in achieving a similar sense of enlightenment as does its eponymous character. The specific circumstances of these characters turn into hazy pursuits for redemption, as the soundtrack hums and whirs with the sound of lofty goals revealed to be little more than so much noise.

Mark Dujsik

CREDITS

Gerald "Stone" Creeson: Edward Norton
Jack Mabry: Robert De Niro
Lucetta Creeson: Milla Jovovich
Madylyn Mabry: Frances Conroy
Young Jack: Enver Gjokaj
Young Madylyn: Pepper Binkley
Origin: USA
Language: English
Released: 2010
Production: Jordan Schur, Holly Wiersma, David Mimran PROD; Millenium Films, Stone Productions; released by Overture Films
Directed by: John Curran
Written by: Angus MacLachlan
Cinematography by: Maryse Alberti
Music by: Jon Brion, Selena Arizanovic
Sound: Jay Meagher
Editing: Alexandre De Francheschi
Art Direction: Kerry Sanders
Costumes: Victoria Farrell
Production Design: Tim Grimes
MPAA rating: R
Running time: 105 minutes

REVIEWS

Berardinelli, James. *ReelViews.* October 20, 2010.
Buckwalter, Ian. *NPR.* October 7, 2010.
Childress, Erik. *Cinematical.* September 10, 2010.
Dargis, Manohla. *New York Times.* October 7, 2010.
Ebert, Roger. *Chicago Sun-Times.* October 13, 2010.
Olszewski, Tricia. *Washington City Paper.* October 15, 2010.
Phillips, Michael. *Chicago Tribune.* October 7, 2010.
Strout, Justin. *Orlando Weekly.* October 21, 2010.
Tallerico, Brian. *HollywoodChicago.com.* October 15, 2010.
Tobias, Scott. *AV Club.* October 7, 2010.

TRIVIA

All of the prison scenes were filmed at the State Prison of Southern Michigan, one of the largest walled prisons in the world.

SURVIVAL OF THE DEAD
(George A. Romero's Survival of the Dead)

Survival isn't just for the living.
—Movie tagline
Death isn't what it used to be.
—Movie tagline

Hardcore fans greet the release of zombie films by George A. Romero with a single-minded zeal reserved for big events. Of course, Romero is the patron saint of the zombie film. The first three films in his unofficial undead series *Night of the Living Dead* (1968), *Dawn of the Dead* (1977), and *Day of the Dead* (1981) are rightly considered some of the best and most important horror films ever made. Yet many would argue that since the underrated *Land of the Dead* (2005), Romero's undead series has lacked clear direction. *Diary of the Dead* (2008) was an interesting but not very compelling experiment in both digital filmmaking and use of the found footage format. *Survival of the Dead* is far less experimental and more entertaining, but for fans awaiting the capstone on arguably the most important film series in horror film history the wait is not yet over. *Survival of the Dead* survives viewing but fails to add anything new to the zombie-verse.

The film tells the story of two feuding Irish patriarchs and a group of American National Guardsmen deserters were met briefly during *Diary of the Dead.* Led by Sarge "Nicotine" Crockett (Alan Van Sprang), a gruff mix of likeable rogue and mercenary, the group survives by waylaying whoever they come across for supplies. They do not kill the people they meet and seem to live by a loose code, conducting themselves like a closed circle of fast friends. After picking up a young man (Devon Bostick) during a raid, the group learns on the internet of an island off the East Coast offering a safe haven for survivors.

Crocket is immediately suspicious and proven right when, upon arriving at the dock, they are threatened by a man who demands they hand over everything. After a gun battle in which Crocket's group is able to commandeer a boat, they force the now captured leader, exiled islander Patrick O'Flynn (Kenneth Welsh), to take them to the island. O'Flynn proves a not-altogether unlikeable man. He is, in fact, the quintessential Irish caricature full of quips and stubbornness, and undying in his hatred for Muldoon (Richard Fitzpatrick), who exiled him. O'Flynn and Muldoon have taken opposite sides of the zombie war since day one. O'Flynn is content to lay the dead to rest to prevent the spread of infection. Muldoon is determined they be rehabilitated. Caught in the middle is O'Flynn's daughter Janet (Kathleen Munroe), the lone survivor of a pair of twins; the other being Jane, (also played by Munroe) who, undead, rides across the island on horseback. When Crocket and his team are captured and the situation on the island begins to decay, Muldoon and O'Flynn's feud may prove the end of everyone.

Welsh and Fitzpatrick are so good in their roles and so able to handle the broad aspects of them that the film could have been truly memorable as a fablesque look at war using only the Muldoon and the O'Flynn factions. There really is no need at all for the presence of the Crocket character who is simply the typical good guy in the rough albeit well-played by Allen Van Sprang. Romero himself has said in supplemental materials that he was simply unsure what this film would be about and his lack of sureness is all over it. One moment, O'Flynn hands a zombie some dynamite causing a zany wide-eyed double-take that would be at home in a Warner Brothers cartoon and the next offers a series of haunting shots of the horseback riding undead Jane that feel lifted from something like a Mario Bava film. Some characters are mourned while the audience is asked to simply laugh at the death of others. It is every bit as chaotic as the war it seems to want to comment on, but ultimately lacks a point. *Survival of the Dead* is the funniest entry in the series since *Day of the Dead* but rather than clarify any satirical intent the series of inventive zombie sight gags seem sadly like corpse leftovers.

Another major problem in both *Survival of the Dead* and *Diary of the Dead* is the use of CGI imagery in place of practical effects. Like any good special effect, CGI should be basically invisible, leaving the viewer to either question how it was done or, at best, have a strong connection with whatever feeling the filmmaker was trying to provoke. The CGI effects here, especially those using blood and flesh, stick out like a sore thumb when they need to be visceral.

George A. Romero has never stopped being relevant. He needs to keep making films but he would be wise to wait until he has a film solidly in mind before he gets back behind the camera. There are some wonderful ideas here, some great performances and echoes of the past glory that has led to the zombie becoming the world's most prominent movie monster. Romero has spoken to the nameless dread of meaninglessness in modern culture, racism, consumerism, and the plight of the poor. What he speaks about next should be listened to even if this time around he did not have much to say.

Dave Canfield

CREDITS

Sarge "Nicotine" Crockett: Alan Van Sprang
Kenny: Eric Woolfe
Patrick O'Flynn: Kenneth Welsh
Seamus Muldoon: Richard Fitzpatrick
Janet/Jane O'Flynn: Kathleen Munroe
Francisco: Stefano di Matteo
Chuck: Joris Jarsky
Boy: Devon Bostick
Origin: Canada
Language: English
Released: 2009
Production: Paula Devonshire; Romero-Grunwald; released by Artfine Films
Directed by: George A. Romero
Written by: George A. Romero
Cinematography by: Adam Swica
Music by: Robert Carli
Editing: Michael Doherty
Sound: Greg Chapman
Art Direction: Joshu De Cartier
Costumes: Alex Kavanagh
Production Design: Art Greywal
MPAA rating: R
Running time: 88 minutes

REVIEWS

Alexander, Chris. *Fangoria.* April 24, 2010.
Biodrowski, Steve. *Cinefantastique.* May 6, 2010.
Butane, Johnny. *Dread Central.* October 7, 2009.
Ebert, Roger. *Chicago Sun-Times.* May 26, 2010.
Edelstein, David. *New York Magazine.* June 1, 2010.
Felperin, Leslie. *Variety.* July 7, 2010.
Graham, Jamie. *Total Film.* March 26, 2010.
Miska, Brad. *Bloody Disgusting.* April 26, 2010.
Murray, Noel. *AV Club.* May 27, 2010.
Soullis, Jeannette. *New York Times.* May 28, 2010.

QUOTES

Patrick O'Flynn: "Well, I'm always the type of person who has something up his sleeve. I could kill you right now if I wanted to."

SWEETGRASS

The last ride of the American cowboy.
—Movie tagline

If you just read its single-sentence logline description, *Sweetgrass* seems more or less like a film-within-a-film joke—the sort of insufferably pretentious documentary that a stuffy, erudite in-law or spouse of a pal would be viewing in an Adam Sandler movie, and get clowned on for watching. Yes, you see, *Sweetgrass* is a largely silent nonfiction film about Montana sheepherders. And yet despite the almost reflexive yawn that summary provokes, the movie is also a uniquely engaging cinematic experience.

Co-directed by Lucien Castaing-Taylor and Ilisa Barbash, *Sweetgrass* follows a group of shepherd-cowboys as over the course of several months in 2003 they first tend to the care of their flock and then drive their teeming herd of sheep on a trek of over 185 miles across the Beartooth Mountains, to greener pastures. The filmmakers are not at all concerned, however, with the personalities of their human participants. In fact, they are not much concerned with any sort of interpersonal inquiry, let alone subjective perspective. Instead, *Sweetgrass* merely unfolds in almost doggedly submissive fashion. There is no real narrative imposed here, just the occupational particulars that happen between points A and B, and all the beaten-up items—canvas bags, well-worn traveling stoves, homemade teepees—that entails. Apart from the occasional use of walkie-talkies—and, late in the movie, a cell phone which allows for a hired hand's frustrations to spill over almost comically in a one-sided conversation with his mother—the movie has an eerie timeless quality to it.

This may well be the only review of *Sweetgrass* to also make mention of *Jackass 3-D* (2010), and not merely because of the chasm in their commercial acceptance. (Released by boutique distributor Cinema Guild, *Sweetgrass* pulled in just over $200,000 during its theatrical run, which the latest *Jackass* sequel probably grossed in Manhattan alone on the afternoon of its opening day.) The reason is that, in a weird way, the two movies are decidedly opposite sides of the same coin, each challenging and expanding traditional notions about what constitutes nonfiction American cinema. And while documentaries that illuminate a particular social issue or concern are important, so too is a pinch of intra-genre variety. The gonzo-vaudevillian antics of Johnny Knoxville and his motley crew of merry pranksters serve to highlight some of the baser impulses that bind us all together. As a remarkable experiential work, meanwhile, *Sweetgrass*' monastic passivity seeks to remind its audience that we all share this space, this Earth, regardless of where we individually live.

While the movie's digital video capturing (blown up to 35mm for its theatrical presentation) occasionally leaves something to be desired, compositionally, Castaing-Taylor's cinematography is driven by a very earthy attitude, neither grasping wildly at epic overviews attempting to convince the audience of nature's stark beauty, nor rooting around in extreme close-up in an effort to arouse sympathetic identification with the animals. Most of the film unfolds at a certain staid, almost academic, remove; a grasp of actual herder technique and intent develops slowly, in elliptical fashion. Instead, the jostling neck-bells and constant bleating of the thousands of sheep (sure to arouse the suspicion of neighbors for anyone undertaking a home viewing with THX surround sound) eventually come to represent its own lulling sort of white noise, though a viewer might swear they are able to discern some emotional feeling if not meaning in the sheep's plaintive baying.

All of this may sound tedious, and there is a sense of panic akin to being tossed in the deep end of a pool when one first realizes there are essentially no human characters or guides to *Sweetgrass*. Yet there is a weird and fascinating sense of almost guilty disconnect that eventually envelops a more reflective viewer—presumably the sort of person who would be watching a near-wordless documentary about sheepherders in the first place. Observing the pliant sheep being sheared clean of their wool, or quivering newborn lambs being literally tugged out of their mothers' bodies, one is reminded again how separated most of us in the modern day are from the animals over which humans have dominion. Sheep give us food, clothing, and much more, but as with cows, chickens and so many other animals, this is a foreign and purely one-way, transactional relationship, unless one owns or works at a farm.

Truth be told, *Sweetgrass* could conceivably work equally well as a short-form documentary, trimmed by about half of its 101-minute running time. It is not that any one particular portion of the movie cries out for excising over any other, but that it reaches a point of fairly diminishing return, so wedded is it to directorial non-engagement. Still, the film intimately showcases a dependency between humankind and animal that, in today's world, is easy to dismiss or forget outright. It is an interesting thing to ponder, and, like a master, zen sheepherder itself, *Sweetgrass* leads one to such consideration all in a non-confrontational way.

Brent Simon

CREDITS

Origin: USA, France, United Kingdom
Language: English
Released: 2009
Production: Ilisa Barbash; released by The Cinema Guild
Directed by: Lucien Castaing-Taylor, Ilisa Barbash
Cinematography by: Lucien Castaing-Taylor
Sound: Ernst Karel
Editing: Lucien Castaing-Taylor, Ilisa Barbash
MPAA rating: Unrated
Running time: 101 minutes

REVIEWS

Anderson, Melissa. *Village Voice.* January 5, 2010.
Burr, Ty. *Boston Globe.* April 1, 2010.

Dargis, Manohla. *New York Times.* January 6, 2010.
Gleiberman, Owen. *Entertainment Weekly.* January 20, 2010.
Hartlaub, Peter. *San Francisco Chronicle.* March 12, 2010.
O'Hehir, Andrew. *Salon.com.* January 5, 2010.
Stevens, Dana. *Slate.* January 22, 2010.
Tallerico, Brian. *MovieRetriever.com.* June 28, 2010.
Turan, Kenneth. *Los Angeles Times.* March 25, 2010.
Vognar, Chris. *Dallas Morning News.* April 23, 2010.

AWARDS

Nomination:

Ind. Spirit 2011: Truer than Fiction Award, Feature Doc.

THE SWITCH

The most unexpected comedy ever conceived.
—Movie tagline

Box Office: $28 million

Two-thousand and ten has seen the highs and lows of artificial insemination comedies. That it has seen any high whatsoever with *The Kids Are All Right* (2010) is a little miracle in itself for a genre that has seen such lows as *The Back-Up Plan* (2010), just about every straight-to-video vehicle starring Heather Graham, and *Frozen Assets* (1992), once dubbed by Roger Ebert as "perhaps the worst comedy ever made." It is doubtful that even women and their biological clocks can defend the bizarre lengths to which their ilk in these films go to get pregnant, coupled with comedic overtones that hammer the grotesque unreality of their situation and make light of real sociological fears. In the middle of all this mis-shapen wackiness arrives *The Switch,* a film founded on the institute of an unbelievable premise that nevertheless looks away from its screwball nature and surprises in becoming a funny and thoughtful look at unexpected fatherhood.

Wally Mars (Jason Bateman) is not exactly connected to the bright side of life. Stockbroker by day and hypochondriac the rest of the time, his commentary on the world often shifts to the negative when impulsive behavior is involved. Two people are able to size Wally up and challenge his way of life. One is a mentally-challenged New Yorker who sees a "man-boy" trying to cross the street. The other is his longtime gal pal, Kassie Larson (Jennifer Aniston), who breaks the big news that she wants to have a baby. Unmarried and single, Kassie hears the proverbial clock ticking and wants to try while she can. Wally is taken aback; not just at the announcement but that his donation was never in the running since it would be a weird request between best friends and his "dark side" would be an unfortunate side effect to the genes she is hoping to catch in a bottle.

Kassie's friend, Debbie (Juliette Lewis) throws her a very gauche "getting pregnant" party where Wally meets married donor, Roland (Patrick Wilson). He is just in it for the money to support his wife and not quite like the other "douches" Wally has been protecting her from. That still does not stop Wally from getting drunk and accidentally depositing Roland's sample into the bathroom sinkhole. Realizing his epic faux pas, Wally secretly replaces the contents with his own swimmers. Kassie gets pregnant and moves away to raise her child in a quieter landscape, but returns seven years later with little Sebastian (Thomas Robinson) in tow. Wally is happy to have Kassie back in his life, having forgotten all about his switcheroo at her party, but now notices that her son's outlook on life mirrors his own a bit too closely.

For its first half-hour, *The Switch* glides along on the natural presences of Bateman and Aniston. They may be glum characters by romantic comedy standards but it is interesting that we are not being goaded into liking their decisions; just understanding why they are making them. Once the switch is made, years and years of bad mistaken identity comedies have audiences prepared for circumstances where characters must avoid saying the right thing and react like fools while the script makes them jump through situations best summed up in the TV guide of shows destined for cancellation. Allan Loeb's screenplay does corner the audience into accepting this premise wholesale and then the belief that Kassie would not recognize direct genetic details that fail to match up with her or Roland and point directly to Wally. Even suspending our disbelief so far as Sebastian's hair and depressive demeanor, how Kassie never noticed the kid's yummy moaning signs during chow time as one of Wally's definitive traits makes for either an inattentive mommy or a genetic flaw in the script.

These are leaps of logic that Wally himself would shoot down on sight. But this being Wally's story and all, it is one of looking past such flaws and reinventing oneself to the opportunity to give another a brighter view of the world. *The Switch* is Jason Bateman's film from start to finish. One of the actors who has made sardonic condescension to an art form on TV's *Arrested Development* and films, Bateman has become a standout player in supporting roles and cameos on screen. With this film, he has been given a kind of defacto sequel to *Juno* (2007) where his character was not ready to be a father and lost a marriage because of it. Now, with nothing but a nice-but-uninspiring brokerage job and a friendship in Kassie he wishes was more, Bateman's Wally can now see himself in Sebastian. He may not be capable of changing himself, but he can help this new version. Bateman has never been so vulnerable, especially in a wonderfully played scene with Robinson where Sebastian reveals his inner passion for picture frames and Wally counters with a fact from his past that may explain everything we need to know about him.

Bateman gets occasional support from a trio of actors familiar with dealing with unwanted pregnancies on screen. Patrick Wilson played a guy missing his family jewels after a drunken one-night stand in *Barry Munday* (2010) and now plays a guy with perhaps too much testosterone for his own good. Juliette Lewis was artificially inseminated and then kidnapped in *The Way of the Gun* (2000) so forgive her if she cuts loose as the outspoken dance-happy best friend here. Jeff Goldblum may have implanted a mutated seed in *The Fly* (1986), but in *The Switch* is having a lot of fun replaying his single guy confidant from *Nine Months* (1995) and finds a way in every scene he is in to playfully mock that very thankless role to maximum laughs.

The Switch occasionally tries too hard to clue us into its very earnestness. Narration by Bateman involving fate, the craving of connection, and "why we call it the human race" unnecessarily bookends a story that is supposed to be more personal than universal. Not a scene goes by without Alex Wurman's score or some background song underlining it. Still, the film is certainly more *About a Boy* (2002) than *The Back-Up Plan* (2010) and is dependent on the actor behind that "man-boy face" to overlook those flaws. *The Switch* is truly an unexpected little surprise that can make critics feel like proud papas after a myriad of efforts that could never quite take.

Erik Childress

CREDITS

Kassie Larson: Jennifer Aniston
Wally Mars: Jason Bateman
Roland: Patrick Wilson
Declan: Scott Elrod
Leonard: Jeff Goldblum
Sebastian Larson: Thomas Robinson

Debbie: Juliette Lewis
Origin: USA
Language: English
Released: 2010
Production: Albert Berger, Bradley Thomas, Ron Yerxa, Allan Loeb; Mandate Pictures, BonaFide Productions, Echo Film Productions; released by Miramax Films
Directed by: Will Speck, Josh Gordon
Written by: Allan Loeb
Cinematography by: Jess Hall
Music by: Alex Wurman
Sound: James Bolt, Nerses Gezalyan, Thomas Gregory Varga
Music Supervisor: Steven Baker
Editing: John Axelrod
Art Direction: Larry M. Gruber
Costumes: Kasia Walicka-Maimone
Production Design: Adam Stockhausen
MPAA rating: PG-13
Running time: 101 minutes

REVIEWS

Honeycutt, Kirk. *Hollywood Reporter.* August 17, 2010.
Hornaday, Ann. *Washington Post.* August 20, 2010.
Judy, Jim. *Screen It!* August 20, 2010.
Longworth, Karina. *Village Voice.* August 17, 2010.
O'Hehir, Andrew. *Salon.com.* August 19, 2010.
Phillips, Michael. *Chicago Tribune.* August 19, 2010.
Rocchi, James. *MSN Movies.* August 19, 2010.
Roeper, Richard. *RichardRoeper.com.* August 20, 2010.
Schager, Nick. *Slant Magazine.* August 19, 2010.
Snider, Eric D. *Film.com.* August 20, 2010.

QUOTES

Kassie Larson: "Would you please stop having sex with your food?"
Wally Mars: "Neurotic is simply an intense form of introspection."

AWARDS

Nomination:

Golden Raspberries 2010: Worst Actress (Aniston).

T

TAKERS

Who's taking who?
—Movie tagline

Everyone's after something.
—Movie tagline

Box Office: $58 million

"We're takers. That's what we do. We take!" So goes the mantra of the Gordon Jennings crew; not exactly something one wants to put on a business card when what one is taking belongs to banks, but a gentle reminder to the audience that these are not nine-to-five type of guys. Neither are those behind the motion picture *Takers* who, truth be told, certainly cannot be accused of hypocrisy. Without shame they have jumbled together a screenplay full of ideas, dialogue, and consequences directly from other heist pictures. A dash of *Butch Cassidy and the Sundance Kid* (1969), a splash of *Point Break* (1991), a pinch of *The Score* (2001), and a whole fistful of *Heat* (1995), *Takers* even has one character preface their big plan by proudly exclaiming, "we're gonna get all Italian Job up on this" and then execute their own job in exactly the same manner.

The "Jennings Five" open the film with an old-fashioned bank heist: large guns, ski masks, the whole works. If it is not the most cunning in-and-out plan of all time, but they pull it off by escaping in a stolen helicopter and then blowing it up on a rooftop. After a job like that, Gordon (Idris Elba) likes to hit the town with his boys including John Rahway (Paul Walker), unfortunately-named club owner Jake Attica (Michael Ealy), his brother Jesse (Chris Brown), and goofy hat wearin' A.J. (Hayden Christensen).

Evidently they were once the "Jennings Six" though as Ghost (Tip "T.I." Harris) took the fall in one of their gambits. Now out of jail he has a quick job for them as part of payback for not giving them up: five days, armored trucks, a crowded city street, and a sewer full of C-4. There is a pair of detectives on the case—Jack Welles (Matt Dillon) and Eddie Hatcher (Jay Hernandez) are following the trail left of big crumbs left behind by this stellar crew including Ghost's recent release and Jennings' junkie sister (Marianne Jean-Baptiste) that he foolishly gave marked bills to. Jack is so obsessed with taking them down he even turns a day with his daughter into a ride-along as he tails their leaders. And just why is an internal affairs officer (Steve Harris) tailing Jack and insisting on a meeting?

Sketched out in not even the simplest of classifications since each person's specialty is a blur in their preparation, the entirety of *Takers* features one punk trying to take down five other punks. T.I. plays Ghost with a cocky scowl leaving all chance that viewers would sympathize with this spurned criminal off the table. Watching the J. Crew (Jesse, Jake, John, Jennings, and A.J.) play dress up like a boy band and be led into slow-motion walking montages by Elba, who swings his arms like a remedial student in swagger school just makes you want to snuff them all out with Hayden's hat. If the four screenwriters (Peter Allen, Gabriel Casseus, Avery Duff, and John Luessenhop, evidently needed to grab something from one previous heist movie apiece) had invented an outsider to the crew to serve as the audience's eye, some fun may have sneaked into this uber-serious exercise as he called out their methods of being archaic and counterproductive. Of course, that would have meant the writers actually inventing something.

"The heat's gonna be coming down now," Jennings is told as things begin to go badly for them. That tends to happen when you ignore your own philosophy on shooting cops. Apparently it is okay to fire upon them with machine guns when stealing from them, but keeping yourself from being caught in a foot chase is a big no-no. Perhaps on their next job they can avoid making identifiable gestures directly into the security cameras. Thankfully it is not a full moon like the Ex-Presidents of *Point Break* (1991), yet one can practically hear the spirit of Gary Busey saying "forget it kid, they're ghosts" as the detectives make the same sort of connection. Too bad Dillon's cop failed to see *The Italian Job* (1969) as he may have recognized the crew's control of traffic lights to their liking. He was probably too busy graduating to the right side of the law from twisty criminal plots in *Wild Things* (1998), *Employee of the Month* (2004), and *Armored* (2009). If viewers have learned anything from cops-and-robbers movies over the years, rule number one is no phones. So is it really a good idea to be utilizing traceable Bluetooth technology during the L.A. job with T.I.'s Ghost narrating their every move as if he were Nick Cannon on TV's *America's Got Talent*?

From the lifted-wholesale script to the understudy cast populating it, co-writer and director Luessenhop had very little going for him outside of his own skills, which amounted to even less. He brings no particular flair to the heist scenes. A lengthy chase sequence that emboldens one character with sudden parkour skills is so hastily cut and out-of-focus it is like watching a 3-D movie without glasses. When one of the J. Crew marks Jack as "that cop with the little girl," Luessenhop forgets that he never gave them or the audience a line-of-sight shot for that correlation to ever be made. Films that build towards a hotel shootout straight out of *True Romance* (1993) may want to rethink that PG-13 rating since they may end up with a muddled mash-up of bloodless bullet strikes and the proverbial "good-looking corpse" that one can actually catch breathing. The overly operatic score that plays over this massacre echoes one of the themes from *The Insider* (1999), proving that even when the filmmakers steal they cannot even do it from the right Michael Mann film.

Erik Childress

CREDITS

Det. Jack Welles: Matt Dillon
John Rahway: Paul Walker
Gordon "Jennings" Cozier: Idris Elba
Eddie Hatcher: Jay Hernandez
Ghost: Tip "T.I." Harris
Jake Attica: Michael Ealy
Jesse Attica: Chris Brown
Scott: Johnathon Schaech
A.J.: Hayden Christensen
Rachel Jansen: Zoe Saldana
Naomi Cozier: Marianne Jean-Baptiste
Lt. Carver: Steve Harris
Origin: USA
Language: English
Released: 2010
Production: Will Packer, Jason Peter; Rainforest Films, Screen Gems; released by Sony Pictures Entertainment
Directed by: John Luessenhop
Written by: John Luessenhop, Peter Allen, Gabriel Casseus, Avery Duff
Cinematography by: Michael Barrett
Music by: Paul Haslinger
Sound: Shawn Holden
Editing: Armen Minasian
Art Direction: Chris Cornwell
Costumes: Maya Lieberman, Steve Harris
Production Design: Jon Gary Steele
MPAA rating: PG-13
Running time: 107 minutes

REVIEWS

Anderson, John. *Washington Post.* August 27, 2010.
Bell, Josh. *Las Vegas Weekly.* August 26, 2010.
Burr, Ty. *Boston Globe.* August 26, 2010.
Lowry, Brian. *Variety.* August 16, 2010.
Novikov, Eugene. *Film Blather.* August 26, 2010.
Orndorf, Brian. *BrianOrndorf.com.* August 26, 2010.
Pais, Matt. *Metromix.com.* August 26, 2010.
Rabin, Nathan. *AV Club.* August 26, 2010.
Snider, Eric D. *Cinematical.* August 27, 2010.
Swietek, Frank. *One Guy's Opinion.* August 26, 2010.

QUOTES

Gordon Jennings: "We're takers, gents. That's what we do for a living. We take."

TRIVIA

The film was sent to theaters with the code name "Wide Ranging."

TAMARA DREWE

It all starts with a nose job. Well, that is not the first thing that happens in *Tamara Drewe,* director Stephen Frears' spunky adaptation of Posy Simmonds' weekly comic strip-turned-graphic novel. Yet the nose job may be the film's smallest action that has the largest results. That is because when she was growing up in a small English country town, Tamara Drewe (Gemma Arterton) had one identifying characteristic: Her large nose. Many years later, when Tamara returns after her mother's death to sell the family house, rhinoplasty has taken care of that distinguishing characteristic. Now, her most noticeable attributes peek out of tight shirts and short shorts, assets that are not exactly ignored by residents and employees of the writers' retreat at the adjacent farm.

Overseeing that retreat is Nicholas Hardiment (Roger Allam), a popular author who does not help out at the retreat so much as pay the bills. Nicholas' wife Beth (Tamsin Greig) tends to the guests who come to the retreat to work in peace and assists with the business affairs of her husband, who is far less considerate. In fact, as the film opens, Nicholas is preparing to leave his wife for his latest mistress, and the film offers the first of several tart gags by depicting a cow urinating in the face of another cow just after Nicholas lies to his wife. This is a fitting image: Nicholas is an animal more concerned with relieving his own urges than with who gets hurt in the process, so it is no surprise later in the film when the middle-aged philanderer takes a liking to the younger, far better-looking Tamara.

Yet Tamara's most meaningful reunion upon returning is with Andy (Luke Evans), a muscular handyman who helps out around the Hardiments' estate and regretfully broke up with Tamara years ago when he was twenty. (It is questionable how much he regretted this before seeing Tamara and her new nose.) Soon after Tamara's return, Andy notes her new appearance and exclaims that she is completely different. Clearly the beautiful, well-proportioned woman in front of him, who now works as a journalist and aspires to write a novel about her life, possesses strength and confidence that the young Tamara did not. One of the film's biggest limitations, in fact, is that at no point does it really offer much of a sense of who Tamara was then or truly is now. It would be interesting to examine how someone's personality does or does not change based on the way he or she looks, but to tackle that idea a film has to present a much more well-defined character than Tamara Drewe.

Rather than offer many details about its title character, *Tamara Drewe* focuses on the impact that Tamara's return has on the small community. Immediately her presence sparks old feelings in Andy, who was born in the home Tamara is trying to sell; his feelings turn to jealousy when Tamara shacks up with, and then becomes engaged to, arrogant indie rock drummer Ben Sergeant (Dominic Cooper). Initially Tamara was

supposed to interview Ben for an article, but she barely gets any information out of him before he gets her clothes off. How Tamara supposedly maintains a successful career as a professional journalist with such shaky ethical standards is not an issue the film seeks to explore. Much more time is spent on Jody (Jessica Barden) and Casey (Charlotte Christie), two local fifteen-year-old girls with such a totally wicked crush on Ben that they frequently hide outside his and Tamara's house to get a glimpse. Eventually the girls, who call Tamara "Plastic" and serve as a sort of Greek Chorus for the film, resort to breaking into the house and cause a whole mess of trouble for practically every character in the movie.

Fortunately, Frears, working from a script by Moira Buffini, corrals all of this emotional upheaval into a pleasantly linear storyline that does not feel overly episodic the way that graphic novel adaptations sometimes do. *Tamara Drewe* is a comedy of errors, and its strongest weapon is dialogue that constantly winks at the pretentiousness of stuffy authors, obnoxious musicians and anyone who thinks they are simply better than someone else. For example: "We're surrounded by novelists!" cries Nicholas foolishly as he tries to calm down Beth after the first time she discovers his affairs. "When the hat's on," one author says snootily, pleading for a quiet work environment, "It means don't speak." And, after telling Nicholas that he read some of his work, American author Glen McCreavy (Bill Camp) adds insincerely, "I thought it was decent stuff." Fundamentally *Tamara Drewe* is a critique of artists who take themselves too seriously. When Nicholas pompously declares that all storytellers are thieves and liars, Glen counters the statement by quoting Samuel Johnson, an author far more famous than Nicholas: "The best of all excellence is truth."

This sharp wit shines through well-pitched performances by Allam and Camp, as well as a cleverly self-satisfied turn by Cooper—who follows *An Education* (2009) by showing again the impact a supporting actor can make by appearing more or less mysterious than his character actually is inside. Arterton suggests that Tamara's newfound, beauty-driven self-confidence results in her tendency towards impulsive decisions, and the film speculates but does not fully address the notion that Tamara's poor judgment may result from her dad leaving her and her mom many years before. Time and again, though, the film shows more of an interest in how others perceive Tamara. "Life sure comes easy for the beautiful," says Glen well before he has known Tamara enough to make a comment like that. He says it because he is a reserved guy who has long believed in the cliché that nice guys finish last, and he is frustrated, particularly after he develops a connection with Beth, to be left out in the cold while the rest of the more outgoing, less kind society seems to have more success in love and career.

Not surprisingly, this moves the film into expected territory as selfish characters get their comeuppance and honest ones see karma come back around on their side. Yet *Tamara Drewe* possess a playful, intelligent charm that makes it funny and appealing despite a number of superficial relationships and characterizations. Besides, sometimes all it takes to understand a person is hearing them repeat something they do not mean, like when Nicholas insincerely tells Beth, "You're a marvel," which is really his way of appreciating that she trusts him enough not to be more suspicious of his dalliances. And while Tamara never contributes any revealing words of her own, the continually amusing script recognizes the power of one smart, tossed-off line of self-awareness: "I don't mean to pry," says bartender Zoe (Josie Taylor) after doing just that. "I'm just really nosy."

Matt Pais

CREDITS

Tamara Drewe: Gemma Arterton
Nicholas Hardiment: Roger Allam
Ben Seargeant: Dominic Cooper
Andy Cobb: Luke Evans
Beth Hardiment: Tamsin Greig
Jody Long: Jessica Barden
Casey Shaw: Charlotte Christie
Penny Upminster: Susan Woolridge
Eustacia: Bronagh Gallagher
Glen McCreavy: Bill Camp
Zoe: Josie Taylor
Origin: United Kingdom
Language: English
Released: 2010
Production: Alison Owen, Paul Trijbits, Tracey Seaward; WestEnd Films, BBC Films, Ruby Films, Notting Hill Films; released by Sony Pictures Classics
Directed by: Stephen Frears
Written by: Moira Buffini
Cinematography by: Benjamin Davis
Music by: Alexandre Desplat
Sound: Peter Lindsay Amps
Music Supervisor: Karen Elliott
Editing: Mick Audsley
Art Direction: Christopher Wyatt
Costumes: Consolata Boyle
Production Design: Alan Macdonald
MPAA rating: R
Running time: 110 minutes

REVIEWS

Abele, Robert. *Los Angeles Times.* October 8, 2010.
Corliss, Richard. *TIME Magazine.* October 6, 2010.
Gleiberman, Owen. *Entertainment Weekly.* October 8, 2010.
Hoberman, J. *Village Voice.* October 6, 2010.
Jones, J.R. *Chicago Reader.* October 8, 2010.
Murray, Noel. *AV Club.* October 7, 2010.
Scott, A.O. *New York Times.* October 7, 2010.
Taylor, Ella. *NPR.* October 7, 2010.
Uhlich, Keith. *Time Out New York.* October 7, 2010.
Weitzman, Elizabeth. *New York Daily News.* October 8, 2010.

QUOTES

Glen McCreavy: "Why does the a**hole always get the girl?"

TANGLED

They're taking adventure to new lengths.
   —Movie tagline

Get tangled up.
   —Movie tagline

Box Office: $194 million

While Walt Disney's *Beauty and the Beast* (1991) remains the gold standard of the studio's modern animated features, its fiftieth film, *Tangled,* is as good or perhaps better than many of the other work that Disney (not including the Pixar films) has produced in the last twenty-plus years, including *The Little Mermaid* (1989) and *Aladdin* (1992). A major reason for the success of all four of the aforementioned films is Alan Menken, whose music has left an indelible mark in the ears of audiences in such productions as *Little Shop of Horrors* (1986) and Disney's live-action tribute to its "princess" cartoons, *Enchanted* (2007). With lyrics by Glenn Slater, *Tangled* unleashes nearly a dozen new Menken tunes into the world, including the standout "Mother Knows Best," perhaps the finest ode to overbearing mothers everywhere, performed by Donna Murphy, voicing the villainess Mother Gothel.

Tangled is a clever adaptation of the story of Princess Rapunzel, who, as an infant, was kidnapped from her loving parents by Mother Gothel, who had managed to stay young for years thanks to the healing power of a magic flower that has since been absorbed into the hair of young Rapunzel. Gothel sings a little song, Rapunzel's golden locks glow, and the old lady becomes young again. To make certain Rapunzel is always available to make her young, Gothel locks her in a hidden tower and tells her adopted daughter horror stories about the world outside so that the girl has no interest in leaving her confines, all the while her hair grows to incredible lengths because if it gets cut, the healing powers die out.

The life Rapunzel has carved out for herself is fascinating. She has picked up every hobby known to mankind and has become best friends with a chameleon named Pascal (no, he does not talk, but he is remarkably expressive and funny). This telling of her story does not exactly match the Brothers Grimm account, but it is still fairly faithful. When the now-eighteen-year-old Rapunzel (voiced by singer-actress Mandy Moore) begins to get the urge to leave her confines, Gothel breaks out "Mother Knows Best" and paints an awful account of the world around them. What Murphy pulls off with Gothel is pure, jaw-dropping meanness, as if she is channeling the worst parts of Joan Crawford and Bette Davis. While Moore is the epitome of sweetness, with a liberal sprinkling of stir-crazy.

Tangled is also the story of ne'er-do-well thief Flynn Rider (Zachary Levi), who steals a crown from the king and queen, and accidentally discovers the hidden tower and Rapunzel in it. The two strike a bargain, and Rider agrees to escort her out in the world to witness the kingdom's floating lights ceremony, which occurs every year on her birthday. What she does not know is that the event was initiated by her real parents to commemorate the birthday of their lost daughter. But Flynn has a few troubles of his own: His former partners in crime (one voiced by Ron Perlman, the other silent), who want revenge on him for leaving them to get captured by the king's guards) and a horse named Maximus (no, he does not talk either), the official steed belonging to the Captain of the Guard.

One of the film's many musical highlights takes place in the Snuggly Duckling, a tavern where all manner of ruffians gather. Flynn deliberately takes Rapunzel there, hoping the crowd will scare her enough to return to the tower. Instead, her talk of wanting her dreams to come true sends the thugs into a fantastic pub sing-a-long of "I've Got A Dream." A few famous voices pop up in this sequence, including those belonging to Brad Garrett, Jeffrey Tambor, Paul F. Tompkins, and Richard Kiel.

It may not come as a surprise, but *Tangled* is also a love story, as Flynn and Rapunzel begin to develop feelings for one another. It may be because of the one or two kissing scenes in the film that this is the first of Disney's princess movies to get a PG rating. The studio also opted out of making *Tangled* a hand-drawn animated work, as it did with 2009's *The Princess and the Frog*, but the film still has a free-floating, warm feeling to it that is reminiscent of traditional animation.

Co-director Byron Howard (who also helmed 2008's *Bolt*) and first-time feature filmmaker Nathan Greno have done an admirable job balancing the energy of the vocal performances with the vivid visual style. More importantly, the film never panders to younger audience members. It finds the perfect middle ground to appeal to parents, children, and folks without kids who just enjoy good moviemaking. There is a bit of death, a great deal of peril, and some public displays of affection between the two lead characters, so *Tangled* may not be suited for young children, but the classic storytelling, superior music, and fluid, striking animation combine to make for an uplifting experience. And the added, flawless 3D only heightens the enjoyment.

Steven Prokopy

CREDITS

Rapunzel: Mandy Moore (Voice)
Flynn Rider: Zachary Levi (Voice)
Mother Gothel: Donna Murphy (Voice)
Hookhand: Brad Garrett (Voice)
Lord Jamie: Jeffrey Tambor (Voice)
Vlad: Richard Kiel (Voice)
Short Thug: Paul F. Thompkins (Voice)
Captain of the Guard: M.C. Gainey (Voice)
Stabbington Brother: Ron Perlman (Voice)
Origin: USA
Language: English
Released: 2010
Production: Roy Conli; Walt Disney Animation Studios; released by Walt Disney Pictures
Directed by: Byron Howard, Nathan Greno
Written by: Dan Fogelman
Music by: Alan Menken
Editing: Tim Mertens
Sound: Cameron Frankley
Production Design: Douglas Rogers
MPAA rating: PG
Running time: 100 minutes

REVIEWS

Hornaday, Ann. *Washington Post.* November 24, 2010.
Kois, Dan. *Village Voice.* November 24, 2010.
McCarthy, Todd. *Hollywood Reporter.* November 8, 2010.
Morgenstern, Joe. *Wall Street Journal.* November 26, 2010.
Morris, Wesley. *Boston Globe.* November 24, 2010.
Phillips, Michael. *Chicago Tribune.* November 22, 2010.
Puig, Claudia. *USA Today.* November 26, 2010.
Robinson, Tasha. *AV Club.* November 23, 2010.
Schwarzbaum, Lisa. *Entertainment Weekly.* November 24, 2010.
Travers, Peter. *Rolling Stone.* November 24, 2010.

QUOTES

Repunzel: "Something brought you here, Flynn Rider. Call it what you will…fate…destiny."
Flynn Rider: "I could get used to a view like this. Yep, I'm used to it. Guys, I want a castle."

TRIVIA

This is the first computer-generated Disney "fairytale" film, the first PG rated "princess" film, and at $260 million the most expensive Disney animated film to date.

AWARDS

Nomination:

Oscars 2010: Song ("I See the Light")

Golden Globes 2011: Animated Film, Song ("I See the Light").

THE TEMPEST

Titus (1999), as imagined by Julie Taymor, was a vital organ pumping blood onto the screen by the gallon, a cinematic cry of despair that settled like prime poetry on the heart, a sublime mix of theatricality and magnetic melodramatic cinema. Taymor's *The Tempest* is loud to the point of cacophony, uncomfortably aware of its own attempted revisionist feminism, and perhaps most unexpectedly from such a visual director, overly confident that poor special effects and music video aesthetics will mask the inexperience of key cast members. A glorious and sometimes exhilarating mess that never finds the heart of Shakespeare's play, *The Tempest* comes and goes like a spring shower leaving little to no evidence of its passing.

Prospera (Helen Mirren), a female alchemist, has been exiled to an uncharted island. For twelve years she has raised her daughter Miranda (Felicity Jones) while also plotting her revenge and spinning herself ever deeper into her dark magical skills, aided only by her slaves Ariel (Ben Whishaw), a sprite of unknown gender and Caliban (Djimon Hounsou), who feels his rule over the island has been usurped, Prospera has conjured a mighty storm to shipwreck her enemies upon the island. With them is Prince Ferdinand (Reeve Carney), who falls in love with Miranda. Soon, Prospera finds herself amidst complex plots, counterplots, and the usual misunderstandings that mark Shakespearean storytelling.

The idea of Shakespeare writ large has challenged writers, actors, and especially directors, to bring the fullness of his fantastic words to modern visual life. Notable examples would be *Richard III* (1995) and Baz Lurhmann's *Romeo + Juliet* (1996), which both offered intense visual re-imaginings. *The Tempest* has been adapted to a number of genres, perhaps the weirdest being the Western *Yellow Sky* (1979) and the decidedly strange *Prospero's Books* (1991). But, in an age where special effects make almost any image possible, Taymor must have found it simply too tempting to reign herself in and ends up with the award for the gaudiest Shakespeare film ever made.

CGI was a good choice here and could have produced a truly remarkable aesthetic, but too often it is the only choice. One would think that Taymor's own natural theatricality, and the critical drubbing she was given over the excesses in *Across the Universe* (2007) would have led her in other directions visually. She fails the story, plain and simple, in pursuit of music video moments and been-there-done-that effects sequences that have been executed far more successfully in other films. Gone is the sense of dire pageantry that an updated *Titus* enjoyed in Taymor's hands. Gone is the same sort of magic that brought *The Lion King* (1994) to splendid life on Broadway. It is almost as if Taymor has decided that those past successes only paved the way for her to tinker with pixels like some avant-garde George Lucas.

The pedigree here is a mile long and the failure that much more confusing. It is clearly difficult to blame anyone but Taymor for producing something that has so little sense of direction. Dame Helen Mirren, Oscar® winner for Best Actress for *The Queen* (2006), is perfect for the role of Prospera, but is forced to mouth lines that have had their gender-changed. This would be fine if Taymor had left good enough alone and changed "father" to "mother." But instead Mirren must refer to "mom." Shakespeare simply never sounded so un-Shakespearean.

Other casting choices seems inspired or at least collectively dazzling: King Alonso (David Strathairn), Gonzalo (Tom Conti), Sebastian (Alan Cumming), Antonio (Chris Cooper), Trinculo (Russell Brand), and Stephano (Alfred Molina). From this largely-male list it is pretty easy to separate the men from the boys. Completely lost is Russell Brand, who barely seems able to demonstrate a connection to any of the other actors who surely had to ignore his performance in order to bring forth theirs. Also in over their heads are Felicity Jones and Reeve Carney. None of these performers tend to function well outside their element, and Shakespeare is simply not it.

Perhaps the biggest reason to watch is Djimon Hounsou (*Amistad* [1997], *Gladiator* [2000], *In America* [2003]). Hounsou always brings a dynamic presence to any role even in cheap genre stuff. But when he has the chance to sink his teeth into something substantial he reminds one constantly of why he is in so much demand. Bold, beautiful, and completely majestic in a role that many would play as simply monstrous and grotesque, his Calaban may be one for the ages.

Everyone else acquits themselves admirably enough. It is a pleasure to watch such a luminous group invited to a party where any one of them could be the guest of honor. Molina revels as the drunk, Alan Cumming seethes as Sebastian. But none of it feels of a piece. The cast seems individually disconnected by the very nature of the type of film Taymor is striving to create.

The Tempest is hardly regarded as Shakespeare's greatest play in terms of plotting or characterization. As a later work, it even seems a bit derivative of stronger stuff like *Hamlet, Macbeth,* and *The Merchant of Venice.* But, unlike those plays, *The Tempest* has endured mainly in the service of Shakespeare's larger body of work. Sadly, Julie Taymor's *The Tempest* will have to settle for the same thing.

Dave Canfield

CREDITS

Prospera: Helen Mirren
Miranda: Felicity Jones
Caliban: Djimon Hounsou
Ariel: Ben Whishaw
Ferdinand: Reeve Carney
Sebastian: Alan Cumming
Trinculo: Russell Brand
Alonso: David Strathairn
Stephano: Alfred Molina
Gonzalo: Tom Conti
Antonio: Chris Cooper
Origin: USA
Language: English
Released: 2010
Production: Robert Chartoff, Lynn Hendee, Jason K. Lau, Julia Taylor-Stanley, Julie Taymor; Touchstone Pictures; released by Touchstone Pictures
Directed by: Julie Taymor
Written by: Julie Taymor
Cinematography by: Stuart Dryburgh
Music by: Elliot Goldenthal
Editing: Francoise Bonnot
Production Design: Mark Friedberg
Sound: Blake Leyh
Costumes: Sandy Powell
MPAA rating: PG-13
Running time: 110 minutes

REVIEWS

Denby, David. *New Yorker.* December 27, 2010.
Duralde, Alonso. *HitFix.* December 9, 2010.
Ebert, Roger. *Chicago Sun-Times.* December 16, 2010.
Edelstein, David. *New York Magazine.* December 13, 2010.
Howell, Peter. *Toronto Star.* December 16, 2010.
LaSalle, Mick. *San Francisco Chronicle.* December 9, 2010.
Lemire, Christy. *Associated Press.* December 8, 2010.
MacDonald, Moira. *Seattle Times.* December 16, 2010.
Scott, A.O. *New York Times.* December 9, 2010.
Young, Deborah. *Hollywood Reporter.* September 14, 2010.

QUOTES

Stephano: "Out of the moon, I do assure thee."

TRIVIA

This is Julie Taymor and Alan Cummings second collaboration since the film, *Titus.*

AWARDS

Nomination:
Oscars 2010: Costume Des.

35 SHOTS OF RUM
(35 Rhums)

The masterful French filmmaker Claire Denis makes movies for which the word minimal seems to apply but she does so with such grace and depth of character that one would not want such an appellation to diminish her accomplishments. Yes, her works, including the excellent *35 Shots of Rum* (and the even-better same-year follow-up *White Material* [2010]) are sparse on dialogue and do not feature hook-driven plots but the way she chronicles honest human behavior to dramatic effort has awarded her a loyal international following for good reason. One of two films to be released in 2010 stateside, *35 Shots of Rum* is an undeniably slow, often silent affair, but it culminates in a dialogue-free scene of such power that it causes one to reconsider the accomplishments of the film that came before it.

35 Shots of Rum is a melancholy drama about loneliness, depression, isolation, and change. Denis makes films that are often about attempts to keep connections in a world that often makes honest human interaction difficult. Her film opens with five minutes of no dialogue and shots of trains running in and out of a station. The effect is two-fold: One, the pace of the film is set in that it is instantly clear that this will be a slow, meditative piece. Two, this is a story in which life is going on all around our characters. Their story is not going to be remarkable or unique. Theirs is merely one of many stories in the city.

Josephine (Mati Diop) lives with her father Lionel (Alex Descas) in a Parisian apartment building right on the edge of poverty. She works at a music store and goes to school while Lionel drives a train. Lionel's weathered face makes it clear that he has worked a hard life but his eyes portray a gentle soul. Josephine and Lionel are each other's support system but not in a manipulative or impractical way. The film's main quartet of characters also include two other denizens of the same apartment building—Gabrielle (Nicole Dogue), Lionel's ex-girlfriend, and a family friend named Noe (Gregoire Colin). Noe and Jo clearly have strong chemistry that will change the friend and family dynamic soon.

These people do not live complex lives. Jo studies and Lionel goes to work. They eat dinner together. They are creatures of habit and Denis expresses their affection for each other in very subtle, matter-of-fact ways, such as in how Jo brings her father his Alka-Seltzer before he goes to bed. Drama works its way slowly into their lives when Lionel's co-worker Rene (Julieth Mars Toussaint) retires. As his formerly vibrant colleague becomes a shell of a man, Lionel worries that he will someday bring sadness into his daughter's life. So, as she begins to drift away from him, possibly to Noe, he lets her go in a series of sweet, gentle moments that culminate in one of the best scenes of 2010 (or 2008 or 2009, depending on when one was lucky enough to see it). As the characters dance (to the brilliantly-chosen "Nightshift" by The Commodores), they slowly shift alliances. Without words, they come to clear realizations about the next chapter in their lives. It is a masterful short film of its very own that serves as the centerpiece of *35 Shots of Rum*.

The cast is uniformly strong thanks in large part to Denis' emphasis on realism over artifice. Descas never feels anything less than genuine and it is the level of believability in his performance that makes his story mesmerizing, not the action of the drama. Denis' has developed such a following by virtue of her amazing ability to write and direct performers through actions that feel one hundred percent real. And she shades most of her work in political subtext, most prevalent in this one through heated discussion in one of Jo's classes.

Denis does not make easily digestible films, even for Francophiles. *35 Shots of Rum* played at the 2008 Toronto Film Festival but did not open in most American markets until 2010, and even then only played major markets. Sadly, the diversity in delivery systems (such as On Demand services, Netflix, etc.) that have created a movie marketplace with a wide variety of product for Americans has done little to increase the accessibility of foreign films like *35 Shots of Rum,* which made less than $200k domestically. Claire Denis may have critics proclaiming her prodigious talents but it feels like audiences have yet to hear one of the most impressive voices in international cinema.

Brian Tallerico

CREDITS

Lionel: Alex Descas
Noe: Gregoire Colin
Josephine: Mati Diop
Gabrielle: Nicole Dogue
Rene: Julieth Mars Toussaint
Origin: France, Germany
Language: French, German
Released: 2008
Production: Bruno Pesery; Soudaine Compagnie, Pandora Film, Arte France Cinema; released by The Cinema Guild
Directed by: Claire Denis
Written by: Claire Denis, Jean-Pol Fargeau
Cinematography by: Agnes Godard
Music by: Tindersticks
Sound: Martin Boissau, Christophe Winding
Editing: Guy Lecorne, Dominique Hennequin
Costumes: Judy Shrewsbury
Production Design: Arnaud de Moleron
MPAA rating: Unrated
Running time: 99 minutes

REVIEWS

Anderson, Melissa. *Village Voice.* September 15, 2009.
Bradshaw, Peter. *The Guardian.* July 10, 2009.
Butler, Robert W. *Kansas City Star.* March 12, 2010.
Doerksen, Cliff. *Chicago Reader.* January 26, 2010.
Ebert, Roger. *Chicago Sun-Times.* January 21, 2010.
Musetto, V.A. *New York Post.* September 18, 2009.
Phillips, Michael. *Chicago Tribune.* January 22, 2010.
Scott, A.O. *New York Times.* September 16, 2009.
White, Armond. *New York Press.* September 16, 2009.
Wilson, Calvin. *St. Louis Post-Dispatch.* February 11, 2010.

THE TILLMAN STORY

A mystery. A cover up. A crime. One family will risk everything for the truth.
—Movie tagline

Amir Bar-Lev's highly-acclaimed documentary about the life and tragic death of Pat Tillman works as well as it does by avoiding politicizing its subject in the way that so many attempted to do in the weeks and months after his death. Pat Tillman was undeniably used as political currency and it was surely tempting and would have been easy to turn him into the same kind of device in the other direction. But to use his story as a commentary on the failure of the conflict in the Middle East or as a condemnation of the Bush administration would have done Tillman's legacy the same disservice. With the utmost respect for his subject matter, Bar-Lev outlines the concept of heroism, the marketing machine of government, the power of the military complex, and the sad state of journalism, but he does so with no preaching and just enough politicizing to start the discussion amongst the people who see it. *The Tillman Story* was the best documentary of a very good year for the form that included *Inside Job, Exit Through the Gift Shop, Joan Rivers: A Piece of Work, Restrepo, Waiting For 'Superman,'* and *Cropsey.*

Pat Tillman was an NFL superstar for the Arizona Cardinals. He very likely would have been a multi-millionaire by the time that the film that bore his name was released if he had not forever changed his course after the events of 9/11. Like a lot of young men did upon seeing the towers fall, Tillman answered a perceived call to serve his country. He gave up his increasingly-lavish lifestyle to fight and, far too shortly after he landed in country, he was killed in an ambush and died valiantly in the line of fire. Or so the government wanted people to believe. The truth was that Pat Tillman died in a dangerous valley under fire from his own men, cowering and screaming "I'm Pat F**king Tillman!!!" until one of his fellow soldiers mistakenly put a bullet in his head. Friendly fire is a tragic fact of war but rather than investigate the situation that caused the tragedy, the machine went to work and not only covered it up but began to use Tillman's death as a symbol for the evil overseas that needed vanquishing. Who could oppose a war against an enemy that could kill a hero like Pat Tillman?

Pat Tillman made his desire for privacy well-known. He never gave a single interview, despite what must have been numerous requests from sports shows and news networks, about why he left the NFL behind to join the military. He even filled out paperwork with the aware-ness that he could be used as a martyr and sent his desire to not have a military funeral to his wife. When the government ignored that paperwork and tried to schedule an event to sell an increasingly-popular war, the marketing hook was exposed. Bar-Lev focuses his documentary on Tillman's family, the underestimated element of the men who wanted to use the man's death to drum up support to defeat an enemy who could kill a soldier as All-American as the NFL star. The one thing that everyone should equally take away from *The Tillman Story* is that all soldiers should be as lucky as to have Pat's family on their side. They are intelligent, passion-ate, driven people who did not take the pills that so many others would have in their days of grief. Like their son, they knew what was right. And the title of the film refers to them as much as Pat. The men and women who refused to let their son, brother, or husband be used in ways that he never wanted to be are all heroes in their own way.

Amir Bar-Lev structures *The Tillman Story* through a series of one-on-one interviews with the men who served with Tillman about his death intercut with the family's actions after it. The film builds through the narrative about his passing and the men who knew the truth while also paralleling it with the lies being told stateside. Bar-Lev pulls no punches; clearly implying that powerful men like George Bush and Donald Rumsfeld, despite their later denials, knew the truth about how Pat Tillman had died. Despite adding a bit of fuel to the fire regarding the overall mismanagement of the war, *The Tillman Story* avoids turning off war supporters and serious Conservatives by making clear that this could have happened to anyone. Pat Tillman supported the war too. Bar-Lev's flawless film does not turn him into the symbol he never wanted to be. Instead, he merely pulls at the torn seams of shoddy journalism (that first bought the story hook-line-and-sinker and never asked the right questions), governmental mistruths, and straight-up lies that turned a man who never wanted to be one into a hero. The amazing dramatic irony is that the true story of the Tillmans made it more clear that all of them were actual heroes in ways that the fiction never could.

Brian Tallerico

CREDITS

Narrator: Josh Brolin
Origin: USA
Language: English
Released: 2010
Production: John Battsek; Passion Pictures, Axis Films International; released by Weinstein Company
Directed by: Amir Bar-Lev
Written by: Amir Bar-Lev, Mark Monroe, Joe Bini
Cinematography by: Sean Kirby, Igor Martinovic
Music by: Philip Sheppard
Sound: Tom Efinger
Music Supervisor: Liz Gallacher
Editing: Joe Bini, Josh Altman, Gabriel Rhodes
MPAA rating: R
Running time: 94 minutes

REVIEWS

Anderson, Melissa. *Village Voice.* August 17, 2010.
Childress, Erik. *eFilmCritic.com.* February 1, 2010.
Harvey, Dennis. *Variety.* January 26, 2010.
Holden, Stephen. *New York Times.* August 20, 2010.
Lemire, Christy. *Associated Press.* October 29, 2010.
Morgenstern, Joe. *Wall Street Journal.* August 27, 2010.
Pais, Matt. *Metromix.com.* September 2, 2010.
Phillips, Michael. *Chicago Tribune.* September 2, 2010.

Rodriguez, Rene. *Miami Herald*. September 16, 2010.
Turan, Kenneth. *Los Angeles Times*. August 19, 2010.

TOOTH FAIRY

You can't handle the tooth.
—Movie tagline
The tooth hurts.
—Movie tagline

Box Office: $60 million

Following in the less-than-hallowed footsteps of such epics as *Kindergarten Cop* (1990), *Cop and a Half* (1993), and *The Pacifier* (2005), *Tooth Fairy* offers up the grim spectacle of a tough guy movie star attempting to tap into the lucrative family film audience by appearing in a project that has him subverting his image by appearing opposite adorable kids and/or animals, taking any number of pratfalls and parading around in some kind of embarrassing outfit. Unfortunately, the problem with most of these movies is that all the creative inspiration tends to have been squandered on coming up with the concept—the films themselves are so threadbare and pedestrian that they barely have enough going for them to sustain a 30-second commercial, let alone a feature-length story. That is certainly the case with this film, an utterly witless and banal family comedy.

Derek Thompson (Dwayne Johnson) is a former hockey star now reduced to running out the final days of his career on a minor league team as a goon whose primary objective is to take opponents out of the game via body checks hard enough to send their bicuspids flying into the audience, a tactic that has earned him the nickname "The Tooth Fairy." Off the rink, he enjoys crushing the dreams and aspirations of any little child whose comes across his path—when a little autograph seeker says that he wants to be a hockey player when he grows up, Derek explains in excruciating detail why that will never happen—but when he dares to suggest the same to adorable moppet Tess (Destiny Whitlock), the youngest child of girlfriend Carly (Ashley Judd), he has simply gone too far and he is forcibly summoned to Fairy Land and informed by the head fairy (Julie Andrews) that he is to assume the role of Tooth Fairy for a week to pay for his sins. After learning the ropes from his fairy handler (Stephen Merchant), Derek is sent out into the world to collect discarded dentata, usually at the most inopportune time imaginable, and while he is an epic fail at first, he gradually gets the hang of it and winds up learning to become a better person as a result—he becomes more of a team player on the rink and even encourages Carly's other kid, sullen twerp Randy (Chase Ellison) to embrace his dreams of playing guitar in the junior high talent show. Of course, the moment that the script require him to do so, he forgets all of this and begins acting like a jerk again—the down side is that this drives Carly and the kids away from him but the up side is that it allows him to suddenly remember everything that he forgot just in time for the allegedly-triumphant finale.

The fundamental problem with *Tooth Fairy* is that while it has what sounds like an irresistible premise for a family comedy, it is the kind of premise that offers up much less than one might think. Face it, the mythology of the tooth fairy is one that is somewhat limited and once the initial gimmick of someone with a tough guy persona prancing around in tights and wings has worn off, there really isn't anywhere for the story to go. In a perfect world, the platoon of screenwriters employed here would have accepted that sad fact early on in the writing process and just abandoned the whole thing for good. Instead, they seem to have decided that if they could not come up with one decent plot that could sustain a full-length narrative, they could at least jam it up with enough unnecessary subplots to stretch it out to an acceptable length. As a result, we have a film that is ostensibly about an ordinary guy charged with becoming a tooth fairy that is now cluttered with pointless diversions about the budget troubles in Fairy Land, Derek's dream of reestablishing himself as a real hockey player, his conflicts with a young hotshot teammate, the status of his relationship with Carly and whether her son will take that big chance and appear in the junior-high talent show. There is not a single member of the target audience for this film—which is presumably limited to those still in possession of the majority of their baby teeth—who will find any of this stuff remotely interesting and since they have been handled in such a flat and sitcomish manner by director Michael Lembeck, it is unlikely that parents or older siblings roped into attending will care about them either. What is especially annoying is that the film wastes so much time and energy on this stuff, but, at the same time, it utterly ignores one question that could have inspired something genuinely amusing—what is it that the tooth fairy conglomerate actually does with all the teeth that they collect?

Adding to the grisliness of *Tooth Fairy* is the grim experience of seeing good actors trying and failing to make something out of the decidedly substandard material that they are working with. Johnson is game enough, but the role does not give him anything to do other than stand around in a funny outfit and the decision to make his character a self-absorbed boor means that his chief asset as an actor—his intense likeability—is unfortunately sidelined for long periods of time. As for Ashley Judd, words cannot begin to describe how depressing it is to witness an actress as talented as her going through the motions in such a thinly written role, especially after the one-two punch of *Bug* (2006) and *Come Every Morning* (2006) that suggested a renewed commitment to acting after a string of increasingly formulaic thrillers. Billy Crystal pops up as the Fairy World equivalent of Q in one scene that is a blatant retread of his bit in *The Princess Bride* (1987) and which will have most people wishing that they were spending their time watching that film again instead of this one. The only cast member who comes away from this film without completely embarrassing herself is the inimitable Julie Andrews as the chief fairy. Granted, it will not go down as one of her great performances and there is nothing that she does here that she has not done better in any number of her past movies. However, there are very few actresses out there capable of appearing in a movie that has her making a grand entrance by floating into a room, delivering sage life lessons to The Rock, eventually receive a big bear hug from him in return and appearing in a scene opposite a kibitzing Billy Crystal—all while wearing a pair of wings—and still walk away with a shred of personal dignity and if this film does nothing else (and it does not), it proves that she is one of them. If the rest of *Tooth Fairy* is one long and painful cinematic cavity, she serves as a dab of Benzocaine that serves to briefly take the agony away.

Peter Sobczynski

CREDITS

Derek Thompson: Dwayne Johnson
Lily: Julie Andrews
Tess: Destiny Whitlock
Tracy: Stephen Merchant
Mick Donnelly: Ryan Sheckler
Carly: Ashley Judd
Jerry: Billy Crystal
Ziggy: Seth MacFarlane
Randy: Chase Ellison
Origin: USA, Canada
Language: English
Released: 2010
Production: Jason Blum, Mark Ciardi, Gordon Gray; Mayhem Pictures, Walden Media, Blumhouse Productions,; released by 20th Century Fox
Directed by: Michael Lembeck
Written by: Lowell Ganz, Babaloo Mandell, Joshua Sternin, Jeffrey Ventimilia, Randi Mayern Singer
Cinematography by: David Tattersall
Music by: George S. Clinton
Sound: John Morris

Music Supervisor: Mike Flicker
Editing: David Finfer
Costumes: Angus Strathie
Production Design: Marcia Hinds
MPAA rating: PG
Running time: 101 minutes

REVIEWS

Ebert, Roger. *Chicago Sun-Times.* January 21, 2010.
Holden, Stephen. *New York Times.* January 22, 2010.
Lumenick, Lou. *New York Post.* January 22, 2010.
Pais, Matt. *Metromix.com.* January 21, 2010.
Phillips, Michael. *Chicago Tribune.* January 21, 2010.
Puig, Claudia. *USA Today.* January 21, 2010.
Robinson, Tasha. *AV Club.* January 21, 2010.
Scott, A.O. *At the Movies.* February 1, 2010.
Snider, Eric D. *Film.com.* January 21, 2010.
Tallerico, Brian. *MovieRetriever.com.* January 22, 2010.

QUOTES

Derek Thompson: "You can't handle the Tooth! And that's the Tooth, the whole Tooth and nothing but the Tooth! I pledge allegiance to the Tooth."

TRIVIA

This film includes Billy Crystal's first live action movie role since the 2002 film *Analyze That.*

THE TOURIST

> *It all started when he met a woman.*
> —Movie tagline
> *The perfect trip—the perfect trap.*
> —Movie tagline

Box Office: $67 million

By the end of *The Tourist,* Scotland Yard Inspector John Acheson (Paul Bettany) is scratching his head in bewilderment and so too is the viewer. Unlike Acheson however, the viewer's confusion is not due to having been thoroughly outfoxed by the elusive Alexander Pierce but rather plot holes large enough to sail a gondola through, dialogue that thinks it is far more sophisticated and witty than it actually is, and a climactic "twist" that makes no sense and leaves the viewer feeling cheated. *The Tourist* wants to be one part Blake Edward's farce and two parts Alfred Hitchcock thriller but fails on both counts due to its lazy and lackluster script.

The film opens in Paris with the elegant Elise Clifton-Ward (Angelina Jolie) under the surveillance of a French espionage team who is in turn under the supervision of Acheson. Elise, though simply walking a few blocks to a local café for morning coffee, is dressed like a runway model, resembling nothing less than a 1960s Italian film goddess as she leisurely struts down the street in high heels. Elise is under surveillance because twelve months earlier she was romantically involved with an accountant named Alexander Pierce, who embezzled some two billion dollars from his employer, criminal and murderer Reginald Shaw (Steven Berkoff), and promptly disappeared. British agents are following Elise in the hope that Alexander will contact her and allow them to apprehend him and recover the embezzled funds for the British government.

Alexander does exactly that that very morning: A courier arrives at the café and delivers a note to Elise reading: "I know the police are watching you, we have to throw them off the trail. Board the eight-twenty-two, the Gare de Lyon, pick someone my height and build and make them believe it is me." Elise immediately burns the note and leaves the cafe. "Save that letter. Go in now, save that letter," Acheson orders. This is a rather optimistic request since the note is already on fire and the nearest agent is across the street, inside a van when the order comes through. The agent does his best but is forced to glumly report to an exasperated Acheson that the letter is "burnt to sh*t," establishing both the bumbling nature the agents will display throughout the rest of the film and the general level of wit and sophistication of the script.

Elise easily eludes her followers, even pausing at the mouth of the subway station to taunt them. Soon she is on the train looking for an innocent schlub with the requisite height and build per Alexander's orders. She finds him in the person of tourist Frank Tupelo (Johnny Depp), a supposedly nebbish mathematics professor from Wisconsin. Frank does not look or sound much like a math professor (indeed with his long hair and goatee he resembles nothing less than a *Saturday Night Fever* era Barry Gibb) and he cannot believe his good fortune to be sitting next to and talking with a goddess. The two exchange dialogue that is supposed to be cute, witty and laden with double entendres but does not cut the mustard. With an innocent man caught up in events beyond his understanding and a beautiful woman of mystery who knows more than she reveals meeting on a train, *The Tourist* is clearly, and unwisely, courting comparison to *North by Northwest* (1959). The comparison is unfortunate because the limp dialogue Depp and Jolie are given to exchange pales in comparison to Cary Grant and Eva Marie Saint's electric banter in Hitchcock's classic.

By the time Frank and Elise reach Venice, they are under surveillance by three parties: an Italian espionage team under the supervision of Bettany, Reginald Shaw, Alexander's murderous former employer, and a mysteri-ous man (Rufus Sewell) who has been following Elise since Paris. Elise invites Frank to stay with her in the luxurious hotel room Alexander has reserved for her and invites him to dinner. After dinner, Frank decides to try his luck at getting a goodnight kiss and Elise decides to give it to him although this decision seems to be generated by plot requirements, not a convincingly developed romance between the two. When Elise kisses Frank, Shaw and his thugs take that as confirmation that Frank is a disguised Alexander and decide to move in. The next day while Elise is out, two of Shaw's thugs appear in the hotel room to kidnap Frank. Surprised and standing in his pajamas, Frank comically attempts to explain that he is not Alexander, whoever that is. When the thugs start shooting, Frank flees out the bathroom window which leads to a supposedly comic chase on the rooftops. The chase ends when, in pure Warner Brothers style, Frank falls off the roof and knocks a policeman into the canal (trying to maintain his balance before the fall, Depp actually swings his arms in circles). This leads to his arrest and one of the few genuinely funny scenes in the film in which Frank amusingly attempts to persuade a skeptical Italian detective (Christian de Sica) of his crazy predicament.

The rest of the film consists of a very poor man's variation of Hitchcock's "the wrong man" theme. Acheson and his agents continue to watch Frank and Elise, waiting for Alexander to appear while Shaw and his thugs, convinced Frank is Alexander, pursue the couple with the intent of torturing out of Frank the location of Shaw's embezzled money. Along the way several characters are revealed to not be who they say they are culminating in a climactic plot twist that is supposed to stunningly recast the viewer's experience of the entire film but instead succeeds only in infuriating the viewer and rendering much of the film nonsensical. An earned plot twist is a clever, surprising development that, when the viewer reexamines the plot developments leading up to it will make perfect sense and seems organic. An unearned plot twist is a lazy, thrown-in surprise that seeks to end the movie on a " whoa" note without putting in the hard work of making that twist believable in relation to the rest of the film. *The Tourist*'s plot twist falls very much into the latter category and ruins what little suspense and charm the script had managed to establish.

That is a shame because, aside from its inadequate script, *The Tourist* gets just about everything else right. Despite the limitations of their dialogue, there are some amusing interactions between Depp and Jolie (who cares if they appear to be acting in two separate films: he a farce and she a thriller?). Depp, in scenes like the one with the skeptical detective, does the bewildered man in over his head quite well. Jolie, playing it straight, comes closest to anyone in the film to establishing a compelling, real life person. The sets, costumes, and locations are exquisite as is the setting. There are few places as beautiful as Venice and cinematographer John Seale renders it sublimely. The visual beauty of the film is matched by a lush and romantic score by James Newton Howard. And the film is packed with a great supporting cast: Paul Bettany, Timothy Dalton, Steven Berkoff, Rufus Sewell, and Christian de Sica, excellent actors all, who simply need a script that gives them more to do and cleverer dialogue to deliver. Indeed, although *The Tourist* is a remake of an earlier film—*Anthony Zimmer* (2005)— and its script was presumably in final form before the leads were cast, it is hard to shake the feeling that director/writer Florian Henckel von Donnersmarck and his co-writers Julian Fellowes and Christopher McQuarrie seem to have concluded, "we've got two of the biggest stars in the world and a beautiful, romantic setting, let's just laze our way through a plot."

Donnersmarck and his co-writers deserve credit for the comic, lighthearted tone they try to achieve with *The Tourist*. It is a difficult enough task to succeed in making a straightforward thriller or a straightforward comedy, let alone both at the same time. Few films attempt to do so but when they succeed the results can be delightful (*Get Shorty* [1995], *The Thomas Crown Affair* [1999]). Unfortunately, *The Tourist* fails to deliver a script capable of sustaining its desired tone. With its unremarkable dialogue and lazy plot twists, *The Tourist* ends up being a beautiful but intellectually empty affair, a coffee table movie with two of the world's biggest stars.

Nate Vercauteren

CREDITS

Frank Tupelo: Johnny Depp
Elise Clifton-Ward: Angelina Jolie
Inspector John Acheson: Paul Bettany
Chief Inspector Jones: Timothy Dalton
The Englishman: Rufus Sewell
Reginald Shaw: Steven Berkoff
Lombardi: Christian de Sica
Origin: USA
Language: English
Released: 2010
Production: Graham King, Tim Headington, Roger Birnbaum, Gary Barber, Jonathan Glickman; Spyglass Entertainment, GK Films, Columbia Pictures; released by Sony Pictures Entertainment
Directed by: Florian Henckel von Donnersmarck
Written by: Florian Henckel von Donnersmarck, Christopher McQuarrie, Julian Fellowes

Cinematography by: John Seale
Music by: James Newton Howard
Sound: Mark Ulano
Editing: Joe Hutshing, Patricia Rommel
Art Direction: Marco Tretini
Costumes: Colleen Atwood
Production Design: Jon Hutman
MPAA rating: PG-13
Running time: 103 minutes

REVIEWS

Anderson, John. *Washington Post.* December 9, 2010.
Baumgarter, Marjorie. *Austin Chronicle.* December 15, 2010.
Chang, Justin. *Variety.* December 8, 2010.
Dargis, Manohla. *New York Times.* December 9, 2010.
Ebert, Roger. *Chicago Sun-Times.* December 8, 2010.
Morris, Wesley. *Boston Globe.* December 9, 2010.
Pols, Mary. *Time Magazine.* December 13, 2010.
Rea, Stephen. *Philadelphia Inquirer.* December 9, 2010.
Tobias, Scott. *AV Club.* December 9, 2010.
Travers, Peter. *Rolling Stone.* December 10, 2010.

QUOTES

Frank Taylor: "Why is everyone trying to kill me?"

TRIVIA

The film originally included Tom Cruise and Charlize Theron in the leading roles.

AWARDS

Nomination:

Golden Globes 2011: Actor—Mus./Comedy (Depp), Actress—Mus./Comedy (Jolie), Film—Mus./Comedy.

THE TOWN

Welcome to the bank robbery capital of America.
—Movie tagline

Box Office: $92 million

If the Boston setting helps Ben Affleck make films as exciting and efficient as *Gone Baby Gone* (2007) and the remarkably assured genre piece *The Town*, no one will rag on the guy for sticking around the city in which he was raised. In fact, movie fans may beg him not to leave. With just two films under his belt as a director, Affleck has already proven to have a keen eye for detail and an all-important understanding of how to nudge a good cop movie towards greatness. Doing so takes action sequences with propulsion and clarity. It takes an understanding that the sensational appeal of crime and other illegal behavior on the big screen ends once people start getting shot and killed. It takes morally complicated and sometimes conflicted characters on both sides of the law. *The Town* offers all of these; the film may not rival the scope and ambition of Michael Mann's *Heat* (1995), but, released just three weeks after the massively inferior *Takers* (2010), *The Town* does restore a crisp, bare-knuckled proficiency to the heist genre.

Affleck, who shares a writing credit with Peter Craig and Aaron Stockard in adapting Chuck Hogan's novel *Prince of Thieves,* (2005) stars as Doug, the latest in a long line of cinematic criminals looking to get out of their dangerous line of work. Except Doug is not just the average baddie looking to go straight. He is a man with a loaded past, to say the least. Doug's mother left when he was six, and his dad (Chris Cooper) has been in jail for most of Doug's life. There was a time that Doug was a hockey star on the rise, when newspapers ran stories about him and used terms like "local hero." Of course, that was before Doug's temper and vices got the best of him; a few fights with his teammates and some dabbling in cocaine and Oxycontin later, the aspiring hockey star has transformed into a career criminal, aided most by James (Jeremy Renner), whose family took in Doug many years ago when his dad went to prison.

That back story, along with Doug's previous relationship with James' drug-dealing, single-mother sister Krista (Blake Lively), provides *The Town* with important emotional context as situations start to get sticky. When the film opens, Doug and James lead a crew in a bank robbery—not unusual around here; opening on-screen slides identify the Boston-area city of Charlestown as the bank robbing capital of the world—that goes right, mostly. They get away with a big stash of cash, but as the heat comes their way James takes the bank manager, Claire (Rebecca Hall), as a hostage. The guys let her go physically unharmed but worry that, since the driver's license they stole indicates Claire lives only a few blocks away, she may soon recognize their voices and turn them in to the chief FBI investigator on the case, Adam Frawley (Jon Hamm). James, a violent guy who has already done nine years in jail, considers roughing her up or worse. Doug believes in retaliation but is far more averse to murder. So he takes it upon himself to get close to Claire and ensure she is not planning on squealing. Soon the two meet at a Laundromat and she is opening her heart to Doug and the bank robber has begun a romantic relationship with the one woman who can identify him and his colleagues to the feds.

The relationship between Doug and Claire never quite escapes its credibility stretching set-up. However, Affleck handles this plotline so that it never becomes

stale or that anyone watching wishes Claire would just find out the truth so the movie could move things along. Instead, Doug and Claire bond over old and new wounds, and considerable tension comes from Doug's fear that the woman he has grown to care about will recognize him as taking part in an event that has left her permanently shaken. That anxiety hits a peak as James unexpectedly drops in on the couple's date. He does not know that Claire has told Doug she spotted one of the robber's tattoos, a small Irish logo as seen on T-shirts for the University of Notre Dame, on the back of his neck. So as James introduces himself to Claire, Doug eyes that very tattoo on James' neck, silently praying that Claire will not notice. The scene is a terrific demonstration of how much can hang at stake in the air while very little is said at all. The same sense of quiet intensity comes much later, when Frawley approaches Krista in a bar and what seems like flirtation quickly becomes a situation in which the beautiful girl sitting at the bar no longer has the power. Instead, she fears what the guy sitting on the next stool can do to her if she does not do and say the right things.

These scenes are all acted with tremendous care. In *Gone Baby Gone* Affleck proved his skill with actors by generating a terrific lead performance from his brother Casey and a devastating supporting turn from Amy Ryan that earned her a Best Supporting Actress Oscar® nomination. In *The Town,* on top of delivering a commanding lead performance of his own and the expected top-tier turns from recent Oscar® nominee Renner, Affleck does it again as director. He generates very strong work from two stars known mostly for TV: Hamm, the star of AMC's *Mad Men,* and Lively, whose work on the teen-oriented soap *Gossip Girl* does not come close to foretelling the kind of work she does in *The Town* as a woman who recognizes her place in her community but has not fully given up on getting out.

The scene between Frawley and Krista is just one of the film's many memorable sequences delivered with the sort of crackling urgency not found in more generic installments of the heist genre. At one point in the film's second robbery sequence, Doug and company don creepy-looking masks attached to nun's habits. Just before the robbery, a child spots the armed criminals through their van window, and it is a haunting portrait of the town's ever-present threat of violence and a waking nightmare for a young kid on a public street. Later, after the robbery, a cop spots the guys, still holding their guns and wearing their masks. The unspoken showdown is clear: The cop can radio in the sighting and be killed instantly, likely by James or their cohorts Albert Magloan (Slaine) or Desmond Elden (Owen Burke). Or he can do nothing. The cop slowly turns away, and no bullets are fired. It is a powerful moment of criminals in complete control and cops exposed as vulnerable people who do not want to die.

The film is more than just action, though, and certain lines of dialogue can be taken completely out of context and still strongly reflect different personalities. "Anyone who lawyer's up is guilty," says Frawley, who is always playing his hand while hiding his cards. "We're hittin' pause after this one," says Doug, convincing James as much as he is convincing himself. These are smart, meaningful quips, strewn throughout a film that realizes well-established characters in a cops-and-robbers movie have to develop through their conversations and not just based on who does the running and who does the chasing.

The Town does not address why Charlestown has such a long history of bank robberies. The film does, however, get a lot of mileage from smart uses of audio. At times during robberies, the criminals are seen on black-and-white security monitors without any sound, a reminder of how that terror looks to someone working surveillance in real time. At other times, nothing can be heard but the sound of the robbery itself as drawers are opened and closed, cash is snatched and stuffed away, and bleach is poured to eliminate the presence of DNA that could identify the crooks. This is exciting, well-executed action. The same goes for when Doug and his colleagues speed away from police cars giving chase, and Affleck reminds action fans tired of the over-the-top chaos of Michael Bay movies just how much more is felt when it is clear what is going on and where the heroes are in proximity to the villains.

Actually, *The Town* does not feel like a story of heroes and villains thanks to the shading of the film's perceptive if slightly overlong script. Frawley may be the good guy on the right side of the law, but there is also reason to root for Doug, who is not a hardened criminal but a guy who made some bad choices and now constantly tries not to let anything get out of hand. That Doug ultimately commits several acts of brutal violence suggests not that he is actually a much worse person than previously believed but that he truly is willing to do anything to escape the life he has built for himself. After all, that is fundamentally what *The Town* is about: People who do what they do because they think there is nothing else that they can do.

Matt Pais

CREDITS

Doug MacRay: Ben Affleck
Claire Keesey: Rebecca Hall
Adam Frawley: Jon Hamm
James Coughlin: Jeremy Renner
Krista: Blake Lively
Dino Ciampa: Titus Welliver
Fergus "Fergie" Colm: Pete Postlethwaite
Stephen MacRay: Chris Cooper
Albert "Gloansy" Magloan: Slaine
Desmond Elden: Owen Burke
Agent Quinlan: Corena Chase
Rusty: Dennis Mclaughlin
Origin: USA
Language: English
Released: 2010
Production: Basil Iwanyk, Graham King; Legendary Pictures, GK Films, Thunder Road Productions; released by Warner Bros.
Directed by: Ben Affleck
Written by: Ben Affleck, Aaron Stockard, Peter Craig
Cinematography by: Robert Elswit
Music by: Harry Gregson-Williams, David Buckley
Sound: David J. Schwartz
Editing: Dylan Tichenor
Art Direction: Peter Borck
Costumes: Susan Matheson
Production Design: Sharon Seymour
MPAA rating: R
Running time: 125 minutes

REVIEWS

Catsoulis, Jeanette. *NPR.* September 16, 2010.
Ebert, Roger. *Chicago Sun-Times.* September 15, 2010.
Jones, Kimberley. *Austin Chronicle.* September 17, 2010.
Lumenick, Lou. *New York Post.* September 17, 2010.
Moore, Roger. *Orlando Sentinel.* September 15, 2010.
Puig, Claudia. *USA Today.* September 17, 2010.
Salisbury, Mark. *Premiere.* September 17, 2010.
Schwarzbaum, Lisa. *Entertainment Weekly.* September 21, 2010.
Scott, Mike. *New Orleans Times-Picayune.* September 17, 2010.
Stevens, Dana. *Slate.* September 17, 2010.

QUOTES

Doug MacRay: "No matter how much you change, you still have to pay the price for the things you've done. So I got a long road. But I know I'll see you again—this side or the other."

TRIVIA

Ben Affleck, a devoted Red Sox fan, decided to premiere the film at Fenway Park in Boston.

AWARDS

Nomination:

Oscars 2010: Support. Actor (Renner)

British Acad. 2010: Support. Actor (Postlethwaite)
Golden Globes 2011: Support. Actor (Renner)
Screen Actors Guild 2010: Support. Actor (Renner)
Writers Guild 2010: Adapt. Screenplay.

TOY STORY 3

The great escape.
—Movie tagline
No toy gets left behind.
—Movie tagline

Box Office: $415 million

There was no mystery as to why many moviegoers were slow in taking off their 3D glasses when the lights went back up at the end of *Toy Story 3*: they did not find themselves feeling surprisingly stylish, but surprisingly moved. The delay gave a little extra time for the tears to dry; a minute or two during which that lump in the throat that had nothing to do with improperly-swallowed popcorn might also disappear. What audiences saw through those glasses did not just possess a greater depth of field but also of feeling, and viewers left unaffected by the *Toy Story* trilogy's profoundly-poignant final bow must surely be made of stone.

They certainly could not have been made of fabric or plastic, as those comprised of such materials have certainly not remained unfazed when it comes to people moving on and leaving toys behind. Through the hauntingly beautiful, bittersweet song "When She Loved Me" in *Toy Story 2* (1999), it was shown that toys too can be torn apart by separation, increasingly pining to be played with as their beloved owners first outgrow and then, much to their incredulity, abandon them. The sad plight of cowgirl Jessie (Joan Cusack) gave Sheriff Woody (Tom Hanks) pause, having already been shaken by a nightmare about his own obsolescence. However, he ended up at peace with whatever might loom somewhere down the road, as long as he had Space Ranger Buzz Lightyear (Tim Allen) and his other pals to travel toward it with him. The reaching of that pivotal fork in the road causes a crisis for all in *Toy Story 3,* which mixes heartfelt emotional material, exciting (and sometimes unexpectedly harrowing) action sequences, and the usual delightful mirth. Worth the eleven-year wait, it is one of the best productions of 2010—animated or otherwise.

The film begins with a vibrant mish-mash of frenetic, fantastic mayhem, which turns out to be a vivid reminder of why it had always been such fun to be a treasured toy of the exhaustively-imaginative Andy. A subsequent montage reveals that time has passed and a lot has changed since the days of such fever-pitched flights of fancy. Andy is now a gangly seventeen-year-old (once again voiced—but more deeply now—by John Morris) who is about to leave home for college. What he reaches for these days are the mouse attached to his computer, his cell phone, or the keys to his car. While the toys remain eager to be played with (which is, of course, their raison d'être), that has not happened in ages. Woody reassuringly asserts to his forlorn friends that simply "being there for Andy is what's important," even if it means dutifully and devotedly biding their time up in the attic until the young man retrieves them for his own children to embrace. It is a sweet notion, but these loyal words from their leader do not make Andy's other favorites feel any less forsaken.

This prevailing air of dejection and uncertainty is reflected in the lighting of the room the toys have shared with Andy for so long, which no longer possesses the sunbeam-drenched, cozy warmth of halcyon days gone by. One cannot help but also notice that his crayon-scrawled drawings from childhood have been supplanted by more grown-up examples of his artwork, as well as various teen-themed posters. The toys' concern about what the future holds becomes acute when Andy's mom (Laurie Metcalf) announces that everything in the wagon wheel chest must be stored in the aforementioned attic, sent to a day care center, or simply thrown away. Andy does not mean it when he dismissively pronounces them as "junk" that no one would want—he is merely asserting his maturity—but it surely does nothing to reassure his beleaguered old belongings.

It is Woody's fondest wish come true when Andy cannot part with him, and he is put in a box earmarked for college. Woody (and the audience) is briefly horrified when the others are put in a trash bag, but they are actually still valued and headed to the attic for safekeeping. Due to a mix-up, however, the toys narrowly escape being carted away as garbage, and subsequently ignore Woody's protestations that Andy had indeed wanted to hang onto them. Instead, they hop into a box heading for Sunnyside Daycare, where the gang will have no shortage of kids with which they can play day after day, year after year, to infinity and beyond. However, what initially seems like a heavenly haven turns out to be more like a hell, as a shrieking, slobbering plague of terrifying toddlers descends upon the toys and proceeds to treat them most unkindly. (Don Rickles' Mr. Potato Head gets especially mashed.)

Life at Sunnyside is even less a bowl of cherries thanks to strawberry-scented, enormous Lots-o'-Huggin' Bear (Ned Beatty), whose benevolent, glad-handing Southern courtliness ends up masking malevolent, bitterness-fueled, iron-fisted oppression. Lotso's charmingly-concealed ill will reminds one of characters like Andy Griffith's Larry Rhodes in *A Face in the Crowd* (1957) and Burl Ives as Big Daddy Pollitt in *Cat on a Hot Tin Roof* (1958). This teddy became twisted and his heart hardened when his owner lost and then replaced him. To Lotso, if a loved one ever leaves, then the closeness that was shared was in actuality meaningless, without value, and a lie while it lasted. He has since callously ruled Sunnyside, helped by henchmen like a big, creepy, zombie-like baby doll with one droopy eye and multiple pen tattoos, and an ascot-adorned Ken doll (Michael Keaton) who seems to be in the closet along with his extensive wardrobe.

With the toys (sans Woody) under Lotso's plush, pink thumb in a daycare that turns into a grim, locked-down penitentiary for playthings at night (the filmmakers visited Alcatraz for inspiration), it is time for yet another *Toy Story* rescue mission. Despite his imminent departure to adorn Andy's dorm room, all-for-one-and-one-for-all Woody hatches a bold, intricate plan to break his pals out of prison. This is when *Toy Story 3* begins firing on an uncommon number of cylinders, a highly-inventive, action-packed, nail-biter of a sequence that pays homage to films like *Cool Hand Luke* (1967) and *The Great Escape* (1963). The toys' getaway is deliciously aided by a film noir-ish Fisher Price Chatter Phone informant (Teddy Newton), as well as the help Barbie (Jodi Benson) hilariously elicits from Ken, who practically unravels when she threatens to rip apart his treasured threads. Things are also complicated by Buzz exhibiting multiple personalities—all of them hard to handle—due to the manipulation for good and evil of his controls. His potently suave, Spanish-spouting Latin lover mode is sublimely loopy.

While Woody's fervently-clung-to dream of accompanying Andy when he matriculates seems about to be realized, *Toy Story 3* also brings him face-to-face with his previously-mentioned worst nightmare, as the escape route from Sunnyside takes an unexpected detour toward what looks like the end of the line at the city dump. Many viewers were aghast at the overpoweringly-grim sight of theses much-loved characters resignedly holding hands as they slide downward toward the glowing, gaping mouth of an incinerator. The youngest audience members may very well have resultantly had nightmares of their own, but it is a testament to the skill of the people at Pixar that even adults watched the near-death experience of animated objects with such acute dread—and subsequent relief.

The scene that packs the most powerful emotional wallop, however, is the film's final one, in which Andy proves his caring by ensuring that these prized possessions just back from the brink of annihilation enjoy a fulfilling renaissance. They will become the cherished playmates of beguiling little Bonnie (Emily Hahn), who

will utilize them with as much care and imagination as he had. As Andy tenderly hands over each old friend, every introduction doubles as a heartfelt expression to the toy of all that it has meant—actually, will always mean—to him. The camera holds on each one, giving the impression that the toy is basking in his affectionate gratitude. This also allows viewers one last chance to say their own goodbyes. Andy says a soft "Thanks guys," and his voice catches as Bonnie enables Woody to wave so long in return, a moment which surely made even the iciest of audience members melt into tears. Viewers realize that Andy is not just bidding farewell to childhood toys but to childhood itself, which will wrench the hearts of both young adults teetering on the same uncertain cusp and wistful parents to whom it seems that the stork just brought what is now spreading its wings to fly away. Before departing, with none of his too-cool friends around to probably razz him, Andy allows himself to revert back to being a kid for one last joyous, free-spirited romp for old time's sake. As the camera pans up to a bright blue sky with puffy white clouds, the audience is able to let out a collective sigh of contentment. Anyone who dared to break the spell on the way out of the theater by pondering aloud what might befall the toys as Bonnie matures was, it is fervently hoped, slapped silly.

It was surely daunting to try to remain on par with not only a groundbreaking feature that was named to the National Film Registry and made the American Film Institute's list of the 100 greatest motion pictures, but also an acclaimed sequel that surpassed its predecessor's earnings with a worldwide gross of $1 billion. Nevertheless, *Toy Story 3,* made on a budget of $200 million, was itself embraced by critics and passed the $400 million mark to become the top-grossing animated film of all time. "In *Toy Story 3,* we deal with the point in time that concerns toys the most," said John Lassetter, the current head of Pixar and Disney Animation Studios who directed *Toy Story* (1995) and then shared the reins with this film's director, Lee Unkrich, for *Toy Story 2* (1999). "When you're broken, you can be fixed. When you're lost, you can be found. When you're stolen, you can be recovered. But there's no way to fix being outgrown by a child." There is also no way of fixing the fact that children outgrow the need for their parents in their day-to-day existence. However, when Woody overhears Andy comfortingly telling his mother that she will in a sense always be with him, the sheriff comes to the realization that he will indelibly be a part of Andy and Andy of him—and he will not need to look at the magic-markered name on the bottom of his boot to remember that warming fact.

David L. Boxerbaum

CREDITS

Woody: Tom Hanks (Voice)
Buzz Lightyear: Tim Allen (Voice)
Jessie: Joan Cusack (Voice)
Rex: Wallace Shawn (Voice)
Hamm: John Ratzenberger (Voice)
Mr. Potato Head: Don Rickles (Voice)
Mrs. Potato Head: Estelle Harris (Voice)
Slinky Dog: Blake Clark (Voice)
Sergeant: R. Lee Ermey (Voice)
Ken: Michael Keaton (Voice)
Barbie: Jodi Benson (Voice)
Lots-O'Huggin' Bear: Ned Beatty (Voice)
Mr. Pricklepants: Timothy Dalton (Voice)
Mrs. Davis: Laurie Metcalf (Voice)
Andy Davis: John Morris (Voice)
Dolly: Bonnie Hunt (Voice)
Buttercup: Jeff Garlin (Voice)
Trixie: Kirsten Schaal (Voice)
Peter: Lou Romano (Voice)
Lenny: Richard "Cheech" Marin (Voice)
Stretch the Octopus: Whoopi Goldberg (Voice)
RC: Frank Welker (Voice)
Molly Davis: Beatrice Miller (Voice)
Jack in the Box: Lee Unkrich (Voice)
Bookworm: Richard Kind (Voice)
Chatter Telephone: Teddy Newton (Voice)
Spanish Buzz: Javier Fernandez Pena (Voice)
Bonnie: Emily Hahn (Voice)
Origin: USA
Language: English
Released: 2010
Production: Darla K. Anderson; Pixar Animation Studios; released by Walt Disney Pictures
Directed by: Lee Unkrich
Written by: Michael Arndt
Music by: Randy Newman
Editing: Ken Schretzmann, Lee Unkrich
Sound: Tom Myers
Production Design: Bob Pauley
MPAA rating: G
Running time: 103 minutes

REVIEWS

Debruge, Peter. *Variety.* June 14, 2010.
Denby, David. *New Yorker.* July 5, 2010.
Edelstein, David. *New York.* June 28, 2010.
Gleiberman, Owen. *Entertainment Weekly.* June 25, 2010.
Morgenstern, Joe. *Wall Street Journal.* June 18, 2010.
Romney, Jonathan. *Sight & Sound.* August 2010.
Scott, A.O. *New York Times.* June 18, 2010.
Travers, Peter. *Rolling Stone.* July 8, 2010.

Wheat, Alynda. *People.* June 28, 2010.
Wloszczyna, Susan. *USA Today.* June 22, 2010.

QUOTES

Buzz Lightyear: "Hold on, this is no time to be hysterical!"
Mr. Pricklepants: "Sunnyside is a place of ruin and despair, ruled by an evil bear who smells of strawberries!"
Andy: "Now Woody, he's been my pal for as long as I can remember. He's brave, like a cowboy should be...and kind and smart. But the thing that makes Woody special is he'll never give up on you...ever. He'll be there for you, no matter what."

TRIVIA

An early draft of the script included the toys shipping themselves to Taiwan in order to save Buzz Lightyear after he was returned to his manufacturer to fix a defect.

Toy Story 3 is the first sequel to be nominated for the Best Picture Oscar® when none of its predecessors were nominated.

AWARDS

Oscars 2010: Animated Film, Song ("We Belong Together")
British Acad. 2010: Animated Film
Golden Globes 2011: Animated Film
Nomination:
Oscars 2010: Adapt. Screenplay, Film, Sound FX Editing
British Acad. 2010: Adapt. Screenplay, Visual FX.

TRON: LEGACY

The game has changed.
—Movie tagline
The only way to win is to survive.
—Movie tagline

Box Office: $171 million

It's impossible to look at a movie like *TRON: Legacy* and not think about how strange and amorphous the concept of "nostalgia" truly is. To be frank, *TRON: Legacy* wouldn't exist without nostalgia. And while there have been many, many films that have structured themselves almost completely around the idea of nostalgia—George Lucas' *American Graffiti* and Barry Levinson's *Diner* come to mind—the fact that Disney released a sequel to Steven Lisberger's *TRON* twenty-eight years after the original really speaks to the often-odd impact that nostalgia can have on the critical and popular legacy of a motion picture. Because, let's be honest, it's downright strange that *TRON* even got a sequel.

The original *TRON* was a movie that had a lot going for it conceptually, but, in the end, it simply didn't work. It was not the hit that Disney had hoped for back in 1982 and, for most of the following twenty-odd years, *TRON* was considered to be a flop. It was a movie that was mocked in pop culture—on an episode of *The Simpsons*, Chief Wiggum once tripped over himself to deny that he'd ever even seen *TRON*—and the film had less of a cult following than many low-budget horror films of the same era. However, as we entered the 2000s, the cult of *TRON* began to grow. The *TRON* Guy became a popular YouTube meme, the *TRON* Wikipedia called the film "a box office success," despite twenty years of evidence to the contrary. *TRON* suddenly became a film that was appreciated retroactively. Perhaps it was just a resurgence of 1980s nostalgia. Perhaps it was the growing popularity of CGI animation, fostered by the virtuosity of Pixar and their animators. Perhaps the sheer concept of *TRON*—the first real video game movie—just seemed too impossibly attractive to modern gamer culture. Whatever the reason, thanks to this building nostalgia, the brand of *TRON* finally became the hot ticket item that Disney was hoping for back in 1982 and, thus, a sequel was born.

Nevertheless, this history-warping wave of nostalgia is a dual-edged sword. It helps *TRON: Legacy* because it's the primary reason the film exists and many of its strongest aspects—the design aesthetic, actors like Jeff Bridges and Bruce Boxleitner, etc.—can be traced back to the original *TRON*. But it hurts *TRON: Legacy* in fatal ways because director Joseph Kosinski apparently views the first *TRON* through such rose-colored glasses that he made his sequel into a gigantic, unquestioning tribute to the original film—even the parts that didn't work. *TRON* the brand might be uber-cool, but *TRON* the 1982 film had major flaws, and *TRON: Legacy*, unfortunately, reproduces and magnifies those flaws with loving reverence.

TRON: Legacy opens with a series of flashbacks, filling in the twenty-eight years of history since the original. Kevin Flynn (Jeff Bridges), the software and video game genius protagonist of the first film, became the CEO of the ENCOM corporation following the events of *TRON*. After alluding to his friends and his young son Sam that he was on the verge of a major technological breakthrough, Flynn disappears one night in 1989 and never returns, leaving ENCOM to evolve into a soulless corporate entity and Sam without a father. Jump ahead to the present where the grown and disillusioned Sam (Garrett Hedlund) carries out acts of corporate mischief against the growing-more-evil-by-the-day ENCOM—even though he's still the company's majority stakeholder. Following one of these stunts, Sam is visited by his dad's old pal and ENCOM executive Alan Bradley (Bruce Boxleitner), who lets Sam know that he just received a message originating from Flynn's abandoned arcade from a phone number that's been disconnected for twenty years. Sam, eager to discover more about his father's disappearance, explores the dilapidated arcade until he stumbles upon his father's secret laboratory and accidentally transports himself into the virtual world of the Grid, the computer-generated miniature universe Flynn explored in the original *TRON*.

It has to be said that Kosinski definitely has a strong visual style, and Sam's disorientated transition into the Grid is one of the cinematic highlights of *TRON: Legacy*. (The scene is greatly helped by Daft Punk's pulsing, electronica soundtrack, which is easily one of the best parts of the film.) However, while the look of *TRON: Legacy* is quite slick and refined, it's almost too architectural and cold and lacks the sheer alien visual grab of the original *TRON*. The original *TRON* looked like nothing you'd ever seen before. *TRON: Legacy* looks like a really cool Super Bowl commercial. As Sam stumbles into the Grid, he's immediately thrown into the game arena, where he quickly runs through revamps of probably the two most iconic scenes from the original *TRON*—the disc war gladiator showdown and the light-cycle battle. While these two scenes are easily the strongest action sequences in *TRON: Legacy*, they're both more choppy homage than anything new and, once they're over, as an audience member, you've pretty much been given everything you'd expect from a *TRON* sequel. The problem is—there's still an hour or so of movie left and this is where Kosinski really falters. After giving us loving, modernized tributes to the best, most memorable scenes from the original *TRON* in the first act of *TRON: Legacy*, he has almost nothing left to draw from for the final two-thirds of the film. And rather than creating new and exciting images and story ideas to explore in the TRON universe, Kosinski instead just gives us a retread of the truly underwhelming elements from the 1982 *TRON*—namely, the slow-as-molasses storytelling and the paper-thin characterizations.

After Sam survives the disc wars and the living programs within the Grid realize that he's a User (i.e. a real person) as opposed to a Program, he's taken by the mysterious cyber-warrior Rinzler (Anis Cheurfa) for an audience with Clu, the evil overlord of the Grid who's a digital doppelganger of Kevin Flynn. Clu throws Sam into a light-cycle battle and, after proving that he's a digital racing pro, Sam is rescued from the arena by Quorra (Olivia Wilde), a protégé of his father. The earnest and tough Quorra takes Sam into the Outlands of the Grid, where his father, Flynn, has been hiding for years. After an astonished reunion with his son, Flynn gives Sam the sordid history of the now-totalitarian Grid. Back in 1989, Flynn, Clu, and Tron—the anthropomorphized security program hero of the first film—entered the virtual world of the Grid intent on creating a "perfect" system, a utopian digital universe. While Flynn became obsessed with the unexplained appearance of ISOs (isomorphic algorithms)—i.e. sentient digital life-forms that spontaneously evolved in their "perfect" grid—Clu himself became obsessed with the concept of purity and perfection and saw the ISOs as an imperfect blight on the Grid. As such, Clu seized control of the Grid, ambushed Tron, exterminated the ISOs, and trapped Flynn in the digital universe.

Ever since, Flynn has been hiding in the Outlands of the Grid, waiting for a chance to escape and free the Grid from Clu's fascist clutches. (In the outside world, defeating Clu would be as easy as hitting the "delete" button.) Meanwhile, Clu desperately wants to find Flynn in order to steal his creator's identity disc, which acts as a sort of skeleton key/cheat code for the entire Grid. Thus, determined to escape, Sam, Flynn, and Quorra head back into the Grid's central metropolis to find a program named Zuse, who may or may not be able to get the trio to the portal back to the outside, non-digital world. After a showdown at the Grid's End of Line Club, owned by the Program Castor (played by Michael Sheen with ill-advised, scenery-chewing abandon), our heroes embark on a long trek to the mystical portal as they're relentlessly pursued by Clu and Rinzler.

As you can see, a lot happens following the aforementioned games arena scenes in *TRON: Legacy*, but it's startling how inert the rest of the film is. Sam's reunion with his father is brisk and unsatisfying and is followed by an overload of interminable exposition. As a storyteller, Kosinski has little skill at creating nuanced relationships between his characters and, it doesn't help that his two leads, Sam and Kevin Flynn, are such unsatisfying protagonists. Garrett Hedlund has moments of charisma, but Sam is more of a reactionary cipher than a real-life character with lost-daddy issues. And, while Jeff Bridges is an acting icon unto himself these days, his Kevin Flynn comes across as more of a riff on the Jeff Bridges persona rather than the earnest, optimistic computer programmer he originally played back in 1982. In fact, there are moments where Bridges seemingly lapses into a Jeff Lebowski caricature, where Flynn is momentarily replaced by The Dude, which almost makes Bridges' whole performance seem like a parody of himself. There just isn't enough going on with the Flynns, internally or externally, to make their quest for the portal engaging, even when paired with Olivia Wilde's Quorra, who's probably the film's most endearing character.

Beyond his disengaged leads, Kosinski only has one other trick up his sleeve for the final two-thirds of the movie—homage after homage after homage. Regrettably, Kosinski seems most interested in delivering references to one of two films—the original *TRON* or George Lu-

cas' *Star Wars*—two movies that are such frequently referenced sci-fi icons that Kosinski's constant tributes border on cliché. The visit to the End of the Line Club is a low-rent Mos Eisley Cantina scene, there's a scene where Sam becomes a young Luke Skywalker acting as a gunner on the Millennium Falcon—it's nothing you haven't seen before and seen better. It's hard to know whether to blame these storytelling flaws on the director or the screenwriters, Adam Horowitz and Edward Kitsis, but the inescapable truth is that *TRON: Legacy* is a film with almost nothing new to say, which is a shame, particularly when the forces of nostalgia keep telling us that the original *TRON* is such a "groundbreaking" film.

Perhaps the problem is that pop culture has confused its nostalgia for TRON the brand with *TRON* the film. Modern audiences wanted a return to the exciting visual world of the Grid. They fondly remembered moments, the video game tie-ins, the imagery, the descendents of *TRON*, and so on. But it's hard to think that people really yearned for a return to the characters and stilted storytelling of Steven Lisberger's original narrative. A return to the world of *TRON* was an exciting proposition, but only if the flaws of the original could be ignored or abandoned. Regrettably, the person who seems most confused with the "TRON the brand vs. the movie" conflict is Joseph Kosinski, who, with *TRON: Legacy*, delivered a movie that aspired to be nothing more than a retread of what had come before. Kosinski blindly embraced every aspect of the original *TRON*—the good and the bad—and the result is a film that not only squanders the Grid's second chance, but also fails to live up to the ambition of its predecessor.

Tom Burns

CREDITS

Sam Flynn: Garrett Hedlund
Kevin Flynn/Clu: Jeff Bridges
Quorra: Olivia Wilde
Alan Bradley: Bruce Boxleitner
Jarvis: James Frain
Siren Jem: Beau Garrett
Castor: Michael Sheen
Rinzler: Anis Cheurfa
Origin: USA
Language: English
Released: 2010
Production: Sean Bailey, Steven Lisberger, Jeffrey Silver; Live Planet; released by Walt Disney Pictures
Directed by: Joseph Kosinski
Written by: Edward Kitsis, Adam Horowitz
Cinematography by: Claudio Miranda

Editing: James Haygood
Music by: Daft Punk
Sound: Christopher Boyes
Costumes: Michael Wilkinson
Production Design: Darren Gilford
MPAA rating: PG
Running time: 125 minutes

REVIEWS

Debruge, Peter. *Variety.* October 16, 2010.
Edelstein, David. *New York Magazine.* December 13, 2010.
Fowler, Matt. *IGN Movies.* December 2, 2010.
Howell, Peter. *Toronto Star.* December 16, 2010.
Lemire, Christy. *Associated Press.* December 15, 2010.
McCarthy, Todd. *Hollywood Reporter.* December 3, 2010.
Phillips, Michael. *Chicago Tribune.* December 16, 2010.
Rich, Katey. *CinemaBlend.com.* December 7, 2010.
Simon, Brent. *Screen International.* December 9, 2010.
Young, Graham. *Birmingham Post.* December 15, 2010.

QUOTES

Kevin Flynn: "The Grid. A digital frontier. I tried to picture clusters of information as they moved through the computer. What did they look like? Ships, motorcycles? Were the circuits like freeways? I kept dreaming of a world I thought I'd never see. And then, one day…"

Clu: "Out there is a new world! Out there is our victory! Out there is our destiny!"

TRIVIA

While the shoot lasted only 64 days, post production took an additional 68 weeks to create the special effects.

Daft Punk not only created the soundtrack but made a brief cameo appearance as DJs in the film.

AWARDS

Nomination:

Oscars 2010: Sound FX Editing.

TRUE GRIT

Punishment comes one way or another.
—Movie tagline

Box Office: $165 million

The Coen brothers open their highly-anticipated and incredibly-lauded remake of the Oscar®-winning *True Grit* with a quote from Proverbs, "The wicked flee when none pursueth." It is followed by an equally-important quote from its narrator/heroine, who says, "You must pay for everything in this world in one way or another. There is nothing free except for the grace of God." Joel and Ethan Coen's accomplished adaptation of the same novel that inspired the beloved film that earned John Wayne his only Oscar® is a traditional coming-of-age adventure unafraid of issues like justice, wickedness, and the grace of God. It is defiantly old-fashioned in its sensibility, something that helped it become the highest box office grosser of the Coen brothers' amazing career and a ten-time Oscar® nominee, including for Best Picture, Best Actor, Best Supporting Actress, and Best Director. *True Grit* was one of the most beloved films of 2010, a film that does not necessarily break any of the rules of the Western as much as follow them in more remarkable ways than typically seen. With excellent performances and rock-solid production values, *True Grit* is a film that holds up well to repeat viewing, revealing itself as a solid adventure tale, even if it does sometimes drift into the unemotional territory that has sometimes left Coen films more ineffective than they would have been in other hands.

True Grit opens with a description of the murder of the father of Mattie Ross (Hailee Steinfeld, giving one of the most acclaimed debuts in years) and her arrival to claim his body and begin her quest for vengeance. A headstrong young lady, Mattie has no difficulty negotiating the final effects of her father's life and is determined to bring Tom Chaney (Josh Brolin), the man who shot him, to justice as it appears no one else cares enough to do so. She seeks out U.S. Marshal Rooster Cogburn (Jeff Bridges) after a recommendation and hears him testifying a case where it makes clear that this man has the killer instinct to survive a dangerous situation and keep her safe at the same time (although her confident exterior hides the girl who would surely be terrified by chasing a murderer into Indian Territory). Cogburn first denies Mattie's request and the young lady then encounters a Texas Ranger named LaBoeuf (Matt Damon) who happens to be tracking Chaney himself. After Cogburn and LaBoeuf first attempt to head out after Chaney on their own, the Ranger breaks from the group when Mattie chases the pair down and demands she accompany them. It is not long before, Mattie and Cogburn are on the trail of the "Lucky" Ned Pepper (Barry Pepper) Gang, who they believe that Chaney has hooked up with in Choctaw Territory. LaBoeuf eventually returns, the group catches up with the men in question, gunfire is exchanged, threats are made, and a snakebite even plays a major role in the final act.

True Grit hits common beats of the old-fashioned Western and contains some elements of the coming-of-age tale in that Mattie goes from determined to near-death and is shown at the end as an adult who has been forever changed by the experience. The story has the potential for intense melodrama and heartfelt emotion. It is about a young girl seeking justice for her father's murder. Anyone familiar with the Coen brothers' work knows that they do not traffic in easy emotion or rarely any emotion at all. Consequently, *True Grit* is often as cold as the snowy landscapes that Rooster and Mattie cross. There is little emotional investment here and little arc to the characters. One is left wondering what exactly Rooster and LaBoeuf got out of the journey other than a good story for the next campfire and Mattie's character starts off so intensely "full of grit" that her adventure seems merely to confirm her backbone more than build it. One has to wonder if the Coens cold approach to characters has not hurt them a bit in this case, leaving the story and its character at a bit more arms-length than they needed to be. In some ways, the film does not really develop a personality until the group catches up with Chaney and Pepper, as the two great actors playing the roles clearly relish the assignment to chew some scenery as bad guys.

If the Coens approach was a bit too calculated and cold for this critic, it still resulted in a film of technical brilliance. Once again, the Coens edited under the pseudonym Roderick Jaynes and the piece is perfectly composed and paced (although it was one of the few Oscar® nominations that the film surprisingly missed). Carter Burwell, a regular Coen collaborator, delivers another beautiful score. Most notably, Roger Deakins once again finds ways to make the Old West feel new, as he did so beautifully in *The Assassination of Jesse James by the Coward Robert Ford* (2007). Shockingly, Deakins had never won an Oscar® for Best Cinematography despite notching his ninth nomination this year for such incredible work as *The Shawshank Redemption* (1994), *Fargo* (1996), and many more. Most assumed he would finally take home the statue, deservedly so, for *True Grit*, undeniably one of the most visually sumptuous films of 2010.

As for performances, Hailee Steinfeld gives a confident, excellent one in what is truly the lead role of the film—it opens and closes with her narration and if it features any arc, it is Mattie's—despite winning several awards, including a nomination for Oscar®, for Best Supporting Actress. Steinfeld never falters, giving a performance that feels completely in the moment and genuine. Bridges is strong as Cogburn although one does not sense much of a challenge in the part for an actor of his caliber. Damon is actually better, disappearing so completely into his role that many did not even recognize the Oscar® winner.

As film journalists get lazy and run out of viable article topics, they often turn to the old chestnut that the movie Western is dead. And yet there are regular examples to prove otherwise. Clearly it is not as prominent a genre in the marketplace as it once was but the success of *True Grit* makes one wonder why.

Brian Tallerico

CREDITS

Mattie Ross: Hailee Steinfeld
Reuben J. "Rooster" Cogburn: Jeff Bridges
LaBoeuf: Matt Damon
Tom Chaney: Josh Brolin
"Lucky" Ned Pepper: Barry Pepper
Moon: Domhnall Gleeson
Bear Man: Ed Corbin
Adult Mattie Ross: Elizabeth Marvel
Harold Parmalee: Bruce Green
Emmett Quincy: Paul Rae
Colonel Stonehill: Dakin Matthews
Coke Hays: Brian Brown
Sullivan: Nicholas Sadler
Origin: USA
Language: English
Released: 2010
Production: Ethan Coen, Scott Rudin, Steven Spielberg, Joel Coen; Skydance Prods.; released by Paramount
Directed by: Joel Coen, Ethan Coen
Written by: Joel Coen, Ethan Coen
Cinematography by: Roger Deakins
Music by: Carter Burwell
Sound: Peter Kurland, Douglas Axtell
Editing: Roderick Jaynes
Art Direction: Christina Wilson
Costumes: Mary Zophres
Production Design: Jess Gonchor
MPAA rating: PG-13
Running time: 110 minutes

REVIEWS

Ebert, Roger. *Chicago Sun-Times.* December 21, 2010.
Edelstein, David. *New York Magazine.* December 13, 2010.
Hornaday, Ann. *Washington Post.* December 21, 2010.
Kohn, Eric. *indieWIRE.* December 17, 2010.
Lemire, Christy. *Associated Press.* December 21, 2010.
Morris, Wesley. *Boston Globe.* December 21, 2010.
Phillips, Michael. *Chicago Tribune.* December 21, 2010.
Phipps, Keith. *AV Club.* December 21, 2010.
Schager, Nick. *Slant Magazine.* December 20, 2010.
Smith, Kyle. *New York Post.* December 21, 2010.

QUOTES

Mattie Ross: "You must pay for everything in this world, one way and another. There is nothing free except the grace of God."

TRIVIA

This is the Coen Brothers first film to gross over $100 million in the United States.

Rooster Cogburn's eye-patch switched from covering the left eye of John Wayne in the original version to covering the right eye of Jeff Bridges in the remake.

AWARDS

British Acad. 2010: Cinematog

Nomination:

Oscars 2010: Actor (Bridges), Adapt. Screenplay, Art Dir./Set Dec., Cinematog., Costume Des., Director (Coen, Coen), Film, Sound, Sound FX Editing, Support. Actress (Steinfeld)

British Acad. 2010: Actor (Bridges), Actress (Steinfeld), Adapt. Screenplay, Costume Des., Film, Prod. Des., Sound

Screen Actors Guild 2010: Actor (Bridges), Support. Actress (Steinfeld)

Writers Guild 2010: Adapt. Screenplay.

TWELVE

No one needs anything here. It's all about want.
—Movie tagline

Back in the 1980s, Joel Schumacher's forays into youth-oriented soap operas had always been commercially-successful, even if not so artistically. The results of delving into the minds of young adults have ranged from the slightly off-putting (*Flatliners* [1990]) to fun-yet-cheesy (*The Lost Boys* [1987]) to the God-awful (*St. Elmo's Fire* [1985]). For whatever reason, decades later, Schumacher decided to return to the youth-oriented drama with *Twelve,* a meandering mess that echoes *Less Than Zero* (1987) and *Bright Lights, Big City* (1988), but without the relevance of the time period. It tries in earnest to paint a portrait of troubled, drug-addled youth in Upper East Side Manhattan, but ends up over-explaining to its audience why everyone is so damn whiny.

This is a multi-character piece and if there is any confusion on the part of the viewer as to how everyone is related to each other, narrator Kiefer Sutherland is on hand to provide detailed narration as though he were reading the audio book (this film is based on the novel by Nick McDonnell). No world-weary observation is left without being expounded upon ad nauseam, even when directly addressing the viewer. "Everyone wants something. What do you want? Because if you don't want anything, you got nothing." It goes on like that for ninety minutes.

The story, which takes place during spring break, centers mainly around a drug dealer who goes by the name of White Mike (Chace Crawford), who dropped out of the boarding school that most of the other characters attend. White Mike's cousin Charlie gets shot during a bad drug deal by Lionel (Curtis Jackson, a.k.a. rapper 50-Cent). Another youth, Nana (Jermaine Crawford), witnessed it and has all but disappeared, while White Mike's other cousin, Hunter (Philip Ettinger), has been labeled as the prime suspect. White Mike spends much of the film trying to find Charlie and Hunter while hooking up a party socialite named Jessica (Emily Meade) with Lionel, who is the sole dealer of a drug called "twelve," which is the new drug of choice.

Meanwhile, brothers Chris (Rory Culkin) and Claude (Billy Magnussen) live in their parents' penthouse where they throw big parties, but the two brothers could not be any more different. Chris is a virgin and a little too nice for this crowd. He throws the parties to try and establish himself in a social light, while Claude is home from rehab, jacked-up and more than a little on-edge. It is only a matter of time before he relapses. Chris gets seduced by Paris Hilton wannabe Sara (Esti Ginzburg) into throwing the biggest party in the world for her eighteenth birthday.

Almost every main character in the piece gets to have an out-of-body, fantasy or flashback sequence that takes place in an all-white room. White Mike, naturally, has visions of his dead mother while remembering the good times he used to spend with his cousins. One of White Mike's friends, Molly (Emma Roberts), seems all but oblivious to his new lifestyle choice, but clearly remembers him as a bright, idealistic student before he dropped out. But Jessica has the most memorable hallucination as she trips on "twelve." While flying high on the drug, she surrounds herself with her vast teddy bear collection, all of whom begin talking to her in harsh, taunting tones, a scene that borders on parody.

None of the performances here are particularly bad. The talented cast has a way of rising above the material they've been saddled with. *Twelve* even has moments that would work in a much better movie. The movie's best moment comes when socialite Sara, who is dying to have one of the biggest parties ever thrown in her honor in hopes of being hugely popular, comes clean and admits that if she met herself, she would hate herself. The same is probably true of most of these characters, yet it is not to the movie's benefit that the audience feels the same way having met everyone here. Molly is the only really likable person in the ensemble and even she is a bit of a bore.

The main problem with *Twelve,* other than its shallow, narcissistic characters, is that it lacks a point of view. There seems to be no purpose for telling this story other than to force feed its audience a tome on the dangers of high society drug use and parental abandonment. The movie builds up to the big party and it becomes plainly obvious as every storyline is laid out what each tragic outcome will be. Those who are less deserving of a horrible fate will probably be met with one regardless, while the dealers of such dead ends will continue to wallow in self pity and remorse for the rest of their lives.

Schumacher is not working outside of his element, but one feels when watching this movie that he is definitely repeating himself. He clearly loved and admired his characters in *St. Elmo's Fire,* and he obviously sympathizes with the doomed souls in *Twelve.* His problem is that he and screenwriter Jordan Melamed cannot get the audience on their side. "That's the way it is," Sutherland keeps reiterating in the narration. By the end, the viewer is left with little more insight than: A. There are rich prep school kids in New York whose parents do not pay attention to them. B. They are drug-addled. C. Don't do drugs. Whatever the message, there is something about *Twelve* that still makes it compulsively watchable, but the overall experience is tantamount to drinking lots of alcohol-free beer and still having a hangover.

Collin Souter

CREDITS

White Mike: Chace Crawford
Lionel: Curtis "50 Cent" Jackson
Molly: Emma Roberts
Chris: Rory Culkin
Charlie: Jeremy White
Claude: Billy Magnussen
Jessica: Emily Meade
Sara: Esti Ginzburg
Mark: Charlie Saxton
Andrew: Maxx Bauer
Nana: Jermaine Crawford
Hunter: Philip Ettinger
Narrator: Kiefer Sutherland
Origin: USA
Language: English
Released: 2010
Production: Ted Field, Charlie Corwin, Robert Salerno, Sidonie Dumas, Jordan Melamed; Radar Pictures, Original Media, Artina Films; released by Hannover House
Directed by: Joel Schumacher
Written by: Jordan Melamed
Cinematography by: Steven Fierberg
Music by: Harry Gregson-Williams
Sound: Richard Mader
Editing: Paul Zucker
Art Direction: Katya Debear
Costumes: David C. Robinson

Production Design: Ethan Tobman
MPAA rating: R
Running time: 94 minutes

REVIEWS

Abele, Robert, *Los Angeles Times.* August 6, 2010.
Anderson, Melissa. *Village Voice.* August 3, 2010.
Ellingston, Annlee, *Moving Pictures Magazine.* August 6, 2010.
Fry, Ted. *Seattle Times.* August 6, 2010.
Holden, Stephen. *New York Times.* August 6, 2010.
O'Hehir, Andrew. *Salon.com.* August 5, 2010.
Schenker, Andrew. *Slant Magazine.* August 3, 2010.
Schwarzbaum, Lisa. *Entertainment Weekly.* August 4, 2010.
Smith, Kyle. *New York Post.* August 6, 2010.
Whitty, Stephen. *Newark Star-Ledger.* August 6, 2010.

QUOTES

Sara Ludlow: "I have lots of boyfriends. I mean, I'm not a slut. But, different guys are interesting for different reasons. You're interesting for a very specific reason."

THE TWILIGHT SAGA: ECLIPSE

It all begins...with a choice.
   —Movie tagline

Box Office: $301 million

The *Twilight* films have two obvious angles to work when it come to attracting and keeping viewers: Make them care about the relationships between the characters or merely revel in the special effects that go hand-in-hand with movies featuring vampires and werewolves. *The Twilight Saga: Eclipse* accomplishes neither of these things. In a sense, far more than most adaptations of popular books into films, it is not a film in any real sense, playing instead like an overlong commercial for a CW made-for-TV movie event. This is cinema made especially for those who will invest in it for no other reason than it can be ignored as they use aspects of it to leap off into their own imaginative agendas.

The story opens with a cloying marriage proposal in a sunny meadow. Bella (Kristen Stewart) thinks marriage is just a piece of paper and wants Edward (Robert Pattinson) to simply bring her over to the vamp side. Edward has grave questions about whether she should become a vampire at all. The situation itself is adequately motivated but the dialogue is so bad here that right off the bat any geek worth their salt will make a comparison to the similar sickeningly sweet picnic scene featuring Padme and Anakin in *Star Wars: Episode II—Attack of the Clones* (2002). While the young couple navigates the dangers of their own uncertainty, other complicating factors arise. Bella is being hunted by Victoria (Bryce Dallas Howard) a vampire hungry for revenge against Edward, who killed her mate. She has turned a young man named Riley (Xavier Samuel) to help her create a small but incredibly vicious newly-undead army and it is only a matter of time before everyone Bella and Edward know is in the line of fire. To protect Bella, Edward and the other vampires, must enlist the aid of the were-wolves whose unwilling leader Jacob Black (Taylor Lautner) struggles with his own feelings of love for Bella. Deciding to use Bella and her scent as bait to draw out the newborns, the stage is set. No matter who wins this battle, Bella and Edward will have to live with decision of the Volturi, the law-givers and enforcers of the vampire clans who have come to pass judgment on the participants. Led by Jane (Dakota Fanning) the Volturi have the power of life and death. A battleground is chosen and a fierce and final confrontation will once and for all settle Bella's romantic fate.

Adapted by Melissa Rosenberg (as have been *Twilight* [2008], *The Twilight Saga: New Moon* [2009], and the upcoming *The Twilight Saga: Breaking Dawn* parts I [2011] and II [2012]) the TV feel of the film should come as no surprise. Rosenberg has made her living writing and producing a wide range of TV programming including a slightly interesting stint on *Dexter* (during what most critics consider a decline). The bulk of her work however is on decidedly less interesting stuff like *The O.C.* (2003-2004), *Birds of Prey* (2002-2003), and a screenplay for the dance film *Step Up* (2006). As viewers will imagine base on those credits this screenplay for *Eclipse* barely plays at all, never feeling like more than an inadequate expository scrunching together of the major plot points.

The performances here range from solid to almost unbearably bad. Pattinson and Stewart are excellent leads but they are playing through such a weak script that they seem horribly wooden. They are given little to do but drone on endlessly about the difficulties of their love and exposit the necessary bits of information that will allow filmmakers to get on to the next action sequence and the next film in the series. Kristen Stewart has been working steadily since her early teens and hardly needed the breakthrough offered by the *Twilight* series to maintain an uphill climb. The roles that best demonstrated her true range were well-reviewed films including *Panic Room* (2002), *Undertow* (2004), and *Into the Wild* (2007). Since the success of the *Twilight* franchise, she has continued to be involved in worthwhile projects such as the very funny and surprisingly poignant *Adventureland* (2009) and *Welcome to the Rileys* (2010). There is hope she will continue the trend of using her clout to develop her craft.

Prior to the *The Twilight Saga,* Robert Pattinson was easily best known for his role of Cedric Diggory in *Harry Potter and The Goblet of Fire* (2005). A recent attempt to do something outside the mainstream market, playing a young Salavador Dali in *Little Ashes* (2009), received solid reviews and Pattison generally shows himself to be a capable actor. Arguably, *Twilight* leaves him nowhere to go but up in all things except box office. Taylor Lautner is simply awful as Jacob Black, projecting nothing except his bare chest. It is notable that since his role of Sharkboy in *The Adventures of Sharkboy and Lava-Girl* (2005) he has continued to astound critics by being asked to appear in movies and act. Lautner has done nothing else substantial in his career except the not-very-good *Valentine's Day* (2010), which does not bode well for future employment in a profession for which he is clearly unsuited. Bryce Dallas Howard (*The Village* [2004], *Manderlay* [2005], *Lady in the Water* [2006]) has a very nice turn as the vengeful Victoria and, lastly, the amazing child actor Jodelle Ferland (*Tideland* [2005], *Silent Hill* [2006], *Case 39* [2009]) delivers a promising performance as Bree, a captured newborn who has been reprieved by Edward and his clan only to fall into the merciless hands of the Volturi.

Despite the range of success and failure, these are all young actors being asked to breathe life into an undead script. One can barely blame director David Slade for trying his hand here. His first feature was the brilliant *Hard Candy* (2005) and he followed it with the solid-if-dumbed-down *30 Days of Night* (2007). Prior to that, he was making music videos for Stone Temple Pilots and Aphex Twin, which is ironic considering most of his music video work has more substance to offer than a single scene in this lifeless gothic romance. The special effects here, something that Slade should have exerted more control over, are almost as disappointing as the script. CGI is badly used, making miracles that should seem seamless constantly jarring. There is barely an effect in this film that feels or looks natural.

Almost from the get-go, fans have been using phrases like "mindless entertainment" and "harmless eye-candy" to defend the *Twilight* series of books and films and the third film does not break the pattern. Romance (something different from love) is offered up as an emotional panacea in an age of exploding divorce rates, setting forth a story in a land where boobs will never sag, impotency is nonexistent, and real, inconvenient, painful, messy love, is almost completely beside the point. As a love story, this film is tepid and even offensive. As a supernatural drama the only thing creepy about *Eclipse* is the invitation to ogle the underage cast. The only moving thing about it is the sense that some talented people are contractually obligated to go make the next film in the series.

Dave Canfield

CREDITS

Bella Swan: Kristen Stewart
Edward Cullen: Robert Pattinson
Jacob Black: Taylor Lautner
Alice Cullen: Ashley Greene
Dr. Carlisle Cullen: Peter Facinelli
Esme Cullen: Elizabeth Reaser
Emmet Cullen: Kellan Lutz
Rosalie Hale: Nikki Reed
Jasper Hale: Jackson Rathbone
Victoria: Bryce Dallas Howard
Charlie Swan: Billy Burke
Jessica: Anna Kendrick
Jane: Dakota Fanning
Bree: Jodelle Ferland
Mike Newton: Michael Welch
Billy Black: Gil Birmingham
Angela: Christian Serratos
Leah Clearwater: Julia Jones
Alec: Cameron Bright
Lucy: Kirsten Prout
Renee Dwyer: Sarah Clarke
Maria: Catalina Sandino Moreno
Sam Uley: Chaske Spencer
Nettie: Leah Gibson
Paul: Alex Meraz
Riley: Xavier Samuel
Origin: USA
Language: English
Released: 2010
Production: Wyck Godfrey, Greg Mooradian, Karen Rosenfelt; Temple Hill Productions, Maverick Films, Imprint Entertainment, Sunswept Entertainment; released by Summit Entertainment
Directed by: David Slade
Written by: Melissa Rosenberg
Cinematography by: Javier Aguirresarobe
Music by: Howard Shore
Sound: James Kusan
Music Supervisor: Alexandra Patsavas
Editing: Art Jones, Nancy Richardson
Art Direction: Catherine Ircha
Costumes: Tish Monaghan
Production Design: Paul Denham Austerberry
MPAA rating: PG-13
Running time: 124 minutes

REVIEWS

Biodrowski, Steve. *Cinefantastique.* July 1, 2010.
Ebert, Roger. *Chicago Sun-Times.* June 29, 2010.
Gibron, Bill. *PopMatters.* June 30, 2010.
Howell, Peter. *Toronto Star.* June 29, 2010.
Kennedy, Lisa. *Denver Post.* June 30, 2010.
Kois, Dan. *Village Voice.* June 30, 2010.
Lybarger, Dan. *eFilmCritic.com.* June 30, 2010.
McDonagh, Maitland. *Miss FlickChick.* June 30, 2010.
Mondello, Bob. *NPR.* June 30. 2010.
Stevens, Dana. *Slate.* June 30, 2010.

QUOTES

Edward Cullen: "I know the consequences of the choices you're making. After a few decades, everyone you know will be dead."
Edward Cullen: "Bella, would you please stop trying to take your clothes off?"
Bella Swan: "This wasn't a choice between you and Jacob. It was a choice between who I am and who I should be."

TRIVIA

After she cut her hair to portray Joan Jett in the film *The Runaways*, Kirsten Stewart was forced to wear a wig to portray Bella Swan.

AWARDS

Golden Raspberries 2010: Worst Support. Actor (Rathbone)
Nomination:
Golden Raspberries 2010: Worst Picture, Worst Actor (Lautner, Pattinson), Worst Actress (Stewart), Worst Director (Slade), Worst Screenplay, Worst Couple/Ensemble (Cast), Worst Sequel/Prequel.

U–V

UNSTOPPABLE

1 million tons of steel. 100,000 lives at stake.
100 minutes to impact.
—Movie tagline

Box Office: $81 million

We interrupt this program for a special bulletin from the Metropolis news center: Reports indicate a speeding train containing hazardous chemicals is out of control. Children's lives are at stake! There are animals on the tracks! Corporate America does not care about the common citizen! This sounds like a job for Superman!

If only *Unstoppable* were a task for Superman. Then the movie would be entertainingly tongue-in-cheek instead of straight-faced and dull. In actuality, the guy trying to prevent disaster when an unmanned, 39-car Pennsylvania freight train rockets towards certain destruction is Frank (Denzel Washington), a 28-year railroad veteran who, like his blue-collar contemporaries, feels a bunch of young, undeserving kids are about to come in and take their jobs. Today Frank is teamed up with one of those very youngsters: Will (Chris Pine), an arrogant rookie who has only been on the job four months and is tired of being picked on for being green. Perhaps they are just the right odd couple to trade some banter and rise to the occasion when there is no other hope to stop train 777 from plummeting into Stanton, Pennsylvania, a town whose population of 752,000 includes Will's son and wife—who, for reasons Will absurdly explains during life-saving crunch time, has a restraining order out against him.

Nearly all of the circumstances about this deadly scenario, inspired by an actual runaway train in Ohio in 2001, unfold with cartoonish, clichéd extremeness that removes any sense that the film comes from reality. Of course, today is the day Will is supposed to have a hearing about reconnecting with his wife. Of course, today is the day Frank realizes he has yet to wish a happy birthday to one of his two daughters, both of whom work at Hooters in what seems like a gratuitous attempt to inject the film with a few seconds of sex appeal. Other blunt attempts at evoking drama and danger: A train packed with schoolchildren taking a field trip to learn about railway safety nearly collides with 777 in a sequence that Tony Scott fails to milk for suspense. (Scott shows the eyes of the concerned conductor but does not address the fear of the children or anyone else on board.) Horses and a horse trailer must be moved out of the way at the last minute to avoid the runaway locomotive, which train dispatcher Connie (Rosario Dawson) laughably refers to as "a missile the size of the Chrysler building." The train also has none of its usual hoses connected or air breaks activated thanks to the incompetence of railroad employee Dewey (Ethan Suplee), whose conspicuously aw-shucks name should have been the first sign that he would eventually execute a hapless screw-up like this.

Most of *Unstoppable* evokes more rolls of the eyes than gasps of suspense. This seems particularly inexcusable considering Scott and Washington already had a warm-up with their last film, the train-set remake of *The Taking of Pelham 123* (2009). That movie, based on the 1974 original, felt stale and outdated. *Unstoppable,* on the other hand, feels uninspired and trapped both by its commitment to action flick conventions and its circumstances. Because the train, unless it derails, must stay along the track, there is only so many times that Scott can show the train flying along and Frank and Will, eventually trying to hook their train to 777 to slow it down, figuring out how to get the job done. It just is not entertaining to watch someone drive a train, even in an urgent situation. Conversely, a runaway bus movie like *Speed* (1994) is able to draw considerable excitement from the swerving maneuvers of the star vehicle. To fill time away from the action, *Unstoppable* resorts to Connie unconvincingly and unprofessionally shouting empty directions like "Will, you can do this!" from headquarters while a safety expert (Kevin Corrigan) spouts train terminology like "trip a relay." This would be boring even if it seemed like the actors cared about what they were doing, but the dryness in their voices suggests otherwise. Dawson obviously knows she is saddled with a thankless role in a totally unnecessary movie, and she is too honest an actress to fake conviction she does not believe. Even Pine, who possessed a lot of cocky swagger in *Star Trek,* cannot muster the spark to make Will a hero worth rooting for.

Washington, however, could play a role like Frank in his sleep, but he is the film's one human element that does not coast. Like so many unlikely heroes, Frank knows it all and knows he can ultimately prove that everyone else is wrong, but Washington's charisma and million-dollar smile make it hard not to like this seasoned railroader anyway. Except for too long all Frank has to do is bark orders about what should be done. When he ultimately runs across the top of the train as it speeds along, the scene just seems like a last-ditch attempt at something pulse-pounding in a film that makes explosions and 10 million runaway pounds of train at best shrug-worthy and at worst accidentally funny.

These unintended laughs occur throughout, whether troopers foolishly fire at train 777 and nearly ignite a fuel tank or corporate fat cats care more about playing golf and their stock status than the lives at risk if the deadly train crashes into Stanton and other towns on the way. It is fine for a thriller to deliver a few chuckles, but they have to be on purpose. When viewers laugh at an action movie, not with it, any hope for thrills has likely disappeared, whether or not the director knows how to competently stage a chase scene. Scott does know this, but he does not know the difference between organic tension and forced tension. That is why frequent notes about how there is a high school right next to the tracks or that the train contains a toxic, combustible chemical used to make glue sound ridiculous and diffuse, not amplify, the mayhem. *Unstoppable* boasts a promisingly straightforward concept for an action

blockbuster, but its execution falls somewhere closer to a *South Park* parody of the genre.

Matt Pais

CREDITS

Frank Barnes: Denzel Washington
Will Gordon: Chris Pine
Connie Hooper: Rosario Dawson
Bunny: Kevin Chapman
Dewey: Ethan Suplee
Oscar Galvin: Kevin Dunn
Ins. Scott Werner: Kevin Corrigan
Origin: USA
Language: English
Released: 2010
Production: Eric McLeod, Mimi Rogers, Tony Scott, Julie Yorn, Alex Young; released by 20th Century Fox
Directed by: Tony Scott
Written by: Mark Bomback
Cinematography by: Ben Seresin
Music by: Harry Gregson-Williams
Costumes: Penny Rose
Production Design: Chris Seagers
Editing: Robert Duffy, Chris Lebenzon
Sound: Mark P. Stoeckinger
MPAA rating: PG-13
Running time: 98 minutes

REVIEWS

Berardinelli, James. *Reelviews.* November 10, 2010.
Dargis, Manohla. *New York Times.* November 11, 2010.
Ebert, Roger. *Chicago Sun-Times.* November 11, 2010.
Goodykoontz, Bill. *Arizona Republic.* November 10, 2010.
Morgenstern, Joe. *Wall Street Journal.* November 11, 2010.
Rea, Stephen. *Philadelphia Enquirer.* November 12, 2010.
Rodriguez, Rene. *Miami Herald.* November 10, 2010.
Smith, Kyle. *New York Post.* November 11, 2010.
Williams, Joe. *St. Louis Post-Dispatch.* November 11, 2010.
Zacharek, Stephanie. *Movieline.* November 12, 2010.

QUOTES

Frank: "This ain't training. In training they just give you an F. Out here you get killed."

TRIVIA

This is Tony Scott's fifth time directing Denzel Washington.

The plot is based on an actual runaway train incident that occurred in Ohio in 2001.

AWARDS

Nomination:

Oscars 2010: Sound FX Editing.

VALENTINE'S DAY

A love story. More or less.
—Movie tagline

Box Office: $110 million

The wonderful romantic drama *Once* (2007) did not suffer for its lack of big Hollywood stars. Likewise, the excruciatingly earnest ensemble love story *Valentine's Day* is not improved just because nearly everyone in the cast has a recognizable face.

Not only are they familiar actors who may know each other off-screen; the characters in *Valentine's Day* are so absurdly interconnected that viewers who do not know any better may suspect that only nineteen people live in Los Angeles. They may also wonder if anyone knew the camera was running; in a cast populated by huge movie stars like Julia Roberts and Jamie Foxx (cough, both Oscar® winners, cough) and big television stars like Patrick Dempsey, Ashton Kutcher, and Jennifer Garner, only singer Taylor Swift delivers a performance of any comic cleverness. Yes, that Taylor Swift, who sings songs with deep messages like "Today Was a Fairytale," which even plays in the background late in *Valentine's Day* as Felicia (Swift) makes out with Willy (Taylor Lautner).

The film is the sort of overcrowded ensemble piece that needs more than a half-hour to introduce all its characters. It is a movie featuring people with names like Morley, Edison, Holden, and Reed; names that have been scientifically proven to never exist together in one group of people, except maybe as contestants on *The Bachelor*. *Valentine's Day* uses clichés like "head over heels" without even considering the lack of meaning behind them. Most painfully, the movie is about absolutely nothing other than love, despite the fact that the film knows virtually nothing about the subject. Possibly less.

Out of the approximately 3,412 subplots, the one given priority is the emotional rollercoaster for flower shop owner Reed (Kutcher). The morning of Valentine's Day, he is elated after getting engaged to Morley (Jessica Alba), whose hesitation makes it less than surprising when she breaks things off a few hours later. Of course, Reed does not react to this the way most jilted fiancées would. No, he must provide one of the film's many romantic clichés and rush to the airport to stop his best friend Julia (Garner) from boarding a plane. If he fails, she may discover that her boyfriend, Dr. Harrison Copeland (Dempsey), is still married. Luckily, none of these heartbreaking episodes is apparently enough to prevent Reed or Julia from finding love by the end of the day. Anyone who thinks that is a spoiler should remind themselves that this is a movie called *Valentine's*

Day, directed by Garry Marshall, who previously labored to make prostitution (*Pretty Woman* [1990]) and sexual abuse (*Georgia Rule* [2007]) lighthearted and charming for mainstream audiences.

It is thus no surprise that Marshall strains to squeeze lovey-dovey nonsense into every frame of *Valentine's Day*, which will unite romantics and non-romantics in that both camps will find the movie irritating. Writer Katherine Fugate, on the other hand, does not know the difference between real love and phony sentimentality. That is why Reed makes hollow statements like "Love is the only shocking act left on the planet" that are based on absolutely nothing. That does not come across as a profound statement of feeling. It sounds more like a fortune cookie message that even the most superstitious diner would shrug off and throw away.

A brief run-through of the many other groan-worthy moments from other characters: Publicist Kara (Jessica Biel) binges on candy because, obviously, someone as beautiful and well-connected as her cannot possibly find a companion. Liz (Anne Hathaway) moonlights as a phone sex operator during her job as a receptionist, and, amazingly, her boss Paula (Queen Latifah) does not mind, as long as Liz answers Paula's calls first. On live TV, Kelvin (Foxx) says to a gay football player who just came out of the closet, "I stand behind you. Metaphorically." In real life, that kind of blatant homophobia would get a television reporter suspended, maybe even fired. In the far-fetched, laugh-free world of *Valentine's Day*, Kelvin's boss (Kathy Bates) praises and supports him.

Romantic comedies are not always believable, and they do not necessarily need to be. However, *Valentine's Day* never delivers any clever dialogue or interesting conflict to suggest that the film qualifies as an entertaining snack. Its revolving door of insignificant and childish dramas is more akin to fattening, regrettable rubbish, like eating a week-old chocolate heart out of the garbage. In breezily enjoyable films, the musical cues are not so noticeably lazy, such as when Foreigner's "Feels like the First Time" plays while Alex (Carter Jenkins) prepares to have sex with his girlfriend Grace (Emma Roberts) for the, ahem, first time. Effortless crowd pleasers also create likable characters that speak like real people, not as if their words are a result of a writer trying and failing to be clever. When young Edison (Bryce Robinson) compliments a girl in his class because "She's the only other fifth grader that has Frank Zappa on her iPod," it does not sound cute. It comes off as a hard-to-believe detail offered for characters about who viewers know very little in the first place.

A few sweet moments would be enough to justify all this cheesiness in a film as obvious in its intentions as one titled *Valentine's Day*. Yet, by never establishing any of its characters as relatable people—as opposed to one-dimensional movie character types—*Valentine's Day* prevents its audience from caring about anyone's big-screen love life. Particularly when Estelle (Shirley MacLaine) informs her husband Edgar (Hector Elizondo), whom she just confessed to cheating on, that "When you love someone, you love all of them; that's the job." In other words, she speaks generally to imply that infidelity is just a small matter of which love requires understanding, which goes against most marital vows. Nope, for lessons in love, the best thing *Valentine's Day* has to offer is Liz noting that V-Day is the busiest day of the year for phone sex. How profound.

Matt Pais

CREDITS

Captain Kate Hazeltine: Julia Roberts
Liz: Anne Hathaway
Morley Clarkson: Jessica Alba
Kara Monahan: Jessica Biel
Julia Fitzpatrick: Jennifer Garner
Estelle: Shirley MacLaine
Paula Thomas: Queen Latifah
Holden: Bradley Cooper
Reed Bennett: Ashton Kutcher
Kelvin Moore: Jamie Foxx
Jason: Topher Grace
Grace: Emma Roberts
Felicia: Taylor Swift
Edgar: Hector Elizondo
Alphonso: George Lopez
Dr. Harrison Copeland: Patrick Dempsey
Sean Jackson: Eric Dane
Susan: Kathy Bates
Willy: Taylor Lautner
Alex: Carter Jenkins
Edison: Bryce Robinson
Origin: USA
Language: English
Released: 2010
Production: Mike Karz, Josie Rosen, Wayne Allan Rice; Karz Entertainment, Rice Films; released by New Line Cinema
Directed by: Garry Marshall
Written by: Katherine Fugate
Cinematography by: Charles Minsky
Music by: John Debney
Sound: Jeff Wexler
Music Supervisor: Julianne Jordan
Editing: Bruce Green
Art Direction: Adrian Gorton

Costumes: Gary Jones
Production Design: Albert Brenner
MPAA rating: PG-13
Running time: 125 minutes

REVIEWS

Ebert, Roger. *Chicago Sun-Times.* February 10, 2010.
Jones, Kimberley. *Austin Chronicle.* February 12, 2010.
Lumenick, Lou. *New York Post.* February 13, 2010.
Morris, Wesley. *Boston Globe.* February 12, 2010.
Phillips, Michael. *Chicago Tribune.* February 11, 2010.
Rabin, Nathan. *AV Club.* February 11, 2010.
Rickey, Carrie. *Philadelphia Inquirer.* February 12, 2010.
Rodriguez, Rene. *Miami Herald.* February 11, 2010.
Schwarzbaum, Lisa. *Entertainment Weekly.* February 12, 2010.
Stevens, Dana. *Slate.* February 11, 2010.

QUOTES

Kara Monahan: "My closest relationship is with my Blackberry, thank God it vibrates!"

TRIVIA

The cast featured six previous Oscar® nominees including Julia Roberts, Kathy Bates, Jamie Foxx, Anne Hathaway, Queen Latifah, and Shirley MacLaine.

AWARDS

Golden Raspberries 2010: Worst Actor (Kutcher), Worst Support. Actress (Alba)

Nomination:

Golden Raspberries 2010: Worst Actor (Lautner), Worst Support. Actor (Lopez).

VALHALLA RISING

In his book, *The Idea of the Holy*, Rudolf Otto talks about God in terms of the ineffable—a sort of natural terror and inability to speak that man feels on encountering the divine. It is an idea that seems especially relevant and urgent at a time when war and religion seem almost joined at the hip. In *Valhalla Rising*, writer-director Nicolas Winding Refn takes both subjects head on, utilizing a character who does not speak, transcending war and religion through revelation. In Refn's ancient Viking vision, man must meet the ineffable to encounter meaning or risk destruction amidst an almost alien landscape of war-torn natural wonders.

Refn chooses to tell his story in six clearly labeled sections. "Part I: Wrath" introduces us to a one-eyed warrior prisoner forced to fight for money by a Norse tribe. He is a silent deadly adversary to all who are unfortunate enough to face him and the tribe's only real source of income. His long years of imprisonment come to an end when he overpowers his keepers and escapes only to find himself followed by a young child. In "Part II: Silent Warrior," the pair's journey is interrupted when they stumble upon a small band of Christian warriors who invite them to join them in their mission to visit the Holy Land and convert unbelievers. In "Part III: Men of God," the travelers find themselves afloat, lost in an unforgiving glassy sea with no wind and provisions running low. They argue amongst themselves regarding who is to blame, wondering if One Eye and/or the boy have brought a curse with them. In "Part IV: The Holy Land," the boat drifts ashore to a place that the group's leader proclaims as the Holy Land. In "Part V: Hell," they realize that this new found land has nothing for them to eat and they face starvation as well as hostile unseen natives. Convinced that One Eye has indeed brought them to hell they turn on one another. In "Part VI: Sacrifice," One Eye and the boy, having escaped the other warriors, find themselves face-to-face with the mysterious natives. Unable to communicate, One Eye realizes he must sacrifice himself for the child.

Mads Mikkelsen is absolutely riveting as One Eye. Mikkelsen first became widely known for his appearance in the Dogma film *Open Hearts* (2002). His follow-up, *Wilbur Wants to Kill Himself* (2002) only solidified his appeal to a wider audience signaling that he was a talent to watch. Since then he has appeared in the widest variety of roles possible, distinguishing himself each time. Those interested in more of his work will enjoy *Coco Chanel & Igor Stravinsky* (2009) and the American Bond films *Quantum of Solace* (2008) and *Casino Royale* (2006), but by no means should viewers miss the less-renowned *Flame and Citron* (2008), *After the Wedding* (2006), or especially the grim and hilarious *The Green Butchers* (2003).

Valhalla Rising will be a love or hate affair for most viewers but that makes it little different than most of writer-director Nicolas Winding Refn's work. His much acclaimed *Pusher Trilogy* (*Pusher* [1999], *With Blood on My Hands: Pusher II* [2004], *I'm The Angel of Death* [2005]) and *Bronson* (2008) certainly pushed the limits of what most would want to watch in the name of entertainment. But, then again, Refn has always clearly been about more than envelope-pushing than straightforward narratives. This is hardly some half-baked exercise in genre-posing as thought piece. Instead, *Valhalla Rising* almost comes across as a meditation. No doubt some will charge the film with being too simple, boring in fact, due to the stark nature of the imagery and the overtly symbolic cinematography. The many foreboding dream sequences for instance utilize primary-colored, often motionless figures set against nearly black-and-

white backgrounds. *Valhalla Rising* is almost devoid of dialogue, Refn choosing instead to tell his story through the starkest possible means like close-ups and long takes. Reviewers have invoked Lynch, Malick, and even Bergman in their attempts to come to grips with the power here and while Refn is certainly no Bergman, he has demonstrated he is much more than some one-trick-pony over the course of his career. Even his lesser known films like *Fear X* (2003) showcase a profound sense of cinema and of the mise-en-scène that makes for truly memorable storytelling.

Far from being self indulgent, Refn is instead employing the most basic of artifice in an attempt to bring up a sense of the primal, the quiet stillness, the horror of a fallen world and of revelation. Man, intent on saving himself in order to gain the world, finds only the barren landscape, the blood, and the fruitless struggle. His attempts to clothe himself in the righteousness of a religious cause lead only to his destruction. *Valhalla Rising* says that it is only when man truly sacrifices himself to the transcendent that man matters because, in a violent world, man must love even in the face of death.

Dave Canfield

CREDITS

One Eye: Mads Mikkelsen
Are: Maarten Stevenson
Hagen: Gordon Brown
Duggal: Andrew Flanagan
Kare: Gary Lewis
Hawk: Gary McCormack
Barde: Alexander Morgan
Gorm: Jamie Sieves
Origin: Denmark
Language: English
Released: 2009
Production: Johnny Anderson, Bo Ehrhardt, Henrik Danstrup; Nimbus Film, Blind Eye Prods., La Belle Allee Prods., Scanbox; released by IFC
Directed by: Nicolas Winding Refn
Written by: Nicolas Winding Refn, Roy Jacobsen
Cinematography by: Morten Soborg
Music by: Peter Kyed
Sound: Cameron Mercer
Editing: Mat Newman
Costumes: Gill Horn
Production Design: Maurel Wear
MPAA rating: Unrated
Running time: 90 minutes

REVIEWS

Abele, Robert. *Los Angeles Times.* July 23, 2010.
Austwick, Ben. *Quiet Earth.* October 23, 2010.

Cabin, Chris. *FilmCritic.com.* July 16, 2010.
Chang, Dustin. *Twitch Film.* July 16, 2010.
Hale, Mike. *New York Times.* July 16, 2010.
Halligan, Fionnuala. *Screen Daily.* September 6, 2010.
Knoll, Paul. *Metro Times.* September 15, 2010.
Kohn, Eric. *indieWire.* July 12, 2010.
Ramos, Steve. *Box Office Magazine.* July 16, 2010.
Rizov, Vadim. *Village Voice.* July 13, 2010.

QUOTES

Kare: "I am going to show them that a man of God has arrived."

Viking chief: "They only have one God. We have many."

TRIVIA

Mads Mikkelsen has no dialogue film and the other characters combined have only around 120 lines.

VAMPIRES SUCK

Some sagas just won't die.
—Movie tagline

Box Office: $37 million

It is difficult to believe that a parody of the *Twilight* (2008) franchise would be that difficult to pull together. The vampire romance series openly and flagrantly mocks everything that is good and right about vampire movies all by itself without the assistance of joke writers and celebrity impersonators. Still, the ever-reliable comedy writer-director team of Jason Friedberg and Aaron Seltzer, whose writing partnership includes the far better *Scary Movie* (2000) series, have coughed up *Vampires Suck,* another in a interminably long string of movies that barely seem timely when they are released and certainly feel dated by the time their next 'masterpiece' arrives in theaters a year later. What Friedberg and Seltzer fail to understand is that simply recognizing which movies they are parodying does not mean that the joke is in any way funny. With film after film— including *Date Movie* (2006), *Epic Movie* (2007), *Meet the Spartans* (2008), *Disaster Movie* (2008)—this terrible twosome has drifted further and further away from what parody and righteous silliness used to be about, as established in the king of all films of this ilk, *Airplane!* (1980).

Perhaps the biggest let-down regarding *Vampires Suck* is that some of the key cast members seem up to the task of doing something worthy of a laugh or two. In particular, Jenn Proske's Becca is a dead-on impersonation of Kristen Stewart's Bella from the *Twilight* saga. Proske has Stewart's mannerisms, vocal quirks and posture absolutely perfect. If someone had taken the time to write her some humorous dialogue then this movie might have at least garnered some positive reactions. Instead, the filmmakers toss Becca into the *Twilight* story of being caught in a love triangle between moody vampire Edward Sullen (Matt Lanter) and a muscle-bound werewolf Jacob White (Chris Riggi). Apparently, changing the last names Cullen to Sullen and Black to White is someone's idea of actual comedy prose.

Instead of *Scary Movie*-style, R-rated humor that actually plays with the idea of pent-up teen hormones, we get jokes about werewolves scratching and licking themselves inappropriately, and cameos by or references to celebrities such as the Kardashians, the cast of *Jersey Shore,* and Tiger & Elin Woods. But the best of the look-a-likes are saved for those parodying the various actors in the *Twilight* movies. With so little time spent with peripheral characters, the audience is left with fleeting glimpses of somewhat familiar faces and are stuck thinking, "Oh, there's the red-headed vampire" or "There's the one with dreadlocks." What is also strange about the film is that it seems to focus only on the first two films in the franchise, *Twilight* (2008) and *The Twilight Saga: New Moon* (2009), despite the fact that it was released about two months after the third film, *The Twilight Saga: Eclipse* (2010), making *Vampires Suck* feel all the more out of touch.

Becca leaves her mother's house and ends up living with her father in the Pacific Northwest supernatural epicenter Sporks. (See, how they changed the name from Forks? Comedy gold.) There she meets Edward and his family of pasty vampires. Naturally the filmmakers play with *Twilight* writer Stephenie Meyer's philosophies on celibacy, as well as the franchise's vampire sparkle when the sun hits their skin. And none of it will bring a laugh. About the only laughs in *Vampires Suck* come from Ken Jeong as Daro, leader of the Zolturi, but most of that humor comes from Jeong being an inherently funny guy and not from any of the words in this flaccid screenplay. It is eerie how unnatural pauses in the dialogue can be sensed as the characters wait for laughter that will never come.

Terrible, cheap-looking sight gags, which tend to amount to little more than someone putting on a bad wig, stand side by side with miserable one-liners, toilet humor, and sex jokes that get about as explicit as a PG-13 rating will allow will make audiences long for the days when Anna Farris led the *Scary Movie* franchise into some seriously risque territory. Perhaps the worst thing about *Vampires Suck* is how terribly safe everything is played. The times when the parody elements seem to work the best is when Friedberg and Seltzer are not trying so hard. The closer they mimic the *Twilight* stories, the more idiotic the source material appears, not that it needed much help. If only the cast had gone the extra mile and really tore into just how poor Pattinson and Lautner are as actors. And while it seems like the better idea to target one movie and dissect it down to its shallow core, the filmmakers cannot resist the opportunity to go broad and include name-checks of reality-show stars and recreate scenes from other horror films in the year prior to *Vampires Suck*'s release.

The question needs to be asked: What do fans of the *Twilight* movies think of *Vampires Suck*? In a perfect world, they would acknowledge the shortcomings of the books and movies, and as a result would get more out of this parody than the average filmgoers. It is difficult to imagine that even the most passionate fan would react any differently to a movie loaded with dreadful vampire puns, with Friedberg and Seltzer never missing an opportunity to grab for the lowest-hanging fruit. Even then, they miss the mark most of the time. Rather than openly mock the faux angst and melodrama of the *Twilight* saga, the filmmakers suffocate the audience with dreck disguised as humor. If they had waited to make this movie until after the *Twilight* films had run their course, the makers of *Vampires Suck* might have had the true last word on this series. But easy money trumps their version of art, and this sad little movie is proof.

Steven Prokopy

CREDITS

Edward Sullen: Matt Lanter
Frank Crane: Diedrich Bader
Daro: Ken Jeong
Jennifer: Anneliese van der Pol
Fisherman Sulley: David DeLuise
Principal Smith: Dave Foley
Rachel: Arielle Kebbel
Becca Crane: Jenn Proske
Jacob White: Chris Riggi
Iris: Kelsey Ford
Dr. Carlton: Jeff Witzke
Origin: USA
Language: English
Released: 2010
Production: Peter Safran, Jason Friedberg, Aaron Seltzer; Regency Enterprises, New Regency, Three in the Box; released by 20th Century Fox
Directed by: Jason Friedberg, Aaron Seltzer
Written by: Jason Friedberg, Aaron Seltzer
Cinematography by: Shawn Maurer
Music by: Christopher Lennertz
Sound: Steve Aaron

Music Supervisor: Dave Jordan, JoJo Villanueva
Editing: Peck Prior
Art Direction: Kevin Hardison
Costumes: Alix Hester
Production Design: William A. "Bill" Elliott
MPAA rating: PG-13
Running time: 82 minutes

REVIEWS

Abrams, Simon. *SlantMagazine.com*. August 18, 2010.
Biodrowski, Steve. *CinefantastiqueOnline.com*. August 18, 2010.
Catsoulis, Jeannette. *New York Times*. August 18, 2010.
Hartlaub, Peter. *San Francisco Chronicle*. August 19, 2010.
Minzey, Lisa. *TheRealCritic.com*. August 17, 2010.
Orndorf, Brian. *BrianOrndorf.com*. August 18, 2010.
Rogne, Marit. *MovieRetriever.com*. August 21, 2010.
Savlov, Marc. *Austin Chronicle*. August 27, 2010.
Propes, Richard. *TheIndependentCritic.com*. August 18, 2010.
Tyler, Josh. *CinemaBlend.com*. August 18, 2010.

QUOTES

Edward Sullen: "Every time I bring a girl over, you try to eat her! It's not fair!"

AWARDS

Nomination:

Golden Raspberries 2010: Worst Picture, Worst Director (Friedberg, Seltzer), Worst Screenplay, Worst Sequel/Prequel.

VINCERE
(Victory)
(Win)

The lingering, nagging question left at the end of *Vincere* (translated from Italian as "Win") is not an easy one to dismiss, as it relates to perhaps the most vital element for the account to work: authenticity. Conveying the story of Ida Dalser (Giovanna Mezzogiorno), the alleged first wife of Italian dictator and one of the key originators of Fascism, Benito Mussolini (Filippo Timi), the director Marco Bellocchio and co-screenwriter Daniela Ceselli play fast and loose with facts. The primary reason is because—as is stated directly at the movie's coda—there are none known to fully support this tale.

Aside from its lack of a solid historical foundation, *Vincere* falters as drama. The movie opens with Mussolini, then a union representative and member of the Socialist Party, proposing a theological argument: He will give God five minutes to kill him, otherwise it proves that a higher power does not exist. Dalser looks on in awe as her lover stands in defiance against religious leaders and what they represent. Mezzogiorno spends most of the movie's opening act staring at her romantic opposite with wide-eyed reverence and amour, while Timi, a staunch presence, implies an unwavering ambition with his own gaze. The contrast is established firmly in a sex scene between Dalser and Mussolini, in which she begs him to say he loves her. He looks not at but beyond her—to war and the promise of power.

Bellocchio incorporates archival footage of the era (1907-1945) into the narrative as newsreel footage and exposition ("War," cries the flying text as Italy enters World War I), and a few brief images of animation (soldiers goose-stepping, for example) have the effect of entering Mussolini's mind as he envisions his own future. They compliment Daniele Ciprì's stark cinematography, washed out in certain scenes to a near lack of color.

The opening act, which details Mussolini's move from Socialism toward nationalism, is when the movie works. Bellocchio and Ceselli show a man who arranges events in his life to act in his favor. The threat of war is an opportunity to ride the wave of populism—a sense of national pride—and hence eradicate his political views and ties. Mussolini starts critical of the Catholic Church and King Victor Emmanuel III in protest and rallies ("With the guts of the last Pope we'll strangle the last King!"). He launches his own newspaper (*Il Popolo d'Italia,* keeping the word of still being one with the people, if not the spirit) for the purposes of warmongering and to inflate his own persona, including misreporting about a duel he loses.

Meanwhile, Dalser sells everything she owns, gives birth to Mussolini's first son, and continues to look upon him with adoration. After the war, he marries Rachele (Michela Cescon), abandoning Dalser and his namesake to a life of poverty and shame.

Mezzogiorno's performance here shifts to unblinking detachment, and Dalser, later confined to an asylum for women after she refuses to deny her marriage to Mussolini (seen in flashback) or produce the marriage certificate she claims to possess (she hides it before any of Mussolini's government cronies can steal and destroy it), quickly becomes unsympathetic in her stubbornness. Despite a cavalcade of people who offer to help, including her brother-in-law (Fausto Russo Alesi), who maintains guardianship of young Benito (Fabrizio Costella) until the boy to sent to his own exile at a private school, and a doctor (Corrado Invernizzi), who offers to help free her, she will not back down.

The scene with the doctor is key. Here is a man who is critical of Mussolini and Fascism but deems it necessary to play a role for the moment. The Dalser of Bellocchio and Ceselli's script is neither fighting the man nor the government; she is simply yelling to be heard. Given the opportunity to state her case and gain her freedom, she figuratively throws her hands up in rebellion by literally throwing her body across the evaluators' table. Young Benito, meanwhile, offers a similar, useless revolt by knocking the bust of his father's likeness off its pedestal at the school and later, as a young man (also played by Timi), aping Mussolini's speech in brash caricature.

As an allegory for the control of Mussolini's government over its people—even and especially those who supported him at the start—the movie is clear. Playing that allegory out as a personal drama is its misstep. The story becomes repetitive; the drama becomes more about gestures than characters. Carlo Crivelli's bombastic score of trilling woodwinds playing sliding scales underneath operatic vocals mirrors the reliance on affectation. *Vincere* moves beyond its natural climax after Dalser's outburst and self-condemnation. By the time Bellocchio suggests through a final montage that Mussolini's treatment of her is a precursor to World War II, the movie has lost even its political nuance.

Mark Dujsik

CREDITS

Rachele Giudi: Michela Cescon
Pietro Fedele: Piergiorgio Bellocchio
Giulio Bernardi: Paolo Pierobon
Benito Albino: Fabrizio Costella
Ida Dalser: Giovanna Mezzogiorno
Benito Mussolini: Filippo Timi
Ricardo Paicher: Fausto Russo Alesi
Giudice: Bruno Cariello
Adelina: Francesca Picozza
Dottor Cappelletti: Corrado Invernizzi
Origin: Italy, France
Language: Italian
Released: 2009
Production: Mario Gianani; RAI Cinema, Celluloid Dreams, Offside; released by IFC Films
Directed by: Marco Bellocchio
Written by: Daniela Ceselli, Marco Bellocchio
Cinematography by: Daniele Cipri
Music by: Carlo Crivelli
Sound: Gaetano Carito
Editing: Francesca Calvelli
Costumes: Sergio Ballo
Production Design: Marco Dentici

MPAA rating: Unrated

Running time: 128 minutes

REVIEWS

Berardinelli, James. *Reelviews.net.* April 1, 2010.
Covert, Colin. *Star Tribune.* April 9, 2010.
Ebert, Roger. *Chicago Sun-Times.* March 31, 2010.

Hartl, John. *Seattle Times.* April 1, 2010.
Martin, Philip. *Arkansas Democrat-Gazette.* May 14, 2010.
Morris, Wesley. *Boston Globe.* April 2, 2010.
Pulver, Andrew. *Guardian.* May 13, 2010.
Rea, Steven. *Philadelphia Inquirer.* April 2, 2010.
Robey, Tim. *Daily Telegraph.* May 13, 2010.
Sharkey, Betsy. *Los Angeles Times.* March 26, 2010.

W–Y

WAITING FOR 'SUPERMAN'

The fate of our country won't be decided on a battlefield, it will be determined in a classroom.
—Movie tagline

Box Office: $6 million

In 1999, documentary filmmaker Davis Guggenheim made a documentary called *The First Year,* in which he followed five different public school teachers during their very first year at teaching, which many say is the hardest year of them all. Now, eleven years later, Guggenheim finds himself the father of a child with a choice between a public school education and a private school one. Guggenheim says at the beginning of his documentary *Waiting for 'Superman'* that he has enrolled his kids into a private school and that he is fully aware how lucky he is to be able to afford that choice. This education, he believes, will ensure his kids a brighter and better future and will allow them to move on to better, more reputable schools as they get older. Thus begins the documentary's central question: Just what is wrong with public education and why does the alternative seem so unattainable?

The questions have endless answers and Guggenheim does the best he can to tackle most of them. Much like he did with *The First Year,* he intercuts many facts, figures and testimonials with narrative arcs (such as they are). Six kids spread throughout the United States and with varying degrees of status (from a well-off teenager in San Francisco to a fifth grader in Washington, D.C.,

which has the worst education record in the country), Guggenheim essentially tells the same story several times over: These kids are at the mercy of a lottery, whereby the luck of the draw determines whether or not they can go to a more prestigious school and get out of their somewhat doomed situation in a public school. They have the grades, the determination and the desire. They just need to be lucky enough to have their numbers drawn. Odds are against them, of course. Summit Prep School, for example, has only 135 open spaces with 455 applicants.

What the movie lacks in narrative momentum, though, it more than makes up for in compelling testimonials and startling revelations. Guggenheim takes on the problems of teacher unions and how they tend to protect their own at any cost. New York, it is said, spends $800,000 a year on its teacher's trials for whatever crimes they committed while these same teachers sit in a room all day doing nothing while still collecting paychecks. Guggenheim often employs animation to illustrate such statistics, such as the Turkey Trots or Lemon Dances, whereby public schools will often trade out their worst performing teachers to other schools in the area in exchange for better ones, while those poor teachers still get jobs within the system. Thanks to the inflexibility of the teachers union, it is almost impossible to lose a job as a teacher.

There are those out there, of course, who are doing their damndest to make a difference, the most controversial being Michelle Rhee, a newly appointed 37-year-old Chancellor of Education in Washington D.C. Rhee took it upon herself to take drastic measures by closing several schools and laying off countless teachers, much to the dismay of the many communities who depended on those schools for their children, no matter how bad they were. In a political climate that demands quick results, Rhee's measures and policies would take a lot of time before the effects would be seen. She eventually became vilified for her actions. Guggenheim forgets to mention that such measures also lead to over-crowding classrooms, which just makes things worse for everyone involved.

There are also the matters of tenure, massive school boards (also known as "the blob") and communities that produce "drop-out factories" rather than educational institutions. The chances of getting a solid education in a public school setting are random and remote. There is no telling what kind of teacher a student might get in any given year in any given subject. Guggenheim asks the question: Do failing neighborhoods automatically produce failing schools? Not necessarily. A school can have all the money and resources at its disposal, but a teacher with tenure can just as well read to the students from an old textbook and pass them through the system without the slightest bit of interest in engaging them or taking an active interest in the ones who do not understand the lessons. Some of Guggenheim's findings lack a truly relevant punch (of course it costs more to run a prison than a private school), but the end results of the narratives—particularly Rhee's attempt at a wage reform in the teachers union—are true eye-openers. The "Superman" in the title refers to an elusive, make-believe savior of the education system that does not really exist.

Obviously, the climax of the film are the various lotteries and the fate of the students that Guggenheim has been following. The tension and suspense is earned and the kids are likable and interesting enough to get to know. But getting into these schools has a personal cost as well as an educational reward. Anthony, a fifth grader who lives with his grandmother, needs to get out of the Washington D.C. school district, but that will mean leaving his grandmother and friends. "It will be bittersweet if I get in," he says.

Most documentaries fly under the radar and end up at maybe one or two art houses per major metropolitan area, but Paramount Vantage went all out on a marketing campaign for this film, and with good reason. Guggenheim won the Academy Award® in 2006 for filming Al Gore's environmental power point presentation in *An Inconvenient Truth*. The subject of education is almost universal and Guggenheim effectively engages his audience until the very end when the film dissolves into vague platitudes and constant requests for the audience to text a number, so as to land on the movie's text message list while playing not one, but two cloying John Legend songs (*An Inconvenient Truth* also won the Academy Award® for Best Song, a feat this movie is trying for two-fold). Time will tell if the marketing campaign worked, but as a movie, *Waiting For 'Superman'* is as good a movie as one could hope for on an endless subject.

Collin Souter

CREDITS

Origin: USA
Language: English
Released: 2010
Production: Leslie Chilcott; Participant Media, Electric Kinney; released by Paramount Vantage
Directed by: Davis Guggenheim
Written by: Davis Guggenheim, Billy Kimball
Cinematography by: Erich Roland
Music by: Christophe Beck
Sound: Skip Lievsay
Music Supervisor: John Houlihan
Editing: Greg Finton, Jay Cassidy, Kim Roberts
MPAA rating: PG
Running time: 102 minutes

REVIEWS

Denby, David. *New Yorker*. October 11, 2010.
Ebert, Roger. *Chicago Sun-Times*. September 30, 2010.
Edelstein, David. *New York Magazine*. September 20, 2010.
Holden, Stephen. *New York Times*. September 24, 2010.
Jones, J.R. *Chicago Reader*. October 8, 2010.
Long, Tom. *Detroit News*. October 8, 2010.
Morgenstern, Joe. *Wall Street Journal*. September 23, 2010.
Null, Christopher. *Filmcritic.com*. October 14, 2010.
Rodriguez, Rene. *Miami Herald*. October 7, 2010.
Weinberg, Scott. *Cinematical*. April 6, 2010.

AWARDS

Nomination:

Directors Guild 2010: Director (Guggenheim).

WALL STREET: MONEY NEVER SLEEPS

Box Office: $52 million

Though Oliver Stone's filmmaking is primarily associated with some of the most tumultuous moments in America's past (*Platoon* [1986], *JFK* [1991] and *Nixon* [1995]), in recent years, he has turned his eye toward the present tense and increasingly-topical subjects. His last three projects focused on the events of 9/11 (2006's *World Trade Center*), the 43rd U.S. President (2008's *W.*) and the misunderstood sociopolitical climate of

South America (the 2009 documentary, *South of the Border*). So in 2008, when the financial industry's unchecked greed sent the planet's economy into a near tailspin, Stone chose to resurrect one of his most lovingly despised characters, crooked Wall Street maverick Gordon Gekko, from one of his most revered films, *Wall Street* (1987). More than twenty years later, Michael Douglas's iconic, Oscar®-winning turn as Gekko still symbolizes the wanton ways of the 1980's financial industry better than any other character, fictional or otherwise. In *Wall Street: Money Never Sleeps,* Stone makes expert use of the man to illustrate just how far down the rabbit hole the industry and its inhabitants have fallen.

Money Never Sleeps wastes no time in setting up its central theme and premise. The film opens with Gekko recollecting his possessions upon his release from prison, after doing eight years of time for insider trading and securities fraud, a lengthy stint for someone guilty of white collar crime. Among the items he is handed are a laughably-oversized, antiquated cellular phone and a gold money clip "with no money in it," as the prison employee is happy to point out. Stone sets up the movie's primary question: Can the old brand of Wall Street greed hold its own in a world infected by the industry's newer, jacked-up strain?

Gekko may be the face of the film, but its protagonist is the young Jake Moore (Shia LaBeouf), a hot-shot broker at the major investment bank Keller Zabel, with the the skills to kill, but the moral instincts to stop short. Jake specializes in long-term investments concerning alternative energy technology. But his levelheadedness is tested when his boss, mentor and father figure, the gentle, bow-tied Louis Zabel (Frank Langella), is forced to sell-off his company at a ludicrously-low price-per-share, due to nasty, circulating rumors regarding its instability. The boardroom scene in which that takes place likely bears no small resemblance to the fateful 2008 meeting at which real-world, investment bank Bear Stearns was sold in similar fashion. It is there that we meet Bretton James (Josh Brolin), the cocksure CEO of the competing bank that appears all too eager to absorb Keller Zabel (and Jake's job). Already worn out by an out-of-control industry he barely recognizes, the humiliation proves too much for the aging Zabel, who throws himself in front of a subway train. Jake is crushed by the death and becomes determined to learn who lies behind the rumors that set the wheels in motion.

But Jake also happens to be in love with—and preparing to marry—Winnie Gekko (Carey Mulligan), Gordon's estranged daughter, who did most of her growing up while her father was busy fighting legal battles and doing time. Winnie, now a successful liberal blogger, has done everything within her power to separate herself from her father's reputation, even going so far as to ignore a great fortune he had set aside for her. Without Winnie's knowledge, Jake attends a lecture by Gordon, who is promoting a book he has written in prison entitled "Is Greed Good?" (a sly twist on the "Greed Is Good" speech famously delivered in *Wall Street*). Although Gekko is far from reformed, he is disgusted by the current culture on Wall Street and positions himself and the old guard as the much lesser of two evils. The audience is treated to a fairly large portion of the lecture, which not only presents Gekko's view of the world into which he was released, but also doubles as Stone's crash-course for viewers unfamiliar with the causes of the recent financial meltdown. He describes the financial industry's problems as systemic, malignant and global, citing Wall Street's risky practices, lack of anyone to whom it must answer, and, most of all, its insatiable greed.

Jake is impressed enough by Gordon's take on things and decides that he is no longer the man Winnie fears him to be. So Jake introduces himself and explains that he would like to help him reconnect with her. Gordon insists that he has developed enormous regrets about his relationship with Winnie and seems genuinely interested in this prospect, though skeptical. In return for his help, Jake taps Gordon's financial expertise in an effort to discover more about the scheme that brought down Keller Zabel. And, for a moment, the two of them seem to be forming a symbiotic relationship and perhaps even something slightly resembling a family. Though once Jake gathers enough information to place blame for Zabel's death, he begins to fall victim to vengeance. His plan to reintroduce Gordon into Winnie's life looks destined for failure as it meets with great resistance from a woman who's determined to protect herself from further abandonment. Gordon, of course, is surprised by none of this and unbeknownst to Jake and Winnie, has already started preparing for his dramatic return to "the game," as he calls it.

As of late, Shia LaBeouf has spent the bulk of his time in the big budget action franchises *Transformers* (2007, 2009) and *Indiana Jones and the Crystal Skull* (2008), so he is not often in a position to show off his acting chops. While most actors his age seem to think that the key is making the job look effortless, Shia seems to take pride in the fact that he is working hard—his smart, but scrappy, performance here is his strongest to date. It truly feels like he is thinking on his feet and reacting for the first time, to the things happening around him. It should come as no surprise that Michael Douglas has no trouble slipping back into Gekko's shoes after all these years. Keeping in mind the fact that his character has had eight years of jail time with which to think things over, Douglas plays him with just a bit less intensity and a touch more tranquility this time. Carey Mulligan is also good, though her part is a bit underwritten. Winnie's love for Jake feels deep, as does her resentment for her father, which are the two most important things. To be honest, the fact that these characters feel at all like real people, rather than talking heads, when one considers the amount of complicated financial information that has to be tossed about, is a real tribute to screenwriters Allan Loeb and Stephen Schiff. The dialogue is sufficiently dense enough, so as to be believable coming from fast talking Wall Street types, while also being straightforward enough so as to allow viewers to follow what is going on.

As director, Oliver Stone is clearly energized by his return to the helm of this familiar world. Throughout, director of photography Rodrigo Prieto's camera rarely stands still; even in scenes of tension, it is often inching forward or sideways ever so slightly. And in scenes where the already kinetic film requires even more energy—such as those in which Jake is dueling in one sense or another with either Gekko or James—Stone ups the ante by placing them on a barreling subway car, in the back of a careening cab or atop speeding motorbikes. As in the original movie, the playfully quirky music of Brian Eno and ex-Talking Head David Byrne is again featured prominently, often set to footage of regular New Yorkers hustling and bustling through life. Despite the highly serious nature of the stakes, something about Stone's tone also suggests that regardless of how this plays out, life will go on.

As with most Stone films, his scope is epic and he attempts to touch on each and every piece of the puzzle. Jake's mother, played comfortably by Susan Sarandon, is a real estate agent who is turning a blind eye to the impending collapse of the housing market. Her rapport with LaBeouf is nice and relaxed, but the fact that their conversations always steer their way back to the subject of finances feels a bit forced. Along those same lines, Jake's quest for alternative energy solutions is an important part of his idealistic character, but computer-animated demonstrations and explanations as to the process of fusion are unnecessary. The moments when Stone reaches for these sorts of things are generally short, so at the time, they are mere distractions. Over the course of a long movie such as this one, they add up, and, as a result, the film loses steam by the final act.

For the most part, *Wall Street: Money Never Sleeps* is a very good film. However, it does have its shortcomings and unfortunately, they reveal themselves in a series of fast and loose plot developments which happen during the film's final fifteen minutes. After spending the first two hours witnessing the strengthening of Gordon's dedication to Winnie and Winnie's dedication to Jake, everything unravels without much provocation, only to

be tied up neatly a few scenes later. The hope was that this might lend the film some extra—albeit unnecessary—emotional gravitas. Thankfully, these occurrences feel so artificially tacked on, that as strange as this may sound, it actually is not too difficult to mentally remove them again, when recalling the experience of viewing the movie. What is left is a highly-entertaining piece of historical fiction that also serves as an intriguing meditation on the current state of the financial industry. Using as a point of reference an iconic character who once represented the very essence of 1980's greed, it deftly asks us whether the greed of today is truly the entirely new beast it seems to be or perhaps just the same old dog with a new set of tricks.

Matt Priest

CREDITS

Gordon Gekko: Michael Douglas
Jake Moore: Shia LaBeouf
Winnie Gekko: Carey Mulligan
Lewis Zabel: Frank Langella
Bretton James: Josh Brolin
Sylvia Moore: Susan Sarandon
Audrey: Vanessa Ferlito
Julie Steinhardt: Eli Wallach
Dr. Masters: Austin Pendleton
Origin: USA
Language: English
Released: 2010
Production: Edward R. Pressman Film, Eric Kopeloff; Dune Entertainment; released by 20th Century Fox
Directed by: Oliver Stone
Written by: Allan Loeb, Stephen Schiff
Cinematography by: Rodrigo Prieto
Music by: Craig Armstrong
Sound: Tod A. Maitland
Editing: Julie Monroe, David Brenner
Art Direction: Paul D. Kelly
Costumes: Ellen Mirojnick
Production Design: Kristi Zea
MPAA rating: PG-13
Running time: 133 minutes

REVIEWS

Bowles, Scott. *USA Today.* September 23, 2010.
Chang, Justin. *Variety.* May 14, 2010.
DeVore, John. *Premiere.* September 27, 2010.
Ebert, Roger. *Chicago Sun-Times.* September 22, 2010.
Neumaier, Joe. *New York Daily News.* September 24, 2010.
Rodriguez, Rene. *Miami Herald.* September 22, 2010.
Schwarzbaum, Lisa. *Entertainment Weekly.* September 25, 2010.

Scott, A.O. *New York Times.* September 23, 2010.
Travers, Peter. *Rolling Stone.* September 24, 2010.
Turan, Kenneth. *Los Angeles Times.* September 24, 2010.

QUOTES

Gordon Gekko: "Someone reminded me I once said 'Greed is good.' Now it seems it's legal. Because everyone is drinking the same Kool Aid."

Gordon Gekko: "Idealism kills every deal."

TRIVIA

Javier Bardem was the original choice to play the Bretton James character but after he turned it down the studio considered Edward Norton, Mark Wahlberg, Aaron Eckhart, and James Franco among others before settling on Josh Brolin.

This is Oliver Stone's first sequel, being made twenty-three years after the original *Wall Street*.

AWARDS

Nomination:

Golden Globes 2011: Support. Actor (Douglas).

THE WAY BACK

Their escape was just the beginning.
—Movie tagline

Box Office: $3 million

Australian director Peter Weir has often let the physical environment of the characters play a central role in the story itself. Whether the characters are trying to adapt to new surroundings, fish out of water style (*Witness* [1985], *Greencard* [1990]), survive harsh terrain (*Master and Commander: The Far Side of the World* [2003]), make the land their own (*The Mosquito Coast* [1986]), trying to make sense of it while yearning for escape (*The Truman Show* [1998]) or are at a loss on how to solve its ethereal mysteries (*Picnic at Hanging Rock* [1975] and to a certain extent, *Fearless* [1993]), Weir's characters are often at odds with their own worlds. Sometimes the conflict works out in the characters' favor, sometimes not. Weir's latest, *The Way Back,* has it both ways and is certainly the most-challenging journey the director has yet presented.

The story begins in 1939 in Poland. Janusz (Jim Sturgess), a young Polish soldier has been sent to a Serbian gulag after being incriminated by his wife (presumably after much torture). Janusz refuses to sign the confession, a fact that garners some attention from one of his fellow prisoners, Khabarov (Mark Strong), who has a plan to escape the prison, which is stationed in the middle of nowhere in an unforgiving winter landscape.

The guards tell them up front that it is not their guns, their dogs, or their wire that make the prison. "Siberia is your prison," they say. "All five million square miles of it. Nature is your jailer, and she is without mercy." The plan to escape this prison clearly requires strength of character, people who will not cave in easily.

Janusz wants to bring a few more soldiers and it is decided during one intense blizzard to carry through with the plan so the snow will cover their tracks. To Janusz's dismay, Khabarov does not accept Janusz's sudden plan and stays behind. Janusz's sudden urge to escape is triggered by what is either a flashback or a flash-forward of him in another place reaching for a small rock on a ledge of a house. Whatever the image means, it propels him to carry through with the plan under penalty of death either by the guards or the land itself. Seven men follow Janusz through the deadly tundra, including an American expatriate who insists on going by the name of "Mr. Smith" (Ed Harris), a Russian named Valka who has tattoos of Stalin on his chest (Colin Farrell), a teenager with night blindness (Sebastian Urzendowsky), an artist (Alexandru Potocean), and a priest (Gustaf Skarsgard).

The plan, for the most part, appears to have worked. Never once does Weir go back to check in with the guards to see if they have a plan for finding the prisoners and bringing them back. The movie is the journey and nothing else. Every character is, in his own way, resourceful. They only have two sacks of food between the five of them. Their overall sense of direction eventually becomes muddled. There are wolves, blizzards, thigh-deep snow, and mountains beyond mountains. Hallucinations of having completed the journey become commonplace. The plan is to head south towards a lake near the Mongolian border.

Weeks become months and months. Nothing appears inedible. Valka predicts who will die next. After one dies, his only remark is "Still…one less mouth to feed." Echoes of the Donner Party plight begin to surface as Valka states matter-of-factly to Janusz that the only reason that so many were brought on this journey was that there would be more flesh to eat when the time comes. Upon their first destination, they encounter a young orphan girl named Irena (Saoirse Ronan) who is also a Russian escapee. After much deliberation and skepticism, they decide to let her join them.

The journey to the lake is really only the first act of the film. There are still deserts to conquer and many more mountains to climb. They come across small villages, but avoid contact with the citizens for fear of being found by the wrong people. The rest of the story from here on in involves more destinations, more celebratory moments when they are reached, more starvation and, ultimately, more death. There is a repetitiveness that Weir is unable to escape, but the story is never less compelling. Still, it is quite an endurance test for the audience. This is a tough film to watch, but certainly a rewarding one and not without its humorous moments.

Weir is able to place the viewer in the thick of it no matter the locale. The merciless chill of Siberia is felt deep beneath the skin while the still dryness of the deserts will have the viewer craving gallons of Gatorade. In typical form, Weir keeps the audience at just enough of an emotional distance so as not to be manipulative (*Dead Poets Society* [1989] remains the one film of his that clearly yanks at the heartstrings). The long, silent passages in the desert are enough to underline the sorrowful, yet calm moment of one's expiration. No overbearing film score is necessary. Likewise, the strength of Russell Boyd's cinematography depends more on making the journey look too daunting to fathom more than on capturing breathtaking vistas. He manages to succeed at both.

The performances are all flawless. Ed Harris' world-weary sternness is a typical note for him to play, but he does it here without ever once seeming like he believes he matters the most in the story. Farrell continues to be an underrated actor (no doubt brought on because of the over documentation of his off-screen bad boy behavior). He is the perfect choice to play the dedicated Russian hooligan who calls every situation as he sees it, even if undesirable. Jim Sturgess is a curious choice for the lead. His persona has not yet been burned into the public consciousness and while he does give a great performance, the viewer's eyes are often drawn elsewhere. Weir makes a point of never casting him as the "hero" character even if he is the catalyst.

The issue of "kindness" often comes up in Keith R. Clarke and Weir's smartly-written screenplay. The relationship between Janusz and Mr. Smith is one based on a give and take. Mr. Smith tells Janusz that kindness is the one thing that can kill a man in a prison camp, but yet that same kindness can be used to an advantage when trying to survive in the wilderness. Mr. Smith often rejects Janusz's acts of kindness as a way of punishing himself for a mistake he made in the past. "In the camp, some saw death as freedom," Mr. Smith says. "Why didn't you just kill yourself then?" asks Janusz. "Survival was a kind of protest. Being alive was my punishment."

While it may not be entirely clear what is keeping everyone else's will to live afloat under these unthinkable circumstances, once the men reach their final destination, the weight and meaning of the moment is clearly felt as a whole. The repetitiveness in the duration works in the film's favor in the long run. Having an outside character find these men will feel like a welcome relief to any viewer who has grown tired of looking at vast mountains and horizon-less vistas.

The book upon which the film is based, *The Long Walk: The True Story of a Trek to Freedom,* by Slavomir Rawicz (for whom Janusz serves as a substitute), has been called into question by historians and researchers. Some have claimed the journey never took place and that many of these characters never existed in the first place. Whether valid of not, *The Way Back* stays true to the idea of survival in a harsh landscape that eventually becomes a way of life until one does not know how to stay put in comfortable surroundings. Eventually, the feet have to keep moving again, regardless of what lays ahead. The coda at the end does not try to sell the viewer on the validity of the story by giving a where-are-they-now wrap-up, but instead delves into a history lesson on the fall of Communism. Weir himself does not believe the entire story of these men is true. But he makes a compelling case that the legend should at least be explored, if only to use it as a metaphor for all journeys, either personal or as a human collective.

Collin Souter

CREDITS

Janusz: Jim Sturgess
Valka: Colin Farrell
Mr. Smith: Ed Harris
Irena: Saoirse Ronan
Khabarov: Mark Strong
Voss: Gustaf Skarsgard
Tomasz: Alexandru Potocean
Kazik: Sebastian Urzendowsky
Origin: USA
Language: English
Released: 2010
Production: Duncan Henderson, Joni Levin, Nigel Sinclair, Peter Weir; Exclusive Films, National Geographic Films, Imagenation Abu Dhabi FZ; released by Newmarket Films
Directed by: Peter Weir
Written by: Peter Weir, Keith R. Clarke
Cinematography by: Russell Boyd
Music by: Burkhard von Dallwitz
Editing: Lee Smith
Sound: Richard King
Costumes: Wendy Stites
Production Design: John Stoddart
MPAA rating: PG-13
Running time: 132 minutes

REVIEWS

Burr, Ty. *Boston Globe.* January 20, 2011.
Dargis, Manohla. *New York Times.* January 20, 2011.

Debruge, Peter. *Variety.* September 8, 2010.
Farber, Stephen. *Hollywood Reporter.* September 7, 2010.
MacDonald, Moira. *Seattle Times.* January 20, 2011.
Mitchell, Elvis. *Movieline.* January 20, 2011.
Pais, Matt. *Metromix.com.* January 20, 2011.
Phillips, Michael. *Chicago Tribune.* January 20, 2011.
Rich, Katey. *CinemaBlend.com.* January 19, 2011.
Rickey, Carrie. *Philadelphia Inquirer.* January 20, 2011.

TRIVIA

On the set of the film, actress Saiorse Ronan celebrated her sixteenth birthday.

AWARDS

Nomination:

Oscars 2010: Makeup.

WELCOME TO THE RILEYS

If all of the movies from 2010 were in a room together, yelling and arguing and saying whatever each had to say, *Welcome to the Rileys* would be the wallflower in the corner without anything to contribute. That is not to suggest that the indie drama from director Jake Scott (son of Ridley) and writer Ken Hixon (*City by the Sea* [2002]) is an awful movie. It is merely a tentative, unnecessary one, which handles a messy situation far too cleanly.

New Jersey native James Gandolfini and his distractingly heavy Midwestern accent star as Doug Riley, a large, unhappy Indianapolis man in the plumbing supply business. When Doug goes to New Orleans for a conference—fortunately Scott shows none of the conference itself, confident that no one wants to hear much about plumbing supplies—he realizes he cannot bring himself to return home. There, his wife Lois (Melissa Leo) has not left the house since their daughter's death eight years before and his mistress Vivian (Elsa Davis) recently passed away. In New Orleans, Doug meets Mallory (Kristen Stewart), a teenage stripper who ran away from her home in Florida, and Doug would rather watch over her as a replacement daughter than try to get his marriage back on the right track.

The characters are straight out of the indie drama textbook. Doug is big and protective and old-fashioned, refusing Mallory's sexual advances both at the strip club in which she works and at her home, where Doug eventually pays her $100 per day for him to stay. (This certainly reflects Doug's generosity. Even $10 per day would be a high rate for the sort of unpleasant place

Mallory lives, which still boasts post-Hurricane Katrina markings on its worn-down exterior.) Mallory, on the other hand, is small and alone and reckless. She calls herself a dancer but knows that she is actually a prostitute, turning tricks because, as she says, it is the only way she can have enough money to eat. Doug hates profanity; Mallory swears constantly, and eventually Doug insists on charging her $1 every time she drops an F-bomb. These two are the sort of lost polar opposites that frequently combine on the big screen to teach each other lessons and become the unlikeliest of friends.

Except one of the film's many problems is that the relationship between Doug and Mallory is mostly one-sided, not to mention fundamentally unsettling. Mallory needs discipline and looking after, and Doug disciplines and looks after her. This exchange should be much more complicated, but it does not play out that way. Mallory does not care terribly about Doug's motivations; she desperately needs the money and he does not beat her or steal from her, which is more than can be said for most of the guys she encounters. So, ultimately, when the movie needs Mallory to teach Doug something, it feels like a narrative inevitability rather than a place to which the story naturally leads.

Though she looks too old to be the damaged 16-year-old she is playing, Stewart gives a performance that makes Mallory more than just a lazy choice for a screenwriter who needed a wounded object for the film's subject to watch over. Gandolfini, lost in a part that feels like condescension to the Midwest, never clicks with Stewart. The filmmakers need to demonstrate that Doug and Mallory are establishing a meaningful father-daughter relationship. Instead, they never interact in any interesting or unexpected ways; merely predictable, shallow encounters of Doug protecting Mallory from a variety of creeps and Mallory getting Doug high for the first time in more than twenty years. Throughout the film, Hixon takes a paint-by-numbers approach to these characters and never colors outside the lines.

The relationship between Doug and Mallory, however, works far better than practically everything involving Lois, who decides to drive down to New Orleans to see her husband even though she has not been behind the wheel in years. *Welcome to the Rileys* tries to position this as proof of her undying devotion, but it feels like halfway through the writing process Hixon decided that Lois needed to be more involved in the story. Before that, very little is revealed about her, so the notion that she would suddenly overcome her agoraphobia to try to drive—the scene in which she gets in the car and accidentally crashes into a garbage can and basketball pole has a misguided, strangely comic tone—just seems out of character. It is more likely that Lois, who later tells Doug, "You can leave me if you have to, but I will never leave you," would remain in the house and wait for her man to come home. This is a woman who made no fuss when she discovered her husband was cheating on her. If Lois' choice to drive to New Orleans is meant as a woman snapping back into her life, *Welcome to the Rileys* fails to depict it that way.

The film also winds up suggesting, no matter how much everyone acknowledges that Doug and Lois are not actually a mom and dad to Mallory (whose real name is Allison), that their attempt to fill the void of their own daughter with a stranger was psychologically wise. Mallory is someone who could be expected to be filled with trust issues, yet she takes to her new caretakers without nearly as much resistance or incident as viewers might anticipate. The role she plays in bringing Doug and Lois back together also far underplays the lingering effects of tragedy and the importance of marital communication. Doug and Lois have been married nearly thirty years but distant for almost a decade, and the notion that all they needed to feel better was to attach themselves to another teenage girl comes off as more disturbing and less moving than the film intends.

Certainly, there is legitimate feeling in these characters' painful histories, but *Welcome to the Rileys* spends less time exploring the similarities that bind even the most different people than piling up forced symbolism and melodramatic situations. Early in the film, Doug becomes angry when he sees that Lois has already purchased a tombstone with their names on it. After he tells her he is not returning to Indianapolis, he says, "I know I'm not dead yet." Later, a hysterical argument between Mallory and Lois leads to a slapping incident that is not a case of repressed people unraveling at each other. It is just a movie that has no ideas of its own deciding to include yet another cliché: an unhappy mom lashing out against her rebellious child without any long-lasting effects or re-opening of old wounds.

To achieve the sort of catharsis it seeks, *Welcome to the Rileys* should force its characters to break down each other's emotional walls in raw, honest ways to recognize their pain and come out better on the other side, together. The drama is too safe and familiar, though, featuring people who are always running or chasing but never believably finding. Meanwhile, Doug, who has plenty of money and little emotional release after the film's first few minutes, remains too far above it all. He spends most of the movie giving advice and offering lessons instead of demonstrating his own instability and need for change. When he first arrives in Mallory's house, he says he feels like he landed on Mars. For such a naïve, upstanding fish-out-of-water, the film never lets him flop around.

Matt Pais

CREDITS

Doug Riley: James Gandolfini
Lois Riley: Melissa Leo
Mallory: Kristen Stewart
Vivian: Eisa Davis
Origin: USA
Language: English
Released: 2010
Production: Giovanni Agnelli PRO, Argonaut Pictures, Michael Costigan; Scott Free, Argonaut Pictures; released by Samuel Goldwyn Films
Directed by: Jake Scott
Written by: Ken Hixon
Cinematography by: Christopher Soos
Music by: Marc Streitenfeld
Sound: Noah Vivekanand Timan
Editing: Nicolas Gaster
Costumes: Kim Bowen
Production Design: Happy Massee
MPAA rating: R
Running time: 110 minutes

REVIEWS

Burr, Ty. *Boston Globe.* October 28, 2010.
Catsoulis, Jeannette. *NPR.* October 28, 2010.
Dargis, Manohla. *New York Times.* October 28, 2010.
Debruge, Peter. *Variety.* October 24, 2010.
Goodykoontz, Bill. *Arizona Republic.* November 13, 2010.
Puig, Claudia. *USA Today.* October 28, 2010.
Rabin, Nathan. *AV Club.* October 28, 2010.
Scott, Mike. *New Orleans Times-Picayune.* November 12, 2010.
Sharkey, Betsy. *Los Angeles Times.* October 28, 2010.
Zacharek, Stephanie. *Movieline.* October 28, 2010.

QUOTES

Mallory: "I'm nobody's little girl! It's too late for that sh*t."

WHEN IN ROME

Did you ever wish for the impossible?
    —Movie tagline
All is fair in love and Rome.
    —Movie tagline

Box Office: $33 million

When in Rome is yet another lackluster romantic comedy about a workaholic woman who has ostensibly chosen career over passion and finds herself swept up by a charming beau. Forgetting simple things like chemistry, honest laughs, and true emotion, *When in Rome* is a romantic comedy that is neither romantic nor comedic. It exists only to remind viewers that its sometimes-charming stars can be completely miscast and misused, especially when they either have zero chemistry or have been reduced to cardboard cut-out supporting roles. 2010 represented a new low for the romantic comedy with worthless junk like *Leap Year* (2010), *Valentine's Day* (2010), and *She's Out of My League* (2010) littering the marketplace in the first few months of the year. *When in Rome* seemed practically designed to join the chorus.

Kristen Bell proved to be a charming, engaging lead on the highly-acclaimed TV series *Veronica Mars* but she has yet to find a single film role to translate the small-screen talents she showed to the big one (other than perhaps effective supporting work in *Forgetting Sarah Marshall* [2008]). The lovely young star probably saw *When in Rome* as her ticket to romantic comedy glory but she is woefully miscast as Beth, an unlucky-in-love workaholic who cannot manage to have much of a personal life due to the stress of her professional one (at which she is bossed by a slumming Anjelica Huston). Beth's sister (Alexis Dziena) goes through a whirlwind engagement and ends up getting married in Rome at short notice. Beth flies out there for the nuptials and meets Nick (Josh Duhamel), a charming American in a tuxedo who comes to Beth's rescue after a tribute and toast goes wrong. Beth and Nick flirt, dance, and seem ready for love but the poor girl sees Nick making out with a young lady and kind of snaps. She dives into "La Fontana de Amore," clearly inspired by The Fountain of Trevi, for a swim and ends up absconding with several of the coins dropped in there as wishes for love. The legend goes that if one takes the coins from the fountain, they then become the object of intense obsession of the people who originally threw them. So, Beth essentially gets stalked by an obnoxious painter (Will Arnett), an egotistical model (Dax Shepard), a sausage magnate (Danny DeVito), and a moronic magician (Jon Heder). Instead of being allowed to merely return the coins to this ensemble of idiocy, Beth's secretary (Kate Micucci) steals the coins. Wacky hijinks ensue.

Naturally, it is merely a matter of time before Beth and Nick end up united in love but *When in Rome* goes through bizarre machinations to get there even for the beleaguered romantic comedy genre. The quartet of losers chasing after Beth that is clearly intended as comic relief merely disturbs more than provide humor. A scene in which Jon Heder attempts a magic trick in which he rips his heart from his chest falls flat in every way, as does literally every scene the overcooked Will Arnett appears in. Danny DeVito running after Bell screaming about sausages is just creepy. Shepard fares the best of the suitors merely by virtue of being given the least embarrassing material to perform, but that is faint praise indeed. Of course, Beth fished five coins out of the fountain, including a poker chip she believes belongs to the gambler Nick. Is he interested in Beth because of the chip/fountain or for true love?

When in Rome simply never gives the viewer a reason to care. If Bell and Duhamel had stronger chemistry, perhaps it would be easier to wade through the stalker comedy that surrounds their courtship but they offer no romantic antithesis to the physical comedy of the rest of the piece. Both Bell and Duhamel are relatively likable stars in general but they just do not work together here. The modern romantic comedy seems to have forgotten the most important ingredient of the genre—two leads that the audience does not just want to see get together but virtually needs to see together by the end of the film. *When in Rome* is so poorly written that one has absolutely nothing invested in what happens to Beth or which one of her twisted suitors ends up being the man for her. And the film crosses into that uncomfortable territory of misogyny that so often suggests in films like this that women cannot find love and be professionally accomplished as well. Of course, reading something like that into a forgettable trip like *When in Rome* is probably giving the film more credit than it deserves, which is to say any credit at all.

Brian Tallerico

CREDITS

Beth Harper: Kristen Bell
Nick Beamon: Josh Duhamel
Antonio: Will Arnett
Lance: Jon Heder
Celeste: Anjelica Huston
Joan: Alexis Dziena
Priscilla: Peggy Lipton
Father Dino: Keir O'Donnell
Stacy Harper: Kate Micucci
Puck: Bobby Moynihan
Gale: Dax Shepard
Al Russo: Danny DeVito
Origin: USA
Language: English
Released: 2009
Production: Gary Foster, Mark Johnson, Andrew Panay, Ezra Swerdlow, Rikki Lea Bestall; Touchstone Pictures, Krasnoff Foster Productions; released by Walt Disney Pictures
Directed by: Mark Steven Johnson
Written by: David Diamond, David Weissman
Cinematography by: John Bailey
Music by: Christopher Young
Sound: Andrew Decristofaro
Music Supervisor: Dave Jordan

Editing: Ryan Folsey, Andrew Marcus
Art Direction: John J. Kasarda, Stefano Ortolani
Costumes: Sarah Edwards
Production Design: Kirk M. Petruccelli
MPAA rating: PG-13
Running time: 91 minutes

REVIEWS

Anderson, Jeffrey. *Combustible Celluloid.* January 28, 2010.
Barnard, Linda. *Toronto Star.* January 29, 2010.
Biancolli, Amy. *Houston Chronicle.* January 28, 2010.
Dujsik, Mark. *Mark Reviews Movies.* January 28, 2010.
Farber, Stephen. *Hollywood Reporter.* January 29, 2010.
Long, Tom. *Detroit News.* January 29, 2010.
MacDonald, Moira. *Seattle Times.* January 28, 2010.
Rickey, Carrie. *Philadelphia Inquirer.* January 28, 2010.
Roeper, Richard. *RichardRoeper.com.* January 29, 2010.
Schager, Nick. *Slant Magazine.* January 28, 2010.

QUOTES

Beth's Dad: "You could get your heart broken or…you could have the greatest love affair the world has ever known. But you're never gonna know unless you try."

TRIVIA

All the change that appears in the Fountain of Love is actually American currency despite being set in Rome.

WHITE MATERIAL

In the African heat, one woman stands alone.
—Movie tagline

Clare Denis' *White Material* is a deceptively simple film that feels like a puzzle. Much of that has to do with Denis' characteristically-stoic presentation and her refusal to sentimentalize or express her characters in a straightforward manner. The audience is left to put the pieces of the story together as it unfolds in an almost directionless fashion. It is, for the most part, a linear story even if it seems to forego simple narrative conventions.

The film, which takes place in post-colonial Africa, opens in the middle of the story (as so many films often do these days) with an African military search party wandering through a dark house and eventually finding the dead body of "the Boxer" (Isaach De Bankolé). Post credits, the movie flashes back to Maria Vial (Isabelle Huppert), a French coffee plantation owner hitching a ride on the back of a crowded bus. Later, as she wanders her own plantation, seemingly alone, a helicopter flies over her with a French soldier pleading with her to get out of this unnamed African country. The French army

is pulling out and she will have few, if any, allies to help her out should she need it.

Something is making her stay, but it is not made very clear. Her reason could be stubbornness. It could be a small act of rebellion against the French, who have all but destroyed this beautiful land. It could be a sense of duty to the African people (yet they are also at war with insurgents as well as the colonialists). Maybe it is all of the above and more. Denis keeps her lead's intentions clouded in quiet passages as she explores a land that is in a state of uncertain calmness. Soldiers are waiting for something, ready for anything, but never quite sure what. Without the colonialists permeating the landscape, it is a place that is ravaged in post-war ruins with only citizens eager to leave to put it all back together.

Maria tries to keep her plantation afloat for at least five more days and must plead with her workers to stay rather than flee. "We might be more safe," she says. "We don't have to be terrorized. We can fight back." The armies are made up of adults and kids, all of them armed and suspicious. Men she knows well now demand she pay outrageous toll fees in order to be granted passage onto the land. Surprisingly, she does not react with any fear, but calm rationale. Maria's ex-husband, André (Christopher Lambert), is the real owner of the plantation and is trying to sell it. "I'm trying to save her from herself," he says.

She has a stepson and a son of her own. She tries to enlist the help of her stepson first, but he is soon whisked away be André. Her son Manual (Nicolas Duvauchelle) has all but lost interest in everything and spends most of his days laying around being useless until something unsettling in him starts to surface. Soon, after an encounter with a pair of young thieves who hold him at knife and gunpoint and leave him naked in the middle of a field, he transforms himself into an unrecognizable and hateful figure.

Denis is returning to familiar territory here. A French woman who grew up in Africa, Denis knows her way around this material and perhaps this is something of a personal statement for her. She has explored Africa in her previous films (*Chocolate* [1988] and most recently *35 Shots of Rum* [2010]) and they are not angry political statements. They are, instead, matter-of-fact perceptions of the land, its people and their personal struggles. She seems to care very deeply about her characters, especially here, but she is careful not to divulge too much information about them.

Stuart Staples' almost monotone score helps keep the material from reaching overbearing dramatic heights. It is subdued and exists to keep every character on the same playing field, never used to underscore an event, only to bridge scenes and convey a combination of calm and dread. Yves Cape's cinematography, likewise, has a neutral feel about it. Rather than try and make the most of the African landscape (which would be hard for any cinematographer to resist), Cape keeps everything a little on edge, careful to remember that this is a land whose beauty has been ravaged and will continue to be so for some time.

The anchor of the film is, of course, Huppert, whose fierce performance keeps the viewer guessing as to what she is thinking, which turns out to be more of a strength than a weakness. Maria is full of mysteries and Huppert is the perfect choice for the role. A more conventional director would have found a way for Huppert to finally cave in and open up about her situation, perhaps through a tearful monologue. No such pay-offs exist here. Instead, it is Huppert carrying a movie with as much confidence as she has ever had, even if the story does not allow for a full explanation of her actions.

Like many of Denis' films, *White Material* is easier to admire than it is to love and it works better upon a repeat viewing. Its detachment from conventional story structure, character development and sentimentality will not be for all tastes and Denis does not have a political axe to grind (nothing overt anyway). Perhaps she simply sees herself in Maria's eyes, a determined spirit who cannot bring herself to leave the landscape, no matter the risk. It might not be a practical, spiritual or even artistic need to prove herself, but rather a divine right to exist and simply be.

Collin Souter

CREDITS

Maria Vial: Isabelle Huppert
Andre Vail: Christopher Lambert
Manuel Vial: Nicolas Duvauchelle
Henri Vial: Michel Subor
The Boxer: Isaach De Bankole
Lucie Vial: Adele Ado
Jeep: Ali Barkai
Jose: Daniel Tchangang
The Mayor: Marie N'Diaye
Origin: France
Language: French
Released: 2010
Production: Pascal Caucheteux; Why Not Productions, Wild Bunch, France 3 Cinema; released by IFC Films
Directed by: Claire Denis
Written by: Claire Denis
Cinematography by: Yves Cape
Music by: Stuart S. Staples

Sound: Jean-Paul Mugel, Christophe Wilding
Editing: Guy Lecorne
Costumes: Judy Shrewsbury
Production Design: Saint Pere Abiassi, Alain Veissier
MPAA rating: Unrated
Running time: 106 minutes

REVIEWS

Dargis, Manohla. *New York Times*. November 18, 2010.
Ebert, Roger. *Chicago Sun-Times*. November 18, 2010.
Harley, Kevin. *Total Film*. June 30, 2010.
Hoberman, J. *Village Voice*. November 16, 2010.
Long, Tom. *Detroit News*. December 17, 2010.
O'Hehir, Andrew. *Salon.com*. November 19, 2010.
Phillips, Michael. *Chicago Tribune*. November 19, 2010.
Schwartzbaum, Lisa. *Entertainment Weekly*. November 18, 2010.
Tobias, Scott. *AV Club*. November 18, 2010.
Turan, Kenneth. *Los Angeles Times*. December 2, 2010.

WHY DID I GET MARRIED TOO?
(Tyler Perry's Why Did I Get Married Too?)

Marriage is an institution they're committed to.
    —Movie tagline
Together. Forever.
    —Movie tagline

Box Office: $60 million

Where no one else saw a consistently underserved demographic hungry for colorful familial dramedies, regional playwright Tyler Perry—with the assistance of Lionsgate, who have served as the financier and distributor on all of his films ever since *Madea's Family Reunion* (2006), his theatrical debut—made a bet that predominantly African American audiences would turn out to theaters to see a circus-funhouse mirror held up to their love, strife, fumblings, and aspirations, in the form of his garrulous homilies. Perry's calculations have paid off, and then some. His eight commercially released films as a writer-director—many of which are recast remakes of previous productions that went straight-to-video—have been reliable mid-eight-figure moneymakers, grossing a cumulative $430 million.

The follow-up to his $55-million-grossing relationship dramedy *Why Did I Get Married?* (2007), featuring the same cast, *Why Did I Get Married Too?* centers on four couples who reunite on a child-free vacation in the Bahamas to catch up, and ostensibly talk about and work on their marriages. Terry (Perry) and lawyer wife

Dianne (Sharon Leal) are seemingly the most grounded, but suspicions of an affair soon arise. Voluble Angela (Tasha Smith) has major trust issues with Marcus (Michael Jai White), a TV sports talk show host. Having lost a child, relationship book author Patricia (Janet Jackson) and husband Gavin (Malik Yoba) find themselves hitting a rut that may have been there all along. Meanwhile, newlyweds Troy (Lamman Rucker) and Sheila (Jill Scott), who have recently relocated to Atlanta from Colorado, find themselves dealing with a new baby, as well as a rift born of Troy's frustration with his ongoing job search. There is also a disruptive interloper, in the form of Sheila's ex-husband Mike (Richard T. Jones).

The first half-hour of the movie unfolds in a fairly straightforward fashion, albeit one pitched at a somewhat hyper-realistic level. With its tropical setting and focus on the various pitfalls of adult relationships, this portion of the movie could easily be a cousin of *Couples Retreat* (2009). This is easily the strongest part of *Why Did I Get Married Too?*, as a series of extended scenes help its ensemble believably locate a jocular rapport between old friends.

This goodwill does not last long, however. The film narratively treads water for a while, though mostly rooted in some understandably human anxieties, like Troy's irritation at having Sheila share details of their financial situation with their friends. In its final hour, though, the movie takes a full-on tumble down Crazy Mountain. The motivations of characters become secondary to provocation within scenes, and they sometimes do things that would have likely gotten them arrested or otherwise detained. It becomes manifestly clear that, despite the putative focus of its dialogue about keeping open the lines of communication in relationships, Perry's movie is not rooted in any sort of honest discourse between men and women. Neither is it really interested in believably assaying modern married life. Instead, *Why Did I Get Married Too?* is constructed to supply a steady stream of charged, "shocking" moments, which includes a discharged firearm, the interruption of a live TV show, a character coated in the ashes of a cremated stranger, and a full minute-plus of Janet Jackson, seemingly exorcising the demons of her off-screen childhood, smashing two dozen glass surfaces with a golf club.

At fault equally are subpar direction and a messy, uneven script. The former is evident in poor staging and shot selection, as well as small details, like the manner in which characters blithely handle coffee cups supposedly filled to the brim with hot liquid. Cinematographer Toyomichi Kurita has plenty of experience in capturing interwoven relationship ensembles, having shot both *Waiting to Exhale* (1995) and *Cookie's Fortune* (1999), in addition to this film's predecessor. Yet in his fifth col-

laboration with Perry, the writer-director continues to undercut his director of photography with editorial choices that partition characters, closing them off from one another, and thus draining scenes of their natural pep and liveliness.

Substantiation of the screenplay's shortcomings runs steadily throughout the film. As a writer, Perry's greatest gift is his ability to locate the culturally specific rhythms of genial backbiting amongst friends. While he still is given to certain stagey pitfalls—processing exposition through children's dialogue, for instance—his characterizations are often vivid, and his dialogue is not without snap. Yet Perry seems inescapably tethered to tired (and very shallow) notions of exaggerated, campy melodrama, like a stand-up performer wanly returning to the crutch of an old catchphrase. The movie's best scene—in which Gavin, with a sort of sad fury, accuses Patricia of tolerating him rather than loving him for their entire marriage—is so wildly out of step with most of its stabs at air-quote drama as to both induce whiplash and simultaneously make one wonder what sort of writer Perry could develop into were he to work with other directors, and/or be forced into collaborations with less sycophantic parties.

Even in a film with so many problems, the wildly uneven nature of the performances here ranks highest on the list. The notable exception is Yoba, who locates in Gavin a palpable sense of swallowed aggrievement—the raw emotion of someone who sincerely loves his wife, and yet also feels like a fool for having wasted so much time in a relationship where his affections were not completely reciprocated. Perry, who has always seemed more at home as a performer in the dress-up drag of his nutty Madea character, seems here to channel the interview-circuit mannerisms of Will Smith, with a full litany of laughs, guttural vocalizations and other chirpy asides. He is pantomiming self-assured gregariousness, and it comes across as cloying and phony. Smith, meanwhile, is like an atom bomb to the movie. Her characterization of Angela is that of a screeching sociopath, someone so unhinged that only a deeply disturbed and masochistic individual would continue to tolerate her as a friend, let alone a lover. If the entire movie were pitched at this manic level, that would be one thing, but her performance—with all the wheel-spinning, carnival barker energy of an Eddie Griffin stand-up routine—is a selfish exercise in look-at-me theatrics. Where Smith's performance moves from merely bad and derailing to borderline offensive, however, is in the wearyingly unimaginative manner in which it relies so forcefully on the minstrel stereotyping of African American women's public demonstrativeness.

In the end, despite all its wild story twists, *Why Did I Get Married Too?* is perfectly emblematic of Perry's methodology, which has evolved technically, but only to a point. In its insistent embrace of melodramatic histrionics, and with another late narrative pivot to maudlin reconciliation and artificial uplift, Perry again underscores his polarized cinematic worldview, in which there exists only the grotesque, the sublime or the time-whiling set-up for one or the other.

Brent Simon

CREDITS

Terry: Tyler Perry
Patricia: Janet Jackson
Gavin: Malik Yoba
Dianne: Sharon Leal
Marcus: Michael Jai White
Angela: Tasha Smith
LaToya: Amber Stevens
Mike: Richard T. Jones
Porter: Louis Gossett Jr.
Ola: Cicely Tyson
Sheila: Jill Scott
Troy: Lamman Rucker
Origin: USA
Language: English
Released: 2010
Production: Tyler Perry, Reuben Cannon; Tyler Perry Co.; released by Lionsgate
Directed by: Tyler Perry
Written by: Tyler Perry
Cinematography by: Toyomichi Kurita
Music by: Michael Stern
Sound: Mike Wilhoit
Music Supervisor: Joel High
Editing: Maysie Hoy
Costumes: Keith Lewis
MPAA rating: PG-13
Running time: 121 minutes

REVIEWS

Chaney, Jen. *Washington Post.* April 2, 2010.
Debruge, Peter. *Variety.* April 2, 2010.
Ellingson, Annlee. *Moving Pictures Magazine.* April 4, 2010.
Gronvall, Andrea. *Chicago Reader.* April 2, 2010.
Morris, Wesley. *Boston Globe.* April 2, 2010.
Schaefer, Stephen. *Boston Herald.* April 2, 2010.
Scheck, Frank. *Hollywood Reporter.* April 2, 2010.
Schwarzbaum, Lisa. *Entertainment Weekly.* April 2, 2010.
Snider, Eric. *Cinematical.* April 3, 2010.
White, Armond. *New York Press.* March 31, 2010.

QUOTES

Angela: "You and that book! You just have all the answers, don't you?"

Janet Jackson found out about her brother Michael Jackson's death while filming this movie.

WILD GRASS
(Les herbes folles)

Alain Resnais is no stranger to onscreen love. Widely acclaimed for his contributions to the so called French New Wave, the deeply moving *Hiroshima mon Amour* (1959) and *Last Year At Marienbad* (1961), Resnais offers a complex, emotionally-nuanced look at late-life romanticism with his latest work. It is easy to get lost in *Wild Grass.* Viewers looking for the usual sorts of cinematic or narrative handholds here will find themselves quickly frustrated. There are no genre mechanics at work here, the plot line seems ambiguous, and the film seems uninterested in identifying a clear protagonist. For those willing to hang in there, *Wild Grass* reveals itself as a compelling character study and a telling look at the tension between the human desire to be loved and keep secrets safe. By turns darkly humorous and slightly chilling, but ultimately enigmatic, *Wild Grass* is well-worth viewing by anyone with a taste for sophisticated whimsy, surreal imagery, and a realistic view of what is at risk when one leaves the wild grass behind for flights of fantasy.

Two decidedly odd characters find themselves thrust together in a discomforting quasi-romantic adventure. The aging and secretive Georges (André Dussollier) lives a quiet-if-emotionally frustrated existence which is soundly disrupted when he finds a red wallet belonging to the frizzy red-haired dentist Marguerite, (Sabine Azema) whose aviator license and photo conjures nostalgic reminiscence of the great female pilots.

The problem of how to return the wallet is complicated by two things: Georges believes that he cannot simply give it to the police as he might be recognized for some heinous crime from which he has been forced into hiding and he has an undeniable growing fascination with Marguerite. He feels he must meet her. Marguerite however is more uncertain and even threatened by the idea, especially after Georges slashes her tires and leaves her a written apology. All seems lost for Georges until the most unlikely of things happens: Marguerite, after already having rebuffed his calls and reported his behavior to the police, begins to wonder about him as well. As she waits for him outside a cinema showing *The Bridges at Toko-Ri* (1954) it seems that standard romance is about to bloom. But Resnais has never been interested in simply-styled oddball rom-com, choosing instead to allow his characters to meander beyond the simple roles that genre would define for them. Late in *Wild Grass*, high above the earth in a vintage red spitfire the symbolism becomes chilling indeed. Desire and death, hope and chaos are intermingled here in a manner that is sadly lost on those anxious for a quick cinematic affirmation of love come easy and sentimentality as its own reward. One wants intimacy Resnais seems to say and yet most are totally unprepared whet it is encountered.

The performances here are uniformly compelling. André Dussollier is liable to be recognizable to anyone who has kept up with world cinema over the last decade having been seen in *Amelie* (2001), *A Very Long Engagement,* (2004) and the excellent thriller *Tell No One* (2006) but he is hardly a household name. This seems a shame. His expressive face and gift for subtle interpretation would be welcome indeed on broader cinematic canvases. Resnais' longtime companion Sabine Azema (*Private Fears in Public Places* [2006]) imbues Marguerite with a dangerous twitchiness. Either she or Georges, or both, might ultimately be mad but we remain uncertain of whether that is because they hesitate, or finally leap forward, flirting with disaster. Anne Consigny (*The Diving Bell and the Butterfly* [2007], *A Christmas Tale* [2008], *Mesrine: Public Enemy #1* [2008]) handles the role of long-suffering young wife deftly. She is not lost because her husband is, and she is willing to take her own steps on this journey. It is a powerfully-written, if understated, role that allows her to come across as empowered without seeming ugly or without compassion.

The sparse but effectively longing score by Mark Snow offers a sort of lush, almost-smoky jazz romanticism that upholds the notion that Resnais is as serious about the notion of romance as he is about the things that tend to thwart it. Snow has worked mainly in television and is most famous for his work on *The X-Files* (1993-2002).

Wild Grass will not be for everyone but for those who respond to it a line from Georges may prove especially resonant "After the cinema, nothing surprises you...anything can happen as naturally as possible." Come what may, life is not a movie, love cannot be lived as it is in the movies. Love comes with the possibility of exposure, pain, and even death. Whether or not it was worth it to journey out of the wild grass is something each of us must own, hold close, and ultimately share.

Dave Canfield

CREDITS

Marguerite Muir: Sabine Azema
Georges Palet: André Dussollier

Suzanne Palet: Anne Consigny
Josepha: Emmanuelle Devos
Bernard de Bordeaux: Mathieu Amalric
Lucien d'Orange: Michel Vuillermoz
Elodie: Sara Forestier
Jean-Mi: Nicolas Duvauchelle
Marcelin Palet: Vladimir Consigny
Narrator: Edouard Baer
Origin: France, Italy
Language: French
Released: 2009
Production: Jean-Louis Livi; StudioCanal, France 2 Cinema, Bim Distribuzione; released by Sony Pictures Classics
Directed by: Alain Resnais
Written by: Alex Reval, Laurent Herbiert
Cinematography by: Eric Gautier
Music by: Mark Snow
Sound: Jean-Marie Blondel, Gerard Hardy, Gerard Lamps
Editing: Herve De Luze
Costumes: Jackie Budin
Production Design: Jacques Saulnier
MPAA rating: PG
Running time: 113 minutes

REVIEWS

Bitel, Anton. *Film4.* June 14, 2010.
Brayton, Tim. *Antagony & Ecstacy.* July 22, 2010.
Ebert, Roger. *Chicago Sun-Times.* July 15, 2010.
Hoberman, J. *Village Voice.* June 22, 2010.
Holden, Stephen. *New York Times.* June 25, 2010.
Mintzer, Jordan. *Variety.* May 21, 2009.
O'Sullivan, Michael. *Washington Post.* July 23, 2010.
Savlov, Marc. *Austin Chronicle.* August 20, 2010.
Schenker, Andrew. *Slant Magazine.* June 21, 2010.
Schwarzbaum, Lisa. *Entertainment Weekly.* June 23, 2010.

WINTER'S BONE

Box Office: $6 million

Most 17-year-old girls on the big screen deal with issues common to teenagers: Friendships and dating, peer pressure and body image, college applications and prom. Skinning a squirrel is typically not one of these rites of passage.

Of those issues, however, the latter is the only one of any concern to Ree Dolly (Jennifer Lawrence), who is not like most teen girls in the movies. She does not go to school. She does not have a boyfriend, and she is not looking for one. In the sparsely populated Ozarks of Missouri, Ree lives with her mom Connie (Valerie Richards), who rarely speaks or moves. Ree's father was just released from prison, but no one knows where he is. Ree spends most of her time worrying about putting food on the table for her young siblings, 12-year-old Sonny (Isaiah Stone) and six-year-old Ashlee (Ashlee Thompson), whose sole options for entertainment involve a couple of toys here and there and a trampoline out back. It is an undesirable life that gets even harder and more urgent when Ree learns her father put the family house up for his bond. In other words, if dad, a known drug dealer, does not show for his court date in a week, a near-desperate living situation will become a non-existent living situation for the Dolly family.

This painful truth gives *Winter's Bone,* a drama modeled like a Western and told with documentary-like realism, a gripping tension that is difficult to achieve in film with such a quiet, measured pace. In this world of few words, threats are distributed frequently and softly, which only makes them that much more chilling. "I said shut up already once with my mouth," Ree's uncle Teardrop (John Hawkes) utters to his wife, suggesting that next time he will tell her to shut up through the use of physical force. Throughout the film, characters acknowledge that many of them share the same blood, but family relations among neighbors sure do not create an environment of safety and support. As Ree searches for someone who knows where her father is, she fearlessly confronts a community built on secrecy where women, appearing on porches to prevent entry into the house, frequently serve as bouncers for the scary men in their lives. At one point, Ree suffers a beating at the hands of her cousin Megan (Casey MacLaren), who admits to being afraid of her grandfather Thump Milton (Ron Hall), and several others who likely occupy a branch somewhere on her family tree. This does not matter to them. Here, there is no love, only protection of unwritten rules and the drug trade, which has little competition in the race for the town's most popular profession.

Adapting Daniel Woodrell's 2006 novel, director/co-writer Debra Granik establishes a devastatingly chilly sense of place. At times, the setting almost looks like a depressing postcard, except this is an area where postcards are not sold, and no one would ever brag about visiting. The people of this insular, oft-suspicious place have their own ways and expressions, referring to potatoes as "taters" and cops as "the law." Yet while the police have a very loose grip on the townspeople—in one breathless scene, Sheriff Baskin (Garret Dillahunt) fails to get Teardrop out of his truck when Teardrop holds a gun and suggests that if he gets out, it will likely be the death of both of them—there are still plenty of people who abide a moral code, none more so than Ree. She insists that her young siblings watch her make deer stew, so they know how to do it if she is not around.

(Ree hopes to join the army, basically just for the money.) She knows her family has very little to eat, but when Ashlee asks if they should ask a neighbor for some of their food, Ree advises, "Never ask for what outta be offered." The Dollys may live in a place to which many viewers can not relate, but the experiences and priorities of their family nonetheless apply to anyone watching.

Which is not to say that everyone's actions will be expected. The film's moments of violence and near-horror are so based in everyday, person-to-person conflict that they possess incredible blunt force. This is seen several times, particularly when Teardrop takes an axe to the windshield of men who threaten him, and later when Ree must face an unshakable and disturbing challenge to at last close her investigation into her father and save the house. No matter what is happening, Lawrence and Hawkes are both terrific and deserve any and every accolade that may come their way. *Winter's Bone* is the type of small film that is easily overlooked by all honorees other than the Independent Spirit Awards. Its stark slice of life, though, is likely to connect with anyone who sees it and appreciates the way the elements of a noir can seep themselves into real life, turning brightness into black. After all, in most other parts of America, Ree's looks would probably be an asset. She might be nominated for prom queen; at the very least she would catch the eyes of her classmates. That is not the life she lives. Ree lives in a land of no opportunity, where she chops wood and survives and gives no mind to things like the Internet.

These are experiences that tend to appear once in a while at the Sundance Film Festival, where *Winter's Bone* won the Grand Jury prize for drama in 2010. That award likely came because the film stands out from the pack of similarly-themed stories about desperate people in troubled places. As a look at an unenviable life lived by a strong character to admire, *Winter's Bone* unfolds with an authentic sense of dread that is slightly done in by a too-convenient ending. The final moments achieve considerable power anyway; they resonate like the silence after a gunshot, when it seems, for a little while at least, no more bullets will be fired.

Matt Pais

CREDITS

Ree: Jennifer Lawrence
Teardrop: John Hawkes
Little Arthur: Kevin Breznahan
Merab: Dale Dickey
Sheriff Baskin: Garret Dillahunt
April: Sheryl Lee

Gail: Lauren Sweetser
Mike Satterfield: Tate Taylor
Connie: Valerie Richards
Sonny: Isaiah Stone
Ashlee: Ashlee Thompson
Megan: Casey MacLaren
Thump Milton: Ron Hall
Origin: USA
Language: English
Released: 2010
Production: Anne Rosellini, Alix Madigan; Anonymous Content; released by Roadside Attractions
Directed by: Debra Granik
Written by: Debra Granik, Anne Rosellini
Cinematography by: Michael McDonough
Music by: Dickon Hinchliffe
Sound: James Demer
Editing: Affonso Goncalves
Costumes: Rebecca Hoffher
Production Design: Mark White
MPAA rating: R
Running time: 99 minutes

REVIEWS

Baumgarten, Marjorie. *Austin Chronicle.* June 25, 2010.
Biancolli, Amy. *San Francisco Chronicle.* June 18, 2010.
Burr, Ty. *Boston Globe.* June 18, 2010.
Mohan, Marc. *Portland Oregonian.* June 24, 2010.
Ogle, Connie. *Miami Herald.* July 28, 2010.
Phillips, Michael. *Chicago Tribune.* June 17, 2010.
Scott, Mike. *New Orleans Times-Picayune.* June 23, 2010.
Schwarzbaum, Lisa. *Entertainment Weekly.* June 10, 2010.
Scott, A.O. *New York Times.* June 11, 2010.
Taylor, Ella. *NPR.* June 10, 2010.

QUOTES

Ree: "I'd be lost without the weight of you two on my back. I ain't going anywhere."

TRIVIA

The filmmakers cast many local residents of the Forsyth, Missouri area who had never acted before.

AWARDS

Ind. Spirit 2011: Support. Actor (Hawkes), Support. Actress (Dickey)

Nomination:

Oscars 2010: Actress (Lawrence), Adapt. Screenplay, Film, Support. Actor (Hawkes)
Golden Globes 2011: Actress—Drama (Lawrence)
Ind. Spirit 2011: Actress (Lawrence), Cinematog., Director (Granik), Film, Screenplay

Screen Actors Guild 2010: Actress (Lawrence), Support. Actor (Hawkes).

THE WOLFMAN

When the moon is full the legend comes to life.
    —Movie tagline
Fear what is within.
    —Movie tagline

Box Office: $62 million

The Universal monster collection of the 1930s and 1940s is as revered among cinephiles as it is with horror fans due to its beautiful simplicity of storytelling combined with discolored mood over shock effects and gore. Times do change and all that was once sacred must be retold for new generations. Francis Ford Coppola went back to the diaries for *Bram Stoker's Dracula* (1992) and then helped produce *Mary Shelley's Frankenstein* (1994) for director Kenneth Branagh. Such serious-minded and respectful versions gave way to the very studio who fashioned the originals to let Stephen Sommers turn *The Mummy* (1999) into a matinee-era adventure tale with a CGI-era sensibility. The less said about Sommers' reteaming of all the monsters for his actioner *Van Helsing* (2004) the better. Time heals wounds though and some quicker than others. And despite a troubled history in the making, Universal has made amends with a classy and exciting update of their most infamous werewolf.

As in the 1941 original, Lawrence Talbot (Benicio Del Toro) has returned home circa 1891. Harboring some past issues with his father, John (Anthony Hopkins), the prodigal son arrives to aid in the disappearance of his brother. No sooner than he arrives, the body has already been discovered, ripped to shreds by some kind of animal. While his brother's wife, Gwen Conliffe (Emily Blunt), remains at the family estate to grieve, Lawrence chooses to investigate further, hearing stories of gypsies and curses permeating through England's Blackmoor pubs. Though Sir John warns him to stay inside when the moon is full, Lawrence visits the gypsy Maleva (Geraldine Chaplin) looking for answers and may have found one with teeth.

A true detective has also arrived on the scene. A famous one known as Inspector Abberline (Hugo Weaving), the very man who also investigated another series of brutal slayings linked to Jack the Ripper. He does not subscribe to the local legends either, but having seen what man is capable of is not ready to conclude that it was an animal not found about these parts. Considering Lawrence's history in an asylum in the wake of his mother's death, Abberline sees a person of interest whose return coincides with these slayings. It will not be until the next cycle of the moon when Lawrence becomes a threat.

Werewolf movies, more than any other genre of horror, have suffered over the years thanks to new waves of technology and filmmakers who do not appear to know what makes them tick. John Landis and Joe Dante may have added some cheekier elements to their ground-breaking and still exemplary *An American Werewolf in London* (1981) and *The Howling* (1981), but had enough respect to recognize the elements of physical and psychological terror inflicted upon the ones who carry the curse and those who love them. Most everything now is a simple morph into a creature, or even worse, an actual wolf as if every visual effects artist and creative consultant cannot tell the difference between a shape-shifter and what is supposed to be half-man and half-wolf. This film, at the very least, is a return to the old traditions of makeup transformations, aided by Oscar®-winning artist Rick Baker and, just for good measure, a little CGI that helps enhance the big moments instead of overcoming them.

Whilst some may look away from the ghastlier moments under the light of the moon, *The Wolfman* is still a gorgeous film to look at. Cinematographer Shelly Johnson and a team of art directors have recaptured the look of the period and the feel of those bygone horror films where shadows and surroundings were just as important as the aftermath from what hides amongst them. It helps put a stamp of approval on the script by Andrew Kevin Walker and David Self which treats the material with grave significance. The respective scribes of *Seven* (1995) and *Road to Perdition* (2002) know a little something about man's bestial sides and the struggle between resistance and acceptance. So there are several solemn dialogue passages that draw the viewer into the overall mood of the piece, even when the plotting bears a remarkable resemblance to Zach Braff's *Garden State* (2004)—if the actor with daddy issues sent away after his mother's death met a cute girl and became a Jersey werewolf upon his return.

It also helps to have an actor like Anthony Hopkins capable of selling lines such as "the past is a wilderness of horrors" and "life is much too glorious to the cursed and the damned" with an emphasis towards Shakespear-ean platitudes while still maintaining a gleaming smirk of recognition towards the outlandish. Benicio Del Toro's problem, on the other hand, is not so much that he fails to balance his gloominess in the same way but that there is a sympathetic piece to his performance that is missing. The actor is not exactly known for his warmth on screen and that element, plus his supposed growing affection for Blunt's Gwen suffers for it, lend-ing less credence to the mantra that love can set the beast free. Weaving's Inspector gets to make a grand entrance about forty minutes in and with the character's historical mistrust of actors—one of his chief suspects in the Ripper case helped fuel fear with a performance of *Dr. Jekyll & Mr. Hyde*—the table was set for Walker and Self to have some fun intersecting his cases and establish-ing him as sort of a crossover Sherlock Holmes. Instead of turning into a battle of wills between Lawrence and Abberline, the Inspector does nothing after their first and only conversation but chase the Wolfman through the streets and countryside.

Lawrence and Gwen's relationship is fleshed out a bit more in a director's cut on DVD which also includes a pretty nifty scene featuring Max von Sydow as a mysterious train passenger who gifts Lawrence his iconic wolf's-head cane. One's enjoyment of the film's mood and thrills is not going to be swayed through extended or truncated running times, however. Director Joe Johnston's pacing of the material fails to wane in either version and he remains as adept at ever at handling big special effects sequences. The multiple wolfman attacks are swift and appropriately brutal to satisfy both the animalistic strength on display and the animals in the audience seeking their cinematic bloodlust. For a film that went through numerous production problems including changing directors just weeks before principal photography, late reshoots and a 15-month delay from its originally scheduled release, *The Wolfman* is still a pretty crafty piece of entertainment that is respectable enough to adorn shelves alongside, at the very least, its modern counterparts.

Erik Childress

CREDITS

Lawrence Talbot: Benicio Del Toro
Gwen Conliffe: Emily Blunt
Sir John Talbot: Anthony Hopkins
Aberline: Hugo Weaving
Maleva: Geraldine Chaplin
Singh: Art Malik
Young Ben: Asa Butterfield
Ben Talbot: Simon Merrells
Young Lawrence: Mario Marin-Borquez
Solana Talbot: Cristina Contes
Passenger on train (DVD only): Max von Sydow
Origin: USA
Language: English
Released: 2009
Production: Sean Daniel, Scott Stuber, Rick Yorn, Benicio Del Toro; Relativity Media, Stuber Productions; released by Universal Pictures

Directed by: Joe Johnston
Written by: Andrew Kevin Walker, David Self
Cinematography by: Shelly Johnson
Music by: Danny Elfman
Sound: Karen M. Baker, Per Hallberg
Music Supervisor: Conrad Pope
Editing: Dennis Virkler, Walter Murch, Mark Goldblatt
Art Direction: Andy Nicholson, John Dexter, Phil Harvey
Costumes: Milena Canonero
Production Design: Rick Heinrichs
MPAA rating: R
Running time: 102 minutes

REVIEWS

Bunch, Sonny. *Washington Times.* February 12, 2010.
Burr, Ty. *Boston Globe.* February 11, 2010.
Ebert, Roger. *Chicago Sun-Times.* February 11, 2010.
Jones, J.R. *Chicago Reader.* February 11, 2010.
Phillips, Michael. *Chicago Tribune.* February 11, 2010.
Rechtshaffen, Michael. *Hollywood Reporter.* February 10, 2010.
Rodriguez, Rene. *Miami Herald.* February 11, 2010.
Sharkey, Betsy. *Los Angeles Times.* February 11, 2010.
Smith, Kyle. *New York Post.* February 12, 2010.
Travers, Peter. *Rolling Stone.* February 11, 2010.

QUOTES

Lawrence Talbot: "I am what they say I am...I'm a monster."
Maleva: "Even a man who is pure in heart and says his prayers by night, may become a wolf when the wolfbane blooms, and the autumn moon is bright."

TRIVIA

Depsite passing through the hands of several directors, Benicio Del Toro remained committed to the remake since he is such a huge fan of the original film.

Benicio Del Toro sat through three hours of makeup to create the Wolfman look.

AWARDS

Oscars 2010: Makeup.

YOGI BEAR

Please do not feed the bears.
—Movie tagline
Life's a pic-a-nic.
—Movie tagline

Box Office: $97 million

The problem with *Yogi Bear* is not that it is a bad movie—though it is spectacularly awful in any number of ways—as much as it is a dead one. Simply put, this big-screen translation of the popular Hanna-Barbera animated series has nothing of value to offer audiences—it is not funny, the story is practically nonexistent and the miracle of 3D adds nothing to the proceedings other than a few extra dollars to the theatrical ticket price. It is so relentlessly dull that it is not even worth getting upset about because to do so would require putting more thought into the film than anyone connected with it apparently did. When the film comes to DVD, here is hoping that it includes a making-of documentary so that viewers can see the actors dragging themselves to work every day despite the almost certain knowledge that they are working on one of the most singularly unfulfilling projects to hit the multiplexes in a while.

For those potential viewers who somehow managed to muddle through their lives without ever having been exposed to Yogi Bear, he was a "smarter than the average" bear who talked vaguely like Ed Norton, maintained a slightly questionable man/ward relationship with young sidekick Boo-Boo that made the dynamic between Batman and Robin seem utterly wholesome and spent his days roaming the woods of Jellystone Park concocting elaborate ways of divesting tourists of their picnic baskets and driving the hapless Ranger Smith to distraction at every turn. One might not think that this would be enough to serve as the basis of a feature film and as it plods on for its first half-hour or so, as Yogi (voice of Dan Aykroyd) and Boo-Boo (Justin Timberlake) set about trying (and largely failing) to steal food while exasperating Ranger Smith (Tom Cavanagh) to no end, one would quickly realize that they were right. What passes for conflict comes when the corrupt local mayor (Andrew Daly), looking for a way to cover up a budget shortfall and fund his gubernatorial bid, decides to shut down Jellystone and sell the logging rights to the highest bidder. Ranger Smith is given a week to raise the money needed to save the place but in trying to help out, Yogi only manages to make things worse. In a shocking turn of events, he and Boo-Boo manage to save the day—something about Boo-Boo's pet turtle being an incredibly rare variety—and leave the park open for the hoped-for sequels.

Yogi Bear has a ton of problems working against it but one of the biggest is the fact that the title character is essentially a one-dimensional bore throughout—while he may have enough personality to make it through a six-minute TV cartoon, there is not nearly enough to fill out a full-length film, even one like this where the end credits are rolling before the eighty-minute mark. As the voices of Yogi and Boo-Boo, Aykroyd and Timberlake do vaguely acceptable imitations of the dulcet tones of Daws Butler and Don Messick but bring nothing else to the table—they are essentially doing little more than getting paid huge amounts of money for doing what children used to do in the playground for free. On the bright side, at least are not seen amidst the wreckage of the film, which is the unfortunate plight of Cavanagh and Anna Faris, who is utterly wasted in a nothing role as a documentary filmmaker who arrives at the park to make a film about Yogi. And while no one goes to a film like this for the intricate screenplay, the storyline coughed up here by no less than three writers is utterly bankrupt of anything resembling a fresh idea. Younger viewers will be utterly bored by the stuff involving the closing of the park and the flirtation between Ranger Smith and the documentarian, older viewers will be annoyed by the relentlessly juvenile tone (though they may silently give thanks that it contains only one bit of flatulence-related humor) and both groups may find themselves wondering why Ranger Smith does not raise the money to save the park by putting what would seem to be its central attraction—a fully anthropomorphized bear that not only talks but who could presumably do a credible take on the old "Hello ball" routine from *The Honeymooners*—front and center instead of hiding him in favor of a fireworks display and a mutant turtle.

On the grand scale of patently unnecessary live-action/CGI hybrid films based on old cartoon shows or comic strips, *Yogi Bear* is slightly better than the *Alvin & the Chipmunks* (2007, 2009) movies, largely because they do not involve anyone talking in overly squeaky voices, but not quite as good as the *Garfield* (2004, 2006) movies, which were awful but, unlike his former *Saturday Night Live* colleague Aykroyd, at least Bill Murray managed a droll line reading here and there. It is likely that this film was launched into production immediately after the producers saw the box-office numbers for those movies and only after it was too late did they realize that coming up with a viable plot for a full-length movie about Yogi Bear would be an impossibility. Instead of simply abandoning the idea and going back to the drawing board, they decided to forge ahead by stringing together a bunch of achingly familiar gags in lieu of a story, putting it together in 3D as a way of boosting the gross thanks to the added surcharge, and tossing it out during the Christmas season when parents stuck with little kids on vacation for the holiday are willing to sit through virtually anything to get out of the house for a couple of hours. This is mercenary filmmaking at its most craven and the worst thing about it is that if enough parents wind up going along with the plan, it may mean that *Yogi Bear 2* could be right around the corner, which sounds like a boo-boo if ever there was one.

Peter Sobczynski

CREDITS

Yogi Bear: Dan Aykroyd (Voice)
Boo-boo: Justin Timberlake (Voice)
Ranger Smith: Tom Cavanagh
Mayor Brown: Andrew Daly
Rachel: Anna Faris
Origin: USA
Language: English
Released: 2010
Production: Donald De Line, Karen Rosenfelt; Sunswept Entertainment, De Line Pictures; released by Warner Bros.
Directed by: Eric Brevig
Written by: Brad Copeland
Cinematography by: Peter James
Music by: John Debney
Editing: Kent Beyda
Sound: Christopher S. Aud
Production Design: David Sandefur
MPAA rating: PG
Running time: 80 minutes

REVIEWS

Anderson, Melissa. *Village Voice.* December 14, 2010.
Chang, Justin. *Variety.* December 13, 2010.
Dujsik, Mark. *Mark Reviews Movies.* December 16, 2010.
Honeycutt, Kirk. *Hollywood Reporter.* December 13, 2010.
Minow, Nell. *Beliefnet.* December 16, 2010.
Orndorf, Brian. *BrianOrndorf.com.* December 15, 2010.
Pais, Matt. *Metromix.com.* December 14, 2010.
Phillips, Michael. *Chicago Tribune.* December 16, 2010.
Puig, Claudia. *USA Today.* December 16, 2010.
Tobias, Scott. *AV Club.* December 16, 2010.

TRIVIA

Dan Aykroyd opted to do his own take on the voice of Yogi Bear rather than imitate the original performance by Daws Butler.

YOU AGAIN

What doesn't kill you...is going to marry your brother.
—Movie tagline

Box Office: $26 million

Marni (Kristen Bell) did not have much going for her in high school. She had bad hair, a face full of acne and had the unfortunate initials of M.O.O.. It is practically an invitation for ridicule, which she suffered at the hands of head cheerleader Joanna (Odette Yustman), the self-appointed Marshal of their school. Marni is all grown up now. She has great hair, a glorious complexion worthy of a skin cream commercial and has just received a promotion at her publicity firm. On the plane home for her brother's wedding, Marni discovers from her mother, Gail (Jamie Lee Curtis), that she may actually know the bride-to-be since they went to high school together. When she pieces together that the bride is Joanna she causes a scene in mid-air that gets her restrained by a real life Marshal.

With her past and present converging, Marni is stunned to discover that not only does Joanna appear to have received a personality transplant from the one she remembers, but that her worst enemy does not seem to remember her at all. Keeping herself in check, the stakes get raised for the weekend when Joanna's Aunt Ramona (Sigourney Weaver) shows up. She used to be Gail's best friend growing up, until an incident at prom left one pushing the other into a swimming pool. Gail claims it's all chlorine-laden water under the bridge but still maintains the same kind of anxiety that her daughter is having in confronting old memories. As Marni tests Joanna's own memory of events, not everything is as it appears to be and she is determined to protect her brother from making a big mistake.

For lame-brained plots like this to work, those with the deal-breaking information must be muzzled at every chance they want to spill the beans. What can be said then about a screenplay that is too stupid to acknowledge basic clique politics that even high school dropouts know to be true? If viewers are to agree that Marni's protective brother, Will (horribly played by James Wolk), is left in the dark as to the identity of her chief tormentor, are they really expected to believe that a star basketball player and the head cheerleader do not remember each other, especially when that cheerleader pushed Marni the Mascot into him during the game-winning (or, in this case, losing) shot?

Marni's motivations (sincere or not) to be a better person can be understood, but turning the brother into such a clueless dolt—reinforced when he allows the clearly unstable ex-boyfriend (Kyle Bornheimer) of his fiancé to stay at their rehearsal dinner—qualifies screenwriter Moe Jelline for remedial classes in both drama and comedy. Director Andy Fickman cannot seem to even make heads or tails of who is supposed to be the aggressor in the Gail/Ramona dynamic. Is the underdog of this relationship really deserving of that title if she was the big winner during their teenage years? This flip-flop in the understanding of the situation then doubles back on sympathies for realizing that one's "poor me" routine is rooted more in petty jealousy then something worthy of payback.

If the best revenge is indeed living well, then Marni, Gail, and Ramona have done pretty well for themselves.

Why Marni or Gail would react with such fearful gusto at Joanna or Ramona's reemergence begs questions of insecurity or night terror-like insanity that the script could not possibly confront in a throwaway project like this. Having Weaver and Curtis—two icons who cut their teeth in horror and have become wonderful comic actresses in their own right—together for the first time and wasted here in such miscalculated roles makes Fickman the humiliating bully. The hack helmer of *The Game Plan* (2007) and *Race to Witch Mountain* (2009) focuses more attention on surprise cameos—and fulfilling the federally mandated obligation that Betty White must appear in some media form once-a-week—then putting any of these actresses in scenes that play up to their talent levels than well below them. For a film built upon the theme of second chances, this is hardly an apology for Fickman's own directorial inadequacies. "Are you insane?" is a question that pops up more than once, particularly when the comic madness consists of Marni falling into an anthill causing bite marks that bring her a mirror's view away from her Clearasil-challenged days, plates being thrown, and pea soup being poured over someone's head by someone who may have gone through an exorcism since high school.

Erik Childress

CREDITS

Marni: Kristen Bell
Joanna: Odette Yustman
Gail: Jamie Lee Curtis
Aunt Ramona: Sigourney Weaver
Will: James Wolk
Grandma Bunny: Betty White
Mark: Victor Garber
Monique Leroux: Kristin Chenoweth
Helen: Cloris Leachman
Richie: Patrick Duffy
Kendall: Meagan Holder
Taylor: Christine Lakin
Ben: Billy Unger
Tim: Kyle Bornheimer
Mason Dunlevy: Daryl Hall
Daisy: Catherine Bach
Dana: Staci Keanan
Air Marshal: Dwayne Johnson
Origin: USA
Language: English
Released: 2010
Production: Andy Fickman, Eric Tannenbaum, John J. Strauss; Skydance Prods.; released by Walt Disney Pictures, Paramount

Directed by: Andy Fickman
Written by: Moe Jelline
Cinematography by: David Hennings
Music by: Nathan Wang
Sound: Robert L. Sephton
Editing: David Rennie
Art Direction: Charles Daboub Jr.
Costumes: Genevieve Tyrrell
Production Design: Craig Stearns
MPAA rating: PG
Running time: 105 minutes

REVIEWS

Barker, Andrew. *Variety.* September 23, 2010.
Ebert, Roger. *Chicago Sun-Times.* September 24, 2010.
Gronvall, Andrea. *Chicago Reader.* September 23, 2010.
Holden, Stephen. *New York Times.* September 24, 2010.
Judy, Jim. *Screen It!* September 24, 2010.
Minow, Nell. *Belief.net.* September 24, 2010.
Phipps, Keith. *AV Club.* September 24, 2010.
Roeper, Richard. *RichardRoeper.com.* September 24, 2010.
Swietek, Frank. *One Guy's Opinion.* September 23, 2010.
Verniere, James. *Boston Herald.* September 23, 2010.

QUOTES

Georgia: "Two scoops of crazy with a side of coo-coo-cachoo."

TRIVIA

As an homage to a scene in the film, Jamie Lee Curtis and Sigourney Weaver wore the same dress to the movie's premiere.

YOU WILL MEET A TALL DARK STRANGER

Box Office: $3 million

Woody Allen has been nominated six times for a Best Director Academy Award® and a staggering fourteen times for Best Original Screenplay. An institution unto himself, he remains one of the few American filmmakers who, outside of the Hollywood studio system, can go out and make a movie each year. This is in large part because his films are technically uncomplicated, reasonably budgeted productions that revolve around characters talking rather than aliens attacking or automobiles transforming, but it also has to do with a loyal, largely boomer-aged audience that has, with a few exceptions, made a point of annually tripping back to theaters, hoping to catch a refracted bit of the magic from some of Allen's earliest work, like *Annie Hall* (1977) and *Manhattan* (1979).

But has Allen, now seventy-five years old, either lost or abandoned the desire to work a script up past a first draft, and into something more than merely passable? It seems that way—his fortieth feature film behind the camera unfolds in a characteristically distinct mode, but absent much in the way of actual perspicacious reflection or engagement on the human condition. In fact, *You Will Meet a Tall Dark Stranger* opens with a famous line from *Macbeth,* about "a tale of sound and fury, signifying nothing." It proves eerily prophetic.

An empty farce elevated to only minimal degrees by the shelf life of one's devotion to Allen and the game efforts of several members of its ensemble cast, *You Will Meet a Tall Dark Stranger* tracks a pair of London married couples as their various professional worries, personal anxieties, and romantic temptations lead to some moral missteps. After an out-of-competition premiere at the Cannes Film Festival in May, the movie sputtered a bit upon its autumnal Stateside release but did better overseas, where, like most of Allen's output over the past decade, it earned over seventy percent of its commercial box office tally.

After four decades of marriage, businessman Alfie Shepridge, gripped by panic over thoughts of his own mortality, leaves his wife Helena (Gemma Jones) to pursue his lost youth—a quest that takes the form of a younger woman, of course. Devastated and suicidal, Helena abandons rationality and slowly surrenders to the willfully vague, relentlessly upbeat forecasts of a charlatan fortune teller, Cristal (Pauline Collins). Seized by a desire to have a son in his twilight years, Alfie rushes headlong into a relationship with a free-spirited, unrefined call girl named Charmaine (Lucy Punch), who, not surprisingly, quickly evidences the behavior of someone for whom Madonna's "Material Girl" could serve as unofficial personal theme song.

While successful in her career, Alfie and Helena's adult daughter finds herself at no less nerve-wracking of an intersection. Beset by stress headaches and increasingly unhappy in her own marriage to blocked novelist Roy Channing (Josh Brolin), Sally (Naomi Watts) develops a crush on her handsome art gallery owner boss, Greg Clemente (Antonio Banderas). Still trading on the fading glory of an acclaimed debut novel, meanwhile, Roy nervously awaits his editor's response to his latest manuscript, and fretfully compares his work to the unpublished freshman effort of a poker buddy, Henry (Ewen Bremner). All his sputtering consternation feeds a burgeoning obsession with Dia (Freida Pinto), a mystery woman who catches Roy's gaze in a window across from his apartment. When she does little to dissuade his advances, an affair ensues.

The entire proper narrative of *You Will Meet a Tall Dark Stranger* is one of a shrink-dried fantasy construct, in which people swing in shrugging fashion from one relationship to another, largely absent any of the actual teeth-grinding messy arguments of romantic dissolution. This tack works far better onstage, or in a comedy with a defter touch, where the dialogue has an insightful snap and the direction a sort of loose-limbed, anything-goes energy. Allen, though, has his own particular laidback rhythms, and the set-ups and banter here yield little in the way of amusement or surprise. The fact that the movie is a bit different, in that it does not aim to drive the plot forward by heartily depressing more traditional dramatic keys of marital/relationship discord (lots of blowout arguments, say), does not make it good, however. The less polite way of phrasing this is that without the attachment of Allen's name—and the selected cast that then signs on to work with him—this is not only a script that is not greenlit at a Hollywood studio (which was not the case here), but one that also likely does not make it through the gauntlet of the independent film financing arena.

The laziness of the narrative framework is most robustly evidenced by the movie's disembodied narration from Zak Orth, which adds little to the proceedings other than a repetitive thematic underscoring of what the viewer watches unfold. Absent the pulse-quickening plot injection of murder and other criminal mayhem (as in the recent *Match Point* [2005] and *Cassandra's Dream* [2006]), Allen seems content to wind his characters up and let them drift to and fro in another water-treading comedy of manners with recycled references to Ingmar Bergman. As with all his work, there are some small, glancing moments of literate humor (Charmaine thinks a production of Henrik Ibsen's *Ghosts* is not as scary as it should be), but not enough to recommend the movie. The result is not only the least culturally-specific of Allen's latter-era foreign-filmed canon, which has included *Match Point* (2005), *Scoop* (2006), *Cassandra's Dream* (2008), and *Vicky Cristina Barcelona* (2008), but also the least fun and engaging.

For those that invest in such auteur scrutiny, seeded within the story there is more easygoing, throwaway self-analysis from Allen, in the form of Roy's eroding confidence at ever being able to match his early output. And certainly it is interesting, on a theoretical level, to see a filmmaker so prolific ponder the ultimate end to which we all come. But unlike Clint Eastwood's *Hereafter* (2010), there is not the sense of Allen confronting any of these own jumbled feelings in himself, and stamping the material with it. In fact, for all its acting out, *You Will Meet a Tall Dark Stranger* willfully avoids any deeper considerations. The front-burnered conflict here consists solely of surface emotionalism, and once it becomes ap-

parent that that is all the movie has to offer, its piecemeal charms wane fairly quickly.

The performances are fairly hit-and-miss as well. Banderas lends his character, neither complete cad nor standup gentleman, a bit of nicely layered complexity in addition to a dollop of his trademark charm. In her seriocomic hysteria, Jones locates the panic of discovering life anew as a senior citizen. Brolin, though, telegraphs Roy's rumpled misanthropy, never digging much beyond the surface. Others in the ensemble, like Watts and Hopkins, seem mainly motivated to take *You Will Meet a Tall Dark Stranger* in order to check off another box: worked with Woody Allen.

More forgiving viewers may contort their natural reaction, and assert that Allen mines comedic tension from juxtaposing the cynicism and negativity of several characters (a stand-in for his own well-known habitual pessimistic pose) with the mounting absurdities around them, as if mere formal, on-the-page contrast somehow lively and three-dimensional art makes. But *You Will Meet a Tall Dark Stranger* is a dawdling work, arriving in its end game at a place with its characters and their relationships and predicaments that would have been much more intriguing as a midway point in the movie.

Even its title—taken from the prediction fortune-tellers use to beguile their marks, with a winking, double entendre's nod toward death—is an empty come-on. The only thing *You Will Meet a Tall Dark Stranger* ultimately affirms is that the act of filmmaking offers Allen fleeting delights, a way to keep his mind off the morbid contemplations of obsolescence and death naturally attached to aging. Perhaps those are the very thoughts about which he should be writing, however. They would almost certainly not be less interesting.

Brent Simon

CREDITS

Sally: Naomi Watts
Roy Channing: Josh Brolin
Helena Shepridge: Gemma Jones
Alfie: Anthony Hopkins
Cristal Delgiorno: Pauline Collins
Dia: Freida Pinto
Greg Clemente: Antonio Banderas
Charmaine: Lucy Punch
Jonathan: Roger Ashton-Griffiths
Henry Strangler: Ewen Bremner
Narrator: Zak Orth
Origin: United Kingdom, Spain
Language: English
Released: 2010

Production: Letty Aronson, Stephen Tenenbaum, Jaume Roures; Dippermouth, Antena 3 Films, MediaPro, Versatil Cinema, Gravier Productions; released by Sony Pictures Classics

Directed by: Woody Allen

Written by: Woody Allen

Cinematography by: Vilmos Zsigmond

Sound: Lee Dichter

Editing: Alisa Lepselter

Art Direction: Dominic Masters

Costumes: Beatrix Aruna Pasztor

Production Design: Jim Clay

MPAA rating: R

Running time: 98 minutes

REVIEWS

Chang, Justin. *Variety.* May 17, 2010.
Dudek, Duane. *Milwaukee Journal Sentinel.* October 14, 2010.
Ebert, Roger. *Chicago Sun-Times.* September 30, 2010.
Edelstein, David. *New York Magazine.* September 27, 2010.
Long, Tom. *Detroit News.* October 15, 2010.
Maurstad, Tom. *Dallas Morning News.* October 8, 2010.
Moore, Roger. *Orlando Sentinel.* October 13, 2010.
Morgenstern, Joe. *Wall Street Journal.* September 23, 2010.
Puig, Claudia. *USA Today.* September 22, 2010.
Scott, A.O. *New York Times.* September 22, 2010.

TRIVIA

Both Anna Friel and Celia Imrie filmed their roles in one day.

Woody Allen's first feature film not produced by long time collaborator Charles H. Joffe who passed away in 2008.

YOUTH IN REVOLT

Every "revolution" needs a leader.
—Movie tagline

He wasn't a rebel until he found his cause.
—Movie tagline

Box Office: $15 million

When *Youth in Revolt* made its debut in the early days of 2010 after several postponements, it proved to be a disappointment at the box-office and was pulled from theaters so quickly that it was as if it never existed. Although its inability to catch on with audiences could be attributed to any number of factors, such as the failure of the cash-strapped Weinstein Company to mount a credible marketing campaign and the overwhelming success of the then-current *Avatar* (2009) essentially steamrolling over all the competition, it seemed that much of the blame for viewer apathy could be placed on the slender shoulders of its star, Michael Cera. Having established himself as a fan favorite for his portrayal of the sweetly nerdy and terminally lovelorn George Michael Bluth on the late, great TV series *Arrested Development*, he then proceeded to play slight variations on that basic persona in such films as *Superbad* (2007), *Juno* (2007), *Nick and Norah's Infinite Playlist* (2008), *Paper Heart* (2009), and *Year One* (2009). With all of those films having come out in the space of a couple of years and with the similarly-themed and highly-publicized *Scott Pilgrim vs. the World* (2010) lurking in the wings later in the year, it seemed that people had just grown tired of seeing him doing essentially the same thing over and over again. This was too bad because, as it turns out, *Youth in Revolt* is a film a lot smarter and funnier than the ads let on and one of the chief reasons for its success is the way that it allows Cera to deftly spoof his mild-mannered persona in the service of a raucous teen comedy that plays less like a *Porky's* (1981) knockoff and more like the inspired mating of the subversive cult favorites *Lord Love A Duck* (1966) and *Fight Club* (1999).

Cera plays the unfortunately-named Nick Twisp, an exceptionally-awkward hipster teen who is living with his divorced mother (Jean Smart) and her piggish live-in boyfriend (Zach Galifianakis), seemingly doomed to live in a world in which everyone, no matter how loathsome or slow-witted, seems to be having sex on a regular basis except for him. As the story opens, the boyfriend has run afoul of some Russian sailors and this necessitates an instant "vacation" for the trio to the Restless Axles trailer park. It is here that Nick meets and becomes instantly besotted with Sheeni Saunders (Portia Doubleday), a girl who is smart as a whip, cute as a button, obsessed with all things French, hip enough to understand Nick's cultural references (and even to catch him when he makes a mistake) and decidedly not a virgin. Naturally, she already has a boyfriend but that obstacle does not prevent her from the occasional makeout session. Just when Nick's dream of losing his virginity seems about to come true, it is shattered when he is suddenly forced to return home. Not willing to take this setback lying down, Nick decides to indulge in long-overdue rebellious behavior in the hopes that it will reunite him with Sheeni and even goes so far as to develop an alter ego in the form of mustachioed French bad boy Francois Dillinger (Cera again) to help inspire mayhem that includes car theft, massive property damage, infiltration of a French-language boarding school, public nudity, cross-dressing and various drugs, among other things.

On the surface, *Youth in Revolt* may appear to be virtually identical with all of the other horny teenager movies of the last few years but one of the great pleasures of watching the film is to see how it actually confounds such expectations at virtually every turn. Instead of using the brash, noisy, and borderline cartoonish approach favored by most directors working in this particular sub-genre, Miguel Arteta, making his first feature since *The Good Girl* (2002), has instead gone for a more laid-back and deadpan take that does an effective job of putting viewers in Nick's detached mind and offers up a nice contrast with some of the wilder twists and turns of the material. The screenplay by Gustin Nash is also smarter than one might expect without tripping over the line into precociousness. The casting is also unusually spot-on and effective for this kind of film—in addition to those already mentioned, there are also turns from Steve Buscemi as Nick's creepy dad, Ari Graynor as his much-younger live-in girlfriend, Ray Liotta as a cop who briefly takes up with Nick's mom, Fred Willard as a friendly neighbor and, best of all, M. Emmet Walsh and Mary Kay Place as Sheeni's deeply-devout and deeply-disapproving parents. Even people who have usually proven to be comedic black holes in the past such as Galifianakis and Justin Long, who turns up as Sheeni's mushroom-addled older brother, score a few laughs here. However, the biggest surprise to be found in the film is the hilarious dual performance turned in by Cera. The role of Nick is obviously the sort that he has played many times in the past and, by this point, he could pretty much do it in his sleep, but the secondary role of Francois allows him to spoof those roles and their lack of range while showing that he is capable of scoring laughs without having to constantly play the overly earnest geek.

Youth in Revolt is not without its flaws. The episodic nature of the story makes it feel at times like a collection of sketches instead of a fully formed tale and it loses a certain amount of narrative drive as it goes on as a result. A bigger problem is the fact that, having done its best to give all of its supporting characters a few quirks and twists to keep them from seeming like clichés, the film disappointingly portrays Nick's rival for Sheeni's affections as just another bland William Zabka clone who could have been trucked in from any other ordinary teen movie. For the most part, though, *Youth in Revolt* manages to avoid those pitfalls and while the end result may have turned out to be too odd to make it with a mass audience the first time around, it may eventually develop a cult following over time as more and more people are gradually exposed to its strange charms. This is the kind of movie that even someone as demanding as Nick Twisp himself would wholeheartedly embrace as being right on his particular wavelength.

Peter Sobczynski

CREDITS

Nick Twisp/Francois Dillinger: Michael Cera
George Twisp: Steve Buscemi
Estelle Twisp: Jean Smart
Paul Saunders: Justin Long
Sheeni Saunders: Portia Doubleday
Lance Wescott: Ray Liotta
Lacey: Ari Graynor
Mr. Ferguson: Fred Willard
Jerry: Zach Galifianakis
Lefty: Erik Knudsen
Mr. Saunders: M. Emmet Walsh
Mrs. Saunders: Mary Kay Place
Origin: USA
Language: English
Released: 2010
Production: David Permut; Shangri-La Entertainment; released by Dimension Films
Directed by: Miguel Arteta
Written by: Gustin Nash
Cinematography by: Chuy Chavez
Music by: John Swihart
Sound: Jonathan S. Gaynor
Music Supervisor: Anne Litt
Editing: Andy Keir, Pamela Martin
Costumes: Nancy Steiner
Production Design: Tony Fanning
MPAA rating: R
Running time: 90 minutes

REVIEWS

Dargis, Manohla. *New York Times.* January 8, 2010.
Debruge, Peter. *Variety.* September 4, 2009.
Edelstein, David. *New York Magazine.* January 11, 2010.
Ebert, Roger. *Chicago Sun-Times.* January 7, 2010.
Phillips, Michael. *Chicago Tribune.* January 7, 2010.
Rabin, Nathan. *AV Club.* January 7, 2010.
Schwarzbaum, Lisa. *Entertainment Weekly.* January 6, 2010.
Snider, Eric. *EricDSnider.com.* January 15, 2010.
Tallerico, Brian. *MovieRetriever.com.* January 8, 2010.
Wilonsky, Robert. *Village Voice.* January 5, 2010.

QUOTES

Francois Dillinger: "I want to tickle your belly button...from the inside."
Nick Twisp: "In the movies the good guy gets the girl. In real life it's usually the prick."

TRIVIA

Francois Dillinger's eyes are light blue and Nick Twisp's eye color is brown.

List of Awards

Academy Awards

Film: (*The King's Speech*)
Animated Film: (*Toy Story 3*)
Director: Tom Hooper (*The King's Speech*)
Actor: Colin Firth (*The King's Speech*)
Actress: Natalie Portman (*Black Swan*)
Supporting Actor: Christian Bale (*The Fighter*)
Supporting Actress: Melissa Leo (*The Fighter*)
Original Screenplay: David Seidler (*The King's Speech*)
Adapted Screenplay: Aaron Sorkin (*The Social Network*)
Cinematography: Wally Pfister (*Inception*)
Editing: Kirk Baxter and Angus Wall (*The Social Network*)
Art Direction: Robert Stromberg and Karen O'Hara (*Alice in Wonderland*)
Visual Effects: Chris Corbould, Andrew Lockley, Pete Bebb, and Paul J. Franklin (*Inception*)
Sound: Lora Hirschberg, Gary Rizzo, and Ed Novick (*Inception*)
Sound Editing: Richard King (*Inception*)
Makeup: Rick Baker and Dave Elsey (*The Wolfman*)
Costume Design: Colleen Atwood (*Alice in Wonderland*)
Original Score: Trent Reznor and Atticus Ross (*The Social Network*)
Original Song: "We Belong Together" (Randy Newman *Toy Story 3*)
Foreign Language Film: (*In a Better World*)
Documentary, Feature: (*Inside a Job*)
Documentary, Short Subject: (*Strangers No More*)
Short Film, Animated: (*The Lost Thing*)
Short Film, Live Action: (*God of Love*)

British Academy of Film & Television Awards

Animated Film: (*Toy Story 3*)
Film: (*The King's Speech*)
British Film of the Year: (*The King's Speech*)
Director: David Fincher (*The Social Network*)
Original Screenplay: David Seidler (*The King's Speech*)
Adapted Screenplay: Aaron Sorkin (*The Social Network*)
Actor: Colin Firth (*The King's Speech*)
Actress: Natalie Portman (*Black Swan*)
Supporting Actor: Geoffrey Rush (*The King's Speech*)
Supporting Actress: Helena Bonham Carter (*The King's Speech*)
Editing: Angus Wall and Kirk Baxter (*The Social Network*)
Cinematography: Roger Deakins (*True Grit*)
Production Design: Guy Hendrix Dyas, Larry Dias, and Douglas A. Mowat (*Inception*)
Costume Design: Colleen Atwood (*Alice in Wonderland*)
Makeup: Valli O'Reilly and Paul Gooch (*Alice in Wonderland*)
Sound: Richard King, Lora Hirschberg, Gary A. Rizzo, and Ed Novick (*Inception*)
Visual Effects: Chris Corbould, Paul Franklin, Andrew Lockley, and Peter Bebb (*Inception*)
Music: Alexandre Desplat (*The King's Speech*)
Outstanding Debut by a British Writer, Director, or Producer: Christopher Morris (*Four Lions*)
Outstanding British Film: (*The King's Speech*)
Foreign Film: (*The Girl with the Dragon Tattoo*)
Short Animation: (*The Eagleman Stag*)
Short Film: (*Until the River Runs Red*)

Directors Guild of America Awards

Outstanding Directorial Achievement in Motion Pictures: Tom Hooper (*The King's Speech*)

Outstanding Directorial Achievement in Documentary: Charles Ferguson (*Inside Job*)

Golden Globes

Film, Drama: (*The Social Network*)

Film, Musical or Comedy: (*The Kids Are All Right*)

Animated Film: (*Toy Story 3*)

Director: David Fincher (*The Social Network*)

Actor, Drama: Colin Firth (*The King's Speech*)

Actor, Musical or Comedy: Paul Giamatti (*Barney's Version*)

Actress, Drama: Natalie Portman (*Black Swan*)

Actress, Musical or Comedy: Annette Bening (*The Kids Are All Right*)

Supporting Actor: Christian Bale (*The Fighter*)

Supporting Actress: Melissa Leo (*The Fighter*)

Screenplay: Aaron Sorkin (*The Social Network*)

Score: Trent Reznor and Atticus Ross (*The Social Network*)

Song: "You Haven't Seen The Last of Me" (Diane Warren *Burlesque*)

Foreign Language Film: (*In a Better World*)

Golden Raspberry Awards

Worst Picture: (*The Last Airbender*)

Worst Director: M. Night Shyamalan (*The Last Airbender*)

Worst Actor: Ashton Kutcher (*Killers*) and (*Valentine's Day*)

Worst Actress: The Four "Gal Pals" (*Sex and the City 2*)

Worst Supporting Actor: Jackson Rathbone (*The Last Airbender*) and (*The Twilight Saga: Eclipse*)

Worst Supporting Actress: Jessica Alba (*The Killer Inside Me*), (*Little Fockers*), (*Machete*), and (*Valentine's Day*)

Worst Screenplay: M. Night Shyamalan (*The Last Airbender*)

Worst Screen Couple: The Entire Cast (*Sex and the City 2*)

Worst Remake, Rip-Off or Sequel: (*Sex and the City 2*)

Worst Eye-Gouging Use of 3D: (*The Last Airbender*)

Independent Spirit Awards

Film: (*Black Swan*)

First Film: Aaron Schneider (*Get Low*)

Director: Darren Aronofsky (*Black Swan*)

Actor: James Franco (*127 Hours*)

Actress: Natalie Portman (*Black Swan*)

Supporting Actor: John Hawkes (*Winter's Bone*)

Supporting Actress: Dale Dickey (*Winter's Bone*)

Screenplay: Stuart Blumberg and Lisa Choldodenko (*The Kids Are All Right*)

First Screenplay: Lena Dunham (*Tiny Furniture*)

Cinematography: Matthew Libatique (*Black Swan*)

Foreign Film: (*The King's Speech*)

Documentary: (*Exit Through the Gift Shop*)

Truer than Fiction Award: (*Marwencol*)

Robert Altman Award: (*Please Give*)

Screen Actors Guild Awards

Actor: Colin Firth (*The King's Speech*)

Actress: Natalie Portman (*Black Swan*)

Supporting Actor: Christian Bale (*The Fighter*)

Supporting Actress: Melissa Leo (*The Fighter*)

Ensemble Cast: (*The King's Speech*)

Stunt Ensemble: (*Inception*)

Writers Guild of America Awards

Original Screenplay: Christopher Nolan (*Inception*)

Adapted Screenplay: Aaron Sorkin (*The Social Network*)

Documentary Screenplay: Charles Ferguson, Chad Beck, and Adam Bolt (*Inside Job*)

Obituaries

Danny Aiello III (January 27, 1957–May 1, 2010). Son of character actor Danny Aiello, Danny Aiello III was a stuntman and stunt coordinator who passed away from pancreatic cancer in Hillsdale, California. Aiello worked behind-the-scenes for years, coordinating stunts on such diverse projects as *Sex and the City 2* (2010) and the FX series *Rescue Me*. The stunt professional also worked on soap operas, including twenty episodes of *All My Children* and an amazing 846 episodes of *One Life to Live*. The resume of stunt work coordinated by Mr. Aiello stretches over a hundred credits including such notable entries as *Jacob's Ladder* (1990), *The Last Boy Scout* (1991), *Die Hard: With a Vengeance* (1995), *Cop Land* (1997), *Catch Me If You Can* (2002), *Angels in America* (2003), and *Eternal Sunshine of the Spotless Mind* (2004). He also had a few acting credits and even directed his father in *18 Shades of Dust* (1999).

Corey Allen (June 29, 1934–June 27, 2010). Born Alan Cohen, the son of famed Las Vegas casino owner Carl Cohen, Allen studied acting at UCLA and after graduating, he appeared in numerous plays and had bit parts in films such as *The Mad Magician* (1954), *The Bridges at Toko-Ri* (1954) and *The Night of the Hunter* (1955) before being selected by Nicholas Ray to play the role of doomed driver Buzz Gunderson in the cult classic *Rebel Without a Cause* (1955). For the next ten years, he worked steadily as an actor both in television, including appearances on *The Millionaire, Alfred Hitchcock Presents, Gunsmoke,* and *Bonanza* and on the big screen in *Party Girl* (1958), *Sweet Bird of Youth* (1962) and *The Chapman Report* (1962). After that, he shifted his focus from acting to directing and spent the majority of the remainder of his career behind the camera. Although most of his directing was for television, including episodes of *Mannix, Barnaby Jones, Police Woman, Quincy,* and *Hill Street Blues* (for which he won an Emmy for Outstanding Direction in a Drama Series in 1981), he also helmed a handful of theatrical releases that included the infamous *The Erotic Adventures of Pinocchio* (1971), *Thunder and Lightning* (1974), and *Avalanche* (1978).

Roy Ward Baker (December 19, 1916–October 5, 2010). Born in London, Baker went to work at the Gainsborough Studios and, within the space of three years, went from being a lowly teaboy to working as an assistant director. During World War II, he served in the Army Kinematograph unit under writer/producer Eric Ambler and when the war was over, Ambler gave Baker the opportunity to make his feature film directorial debut with *The October Man* (1947). In the early Fifties, he went to Hollywood and directed a handful of films, the most notable of the bunch being *Don't Bother to Knock* (1952), a suspense thriller featuring Marilyn Monroe in an early lead performance as a dangerously unhinged babysitter. After a few years, Baker returned to England and made the most celebrated film of his career, *A Night to Remember* (1958), a straightforward and melodrama-free look at the sinking of the Titanic. Until retiring in 1992, he would work steadily with most of his efforts being in the fantasy and horror genres, including such films as *Moon Zero Two* (1969), *The Vampire Lovers* (1970), *Scars of Dracula* (1970), *Asylum* (1972), and the infamous vampire/kung-fu hybrid *The Legend of the 7 Golden Vampires* (1974) as well as episodes of the British cult television favorites *The Saint* and *The Avengers*.

Barbara Billingsley (December 22, 1915–October 16, 2010). The legendary TV icon was born Barbara Lillian Combes in Los Angeles, California, and began acting at a young age. The surname with which she would become a household name happened in 1942 when Combes married Glenn Billingsley (who she would divorce in 1947, remarrying in 1953 to Roy Kellino and in 1959 to Dr. William S. Mortensen). Like so many actors and actresses, Billingsley's acting career began on stage, appearing on Broadway and being signed to a contract with MGM Studios in 1945. Billingsley took small roles, often uncredited, in films for years before sitcom and TV work in the 1950s. She would work on and off in television, but the role for which she will forever be remembered is June Cleaver on the iconic family sitcom *Leave it to Beaver*. She was typecast in the mother role for years after that program ended and had essentially retired when she came out of hiding to steal scenes in the comedy classic *Airplane!* (1980). This led to more regular TV and film work in the 1980s and 1990s, including appearances on *Mork & Mindy* and *Roseanne*. Her final film credit was in the film reboot of *Leave it to Beaver* (1997).

Lisa Blount (July 1, 1957–October 25, 2010). Born in Jacksonville, Arkansas, Blount began her career as a child actress in *Sam's Song* (1969) and studied at Jacksonville High School and Valdosta State University. She acted from the 1980s to the 2000s but will be most remembered for one of her first roles opposite Debra Winger in *An Officer and a Gentleman* (1982). Other notable credits include *Prince of Darkness* (1987), *Great Balls of Fire!* (1989), and TV's critically-acclaimed *Profit*. Blount won an Academy Award® in 2001 for the live-action short film *The Accountant* (2001) and suffered from idiopathic thrombocytopenic purpura, a blood-related disease that took her life at a far-too-young age.

Tom Bosley (October 1, 1927–October 19, 2010). He will forever be remembered as one of the most iconic TV patriarchs of all time on ABC's *Happy Days* but Tom Bosley acted regularly for over five decades. Born in Chicago, Bosley served in the Navy in World War II, and began his stage career while attending DePaul University, even performing on the same stage as Paul Newman in Woodstock, Illinois in 1949 and 1950. Less than a decade later, Bosley would win a Tony Award for his work in the musical *Fiorello!* His first film role was a notable one, opposite Natalie Wood in *Love with the Proper Stranger* (1963). He would work regularly over the next several decades, most notably on *Happy Days, Murder, She Wrote,* and *Father Dowling Mysteries*. Other notable credits include *Yours, Mine and Ours* (1968), *The Debbie Reynolds Show, The Love Boat,* and dozens of other TV guest appearances of all kinds. His final credit was opposite Jennifer Lopez in *The Back-Up Plan* (2010).

Robert F. Boyle (October 10, 1909–August 1, 2010). Art director and production designer Robert Francis Boyle was born in Los Angeles, California and worked consistently for decades, including several collaborations with Alfred Hitchcock. He trained at the University of Southern California but struggled to find work during the Depression before art department work at Paramount Pictures in the 1930s and becoming the lead art director at Universal Studios in the 1940s. It was there that he would begin his working relationship with Hitchcock, working on *Saboteur* (1942), *North by Northwest* (1959), *The Birds* (1963), and *Marnie* (1964). Boyle was responsible for one of the most iconic moments in film history, recreating the Mount Rushmore set for the climax of *North by Northwest*. Boyle was nominated four times for the Academy Award® for Best Art Direction and won the Art Directors Guild's Lifetime Achievement Award in 1997 and the Academy's Honorary Academy Award® in 2008. At 98, he was the oldest winner of that award, walking onstage with Nicole Kidman to accept the award. Notable credits of an amazing career include *It Came From Outer Space* (1953), *Cape Fear* (1962), *The Russians Are Coming, the Russians Are Coming, In Cold Blood* (1967), *Fiddler on the Roof* (1971), *Portnoy's Complaint* (1972), *Mame* (1974), *The Shootist* (1976), *Private Benjamin* (1980), and *Staying Alive* (1983).

Jackie Burroughs (February 2, 1939–September 22, 2010). Canadian actress Jacqueline Burroughs was actually born in Lancashire, England in 1939 although she earned her initial reputation by performing at the world-renowned Stratford Festival in Ontario. Burroughs will be most remembered for a series of roles in the early 1980s, including voiceover work in *Heavy Metal* (1981) and crucial roles in *The Dead Zone* (1983) and *The Grey Fox* (1982). She would earn numerous Canadian TV awards and international acclaim for her TV work, most notably in *Road to Avonlea* and she was a crucial part of the highly-acclaimed mini-series *More Tales of the City* (1998) and *Further Tales of the City* (2001). With five decades of consistent work in film and television, other recent notable roles included *Lost and Delirious* (2001), the series premiere of TV's *Smallville, Willard* (2003), *Fever Pitch* (2005), and *First Snow* (2006). She died of stomach cancer at the age of seventy-one.

Ian Carmichael (June 18, 1920–February 5, 2010). English film and television actor Ian Gillett Carmichael was born in Hull, England in 1920 and made his stage debut in London right before the outbreak of World War II. The war interrupted his career as he served in the Royal Armoured Corps but he returned to it after leaving the Army in 1947 and found his most success in the 1950s including roles in *Betrayed* (1954) with Clark Gable and Lana Turner, *The Colditz Story* (1955), *Private's Progress* (1956), *Brothers in Law* (1957), *I'm All Right Jack* (1959), and *School for Scoundrels* (1960). He would work regularly in British television until shortly before his death.

Dixie Carter (May 25, 1939–April 10, 2010). The Southern actress Dixie Carter will be most remembered for her award-winning work on the sitcom *Designing Women* but she had a notable stage and film career as well. Carter made her stage debut in 1960 in a Memphis production of *Carousal* and was on a New York stage just three years later. She would make her TV debut in 1974, filling in for actress Nancy Pinkerton on the hit soap opera *One Life to Live* before landing her own recurring role on the soap *The Edge of Night*. She would find her most success on *Designing Women,* which would define her for the rest of her career, as she went on to also appear on the series *Family Law* and *Desperate Housewives,* for which she was nominated for an Emmy Award. Carter only had a few film roles but one of her final ones was with her husband, Hal Halbrook, in the highly-acclaimed *That Evening Sun* (2009). Holbrook delivered the sad news of her death from endometrial cancer on April 10th.

Claude Chabrol (June 24, 1930–September 12, 2010). Although he was a charter member of the Nouvelle Vague film movement that burst out of France in the late 1950s and revolutionized cinema (a group of critics-turned-filmmakers that also included the likes of Jean-Luc Godard, Francois Truffaut, Jacques Rivette, and Eric Rohmer), Claude Chabrol was not as interested in shaking things up stylistically as his colleagues. Instead, he was more interested in how filmmakers ranging from Alfred Hitchcock (whom he co-wrote a book about with Rohmer in 1957) to otherwise-unheralded Hollywood contract directors were able to imprint whatever material they were working with, good or bad, with traits that made them distinctively their own. Over the course of over sixty films starting off with *Le beau Serge* (1958), he would go on to do just that with a series of films that would offer endless and fascinating variations on his favorite themes of infidelity, guilt, and murder teeming just beneath the well-manicured surfaces of the bourgeois class. Although the prolific nature of his filmography would confound some critics and lead to the occasional artistic dead end, such as the English-language misfire *Blood Relatives* (1978) and a dramatically inert adaptation of *Madame Bovary* (1991), his ability to generate suspense without ever seeming to break a sweat would result in such acclaimed and often blood-curdling works as *Les bonnes femmes* (1960), *Le Boucher* (1969), *Violette* (1977) (the first of many celebrated collaborations with actress Isabelle Huppert), *The Story of Women* (1988), *Betty* (1992), *L'enfer* (1994) (a project originally developed and abandoned two decades earlier by French filmmaker Henri-Georges Clouzot), *La CérÉmonie* (1995), *Merci Pour le Chocolat* (1999) and *The Flower of Evil* (2003). His final feature of his half-century career was *Inspector Bellamy* (2009), a quirky crime drama that would see him working for the first time with another legend of French cinema, actor Gerard Depardieu. Throughout his career, Chabrol would win a number of awards for his individual efforts and in 2004 he would be given the European Film Prize for his entire body of work.

Ronni Sue Chasen (October 17, 1946–November 16, 2010). Chasen was a legendary publicist who had her finger on the pulse of everything happening in Hollywood when she was shockingly gunned down after driving home from the premiere of *Burlesque* (2010) on November 16th in an apparently random act of violence. One of the most popular and professional women in her business, Chasen represented Michael Douglas, Hans Zimmer, Mark Isham, and many others, along with directing Academy Award® campaigns for more than a hundred films including Best Picture winners *Driving Miss Daisy* (1989) and *The Hurt Locker* (2009). She was the Senior Vice President for publicity at MGM in the 1990s and owned the firm Chasen & Co., which represented numerous Hollywood power players.

Maury Chaykin (July 27, 1949–July 27, 2010). The incredibly-recognizable character actor Maury Chaykin was born in Brooklyn in 1949 to Irving J. Chaykin and he would study drama in New York at the State University of New York at Buffalo before moving to Toronto, where he lived until his death. Chaykin had significant success in television playing detective Nero Wolfe on A&E and an obvious riff on the legendary Harvey Weinstein on HBO's *Entourage,* but he will likely be most remembered for a series of blustery supporting character roles in a diverse array of films including *WarGames,* (1983), *Mrs. Soffel* (1984), *Turk 182* (1985), *The Bedroom Window* (1987), *Iron Eagle II* (1988), *Twins* (1988), *Dances with Wolves,* (1990), *My Cousin Vinny* (1992), *Devil in a Blue Dress,* (1995), *The Sweet Hereafter* (1997), *A Life Less Ordinary* (1997), *Being Julia* (2004), *Where the Truth Lies* (2005), *Barney's Version* (2010), and *Casino Jack* (2010).

Jill Clayburgh (April 30, 1944–November 5, 2010). Two-time Academy Award® nominee, Jill Clayburgh was born in New York City to a theatrical production secretary and a manufacturing executive. She did not become an actress until after attending school and started on stage in Boston and in New York City, making her screen debut in *The Wedding Party* (1969), becoming a household name in the 1970s with hits like *Silver Streak* (1976). She scored back-to-back Oscar® nominations for *An Unmarried Woman* (1978) and *Starting Over* (1979) and would arguably never reach the level of fame she had in the 1970s again although she remained a respected actress throughout her career. Clayburgh notoriously dated Al Pacino for a period of time and married playwright David Rabe in 1979. Notable roles outside of her Oscar®-nominated ones include *I'm Dancing as Fast as I Can* (1982), *Whispers in the Dark* (1992), *Rich in Love* (1993), *Fools Rush In* (1997), *Running with Scissors* (2006), TV's *Dirty Sexy Money, Love and Other Drugs* (2010), and her final film, *Bridesmaids* (2011).

Gary Coleman (February 8, 1968–May 28, 2010). Gary Wayne Coleman was born in 1968 in Zion, Illinois and will forever be remembered for playing Arnold Jackson on the sitcom *Diff'rent Strokes* in the 1970s and 1980s. He would struggle in the years after, appearing in B-movies and TV guest appearances but never breaking free of the shadow of the role that defined him or the financial troubles that would haunt him (he would successfully sue his parents in 1989 for misappropriation of the money earned during the peak of his fame). Coleman suffered from an autoimmune kidney disease that limited his height to 4' 8? and forced him to undergo daily dialysis while also being typecast as a child for the rest of his life. Coleman had appeared on *The Jeffersons* and *Good Times* before getting the role that would define him in 1978. He made his feature film debut in *On the Right Track* (1981) and went on to appear, often as himself, in *S.F.W.* (1994), *Dirty Work* (1998), *Dickie Roberts: Former Child Star,* (2003), and *An American Carol* (2008).

Robert Culp (August 16, 1930–March 24, 2010). Born in Oakland, California in 1930, Robert Culp was most widely known for his work in television (particularly the hit *I Spy* with Bill Cosby in the 1960s) but also appeared in film and worked as a screenwriter and voice actor. Before becoming a household name, Culp appeared on several other series including *Trackdown, The Barbara Stanwyck Show, The Man from U.N.C.L.E.,* and *The Outer Limits*. After *I Spy,* Robert Culp would make regular TV appearances for the next several decades, including recurring roles on *Columbo* and *Everybody Loves Raymond,* but his film work was more limited, starting with *PT 109* (1963). His most notable role was as Bob in *Bob & Carol & Ted & Alice* (1969), near the height of his fame. Other film performances include *Turk 182* (1985), *The Pelican Brief* (1993), *Spy Hard* (1996), and *Most Wanted* (1997).

Tony Curtis (June 3, 1925–September 29, 2010). One of the few remaining icons of the golden age of cinema passed away on September 29th, 2010 when Bernard Schwartz (aka Tony Curtis) died due to cardiac arrest in Henderson, Nevada. Tony Curtis was a living legend, a man whose acting career spanned six decades and included over 100 films, many of which fill lists of the best ever made. Born in New York City, Curtis' parents were Hungarian Jewish immigrants and his mother was diagnosed with schizophrenia later in life, leading to a tumultuous upbringing for the future superstar including time in an orphanage. He joined the United States Navy after Pearl Harbor and served in World War II. After the War, he attended City College of New York and studied drama, being placed under contract by Universal Pictures at the age of 23. Curtis made his uncredited screen debut in *Criss Cross* (1949) but, despite regular work throughout the next decade, did not really break through until eight years later with a brilliant performance in *Sweet Smell of Success* (1957), followed by an Oscar®-nominated one with Sidney Poitier in *The Defiant Ones* (1958). Tony Curtis was one of the biggest movie stars alive in the late 1950s and 1960s, appearing in *Some Like It Hot* (1959), *Spartacus* (1960), for which he was Golden Globe-nominated, *The Outsider* (1961), *Sex and the Single Girl* (1964), *The Great Race* (1965), and *The Boston Strangler* (1968). Early in his career, Curtis married another screen legend, Janet Leigh, and the two were together from 1951 to 1962, during which he fathered another legend, Jamie Lee Curtis. He would marry four more times before his death. Other memorable films from the resume of the legend include *Operation Petticoat* (1959), *The Count of Monte Cristo* (1975), *The Last Tycoon* (1976), the B-movie cult classic *The Manitou* (1978), and *Insignificance* (1985).

Dino De Laurentiis (August 8, 1919–November 10, 2010). One of the last of the big-time showmen, De Laurentiis enrolled in film school in Italy at the age of 17 and supported himself by working any number of odd jobs within the industry and by the age of 20, he had already produced his first feature film, *L'amore canta* (1941) before leaving to fight for the Italian Army during World War II. After the war, he returned to the film industry and had his first major international hit with the neo-realist drama *Bitter Rice* (1949). From there, he entered into a partnership with fellow Italian producer Carlo Ponti and had a number of successes that included the Federico Fellini classics *La strada* (1954) (for which he won the Oscar® for Best Foreign-Language Film) and *Nights in Cabria* (1956) and an epic adaptation of *War and Peace* (1956) before they dissolved their relationship. In the 1960s, he embarked on an ambitious plan to create a massive studio complex that would allow him to make the jumbo-sized spectacles that he was increasingly becoming known for, such as *Barabbas* (1961), *The Bible: In the Beginning* (1966), *Anzio* (1968), and *Barbarella* (1968) until a string of expensive flops and a general downturn in the Italian film industry forced him to close it down. In the 1970s, he relocated to America and began producing a string of films that would veer wildly between blatantly commercial endeavors like *Death Wish* (1974), *Mandingo* (1975), *Lipstick* (1976), *King Kong* (1976), *Flash Gordon* (1980), *Conan the Barbarian* (1982), and *Amityville II: The Possession* (1982) and more artistically inclined efforts like *Serpico* (1973), *Three Days of the Condor* (1975), *Buffalo Bill and the Indians* (1976), *The Serpent's Egg* (1977), and *Ragtime* (1981). During that time, he had a number of expensive box-office flops, including two attempts to cash in on the success of *Jaws* (1975), *Orca the Killer Whale* (1977) and *The White Buffalo* (1977), a remake

of *Hurricane* (1979), David Lynch's flawed-but-ambitious adaptation of Frank Herbert's classic sci-fi novel *Dune* (1984) and *Year of the Dragon* (1985). He formed his own production company, De Laurentiis Entertainment Group, in an attempt to replicate what he had done two decades earlier in Italy. Although DEG would finance and distribute two of the best American films of the 1980s in Lynch's *Blue Velvet* (1986) (which De Laurentiis agreed to back in exchange for Lynch directing *Dune*) and Michael Mann's *Manhunter* (1986), neither one made very much money, and that, combined with such expensive money-losers as *Maximum Overdrive* (1986), *Tai-Pan* (1986), and *King Kong Lives* (1986), forced him to shut it down for good in 1988. He continued to produce films such as *Army of Darkness* (1993), *Body of Evidence* (1993), and *U-571* (2000) and would return to box-office glory with a trio of films featuring the erudite cannibalistic serial killer Hannibal Lecter: The non-De Laurentiis-produced *Silence of the Lambs* (1991), *Hannibal* (2001), a remake of *Red Dragon* (2002), and the prequel *Hannibal Rising* (2007). In 2001, just as *Hannibal* was riding high atop the box-office charts, he was awarded the Irving G. Thallberg Memorial Award at that year's Academy Awards® ceremony.

Jimmy Dean (August 10, 1928–June 13, 2010). Jimmy Dean will forever live on as the brand name for a successful sausage line but the man who gave his name to a pork product started as a multi-talented singer, TV host, actor, and businessman, even appearing in a James Bond movie. Born in Plainview, Texas in 1928, Jimmy Ray Dean would go on to personify "good ol' boy" Southern hospitality, starting with a minor radio hit in the 1950s and then moving on hosting a country music program on WARL-AM in Washington, D.C. It was not long before Dean was on television, appearing on *The Jimmy Dean Show* on CBS in the 1950s. He had a few country hits in the 1960s, even winning a Grammy Award, and even hosted *The Tonight Show* on occasion, returning to another incarnation of *The Jimmy Dean Show* on ABC in the mid-1960s. He turned to acting after the end of the show, appearing mostly on television programs like *Daniel Boone* and *Fantasy Island*, but he will also be remembered for playing Willard Whyte in *Diamonds Are Forever* (1971) and he also appeared in a film based on his hit song called *Big Bad John* (1990). He passed away on June 13th from natural causes.

Blake Edwards (July 26, 1922–December 15, 2010). Blake Edwards was born in Tulsa, Oklahoma into a family that even then had show-biz connections—his stepfather's father was a director of silent movies and his stepfather worked as a production manager and as a stage director. He got his start in the movie industry as an actor with small parts in a number of films, including uncredited appearances in *Thirty Seconds Over Tokyo* (1944), *The Strange Love of Martha Ivers* (1946), and *The Best Years of Our Lives* (1946), and then moved on to become a screenwriter starting with *Panhandle* (1948). He made his directorial debut with *Bring Your Smile Along* (1955) and had his first big successes with *Operation Petticoat* (1959) and *Breakfast at Tiffany's* (1961). Over the course of his long career, he would come to be thought of strictly as a comedic director thanks to such efforts as *The Great Race* (1965), *The Party*

(1968), *10* (1979), *S.O.B.* (1981) and, perhaps most famously, the *Pink Panther* series, five of which—*The Pink Panther* (1963), *A Shot in the Dark* (1964), *Return of the Pink Panther* (1975), *The Pink Panther Strikes Again* (1976), and *Revenge of the Pink Panther* (1978)—he made in collaboration with Peter Sellers, one (*Trail of the Pink Panther*) which he pieced together out of unused footage featuring Sellers and newly-shot scenes that attempted to tie them together and two (*Curse of the Pink Panther* and *Son of the Pink Panther*) in which he unsuccessfully tried to continue the franchise with the respective likes of Ted Wass and a then-unknown Roberto Benigni. However, he would dabble in numerous genres throughout his career, including straightforward dramas (*Days of Wine and Roses, The Tamarind Seed,* and *That's Life*), thrillers (*Experiment in Terror* and *The Carey Treatment*), musicals (*Darling Lili* and *Victor Victoria*) and even a western (*Wild Rovers*). During his career, he would received only one Academy Award® nomination (a Best Adapted Screenplay nod for *Victor Victoria*) but in 2004, he received an honorary Oscar® "in recognition of his writing, directing, and producing an extraordinary body of work for the screen." He passed away on December 15th of complications from pneumonia.

Eddie Fisher (August 10, 1928–September 22, 2010). Known nearly as much for his off-stage and off-screen dalliances as his professional accomplishments, Eddie Fisher was an icon of his day, climbing the charts while keeping gossip magazines in business. Fisher had a growing singing career when he was drafted into the U.S. Army to serve in the Korean War. After he left combat, his star continued to rise, turning into two variety shows on NBC in the 1950s (*Coke Time with Eddie Fisher* and *The Eddie Fisher Show*). He was one of the most popular singers of the 1950s with seventeen songs in the top ten and thirty-five in the top forty. He married actress Debbie Reynolds in 1955 and the two welcomed future actress Carrie Fisher in 1956. He would star with Reynolds in a musical comedy that year called *Bundle of Joy* (1956). He left Debbie Reynolds in 1959 and appeared with his next wife, Elizabeth Taylor, in 1960's *Butterfield 8*. The two were married for five years and Eddie Fisher would have three more wives, including Connie Stevens, with whom he had two children, including actress Joely Fisher (TV's *'Til Death*). He passed away from complications due to hip surgery on September 22nd.

John Forsythe (January 29, 1918–April 1, 2010). Born Jacob Lincoln Freund in New Jersey, John Forsythe was a square-jawed icon for decade who was most-known for his work in television with three hit series that ran for multiple years and spanned decades—*Bachelor Father, Charlie's Angels,* and *Dynasty.* Forsythe started as a bit player for Warner Bros. in the 1940s, taking small roles until he was forced to suspend his acting career to serve in World War II in the U.S. Army Air Forces. He will likely forever be remembered for his iconic TV roles but he also worked with Alfred Hitchcock and Sidney Lumet in his limited film career. Highlights of his film work include *Destination Tokyo* (1943), *The Trouble with Harry* (1955), *In Cold Blood* (1967), *Topaz* (1969), *...And Justice for All* (1979), *Scrooged* (1988), *Charlie's Angels* (2000), and *Charlie's Angels: Full Throttle* (2003).

James Gammon (April 20, 1940–July 16, 2010). Born in Newman, Illinois in 1940, James Gammon was never a household name but always remained a recognizable character actor throughout his career, probably earning the most adoration for his memorable role as the manager in *Major League* (1989). He worked regularly in TV (and is probably remembered by some for recurring work on *Nash Bridges*) and theatre, founding the Met Theatre in Los Angeles in the 1970s, appearing in Sam Shepard's masterful play *Curse of the Starving Class.* He only appeared on Broadway once, in Sam Shepard's *Broken Child,* and earned a Tony Award nomination for that one performance. Notable film credits include *Cool Hand Luke* (1967), *Urban Cowboy* (1980), *Silverado* (1985), *The Milagro Beanfield War* (1988), *Major League II* (1994), *Wyatt Earp* (1994), *Wild Bill* (1995), *Cold Mountain* (2003), and *Appaloosa* (2008). Gammon passed away from liver cancer on July 16th.

Harold Gould (December 10, 1923–September 11, 2010). Born Harold Goldstein, Harold Gould will be most remembered for regular TV work including recurring roles on *Rhoda, The Mary Tyler Moore Show,* and *The Golden Girls.* He ultimately appeared on more than 300 television shows and was nominated for an Emmy Award five times, but he also appeared in nearly two dozen films including *The Sting* (1973), *The Front Page* (1974), *Love and Death,* (1975), *Silent Movie* (1976), *Patch Adams* (1998), *My Giant* (1998), *Stuart Little* (1999), and *Freaky Friday* (2003). The television programs on which Mr. Gould appeared are too many to list but highlights include *The Outer Limits, Dallas, L.A. Law, St. Elsewhere, Soap, Hawaii Five-O, Gunsmoke, The Fugitive, Get Smart, Mister Ed, The Twilight Zone, The Alfred Hitchcock Hour,* and many, many more. Mr. Gould passed away from prostate cancer on September 11thh and is survived by his wife Lea to whom he was married for six decades.

Peter Graves (March 18, 1926–March 14, 2010). Another actor primarily known for television, Peter Graves will be best-remembered for his iconic starring role on *Mission: Impossible* from 1967 to 1973, but he too had a significant film career. Born Peter Aurness (and younger brother of actor James Arness), Peter Graves started in television after serving in World War II, appearing regularly on several series before landing the role in *Mission: Impossible.* He also worked consistently in film including roles in *Stalag 17* (1953), *The Night of the Hunter* (1955), *Airplane!* (1980), *Savannah Smiles* (1982), *Airplane II: The Sequel* (1982), *The Winds of War* (1983), *Addams Family Values* (1993), *House on Haunted Hill* (1999), *Men in Black II* (2002), and *Looney Tunes: Back in Action* (2003), along with a number of B-movies that would become cult hits through their inclusion in *Mystery Science Theater 3000—SST: Death Flight* (1977), *It Conquered the World* (1956), *Beginning of the End* (1957), and *The Clonus Horror* (1979). Graves also hosted the A&E documentary series *Biography* in the 1990s and received a star on the Hollywood Walk of Fame in 2009. After marriage to his wife Joan for over six decades, Graves passed away from a heart attack on March 14th.

Kathryn Grayson (February 9, 1922–February 17, 2010). Opera singer and actress Zelma Kathryn Elisabeth Hedrick was born in Winston-Salem in 1922 and began her singing career at the age of twelve. By the early 1940s, Grayson was under contract with MGM and worked regularly in musicals for the studio, appearing with Frank Sinatra, Gene Kelly, and Howard Keel, among many others. After months of training with MGM, Grayson made her first appearance in 1941 in the studio's *Andy Hardy's Private Secretary.* She would appear in several films in the 1940s with co-stars including Van Heflin, Abbot and Costello, Gene Kelly, Mickey Rooney, Eleanor Powell, and June Allyson. She worked to entertain the troops during World War II and returned to film with one of her biggest hits, *Anchors Aweigh* (1945). She appeared in several more musicals, singing the Academy Award®-nominated song from *The Toast of New Orleans* (1950), but would not have another major musical hit until 1951 when she appeared with Keel and Ava Gardner in *Show Boat* (1951). After her MGM contract, Grayson went to work for Warner Bros. but would not find the same success again, although she would co-star in MGM's *Kiss Me Kate* (1953). She also appeared on TV in the 1950s but essentially retired after *The Vagabond King* (1956), although she returned for a few episodes of *Murder, She Wrote* in the 1980s. Grayson passed away of natural causes on February 17th.

Bud Greenspan (September 18, 1926–December 25, 2010). Jonah J. Greenspan, who went by his nickname Bud, was a film director, writer, and producer, primarily known for his work in sports documentaries. When he was only twenty-one years old, Greenspan became the sports director of the largest sports radio station in the United States. After he left there, he worked in print and in TV commercials, starting documentary filmmaking with a short called *The Strongest Man in the World* (1952). His film career would not really get going for another decade until a TV movie about the famed athlete Jesse Owens's trip to West Berlin called *Jesse Owens Returns to Berlin* (1964). He worked on dozens of TV specials, sports movies of the week, books, and sports magazine articles. Most of his work appeared on television but theatrical documentaries directed by Grayson included *The Glory of Their Times* (1977) and *16 Days of Glory* (1986).

Bob Guccione (December 17, 1930–October 20, 2010) Inspired by the success of Hugh Hefner's popular men's magazine *Playboy* while running a dry-cleaning business in London and working as a freelance cartoonist, Brooklyn-born Bob Guccione decided to launch a competing title that would offer readers photos of a far-more-explicit nature (often shot by Guccione himself) than even *Playboy* dared to show. The magazine, dubbed *Penthouse*, would debut in London in 1965 and made its first appearance in America in 1969, where it was an instant hit. In the mid-1970s, he decided to expand his horizons into the film world by personally financing *Caligula*, a $17 million dollar sexually-explicit biopic of the decadent Roman emperor featuring direction from Tinto Brass, a screenplay by Gore Vidal and a cast including the likes of Malcolm McDowell, Helen Mirren, Sir John Gielgud, and Peter O'Toole. By the time it was finally released in 1979, Vidal had his name removed from the project and Guccione had fired Tinto Brass for not including enough sex-related material—he would personally shoot several minutes of hardcore pornographic footage for inclusion in the final cut. The film was not well-received by critics and, despite elevated ticket prices, it was not a hit in its theatrical release, though it would prove to be a steady seller on home video. Although he would talk about possible future film projects, including a proposed take on the life of Catherine the Great, none of them ever came to pass. At the same time, he was also battling lung cancer and would succumb to the disease on October 20th.

Corey Haim (December 23, 1971–March 10, 2010). He eventually became a cautionary tale about the pitfalls of the fame that comes with being a teenage star, but there was a time when Corey Haim was one of the most promising stars of his generation, at least at the box office. Years after the peak of his fame, when he was appearing on reality shows and looked like a mere shadow of himself amidst rumors of substance abuse and legal problems, it may have been easier to write off his acting career (it was enough of a fall for the producers of the Academy Awards® to exclude him from their annual montage of the deceased). Haim, most often paired with fellow teen icon Corey Feldman (the two made an amazing seven movies together), was an undeniable movie star of his day; a household name. A child actor from the age of ten, Haim actually got his start on television on *The Edison Twins*, making his film debut in 1984 in *Firstborn*. Bigger and bigger roles followed, including *Secret Admirer* (1985), *Murphy's Romance* (1985), and *Silver Bullet* (1985), but the breakthrough would come the next year in *Lucas* (1986), a heartfelt and surprising hit. It would be followed by a much-bigger hit with Feldman in *The Lost Boys* (1987). Personal problems, including rumored substance abuse starting at the age of fifteen, would begin to haunt Haim but he would have a few more hits including *License to Drive* (1988), *Watchers* (1988), and *Dream a Little Dream* (1989). As fast as his career began, it seemed to crash, as Haim appeared in straight-to-video junk in the 1990s like *National Lampoon's Last Resort* (1994). After relative obscurity for over a decade, he enjoyed a brief bit of reality TV fame and passed away on March 10th from what was ruled a natural death related to pneumonia although years of substance abuse was perceived to have contributed to his weakened state even if it was not confirmed by any official reports.

June Havoc (November 8, 1912–March 28, 2010). Born Ellen Evangeline Hovick in 1912 in Vancouver, June Havoc was a well-known Broadway performer with a film career in the 1940s and 1950s and worked regularly as a child vaudeville star, sometimes with sister Gypsy Rose Lee (and watched her life with her chronicled in the Broadway hit *Gypsy*). June reportedly hit the stage at the ripe old age of two, appearing in a vaudeville act as the "Tiniest Toe Dancer in the World." It was not long after that that Havoc appeared in silent films, but vaudeville was coming to an end and Havoc would not really find national success until 1940 when she earned praise starring in the musical comedy *Pal Joey* (1940) on Broadway. She turned the acclaim there into a film career, appearing in *Four Jacks and a Jill* (1942), *Sing Your Worries Away* (1942), *Brewster's Millions* (1945), *Gentleman's Agreement* (1947), and *Once a Thief* (1950), among others, before essentially sticking to television for the rest of her career, including guest roles all the way up to an appearance on *General Hospital* in 1990. She passed away at the age of 97 in Stamford, Connecticut.

George Hickenlooper (May 25, 1963–October 29, 2010). Acclaimed director George Hickenlooper died suddenly at the age of 47 while he still had a film (*Casino Jack*) about to be released. Hickenlooper will likely most be remembered for the incredible documentary that chronicled the tumultuous production of *Apocalypse Now* (1979) called *Hearts of Darkness: A Filmmaker's Apocalypse* (1991). He alternated between non-fiction and narrative filmmaking throughout his too-brief career, most successfully merging both sides in making fictional films based on real larger-than-life personalities like Edie Sedgwick (*Factory Girl*) and Jack Abramoff (*Casino Jack*). He also directed the initial short film that was developed into the award-winning *Sling Blade* (1996), *Some Folks Call It a Sling Blade* (1994). Other credits in his career as a director include *The Low Life* (1995), *Dogtown* (1996), *The Big Brass Ring* (1999), and *The Man From Elysian Fields* (2001).

Dennis Hopper (May 17, 1936–May 29, 2010). Born in Dodge City, Kansas, Dennis Hopper began his acting career with numerous appearances on shows such as *Medic* (1955), *The Loretta Young Show* (1955), and *The Public Defender* (1955) and segued into features with small roles in such films as *Rebel Without a Cause* (1954), *Giant* (1956), *Gunfight at the O.K. Corral* (1957) and the infamous *The Story of Mankind* (1957), in which he portrayed Napoleon Bonaparte. Over the next decade, he would go back and forth between television, including episodes of *The Defenders*, *Petticoat Junction*, *The Twilight Zone*, *Bonanza*, and *Gunsmoke*, and films, where he appeared in small roles in *The Sons of Katie Elder* (1965), *Cool Hand Luke* (1967), and *True Grit* (1969), before making his breakthrough as the star, director, and co-writer of the hugely influential biker movie hit *Easy Rider* (1969). This film made Hopper a symbol of the counter-culture but his follow-up, the surreal meta-movie *The Last Movie* (1971), proved to be a huge flop with critics and audiences and that, combined with a growing substance abuse problem, led to an erratic career over the next decade or so consisting largely of barely-seen productions made in Europe along with the occasional intriguing performance in the likes of *The American Friend* (1977), *Apocalypse Now* (1979), *Rumble Fish* (1983), and *The Osterman Weekend* (1983). In 1986, a newly cleaned-up Hopper would make a major comeback with celebrated performances in *River's Edge*, *Hoosiers*, for which he would receive an Oscar® nomination for Best Supporting Actor, and David Lynch's *Blue Velvet*, in which he portrayed one of the most terrifying psychos in screen history. For the remainder of his career, he would work steadily in television and films, often in roles that would trade on his counter-cultural notoriety, including *Paris Trout* (1991), *The Indian Runner* (1991), *True Romance* (1993), *Speed* (1994), *George A. Romero's Land of the Dead* (2005), and *Swing Vote* (2008). During this time, he would also return to directing as well with the surprisingly straightforward cop drama *Colors* (1988), the bizarre crime drama *Catchfire* (1990), the outlandish neo-noir exercise *The Hot Spot* (1990) and *Chasers* (1994).

Lena Horne (June 30, 1917–May 9, 2010). With her sultry voice, Lena Horne may be most remembered as a fantastic singer but she was a dancer, actress, and an important civil rights activist as well, so politically active at certain points in her career that she was blacklisted from Hollywood. Lena Mary Calhoun Horne was born on June 30, 1917 in Brooklyn, New York and would be identified with the city she loved for most of her career, passing away in that city at the age of 92. At the age of just sixteen, Horne joined the chorus line of the legendary Cotton Club in New York and had a feature role the next year. She would tour during the 1930s and started to break through nationally when she became a featured vocalist on NBC's *The Chamber Music Society of Lower Basin Street* in the 1940s, really kickstarting her musical career. At that point, she already has a few low-budget movies under her belt, but she was not really discovered until 1943 when MGM signed her as the first black performer to a long-term contract with a major studio. Her first film for the company was *Panama Hattie* (1942) and she made a number of musicals for the company, including *Cabin in the Sky* (1943), but she suffered from the fact that a black woman would not be given a lead role and her parts were even edited out completely in parts of the country that were still severely racist. The problems getting the credit she deserved on the screen sent Horne back to the nightclub circuit in the 1950s, appearing in only two films (*Duchess of Idaho* and *Meet Me in Las Vegas*) that decade. It was then that the red scare forced Horne into being blacklisted and she would only appear on-screen three more times in her career—*Death of a Gunfighter* (1969), *The Wiz* (1978), and *That's Entertainment! III* (1994)—although she would find more success on stage and as a regular guest star on TV. From very early in her career, Lena Horne was an icon of the civil rights movement, refusing to perform for segregated audiences and speaking with Presidents, including John F. Kennedy, about the movement. She passed away from heart failure on May 9th and thousands gathered to mourn a woman who was more than just a performer.

Monica Johnson (February 21, 1946–November 1, 2010). Monica Johnson got her start in show business when her brother, comedy writer Jerry Belson, got her a job typing scripts for the television series he was then working for, *The Odd Couple*. Before long, she wrote a spec script for *The Mary Tyler Moore Show* and soon found herself in demand as a writer for that show as well as for others such as *The Paul Lynde Show* and *Laverne & Shirley*. She made her debut as a screenwriter collaborating with Albert Brooks and Harry Shearer on the script for Brooks' first film, the cult favorite *Real Life* (1978). Over the next two decades, she and Brooks would work together on the screenplays for *Modern Romance* (1981), *Lost in America* (1985), *The Scout* (1994), *Mother* (1996), and *The Muse* (1999). Apart from Brooks, she co-wrote the screenplays for the largely (and justly) forgotten comedies *Americathon* (1979) and *Jekyll and Hyde...Together Again* (1982) and wrote some episodes for the slightly more celebrated TV series *It's Garry Shandling's Show*. She died on November 1st of esophageal cancer.

Irving Kershner (April 29, 1923–November 27, 2010). After graduating from the film school at the University of Southern California, Irving Kershner began his film career producing documentaries for the U.S. Information Service. He became one of the countless young filmmakers who were given a break by maverick B-movie producer Roger

Corman when he was hired to make his directorial debut with the crime drama *Stakeout on Dope Street* (1958) and from then on, he worked steadily on such diverse films as *Hoodlum Priest* (1961), *The Luck of Ginger Coffey* (1964), *A Fine Madness* (1966), *The Flim-Flam Man* (1967), *Up the Sandbox* (1972), and *Eyes of Laura Mars* (1978). During this time, he also work as a teacher at USC and among his students was George Lucas, who later hired Kershner to direct the eagerly awaited sequel to his smash hit *Star Wars* (1977). The resulting film, *The Empire Strikes Back* (1980), was another enormous success and is now generally considered by fans to be the best of the entire franchise. From there, he went on to direct the ersatz James Bond film *Never Say Never Again* (1983), a loose remake of *Thunderball* (1965) that marked Sean Connery's return to the role that made him famous, and *Robocop 2* (1990), a sequel to the 1987 sci-fi smash hit that was panned by critics and largely ignored by audiences. After directing an episode of the television series *Seaquest 2032* in 1993, he retired from directing for good but made the occasional appearance in front of the camera—after making his acting debut as Zebedee in Martin Scorsese's controversial adaptation of *The Last Temptation of Christ* (1988), he would also turn up in *On Deadly Ground* (1994), *Angus* (1995), *Manhood* (2003), and *Berkeley* (2005).

Eleanore Cammack King (August 5, 1934–September 1, 2010). Known as Cammie King, the former child actress is best remembered as one of the young ladies who played Bonnie Blue Butler in *Gone with the Wind* (1939) and for providing the voice of the doe Faline in *Bambi* (1942). King only appeared in movies for four years of her very young life but she is associated with two of the most-beloved films of all time. She joked late in life that she "peaked at 5." King passed away from lung cancer at the age of 76.

Satoshi Kon (October 12, 1963–August 24, 2010). One of the leading names in the field of anime, Satoshi Kon studied at the Musashino College of the Arts and began his career as a manga artist. He then moved into animation and worked as a background artist for a number of films, the most notable being Katsuhiro Otomo's *Rojin Z* (1991). He made his directorial debut with *Magnetic Rose*, a section of the anthology film *Memories* (1995) and followed that up with *Perfect Blue* (1998), a spellbinding psychological thriller about a pop singer-turned-actress being stalked by an obsessed fan and a ghostly figure from her past. Closer in tone to the works of Dario Argento than Walt Disney, the film was an international sensation among animation buffs who looked upon him as the next big thing in the field. Kon proved himself to be anything but a one-hit wonder with his next effort, *Millennium Actress* (2001), a haunting and touching drama about a reclusive actress reflecting back on her life and career that proved to be as gripping and emotionally involving as any live-action film. Kon shifted gears again with his next film, *Tokyo Godfathers* (2003), a sweetly sentimental Christmas-set fable about a trio of homeless misfits on the streets of Tokyo who discover a newborn baby in a dumpster and set off to find its parents. After turning to television in 2004 to direct the 13-part anime series *Paranoia Agent*, Kon returned to the big screen with *Paprika* (2006), a trippy sci-fi mindbender about the theft of a machine that allows people to record and watch their dreams as well as enter the minds of others. At the time of his death from pancreatic cancer, he was at work on his latest feature, *The Dreaming Machine*, and it is currently scheduled to be completed by Yoshimi Itazu, who was already working on the project as its chief animation director and character designer.

Steve Landesberg (November 23, 1936–December 20, 2010). Comedian Steve Landesberg will be most-remembered for his work on TV, especially his co-starring role on the ABC sitcom *Barney Miller*, along with numerous guest appearances from the 1970s through the 2000s. Landesberg's first film credit is the fantastically-titled *You've Got to Walk It Like You Talk It or You'll Lose That Beat* (1971) and while he worked primarily in television, he popped up near the end of his career in small theatrical parts including hit comedies *Wild Hogs* (2007) and *Forgetting Sarah Marshall* (2008). When he passed away on December 20th, many outlets incorrectly reported his age at 65, revealing that Landesberg had been a little deceptive about his real age as he did not truly get started until later in life as a comedian and wanted to have producers and audiences think he was younger.

James MacArthur (December 8, 1937–October 28, 2010). The adopted son of actress Helen Hayes and writer Charles MacArthur, MacArthur got his first big break playing the role of a troubled teen in "Deal a Blow," a 1955 episode of the anthology series *Climax* that was directed by the up-and-coming John Frankenheimer. When Frankenheimer retooled the show as his big-screen directorial debut, he brought MacArthur along to repeat his performance and the film, retitled *The Young Stranger* (1957), was critically acclaimed and earned MacArthur a BAFTA award for Most Promising Newcomer. From there, MacArthur worked steadily in films such as *Kidnapped* (1960), *Swiss Family Robinson* (1960), *The Bedford Incident* (1965), and *Hang 'Em High* (1968) and in episodes of *The Untouchables, Wagon Train, The Alfred Hitchcock Hour,* and *Gunsmoke*. In 1968, he landed the role that would cement his place in the pop-culture firmament when he was cast as Dan "Dan-O" Williams in the long-running television series *Hawaii Five-O*. After that show went off the air in 1979, he would make occasional television guest shots and retired after appearing in the TV movie *Storm Chasers: Revenge of the Twister* (1998).

Simon MacCorkindale (February 12, 1952–October 14, 2010). Born and raised in England, Simon Charles Pendered MacCorkindale appeared on stage and in numerous television roles (including the acclaimed versions of *I Claudius* and *Jesus of Nazareth*) before breaking through in *Death on the Nile* (1978). Acclaim for that role brought MacCorkindale to the United States where he starred in a series of films, even turning his brief time in the spotlight into a starring role on the cult series *Manimal,* which he turned into a long-running role on the 1980s soap hit *Falcon Crest*. He worked in Canadian and British TV and film until he passed away from colorectal cancer at the age of 58 in London, England. Other film credits include *The Riddle of the Sands* (1979), *The Quatermass Conclusion* (1979), *Macbeth* (1981), *The Sword and the Sorcerer* (1982), and *Jaws 3-D* (1983).

Kevin McCarthy (February 15, 1914–September 11, 2010). Perhaps the only actor who could claim a filmography that listed him in films opposite both Marilyn Monroe and "Weird" Al Yankovic, McCarthy originally contemplated going to work as a diplomat but eventually found himself studying acting at the Actors Studio in New York. After appearing in numerous plays, McCarthy made his film debut in the role of Biff Loman in the screen adaptation of Arthur Miller's *Death of a Salesman* (1951), a performance that would earn him an Academy Award® nomination for Best Supporting Actor and launch a career that would see him appear in nearly one hundred films and countless television series. Among his more notable screen credits were *The Misfits* (1961), *The Prize* (1963), *The Best Man* (1964), *Mirage* (1965), *A Big Hand for the Little Lady* (1966), *Kansas City Bomber* (1972), *My Tutor* (1983), and *UHF* (1989). However, he became a part of screen history when he took the lead role in *Invasion of the Body Snatchers* (1956), the sci-fi classic in which he played Miles Bennell, a small-town doctor who discovers that the entire population of his town, and possibly the world, is being replaced by emotionless alien duplicates. The role made him a legend in genre circles and he would go on to sort-of reprise it in later years in two cameo roles, a serious bit in Philip Kaufman's 1978 remake and as a one-off gag in *Looney Tunes: Back in Action* (2003). In later years, he would serve as a sort of good-luck charm for director and noted genre fan Joe Dante by appearing in his films *Piranha* (1978), *The Howling* (1981), *Twilight Zone: The Movie* (1983), *Innerspace* (1987), *Matinee* (1993), *The Second Civil War* (1997), and *Looney Tunes: Back in Action*. He continued acting right up until his death from pneumonia and his last film, *The Ghastly Love of Johnny X,* is scheduled for release in 2011.

Rue McClanahan (February 21, 1934–June 3, 2010). Eddi-Rue McClanahan will forever be remembered as Blanche Devereaux on TV's *The Golden Girls* (or perhaps as Vivian Harmon on *Maude*) but the sassy actress had a notable film career long before the boob tube made her a household name. McClanahan actually started on stage in the 1950s, working in local theaters until she made her Broadway debut in 1969 with Dustin Hoffman. In the meantime, she started her work in film, debuting in *The Rotten Apple* (1961), and going on to appear in, among others, *Walk the Angry Beach* (1968), *The People Next Door* (1970), *They Might Be Giants* (1971), *Dear God* (1996), *Out to Sea* (1997), *Starship Troopers* (1997), and *The Fighting Temptations* (2003). McClanahan never made much of an impact in film but she was a TV icon for two decades, starting with *Another World* from 1970 to 1971, which she parlayed into a lucrative role as the best friend of Bea Arthur's title character on the hit show *Maude* from 1972 to 1978. She appeared on *The Golden Girls* from 1985 to 1992 and won an Emmy for her work on that series. One of her final appearances was on *Law & Order* in 2009. Rue McClanahan passed away after several heath problems led to a final stroke on June 3rd. She was 76.

Grant McCune (March 27, 1943–December 27, 2010). The name may not be overly familiar but his work is beloved by millions as Grant McCune was a special effects designer who not only reportedly created the shark in *Jaws* (1975) (although he was not credited) but would design several of the robots in *Star Wars* (1977), winning an Oscar® for his work on that film. According to some reports, McCune was responsible for the design of one of the most beloved characters in the history of science fiction—R2-D2. McCune would be nominated for Best Visual Effects a second time for his work on another beloved sci-fi franchise with *Star Trek: The Motion Picture* (1979). His design company's work was featured in *Caddyshack* (1980), *Never Say Never Again* (1983), *Big* (1988), and *Die Hard* (1988) and McCune would found a company that worked on numerous films including *Speed* (1994), *Batman Forever* (1995), *Red Planet* (2000), *Spider-Man* (2002), and *Serenity* (2005).

Vonetta McGee (January 14, 1945–July 9, 2010). Vonetta McGee became one of the many iconic actors of the Blaxploitation period of cinema in the 1970s, a series of films featuring African Americans in larger-than-life roles, often as action heroes. McGee starred in *Melinda* (1972), *Blacula* (1972), *Hammer* (1972), *Detroit 9000* (1973), and *Shaft in Africa* (1973) at the arguable height of the craze. Other credits include *The Great Silence* (1968), *The Eiger Sanction* (1975), *Repo Man* (1984), and *To Sleep with Anger* (1990). McGee passed away from cardiac arrest at the age of 65.

Sally Menke (December 17, 1953–September 27, 2010). Following in the tradition of such noted female film editors as Anne Coates, Verna Fields, and Thelma Schoonmaker, Menke studied film at New York University and upon graduating in 1977, she went to work editing documentaries and the occasional feature film such as *Cold Feet* (1983), *Teenage Mutant Ninja Turtles* (1990), and *The Search for Signs of Intelligent Life in the Universe* (1991). Her big breakthrough came when she got word that a fledgling filmmaker was looking for someone to edit his debut feature. That filmmaker was Quentin Tarantino and the film, the stylish and bloody heist-gone-wrong drama *Reservoir Dogs* (1992), was a breakthrough work of the American independent film scene and Menke's work was singled out for praise for her ability to take a screenplay featuring multiple points-of-view, a deliberately fractured timeline, and long scenes consisting of guys in a room talking, and turn it into a tense, funny, and endlessly watchable work that always made sense despite the trickiness of its narrative structure. This began a long collaboration with Tarantino that would see her editing all of his subsequent films—*Pulp Fiction* (1994), *Four Rooms* (1995), *Jackie Brown* (1997), *Kill Bill Vol. 1* (2003), *Kill Bill Vol. 2* (2004), *Grindhouse: Death Proof* (2007), and *Inglourious Basterds* (2009)—and her contributions would be singled out for praise every time, winning Academy Award® nominations for Best Editing for *Pulp Fiction* and *Inglourious Basterds*. In addition to her collaborations with Tarantino, Menke also worked on *Heaven & Earth* (1993), *Mulholland Falls* (1996), *Nightwatch* (1997), *All the Pretty Horses* (2000), *Daddy and Them* (2001), and *Peacock* (2010) and at the time of her death, she was working on *The Green Hornet* (2011).

Augustino Mercurio (August 10, 1928–December 7, 2010). The eldest child of Vincent Mercurio and Cecilia Miller, Gus Mercurio was an Australian character actor who appeared in numerous television series and films in his home country and fathered an Aussie actor of his own in

Paul Mercurio (*Strictly Ballroom*). Selected film credits for the actor include *The Blue Lagoon* (1980), *The Man From Snowy River* (1982), *Crocodile Dundee II* (1988), *Return to the Blue Lagoon* (1991), and *Lightning Jack* (1994). Mr. Mercurio passed away on December 7th during surgery for a chest aneurism.

Mario Monicelli (May 16, 1915–November 29, 2010). Italian director Mario Monicelli was a multiple award winner who helped create the modern cinema in his country, starting with a short film in 1934. The son of journalist, Monicelli became friends with the son of a playwright who happened to be the man that Benito Mussolini had chosen to found cinema in Tirrenia. He produced numerous screenplays in the 1930s and 1940s and earned his first director credit in 1949 with *Toto Cerca Casa* (1949). He directed regularly in the 1950s, helming what many consider the first true commedia all'italiana with Vittorio Gassman, Claudia Cardinale, Toto, and Marcello Mastroianni in *Big Deal on Madonna Street* (1958). *The Great War* (1959) would earn Monicelli the Golden Lion at the Venice Film Festival and a nomination for the Academy Award® for Best Foreign Language Film, an honor he would receive two more times for *The Organizer,* (1963) and *The Girl with a Pistol* (1968). Other notable credits include *For Love and Gold* (1966), *Branca-leone at the Crusades* (1970), *Amici Miei* (1975), and *Caro Michele* (1976), the winner of the Silver Bear for Best Director at the Berlin International Film Festival, a prize he would take home a third time in 1981 for *Il Marchese del Grillo.* Even into his nineties, Monicelli was still directing, helming *The Roses of the Desert* (2006) at the age of 91. In November of 2010, Monicelli was admitted to a hospital in Rome for treatment of prostate cancer, something he had been in and out of care for through his final years, and he jumped from his fifth floor window, committing suicide.

Patricia Neal (January 20, 1926–August 8, 2010). Oscar® winner Patricia Neal gave several iconic performances in her career, including *Hud* (1963), which won her the Academy Award®, *The Day the Earth Stood Still* (1951), and *Break-fast at Tiffany's* (1961). Neal began her career, as so many of her day, on Broadway, winning an award at the inaugural Tony Awards in 1947. She turned her stage success into a film career, starting in 1949 with her debut role in *John Loves Mary.* Notable film appearances besides the aforementioned classics include *The Fountainhead* (1949), *The Breaking Point* (1950), *Operation Pacific* (1951), *A Face in the Crowd* (1957), *In Harm's Way* (1965), *The Subject Was Roses* (1968), *Ghost Story* (1981), and *Cookie's Fortune* (1999). Patricia Neal went through some turbulent times off-camera, including a legendary affair with Gary Cooper and a series of personal tragedies that culminated in three strokes at the age of 39, which put her in a coma for three weeks and forced her to learn how to walk and talk again. She survived that latter tragedy through the help of her husband, legendary author Roald Dahl in 1953. The two had five children, although one passed away at a very young age. Patricia Neal died from lung cancer at the age of 84 in Martha's Vineyard.

Leslie Nielsen (February 11, 1926–November 28, 2010). Born in Regina, Saskatchewan, Nielsen studied at the Academy of Radio Arts in Toronto before relocating to New York to work at the Neighborhood Playhouse. He made his big-screen debut in *Ransom* (1956) and from there went on to appear as Commander J.J. Adams in the sci-fi classic *Forbidden Planet* (1956). For the next quarter-century, he was a familiar face in movies and on television, usually playing either businessmen or bad guys—often both at once. Among the more notable films that he appeared in during this time were *Tammy and the Bachelor* (1957), *Harlow* (1965), *Beau Geste* (1966), *The Poseidon Adventure* (1972), *Day of the Animals* (1977), *Viva Knievel!* (1977), and *Prom Night* (1980). The trajectory of his career would be forever altered when the filmmaking team of Jim Abrahams, David Zucker, and Jerry Zucker were casting their disaster movie parody *Airplane!* (1980) and realized that if they cast actors noted for their seriousness and had them go about their parts in the most straightforward manner possible, the effect would be much funnier than casting pure comedians. The film was a surprise smash hit and Nielsen was generally singled out for his dryly deadpan turn as Dr. Rumack. After *Airplane!,* Nielsen would continue to work steadily until his passing but while there would be the occasional serious-minded role in films like *Creepshow* (1982) and *Nuts* (1987), he would spend the rest of his career appearing in goofball comedies, the best of which was *The Naked Gun: From the Files of Police Squad!* (1988), in which he reunited with his *Airplane!* directors in a big-screen spin-off of *Police Squad!,* a short-lived parody of cop shows from 1982. Unlike the series, the film version was a hit and Nielsen would go on to appear in two sequels, *The Naked Gun 2: The Smell of Fear* (1991) and *The Naked Gun 33 1/3: The Final Insult* (1994). Other films that he appeared in during this time included *Wrong is Right* (1982), *Soul Man* (1986), *All I Want for Christmas* (1991), *Surf Ninjas* (1993), *Dracula: Dead and Loving It* (1995), *Spy Hard* (1996), *Mr. Magoo* (1997), *Wrongfully Accused* (1998), *Scary Movie 3* (2003), and *Scary Movie 4* (2006).

Fess Parker (August 16, 1924–March 18, 2010). Born in Fort Worth, Texas, Parker attended college at the University of Texas at Austin and, while there, made the acquaintance of actor Adolph Menjou, who was at the school serving as a guest artist, and when Parker went to Hollywood after graduating in 1950, the veteran actor helped him out by introducing him around town. He began to steadily appear in small roles in such films as *Untamed Frontier* (1952), *The Kid from Left Field* (1953), *Thunder Over the Plains* (1953), and the sci-fi classic *Them!* (1954). The latter film inadvertently led to his big break in 1955 when Walt Disney screened it in order to check out the performance of James Arness, whom he was considering casting in a role in one of his upcoming TV endeavors. After watching Parker's work in the film, he decided that he was more appropriate and offered him the role of legendary pioneer Davy Crockett in *Davy Crocket: King of the Wild Frontier,* part of his television series *Walt Disney's Wonderful World of Color.* Although the Crockett series lasted for only three episodes, it was an immediate sensation with kids and made Parker an instant celebrity. Parker would work with Disney again on three additional *Davy Crockett* episodes chronicling his earlier adventures and in the films *Westward Ho the Wagons!* (1956), *The Great Locomotive Chase* (1956), the classic tearjerker *Old Yeller* (1957), and *The Light in the Forest*

(1958) but the Davy Crockett fad faded as quickly as it rose and Parker's career cooled down as well. After appearances in *The Hangman* (1959), *Alias Jesse James* (1959), a Bob Hope comedy in which he made an uncredited gag cameo as Crockett, *The Jayhawkers* (1959) and *Hell is for Heroes* (1962), he would spend the rest of his career working in television with his biggest success coming from the long-running series *Daniel Boone,* in which he played yet another legendary figure of the Old West.

Arthur Penn (September 27, 1922–September 28, 2010). Celebrated filmmaker Arthur Penn was born in Philadelphia, Pennsylvania and first made his mark in live television, where he worked on such shows as *The Gulf Playhouse, The Philco-Goodyear Television Playhouse,* and *Playhouse 90* and on Broadway, where he was nominated for the Best Director Tony in 1958 for *Two for the Seesaw* and in 1961 for *All the Way Home* and won the prize in 1960 for *The Miracle Worker.* He made his film directorial debut with the offbeat western *The Left-Handed Kid* (1958) and followed that up with the screen version of *The Miracle Worker* (1962), for which he received his first Oscar® nomination for Best Director. The next few years would be a bit bumpy—he was fired from *The Train* after filming began and was replaced by John Frankenheimer and his next two films, the fascinating *Mickey One* (1965) and the flawed-but-interesting *The Chase* (1966) would flop at the box-office—before striking it big with the controversial hit *Bonnie and Clyde* (1967), for which he received his second Best Director nomination. He followed up this success with such iconoclastic works as *Alice's Restaurant* (1969), *Little Big Man* (1970), for which he received his third and final Best Director nomination, and the cult favorite *Night Moves* (1975). His next project was *The Missouri Breaks* (1976), a heavily hyped Western that featured the first on-screen pairing of Marlon Brando and Jack Nicholson, and when it proved to be a surprise failure at the box-office, he would not direct again until the coming-of-age drama *Four Friends* (1981). In the 1980s, he would work sporadically, helming the thrillers *Target* (1985) and *Dead of Winter* (1987) and the bizarre *Penn & Teller Get Killed* (1989), and would conclude his career by returning to television to direct the TV movies *The Portrait* (1993) and *Inside* (1996) as well as an episode of the cable series *100 Centre Street.*

Dorothy Provine (January 20, 1935–April 25, 2010). Blue-eyed and blonde, actress Dorothy Provine became a star in the 1960s in a series of wacky comedies and crowd-pleasing TV shows. After majoring in drama at the University of Washington, she was hired by Warner Bros. and starred in *The Bonnie Parker Story* (1958) and *The 30 Foot Bride of Candy Rock* (1959). She would appear on a pair of ABC TV series and even have two hit singles in the early 1960s ("Don't Bring Lulu" and "Crazy Words, Crazy Tune") but it would be a string of comedies that would cement her legacy—*It's a Mad, Mad, Mad, Mad World* (1963), *Good Neighbor Sam* (1964), *The Great Race* (1965), *That Darn Cat!* (1965), the 007 spoof *Kiss the Girls and Make Them Die* (1966), *Who's Minding the Mint?* (1967), and *Never a Dull Moment* (1968). She married director Robert Day in 1968 and retired with the exception of a few TV guest roles. Dorothy Provine died from emphysema on April 25th at the age of 75.

Lynn Redgrave (March 8, 1943–May 2, 2010). An essential part of a royal family of acting that included sister Vanessa Redgrave and nieces Joely and Natasha Richardson, Lynn Redgrave began her very notable career training at the Central School of Speech and Drama in London, making her debut in *A Midsummer Night's Dream* at the Royal Court Theatre in 1962. Redgrave was a massive success on the British stage, appearing all over the city and working at the National Theatre with Laurence Olivier, Franco Zeffirelli, and Noel Coward. Her debut film role came around this time with the Best Picture-winning *Tom Jones* (1963). It was not long before Redgrave was one of the more notable film actresses as well, earning an individual Oscar® nomination just a few years later with *Georgy Girl* (1966). Throughout her career, Lynn Redgrave would alternate theatre with film, arguably earning more praise for her stage work than anything else. Having said that, she still amassed a very impressive film resume including *Everything You Always Wanted to Know About Sex (But Were Afraid to Ask)* (1972), *The Turn of the Screw* (1974), *The Happy Hooker* (1975), *Shine* (1996), *Gods and Monsters* (1998), *Spider* (2002), *Kinsey* (2004), and *The White Countess* (2005). Lynn Redgrave died of breast cancer on May 2nd.

Steven Reuther (November 2, 1951–June 5, 2010). A true mailroom-to-boardroom success story, Steven Reuther became an executive at Galactic Films in the 1980s and helped produce some of the most notable films of that decade and the next including *9 Weeks* (1986), *Dirty Dancing* (1987), and *And God Created Woman* (1988). His first solo producer credit came on *Pretty Woman* (1990) but it was only one of many credits as producer or executive producer, including *Love Hurts* (1990), *Guilty by Suspicion* (1991), *The Mambo Kings* (1992), *The Power of One* (1992), *Under Siege* (1992), *Sommersby* (1993), *The Client* (1994), *Boys on the Side* (1995), *Face/Off* (1997), *Pay It Forward* (2000), *Proof of Life* (2000), *Rock Star* (2001), *Collateral Damage* (2002), and *The Ugly Truth* (2009).

Eric Rohmer (March 20, 1920–January 11, 2010). Born Jean-Marie Maurice Scherer in the city of Nancy, Eric Rohmer would move to Paris and work as a literature teacher and as a newspaper reporter. After publishing a novel, *Elizabeth,* in 1946 under the name Gilbert Cordier, he switched his interest to film criticism and soon fell in with such fellow cinema enthusiasts as Jean-Luc Godard, Francois Truffaut, Jacques Rivette, and Claude Chabrol. After adopting a pseudonym inspired by director Erich von Stroheim and author Sax Rohmer, he directed his first short film, *Journal d'un scelerat,* and founded the film magazine *Gazette du Cinema* in 1950. The next year, he would join the influential magazine *Cahiers du Cinema,* where he would serve as editor-in-chief from 1956 to 1963. During this time, he also made five additional short films and an uncompleted feature before finally making his feature debut with *The Sign of Leo* (1962). Over the course of the next decade, he would make eleven films but would not achieve international recognition until the release of *My Night at Maud's* (1969). The film, the fourth of his so-called *Six Moral Tales* series devoted to stories of people facing temptation, was a hit across the world and earned numerous awards and two Oscar® nominations. After completing the *Moral Tales* cycle with the equally acclaimed *Claire's*

Knee (1970) and *Love in the Afternoon* (1972), he moved on to a second celebrated series, dubbed *Comedies and Proverbs*, that dealt with various forms of deception and which included *La Femme de l'aviateur* (1980), *Pauline at the Beach* (1983), *Summer* (1986), and *Boyfriends and Girlfriends* (1987). Rohmer's final cycle, *Tales of the Four Seasons*, would deal with emotional isolation and include *A Tale of Springtime* (1990), *A Tale of Winter* (1992), *A Summer's Tale* (1996), and *Autumn Tale* (1998). When not working on his various cycles, Rohmer made a number of one-off films as well including *Four Adventures of Reinette and Mirabelle* (1987), *Rendezvous in Paris* (1995), and *The Lady and the Duke* (2001). His final project would be *The Romance of Astrea and Celadon* (2007), an ambitious medieval-age romantic drama. For a good portion of his career, his films were sometimes dismissed by film scholars for lacking the formal ambitions of the works of his fellow members of the Nouvelle Vague—in Arthur Penn's detective thriller *Night Moves* (1975), Gene Hackman would infamously say "I saw a Rohmer film once. It was like watching paint dry"—but while many of his colleagues would fall in and out of fashion over the years, his subtle and stately approach would stand the test of time and Rohmer's reputation would only increase in stature over the years with even a filmmaker as aesthetically opposite to his own work as Quentin Tarantino singing his praises to new generations of moviegoers.

Zelda Rubenstein (May 28, 1933–January 27, 2010). Diminutive actress Zelda Rubenstein would make a permanent impact on the world of horror by playing a prophetic medium named Tangina Barrons in *Poltergeist* (1982), *Poltergeist II: The Other Side* (1986), and *Poltergeist III* (1988). It was a deficiency of her anterior pituitary gland that forced Rubenstein to stand only 4' 3? but it did not stop her from pursuing an acting career by studying at the University of California. She would never break out of her role in *Poltergeist,* playing psychics and mediums throughout her career. Other film roles included *Frances* (1982), *Sixteen Candles* (1984), and *Southland Tales* (2006). Rubenstein also played a recurring role for 44 episodes of the hit TV series *Picket Fences* in the 1990s and appeared regularly as a TV guest star.

Erich Segal (June 16, 1937–January 17, 2010). Erich Wolf Segal wrote the book and screenplay adaptation for one of the most notable romantic hits of its era, *Love Story* (1970), starring Ryan O'Neal and Ali MacGraw. *Love Story* was actually Segal's second notable credit after writing the screenplay for the Beatles' 1968 motion picture, *Yellow Submarine.* He would write a book sequel to *Love Story* called *Oliver's Story* (and shared writing credit on the film adaptation of the same name) but he would never find the fame again that his most notable credit gave him, turning to teaching at University of Munich, Princeton University, and Dartmouth College. He passed away from a heart attack at the age of 72.

Glenn Shadix (April 15, 1952–September 7, 2010). William Glenn Shadix was born in Bessemer, Alabama, and will perhaps most be remembered for a memorable role in Tim Burton's cult favorite *Beetlejuice* (1988). Burton would use Shadix again in *The Nightmare Before Christmas* (1993) and *Planet of the Apes* (2001). Other film roles included parts in

Heathers (1989), *Meet the Applegates* (1991), *Sleepwalkers* (1992), *Demolition Man* (1993), *Love Affair* (1994), *Multiplicity* (1996), and the upcoming *Frankenweenie* (2012). Shadix passed away after blunt trauma on September 7th at the age of 58.

Jean Simmons (January 31, 1929–January 22, 2010). Born in London, England, Jean Merilyn Simmons began acting at the age of fourteen, appearing with Margaret Lockwood in *Give Us the Moon* (1944) and starred in David Lean's *Great Expectations* (1946), Powell and Pressburger's *Black Narcissus* (1947), and Laurence Olivier's *Hamlet* (1948) before moving to Hollywood and working for Howard Hughes at RKO. Simmons would work with many of the icons of the day, appearing in Otto Preminger's *Angel Face* (1952) with Robert Mitchum, *The Actress* (1953) with Spencer Tracy, *The Robe* (1953) with Richard Burton, *Guys and Dolls* (1955) with Frank Sinatra and Marlon Brando, *The Big Country* (1958) with Gregory Peck, *Elmer Gantry* (1960) with Burt Lancaster, *Spartacus* (1960) with Kirk Douglas, and *All the Way Home* (1963) with Robert Preston. Simmons moved to the stage and TV in the 1970s and 1980s. She passed away from lung cancer at the age of 80 in Santa Monica, California.

Gloria Stuart (July 4, 1910–September 26, 2010). Born in Santa Monica, California, Stuart studied acting at the University of California at Berkeley and after appearing in some local stage productions, she came to the attention of Universal Pictures and was signed to a contract. Although she appeared in a trio of well-regarded films directed by James Whale—*The Old Dark House* (1932), *The Invisible Man* (1933), and *The Kiss Before the Mirror* (1933)—she found herself mostly appearing in undistinguished programmers and when a stint at 20th Century Fox yielded the same dire results—including a version of *The Three Musketeers* (1939) co-starring the Ritz Brothers—she retired from the screen in the mid-1940s. In the mid-1970s, she returned to acting with appearances in numerous television shows and movies, including a memorable bit as a besotted fan dancing with matinee idol Peter O'Toole in *My Favorite Year* (1982). In an unexpected twist, the stardom that had previously eluded her finally arrived when James Cameron cast her as the older version of Rose in the modern-day scenes of his blockbuster epic *Titanic* (1997). The only member of the cast who was alive at the time of the actual disaster, Stuart would go on to be nominated for the Best Supporting Actress Oscar® for her performance, making her the oldest person ever to be nominated for an Academy Award®. After that, she continued to make television appearance and also acted in such films as *The Love Letter* (1999), *The Million Dollar Hotel* (2000), and *Land of Plenty* (2004) before passing away from lung cancer.

Marie Osborne Yeats (November 5, 1911–November 11, 2010). She would be simply known as Baby Marie when she became the first major child star of the silent film era even though she was born Helen Alice Myres only to be adopted by Leon and Edith Osborn and have her name changed. Baby Marie made her debut in *Kidnapped in New York* (1914) and was signed to a contract at the age of five. Her most beloved film is *Little Mary Sunshine* (1916) and many of her early films never survived the test of time, as so many early era films were destroyed or not preserved enough. Baby Marie starred in twenty-nine films in a six-year period and actually returned to film later in life, starring in *Carolina* (1934) and appearing as an extra in the 1930s and 1940s. She lived to the age of 99 and passed away in San Clemente, California.

Selected Film Books of 2010

Alessandra, Pilar. *The Coffee Break Screenwriter: Writing Your Script Ten Minutes at a Time.* Michael Wiese Productions, 2010. The time-saving approach to screenwriting is espoused by the author who claims that with every ten minutes to spare one can be working on their screenplay. The book contains ten-minute exercises to help the reader build a sellable screenplay in installments.

Ball, James, Robbie Carman, Matt Gottshalk, and Richard Harrington. *From Still to Motion: A Photographer's Guide to Creating Video With Your DSLR (Voices That Matter).* New Riders Press, 2010. A guide to using the DSLR that includes an accompanying DVD with over six hours of video training about how to use DSLR cameras in every aspect of filmmaking.

Beck, Jerry and Leonard Maltin. *The 100 Greatest Looney Tunes Cartoons.* Insight Editions, 2010. Historians, animators, and cartoon fans were asked to name their favorite Looney Tunes cartoons and the results were compiled along with history, anecdotes, and insights into the production of the chosen hundred.

Bible, Karie, Marc Wanamaker, and Harry Medved. *Location Filming in Los Angeles.* Arcadia Publishing, 2010. A photograph-heavy book that focuses on memorable locations in the city of angels through the history of film.

Biskind, Peter. *Star: How Warren Beatty Seduced America.* Simon & Schuster, 2010. Legendary Hollywood writer Biskind attempts to balance the public persona of the Oscar®-winning actor Warren Beatty as a notorious womanizer along with his film career as a heartthrob actor and accomplished director.

Block, Alex Ben and Lucy Autrey Wilson. *George Lucas's Blockbusting: A Decade-by-Decade Survey of Timeless Movies Including Untold Secrets of Their Financial and Cultural Success.* It Books, 2010. At nearly a thousand pages, the author examines three hundred of the most successful (financially or critically) motion pictures in history. The history of the production of each film is explored in detail.

Bloom, Ken. *Hollywood Musicals: The 101 Greatest Song-and-Dance Movies of All Time.* Black Do & Leventhal Publishers, 2010. From 1927 to present day, organized alphabetically, the author selects and profiles the best movie musicals in history with a foreword by Jane Powell.

Blount, Roy Jr. *Hail, Hail Euphoria!: Presenting the Marx Brothers in Duck Soup, the Greatest War Movie Ever Made.* It Books, 2010. The humorist author deconstructs one of the most famous comedies of all time with an eye on its production and stars and how it was re-appreciated as an anti-war movie in the 1960s.

Bouzereau, Laurent and Patricia Hitchcock. *Hitchcock, Piece by Piece.* Abrams, 2010. With a foreword by Alfred Hitchcock's daughter, Patricia Hitchcock O'Connell, this coffee table book spans the entire career of the master with an emphasis on removable memorabilia—facsimiles of letters, memos, and snapshots from the filmography of one of the form's most influential directors.

Caine, Michael. *The Elephant to Hollywood.* Henry Holt and Co., 2010. An autobiography by the Oscar®-winning actor that focuses on all five decades of the actor's career, including details about Caine's poverty-stricken upbringing in the Elephant and Castle area of London. Caine also served in the military, writes about his family life, and offers numerous anecdotes of his life in film.

Carlson, Zack and Bryan Connolly. *Destroy All Movies!!! The Complete Guide to Punks on Film.* Fantagraphic Books, 2010. A gigantic, comprehensive guide to every appearance by a punk in film history with mention of over 1,100 films from around the world. The book includes popular fare along with obscure cult classics and features color posters and stills for both.

Carroll, Mike. *Naked Filmmaking: How to Make a Feature-Length Film—Without a Crew—For $10,000 Or Less.* CreateSpace, 2010. The author, an award-winning filmmaker and cameraman-editor for twenty-five years, details the low-budget filmmaking process with an eye on a young screenwriter shooting their own film instead of trying to get one green-lit by someone else. The focus is on the practical step-by-step advice from an idea that can work on a low budget to making it happen.

Coleman, Lori and Diana Friedberg. *Make the Cut: A Guide to Becoming a Successful Assistant Editor in Film and TV.* Focal Press, 2010. The authors, successful Hollywood editors themselves, detail the industry through first-hand experience, even including a Q&A section with established editors and what they require of their assistant editors.

Cyphers, Eric, Sarah Jessica Parker, and Michael Patrick King. *Sex and the City 2: The Stories. The Fashion. The Adventure.* Running Press, 2010. An official companion to the sequel of the hit movie with a focus on the costumes, jewelry, and accessories worn by the stars of the film. The book also includes interviews with the cast and crew and details about its production with over 500 photos.

D'Arc, James V. *When Hollywood Came to Town: The History of Moviemaking in Utah.* Gibbs Smith, 2010. A library curator at Brigham Young University details the use of the school's state in filmmaking from such diverse movies as *The Searchers* (1956), *Butch Cassidy and the Sundance Kid* (1969), *Footloose* (1984), and *Planet of the Apes* (1968).

Duncan, Jody and Lisa Fitzpatrick. *The Making of Avatar.* Abrams, 2010. The editor of *Cinefex* magazine, a leading publication on special effects, details the behind-the-scenes challenges of the technical difficulties of one of the biggest blockbusters of all time.

Ebert, Roger. *Roger Ebert's Movie Yearbook 2011.* The Pulitzer Prize-winning Chicago film critic releases another of his annual collections, updated with new reviews.

Eiss, Jennifer, JP Rutter, and Steve White. *500 Essential Cult Movies: The Ultimate Guide.* Sterling, 2010. A reference guide to films with "a devoted and growing audience," including *A Clockwork Orange* (1971), *Harold and Maude* (1971), *This is Spinal Tap* (1984), *Dr. Strangelove* (1964), *The Big Lebowski* (1998), *Freaks* (1932), and hundreds more.

Eliot, Marc. *American Rebel: The Life of Clint Eastwood.* Three Rivers Press, 2010. The life and career of one of the most beloved filmmakers is chronicled from his early years with uncredited appearances to his TV work to his Westerns and, finally, his incredible work as a director from the 1970s through the 2000s.

Epstein, Edward Jay. *The Hollywood Economist: The Hidden Financial Reality Behind the Movies.* Melville House, 2010. The author, an investigative reporter, revisits themes he has researched in previous works about the financial side of Hollywood while adding the two essential new ingredients to the equation—the economic impact on the independent film market in present day and the availability of illegal downloads and new delivery systems for entertainment.

Eyman, Scott. *Empire of Dreams: The Epic Life of Cecil B. DeMille.* Simon & Schuster, 2010. The life and films of the legendary director of *The Ten Commandments* (1956) and *King of Kings* (1961) is examined as an epic parallel to the movies that made him a household name in the golden age of cinema.

Falconer, Daniel. *The Art of District 9: Weta Workshop.* Harper Design, 2010. With never-before-seen images, this coffee table book focuses on the design of the Best Picture nominee with a foreword by director Neill Blomkamp and an introduction by special effects master Richard Taylor.

Fontana, Ellen. *Audrey 100.* Sterling, 2010. Compiled by her family, these hundred images of Audrey Hepburn have been collected as a tribute to one of Hollywood's most recognizable icons. The book also includes a 9″ by 11″ print, suitable for framing.

Frey, James N. *How to Write a Damn Good Thriller: A Step-by-Step Guide for Novelists and Screenwriters.* St. Martin's Press, 2010. The fifth book by the writer of guides to fiction writing defines the key elements of the thriller genre and guides the reader through the process of creating their own. He uses a practical approach, referencing well-known thrillers as guide posts to light the path for the aspiring novelist or screenwriter.

Fuchs, Leo, Alexandre Fuchs, and Bruce Weber. *Leo Fuchs: Special Photographer From the Golden Age of Hollywood.* Powerhouse Books, 2010. The forty-year career of the world-famous photographer is chronicled from his days as a freelance magazine photographer to a fixture on movie sets in the 1950s and 1960s, where he shot some of the most iconic stars of the day. The book includes the well-known shots along with never-before-seen, behind-the-scenes photographs and memories of details of the shots from Fuchs himself.

Giddins, Gary. *Warning Shadows: Home Alone with Classic Cinema.* W. W. North & Company, 2010. A collection of essays from the author's newspaper reviews of DVD collections serve as the foundation for this piece, which can be viewed as an examination of the positives and negatives associated with DVD box sets or just as a useful buyer's guide.

Gora, Susannah. *You Couldn't Ignore Me If You Tried: The Brat Pack, John Hughes, and Their Impact on a Generation.* Three Rivers Press, 2010. Teen cinema of the 1980s is the focus of this book by the former editor of *Premiere*, which includes interviews with over two dozen actors, plus the directors and producers behind some of the most memorable films of the era, including *The Breakfast Club* (1985), *Fast Times at Ridgemont High* (1982), *Sixteen Candles* (1984), and *Pretty in Pink* (1986).

Hanson, Peter and Paul Robert Herman. *Tales From the Script: 50 Hollywood Screenwriters Share Their Stories.* It Books, 2010. With interviews with fifty writers, including William Goldman, Antwone Fisher, and Nora Ephron, the editors chart the course from concept to production with all the rejections along the way.

Hearn, Marcus. *The Art of Hammer: The Official Poster Collection From the Archive of Hammer Films.* Titan Books, 2010. The most iconic and memorable movie posters of the prime era of the Hammer studio are collected in a hardcover coffee table book, featuring rare artwork from around the world for such timeless films as *The Curse of Frankenstein* (1957) and the *Dracula* movies with Christopher Lee.

Hofler, Robert. *Party Animals: A Hollywood Tale of Sex, Drugs, and Rock 'n' Roll Starring the Fabulous Allan Carr.* Da Capo Press, 2010. Allan Carr threw some of the most notorious parties of the 1970s and the book about him offers some juicy details about celebrity soirees but also serves as a tale of the rise and fall of a man who went from the fringe of the industry to the heart of it (making *Grease*) and then back again.

Hotchner, A.E. *Paul and Me: Fifty-Three years of Adventures of Misadventures with My Pal Paul Newman.* Nan A. Talese, 2010. The author, a playwright, met Paul Newman in 1955 and the two remained friends until the actor's death in 2008. He chronicles his time with one of the most beloved actors of all time through stories about their adventures together fishing, traveling, and even helping to develop the Newman's Own brand.

Huang, Yunte. *Charlie Chan: The Untold Story of the Honorable Detective and His Rendezvous with American History.* W. W. Norton & Company, 2010. The social and cultural impact of the legendary film character is examined from the personal perspective of a Chinese immigrant who uses the icon to examine racism, exploitation, and assimilation.

Iandolo, Nicholas. *Cut the Crap and Write That Damn Screenplay!* lulu.com, 2010. A straightforward lesson on the basics of screenwriting, focusing on the ways in which writers constantly delay actually sitting down and doing the work required to go from concept to screenplay.

Jacey, Helen. *The Woman in the Story: Writing Memorable Female Characters.* Michael Wiese Productions, 2010. A professional screenwriter with more than ten years experience writing numerous screenplays for dozens of European film production companies turns a two-day seminar (Helen Jacey's "Writing the Heroine's Story") into a book.

Jackson, Jonathon. *The Making of Slap Shot: Behind the Scenes of the Greatest Hockey Movie.* Wiley, 2010. Interviews with over fifty cast members, production staff, and those who love the film *Slap Shot* (1977) serve as the structure for a companion book to the beloved hockey fan classic.

Jorgensen, Jay. *Edith Head: The Fifty-Year Career of Hollywood's Greatest Costume Designer.* Running Press, 2010. Costume designer Edith Head (1897-1981) helped define the look of not just film's golden age but fashion in general with her work on timeless films like *All About Eve* (1950), *Funny Face* (1957), *Rear Window* (1954), *Sabrina* (1954), *The Ten Commandments* (1956), and hundreds more film credits over a career that also included thirty-five Oscar® nominations. The book includes never-before-seen material from the Edith Head Archives of the Academy of Motion Picture Arts and Sciences.

Kashner, Sam and Nancy Schoenberger. *Furious Love: Elizabeth Taylor, Richard Burton, and the Marriage of the Century.* Harper, 2010. One of the rockiest and yet most iconic relationships of the golden age of cinema is elevated to the pedestal of marriage of the century in no small part due to how its ups and downs were spotlighted through the films they worked on together including *Cleopatra* (1963), *The Taming of the Shrew* (1967), and *Who's Afraid of Virginia Woolf?* (1966).

Kurtti, Jeff, John Lasseter, Nathan Greno, and Byron Howard. *The Art of Tangled.* Chronicle Books, 2010. A companion piece to the Disney hit, based on the fairy tale *Rapunzel* by the Brothers Grimm, including interviews with the artists, animators, and production team.

Landau, Neil and Matthew Frederick. *101 Things I Learned in Film School.* Grand Central Publishing, 2010. A writer and producer for major companies like Disney and Columbia Pictures, who currently serves as a faculty advisor in the MFA Writing Program at Goddard College and teaches at the UCLA School of Theatre, Film and Television offers insight into what is learned in film school and how to use it to get ahead in a competitive industry.

Laporte, Nicole. *The Men Who Would Be King: An Almost Epic Tale of Moguls Movies, and a Company Called Dream-Works.* Houghton Mifflin Harcourt, 2010. The author chronicles the rise and arguable fall of DreamWorks in an unauthorized saga of the legendary company founded by Steven Spielberg, Jeffrey Katzenberg, and David Geffen and how the combative personalities of the three men often clashed in ways that led to some problem years for the company.

Lethem, Jonathan and Sean Howe. *They Live.* Soft Skull Press, 2010. John Carpenter's 1988 sci-fi action satire has become a cult classic and the film is analyzed as a part of a new series of books called Deep Focus. The film is picked apart, scene-by-scene by the respected essayist and author of *The Fortress of Solitude.*

Maltin, Leonard. *Leonard Maltin's Classic Movie Guide: From the Silent Era Through 1965.* Plume, 2010. The author of the best-selling guide focuses on films that may be overlooked in his annual guide including a comprehensive look at the films of the silent era until the 1960s. The guide is pitched as a handy companion to discovering vintage works on DVD or cable.

Maltin, Leonard. *Leonard Maltin's 151 Best Movies You've Never Seen.* It Books, 2010. One of the most notable film critics chooses a series of smaller films for his signature succinct style with an emphasis on underrated gems from the last twenty years, focusing on independent, foreign, and documentary films including *Idiocracy* (2006), *Fast, Cheap, and Out of Control* (1997), and *The Devil's Backbone* (2001).

Maltin, Leonard. *Leonard Maltin's 2011 Movie Guide.* Signet, 2010. The man who holds the Guinness World Record for the shortest review trains his signature succinct style in his annual tome of reviews mostly for reference with more than 17,000 entries, including more than 300 new ones.

Marriot, James and Kim Newman. *Horror!: 333 Films to Scare You to Death.* Carlton Books, 2010. A definitive volume for horror fans that tracks the genre decade-by-decade with an examination of films from around the world and accompanying images from some of the most iconic scenes in horror history.

Matzen, Robert. *Errol & Olivia: Ego & Obsession in Golden Era Hollywood.* Paladin Communications, 2010. The title refers to Errol Flynn and Olivia de Havilland, who shared a complex personal and professional relationship on-screen and off and this book about them details their dynamic with many previously-unpublished photos.

McDonald, Brian. *Invisible Ink: A Practical Guide to Building Stories That Resonate.* Libertary Co., 2010. A screenwriter's guide to the elements of storytelling from an award-winning screenwriters that focuses on "invisible" elements like structure and technique so the reader can building a compelling story around a theme.

Mercado, Gustavo. *The Filmmaker's Eye: Learning (and Breaking) the Rules of Cinematic Composition.* Focal Press, 2010. With hundreds of photos and stills, the author explains the principles of cinematography by deconstructing the basic principles of the form.

Michaud, Michael Gregg. *Sal Mineo: A Biography.* Crown Archetype, 2010. The life of the beloved actor, who made twenty-one films before his brutal 1976 murder and was the youngest performer ever nominated for a Best Supporting Actor Oscar® for *Rebel Without a Cause* (1955), is chronicled from its early days to its bitter end.

Miller-Zarneke, Tracey and Cressida Cowell. *The Art of How to Train Your Dragon.* Newmarket Press, 2010. A companion book to the hit DreamWorks film with over 350 images including early character designs, story sketched, and concept paintings that had never been released before.

Monetti, Sandro. *Mickey Rourke: Wrestling With Demons.* Transit Publishing, 2010. A portrait of the Oscar® nominee from his early days as a boxer to his heartthrob status in the 1980s to his return to the ring in the 1990s and then back to the height of fame with *The Wrestler* (2008).

Monroe, Marilyn, Bernard Comment, and Stanley Buchthal. *Fragments: Poems, Intimate Notes, Letters.* Farrar, Straus and Giroux, 2010. The private life of the publicly-beloved star is chronicled with a collection of written artifacts in her own handwriting, including many never before published, along with rarely seen photos.

Morton, Andrew. *Angelina: An Unauthorized Biography.* St. Martin's Press, 2010. A no-holds-barred look at the tumultuous life of Angelina Jolie that focuses on her numerous marriages (Jonny Lee Miller, Billy Bob Thornton, Brad Pitt), her oft-reported feud with her father Jon Voight, her adoptions, and her drive to become more than just an actress in her role as philanthropist around the world.

Nichols, Bill. *Engaging Cinema: An Introduction to Film Studies.* An examination of the interaction between society and cinema as it is studies by scholars and critics that serves as a starting point for introductory film students; written by a Professor of Cinema at San Francisco State University.

Nolan, Christopher. *Inception: The Shooting Script.* Insight Editions, 2010. A companion piece to the blockbuster film that features a paperback edition of the screenplay, eight pages of color concept art, and production details like storyboards, notes, and diagrams. The introduction to the book is an interview with Nolan by his brother Jonathan.

Okun, Jeffrey A. and Susan Zwerman. *The VES Handbook of Visual Effects: Industry Standard VFX Practices and Procedures.* A massive (nearly 1,000 pages) reference guide for visual effects with techniques and procedures for artisans of the craft from eighty-eight top leading visual effects practitioners, covering every aspect of the filmmaking process.

Palmer, Scott. *Shooting in the Wild: An Insider's Account of Making Movies in the Animal Kingdom.* Sierra Club/Counterpoint, 2010. A producer writes about covering animals on film, particularly in the pursuit of wildlife

documentaries like those featuring Marlin Perkins, Jacques Cousteau, and Steve Irwin. The writer also examines how films about the animal kingdom influence preset conclusions about animal behavior and suggests changes in the wildlife filmmaking process for ethical reasons.

Penniston, Penny. *Talk the Talk: A Dialogue Workshop for Scriptwriters.* Michael Wiese Productions, 2010. A screenwriting guide with an emphasis on dialogue with twenty lessons for screenwriters and playwrights to master the art of the spoken word.

Pippin, Robert B. *Hollywood Westerns and American Myth: The Importance of Howard Hawks and John Ford for Political Philosophy.* Yale University Press, 2010. A philosophical study of three of the genre's most beloved Westerns: Howard Hawks' *Red River* (1948), John Ford's *The Man Who Shot Liberty Valance* (1962), and Ford's *The Searchers* (1956).

Porter, Darwin. *Humphrey Bogart: The Making of a Legend.* Blood Moon Productions, 2010. Yet another volume about the legendary star that traces his life through three unhappy marriages until he met Lauren Bacall, claiming that the iconic actor had bedded 1,000 women before the legendary marriage settled him down. The author is a journalist from Hollywood in the 1960s who uses interviews with some of Bogart's contemporaries as a source along with unpublished memoirs of the actor.

Porter, Darwin and Danforth Pince. *Hollywood Babylon Strikes Again!: More Exhibitions! More Sex! More Sin! More Scandals Unfit to Print.* Blood Moon Productions, 2010. Another volume in the series that seeks to unearth outrageous secrets from Hollywood's past.

Rabin, Nathan and A.V. Club. *My Year of Flops: The A.V. Club Presents One Man's Journey Deep Into the Heart of Cinematic Failure.* Scribner, 2010. A critic from *The A.V. Club* revisited one notorious flop every week for a year for a column and the contributions are collected into one volume for this release.

Ringwald, Molly. *Getting the Pretty Back: Friendship, Family, and Finding the Perfect Lipstick.* It Books, 2010. The star of films like *Pretty in Pink* (1986) and *Sixteen Candles* (1984) becomes a source for advice for young women but eschews much commentary or insight into her career in favor of relationship advice.

Rinzler, J.W. and George Lucas. *Star Wars Art: Visions.* Abrams, 2010. A collection of artwork inspired by *Star Wars* (1977) from 100 well-known and promising artists that serves as a tribute to one of the most-beloved films ever made.

Rinzler, J.W. and Ridley Scott. *The Making of Star Wars: The Empire Strikes Back.* Lucasbooks, 2010. A book timed with the 30th anniversary of *The Empire Strikes Back* (1980) that provides an in-depth account of the production of one of the most beloved films ever made. The author explores every aspect of the production along with interviews, archival records, books, magazine articles, and includes preproduction sketches, on-set photos, script drafts, notes, and more.

Rocca, Vincent and Kevin Smith. *Rebel Without a Deal: or, How a 30-year-old Filmmaker With $11,000 Almost Became* *a Hollywood Player.* CreateSpace, 2010. The author kept a journal about his attempt to become the next low-budget phenomenon and actually made a movie in five days for $11,000, landed and lost a multi-million dollar deal, and somehow kept the deal alive long enough for it to be released on DVD. Writer/Director Kevin Smith offers commentary and relates his own experiences in the low-budget comedy world.

Rosenbaum, Jonathan. *Goodbye Cinema, Hello Cinephilia: Film Culture in Transition.* University of Chicago Press, 2010. The legendary critic argues against the idea that serious film criticism has died and posits that it has merely moved to the online world through over fifty pieces collected in this volume.

Ryan, Maureen A. *Producer to Producer: A Step-by-Step Guide to Low Budget Independent Film Producing.* Michael Wiese Productions, 2010. A guide for low-budget, independent film producing from the co-producer of *Man on Wire* (2008) that outlines the entire production process along with checklists and templates for practical use.

Salisbury, Mark, Leah Gallo, and Holly Kempf. *Disney: Alice in Wonderland: A Visual Companion.* Disney Editions, 2010. A companion book to the hit film by Tim Burton with photos and details about the production of the fantasy adaptation.

Schatz, Thomas and Steven Bach. *The Genius of the System: Hollywood Filmmaking in the Studio Era.* University of Minnesota Press, 2010. A Professor at the University of Texas examines the period when he argues that writers, directors, and stars most creatively fused with the desires of studio management in the golden era of MGM, Warner Bros., Paramount, Universal, and RKO.

Schickel, Richard and Clint Eastwood. *Clint: A Retrospective.* Sterling, 2010. *TIME* film critic Schickel, who has written about Clint Eastwood before and openly expressed admiration for the filmmaker on numerous occasions, having known him for thirty-three years, focuses on his career with a film-by-film account, including 300 photos, many from behind-the-scenes.

Schochet, Stephen. *Hollywood Stories: Short, Entertaining Anecdotes About the Stars and Legends of the Movies!* BCH Fulfillment & Distribution, 2010. A collection of brief, anecdotal stories about iconic stars including John Wayne, Charlie Chaplin, Walt Disney, Jack Nicholson, Johnny Depp, Shirley Temple, Marilyn Monroe, Marlon Brando, Errol Flynn, and many more.

Shearer, Stephen Michael. *Beautiful: The Life of Hedy Lamarr.* Thomas Dunne Books, 2010. From her early days as Hedwig Eva Maria Kiesler in Vienna through her work in German films to the moment Louis B. Mayer offered her a contract with MGM, the life of movie star Hedy Lamarr was an unusual one. The biographer attempts to chronicle a very unique life that included five marriages, the biggest hit for Paramount of its time (*Samson and Delilah*), various lawsuits, and work in radio, TV, and film.

Shumate, Nathan. *The Golden Age of Crap: 77 B-Movies From the Glory Days of VHS.* CreateSpace, 2010. A sampling of the "best" films of the day when video stores offered sleeper hits, foreign horror films, and cult favorites for fans outside

of major cities to discover on their own. The author covers well-known cult hits like *Phantasm II* (1988) but also delves deeper for underground titles like *Plutonium Baby* (1987).

Sibley, Brian. *Harry Potter Film Wizardry.* Harper Design, 2010. With removable props and paper facsimiles, this companion book provides an interactive experience for fans who desire to dive deeper into the world of the beloved film series based on the J.K. Rowling fantasy tomes.

Solomon, Charles. *Tale as Old as Time: The Art and Making of Beauty and the Beast.* Disney Editions, 2010. An authoritative history of one of Disney's most beloved films from its history back in the late 1930s when Walt Disney first considered animating it through some false starts in the 1980s to a tumultuous production process to becoming the first animated film ever nominated for Best Picture.

Solomon, Charles, John Lasseter, Lee Unkrich, and Darla K. Anderson. *The Art of Toy Story 3.* Chronicle Books, 2010. A companion book to the #1 film of 2010 with photos and behind-the-scenes details as to its production.

Spies, Werner, Peter-Klaus Schuster, Dietmar Dath, and David Lynch. *David Lynch: Dark Splendor.* Hatje Cantz, 2010. An examination of the legendary director's non-film work in paintings, drawings, prints, photographs, and musical compositions. While not necessarily a film book, Lynch's art is creatively parallel to the films he has directed and should be of interest to fans of his movies.

Spivak, Jeffrey. *Buzz: The Life and Art of Busby Berkeley.* The University Press of Kentucky, 2010. Busby Berkeley was a legendary choreographer and director in the golden age of Hollywood whose style became iconic, but he was also a workaholic who went through multiple marriages and parties fueled by alcohol. This biography examines both the influence of Berkeley's work on the screen and the life off-screen that produced it.

Spoto, Donald. *Possessed: The Life of Joan Crawford.* William Morrow, 2010. Using exclusive interviews and archival documents, the biographer pieces together the reclusive life of Joan Crawford's early life through the days she was discovered by MGM and became a household name.

Stephens, E.J. and Marc Wanamaker. *Early Warner Bros. Studio.* Arcadia Publishing, 2010. A photo-heavy book that concentrates on the Warner Bros. golden era of the 1920s through the 1950s—the era where *Casablanca* (1942), *The Maltese Falcon* (1941), *East of Eden* (1955), and many more all came to life on the same 110-acre film factory in Burbank.

Sumner, Don. *Horror Movie Freak.* Krause Publications, 2010. A guide to the genre with films divided into unique categories like "zombie invasion" and "homicidal slashers" that also includes a DVD of George A. Romero's beloved and influential *Night of the Living Dead* (1968).

Terrell, Marshall. *Steve McQueen: The Life and Legend of a Hollywood Icon.* Triumph Books, 2010. With 32 pages of intimate photographs, the author builds on the foundation of his own 1993 biography of Steve McQueen by going into more detail about his subject's life, from his turbulent childhood to his time in the Marines to theater, TV, and film stardom.

Thomas, John Rhett. *Iron Man: The Art of Iron Man the Movie.* Marvel, 2010. A close-up look at the hit film that details the process behind its production with photos, storyboards, and details about the animatics and pre-visualization techniques for a blockbuster.

Von Busack, Richard. *The Art of Megamind.* Insight Editions, 2010. A companion piece to the hit DreamWorks movie that includes exclusive photos and behind-the-scenes details about its production that is broken down into three distinct sections—characters, locations, and technology.

Walter, Richard. *Essentials of Screenwriting: The Art, Craft, and Business of Film and Television Writing.* Plume, 2010. A respected teacher for almost thirty years at the prestigious UCLA Film School offers a window into his class, one that has produced two recent Oscar® winners for Best Screenplay (*Milk* and *Sideways*). The result is an essential guide for the aspiring screenwriter.

Wasson, Sam. *Fifth Avenue, 5 A.M.: Audrey Hepburn, Breakfast at Tiffany's, and the Dawn of the Modern Woman.* Harper, 2010. With interviews with director Blake Edwards and others, the author details the making of the timeless *Breakfast at Tiffany's* (1961) through pre-production to the drama on-set into the fashion impact of Hepburn's signature style.

Weber, Karl. *Waiting For 'SUPERMAN': How We Can Save America's Failing Public Schools.* PublicAffairs, 2010. A companion book to the film by Davis Guggenheim that further outlines the issues, challenges, and opportunities facing America's public schools with a focus on hands-on suggestions as to what the reader can do to enact change.

Weintraub, Jerry and Rich Cohen. *When I Stop Talking, You'll Know I'm Dead: Useful Stories from a Persuasive Man.* Twelve, 2010. The legendary manager of icons like Elvis Presley, Frank Sinatra, and John Denver details his incredible rise to power in Hollywood, where he was a major producer of TV and film for five decades in the entertainment industry.

Wexler, Bruce. *John Wayne's Wild West: An Illustrated History of Cowboys, Gunfights, Weapons, and Equipment.* Skyhorse Publishing, 2010. An examination of what was genuine in the Westerns of John Wayne and what was not with a focus on the equipment Wayne's characters used with hundreds of illustrations.

Whitlock, Cathy. Designs on Film: A Century of Hollywood Art Direction. It Books, 2010. An invaluable look at the art of design that attempts to capture a century of filmmaking art direction in one tome from *Top Hat* (1935) to *Avatar* (2009).

Director Index

Ben Affleck (1972-)
   The Town *391*
Casey Affleck (1975-)
   I'm Still Here *187*
Alexandre Aja (1978-)
   Piranha 3D *308*
Fatih Akin (1973-)
   Soul Kitchen *364*
Patrick Alessandrin (1965-)
   District 13: Ultimatum *93*
Daniel Alfredson (1959-)
   The Girl Who Kicked the Hor-
      net's Nest *144*
   The Girl Who Played with
      Fire *145*
Elizabeth Allen
   Ramona and Beezus *319*
Woody Allen (1935-)
   You Will Meet a Tall Dark
      Stranger *435*
Christian Alvart
   Case 39 *43*
Alejandro Amenabar (1972-)
   Agora *2*
Jon Amiel (1948-)
   Creation *73*
Paul W.S. Anderson (1965-)
   Resident Evil: Afterlife *331*
Nimród Antal (1973-)
   Predators *311*
Steve Antin (1956-)
   Burlesque *35*
Michael Apted (1941-)
   The Chronicles of Narnia: The

   Voyage of the Dawn
      Treader *54*
Andrea Arnold
   Fish Tank *122*
Darren Aronofsky (1969-)
   Black Swan *26*
Miguel Arteta (1965-)
   Youth in Revolt *437*
Kevin Asch (1975-)
   Holy Rollers *169*
Katie Aselton (1978-)
   The Freebie *130*
Olivier Assayas (1955-)
   Carlos *41*
Jacques Audiard (1952-)
   A Prophet *315*
Jaume Balagueró
   [Rec] 2 *320*
Thomas Balmes
   Babies *19*
Banksy
   Exit Through the Gift
      Shop *109*
Ilisa Barbash
   Sweetgrass *374*
Daniel Barber
   Harry Brown *161*
Amir Bar-Lev
   The Tillman Story *386*
Noah Baumbach (1969-)
   Greenberg *154*
Samuel Bayer
   A Nightmare on Elm
      Street *288*

Anthony Bell
   Alpha and Omega *10*
Marco Bellocchio (1939-)
   Vincere *411*
Bruce Beresford (1940-)
   Mao's Last Dancer *258*
Greg Berlanti
   Life As We Know It *239*
J. Blakeson
   The Disappearance of Alice
      Creed *92*
Anna Boden
   It's Kind of a Funny Story *194*
Joon-ho Bong
   Mother *273*
Derrick Borte (1967-)
   The Joneses *203*
Danny Boyle (1956-)
   127 Hours *298*
Barbara Brancaccio
   Cropsey *74*
Eric Brevig (1957-)
   Yogi Bear *432*
James L. Brooks (1940-)
   How Do You Know *172*
Nanette Burstein
   Going the Distance *148*
Tim Burton (1960-)
   Alice in Wonderland *6*
Juan Jose Campanella (1959-)
   The Secret in Their Eyes *344*
Martin Campbell (1940-)
   Edge of Darkness *105*

Yael Heronski
    A Film Unfinished *121*

Werner Herzog (1942-)
    My Son, My Son, What Have Ye
        Done *276*

Tim Hetherington (-2011)
    Restrepo *332*

George Hickenlooper (1964-2010)
    Casino Jack *44 *

Philip Seymour Hoffman (1967-)
    Jack Goes Boating *197*

Nicole Holofcener (1960-)
    Please Give *310*

Tom Hooper
    The King's Speech *216*

Byron Howard
    Tangled *382*

Albert Hughes (1972-)
    The Book of Eli *30*

Allen Hughes (1972-)
    The Book of Eli *30*

Patrick Hughes
    Red Hill *323*

Alejandro González Iñárritu (1963-)
    Biutiful *25*

James Ivory (1928-)
    The City of Your Final Destina-
        tion *57*

Andrew Jarecki
    All Good Things *8*

Eugene Jarecki
    Freakonomics *128*

Julian Jarrold
    Red Riding: 1974 *326*

Jean-Pierre Jeunet (1955-)
    Micmacs *265*

Mark Steven Johnson (1964-)
    When in Rome *422*

Joe Johnston (1950-)
    The Wolfman *430*

Henry Joost
    Catfish *47*

Neil Jordan (1950-)
    Ondine *296*

Sebastian Junger
    Restrepo *332*

Jee-woon Kim
    The Good, the Bad, the
        Weird *150*

Michael Patrick King
    Sex and the City 2 *349*

Josh Klausner
    Date Night *79*

Brian Koppelman
    Solitary Man *359*

Joseph Kosinski
    TRON: Legacy *396*

Roger Kumble (1966-)
    Furry Vengeance *134*

Neil LaBute (1963-)
    Death at a Funeral *84*

Yorgos Lanthimos
    Dogtooth *94*

Mike Leigh (1943-)
    Another Year *15*

Michael Lembeck (1948-)
    Tooth Fairy *388*

Louis Leterrier (1973-)
    Clash of the Titans *59*

Rob Letterman
    Gulliver's Travels *158*

Brian Levant (1952-)
    The Spy Next Door *367*

Shawn Levy (1968-)
    Date Night *79*

Richard J. Lewis
    Barney's Version *22*

Doug Liman (1965-)
    Fair Game *115*

David Lindsay-Abaire
    Rabbit Hole *317*

John Luessenhop
    Takers *379*

Robert Luketic (1973-)
    Killers *215*

James Mangold (1964-)
    Knight and Day *220*

Ethan Maniquis
    Machete *254*

Samuel Maoz
    Lebanon *231*

James Marsh (1963-)
    Red Riding: 1980 *326*

Garry Marshall (1934-)
    Valentine's Day *407*

Neil Marshall (1970-)
    Centurion *50*

Tom McGrath
    Megamind *261*

Adam McKay (1968-)
    The Other Guys *300*

Conor McPherson (1971-)
    The Eclipse *104*

Roger Michell (1957-)
    Morning Glory *270*

David Michôd
    Animal Kingdom *13*

Radu Mihaileanu (1958-)
    The Concert *63*

John Cameron Mitchell (1963-)
    Rabbit Hole *317*

Mike Mitchell
    Shrek Forever After *352*

Stephen R. Monroe (1964-)
    I Spit on Your Grave *184*

Tomm Moore
    The Secret of Kells *346*

Pierre Morel (1964-)
    From Paris With Love *131*

Christopher Morris (1965-)
    Four Lions *125*

Ryan Murphy (1966-)
    Eat Pray Love *103*

Ruba Nadda
    Cairo Time *39*

Vincenzo Natali (1969-)
    Splice *366*

Tim Blake Nelson (1965-)
    Leaves of Grass *230*

Mike Newell (1942-)
    Prince of Persia: The Sands of
        Time *313*

Gaspar Noe (1963-)
    Enter the Void *107*

Christopher Nolan (1970-)
    Inception *188*

Phillip Noyce (1950-)
    Salt *339*

Niels Arden Oplev (1961-)
    The Girl with the Dragon Tat-
        too *147*

Jacques Perrin (1941-)
    Oceans *295*

Tyler Perry (1969-)
    For Colored Girls *123*
    Why Did I Get Married
        Too? *425*

Brad Peyton (1979-)
    Cats & Dogs: The Revenge of
        Kitty Galore *48*

Todd Phillips (1970-)
    Due Date *98*

Steve Pink (1966-)
    Hot Tub Time Machine *170*

Paco Plaza
    [Rec] 2 *320*

Roman Polanski (1933-)
    The Ghost Writer *140*

Alan Poul (1958-)
    The Back-Up Plan *20*

Matt Reeves (1966-)
    Let Me In *235*

Joshua Zeman
  Cropsey *74*

Harald Zwart (1965-)
  The Karate Kid *207*

Edward Zwick (1952-)
  Love and Other Drugs *247*

Screenwriter Index

Ben Affleck (1972-)
  The Town *391*

Alexandre Aja (1978-)
  Piranha 3D *308*

Fatih Akin (1973-)
  Soul Kitchen *364*

Barbara Alberti (1943-)
  I Am Love *181*

Peter Allen
  Takers *379*

Woody Allen (1935-)
  You Will Meet a Tall Dark
    Stranger *435*

Christian Alvart
  Case 39 *43*

Alejandro Amenabar (1972-)
  Agora *2*

Amy Andelson
  Step Up 3D *370*

Sean Anders
  She's Out of My League *350*

Paul W.S. Anderson (1965-)
  Resident Evil: Afterlife *331*

Kate Angelo (1958-)
  The Back-Up Plan *20*

Steve Antin (1956-)
  Burlesque *35*

Nicolaj Arcel (1972-)
  The Girl with the Dragon Tat-
    too *147*

Jesse Armstrong
  Four Lions *125*

Michael Arndt
  Toy Story 3 *394*

Andrea Arnold
  Fish Tank *122*

Katie Aselton (1978-)
  The Freebie *130*

Olivier Assayas (1955-)
  Carlos *41*

Jacques Audiard (1952-)
  A Prophet *315*

Michael Bacall
  Scott Pilgrim vs. the
    World *343*

Sam Bain
  Four Lions *125*

Julia Baird
  Nowhere Boy *291*

Jaume Balagueró
  [Rec] 2 *320*

Amir Bar-Lev
  The Tillman Story *386*

Odile Barski
  The Girl on the Train *142*

Noah Baumbach (1969-)
  Greenberg *154*

Travis Beacham
  Clash of the Titans *59*

Simon Beaufoy (1967-)
  127 Hours *298*

Marco Bellocchio (1939-)
  Vincere *411*

Steve Bencich
  Cats & Dogs: The Revenge of
    Kitty Galore *48*

Peter Berg (1964-)
  The Losers *244*

Carlo Bernard
  Prince of Persia: The Sands of
    Time *313*
  The Sorcerer's Apprentice *362*

Jonathan Bernstein
  The Spy Next Door *367*

Jean-Marie Besset
  The Girl on the Train *142*

Luc Besson (1959-)
  District 13: Ultimatum *93*

Thomas Bidegain
  A Prophet *315*

Joe Bini
  The Tillman Story *386*

Steve Blair
  Frankie & Alice *127*

J. Blakeson
  The Disappearance of Alice
    Creed *92*

Alain-Michel Blanc
  The Concert *63*

Stuart Blumberg (1969-)
  The Kids Are All Right *211*

Armando Bo
  Biutiful *25*

Anna Boden
  It's Kind of a Funny Story *194*

Mark Bomback
  Unstoppable *405*

Joon-ho Bong
  Mother *273*

Derrick Borte (1967-)
  The Joneses *203*

Huck Botko
  The Last Exorcism *225*

Jeff Filgo
  Diary of a Wimpy Kid *89*

Efthimis Filippou
  Dogtooth *94*

Michael Finch
  Predators *311*

Ryan Fleck (1976-)
  It's Kind of a Funny Story *194*

Dan Fogelman
  Tangled *382*

Will Forte (1970-)
  MacGruber *253*

Dan Franck
  Carlos *41*

Adam Freedland
  Due Date *98*

Jason Friedberg
  Vampires Suck *410*

Jeffrey Friedman
  Howl *176*

Ron J. Friedman
  Cats & Dogs: The Revenge of
    Kitty Galore *48*

Jonas Frykberg
  The Girl Who Played with
    Fire *145*

Katherine Fugate (1965-)
  Valentine's Day *407*

George Gallo (1956-)
  Middle Men *266*

Lowell Ganz (1948-)
  Tooth Fairy *388*

Eric Garcia
  Repo Men *329*

Rodrigo Garcia (1959-)
  Mother and Child *275*

Alex Garland (1970-)
  Never Let Me Go *282*

Joe Gayton
  Faster *116*

Tony Gayton (1959-)
  Faster *116*

Nicolas Giabone
  Biutiful *25*

Alex Gibney
  Casino Jack and the United States
    of Money *45*
  Client 9: The Rise and Fall of
    Eliot Spitzer *60*
  Freakonomics *128*

Mateo Gil (1972-)
  Agora *2*

Josh Gilbert
  Furry Vengeance *134*

Bob Glaudini
  Jack Goes Boating *197*

Jake Goldberger (1977-)
  Don McKay *96*

Herbert Golder
  My Son, My Son, What Have Ye
    Done *276*

Jane Goldman
  Kick-Ass *209*

Rick Goldsmith
  The Most Dangerous Man in
    America: Daniel Ellsberg and
    the Pentagon Papers *272*

Seth Gordon
  Freakonomics *128*

Debra Granik
  Winter's Bone *428*

Pamela Gray
  Conviction *65*

Adam Green (1975-)
  Frozen *133*
  Hatchet II *165*

Matt Greenhalgh
  Nowhere Boy *291*

James Greer
  The Spy Next Door *367*

Ted Griffin (1970-)
  Killers *215*

Tony Grisoni
  Red Riding: 1980 *326*
  Red Riding: 1983 *327*
  Red Riding: 1974 *326*

Frederique Gruyer
  For Colored Girls *123*

Luca Guadagnino (1971-)
  I Am Love *181*

Davis Guggenheim (1964-)
  Waiting for 'Superman' *415*

Andrew Gurland
  The Last Exorcism *225*

Derek Haas (1970-)
  The A-Team *17*

Paul Haggis (1953-)
  The Next Three Days *285*

John Hamburg (1970-)
  Little Fockers *242*

Tanya Hamilton
  Night Catches Us *287*

Michael Handelman
  Dinner for Schmucks *90*

Robert Harris (1957-)
  The Ghost Writer *140*

Adi Hasak
  From Paris With Love *131*

Phil Hay
  Clash of the Titans *59*

Josh Heald (1977-)
  Hot Tub Time Machine *170*

Eric Heisserer
  A Nightmare on Elm
    Street *288*

Rasmus Heisterberg
  The Girl with the Dragon Tat-
    too *147*

Brian Helgeland (1961-)
  Green Zone *153*
  Robin Hood *334*
  Salt *339*

Chris Henchy
  The Other Guys *300*

Rupert Henning (1967-)
  North Face *290*

Laurent Herbiert (1961-)
  Wild Grass *427*

Yael Heronski
  A Film Unfinished *121*

Marshall Herskovitz (1952-)
  Love and Other Drugs *247*

Werner Herzog (1942-)
  My Son, My Son, What Have Ye
    Done *276*

Mark Heyman
  Black Swan *26*

Robin Hill
  Down Terrace *97*

Marcus Hinchey
  All Good Things *8*

Ken Hixon
  Welcome to the Rileys *421*

Erich Hoeber
  Red *322*

Jon Hoeber
  Red *322*

Nicole Holofcener (1960-)
  Please Give *310*

Adam Horowitz
  TRON: Legacy *396*

Patrick Hughes
  Red Hill *323*

Alejandro González Iñárritu (1963-)
  Biutiful *25*

Billy Ivory
  Made in Dagenham *256*

Robert Nelson Jacobs
  Extraordinary Measures *112*

Roy Jacobsen
  Valhalla Rising *408*

Mark Jacobson
  Love Ranch *249*

Brian Nelson
Devil *87*

Tim Blake Nelson (1965-)
Leaves of Grass *230*

Mark Neveldine (1973-)
Jonah Hex *202*

Gaspar Noe (1963-)
Enter the Void *107*

Christopher Nolan (1970-)
Inception *188*

Liam O'Donnell
Skyline *355*

Patrick O'Neill
Knight and Day *220*

John Orloff
Legend of the Guardians: The
Owls of Ga'Hoole *232*

Tom Pabst
Paranormal Activity 2 *305*

Eun-kyo Park
Mother *273*

Cinco Paul
Despicable Me *86*

Craig Pearce
Charlie St. Cloud *51*

Anthony Peckham
The Book of Eli *30*

Jacques Perrin (1941-)
Oceans *295*

Michael R. Perry
Paranormal Activity 2 *305*

Tyler Perry (1969-)
For Colored Girls *123*
Why Did I Get Married
Too? *425*

Todd Phillips (1970-)
Due Date *98*

Paco Plaza
[Rec] 2 *320*

Gregory Poirier
The Spy Next Door *367*

Roman Polanski (1933-)
The Ghost Writer *140*

Chris Provenzano
Get Low *139*

Nick Pustav
Ramona and Beezus *319*

Charles Randolph
Love and Other Drugs *247*

Tim Rasmussen
Marmaduke *259*

Matt Reeves (1966-)
Let Me In *235*

Nicolas Winding Refn (1970-)
Valhalla Rising *408*

John Requa
I Love You Phillip Morris *182*

Alex Reval
Wild Grass *427*

Mike Rich (1959-)
Secretariat *347*

Jean-Francois Richet
Mesrine: Killer Instinct *264*
Mesrine: Public Enemy #1 *265*

Jose Rivera
Letters to Juliet *237*

Matthew Robbins (1945-)
The Concert *63*

Kristin Rusk Robinson
Life As We Know It *239*

Billy Roche
The Eclipse *104*

Chris Rock (1966-)
Death at a Funeral *84*

Alvaro Rodriguez
Machete *254*

Robert Rodriguez (1968-)
Machete *254*

George A. Romero (1940-)
Survival of the Dead *373*

Anne Rosellini
Winter's Bone *428*

Melissa Rosenberg
The Twilight Saga: Eclipse *402*

Bert V. Royal (1977-)
Easy A *101*

Ulf Rydberg
The Girl Who Kicked the Hornet's Nest *144*

Eduardo Sacheri
The Secret in Their Eyes *344*

Gabe Sachs
Diary of a Wimpy Kid *89*

Jennifer Salt (1944-)
Eat Pray Love *103*

Christopher Sanders (1960-)
How to Train Your
Dragon *174*

Adam Sandler (1966-)
Grown Ups *156*

Jan Sardi
Mao's Last Dancer *258*

Stephen Schiff
Wall Street: Money Never
Sleeps *416*

Peter Schink
Legion *234*

Alan Schoolcraft
Megamind *261*

David Seidler
The King's Speech *216*

David Self
The Wolfman *430*

Aaron Seltzer
Vampires Suck *410*

Yaron Shani
Ajami *4*

Ally Sheedy (1962-)
Life During Wartime *240*

M. Night Shyamalan (1970-)
The Last Airbender *223*

Floria Sigismondi (1965-)
The Runaways *336*

Christoph Silber (1971-)
North Face *290*

Scott Silver
The Fighter *118*

Brent Simons
Megamind *261*

Randi Mayern Singer
Tooth Fairy *388*

Tom Six
The Human Centipede: First Sequence *177*

Marc Smerling
All Good Things *8*

Norman Snider
Casino Jack *44 *

John Solomon
MacGruber *253*

Todd Solondz (1960-)
Life During Wartime *240*

Aaron Sorkin (1961-)
The Social Network *357*

Nicholas Sparks
The Last Song *226*

Chris Sparling
Buried *34*

Malcolm Spellman
Our Family Wedding *301*

Michael Spierig
Daybreakers *81*

Peter Spierig
Daybreakers *81*

Morgan Spurlock
Freakonomics *128*

Sylvester Stallone (1946-)
The Expendables *110*

Emil Stern
Legend of the Guardians: The
Owls of Ga'Hoole *232*

Cinematographer Index

Michel Abramowicz
    From Paris With Love *131*

Barry Ackroyd (1954-)
    Green Zone *153*

Remi Adefarasin (1948-)
    Little Fockers *242*

Javier Aguirresarobe (1948-)
    The City of Your Final Destina-
      tion *57*
    The Twilight Saga: Eclipse *402*

Maryse Alberti
    Casino Jack and the United States
      of Money *45*
    Client 9: The Rise and Fall of
      Eliot Spitzer *60*
    Stone *371*

Maxime Alexandre (1971-)
    The Crazies *72*

Jerome Almeras
    Babies *19*

Fabienne Alvarez-Giro
    The Secret of Kells *346*

Mitchell Amundsen (1958-)
    Jonah Hex *202*

Junji Aoki
    Freakonomics *128*

Adam Arkapaw
    Animal Kingdom *13*

John Bailey (1942-)
    Country Strong *70*
    The Greatest *151*
    Ramona and Beezus *319*
    When in Rome *422*

Thimios Bakatakis
    Dogtooth *94*

Florian Ballhaus (1965-)
    Red *322*

Lance Bangs
    Jackass 3D *198*

Will Barratt
    Frozen *133*
    Hatchet II *165*

Michael Barrett (1970-)
    Takers *379*

Bojan Bazelli
    Burlesque *35*
    The Sorcerer's Apprentice *362*

Giora Bejach
    Lebanon *231*

Philipp Blaubach
    The Disappearance of Alice
      Creed *92*

Hagen Bogdanski
    Case 39 *43*

Oliver Bokelberg (1964-)
    The Bounty Hunter *31*

David Boyd
    Get Low *139*

Russell Boyd (1944-)
    The Way Back *419*

Kolja Brandt
    North Face *290*

Jennifer Brooks
    See Laurie Rose

Don Burgess (1956-)
    The Book of Eli *30*

Patrick Cady
    Lottery Ticket *246*

Yves Cape (1960-)
    White Material *424*

Russell Carpenter (1950-)
    Killers *215*

Lucien Castaing-Taylor
    Sweetgrass *374*

Vanja Cernjul (1968-)
    City Island *56*

Robert Chappell
    Countdown to Zero *68*

Chuy Chavez
    Youth in Revolt *437*

Enrique Chediak
    Charlie St. Cloud *51*
    127 Hours *298*
    Repo Men *329*

Simon Christidis
    Oceans *295*

Daniele Cipri
    Vincere *411*

Gary Clarke
    Countdown to Zero *68*

Danny Cohen
    The King's Speech *216*

Peter Lyons Collister (1956-)
    Furry Vengeance *134*

Lol Crawley
    Four Lions *125*

Jeff Cronenweth (1962-)
    The Social Network *357*

Dean Cundey (1946-)
    The Spy Next Door *367*

Jeff Cutter
    A Nightmare on Elm
      Street *288*

Svetlana Cvetko
    Inside Job *191*

Editor Index

Joelle Alexis
    A Film Unfinished *121*

John David Allen
    The City of Your Final Destination *57*

Josh Altman
    The Tillman Story *386*

Fabienne Alvarez-Giro
    The Secret of Kells *346*

Jonathan Amos
    Scott Pilgrim vs. the World *343*

Scott Anderson
    Alpha and Omega *10*

Michael Andrews
    Megamind *261*

James Andrykowski
    Little Fockers *242*

Tariq Anwar
    The King's Speech *216*

Mags Arnold
    The Killer Inside Me *213*

Mick Audsley
    Prince of Persia: The Sands of Time *313*
    Tamara Drewe *380*

John Axelrod
    The Switch *376*

Stuart Baird (1947-)
    Edge of Darkness *105*
    Salt *339*

Ilisa Barbash
    Sweetgrass *374*

Luc Barnier
    Carlos *41*

Roger Barton
    The A-Team *17*

Alan Baumgarten
    Dinner for Schmucks *90*

Baxter
    Piranha 3D *308*

Kirk Baxter
    The Social Network *357*

Chad Beck
    Inside Job *191*

Alan Edward Bell
    Gulliver's Travels *158*

Michael Berenbaum
    Sex and the City 2 *349*

Reynald Bertrand
    Babies *19*

Kent Beyda
    Jonah Hex *202*
    Yogi Bear *432*

Joe Bini
    My Son, My Son, What Have Ye Done *276*
    The Tillman Story *386*

Andrew Bird
    Soul Kitchen *364*

Ken Blackwell
    The Expendables *110*

Doug Blush
    Freakonomics *128*

Anna Boden
    It's Kind of a Funny Story *194*

Kristina Boden
    Dear John *82*

Adam Bolt
    Inside Job *191*

Francoise Bonnot
    The Tempest *384*

Michelle Botticelli
    Leaves of Grass *230*

Marc Boucrot
    Enter the Void *107*

Maryann Brandon
    How to Train Your Dragon (V) *174*

David Brenner
    Wall Street: Money Never Sleeps *416*

Sven Budelmann (1973-)
    North Face *290*

Bradley Buecker
    Eat Pray Love *103*

Conrad Buff
    The Last Airbender *223*

Gary Burritt
    Diary of a Wimpy Kid *89*

David Burrows
    Legend of the Guardians: The Owls of Ga'Hoole (V) *232*

Francesca Calvelli
    Vincere *411*

Juan J. Campanella (1959-)
    The Secret in Their Eyes *344*

Malcolm Campbell
    Middle Men *266*

Seth Casriel
    Jackass 3D *198*

Jay Cassidy
    Conviction *65*
    Waiting for 'Superman' *415*

Angus Wall
    The Social Network *357*

Martin Walsh
    Clash of the Titans *59*
    Prince of Persia: The Sands of
        Time *313*

Mark Warner
    Mao's Last Dancer *258*

George Watters
    The Sorcerer's Apprentice *362*

Nicholas Wayman-Harris
    Skyline *355*

Steven Weisberg
    Morning Glory *270*
    Mother and Child *275*

Andrew Weisblum
    Black Swan *26*

Juliette Welfing
    A Prophet *315*

Jeff Werner
    The Kids Are All Right *211*

Dirk Westervelt
    Faster *116*
    Our Family Wedding *301*

Brent White
    The Other Guys *300*

John Wright
    Secretariat *347*

Pamela Ziegenhagen-Shefland
    Despicable Me *86*

Dan Zimmerman
    Predators *311*

Dean Zimmerman
    Date Night *79*

Don Zimmerman
    Marmaduke *259*

Paul Zucker
    Twelve *401*

Art Director Index

Music Director Index

John Adams
  I Am Love *181*
Ishai Adar
  A Film Unfinished *121*
Armand Amar (1953-)
  The Concert *63*
Michael Andrews
  Cyrus *76*
  She's Out of My League *350*
Selena Arizanovic
  Stone *371*
Craig Armstrong (1959-)
  Wall Street: Money Never
    Sleeps *416*
David Arnold (1962-)
  The Chronicles of Narnia: The
    Voyage of the Dawn
    Treader *54*
  Made in Dagenham *256*
  Morning Glory *270*
Cyrille Aufort
  Splice *366*
Chris P. Bacon
  Alpha and Omega *10*
  Love Ranch *249*
Lorne Balfe
  Megamind *261*
Thomas Bangalter
  Enter the Void *107*
Nathan Barr
  The Last Exorcism *225*
Ruth Barrett
  Harry Brown *161*
Geoff Barrow
  Exit Through the Gift
    Shop *109*

Raphael Beau
  Micmacs *265*
Christophe Beck (1972-)
  Burlesque *35*
  Date Night *79*
  Death at a Funeral *84*
  Due Date *98*
  The Greatest *151*
  Hot Tub Time Machine *170*
  Percy Jackson & the Olympians:
    The Lightning Thief *306*
  Red *322*
  Waiting for 'Superman' *415*
Nicolas Becker
  Lebanon *231*
Marco Beltrami (1966-)
  Jonah Hex *202*
  Mesrine: Killer Instinct *264*
  Mesrine: Public Enemy #1 *265*
  My Soul to Take *277*
  Repo Men *329*
Doug Bernheim
  Life During Wartime *240*
Matt Biffa (1969-)
  Harry Potter and the Deathly
    Hallows: Part 1 *162*
Steven Bramson
  Don McKay *96*
Kathleen Brennan
  I'm Still Here *187*
Paul Brill
  Freakonomics *128*
  Joan Rivers: A Piece of
    Work *200*

Jon Brion (1963-)
  The Other Guys *300*
  Stone *371*
Michi Britsch
  Case 39 *43*
Broken Social Scene
  It's Kind of a Funny Story *194*
Michael Brook
  Country Strong *70*
Rabiah Buchari
  Ajami *4*
David Buckley
  From Paris With Love *131*
  The Town *391*
Carter Burwell (1955-)
  Howl *176*
  True Grit *399*
Niall Byrne
  Cairo Time *39*
Joel Cadbury
  The Killer Inside Me *213*
Marc Canham
  The Disappearance of Alice
    Creed *92*
Phil Canning
  Four Lions *125*
Paul Cantelon
  Conviction *65*
Robert Carli
  Survival of the Dead *373*
Teddy Castellucci
  Lottery Ticket *246*
Pasquale Catalano
  Barney's Version *22*

Rayston Langdon
    I'm Still Here *187*

Nathan Larson (1970-)
    The Kids Are All Right *211*

Alexander Lasarenko
    Cropsey *74*

Byeong-woo Lee
    Mother *273*

Christopher Lennertz (1972-)
    Cats & Dogs: The Revenge of
        Kitty Galore *48*
    Marmaduke *259*
    Vampires Suck *410*

Blake Leyh
    The Most Dangerous Man in
        America: Daniel Ellsberg and
        the Pentagon Papers *272*

Andrew Lockington (1974-)
    Frankie & Alice *127*

Deborah Lurie
    Dear John *82*

Evan Lurie (1954-)
    Jack Goes Boating *197*

Alexandre Mahout
    District 13: Ultimatum *93*

Clint Mansell (1963-)
    Black Swan *26*
    Faster *116*

Matthew Margeson
    Skyline *355*

Dario Marianelli (1963-)
    Agora *2*
    Eat Pray Love *103*

Mastodon
    Jonah Hex *202*

Bear McCreary
    Step Up 3D *370*

John McCullough
    Casino Jack and the United States
        of Money *45*

Wendy Melvoin (1964-)
    Just Wright *205*

Alan Menken (1949-)
    Tangled *382*

Lynette Meyer
    The Killer Inside Me *213*

Julia Michels
    Diary of a Wimpy Kid *89*
    Sex and the City 2 *349*

Pete Miser
    Freakonomics *128*

Mark Mothersbaugh (1950-)
    Ramona and Beezus *319*

James Murphy
    Greenberg *154*

John Murphy (1965-)
    Kick-Ass *209*

MJ Mynarski
    Holy Rollers *169*

Peter Nashel
    Client 9: The Rise and Fall of
        Eliot Spitzer *60*
    Freakonomics *128*

Blake Neely (1969-)
    Life As We Know It *239*

David Newman (1954-)
    The Spy Next Door *367*

Randy Newman (1943-)
    Toy Story 3 *394*

John Ottman (1964-)
    The Losers *244*

Melissa Parmenter
    The Killer Inside Me *213*

Antony Partos
    Animal Kingdom *13*

Michael Penn (1958-)
    Solitary Man *359*

Barrington Pheloung (1954-)
    Red Riding: 1983 *327*

Martin Phipps
    Harry Brown *161*

Phoenix
    Somewhere *361*

Rachel Portman (1960-)
    Never Let Me Go *282*

John Powell (1963-)
    Fair Game *115*
    Green Zone *153*
    How to Train Your
        Dragon *174*
    Knight and Day *220*

Trevor Rabin (1954-)
    The Sorcerer's Apprentice *362*

A.R. Rahman (1966-)
    127 Hours *298*

Raphael
    See Raphael Beau

Ernst Reijseger
    My Son, My Son, What Have Ye
        Done *276*

Victor Reyes
    Buried *34*

Trent Reznor (1965-)
    The Social Network *357*

Atticus Ross
    The Book of Eli *30*
    The Social Network *357*

Leopold Ross
    The Book of Eli *30*

Malcolm Ross
    The Illusionist *185*

Anton Sanko
    Rabbit Hole *317*

Gustavo Santaolalla
    Biutiful *25*

Philippe Sarde (1945-)
    The Girl on the Train *142*

Claudia Sarne
    The Book of Eli *30*

Patrick Savage
    The Human Centipede: First Se-
        quence *177*

Brad Segal
    Easy A *101*

Theodore Shapiro (1971-)
    Dinner for Schmucks *90*

Ed Shearmur (1966-)
    Furry Vengeance *134*
    Mother and Child *275*

Philip Sheppard
    The Tillman Story *386*

Howard Shore (1946-)
    Edge of Darkness *105*
    The Twilight Saga: Eclipse *402*

Alan Silvestri (1950-)
    The A-Team *17*

Rob Simonsen
    All Good Things *8*

Mark Snow (1946-)
    Wild Grass *427*

Holeg Spies
    The Human Centipede: First Se-
        quence *177*

Jon Spurney
    Freakonomics *128*

Stuart S. Staples
    White Material *424*

Michael Stern
    Why Did I Get Married
        Too? *425*

Marc Streitenfeld
    Robin Hood *334*
    Welcome to the Rileys *421*

Kjartan Sveinsson
    Ondine *296*

John Swihart
    Youth in Revolt *437*

Bobby Tahouri
    Best Worst Movie *23*

Francois Tetaz
    The Square *368*

Mark Tildesley
    The Killer Inside Me *213*

Performer Index

Danny A. Abeckaser
  Holy Rollers *169*

Lionel Abelanski (1964-)
  The Concert *63*

Whitney Able
  Monsters *268*

Ed Ackerman (1977-)
  Frozen *133*
  Hatchet II *165*

Jason "Wee Man" Acuna (1973-)
  Jackass 3D *198*

Amy Adams (1974-)
  The Fighter *118*
  Leap Year *228*

Mark Addy (1963-)
  Barney's Version *22*
  Red Riding: 1983 *327*
  Robin Hood *334*

Adele Ado
  White Material *424*

Ben Affleck (1972-)
  The Company Men *62*
  The Town *391*

Casey Affleck (1975-)
  I'm Still Here *187*
  The Killer Inside Me *213*

Christina Aguilera
  Burlesque *35*

Anders Ahlbom
  The Girl Who Kicked the Hor-
    net's Nest *144*

Waris Ahluwalia
  I Am Love *181*

Rizwan Ahmed
  Centurion *50*
  Four Lions *125*

Liam Aiken (1990-)
  The Killer Inside Me *213*

Adeel Akhtar
  Four Lions *125*

Gbenga Akinnagbe
  Lottery Ticket *246*

Adewale Akinnuoye-Agbaje (1967-)
  Faster *116*

Jessica Alba (1981-)
  The Killer Inside Me *213*
  Little Fockers *242*
  Machete *254*
  Valentine's Day *407*

Norma Aleandro (1936-)
  The City of Your Final Destina-
    tion *57*

Fausto Russo Alesi
  Vincere *411*

Olly Alexander
  Enter the Void *107*

Arsher Ali
  Four Lions *125*

Mahershalalhashbaz Ali
  Predators *311*

Tatyana Ali (1979-)
  Mother and Child *275*

Roger Allam (1953-)
  Tamara Drewe *380*

Parry Allen
  See Parry Shen

Tim Allen (1953-)
  Toy Story 3 *(V)* *394*

Bruce Altman (1955-)
  The American *12*

Maricel Álvarez
  Biutiful *25*

Mathieu Amalric (1965-)
  Mesrine: Public Enemy #1 *265*
  Wild Grass *427*

Elena Anaya (1975-)
  Cairo Time *39*
  Mesrine: Killer Instinct *264*

Anthony Anderson (1970-)
  The Back-Up Plan *20*

Joe Anderson
  The Crazies *72*

Peter Andersson (1953-)
  The Girl Who Kicked the Hor-
    net's Nest *144*
  The Girl Who Played with
    Fire *145*

Anthony Andrews (1948-)
  The King's Speech *216*

David Andrews (1952-)
  Fair Game *115*

Julie Andrews (1935-)
  Despicable Me *(V)* *86*
  Shrek Forever After *(V)* *352*
  Tooth Fairy *388*

Jennifer Aniston (1969-)
  The Bounty Hunter *31*
  The Switch *376*

Amina Annabi
  Cairo Time *39*

Christina Applegate (1971-)
  Cats & Dogs: The Revenge of
    Kitty Galore *(V)* *48*
  Going the Distance *148*

Mohammad Aqil
  Four Lions *125*

Madeline Carroll (1996-)
The Spy Next Door *367*

Jim Carter (1948-)
Creation *73*

Ariel Casas
[Rec] 2 *320*

Alejandro Casaseca
[Rec] 2 *320*

Vincent Cassel (1967-)
Black Swan *26*
Mesrine: Killer Instinct *264*
Mesrine: Public Enemy #1 *265*

Katie Cassidy (1986-)
A Nightmare on Elm
Street *288*

Kim Cattrall (1956-)
The Ghost Writer *140*
Sex and the City 2 *349*

Tom Cavanagh (1963-)
Yogi Bear *432*

Fulvio Cecere (1960-)
Resident Evil: Afterlife *331*

Michael Cera (1988-)
Scott Pilgrim vs. the
World *343*
Youth in Revolt *437*

Michela Cescon
Vincere *411*

Maury Chakin
Casino Jack *44 *

Jackie Chan (1954-)
The Karate Kid *207*
The Spy Next Door *367*

Delphine Chaneac
Splice *366*

Louis Ozawa Changchien
Predators *311*

Geraldine Chaplin (1944-)
The Wolfman *430*

Kevin Chapman
Unstoppable *405*

Josh Charles (1971-)
After.life *1*

Chevy Chase (1943-)
Hot Tub Time Machine *170*

Corena Chase
The Town *391*

Don Cheadle (1964-)
Brooklyn's Finest *33*
Iron Man 2 *192*

Amari Cheatom
Night Catches Us *287*

Joan Chen (1961-)
Mao's Last Dancer *258*

Taisheng ("Cheng Tai Shen") Cheng
Biutiful *25*

Kristin Chenoweth (1968-)
You Again *433*

Cher (1946-)
Burlesque *35*

Anis Cheurfa
TRON: Legacy *396*

Hayden Christensen (1981-)
Takers *379*

Charlotte Christie
Tamara Drewe *380*

Abigail Chu
Splice *366*

Jamie Chung
Grown Ups *156*

Thomas Haden Church (1960-)
Don McKay *96*
Easy A *101*

Blake Clark (1946-)
Grown Ups *156*
Toy Story 3 (V) *394*

Noel Clarke (1975-)
Centurion *50*

Sarah Clarke (1972-)
The Twilight Saga: Eclipse *402*

Warren Clarke (1947-)
Red Riding: 1980 *326*
Red Riding: 1983 *327*
Red Riding: 1974 *326*

Patricia Clarkson (1959-)
Cairo Time *39*
Easy A *101*
Shutter Island *354*

Claudio
Best Worst Movie *23*

Jill Clayburgh
Love and Other Drugs *247*

Jemaine Clement (1974-)
Despicable Me (V) *86*
Dinner for Schmucks *90*

George Clooney (1961-)
The American *12*

Kim Coates (1959-)
Resident Evil: Afterlife *331*

Bill Cobbs (1935-)
Get Low *139*

Pierre Coffin
Despicable Me (V) *86*

Bern Cohen
Holy Rollers *169*

Gilles Cohen
A Prophet *315*

Oshri Cohen (1984-)
Lebanon *231*

Scott Cohen (1964-)
Love and Other Drugs *247*

Gary Cole (1957-)
The Joneses *203*

Bobby Coleman (1997-)
The Last Song *226*

Gregoire Colin (1975-)
35 Shots of Rum *385*

Pauline Collins (1940-)
You Will Meet a Tall Dark
Stranger *435*

Vince Colosimo (1966-)
Daybreakers *81*

Robbie Coltrane (1950-)
Harry Potter and the Deathly
Hallows: Part 1 *162*

Sean Combs (1969-)
Get Him to the Greek *137*

Common
Date Night *79*
Just Wright *205*

Martin Compston (1984-)
The Disappearance of Alice
Creed *92*

Shelley Conn (1976-)
How Do You Know *172*

Jennifer Connelly (1970-)
Creation *73*

Billy Connolly (1942-)
Gulliver's Travels *158*

Kevin Connolly (1974-)
Secretariat *347*

Frances Conroy (1953-)
Stone *371*

Neili Conroy
Kisses *218*

Paddy Considine (1974-)
Red Riding: 1980 *326*

Anne Consigny
Mesrine: Public Enemy #1 *265*
Wild Grass *427*

Vladimir Consigny
Wild Grass *427*

Mark Consuelos (1971-)
Cop Out *67*

Cristina Contes (1969-)
The Wolfman *430*

Tom Conti (1941-)
The Tempest *384*

Steve Coogan (1965-)
Marmaduke (V) *259*
The Other Guys *300*
Percy Jackson & the Olympians:
The Lightning Thief *306*

Christopher Davis
Red Hill *323*

Eisa Davis (1971-)
Welcome to the Rileys *421*

Essie Davis
Legend of the Guardians: The
Owls of Ga'Hoole *(V)* *232*

Julia Davis
Four Lions *125*

Kristin Davis (1965-)
Sex and the City 2 *349*

Philip Davis (1953-)
Another Year *15*

Viola Davis (1952-)
Eat Pray Love *103*
It's Kind of a Funny Story *194*
Knight and Day *220*

Warwick Davis (1970-)
Harry Potter and the Deathly
Hallows: Part 1 *162*

Rosario Dawson (1979-)
Unstoppable *405*

Charlie Day (1976-)
Going the Distance *148*

Isaach De Bankole (1957-)
White Material *424*

Cecile de France (1975-)
Hereafter *166*
Mesrine: Killer Instinct *264*

Paz de la Huerta (1984-)
Enter the Void *107*

Frances de la Tour
Alice in Wonderland *6*

Robert De Niro (1943-)
Little Fockers *242*
Machete *254*
Stone *371*

Emilie de Ravin (1981-)
Remember Me *327*

Christian de Sica (1951-)
The Tourist *389*

Julia Deakin (1952-)
Down Terrace *97*

Loren Dean (1969-)
Conviction *65*

Marcia DeBonis (1960-)
Letters to Juliet *237*

Adrienne DeFaria
Legend of the Guardians: The
Owls of Ga'Hoole *(V)* *232*

Thomas Dekker (1987-)
A Nightmare on Elm
Street *288*

Benicio Del Toro (1967-)
The Wolfman *430*

Pippo Delbono
I Am Love *181*

David DeLuise (1971-)
Vampires Suck *410*

Patrick Dempsey (1966-)
Valentine's Day *407*

Mathieu Demy (1972-)
The Girl on the Train *142*

Catherine Deneuve (1943-)
The Girl on the Train *142*

David Denman (1973-)
Fair Game *115*

Brian Dennehy (1939-)
The Next Three Days *285*

Gerard Depardieu (1948-)
Mesrine: Killer Instinct *264*

Johnny Depp (1963-)
Alice in Wonderland *6*
The Tourist *389*

Emilie Dequenne (1981-)
The Girl on the Train *142*

Laura Dern
Little Fockers *242*

Alex Descas (1958-)
35 Shots of Rum *385*

Loretta Devine (1949-)
Death at a Funeral *84*
For Colored Girls *123*
Lottery Ticket *246*
My Son, My Son, What Have Ye
Done *276*

Danny DeVito (1944-)
Solitary Man *359*
When in Rome *422*

Emmanuelle Devos (1964-)
Wild Grass *427*

Rosemarie DeWitt (1974-)
The Company Men *62*

Caroline Dhavernas (1978-)
Devil *87*

Stefano di Matteo
Survival of the Dead *373*

Sheryl Lee Diamond
See Sheryl Lee

Cameron Diaz (1972-)
Knight and Day *220*
Shrek Forever After *(V)* *352*

Leonardo DiCaprio (1974-)
Inception *188*
Shutter Island *354*

Dale Dickey
Winter's Bone *428*

August Diehl (1976-)
Salt *339*

Robert Diggs
See RZA

Garret Dillahunt (1964-)
Winter's Bone *428*

Matt Dillon (1964-)
Takers *379*

Peter Dinklage (1969-)
Death at a Funeral *84*

Mati Diop
35 Shots of Rum *385*

Nina Dobrev
Chloe *53*

Nicole Dogue
35 Shots of Rum *385*

Walt Dohrn
Shrek Forever After *(V)* *352*

John Doman (1945-)
Blue Valentine *28*

Yoav Donat
Lebanon *231*

Jean-Claude Donda
The Illusionist *(V)* *185*

Chad Donella (1978-)
Saw 3D: The Final Chap-
ter *341*

Vincent D'Onofrio (1959-)
Brooklyn's Finest *33*

Brendan Donoghue (1977-)
The Square *368*

Brian Donovan
Alpha and Omega *(V)* *10*

Conor Donovan
Conviction *65*

Luke Doolan
The Square *368*

Stephen Dorff (1973-)
Somewhere *361*

Michael Dorman
Daybreakers *81*

Portia Doubleday
Youth in Revolt *437*

Michael Douglas (1944-)
Solitary Man *359*
Wall Street: Money Never
Sleeps *416*

Brad Dourif (1950-)
My Son, My Son, What Have Ye
Done *276*

Robert Downey, Jr. (1965-)
Due Date *98*
Iron Man 2 *192*

Alan Doyle (1969-)
Robin Hood *334*

Ben Drew (1983-)
Harry Brown *161*

Richard Dreyfuss (1947-)
    Leaves of Grass *230*
    Piranha 3D *308*
    Red *322*

Minnie Driver (1971-)
    Barney's Version *22*
    Conviction *65*

Meredith Droeger
    Extraordinary Measures *112*

Michel Duchaussoy (1938-)
    Mesrine: Killer Instinct *264*
    Mesrine: Public Enemy #1 *265*

David Duchovny (1960-)
    The Joneses *203*

Anne-Marie Duff (1970-)
    Nowhere Boy *291*

Patrick Duffy (1949-)
    You Again *433*

Josh Duhamel (1972-)
    Life As We Know It *239*
    Ramona and Beezus *319*
    When in Rome *422*

Clark Duke
    Hot Tub Time Machine *170*
    Kick-Ass *209*

Lindsay Duncan (1950-)
    Alice in Wonderland *6*

Michael Clarke Duncan (1957-)
    Cats & Dogs: The Revenge of
        Kitty Galore (V) *48*

Kevin Dunn
    Unstoppable *405*

Ryan Dunn (1977-)
    Jackass 3D *198*

Kirsten Dunst (1982-)
    All Good Things *8*

Mark Duplass
    Greenberg *154*

Roy Dupuis (1963-)
    Mesrine: Killer Instinct *264*

Kevin Durand (1974-)
    Legion *234*
    Robin Hood *334*

Richard Durden
    From Paris With Love *131*

André Dussollier (1946-)
    Micmacs *265*
    Wild Grass *427*

Charles S. Dutton (1951-)
    Legion *234*

Daniel Duval (1944-)
    District 13: Ultimatum *93*

Clea DuVall (1977-)
    Conviction *65*

Robert Duvall (1931-)
    Get Low *139*

Nicolas Duvauchelle
    The Girl on the Train *142*
    White Material *424*
    Wild Grass *427*

Dale Dye (1944-)
    Knight and Day *220*

Alexis Dziena (1984-)
    When in Rome *422*

Michael Ealy (1973-)
    For Colored Girls *123*
    Takers *379*

Steve Earle
    Leaves of Grass *230*

Rodney Eastman (1967-)
    I Spit on Your Grave *184*

Aaron Eckhart
    Rabbit Hole *317*

Rodney Ed-Haddad
    Carlos *41*

Lori Beth Edgeman
    Get Low *139*

Joel Edgerton (1974-)
    Animal Kingdom *13*
    Legend of the Guardians: The
        Owls of Ga'Hoole (V) *232*
    The Square *368*

Zac Efron (1987-)
    Charlie St. Cloud *51*

Christopher Egan (1984-)
    Letters to Juliet *237*

Jennifer Ehle (1969-)
    The Greatest *151*
    The King's Speech *216*

David Eigenberg (1964-)
    Sex and the City 2 *349*

Hallie Kate Eisenberg
    Holy Rollers *169*

Jesse Eisenberg (1983-)
    Holy Rollers *169*
    The Social Network *357*
    Solitary Man *359*

Chiwetel Ejiofor (1976-)
    Salt *339*

Idris Elba (1972-)
    The Losers *244*
    Takers *379*

Kimberly Elise (1971-)
    For Colored Girls *123*

Hector Elizondo (1936-)
    Valentine's Day *407*

Ronit Elkabetz (1966-)
    The Girl on the Train *142*

Tate Ellington
    Remember Me *327*

Sam Elliott
    Marmaduke (V) *259*

Nelsan Ellis
    Secretariat *347*

Chase Ellison (1993-)
    Tooth Fairy *388*

Daniel Ellsberg (1931-)
    The Most Dangerous Man in
        America: Daniel Ellsberg and
        the Pentagon Papers (N) *272*

Scott Elrod (1975-)
    The Switch *376*

Cary Elwes (1962-)
    Saw 3D: The Final Chap-
        ter *341*

Noah Emmerich (1965-)
    Fair Game *115*

Lena Endre (1955-)
    The Girl Who Kicked the Hor-
        net's Nest *144*
    The Girl Who Played with
        Fire *145*

Dave Englund
    Jackass 3D *198*

Molly Ephraim
    Paranormal Activity 2 *305*

Mike Epps (1970-)
    Faster *116*
    Lottery Ticket *246*

Shareeka Epps (1989-)
    Mother and Child *275*
    My Soul to Take *277*

Jacob Ericksson (1967-)
    The Girl Who Kicked the Hor-
        net's Nest *144*
    The Girl Who Played with
        Fire *145*

R. Lee Ermey (1944-)
    Toy Story 3 (V) *394*

Homayouin Ershadi
    Agora *2*

Raul Esparza (1970-)
    My Soul to Take *277*

Tiffany Espensen
    Repo Men *329*

Michael Esper
    All Good Things *8*

Giancarlo Esposito (1958-)
    Rabbit Hole *317*

Guillermo Estrella
    Biutiful *25*

Philip Ettinger
    Twelve *401*

Topher Grace (1978-)
    Predators *311*
    Valentine's Day *407*

Lauren Graham (1967-)
    It's Kind of a Funny Story *194*

Rupert Graves
    Made in Dagenham *256*

Macy Gray (1967-)
    For Colored Girls *123*

Sprague Grayden
    Paranormal Activity 2 *305*

Ari Graynor (1983-)
    Conviction *65*
    Holy Rollers *169*
    Youth in Revolt *437*

Bruce Green
    True Grit *399*

Ashley Greene (1987-)
    The Twilight Saga: Eclipse *402*

Peter Greene
    The Bounty Hunter *31*

Bruce Greenwood (1956-)
    Barney's Version *22*
    Dinner for Schmucks *90*
    Mao's Last Dancer *258*

Judy Greer (1971-)
    Love and Other Drugs *247*
    Marmaduke *259*

Clark Gregg (1964-)
    Iron Man 2 *192*

Tamsin Greig
    Tamara Drewe *380*

Zena Grey (1988-)
    My Soul to Take *277*

Pam Grier (1949-)
    Just Wright *205*

Jamara Griffin
    Night Catches Us *287*

Kathy Griffin (1960-)
    Shrek Forever After (V) *352*

Rebecca Griffiths
    Fish Tank *122*

Richard Griffiths (1947-)
    Harry Potter and the Deathly
        Hallows: Part 1 *162*

Frank Grillo
    My Soul to Take *277*

Adam Grimes
    The Last Exorcism *225*

Scott Grimes (1971-)
    Robin Hood *334*

Rupert Grint (1988-)
    Harry Potter and the Deathly
        Hallows: Part 1 *162*

Lance Gross
    Our Family Wedding *301*

Dorka Gryllus
    Soul Kitchen *364*

Carla Gugino (1971-)
    Faster *116*

Ann Guilbert (1928-)
    Please Give *310*

Sienna Guillory (1975-)
    Resident Evil: Afterlife *331*

Tim Guinee (1962-)
    Cyrus *76*
    Iron Man 2 *192*

Aleksey Guskov (1958-)
    The Concert *63*

Jake Gyllenhaal (1980-)
    Love and Other Drugs *247*
    Prince of Persia: The Sands of
        Time *313*

Maggie Gyllenhaal (1977-)
    Nanny McPhee Returns *281*

Lukas Haas (1976-)
    Inception *188*

Fouad Habash
    Ajami *4*

Peter Haber (1952-)
    The Girl with the Dragon Tat-
        too *147*

Penne Hackforth-Jones (1943-)
    Mao's Last Dancer *258*

Emily Hahn
    Toy Story 3 (V) *394*

Kathryn Hahn (1974-)
    How Do You Know *172*

Jackie Earle Haley (1961-)
    A Nightmare on Elm
        Street *288*
    Shutter Island *354*

Daryl Hall
    You Again *433*

Irma P. Hall (1937-)
    My Son, My Son, What Have Ye
        Done *276*

Philip Baker Hall (1931-)
    All Good Things *8*

Rebecca Hall (1982-)
    Please Give *310*
    Red Riding: 1974 *326*
    The Town *391*

Regina Hall (1970-)
    Death at a Funeral *84*

Ron Hall
    Winter's Bone *428*

Sam Hall
    Extraordinary Measures *112*

Annika Hallin (1968-)
    The Girl Who Kicked the Hor-
        net's Nest *144*
    The Girl Who Played with
        Fire *145*

Zeid Hamdan
    Carlos *41*

Lisa Gay Hamilton (1964-)
    Mother and Child *275*

Jon Hamm
    The A-Team *17*
    Howl *176*
    Shrek Forever After (V) *352*
    The Town *391*

Armie Hammer
    The Social Network *357*

Evan Handler (1961-)
    Sex and the City 2 *349*

Tom Hanks (1956-)
    Toy Story 3 (V) *394*

Omari Hardwick (1974-)
    The A-Team *17*
    For Colored Girls *123*

Eanna Hardwicke
    The Eclipse *104*

George Hardy
    Best Worst Movie *23*

Tom Hardy (1977-)
    Inception *188*

Kevin Harrington
    Red Hill *323*

Danielle Harris (1977-)
    Hatchet II *165*

Danneel Harris (1979-)
    The Back-Up Plan *20*

Ed Harris (1949-)
    The Way Back *419*

Estelle Harris (1926-)
    Toy Story 3 (V) *394*

George Harris (1949-)
    Harry Potter and the Deathly
        Hallows: Part 1 *162*

Jared Harris (1961-)
    Extraordinary Measures *112*

Neil Patrick Harris (1973-)
    Cats & Dogs: The Revenge of
        Kitty Galore (V) *48*

Rachael Harris (1968-)
    Diary of a Wimpy Kid *89*

Sean Harris
    Red Riding: 1980 *326*
    Red Riding: 1983 *327*
    Red Riding: 1974 *326*

Steve Harris
    Takers *379*

Tip "T.I." Harris (1980-)
  Takers *379*

Nikki Harrup
  Gulliver's Travels *158*

Kevin Hart
  Death at a Funeral *84*

Eddie Hassell
  The Kids Are All Right *211*

Anne Hathaway (1982-)
  Alice in Wonderland *6*
  Love and Other Drugs *247*
  Valentine's Day *407*

Ethan Hawke (1971-)
  Brooklyn's Finest *33*
  Daybreakers *81*

John Hawkes (1959-)
  Winter's Bone *428*

Sally Hawkins (1976-)
  Made in Dagenham *256*
  Never Let Me Go *282*

Salma Hayek (1966-)
  Grown Ups *156*

Anthony Hayes (1977-)
  Animal Kingdom *13*
  The Square *368*

Sean P. Hayes (1970-)
  Cats & Dogs: The Revenge of
    Kitty Galore (V) *48*

Glenne Headly (1955-)
  The Joneses *203*

Amber Heard (1986-)
  The Joneses *203*

Anne Heche (1969-)
  The Other Guys *300*

Jessica Hecht (1965-)
  My Soul to Take *277*

Jamie Hector
  Night Catches Us *287*

Jon Heder (1977-)
  When in Rome *422*

Garrett Hedlund (1984-)
  Country Strong *70*
  TRON: Legacy *396*

Katherine Heigl (1978-)
  Killers *215*
  Life As We Know It *239*

Jonathan Morgan Heit
  Date Night *79*

Liam Hemsworth (1990-)
  The Last Song *226*

Shirley Henderson (1966-)
  Life During Wartime *240*

Christina Hendricks
  Life As We Know It *239*

Georgie Henley
  The Chronicles of Narnia: The
    Voyage of the Dawn
    Treader *54*

Taraji P. Henson (1970-)
  Date Night *79*
  The Karate Kid *207*

Tim Herlihy (1966-)
  Grown Ups *156*

Pee-wee Herman
  See Paul Reubens

Jay Hernandez (1978-)
  Takers *379*

Barbara Hershey (1948-)
  Black Swan *26*

Louis Herthum
  The Last Exorcism *225*

David Hewlett (1968-)
  Splice *366*

Jonah Hill (1983-)
  Cyrus *76*
  Get Him to the Greek *137*
  How to Train Your Dragon
    (V) *174*
  Megamind (V) *261*

Robert Hill
  Down Terrace *97*

Robin Hill
  Down Terrace *97*

Paris Hilton (1981-)
  The Other Guys *300*

Ciaran Hinds (1953-)
  The Eclipse *104*
  Harry Potter and the Deathly
    Hallows: Part 1 *162*
  Life During Wartime *240*

Ingvar Hirdwall (1934-)
  The Girl with the Dragon Tat-
    too *147*

Iben Hjejle (1971-)
  The Eclipse *104*

Ferdinand Hoang
  Mao's Last Dancer *258*

Kane Hodder (1951-)
  Hatchet II *165*

Douglas Hodge
  Robin Hood *334*

Dustin Hoffman (1937-)
  Barney's Version *22*
  Little Fockers *242*

Gaby Hoffman (1982-)
  Life During Wartime *240*

Philip Seymour Hoffman (1967-)
  Jack Goes Boating *197*

Gina Holden (1975-)
  Saw 3D: The Final Chap-
    ter *341*

Meagan Holder
  You Again *433*

Tom Holland (1943-)
  Hatchet II *165*

Willa Holland
  Legion *234*

Ben Hollingsworth
  The Joneses *203*

Adrian Holmes (1974-)
  Frankie & Alice *127*

Anthony Hopkins (1937-)
  The City of Your Final Destina-
    tion *57*
  The Wolfman *430*
  You Will Meet a Tall Dark
    Stranger *435*

Dennis Hopper (1936-2010)
  Alpha and Omega (V) *10*

Anna Maria Horsford (1948-)
  Our Family Wedding *301*

Bob Hoskins (1942-)
  Made in Dagenham *256*

Emil Hostina
  Ondine *296*

Julianne Hough
  Burlesque *35*

Djimon Hounsou (1964-)
  The Tempest *384*

Liam Hourican
  The Secret of Kells (V) *346*

Andrew Howard
  I Spit on Your Grave *184*

Bryce Dallas Howard (1981-)
  Hereafter *166*
  The Twilight Saga: Eclipse *402*

Lisa Howard (1963-)
  Red Riding: 1983 *327*

Kate Hudson (1979-)
  The Killer Inside Me *213*

Julia Hummer
  Carlos *41*

Bonnie Hunt (1964-)
  Toy Story 3 (V) *394*

Bianca Hunter
  The Fighter *118*

Bill Hunter (1940-)
  The Square *368*

Isabelle Huppert (1955-)
  White Material *424*

John Hurt (1940-)
  Harry Potter and the Deathly
    Hallows: Part 1 *162*

William Hurt (1950-)
Robin Hood *334*

Anjelica Huston (1951-)
When in Rome *422*

Danny Huston (1962-)
Clash of the Titans *59*
Edge of Darkness *105*
Robin Hood *334*

Josh Hutcherson (1992-)
The Kids Are All Right *211*

Lauren Hutton (1943-)
The Joneses *203*

Timothy Hutton (1960-)
The Ghost Writer *140*

Stanislav Ianevski (1985-)
Harry Potter and the Deathly
Hallows: Part 1 *162*

Ice Cube (1969-)
Lottery Ticket *246*

Ice-T (1958-)
The Other Guys (N) *300*

Eric Idle (1943-)
Shrek Forever After (V) *352*

Rhys Ifans (1968-)
Exit Through the Gift Shop
(N) *109*
Greenberg *154*
Harry Potter and the Deathly
Hallows: Part 1 *162*
Nanny McPhee Returns *281*

Oscar Isaac
Agora *2*
Robin Hood *334*

Jason Isaacs (1963-)
Green Zone *153*
Harry Potter and the Deathly
Hallows: Part 1 *162*

Giselle Itié (1982-)
The Expendables *110*

Mark Ivanir (1968-)
Holy Rollers *169*

Vlad Ivanov
The Concert *63*

Brandon T. Jackson (1984-)
Lottery Ticket *246*
Percy Jackson & the Olympians:
The Lightning Thief *306*

Curtis "50 Cent" Jackson (1975-)
Twelve *401*

Janet Jackson (1966-)
For Colored Girls *123*
Why Did I Get Married
Too? *425*

Quinton "Rampage" Jackson (1978-)
The A-Team *17*

Samuel L. Jackson (1948-)
Iron Man 2 *192*
Mother and Child *275*
The Other Guys *300*

Oliver Jackson-Cohen (1986-)
Faster *116*

Derek Jacobi (1938-)
The King's Speech *216*

Finley Jacobsen
Marmaduke *259*

Clayton Jacobson
Animal Kingdom *13*

Óscar Jaenada
The Losers *244*

Geraldine James (1950-)
Made in Dagenham *256*

Kevin James (1965-)
Grown Ups *156*

Lennie James (1965-)
The Next Three Days *285*

Allison Janney (1960-)
Life During Wartime *240*

Joris Jarsky
Survival of the Dead *373*

Katie Jarvis (1991-)
Fish Tank *122*

Marianne Jean-Baptiste
Takers *379*

Carter Jenkins
Valentine's Day *407*

Richard Jenkins (1953-)
Dear John *82*
Eat Pray Love *103*
Let Me In *235*

Ken Jeong (1969-)
Despicable Me (V) *86*
Furry Vengeance *134*
Vampires Suck *410*

Ruby Jerins
Remember Me *327*

Derek Jeter
The Other Guys *300*

Ku Jin
Mother *273*

Ebony Jo-Ann
Grown Ups *156*

Scarlett Johansson (1984-)
Iron Man 2 *192*

Aaron Johnson (1990-)
The Greatest *151*
Kick-Ass *209*
Nowhere Boy *291*

Adam Johnson (1973-)
Frozen *133*

Don Johnson (1950-)
Machete *254*

Dwayne Johnson (1972-)
Faster *116*
The Other Guys *300*
Tooth Fairy *388*
You Again *433*

Angelina Jolie (1975-)
Salt *339*
The Tourist *389*

Caleb Landry Jones
The Last Exorcism *225*

Cherry Jones (1956-)
Mother and Child *275*

Felicity Jones (1984-)
The Tempest *384*

Gemma Jones (1942-)
You Will Meet a Tall Dark
Stranger *435*

Julia Jones (1981-)
Jonah Hex *202*
The Twilight Saga: Eclipse *402*

Rashida Jones (1976-)
Cop Out *67*
The Social Network *357*

Richard T. Jones (1972-)
Why Did I Get Married
Too? *425*

Toby Jones (1967-)
Creation *73*

Tommy Lee Jones (1946-)
The Company Men *62*

Milla Jovovich (1975-)
Resident Evil: Afterlife *331*
Stone *371*

Ashley Judd (1968-)
Tooth Fairy *388*

Woo-sung Jung
The Good, the Bad, the
Weird *150*

Ahmad Kaabour
Carlos *41*

Shahir Kabaha
Ajami *4*

Anna Kalaitzidou
Dogtooth *94*

Preeya Kalidas
Four Lions *125*

Mindy Kaling (1979-)
Despicable Me (V) *86*

Melina Kanakaredes (1967-)
Percy Jackson & the Olympians:
The Lightning Thief *306*

Shannon Kane
Brooklyn's Finest *33*

Ramin Karim
  Ajami *4*

Claudia Karvan (1972-)
  Daybreakers *81*

Reda Kateb
  A Prophet *315*

Staci Keanan (1975-)
  You Again *433*

Diane Keaton (1946-)
  Morning Glory *270*

Michael Keaton (1951-)
  The Other Guys *300*
  Toy Story 3 (V) *394*

Arielle Kebbel (1985-)
  Vampires Suck *410*

Toby Kebbell
  Prince of Persia: The Sands of
    Time *313*
  The Sorcerer's Apprentice *362*

Catherine Keener (1961-)
  Cyrus *76*
  Percy Jackson & the Olympians:
    The Lightning Thief *306*
  Please Give *310*

Stella Keitel
  Holy Rollers *169*

Marthe Keller (1945-)
  Hereafter *166*

David Patrick Kelly (1952-)
  Jonah Hex *202*

Sam Kelly
  Nanny McPhee Returns *281*

Mark Kempner
  Down Terrace *97*

Rona Kenan
  A Film Unfinished (N) *121*

Anna Kendrick (1985-)
  Scott Pilgrim vs. the
    World *343*
  The Twilight Saga: Eclipse *402*

Ken Kennedy
  The Freebie *130*

Skander Keynes
  The Chronicles of Narnia: The
    Voyage of the Dawn
    Treader *54*

Nicole Kidman (1966-)
  Rabbit Hole *317*

Richard Kiel
  Tangled (V) *382*

Udo Kier (1944-)
  My Son, My Son, What Have Ye
    Done *276*

Val Kilmer (1959-)
  MacGruber *253*

Hye-ja Kim
  Mother *273*

Randall Duk Kim (1943-)
  The Last Airbender *223*

Richard Kind (1956-)
  Hereafter *166*
  Toy Story 3 (V) *394*

Joey King (1999-)
  Ramona and Beezus *319*

Larry King (1933-)
  Shrek Forever After (V) *352*

Regina King (1971-)
  Our Family Wedding *301*

Ben Kingsley (1943-)
  Prince of Persia: The Sands of
    Time *313*
  Shutter Island *354*

Greg Kinnear (1963-)
  Green Zone *153*
  The Last Song *226*

James Kirk (1986-)
  Frankie & Alice *127*

Dervla Kirwan
  Ondine *296*

Akhiro Kitamura
  The Human Centipede: First Se-
    quence *177*

Keira Knightley (1985-)
  Never Let Me Go *282*

Johnny Knoxville (1971-)
  Jackass 3D *198*

Erik Knudsen
  Youth in Revolt *437*

Boris Kodjoe (1973-)
  Resident Evil: Afterlife *331*

Elias Koteas (1961-)
  The Killer Inside Me *213*
  Let Me In *235*
  Shutter Island *354*

Zoë Kravitz
  The Greatest *151*
  It's Kind of a Funny Story *194*

Alice Krige
  The Sorcerer's Apprentice *362*

Nick Kroll
  Date Night *79*

Lisa Kudrow (1963-)
  Easy A *101*

Jesse Kuhn
  Enter the Void *107*

Mila Kunis (1983-)
  Black Swan *26*
  The Book of Eli *30*
  Date Night *79*

Olga Kurylenko
  Centurion *50*

Ashton Kutcher (1978-)
  Killers *215*
  Valentine's Day *407*

Ryan Kwanten (1976-)
  Legend of the Guardians: The
    Owls of Ga'Hoole (V) *232*
  Red Hill *323*

Shia LaBeouf (1986-)
  Wall Street: Money Never
    Sleeps *416*

Preston Lacy (1969-)
  Jackass 3D *198*

Marika Lagercrantz (1954-)
  The Girl with the Dragon Tat-
    too *147*

Richard Laing
  Gulliver's Travels *158*

Christine Lakin (1979-)
  You Again *433*

Mick Lally (1945-)
  The Secret of Kells (V) *346*

Christopher Lambert (1959-)
  White Material *424*

Michael Landes (1972-)
  Just Wright *205*

Diane Lane (1965-)
  Secretariat *347*

Antony Langdon (1968-)
  I'm Still Here *187*

Frank Langella (1940-)
  All Good Things *8*
  Wall Street: Money Never
    Sleeps *416*

Wallace Langham (1965-)
  The Social Network *357*

Matt Lanter
  Vampires Suck *410*

Gerard Lanvin (1950-)
  Mesrine: Public Enemy #1 *265*

Anthony LaPaglia (1959-)
  Legend of the Guardians: The
    Owls of Ga'Hoole (V) *232*

Alexandra Maria Lara (1978-)
  The City of Your Final Destina-
    tion *57*

Tito Larriva
  Machete *254*

Brie Larson (1989-)
  Greenberg *154*
  Scott Pilgrim vs. the
    World *343*

Ali Larter (1976-)
  Resident Evil: Afterlife *331*

Evanna Lynch (1991-)
    Harry Potter and the Deathly
        Hallows: Part 1 *162*

Hannah Lynch
    The Eclipse *104*

Jane Lynch (1960-)
    Shrek Forever After *(V)* *352*

Melanie Lynskey (1977-)
    Leaves of Grass *230*

Scott Lyster
    Frankie & Alice *127*

Hayes Macarthur
    Life As We Know It *239*

Norm MacDonald (1963-)
    Grown Ups *156*

Matthew Macfadyen (1974-)
    Robin Hood *334*

Seth MacFarlane (1973-)
    Tooth Fairy *388*

Gabriel Macht (1972-)
    Love and Other Drugs *247*
    Middle Men *266*

Anthony Mackie (1979-)
    Night Catches Us *287*

Kyle MacLachlan (1959-)
    Mao's Last Dancer *258*

Shirley MacLaine (1934-)
    Valentine's Day *407*

Casey MacLaren
    Winter's Bone *428*

William H. Macy (1950-)
    Marmaduke *259*

Bailee Madison (1999-)
    Conviction *65*

Stella Maeve
    The Runaways *336*

John Magaro
    My Soul to Take *277*

Billy Magnussen
    Twelve *401*

Matthew Maher
    The Killer Inside Me *213*

Simona Maicanescu
    Splice *366*

Ally Maki
    Step Up 3D *370*

Rick Malambri (1982-)
    Step Up 3D *370*

Art Malik (1952-)
    Sex and the City 2 *349*
    The Wolfman *430*

John Malkovich (1953-)
    Jonah Hex *202*
    Red *322*
    Secretariat *347*

Ambar Mallman
    The City of Your Final Destina-
        tion *57*

Matt Malloy
    Morning Glory *270*

Oliver Maltman
    Another Year *15*

Zosia Mamet
    The Kids Are All Right *211*

Aasif Mandvi (-1966)
    It's Kind of a Funny Story *194*
    The Last Airbender *223*

Costas Mandylor (1962-)
    Saw 3D: The Final Chap-
        ter *341*

Leslie Mann (1972-)
    I Love You Phillip Morris *182*

Thomas Mann
    It's Kind of a Funny Story *194*

Taryn Manning (1978-)
    Love Ranch *249*

Lesley Manville (1956-)
    Another Year *15*

Patrick Mapel
    The Social Network *357*

Kate Mara (1983-)
    Iron Man 2 *192*
    127 Hours *298*

Rooney Mara
    A Nightmare on Elm
        Street *288*
    The Social Network *357*

Alicia Marek
    Machete *254*

Bam Margera (1979-)
    Jackass 3D *198*

Miriam Margolyes (1941-)
    Legend of the Guardians: The
        Owls of Ga'Hoole *(V)* *232*

Julianna Margulies (1966-)
    City Island *56*

Teairra Mari
    Lottery Ticket *246*

Nicolas Marie
    Micmacs *265*

Jean-Pierre Marielle (1932-)
    Micmacs *265*

Cheech Marin (1946-)
    Machete *254*
    Toy Story 3 *(V)* *394*

Mario Marin-Borquez (1999-)
    The Wolfman *430*

Brian Markinson
    Frankie & Alice *127*

Hannah Marks (1993-)
    The Runaways *336*

Chris Marquette (1984-)
    Life During Wartime *240*

Eddie Marsan (1968-)
    The Disappearance of Alice
        Creed *92*
    Red Riding: 1980 *326*
    Red Riding: 1974 *326*

James Marsden (1973-)
    Cats & Dogs: The Revenge of
        Kitty Galore *(V)* *48*
    Death at a Funeral *84*

Lyndsey Marshal
    Hereafter *166*

Logan Marshall-Green
    Devil *87*

Margo Martindale (1951-)
    Secretariat *347*

Elizabeth Marvel
    Holy Rollers *169*
    True Grit *399*

Samantha Mathis (1970-)
    Buried *34*

Dakin Matthews (1933-)
    True Grit *399*

Sinead Matthews
    Nanny McPhee Returns *281*

Helena Mattsson
    Iron Man 2 *192*

Joseph Mawle
    Red Riding: 1980 *326*

Daniel Mays (1978-)
    Made in Dagenham *256*
    Nanny McPhee Returns *281*
    Red Riding: 1983 *327*

Jason Maza (1987-)
    Fish Tank *122*

Joseph Mazzello (1983-)
    The Social Network *357*

Rachel McAdams (1976-)
    Morning Glory *270*

Jack McBrayer
    Cats & Dogs: The Revenge of
        Kitty Galore *48*
    Despicable Me *(V)* *86*

Danny McBride
    Despicable Me *(V)* *86*
    Due Date *98*

Holt McCallany (1964-)
    The Losers *244*

Tom McCamus (1955-)
    Cairo Time *39*

Melissa McCarthy
    The Back-Up Plan *20*
    Life As We Know It *239*

Thomas McCarthy (1969-)
Jack Goes Boating *197*

Gary McCormack
Valhalla Rising *408*

Sierra McCormick
Ramona and Beezus *319*

Gavin McCulley
Dear John *82*

Erica McDermott (1973-)
The Fighter *118*

Malcolm McDowell (1943-)
The Book of Eli *30*
Easy A *101*

Jack McGee (1948-)
The Fighter *118*

Ehren McGhehey
Jackass 3D *198*

Brandon McGibbon
Splice *366*

Bruce McGill (1950-)
Fair Game *115*

Elizabeth McGovern (1961-)
Kick-Ass *209*

Rose McGowan (1975-)
Machete *254*

Tim McGraw (1967-)
Country Strong *70*

Ewan McGregor (1971-)
The Ghost Writer *140*
I Love You Phillip Morris *182*
Nanny McPhee Returns *281*

Evan McGuire
The Secret of Kells (V) *346*

Kevin McKidd (1973-)
Percy Jackson & the Olympians:
The Lightning Thief *306*

Frankie McLaren
Hereafter *166*

George McLaren
Hereafter *166*

Ron McLarty (1947-)
How Do You Know *172*

Dennis Mclaughlin
The Town *391*

Julian McMahon (1968-)
Red *322*

Scoot McNairy
Monsters *268*

Steven R. McQueen
Piranha 3D *308*

Gerald McRaney (1948-)
The A-Team *17*
Get Low *139*

Ian McShane (1942-)
Case 39 *43*

Emily Meade
My Soul to Take *277*
Twelve *401*

Tim Meadows (1961-)
Grown Ups *156*

Colm Meaney
Get Him to the Greek *137*

Leighton Meester (1986-)
Country Strong *70*
Date Night *79*
Going the Distance *148*

Isobel Meikle-Small
Never Let Me Go *282*

Jonathan Mellor
[Rec] 2 *320*

Carlos Mencia (1967-)
Our Family Wedding *301*

Ben Mendelsohn (1969-)
Animal Kingdom *13*

Eva Mendes (1974-)
The Other Guys *300*

Alex Meraz (1985-)
The Twilight Saga: Eclipse *402*

Stephen Merchant (1974-)
Tooth Fairy *388*

S. Epatha Merkerson (1952-)
Mother and Child *275*

Simon Merrells
The Wolfman *430*

Chris Messina (1974-)
Devil *87*
Greenberg *154*

Laurie Metcalf (1955-)
Toy Story 3 (V) *394*

Omar Metwally (1975-)
The City of Your Final Destination *57*

Dina Meyer (1969-)
Piranha 3D *308*

Giovanna Mezzogiorno (1974-)
Vincere *411*

Alyson Michalka (1989-)
Easy A *101*

Amanda Michalka (1991-)
Secretariat *347*

Kate Micucci
When in Rome *422*

Bette Midler (1945-)
Cats & Dogs: The Revenge of
Kitty Galore (V) *48*

R.A. Mihailoff
Hatchet II *165*

Mads Mikkelsen (1965-)
Clash of the Titans *59*
Valhalla Rising *408*

Izabella Miko (1981-)
Clash of the Titans *59*

Beatrice Miller
Toy Story 3 (V) *394*

Ezra Miller
City Island *56*

Jeanette Miller
Legion *234*

Larry Miller (1953-)
Alpha and Omega (V) *10*

T.J. Miller
Gulliver's Travels *158*
How to Train Your Dragon
(V) *174*
She's Out of My League *350*

Wentworth Miller (1972-)
Resident Evil: Afterlife *331*

Max Minghella (1985-)
Agora *2*
The Social Network *357*

Liza Minnelli (1946-)
Sex and the City 2 *349*

Dylan Minnette
Let Me In *235*

Christopher Mintz-Plasse (1989-)
How to Train Your Dragon
(V) *174*
Kick-Ass *209*
Marmaduke (V) *259*

Miou-Miou (1950-)
The Concert *63*

Helen Mirren (1946-)
Legend of the Guardians: The
Owls of Ga'Hoole (V) *232*
Love Ranch *249*
Red *322*
The Tempest *384*

Radha Mitchell (1973-)
The Crazies *72*

Wotan Wilke Möhring
Soul Kitchen *364*

Jay Mohr (1970-)
Hereafter *166*

Alfred Molina (1953-)
Prince of Persia: The Sands of
Time *313*
The Sorcerer's Apprentice *362*
The Tempest *384*

Jordi Molla (1968-)
Knight and Day *220*

Michelle Monaghan (1976-)
Due Date *98*
Somewhere *361*

Janet Montgomery
Black Swan *26*

Christen Mooney
  The Secret of Kells *(V)* *346*

Tony Mooney
  Red Riding: 1980 *326*
  Red Riding: 1983 *327*
  Red Riding: 1974 *326*

Demi Moore (1962-)
  The Joneses *203*

Julianne Moore (1961-)
  Chloe *53*
  The Kids Are All Right *211*

Mandy Moore (1984-)
  Tangled *(V)* *382*

Roger Moore (1927-)
  Cats & Dogs: The Revenge of
    Kitty Galore *(V)* *48*

Yolande Moreau (1953-)
  Micmacs *265*

Catalina Sandino Moreno (1981-)
  The Twilight Saga: Eclipse *402*

Chloe Grace Moretz (1997-)
  Diary of a Wimpy Kid *89*
  Kick-Ass *209*
  Let Me In *235*

Alexander Morgan
  Valhalla Rising *408*

Jeffrey Dean Morgan (1966-)
  Jonah Hex *202*
  The Losers *244*

Tracy Morgan (1968-)
  Cop Out *67*
  Death at a Funeral *84*

Vanessa Morgan
  Frankie & Alice *127*

Cathy Moriarty (1961-)
  The Bounty Hunter *31*

Aksel Morisse
  The Girl Who Kicked the Hor-
    net's Nest *144*

John Morris
  Toy Story 3 *(V)* *394*

David Morrissey (1963-)
  Centurion *50*
  Nowhere Boy *291*
  Red Riding: 1980 *326*
  Red Riding: 1983 *327*
  Red Riding: 1974 *326*

David Morse (1953-)
  Mother and Child *275*

Emily Mortimer (1971-)
  City Island *56*
  Harry Brown *161*
  Shutter Island *354*

Amy Morton
  The Greatest *151*

Pierre-Marie Mosconi
  District 13: Ultimatum *93*

William Moseley
  The Chronicles of Narnia: The
    Voyage of the Dawn
    Treader *54*

Michael Moshonov
  Lebanon *231*

Cullen Moss
  Dear John *82*

Elisabeth (Elissabeth, Elizabeth, Liz)
  Moss (1982-)
  Get Him to the Greek *137*

Bridget Moynahan (1972-)
  Ramona and Beezus *319*

Bobby Moynihan
  When in Rome *422*

Martin Mull (1943-)
  Killers *215*

Peter Mullan (1954-)
  Red Riding: 1980 *326*
  Red Riding: 1983 *327*
  Red Riding: 1974 *326*

Carey Mulligan (1985-)
  The Greatest *151*
  Never Let Me Go *282*
  Wall Street: Money Never
    Sleeps *416*

Kathleen Munroe
  Survival of the Dead *373*

Brittany Murphy (1977-2009)
  The Expendables *110*

Charlie (Charles Q.) Murphy (1959-)
  Lottery Ticket *246*

Cillian Murphy (1976-)
  Inception *188*

Donna Murphy (1958-)
  Tangled *(V)* *382*

Eddie Murphy (1961-)
  Shrek Forever After *(V)* *352*

Bill Murray (1950-)
  Get Low *139*

Mike Myers (1963-)
  Shrek Forever After *(V)* *352*

Khaled Nabawy (1966-)
  Fair Game *115*

Eran Naim
  Ajami *4*

Sydney Mary Nash
  Fish Tank *122*

Naturi Naughton
  Lottery Ticket *246*

Dmitri Nazarov (1957-)
  The Concert *63*

Marie N'Diaye
  White Material *424*

Liam Neeson (1952-)
  After.life *1*
  The A-Team *17*
  Chloe *53*
  The Chronicles of Narnia: The
    Voyage of the Dawn Treader
    (V) *54*
  Clash of the Titans *59*
  The Next Three Days *285*

Sam Neill (1948-)
  Daybreakers *81*
  Legend of the Guardians: The
    Owls of Ga'Hoole *(V)* *232*

Craig T. Nelson (1946-)
  The Company Men *62*

Sean Nelson (1980-)
  The Freebie *130*

Tim Blake Nelson (1965-)
  Leaves of Grass *230*

Franco Nero (1942-)
  Letters to Juliet *237*

Thierry Neuvic
  Hereafter *166*

Teddy Newton
  Toy Story 3 *(V)* *394*

Thandie Newton (1972-)
  For Colored Girls *123*

Thomas Ian Nicholas (1980-)
  Please Give *310*

Jack Nicholson (1937-)
  How Do You Know *172*

Bill Nighy (1949-)
  Harry Potter and the Deathly
    Hallows: Part 1 *162*

Alessandro Nivola (1972-)
  Howl *176*

Cynthia Nixon (1966-)
  Sex and the City 2 *349*

Nick Nolte (1941-)
  Cats & Dogs: The Revenge of
    Kitty Galore *(V)* *48*

Dean Norris
  How Do You Know *172*

Jeremy Northam (1961-)
  Creation *73*

Edward Norton (1969-)
  Leaves of Grass *230*
  Stone *371*

Jim Norton (1938-)
  The Eclipse *104*

Christopher Noth (1956-)
  Sex and the City 2 *349*

Kayvan Novak
  Four Lions *125*

Simon Schwarz
    North Face *290*

Arnold Schwarzenegger (1947-)
    The Expendables *110*

Eric Schweig (1967-)
    Casino Jack *44 *

Catarina Scorsone
    Edge of Darkness *105*

Adam Scott (1973-)
    Leap Year *228*
    Piranha 3D *308*

Jill Scott
    Why Did I Get Married
        Too? *425*

Seann William Scott (1976-)
    Cop Out *67*

Kristin Scott Thomas (1960-)
    Nowhere Boy *291*

Ryan Seacrest
    Shrek Forever After (V) *352*

Steven Seagal (1952-)
    Machete *254*

Nick Searcy (1959-)
    The Expendables *110*
    The Last Song *226*

Amy Sedaris (1961-)
    Shrek Forever After (V) *352*

George Segal (1934-)
    Love and Other Drugs *247*

Jason Segel (1980-)
    Despicable Me (V) *86*
    Gulliver's Travels *158*

David Selby (1941-)
    The Social Network *357*

Tom Selleck (1945-)
    Killers *215*

Rade Serbedzija (1946-)
    Middle Men *266*

Nestor Serrano (1957-)
    Secretariat *347*

Christian Serratos (1990-)
    The Twilight Saga: Eclipse *402*

Matt Servitto
    Going the Distance *148*

John Sessions (1953-)
    Made in Dagenham *256*

Adam G. Sevani
    Step Up 3D *370*

Chloe Sevigny (1975-)
    My Son, My Son, What Have Ye
        Done *276*

Rufus Sewell (1967-)
    The Tourist *389*

Léa Seydoux
    Robin Hood *334*

Amanda Seyfried (1985-)
    Chloe *53*
    Dear John *82*
    Letters to Juliet *237*

Will Shadley
    The Spy Next Door *367*

Garry Shandling (1949-)
    Iron Man 2 *192*

Michael Shannon (1974-)
    The Greatest *151*
    Jonah Hex *202*
    My Son, My Son, What Have Ye
        Done *276*
    The Runaways *336*

Kunal Sharma
    The Kids Are All Right *211*

Alia Shawkat (1989-)
    The Runaways *336*

Wallace Shawn (1943-)
    Toy Story 3 (V) *394*

Ryan Sheckler (1989-)
    Tooth Fairy *388*

Ally Sheedy (1962-)
    Life During Wartime *240*

Robert Sheehan
    Red Riding: 1980 *326*
    Red Riding: 1983 *327*
    Red Riding: 1974 *326*

Michael Sheen (1969-)
    Alice in Wonderland *6*
    TRON: Legacy *396*

Ruth Sheen (1952-)
    Another Year *15*

Parry Shen (1979-)
    Hatchet II *165*

Ben Shenkman (1968-)
    Blue Valentine *28*

Dax Shepard (1975-)
    The Freebie *130*
    When in Rome *422*

Sam Shepard (1943-)
    Fair Game *115*

Rade Sherbedgia
    See Rade Serbedzija

Brooke Shields (1965-)
    Furry Vengeance *134*
    The Other Guys *300*

Columbus Short (1982-)
    Death at a Funeral *84*
    The Losers *244*

Elisabeth Shue (1963-)
    Don McKay *96*
    Piranha 3D *308*

Harry Shum, Jr. (1982-)
    Step Up 3D *370*

Alexander Siddig (1965-)
    Cairo Time *39*

Jamie Sieves
    Valhalla Rising *408*

Johnny Simmons
    The Greatest *151*

Ty Simpkins
    The Next Three Days *285*

Jimmi Simpson
    Date Night *79*

Gustaf Skarsgard
    The Way Back *419*

Stellan Skarsgard (1951-)
    Frankie & Alice *127*

Slaine
    The Town *391*

John Slattery (1963-)
    Iron Man 2 *192*

Joe Slaughter
    Step Up 3D *370*

Lindsay Sloane (1977-)
    The Other Guys *300*
    She's Out of My League *350*

Micah Sloat
    Paranormal Activity 2 *305*

Jean Smart (1959-)
    Youth in Revolt *437*

Michael Smiley
    Down Terrace *97*

Kodi Smit-McPhee (1996-)
    Let Me In *235*

Brooke Smith (1967-)
    Fair Game *115*

Jaden Smith
    The Karate Kid *207*

Lois Smith (1930-)
    Please Give *310*

Maggie Smith (1934-)
    Harry Potter and the Deathly
        Hallows: Part 1 *162*
    Nanny McPhee Returns *281*

Tasha Smith (1971-)
    Why Did I Get Married
        Too? *425*

Jimmy Smits (1956-)
    Mother and Child *275*

Kasia Smutniak
    From Paris With Love *131*

Wesley Snipes (1962-)
    Brooklyn's Finest *33*

Dylan Riley Snyder
    Life During Wartime *240*

Brenda Song (1988-)
    The Social Network *357*

Masto Tanno
Enter the Void *107*

Catherine Tate (1968-)
Gulliver's Travels *158*

Channing Tatum (1980-)
Dear John *82*

Sven-Bertil Taube (1934-)
The Girl with the Dragon Tattoo *147*

Josie Taylor
Tamara Drewe *380*

Lili Taylor (1967-)
Brooklyn's Finest *33*

Renee Taylor (1933-)
Life During Wartime *240*

Tate Taylor
Winter's Bone *428*

Scout Taylor-Compton (1989-)
Love Ranch *249*
The Runaways *336*

Rosie Taylor-Ritson
Nanny McPhee Returns *281*

Daniel Tchangang
White Material *424*

Miles Teller
Rabbit Hole *317*

Juno Temple
Greenberg *154*

Natalia Tena
Harry Potter and the Deathly
Hallows: Part 1 *162*

Emily Tennant
Frankie & Alice *127*

Jon Tenney (1961-)
Legion *234*
Rabbit Hole *317*

David Thewlis (1963-)
Harry Potter and the Deathly
Hallows: Part 1 *162*

Max Thieriot (1988-)
Chloe *53*
My Soul to Take *277*

Olivia Thirlby
Solitary Man *359*

Henry Thomas (1971-)
Dear John *82*

Florence Thomassin (1966-)
Mesrine: Killer Instinct *264*

Ashlee Thompson
Winter's Bone *428*

Emma Thompson (1959-)
Nanny McPhee Returns *281*

Fred Dalton Thompson (1942-)
Secretariat *347*

Jack Thompson (1940-)
Mao's Last Dancer *258*

Scottie Thompson
Skyline *355*

Tessa Thompson (1983-)
For Colored Girls *123*

Ulrich Thomsen (1963-)
Centurion *50*

R.H. Thomson (1947-)
Chloe *53*

Billy Bob Thornton (1955-)
Faster *116*

Otto Thorwarth
Secretariat *347*

David Threlfall (1953-)
Nowhere Boy *291*

Uma Thurman (1970-)
Percy Jackson & the Olympians:
The Lightning Thief *306*

Justin Timberlake (1981-)
Shrek Forever After (V) *352*
The Social Network *357*
Yogi Bear (V) *432*

Filippo Timi
Vincere *411*

Itay Tiran
Lebanon *231*

Stephen Tobolowsky (1951-)
Buried *34*

Tony Todd (1954-)
Hatchet II *165*

Marisa Tomei (1964-)
Cyrus *76*

Paul F. Tompkins
Tangled (V) *382*

Nate Torrence (1977-)
She's Out of My League *350*

Philippe Torreton (1965-)
District 13: Ultimatum *93*

Shaun Toub
The Last Airbender *223*

Julieth Mars Toussaint
35 Shots of Rum *385*

Steve Toussaint
Prince of Persia: The Sands of
Time *313*

Michelle Trachtenberg (1985-)
Cop Out *67*

Stacey Travis
Easy A *101*

John Travolta (1954-)
From Paris With Love *131*

Harry Treadway
Fish Tank *122*

Danny Trejo (1944-)
The Expendables *110*
Machete *254*
Predators *311*

Gilbert Trejo
Machete *254*

Tariq Trotter
Night Catches Us *287*

Verne Troyer (1969-)
My Son, My Son, What Have Ye
Done *276*

Mary Tsoni
Dogtooth *94*

Stanley Tucci (1960-)
Burlesque *35*
Easy A *101*

Jonathan Tucker (1982-)
The Next Three Days *285*

Ulrich Tukur (1957-)
North Face *290*

Aaron Tveit
Howl *176*

Tyrese
See Tyrese Gibson

Cicely Tyson (1933-)
Why Did I Get Married
Too? *425*

Birol Unel
Soul Kitchen *364*

Billy Unger
You Again *433*

Lee Unkrich
Toy Story 3 (V) *394*

Karl Urban (1972-)
Red *322*

Sebastian Urzendowsky
The Way Back *419*

Amber Valletta (1974-)
The Spy Next Door *367*

Michele Valley
Dogtooth *94*

Claire van der Boom
Red Hill *323*
The Square *368*

Anneliese van der Pol
Vampires Suck *410*

Carice van Houten (1976-)
Repo Men *329*

Joyce Van Patten (1934-)
Grown Ups *156*

Melvin Van Peebles (1932-)
Freakonomics (N) *128*

Courtney B. Vance (1960-)
Extraordinary Measures *112*

Olivia Wilde (1984-)
  The Next Three Days *285*
  TRON: Legacy *396*

Tom Wilkinson (1948-)
  The Ghost Writer *140*

Fred Willard (1939-)
  Youth in Revolt *437*

Ashley Williams
  The Human Centipede: First Se-
    quence *177*

Chris Williams
  The Joneses *203*

Katt Micah Williams (1973-)
  Cats & Dogs: The Revenge of
    Kitty Galore (V) *48*

Michael K. Williams
  Brooklyn's Finest *33*
  Life During Wartime *240*

Michelle Williams (1980-)
  Blue Valentine *28*
  Shutter Island *354*

Olivia Williams (1968-)
  The Ghost Writer *140*

Treat Williams (1952-)
  Howl *176*
  127 Hours *298*

Bruce Willis (1955-)
  Cop Out *67*
  The Expendables *110*
  Red *322*

Chandra Wilson
  Frankie & Alice *127*

George Wilson (1921-)
  Mesrine: Public Enemy #1 *265*

Luke Wilson (1971-)
  Death at a Funeral *84*
  Middle Men *266*

Owen Wilson (1968-)
  How Do You Know *172*
  Little Fockers *242*
  Marmaduke (V) *259*

Patrick Wilson (1973-)
  The A-Team *17*
  Morning Glory *270*
  The Switch *376*

Katheryn Winnick (1977-)
  Love and Other Drugs *247*

Katheryn Winnick (1978-)
  Killers *215*

Mary Elizabeth Winstead (1984-)
  Scott Pilgrim vs. the
    World *343*

Ray Winstone (1957-)
  Edge of Darkness *105*

Kristoffer Ryan Winters (1978-)
  Fair Game *115*

Reese Witherspoon (1976-)
  How Do You Know *172*

Jeff Witzke (1970-)
  Vampires Suck *410*

Faith Wladyka (2004-)
  Blue Valentine *28*

Johanna Wokalek
  North Face *290*

Collette Wolfe
  Hot Tub Time Machine *170*

James Wolk
  You Again *433*

Bin Won (1977-)
  Mother *273*

Ellen Wong
  Scott Pilgrim vs. the
    World *343*

Bokeem Woodbine (1973-)
  Devil *87*

Lil Woods
  Nanny McPhee Returns *281*

Eric Woolfe
  Survival of the Dead *373*

Susan Woolridge
  Tamara Drewe *380*

Sam Worthington (1976-)
  Clash of the Titans *59*

Bonnie Wright (1991-)
  Harry Potter and the Deathly
    Hallows: Part 1 *162*

Janet Wright (1945-)
  Ramona and Beezus *319*

Sophie Wu
  Kick-Ass *209*

Daniel Wyllie
  Animal Kingdom *13*

Hichem Yacoubi
  A Prophet *315*

Ashlynn Yennie
  The Human Centipede: First Se-
    quence *177*

Malik Yoba (1967-)
  Why Did I Get Married
    Too? *425*

Chris York
  Frozen *133*

Aden Young (1972-)
  Mao's Last Dancer *258*

Bellamy Young
  The Freebie *130*

Damian Young
  Edge of Darkness *105*

Karen Young (1958-)
  Conviction *65*

Elodie Yung (1981-)
  District 13: Ultimatum *93*

Odette Yustman
  You Again *433*

Grace Zabriskie (1938-)
  My Son, My Son, What Have Ye
    Done *276*

Jonathan Zaccai
  Robin Hood *334*

Mattia Zaccaro
  I Am Love *181*

Oscar Sanchez Zafra (1969-)
  [Rec] 2 *320*

Steve Zahn (1968-)
  Diary of a Wimpy Kid *89*

Wasim Zakir
  Four Lions *125*

David Zayas
  The Expendables *110*
  Skyline *355*

Natalie Zea
  The Other Guys *300*

Kevin Zegers (1984-)
  Frozen *133*

Renee Zellweger (1969-)
  Case 39 *43*

Yu Qi Zhang
  Mao's Last Dancer *258*

Subject Index

Action-Adventure
The American *12*
The A-Team *17*
Carlos *41*
Centurion *50*
Clash of the Titans *59*
District 13: Ultimatum *93*
The Expendables *110*
Faster *116*
From Paris With Love *131*
The Ghost Writer *140*
Gulliver's Travels *158*
Iron Man 2 *192*
The Losers *244*
Machete *254*
North Face *290*
127 Hours *298*
Prince of Persia: The Sands of
    Time *313*
Robin Hood *334*
Salt *339*
Takers *379*
The Tourist *389*
Unstoppable *405*
Valhalla Rising *408*
The Way Back *419*

Action-Comedy
Kick-Ass *209*
Killers *215*
Knight and Day *220*
MacGruber *253*
The Other Guys *300*
Red *322*
Scott Pilgrim vs. the
    World *343*
The Spy Next Door *367*

Adapted from a Book
Barney's Version *22*
Gulliver's Travels *158*
Hereafter *166*
The Killer Inside Me *213*
Shrek Forever After *352*
Tamara Drewe *380*

Adapted from a Cartoon
The Last Airbender *223*

Adapted from a Fairy Tale
Tangled *382*

Adapted from a Game
Prince of Persia: The Sands of
    Time *313*
Resident Evil: Afterlife *331*

Adapted from a Play
The Girl on the Train *142*
Jack Goes Boating *197*
Rabbit Hole *317*
The Tempest *384*

Adapted from a Poem
Howl *176*

Adapted from a Story
The Eclipse *104*
The Switch *376*

Adapted from Comics
Kick-Ass *209*
Marmaduke *259*
Scott Pilgrim vs. the
    World *343*
Tamara Drewe *380*

Adapted from Memoirs or Diaries
Eat Pray Love *103*
Mesrine: Killer Instinct *264*
Mesrine: Public Enemy #1 *265*

Adapted from Television
The A-Team *17*
The Last Airbender *223*
Yogi Bear *432*

Adolescence
Fish Tank *122*
Nowhere Boy *291*

Adoption
Despicable Me *86*
Mother and Child *275*

Advertising
The Joneses *203*

Africa
Babies *19*
White Material *424*

Aging
Harry Brown *161*
Please Give *310*
Red *322*
Wild Grass *427*

Alien Beings
Monsters *268*
Predators *311*
Skyline *355*

American Heartland
Leaves of Grass *230*

American Remakes of European Films
Let Me In *235*

American Remakes of French Films
Chloe *53*
The Next Three Days *285*

American South
Get Low *139*
The Last Song *226*
Secretariat *347*

Angels
Legion *234*

Animals
Alpha and Omega *10*
Furry Vengeance *134*
Sweetgrass *374*

Animation & Cartoons
Alpha and Omega *10*
How to Train Your
   Dragon *174*
The Illusionist *185*
Legend of the Guardians: The
   Owls of Ga'Hoole *232*
Megamind *261*
The Secret of Kells *346*
Shrek Forever After *352*
Tangled *382*
Toy Story 3 *394*
Yogi Bear *432*

Arctic or Antarctic Regions
Frozen *133*
North Face *290*

Art or Artists
Exit Through the Gift
   Shop *109*

Asia
Babies *19*
Eat Pray Love *103*
Mother *273*

Australia
Animal Kingdom *13*
Red Hill *323*

Babysitting
The Spy Next Door *367*

Baseball
How Do You Know *172*

Basketball
Grown Ups *156*
Just Wright *205*

Behind the Scenes
Burlesque *35*
Country Strong *70*
Morning Glory *270*

Biography
Carlos *41*
Mao's Last Dancer *258*

Biography: Music
The Runaways *336*

Biography: Show Business
I'm Still Here *187*
Nowhere Boy *291*

Birds
Legend of the Guardians: The
   Owls of Ga'Hoole *232*
My Son, My Son, What Have Ye
   Done *276*

Black Culture
For Colored Girls *123*
Frankie & Alice *127*
Just Wright *205*
Lottery Ticket *246*
Night Catches Us *287*
Our Family Wedding *301*
Why Did I Get Married
   Too? *425*

Blackmail
Death at a Funeral *84*
The Girl Who Played with
   Fire *145*
The Square *368*

Boats or Ships
The Chronicles of Narnia: The
   Voyage of the Dawn
   Treader *54*
Valhalla Rising *408*

Books or Bookstores
The Book of Eli *30*

Boston
The Company Men *62*
Edge of Darkness *105*
The Town *391*

Bounty Hunters
The Bounty Hunter *31*
The Good, the Bad, the
   Weird *150*
Jonah Hex *202*

Boxing
The Fighter *118*
Love Ranch *249*

Broadcast Journalism
Morning Glory *270*

Business or Industry
Daybreakers *81*
Edge of Darkness *105*
How Do You Know *172*
Iron Man 2 *192*
Micmacs *265*
Solitary Man *359*

Canada
Alpha and Omega *10*
Mesrine: Killer Instinct *264*

Cancer
Love Ranch *249*

Cats
Cats & Dogs: The Revenge of
   Kitty Galore *48*
Marmaduke *259*

Child Abuse
A Nightmare on Elm
   Street *288*

Child Care
Toy Story 3 *394*

Childhood
The Karate Kid *207*
Kisses *218*
The Last Airbender *223*
The Secret of Kells *346*
Tooth Fairy *388*

Children
Waiting for 'Superman' *415*

China
The Good, the Bad, the
   Weird *150*
The Karate Kid *207*
Mao's Last Dancer *258*

Classical Music
The Concert *63*

Clergymen
Creation *73*
Get Low *139*
Red Riding: 1974 *326*

Title Index

This cumulative index is an alphabetical list of all films covered in the volumes of the *Magill's Cinema Annual*. Film titles are indexed on a word-by-word basis, including articles and prepositions. English leading articles (A, An, The) are ignored, as are foreign leading articles (El, Il, La, Las, Le, Les, Los). Acronyms appear alphabetically as if regular words. Common abbreviations in titles file as if they are spelled out. Proper names in titles are alphabetized beginning with the individual's first name. Titles with numbers are alphabetized as if the numbers were spelled out. When numeric titles gather in close proximity to each other, the titles will be arranged in a low-to-high numeric sequence. Films reviewed in this volume are cited in bold with an Arabic number indicating the page number on which the review begins; films reviewed in past volumes are cited with the *Annual* year in which the review was published. Original and alternate titles are cross-referenced to the American release title. Titles of retrospective films are followed by the year, in brackets, of their original release.

A

A corps perdu. *See* Straight for the Heart.

A. I.: Artificial Intelligence 2002

A la Mode (Fausto) 1995

A Lot Like Love 2006

A Ma Soeur. *See* Fat Girl.

A nos amours 1984

Abandon 2003

ABCD 2002

Abgeschminkt! *See* Making Up!.

About a Boy 2003

About Adam 2002

About Last Night... 1986

About Schmidt 2003

Above the Law 1988

Above the Rim 1995

Abrazos rotos, Los. *See* Broken Embraces.

Abre Los Ojos. *See* Open Your Eyes.

Abril Despedacado. *See* Behind the Sun.

Absence of Malice 1981

Absolute Beginners 1986

Absolute Power 1997

Absolution 1988

Abyss, The 1989

Accepted 2007

Accidental Tourist, The 1988

Accompanist, The 1993

Accordeur de tremblements de terre, L'. *See* Piano Tuner of Earthquakes, The.

Accused, The 1988

Ace in the Hole [1951] 1986, 1991

Ace Ventura: Pet Detective 1995

Ace Ventura: When Nature Calls 1996

Aces: Iron Eagle III 1992

Acid House, The 2000

Acqua e sapone. *See* Water and Soap.

Across the Tracks 1991

Across the Universe 2008

Acting on Impulse 1995

Action Jackson 1988

Actress 1988

Adam 2010

Adam Sandler's 8 Crazy Nights 2003

Adam's Rib [1950] 1992

Adaptation 2003

Addams Family, The 1991

Addams Family Values 1993

Addicted to Love 1997

Addiction, The 1995

Addition, L'. *See* Patsy, The.

Adjo, Solidaritet. *See* Farewell Illusion.

Adjuster, The 1992

Adolescente, L' 1982

Adoration 2010

Adventureland 2010

Adventures in Babysitting 1987

Adventures of Baron Munchausen, The 1989

Almost Heroes 1999

Almost You 1985

Aloha Summer 1988

Alone. *See* Solas.

Alone in the Dark 2006

Alone with Her 2008

Along Came a Spider 2002

Along Came Polly 2005

Alpha and Omega pg. 10

Alpha Dog 2008

Alphabet City 1983

Alpine Fire 1987

Altars of the World [1976] 1985

Alvin and the Chipmunks 2008

Alvin and the Chipmunks: The Squeakquel 2010

Always (Jaglom) 1985

Always (Spielberg) 1989

Amadeus 1984, 1985

Amanda 1989

Amantes. *See* Lovers.

Amantes del Circulo Polar, Los. *See* Lovers of the Arctic Circle, The.

Amants du Pont Neuf, Les 1995

Amateur 1995

Amateur, The 1982

Amazing Grace 2008

Amazing Grace and Chuck 1987

Amazing Panda Adventure, The 1995

Amazon Women on the Moon 1987

Ambition 1991

Amelia 2010

Amelie 2002

Amen 2004

America 1986

American, The pg. 12

American Anthem 1986

American Beauty 2000

American Blue Note 1991

American Buffalo 1996

American Carol, An 2009

American Chai 2003

American Cyborg: Steel Warrior 1995

American Desi 2002

American Dream 1992

American Dreamer 1984

American Dreamz 2007

American Fabulous 1992

American Flyers 1985

American Friends 1993

American Gangster 2008

American Gothic 1988

American Haunting, An 2007

American Heart 1993

American History X 1999

American in Paris, An [1951] 1985

American Justice 1986

American Me 1992

American Movie 2000

American Ninja 1984, 1991

American Ninja 1985

American Ninja II 1987

American Ninja III 1989

American Outlaws 2002

American Pie 2000

American Pie 2 2002

American Pop 1981

American President, The 1995

American Psycho 2001

American Rhapsody, An 2002

American Stories 1989

American Splendor 2004

American Summer, An 1991

American Taboo 1984, 1991

American Tail, An 1986

American Tail: Fievel Goes West, An 1991

American Teen 2009

American Wedding 2004

American Werewolf in London, An 1981

American Werewolf in Paris, An 1997

American Women. *See* The Closer You Get.

America's Sweethearts 2002

Ami de mon amie, L'. *See* Boyfriends and Girlfriends.

Amin: The Rise and Fall 1983

Amistad 1997

Amityville Horror, The 2006

Amityville II: The Possession 1981

Amityville 3-D 1983

Among Giants 2000

Among People 1988

Amongst Friends 1993

Amor brujo, El 1986

Amores Perros 2002

Amos and Andrew 1993

Amour de Swann, Un. *See* Swann in Love.

Amours d'Astrée et de Céladon, Les. *See* Romance of Astree and Celadon, The.

Amreeka 2010

Anaconda 1997

Analyze That 2003

Analyze This 2000

Anastasia 1997

Anchorman: The Legend of Ron Burgundy 2005

Anchors Aweigh [1945] 1985

And God Created Woman 1988

...And God Spoke 1995

And Life Goes On (Zebdegi Edame Darad) 1995

And Nothing but the Truth 1984

And Now Ladies and Gentlemen 2004

And the Ship Sails On 1984

And You Thought Your Parents Were Weird 1991

And Your Mother Too. *See* Y tu mama tambien.

Andre 1995

Android 1984

Ane qui a bu la lune, L'. *See* Donkey Who Drank the Moon, The.

Angel at My Table, An 1991

Angel Baby 1997

Angel Dust 1987

Angel Dust (Ishii) 1997

Angel Eyes 2002

Angel Heart 1987

Angel 1984

Angel III 1988

Angel Town 1990

Angel-A 2008

Angela's Ashes 2000

Catch and Release 2008

Catch Me If You Can 1989

Catch Me If You Can (Spielberg) 2003

Catch That Kid 2005

Catfish pg. 47

Catfish in Black Bean Sauce 2001

Cats & Dogs 2002

Cats & Dogs: The Revenge of Kitty Galore pg. 48

Cats Don't Dance 1997

Cat's Meow, The 2003

Cattle Annie and Little Britches 1981

Catwoman 2005

Caught 1996

Caught Up 1999

Cave, The 2006

Cave Girl 1985

Caveman's Valentine, The 2002

CB4 1993

Cease Fire 1985

Cecil B. Demented 2001

Celebrity 1999

Celeste 1982

Celestial Clockwork 1996

Cell, The 2001

Cellular 2005

Celluloid Closet, The 1996

Celtic Pride 1996

Cement Garden, The 1995

Cemetery Club, The 1993

Cemetery Man 1996

Center of the Web 1992

Center of the World, The 2002

Center Stage 2001

Central do Brasil. *See* Central Station.

Central Station 1999

Centurion pg. 50

Century 1995

Ceravani tanto Amati. *See* We All Loved Each Other So Much.

Cercle Rouge, Le 2004

Ceremonie, La 1996

Certain Fury 1985

Certain Regard, Un. *See* Hotel Terminus.

C'est la vie 1990

Ceux qui m'aiment predont le train. *See* Those Who Love Me Can Take the Train.

Chac 2001

Chain of Desire 1993

Chain Reaction 1996

Chaindance. *See* Common Bonds.

Chained Heat 1983

Chairman of the Board 1999

Challenge, The 1982

Chamber, The 1996

Chambermaid of the Titanic, The 1999

Chameleon Street 1991

Champion [1949] 1991

Champions 1984

Chan Is Missing 1982

Chances Are 1989

Changeling 2009

Changing Lanes 2003

Changing Times 2007

Chansons d'amour, Les. *See* Love Songs.

Chantilly Lace 1995

Chaos 2004

Chaos. *See* Ran.

Chaos Theory 2009

Chaplin 1992

Character 1999

Chariots of Fire 1981

Charlie and the Chocolate Factory 2006

Charlie Bartlett 2009

Charlie St. Cloud pg. 51

Charlie's Angels 2001

Charlie's Angels: Full Throttle 2004

Charlie Wilson's War 2008

Charlotte Gray 2003

Charlotte's Web 2007

Charm Discret de la Bourgeoisie, Le. *See* The Discreet Charm of the Bourgeoisie.

Chase, The 1995

Chasers 1995

Chasing Amy 1988

Chasing Liberty 2005

Chasing Papi 2004

Chateau, The 2003

Chateau de ma mere, Le. *See* My Mother's Castle.

Chattahoochee 1990

Chattanooga Choo Choo 1984

Che 2010

Cheap Shots 1991

Cheaper by the Dozen 2004

Cheaper by the Dozen 2 2006

Cheatin' Hearts 1993

Check Is in the Mail, The 1986

Checking Out 1989

Cheech & Chong Still Smokin' 1983

Cheech & Chong's The Corsican Brothers 1984

Cheetah 1989

Chef in Love, A 1997

Chelsea Walls 2003

Chere Inconnue. *See* I Sent a Letter to My Love.

Chéri 2010

Cherish 2003

Cherry Orchard, The 2003

Cherry Pink. *See* Just Looking.

Chevre, La. *See* Goat, The.

Chi bi. *See* Red Cliff.

Chicago 2003

Chicago Joe and the Showgirl 1990

Chicago 10 2009

Chicken Hawk: Men Who Love Boys 1995

Chicken Little 2006

Chicken Run 2001

Chief Zabu 1988

Chihwaseon: Painted Fire 2003

Child, The 2007

Child's Play 1988

Child's Play II 1990

Child's Play III 1991

Children of a Lesser God 1986

Children of Heaven, The 2000

Children of Men 2007

Children of Nature 1995

Children of the Corn II 1993

Children of the Revolution 1997

Gift From Heaven, A 1995

Gig, The 1986

Gigli 2004

Ginger Ale Afternoon 1989

Ginger and Fred 1986

Ginger Snaps 2002

Gingerbread Man, The 1999

Giornata speciale, Una. *See* Special Day, A.

Giovane Toscanini, II. *See* Young Toscanini.

Girl Cut in Two, A 2009

Girl from Paris, The 2004

Girl in a Swing, The 1988

Girl in the Picture, The 1986

Girl, Interrupted 2000

Girl Next Door, The 2001

Girl Next Door, The (Greenfield) 2005

Girl on the Train, The pg. 142

Girl 6 1996

Girl Talk 1988

Girl Who Kicked the Hornet's Nest, The pg. 144

Girl Who Played with Fire, The pg. 145

Girl with a Pearl Earring 2004

Girl with the Dragon Tattoo, The pg. 147

Girl with the Hungry Eyes, The 1995

Girl with the Red Hair, The 1983

Girlfight 2001

Girlfriend Experience, The 2010

Girls Can't Swim 2003

Girls School Screamers 1986

Girls Town 1996

Give My Regards to Broad Street 1984

Giving, The 1992

Gladiator (Herrington) 1992

Gladiator (Scott) 2001

Glamazon: A Different Kind of Girl 1995

Glamour 2002

Glaneurs et la Glaneuse, Les. *See* Gleaners and I, The.

Glass House, The 2002

Glass Menagerie, The 1987

Glass Shield, The 1995

Gleaming the Cube 1989

Gleaners and I, The 2002

Glengarry Glen Ross 1992

Glimmer Man, The 1996

Glitter 2002

Gloire de mon pere, La. *See* My Father's Glory.

Gloomy Sunday 2004

Gloria (Cassavetes) [1980] 1987

Gloria (Lumet) 2000

Glory 1989

Glory Road 2007

Go 2000

Go Fish 1995

Go Now 1999

Goal! The Dream Begins 2007

Goat, The 1985

Gobots 1986

God Doesn't Believe in Us Anymore 1988

God Grew Tired of Us 2008

God Is Great, I'm Not 2003

God Is My Witness 1993

God Said "Ha"! 2000

Goddess of 1967, The 2003

Godfather, Part III, The 1990

Gods and Generals 2004

Gods and Monsters 1999

Gods Must Be Crazy, The 1984

Gods Must Be Crazy II, The 1990

God's Will 1989

Godsend 2005

Godzilla 1985 1985

Godzilla 1997

Godzilla 2000 2001

Gohatto. *See* Taboo.

Goin' to Chicago 1991

Going All the Way 1997

Going Berserk 1983

Going the Distance pg. 148

Going Undercover 1988

Goin' South 1978

Gold Diggers: The Secret of Bear Mountain 1995

Golden Bowl, The 2002

Golden Child, The 1986

Golden Compass, The 2008

Golden Gate 1995

Golden Seal 1983

Goldeneye 1995

Gomorrah 2010

Gone Baby Gone 2008

Gone Fishin' 1997

Gone in Sixty Seconds 2001

Gone With the Wind [1939] 1981, 1982, 1997

Gong fu. *See* Kung Fu Hustle.

Gonza the Spearman 1988

Good Boy! 2004

Good Burger 1997

Good Bye Cruel World 1984

Good Bye, Lenin! 2005

Good Evening, Mr. Wallenberg 1995

Good German, The 2007

Good Girl, The 2003

Good Hair 2010

Good Luck Chuck 2008

Good Man in Africa, A 1995

Good Marriage, A. *See* Beau Mariage, Le.

Good Morning, Babylon 1987

Good Morning, Vietnam 1987

Good Mother, The 1988

Good Night, and Good Luck 2006

Good Shepherd, The 2007

Good Son, The 1993

Good, the Bad, the Weird, The pg. 150

Good Thief, The 2004

Good Weather, But Stormy Late This Afternoon 1987

Good Will Hunting 1997

Good Woman, A 2007

Good Woman of Bangkok, The 1992

Good Work. *See* Beau Travail.

Good Year, A 2007

Goodbye, Children. *See* Au Revoir les Enfants.

Goodbye Lover 2000

Goodbye, New York 1985

Goodbye People, The 1986

Goodbye Solo 2010

GoodFellas 1990

Goods: Live Hard, Sell Hard, The 2010

Goods: The Don Ready Story, The. *See* Goods: Live Hard, Sell Hard, The.

Goofy Movie, A 1995

Goonies, The 1985

Gordy 1995

Gorillas in the Mist 1988

Gorky Park 1983

Gorky Triology, The. *See* Among People.

Gosford Park 2002

Gospel 1984

Gospel According to Vic 1986

Gossip 2001

Gossip (Nutley) 2003

Gost 1988

Gotcha! 1985

Gothic 1987

Gothika 2004

Gout des Autres, Le. *See* Taste of Others, The.

Gouttes d'Eau sur Pierres Brulantes. *See* Water Drops on Burning Rocks.

Governess 1999

Goya in Bordeaux 2001

Grace Is Gone 2008

Grace of My Heart 1996

Grace Quigley 1985

Gracie 2008

Graffiti Bridge 1990

Gran Fiesta, La 1987

Gran Torino 2009

Grand Bleu, Le. *See* Big Blue, The (Besson).

Grand Canyon 1991

Grand Canyon: The Hidden Secrets 1987

Grand Chemin, Le. *See* Grand Highway, The.

Grand Highway, The 1988

Grand Illusion, The 2000

Grand Isle 1995

Grande Cocomero, Il. *See* Great Pumpkin, The.

Grandfather, The 2000

Grandma's Boy 2007

Grandview, U.S.A. 1984

Grass Harp, The 1996

Gravesend 1997

Graveyard Shift. *See* Stephen King's Graveyard Shift.

Gray Matters 2008

Gray's Anatomy 1997

Grease [1978] 1997

Grease II 1982

Great Balls of Fire! 1989

Great Barrier Reef, The 1990

Great Buck Howard, The 2010

Great Day In Harlem, A 1995

Great Debaters, The 2008

Great Expectations 1999

Great Mouse Detective, The 1986

Great Muppet Caper, The 1981

Great Outdoors, The 1988

Great Pumpkin, The 1993

Great Raid, The 2006

Great Wall, A 1986

Great White Hype, The 1996

Greatest, The pg. 151

Greatest Game Ever Played, The 2006

Greedy 1995

Green Card 1990

Green Desert 2001

Green Mile, The 2000

Green Zone pg. 153

Greenberg pg. 154

Greenfingers 2002

Greenhouse, The 1996

Gregory's Girl 1982

Gremlins 1984

Gremlins II 1990

Grey Fox, The 1983

Grey Zone, The 2003

Greystoke 1984

Gridlock'd 1988

Grief 1995

Grievous Bodily Harm 1988

Grifters, The 1990

Grim Prairie Tales 1990

Grind 2004

Grindhouse 2008

Gringo 1985

Grizzly Man 2006

Grizzly Mountain 1997

Groomsmen, The 2007

Groove 2001

Gross Anatomy 1989

Grosse Fatigue 1995

Grosse Pointe Blank 1997

Ground Truth, The 2008

Ground Zero 1987, 1988

Groundhog Day 1993

Grown Ups pg. 156

Grudge, The 2005

Grudge 2, The 2007

Grumpier Old Men 1995

Grumpy Old Men 1993

Grune Wuste. *See* Green Desert.

Guardian, The 1990

Guardian, The 2007

Guarding Tess 1995

Guatanamera 1997

Guelwaar 1995

Guerre du Feu, La. *See* Quest for Fire.

Guess Who 2006

Guess Who's Coming to Dinner? [1967] 1992

Guest, The 1984

Guests of Hotel Astoria, The 1989

Guilty as Charged 1992

Guilty as Sin 1993

Guilty by Suspicion 1991

Guinevere 2000

Gulliver's Travels pg. 158

Gummo 1997

Gun in Betty Lou's Handbag, The 1992

Gun Shy 2001

Gunbus. *See* Sky Bandits.

Guncrazy 1993

Gunfighter, The [1950] 1989

Gung Ho 1986

Gunmen 1995

Gunner Palace 2006

Guru, The 2004

Guy Named Joe, A [1943] 1981

Guy Thing, A 2004

Guys, The 2003

Gwendoline 1984

Gwoemul. *See* Host, The.

Gyakufunsha Kazoku. *See* Crazy Family, The.

Gymkata 1985

H

H. M. Pulham, Esq. [1941] 1981

Hable con Ella. *See* Talk to Her.

Hackers 1995

Hadesae: The Final Incident 1992

Hadley's Rebellion 1984

Hail Mary 1985

Hairdresser's Husband, The 1992

Hairspray 1988

Hairspray 2008

Haizi wang. *See* King of the Children.

Hak hap. *See* Black Mask

Hak mau. *See* Black Cat.

Half-Baked 1999

Half Moon Street 1986

Half of Heaven 1988

Halfmoon 1996

Hall of Fire [1941] 1986

Halloween (Zombie) 2008

Halloween II 2010

Halloween III: Season of the Witch 1982

Halloween IV 1988

Halloween V 1989

Halloween VI: the Curse of Michael Myers 1995

Halloween H20 1999

Halloween: Resurrection 2003

Hamburger 1986

Hamburger Hill 1987

Hamlet (Zeffirelli) 1990

Hamlet (Branagh) 1996

Hamlet (Almereyda) 2001

Hamlet 2 2009

Hammett 1983

Hana-Bi. *See* Fireworks.

Hancock 2009

Hand That Rocks the Cradle, The 1992

Handful of Dust, A 1988

Handmaid's Tale, The 1990

Hangfire 1991

Hanging Garden, The 1999

Hanging Up 2001

Hangin' with the Homeboys 1991

Hangover, The 2010

Hanky Panky 1982

Hanna K. 1983

Hannah and Her Sisters 1986

Hannah Montana: The Movie 2010

Hannibal 2002

Hannibal Rising 2008

Hanoi Hilton, The 1987

Hans Christian Andersen's Thumbelina 1995

Hansel and Gretel 1987

Hanussen 1988, 1989

Happening, The 2009

Happenstance 2002

Happily Ever After 1993

Happily Ever After 2006

Happily N'Ever After 2008

Happiness 1999

Happy Accidents 2002

Happy End 2001

Happy Endings 2006

Happy Feet 2007

Happy '49 1987

Happy Gilmore 1996

Happy Hour 1987

Happy New Year 1987

Happy, Texas 2000

Happy Times 2003

Happy Together 1990

Happy Together 1997

Happy-Go-Lucky 2009

Hard Candy 2007

Hard Choices 1986

Hard Core Logo 1999

Hard Eight 1997

Hard Hunted 1995

Hard Promises 1992

Hard Rain 1999

Hard Target 1993

Hard Ticket to Hawaii 1987

Hard Times 1988

Hard to Hold 1984

Hard to Kill 1990

Hard Traveling 1986

Hard Way, The (Badham) 1991

Hard Way, The (Sherman) 1984

Hard Word, The 2004

Hardball 2002

Hardbodies 1984

Hardbodies II 1986

Hardware 1990

Harlem Nights 1989

Harley Davidson and the Marlboro Man 1991

Harmonists, The 2000

Harold & Kumar Escape from Guantanamo Bay 2009

Harold & Kumar Go to White Castle 2005

Harriet Craig [1950] 1984

Harriet the Spy 1996

Harrison's Flowers 2003

Harry and Son 1984

Harry and the Hendersons 1987

Harry Brown pg. 161

Harry, He's Here to Help. *See* With a Friend Like Harry.

Harry Potter and the Chamber of Secrets 2003

Harry Potter and the Deathly Hallows: Part 1 pg. 162

Harry Potter and the Goblet of Fire 2006

Harry Potter and the Half-Blood Prince 2010

Harry Potter and the Order of the Phoenix 2008

Harry Potter and the Prisoner of Azkaban 2005

Harry Potter and the Sorcerer's Stone 2002

Hide and Seek 2006

Hideaway 1995

Hideous Kinky 2000

Hiding Out 1987

Hifazaat. *See* In Custody.

High Art 1999

High Crimes 2003

High Fidelity 2001

High Heels 1991

High Heels and Low Lives 2002

High Hopes 1988, 1989

High Lonesome: The Story of Blue-grass Music 258

High Risk 1995

High Road to China 1983

High School High 1996

High School Musical 3: Senior Year 2009

High Season 1988

High Spirits 1988

High Tension 2006

High Tide 1987

Higher Learning 1995

Highlander 1986

Highlander 2: The Quickening 1991

Highlander 3: The Final Dimension 1995

Highlander: Endgame 2001

Highway Patrolman 1995

Highway 61 1992

Highway to Hell 1992

Hijacking Hollywood

Hijo se la Novia, El. *See* Son of the Bride.

Hi-Lo Country, The 2000

Hilary and Jackie 1999

Hills Have Eyes, The 2007

Hills Have Eyes II, The 2008

Himmel uber Berlin, Der. *See* Wings of Desire.

Histories d'amerique. *See* American Stories.

History Boys, The 2007

History Is Made at Night [1937] 1983

History of Violence, A 2006

Hit, The 1985

Hit and Runway 2002

Hit List 1989

Hit the Dutchman 1995

Hitch 2006

Hitcher, The 1986

Hitcher, The (Meyers) 2008

Hitchhiker's Guide to the Galaxy, The 2006

Hitman 2008

Hitman, The 1991

Hoax, The 2008

Hocus Pocus 1993

Hoffa 1992

Holcroft Covenant, The 1985

Hold Back the Dawn [1941] 1986

Hold Me, Thrill Me, Kiss Me 1993

Holes 2004

Holiday [1938] 1985

Holiday, The 2007

Holiday Inn [1942] 1981

Hollow Man 2001

Hollow Reed 1997

Hollywood Ending 2003

Hollywood Homicide 2004

Hollywood in Trouble 1986

Hollywood Mavericks 1990

Hollywood Shuffle 1987

Hollywood Vice Squad 1986

Hollywoodland 2007

Holy Blood. *See* Santa Sangre.

Holy Innocents, The 1985

Holy Man 1999

Holy Rollers pg. 169

Holy Smoke 2000

Holy Tongue, The 2002

Hombre [1967] 1983

Home Alone 1990

Home Alone II: Lost in New York 1992

Home Alone III 1997

Home and the World, The 1985

Home at the End of the World, A 2005

Home for the Holidays 1995

Home Free All 1984

Home Fries 1999

Home Is Where the Heart Is 1987

Home of Our Own, A 1993

Home of the Brave 1986

Home on the Range 2005

Home Remedy 1987

Homeboy 1988

Homegrown 1999

Homer and Eddie 1990

Homeward Bound 1993

Homeward Bound II: Lost in San Francisco 1996

Homework 1982

Homicide 1991

Homme et une femme, Un. *See* Man and a Woman, A.

Hondo [1953] 1982

Honey 2004

Honey, I Blew Up the Kid 1992

Honey, I Shrunk the Kids 1989

Honeybunch 1988

Honeydripper 2008

Honeymoon Academy 1990

Honeymoon in Vegas 1992

Honeymooners, The 2006

Hong Gaoliang. *See* Red Sorghum.

Honky Tonk Freeway 1981

Honkytonk Man 1982

Honneponnetge. *See* Honeybunch.

Honor Betrayed. *See* Fear.

Honorable Mr. Wong, The. *See* Hatchet Man, The.

Honour of the House 2001

Hoodlum 1997

Hoodwinked 2007

Hook 1991

Hoop Dreams 1995

Hoosiers 1986

Hoot 2007

Hope and Glory 1987

Hope and Pain 1988

Hope Floats 1999

Horror Show, The 1989

Hors de prix. *See* Priceless.

Hors la Vie 1995

Horse of Pride, The 1985

Horse Whisperer, The 1999

Loophole 1986

Loose Cannons 1990

Loose Connections 1988

Loose Screws 1986

L'ora di religione: Il sorriso di mia madre. *See* My Mother's Smile.

Lord of Illusions 1995

Lord of the Flies 1990

Lord of the Rings: The Fellowship of the Ring 2002

Lord of the Rings: The Return of the King 2004

Lord of the Rings: The Two Towers 2003

Lord of War 2006

Lords of Discipline, The 1983

Lords of Dogtown 2006

Lords of the Deep 1989

Lorenzo's Oil 1992

Loser 2001

Losers, The pg. 244

Losin' It 1983

Losing Isaiah 1995

Loss of a Teardrop Diamond, The 2010

Loss of Sexual Innocence 2000

Lost and Delirious 2002

Lost and Found 2000

Lost Angels 1989

Lost Boys, The 1987

Lost City, The 2007

Lost Highway 1997

Lost in America 1985

Lost in La Mancha 2004

Lost in Siberia 1991

Lost in Space 1999

Lost in Translation 2004

Lost in Yonkers. *See* Neil Simon's Lost in Yonkers.

Lost Moment, The [1947] 1982

Lost Prophet 1995

Lost Souls 2001

Lost Weekend, The [1945] 1986

Lost Words, The 1995

Lost World, The 1997

Lottery Ticket pg. 246

Lou, Pat, and Joe D 1988

Louis Bluie 1985

Louis Prima: The Wildest 2001

Loulou 1981

Love Actually 2004

Love Affair 1995

Love After Love 1995

Love Always 1997

Love and a .45 1995

Love and Basketball 2001

Love and Death in Long Island 1999

Love and Human Remains 1995

Love and Murder 1991

Love and Other Catastrophes 1997

Love and Other Drugs pg. 247

Love & Sex 2001

Love at Large 1990

Love Child, The 1988

Love Child: A True Story 1982

Love Come Down 2002

Love Crimes 1992

Love Don't Cost a Thing 2004

Love Field 1992

Love Guru, The 2009

Love Happens 2010

Love in Germany, A 1984

Love in the Afternoon [1957] 1986

Love in the Time of Cholera 2008

Love in the Time of Money 2003

Love Is a Dog from Hell 1988

Love Is the Devil 1999

love jones 1997

Love/Juice 2001

Love Letter, The 2000

Love Letters 1984

Love Liza 2004

Love Potion #9 1992

Love Ranch pg. 249

Love Serenade 1997

Love Song for Bobby Long, A 2006

Love Songs 2009

Love Stinks 2000

Love Story, A. *See* Bound and Gagged.

Love Streams 1984

Love the Hard Way 2004

Love, the Magician. *See* Amor brujo, El.

Love! Valour! Compassion! 1997

Love Walked In 1999

Love Without Pity 1991

Loveless, The 1984, 1986

Lovelines 1984

Lovely & Amazing 2003

Lovely Bones, The 2010

Lover, The 1992

Loverboy 1989

Loverboy 2007

Lovers 1992

Lovers of the Arctic Circle, The 2000

Lovers on the Bridge 2000

Love's a Bitch. *See* Amores Perros.

Love's Labour's Lost 2001

Loves of a Blonde [1965] 1985

Lovesick 1983

Loving Jezebel 2001

Low Blow 1986

Low Down, The 2002

Low Down Dirty Shame, A 1995

Low Life, The 1996

Lucas 1986

Lucia, Lucia 2004

Lucia y el Sexo. *See* Sex and Lucia.

Lucie Aubrac 2000

Luckiest Man in the World, The 1989

Lucky Break 2003

Lucky Number Slevin 2007

Lucky Numbers 2001

Lucky Ones, The 2009

Lucky You 2008

Luftslottet som sprängdes. *See* Girl Who Kicked the Hornet's Nest, The.

L'Ultimo Bacio. *See* Last Kiss, The.

Luminous Motion 2001

Lumumba 2002

Lumumba: Death of a Prophet 1995

Luna Park 1995

Lunatic, The 1992

Lunatics: A Love Story 1992

Milk Money 1995

Millennium 1989

Millennium Mambo 2003

Miller's Crossing 1990

Million Dollar Baby 2005

Million Dollar Hotel, The 2002

Million Dollar Mystery 1987

Million to Juan, A 1995

Millions 2006

Mimic 1997

Mina Tannenbaum 1995

Mindhunters 2006

Mindwalk 1991

Ministry of Vengeance 1989

Minner. *See* Men.

Minority Report 2003

Minotaur 1995

Minus Man, The 2000

Mio Viaggio in Italia. *See* My Voyage to Italy.

Miracle 2005

Miracle, The 1991

Miracle at St. Anna 2009

Miracle Mile 1988, 1989

Miracle on 34th Street 1995

Miracle Woman, The (1931) 1982

Mirror, The 2000

Mirror Has Two Faces, The 1996

Mirrors 2009

Misadventures of Mr. Wilt, The 1990

Mischief 1985

Miserables, The 1995

Miserables, The 1999

Misery 1990

Misfits, The [1961] 1983

Mishima 1985

Misma luna, La. *See* Under the Same Moon.

Misplaced 1995

Misplaced 1989

Miss Congeniality 2001

Miss Congeniality 2: Armed and Fabulous 2006

Miss Firecracker 1989

Miss March 2010

Miss Mary 1986

Miss Mona 1987

Miss...or Myth? 1987

Miss Pettigrew Lives for a Day 2009

Miss Potter 2008

Missing 1982, 1988

Missing, The 2004

Missing in Action, 1984

Missing in Action II 1985

Mission, The (Joffe) 1986

Mission, The (Sayyad) 1983

Mission: Impossible 1996

Mission: Impossible 2 2001

Mission: Impossible III 2007

Mission to Mars 2001

Missionary, The 1982

Mississippi Burning 1988

Mississippi Masala 1992

Mist, The 2008

Mr. and Mrs. Bridge 1990

Mr. & Mrs. Smith 2006

Mr. Baseball 1992

Mr. Bean's Holiday 2008

Mr. Brooks 2008

Mr. Death: The Rise and Fall of Fred A. Leuchter, Jr. 2000

Mr. Deeds 2003

Mr. Deeds Goes to Town [1936] 1982

Mr. Destiny 1990

Mr. Frost 1990

Mr. Holland's Opus 1995

Mr. Jealousy 1999

Mister Johnson 1991

Mr. Jones 1993

Mr. Love 1986

Mr. Magoo 1997

Mr. Magorium's Wonder Emporium 2008

Mr. Mom 1983

Mr. Nanny 1993

Mr. Nice Guy 1999

Mr. North 1988

Mr. Payback 1995

Mister Roberts [1955] 1988

Mr. Saturday Night 1992

Mr. Smith Goes to Washington [1939] 1982

Mr. 3000 2005

Mr. Wonderful 1993

Mr. Woodcock 2008

Mr. Write 1995

Mr. Wrong 1996

Mistress 1992

Mrs. Brown 1997

Mrs. Dalloway 1999

Mrs. Doubtfire 1993

Mrs. Henderson Presents 2006

Mrs. Palfrey at the Claremont 2007

Mrs. Parker and the Vicious Circle 1995

Mrs. Soffel 1984

Mrs. Winterbourne 1996

Misunderstood 1984

Mit Liv som Hund. *See* My Life as a Dog.

Mitad del cielo, La. *See* Half of Heaven.

Mixed Blood 1985

Mixed Nuts 1995

Mo' Better Blues 1990

Mo' Money 1992

Moartea domnului Lazarescu. *See* Death of Mr. Lazarescu, The.

Mobsters 1991

Mod Squad, The 2000

Modern Girls 1986

Modern Romance 1981

Moderns, The 1988

Mogan Do. *See* Infernal Affairs.

Mois d'avril sont meurtriers, Les. *See* April Is a Deadly Month.

Moitie Gauche du Frigo, La. *See* Left Hand Side of the Fridge, The.

Moll Flanders 1996

Molly 2000

Mom and Dad Save the World 1992

Môme, La. *See* Vie en Rose, La.

Mommie Dearest 1981

Mon bel Amour, Ma Dechirure. *See* My True Love, My Wound.

Mon meilleur ami. *See* My Best Friend.

Night of the Shooting Stars, The 1983

Night on Earth 1992

Night Patrol 1985

Night Shift 1982

Night Song [1947] 1981

Night Visitor 1989

Night Watch 2007

Night We Never Met, The 1993

Nightbreed 1990

Nightcap. *See* Merci pour le Chocolat.

Nightfall 1988

Nightflyers 1987

Nighthawks 1981

Nighthawks II. *See* Strip Jack Naked.

Nightmare at Shadow Woods 1987

Nightmare Before Christmas, The 1993

Nightmare on Elm Street, A pg. 288

Nightmare on Elm Street, A 1984

Nightmare on Elm Street: II, A 1985

Nightmare on Elm Street: III, A 1987

Nightmare on Elm Street: IV, A 1988

Nightmare on Elm Street: V, A 1989

Nightmares III 1984

Nights in Rodanthe 2009

Nightsongs 1991

Nightstick 1987

Nightwatch 1999

Nil by Mouth 1999

Nim's Island 2009

9 2010

Nine 2010

9 1/2 Weeks 1986

9 Deaths of the Ninja 1985

Nine Months 1995

Nine Queens 2003

976-EVIL 1989

1918 1985

1969 1988

1990: The Bronx Warriors 1983

1991: The Year Punk Broke 1995

Ninety Days 1986

Ninja Assassin 2010

Ninja Turf 1986

Ninotchka [1939] 1986

Ninth Gate, The 2001

Nixon 1995

No 1999

No Country for Old Men 2008

No End in Sight 2008

No Escape 1995

No Fear, No Die 1995

No Holds Barred 1989

No Looking Back 1999

No Man of Her Own [1949] 1986

No Man's Land 1987

No Man's Land 2002

No Mercy 1986

No News from God 2003

No Picnic 1987

No Reservations 2008

No Retreat, No Surrender 1986

No Retreat, No Surrender II 1989

No Secrets 1991

No Small Affair 1984

No Such Thing 2003

No Way Out 1987, 1992

Nobody Loves Me 1996

Nobody's Fool (Benton) 1995

Nobody's Fool (Purcell) 1986

Nobody's Perfect 1990

Noce en Galilee. *See* Wedding in Galilee, A.

Noche de los lapices, La. *See* Night of the Pencils, The.

Nochnoi Dozor. *See* Night Watch.

Noel 2005

Noises Off 1992

Nomads 1986

Non ti muovere. *See* Don't Move.

Nora 2002

Norbit 2008

Nordwand. *See* North Face.

Normal Life 1996

Norte, El 1983

North 1995

North Country 2006

North Face pg. 290

North Shore 1987

North Star, The [1943] 1982

Northfork 2004

Nostalgia 1984

Nostradamus 1995

Not Another Teen Movie 2002

Not Easily Broken 2010

Not for Publication 1984

Not of This Earth 1988

Not Quite Paradise 1986

Not Since Casanova 1988

Not Without My Daughter 1991

Notebook, The 2005

Notebook on Cities and Clothes 1992

Notes on a Scandal 2007

Nothing but Trouble 1991

Nothing in Common 1986

Nothing Personal 1997

Nothing to Lose 1997

Notorious 2010

Notorious Bettie Page, The 2007

Notte di San Lorenzo, La. *See* Night of the Shooting Stars, The.

Notting Hill 2000

Nouvelle Eve, The. *See* New Eve, The.

November 2006

Novocaine 2002

Now and Then 1995

Nowhere 1997

Nowhere Boy pg. 291

Nowhere in Africa 2004

Nowhere to Hide 1987

Nowhere to Run 1993

Nowhereland. *See* Imagine That.

Nueve Reinas. *See* Nine Queens.

Nuit de Varennes, La [1982] 1983, 1984

Nuits Fauves, Les. *See* Savage Nights.

Nuits de la pleine lune, Les. *See* Full Moon In Paris.

Number One with a Bullet 1987

Number 23, The 2008

Nuns on the Run 1990

Nurse Betty 2001

Nutcracker Prince, The 1990

Operation Condor 1997

Operation Dumbo Drop 1995

Opportunists, The 2001

Opportunity Knocks 1990

Opposite of Sex, The 1999

Opposite Sex, The 1993

Orange County 2003

Orchestra Seats. *See* Avenue Montaigne.

Ordeal by Innocence 1985

Order, The 2004

Orfanato, El. *See* Orphanage, The.

Orgazmo 1999

Original Gangstas 1996

Original Kings of Comedy, The 2001

Original Sin 2002

Orlando 1993

Orphan 2010

Orphan Muses, The 2002

Orphanage, The 2009

Orphans 1987

Orphans of the Storm 1984

Osama 2005

Oscar 1991

Oscar & Lucinda 1997

Osmosis Jones 2002

Ososhiki. *See* Funeral, The.

Osterman Weekend, The 1983

Otac Na Sluzbenom Putu. *See* When Father Was Away on Business.

Otello 1986

Othello 1995

Other Boleyn Girl, The 2009

Other Guys, The pg. 300

Other People's Money 1991

Other Side of Heaven, The 2003

Other Sister, The 2000

Other Voices, Other Rooms 1997

Others, The 2002

Our Family Wedding pg. 302

Our Lady of the Assassins 2002

Our Relations [1936] 1985

Our Song 2002

Out Cold 1989

Out for Justice 1991

Out in the World. *See* Among People.

Out of Africa 1985

Out of Bounds 1986

Out of Control 1985

Out of Life. *See* Hors la Vie.

Out of Order 1985

Out of Sight 1999

Out of Sync 1995

Out of the Dark 1989

Out of the Past [1947] 1991

Out of Time 2004

Out-of-Towners, The 2000

Out on a Limb 1992

Out to Sea 1997

Outbreak 1995

Outfoxed: Rupert Murdoch's War on Journalism 2005

Outing, The 1987

Outland 1981

Outrage 2010

Outrageous Fortune 1987

Outside Providence 2000

Outsiders, The 1983

Over Her Dead Body 1995

Over Her Dead Body 2009

Over the Edge [1979] 1987

Over the Hedge 2007

Over the Hill 1995

Over the Ocean 1995

Over the Top 1987

Overboard 1987

Overexposed 1990

Overseas 1991

Owning Mahowny 2004

Ox, The 1992

Oxford, Blues 1984

Oxygen 2000

P

P.O.W. the Escape 1986

P.S. 2005

Pacific Heights 1990

Pacifier, The 2006

Package, The 1989

Pacte des Loups, Le. *See* Brotherhood of the Wolf.

Pagemaster, The 1995

Paint Job, The 1995

Painted Desert, The 1995

Painted Veil, The 2008

Palais Royale 1988

Pale Rider 1985

Palindromes 2006

Pallbearer, The 1996

Palmetto 1999

Palombella Rossa. *See* Redwood Pigeon.

Palookaville 1996

Panama Deception, The 1992

Pandorum 2010

Pane e Tulipani. *See* Bread and Tulips.

Panic 2001

Panic Room, The 2003

Pan's Labyrinth 2007

Panther 1995

Papa's Song 2001

Paparazzi 2005

Paper, The 1995

Paper Heart 2010

Paper Hearts 1995

Paper Mask 1991

Paper Wedding, A 1991

Paperback Romance 1997

Paperhouse 1988

Paprika 2008

Paradise (Donoghue) 1991

Paradise (Gillard) 1982

Paradise Lost 1996

Paradise Now 2006

Paradise Road 1997

Paranoid Park 2009

Paranormal Activity 2010

Paranormal Activity 2 pg. 305

Parasite 1982

Parde-ye akhar. *See* Last Act, The.

Parent Trap, The 1999

Parenthood 1989

Parents 1989

Paris, I Love You. *See* Paris, je t'aime.

Paris, Texas 1984

Paris Blues [1961] 1992

Tap 1989

Tape 2002

Tapeheads 1988

Taps 1981

Target 1985

Target 1996

Tarnation 2005

Tarzan 2000

Tarzan and the Lost City 1999

Tasogare Seibei. *See* Twilight Samurai, The.

Taste of Others, The 2002

Tatie Danielle 1991

Taxi 2005

Taxi Blues 1991

Taxi nach Kairo. *See* Taxi to Cairo.

Taxi to Cairo 1988

Taxi to the Dark Side 2009

Taxi to the Toilet. *See* Taxi Zum Klo.

Taxi Zum Klo 1981

Taxing Woman, A 1988

Taxing Woman's Return, A 1989

Tea in the Harem 1986

Tea With Mussolini 2000

Teachers 1984

Teacher's Pet: The Movie. *See* Disney's Teacher's Pet.

Teaching Mrs. Tingle 2000

Team America: World Police 2005

Tears of the Sun 2004

Ted and Venus 1991

Teen Witch 1989

Teen Wolf 1985

Teenage Mutant Ninja Turtles 1990

Teenage Mutant Ninja Turtles (2007). *See* TMNT.

Teenage Mutant Ninja Turtles II 1991

Teenage Mutant Ninja Turtles III 1993

Teeth 2009

Telephone, The 1988

Tell No One 2009

Telling Lies in America 1997

Témoins, Les. *See* Witnesses, The.

Temp, The 1993

Tempest 1982

Tempest, The pg. 384

Temporada de patos. *See* Duck Season.

Temps qui changent, Les. *See* Changing Times.

Temps qui reste, Les. *See* Time to Leave.

Temps Retrouve. *See* Time Regained.

Temptress Moon 1997

Ten 2004

Ten Things I Hate About You 2000

10,000 B.C. 2009

10 to Midnight 1983

Tenacious D in the Pick of Destiny 2007

Tender Mercies 1983

Tenebrae. *See* Unsane.

Tenue de soiree. *See* Menage.

Tequila Sunrise 1988

Terminal, The 2005

Terminal Bliss 1992

Terminal Velocity 1995

Terminator, The 1984

Terminator Salvation 2010

Terminator 2 1991

Terminator 3: Rise of the Machines 2004

Termini Station 1991

Terminus. *See* End of the Line.

Terms of Endearment 1983

Terror Within, The 1989

Terrorvision 1986

Tess 1981

Test of Love 1985

Testament 1983

Testimony 1987

Tetro 2010

Tetsuo: The Iron Man 1992

Tex 1982, 1987

Texas Chainsaw Massacre, The (Nispel) 2004

Texas Chainsaw Massacre, Part II, The 1986

Texas Chainsaw Massacre: The Beginning, The 2007

Texas Comedy Massacre, The 1988

Texas Rangers 2003

Texas Tenor: The Illinois Jacquet Story 1995

Texasville 1990

Thank You and Good Night 1992

Thank You for Smoking 2007

That Championship Season 1982

That Darn Cat 1997

That Night 1993

That Old Feeling 1997

That Sinking Feeling 1984

That Thing You Do! 1996

That Was Then...This Is Now 1985

That's Entertainment! III 1995

That's Life! 1986, 1988

The au harem d'Archi Ahmed, Le. *See* Tea in the Harem.

Thelma and Louise 1991

Thelonious Monk 1988

Then She Found Me 2009

Theory of Flight, The 1999

There Goes My Baby 1995

There Goes the Neighborhood 1995

There Will Be Blood 2008

There's Nothing Out There 1992

There's Something About Mary 1999

Theremin: An Electronic Odyssey 1995

They All Laughed 1981

They Call Me Bruce 1982

They Drive by Night [1940] 1982

They Live 1988

They Live by Night [1949] 1981

They Might Be Giants [1971] 1982

They Still Call Me Bruce 1987

They Won't Believe Me [1947] 1987

They're Playing with Fire 1984

Thiassos, O. *See* Traveling Players, The.

Thief 1981

Thief, The 1999

Thief of Hearts 1984

Thieves 1996

Thin Blue Line, The 1988

Thin Line Between Love and Hate, A 1996

Vince Vaughn's Wild West Comedy Show: 30 Days & 30 Nights—Hollywood to the Heartland 2009

Vincent and Theo 1990

Vincere pg. 411

Violets Are Blue 1986

Violins Came with the Americans, The 1987

Violon Rouge, Le. *See* Red Violin, The.

Viper 1988

Virgen de los Sicanos, La. *See* Our Lady of the Assassins.

Virgin Queen of St. Francis High, The 1987

Virgin Suicides, The 2001

Virtuosity 1995

Virus 2000

Vision Quest 1985

Visions of Light 1993

Visions of the Spirit 1988

Visit, The 2002

Visiting Hours 1982

Visitor, The 2009

Visitor, The. *See* Ghost.

Vital Signs 1990

Volcano 1997

Volere, Volare 1992

Volunteers 1985

Volver 2007

Volver a empezar 1982

Vor. *See* Thief, The.

Voyage du ballon rouge, Le. *See* Flight of the Red Balloon.

Voyager 1992

Voyages 2002

Voyeur 1995

Vroom 1988

Vulture, The 1985

Vzlomshik. *See* Burglar, The.

W

W. 2009

Wackness, The 2009

Waco: The Rules of Engagement 1997

Wag the Dog 1997

Wagner 1983

Wagons East! 1995

Wah-Wah 2007

Waist Deep 2007

Wait for Me in Heaven 1990

Wait Until Spring, Bandini 1990

Waiting… 2006

Waiting for Gavrilov 1983

Waiting for Guffman 1997

Waiting for 'Superman' pg. 415

Waiting for the Light 1990

Waiting for the Moon 1987

Waiting to Exhale 1995

Waitress 1982

Waitress (Shelly) 2008

Waking Life 2002

Waking Ned Devine 1999

Waking the Dead 2001

Walk Hard: The Dewey Cox Story 2008

Walk in the Clouds, A 1995

Walk Like a Man 1987

Walk on the Moon, A 1987

Walk on the Moon, A (Goldwyn) 2000

Walk the Line 2006

Walk to Remember, A 2003

Walker 1987

Walking and Talking 1996

Walking After Midnight 1988

Walking Dead, The 1995

Walking Tall 2005

Wall, The 1986

Wall Street 1987

Wallace & Gromit: The Curse of the Were-Rabbit 2006

WALL-E 2009

Wall Street: Money Never Sleeps pg. 416

Waltz Across Texas 1983

Waltz with Bashir 2009

Wandafuru raifu. *See* After Life.

Wannsee Conference, The 1987

Wannseekonferenz, Die. *See* Wannsee Conference, The.

Wanted 2009

Wanted: Dead or Alive 1987

War 1988

War (Arwell) 2008

War, The 1995

War Against the Indians 1995

War and Love 1985

War, Inc. 2009

War at Home, The 1997

War of the Buttons 1995

War of the Roses, The 1989

War of the Worlds 2006

War Party 1988

War Room, The 1993

War Tapes, The 2007

War Zone, The 2000

WarGames 1983

Warlock 1989, 1990

Warlock: The Armageddon 1993

Warm Nights on a Slow Moving Train 1987

Warm Summer Rain 1989

Warm Water Under a Red Bridge 2002

Warning Bandits 1987

Warning Sign 1985

Warrior Queen 1987

Warriors of Heaven and Earth 2005

Warriors of Virtue 1997

Wash, The 1988

Washington Heights 2004

Washington Square 1997

Wassup Rockers 2007

Watch It 1993

Watcher, The 2001

Watchers 1988

Watchmen 2010

Water 1986

Water 2007

Water and Soap 1985

Water Drops on Burning Rocks 2001

Water Horse: Legend of the Deep, The 2008

Waterboy, The 1999

Waterdance, The 1992

Waterland 1992

Waterloo Bridge [1940] 1981

For Reference

Not to be taken from this room